SECOND EDITION

Advertising
Principles and Practice

William Wells
DDB Needham Worldwide

John Burnett
University of Denver

Sandra Moriarty
University of Colorado

Prentice Hall, Englewood Cliffs, New Jersey 07632

Library of Congress Cataloging-in-Publication Data

Wells, William (date)
   Advertising: principles and practice / William Wells, John
Burnett, Sandra Moriarty.—2nd ed.
     p.   cm.
   Includes bibliographical references and index.
   ISBN 0-13-016205-1
    1. Advertising. I. Burnett, John (date). II. Moriarty,
Sandra E. (Sandra Ernst) III. Title.
   HF5823.W455   1992
   659.1—dc20   91-36573
                                 CIP

Editorial/production supervision: Patrick Reynolds and Barbara Grasso
Permissions/production: Lisa Kinne
Design supervisor: Christine Gehring-Wolf
Interior design: Aurora Graphics
Development editor: Rachel Nelson
Acquisitions editor: Jennifer Young
Cover design: Aurora Graphics
Prepress buyer: Trudy Pisciotti
Manufacturing buyer: Robert Anderson
Page layout: Nancy Field, Meryl Poweski, and Maureen Eide
Photo research: Eileen Cherna
Photo editor: Lorinda Morris-Nantz
Ad permission researcher: Karen Eisen
Chapter opening photos: Chapter 1: BAKER'S is a registered trademark of Kraft General Foods,
Inc. Reproduced with permission.   Chapter 2: Bob Daemmrich/The Image Works   Chapter
3: Jacques Chenet/Woodfin Camp & Associates   Chapter 4: Jeff Persons/Stock Boston
Chapter 5: Sepp Seitz/Woodfin Camp & Associates   Chapter 6: Bob Daemmrich/The Image
Works   Chapter 7: (no credit)   Chapter 8: © 1990 The Estate and Foundation of Andy
Warhol/ARS, N.Y.   Chapter 9: DDB Needham   Chapter 10: Michael S. Yamashita/
Woodfin Camp & Associates   Chapter 11: Michael Hayman/Photo Researchers   Chapter
12: Frank Siteman/Stock Boston   Chapter 13: Comstock   Chapter 14: Dan McCoy/
Rainbow   Chapter 15: David W. Hamilton/The Image Bank   Chapter 16: Mark Antman/
The Image Works   Chapter 17: Michael Hart/FPG International   Chapter 18: Richard
Pasley/Stock Boston   Chapter 19: Tannenbaum/Sygma   Chapter 20: Thomson
Consumer Electronics   Chapter 21: Spencer Grant/Stock Boston   Chapter 22: Michael
Hart/FPG   Chapter 23: John Marmaras/Woodfin Camp & Associates

 © 1992, 1989 by Prentice-Hall, Inc.
A Simon & Schuster Company
Englewood Cliffs, NJ 07632

Printed in the United States of America
10 9 8 7 6 5 4 3 2 1

ISBN 0-13-016205-1

Prentice-Hall International (UK) Limited, *London*
Prentice-Hall of Australia Pty. Limited, *Sydney*
Prentice-Hall Canada Inc, *Toronto*
Prentice-Hall Hispanoamericana, S.A., *Mexico*
Prentice-Hall of India Private Limited, *New Delhi*
Prentice-Hall of Japan, Inc., *Tokyo*
Prentice-Hal of Southeast Asia Pte. Ltd., *Singapore*
Editora Prentice-Hall do Brasil, Ltda., *Rio de Janeiro*

CONTENTS

PART ONE

ADVERTISING FOUNDATIONS AND ENVIRONMENT

4 *Advertising Agencies*   96

7 *Strategy and Planning 200*

8 *How Advertising Works 236*

PART THREE

ADVERTISING MEDIA

9 *Media Strategy and Planning   264*

10 *Broadcast Media   298*

11 *Print Media   330*

12 *Media Buying   356*

PART FOUR

CREATING ADVERTISING

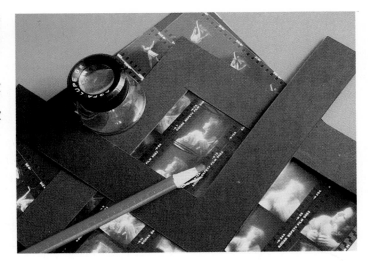

17 Creating Directory and Out-of-home Advertising 506

PART FIVE

ADVERTISING OPERATIONS

20   *Advertising Campaigns   584*

21   *Evaluative Research   602*

PART SIX

MISCELLANEOUS ADVERTISING

22 Business-to-Business and Retail Advertising   628

PREFACE

*A*DVERTISING AND THE REAL WORLD

Advertising professionals often question whether this field can be taught from a book. Although nothing compares with the experience of "being there," it is obvious that all college students who want an introduction to advertising cannot work in an advertising agency. The solution, then, is to create a textbook and a teaching package that will bring the real-world experience of advertising alive using paper, ink, pictures, slides, overheads, audiotapes, and videotapes. That is the goal of this textbook.

A World of Experience

The secret to capturing the real world of advertising does not lie in a book or any of the other media involved in this project, but rather in *people and their experiences*—a wide variety of people representing all the different aspects of the diverse field of advertising. In order to provide a real-life view of advertising for a student who wants an introduction to the field, it is necessary to consult and involve specialists from all the different areas, to bring their stories to life, and to record their insight and wisdom. That's what this book attempts to do.

A World of Diversity

Another secret to capturing the real world of advertising is to present the breadth as well as depth of the field. An introductory textbook has an obligation to cover the field as accurately as possible. That does not mean writing about advertising from a business viewpoint, from a marketing viewpoint, or from a creative viewpoint, but instead writing about advertising from an *advertising* viewpoint.

Advertising includes *a variety of disciplines and specialties.* For example, advertising is a major element in a company's marketing plan, so it must dovetail with corporate marketing practices. Furthermore, the field of advertising itself contains such specialties as research, media buying and planning, copywriting, art direction, print and broadcast production, media sales, sales promotion and product publicity, strategic planning, personnel management, budgeting, scheduling, negotiating, and even business presentations. This book will introduce the advertising student to the richness and the variety of the real world of advertising.

The Focus

In the field of advertising you find writers, artists, producers, performers, composers and arrangers, researchers, accountants, salespeople, and managers, to name a few—and all of them are important. The focus of all their efforts, regardless of their professional area of expertise, is on the most effective way to present a sales message to a potential consumer. This is the focus of advertising departments and advertising agencies, of media sales departments and consumer behavior researchers, of national brand advertising managers as well as local entrepreneurs and retailers, of huge global mega-agencies and small creative boutiques. All of these activities are ultimately directed at producing *a message that sells something to someone,* and that, too, is the focus of this book.

Science and Art

No single area in the real world is called "advertising." Instead, advertising is an amalgamation of specialized skills and professions that utilize a number of approaches and philosophies, including scientific, or numbers-oriented; or problem/solution-oriented; and artistic, or aesthetically-oriented. An introduction to advertising is an introduction to all sides of the advertising field and to the processes—quantitative, strategic, and aesthetic—by which the sales message is planned and produced. This book will attempt to present both *the science and the art* of advertising.

Real World Insights

This book is built upon the work and insights of the stars and giants in the world of advertising. It reflects *advertising as professionals see it*—their theories, their styles and approaches, their rules of thumb, their hindsights and foresights, and their visions. Of course, because not everyone agrees with everyone else in the field, this book presents a variety of approaches, styles, and theories.

An approach upon which advertising professionals seem to agree is presented in this book as *a principle.* Advertising is still a young field, so these principles are evolving and changing as the field develops. The principles, do, however, reflect the current wisdom.

Professionals and Basic Philosophies

Some basic philosophies guide the direction of this book. For example, *the bottom line of advertising,* according to Lou Hagopian, chairman of the N.W. Ayer agency, is to sell more of something. Furthermore, advertising, and the diversity and variety of products that it supports, is an important part of a free-market economy. According to John O'Toole, of the American Association of Advertising Agencies in New York, advertising is an important factor in our economic freedom of choice. This book realizes, therefore, that advertising is not only a business itself, but it is an important aspect of business in general.

But advertising is more than just a sales pitch. Bill Bernbach, one of the founders of Doyle, Dane and Bernbach (now DDB Needham Worldwide), brought style and flair to advertising when he insisted that *what* is said is only the beginning: "*How* you say it makes people look and listen." Advertising is an art form because it is able to motivate people and move them emotionally. When it is done well—and admittedly not all advertising is done well—it touches common chords in all of us with carefully composed messages. So an important premise of this book is that *although what is said is important, how it is said is equally as important.*

Advertising professionals can create and deliver sales messages that touch us because they are students of human behavior, the most complicated and fascinating area of study in the world. *Insights into human behavior and respect for people* are absolutely fundamental to good advertising. Unfortunately, not all advertising is good, and not all advertising respects the people it tries to reach, but that is still the goal of the true professionals in the business—and another premise of this book.

John O'Toole explains it best in his book, *The Trouble with Advertising . . . ,* when he says you have to respect the critical faculties of the contemporary consumer. He points to the fact that 66 percent of new products do not make it. They are purchased and evaluated by the public and not bought again, no matter how powerful the advertising might be. He calls the public "these formidable folks whose wrath is so fearful." He describes the implicit contract, or at least understanding, between the advertiser and the public that makes advertising work in a free-market economy:

> I promise you this. My advertising won't lie to you, and it will not deliberately try to mislead you. It won't bore the hell out of you or treat you as though you were a fool or embarrass you or your family. But remember, it's a salesman. Its purpose is to persuade you to trade your hard-earned cash for my product or service.

This then is the purpose of this book—to introduce the real world of advertising—its diversity, its processes and principles, its people, and their professional experiences and ways of thinking.

*L*EARNING AIDS

Many aids are provided within this book to help students learn about advertising. The main ones are:

- *Chapter Objectives.* Each chapter begins with objectives that prepare the student for the chapter material and point out learning goals.
- *Chapter Outline.* A chapter outline is included at the beginning of each chapter.
- *Opening Examples.* Most of the chapters start with a dramatic advertising story that introduces the chapter material and arouses student interest.
- *Full-Color Advertisements, Photographs, and Illustrations.* Throughout the text, key concepts and applications are illustrated with strong, full-color visuals, including over 200 full-color advertisements and 100 color photographs and graphic illustrations.
- *Principles.* Throughout the text, principles are presented that reflect the current wisdom in the industry, giving students some memorable thoughts about advertising.
- *Inside the Advertising World.* These boxed materials reflect the thoughts and day-to-day activities of advertising professionals in "real-world" terms.
- *Concepts and Controversies.* Through the text, controversial issues in advertising are presented in a boxed format.
- *Issues and Applications.* These boxes examine real world issues in advertising and relate them to relevant text material.
- *Lifestyle.* Based upon studies conducted by DDB Needham, short profiles of typical consumers are presented throughout the text.
- *Video Cases.* Every chapter ends with a video case detailing an ABC video clip or an EFFIE award winning ad campaign.
- *Case Studies.* Case studies are presented at the end of each section of the text, illustrating the concepts in preceding chapters.

- *Margin Definitions.* Definitions of key terms are presented in the margins where these terms appear.
- *Careers in Advertising.* The career appendix at the end of the book gives students valuable insights and advice for obtaining a job in advertising.

SUPPLEMENTS

A successful advertising course involves more than a well-written, well-illustrated book. It requires a dedicated teacher and a complete set of supplemental learning and teaching aids. The supplementary materials that have been developed to accompany *ADVERTISING: PRINCIPLES AND PRACTICE* are designed to enhance the classroom experience and to reflect the "real world" of advertising.

- **Annotated Instructor's Edition:** The entire text is annotated with additional examples and applications.
- **Instructor's Resource Manual:** The IRM contains suggested activities, lecture outlines, and recommended audiovisual materials and outside readings for each chapter. The IRM also provides lecture suggestions, answers to discussion questions and case questions and teaching suggestions.
- **Test Item File:** The test item file contains about 2,500 multiple-choice, true-false, and essay questions. These questions are available on floppy disks and through the Prentice Hall Telephone Testing Service.
- **Prentice Hall Videos for Advertising:** A dynamic video program is available to adopters, featuring exciting vignettes from ABC News, a full complement of broadcast commercials from the 1991 EFFIE-winning campaigns, and videos from the Advertising Education Foundation and international sources.
- **Video Guide for Advertising:** Along with the supplemental video series, a video guide is available with descriptions of each of the videos available and helpful teaching tips for incorporating the audiovisual material into your lectures, including teaching objectives, study questions, and teaching suggestions.
- **Prentice Hall Slides for Advertising Series III:** A set of over 100 slides is available to adopters. Updated through early 1991, the slides feature advertisements as well as tours of advertising agencies, television stations, radio stations, newspapers, and the personnel who work within them.
- **Color Transparencies:** Key tables, figures, and diagrams, and visually appealing advertisements and photos have been chosen from the text and made into a set of color overhead transparencies to aid in classroom lectures and discussions.
- **WHEATIES Case Study:** Each student will receive a comprehensive case study prepared by WHEATIES and DDB Needham Worldwide. This study illustrates all of the major concepts presented in the text and includes questions for discussion.

ACKNOWLEDGMENTS

ADVERTISING: PRINCIPLES AND PRACTICE 2/E has benefitted from an outstanding team of authors and contributors. We wish to acknowledge the assistance of many academics and professionals in bringing the real world of advertising into the text.

Various experts in the industry contributed to the development of parts of the text. We are indebted to Peter Turk of the University of Akron for lending his expertise to the media sections of the text. Norval Stephens of the Norval Stephens Company provided a wealth of experience in the areas of advertising agencies and international advertising. Ann Pasanella wrote the Lifestyle boxes featured throughout the text, and Brad Haley wrote the chapter-ending video cases. We would also like to thank Kris Hartzell and Susan Fignar of DDB Needham for their help in obtaining artwork and photographs, and we extend our deepest gratitude to Charles Pearce for his insightful annotations.

Numerous people assisted in the preparation of the case studies. The Honda case was provided by Sanford Edelstein of Rubin Postaer. The Discover Card case was provided by Ray Gillette of DDB Needham. The Disney case study was provided by Vicki Mondae of DDB Needham. The Lands' End case study was provided by Jill Palamountain of Lands' End. The Cancer Treatment Centers of America case study was provided by Roger O'Connor and Vicki Lorenz of Cancer Treatment Centers of America. The Brooke Bond PG Tips case study was provided by Paul Feldwick of BMP DDB Needham Worldwide. The material on the RCA campaign in Chapter 20 was provided by Sunil Mehrotra and Bruce Hutchison of Thomson Consumer Electronics.

Many thanks to Colleen Boselli, Chris Iannuccilli, Robert Klein, and Fran Sussman of DDB Needham and Scott Rice and Jeff Swenson of General Mills for preparing the WHEATIES Case Study that supplements this text.

No text can be successfully developed without a supportive publisher. The team at Prentice Hall helped to develop both the text and the supplementary package. We express our gratitude to Rachel Nelson, for her unfailing dedication to development; Chris Trieber, for putting the team together; Tim Kent and Jennifer Young, for overseeing the project; Pat Reynolds and Barbara Grasso, for patience during a hectic production process; Karen Eisen, for help with the endless permission requests and art program; Christine Wolf, for design; Lorinda Morris-Nantz and Eileen Cherna, for photo research; Lisamarie Brassini, for coordinating the supplements package; and Rob McCarry, Carol Carter, and Lori Cowen, for developing the promotional program.

Many reviewers provided helpful comments on the drafts of the original chapters for the first edition and the revised drafts in the second edition. Their time and thoughtful comments are appreciated.

Edd Applegate
Middle Tennessee State University

David Andrus
Kansas State University

Linda Baker
Highline Community College

Ann Marie Barry
Boston College

Jack Bell
Metropolitan State College

Tim Bengston
University of Kansas

William Bigelow
University of Wisconsin

Lucia Blinn
DDB Needham Worldwide

Lawrence Bowen
University of Washington

Thomas Bowers
University of North Carolina

John Buckley
Orange County Community
College

James Camerius
Northern Michigan University

Donald Cappa
Charbat College

Howard Cogan
Ithaca College

Hugh Daubek
Central Michigan University

Michael Dotson
Appalachian State University

Lou Harmin
Sullivan County Community
College

Nathan Himelstein
Essex County College

John Holmes
Skidmore College

Thomas Kelly
Rider College

Lawrence Knight
Indiana State University

Darwin Krumrey
Kirkwood Community College

Priscilla LaBarbera
New York University

Gerald Leadham
Clackamus Community College

C. David Light
University of San Diego

John W. Lloyd
Monroe County Community College

William Lundstrom
Old Dominion University

Harry Marsh
Kansas State University

David G. Moore
University of Michigan

H. Neal
County College of Morris

Charles Pearce
Kansas State University

Richard Semenick
University of Utah

Kathy Smith
Towson State University

Margery Steinberg
University of Hartford

James Taylor
California State University—
Fullerton

Donald Vance
University of Miami

Joan Weiss
Bucks County Community College

Gary Wilcox
University of Texas—Austin

Anthony Zahorik
Vanderbilt University

ABOUT THE AUTHORS

William Wells

WILLIAM WELLS—Bill Wells, Former Executive Vice President and Director of Marketing Services at DDB Needham Chicago, is one of the industry's leading market and research authorities. He is, in fact, the only representative of the advertising business elected to the Attitude Research Hall of Fame. He earned a Ph.D. from Stanford University and was formerly Professor of Psychology and Marketing at the University of Chicago. He then joined Needham, Harper, Chicago as Director of Corporate Research. He is author of the Needham Harper Lifestyle Study as well as author of over sixty books and articles. In addition to *Advertising: Principles and Practice,* he also published *Planning for R.O.I.: Effective Advertising Strategy* (Prentice Hall) in 1989.

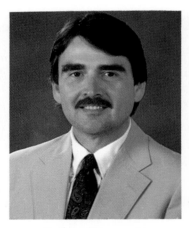

John Burnett

JOHN BURNETT is a Professor of Marketing at the University of Denver. He holds a D.B.A. Degree in Marketing from the University of Kentucky. He is author of *Promotion Management,* now in its third edition. In addition, he has authored numerous articles and papers in a wide variety of professional and academic journals. In particular, his research has examined the effectiveness of emotional appeals in advertising and how various segments respond to such strategies. He is an active consultant in marketing and advertising and has served as a consulting professor for AT&T, the Dallas Mart, the AAFES organization, and Scott & White Hospitals. He has won several teaching awards and serves as faculty advisor for student chapters of the American Marketing Association.

Sandra Moriarty

SANDRA MORIARTY—Formerly a copywriter, and then owner of her own agency, Sandra has been teaching at the university level since 1968. A journalism major at the University of Missouri, she worked in advertising and public relations before moving into academics. She started teaching part time while directing a program in university relations at Kansas State University, then moved to full-time teaching after completing her Ph.D. in educational communication. Before moving to the University of Colorado, she taught at the University of Kansas and Michigan State University. She is author of seven books, including *Creative Advertising* (1991) and *Principles of Marketing* (1992), and many professional articles in such areas as typography, the creative side of advertising, advertising presentations, agency approaches to effective advertising, and advertising management. She also has published numerous scholarly research reports in such areas as creative thinking, cognitive theory and communication, typography, graphic design, and visual communication.

Norval B. Stephens, Jr.

NORVAL STEPHENS provided assistance for the advertising agency and international chapters. His 40 years in marketing include management of the New York office and of the international division of a worldwide agency. He is a consultant and executive director of the International Federation of Advertising Agencies.

Peter B. Turk

DR. TURK is a professor of marketing at the University of Akron. With ten years of professional experience in media research and strategic planning, he continues to write in this area, including two books, *Advertising Media Research Sourcebook* (NTC Books) and *Advertising Media: Strategy and Tactics* (William Brown), as well as an invited article on research developments for *Current Issues in Research and Advertising,* 1992.

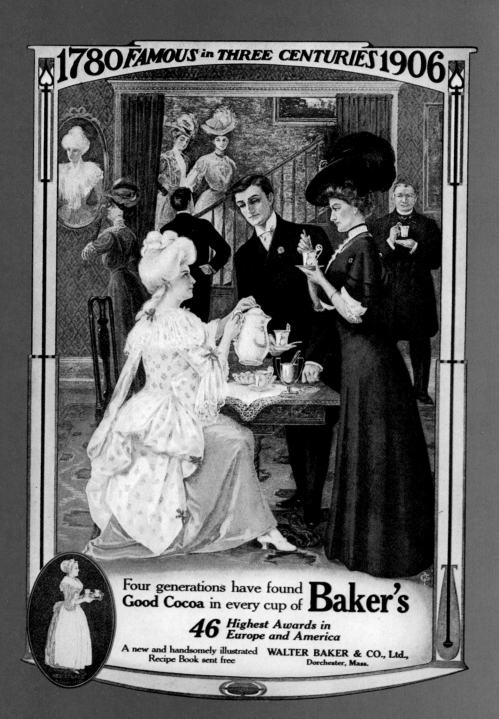

1

Introduction to Advertising

Chapter Outline

What Does *Fahrvergnügen* Mean Anyhow?
What Makes an Ad Great?
The World of Advertising
The Three Players
The Evolution of Advertising

Chapter Objectives

When you have completed this chapter, you should be able to:

- Define advertising and discuss its component parts
- Identify the eight types of advertising
- Explain the four roles of advertising
- Identify the three key players in the advertising world
- Explain the impact on advertising of the invention of new media forms such as print, radio, and television
- Relate key figures in the history of advertising to their contributions to the field

WHAT DOES *FAHRVERGNÜGEN* MEAN ANYHOW?

It doesn't bother Volkswagen U.S. executives that so few people know what *fahrvergnügen* means. They're just happy that people are talking about it. Since the German word became the cornerstone of the company's advertising and marketing campaign in January 1990, it has been the subject of a comic strip and used in jokes by many comedians. Volkswagen U.S. and DDB Needham introduced the advertising and marketing campaign that is wrapped around the tongue twister, a German word that literally means "pleasure of driving." The word was used as a concept to give the car company a new image in the early 1990s.

Volkswagen's sales had increased in the 1960s as the Beetle (Bug) became known as the counterculture car that provided affordable transportation. The reputation of Volkswagen's agency, Doyle Dane Bernbach (now DDB Needham) had grown strong as well. During the last 15 years, however, the car maker had lost its niche and market share to the Japanese companies, which offered Americans low-priced, efficient cars with more style than the Bug afforded. Volkswagen's decline had reached the point where some consumers even thought the company had stopped selling cars in the United States altogether.

Revitalizing the Volkswagen name became important to both the company and the agency, which had established a great deal of its reputation through the early success of VW. The agency involved its top executive in the project, including chairman/CEO Keith Reinhard, and tapped into both the New York and Detroit offices for talent.

Now Volkswagen says it is making a comeback. Consumer awareness of the car company has increased, and there have been shifts in consumer attitudes about the auto maker, according to consumer-tracking studies commissioned by Volkswagen. Tracking has shown, for instance, that in the third quarter of 1990, 48 percent of consumers believed that the company offered contemporary and up-to-date vehicles, compared to only 35 percent in the fourth quarter of 1989; 68 percent recognized the company as offering well-made vehicles, compared to 51 percent in 1989; and 34 percent saw Volkswagen as offering outstanding passenger safety, compared to 20 percent in 1989.

The apparent change in consumer attitudes, albeit gradual, gave Volkswagen enough confidence to keep going with the campaign. New television ads for the Passat and Jetta cars and a variety of radio and print ads were produced in 1991. The black-and-white imagery and the stick figure *Otto Bahn* appeared in dealer displays and other marketing efforts, as well as in the ads themselves (see Figure 1.1).

Has the campaign improved sales? In 1990 Volkswagen sold 136,357 cars in the United States, up from 133,650 in 1989. Although this increase of 2,707 (or about 2%) cars is not very impressive, it is the first increase for Volkswagen in 7 years. Industry experts suggest that the campaign is the primary reason for this reversal and that it has been stemming the decline in sales that the car manufacturer has experienced in recent years.*

FIGURE 1.1
The *Otto Bahn* logo. (Courtesy of Volkswagen United States Inc.)

---

*Adapted from Kim Kinter, "Fahrvergnügen: Few Understand It, But It's Working," *Adweek* (October 29, 1990):28.

WHAT MAKES AN AD GREAT?

Is the Volkswagen *Fahrvergnügen* ad campaign great? Not yet. Will it be eventually? Maybe. The difficulty is in defining "great." Clearly the Volkswagen ads created in the 1960s by Bill Bernbach were great. They won many awards, elicited praise from consumers, and contributed significantly to increased sales. When did they stop being great? Some argue this happened when Bernbach died, and that's why Volkswagen sales went into a decline. But others contend that advertising had little to do with the decline; it was new and better competition that put Volkswagen products at a serious disadvantage. Essentially, advertising—even the greatest advertising—cannot save a product the consumer doesn't want.

Often the determination of great advertising is reduced to a popularity contest. We all have our favorite ads. Which television commercials do you remember? Which radio commercials? Magazine ads? Why are they your favorites? Do you prefer funny ads to serious ones? Most people do. Table 1.1 lists the most popular commercials of 1990.

Several companies ask people questions such as these. *Advertising Age,* working with the SRI Research Center, conducts a monthly "Ad Watch" survey of advertising awareness. Video Storyboard Tests asks consumers to list the most outstanding print advertisements and television commercials. *Advertising Age* also regularly interviews top creative people to identify those ads that professionals think are most effective. The advertising industry evaluates its work through such award programs as the Clios, the EFFIES, and the Addy Awards. Achieving consumer recognition and winning prizes do not necessarily mean an ad is great, however. The box in Chapter 13 entitled "Curse of the Clio" examines the function of award programs. Many agencies that have developed award-winning campaigns

TABLE 1.1
Most Popular Commercials of 1990

1990 Rank	1989 Rank	Brand	Agency
1	2	Pepsi/Diet Pepsi	BBDO
2	10	Nike	Wieden & Kennedy
3	4	Energizer	Chiat/Day/Mojo
4	7	Coca-Cola	McCann-Erickson
5	1	McDonald's	Leo Burnett[1]
6	17	Little Caesar	Cliff Freeman & Partners
7	8	Miller Lite	Backer Spielvogel Bates
8	3	California Raisins	Foote, Cone & Belding
9	15	Budweiser	DMB&B
10	9	Infiniti	Hill, Holiday, Connors, Cosmopulos
11	—	Reebok	Chiat/Day/Mojo[2]
12	6	Bud Light	DDB Needham
13	5	Isuzu	Della Femina, McNamee
14	24	Partnership for a Drug Free America	Various Agencies
15	20	Burger King	Saatchi & Saatchi Advertising and DMB&B

[1] A portion of the McDonald's account was moved to DDB Needham in November 1990.

[2] Account was moved to Hill, Holiday, Connors, Cosmopulos in April 1990.

Source: Video Storyboard Tests' Commercial Break newsletter.

have been dropped by their clients because the ads did not increase sales for the company.

Although awards are still considered a necessary morale booster for creative staffs, a survey of advertising agencies shows that many have pulled back from entering advertising competitions, reserving entries for those shows that have greater acclaim, such as the Clios, the New York Art Directors, the One Show, and the International Advertising Film Festival in Cannes, France. For example, BBDO, which annually enters 14 shows, is getting pickier about its choices. "The rising costs are outrageous and I don't think they're warranted," says creative administrator June Baloutine.

Agencies are not entering competitions for other reasons as well. In these days of awards proliferation, awards no longer seem to impress clients. Michael Lollis, executive vice president and executive creative director at J. Walter Thompson in Atlanta, states, "As there are more and more shows, they become less meaningful. If you enter often enough, you can win something someplace." According to Richard Kirshenbaum, creative director of Kirshenbaum & Bond, "Shows are necessary to keep the creative staff happy. But the costs are so high, it's just not worth entering unless I know the work is brilliant."*

If awards are not reliable measures of great advertising, then what is?

Classics

There are few ads that have stood the test of time. This chapter will discuss the objective and subjective criteria for greatness that these ads have consistently met. Certain ads are simply outstanding; they are classics. Some are from campaigns that have been running for a long time; others are single ads or campaigns that have been around for only a short time. What do all these ads have in common? Good ads work on two levels: They engage the mind of the consumer and at the same time deliver a selling message.

The California Raisins "I Heard It Through the Grapevine" commercials, for example, dominated the AdWatch awareness studies in the late 1980s (see Ad 1.1). The catchy music and the parody of a rhythm-and-blues singing group performing a 1960s hit have made this campaign a favorite of consumers and professionals alike.

The campaigns for Obsession, Nike, and Levi's 501 have each achieved a considerable level of success. Targeted primarily at young men, these ads reflect this group's interests and needs. Moreover, they have used a variety of techniques, such as humor, action, and sex, effectively enough to attract the attention of young males and keep it.

Spokespersons and celebrities have been an important part of many classic ads. Bill Cosby is a successful presenter for a number of companies, and his long-standing relationship with Jell-O has produced a number of winning ads. Ed and Frank, two invented but believable characters for Bartles and Jaymes Wine Coolers, became well-loved stars in their own continuing miniseries. Their "Baseball Tips" commercial, which ran for 2 weeks around the time of the 1988 World Series, reached and affected three times as many people as the average commercial.

These campaigns are widely remembered, not only because they are entertaining, but also because they involve viewers and make them wonder what the campaigns' creators will come up with next. The campaigns also use humor, ranging from soft and gentle to outrageous. Humor is an impor-

*Kathy Ruehle and Barbara Holsonback, "Some Agencies Deciding Awards Not Worth the Cost," *Adweek* (April 30, 1990):1, 10.

AD 1.1
This popular commercial for California raisins was created through a process called claymation. (Courtesy of THE CALIFORNIA RAISINS™, © 1987 CalRab. Licensed by Applause Licensing.)

tant part of some of the other all-time great ads, such as the Federal Express ad featuring the fast-talking executive. Underneath the funny characterizations, however, the Federal Express ads carry a hard-hitting message of dependability: "When it absolutely, positively has to be there overnight."

Great ads often touch emotions other than humor. The AT&T/Long Distance Service "Reach Out and Touch Someone" campaign has been touching emotions since 1979. The messages are warm and sentimental, but more than that, they communicate the idea that it is easy and rewarding to call friends and family at any time.

Other outstanding ads have created memorable characters. Inspector 12 has been holding up the standards for Hanes underwear since 1980. Mikey, the finicky little boy who doesn't like anything, made viewers like Life cereal. The original commercial first ran in 1971 and was brought back in 1981. Even though the original Mikey is now grown up, the commercial has maintained its appeal for several generations of Life consumers.

Children, cats, and puppy dogs are lovable and give a product warm associations. The Oscar Mayer kids have been singing the product's theme song since 1973. The sing-along music contributes to the Oscar Mayer success story.

Often the characters are fictional, like Ed and Frank and Inspector 12. The Concepts and Controversies box entitled "The Demise of Joe Isuzu" takes a look at one of the popular fictional characters of advertising in the late 1980s. Some of these characters, like Charlie the Tuna and the Jolly Green Giant, are total fantasy. But all of them capture the "inherent drama" of the product. Imagine yourself an advertiser who wants to position vegetables to make them acceptable to children. Why not use a cartoon character like a giant to promote them? But giants are fearsome, you think, so how do I make this character appealing to kids? Make him "Jolly." This way a complex message is built into a single cartoon character.

Drama is often an important aspect of successful advertising. One of the most dramatic advertisements ever produced was a commercial for the launch of the Apple Macintosh computer that took on Apple's most serious competitor, IBM. The stark images of the classic George Orwell novel *1984* (Ad 1.2) came alive in this commercial, which only ran once, on the 1984

AD 1.2
This award-winning Apple ad for the Macintosh computers changed America's attitude toward PCs.
(Photo courtesy of Apple Computer, Inc.)

Super Bowl before 100 million viewers. Not only was this ad a captivating drama, it also demonstrated the power of an effective media buy.

Significant images are another important part of advertising. The Mountain Dew campaign (Ad 1.3) has used a stream of successful commercials that depict the lifestyle of the intended audience—teenagers. Since 1980, these commercials have been showing active, lively, appealing teens having fun. But more than that, the water-oriented recreation scenes also say "refreshing," and the imagery is heightened by excellent photography and slow-motion shots of attractive young people in water. An even more effective visual was the Nestea "plunge" that overwhelmed the viewer with the feeling of refreshment.

Perhaps the most successful image advertising of all time, however, is the Marlboro campaign, which has been running since 1955. With overwhelming single-mindedness the campaign has focused on western imagery with cowboys, horses, and ranching. The cowboy myth is a strong and compelling image. This campaign has been successful both as communi-

AD 1.3
One of a series of Mountain Dew ads that were directed toward a teenage audience. (Courtesy of Pepsi Cola Company.)

BO KNOWS GREAT ADVERTISING

Most great ad campaigns require trial-and-error, time, patience, and a good number of scratched ideas until the great idea finally hits. But sometimes a great idea can develop overnight—or over drinks. That is precisely how the popular "Bo Knows" campaign, one of the most visible, talked-about, and hyped celebrity endorsements of the late 1980s, came to be. A few marketing directors from Nike were drinking beer with some creatives from Wieden & Kennedy in a local pub when the inspiration hit. Scott Bedbury, Nike ad director, recalls, "We were talking about the back-to-school [1989] campaign and somehow the conversation got onto the Bos of the world." Bo Derek, Beau Geste, Bo-dacious—they were all tossed out in this casual brainstorming session, when Tom Clark, Nike vice president and marketing director, said "Bo Diddley." By 10:00 the next morning, the concept had been established.

The idea to use Bo Jackson as the Nike spokesperson in this campaign was logical. According to Bedbury, "Bo is probably the athlete most uniquely qualified to promote cross-training." This logic escalated into the popular 60-second spot that featured Bo Jackson's prowess in baseball, football, tennis, hockey, basketball, cycling, running, and weight lifting, and ended with a jam session with rock great Bo Diddley: "Bo, you don't know diddley." Getting Diddley to agree to make the commercial was easy. According to Tim O'Kennedy, Wieden & Kennedy's management supervisor, Bo Diddley is very proud of his name and liked the idea of working with someone else with the same name. Bedbury added that Diddley saw the commercial as an opportunity to expose his music to a younger audience because Nike targets males aged 15 to 24.

The spot only took 4 or 5 days to shoot. The last sequence—5 to 8 seconds of Jackson and Diddley on guitars—took over 3 hours to shoot because, according to Bedbury, "Bo [Jackson] actually began to believe he could play." This gave Bedbury the idea for the next spot in the campaign—the same ad with the ending changed. The new ending is introduced "Six months later," at which time Jackson has learned to play the guitar and earns Bo Diddley's praise: "Bo, you *do* know Diddley." The second ad was developed so that the campaign would not disappear without some kind of style.

The Wieden & Kennedy agency has a policy by which clients who submit creative ideas have to attach $1 to their idea. If the idea is used, the client gets $10 back from the agency. It is unknown whether Bedbury ever really got $10 for the Bo Diddley idea, but he did come up with a "Big Idea" for Nike, and he did so with "a flash of inspiration" —the stuff great advertising is made of.

Source: Adapted from Marcy Magiera, "How Bo Learned Diddley," *Advertising Age* (March 5, 1990):S-2, S-7.

cation and as a marketing effort. It has helped to make Marlboro the best-selling cigarette in the world.

Characteristics of Great Ads

What do you think makes an ad great? And what turns great ads into classics? What makes certain ads stand out in people's minds? And why do some ads continue to run for years, sometimes even for decades? From this discussion it should be clear that great advertising employs a variety of techniques: celebrities and spokespersons, fantasy characters, children and puppies, music, drama, significant imagery, and creative media buying. Advertising is complicated, and the rest of this book will try to explain how all of these factors are interwoven to create great advertising. The premise of this book, however, is that three broad dimensions characterize great advertising: strategy, creativity, and execution (See Ad 1.4). This book is built around these three dimensions.

Strategy. Every great ad is strategically sound. In other words, it is carefully directed to a certain audience, it is driven by specific objectives, its message is crafted to speak to that audience's most important concerns, and it is run in media that will most effectively reach that audience. The measure of an ad's success is how well it achieves its goals, whether they be increased sales, memorability, attitude change, or brand awareness.

The Mountain Dew commercials, for example, are perfectly on target for the teenage audience. The crazy characters and situations in the Federal Express ads bring to life a very important selling premise about the essence of dependability. Mikey likes Life, so it must be good.

Creativity. The *creative concept* is a central idea that gets your attention and sticks in your memory. Every one of the ads we've discussed has a Big Idea that is creative and original. Frank and Ed are unique characters, as is the Jolly Green Giant. Isuzu took the stereotype of the untrustworthy car salesman and created the unforgettable Joe Isuzu.

AD 1.4
The fast-talking executive ads for Federal Express are examples of great advertising (©1981 Federal Express Corporation.)

Ally & Gargano

CLIENT: FEDERAL EXPRESS CORP.
PRODUCT: AIR FREIGHT
TITLE: "FAST PACED WORLD"
COMMERCIAL NO.: QFAS 1326 (:30)
DATE APPROVED: 7/14/81

1. MR. SPLEEN: (OC) Okay Eunice, travel plans, I need to be in New York on Monday, LA on Tuesday, New York on Wednesday, LA on Thursday,

2. and New York on Friday. Got it? So you want to work here, well what makes you think you deserve a job here?

3. GUY: Well sir I think on my feet, I'm good with figures and I have a sharp mind.

4. SPLEEN: Excellent, can you start Monday?

5. (OC): And in conclusion, Jim, Bill, Bob and Ted,

6. business is business so let's get to work. Thank you for taking this meeting.

7. (OC): Peter you did a bang-up job, I'm putting you in charge of Pittsburgh.

8. PETER: (OC) Pittsburgh's perfect. SPLEEN: I know it's perfect, Peter, that's why I picked Pittsburgh. Pittsburgh's perfect, Peter, May I call you Pete?

9. (OC): Congratulations on your deal in Denver David.

10. I'm putting you down to deal in Dallas. ANNCR: (VO) In this fast moving, high pressure, get-it-done yesterday world,

11. aren't you glad there's one company that can keep up with it all?

12. Federal Express. (SFX) When it absolutely, positively has to be there overnight.

THE DEMISE OF JOE ISUZU

For every classic ad there is a time when it must be quietly, calmly laid to rest. And that's no lie. On August 13, 1990, American Isuzu Motors aired a new ad campaign, the first in 4 years not to feature its lying "Joe Isuzu" pitchman. Venturing out without Joe, a likable but insincere guy who distorted the benefits of Isuzu cars and trucks, was a risky move. The character, played by comic actor David Leisure, established little-known Isuzu in the minds of American car buyers. The humorous, clever commercials routinely topped consumer polls of favorite ad campaigns.

Starting with the simple premise that nobody believes a car salesman, Della Femina, Travisano & Partners in Los Angeles created a sort of cult figure in Joe Isuzu, who first appeared in a regional dealer spot for American Isuzu Motors in 1985. In "Liar," "Mom," and other famous spots, Joe Isuzu made outrageous claims, such as "you will get a free house when you buy a car." In the later Joe Isuzu ads the focus was more on the car itself. For example, in "Bullet" Isuzu's Turbo Impulse surpasses a speeding bullet, and in "The Queen" Joe stands outside Buckingham Palace, quoting the price of the small, inexpensive I Mark as "seven pounds, nine ounces."

In an interview at Della Femina McNamee's office, where Isuzu's ads are cooked up, executives involved in the launch of the new campaign described why Joe got the ax: Isuzu Cars—unlike Isuzu trucks —don't sell well, and Joe's getting the blame. "It was our judgment that Joe doesn't do as good a job selling passenger cars as he does trucks. Isuzu's sporty Impulse car, for example, is a pretty serious car. It's in a highly competitive segment, and the people who are interested in it see a dichotomy between the Joe Isuzu character and that kind of product," says Fritz Kern, senior vice president at American Isuzu.

Some marketing specialists say dropping Joe is a mistake, that although Isuzu has tired of the campaign, consumers haven't. "I don't think they should be chucking the whole concept. They have spent 4 years establishing him. If he's doing a good job selling trucks, why not keep him?" says David Vadehra, president of Video Storyboard Tests, Inc. "To get through the clutter of auto advertising is a horrendous challenge. These people did it brilliantly," says Clive Chajet, chairman and chief executive officer at Lippincott & Margulies. "I'm surprised that they are walking away from all that equity."

But Peter Stranger, president of Della Femina, insisted that the decision to drop Joe wasn't made lightly. "There was no grand scheme to assassinate Joe Isuzu," he said. "Every year we assessed how successful he was being. You don't want to stay too long and you don't want to get out too early. The bigger mistake would be to stay too long."

Source: Adapted from Thomas R. King, "Isuzu Ends Its Popular Liar Campaign," *The Wall Street Journal* (August 2, 1990):B4.

A concern for creative thinking drives the entire field of advertising. Planning the strategy calls for creative problem solving; the research efforts are creative; the buying and placing of ads in the media are creative. Advertising is an exciting field because of the constant demand for creative solutions to media and message problems.

PRINCIPLE
Great ads are original, strategically sound, and perfectly executed.

Execution.   Finally, every great ad is well executed. That means the craftsmanship is impressive. The details, the techniques, and the production values have all been fine-tuned. Many of these techniques are experimental, such as the dancing claymation raisins. There is more to execution than technology, however. The warm touch in the AT&T commercials is a delicate emotional effect. It is sensitive without being overly sentimental or manipulative.

Good advertisers know that how you say it is just as important as what you say. *What you say* comes from strategy, whereas *how you say it* is a product of creativity and execution. The great ads, then, are ads that (1) are strategically sound, (2) have an original creative concept, and (3) use exactly the right execution for the message. Strategy, creativity, and execution —these are the qualities that turn great ads into classics.

THE WORLD OF ADVERTISING

Defining Advertising

advertising *Paid nonpersonal communication from an identified sponsor using mass media to persuade or influence an audience.*

What is advertising? What are its important dimensions? The standard definition of advertising includes six elements. Advertising is a *paid form of communication,* although some forms of advertising, such as public service, use donated space and time. Not only is the message paid for, but the *sponsor is identified.* In some cases the point of the message is simply to make consumers aware of the product or company, although most advertising tries to *persuade or influence* the consumer to do something. The message is conveyed through many different kinds of *mass media* reaching a large *audience* of potential consumers. Because advertising is a form of mass communication, it is also *nonpersonal.* A definition of **advertising,** then, would include all six of those features:

> Advertising is *paid nonpersonal communication* from an identified *sponsor* using *mass media* to *persuade or influence* an *audience.*

In an ideal world every manufacturer would be able to talk one-on-one with every consumer about the product or service being offered for sale. Personal selling approaches that idea, but it is very expensive. Calls made by salespeople can cost well in excess of $150.

Marketers who have products and services for sale avoid the enormous expense of personal contact by using mass media to convey their messages. There the costs, for *time* in broadcast media and for *space* in print media, are spread over the tremendous number of people that these media reach. For example, $650,000 may sound like a lot of money for one ad on the Super Bowl, but when you consider that the advertisers are reaching over 100 million people, the cost is not extreme.

Types of Advertising

Advertising is complex because so many diverse advertisers try to reach so many different types of audiences.

Brand Advertising. The most visible type of advertising is *national consumer advertising.* Another name for this is *brand advertising,* which focuses on the development of a long-term brand identity and image. It tries to develop a distinctive brand image for a product.

Retail Advertising. In contrast, *retail advertising* is local and focuses on the store where a variety of products can be purchased or where a service is offered. The message announces products that are available locally, stimulates store traffic, and tries to create a distinctive image for the store. Retail advertising emphasizes price, availability, location, and hours of operation.

Political Advertising. *Political advertising* is used by politicians to persuade people to vote for them and therefore is an important part of the political process in the United States and other democratic countries that permit candidate advertising. Although it is an important source of communication for voters, some critics are concerned that political advertising tends to focus more on image than on issues.

Directory Advertising.   Another type of advertising is called directional because people refer to it to find out how to buy a product or service. The best-known form of *directory advertising* is the Yellow Pages, although there are many different kinds of directories that perform the same function.

Direct-Response Advertising.   *Direct-response advertising* can use any advertising medium, including direct mail, but the message is different from that of national and retail advertising in that it tries to stimulate a sale directly. The consumer can respond by telephone or mail, and the product is delivered directly to the consumer by mail or some other carrier.

Business-to-Business Advertising.   *Business-to-business advertising* includes messages directed at retailers, wholesalers, and distributors, as well as industrial purchasers and professionals such as lawyers and physicians. Business advertising tends to be concentrated in business publications or professional journals.

Institutional Advertising.   *Institutional advertising* is also called *corporate advertising.* The focus of these messages is on establishing a corporate identity or on winning the public over to the organization's point of view.

Public Service Advertising.   *Public service advertising* communicates a message on behalf of some good cause, such as a drug-free America or preventing child abuse. These advertisements are created for free by advertising professionals, and the space and time are donated by the media.

As you can see, there isn't just one kind of advertising; in fact, advertising is a large and varied industry. All of these areas demand creative, original messages that are strategically sound and well executed. In the chapters to come, all of these types of advertising will be discussed in more depth.

Roles of Advertising

Advertising can also be explained in terms of the roles it plays in business and in society. Four different roles have been identified for advertising:

1. Marketing role
2. Communication role
3. Economic role
4. Societal role

The Marketing Role.   Marketing is the strategic process a business uses to satisfy consumer needs and wants through goods and services. The particular consumers at whom the company directs its marketing effort constitute the *target market.* The tools available to marketing include the product, its price, and the means used to deliver the product, or the place. Marketing also includes a mechanism for communicating this information to the consumer, which is called *marketing communication,* or promotion. These four tools are collectively referred to as the *marketing mix* or the *4 Ps.* Marketing communication is further broken down into four related communication techniques: advertising, sales promotion, public relations, and personal selling. Thus advertising is only one element in a company's overall marketing communication program, although it is the most visible. The marketing role will be discussed in depth in Chapter 3.

PRINCIPLE
Advertising provides information that helps match buyers and sellers in the marketplace.

The Communication Role.   Advertising is a form of mass communication. It transmits different types of market information to match buyers and sellers in the marketplace. Advertising both informs and transforms the product by creating an image that goes beyond straightforward facts. Specific suggestions about how to accomplish these tasks will be discussed in later chapters on creating messages.

The Economic Role. The two major schools of thought concerning the effects of advertising on the economy are the market power school and the market competition school.* According to the market power school, advertising is a persuasive communication tool used by marketers to distract consumers' attention from the price of the product. In contrast, the market competition school sees advertising as a source of information that increases consumers' price sensitivity and stimulates competition.

Actually, little is known about the true nature of advertising in the economy. Charles Sandage, an advertising professor, provides a different perspective. He sees the economic role of advertising as "helping society to achieve abundance by informing and persuading members of society with respect to products, services, and ideals."† In addition, he argues that advertising assists in "the development of judgment on the part of consumers in their purchase practices."

The Societal Role. Advertising also has a number of social roles. It informs us about new and improved products and teaches us how to use these innovations. It helps us compare products and features and make informed consumer decisions. It mirrors fashion and design trends and contributes to our aesthetic sense.

Advertising tends to flourish in societies that enjoy some level of economic abundance, that is, in which supply exceeds demand. It is at this point that advertising moves from being a simple informational service (telling consumers where they can find the product) to being a message designated to create a demand for a particular brand.

The question is: Does advertising follow trends or does it lead them? At what point does advertising cross the line between *reflecting* social values and *creating* social values? Critics argue that advertising has repeatedly crossed this line and has evolved into an instrument of social control. Although these concerns are not new, the increasing power of advertising, both in terms of money (we spend more annually educating consumers than we spend education our children) and in terms of communication dominance (the mass media can no longer survive without advertising support), has made these concerns more prominent than ever.

Advertising and Manipulation Can advertising manipulate people? Some critics argue that advertising has the power to dictate how people behave. They believe that, even if an individual ad cannot control our behavior, the cumulative effects of nonstop television, radio, print, and outdoor ads can be overwhelming.

Although certain groups of people, such as young children, the less educated, and the elderly, might be more susceptible to certain kinds of advertising, it is hard to conclude that a particular ad or series of ads caused, tricked, or coerced anyone into making a particular buying decision. There is no solid evidence for the manipulative power of advertising because so many other factors contribute to the choices we make.

Although advertising does attempt to persuade, most people are

---

*John M. Vernon, "Concentration, Promoting, and Market Share Stability in the Pharmaceutical Industry," *Journal of Industrial Economics.* (July 1971):146–266.
†Charles H. Sandage, "Some Institutional Aspects of Advertising," *Journal of Advertising,* Vol. 1, No. 1 (1973):9.

aware that advertisers are biased in favor of their own products and learn how to handle persuasive advertising in their daily lives. Manipulation and other ethical issues will be discussed in more detail in Chapter 2.

Functions of Advertising

Not all advertising attempts to accomplish the same objectives. Although each ad or campaign tries to reach goals unique to its sponsor, there are two basic functions that advertising performs, along with several subfunctions.

Product advertising aims to inform or stimulate the market about the sponsor's product(s). The intent is clearly to sell a particular product, to the exclusion of competitors' products. Conversely, *institutional advertising* is designed to create a positive attitude toward the seller. The intent is to promote the sponsoring organization rather than the things it sells.

Direct Action versus Indirect Action. Product advertising may be either direct-action or indirect-action advertising. *Direct-action advertising* is intended to produce a quick response. Ads that include a coupon with an expiration date, or a sale with an expiration date, or an 800 number, or a mail-in order blank fall under this heading. *Indirect-action advertising* is designed to stimulate demand over a longer period of time. These advertisements inform customers that the product exists, indicate its benefits, state where it can be purchased, remind customers to repurchase, and reinforce this decision.

Primary versus Selective. Product advertising can also be primary or selective. *Primary adverting* aims to promote demand for a generic product. Thus ads by the American Raisin Growers Association emphasize raisins; it really doesn't matter to the association which brand of raisins you purchase. *Selective adverting* attempts to create demand for a particular brand. It typically follows primary advertising, which more or less sets the stage for selective advertising.

Commercial versus Noncommercial. Finally, product advertising can serve either a commercial or a noncommecial function. *Commercial advertising* promotes a product with the intent of making a profit. Most of the advertising you see in the mass media falls under this heading. In contrast, *noncommercial advertising* tends to be sponsored by organizations that are not in business to make money. Charities and nonprofit organizations such as museums produce this type of advertising. Although the goal may be to raise money for a particular cause, it could just as easily be the donation of time or ideas.

As noted, rather than selling a particular product, institutional advertising aims to establish a high level of goodwill. *Public relations institutional advertising* attempts to create a favorable image of the firm among employees, customers, stockholders, or the general public. Texaco Petroleum, for example, runs ads that highlight the company's attempts to protect the environment.

*T*HE THREE PLAYERS

In addition to the types of advertising and their various roles and functions, advertising can be defined in terms of those who play important roles in bringing ads to the consumer. The three primary players in the advertising world are:

1. The advertiser
2. The advertising agency
3. The media

The Advertiser

advertiser *The individual or organization that initiates the advertising process.*

Advertising begins with the **advertiser**—the individual or organization that usually initiates the advertising process. The advertiser also makes the final decisions about whom the advertising will be directed to, the media in which it will appear, the size of the advertising budget, and the duration of the campaign.

We can only estimate how much money is spent annually by advertisers. In 1991 expenditures were expected to exceed $132 billion, more than double the figure of 1980 but less than the $136 billion forecast the previous December. The final ad expenditures for 1990 showed 3.8 percent growth instead of the 4.9 percent gain estimated earlier. This slowdown was attributed to the drastic trimming of ad budgets as a result of the Mideast situation and the beginning of the recession. Newspapers experienced their worst year in 1990 since 1961 due to the retail slump and decline in help-wanted and real estate ads. In addition, many marketers cut back on their usual level of holiday promotions due to the economic slowdown. Ads for toys, perfumes, expensive watches, and cameras were particularly below previous levels. This downward trend was expected to be temporary, however. Early forecasts for 1992 were optimistic. Economic recovery, pent-up consumer demand, political elections, and the Olympics were all expected to fuel a reexpansion in advertising.*

Types of Advertisers. There are a number of different types of advertisers. Some manufacture the product or service; others sell manufacturers' products to the ultimate consumer; some use advertising to represent themselves and the services they provide; and others provide a service to the public. The various businesses that perform these tasks fall into four categories: manufacturers, resellers, individuals, and institutions.

Manufacturers *Manufacturers* actually make the product or service and distribute it to resellers or ultimate users for a profit. They usually build their advertising around a product brand name. Because so much money is spent on advertising sponsored by manufacturers, we are most familiar with this type of advertising.

Resellers *Resellers* are wholesalers and retailers who distribute the manufacturers' products to other resellers or to the ultimate user. Wholesalers promote their goods through personal selling and possess little expertise in advertising. Conversely, retailers advertise a great deal, either cooperatively with manufacturers or independently.

Individuals An *individual* advertiser is a private citizen who wishes to sell a personal product for a profit, to request a particular need, or to express a perspective or an idea. For example, a college student selling a motorcycle would place a classified ad in the school newspaper. This same student may advertise for collector baseball cards in a hobby magazine. Politicians often advertise to voters to express their position on certain issues.

---

*Robert J. Coen, "Coen: Little Ad Growth," *Advertising Age* (May 6, 1991):1, 16.

PAT CAFFERATA, PRESIDENT AND CEO, YOUNG & RUBICAM CHICAGO

As chief executive officer of the advertising firm of Young & Rubicam Chicago, Pat Cafferata becomes involved in various advertising activities with clients throughout the country. Here she describes a typically hectic day in the world of advertising.

5:30 A.M.   Arose.

Picked up *Chicago Tribune* on way to Evanston Athletic Club. Did workout and, while riding Life Cycle, read *The Tribune's* Business Section with special attention to George Lazarus's column on marketing and advertising. Returned home to get ready for work.

7:45 A.M.   Arrived at my office. Made calls to Y&R corporate offices in New York regarding account executive training program and my Chicago office Business Plan for 1991.

8:30 A.M.   Chaired Membership Committee meeting for the Chicago Advertising Federation. Focus was on how to encourage more corporate memberships, based on the Federation's government lobbying efforts on tax and free speech issues.

9:30 A.M.   Reviewed print and television campaigns to be presented to our Jenn-Air client later this week.

10:30 A.M.   Met with my assistant to resolve a number of issues: my travel arrangements for trip to Y&R New York; signed salary increase approval forms for three employees; discussed timing for our Executive Committee meeting; decided on restaurant for prospective client dinner; selected gift for employee in the hospital. (We were interrupted by phone calls from a client to discuss a television production estimate and by the President of Y&R New York to discuss a client conflict issue.)

11:30 A.M.   Did final preparation for a new business presentation at 1:30 in the afternoon. (Revised the agenda; suggested final changes to storyboards; rehearsed the Media Director's presentation; rearranged the conference room tables and chairs; checked the videotape of commercials to be shown in the credentials part of the meeting.)

12:45 P.M.   Ate salad while adding final touches to my part of new business presentation. Returned two phone calls.

1:30 P.M.   Participated in new business presentation. Conducted a short debriefing with Y&R Chicago's participants to evaluate the meeting and determine next steps in soliciting the prospective client.

3:30 P.M.   Conducted an interview with a prospective account supervisor to work on our Brach's account.

4:30 P.M.   Returned five phone calls. Reached only one person. Left messages for the other four.

5:00 P.M.   Met with our Director of Client Services and Executive Creative Director to review strategies and creative development progress for Adidas and Hartmarx accounts.

6:15 P.M.   Read day's mail and wrote memo to staff on upcoming Christmas party.

7:00 P.M.   Met my husband and a client and his wife for dinner at the Everest Room.

Source: Courtesy of Pat Cafferata

TABLE 1.2
Who's on Top in 1990 Gross Income

	Top 10 Advertising Organizations				Top 10 U.S. Agency Brands		
Rank	Organization	Worldwide Gross Income	% Change	Rank	Agency	U.S. Gross Income	% Change
1	WPP Group	$2,712.0	12.9	1	Leo Burnett Co.	$299.3	3.7
2	Saatchi & Saatchi Co.	1,729.3	9.7	2	Saatchi & Saatchi Advertising Worldwide	270.7	10.1
3	Interpublic Group of Cos.	1,649.8	10.4	3	Foote, Cone & Belding Communications	262.7	4.6
4	Omnicom Group	1,335.5	13.4	4	Grey Advertising	256.3	6.5
5	Dentsu Inc.	1,254.8	(0.6)	5	J. Walter Thompson Co.	251.7	7.1
6	Young & Rubicam	1,073.6	16.0	6	Ogilvy & Mather Worldwide	229.7	2.5
7	Eurocom Group	748.5	58.5	7	Young & Rubicam	216.6	2.7
8	Hakubodo Inc.	586.3	0.1	8	McCann-Erickson Worldwide	210.1	0.5
9	Grey Advertising	583.3	19.1	9	BBDO Worldwide	207.1	10.8
10	Foote, Cone & Belding Communications	536.2	5.9	10	D'Arcy Masius Benton & Bowles	204.4	14.6

Note: Dollars are in millions.

Source: Advertising Age (March 25, 1991):S-1. Copyright Crain Communications Inc.

Institutions   The last group of advertisers includes *institutions, government agencies,* and *social groups.* They are distinguished from the other categories in that their primary objective is not to sell a product or generate profits but rather to raise issues, influence ideas, affect legislation, provide a social service, or alter behavior in ways that are seen as socially desirable. Examples are Mothers Against Drunk Drivers (MADD), the Southern Baptist Convention, the Metropolitan Museum of Art, a local school board, the U.S. Army, the Teamsters Union, and a government-sponsored campaign telling us to "get out and vote."

The Advertising Agency

PRINCIPLE
The agency-client partnership is the dominant organizational arrangement in advertising.

The second key player in the advertising world is the advertising agency. Advertisers hire independent agencies to plan and implement part or all of their advertising effort. The agency-client partnership is the dominant organizational arrangement in advertising.

There are approximately 10,000 advertising agencies in the United States. One report indicated that fewer than 12 percent of these agencies accounted for over 84 percent of agency gross income.* Ongoing mergers and acquisitions are continually changing the rankings, but Young & Rubicam was the top agency worldwide in 1990, with gross income of over $1 billion. (see Table 1.2).† Rankings change when you look at agency megagroups. As listed in Table 1.3, WPP Group PLC was the industry leader in

*Gary Levin, "Agency Staffing Keeps Even Keel in '90," *Advertising Age* (January 21, 1991): S-1.
†*Advertising Age* (March 25, 1991):S-1.

TABLE 1.3
World's Top 10 Advertising Organizations
Ranked by Equity Gross Income

Rank '90	Rank '89	Advertising Organization, Headquarters	U.S.-Based Agencies Included	Worldwide Capitalized Billings 1990	1989	% Change
1	1	*WPP Group,* London	Ogilvy & Mather Worldwide; Ogilvy & Mather Direct Response; J. Walter Thompson Co.; Thompson Recruitment; Brouillard Communications; Scali, McCabe, Sloves; Fallon McElligott; Martin Agency.	$18,095.0	$16,052.0	12.7
2	2	*Saatchi & Saatchi Co.,* London	Saatchi & Saatchi Advertising Worldwide; AC&R Advertising; Cadwell Davis Partners; Cliff Freeman & Partners; Conill Advertising; Klemtner Advertising; Rumrill-Hoyt; Team One; Backer Spielvogel Bates Wordwide; Campbell-Mithun-Esty; Kobs & Draft.	11,861.7	10,802.4	9.8
3	3	*Interpublic Group of Cos.,* New York	McCann-Erickson Worldwide; Lintas:Worldwide; Dailey & Associates; Laurence, Charles, Free & Lawson; Lowe & Partners; Fahlgren Martin.	11,025.3	9,984.6	10.4
4	5	*Omnicom Group,* New York	BBDO Worldwide; Baxter, Gurian & Mazzei; Frank J. Corbett Inc.; Doremus & Co.; Lavey/Wolff/Swift; Tracy-Locke; Rapp Collins Marcoa; DDB Needham Worldwide; Bernard Hodes Group; Kallir, Philips, Ross.	9,699.6	8,405.3	15.4
5	4	*Dentsu, Inc.,* Tokyo	DCA Advertising	9,671.6	9,695.5	(0.2)
6	6	*Young & Rubicam,* New York	Young & Rubicam; Cato Johnson Worldwide; Chapman Direct; Sudler & Hennessey; Creswell, Munsell, Fultz & Zirbel; Wunderman Worldwide; Dentsu, Young & Rubicam Partnerships (including Y&R's 50% equity in Lord, Dentsu & Partners).	8,000.7	6,652.0	20.3
7	11	*Eurocom Group,* Paris	Della Femina, McNamee	5,065.7	3,195.5	58.5
8	7	*Hakuhodo Inc.,* Tokyo	Hakuhodo Advertising America	4,529.4	4,449.2	1.8
9	9	*Grey Advertising,* New York	Grey Advertising	3,910.4	3,267.4	19.7
10	8	*Foote, Cone & Belding Communications,* Chicago	Foote, Cone & Belding Communications; Albert Frank-Guenther Law; IMPACT; Vicom/FCB; Publicis-FCB Communications (49%).	3,554.8	3,371.8	5.4

Notes: Dollars are in millions. Some of the top 50 hold minority equity in each other as follows: Publicis-FCB Communications is 49% owned by Foote, Cone & Belding Communications; Omnicom Group owns 46.67% of Clemenger/BBDO; BDDP Worldwide own 40% of Wells, Rich, Greene; Young & Rubicam and Dentsu Inc. each own 50% of Dentsu, Young & Rubicam Partnerships.

Source: Advertising Age (March 25, 1991):S-8. Copyright Crain Communications Inc.

1990, with worldwide billings of over $18 billion.* These megagroups are actually holding companies that include the parent agency and all of its subsidiaries.

An advertiser uses an outside agency because it believes the agency will be more effective and efficient in creating an individual commercial or a complete campaign. The strength of an agency is its resources, primarily in the form of creative expertise, media knowledge, and advertising strategy. Chapter 4 will discuss agencies in more detail.

Large advertisers—either companies or organizations—are involved in the advertising process in one of two ways: (1) through their advertising department or (2) through their in-house agency.

The Advertising Department. The most common organizational arrangement in a large business is the *advertising department.* The primary corporate responsibility for advertising lies with the *advertising manager,* or *advertising director,* who usually reports to the *director of marketing.* In the typical multiple-brand, consumer-products company, responsibility is divided by brand, with each brand managed by a *brand manager.* The brand manager is the business leader for the brand and has the ultimate responsibility for sales, product development, budget, and profits, as well as for advertising and other promotions. The brand manager, or advertising director, along with the advertising agency, develops the advertising strategy.

The advertising is usually presented by the agency to the brand manager and the director of advertising. The director of advertising, a specialist in recognizing and supporting effective advertising, advises the brand manager. Frequently the advertising director is responsible for approving advertising before it undergoes preliminary testing with real consumers.

PRINCIPLE ——————
The advertiser's ad manager is in charge of the total advertising program.

The advertising manager organizes and staffs the advertising department, selects the advertising agency, and coordinates efforts with other departments within the company and businesses outside the organization. The advertising manager is also in charge of advertising control, which involves checking on such things as: Have the ads been run? At the right time, the right size, and in the right place? Was the ad produced exactly the way the company wanted? Was the work done within the budget? Most importantly, did the advertisement reach its objectives?

Who performs these tasks varies within the industry and the size of the business. The small retailer, for example, might have one person (often the owner) laying out the ad, writing the copy, and selecting the media. Physical production of the ad may be farmed out to freelancers or to the local media. Large retailers have more complete advertising departments and may have specialists on staff to do much of the work in house. Manufacturers tend to rely more on ad agencies to perform these tasks, with the advertising manager acting as a liaison between the company and the agency.

in-house agency *An advertising department on the advertiser's staff that handles most, if not all, of the functions of an outside agency.*

The In-House Agency. Companies that need closer control over the advertising have their own in-house agencies. Large retailers, for example, find that doing their own advertising provides cost savings as well as the ability to make fast-breaking local deadlines. An **in-house agency** performs most, and sometimes all, of the functions of an outside advertising agency. According to the American Association of Advertising Agencies (AAAA), the percentage of total business handled by in-house agencies remained fairly constant in the late 1980s at about 5 percent.†

Advertising Age (March 25, 1991):S-8.
†C. Craig Endicott, "Sales Surge 11% for Media Giants," *Advertising Age* (June 29, 1987):S-1.

Media	Billings reported by 476 agencies			Media by percent of total	
PRINT	**1990**	**1989**	**% chg**	**1990**	**1989**
Newspaper	$2,807.7	$2,850.2	(1.5)	8.3	9.1
Magazine	4,854.5	4,635.5	4.7	14.4	14.8
Sunday newspaper magazine	111.2	91.6	21.4	0.3	0.3
Business publication	889.8	894.4	(0.5)	2.6	2.9
Medical journal	468.8	486.6	(3.7)	1.4	1.6
Farm publication	47.5	47.1	0.8	0.1	0.2
Subtotal print	9,179.5	9,005.4	1.9	27.1	28.8
BROADCAST					
Spot TV*	8,490.7	7,680.7	10.5	25.1	24.6
Network TV	10,208.8	9,704.7	5.2	30.2	31.1
Cable TV	1,020.0	723.3	41.0	3.0	2.3
Syndicated TV	599.7	440.4	36.2	1.8	1.4
Spot radio*	2,211.1	2,126.4	4.0	6.5	6.8
Network radio	487.4	NA	NA	1.4	NA
Subtotal broadcast	23,017.6	20,863.2	10.3	68.1	66.8
OTHER					
Outdoor	729.6	654.1	11.5	2.2	2.1
Transit	29.2	26.0	12.3	0.1	0.1
Yellow pages	866.2	691.2	25.3	2.6	2.2
Subtotal other	1,625.1	1,371.3	18.5	4.8	4.4
TOTAL	33,822.2	31,239.9	8.3	100.0	100.0

* Figures may be slightly high because some agencies combine network, syndicated and cable TV billings into spot, and network radio into spot radio.
NOTES: Dollars are in millions. Information in this chart is compiled from media breakouts supplied by 476 of 558 U.S.-based agencies. Not all agencies break out media for AA.

FIGURE 1.2
U.S. media billings by category.   *Source: Advertising Age* (March 25, 1991):S.54. Copyright Crain Communications Inc.

Most in-house agencies are found in retailing, for several reasons. First, retailers tend to operate under small profit margins and find they can save money by doing their own advertising. Second, retailers often receive a great many advertising materials either free or at a reduced cost from manufacturers and trade associations. Local media, for example, will provide creative and production assistance for free. Third, the timetable for retailing tends to be much tighter than that for national advertising. Retailers often create complete campaigns in hours, whereas advertising agencies may take weeks or months.

The Media

The third player in the advertising world is the media used by advertisers. The **media** are the channels of communication that carry the messages from the advertiser to the audience. Media organizations are organized to sell space (in print media) and time (in broadcast media). A media representative meets with the agency media buyers to convince them that the medium is a good advertising vehicle for their client's message. The most frequently used advertising media are newspapers, television, radio, magazines, out-of-home media such as outdoor and transit, and direct response. The primary media used in advertising are shown in Figure 1.2.

Media must deliver advertising messages in a way that is consistent with the creative effort. Media staff gather relevant information about their audiences so the message can be matched with the medium. Media also need to sell the product to prospective advertisers. Media representatives negotiate directly with the advertiser or work through the agency and its media department. They usually initiate the selling effort and personally call on the decision makers.

THE EVOLUTION OF ADVERTISING

Now that we have discussed the factors of great advertising and introduced the roles and functions of advertising, advertisers, agencies, and the media,

FIGURE 1.3
The evolution of advertising.

	People	Time	Events		People	Time	Events
Ancient Period			Signs	**Modern Period**	E.E. Calkins	1895	Image Copy
			Criers		John B. Kennedy	1904	Hard-Sell Copy
			Sequis		Claude Hopkins	1910	Reason-Why Copy
	Johannes Gutenberg	1441	Movable Type		Albert Lasker	1904 to 1944	Great Advertising Executive
	Wm. Claxton	1477	First Ad in English		Theodore MacManus	1910	Atmosphere Advertising
		1625	First Ad in English Newspaper			1914	FTC act Passed
		1655	Term Advertising Introduced			1917	Am. Assoc. of Advt. formed
		1704	First U.S. Newspaper to Carry Ads.		Stanley/Helen Resor	1920	Intro. Psych./Res.
	Volney Palmer	1841	First Ad Sales Agent		Raymond Rubicam	1923	Y&R Formed
Formative Period	George Rowell	1850	First Ad W/S			1926	Commercial Radio
	Charles Bates	1871	First Formal Agency			1940	Selling Strategems
	Francis Ayer	1875	Fixed Commission			1947	Commercial Television
	John Powers	1880	First Great Copywriter		Rosser Reeves Marion Harber	1950s	Mergers, Research and Hard Sell
	E.C. Allen	1887	Magazine Advertising		Leo Burnett David Ogilvy	1960s	High Creativity
	J. Walter Thompson	1891	First Account Executive		William Bernbach	1970s	Back to the 50s
						1980s	Mergers and Creativity
						1990s	Accountability and Globalization

let's look at how these roles and players developed historically.* The key players and events that influenced the development of advertising are listed in Figure 1.3.

The Ancient Period

Persuasive communication has been around since early times. Inscriptions on tablets, walls, and papyrus from ancient Babylonia, Egypt, and Greece carry messages listing available products and upcoming events and announcing rewards for the return of runaway slaves.

Because of widespread illiteracy before the age of print, most messages were actually delivered by *criers* who stood on street corners shouting the wares of the sponsor. Stores, and the merchandise they carried, were identified by signs. Information rather than persuasion was the objective of the early commercial messages.

The Age of Print

The invention of movable type by Johannes Gutenberg around 1440 moved society toward a new level of communication—mass communication. No longer restricted by the time required by a scribe to hand-letter a single message, advertising could now be mass-produced. The availability of printed media to a greater number of people increased the level of literacy, which, in turn, encouraged more businesses to advertise. In terms of media, the early printed advertisements included posters, handbills, and classified advertisements in newspapers. Ad 1.5 is an example of an early print ad from the fifteenth century. The first printed advertisement in English appeared in London around 1472 tacked to church doors. The product advertised was a prayer book for sale.

The word *advertisement* first appeared around 1655. It was used in the Bible to indicate notification or warning. Book publishers, for example, headed most of their announcements with the term, and by 1660 it was generally used as a heading for commercial information, primarily by store owners. The messages continued to be simple and informative through the 1700s and into the 1800s.

*Much of this historical review was adapted from Stephen Fox, *The Mirror Makers* (New York: Vintage Books, 1985).

PRINCIPLE _____
Information rather than persuasion was the objective of early commercial messages.

PRINCIPLE _____
The invention of movable type ushered in mass literacy, mass communication, and, ultimately, advertising.

AD 1.5
An early English ad written by William Caxton in 1477. *Source:* Alex Groner, *The American Heritage History of American Business and Industry* (New York: American Heritage Publishing Co., 1972);19. (Courtesy of Bodleian Library, Oxford, U.K.)

The culmination of the age of print was the development of the news-paper. The very first U.S. newspaper was titled *Public Occurrences both Forreign and Domestick;* it appeared in 1690 and only lasted one issue. In 1704 the *Boston Newsletter* was the first paper to carry an ad, which offered a reward for the capture of a thief. James and Benjamin Franklin, early Colonial printers, started the *New England Courant* in 1721. By the time of the American Revolution, there were over 30 newspapers in the United States. The first daily newspaper was *The Pennsylvania Evening Post and Daily Advertiser,* which appeared in 1783.

The Formative Years

The mid-1800s marked the beginning of the development of the advertising industry in the United States. The emerging importance and growth of advertising during this period resulted from a number of social and technological developments associated with the Industrial Revolution.

The Age of Mass Marketing.

Because of inventions that increased productivity, such as the internal combustion engine and the cotton gin, manufacturers were able to mass-produce goods of uniform quality. The resulting excess production, however, could be profitable only if it attracted customers living beyond the local markets. Fortunately, the long-distance transportation network of rivers and canals was being replaced in mid-century by a much speedier system of roads and railroads.

All that remained for modern advertising to do was to devise an effective and efficient communication system that could reach a widely dispersed marketplace. National media developed as the country's transportation system grew. At about the same time a number of new technologies emerged that greatly facilitated mass marketing and mass communications. Most notably, the telegraph, the telephone, and the typewriter provided dramatic improvements in mass-message delivery. The early advertising experts, such as Volney Palmer, the first "adman," functioned strictly as *media brokers.* Palmer established himself as an "agent" in 1841 in Philadelphia, and opened a branch office in Boston in 1845 and New York in 1849, charging a commission for placing ads in newspapers. Thoroughly familiar with all the periodicals and their rates, these early media brokers had a keen ability to negotiate. They received their commissions out of the fees paid by publishers. The messages were prepared primarily by the advertisers or writers they hired directly and often featured exaggerated and outrageous claims.

By the late nineteenth century the advertising profession was more fully developed. Agencies had taken on the role of convincing manufactures to advertise their products. Ads had assumed a more complete informational and educational role. Copywriting had become a polished and reputable craft. Ad 1.7 is an example of an ad for an early advertising agency.

The Growth of the Retailer.

In the late 1800s John Wanamaker revolutionized retailing. Before the Civil War there were no set prices for merchandise sold in retail outlets. As a result, store owners bartered and changed prices depending on the perceived wealth of the customer being served or on their own need for cash that day. Wanamaker, who owned a dry-goods store in Philadelphia, changed this tradition by standardizing the prices on all the merchandise he sold. Furthermore, he established even greater credibility by offering a money-back guarantee. This strategy of

Most people attribute to John Wanamaker the quote: "I know that half of my advertising money is wasted—trouble is, I don't know which half."

Atlantic Monthly Advertiser. 5

G. P. Rowell & Co.'s Advertising Agency,
No. 40 Park Row, New York.
Send for a Circular giving lists of 1000 leading Newspapers and advertising rates.

THE LIST SYSTEM.

The firm whose letter we Print below, gave us in 1867 what was then the largest contract we had ever received for our "LISTS OF 100 NEWSPAPERS." The fact that they this year renew the order and increase the amount, is the best argument we can give that these "Lists" are good advertising mediums.

NEW YORK, Dec. 5th, 1868.   GEO. P. ROWELL & CO.

Office of Lippincott & Bakewell, Manufacturers of Axes, Shovels, Saws, &c.
NO. 118 WATER STREET.

PITTSBURG, PA., Dec. 24, 1868.

MESSRS. GEO. P. ROWELL & CO. — GENTLEMEN : — One year ago, with much hesitation, we gave you an advertisement for one of your Lists of One Hundred Local Papers ; a very short time thereafter we unhesitatingly added two more lists of One Hundred papers.

But a short time elapsed before we were inquired of on every side for "Colburn's Patent Red Jacket Axe," proving to us that your plan of Lists had reached the very parties to whom we wanted to introduce the new patent Axe.

The year having now nearly gone by, we cannot but believe your system of advertising by "Lists of Local Papers" is just the kind of advertising we want, and we to-day forward you an order, still adding one more List of One Hundred papers, making the number now altogether four (4) Lists of One Hundred (100) local papers.

The more we talk with newspaper agents and editors' agents, the more satisfied we are that the arrangement we have made with you is preferable to any we have ever heard of. The merit of the Axe itself has, of course, something to do with the great demand for it, but we are satisfied that by your system of advertising by "Lists" we have accomplished in one year what would have ordinarily taken five years to accomplish. Respectfully,

LIPPINCOTT & BAKEWELL.

☞ *Send for a Circular.* **G. P. ROWELL & CO.,** Advertising Agents, 40 Park Row, New York.

AD 1.6
In an 1869 advertisement for itself, George P. Rowell's ad-wholesaling agency made use of a testimonial from a satisfied customer—an advertising device as popular now as it was then. (Courtesy of Warshaw Collection, Smithsonian Institution.)

honest dealings and straight talk was so successful that Wanamaker built two more outlets and the huge Philadelphia Grand Depot department store.

Wanamaker also hired the first great copywriter, John E. Powers. In 1880 Powers was hired to communicate Wanamaker's philosophy to the public. Powers "journalized" advertising by writing ads that were newsy and informationally accurate. He also made the ad more up-to-date with new copy every day. "My discovery," as Powers explained it, was to "print the news of the store."* With Powers's assistance, the sales volume in Wanamaker's stores doubled in just a few years.

The Advent of Magazines. During the 1800s most advertising was placed in newspapers or appeared on posters and handbills. Until the late 1880s magazines were a medium strictly for the wealthy and well-educated, containing political commentaries, short stories, and discussions of art and fashion. This changed with the introduction of the *People's Literary Companion* by E. C. Allen, which appealed to a large group of general readers. Also, about this time Congress approved low postage rates for periodicals, which allowed magazines to be distributed economically by mail. The first magazine advertising appeared in July 1844 in the *Southern Messenger,* which was edited for a short time by Edgar Allan Poe.

Magazines offered a medium for longer, more complex messages. They also had enough lead time to permit the production of art such as engravings to illustrate articles and ads. As the production processes improved, photographs were introduced, and magazine advertisements

Printer's Ink (October 23, 1895).

Claude Hopkins, considered by some people to be the greatest copywriter of all times. (Courtesy of FCB/Leber Katz Partners.)

Copywriter John E. Kennedy explained that "Advertising is salesmanship in print." (Courtesy of FCB/Leber Katz Partners.)

PRINCIPLE —————
"Advertising is salesmanship in print."

PRINCIPLE —————
Soft-sell advertising creates messages through a slow accumulation of positive images.

became highly visual. Some of the earliest magazines to include advertising are still around today, including *Cosmopolitan, Ladies' Home Journal,* and *Reader's Digest.*

Modern Advertising

By the beginning of the twentieth century the total volume of advertising had increased to $500 million from $50 million in 1870. The industry had become a major force in marketing, and had achieved a significant level of respect and esteem.*

The Era of Professionalism.

Calkens and Graphics   The twentieth century also witnessed a revolution in advertising. Earnest Elmo Calkens of the Bates agency created a style of advertising that resembled original art and adapted beautifully to the medium of magazines. Calkens's ads not only attracted the viewer's attention but also increased the status and image of the advertiser. His work represented the first venture into image advertising.

Lord & Thomas Salesmanship   Advertising took a dramatic detour when John E. Kennedy and Albert Lasker formed their historic partnership in 1905 at the powerful Lord & Thomas agency. Lasker was a partner in the firm and the managerial genius who made Lord & Thomas such a force in the advertising industry. Ads that sold the product were all that mattered to him. Because of Lasker's philosophy, the agency was able to make a profit when others were losing money.

In 1905 Lasker was pondering the question: What is advertising? Like Powers, he had been approaching advertising as news. John E. Kennedy, who had worked for a variety of retailers and patent-medicine clients, responded with a note that said, "I can tell you what advertising is." When the two met, Kennedy explained, "Advertising is salesmanship in print."†

Thus was born the "sales" approach to advertising copy. Kennedy's style was simple and straightforward, based on the belief that advertising should present the same arguments a salesman would use in person. This "reason-why" copy style became the hallmark of Lord & Thomas ads. Lasker, referring to his meeting with Kennedy in 1905, said, "The whole complexion of advertising for all America was changed from that day on."

Hopkins and Testing   At the height of his career in the early 1930s Claude Hopkins was Lord & Thomas's best-known copywriter and made the unheard-of-salary of $185,000. Sometimes called "the greatest copywriter of all time," he was also the most analytical.

Hopkins worked with direct mail and used that medium to test and refine his techniques. In his 1923 book *Scientific Advertising,* he discussed the principles and laws he had discovered as a result of his constant copy testing: "One ad is compared with another, one method with another. . . . No guesswork is permitted. One must know what is best. Thus mail-order advertising first established many of our basic laws."‡

MacManus and Soft-Sell   Theodore F. MacManus was a copywriter for the young General Motors company, where he produced an image style of advertising resembling that of Calkens. He felt that a "soft-sell" rather than a "hard-sell" copy style would better create the long-term relationship con-

---

* *Printer's Ink* (October 23, 1953).
†Merrill DeVoe, *Effective Advertising Copy* (New York: Macmillan Co., 1956):21.
‡DeVoe, *Effective Advertising Copy,* 22.

sidered necessary between a car manufacturer and its customers. Image was everything. The only way to penetrate the subconscious of the reader was through a slow accumulation of positive images.* The positive illusions crated by MacManus for Cadillac and Buick had much to do with their early successes

War and Prosperity. With the outbreak of World War I, the advertising industry offered its services to the Council of National Defense. The Division of Advertising of the Committee of Public Information was formed. This volunteer agency created advertising to attract military recruits, sell Liberty Bonds, and support the Red Cross and the war effort in general (see Ad 1.7). Thus was born public service advertising that relied on volunteer professionals and donated time and space.

J. Walter Thompson and the Postwar Boom

After the war consumers were desperate for goods and services. New products were emerg-

* *Printer's Ink* (January 31, 1918).

AD 1.8
Following World War I, "I want to be happy" was the call of consumers, and jazz and dancing became popular, as this 1922 ad for the Victor Talking Machine Company illustrates. (Courtesy of William Heinemann)

ing constantly (see Ad 1.8). A great boom in advertising was led by the J. Walter Thompson agency (JWT) through the innovative copy and management style of the husband-and-wife team Stanley and Helen Resor. Stanley administered the agency and developed the concept of account services.

The JWT agency was known for many innovations in advertising. The Resors coined the concept of *brand names* to associate a unique identity with a particular product. They also developed the status appeal by which they persuaded nonwealthy people to imitate the habits of richer people. JWT advertising introduced modern marketing research to advertising. Stanley Resor also built a network of agencies, including some outside the United States.

Dealing with the Depression. Advertising diminished drastically after the October stock market crash and the onset of the Great Depression in 1929. Advertising budgets were slashed in an attempt to cut costs, and advertisers and consumers alike began to question the value and legitimacy of advertising. Clients demanded more service and special deals. The Depression brought back the hard-sell, reason-why copy approach of Lasker and Hopkins and gave rise to the consumer movement and tighter government regulation. The Federal Trade Commission (FTC), which was established in 1914 to prevent unfair or anticompetitive business practices, was amended at this time to give the agency more consumer-oriented power. The Wheeler-Lea Amendment gave the FTC the power to curb "deceptive" or "unfair" advertising. The FTC was also given authority over false advertising of food, drugs, cosmetics, and therapeutic devices.

Helen and Stanley Resor.

PRINCIPLE _____
The value of an idea is measured by its originality.

Rubicam and Originality   During and after the Depression Raymond Rubicam emerged as one of the giants of advertising. In the spring of 1923 he launched his own agency with John Orr Young, a Lord & Thomas copywriter. Young & Rubicam created unique ads with intriguing headlines. Rubicam emphasized fresh, original ideas. He also hired the researcher George Gallup and made research an essential part of the creative process. Research became an important part of advertising as research organizations founded by Daniel Starch, A. C. Nielsen, and George Gallup, gave rise to the research industry.

Caples and Headlines   John Caples, a vice president of Batten, Barton, Durstine and Osborn (BBDO), made a major contribution to the field in 1932 when he published *Tested Advertising Methods.* His theories about the "pulling power" of headlines were based on extensive mail-order and inquiry testing. Caples was also known for changing the style of advertising writing, which had been wordy and full of exaggerations. He used short words, short sentences, and short paragraphs.*

The Advent of Radio.   Radio offered the Depression-weary consumer an inexpensive form of entertainment. The tremendous potential of radio created two serious problems for advertising, however. First, it meant that advertising agencies had to find or train staff who could write copy for the ear. The second problem was financial. In the early days of radio sponsors underwrote the programming, which involved a much greater financial commitment than a single ad. The growth of radio, however, was phenomenal. Twelve years after its first commercial broadcast, radio surpassed magazines as the leading advertising medium.

*DeVoe, *Advertising Copy,* pp. 25–26.

World War II. During World War II the advertising industry once again served as mass communicator for America. The War Advertising Council (WAC) used advertising to enlist recruits, sell war bonds, and encourage the planting of victory gardens and the sending of V-mail letters. Ad 1.9 is an example of a 1944 ad encouraging the purchase of war bonds. Over $1 billion was spent on the most extensive advertising campaign ever created. The effort was so successful that after the war, instead of disbanding, the WAC simply changed its name to the Advertising Council and has remained a very effective public service effort to this day.

Postwar Advertising. During the 1950s markets were inundated with "me too" products with similar features. "Keeping up with the Joneses" was the attitude among consumers, and many products stressing style, luxury, and social acceptance were forced to compete. The primary difference between many of these products was the image created by the advertising.

AD 1.9
Many companies openly supported the World War II effort through their advertisements. (Courtesy of William Heinemann)

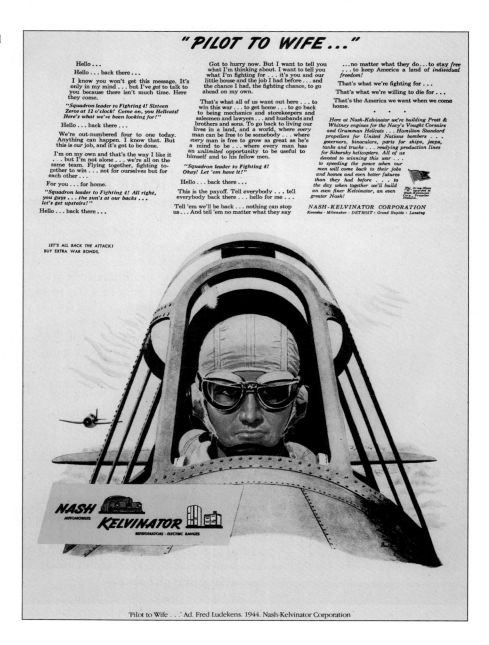

'Pilot to Wife . . .' Ad. Fred Ludekens. 1944. Nash-Kelvinator Corporation

AD 1.10
Popular actors often served as spokespersons for brand-name products in the 1950s. (Courtesy of Liggett Group Inc.)

Rosser Reeves and the USP One person who was able to cut through this clutter of products was Rosser Reeves of the Ted Bates agency. Reeves proposed that an effective ad had to offer a "unique selling proposition" (USP) containing a benefit that was important to consumers and that no other competitor offered. "M&M's melt in your mouth, not in your hands" and "Double your pleasure, double your fun" are two USPs made famous by Reeves.

Bedell and selling stratagems Like Caples, Clyde Bedell was a student and a master of mail-order copy. In a 1940 book *How to Write Advertising That Sells* he expressed his philosophy of advertising, which focused on the selling aspects. He developed a set of "31 Proved Selling Stratagems" that defined the relationship between product features and selling points.*

The Advent of Television. In 1939 NBC became the first television network to initiate regular broadcasting. Not until the 1950s, however, did television become a major player in advertising. By the end of that decade television was the dominant advertising medium. Its total advertising revenues grew from $12.3 million in 1949 to $128 million in 1951.† Ad 1.10 is an example of a popular ad from the 1950s.

*DeVoe, *Advertising Copy,* p. 27.
†Stephen Fox, *The Mirror Makers: A History of American Advertising and Its Creators* (New York: Vintage Books, 1985):211.

The Era of Creativity.
The 1960s saw a resurgence of art, inspiration, and intuition in advertising. This revolution was inspired by three creative geniuses: Leo Burnett, David Ogilvy, and William Bernbach.

Burnett and Middle America Leo Burnett was the leader of the "Chicago School" of advertising. He believed in finding the "inherent drama" in every product and then presenting it as believably as possible. The Leo Burnett agency created mythical characters who represented American values, such as the Jolly Green Giant, Tony the Tiger, Charlie the Tuna, and Morris the Cat. The most famous campaign, which was discussed in the introduction to this chapter, is the "Marlboro Man," which has built the American cowboy into the symbol of the best-selling cigarette in the world. Burnett never apologized for his common-touch approach. He took pride in his ability to reach the average consumer.

Ogilvy: Discipline and Style David Ogilvy, founder of the Ogilvy & Mather agency, is a paradox because he represents both the "image" school of MacManus and Rubicam and the "claim" school of Lasker and Hopkins. Although Ogilvy believed in research and mail-order copy with all of its testing, he had a tremendous sense of image and story appeal. He created enduring brands with campaign symbols like the eyepatch on the Hathaway man. Among the other products he handled were Rolls-Royce, Pepperidge Farm, and Guinness.

The Art of Bernbach Doyle, Dane, and Bernbach opened in 1949. From the beginning, William Bernbach was the catalyst for the agency's success. A copywriter with an acute sense of design, he was considered by many to be the most innovative advertiser of his time. His advertising touched people by focusing on feelings and emotions. He explained: "There are a lot of great technicians in advertising. However, they forget that advertising is persuasion, and persuasion is not a science, but an art. Advertising is the art of persuasion."*

PRINCIPLE _____
"Advertising is the art of persuasion."

The Era of Accountability.
The Vietnam War and the economic downturn of the 1970s led to a reemphasis on hard-sell advertising. Clients wanted results, and agencies hired marketing MBAs who understood strategic planning and the elements of marketing. Advertising increasingly reflected the safe 1950s "formula ads"—vignettes and slice-of-life commercials showing people enjoying the product. Despite the lack of fresh approaches, but bolstered by runaway inflation, 11 agencies—led by Y&R at $2.3 billion—had reached the billion-dollar mark by the end of the decade, compared to none in 1970.†

In response to the intense emphasis on performance and profit in the 1970s and 1980s, many consumer-product companies shifted their budgets from traditional media to *sales promotion,* which uses strategies such as coupons, rebates, and sweepstakes to generate short-term sales gains. Agencies either learned to create sales promotions or acquired firms that specialized in doing so.

Mergers.
Another trend of the 1980s was mergers, both on the client side and among advertising agencies. In order to serve the global needs of major clients, agencies embarked on a spree of national and international

* *Printer's Ink* (January 2, 1953).
†Fox, *Mirror Makers,* p. 262.

mergers. The new super-agencies, which are basically holding companies for a group of merged agencies, promised more efficiency, more specialization, and better global service. Many of the old agencies, and the names of the giants who built them, are now buried in these conglomerates.

The 1990s and Beyond. What advertising will be like in the 1990s and into the twenty-first century is still unclear. The advertising industry has come to realize just how vulnerable it is to the outside world, however. Many agencies closed when poor economic conditions in the late 1980s and early 1990s severely reduced advertising budgets. The war in the Middle East in early 1991 turned the public's attention away from spending and cost the television networks millions of dollars.

Marketers are expecting a great deal more from advertising than they did a decade ago. Advertising must pay its own way—and quickly. Sales promotions, which directly affect sales, have replaced advertising in many cases. Moreover, clients are demanding more value-added services from agencies, at no extra charge. To cope with these new demands agencies have reduced staff size and carefully pruned services that are not cost-effective. They have also placed tremendous pressure on media companies to reduce their rates and to provide better measures of effectiveness.

Another trend that is sure to continue is the globalization of advertising. In the early 1990s the trade barriers throughout much of Europe came down, making it the largest contiguous market in the world. Eastern Europe, Russia, and China have at least partially opened their markets to Western businesses. Advertisers are moving into these markets, and ad agencies are forming huge multinational agencies with international research and media-buying capabilities.

Along with the trend toward globalization is a move toward tighter and tighter "niche" marketing to market segments and even to individuals. The direct-marketing chapter (Chapter 16) chronicles this move from mass marketing to individualized or personalized marketing.

The byword for advertising in the future will be "accountability." Advertising will be forced to walk the precarious tightrope between creativity and profitability, and survival will go to the fittest.

SUMMARY

- Great advertisements have (1) a strong, original creative concept that (2) is strategically sound and (3) has exactly the right execution for the message and audience.
- The definition of advertising has six elements: (1) paid communication (2) that is nonpersonal (3) from an identified sponsor (4) using mass media (5) to persuade or influence (6) an audience.
- Advertising fulfills (1) a marketing role, (2) a communication role, (3) an economic role, and (4) a societal role.

- The three key players in the advertising industry are (1) advertisers, (2) advertising agencies, and (3) media.
- Advertising is handled either internally by an in-house agency or externally by an advertising agency.
- The development of each of the major media—print, media, and television—has transformed advertising.
- Advertising styles have alternated between periods of hard sell (information and salesmanship) and periods of soft sell (image and emotion).

QUESTIONS

1. Critics charge that advertising seeks to manipulate its audience, whereas advertising's supporters claim that it merely seeks to persuade. Which interpretation do you agree with? Why?

2. "I'll tell you what great advertising means," Bill Slater said during a heated dorm discussion. "Great advertising is the ability to capture the imagination of the public—the stuff that sticks in the memory, like Dancing Raisins, or Levi's jeans commercials, or that rabbit with the drum—that's what great is," he says. "Bill, you missed the point," says Phil Graham, a marketing major. "Advertising is a promotional weapon. Greatness means commanding attention and persuading people to buy something. It's what David Leisure did for Isuzu. No frills, no cuteness—great advertising has to sell the public and keep them sold," he adds. How would you enter this argument? What is your interpretation of "great advertising?"

3. Walt Jameson has just joined the advertising department faculty in a university after a long professional career. In an informal talk with the campus advertising club, Jameson is put on the spot about career choices. The students want to know which is the best place to start in the 1990s—with an advertiser (a company) or with an advertising agency. How should Jameson respond? Should he base his answer on the current situation or on how he reads the future?

4. A strong debate continues at Telcom, a supplier of telephone communication systems for business. The issue is whether the company will do a better communication job with its budget of $15 million by using an "in-house" advertising agency or by assigning the business to an independent advertising agency. What are the major issues that Telcom should consider?

5. The chapter discussed a number of creative approaches that are honored in the history of advertising. When you think of Reeves, Burnett, Ogilvy, and Bernbach, do any of their styles seem suited to the 1990s? Do the years ahead seem to require hard-sell or soft-sell advertising strategies? Explain your reasons.

6. Identify five major figures in the history of advertising and explain their contributions to the field.

7. How did the advertising field change after the invention of movable type, radio, and television?

FURTHER READINGS

AAKER, DAVID A., and JOHN G. MEYERS, *Advertising Management* (Englewood Cliffs, NJ; Prentice Hall, 1975).

FOX, STEPHEN, *The Mirror Makers: A History of American Advertising and Its Creators* (New York: Vintage Books, 1985).

"How Advertising Is Reshaping Madison Avenue," *Business Week,* (September 15, 1986):147.

JAFFE, ANDREW "Entrepreneurs Fashion Lean, Mean Shops," *Adweek,* (January 19, 1987):34.

OGILVY, DAVID, *Ogilvy on Advertising* (New York: Vintage Books, 1985).

ORNSTEIN, STANLEY I., *Industrial Concentration and Advertising* (Washington, DC: American Enterprise Institute, 1977).

ROTZELL, KIM B., and JAMES E. HAEFNER, *Advertising in Contemporary Society* (Cincinnati, OH: South-Western Publishing Co., 1986).

VIDEO CASE

Secondary Uses: Avon's Skin So Soft

read ↓

Whether by chance or by design, many firms' products have experienced significant sales increases as a result of "secondary" or "alternative uses." Secondary uses are simply any use of a product other than the one for which it was originally intended. Though most good marketing firms will perform extensive product research in an attempt to identify potential secondary uses for their products, many of the most noteworthy examples of secondary uses have been identified by consumers themselves and communicated via word-of-mouth.

Undoubtedly, the most widely known examples of multiple secondary uses are those for Arm and Hammer's Baking Soda. Originally sold as an ingredient essential to baking, Arm & Hammer's Baking Soda eventually found its way into million of refrigerators as a deodorant, into medicine cabinets as a tooth polish, and into washing machines as a laundry additive. As women increasingly joined the work force and, therefore, had less time for traditional baking, Arm & Hammer was glad to see alternative uses surface for its flagship product. In fact, the broadly held consumer belief in baking soda as a universal cleanser and deodorizer has led Arm & Hammer to develop a variety of baking soda-based cleaning and personal-hygiene products, including detergents, oven cleaners, litter-box deodorizers, and toothpastes and powders.

Generally, those products that have been on the market for the longest period of time have experienced the greatest incidences of alternative uses. Undoubtedly, this was a result of consumer necessity, as consumers were faced with a limited selection of brands of household cleaning products during the first half of this century. Consequently, those brands that were available at the time often served a variety of purposes.

Thus, it is not surprising that older Clorox Liquid Bleach consumers, for example, use the product for a variety of purposes Clorox never anticipated or intended. Since the product's introduction shortly after the turn of the century, Clorox has received testimonials from consumers relating how they use Liquid Bleach as a water purifier, an insecticide, a wound cleaner, a cure for rashes, a general-purpose household cleaner/disinfectant, and, of course, a laundry additive. Similarly, Vaseline Petroleum Jelly has developed a wide range of uses, from a skin balm and ointment to a multipurpose household lubricant.

With the broad range of specialized product choices facing today's consumers, it is rare for a relatively new product to have secondary uses at all, much less any that rival the product's original use. Consequently, Avon was pleasantly surprised when the company began receiving reports from consumers that one of its bath oils, Skin So Soft, was being broadly used in the Northeast as an insect repellent. Advertising for products that provide a medicinal or pesticidal benefit is closely regulated by the government, however, so Skin So Soft's secondary use as an insect repellent could not be advertised by Avon without expensive, lengthy testing and EPA approval. Thus, although Avon benefitted from the media coverage of Skin So Soft's unique alternate use, they could not overtly promote the use.

Often companies faced with this situation find creative and legally acceptable methods of promoting their products' alternative uses without drawing the attention of state or federal regulators. Generally, this is achieved via public relations efforts. For example, a press release or, more subtly, a telephone call placed to a major newspaper or television station can stimulate free media coverage of the brand and its secondary use. Obviously, as with any public relations effort, it is very difficult to control the editorial content of media coverage, and thus the resulting publicity a product receives could be negative rather than positive. For the savvy marketing and public relations professionals, however, the risks can be minimized, particularly if the brand has a favorable existing perception among the public and the secondary use is unique enough to create a "media hook."

Whether or not Avon solicited media coverage of Skin So Soft's alternate use as an insect repellent may never be known because Avon has refused to respond to inquires on the subject. Yet, in today's increasingly competitive consumer marketplace, any firm that is not actively researching secondary or alternative uses for its products either has very few potential end uses for its products or is not doing its job completely.

QUESTIONS

1. List five common household products that are frequently used for purposes other than their originally intended use. Provide both the originally intended use as well as the alternative or secondary use(s).

2. Besides the lengthy, costly EPA testing required to register Skin So Soft as an insect repellent, what other reasons may have prompted Avon to avoid vigorously promoting Skin So Soft's use as an insect repellent?

3. Identify a situation in which a product's secondary use may have had a detrimental effect on demand for its primary use and explain why.

Source: ABC News *Business World,* #149 (September 3, 1989).

2

Advertising and Society: Ethics and Regulation

Chapter Outline

Chapter Objectives

When you have completed this chapter, you should be able to:

- Explain the current judicial position concerning the First Amendment rights of advertisers
- List the major federal agencies that regulate advertising
- Define the concept of self-regulation as it applies to advertising
- Discuss the major ethical issues that advertisers and government regulatory agencies must address
- Explain the remedies available to different groups when an ad is judged deceptive or offensive

THERE'S A WAR OUT THERE

To the casual observer it would appear that advertisers and consumers are at war. Consumers charge that advertisers have permeated every inch of their personal space with offensive and irrelevant messages—ads in toilet stalls on the ground and in flight; ads on parking meters and garbage cans; ads on grocery store shopping carts; commercials on movie screens, rented video-cassettes, giant screens at sporting events, and airport television monitors; ads sent to fax machines; commercials on the telephone when people are put on hold; and a wealth of specialty items from T-shirts to sunshades for car windshields to fortune cookies.

Groups are also responding angrily to individual ad messages. On the day before Easter in April 1990, the Reverend Calvin O. Butts, pastor of New York's Abyssinian Baptist Church, painted over nine liquor and tobacco billboards in Harlem with black paint. His reason: "We are saying to Corporate America that you do not have the right to sell products that destroy human life." One of the billboards the reverend covered over was an ad for Christian Brothers Brandy displaying the slogan "Jazzin with the Brothers." Although the rate of smoking has declined among the American population overall, it continues to rise among blacks, and this higher incidence of smoking brings a higher mortality rate for the black population. For this reason black clergymen and activists in Chicago, Detroit, and Dallas are following Butts's lead and acting out against the advertising of harmful products.

Advertising executives harshly condemn Butts's crusade. "He may call it civil disobedience in the spirit of Martin Luther King, but I call it book-burning in the spirit of Adolf Hitler," says John O'Toole, president of the American Association of Advertising Agencies (AAAA).

The advertising industry is worried that a consumer revolt against advertising is taking shape. The immediate fear is that Butts and others like him will prompt a legislative clampdown, banning all tobacco and liquor advertising and restricting other types of ads. The longer-term fear is that consumers, fed up with being bombarded by up to 3,000 marketing messages a day, are becoming less receptive to the strategies of all advertisers.*

Chapter 1 discussed some of the major social criticisms of advertising. Because advertising is so visible, it draws a great deal of attention from citizens and the government. This chapter will examine the ethical questions advertisers face as well as the regulations imposed by government and by the industry itself

ADVERTISING ETHICS

Advertising is a dynamic public forum in which business interests, creativity, consumer needs, and government regulation meet. Advertising's high visibility makes it particularly vulnerable to criticism. For example, a 1989 Opinion Research survey found that approximately 80 percent of respondents felt that advertising was a "deceptive persuader." This is an increase

*Adapted from Nina Lentini, "Junk Fax: Advertisers May Have Worn Out Their Welcome," *Adweek* (August 7, 1989); Rod Miller, "No Escaping Ads," *Advertising Age* (December 11, 1989):34: "Consumers Are Getting Mad, Mad, Mad, Mad at Mad Ave.," *Business Week* (April 30, 1990):70–71; and Steven W. Colford, "Ad-Bashing Is Back in Style," *Advertising Age* (April 30, 1990):4, 58.

from 1964, when only 54 percent of respondents held such a negative opinion. The survey also indicated that television advertising was the most believable, informative, and entertaining form of media advertising, although 47 percent of the respondents also rated it the most annoying.*

There is some new evidence that this general distrust of advertising is changing, however. According to a 1989 Roper Organization Survey, 80 percent of consumers say that advertising provides useful information about products and services.† However, advertising does elicit a range of opinions: 74 percent of respondents in the Roper survey believed advertising encouraged people to use products they don't need; 59 percent thought that advertising increases the cost of products and services; 68 percent said it encourages people to use products that are bad for them; and 65 percent considered advertising fun or interesting.‡

It is doubtful that negative attitudes toward advertising will ever disappear, so it is worthwhile to be aware of the social issues facing advertisers. Each of these issues is complex, and each involves the public welfare as well as freedom of speech. The collective advertising industry, including agencies, advertisers, and the media, has an important stake in how these social issues are viewed both by the public and by those in a position to pass legislation to regulate the industry.

Ethical Criteria

Although advertisers face extensive regulation, every issue is not covered by a clear, written rule. Many advertising-related issues are left to the discretion of the advertiser. Decisions may be based on a variety of considerations, including the objective of the advertising campaign, the attitudes of the target audience, the philosophies of the agency and the advertiser, and legal precedent. Many decisions are based on ethical concerns. Three issues are central to an ethical discussion of advertising: advocacy, accuracy, and acquisitiveness.§

Advocacy. The first issue is *advocacy*. Advertising, by its very nature, tries to persuade the audience to do something. Thus it is not objective or neutral. This fact disturbs critics who think that advertising should be objective, informative, and neutral. They want advertising to provide information and to stop there. Most people, however, are aware that advertising tries to sell us something, whether it be a product, a service, or an idea.

Accuracy. The second issue is *accuracy*. Beyond the easily ascertainable claims in an advertising message (for example, does the advertised automobile have a sun roof and an AM/FM radio, and is it available in different colors?) are matters of perception. Will buying the automobile make me the envy of my neighbors? Will it make me more attractive to the opposite sex? Such messages may be implied by the situations pictured in the advertisements. Ad 2.1 for Dewar's White Label, for example, appeals to "quiet,

*"For More Consumers, Advertising Is the 'Deceptive Persuader,' " *Adweek's Marketing Week* (March 5, 1990):40.

†"Roper's America on Advertising: More Good Than Bad," *Adweek's Marketing Week* (August 7, 1989):11.

‡Jan Berry, "Consumers Find Ads Useful, Says Roper," *Adweek's Marketing Week* (June 4, 1990):48.

§John Crichton, "Morals and Ethics in Advertising," in *Ethics, Morality & the Media,* Lee Thayer, ed. (New York: Hastings House, 1980):105–15.

AD 2.1
Dewar's profile ads target their messages at consumers who see themselves as a certain type of person. (Courtesy of Schenley Imports Co.)

committed, and independent'' consumers. Most of us are realistic enough to know that buying a car or drinking a certain brand of scotch won't make us a new person, but innuendos in the messages we see cause concern among advertising critics. The subtle messages coming across are of special concern when they are aimed at particular groups with limited experiences, such as children and teenagers.

Acquisitiveness. The third issue is *acquisitiveness*. Some critics maintain that advertising is a symbol of our society's preoccupation with accumulating material objects. Because we are continually exposed to an array of changing, newer-and-better products, critics claim we are ''corrupted'' into thinking that we must have these products. The rebuttal of this criticism is that advertising allows a progressive society to see and choose among different products. Advertising gives us choices and incentives for which we continue to strive.

Ultimately, it is the consumer who makes the final decision. If advertising for a product is perceived as violating ethical standards, consumers can exert pressure by refusing to buy the product or by complaining to the company and to a variety of regulatory bodies. However, decisions about advertising campaigns start with the advertiser.

The Problem of Being Ethical

Although advertisers can seek help in making decisions about questionable advertising situations from such sources as codes of ethics (see the box entitled ''Advertising Principles''), these codes provide only general guidance. When advertising decisions are not clearly covered by a code, a rule, or a regulation, someone must make an ethical decision. That person must

"ADVERTISING PRINCIPLES OF AMERICAN BUSINESS" OF THE AMERICAN ADVERTISING FEDERATION (AAF)

1. **Truth**—Advertising shall reveal the truth, and shall reveal significant facts, the omission of which would mislead the public.

2. **Substantiation**—Advertising claims shall be substantiated by evidence in possession of the advertiser and the advertising agency prior to making such claims.

3. **Comparisons**—Advertising shall refrain from making, false, misleading, or unsubstantiated statements or claims about a competitor or his products or services.

4. **Bait Advertising**—Advertising shall not offer products or services for sale unless such offer constitutes a bona fide effort to sell the advertised products or services and is not a device to switch consumers to other goods or services, usually higher priced.

5. **Guarantees and Warranties**—Advertising of guaran-

tees and warranties shall be explicit, with sufficient information to apprise consumers of their principal terms and limitations or, when space or time restrictions preclude such disclosures, the advertisement shall clearly reveal where the full text of the guarantee or warranty can be examined before purchase.

6. **Price Claims**—Advertising shall avoid price claims which are false or misleading, or savings claims which do not offer provable savings.

7. **Testimonials**—Advertising containing testimonials shall be limited to those of competent witnesses who are reflecting a real and honest opinion or experience.

8. **Taste and Decency**—Advertising shall be free of statements, illustrations, or implications which are offensive to good taste or public decency.

Source: Courtesy of the American Advertising Federation.

weigh the pros and cons, the good and the bad, the healthy and harmful effects, and make a value judgment about an unfamiliar situation. These kinds of decisions are complex because there is no clear consensus about what constitutes ethical behavior and also because of the potential conflict between personal ethics and what might be good for the business. Even though it might increase sales of your product, do you use copy that has an offensive double meaning? Do you use illustrations that portray people in stereotypical situations? Do you stretch the truth when making a claim about the product? Do you malign the competitor's product even though you know it is basically the same as your own?

The complexity of ethical issues requires us to make a conscious effort to deal with each situation. We should develop personal standards of what is right and wrong so that we will be less likely to behave unethically. Remember, it is people who create the ethical atmosphere of the organization. Advertising people in particular must address the following questions:

- Who should, and should not, be advertised to?
- What should, and should not, be advertised?
- What should, and should not, be the content of the advertising message?
- What should, and should not, be the symbolic tone of the advertising message?
- What should, and should not, be the relationship between advertising and the mass media?
- What should, and should not, be advertising's conscious obligation to society?*

Unfortunately, answers to these questions are not always straightforward. Rather, the advertiser must consider a number of related factors, such as the company, mission, marketing objectives, reputation, available resources, and competition.

*Kim B. Rotzoll and James G. Haefner, "Advertising and Its Ethical Dimensions," in *Advertising in Contemporary Society* (Cincinnati, OH: South-Western Publishing Co., 1986):137–49.

*E*THICAL ISSUES IN ADVERTISING

Advertising involves many ethical issues. The predominant issues concern puffery, taste, stereotyping, advertising to children, advertising controversial products, and subliminal advertising.

Puffery

Because the federal government does not pursue cases involving obviously exaggerated, or "puffing," claims, the question of puffery has become an ethical issue. The following familiar slogans are examples of puffery:

- Bayer works wonders.
- When you say Budweiser, you've said it all.
- Nestlé's makes the very best chocolate.
- If it's Borden's, it's got to be good.
- Keebler—uncommonly good.
- You can be sure if it's Westinghouse.
- Things go better with Coke.*

puffery *Advertising or other sales representation that praises the item to be sold using subjective opinions, superlatives, and similar mechanisms that are not based on specific fact.*

Puffery is defined as "advertising or other sales representations which praise the item to be sold with subjective opinions, superlatives, or exaggerations, vaguely and generally, stating no specific facts."[†] Critics contend that puffery is misleading and should be regulated by the Federal Trade Commission (FTC). Defenders counter that reasonable people know puffery is just a way of showing enthusiasm for a product and consumers understand this aspect of selling. Nobody really believes that Exxon will "put a tiger in your tank." One study lent support for this position. A test of 50 automobile advertisements, some using puffery and others not, found no difference in readership between the two types of ads. The researchers concluded that puffery did not enhance the attention-getting ability of the magazine message.[‡]

Taste and Advertising

We all have our own ideas as to what constitutes good taste. Unfortunately, because these ideas vary so much, creating general guidelines for good taste in advertising is difficult. Different things offend different people. What is in good taste to some people is objectionable to others. Although Mel Tillis, a country-and-western singer who stutters, did not mind saying "They're my kind of f-f-folks at Fina" in American Petrofina's gasoline advertising campaign, the American Speech Language Hearing Association objected. They urged their members to complain about the campaign, including accompanying billboards that read "Fffffillerup" and bumper stickers with the message "H-honk if you're f-folks."[$] They felt the campaign exploited Mr. Tillis's handicap and thus was not in good taste. That possibility probably did not occur to many others who saw the ads.

---

*Ivan L. Preston, *The Great American Blow-up* (Madison: The University of Wisconsin Press, 1975):3.

[†]"The Image of Advertising," *Editor and Publisher* (February 9, 1985).

[‡]Bruce G. Vanden Bergh and Leonard N. Reid, "Puffery and Magazine Ad Readership," *Journal of Marketing* (Spring 1980):78–81.

[$]Neil Maxwell, "Fina's New Ads Are Criticized for Making Use of a Stutterer," *The Wall Street Journal* (July 29, 1981):21.

Product Categories and Taste. One dimension of the taste issue concerns the product itself. Television advertising for certain products, such as designer jeans, pantyhose, bras and girdles, laxatives, and feminine hygiene aids, produces higher levels of distaste than do ads for other product categories.* The fact that television has the ability to bring a spokesperson into our living rooms to "talk" to us about such "unmentionables" embarrasses many people, who then complain that the advertisements are distasteful. Although certain ads might be in bad taste in any circumstances, viewer reactions are affected by such factors as sensitivity to the product category, the time the message is received (for example, in the middle of dinner), and whether the person is alone or with others when viewing the message.

In addition, taste changes over time. What is offensive today may not be considered offensive in the future. In 1919 a *Ladies' Home Journal* deodorant advertisement that asked the question, "Are you one of the many women who are troubled with excessive perspiration?" was so controversial that 200 readers immediately cancelled their subscriptions.† By today's standards that advertisement seems pretty tame. Ad 2.2 is an example of a current ad that would once have been considered offensive.

*Bill Abrams, "Poll Suggests TV Advertisers Can't Ignore Matters of Taste," *The Wall Street Journal* (July 23, 1981):25.
†Julian Lewis Watkins, *100 Greatest Advertisements. Who Wrote Them and What They Did* (New York: Moore Publishing Co., 1949):201.

AD 2.2
Ads like this one for Jockey underwear were once considered too risqué and offensive to be run in publications. (Courtesy of Jockey International, Inc.)

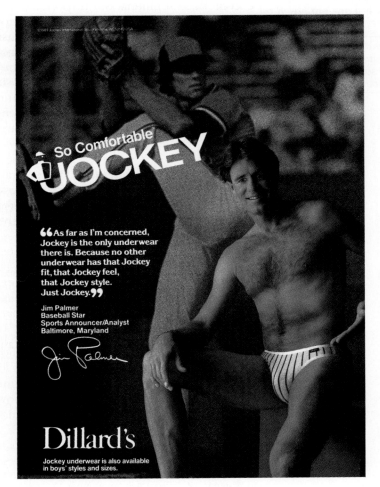

Current Issues. Today's questions of taste center around the use of sexual innuendo, nudity, and violence. Although the use of sex in advertising is not new, the blatancy of its use is. The fashion industry has often been criticized for its liberal use of sex in advertising. Calvin Klein was one of the first to employ sexual innuendo in his advertising messages. A 1980 advertisement for his designer jeans featured model Brooke Shields coyly asking, "Do you want to know what comes between me and my Calvins? Nothing." More recently Guess jeans created a stir with a series of black-and-white ads featuring a variety of scenes. The ads contained virtually no copy, which left them open to individual interpretation. Some of the ads contained a view of two girls in a field in an embrace that many found disconcerting. Another showed a sinister-looking man dressed in black kissing one woman while another watched.

It is to the advantage of the advertiser to be aware of current standards of taste. The safest way to make sure that you are not overlooking some part of the message that could be offensive is to pretest the advertisement. Pretest feedback should minimize the chances of producing distasteful advertising.

Stereotyping in Advertising

stereotyping *Presenting a group of people in an unvarying pattern that lacks individuality and often reflects popular misconceptions.*

PRINCIPLE
Debates about advertising ethics begin with the question: Does advertising shape society's values or simply mirror them?

Stereotyping involves presenting a group of people in an unvarying pattern that lacks individuality. Critics claim that many advertisements stereotype large segments of our population, particularly women, minorities, and the elderly. The issue of stereotyping is connected to the debate about whether advertising shapes society's values or simply mirrors them. Either way, the issue is very important. If you believe that advertising has the ability to shape our values and our view of the world, you will believe it essential that advertisers become aware of how they portray different groups. Conversely, if you believe that advertising mirrors society, you will think that advertisers have a responsibility to ensure that what is portrayed is accurate and representative. Advertisers struggle with this issue every time they use people in an ad.

Women in Advertisements. The portrayal of women in advertisements has received much attention over the years. Initially, critics complained that ads showed women as preoccupied with beauty, household duties, and motherhood. Advertising executives were accused of viewing women as zealous homemakers who were

> in endless pursuit of antiseptic cleanliness. Television ads for Lysol, Spic and Span, and Lemon Pledge, for example, show these ladies frantically spraying and polishing everything in sight—from refrigerator doors to dining-room tables to kitchen floors.*

Although there is still some concern about this stereotype, more advertisers are recognizing the diversity of women's roles. However, with the effort to portray women as more than obsessive housewives came a different problem. Suddenly advertisements focused on briefcase-toting professional women (see Ad 2.3). Consider the commercial where a woman discusses the benefits of serving her children a powdered breakfast drink. She is a NASA engineer. The image of "Supermom" has been displaced by the image of "Superwoman."†

*William Miles, *The Image Makers* (Metuchen, NJ: Scarecrown Press, 1979).
†Jim Auchmutey, "Graphic Changes Charted in the Middle Class," Special Report: Marketing to Women, *Advertising Age* (September 12, 1985):15–17.

AD 2.3
This ad for Hyatt Hotels & Resorts portrays a more modern image of women in society. (Courtesy of Hyatt Hotels & Resorts.)

In 1988 *Adweek* conducted a survey of 3,000 women, which posed a number of questions about how women are depicted in advertising. Asked whether they agree that "The images of women in ads tend to be reasonable reflections of reality," less than 2 percent of respondents said they strongly agree whereas 32 percent strongly disagreed. The survey also offered the statement "There are still too many dumb housewifes in ads." Approximately 30 percent of respondents strongly agreed with this statement, whereas only 3 percent strongly disagreed. Finally, when asked whether "Working mothers in ads are too often portrayed as 'superwomen' with standards no one could live up to," 27.8 percent of the respondents strongly agreed.*

In early 1991 Maidenform introduced a new ad campaign featuring what some call "antiquated stereotypes" of women. After 3 years, the company has decided to drop its celebrity campaign, which featured male stars whispering about women and lingerie and replace it with a new campaign that laments the negative stereotypes of women. Some critics charge that the new ads will actually perpetuate these stereotypes. The ads criticize the stereotypes with a touch of humor in an attempt to confront them head on. In one ad, a female voice says, "Somewhere along the line, someone decided to refer to a woman as this," as images of a chick, a tomato, a fox, a cat,

*Thomas R. King, "Maidenform Ads Focus on Stereotypes," *The Wall Street Journal* (December 10, 1990).

and a dog flash on the screen. The announcer concludes by saying, "While these images are simple and obvious, women themselves rarely are. Just something we like to keep in mind when designing our lingerie."

Ad executives for the campaign claim that the ads are saying that Maidenform understands women, an approach more appropriate for the "back-to-basic" 1990s than the 1980s, which emphasized romance and glitz. The television ads will run in programs that portray women positively, such as *Murphy Brown* and *Designing Women.* The hope is that consumers will see the company as one that understands and stands behind women's concerns.*

The challenge facing advertisers today is to portray woman realistically, in diverse roles, without alienating any segment of women. Experts agree that today's woman wants to see women portrayed with a new freedom, but also as mature, intelligent people with varied interests and abilities.†

Racial and Ethnic Stereotypes.   Racial and ethnic groups also complain of stereotyping in advertising. The root of most complaints is that certain groups are shown in subservient, unflattering ways. Many times minorities are the basis of a joke or, alternatively, consigned to a spot in the background. Other critics complain about underrepresentation of minorities in advertisements. A review of magazine and television advertising determined that blacks account for between 2 and 6 percent of models in print ads and about 13 percent in television advertisements. (Blacks constitute about 13 percent of the total U.S. population.)‡

Senior Citizens.   Another group frequently mentioned with regard to stereotyping is senior citizens, a growing segment of the population with increasing disposable income (see Chapter 5). Critics often object to the use of older people in roles that portray them as slow, senile, and full of afflictions. Although Clara Peller achieved success in the Wendy's hamburger commercials, some critics charged that these ads were too cutsey.§ Others were offended by the shrill "Where's the beef?" and felt that the tone of the commercial portrayed older people as hard to get along with, obstinate, and unattractive.

Baby Boomers.   Few groups in our society have been more extensively stereotyped than baby boomers. Born between 1946 and 1964, these 76 million people represent the largest of all markets. Of the original baby boomers, approximately 68 million are still alive, and they represent over one-fourth of the total population of the United States. Although the total bulk of the economic resources possessed by this group is impressive, the assumption that all baby boomers are wealthy and seek material possessions is inaccurate. Though nurtured through prosperous times, the baby boomers are considered an unlucky generation. Their unprecedented large numbers had to compete for college admission, interesting jobs, and hous-

---

*Mark Dolliver, "The Sixth Annual Woman's Survey," *Adweek Special Report* (July 11, 1988): W4–W8.

†Lynn Folse, "Workers Labor to Raise Women's Status," Special Report: Marketing to Women, *Advertising Age* (September 12, 1985):36–38.

‡Lynette Unger and James M. Stearns, "The Frequency of Blacks in Magazine and Television Advertising: A Review and Additional Evidence," *Southern Marketing Association Proceedings,* Robert L. King, ed. (1986):9–13.

§Laurie Freeman and Nancy Giges, "Ads Giving Older Consumers Short Shrift," *Advertising Age* (November 3, 1986):92.

"I CAN'T COME RIGHT NOW, MOM ... I'M WATCHING A COMMERCIAL SPECIFICALLY TARGETED AT MY DEMOGRAPHIC SEGMENT OF THE POPULATION."

(Courtesy of Bill Whitehead.)

ing. In a reversal of historic trends, boomers so far have experienced lower economic status than their parents.

Nevertheless, advertising has often been blamed for perpetuating the baby-boom myth of the "American Dream." The American Dream is to have it all: a beautiful car, a fancy home, a swimming pool, a beautiful body, and the money to travel and entertain. Clearly, it is a dream attainable for a very small percentage of baby boomers. This issue of the American Dream is addressed more fully in the box entitled "Taking Advantage of People in Crisis."

Advertising to Children

Advertising to children was one of the most controversial topics of the 1970s. In 1977 experts estimated that the average child watched more than 1,300 hours of television annually, which resulted in exposure to over 20,000 commercials.* Proponents of regulating children's advertising were concerned that children did not possess the skills necessary to evaluate advertising messages and to make purchase decisions. They also thought that certain advertising techniques and strategies appropriate for adults were confusing or misleading to children. Two groups in particular, Action for Children's Television (ACT) and the Center for Science in the Public Interest (CSPI), petitioned the FTC to evaluate the situation.

In 1978 the FTC initiated proceedings to study possible regulation of children's television. Several regulations were suggested, including the

*National Science Foundation, *Research on the Effects of Television Advertising on Children* (1977):45.

banning of some types of advertising directed at children. Opponents of the proposed regulations argued that many self-regulatory mechanisms were already in place and that, ultimately, the proper place for restricting advertising to children was in the home.*

After years of debate over the issue, the proposed FTC regulations were abandoned. This did not mean, however, that advertisers to children had unlimited freedom. Advertising to children was carefully monitored by self-regulation. The National Advertising Division (NAD) of the Council of Better Business Bureaus, Inc., set up a group charged with helping advertisers deal with children's advertising in a manner sensitive to children's special needs. (The NAD is discussed in more detail later in the chapter.) The Children's Advertising Review Unit (CARU) was established in 1974 to review and evaluate advertising directed at children under the age of 12.

Then, on October 2, 1990, the House of Representatives and the Senate approved the Children's Television Advertising Practice Act, which restored 9.5-minute-per-hour ceilings for commercials in weekend children's television programming and 12-minute-per-hour limits for weekday programs. The act also restored rules requiring that commercial breaks be clearly distinguished from programming and barring "host selling," tie-ins, and other practices that involve the use of program characters to promote products.

Advertising Controversial Products

Alcohol and Tobacco. One of the most heated advertising issues in recent years is the proposed restrictions on advertising such product categories as alcohol and tobacco. Restrictions on products thought to be unhealthy or unsafe are not new. Cigarette advertising on television and radio has been banned since January 1, 1971. In 1987 the issue was the advisability of a total ban of every form of media advertising of tobacco and alcohol products. A 1986 Tobacco-Free Young American Project poll of 1,025 Americans—70 percent nonsmokers and 30 percent smokers—found that most respondents favored tougher restrictions on public smoking and tobacco-related promotional activities.†

Proponents of such a ban argued that advertising tobacco or alcohol products might result in sickness, injury, or death for the user and possibly others. Restricting advertising of those products would result in fewer sales of the products and consequently would reduce their unhealthy effects.

Opponents of an advertising ban countered that banning truthful, nondeceptive advertising for a legal product is unconstitutional. As attorney and First Amendment authority Floyd Abrams pointed out, "Censorship is contagious and habit-forming . . . even for commercial speech. . . . What we need is more speech, not less. There would be a precedential effect for all other lawful products . . . that are said to do harm." Opponents also cited statistics demonstrating that similar bans in other countries had proved unsuccessful in reducing sales of tobacco and alcohol.‡

The tobacco and alcohol industries have maintained that their intent

*"The Positive Case for Marketing Children's Products to Children," Comments by the Association of National Advertisers, Inc., American Association of Advertising Agencies and the American Advertising Federation Before the Federal Trade Commission (November 24, 1978).

†Joe Agnew, "Trade Groups Align to Counter Public, Government Ban Efforts," *Marketing News* (January 30, 1987):1, 18.

‡Steven W. Colford, "Tobacco Ad Foes Press Fight," *Advertising Age* (February 23, 1987):12; and "Strict Ad Bans Not Effective," *Advertising Age* (August 8, 1986).

TAKING ADVANTAGE OF PEOPLE IN CRISIS

A commercial for the Northern California Honda Dealers Association depicts a yuppified young man talking about his life accomplishments. In his 30s he invented a computer and made a great deal of money, he says. This declaration is followed by remorse—along the way he turned into a jerk and now he feels lost. "I want to simplify . . . You know? Get back to my values." This is the type of confession usually shared with a therapist or member of the clergy. But this man is talking to a car dealer—a Honda car dealer—who assures him that he has come to the right place.

Honda is just one of many advertisers who have based their appeal on the popular midlife crisis. Mazda Miata has built a successful advertising campaign around the desire to return to the simple life of the 1960s (see Ad 2.4). Harley-Davidson has targeted its ads at middle-aged "born-again" motorcycle buyers. Vacation spots and health clubs also appeal to the middle-aged population's desire to escape from routine and responsibility—if only temporarily.

This new approach is grounded in some rather interesting statistics. According to the Roper Organization, only 33 percent of Americans are satisfied with their jobs, a 5 percent decrease from 1973. A similar study by the J. Walter Thompson advertising agency found that people are experiencing midlife crises at younger ages than ever. Ross Goldstein, co-founder of Generational Insights, a consulting firm, cites studies indicating that as many as one-third of the baby-boom generation feel they have not accomplished the goals they set for themselves when they were in high school.

These reports all seem to say the same thing: For the first time in well over a decade, the number of Americans who value leisure time over work is surpassing the number who give work the highest priority. The findings do not negate the American addiction to materialism, however. People are not willing to sacrifice the *fruits* of labor—it's only the labor itself they are disenchanted with. According to Roper's index of tangible measures of "the good life," those values that have shown the most growth since 1981 have been making "a lot" of money (up 21 percent), owning a second car (up 18 percent), buying a vacation home (up 17 percent), and having a high-paying job, two color televisions, and a swimming pool (each up 16 percent). Greed, it seems, is quite alive and well.

Advertisers have responded to these seemingly contradictory values by implementing what critics call "fantasy marketing." For example, the Foote, Cone & Belding advertising agency originally considered developing commercials of people suffering from midlife crises to launch the Miata campaign. The ads would have appealed to those who had once owned, or were attracted to, the mid-1960s sports car, but had grown up and now owned a family sedan instead. In the end the agency decided to create ads that appeal to the nostalgia of the past rather than the despondency of the past: "It was one of those summer evenings you wished would never end . . ."

The ethical question these types of campaigns raise is: Should advertisers cash in on the frailty of people in midlife crises? It will be interesting to monitor what advertisers do.

AD 2.4
(Courtesy of Foote, Cone, and Belding.)

Source: Adapted from Jon Berry, "It's Hip, It's Intense—The Midlife Crisis," *Adweek* (June 25, 1990):54–55.

is to advertise only to those who have already decided to use their products and not to persuade nonusers to try them. R. J. Reynolds defends its position in messages explaining that they do not advertise to children. In late 1989 tobacco companies received negative publicity for marketing Uptown, a new cigarette designed to appeal to black men. Adolph Coors Company sponsored a "Gimme the Keys" television commercial intended to remind people to be responsible drinkers. They also developed a public service campaign using the movie character "E.T." to deliver the message, "If you go beyond your limit, please don't drive. Phone home." More recently, Coors ran a television commercial for Coors' Light that used the tag line "right beer now—but not now" to depict safe times for drinking, such as a social gathering, and unsafe times, such as before getting into a car.

The outcome of the proposed advertising bans has far-reaching implications for advertisers, advertising agencies, and the general public. For example, magazine publishers could be financially devastated if print tobacco ads were banned (see Figure 2.1). According to one report, as many as 165 magazines would fold without tobacco advertising.*

Condoms. Another topic of controversy is whether condoms should be advertised and, if so, in what media. Magazines have been more receptive to condom ads than television. Even though the National Association of Broadcasters repealed its ban on the broadcast of contraceptive ads in 1982, the major networks have hesitated to accept condom ads because of the sensitive nature of the product. Supporters of such advertising contend that the growing number of sexually transmitted diseases, including AIDS, makes such advertising necessary. They further argue that such messages can be done in good taste and at appropriate times, so that few groups would be offended. This issue raises difficult questions that will not be easily resolved.

*Scott Donaton, "Publishers Bracing for Smoke-Free Pages," *Advertising Age* (March 12, 1990):3.

FIGURE 2.1
Percentage of overall advertising revenue from tobacco advertising.

Magazine	Tobacco advertising (in millions)	Tobacco advertising as a % of overall ad revenue
Star	$6.7	43.4
Penthouse	5.1	25.3
Field & Stream	5.9	15.9
Life	6.2	12.7
McCall's	7.0	11.2
Sports Illustrated	35.0	10.8
TV Guide	30.5	10.8
Redbook	7.0	10.2
Popular Science	2.0	9.3
People	27.5	9.0
Playboy	7.7	8.9
Ladies' Home Journal	7.0	8.4
Glamour	6.2	7.1
Cosmopolitan	7.9	6.9
Newsweek	16.6	6.9
U.S. News & World Report	8.6	6.7
Better Homes & Gardens	10.1	6.6
Time	22.9	6.5
Family Circle	8.3	6.2
Woman's Day	6.9	6.0
Southern Living	3.1	5.0

Note: Four magazines in the top 25 do not accept tobacco advertising.
Source: 1990 Leadership Council on Advertising Issues.

Subliminal Advertising

Generally when we think of messages we consider symbols that are consciously seen and heard. However, it is possible to transmit symbols in a manner that puts them below the threshold of normal perception. These kinds of messages are termed "subliminal." A **subliminal message** is one that is transmitted in such a way that the receiver is not consciously aware of receiving it. This usually means that the symbols are too faint or too brief to be clearly recognized. The furor over subliminal perception began with a 1958 study by James Vicary in a movie theater in Fort Lee, New Jersey, where the words "Drink Coke" and "Eat Popcorn" were flashed on the screen, allegedly resulting in increased sales of popcorn and Coke. The issue was further publicized by Vance Packard in his book *The Hidden Persuaders,* and more recently, Wilson Bryan Key discussed the subject in his books *Subliminal Seduction* and *Media Sexploitation.* Key maintains that subliminal "embeds" are placed in ads to manipulate purchase behavior, most frequently through appeals to sexuality. For example, he suggests that 99 percent of ads for alcoholic beverages employ subliminal embeds. Key contends that the messages are buried so skillfully that the average person does not notice them unless they are pointed out. He believes the subliminal embeds are the work of airbrush touch-up artists*. Ad 2.5, sponsored by the American Association of Advertising Industries, reflects the industry's opinion of the subliminal advertising theory.

*Walter Weir, "Another Look at Subliminal Facts," *Advertising Age* (October 15, 1984):46.

AD 2.5
The advertising industry considers accusations of subliminal advertising to be both damaging and totally untrue. (Courtesy of American Association of Advertising Agencies.)

PEOPLE HAVE BEEN TRYING TO FIND THE BREASTS IN THESE ICE CUBES SINCE 1957.

The advertising industry is sometimes charged with sneaking seductive little pictures into ads.

Supposedly, these pictures can get you to buy a product without your even seeing them.

Consider the photograph above. According to some people, there's a pair of female breasts hidden in the patterns of light refracted by the ice cubes.

Well, if you really searched you probably *could* see the breasts. For that matter, you could also see Millard Fillmore, a stuffed pork chop and a 1946 Dodge.

The point is that so-called "subliminal advertising" simply doesn't exist. Overactive imaginations, however, most certainly do.

So if anyone claims to see breasts in that drink up there, they aren't in the ice cubes.

They're in the eye of the beholder.

ADVERTISING
ANOTHER WORD FOR FREEDOM OF CHOICE.
American Association of Advertising Agencies

GUIDELINES FOR CHILDREN'S ADVERTISING

The controversy surrounding the issue of children's advertising has encouraged the advertising industry to regulate this practice carefully. In the 1970s the industry issued written guidelines for children's advertising and established the Children's Advertising Review Unit within the Council of Better Business Bureaus to oversee the self-regulatory process. The Unit revised the written guidelines in 1977 and again in 1983. The following are the five basic principles on which guidelines for advertising directed at children are based.

1. Advertisers should always take into account the level of knowledge, sophistication, and maturity of the audience to which their message is primarily directed. Younger children have a limited capability for evaluating the credibility of what they watch. Advertisers, therefore, have a special responsibility to protect children from their own susceptibilities.
2. Realizing that children are imaginative and that make-believe play constitutes an important part of the growing up process, advertisers should exercise care not to exploit that imaginative quality of children. Unreasonable expectations of product quality or performance should not be stimulated either directly or indirectly by advertising.
3. Recognizing that advertising may plan an important part in educating the child, information should be communicated in a truthful and accurate manner with full recognition by the advertiser that the child may learn practices from advertising which can affect his or her health and well-being.

(Courtesy of Elizabeth Hathon/The Stock Market.)

4. Advertisers are urged to capitalize on the potential of advertising to influence social behavior by developing advertising that, wherever possible, addresses itself to social standards generally regarded as positive and beneficial, such as friendship, kindness, honesty, justice, generosity, and respect for others.
5. Although many influences affect a child's personal and social development, it remains the prime responsibility of the parents to provide guidance for children. Advertisers should contribute to this parent-child relationship in a constructive manner.

Source: "Self-Regulatory Guidelines for Children's Advertising," 3rd ed. Children's Advertising Review Unit, National Advertising Division, Council of Better Business Bureaus, Inc. (1983):4–5.

Whether subliminal stimuli can cause some types of minor reactions has never been the advertising issue. In tightly controlled laboratory settings subliminal stimuli have been shown to produce some reactions, such as a "like/dislike" response. The advertising issue is whether a subliminal message is capable of affecting the public's *buying behavior.*

Research in this field has uncovered several practical difficulties with the theory that subliminal embeds can be used to influence buying behavior. To begin with, perceptual thresholds vary from person to person and from moment to moment. Symbols that are subliminal to one person might be consciously perceived by another. A message guaranteed to be subliminal to an entire audience would probably be so weak that any effect would be limited. Another problem is the lack of control that the advertiser would have over the distance and position of the message receiver from the message. Differences in distances and position could affect when the stimulus is subliminal and when it is recognizable. The third problem comes from the effect of recognizable (supraliminal) material, such as the movie or commercial, used in conjunction with the subliminal message. The supraliminal stimulus might overpower the subliminal material.

Besides the physiological limitations that make it questionable that subliminal messages can cause certain behaviors, there are several pragmatic issues. Most importantly, consumers normally will not buy products they don't need or can't afford to purchase, regardless of the advertising message and whether it is presented subliminally or directly. There will always be freedom of choice. Furthermore, there are many factors besides the advertising message itself that induce consumers to purchase a product. (These influences will be discussed in more detail in Chapter 5.)

Nonetheless, many people still believe subliminal advertising is used frequently, widely, and successfully. Little evidence exists to support this belief, however. A survey of advertising agency art directors found that over 90 percent claimed no personal knowledge of the use of subliminal advertising. Timothy Moore concluded after his overview of the subliminal area, "In general, the literature on subliminal perception shows that the most clearly documented effects are obtained in only highly contrived and artificial situations. These effects, when present, are brief and of small magnitude. . . . These processes have no apparent relevance to the goals of advertising."*

ADVERTISING AND THE LAW

Few elements of business have been more heavily legislated than advertising. This section discusses the most important federal legislation as well as advertisers' attempts at self-regulation (see Figure 2.2).

Advertising and the First Amendment

Freedom of expression in the United States is protected from government control by the Bill of Rights to the Constitution. In particular, the First Amendment states that Congress shall make no law "abridging the freedom of speech, or of the press; or the right of people peaceably to assemble, and to petition the Government for a redress of grievances." Initially, the Court ruled that freedom of expression is not absolute, although only the most compelling circumstances justify prior restraint on the spread of information. Specifically the Court held that the First Amendment applied to most media, including newspapers, books, magazines, broadcasting, and film. However, since Congress adopted the amendment in 1791, the Supreme

*Timothy Moore, "Subliminal Advertising: What You See Is What You Get," *Journal of Marketing* (Spring 1982):38–47.

FIGURE 2.2
Regulatory factors affecting advertising.

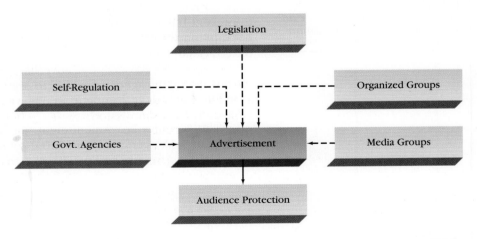

TABLE 2.2
First Amendment Legislation

> **Valentine v. Christensen (1942)**
> First Amendment does not protect purely commercial advertising because that type of advertising does not contribute to decision making in a democracy.
>
> **Virginia State Board of Pharmacy v. Virginia Citizens Consumer Council (1976)**
> States cannot prohibit pharmacists from advertising prices of prescription drugs because the free flow of information is indispensible.
>
> **Central Hudson Gas & Electric Corporation v. Public Service Commission of New York (1980)**
> Public Service Commission's prohibition of promotional advertising by utilities is found to be unconstitutional, placing limitations on government regulation of unlawful, nondeceptive advertising.
>
> **Posadas de Puerto Rico Associates v. Tourism Company of Puerto Rico (1986)**
> Puerto Rican law banned advertising of gambling casinos to residents of Puerto Rico.

Court has continued to reinterpret it as it applies to different situations. Table 2.2 lists some of the important First Amendment legislation.

The First Amendment has been used to strike down many statutes prohibiting commercial expression. For example, as a result of the *Virginia Pharmacy* ruling, states no longer can bar attorneys from advertising the prices of "routine" legal services, home owners from advertising their houses by placing "For Sale" signs in their yards, drugstores from advertising contraceptives, or utilities from promoting the use of electricity.*

Can advertisers now assume they are free from government regulation? Hardly. Although the Supreme Court has ruled that some very limited forms of advertising content merit First Amendment protection, it has not said that a business has the same First Amendment right of expression as a private individual or a newspaper. Nor has the Court accorded the same degree of protection to commercial advertising that it insists on for other protected content. Although the Court's interpretation of constitutional protection for advertising remains unsettled, it does appear to be moving in a direction that favors advertising.

THE FEDERAL TRADE COMMISSION

Federal Trade Commission (FTC) *A federal agency responsible for interpreting deceptive advertising and regulating unfair methods of competition.*

The **Federal Trade Commission** (FTC) is the government agency responsible for regulating much of American business. It was established in 1914 to prevent business activities that were unfair or anticompetitive. Its original mission was to protect business rather than the consumer, and its enabling act contained no statement about advertising. In 1922 a Supreme Court ruling placed deceptive advertising within the scope of the FTC's authority, giving the agency the right to regulate false labeling and advertising as unfair methods of competition. Figure 2.3 shows the organization of the Federal Trade Commission.

The Wheeler-Lea Amendment, passed in 1938, extended the FTC's powers, and the agency became more consumer-oriented. This amendment added "deceptive acts and practices" to the list of "unfair methods of com-

---

*Ivan L. Preston, "A Review of the Literature on Advertising Regulation," in *Current Issues and Research in Advertising* (1983), James H. Leigh and Claude L. Martin, eds. (Ann Arbor: University of Michigan, 1983):2–37.

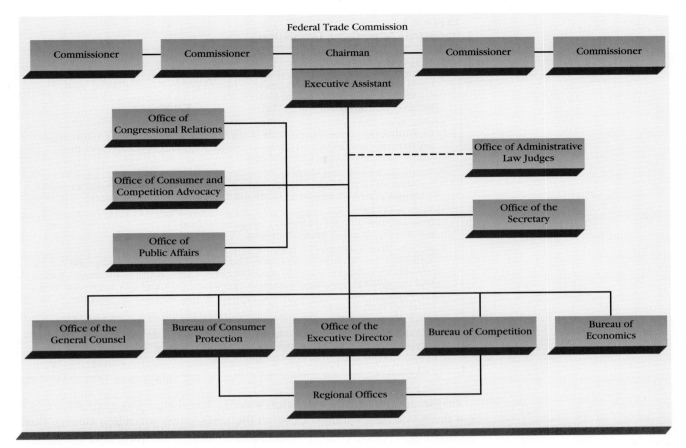

FIGURE 2.3
The Federal Trade Commission Organization. *Source:* Office of the Federal Register National Archives and Records Administration, *The United States Government Manual 1989/90.*

petition." In addition, the Wheeler-Lea Amendment gave the FTC authority to (1) initiate investigations against companies without waiting for complaints, (2) issue cease-and-desist orders, and (3) fine companies for not complying with cease-and-desist orders. The FTC was also given jurisdiction over false advertising of foods, drugs, cosmetics, and therapeutic devices. False advertising was defined as "any false representation, including failure to reveal material facts".*

The FTC acquired increased authority during the late 1960s and mid-1970s through a series of important acts, which are listed in Table 2.3, along with other advertising legislation. An issue of high concern to the advertising industry was winning Congressional reauthorization of the FTC, a feat last accomplished in 1982. The U.S. Senate passed the reauthorization bill in 1989. In addition to appropriating a substantial budget increase, the Senate also commissioned a study identifying those areas under the FTC's jurisdiction that might be appropriate for state enforcement and eliminate the agency's ability to make new rules regulating commercial advertising on the basis of unfairness. Unfortunately, the House and Senate have been unable to reconcile difference over the FTC's ability to use unfairness as the basis for rule-making, and as of early 1991, there was still debate about a reauthorization bill.

In addition, the political climate of the 1980s resulted in new appointees to the FTC who were less aggressive in regulating advertising. The

* *Bates v. State Bar of Arizona,* 433 U.S. 350 (1977); *Linmark Associates, Inc. v. Township of Willingboro,* 431 U.S. 85 (1977); *Carey v. Population Services International,* 431 U.S. 678 (1977); *Central Hudson v. Public Services Commission,* 6 Med. L. Reptr. 1497 (U.S. 1980).

TABLE 2.3
Important Advertising Legislation

> Pure Food and Drug Act (1906)
> Forbids the manufacture, sale, or transport of adulterated or fraudulently labeled foods and drugs in interstate commerce. Supplanted by the Food, Drug, and Cosmetic Act of 1938; amended by Food Additives Amendment in 1958 and Kefauver-Harris Amendment in 1962.
>
> Federal Trade Commission Act (1914)
> Establishes the commission, a body of specialists with broad powers to investigate and to issue cease-and-desist orders to enforce Section 5, which declares that "unfair methods of competition in commerce are unlawful."
>
> Wheeler-Lea Amendment (1938)
> Prohibits unfair and deceptive acts and practices regardless of whether competition is injured; places advertising of foods and drugs under FTC jurisdiction.
>
> Lanham Act (1947)
> Provides protection for trademarks (slogans and brand names) from competitors and also encompasses false advertising.
>
> Magnuson-Moss Warranty/FTC Improvement Act (1975)
> Authorizes the FTC to determine rules concerning consumer warranties and provides for consumer access to means of redress, such as the "class action" suit. Also expands FTC regulatory powers over unfair or deceptive acts or practices and allows it to require restitution for deceptively written warranties costing the consumer more than $5.
>
> FTC Improvement Act (1980)
> Provides the House of Representatives and Senate jointly with veto power over FTC regulation rules. Enacted to limit FTC's powers to regulate "unfairness" issues in designing trade regulation rules on advertising.

Reagan administration's position was that regulation was justifiable only if it produced benefits that outweigh the costs. However, when George Bush succeeded Reagan as president in 1989, the FTC once again became more rigorous in enforcing business trade regulations. The FTC of the Bush administration is expected to be especially aggressive in enforcing regulation on advertising, including health claims or promotions for alcohol and tobacco products.*

Some people think that the end of the Reagan era signaled a change in the hands-off attitude that insulated marketers from regulation. In her coming-out speech in 1990, FTC Chairman Janet Steiger warned agencies that they will be held accountable for ads or practices deemed unfair or deceptive. The response of one advertising executive was typical of the industry: "We haven't heard that from the FTC for years, and I think a lot of agencies don't understand their liability."

Another outcome of the soft FTC years was the development of the National Association of Attorneys General, an organization determined to regulate advertising at the state level. Members of this organization have been successfully bringing suits in their respective states against such advertising giants as Coca-Cola, Kraft, and Campbell Soup.†

The FTC and Advertisers

Regardless of the philosophy of a given administration, the very existence of a regulatory agency like the FTC influences the behavior of advertisers.

Although most cases never reach the FTC, advertisers prefer not to run

---

*Steven W. Colford, "Bush FTC May Clamp Down on Ads," *Advertising Age* (April 17, 1989): 63.

†Steven W. Colford, "FTC Warns Agencies; Eyes Tobacco, Cable," *Advertising Age* (March 12, 1990):6; "Attorney General's Office Investigates Advertising Claims," *Marketing News* (February 29, 1988):16.

the risk of a long legal involvement with the agency. Advertisers are also conscious that competitors, with a lot of consumer dollars at stake, may be quick to complain to an appropriate agency about a questionable advertisement (see Ad 2.6). As was suggested in an editorial in *Advertising Age:*

> We've long since agreed that lies, deception, and fraud are beyond debate. No, ethics in advertising goes far beyond that. To the study of fine-linesmanship of what constitutes "weasel-wording" and what constitutes the whole truth. . . . If the copy stretches the truth even by a hair, or can be misinterpreted by anyone exposed to it, find another way. Chances are you'll end up with a stronger, more believable, more persuasive product presentation. And isn't that what good advertising is all about anyway?*

Ultimately, most advertisers want their customers to remain happy and pleased with their products and advertising, so they take every precaution to make sure their messages are not deceptive.

*F*TC CONCERNS WITH ADVERTISING

Deception

PRINCIPLE

Data must be on file to substantiate claims made by advertisers.

Deceptive advertising is a major focus of the FTC. Some of the activities that the commission has identified as deceptive are deceptive pricing, false criticisms of competing products, deceptive guarantees, ambiguous statements, and false testimonials. Until recently, the legal standard of deceptiveness involved judging only that an advertisement had the *capacity* to deceive consumers, not that it had actually done so. In 1983 the FTC changed the standard used to determine deception. The current policy contains three basic elements:

1. Where there is representation, omission, or practice, there must be a high probability that it will mislead the consumer.
2. The perspective of the "reasonable consumer" is used to judge deception. The FTC tests "reasonableness" by looking at whether the consumer's interpretation or reaction to an advertisement is reasonable.
3. The deception must lead to material injury. In other words, the deception must influence consumers' decision making about products and services.†

This new policy makes deception more difficult to prove. It also creates uncertainty for advertisers, who must wait for congressional hearings and court cases to discover what the FTC will permit. An ad for Volvo is an example of advertising that was found to be deceptive. In November 1990 the Texas attorney general charged that both the print and broadcast versions of the ad depicting a Volvo withstanding the weight of a 6¾-ton truck was deceptive in two ways. First, the roof of the Volvo was actually reinforced with steel and plywood, and second, the ad failed to specify that the scenario was a staged event rather than an actual contest. In response to these allegations Volvo confessed that the advertising was rigged and agreed to stop running the ads. The car company was also charged $300,000 in investigative costs and ran ads in Texas newspapers explaining the settlement. Furthermore, Scali, McCabe, Sloves, the agency that had been responsible for handling Volvo's advertising for over 20 years, resigned the $40 million account. A discussion of possible deception is presented in the box entitled "It's a Mirage!"

*Win Roll, "A Valuable Lesson in Integrity," *Advertising Age* (May 25, 1987):18.
†Letter to Congress Explaining FTC's New Deception Policy," Advertising Compliance Service (Westport, CN: Meckler Publishing, November 21, 1983) and Ivan Preston, "A Review of the Literature":2–37.

Benetton has stirred up controversy with its interracial campaign, but it has always remained in the realm of honest advertising. (Courtesy of Benetton/ph. Tosan)

Reasonable Basis for Making a Claim

The advertiser should have a reasonable basis for making a claim about product performance. This involves having data on file to substantiate any claims made in the advertising.

Determining the reasonableness of a claim is done on a case-by-case basis. The FTC has suggested that the following factors be examined:

1. Type and specificity of claim made
2. Type of product
3. Possible consequences of the false claim
4. Degree of reliance by consumers on the claims
5. The type and accessibility of evidence available for making the claim*

RICO Suits

One of the most serious legal issues facing advertisers has been the recent application of the Racketeer Influenced and Corrupt Organizations Act (RICO) to false advertising lawsuits. Originally designed in 1970 to help curb fraud and organized crime, the broadly worded statute became an increasingly attractive legal weapon against advertisers in late 1989 after it was used in a false advertising suit against Ralston-Purina. Because losing a RICO suit means triple damages, legal costs, and the stigma of being labeled a "mobster," Ralston-Purina agreed to settle.

As of early 1991 there were at least a half-dozen RICO suits pending against companies. Coors was charged with falsely advertising Coors beer as being made from Rocky Mountain spring water, and CPC International was charged with false claims that Mazola corn oil products could lower serum cholesterol. Mobil Corporation was charged with false package labeling, advertising and promoting Hefty trash bags as biodegradable, and using sales proceeds to continue a faulty marketing campaign. The charge

* Federal Trade Commission v. Raladam Company, 283 U.S. 643 (1931).

was dismissed, as was the claim that the relationship between Mobil and its ad agency Wells, Rich, Greene, New York (WRG) was unlawful. According to the RICO criterion, it is unlawful for someone employed or associated with an enterprise affecting interstate commerce to participate in the enterprise's affairs through racketeering activity. Mobil's relationship with WRG did not satisfy the definition of an enterprise.

RICO was enacted to prevent organized crime from taking illegal money and putting it into a legal enterprise and the taking of control of an innocent enterprise by racketeers. The Mobil ruling may be an indication that the proliferation of such suits may be decreasing. The concern over RICO suits is that they may reduce advertisers' inclination to settle regulatory disputes with federal or state agencies through consent decrees. Advertisers fear that the terms and admissions from these settlements will be used against them in subsequent RICO suits. Congress has attempted to stem the use of RICO suits with legislation, based on the shakiness of the argument that the ads in questions, and only the ads, caused the consumers to purchase the product or service.*

Comparative Advertising

PRINCIPLE ——————
Comparative advertising is supported as a means of providing more information to consumers.

The FTC supports comparative advertising as a way of providing more information to consumers. A substantial percentage of all television commercials use a comparative strategy. The Commission requires that comparative claims, like other claims, be substantiated by the advertiser. Comparative advertising is considered deceptive unless the comparisons are based on fact, the differences advertised are statistically significant, the comparisons involve meaningful issues, and the comparisons are to meaningful competitors (see Table 2.4).

*Steven W. Colford, "Mobil's RICO Victory Bolsters Ad Industry," *Advertising Age* (December 10, 1990):1, 59; Steven W. Colford and Ira Teinwitz, "Coors, CPC to Fight RICO Ad Charges," *Advertising Age* (October 22, 1990); and Barbara Hobsonback, "RICO Suit Looms: Volvo Probes Slow," *Adweek* (December 3, 1990):21.

TABLE 2.4
American Association of Advertising Agencies' Ten Guidelines For Comparative Advertising.

1. The intent and connotation of the ad should be to inform and never to discredit or unfairly attack competitors, competing products, or services.
2. When a competitive product is named, it should be one that exists in the marketplace as significant competition.
3. The competition should be fairly and properly identified but never in a manner or tone of voice that degrades the competitive product or service.
4. The advertising should compare related or similar properties or ingredients of the product, dimension to dimension, feature to feature.
5. The identification should be for honest comparison purposes and not simply to upgrade by association.
6. If a competitive test is conducted, it should be done by an objective testing service.
7. In all cases the test should be supportive of all claims made in the advertising that are based on the test.
8. The advertising should never use partial results or stress insignificant differences to cause the consumer to draw an improper conclusion.
9. The property being compared should be significant in terms of value or usefulness of the product to the consumer.
10. Comparisons delivered through the use of testimonials should not imply that the testimonial is more than one individual's thought unless that individual represents a sample of the majority viewpoint.

Source: James B. Astrachan, "When to Name a Competitor," *Adweek* (May 23, 1988):24.

ISSUES AND APPLICATIONS

IT'S A MIRAGE!

In 1990 Sanka aired an impromptu taste test that took place at the Hudson Street train station in New Jersey. The responses to the test were encouraging: "This is great!" one commuter exclaimed. "No way, this isn't Sanka," declared another.

The reactions seemed too good to be true—which was exactly the problem. After the commercial was aired, General Foods acknowledged that the "commuters" were actually paid actors, their lines had been memorized from a script, and the commercial had been filmed at the Hoboken train station ("Hudson Street" was a fictitious name). After Mary Ann Walsch, Massachusetts' Secretary of Consumer Affairs and Business Regulations, criticized the misleading nature of the ad, claiming that it resembled a man-on-the-street taste test closely enough to raise the question of deception, the commercial was modified to superimpose the word "dramatization" for the first 3 seconds.

General Foods is not the only company to come under scrutiny. In the mid-1980s, for example, Drexel Burnham Lambert aired an ad describing how its junk bonds had helped revitalize Vidalia, Louisiana, after the town suffered from a gas leak disaster. The company was attacked for deceiving consumers when it turned out that the images of the windswept town in the commercial had been filmed in Fort Smith, Arkansas, more than 300 miles away from Vidalia.

Some network executives concede that the line between real-people ads and dramatizations is becoming very hazy. The issue is: At what point does a commercial strive so hard for realism that it crosses the line into deception? Should a commercial have to air a disclaimer every time an actor says that something tastes good or praises the effectiveness of a certain product? Do you agree that the line between real-people ads and dramatizations has become obscure? Why or why not? Can you think of other ads that misrepresent reality?

Source: Adapted from Joanne Lipman, "Sanka TV Spot Rekindles Issue of Ads Pretending to Be Real," *The Wall Street Journal* (January 10, 1990): B4.

Endorsements

A popular advertising strategy involves the use of a spokesperson who endorses the brand (see Chapter 8). Because consumers often rely on these endorsements when making purchase decisions, the FTC has concentrated on commercials that use this approach. Endorsers must be qualified by experience or training to make judgments, and they must actually use the product. If endorsers are comparing competing brands, they must have tried those brands as well. Those who endorse a product improperly may be liable if the FTC determines there is a deception.

Demonstrations

Product demonstrations in television advertising must not mislead consumers. A claim that is demonstrated must be accurately shown. This mandate is especially difficult for advertisements containing food products because such factors as hot studio lights and the length of time needed to shoot the commercial can make the product look quite unappetizing. For example, because milk looks gray on television, advertisers often substitute a mixture of glue and water. The question is whether the demonstration falsely upgrades the consumer's perception of the advertised brand. The FTC evaluates this kind of deception on a case-by-case basis.

One technique some advertisers use to sidestep restrictions or demonstrations is to insert **disclaimers** or **supers,** verbal or written words that appear in the ad that indicate exceptions to the claim being made. One recent example is a 30-second spot for Chrysler's Jeep Cherokee that starts out cleanly and concisely, with bold shots of the vehicle and music swelling in the background. Suddenly the message is less clear; for several seconds five different, often lengthy disclaimers flash on the screen in tiny, eyestraining type, including "See dealers for details and guaranteed claim form" and "Deductibles and restrictions apply."*

REMEDIES FOR DECEPTIVE AND UNFAIR ADVERTISING

consent decree *An order given by the FTC and signed by an advertiser, agreeing to stop running a deceptive ad.*

The most common sources of complaints concerning deceptive or unfair advertising practices are competitors, the public, and the FTC's own monitors. If a complaint is found to be justified, the Commission can follow several courses of action. Until 1970 cease-and-desist orders and fines were the FTC's major weapons against deception, but the Commission has developed alternative remedies since then, including corrective advertising, substantiation of advertising claims, and consumer redress.

Consent Decrees

A **consent decree** represents the first step in the regulation process after the FTC determines that an ad is deceptive. The FTC simply notifies the advertiser of its finding and asks the advertiser to sign a consent decree agreeing to stop the deceptive practice. Most advertisers do sign the decree, thereby avoiding the bad publicity and the possible fine of $10,000 per day for refusing to do so.

Cease-and-Desist Orders

cease-and-desist order *A legal order requiring an advertiser to stop its unlawful practices.*

When the advertiser refuses to sign the consent decree and the FTC determines that the deception is substantial, a **cease-and-desist order** will be issued. The process leading to an issuance of a cease-and-desist order is similar to a court trial. An administrative law judge presides, FTC staff attorneys represent the Commission, and the accused parties are entitled to representation by their lawyers. If the administrative judge decides in favor of the FTC, an order is issued requiring the respondents to "cease and desist" their unlawful practices. The order can be appealed to the full five-member Commission.

Corrective Advertising

corrective advertising *A remedy required by the FTC in which an advertiser who produced misleading messages is required to issue factual information to offset these messages*

PRINCIPLE _____
Corrective advertising is required when the FTC determines that an ad has created lasting false impressions.

Corrective advertising is required by the FTC when consumer research determines that lasting false beliefs have been perpetuated by an advertising campaign. Under this remedy, the offending firm is ordered to produce messages that correct any deceptive impressions created in the consumer's mind. The purpose of corrective advertising is not to punish a firm but to prevent that firm from continuing to deceive consumers. The FTC may require a firm to run corrective advertising even if the campaign in question has been discontinued.

The landmark case involving corrective advertising was *Warner-Lambert v. FTC* in 1977. According to the FTC, Warner-Lambert's 50-year-old

*Thomas R. King, "More Fine Print Clouds Message of Commercials," *The Wall Street Journal* (July 12, 1990):B1.

campaign for Listerine mouthwash had been deceiving customers into thinking that Listerine was able to prevent sore throats and colds or to lessen their severity. The company was ordered to run a corrective advertising campaign, mostly on television, for 16 months at a cost of $10 million. Interestingly, even after the corrective campaign ran its course, 42 percent of Listerine users continued to believe the mouthwash was being advertised as a remedy for sore throats and colds, and 57 percent of users rated cold and sore throat effectiveness as a key reason for purchasing the brand.* These results raised doubts about the effectiveness of corrective advertising. However, the *Warner-Lambert* case remains significant because for the first time the FTC was given the power to apply retrospective remedies and to attempt to restrict future deceptions. In addition, the Supreme Court rejected the argument that corrective advertising violates the advertiser's First Amendment rights.

The Legal Responsibility of the Agency

With the resurgence of the FTC has come a new solution for deception—making the ad agency liable. To quote FTC Chairman, Janet Steiger, "An agency that is involved in advertising and promoting a product is not free from responsibility for the content of the claims, whether they are express or implied. You will find the commission staff looking more closely at the extent of advertising agency involvement."†

Two recent examples point to the extent to which the FTC has taken this warning seriously. In 1990 the FTC slapped sanctions on Lewis Galoob Toys and its agency for ads that the FTC said showed toys doing things they really couldn't do. Under terms of the consent agreement, Galoob and its agency, Towne, Silverstein, Rotter, of New York, are prohibited from misrepresenting a toy's ability to move without human assistance. In addition, future ads must disclose that assembly is required when such a toy is shown fully assembled in a commercial.‡

In 1991 a group of state attorney generals reached a settlement with Pfizer and ad agency Ally & Gargano. Pfizer and Ally agreed to stop making a number of deceptive claims in their advertising about the plaque-reducing qualities of Pfizer's Plax mouthwash, and Pfizer agreed to pay the states a total of $70,000 in investigative costs.§

The following is a list of tips one law firm offers agencies to avoid legal pitfalls in advertising:

1. Early in the creative process, get written permission from the appropriate people if an ad carries the potential to violate copyright and/or privacy laws.
2. During production, make sure no one hires a person to sound like, look like, or otherwise represent a celebrity.
3. Before the shoot, get the producers' affidavit signed to substantiate that demonstrations are not mockups.
4. Have regular seminars with a lawyer to update staff on specifically how to stay within the limits of advertising law.‖

*William Wilke, Dennis L. McNeil, and Michael B. Mazis, "Marketing's 'Scarlett Letter': The Theory and Practice of Corrective Advertising," *Journal of Marketing* (Spring 1984):26.

†Steven W. Colford, "FTC Warns Agencies; Eyes Tobacco, Cable," *Advertising Age* (March 12, 1990):6.

‡Steven W. Colford, "FTS Hits Galoob, Agency for Ads," *Advertising Age* (December 10, 1990):62.

§"Ally in Plax Settlement," *The Wall Street Journal* (February 12, 1991):B4.

‖Barbara Holsomback, "Ad Agencies Feel Piercing Glare of Watchdogs," *Adweek* (December 3, 1990):18.

Substantiating Advertising Claims

In 1971 the FTC initiated a policy that required advertisers to validate any claims when requested by the Commission. Advertisers must have a "reasonable basis" for making a claim. It is the responsibility of the advertiser to show the reasonableness of claim; it is *not* up to the FTC to disprove a claim's validity. Documentation may be based on a variety of sources, including scientific research and the opinions of experts.

Consumer Redress

The Magnuson-Moss Warranty—FTC Improvement Act of 1975 empowers the FTC to obtain consumer redress in cases where a person or a firm engages in deceptive practices. The Commission can order any of the following: cancellation or reformation of contracts; refund of money or return of property; payment of damages; and public notification.

Food and Drug Administration

Food and Drug Administration (FDA) *A federal regulatory agency that oversees package labeling and ingredient listings for food and drugs.*

Two other major government agencies deal with advertising-related concerns: the **Food and Drug Administration** (FDA) and the **Federal Communications Commission** (FCC). The FDA is the regulatory division of the Department of Health and Human Services. It oversees package labeling and ingredient listings for food and drugs and determines the safety and purity of foods and cosmetics. Although not directly involved with advertising, the FDA provides advice to the FTC and has a major impact on the overall marketing of food, cosmetics, and drugs.

Federal Communications Commission

Federal Communications Commission (FCC) *A federal agency that regulates broadcast media and has the power to eliminate messages, including ads, that are deceptive or in poor taste.*

The FCC was formed in 1934 to protect the public interest with regard to broadcast communication. It has limited control over broadcast advertising through its authority to issue and revoke licenses to broadcasting stations. The FCC is concerned with radio and television stations and networks, and it has the power to eliminate messages, including ads, that are deceptive or in poor taste. The agency monitors only those advertisements that have been the subject of complaints and works closely with the FTC with regard to false and deceptive advertising. The FCC takes action against the media, whereas the FTC is concerned with advertisers and agencies.

Other Federal Agencies

Other federal agencies are involved in the regulation of advertising, although most are limited by the type of advertising, product, or medium. For example, the Postal Service regulates direct-mail and magazine advertising and has control over the areas of obscenity, lottery, and fraud. Consumers who receive advertisements in the mail that they consider sexually offensive can request that no more mail be delivered from that sender. The postmaster general also has the power to withhold mail that promotes a lottery. Fraud can include any number of activities that are questionable, such as implausible get-rich-quick schemes.

The Bureau of Alcohol, Tobacco, and Firearms within the Treasury Department both regulates deception in advertising and establishes labeling requirements for the liquor industry. This agency's power comes from its authority to issue and revoke annual operating permits for distillers, wine merchants, and brewers. Because there is a danger that public pressure could result in banning all advertisements for alcoholic beverages, the liquor industry strives to maintain relatively tight control on its advertising.

The Patent Office, under the Lanham Trade-Mark Act of 1947, oversees registration of trademarks, which include both brand names and corporate or store names as well as their identifying symbols. This registration process protects unique trademarks from infringement by competitors. Because trademarks are critical communication devices for products and services, they are important in advertising.

Finally, the Library of Congress provides controls for copyright protection. Legal copyrights give creators a monopoly on their creations for a certain time. Advertising is a competitive business where "me too" ads abound. Copyrighting of coined words, illustrations, characters, and photographs can offer some measure of protection from advertisers who borrow too heavily from their competitors.

Certain state laws also regulate unfair and deceptive business practices. These laws are important supplements to federal laws because of the sometimes limited resources and jurisdiction of the FTC and the Justice Department. Because these laws are so numerous and diverse, we cannot begin to examine them in this chapter.

SELF-REGULATION

societal marketing concept *A concept that requires balancing the company, consumer, and public interests.*

Based on the discussion thus far, it would appear that all advertising and advertisers must be carefully governed because without that control all ads would be full of lies. Nothing could be further from the truth, however. For the great majority of advertisers, a societal marketing approach is followed. Philip Kotler defines the **societal marketing concept** as follows. The organization's task is to determine the needs, wants, and interests of target markets and to deliver the desired satisfactions more effectively and efficiently than its competitors in a way that preserves or enhances the consumer's and society's well-being. This requires a careful balance between company profits, consumer-want satisfaction, and public interest.*

Admittedly, this is not an easy balance to maintain. Yet, advertisers realize that everything they do is carefully scrutinized by millions of consumers and a host of agencies. Therefore, it has become necessary for advertisers to regulate themselves even more stringently than do the agencies discussed earlier. Using this system of self-regulation ensures that societal marketing is more likely to become a reality.

PRINCIPLE
Self-regulation encourages voluntary withdrawal of deceptive advertising.

In addition to governmental controls, the advertising industry has created a self-regulating mechanism in an attempt to deal with such issues as deception. The rationale is that if the industry polices itself better, it will avoid confrontations with the government.

National Agencies

In the case of both advertisers and advertising agencies, the most effective attempts at self-regulation have come through the Advertising Review Council and the Better Business Bureau. In 1971 the National Advertising Review Council was established by several professional advertising associations in conjunction with the Council of Better Business Bureaus. The main purpose of the Council is to negotiate voluntary withdrawal of national ad-

*Philip Kotler, *Marketing Management: Analysis, Planning, Implementation, and Control,* 7th ed. (Englewood Cliffs, NJ: Prentice Hall, Inc. 1991):25-26.

vertising that professionals consider to be deceptive. The National Advertising Division (NAD) of the Council of Better Business Bureaus and the National Advertising Review Board (NARB) are the two operating arms of the National Advertising Review Council.

NAD The NAD is a full-time agency made up of people from the field of advertising. It evaluates complaints that are submitted by consumers, consumer groups, industrial organizations, and advertising firms. The NAD also does its own monitoring. After a complaint is received, the NAD may ask the advertiser in question to substantiate claims made in the advertisement. If such substantiation is deemed inadequate, the advertiser is requested either to change or to withdraw the offending ad. When a satisfactory resolution cannot be found, the case is referred to the NARB.

NARB The NARB is a 50-member regulatory group that represents national advertisers, advertising agencies, and other professional fields. When a case is appealed to the NARB, a five-person panel is formed that consists of three advertisers, one agency person, and one public representative. This panel reviews the complaint and the NAD staff findings and holds hearings to let the advertiser present its case. If the case remains unresolved after the process, the NARB can (1) publicly identify the advertiser and the facts about the case and (2) refer the complaint to the appropriate government agency (usually the FTC). Although neither the NAD nor the NARB has any real power other than threatening to invite governmental intervention, these groups have been relatively effective in controlling cases of deception and misleading advertising.

Local Regulation: BBB

At the local level self-regulation has been supported by the Better Business Bureau (BBB). The BBB functions much like the national regulatory agencies, and in addition provides local businesses with advice concerning the legal aspects of advertising. The origin of the Bureau can be traced to the "truth in advertising campaign" sponsored by the American Advertising Federation in 1911. Since that time more than 240 local and national bureaus, made up of advertisers, agencies, and media, have screened hundreds of thousands of advertisements for possible violation of truth and accuracy. Although the BBB has no legal power, it does receive and investigate complaints and maintain files on violators. It also assists local law enforcement officials in prosecuting violators.

Media Regulation and Advertising

PRINCIPLE
Media can refuse to accept advertising that violates standards of truth or good taste.

The media attempt to regulate advertising by screening and rejecting ads that violate their standards of truth and good taste. For example, _Reader's Digest_ does not accept tobacco and liquor ads, and many magazines and television stations will not show condom ads. Each individual medium has the discretion to accept or reject a particular ad. In the case of the major television networks, the ABC's advertising standards and guidelines serve as the primary standard.

A Final Thought

It is clear that advertising, as a high-profile industry, will remain extremely susceptible to controlling legislation and the criticisms of the general public. Rather than lamenting such scrutiny and becoming defensive, advertisers would be wise to take the initiative and establish individual ethical parameters that anticipate and even go beyond the complaints. Such a proactive stance will facilitate the creative process and avoid the kind of disasters that result from violating the law or offending certain publics. The smart advertiser follows the advice given by David Ogilvy of Ogilvy & Mather: Never run an advertisement you would not want your family to see.

SUMMARY

- Federal courts have ruled that advertising is protected under the First Amendment.
- The primary regulatory agencies that govern advertising are the Federal Trade Commission, the Food and Drug Administration, and the Federal Communications Commission. They are concerned with the following advertising issues: deception, reasonable basis for making a claim, comparative advertising, endorsements, demonstrations, and children's advertising.

- Regulatory agencies have a variety of remedies for deception and unfair advertising practices.
- Because of legislative pressure and the costs of defending themselves in legal actions, advertisers and the media have set up a variety of self-regulation systems.
- Advertisers have been very active in addressing the ethical issues in advertising that are not governed by specific legislation.

QUESTIONS

1. Two local agencies are in fierce contention for a major client in Hillsboro. The final presentations are 3 days away when Sue Geners, an account executive for the Adcom Group, learns from her sister-in-law that the creative director for the rival agency has serious personal problems. His son has entered a drug rehabilitation program and his wife has filed for a divorce. Because this information comes from inside the clinic, Sue knows it's very unlikely that anyone in the business side of Hillsboro has any knowledge of this. Should she inform Adcom management? If she does, should Adcom warn the prospective client that a key person in the rival's agency's plans will be seriously limited for months to come?

2. Sue Geners, our account executive from the last question also has a quandry of her own. Adcom keeps very strict hourly records on its accounts for billing and cost accounting purposes. Sue has an old friend with an Adcom client that needs some strong promotional strategy. The client, however, is very small and cannot afford the hours that Sue would have to charge. Should Sue do the work and charge those hours to one of her large clients? Should she turn down her friend? What should she do?

3. Zack Wilson is the advertising manager for the campus newspaper. He is looking over a layout for a promotion for a spring break vacation package. The headline says "Absolutely the Finest Deal Available

This Spring—You'll Have The Best Time Ever if you'll join us in Boca." The newspaper has a solid reputation for not running advertising with questionable claims and promises. Should Zack accept or reject this ad?

4. The Dimento Game Company has a new video game on basketball. To promote it, "Slammer" Aston, an NBA star is signed to do the commercial. In it Aston is shown with the game controls as he speaks these lines: "This is the most challenging court game you've ever tried. It's all here—zones, man-to-man, pick and roll, even the alley oop. For me, this is the best game off-the-court." Is Aston's presentation an endorsement or is he a spokesperson? Should the FTC consider a complaint if Dimento uses this strategy?

5. What are the central issues in ethical decision making? Write a short evaluation of a current ad campaign utilizing three ethical criteria.

6. Think of an ad you have found deceptive or offensive. What bothered you about the ad? Should the media have carried it? Is it proper for the government or the advertising industry to act in cases like this? Why or why not?

7. There is a great deal of controversy surrounding subliminal advertising. Do you think subliminal advertising exists? If so, what do you believe are risks associated with this technique?

FURTHER READINGS

ARMSTRONG, GARY M., AND JUDITH L. OSANNE, "An Evaluation of NAD/NARB: Purpose and Performance," *Journal of Advertising 12* (1983):15–26.

BUCHANAN, BRUCE, AND DORON GOLDMAN, "U.S. vs. Them: The Mindfold of Comparative Ads," *Harvard Business Review,* June 1989, pp. 38–50.

ROTZELL, KIM G., AND JAMES E. HAEFNER, *Advertising in Contemporary Society* (Cincinnati, OH: South-Western Publishing, 1990).

SCHUDSON, MICHAEL, *Advertising: The Uneasy Persuasion* (New York: Basic Books, 1984).

VIDEO CASE

 Infomercials: Opportunity or Threat

With the advent of numerous alternatives to traditional network television programming, such as cable, television stations across the country have been forced to utilize less orthodox techniques to generate acceptable revenues. One of the most notable examples of this trend is the increase use of "infomercials."

Infomercials are, in theory, informational videos featuring and sponsored by branded products or services. For example, Clorox produced an infomercial in the mid-1980s, which showed how its cleaning products could be used to clean up smoke damage after a fire. Originally conceived by advertisers as an acceptable way to slip product messages into a commercial-free environment of public television, infomercials have evolved to the point where they are now often merely 30- to 60-minute ads for products. However, for those viewers who tune in late or slip out of the room during the brief disclaimer that differentiates infomercials from true entertainment-based programming, infomercials can easily be mistaken for "normal" programs. Whether because of this confusion or because of the inherent effectiveness of infomercials as a marketing technique, they have been extremely successful.

Unfortunately for the unwary consumer, infomercials lack even the types of cursory guidelines and regulations that limit traditional advertising's use of false or deceptive claims. Nonetheless, the advertising community has thus far failed to single out infomercials for increased regulation.

The newspaper industry has grappled and dealt with a similar issue. Long ago advertisers recognized the credibility advantage of advertising in newspapers, particularly if the ads could be structured in such a way to look like regular newspaper editorial features. The newspaper industry has chosen to accept advertising that is formatted and typeset in such a way as to resemble the paper's editorial content. However, the advertising is generally identified by printing the word "advertisement" somewhere on the ad and often setting it apart in some graphic fashion to further separate it from the true editorial content of the paper.

In television, a fixed disclaimer such as "advertisement" on an infomercial is somewhat more problematic. A simple solution would be to superimpose the word on the screen during the entire running of the infomercial. Obviously, producers of infomercials would be reluctant to allow networks to damage the credibility of their property in such a fashion without station policy or other regulations requiring it.

Independent and network television also stand to lose in the long run if infomercials continue to proliferate. Just as advertisers fear that infomercials that make false claims could damage the credibility of advertising as a whole, television station owners must address the issue of whether infomercials that look like entertainment-based programming could damage the credibility of their regular programs. Television stations can profit from this type of advertising, however, because they can simply sell the entire 30- to 60-minute time period in which the infomercial runs to the infomercial producers rather than buying regular programming and trying to sell commercial space during the traditionally low viewership periods late at night. Although this had obvious short-term benefits, if the credibility and authenticity of regular entertainment-based programming is questioned by the public, viewership will drop as will the price that stations can charge for commercial time.

The issue is more complex for advertisers. Anything that negatively affects the credibility of advertising can jeopardize that technique's long-term ability to sell products. However, the competitive nature of most industries is such that any new marketing tool that has proven itself effective cannot be summarily dismissed. Firms that pursue those new techniques could have a competitive advantage over those that do not. As long as television viewing options continue to increase and viewership of individual stations continue to decline, a strong market for infomercials will exist. To what extent, if at all, manufacturers, advertising agencies, and the television industry itself will seek to regulate infomercials remains to be seen.

QUESTIONS

1. Explain how infomercials can actually be good for consumers in some situations.
2. As advertising costs have increased, advertisers have responded by producing shorter and shorter commercials. Given this trend, how can infomercials actually benefit advertisers?
3. a. Explain how and why infomercials should be regulated.
   b. Explain why infomercials should not be regulated.

Source: "It's Really a Commercial," *20/20* (September 18, 1990).

3

Advertising and the Marketing Process

Chapter Outline

Meet the McDonald's of Video Stores
The Concept of Marketing
The 4Ps of Marketing
Advertising and the Marketing Mix

Chapter Objectives

When you have completed this chapter, you should be able to:

- Understand the marketing concept and how it differs from production-oriented marketing
- Explain how a company's market philosophy is expressed
- Identify four types of markets
- Define and explain the 4Ps of the marketing mix
- Explain the four stages in a product's life cycle
- Identify the key elements involved in establishing a brand

MEET THE MCDONALD'S OF VIDEO STORES

A visit to a Blockbuster video store is similar to eating out at a McDonald's restaurant. Both offer fast service, convenient location, family orientation, and kid appeal. This isn't too surprising considering that the chief marketing officer at Blockbuster, Tom Gruber, is a former McDonald's marketing executive. According to Gruber, marketing concepts and techniques are universal. What works for McDonald's should also work at Blockbuster, particularly because both franchises have the same target audience in mind: the family.

Blockbuster has experienced great success with the marketing strategies developed for the company by Bernstein-Rein Advertising. (The Kansas City–based agency also serves as a regional agency for McDonald's.) The first Blockbuster store opened in 1985, and by 1988 there were 415 stores. This number increased to over 1,000 in 1990, and the video store chain captured 133 television markets that year, reaching between 75 to 85 percent of the U.S. population. Revenue for 1990 was over $600 million, compared to only $66 million in 1988.

Blockbuster's successful marketing strategy emphasizes product, location, and advertising. The company bills itself as "America's Family Video Store" and attributes much of its success to the fact that its stores don't carry X-rated videos. This principle serves as a central theme in Blockbuster's advertising efforts and has given the company a wholesome image with customers.

The blockbuster location strategy is referred to as "the cluster concept." Before the emergence of Blockbuster, each market was served by a regional chain of video stores and a variety of mom-and-pop stores. The cluster concept allows for a concentration of outlets in a given target market, one market at a time. For example, Blockbuster clustered four stores in the southern and northern parts of Dallas before moving to the western side of the city and, finally, the eastern side. Blockbuster stores are most often sited near routes that are well traveled by commuters.

As far as Blockbuster's advertising strategies are concerned, in the past advertising was primarily concentrated in regional television and radio buys, with newspaper, magazine, and outdoor advertising used to a lesser extent. In 1990, however, Bernstein-Rein realized that Blockbuster's market coverage justified a national television campaign. Two television spots were produced and aired on *The Tonight Show, The Pat Sajak Show,* and *The Arsenio Hall Show.* The budget for the national campaign was $25 million. In 1991 the media budget was doubled, with 65 percent going to television advertising. The increase in Blockbuster's budget, audience, and revenues indicate that the marriage between marketing and advertising is working very well for the video store franchise.*

THE CONCEPT OF MARKETING

marketing *Business activities that direct the exchange of goods and services between producers and consumers*

The American Marketing Association defines **marketing** as "the process of planning and executing the conception, pricing, promotion, and distribution of ideas, goods, and services to create exchanges that satisfy individual

*Adapted from Greg Clarkin, "Fast Forward," *Marketing & Media Decisions* (March 1990): 57–59.

Mission

To become the premiere source of residential and commercial services and products to consumers in the United States and selected international markets. These services and products will be ones that improve the quality of life and assist the consumers in maintaining their property and surrounding.

Objectives

1. To develop the [Company] Quality Service Network, which will be made up of several service companies, each being specialists in their own field, which the consumer can access through one source.
2. To build market share in each of the operating units.
3. To maintain a minimum of X% annual increase in both revenues and profits.

The operational objectives are:

1. To make available the entire range of consumer services in a profitable and timely manner in all major markets in the U.S.
2. To establish and enforce quality standards among all the operating units.
3. To introduce some of the services into selected foreign markets.

The major marketing objectives of the [Company] Quality Service Network are:

1. Cross sell to existing customers of one [Company] operating unit the services of the other operating units.
2. Expand the customer base of the [Company] Network to include customers who have no services with any operating unit.
3. Increase customer loyalty and retention.
4. Expand the number of services available through the [Company] Quality Service Network.

Strategy

1. Each operating unit will continue to build brand awareness for its own service or product. [X], [Y], and [Z} will be promoted under their respective brand names.
2. All the different services and products will be linked together by the 1-800-XXX-XXXX number and the Partners Logo Block.
3. Channels of distribution will be increased by expansion of the services into all markets. Certain segments of the business may be more suitable to franchising while others should be company owned.
4. Foreign markets will be pursued with a minimum investment strategy. A foreign partner will be selected to license the know-how from [Company]. [X] will be the entering brand in the [foreign] markets.
5. The *Partners Pledge* will represent the minimum standards by which all operating units are measured. All [Company] service centers must agree to abide by the pledge before they will be certified to operate under the [Company] Quality Service Network umbrella. This Partners Pledge will be the network's guarantee to the customer that service will be delivered on time and that the job will be done right.

Summary of Mission and Objectives by Operating Units

[Company] currently provides the following services:
Residential and commercial cleaning of carpets, upholstery, and drapes; residential disaster restoration; contract cleaning services; residential home cleaning service; lawn care service; termite and pest control; home system care; and consumer products.

FIGURE 3.1
Consumer Services and Products Strategic Plan Courtesy of The Conference Board, *The Marketing Board in the 1990's,* Report No. 951 (1990):34–35.

(customer) and organizational objectives.* Although the exchange is the focus of the effort, marketing is a complicated process operating in a complex business environment.

PRINCIPLE
Advertising is a component of marketing.

Marketing is an important business function because its purpose is to find, satisfy, and retain customers. The success of a given marketing effort depends on whether a *competitive advantage* can be established in the minds of these customers. A competitive advantage is simply a judgment made by a consumer on how close one product, service, or idea comes to satisfying his or her needs versus a competitor's product, service, or idea. A human need is a state of felt deprivation, such as hunger, or a need for af-

*"AMA Board Approves New Marketing Definition," *Marketing News* (March 1, 1985):1.

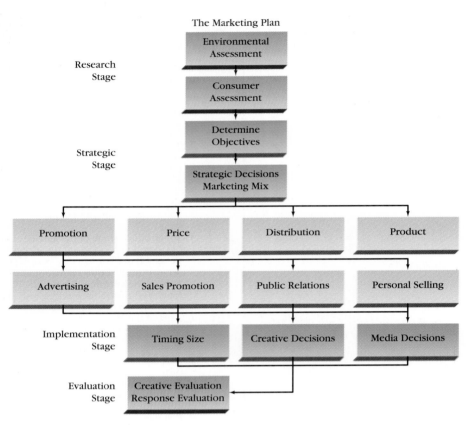

The Marketing Plan

FIGURE 3.2
The place of advertising in the marketing plan.

fection, knowledge, or self-expression. Sometimes the consumer decides that none of the choices provided by advertisers are acceptable, and so makes no purchase. At other times, one choice is perceived to be superior, and the consumer does make a purchase. This is referred to as *exchange*—the act of obtaining a desired object from someone by offering something in return. The process of creating an exchange is not random, and it requires a great deal of marketing effort—in other words, it revolves around a marketing plan. As we will discuss in Chapter 7, a *marketing plan* involves different stages: a research stage, during which the marketing environment, including the consumer, is analyzed; a strategic stage, during which objectives are developed, along with the enduring strategy for achieving them; an implementation stage, which involves the coordination of the marketing strategy with actual marketing activities; and the evaluation stage, when it is determined to what extent the objectives were achieved. Figure 3.1 is a sample marketing plan. Figure 3.2 illustrates advertising's place in the marketing plan.

Advertising is an integral but relatively small part of the marketing plan. It is one of the strategic alternatives available to the marketer. Traditionally, the hierarchy of strategies starts with the **marketing mix,** which involves design of the product, including its package; pricing of the product, as well as terms of sale; distribution of the product; and promotion of the product. *Promotion,* or *marketing communication,* consists of advertising, sales promotion, public relations, direct-response marketing, packaging, and personal selling. Advertising is a special type of marketing communication that has characteristics not possessed by the other types. For example, advertising is capable of reaching a mass audience simultaneously and repeatedly. It is also an excellent device for informing customers about new products or changes in existing products. Reminding customers

marketing mix *A plan that identifies the most effective combination of promotional activities.*

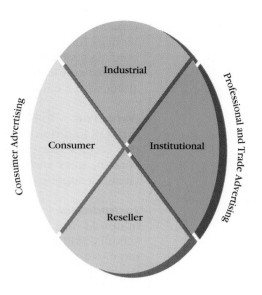

FIGURE 3.3
The four principle types of markets.

to buy and reinforcing past purchases are two other strengths of advertising. Finally, advertising can persuade customers to change their attitudes, beliefs, or behavior.

Superior advertising cannot save an inferior product—at least not for long—but inferior advertising can destroy an excellent product. Therefore it is just as important for the advertising director to have a thorough understanding of marketing and all its facets as it is for the marketing manager to understand how advertising works. This chapter provides only an overview of marketing. In the real world of advertising, a much deeper understanding of marketing in general, as well as of the specific marketing strategy employed by the client, would be required. The starting point for our overview is the market itself.

The Idea of a Market

market *An area of the country, a group of people, or the overall demand for a product.*

The word *market* originally meant the place where the "exchange" between seller and buyer took place. The term has taken on several additional meanings. Today we speak of a **market** as either a region where goods are sold and bought or a particular type of buyer.

The term implies that the buyer and seller are not paired at random, but rather are engaged in negotiation because each has evaluated the likelihood that the other will be able to satisfy his or her needs and wants. How is this accomplished? Businesses are able to locate the best market for an existing or potential product through experience and market research. Likewise, customers rely on experience, market information, and many other factors (including advertising) to identify markets where they feel they will find the best value.

Types of Markets

When marketing strategists speak of markets they are generally referring to groups of people or organizations. The four primary types of markets are (1) consumer, (2) industrial, (3) institutional, and (4) reseller (see Figure 3.3).

Consumer.   Consumer markets consist of people who buy products and services for their own personal use or for the use of others in the household. As a student, you are considered a member of the market for companies that sell jeans, sweatshirts, pizza, textbooks, backpacks, and bicycles, along with a multitude of other products.

Industrial.   Industrial markets consist of companies that buy products or services to use in their own businesses or in making other products. General Electric, for example, buys computers to use in billing and inventory control, steel and wiring to use in the manufacture of its products, and cleaning supplies to use in maintaining its buildings.

Institutional.   Institutional markets include a wide variety of profit and nonprofit organizations, such as hospitals, government agencies, and schools, which provide goods and services for the benefit of society at large. Universities, for example, are in the market for furniture, cleaning supplies, computers, office supplies, groceries and food products, audio-visual materials, and tissue and toilet paper, to name just a few.

Reseller.   The reseller market includes what we often call "the middlemen." These are wholesalers, retailers, and distributors who buy finished or semifinished products and resell them for a profit. Resellers are considered a market by companies that sell such products and services as trucks, cartons, crates, and transportation services (airlines, cruise ships, and rental car agencies).

Of the four markets, the consumer market is probably the largest in terms of dollars spent on advertising. Marketing to this group is generally done through mass media such as radio, television, newspapers, general consumer magazines, and direct-response advertising media. The other three markets—industrial, institutional, and reseller—are reached through trade and professional advertising in specialized media such as trade journals, professional magazines, and direct mail.

The Marketing Concept

The post-1950 "Marketing Era" is considered to be the true beginning of contemporary marketing. Technology could produce more products than the market demanded, and people had more *discretionary income* to buy these products. In addition to necessities, people could choose among a number of "luxury" items. Therefore it became necessary to *appeal* to consumers in areas other than basic needs to stimulate demand. It wasn't enough to produce a product efficiently and offer it for sale. In a competitive situation it became necessary to identify and speak to consumers' needs and preferences. This approach is now called *the marketing concept.*

PRINCIPLE ─────────
The "marketing concept" turns the focus from the seller's product to the buyer's needs.
─────────

Consumer-Centered Marketing.   The marketing concept changes the focus in commerce from the seller's product to the buyer's needs. It recognizes that in times of scarcity people buy what is available; in times of plenty buyers have choices, and the seller has to make special efforts to provide what buyers want and need.

This concept was explained by Philip Kotler in *Principles of Marketing.* According to Kotler, the "marketing concept starts with the needs and wants of the company's targeted customers." In addition to focusing exclusively on more efficient manufacturing processes, companies should focus

We haven't changed a thing.

Over the years our cars have gotten bigger, smoother and more sophisticated. But, one thing has stayed the same. The reputation for quality.
Which is why for the 12th straight year Honda is still number one in Import Owner Loyalty.*
And it's not just the cars that bring people back to Honda. It's also the hard work from our reliable Honda dealers all over the country.
Why change a good thing.

HONDA

#1 in Import Owner Loyalty for 12 years running.

AD 3.1
Honda's appeal to the consumer's desire for quality and commitment comes across in this ad addressing owner loyalty. (Courtesy of American Honda Motor Co., Inc./Rubin Postaer and Associates.)

on consumer problems and try to develop products to solve them.* This means working from the customer backward rather than from the factory forward. The marketing concept states, "First determine what the customer needs and wants, and then develop, manufacture, and market the goods and services that fill those particular needs and wants."

Adopting the marketing concept affects advertising as well. Primarily, advertising is employed as a mechanism for delivering information. Through research, the marketer understands how the consumer makes decisions most efficiently and satisfactorily. This information is then incorporated within advertising messages. The intent is for advertising to facilitate decision making. More importantly, the goal is to create advertising that is honest, useful, and matches the needs of the customer so that the customer is satisfied with the choices made. When advertising is guided by the marketing concept, there is a central goal—satisfying the customer—that helps coordinate advertising with the other marketing functions and increases the likelihood that a particular advertisement will be successful.

That is exactly the philosophy that has made Honda so successful in the American market. When consumers wanted fuel efficiency, Honda brought out the Civic. When they wanted roominess, comfort, and performance, Honda brought out the Accord. Ad 3.1 shows how Honda has maintained this high level of quality and integrity.

*Philip Kotler, *Principles of Marketing,* 3rd ed. (Englewood Cliffs: Prentice Hall, 1986): 15–16.

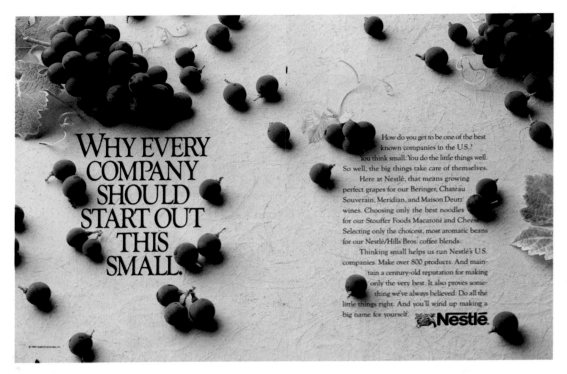

AD 3.2
Nestlé expresses a market philosophy of "thinking small" while maintaining a reputation for making the best products available. (Courtesy of Nestlé Chocolate and Confection Co.)

market philosophy *The general attitude of the marketer toward the customer.*

Market Philosophies. A **market philosophy** is the general perspective or attitude the marketer has toward the customer. Successful companies seem to have an explicit philosophy that is communicated clearly to employees and customers alike. This philosophy is developed by paying careful attention to the customer. Companies following this philosophy know more about their customers and therefore tend to produce more successful products and advertising. The Nestlé ad (Ad 3.2) demonstrates the company's market philosophy in a manner that is clear to anyone who reads it.

THE 4PS OF MARKETING

In his book *Basic Marketing* Jerome McCarthy popularized the classification of the various marketing elements into four categories that have since been known in the marketing industry as the "4Ps"* (see Figure 3.4). They are:

1. *Product:* Includes product design and development, branding, and packaging.
2. *Place* (or Distribution): Includes the channels used in moving the product from the manufacturer to the buyer.
3. *Price:* Includes the price at which the product or service is offered for sale and establishes the level of profitability.
4. *Promotion:* Includes personal selling, advertising, public relations, and sales promotion.

*E. Jerome McCarthy and William D. Perreault, Jr., *Basic Marketing* (Homewood, IL: Irwin, 1987):37.

FIGURE 3.4
The 4Ps of marketing.

It is the job of the marketing or product manager to manipulate these elements to create the most efficient and effective *marketing mix*.

Product

The product is both the object of the advertising and the reason for marketing. Marketing begins by asking a set of questions about the product offered. These questions are always asked from the consumer's perspective: What product attributes and benefits are important? What segments will be attracted? How is the product perceived relative to competitive offerings?

Customers view products as "bundles of satisfaction" rather than just physical things. For example, in the United States, some car buyers perceive automobiles made in Germany and Japan as offering superior quality, better gas mileage, and less costly service and maintenance than American cars. At the luxury level, cars such as Porsche, BMW, Audi, and the Mazda RX-7 now offer the status and prestige once associated with Cadillac and Lincoln (see Ad 3.3). Thus the intangible, symbolic attributes foreign-made automobiles now possess over and above the tangible ones perform psy-

AD 3.3
The copy in this ad for the Porsche 911 describes the type of personal commitment to detail that makes it **a luxury car**. (Courtesy of Porsche.)

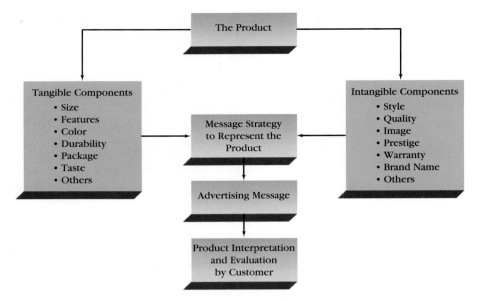

FIGURE 3.5
Tangible and intangible characteristics of a product.

chological and social functions for the buyer. Figure 3.5 portrays both tangible and intangible product characteristics.

To have a practical impact on consumers, managers must translate these product characteristics into concrete attributes with demonstrable benefits. In other words, they must develop message strategy. Consider packaged cookies. The physical ingredients might include sugar, flour, chocolate, and baking powder. The intangible features might be an implied return policy and a reputable brand name. However, these characteristics are too far removed from the real attributes or benefits customers perceive. A customer looks for descriptive phrases such as "tastes like homemade" or "a great afternoon snack," so these are the real pieces of information the marketer desires to communicate. Stressing the most important attributes is the key to influencing customer choices and serves as the foundation for much of advertising.

Product Life Cycle.   The concept of **product life cycle** was introduced by Theodore Levitt in an article in the *Harvard Business Review* in 1965.* It is based on a metaphor that treats products as people and assumes they are born (or introduced), develop, grow old, and die.

A newly developed product is introduced to its market in the *introductory stage,* either representing a new category or improving an old product. Product trial is very important in this stage, and building this necessary level of awareness is often costly.

The hope is that those consumers who try the new product become repeat customers during the *growth stage,* but competition is likely to develop with the success of a new product. As a result, advertising must carve out a distinctive position for the product in a cluttered market. Such advertising is critical during the *maturity stage* as the company shares the market with successful and vigorous competitors and sales increase more slowly and eventually level off. **Line extensions**—new or reformulated products that carry existing brand names—are introduced in an attempt to trade on

product life cycle *The history of the product from its introduction to its eventual decline and withdrawal.*

PRINCIPLE
The stage in the product life cycle affects the advertising message.

line extensions *New products introduced under existing brand names.*

*Theodore Levitt, "Exploit the Product Life Cycle," *Harvard Business Review* (November–December 1965):81–94.

the brand's already established reputation. The maturity stage can be an extremely competitive period, with comparisons, challenges, and counter-challenges, such as the taste-test battles between Pepsi and Coca-Cola.

Finally, many products face a period of obsolescence when they no longer sell as well as they previously did. During this *decline stage,* advertising may be reduced or eliminated altogether. Not all products have to decline, however, and a product may be reformulated or turned around, and the product life cycle begins again.

These stages can vary from several days to many years, depending on the product. The point that the product occupies in its life cycle has a major effect on the advertising strategy for that product. The messages for new products are considerably different from those for products that have been around for many years.

Branding. When you think of bread, what product name comes to mind? When you think of facial tissues, what product name occurs to you? What name comes to mind when you picture a copy machine? Do you think of a product name when you think of salt?

Wonder Bread, Kleenex, Xerox, and Morton's have been extensively advertised over many years. **Branding** makes a product distinctive in the marketplace. As Bogart explained, "Where products are very similar, brand identity—based on the name, packaging, or advertising themes and techniques—produces the illusion of difference that is vital to competitive selling."* Some 29,000 different brands are advertised nationally in the United States, according to Bogart. Although none of us knows all of them, most of us have a large and varied group of brand names anchored in our memories.

Although brand names continue to be powerful, the introduction of **generic products** in the 1970s has made them somewhat less attractive. The issues involved in establishing a brand name are examined in the box entitled "Establishing a Brand Name: The Jeans Industry" and are discussed in more detail in Chapter 8.

Packaging. The package is another important communication device. In today's marketing environment a package is much more than a container. The self-service retailing phenomenon means that the consumer in the typical grocery store or drugstore is faced with an endless array of products. In such a situation the package is the message. When the package works in tandem with consumer advertising, it catches attention, presents a familiar brand image, and communicates critical information. Many purchase decisions are made on the basis of how the product looks on the shelf.

An article in *Advertising Age* explained the importance of the package as a communication medium: "Even if you can't afford a big advertising budget, you've got a fighting chance if your product projects a compelling image from the shelf."† For products that are advertised nationally, the package reflects the brand image developed in the advertising. It serves as a very important reminder at that critical moment when the consumer is choosing among several competing brands. As an advertising medium, the package has to be an eye-catcher as well as an identifier. Most of us carry around in our minds some kind of visual image of our most familiar products. That image is usually the package.

---

branding *The process of creating an identity for a product using a distinctive name or symbol.*

PRINCIPLE _____
Branding makes a product distinctive in the marketplace.

generic products *Products that are marketed without any identifying brand; they are usually less expensive than branded products.*

PRINCIPLE _____
The package stimulates the purchase at the critical moment when the consumer is making a choice.

---

* (Chicago, IL: Crain Books, 1984):26–27. Bogart, *Strategy in Advertising,* 2nd ed.
†Lori Kesler, "Shopping Around for a Design," *Advertising Age* (December 28, 1981):2–4, 2–8.

ESTABLISHING A BRAND NAME:
THE JEANS INDUSTRY

In 1989 the jeans industry sold 350 million pairs of jeans, according to the KSA/NOD Purchase Panel. The four leading brands—Levi's, Wrangler, Lee, and Gitano—controlled slightly over one-half of the $6 billion jeans market. Levi's has 22 percent, Wrangler 13 percent, Lee 11 percent, and Gitano 5 percent. Total advertising spending by the four brands was $64.7 million in the 12-month period ending June 1990, with $52.8 million spent on television advertising, $8.3 million on magazine ads, and $2.5 million on spot radio commercials.

With the 14- to 24-year-old market shrinking, the leading jeans companies are altering their advertising and marketing strategies in order to establish brand recognition among a changing market of consumers while maintaining recognition among the traditional youth market.

According to Dan Chew, a corporate marketing manager for Levi's, the company has broadened its strategy to include a many-markets, one-brand strategy rather than the single national image campaign of a decade ago. In 1989 sales of Levi's jeans were estimated to be $1.3 billion, or 22 percent of the market. Levi's segments its target markets by age, region, and ethnic group. The company's "501" campaign is aimed at their primary target of 14- to 24-year-olds. Levi's has both a national campaign, directed by Spike Lee, and a regional campaign, "Levi's 501 Button Fly Guys," which runs in seven eastern and midwestern cities and markets.

Levi's concentrates its advertising in their "501" television campaign. Spending for television advertising reached $38.2 million in the 12-month period ending June 1990. The company advertised on such programs as *Late Night with David Letterman, Star Trek,* and *Alien Nation.* Print advertising was not used because television advertising was found to be much more efficient.

Total advertising spending by Wrangler, which has captured 7 percent of the jeans market, was $6.6 million. Wrangler chose to concentrate on promoting its Wrangler Rugged Wear brand in markets east of the Mississippi. The company used sports television and rock and country radio stations to reach blue-collar men aged 25 to 49 who enjoy the outdoors. In promoting its Western Wear brand the company developed an advertising campaign featuring rodeo stars and other celebrities admired by the 18- to 34-year-old audience. In contrast to Levi's, Wrangler concentrated its Western Wear advertising in print *(Rolling Stone, Sports Illustrated,* and *Playboy)* and radio (album-oriented rock, country, and contemporary hit stations).

Lee gears its advertising toward the women's market. The company captured an estimated 11 percent of the market by spending $13 million on advertising in 1989, most of which was designated for network television advertising. Lee appealed to the

Packaging is one of the most innovative areas in modern marketing. Inventions are continuous, and one reason packaging is such a big industry is that marketers have to keep up with the competition in new packaging ideas. The package itself becomes a selling point. Morton Salt has retained the same basic package design over the years in order to establish product identification (see Ad 3.4).

Some recent ideas are plastic squeeze bottles, boil-in-bags, crush-proof bags for fragile products like potato chips, ziplock bags, unbreakable bottles like those used with shampoos, shrink wrapping, vacuum-seal plastic lids and bags, and "blister cards," which seal the product under a clear plastic bubble.

Some packages have windows, like the back of a bacon package, because some products are bought only after the consumer has had the opportunity to inspect them visually. Decorator packages are being used for commonplace household items like facial tissue. Reusable packages in-

25- to 44-year-old age group through advertisements on soap operas and prime-time and late-night programs, including *Thirtysomething, Late Night with David Letterman,* and *The Arsenio Hall Show.* It advertised the company's Relaxed Riders brand in a print campaign run in *Cosmopolitan, Elle, Seventeen,* and *YM.* Lee's total print spending in 1989 was $3.6 million.

Lee's 1990 advertising campaign emphasized product benefits, such as comfort, fit, and finish. The company differentiated its brand from others by labeling their jeans in the stores to emphasize fit, an important criterion in the women's market. The company targeted men through print ads for its Easy Riders and Lee Riders brands, which appeared in *Sports Illustrated, GQ,* and *Playboy,* among other magazines. According to Lee's vice president of marketing, Joe Pacifico, the company prides itself on its "competitive advantage" as a "family brand."

In 1990 Gitano launched an $8 million brand campaign for July through September. The company's "Spirit of Family" campaign was targeted at mothers and teenage girls and consisted of print advertising and five 30-second and two 15-second television spots. John Amodeo, president of The Ad Group, Gitano's in-house agency, describes the campaign as "extremely wholesome." The commercials geared toward mothers were run during soap operas and prime-time programs, including *Mac-*

Levi's "501" campaign is targeted at a young audience of 14- to 24-year-olds. (Courtesy of Levi Strauss & Co.)

Guyver, Roseanne, and *The Simpsons.* The company also ran a radio campaign called "Singing the Blues," which encouraged teenagers to call in and sing their favorite summertime blues songs for prizes.

Each of these four leading brands of jeans uses advertising that will enhance the company image, emphasize brand awareness, and capture those target markets most likely to purchase particular kinds of jeans. The medium and type of advertising each chooses to employ depends on who the target market is and what kind of image the company wants to project. The $6 billion jeans industry is quite profitable, and the fact that only four brands control over half of those profits indicates that they have each been very successful in establishing a well-known and -liked brand of jeans in the minds of consumers.

Source: Adapted from Brian Bagot, "Slow Fads," *Marketing & Media Decisions* (October 1990):61–67.

---

clude jelly sold in glasses and teabags sold in decorative tins. Liquor at holiday time is packaged in fancy bottles that serve as decanters.

Package design is very important to advertisers because it is such a vital part of brand image and product identity. For this reason the design needs to be coordinated with the overall advertising program.

Place (The Channel of Distribution)

It does little good to manufacture a fantastic product that will meet the needs of the consumer unless there is a mechanism for delivering and servicing the product and receiving payment. Those individuals and institutions involved in moving products from producers to customers make up the **channel of distribution.** Resellers, or intermediaries, are primary members of the channel who may actually take ownership of the product and participate in its marketing. Wholesalers, retailers, and modes of trans-

channel of distribution *People and organizations involved in moving products from producers to consumers.*

Whenever we start to show our age, we do a little face lifting. Isn't that just like a woman?

No salt salts like Morton Salt salts.

AD 3.4
One major role of the package is to help consumers identify the product. Although the box for Morton Salt has changed over the years, the basic design has remained similar so that customers will not become confused. (Courtesy of Morton Salt Division of Morton Thiokol, Inc.)

portation are typical channel members. Each is capable of influencing and delivering advertising messages.

Other channel-related decisions influence advertising as well. Is the channel direct or indirect? Companies that distribute their products without the use of a reseller engage in *direct marketing.* Companies such as Lands' End, Spiegel, and Burpee Seeds all use direct-marketing channels. In place of stores or personal salespeople, direct marketing relies on advertising media to inform and stimulate customer purchase responses. Direct marketing will be discussed in more detail in Chapter 16.

In *indirect marketing* the product is distributed through a channel structure that includes one or more resellers. A key decision in indirect marketing concerns resellers' involvement in advertising. Wholesalers and especially retailers are often expected to participate in the advertising programs offered by producers. Through **cooperative advertising** allowances the producer and reseller share the cost of placing the advertisement. This activity not only saves money (because local advertising rates are less expensive than national rates), but also creates an important tie-in with local retailers, who often have a much greater following than the producer's brand does.

Wholesalers and retailers also initiate their own advertising campaigns, which often highlight the items of various manufacturers. Few manufacturers can match the advertising impact of retailers such as Sears, J.C. Penney, or Federated Stores. Rather, manufacturers attempt to penetrate these outlets in order to take advantage of their advertising strength.

A final channel-related decision influencing advertising concerns the *market coverage* desired. Three strategies are possible: exclusive distribution, selective distribution, and intensive distribution. With *exclusive distribution,* only one distributor is allowed to sell the brand in a particular market. Two examples of companies that employ exclusive distribution are Rolls-Royce and Ethan Allen Furniture. The retailer is expected to provide a strong personal selling effort, effective merchandising, and heavy participation in cooperative (co-op) advertising. *Selective distribution* expands the number of outlets but restricts participation to those outlets that prove most profitable to the manufacturer. Florsheim Shoes, Farrah Fashions, and Timex all engage in selective distribution. The role of advertising is quite varied under this arrangement, but normally the manufacturer does some mass advertising and offers co-op possibilities. *Intensive distribution* involves placing the product in every possible outlet (including vending machines) in order to attain total market coverage. Intensive distribution is used to advertise soft drinks, candy, and cigarettes. Advertising is paramount in this situation. Because little personal selling can be expected from the retailer, it is up to mass advertising to create brand awareness and preference.

Pricing

The price a seller sets for a product is based not only on the cost of making and marketing the product but also on the seller's expected level of profit. Certain psychological factors also affect the price. For example, it has long been assumed that price suggests quality in the consumer's mind.

With the exception of price information delivered at the point of sale, advertising is the primary vehicle for telling the consumer about the price and associated conditions of a particular product. The term *price copy* has been coined to designate advertising copy devoted primarily to this information.

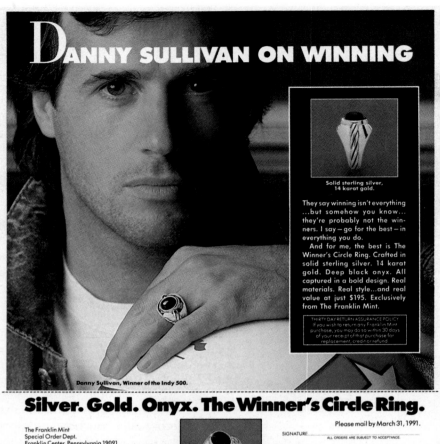

AD 3.5
An example of prestige pricing. A high price is given, with the knowledge that the quality justifies the cost. (Courtesy of The Franklin Mint.)

In turn, there are a number of pricing strategies that influence the specific creative strategy employed in a particular ad. For example, *customary* or *expected* pricing involves the use of a single well-known price for a long period of time. Movie theaters, the U.S. Post Office, and manufacturers of candy and other products sold through vending machines use this pricing strategy. Only price changes would be made explicit in advertising.

Psychological pricing techniques are intended to manipulate the judgment process employed by the customer. A very high price—for example, prestige pricing, where a high price is set to make the product seem worthy or valuable—would be accompanied by photographs of an exceptional product or a copy platform consisting of logical reasons for this high price. Ad 3.5 for the Winner's Circle Ring exemplifies a typical prestige pricing strategy. Conversely, a dramatic price reduction is translated through terms such as "sale," "special," and "today only."

Finally, *price lining* involves offering a number of variations of a particular product and pricing them accordingly. Sears Roebuck, for example, offers many of their products on a "good," "better," and "best" basis. Price lining requires that the ad show the various products so that consumers can assess the relative differences.

It is important that advertising clearly and consistently reflect the

Promotion Type	Intended Effect	Customer Contact	Timing
Personal Selling	Sales	Direct	Short
Advertising	Attitude Change Behavior Change	Indirect	Moderate-Low
Sales Promotion	Sales	Semidirect	Short
Direct Response	Behavior Change	Semidirect	Short
Public Relations	Attitude Change	Semidirect	Long

FIGURE 3.6
Promotional-mix comparison.

product's pricing strategy. For many consumers, this ad-price tandem represents the initial decision to purchase.

Promotion

promotion *The element in the marketing mix that encourages the purchase of a product or service.*

Advertising, personal selling, sales promotion, and public relations constitute the area called **promotion,** or marketing communication. Marketing promotion is defined as "persuasive communication designed to send marketing-related messages to a selected target audience." With the refocusing of commerce from product-centered to consumer-centered strategies, the revolution in marketing brought together a group of activities that had existed on the fringe of the manufacturing process. Bogart explains that "when American business was reorganized in the postwar years, marketing emerged as a major function" that coordinated previously separate specialties—such as product development, sales promotion, merchandising, advertising, and market research; "great emphasis was placed on the integrated marketing plan."*

The idea of coordination suggests that there are a number of elements involved in the marketing process, including the product, the distribution channel, the sales force, and the marketing communication program. These elements can also be viewed as *activities,* such as product design and development, branding, packaging, pricing, distribution, personal selling, advertising, sales promotion, and public relations. Combining these four communication devices in a way that produces a coordinated message structure is called the **promotion mix.**

promotion mix *The combination of personal selling, advertising, sales promotion, and public relations to produce a coordinated message structure.*

The Promotion Mix.   The basic elements of the promotion mix—personal selling, advertising, sales promotion, direct response, and public relations—appear in most marketing plans. These elements differ in terms of their intended effect, the type of customer contact, and the time element (see Figure 3.6).

PRINCIPLE
Advertising helps the salesperson by laying the groundwork and preselling the product.

Personal Selling   *Personal selling* is face-to-face contact between the marketer and a prospective customer. The intention is to create both immediate sales and repeat sales. There are several different types of personal selling, including sales calls at the place of business by a field representative (field sales), assistance at an outlet by a sales clerk (retail selling), and calls by a representative who goes to consumers' homes (door-to-door selling). Personal selling is most important for companies that sell products re-

*Bogart, *Strategy in Advertising*:3.

LAUREN BERGER
SENIOR VICE PRESIDENT/MANAGEMENT SUPERVISOR
DDB NEEDHAM WORLDWIDE

Courtesy of Lauren Berger.

Time/Place	Attendees	Issues
8:30–9:00 A.M. Office	—	Organize for the day.
9:00–9:15 A.M. Office	Two Account Supervisors	Meet to discuss important issues of the day that may need my involvement.
9:15–9:45 A.M. AMD's Office	Associate Media Director (AMD) Senior Planner Account Supervisor	Review Metroliner Service media plan for special promotion period.
9:45–10:30 A.M. CD's Office	SVP Creative Director Creative Team Account Supervisor	Review roughcut of two commercials and address client comments.
10:30–11:00 A.M. BUD's Office	Business Unit Director (BUD)	Brief Business Unit Director on creative meeting and other key issues.
11:00–11:45 A.M. Office	Director of Career Development	Discuss agency training programs designed for Account Management personnel.
11:45–12:30 P.M. Office	As needed	Return phone calls, review mail, meet with account people as needed.
12:30–2:00 P.M. Local Restaurant	Strategic Planning Supervisor (DDBN-Chicago)	Discuss Amtrak's use of integrated marketing as input for agency's integrated marketing planning program.
2:00–3:30 P.M. 10th floor Conference Room	Task Force (Account Management, Research, Creative, Media Groups)	Business review of Auto Train and discussion of agency point of view on new competitive airline pricing strategies.
3:30–3:45 P.M. via phone	Client	Brief agency on new service introduction between Boston and New York, which will require special program.
3:45–4:15 P.M. Office	Research Planning Director	Discuss recommended changes to Amtrak's tracking study based on new advertising strategies.
4:15–5:00 P.M. Office	Account Group	Follow up on client direction on new service, discuss responsibilities, timetables.
5:00–5:15 P.M. Office	—	Return phone calls.
5:15–6:00 P.M. Office	As needed	Write memos, meet with account people *re:* personnel issues, client projects, internal issues, etc.

quiring explanation, demonstration, and service. Such products tend to be higher-priced.

Advertising   *Advertising* has already been defined in Chapter 1, and several of its key characteristics were discussed at the beginning of this chapter. It differs from the other promotional elements in several ways. Although advertising has a greater ability to reach a larger number of people simultaneously than do the other elements, it has less ability to prompt an immediate behavioral change. Furthermore, the contact between the advertiser and the audience is indirect, and it takes a longer period of time to deliver information, change attitudes, and create a rapport or trust between the two parties.

PRINCIPLE
Sales promotion activities are used to generate immediate sales.

Sales Promotion   *Sales promotion* includes a number of communication devices offered for a limited period of time in order to generate immediate sales. Simply stated, sales promotion is an extra incentive to buy *now*. Examples are price discounts, coupons, product sampling, contests or sweepstakes, and rebates. Sales promotion will be discussed in greater detail in Chapter 18.

Advertising is used to promote sales promotion activities such as sweepstakes and contests. Sales promotions can also be used in support of advertising campaigns. Advertising and sales promotion can work together to create a *synergy* in which each makes the other more effective.

Direct Response   *Direct-response* advertising is a type of marketing communication that accomplishes an action-oriented objective as a result of the advertising message. It can use any medium to achieve this objective. Direct-response advertising has less waste than other mass-media advertising because it reaches a specific target audience—those who are most likely to be interested in the product or service. These prospects typically are reached through direct mail. Direct-order marketing is another form of direct marketing that focuses attention on distribution. Direct-response advertising will be discussed in more detail in Chapter 16.

Public Relations   *Public relations* encompasses a set of activities intended to enhance the image of the marketer in order to create goodwill. Public relations includes publicity (stories in the mass media with significant news value), news conferences, company-sponsored events, open houses, plant tours, donations, and other special events.

Rather than attempt to sell the product, public relations seeks to influence people's attitudes about the company or product. In most cases the lag effect associated with public relations is quite long, making any relationship between promotion and sales difficult to determine.

Advertising interacts with public relations in several ways. A public relations event or message can serve as part of an advertising campaign. Product publicity can also be used in support of an advertising campaign. For example, Kingsford charcoal sponsors a Ribfest in Chicago that includes giving free charcoal to all contestants. This event reinforces the association between Kingsford and outdoor activities. Public relations is discussed in greater detail in Chapter 19.

ADVERTISING AND THE MARKETING MIX

Having examined the elements that make up the marketing mix, you are now better prepared to understand how advertising and marketing interact. As noted at the beginning of this chapter, advertising is a subset of marketing that relies on the evaluation and coordination of product-centered and consumer-centered strategies. The product must come first. Its characteristics, its strengths and weaknesses, and its position in the marketplace all dictate the rest of the marketing mix. Advertising must account for all these factors plus the price of the product and the way it is distributed. For a

THE POLITICALLY CYNICAL AMERICAN

Under the powerful reign of television, many a viewer has chosen to take commercials or political campaigns with a grain of salt. Now research shows that some such people are considerably more skeptical than others. The question is, then, what can advertisers do about these Doubting Thomases? How should a political campaign be promoted to appeal to such skeptics? The first step is to identify who the politically cynical Americans are.

One strategy is simply to learn more about the kinds of people they are and the kinds of attitudes and values they espouse. For example, a lifestyle study compared those Americans who either agreed or disagreed with the statement that "An honest man cannot get elected to high office." The 46 percent of the sample who *concurred* with the statement were dubbed the "political cynics." Those who *disagreed* were labelled the "political optimists." Generally speaking, men were more dubious about the possibilities of honest politicians than the women.

Doubters and faith-keepers differ mainly in matters of degree rather than direction of opinion. At the same time, a skeptic in one arena of life, such as politics, is apt to be a skeptic in many other areas as well. For example, doubters are more likely than optimists to feel that American businesses are out for themselves, unions have too much power, our educational system is inadequate, and deregulating the telephone company was definitely a tactical blunder.

When we look at their social and economic characteristics, distrusters are a little older, less likely to have earned college degrees or to occupy white-collar jobs, and more likely to earn lower incomes than their more hopeful counterparts. Furthermore, these differences between the two groups are more marked among the women than the men.

Political doubters are also less interested in politics and are less apt to vote, especially the females. Cynics tend to be more conservative than are political trusters. Thus, the former are more ready to agree that there is too much emphasis on sex on television and in advertising, and they favor greater use of force by the police (almost half the male cynics advocate keeping a gun in every home). Politically cynical women tend to be more supportive of governmental control over television content than male cynics.

Cynics do not view themselves as more patriotic than other people. Still, when given a choice, the pessimists think American products are superior, seek protectionist trade policies, and prefer to travel in the United States rather than abroad.

Curiously enough, although doubters criticize the political system, they also seem to distance themselves from it. As a group, they not only vote

highly technical product, advertising will probably take a backseat to personal selling and support services. Such advertising would tend to be laden with facts and restricted to trade magazines targeted at a very well-defined audience. For a product such as Peter Pan peanut butter, advertising would play a much more important role. A wide range of media would be used. Advertising copy would attempt to instill an emotional appeal for a product that is inherently unexciting. Because price is important to consumers who buy peanut butter, print ads would probably carry coupons.

Even products that have a similar marketing mix may use very different advertising strategies. A case in point is the computer industry. When Apple Computer entered the market, they realized that they faced a serious competitive disadvantage. They attacked IBM through their product innovations and breakthrough advertising. IBM and Apple followed very different creative strategies to achieve comparable objectives. Both were driven by their own unique marketing mix.

less than the believers, but they are less involved in community or civic activities. Perhaps they feel that their opinions don't really count for very much.

Cynics are not very sanguine about either their futures or their pasts. Compared to optimists, they are fearful of the very changes they perceive on the horizon and often wish for the "good old days." They know they are tense about their lives, wish they could somehow live them differently, but just don't know how to wrest control over them. Most of the respondents to the lifestyle study felt the pace of change was too rapid, and female cynics, in particular, were unsettled by this. Both male and female distrusters felt that no matter how fast their incomes increased, they just never seemed to get out from under, and they don't think their family incomes are very likely to improve over the next 5 years.

Not surprisingly, cynics are more likely to prefer the safe and secure than are the trusters. To the nonbelievers, job security is more important than money, and investment safety counts more than high interest rates. Taking chances just isn't a style that appeals to cynics. They seem to regard themselves as homebodies, feeling safer in their familiar surroundings. Even there, however, they wish they knew how to relax, and they would like to have firmer locks on their doors.

Male cynics in particular lean toward more traditional views about women's place in these homes than do their fellow optimists. Father should more or less serve as boss and should definitely handle financial investments. In fact, male cynics are the most dubious of all about whether women are as smart as men. Yet both cynics and optimists hold that marriage means shared responsibilities and that women's lib "is a good thing."

As we mentioned earlier, skeptics don't take very kindly to television advertising, and their purchasing behavior reflects this. Thus, cynical men and women are more likely to refuse to buy products whose advertising they dislike than are optimists. Female doubters feel that television advertising is condescending toward them, and male cynics complain that advertising insults their intelligence. Both male and female cynics distrust advertising that claims to show how tests prove that one company's product is better than the competitor's. Yet despite these negative attitudes, data from the study suggest that television does play a stronger role in the lives of skeptics than of optimists.

Exercise: As a member of the advertising profession, how would you go about trying to reassure political skeptics about that profession? What fears seem paramount? What safeguards could you mention, and what themes would be convincing to them —and to you? Now that you know who the politically cynical American is, how would you promote a political campaign to appeal to this market?

Source: DDB Needham Worldwide, *A Lifestyle Profile of the Politically Cynical American* (October 1988).

SUMMARY

- The marketing concept focuses on the needs of the consumer rather than on the marketer's production capabilities.
- Advertising is a category within the promotion mix and promotion is a category within the marketing mix.
- The marketing mix identifies the most effective combination of four variables: product, price, place (distribution), and marketing communication.
- The typical product moves through the following stages in its life cycle: introduction, growth, maturity, and decline.
- The package is the last chance to affect consumer choice.

- There are three market coverage strategies: exclusive distribution, selective distribution, and extensive distribution.
- There are various pricing strategies, including customary pricing, psychological pricing, and price lining.
- The promotion mix identifies the optimum level of sales promotion, personal selling, public relations, and advertising.
- The amount of emphasis given to each promotional element in the marketing mix determines its budget level.

QUESTIONS

1. Find examples of three advertisements that demonstrate the marketing concept. What elements of these ads reflect this approach?

2. How would you advertise a toothpaste at the four different stages in its life cycle?

3. Imagine you are starting a company to manufacture fudge. Consider the following decisions:
   a. Describe the marketing mix you think would be most effective for this company.
   b. Describe the promotion mix you would recommend for this company.
   c. How would you determine the advertising budget for your new fudge company?
   d. Develop a plan for a brand image for this fudge.

4. Professor Baker tells his advertising class that advertising's relationship to marketing is like the tip of an iceberg. As the class looks puzzled he explains that most (80 percent) of the iceberg cannot be seen. "It's the same with consumer's perception of how much of marketing is advertising-related," Baker explains. What is Baker trying to illustrate with the iceberg analogy?

5. In the 1980s marketers began to look for short-run marketing strategies. This often meant investment in activities other than advertising. Advertising professionals warned companies about ignoring the need for long-run investment through advertising. What activities would marketers use for short-run results? What is the connection between advertising and long-run marketing objectives?

6. The chapter stressed integration of advertising with other components of the "marketing mix." If you were in marketing management for Kellogg cereals how would you see advertising supporting "product," "price," and "place"? Could advertising improve each of these functions for Kellogg? Explain your answer.

7. Angie Todd, an account assistant at a local advertising agency, is upset at the comments of a marketing consultant during a media reception. The consultant is telling listeners that consumer advertising has lost its edge and does not have credibility. He claims consumers pay no attention to glitter or glitz (advertising); they just want a deal on price. "I'll bet none of you can name even two consumer products last year with ad campaigns that made any difference to the target consumer," he challenged. If you were Angie how would you respond?

FURTHER READINGS

HARDY, KENNETH G., AND ALLAN J. MAGRATH, *Marketing Channel Management* (Glenview, IL: Scott, Foresman, 1988).

LODISH, LEONARD M., *The Advertising and Promotion Challenge* (New York: Oxford University Press, 1986).

MONROE, KENT B., *Pricing: Making Profitable Decisions* (New York: McGraw-Hill, 1979).

SHIMP, TERENCE, *Promotion Management and Marketing Communications* (Chicago: Dryden, 1990).

WIND, YORAM J., *Product Policy: Concepts, Methods, and Strategy* (Reading, MA: Addison-Wesley, 1982).

VIDEO CASE

 ## On the Wrong Scent: BiC Parfum

Long known in the United States primarily for its low-cost disposable pens, the BiC Corporation began to branch out into other product areas in the 1970s. BiC's newfound aggressiveness in the marketplace increased the company's strengths in low-cost plastic production to bring consumers the convenience of disposability and affordability.

BiC's first successful new-product venture was the Clic, a disposable plastic lighter that retailed for under 1 dollar. The Clic made fumbling with matches and the messy refilling of fluid-fuel lighters a thing of the past by providing a reliable, adjustable butane gas flame. As the popularity of Clic expanded, other manufacturers began producing attractive sleeves and holders to make the lighter suitable for almost any social occasion.

Buoyed by the success of the Clic, BiC caught Gillette, Schick, and Wilkenson off guard by introducing its next new product—the disposable plastic razor. The old adage of "give them the razor and sell them the blades" had served the industry well until BiC began selling razor *and* the blades for the price of the other manufacturers' blades alone. The industry has never been quite the same since the disposable razor made its appearance. Some manufacturers, such as Gillette and Schick, responded by rushing to develop their own disposable razors, while investing heavily in new technology to make their replacement blade cartridges more effective and more competitive against the disposables. Other manufacturers, like Wilkenson and its Sword blades, have yet to regain the market share they enjoyed before disposable razors were introduced.

The late 1980s and early 1990s were not as good for BiC as the early years. The media reported incidents of burn injuries resulting from leaking and exploding Clic lighters, culminating in a story on *60 Minutes*. Although

BiC denied any problems with the Clic, the persistent media coverage nonetheless had a significant effect on sales of the disposable lighter. Sales of BiC's disposable razors suffered as well as the competition gained market share at BiC's expense. Meanwhile, Gillette readied its long-awaited Sensor razor and blades, which offered a new innovation in shaving that disposable razors could not match. Schick was rumored to be developing a similar product.

Perhaps most concerning of all for BiC was increased environmental consciousness emerging among consumers in the late 1980s. This "green consumerism" emphasized reusability and recyclability, threatening to give disposability, BiC's original strength, a bad name. It was therefore no surprise when BiC announced the introduction of yet another new product, this one providing the affordability that was the company's hallmark but deemphasizing disposability: BiC parfum (perfume). BiC reportedly chose to target the fragrance category because the industry lacked a quality, affordable product. Because quality and price had always been synonymous in the fragrance industry, BiC earmarked $20 million in advertising and promotional support for Parfum to help change existing consumer perceptions. Deemphasizing disposability did take some of the pressure off of BiC to price the product at a minimum, so BiC Parfum was introduced at $5 a bottle, a bold price by the company's usual standards. Although other manufacturers, such as Avon, had been offering low-cost perfumes for several years, BiC became the most notable recent case of a firm with a reputation for low-cost products entering the fragrance industry.

Despite BiC's extensive marketing efforts, however, Parfum failed, forcing the company to drop the product within 2 years of its introduction.

QUESTIONS

1. Explain the factors you think contributed to the failure of BiC Parfum.
2. What does the following statement by Charles Revson say about the intangible nature of cosmetics: "In the factory we make cosmetics; in the store we sell hope"? How did BiC's failure to consider it doom Parfum?

3. What parallels can be drawn between consumer perceptions in the fragrance industry and the wine industry?

Source: "BiC Markets New Perfume," *Business World* #125 (March 5, 1989).

Appendix:
Integrated Marketing Communications

The concept of **integrated marketing communications (IMC)** brings together all the various promotional activities traditionally planned and implemented separately and attempts to integrate the various programs and activities. The shift of marketing resources from mass-media advertising to sales promotion, direct marketing, and other forms of marketing communication has convinced many agency CEOs that they must extend the product line to include all major marketing communications media. The alternative —an exhausting battle for share within a declining market—seems overwhelmingly unattractive.

The logical case for integrated marketing communications is very persuasive. In one of his last speeches as President of the American Association of Advertising Agencies, Len Matthews observed that IMC has already become second nature in a great many small and midsized agencies:

"I noticed just the other day that Keller-Crescent, a medium-sized agency with offices in Evansville, Indiana, and Dallas, Texas, had won a new $10 million account for whom it would be developing television and radio advertising, direct marketing, and sales promotion campaigns.

That is nothing new for them. It's just the way they've been doing business for years—providing every communications service their clients need, including public relations, outdoor, and Yellow Pages advertising.

In these agencies, the various functions are so inextricably intertwined, it would be impossible to separate them out. It's like the marbling in a fine steak; you can't remove it without demolishing the steak."*

Laurie Goldberger, a financial analyst for Shearson Lehman Hutton, concluded:

"In 2 or 3 years we (Shearson) would be concerned about companies that make no visible effort to address this area, that reject the idea that the industry is moving toward integrated service, or that have neither good skills nor strong organizational efforts. We would then have to question whether they will remain industry leaders going into the mid-1990s."†

All signs point to integrated marketing communications as the road to survival for the agency of the 1990s. According to a DDB Needham Worldwide internal memo, to acquire an acceptable level of competence in integrated marketing communications, agency managers need to acquire three attributes: knowledge, trust, and incentive. Agencies that foster these attributes and provide help and serve as partners to their clients will become what they have always wanted to be: their client's marketing partners. In contrast, agencies that remain fixated on mass media advertising will continue to be regarded by their clients with fully justified suspicion. Without integrated marketing communications, when a client tells an advertising agency about a serious marketing problem, the agency's knee-jerk response is, "We have the answer: great creative." Clients wince when they hear that. To them it means that the agency is either unbelievably naive or unforgivably deceptive.

Courtesy of Keith Reinhard.

*Len Matthews, "Reinventing the Advertising Agency Business," address to an advertising sales conference, Williamsburg, Virginia, September 26, 1988.
†Laurie Goldberger, "Advertising: Diversification Begets Integration," Shearson Lehman Hutton, April 20, 1989.

The Role of Media in Integrated Marketing Communications

Keith Reinhard, CEO of DDB Needham Worldwide, provides an in-depth look at integrated marketing communications in action. He quotes Bill Bernbach as saying, "You can't sell a man who isn't listening," and takes this one step further in pointing out the difficulty of merely finding anybody to listen; this, in itself, calls for a new dimension of creativity. In Bernbach's time it was possible to reach 70 percent of U.S. homes with an advertising schedule in *Life, Look,* and *The Saturday Evening Post,* the three major weeklies of the time. Today, there are more than 22,000 magazines, newspapers, and periodicals in publication in the United States alone.

The explosion is every bit as dramatic in the broadcast media. Today, the average household in the United States can receive 33 television channels, as opposed to only ten channels in 1980. Perhaps even more troubling is that the number of daily television commercials—both network and spot—in the average television market has increased from approximately 400 to 2,000 between 1969 and 1990. As you can see, what has changed dramatically is not the consumer, but the media landscape.

Given the media explosion, the new creativity will have to start with an integrated media program. As the advertising industry developed in decades past, such giants of the business as David Ogilvy and Rosser Reeves (see Chapter 1) taught us the importance of what to say, leaving the impression that this was the end of our creative responsibility. Then, in the late 1950s, Bill Bernbach came along and, although he acknowledged the importance of "what" to say as a necessary starting point, he observed that intelligent people with equal access to the marketplace would invariably arrive at the same answer to the question. "How" to say it would be the great differentiator, said Bernbach, and he started a creative revolution by saying things freshly and surprisingly, in ways they had never been said before.

Given today's media jungles, however, more and more the questions of "what" and "how" beg an entirely new set of questions: where to say it and when. The demands of the media and marketing dilemma that confronts us require us to change our approach to the entire ad-making process. The "old way" of advertising is illustrated in Figure 1.

FIGURE 1
The "old way" of advertising.

FIGURE 2
The "new way" of advertising.

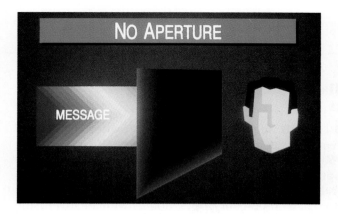

FIGURE 3
Closed aperture.

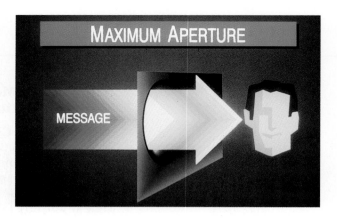

FIGURE 4
Open aperture.

Traditionally we began by establishing the *marketing objective.* Then we selected our *target audience.* Following this step, we set about devising a *copy strategy,* which led quite naturally to *creative executions,* and finally, at the end of the process, we concerned ourselves with *media placement.*

Quite understandably, under this system, creativity was pretty much limited to the creation of print ads and broadcast commercials.

In the new definition of the creative task, this order will change (see Figure 2).

As always, we will first determine the marketing objective and then select the audience. According to the new definition, however, before determining what to say and how to say it, we will first select those times and places that provide the best opportunity for reaching the prospect, and they will guide our media planning. Following that, we will develop communication strategies for each media channel and from those, we will fashion the creative executions themselves.

The first task of the new media function will therefore be to locate prospects and reach them at the most opportune time and place. This process involves delivering our message at a time when the prospect's "aperture of receptivity" is most open to receiving and digesting that message. (For a more detailed discussion of aperture, see Chapter 9.) This process is illustrated in Figure 3.

When the prospect's aperture is closed, the message doesn't get through and nothing registers. In contrast, when we communicate with a prospect at a time and in a place where the mind is open to suggestion, our message gets through and we can hope for a sale, as Figure 4 illustrates.

Amtrak Auto Train. Amtrak provides a real-world example of aperture. Amtrak had very little money with which to introduce a new train called Auto Train, which was designed to take passengers and their cars comfortably to Florida and back from a location just outside Washington, D.C.

The high cost of media (especially television) in the northeast was prohibitive. So the creative media strategists assigned to the task came up with a better idea: They actually drove the entire distance to Florida, making a judgement as to when driver fatigue would most likely set in. They determined that this point would be somewhere near the border between North and South Carolina. At that point, they contracted for a series of outdoor billboards (See Ad 1). The boards showed a relaxed family on board a

AD 1
An outdoor billboard advertising Amtrak's Auto Train.

train and asked road-weary drivers the pertinent question: "Don't you wish you'd taken Auto Train to Florida?" The outdoor advertising was supported by committing scarce television dollars to the task of selling the northward trip on lower-cost Florida television during the 2 weeks following heaviest migration, while the mind-numbing fatigue of the southward drive was still fresh in the motorists' minds. As a result, trip sales increased 386 percent.

As the Amtrak example illustrates, there is a sequential aspect to the new creativity of integrated marketing communications as well. It will have to link messages in a logical way and deliver them along predictable paths. By tracking a prospect through a media day or week, messages can be "programmed" on the "network" of media vehicles the prospect is most loyal to and "programmed" in a sequence that matches the prospect's daily routine.

The New York State Lottery. Figure 5 illustrates the "personal media network" of a prospect for the New York State Lottery. As you can see, the messages are linked and the time and place of media contact often have a direct influence on what is said.

The advertising premise for the Lottery is simply that, for 1 dollar, you have the privilege of dreaming about what you would do if you actually won the jackpot. Using quotes from real New Yorkers, the advertising is crafted to tempt consumers to buy lottery tickets, by using a variety of media, including radio, the morning paper, subway platforms, entrances (see Ad 2), and subway cars, and bus stops.

The messages presented are appropriate to the surroundings and the prospects' reactions to them. Ten-second television spots were also aired

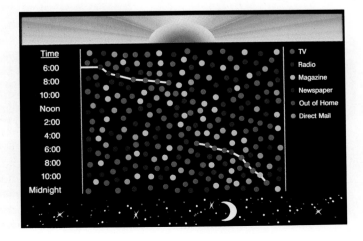

FIGURE 5
The personal media network of a prospect for the New York State Lottery.

AD 2
A subway entrance carrying a New York State lottery ad.

on game shows and later in the evening, 30-second television spots were aired on shows with high fantasy content. In other words, the advertising is with the prospect—both in the media he or she consumes during the day and also in the spirit in which those media are consumed.

Product and Package Design

More and more, the new creativity will need to expand beyond conventional media to include product and package design, public speeches, sales presentations, sales promotion, in-store communications, video cassettes, direct marketing, and a whole host of new media not yet imagined. In short, the new creativity will take advantage of all the voices available to speak in the brand's behalf.

When you approach each contact with the consumer as a media opportunity, you start thinking about a big, overriding idea instead of thinking only of a television commercial or a magazine campaign. For example, the milk producers of Sweden needed to increase the consumption of milk among young people, 14 to 20 years old, who perceived of this beverage as childish or old-fashioned. The overriding idea of the new campaign was to

FIGURE 6
The new milk logo.

A RESULT OF THE MILK ENERGY PROCESS EVALUATION	
Compared with other established "youth brands"	
1. Coca Cola	99%
2. Juicy Fruit	95%
3. Milk Energy	93%
4. Levis	92%
5. Sprite	90%

FIGURE 7
A result of the milk energy process evaluation.

FIGURE 8
Premiums incorporating the Fahrvergnügen logo.

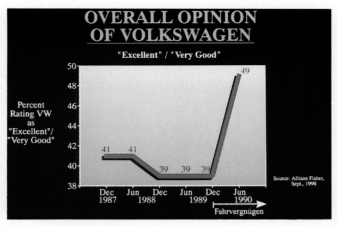

FIGURE 9
Overall opinion of Volkswagen.

brand the commodity—to make milk a brand every bit as viable and contemporary as Coke or Pepsi. As a first step, a new logo was designed to give milk a competitive brand personality (see Figure 6).

This bright, contemporary logo was put on everything to do with the product from its inception to its consumption. It was applied to cartons, delivery trucks, and even became fashionable as a line of clothing.

Before long, milk, as a brand, had become almost as popular as Coke and Juicy Fruit and even more popular than Levi's or Sprite (see Figure 7).

Volkswagen Fahrvergnügen. In order to mobilize communications behind one concept, agency managers need to be much more skilled in the development and use of brand symbols, which, if possible, begin with the product and package itself and become a prominent part of every communication. In the case of the Volkswagen Fahrvergnügen campaign, for example, a strong symbol tied to an intriguing word quickly lent continuity and cohesiveness to a most complex, multichannel campaign.

A symbol can also give a campaign impact out of proportion to its media budget. The Fahrvergnügen graphic for Volkswagen not only appeared in print advertising but in television and show room displays as well.

The distinctive graphic also lent itself to premiums of every kind, such as the watch in Figure 8.

Volkswagen planners also considered every respectable-looking Volkswagen in America not only as a motor vehicle providing an uniquely enjoyable driving experience but as a media vehicle as well. The results of the Fahrvergnügen campaign are indicated in Figure 9, which shows a surge in the general public's positive impression of Volkswagen after a very short span of time.

In summary, the new creativity will start with media. It will then find expression in simple, surprising executions that are linked to one another and programmed to track the consumer and communicate at the most opportune time and place. Most importantly, the new creativity of integrated marketing communications will arrive when we stop looking back and when we stop developing individual ads and commericals in a vacuum and testing them individually, as if nothing in the world has changed. The very nature of creativity is to move on, to be impatient with the past, even as we honor it and draw inspiration from it for a new creative revolution.

Photos courtesy of DDB Needham Worldwide.

4

Advertising Agencies

Chapter Outline

Major Advertiser Appoints Small Agency
Essence of the Business: Value-Adding Ideas
Why Hire an Advertising Agency?
The Agency World: Types of Advertising Agencies
How Agencies Are Organized
How Agencies Are Paid
Changes in the Agency World
Perils of the Business

Chapter Objectives

When you have completed this chapter, you should be able to:

- Explain the four primary functions in an agency: account management, creative services, media services, and research
- Explain which support services are provided by departments such as traffic, print production, accounting, and personnel
- Explain the difference between the commission and the fee system
- Explain why advertisers hire agencies rather than do the work themselves
- Analyze the pros and cons of the trend toward megamergers
- Understand what a "high productivity" agency means.

*M*AJOR ADVERTISER APPOINTS SMALL AGENCY

In 1990 a small New York advertising agency engineered the kind of major coup most small agencies only dream about. Partners & Shevak succeeded in seizing a major client from Young & Rubicam, the largest U.S. advertising agency. The creators of advertising campaigns for Black Flag insecticides and Arm & Hammer baking soda, Partners & Shevak are proud to have added American Home Products' $17 million Anacin account to its lineup of clients.

Although the agency has billings of only about $160 million, its services are of the same caliber as the larger firms'. The staff devotes a great deal of time and energy to research and media-buying operations, two critical services most small agencies neglect. In addition, Partners & Shevak has established a reputation for quality and dedication, which includes making clients feel comfortable and important, being willing to work on special marketing assignments, and coming up with money-saving strategies for their clients.

Executives at the agency pride themselves on creating ads that build brand equity or value. According to the agency's president and chief executive, Brett Shevak, "We have no special creative style. Our ads always take on the client's character." Today that client is American Home Products. Partners & Shevak has already created an advertising campaign for the company's smaller product, Anacin III, using the theme "Pain relief for today's tough headaches." Working with the stronger pain reliever will prove an even greater challenge.*

American Home Products is not unusual in its decision to switch agencies. In May 1989, for example, N W Ayer was dropped as the agency for Burger King and replaced by both D'Arcy Masius Benton & Bowles and Saatchi & Saatchi Advertising. In March 1991, when the man responsible for this move—Burger King's top marketing executive, Gary Langstaff—resigned, several agencies announced plans to pursue the Burger King business, including Ayer and J. Walter Thompson. At the time, J. Walter Thompson was also competing against Grey Advertising, Bayer Bess Vanderwacker, and Group 243 for the $50 million-plus Domino's Pizza account.†

What makes companies switch from one agency to another? What is it that they look for in an agency, and why would they choose to hire an outside firm to handle their advertising rather than doing it themselves?

*E*SSENCE OF THE BUSINESS: VALUE-ADDING IDEAS

In this chapter we will examine the organization, scope, and work that takes place in an advertising agency. Before discussing what an advertising agency does, however, it is appropriate to consider *why* agencies exist. Advertisements can be written by people outside of agencies or they can be written by the clients themselves. Media can be bought through media-buying companies or directly by the clients. Research projects can be carried out by research companies. So what does the advertising agency do

*Adapted from Kim Foltz, "Shevak's Attraction to Big Clients," *The New York Times* (August 23, 1990):C6.
†Gary Levin, "Agencies Hungry for a Bite of BK," *Advertising Age* (March 11, 1991):41.

that has caused this organizational form to dominate the industry worldwide?

Basic marketing wisdom and business intuition have told us for years that "in order to achieve consumer loyalty, communication (not just advertising) must do more than merely "transmit" some set of data. Rather, it must tailor the product story to a potential customer."* Communication at this level converts data into perceptions, and perceptions are key facts in differentiating between products.†

The perceived value of a brand was raised to new heights when British companies (and then others) began to recognize on their balance sheets the value of brands that they owned, presumably the market value or value to another corporate buyer. These brand values, or equities, were largely the contribution of advertising—more specifically, of advertising created by agencies.

The goal each agency strives to achieve is to add perceived value to the product or service of its client. It does this in four ways: (1) by giving the product a personality, (2) by communicating in a manner or tone that shapes the basic understanding of the product, (3) by creating an image or memorable picture of the product, and (4) by setting the product apart from its competitors.

The essence of the business—the value of the agency—is derived from creating and directing the communication about a product or service so that the product is perceived to have a unique value—so much so that the advertising becomes part of the product.

Does the agency always succeed? No. But success of this sort is the dream that drives every advertising agency. It is also the hope, or at least one of the hopes, each client has when it appoints a new ad agency. What follows is a discussion of how an advertising agency organizes to accomplish this goal.

Although reports of comings and goings of notable clients from one agency to another are numerous, the fact is that the average tenure of a client with an agency is 7 years. Many have lasted 50 years. Why do advertisers establish such long-term relationships with agencies?

WHY HIRE AN ADVERTISING AGENCY?

To people in the advertising agency business, this is a naive question. To clients who have reaped the benefits of a talented and committed advertising agency, it is irrelevant. The box entitled "What Do Clients Really Want from Their Agency?" provides an inside look at what clients expect—and don't expect—an advertising agency to deliver. Why, indeed, hire an advertising agency?

Expertise and Objectivity

An advertising agency brings together the talents and experience of practitioners in the field of communication, molds them into a team, and bundles their talents and associated skills in order to deliver them more rapidly,

*The Committee on the Value of Advertising, American Association of Advertising Agencies, *The Value Side of Productivity* (1989):16.
†Ibid.

CONCEPTS AND CONTROVERSIES

WHAT DO CLIENTS REALLY WANT FROM THEIR AGENCIES?

Les J. Hauser, vice president of marketing for Hospital Building & Equipment Company in St. Louis, does business with advertising agencies all the time. He acknowledges that most agencies know what their clients want, but they don't always know what clients *don't* want. He offers 20 basic ground rules for agencies in dealing with clients:

1. *Don't ignore the client's instructions.* New ideas can be discussed after the agency has done what the client asked for.
2. *Don't hand in material with errors.* Clients pay a great deal of money for an agency's services, and they expect quality work in return.
3. *Don't brag about awards.* A client wants to generate new business, not see its ads win awards.
4. *Don't let the agency's creative people run the client's business.* Creative input is fine, but the client knows best how certain things need to be done.
5. *Don't trivialize the client's business.* No client will believe that one good ad will solve all the company's problems.
6. *Don't sell a client an approach just because it worked for another client.* Clients demand and deserve fresh ideas and the courtesy of being treated as individuals.
7. *Don't recommend strategies that will only generate agency revenue.* The agency's first priority should be what's best for the client, not for the agency.
8. *Don't let kids handle the account.* Clients want someone mature enough to deal with their problems to represent their business.
9. *Don't try to buy a client with favors or gifts.* Clients know when their business is being "bought" and resent the insult.
10. *Don't force a tour of the agency on the client.* Most clients are too busy for such impressions and would rather see results than the agency's wall hangings.

11. *Don't try to take additional responsibilities without being asked.* Clients will let their agencies know when they want to include them in other areas of their operation.
12. *Don't tell the client how hard the agency's people worked to deliver on time.* Clients expect their agencies to work hard for them to get the job done right.
13. *Don't change account executives without the client's permission.* "Just anyone" is not acceptable to a client who is paying for quality work.
14. *Don't badger the client about the advertising budget.* Clients require results before they are willing to allocate more money.
15. *Don't rely only on readership measures to evaluate the client's advertising.* Clients are smart enough to know that reading an ad is not the same as purchasing the product or service.
16. *Don't go over the client's head.* Going to the person's boss in the case of a disagreement is both insulting and damaging to the relationship.
17. *Don't drag out the time needed to get the job done.* Clients know typically how long things should take and are unimpressed by long production schedules.
18. *Don't push advertising on a client.* Scare tactics that point out what the competition is doing seldom work.
19. *Don't expect favors in getting into other divisions of the client company.* Many clients will be happy to put in a good word for an agency that does a good job, but other divisions often choose their own agencies independently.
20. *Don't ask to be sent somewhere where you have people to visit.* If it works out that way, fine, but clients will not modify their plans for an agency's personal preferences.

Source: Adapted from Les J. Hauser, "You Can Always Get What You Don't Want," *Marketing News* (March 4, 1991):4.

more efficiently, or in greater depth than a company could on its own. The people who work in an advertising agency are professionals. It is their job to know the business and to apply their expertise, sense of objectivity, and commitment to every client who hires them.

An agency acquires experience by working with a variety of clients and can apply lessons learned with one client to another. Applying a broad perspective and the varied background skills of its employees is often the key to solving difficult advertising problems.

Agency objectivity is also a necessary part of the client-agency relationship. Someone from outside the client company is more likely to speak up frankly and is better able to maintain an independent and detached view of the marketplace and the consumer. At the same time, the agency becomes very much a part of the client team. The relationship serves as an incentive for the agency to produce the extra effort, take an interest in every aspect of the client's business, and refuse to be satisfied with "good enough."

Cost Efficiency

Companies examine their costs carefully. The fact that the overwhelming majority of companies all over the world consistently use advertising agencies for their global, national, and often local advertising testifies to the economic utility of advertising agencies.

The worth of an agency, however, cannot be measured in dollars and cents alone. If clients believed that they could hire, organize, and manage the skills required to produce an advertising campaign, they would do so. Just as they choose to retain outside legal, accounting, design, or engineering consultants and specialists, so do they choose to take advantage of the ability of advertising agency managements to deliver the skills of their professionals. They decide to engage an advertising agency in the hope of reaping the intangible value from advertising that builds awareness and preference.

Creating Brand Value

The success of advertising, which indirectly reflects the work of the agency, is embodied in the concept of brand value. Central to some of the buying and selling of U.S. companies in the late 1980s was the value attached to the brands a company owned or had developed. This was certainly true in the case of RJR Nabisco, the purchase of Pillsbury Company by Grand Metropolitan PLC, and the purchase of Kraft and General Foods by Philip Morris. These companies not only had established recognition and consumer acceptance but were also considered to have brand equity that could be translated into market value. The added value of advertised brands is certainly not the result of advertising alone, but consistent, powerful, and compelling advertising clearly enhances brand values in the minds of consumers in a way that can be measured economically.

Establishing Client-Customer Relations

Although agencies work on a close, collaborative basis with their clients, they are expected to represent the interests and needs of the client's customers to the client. Agencies pride themselves on their ability to interpret the attitudes and reactions of customers into strategies and communication that will motivate those customers to select the client's brand over a competitor's product. By successfully carrying on a dialogue with customers, advertising agencies have been able to infuse that customer relationship with a personality and to establish a rapport between consumer and product. They have provided clients with a means of elevating a commercial transaction into a more responsive and trusting relationship.

Research has indicated that the best-known brands truly have created human-type personalities in the minds of consumers. Certainly this is true of the Nike campaign by Weiden & Kennedy (see Ad 4.1), the Apple Computer and Pepsi campaigns by BBDO, the "Heartbeat of America" campaign for Chevrolet by Lintas: Campbell-Ewald, the Marlboro campaign by Leo

AD 4.1
Weiden & Kennedy's campaign for Nike has been successful in establishing a brand
name with an image consumers are not likely to forget. (Courtesy of Nike and Weiden &
Kennedy)

Burnett, the Coca-Cola campaign by McCann-Erickson, the California Raisin Board campaign by Foote, Cone & Belding, and the Volkswagen campaign by DDB Needham.

Every client hopes that the advertising presented by its advertising agency will result in the kind of value-added communication that builds brands, heightens customer preferences, and rewards the client with customer loyalty. Agency-client communication is just as crucial as client-customer relations and is discussed in more detail in the box entitled "Agency-Client Communication During the Persian Gulf War."

Creating an Impression

How does an advertising agency conceive of itself? The truly difficult and intellectually stimulating work of the advertising agency is not the process of getting the advertising out the door, but the commitment to finding a better way for the client to communicate with its customers. The agency crafts a compelling selling message for the client's product or service. It creates a new and often surprising personality for the client. The advertising agency constantly seeks to make its client special—even unique—and it does so by employing talented people to provide specialized services, such as statisticians, network negotiators, and special-events coordinators, and by coordinating the creative minds of artists, writers, and television producers.

Staffing and Management

Client advertising budgets fluctuate, and as they do, so does the number of people employed in creating their advertising. Because agencies handle a number of clients, they are better able to cope with the ups and downs of advertising budgets. Clients would find it difficult to accommodate their staffing levels to the condition of the marketplace and to hire or fire employees as their advertising budget increases or decreases. Agencies can spread the effects of budget fluctuations among a roster of clients and build personnel policies that adjust to, and compensate for, these risks.

TABLE 4.1
Agency Employment Rankings

Staffing levels at the top 10 agency employers rose slightly in 1990 despite a generally weaker ad environment.				
Rank	Agency	April 1990	December 1990	% Change
1	Young & Rubicam	3,091	3,109	0.6
2	J. Walter Thompson USA	2,564	2,515	(1.9)
3	Foote, Cone & Belding	2,380	2,411	1.3
4	Leo Burnett USA	2,174	2,270	4.4
5	Ogilvy & Mather	2,096	1,991	(5.0)
6	Grey Advertising	1,916	1,963	2.5
7	Lintas:USA	1,900	1,930	1.6
8	D'Arcy Masius Benton & Bowles	1,874	1,872*	(0.1)
9	McCann-Erickson	1,763	1,709	(3.1)
10	Saatchi & Saatchi	1,680	1,706	1.5
	Totals	**21,438**	**21,476**	**0.2**

*As of November 1990.
Source: Advertising Age (May 14, 1990):16. Copyright Crain Communications, Inc.

The size of agency staffs, however, has been declining in recent years. Between October 1, 1989, and April 1, 1990, advertising-related jobs with the top ten U.S. agencies decreased by 0.4 percent. This level increased slightly in the second half of 1990, but the downward trend is expected to resume (see Table 4.1). According to the American Association of Advertising Agencies (AAAA), the average number of employees per million dollars in billings continued its long decline by dropping from 2.37 in 1984 to 1.73 in 1988, both because of increased pressures from clients on compensation paid to agencies and because the agencies themselves are reducing corporate overhead and support staffs for greater efficiency and productivity.*

*T*HE AGENCY WORLD: TYPES OF ADVERTISING AGENCIES

Advertising agencies range in size from one-person shops to giant businesses that employ thousands. The smallest agencies usually have up to a dozen employees. In smaller markets these agencies tend to offer a range of services. For example, Lewis Advertising in Mobile, Alabama, has its own public relations department; a collateral production unit, which produces brochures, point of sales, and newsletters for clients; and a department that specializes in hospital and health-care advertising. Goudelock Advertising in Greenville, South Carolina, has a relatively large number of clients (22 clients billing approximately $7 million) and has created a detailed time-management system that can report to a client the hours and expenditures invested in an individual product to date every day. Hood, Light & Geise agency in Harrisburg, Pennsylvania, billing $5 million, has three divisions: advertising, public relations, and association management. In larger markets smaller agencies usually specialize either in a type of service, such as media buying or creative work, or in a particular type of market, such as health care, agribusiness, or the upscale market. For example, Sandven

*Gary Levin and John Lafayette, "Agency Employment Decline Continues," *Advertising Age* (May 14, 1990):16.

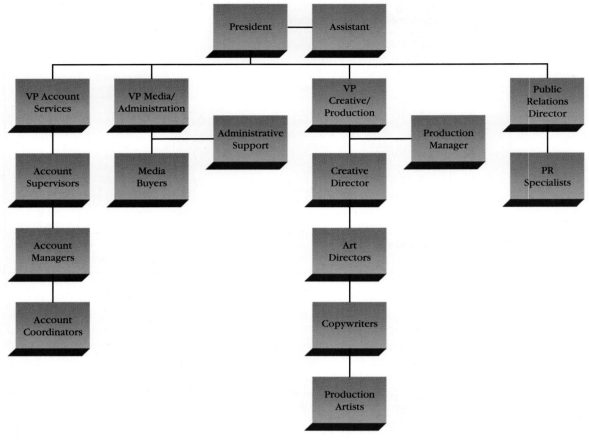

FIGURE 4.1
Turtledove Clemens Inc. organization chart.
Source: Courtesy of Turtledove Clemens Inc., Portland, Oregon

and Associates in Overland Park, near Kansas City, Missouri, is a leader in direct-response advertising.

The forms agencies take, the services they provide, and the types of agencies that exist are constantly changing. Entry to the advertising business is virtually unimpeded. The boundaries defining one type of service are not fixed. The following discussion of types of agencies, although not exhaustive, is intended to show the variety found in the advertising agency business.

Functions

There are standard functions around which most agencies, large and small, organize. The following are the four primary functions of most agencies:

1. Account management
2. Creative development and production
3. Media planning and buying
4. Research services

In addition to these major functional areas, most agencies offer internal support services, such as traffic, print production, financial services, personnel, and, increasingly, direct marketing. Figure 4.1 illustrates the organization of a smaller advertising agency.

AGENCY-CLIENT COMMUNICATION DURING THE PERSIAN GULF WAR

In January 1991 advertising agencies and their clients faced an unexpected dilemma—whether or not to run their commercials during coverage of a war. Many agencies had been discussing their options with their clients before the war broke out. According to Jay Chiat, chairman of Chiat/Day/Mojo of Venice, California, the agency had an ongoing dialogue about contingency plans with their clients during the week and a half before the war. Once the war began, "we called everybody very early to talk about our recommendations, particularly in the media sense. [Those recommendations were], depending on the product areas, to remove ourselves from any of the news and live-action coverage of the war."

Other agencies responded differently to the unusual situation. According to Edward Wax, president of Saatchi & Saatchi North America, his clients felt that life "must go on." The overriding hope was that the war would end soon, "but in the meantime, the economy is important and you've got to keep going, so you've got to keep selling your products."

Some clients were concerned with how much advertising they should do in the weeks immediately following the war. "It's more a question of how much of the current schedule they might change, if at all, and less a question of changing the advertising [itself]," said Allen Rosenshine, chairman-CEO of BBDO Worldwide. Other clients and agencies consulted on the appropriate nature of the advertising itself. For example, John Dooner, president of McCann-Erickson North America, felt that advertis-

ing soft drinks during the war news was inappropriate, but AT&T commercials might be different. "You have to use your judgment."

Judgment was required on the part of both clients and their agencies. Choosing how to handle the situation demanded open communication between both parties. William Weithas, the chairman-CEO of Lintas: Worldwide, said, "Most of the things we're discussing with our clients is making sure at the particular point we're not running anything that would be inappropriate, 'inappropriate' meaning frivolous at a very serious time." Agencies examined their advertisers' commercials for consideration. Sometimes creative changes were made. More often, advertising underwent a temporary interruption in scheduling. As Joe Mark, chairman of Saatchi & Saatchi Advertising, stated, "Our advertising grows out of consumer need. It doesn't grow out of war. So if the advertising is smart and responsive to consumer needs, we shouldn't have to change it."

The networks, particularly CNN, also exercised judgment on when they ran advertising. During the first hours of the air war the networks kept their reporters and analysts on the air without commercial interruption. According to CNN, the network ran only about half as many commercials as it normally would have during the month of January after January 16.

Source: Adapted from John Lafayette, "Agencies Revise Tactics as War Unfolds," *Advertising Age* (January 21, 1991):23.

Full-Service Agencies

A full-service advertising agency is one that provides the four major staff functions. Young & Rubicam, headquartered in New York, is an example of a full-service agency. In addition, a full-service advertising agency will have its own accounting department, a traffic department to handle internal tracking and completion of projects, departments for broadcast and print production (usually organized within the creative department), and a personnel or human-resources department. Two key distinctions of a full-service agency are that the personnel work full-time and the services provided are extensive. They are also unlimited to the extent that they can negotiate a

THE GOLDEN ADVANTAGE.
CASH BACK SAVINGS ON
AMERICA'S GOLD STANDARDS.

Jeep Cherokee: $1,000 or $2,500 cash back.

Dodge Caravan and Plymouth Voyager: $500 or $1,000 cash back.

Save $300 to $3,000 on the world's favorite 4x4s, minivans, and other gold standards.

Savings end soon.

Advantage: Chrysler.

AD 4.2
Full-service agencies provide account management and creative, media, and research services to their clients, as Bozell Advertising does for Chrysler in handling its account. (Courtesy of Chrysler Corporation.)

fee for special services, such as event sponsorship. Ad 4.2 for Chrysler is an example of an ad developed by a full-service agency.

Traditionally, a full-service agency/client agreement states that the agency will analyze market data, propose a strategy, prepare a recommendation, produce the advertising, place it in approved media, verify the advertising's appearance as ordered, invoice the client against the approved budget, collect funds from the client, and disburse those funds to media and suppliers—all for the commission received on media and production services. The ways an agency makes money will be discussed in detail later in the chapter. Such extras as public relations work, research projects, direct marketing, event marketing, and sales promotion are not normally included in the basic agreement, nor are they covered by the revenue the agency receives. Clients can purchase these services from other agencies with departments or subsidiaries that render the specific service, or they can use specialty agencies for these activities. The largest full-service agencies are shown in Table 4.2.

Creative Boutiques

Creative boutiques are relatively small agencies (two or three people to a dozen or more) that concentrate entirely on preparing the creative execution of client communications. Two examples of creative boutiques are Paula Green Associates in New York and Jan Zechman in Chicago. A creative boutique differs from a freelance creative person in the nature of the employment and the extent of the service. A freelance creative writer may work with a freelance artist and together they might present their creative recommendation to a client. They are each individual practitioners, however. A creative boutique will have one or more writers and artists on staff who habitually work together. The organization typically is capable of preparing advertising to run in print media, outdoor, radio, and television. The focus of the creative boutique is entirely on the idea—the creative product. There is no staff for media, research, strategic planning, or annual plan-writing.

Creative boutiques usually are hired by clients but are sometimes re-

TABLE 4.2
U.S. Agencies Ranked by Billing

Rank	Agency	Parent Headquarters	Parent Company	1989 U.S. Millions	1990 U.S. Millions	Change
1	Young & Rubicam	New York	—	3,114.8	3,696.4	18.7
2	Saatchi & Saatchi	London	Saatchi	2,624.7	2,740.7	8.6
3	BBDO Worldwide	New York	Omnicom	2,656.0	2,672.8	0.6
4	DMB & B	New York	—	2,055.3	2,510.9	22.2
5	DDB Needham	New York	Omnicom	2,276.3	2,407.9	5.8
6	Ogilvy & Mathers	London	Saatchi	2,104.4	2,219.7	5.5
7	Barber Speilvogel Bates	London	WPP	2,158.0	2,162.8	0.2
8	Leo Burnett	Chicago	—	1,945.3	2,035.2	4.6
9	J. Walter Thompson	London	WPP	1,851.0	2,010.7	8.6
10	Foote, Cone & Belding	Chicago	—	1,871.2	1,950.3	4.2
11	Grey Advertising	New York	—	1,605.3	1,710.0	6.5
12	Lintas: Worldwide	New York	Interpublic	1,655.1	1,687.6	2.0
13	McCann-Erickson	New York	Interpublic	1,394.8	1,401.4	0.5
14	Bozell	New York	—	1,165.0	1,175.0	0.9
15	Ketchum	Pittsburgh	—	854.9	944.0	10.4

Source: Advertising Age (March 25, 1991):S–6. Copyright Crain Communications, Inc.

tained by an advertising agency when the agency is "stuck" or has an overload of work.

Creative boutiques are not as long-lived as full-service agencies. They depend on one person, or on a small group of people, frequently organized as a partnership. If a key person leaves, retires, or is hired by another firm, the creative boutique may disband. Some of the most successful boutiques, in contrast, have become full-service agencies. Grace & Rothchild in New York, for example, started as a "creative service" and has grown to $70 million in capitalized billing—a size that suggests it is now a full-service agency.

Medical Agencies

Medical agencies concentrate on advertising for health-care orgainizations and pharmaceutical companies such as Abbott, Pfizer, Hoffman-LaRoche, and Upjohn. These agencies require their staff members to have a detailed knowledge of chemistry and pharmacology as well as an understanding of medical practices and the laws relating to health-care advertising. People with advanced scientific degrees are often hired or retained by medical agencies as consultants. This type of agency carries out most of the functions a full-service agency performs but concentrates in the medical field. Seminars, symposia, and the writing and publication of technical papers relating to the business are often planned and managed by pharmaceutical agencies. These agencies may be small, as is Durot, Donahoe & Purohit of Rosemont, Illinois, with 12 employees, or large, such as Kallir Philips Ross, Sudler & Hennessey, and Medicus Intercom of New York, each with well over 100 employees.

Medical agencies have been growing more rapidly than the total industry. This has caused many full-service agencies and holding companies (a company that owns the stock of other corporations) to buy medical agencies. Eight of the top ten medical shops are now owned by full-service agencies.*

Minority Agencies

Agencies that focus on one ethnic group grew substantially in the 1980s as marketers realized that blacks and Hispanics, the two largest U.S. minorities, had different preferences and buying patterns from the general public. Minority agencies are organized much the same as are full-service agencies, but they are specialists in reaching and communicating with their market.

Black and Hispanic Agencies. Burrell Advertising of Chicago, Illinois, is one of the largest and most successful black agencies. The agency's founder, Tom Burrell, worked for several general market agencies before starting his own agency in 1971. With over 100 employees, Burrell Advertising works for such clients as Brown-Forman Beverage Company, Ford Motor Company, McDonald's Corporation, Polaroid, Procter & Gamble, Coca-Cola USA, the Stroh Brewery Company, Quaker Oats, Kraft General Foods, and Blockbuster Video.

Bermudez & Associates, headquartered in Los Angeles, California, is representative of most Hispanic agencies. Bermudez is minority-owned and -controlled and handles national accounts. The agency maintains full-

---

*Meryl Davids, "Taking the Pulse of Medical Agencies," *Adweek's Marketing Week* (March 12, 1990):RC27.

service offices in Los Angeles and New York. Clients include AT&T, Bank of America, Pepsico USA, R. J. Reynolds, and Southern California Edison.

The market for Hispanic advertising has attracted agencies from outside the continental United States. Noble & Asociados of Mexico City opened an office in Irving, California, and is billing over $20 million. Premier Maldonado, the leading independent agency in San Juan, Puerto Rico, opened an office in Miami in the late 1980s, capitalizing on its Hispanic marketing experience to serve its clients in the continental United States.

Targeting minorities is not without problems. Black groups in New York and Chicago have tried to remove billboards advertising alcohol and cigarettes from their neighborhoods (see the opening vignette in Chapter 2). Public pressure that was touched off by criticism from Health and Human Services Secretary Louis Sullivan forced R. J. Reynolds to withdraw Uptown cigarettes, a brand aimed primarily at blacks, from testing. In 1990 operation PUSH boycotted Nike shoes because the organization felt that Nike was not returning enough of its revenue to the black community, to which the brand was presumably marketed. Nike had used black athletes extensively in its advertising but did not use a black advertising agency. In 1990 it appointed Muse Cordero Chen of Los Angeles, an agency employing 15 people, earning $12 million in revenue.

The ethical side of the issue is that so-called "sin products," such as alcohol and tobacco, which can lead to addiction and health problems, are more heavily advertised in black and Hispanic neighborhoods than to the general population. Activists argue that this focus is leading to greater usage of the products. Marketers counter that advertising follows usage patterns and that they are just putting their marketing efforts where their customers are.

In-House Agencies

In-house agencies are advertising agencies that are owned and supervised by the advertisers themselves. They are organized similarly to independent agencies but can take a variety of forms. The advertising director of the company is usually the chief executive officer (CEO) of the agency, and he or she supervises account managers, who are responsible for brands or business groups. The in-house agency employs writers and artists, traffic personnel, and media specialists, all of whose functions will be explained later in this chapter. If the company has a separate research department, this specialty will probably not be duplicated in the in-house unit. The in-house agency may handle its own billing, paying, and collecting but is more likely to use the company's accounting department.

The publishing company R. R. Donnelly has both an in-house agency and a relationship with a Chicago advertising agency to help keep in-house staffers current and to provide stimulation. This use of an outside agency helps to ensure that in-house agency employees don't go stale or lose touch with developments outside their specific company category. A number of retail organizations will retain an advertising agency to do television advertising or image advertising but do their own promotion or retail advertising in-house. In this case the advertising agency may help design a format for the retail advertising, but the in-house advertising department will drop in the various specials and prices according to market or region. Walgreen is one company that works this way. Because prices are set in the merchandising department of the chain and completion of the ads is largely routine, its advertising is handled by the in-house staff.

Why Use an In-House Agency? There are many reasons for using an in-house agency, including cost, the technical nature of advertising, and service.

1. *Savings.* An in-house agency eliminates the expense incurred when the agency duplicates the staffing of a client. Probably the most appealing reason to use an in-house agency is that every agency seeks to make a profit on a client's business. They all have overheads that must be recovered from the prices they charge. By taking the work in-house and thus reducing overhead, the advertiser may be able to save that profit. Actually, though, the failure to realize this profit is one reason many companies return to using an outside agency.

2. *Specialization.* Clients in a highly technical field often find it difficult to get scientifically correct copywriting from an agency. Copywriters and art directors familiar with molecular biology, plasma, electronics, or nuclear microscopy may be hard to find. By the time copywriters do master the field, they are often promoted or transferred to another account. It is therefore better to have someone on staff in the in-house agency who knows the business inside out. The negative side of this solution is the burnout a copywriter may experience working in one field without any variety.

3. *Priority Service.* Clearly the in-house agency works only for the client and is available immediately for high-priority projects. There is no competition with other clients for the use of key personnel or the time of agency management.

Media-Buying Services

Media-buying services first flowered in the 1970s. These media-buying services called on clients and proposed charging rates as low as 1 percent of spending for network television, 2 to 3 percent for national magazines, and up to 5 percent for local newspapers or radio on a nationwide basis.

The relative popularity of the creative boutique also augmented the breakup of services normally provided by full-service agencies. When a client appointed a creative boutique to handle a product, that boutique did not plan or buy media, so the client either turned that assignment over to a media-buying service or planned the media internally and paid a buying service to execute the plan.

As media planning and buying became more and more complex because of additional media choices, the growth of cable, the specialization of magazines, and the wide variety of AM and FM radio stations, the cost of maintaining an informed and competent media department caused some smaller agencies to turn to media-buying services as well. Because these services often bought in more markets or in greater quantities than many advertising agencies, they could deliver media more efficiently. Although media-buying services seldom can beat the top 25 agencies in buying clout, they can usually outdo smaller agencies, especially in spot television and spot radio buying in markets with which the smaller agencies are not familiar.

Dennis Holt is generally credited with starting the first media-buying service in New York in 1965. After that company was sold, Holt moved in 1969 to Los Angeles and founded Western International Media Corporation. At $900 million in annual media buying, it is the largest of the media-buying services, with offices in more than 25 cities in the United States and Canada. Staffed by 728 media professionals, Western Media is the largest purchaser of local television, radio, and outdoor in the United States. Western Media works exclusively for advertising agencies; it does not service clients directly. The company maintains one of the largest secondary research bases available. It has expanded its services to agencies by offering primary and custom market research; print, outdoor, Yellow Pages, television, and radio production; Hispanic and Asian media and marketing; direct-response services; premiums and employee incentives; and syndication and promotional broadcast placement.

HOW AGENCIES ARE ORGANIZED

As an agency grows larger, there is a division of labor. As we mentioned earlier, most full-service agencies employ specialists who provide specific functions. Smaller agencies offer the same basic functions, but they employ a smaller number of people who are less specialized and may perform more than one function. For the purpose of giving a full explanation, the following description of agency organization is based on larger agencies. Figure 4.2 offers a humorous look into the inner workings of an advertising agency.

Rather than organizing around a business unit, as marketers do, an agency organizes around a client's account. Because clients come and go

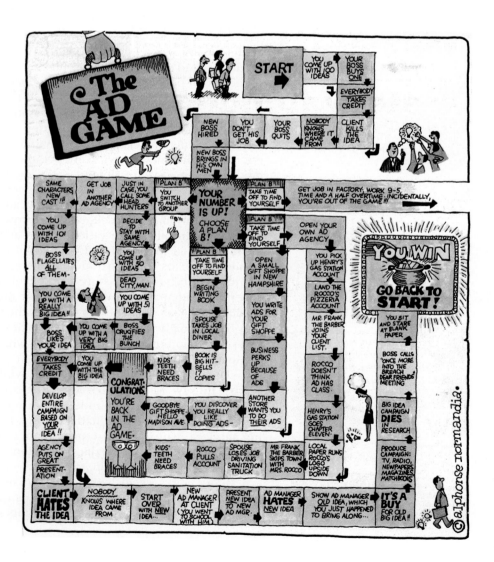

FIGURE 4.2
The Ad Game *Source: Advertising Age* (December 21, 1987):18. Copyright Crain Communications, Inc.

and account needs change, agencies must be adaptable. The agency must encourage new ideas and protect them as they are refined. Openness and flexibility are more important than organizational structure is in most agencies. Furthermore, agencies must organize internally to function as a business, as well as externally to work with their clients.

Unlike corporations, agencies often change structure to accommodate the needs of new clients or the talents of their people. For example, an agency might have one client that advertises a leading brand on a national basis, using primarily television and national magazines. For this client, the emphasis in staffing might be in the creative and research departments. Young & Rubicam would have staffing such as this for American Home Products and Colgate. Another client in the fast-service restaurant field, which has local cooperatives of owner-operators in major markets, would need field service account executives to work with both the co-ops and the local agencies these co-ops use. This is true of Leo Burnett and DDB Needham, both of which handle McDonald's.

Account Management

account management *The function in an agency which serves as a liaison between the agency and the client.*

The role of **account management** is to serve as a liaison between the client and the agency in order to ensure that the agency focuses its resources on the needs of the client. At the same time, the agency also develops its own point of view, which is presented to the client. Once the client (or the client and the agency together) establishes the general guidelines of the advertising campaign, the account management department supervises the day-to-day development of the account within these guidelines, which include:

1. What is the purpose of the advertising?
2. Who is the target audience?
3. What is the promise (claim or benefit) the advertising will make?
4. What is the support for this promise? Are there secondary support points for specific target audiences or models of the product?
5. What media will deliver the message?
6. What is the tone or personality of the advertising?
7. Are there unique opportunities in terms of timing, competitive weaknesses, technological leadership, customer loyalties, or brand equities that must be considered?

Furthermore, agency clients come from all different fields, and the account manager must recognize that strategies that work for one client may not work for another (see Ad 4.3).

PRINCIPLE
The account management role focuses on agency initiative and responsibility rather than on subservience to the client.

The original title for this client liaison function, "account service," has been changed in most agencies because it suggests that the agency should be subservient to the client rather than provide an independent professional viewpoint. "Account management," in contrast, suggests initiative and responsibility by the agency.

Handling the Brand Manager. The client's *brand manager* typically is the account manager's contact at the client company. A client brand is assigned to a brand manager, who is responsible for supervising all aspects of the brand's marketing: manufacturing, packaging, distribution, improvements, changes occasioned by environmental or safety laws, trade relations, promotions, public relations, profits, and advertising. This person takes on many roles, including boss, "God," tyrant, friend, partner, and guardian of the relationship with the agency.

How do you fit five elephants in a box?

First find someone who'll do the killing. Arm him with a machine gun and an axe. Send him off to slaughter elephants. Pay him for the tusks. And ship them away to be carved into bracelets and necklaces.

The African elephant is being driven from the face of the earth for the sake of consumer demand for ivory trinkets. In just 10 years, the population of African elephants has been more than halved. If this rate of killing continues, the African elephant could be extinct in just 25 years. The killers and the people who pay them don't care about elephant deaths. They don't hear the world's outrage. They just want money. They're the people we must stop.

Please join World Wildlife Fund's Elephant Action Campaign. Help us put these killers and the people who finance them out of business. Your donation of $15 or more will help us support increased anti-poaching patrols. And supply equipment to those rangers who are already in the field – desperately trying to stop the senseless slaughter of one of the world's great species.

Time is running out. 143 African elephants are dying every day. So their tusks can be turned into jewelry. You can stop this. Before it's too late.

Call 1-800-453-6100 to make a donation.

AD 4.3
Agency clients come from all different fields. This public service ad for the World Wildlife Fund was produced by W. B. Doner & Company. (Courtesy of World Wildlife Fund.)

Handling the brand manager and the client in general can be a difficult role for the account manager. Deadlines are sometimes missed. An ad may not produce anticipated results. Agency profitability requirements may cause conflicts between the levels of staffing a client wants and those the agency is willing to provide. The agency recommendation may be unusually blunt or even critical. The agency must maintain its independence and honestly express its point of view, however. Paul Harper, chairman emeritus of DDB Needham, put the role in perspective in this way in a *Memorandum to All Our Account Executives:*

> Most good clients have strong views of their own. You will win client respect for yourself and the agency mainly for two things: (1) for forthrightness and thoroughness in presenting the agency's views, and (2) for respectful knowledge of the problems the client faces as he makes his own often difficult decisions. When his answer is "No," as it will sometimes be, this may be a professional defeat. But it will never be a moral defeat if the agency's position has been well presented and stoutly defended.

Account management in a major agency typically has four levels: management representative or supervisor, account supervisor, account executive, and assistant account executives. Sometimes there is a fifth level, the account director, who is above the account supervisor. A smaller agency may combine some of these levels.

Management Supervisor. The *management supervisor* reports to the upper management of the agency. This person provides leadership on strategic issues, looks for new business opportunities, promotes personnel growth and development within the account team, keeps agency management informed, and ensures that the agency is making a realistic profit on the account. The management supervisor is the agency spokesperson for the client and is responsible for delivering the agency's service and for providing an objective outside point of view. The position normally carries the title of senior vice president and is offered to someone who has been working in account management for 10 to 15 years.

Account Supervisor. The *account supervisor* usually is the key working executive on the client's business and the primary liaison between the client and the agency. This person directs the preparation of strategic plans, assigns priorities, reviews and approves all recommendations before they are taken to the client, supervises the presentation of annual plans and other major recommendations to the client, and ensures agency adherence to plans and schedules. The client sees this person as the working manager from the agency—the one who provides the working contact with the client. Account supervisors usually carry the title of vice president.

Account Executive. The *account executive* is responsible for day-to-day activities, including keeping the agency team on schedule and delivering the services as promised to the client. Other functions of the account executive are seeing that all assignments are completed on time and within budget, maintaining the operating records of the account, preparing status and progress reports, supervising the production of materials, and securing legal or network approval of all advertising before production begins. This is the person who is there for the client every time there is work to be assigned or delivered.

Assistant Account Executive. *Assistant account executive* is normally the entry-level position in the agency's account management department. The focus is on learning the business and helping the account executive with records and schedules. In most agencies, computer literacy is required at least through the account supervisor level because records are stored and reports are written on computer terminals that are shared within the account group or even the entire agency. Some agencies are so computerized that computer literacy is required to function at all within the agency.

Creative Development and Production

To some people "creative organization" is a self-contradiction because they believe that creativity can only occur in an unstructured environment. In an agency, however, management must take into consideration how people work together and what assignments are flowing through the agency. The wisest agency managers are flexible in terms of organization but strict in terms of quality and deadline control.

The creative members of the agency typically hold one of the following positions: creative director, creative department manager, copywriter, art director, or producer. In addition to these positions, the broadcast production department and the studio are two other areas where creative personnel can apply their skills. Ad 4.4 for Young & Rubicam describes the creative advertising the agency develops for its clients.

Creative Director. Most agencies have one senior executive called the *creative director*, or executive creative director, who serves as the agency's creative conscience. (Another comparable title is director of creative services.) This person stimulates the department to improve its creative work and approves all ideas before they are presented outside the department. Because of the importance of the creative product, the creative director is more and more likely to be a member of the agency's board of directors or senior management group. To the client this individual is the creative spokesperson of the agency and the strategic creative mind.

AD 4.4
Young & Rubicam used this "house ad" to highlight its philosophy of service and creative strategy.
(Courtesy of Young & Rubicam Inc.)

Within the image:
You can really fly
once you know where you're going.

We believe the sharpest advertising strategies provide the greatest creative freedom. Only when you know exactly where you're going can the imagination soar free, without fear or formulas.
YOUNG & RUBICAM INC.

Creative Department Manager. Larger agencies may also have a person who oversees the internal management process, the administrative activities needed to keep the department running. Referred to as the *creative department manager*, this person handles budgeting, salary administration, office assignments, the hiring and supervising of secretarial and support staff, the recruiting of professional staff, and internal accounting. In acknowledgment of the parental and instructive nature of the job, practitioners often refer to the creative department manager as "house mother," "warden," "priest," "rabbi," "confessor," "crying towel," or "punching bag." Creative directors can survive the loss of a senior staff member more easily than the loss of the creative department manager. Clients seldom have contact with this person.

The Creative Group. Two types of people are generally found within the creative department. One is the brilliant, and sometimes eccentric, creator who conceives, writes, and produces innovative advertising. A staff is often the extension of this person's skills.

The second type is the coach, who delegates assignments, works with the staff to find an idea, and then molds, improves, nurtures, and inspires the staff. Agencies organize teams around the coach, who may be called the creative group head, associate creative director, or creative director (if the senior title is executive creative director). Both the creator and the coach can coexist within the creative department—in fact, many people possess some characteristics of both types—but the coach typically supervises the larger team of people.

A *creative group* includes people who write *(copywriters),* people who draw ideas for print ads or television commercials *(art directors),* and people who translate those ideas into television or radio commercials *(pro-*

An agency art director. (Laima Druskis.)

ducers). In many agencies an art director and copywriter who work well together are teamed up and a support group is built around them. Art directors and copywriters are discussed in more detail in Chapter 13. The creative group leader is the person who typically presents the creative recommendation of the agency—except perhaps for a new campaign—when that task is claimed by the creative director.

Broadcast Production. Sometimes the broadcast production department is a separate department (as the print production department usually is), but more often it is part of the creative department. Because the execution of the tone and action of broadcast advertising is so central to its success, the creative team usually works with a broadcast producer, who is directly involved in the filming and editing of the commercial. Clients usually only see these people when final plans are being made for television or radio production, and then on the set or studio during production.

The Art Studio. The art studio, once called the *bullpen* but recently changed because of sexist connotations, is another part of the creative department. The art studio includes artists who specialize in presentation pieces, called comprehensives or "comps," lettering, and paste-up. (Presentation pieces are discussed in more detail in Chapter 14.) Beginning art directors often start in an agency studio.

The computer is increasingly doing some of the work of the artists. When introduced into the creative departments of advertising agencies, the computer was looked at with skepticism and disapproval. At first it was accepted only for writing and revising copy, but the graphic capabilities of the computer, particularly the Apple Macintosh, have steadily broken down the resistance of art directors. Today the computer is commonly used for fast rough layouts, quick changes on storyboards, and even finished production for some black-and-white newspaper ads.

Media Planning and Buying

The media department performs one of the most complex functions in an advertising agency. It must recommend the most efficient means of delivering the message to the target audience. The look of media departments is

INSIDE ADVERTISING

ROBERT KLEIN, MANAGEMENT REPRESENTATIVE FOR BIG "G" CEREALS, DDB NEEDHAM CHICAGO

As a management representative for Big "G" Cereals, Robert Klein is responsible for finding creative ways to promote his client's cereal. At the same time, Klein is involved with the internal affairs of DDB Needham Chicago and the seven-person account group he heads. The following is a typical day in the life of Robert Klein.

Courtesy of Robert Klein

7:29 A.M.	My day gets started on the morning train ride into the city. I begin with a quick read of the *Chicago Tribune*, especially the sports section. Sports has always been a great passion of mine, and with my responsibilities on Wheaties, staying abreast is absolutely essential. I use the last half of the train ride to organize my day and set priorities in order to hit the ground running when I get into the office.
8:15–9:00 A.M.	As soon as I get into my office, I switch on the Macintosh to check the electronic mail. I'll respond to messages and send out notes of my own before most of our task force members have begun their day in the office. I'll also use this time to catch up on reading and correspondence.
9:00–10:00 A.M.	Meetings with Big "G" account supervisors to review and discuss project lists. The supervisors highlight the key issues for the week and detail the action plans to address these topics.
10:00–11:00 A.M.	The entire cereal account group meets with our research and strategic planning team. The research experts have been working on an analysis of quantitative data regarding the long-term business-building impact of promotion versus advertising. Some insightful observations surface and we discuss how to make this information most relevant and actionable for our client. We agree to next steps, which include having the research associate attend a major division-wide promotion key issues meeting at General Mills to gain a more in-depth understanding of the client's issues and needs. Then we'll regroup to further tailor the presentation and set a date to review with the client.
11:00 A.M.–12:00 N.	We've just implemented a new agency-wide performance evaluation system. Today we spend an hour discussing with the codirector of the account management department and group account director appraisals for the seven people in my account group. Our focus is on writing objectives for each employee that are very specific, actionable, and

changing as computer terminals are replacing the printed schedules and rate cards long used for buying media time. Initially, computer printers inundated media departments with paper, but many media departments have turned to computers for storing schedules, rates, changes, and pre- and post-buy analyses. This information is shared with clients on interactive screens instead of paper printouts and is approved by keystroke. The printed version is commanded only when needed. Other members of the agency and the client can be alerted to changes by electronic mail over computer networks.

measurable. We agree to complete the final stage of the appraisal process, including development of and agreement to objectives, within 2 weeks.

12:00–1:00 P.M.   Today is my first day working with the new account supervisor on Wheaties and Raisin Nut Bran. We take advantage of the lunch hour to chat about the account and the challenges we face. We both order the caesar salad . . . a sure indication we'll get along great!

1:00–1:30 P.M.   Personnel-related issues.

1:30–2:00 P.M.   Several telephone messages have accumulated, and this is my first chance to return calls. Most critical is a follow-up conversation with the Wheaties marketing director regarding a major sports sponsorship. This is a multimillion-dollar program that I've asked our associate media director to evaluate. He has done an exhaustive analysis indicating that the proposed pricing is high and will require some hard negotiating should we choose to pursue.

2:00–2:45 P.M.   Meeting to catch up with account supervisor on Golden Grahams. He identifies an important issue on new television creative work that has surfaced with the brand group. We agree to meet with the creative team at 4:00 P.M. to discuss.

3:00–4:00 P.M.   Incoming mail and more phone calls. I spend a half hour reviewing marketing plans documents from the account executives and jotting down brief notes to each individual.

4:00–5:00 P.M.   The Golden Grahams account supervisor and I meet with the group creative director and creative director. The supervisor lays out the central issue that has arisen with the brand manager and offers his own point of view. We discuss options and agree to a strategic approach. The creative team feels good about the resolution and the supervisor agrees to discuss our plan of attack with the brand.

5:00–5:30 P.M.   Update the group account director on account status and key issues.

5:30–6:00 P.M.   Time to clear up my desk and jot down priorities for tomorrow.

6:31 P.M.   Another 45 minutes on the train! *The National, The Wall Street Journal,* and a few pages of a novel make the ride home fly by. Tonight it's the Bulls vs. Celtics (Jordan vs. Bird) on cable. Hope Michael ate his Wheaties!

Marketing Services.   Some agencies have combined media and research under the supervision of one executive and called the resulting function "Marketing Services." Market research is an important component of any media decision. Central to that decision is a clear understanding of the target audience. The same profile of the target audience is needed by the creative department. The practice of combining management of media and research is not universal, however. We will therefore treat those functions separately in the text. How they are organized in each agency is a management decision.

Most media departments basically break down into three functions: planning, buying, and research. These functions will be outlined here and discussed in more detail in Chapters 9 and 12.

The Media Planner. Developing a media plan is a creative skill that involves determining which medium or media to use, when, for what length of time, and at what cost. The *media planner* must be involved in the overall strategy and creative development of the advertising campaign. Most media and creative plans are prepared concurrently so the message and the medium will work together. Clients look to the media planner to present the media strategy and, once the strategy is approved, the media plan.

The Media Buyer. The *media buyer* determines what media coverage is likely to be available at what costs. Buying involves ordering media on behalf of the client, according to the plan approved by the client. Once the client approves the plan, the media buyer acts quickly to negotiate rates and place orders. There is no point in recommending a plan calling for advertising on specific network television programs if those programs are already sold.

Media Research. In addition to media planners and buyers, most media departments have researchers who gather and evaluate media data. The *media research manager* is responsible for preparing the department's forecasts of future prices, ratings of television programs, and audience composition. The media research department often provides entry-level clerical and data-gathering positions.

Research Services

Full-service U.S. agencies usually have a separate department specifically devoted to research. The emphasis in agency research is on assisting the development of the strategy and the advertising message. Most major agencies conduct research before preparing the advertising to ensure that the advertising will be focused and appropriate to the target audience. They also purchase research from companies that specialize in this area. The leading research firms work on projects for both clients and agencies. The leading U.S. firms are shown in Table 4.3.

Most European advertising agencies either do not have a separate research department or have a research director only, who is responsible for commissioning outside research projects and interpreting the results for the agency.

Whether composed of a single person in a small agency or teams of professionals in a large agency, the research department has a number of duties besides helping creative development. It ensures that the agency has reliable information, screens all new research findings to determine if they change the body of information about a brand, company, industry, or market, and provides the agency with accurate information about consumer behavior. When conducting original research, the agency almost always concentrates on consumer attitudes and behavior. Advertising research will be discussed in more detail in Chapters 6 and 21.

An important philosophical consideration is how the research function is positioned in the agency. The research department conducts *copy testing,* but it should not be the judge of the quality of the creative. It should be the scout—the eyes and ears of the agency. By concentrating on preresearch and on evaluating consumer reaction to creative alternatives,

PRINCIPLE

Research should be a partner with the creative side in the development of great advertising.

TABLE 4.3
Top U.S. Research Companies

Rank		Company, Headquarters	Gross U.S. Research Revenues ($ millions)		
1989	1988		1989	1988	% Change
1	1	**A.C. Nielsen Co.,** Northbrook, Ill.	$426.0	$387.0	10.1
2	2	**Arbitron Co.,** New York	290.0	320.0	(9.4)
3	3	**IMS International,** New York	181.0	164.0	10.4
4	4	**Information Resources Inc.,** Chicago	113.8	99.3	14.6
5	5	**Westat,** Rockville, Md.	65.9	64.5	2.2
6	6	**M/A/R/C,** Irving, Texas	53.2	51.1	4.1
7	7	**Maritz Marketing Research,** Fenton, Mo.	46.1	40.6	13.5
8	10	**MRB Group,** New York	44.6	36.8	21.4
9	8	**NFO Research,** Greenwich, Conn.	42.0	39.9	5.3
10	9	**Market Facts,** Chicago	39.0	37.8	3.1
11	12	**Elrick & Lavidge,** New York	38.0	31.5	20.6
12	11	**NPD Group,** Port Washington, N.Y.	34.7	34.5	0.6
13	13	**Burke Marketing Research,** Cincinnati	27.1	28.6	(5.2)
14	16	**Walker Research,** Indianapolis	26.5	21.5	22.8
15	14	**Chilton Research Services,** Radnor, Pa.	21.8	23.7	(8.0)
16	17	**Starch INRA Hooper,** Mamaroneck, N.Y.	20.5	19.0	7.9
17	15	**Research International,** London	19.8	21.3	(7.1)
18	20	**ASI Market Research,** New York	17.4	14.7	18.4
19	19	**Decision Research Corp.,** Lexington, Mass.	15.9	14.9	6.7
20	24	**National Research Group,** Los Angeles	15.3	12.1	26.4

Figures are AA estimates. This table is an updated version from Research Business Report (AA, June 11).

Source: Advertising Age (December 24, 1990):12. Copyright Crain Communications, Inc.

the research department contributes to the development of new ways of thinking about the message and the consumer. Most agencies ask clients to conduct postresearch and to score the advertising after it has run.

Internal Services

The departments discussed in this section—traffic, print production, financial service, personnel, and direct marketing—are the very important backroom operations of an agency. These departments produce the work, get it to the media, handle the finances, and manage relationships with employees.

Traffic Department.   The traffic department is responsible for internal control and tracking of projects to meet deadlines. The account executive works closely with the assigned traffic coordinator or traffic manager to review deadlines and monitor progress. The traffic department is the lifeline of the agency, and its personnel keep track of everything that is happening in the agency. Trafficking requires diligence, tact, and great attention to detail. Diligence is necessary to keep track of the progress of all the elements of a campaign as they come together to ensure that the key jobs—the ones on which other departments depend to meet their deadlines—do not slip behind. Traffic coordinators must possess tact in negotiating with creative people, who are prone to complain they never have enough time or have too many jobs to complete. These creatives appreciate it, however, when a traffic manager pushes the critical assignments and buys a day or two on those assignments that have a cushion in the schedule. Attention to detail is required in this position because it is the responsibility of the traffic coordinator to get the job finished, assemble all the bills and charges, and deliver

Members of the print services department. (Jeff Persons/Stock Boston.)

the proper sign-offs to financial services for billing to the client. Although computers now help trace and program projects, they cannot replace the persistent traffic coordinator who has heard every excuse for delay.

Print Production. Taking a layout, a photograph or an illustration, and a page of copy and turning them into a four-color magazine page or a full-page newspaper advertisement is the work of the print production department.

Because of the technical nature of making the printing plates, adjusting and matching color, and achieving reproduction, print production is not handled within the creative department, as are television and radio production. The art director on the account normally will supervise the illustrator or photographer and will approve the work, but will not supervise the production of the material sent to the publication. The use of computers and computer graphics is returning some newspaper print production to the art director, but most production for print media is still done in the print production department.

Financial Services. Whether large or small, the agency must send its invoices out promptly, pay its bills on time, control its costs, ensure that expenses incurred on behalf of a client are properly invoiced to that client, meet its payroll, pay its taxes, and make a profit within its budget. These functions are managed by the chief financial officer. In a large agency the treasurer is responsible for cash management, seeing that funds are invested until needed, bills are paid just before they are due, cash discounts are taken, and cash reserves are available for peak billing periods. The comptroller is charged with internal procedures, such as conducting internal audits to prevent misuse of agency resources and ensuring that money is not spent without authority, large checks are countersigned, and invoices are approved before they are paid.

Personnel. An operation of any size requires keeping personnel files and records. The larger the agency, the more likely it is to have a professional personnel staff. These people handle the hiring and firing of clerical, secretarial, and support staff. Recruitment of professional staff, although conducted by the head of the department in which the person will work, is normally coordinated by the personnel department. This department is increasingly referred to as Human Resources. Frequently, it is responsible for ensuring that the agency meets equal opportunity guidelines. Both the financial services and personnel departments of advertising agencies function the same way as do comparable departments in corporations.

Other Departments. The increase in the use of direct marketing (see Chapter 16) and the search by clients for direct-marketing counsel have led to the development of direct-marketing departments and direct-marketing subsidiaries. Likewise, agencies either acquire sales promotion and public relations agencies or set up internal departments to handle these functions as part of a coordinated or integrated marketing communication program.

*H*OW AGENCIES ARE PAID

agent *Someone who acts on behalf of someone else, usually for a fee.*

commission *A form of payment in which an agent or agency receives a certain percentage (often 15 percent) of media charges.*

Agencies derive their revenues, and therefore their profits, from two main sources—commissions and fees. To understand these processes, we must first understand the word **agent.** An agent is someone who acts for another. In this case an advertising agency acts for a client in creating advertising.

Early advertising agents acted on behalf of the medium rather than on behalf of the client. Well into the nineteenth century, advertising agents functioned as representatives for newspapers, magazines, and handbill printers. If the agent brought advertising to the publisher, the publisher paid the agent a **commission,** which was justified by the work the agent did in bringing the publisher the business and preparing the advertisement for publication. The agent might write the copy, prepare the layout, set the type, and arrange for any drawings or plates that were part of the advertisement. These efforts saved the publisher both time and work.

As advertising grew in importance, advertisers began to work with fewer and fewer agents and eventually signed with one agent exclusively. In 1901 Clarence Curtis of Curtis Publishing granted a 15 percent commission to advertising agencies—10 percent for preparation of material and 5 percent for prompt payment. This practice changed the entire advertising industry. Instead of representing one medium to many advertisers, the agent now acted on behalf of the client and placed ads with many media.

The Commission System

A 15 percent commission was long considered standard in the sense of being the usual amount most media allowed agencies. (Outdoor typically is 16 2/3 percent.) For example, when a television commercial cost $100,000, the agency billed the client $100,000 but paid the station only $85,000, keeping $15,000 as its commission.

In the 1980s clients began to squeeze the 15 percent commission to reduce their expenses. When advertising accounts were opened for presentation, the client might indicate it intended to pay, say, only 12 percent commission. Agencies' acceptance of that practice undercut the standard 15 percent commission, which is rare now and may be on its way out. Negotiated commission rates, especially for the largest budgets—$10 million and up—are common. In late 1990, for example, TWA awarded its account

TABLE 4.4
How Commission Is Paid

		To Billing (%)	To Revenue (%)
Billings placed in media	$5,000,000	100	
15% commission (agency revenue)	750,000	15.0	100
Expenses			
Direct salaries*	250,000	5.0	33.3
Indirect salaries†	165,000	3.3	22.0
Social Security, health benefits	125,000	2.5	16.7
Rent	45,000	0.9	6.0
Travel	10,000	0.2	1.3
Telephone, postage, etc.	10,000	0.2	1.3
Supplies	10,000	0.2	1.3
All other	20,000	0.4	2.7
Profit sharing	50,000	1.0	6.7
Gross profit	65,000	1.3	8.6
Tax	20,000	0.4	2.7
Net profit after tax	45,000	0.9	6.0

*Direct salaries apply to people who work directly on client business.
†Indirect salaries apply to people who do not work directly on client business: senior management, accounting, telephone operators, studio, mailroom, receptionist.

to Avrett, Free & Ginsberg in New York at a reported commission rate of 5 percent.

In some places, however, the standard exceeds 15 percent. The commission allowed by media in New Zealand, for example, is 20 percent. The rationale for this higher rate is that New Zealand is a small country and its agencies have to do as much work to prepare a campaign to reach 3.5 million New Zealanders as would a U.S. agency whose campaign will reach a much larger audience. In Australia, which is five times as populous as New Zealand, the commission allowed by media is 16 percent. Throughout the world, although the commission rate allowed by media most commonly is 15 percent, clients are increasingly negotiating to get some of that commission back. Very large clients frequently negotiate sliding scales on commission, for example, 15 percent up to $10 million, 12 percent from $10 million to $25 million, and 10 percent above that.

How the Commission System Works.   We will now discuss how the commission system works and how agencies derive their profits. Our example uses the standard 15 percent commission, but the principle would be the same regardless of the percentage used. The two columns in Table 4.4 relate the typical expense categories to two key financial descriptions: the total billing in media; and the revenue, the money the agency gets to keep.

The percentages shown in Table 4.4 are within the range the industry considers typical. In the late 1980s the rate of profit of the public agencies was slightly below 6 percent. In 1989 the five largest public agencies (Foote, Cone & Belding, Grey, Interpublic, Omnicom, and WPP) had combined after-tax profits of 5.4 percent. Saatchi lost nearly $123 million in 1989.*

What happens when the commission is lower than 15 percent and how is that lower rate set? The rate is negotiated between client and agency, including what work will be done by the agency and what will be charged for separately.

*Kevin McCormack, "A Look at the Publicly Held Concerns," *Adweek's Marketing Week* (March 12, 1990):RC30.

To the degree that the agency does not charge for items in the "Sometimes Included" column or for items usually charged separately from commission, the agency effectively lowers its commission rate.

Marketing Services   Advertising agencies are increasingly asking clients to pay for services traditionally provided for free. Marketing strategies, for instance, are costly services when marketing consultancies are used. Martin Sorrell, chief executive of WPP Group, argues that agencies should charge for the costs of these services.*

For example, if the agency agrees to a commission of 10 percent, here is how the payment works:

Billing placed in media	$5,000,000
Agency pays media on behalf of client	4,250,000
15 percent commission from media	750,000
10 percent commission rate from media	500,000
Rebated to client	250,000

The media will accept the order for $5,000,000 and bill the agency $4,250,000. The agency will charge the client $4,750,000, not $5,000,000, and make a commission of 10 percent on the $5,000,000 budget.

Markups

Some media and most production houses (those that make printing plates or produce television commercials), do not allow agency commissions. The agency then will "mark up" or "gross up" the outside charge to reflect the commission. Here is how that works.

		Net (%)	Grossed Up (%)
Media cost	$100,000		
15 percent commission	15,000		
Net cost to agency	85,000	85	100
Equivalent commission	15,000		17.65

If the $85,000 cost of service to the agency has no commission allowance and the client agrees to a 15 percent commission, the agency will add $15,000 (17.65 percent) to the $85,000 when billing the client. If the agreed commission is 10 percent, the $85,000 represents 90 percent of what the agency will charge the client. The agency then will add $9,444 (11.1 percent) to gross up the amount so that its final charge to the client ($94,444) contains a 10 percent ($9,444) commission.

The Fee System

fee *A mode of payment in which an agency charges a client on the basis of the agency's hourly costs.*

A third form of compensation is the fee system. This system is comparable to that used by lawyers and accountants. The client and agency agree on an hourly **fee,** or charge. This fee can vary according to department or levels of salary within a department. In other cases a flat hourly fee for all work is

Advertising Age (March 19, 1990):1.

TABLE 4.5
Incentive-Based Agency Compensation Plans

These major marketers have implemented agency pay systems that are based on product performance incentives or similar criteria.

Marketer	Agencies	Date Implemented	System
Campbell Soup Co.	BBDO Worldwide Backer Spielvogel Bates FCB/Leber Katz Partners Ogilvy & Mather	August 1990	Compensation is based on a 14%-15%-16% sliding rate. Agencies meeting sales goals agreed on at beginning of fiscal year earn 15%, those failing to meet objectives earn 14%, and those exceeding objectives get 16%.
R.J. Reynolds Tobacco	FCB/Leber Katz Partners Young & Rubicam Long, Haymes & Carr	January 1987	Agencies given a base compensation rate of "below 15%," and then rewarded for "outstanding results" with an additional 20% incentive bonus, a 10% bonus for "very good" work, and a flat fee for average or poor evaluations. Evaluations based on creative development, marketing counsel, promotion counsel, and budget administration.
Nabisco Brands	McCann-Erickson FCB/Leber Katz Partners Lowe & Partners	January 1989	Agencies compensated on a set commission rate of "no less than 10% but no higher than 15%" with bonuses ranging from 5% to 20%, depending on how the agency meets sales goals set at the beginning of each year.
Carnation Co.	Daily & Associates McCann-Erickson	March 1989	Agencies paid 11% commission plus fees, based on whether brands are established or under development, and plus incentives, based on various factors, including whether ads meet objectives in consumer pretesting.

Source: Advertising Age (October 22, 1990):58. Copyright Crain Communications, Inc.

agreed on regardless of the salary level of the person doing the work. Charges are also included for out-of-pocket expenses, travel, and any items normally charged separately under a commission system. These are charged net, without any markup or commission. All media are billed to the client net of any commission.

Trust is the critical element in a fee system. The client must believe that each person in the agency is keeping track of his or her time accurately and charging that time correctly to a particular brand or project. The client must also believe that the agency's hourly charge for salary, overhead, and profit is fair.

Calculating the Agency Fee. How is the agency fee calculated? The agency assigns costs for salary, rent, telephone, postage, internal operations, equipment rentals, taxes, and other expenses, and then determines what hourly charge will recover all of these costs and also provide the agency with a profit. A common rule of thumb in setting a fee is to charge three times the person's annual salary divided by the number of hours that person worked.

Here is how the agency profit and loss statement might look compared to the commission system. In this example there is equivalent billing of $5,000,000 and 1.7 people per million dollars of billing working on the business. The client, therefore, has the services of 8.5 people, approximately 5 of whom are working directly on the account. Because the agency using the fee system is seeking substantially the same revenue ($750,000 or 15 percent of $5,000,000), and is charging only for the five people who work on the business (direct salaries), the fee would be three times the direct salaries ($750,000 ÷ $250,000). Assume an 1800-hour work year and an average salary of $50,000 per year of those working on the account.

Average salary	$50,000
Divided by 1800, direct cost per hour	$27.77
Times 3, fee charge per hour	$83.33
9000 hours × $83.33 per hour	$750,000

If the other costs remain the same, the agency will achieve a profit after taxes of $45,000.

The fee system has many supporters within the field. Those who favor it over the commission system believe that an agency's payments should not be based on the price a medium charges. The commission system has survived, however, because it is simple, easy to understand, and puts pressure on an agency to keep its costs down.

Incentive-Based Agency Compensation. A variation on the fee system is incentive-based agency compensation, which is shown in Table 4.5. An incentive-based system pays the agency a basic amount, either a percentage of media billing or a fixed fee, for basic services. If the agency's work is judged superior, either subjectively or by some objective measure (sales, share), the agency gets a bonus or incentive payment. Failure to reach goals probably means loss of the account. The DDB Needham agency, for example, sensing a movement toward sales-based incentives, announced a "guaranteed results" plan. Its caveat is that the agency must have control over the "consistency of messages."*

CHANGES IN THE AGENCY WORLD

Many changes have occurred within the advertising industry in recent years. Agencies have merged to form large, multibillion-dollar corporations. Companies have consolidated all their divisions under the care of just one agency. These and other changes in the structure of the agency world are the focus of this discussion.

Megamergers

megamergers *Combinations of large international agencies under a central holding company.*

In April 1986 three agencies announced what was called the "Big Bang." Batten, Barton, Durstine, and Osborne (BBDO), Doyle Dane Bernbach, and Needham Harper Worldwide joined together in a **megamerger** to form Omnicom, Inc., a $5 billion giant. The three agencies realigned into two international agencies, BBDO and DDB Needham (see Ad 4.5) and placed most of their specialist agencies into a third group, Diversified Agency Services, which included public relations, direct response, several midsized agencies, recruitment, and medical services. Merging these functions helped the firm to offer **integrated marketing communications** (IMC), a philosophy that stresses bringing together all the variables of the marketing mix and integrating their programs and activities. Shortly after this merger, Saatchi & Saatchi of London acquired the Ted Bates Agency, which owned, among others, the William Esty Agency. The new Saatchi giant is even larger than Omnicom. It operates two international networks: Saatchi & Saatchi and Backer Spielvogel Bates.

integrated marketing communications *Promotional planning that focuses on integrated communication based on an analysis of consumer behavior.*

Merger activity increased greatly in the late 1980s and early 1990s. In 1987 the Saatchi & Saatchi acquisition was followed by the first unfriendly

Advertising Age (October 22, 1990):58.

Fasten your seatbelts.

AD 4.5
This ad was specially prepared to announce the formation of DDB Needham Worldwide. (Courtesy of DDB Needham Worldwide.)

holding company *A company that owns the stocks of other corporations.*

conflict of interest *An agency dilemma of having a client's two competing companies.*

takeover in the industry when J. Walter Thompson (JWT) was acquired—against the wishes of agency management—by the **holding company** WPP Group PLC, also of London.

International Agencies. In 1988 WPP bought Ogilvy & Mather, a respected agency that had lost momentum. Each of the three groups, Omnicom, Saatchi & Saatchi, and WPP, now had two international agencies under its banner.

The new agency groups claimed that their size and geographic scope were not only necessary to serve large global clients but were also brought on by the mergers and increases in size of clients.

International agencies typically are kept separate and competitive in the holding company. Conflicts of interest are avoided by steering one client to one subsidiary and a competing client to the second. A **conflict of interest** occurs when an agency is faced with serving two competing clients. The detergent, automotive, beer, and food giants have made some agency realignments within the mega-agencies but have frowned on or avoided placing assignments within mega-agencies that handle a competitor anywhere in the holding company. Over $700 million in billings have switched hands or had to be resigned because of conflicts following the megamergers. For a closer look at the implications of conflicts of interest, see the Concepts and Controversies box entitled "Conflicts of Loyalty."

At least partly in response to the global scope and dual networks created by the megamergers and holding companies, Young & Rubicam joined with the Japanese giant Dentsu, the world's largest agency, and Havas Conseil, a French advertising conglomerate, to form HDM. The new corporation provided the parent companies with a dual option for clients. By the end of 1990 this joint venture had come apart when Havas Conseil withdrew to concentrate on its own growth.

Concepts and Controversies

Conflicts and Loyalty

The standard industry contract states that the agency agrees not to handle different products or companies in the same category or industry. For example, an agency that represents Coca-Cola will not represent Pepsi. In contrast to lawyers and accountants, who may specialize in a sector or an industry and handle a number of clients in the same field, advertising agencies agree not to work for a competing product or company because this would cause a conflict of interest. ("How can you work for a competitor and assure me I am getting your best ideas and the best media buys?") In theory, the conflict clause is simple. In practice, it has become one of the major controversies in the industry for several reasons: client mergers, agency internationalization, and agency megamergers.

The mergers of clients presented both agencies and clients with new complexities. When a client acquires a new division, it may ask the agency to take on the new assignment. If the agency is already representing the leading product in the category for another very important client, either accepting or rejecting the new assignment risks offending one client. In a worst case scenario, both clients may insist that the agency resign the other company. Usually, goodwill and loyalty resolve these conflict-interpretation problems. Clients will often agree that the agency can handle divisions of competing companies as long as the agency keeps the people working for one multidivision client from working on any division of another multidivision client. For example, the 1987 merger of Doyle Dane Bernbach, the agency for Weight Watchers International, with Needham Harper Worldwide, the agency for the Mrs. Paul product line, created a potential conflict because both companies produce frozen fish. However, the Campbell Soup Company, which produces the Mrs. Paul line, did not ask the new agency to drop either product.

Loyalty is important. Agencies develop loyalties to clients and vice versa. Out of loyalty to a client, an agency might keep itself free of direct conflicts (product-to-product) anywhere in the world and avoid indirect conflicts (the two companies have only similar divisions, but the agency avoids the second company altogether). In the late 1980s companies rewarded this loyalty by avoiding using agencies that served their competitors anywhere. This is especially true with soap and detergent products (Procter & Gamble, Colgate, Lever, and Henkel), automobiles (General Motors, Ford, Chrysler, Toyota, and Nissan), and beer (Anheuser-Busch, Miller, and Stroh's), and is increasingly true with food products (Nestlé, Kraft General Foods, RJR Nabisco, and Mars). Agencies that have one client in each of these categories will not accept (or be cleared to accept) another client in this category. Client nationalities even come into play in interpreting loyalty. One case involved a Japanese client's U.S. division and a U.S. company. Merely inquiring about the Japanese client's reaction to soliciting the U.S. company would have been taken by the Japanese client as a lack of loyalty, though the U.S. client was comfortable that the inquiry be made.

Internationalization creates further complexities. Suppose a client has no European distribution or plans to enter the European market. Could its U.S. agency safely take a competitive product in its client's category in Germany? Usually the answer is yes, but in one recent instance the U.S. client was bought by a European company, and the agency found itself with an unanticipated conflict problem in Europe. Mergers in the United States and the continuing acquisition of companies by the large global corporations have created a need for agencies and clients to maintain communication on what the policy is and how it will be interpreted.

These are particularly nettlesome problems. What if two clients the agency has successfully kept separate decide the same week to ask the agency to begin work in the same new-product area? The agency suddenly is in possession of a valuable piece of competitive intelligence. The best solution is to keep the decision at the highest level and make an informed judgment quickly.

Pros and Cons of Megamergers. Agencies have defended the megamergers by claiming they were forced to merge to match the scope and geographic reach of the new global megacorporation. For example, in 1989 Foote, Cone & Belding and Publicis, a large French agency group, merged their European networks to increase their scope of operations in the Common Market. Tatham, Laird & Kudner merged with RSCG, another large French multinational agency, as both sought greater presence in the general marketplace. The large Japanese agencies, comparatively unsuccessful outside their home markets, are seeking alignments or equity positions (ownership of a portion of an agency's stock) to increase their participation in the European, North American, and Pacific markets.

Some clients agree with the agencies' defense of the mergers. Others do not. According to Roger Smith of General Motors, stronger, more global agencies are better able to support a client's worldwide marketing plans. On the other side, the late Robert Goldstein of Procter & Gamble argued that the agencies have not been merging to benefit their clients, but to benefit their stockholder-managers. He may have been right, but only to an extent. Even though some stockholder-managers do make a great deal of money on mergers, the surviving agencies do emerge as stronger and more valuable resources for their clients. Although the argument may never be settled, it is clear that the megamerger has changed the nature of the advertising business.

What options does a local or national agency have if it wishes to retain its independence and not be swallowed by one of the large multinational agencies? One strategy is to concentrate in specialized market segments. Another is to join a voluntary network. These groups, several of which have over 30 agencies with offices in 50 or more world markets, provide management assistance, joint purchasing of services, and international client management. The largest of these networks are Affiliated Advertising Agencies International, Advertising and Marketing International Network, International Federation of Advertising Agencies, and the National Advertising Agency Network. Similar groups are appearing in Europe.

Consolidation

Consolidation is one of the cruelest words in the advertising industry for those who lose an account because of the transaction. But it is a joyous word for the victors—usually large, multioffice agencies. **Consolidation** occurs when a client, frequently one with a number of divisions, decides to appoint one agency to handle all its advertising. In August 1990, for example, Square D Company, a worldwide manufacturer of electrical controls headquartered in Palatine, Illinois, dismissed 30 agencies and appointed Young & Rubicam and its subsidiary Creswell, Munsell, Fultz & Zirbel to handle the entire account. Agencies sometimes will offer a discount to induce the consolidation.

consolidation *The appointment of one agency to handle all the advertising of a client's divisions.*

The Pros and Cons of Consolidation.   The reasons given for consolidation are to achieve one "look" in the company's advertising, to increase impact, to use the clout of a single negotiator to get better rates from media, and to reduce the complexity of managing the marketing effort by dealing with one outside source.

The arguments against consolidation have more to do with the quality of the advertising. Agencies develop a "feel" for a client product or service and, over time, refine and improve the selling proposition. This experience can be lost in consolidation because of the quantity of the services the agency must perform. Agencies that are "consolidated out" usually are geographically closer to the client's divisional offices. Increased travel time and expense to serve divisional offices from a central location may be a hidden cost of consolidation. A client division that is the most important client of a local agency becomes a small and demanding account to the consolidating agency. If a few division managers complain about lack of service, the consolidation can come apart. The agencies that are not chosen to represent a client's advertising—the losers—point out the unforeseen and substantial costs to the client of briefing the new agency, of "paying while the new agency moves up the learning curve," and of undertaking the central coordination of approvals for what had been decentralized.

*P*ERILS OF THE BUSINESS

Now that we have examined the numerous changes the advertising industry has undergone, the question remains: Is the advertising agency an endangered species? Seldom in its less-than-200-year history (although one Japanese agency claims to be 400 years old) has the advertising agency been in such turmoil as in these last years of the twentieth century. Traditional means of payment, organization, services, competition, and market segmentation are changing. Clients are being squeezed financially and are searching for savings, as Kodak did in January of 1990 by calling a conference with its 28 agencies and asking them for more "bang for the buck."* Agency staffs have been reduced, and revenues are down.

Growth in the advertising world has occurred among both the largest and the smallest agencies, but the agencies in the middle are being squeezed. Too small to compete for the major accounts but too large to grow by adding small accounts, many of these agencies have merged with others to vault into the top rank, as in the Saatchi mergers. Others have turned to specialization as a survival technique.

Despite the emergence of these difficulties, the basic structure of advertising is unlikely to change. The organizational structure of agencies, methods of payment, and reasons for hiring agencies are all relatively stable. In times of stress, however, an organization's structures and innovations are put to the test. The agency's response to such tensions will either renew the life of the organization or signal its demise. The most successful advertising agencies are those that have been willing to be flexible and to adjust to the times, and they are likely to remain successful.

To survive in these competitive times, agencies have been compelled to innovate by expanding services to include such disciplines as public relations, direct marketing, sales promotion, client marketing, and sports sponsoring. Some agencies may stop offering certain services or reduce the priority of the activity. Agencies have begun to form marketing consultancies to advise clients on the optimum mix of agency and outside services.

The 1960s and 1970s were times of expansion for the big agencies. The 1980s saw megamergers, acquisitions, and the growth of the mega-agencies and holding companies. The 1990s almost surely will be a time of testing economies of scale, contributions of service, and ways to build client trust and reliance. Agencies have a new concern as the Federal Trade Commission has become more vigorous in bringing suits for deceptive advertising against clients *and agencies.* Agencies are now being held accountable for false advertising they should have questioned even after a client supplied support and approved the advertising.†

An endangered species? Without necessary adaptations, that certainly is at risk. The creativity that is such an essential product of the advertising

---

Advertising Age (January 29, 1990):56.
†Thomas R. King, "Agencies Give Legal Matters New Emphasis," *The Wall Street Journal* (December 31, 1990):9.

agency, however, will almost certainly serve the best agencies well as they face these new challenges. The creativity characteristic of the field may also generate innovations in structure, means of payment, and client relations. The advertising agency, even in modified form, will continue to be an exciting place to work.

SUMMARY

- When functioning at their best, advertising agencies develop campaigns that enhance the value of the brands they handle.
- Agencies usually have four basic functions: account management, creative development and production, media planning and buying, and research.
- Support departments typically include traffic, print production, financial services, and personnel or human resources. Many agencies are exploring other services as sources of profit.
- The account management function acts as the primary liaison between the agency and the client.

- U.S. agencies traditionally have received a 15 percent commission from media placed, but the commission rate is increasingly being negotiated and varies not only from client to client but from country to country.
- Under the fee system, agencies' charges are computed on the basis of actual time and services provided.
- The late 1980s and early 1990s have seen the advent of megamergers and the proliferation of holding companies.

QUESTIONS

1. Why does the advertising agency form dominate the industry when it is possible for clients to purchase separately agency-type services from other services?

2. Doug Hammond, a dual major in marketing and advertising, has just finished a career-counseling interview. In his discussion with an in-house agency executive, Doug was sorry to hear the man say that account management at agencies is an "overrated" job, filled with "know-nothings" who trade on other people's ideas. The man also told Doug that account managers would disappear by the end of the 1990s. Doug wanted to be an account executive, so the comments have really troubled him. Should he reconsider his goal? What advice would you give Doug?

3. Stark Industries is a fast-climbing prospective client for Anders-Johnson Advertising Agency. Stark management has told A-J partners that it will pay a standard commission on its yearly media billing of $300,000, or it will consider a monthly fee of $3,000. Which is the better dollars-and-cents arrangement for A-J? Which payment is the better incentive for the agency in the long run?

4. Why are agencies under such pressure that their structure and form may have to change?

5. Kim Sessions is an ad director in a quandary. The development of a new division has prompted a need to increase advertising and promotion activities by 50 percent and to increase the number of people who handle it. In discussing the personnel considerations with her management, Kim found them resistant to the idea of hiring an outside ad agency. Most of the board thought "in-house" was best. Kim said she would make her recommendation today. What, if anything, should she say on behalf of the independent agency option?

6. The Wilcox group, a young agency with great potential, has just merged with two other agencies with similar prospects. This action has put the Bannon Company in a very tough position. It seems that Bannon has just developed a product that will directly compete with a major client handled by one of the new agencies associated with Wilcox. Bannon greatly admires Wilcox, but wonders if it shouldn't let the agency go rather than face a period of distractions and the threat of broken confidence. What should Bannon management do? What should Wilcox do?

FURTHER READINGS

DUBOFF, ROBERT S., "Can Research and Creative Coexist?" *Advertising Age* (March 17, 1986):18, 22.

"U.S. Advertising Agency Profiles: 1988 Edition," *Advertising Age* (March 30, 1988). (Special edition.)

MAYER, MARTIN, *Whatever Happened to Madison Avenue?* (Little Brown & Co., 1991).

Chiat/Day/Mojo and the Nissan Stanza Challenge

Founded in 1968 by Jay Chiat and Guy Day, Chiat/Day (now Chiat/Day/Mojo) has grown into one of the largest advertising agencies in the United States and has been responsible for some of the most memorable advertising ever produced by a domestic agency. Yet, Chiat/Day's rapid rise to fame encompassed many of the painful challenges currently facing the industry as a whole.

As do many agencies, Chiat/Day started out as a small boutique operation and quickly began producing notable work for increasingly larger clients. It wasn't until the early 1980s, however, Chiat/Day began to gain the attention and, often, the notoriety of both the industry and advertisers with its visible work for Apple, California Coolers, Nike, and others. Then, in the late 1980s, Chiat/Day lost virtually all of its most visible accounts but successfully won what was at the time the largest single account move in the history of advertising in the United States: Nissan Motor Corporation.

As the agency struggled to absorb the Nissan account, which more than doubled Chiat/Day's billings overnight, it also pursued an aggressive acquisitions and expansion program. In addition to opening new offices and acquiring packaging graphics, public relations, and direct-mail firms, Chiat/Day merged with an Australian agency, resulting in its present title, Chiat/Day/Mojo. The agency's formula for success is actually fairly simple: Hungry, talented, young creative people working below average pay levels for the opportunity to be part of a "hot creative shop," housed in utilitarian environments, empowered with an overriding mission statement of "good enough is not enough," all coupled with the relatively new concept of account planning. The result has been consistently startling and successful creative ads for over 2 decades. Clients frequently have been shocked to find that Jay Chiat's office cubical was no larger than that of any secretary in the agency. Account Planning, which emphasizes frequent informal contact with consumers in focus groups conducted by the account planners themselves, has also surprised many clients. The agency attributes this concept, common in European agencies, to its ability to produce its breakthrough work.

Despite its exceptional creative track record, Chiat/Day was frequently plagued by controversy throughout the 1980s. Often, Chiat/Day creative was attacked by the industry press for emphasizing creativity for creativity's sake, even at the expense of clients' product sales. However, the agency's recent work for Nissan and others demonstrate that the agency has continued to use its creativity effectively to sell products.

When Nissan asked Chiat/Day/Mojo to develop a campaign that would more than double sales of its Stanza model from an average of 3,500 units per month to over 8,000 per month, the agency knew that it had to develop a hard-hitting sales message. To accomplish this feat, it not only had to raise Stanza's familiarity with the public dramatically, but to position the Stanza against its key competitors, the Accord and Camry, while providing a compelling reason for consumers to consider the Stanza seriously. With familiarity of the Stanza at relatively low levels after virtually no advertising since the car's launch in October 1989, Chiat/Day/Mojo determined that the best way to appeal to the smart, practical automobile purchasers in the lower-middle category was to create a challenge. Thus, the advertising strategy for the "Stanza Challenge" was summarized as "We're so sure you will like the Stanza's performance that it you test drive a Stanza and still buy an Accord or Camry, we will pay you $100."

Despite media spending that represented only 14 percent of total media in the lower-middle automobile category and only 2 percent of total car spending, the challenge campaign was extremely successful. Stanza sales increased by 91 percent in the first month alone and maintained that level throughout the model year. Stanza's share of the lower-middle category rose by 147 percent, compared to only an 8 percent increase for Accord and a 13 percent increase for the category as a whole. Tracking research showed that recognition for the Challenge commercials reached an extremely high level of 88 percent.

From its classic "1984" spot for Apple's Macintosh to the work for Nissan and Energizer, Chiat/Day/Mojo advertising has manifested two consistent characteristics that separate it from the bulk of domestic advertising work being done today: it not only communicates a clear selling message, but it evokes strong emotions that never fail to entertain.

QUESTIONS

1. Though Chiat/Day is responsible for producing some of the most memorable advertising created in the United States, it is also responsible for some of the most noteworthy advertising bombs, such as the Apple "Lemmings" spot featuring business professionals marching off a cliff, the indecipherable Reebok "U.B.U." campaign, and the cloyingly yuppie initial Nissan "Built For The Human Race" efforts. Why do you think it is possible for an agency to produce both brilliant work and work that flops rather than producing more consistent creative quality?

2. Why do you believe a bureaucratic environment is more difficult for the creative process to thrive in?

3. Many of the hottest creative agencies in the country did not exist more than 20 years ago. Why would the age of an agency influence its creative ability?

Sources: Courtesy of Chiat/Day/Mojo and *Chiat/Day: The First Twenty Years* (Kessler); Rizzoli, 1990.

CASE STUDY

The Honda Way

In the fall of 1969 Honda produced the top-selling motor-cycle in America. Honda automobiles, however, had not yet appeared in this country. Over 7,000 miles away at Honda corporate headquarters in Tokyo, plans were being made to change that.

The plans were successful. By the 1980s Honda cars were some of the most popular in the United States, and in 1989 the Honda Accord was the number-one selling car in America. What took the company from zero to 717,000 cars a year in record time? It was a combination of engineering prowess, technological innovation, commitment, and good timing, all driven by a company philosophy known as "The Honda Way." This philosophy included a consistent, yet flexible, marketing and advertising strategy.

From the beginning, Honda's marketing philosophy stresses supplying high-efficiency products at a reasonable price. The company has continually emphasized customer satisfaction. Honda Associates were encouraged to be ambitious and daring, to develop fresh ideas, to embrace challenges, and to respond quickly to unforeseen changes and opportunities. In 1969 Honda engineers set the ambitious goal of developing a "world car." This project took them to the center of a profoundly changing automotive marketplace.

At that time over 88 percent of all automobiles sold in the United States came from Detroit. Moreover, the majority of imported cars were European, not Japanese.

Toyota was the leading Japanese import, followed by Datsun (now Nissan). Mazda and Subaru were just making plans to enter the U.S. market.

The popularity of the Volkswagon Beetle convinced Honda executives that a market for a quality small car existed in the United States. In 1970 Honda introduced its first car to America—the N600. Sales were modest. Only a few thousand were sold. Then, in 1973, the company introduced its "world car," the innovative Honda Civic. The Civic was nearly 8 inches longer than the 600 model, and it featured an advanced 4-cylinder engine and front-wheel drive. Available in both a 2-door sedan and a 3-door hatch-back, it was priced at only $2,150.

Although the Civic was well-received by the automotive press and the American public, it was still considered too small. At that point, however, international politics intervened. In October 1973 the Arab oil-producing countries banned oil imports to the West. As gasoline lines grew and prices skyrocketed, Detroit's large engines—some delivering under 12 miles per gallon—began to lose their appeal. Sales of small, fuel-efficient automobiles like the Honda Civic grew rapidly. By the end of 1974 Civic sales had climbed to over 43,000.

Meanwhile, the OPEC embargo produced tough new federal fuel economy regulations. The Environmental Protection Agency (EPA) issued strict new emissions standards. As Detroit carmakers scrambled to meet the new regulations, Honda engineers had already developed

EXHIBIT A

their next big idea: the 1975 Civic CVCC. With its fuel-efficient new engine, the Civic not only met the EPA clean air standards, it also ran on any grade of fuel. At 42 miles per gallon, the Civic was promoted as both the most fuel-efficient and the lowest-priced car in America. The advertising campaign for the Civic positioned the car in the foremost of the move toward economical transportation. The Honda advertising slogan, "What the World Is Coming To," stressed the innovative philosophy behind the Civic. More than 100,000 Civics were sold.

Then Honda's research indicated that the market was about to change once again. As both fuel shortages and gasoline prices eased somewhat, car buyers began to favor values like quality, roominess, performance, and comfort. Honda developed a car to meet this need and in June 1976 launched what would become its most popular model—the Accord.

Honda advertising emphasized the roominess and lively performance of the Accord. The automotive press praised its clean design and advanced engineering. The public reception was remarkable: By the end of 1978 Honda sales had climbed to over 274,000 cars.

During this time, car buying had become more complex. There was a growing number of manufacturers and car models. Financing was more complicated, and Detroit was offering an expanded array of optional equipment. Amid this confusion, Honda's marketing approach was clear and simple: Honda builds quality cars that are simple to drive, simple to park, simple to understand, and simple to own. The message was summed up in Honda's slogan, used in print ads, brochures, on television and even on shopping bags, "We Make It Simple" (see Exhibit A). It was The Honda Way—and it worked.

By the end of 1978 Honda was number three in import car sales, behind Toyota and Nissan. Over the next few years, the company increased its momentum by refining and expanding it's product line. Honda's third series, the Prelude, was introduced in 1979. In 1980, the second generation Civic was named *Motor Trend* magazine's "Import Car of the Year." Annual sales were now well over 375,000. In 1984 Honda launched it's newest idea—the CRX. Conceived as a sporty commuter car with high gas mileage, it too was named *Motor Trend*'s "Import Car of the Year." In addition, the Honda Prelude and Civic Hatchback captured the first and second runner-up spots, making it the first time ever that a single manufacturer had won the top three spots in the long history of this prestigious competition.

Honda was now selling 12 different models in the United States, at the rate of over half a million cars per year. For the first time, Honda advertising began to focus on the particular personality of each model instead of using a unifying corporate slogan. Honda portrayed its luxury Accord as the benchmark in it's class and the Pre-

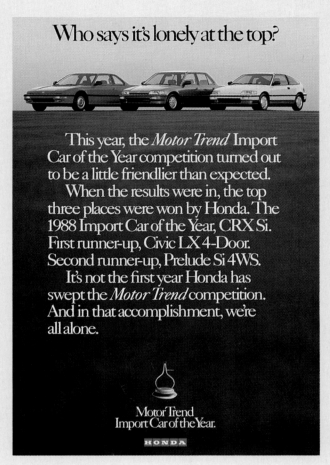

Who says it's lonely at the top?

This year, the *Motor Trend* Import Car of the Year competition turned out to be a little friendlier than expected.

When the results were in, the top three places were won by Honda. The 1988 Import Car of the Year, CRX Si. First runner-up, Civic LX 4-Door. Second runner-up, Prelude Si 4WS.

It's not the first year Honda has swept the *Motor Trend* competition. And in that accomplishment, we're all alone.

Motor Trend
Import Car of the Year.

HONDA

EXHIBIT B

lude Sports Coupe as "a sports car for adults." Its second-generation Civics were marketed as being larger and more stylish than their predecessors while still keeping earlier fuel economy and value. Ironically, "We Make It Simple" was no longer the way to advertise an increasingly sophisticated product line, which now appealed to a wide variety of buyers.

Customer satisfaction has always been emphasized as part of The Honda Way. In 1986 Honda outperformed Mercedes-Benz to become number one in overall customer satisfaction, based on owners' ratings of both the quality of their cars and of the dealerships that service them. Honda spotlighted this success by announcing in print advertising, "We're Happy You're Happy."

When it came time for *Motor Trend*'s 1988 "Import Car of the Year" competition, Honda once again captured the top three spots. The redesigned CRX Si won the top

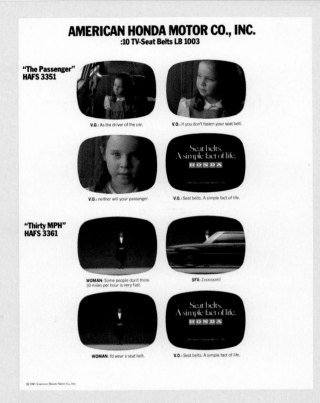

EXHIBIT C

EXHIBIT D

honors, followed by the Prelude Si with 4-wheel steering and the Civic 4-door sedan. In typical Honda fashion, advertisements announcing the award stated simply, "Who says it's lonely at the top?" (see Exhibit B).

One reason for Honda's consistently strong performance in customer satisfaction is its dealer network. Honda works closely with its dealers to insure that their operations—sales, service, parts, and accessories—reflect the quality of the cars themselves. Honda provides its dealers with support materials, from sales training and service manuals to full-line product brochures and videos.

Part of Honda's corporate philosophy is to be a good corporate citizen. In this spirit, Honda began another important campaign: saving lives. For 3 consecutive years—long before it became fashionable to do so—Honda sponsored a multimillion-dollar advertising effort to persuade drivers to use their seat belts (see Exhibit C). The company placed ads designed to convince drivers of the importance of seat belts in saving lives on television and in print media.

Responsible corporate citizenship took another form as well. By 1980, with the desire to manufacture products in the market in which they are sold, Honda began work on a new automobile plant in Marysville,

Ohio. The decision posed both problems and opportunities. Research indicated that prospective buyers might perceive an Ohio-built Honda as inferior to one made in Japan. However, many Americans who felt uncomfortable buying an imported car would now consider buying an Accord built in the United States.

Honda decided to use advertising and marketing campaigns to help sell the idea of its Ohio-made cars. These campaigns described the contribution that Honda was making to the U.S. economy (see Exhibit D). The company also ran a series of ads in key business publications, such as *The Wall Street Journal,* emphasizing the quality of Ohio-built Accords.

When the Marysville plant opened in November 1982, the Honda state of mind had been successfully imported to Ohio. Impartial road tests gave the American-built Accord and the imported Accord equal marks on fit, finish, and overall quality. Moreover, Honda began to implement a new five-part strategy for the future of Honda's operations in the United States, which called for Honda's total manufacturing involvement in this country to reach $1.7 billion. This includes the recently completed manufacturing plant in nearby East Liberty, Ohio, which is now producing Civic 4-door sedans at a rate of 150,000 per year. Other facets of the plan called for an increase of research and developmental activities, the expansion of production engineering, the increase of domestic content in American made Hondas to 75 percent, and the export of U.S.-built Honda products.

By the end of 1990 many of these goals had been reached. The Marysville plant was operating ahead of capacity, producing over 360,000 cars per year, and Honda was selling more American-built cars than imported cars in the United States. The Anna, Ohio engine facility had produced its one-millionth Honda engine. In December 1990, building off of the success of their number-one selling Accord model, Honda introduced the Accord Wagon. This vehicle was the first Honda completely designed, engineered, and manufactured in the United States.

Before the introduction of the Accord Wagon, the Accord Coupe, first introduced in 1988, had been the first Honda to be manufactured exclusively in the United States. A special edition of this Accord became the first Japanese nameplate ever exported back to Japan where it immediately became a much sought-after status symbol among the upwardly-mobile Japanese. By 1991 Honda plans to export 70,000 automobiles to Japan and other countries. The new Accord Wagon will be the first U.S.-built Japanese car to be exported to Europe, where Honda plans to sell about 5,000 units in 1991.

From the beginning, perhaps the key factor in Honda's success has been consistency. Honda products have consistently been of the highest quality and value, and they have continued to evolve in terms of engineering innovations, performance, styling, and comfort. Throughout the years Honda has also maintained a consistent image through its advertising and marketing. Honda advertising has always appealed to the intelligence and common sense of its customers. Consistently clever and subtle, often lighthearted and whimsical, but always honest and confident, Honda's advertising treats the buying public with respect by presenting a message that allows consumers to think for themselves and draw their own conclusions.

Created by Rubin Postaer and Associates, Los Angeles, Honda's advertising has received high praise from industry authorities. A commercial for the 1990 Accord called "Art Gallery" (see Exhibit E) emulated the engineering magic that allowed Fred Astaire to dance on the ceiling in the movie *Royal Wedding*. In this spot, a new Accord is driven off the wall of a museum with the line, "You have to drive it to believe it," as the only copy. *Adweek* advertising critic Barbara Lippert stated, "Rubin Postaer endows Honda with another masterpiece." She went on to say that, "Since 1980 few things have been as consistently engaging as Honda commercials. Honda spots are thinking people's car commercials; they're clever, beautifully shot, and never obvious."

This praise was, perhaps, best summed up by automotive expert Chris Cedergren, who said, "Honda's strength is in the fact that they don't radically change their advertising every 6 months like others do. Honda definitely won't tamper with success."

Source: Adapted from "The Honda Way: The Marketing of Honda Automobiles in America." (Courtesy of Sanford Edelstein, Rubin Postaer and Associates.)

Questions for Discussion

1. What themes in Honda's advertising and marketing reflect what you know of social needs and issues in the 1990s?
2. What advertising strategy could be used to position Honda cars in a more competitive market during the 1990s? How can Honda reach the desired audience for these cars?

EXHIBIT E

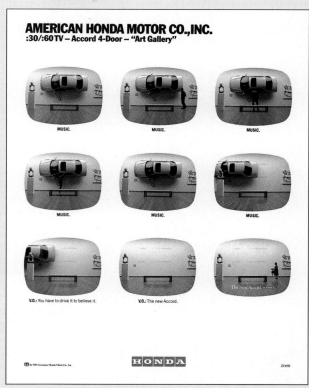

5

The Consumer Audience

Chapter Objectives

When you have completed this chapter, you should be able to:

- Understand the different factors that affect the responses of consumers to advertisements
- Define the concept of culture as it applies to advertising and consumers
- Distinguish between psychographics and demographics and explain how advertisers use each
- Relate such concepts as family, reference groups, and VALS to the practice of advertising

POPEYE THE QUAKER MAN!

In 1990 the Quaker Oats Company and Hearst Corporation's King Features Syndicate, owner of the cartoon character Popeye the Sailor Man, entered an agreement bringing together their company trademarks. The result was a new children's hero—Popeye the Quaker Man. Instead of devouring spinach, however, this Popeye consumes Instant Quaker Oatmeal to acquire the strength needed to fight his enemy Bluto.

Not everyone found this idea clever, entertaining, or tasteful. In particular, 26 Quaker children living in Durham, North Carolina, were not amused. Nonviolence is a central principle of the Quakers, also known as the Society of Friends. In their letter to Quaker Oats the Durham children stated, "We think anyone calling himself a Quaker should act like one and stick with Quaker philosophy." Adults were even more upset. Marty Walton, general secretary of the North American Friends General Conference, said of the cartoon character, "It is totally offensive to Quakers." Elizabeth J. Foley, a Quaker leader in Philadelphia, agreed: "Would anyone advertise 'Popeye the Catholic Man' or 'Popeye the Jewish Man'?"

Ironically, there has never been a direct tie between the Quakers and Quaker Oats. The company was formed in 1891 when seven independent millers joined in what critics called an "oatmeal trust." In 1915 the Society of Friends pressed to ban the commercial use of the Quaker name but they were outlobbied.

The Quaker Oats Company responded swiftly to the recent protest. One Saturday morning television spot shows Popeye saving his hamburger-hankering friend Wimpy by punching out a shark and then singing "I'm Popeye the Quaker Man." A similar ad was aired without the Quaker Man phrase. The company is considering eliminating other print ads, perhaps even the entire campaign.

The Durham children have no problem with the Quaker Man tag as long as Popeye uses his strength in a "Quakerly manner—for example, by rescuing children from a fire or supporting a broken dam."*

CONSUMER BEHAVIOR

Quaker Oats failed to take into account a very important detail in developing its advertising campaign: the consumer audience. The idea for the new cartoon character was clever and imaginative, but it was also offensive to a certain segment of the population.

The goal of advertising is to persuade the consumer to do something, usually to purchase a product. If advertising is to attract and communicate to audiences in a way that produces this desired result, advertisers must first understand their audiences. They must acquaint themselves with consumers' ways of thinking, with those factors that motivate them, and with the environment in which they live. The advertisers involved in the Quaker Oats campaign erred in not foreseeing the negative effect of associating a violent character with the Quaker religion.

This difficult task is further complicated by the fact that the elements advertisers must take into account are constantly changing. Information that is appropriate to consumers today is often invalid tomorrow. Furthermore,

*Adapted from Russell Mitchell, "Will Quaker Oats Bow to Friendly Persuasion?" *Business Week* (March 12, 1990):46.

advertisers must appeal to a complex consumer audience that is affected by many factors. In other words, the breadth of coverage is challenging. Advertisers must draw on input available from fields such as psychology, anthropology, and sociology to learn all they need to know about people.

In this chapter we will restrict our coverage to the specific behaviors people engage in as consumers. At the same time, we recognize that a great deal of what a person does outside the role of consumer is also relevant to advertising.

The Consumer Audience

Consumers are people who buy or use products in order to satisfy needs and wants. There are actually two types of consumers: those who shop for and purchase the product, and those who actually use the product. This distinction is important because the two groups can have different needs and wants. In the case of children's cereals, for example, parents (the purchasers) look for nutritional value, whereas children (the users) look for a sweet taste and a game on the back of the package. Because of the consumer orientation in marketing, consumer behavior is a very important field. Companies need to understand how consumers think and make decisions about products. In order to do this they conduct sophisticated research into consumer behavior. Companies must know who their consumers are, why they buy, what they buy, and how they go about buying certain products. (Consumer research will be discussed in Chapter 6.)

PRINCIPLE —————
Marketers look at people as consumers who buy products; advertisers look at people as an audience for messages.

Market Segmentation/Target Marketing

The advertising manager is responsible for answering many questions about the consumer or industrial customer. This would be an insurmountable task without the framework provided by market segmentation. Kotler and Armstrong define *market segmentation* as the process of dividing a market into distinct groups of buyers who might require separate products or marketing mixes.* Market segmentation divides potential consumers of a particular product into several submarkets or segments, each of which tends to share one or more significant characteristics. For example, in 1990 the banking industry sponsored a study conducted by Teenage Research Unlimited identifying segments of teenagers according to their earning and saving tendencies. The study produced five segments:

- *Energetic socializers* show a high level of energy and sociability, with both sexes likely to have a savings account. Teenage males are more likely to have a checking account than are teenage females.
- *Identity seekers* are the oldest of the five types, bridging the gap between the teen and adult years. This group is most likely to have a checking account as well as credit-card access.
- *Transitional eclectics* compose the largest of the five groups. Members of this group, who sit solidly in the middle teen years, are not big earners or big spenders.
- *Passive introverts* are the "late bloomers." They typically have low energy levels and limited social interaction and are more likely to save money than spend it. Passive introverts are likely to have a savings account but less likely to have a checking account or credit-card access.
- *Emerging participants* are the youngest, but also the most industrious, of the five groups. They are the leaders in getting money from odd jobs.†

*Philip Kotler and Gary Armstrong, *Marketing: An Introduction,* 2nd ed. (Englewood Cliffs, NJ: Prentice Hall, 1990):203.
†Jerry Heisler, "From CDs to CDs: Reaching the Teen Market," *Bank Marketing* (April 1990): 34–35.

As this example illustrates, segmentation enables organizations to design a marketing strategy that matches the market's needs and wants. Advertising, in particular, can be more focused. However, most firms do not have the capabilities to market their product effectively to all viable segments, so they select one or more target markets from the available market segments. The *target market* is a group of people (segment) who are most likely to respond favorably to what the marketer has to offer.

Market segments and target market(s) are based on the consumer characteristics and behaviors discussed in this chapter. (A more complete list of characteristics and behaviors is shown in Table 5.1.) A market segment can be based on geography (domestic vs. foreign), usage level of the product (heavy vs. light), brand loyalty (disloyal vs. highly loyal), and type of customer (ultimate user vs. business user or industrial user). There are a great many characteristics that can be used to separate people into segments and target markets.

The segmentation process begins after the advertiser understands how and why the consumer generally thinks, feels, and behaves in a particular manner. Only then can the advertiser design a campaign that will effectively reach the fade-resistant laundry detergent market, the premium ice cream market, or the frequent business traveler market.

*I*NFLUENCES ON YOU AS A CONSUMER

Your responses to an advertising message are affected by many factors. Study yourself. You are going to be the subject of our field research for this chapter. You are a product of the culture and the society in which you were raised. Many of your values and opinions were shaped by your social environment. Likewise, you are a product of the family in which you were raised, and many of your habits and biases were developed within the family environment.

You are also an individual. As you matured and began to think for yourself, you developed your own individual way of looking at the world, based on such factors as your age, income, sex, education, occupation, and race. Deep within you are factors that influence every decision you make—such things as how you perceive events and other people, how you learn from experience, your basic set of attitudes and opinions, your internal drive and motivation, and the whole bundle of characteristics called your "personality."

Cultural and Social Influences

cultural and social influences *The forces that other people exert on your behavior.*

The forces that other people exert on your behavior are called **cultural and social influences.** They can be grouped into four major areas: (1) culture, (2) social class, (3) reference groups, and (4) family.

culture *The complex whole of tangible items, intangible concepts, and social behaviors that define a group of people or a way of life.*

Culture. **Culture** is defined as a complex of tangible items (art, literature, buildings, furniture, clothing, and music) plus intangible concepts (knowledge, laws, morals, and customs) that define a group of people or a way of life. The concepts, values, and behaviors that make up a culture are learned and passed on from one generation to the next. The boundaries each culture establishes for behavior are called **norms.** Norms are simple rules that we learn through social interaction that specify or prohibit certain behaviors.

norms *Simple rules for behavior that are established by cultures.*

TABLE 5.1
Major Segmentation Variables for Consumer Markets

Variable	Typical Breakdowns
Geographic	
Region	Pacific, Mountain, West North Central, West South Central, East North Central, East South Central, South Atlantic, Middle Atlantic, New England
County size	A, B, C, D
City size	Under 5,000; 5,000–20,000; 20,000–50,000; 50,000–100,000; 100,000–250,000; 250,000–500,000; 500,000–1,000,000; 1,000,000–4,000,000; 4,000,000 or over
Density	Urban, suburban, rural
Climate	Northern, southern
Demographic	
Age	Under 6, 6–11, 12–19, 20–34, 35–49, 50–64, 65 +
Sex	Male, female
Family size	1–2, 3–4, 5 +
Family life cycle	Young, single; young, married, no children; young, married, youngest child under 6; young married, youngest child 6 or over; older, married, with children; older, married, no children under 18; older, single; other
Income	Under $10,000; $10,000–$15,000; $15,000–20,000; $20,000–30,000; $30,000–$50,000; $50,000 and over
Occupation	Professional and technical; managers, officials, and proprietors; clerical, sales; craftsmen, foremen; operatives; farmers; retired; students; homemakers; unemployed
Education	Grade school or less; some high school; high school graduate; some college; college graduate
Religion	Catholic, Protestant, Jewish, other
Race	White, black, Asian, Hispanic
Nationality	American, British, French, German, Scandinavian, Italian, Latin American, Middle Eastern, Japanese
Psychographic	
Social class	Lower lowers, upper lowers, working class, middle class, upper middles, lower uppers, upper uppers
Lifestyle	Belongers, achievers, integrateds
Personality	Compulsive, gregarious, authoritarian, ambitious
Behavioristic	
Purchase occasion	Regular occasion, special occasion
Benefits sought	Quality, service, economy
User status	Nonuser, ex-user, potential user, first-time user, regular user
Usage rate	Light user, medium user, heavy user
Loyalty status	None, medium, strong, absolute
Readiness stage	Unaware, aware, informed, interested, desirous, intending to buy
Attitude toward product	Enthusiastic, positive, indifferent, negative, hostile

Source: Philip Kotler and Gary Armstrong, *Marketing: An Introduction* 2nd ed. (Englewood Cliffs, NJ: Prentice Hall, 1990):204.

values *The source for norms, which are not tied to specific objects or behaviors.*

The source for norms are our **values.** An example of a value is personal security. Possible norms expressing this value range from bars on the window and double-locked doors in Brooklyn, New York, to unlocked cars and homes in Eau Claire, Wisconsin. Values are few in number and are not tied to specific objects or situations. For several decades researchers have attempted to identify *core values* that characterize an entire culture. One simplified list consists of nine core values: (1) a sense of belonging, (2) excitement, (3) fun and enjoyment in life, (4) warm relationships, (5) self-fulfillment, (6) respect from others, (7) a sense of accomplishment, (8) security, and (9) self-respect. Advertisers often refer to core values when selecting their primary appeals. Because values are so closely tied to human behavior, private research firms attempt to monitor values and look for groupings of values and behavioral patterns. Values are discussed in more detail later in the chapter.

Cultural influences have broad effects on buying behavior. For example, the busy working mother of today is not as devoted to meal preparation and household cleaning as was the full-time homemaker of the past. Food marketers have changed their promotional strategies to reach these women, and we now see more advertising for fast foods, convenience foods, and restaurants.

How does culture affect you as a consumer? Can you think of any cultural factors that influence your behavior? How about patriotism and sacrificing for the good of others? Can you see yourself signing up for the Peace Corps? How about materialism? How do you feel about acquiring possessions and making money?

Subcultures   A culture can be divided into *subcultures* on the basis of geographic regions or human characteristics such as age, values, or ethnic background. In the United States, for example, we have many different subcultures: teenagers, college students, retirees, southerners, Texans, blacks, Hispanics, athletes, musicians, and working single mothers, to list just a few. Within subcultures there are similarities in people's attitudes and secondary values.

What subcultures do you belong to? Look at your activities. Do you do anything on a regular basis that might identify you as a member of a distinctive subculture?

social class *A way to categorize people on the basis of their values, attitudes, lifestyles, and behavior.*

Social Class.   A **social class** is the position that you and your family occupy within your society. Social class is determined by such factors as income, wealth, education, occupation, family prestige, value of home, and neighborhood.

Every society has some social class structure. In a rigid society you are not allowed to move out of the class into which you were born. In the United States we like to think we have a classless society because it is possible for us to move into a different class regardless of what social class our parents belonged to. However, even in the United States we speak of an upper class, a middle class, and a lower class.

Marketers assume that people in one class buy different goods from different outlets and for different reasons than people in other classes. Advertisers can get a feel for the social class of a target market by using marketing research or available census data.

In what class do you see yourself? Does social class affect what you buy and how you respond to advertising? Do you know people you would consider to be upper- or lower-class? Do they buy different products than you do? Do they look at products differently in terms of price or quality?

The proliferation of fast-food restaurants is an example of the influence of culture on consumer behaviors. (Courtesy of Dennie Cody/ FPG.)

Reference Groups

reference group *A group of people that a person uses as a guide for behavior in specific situations.*

A **reference group** is a collection of people that you use as a guide for behavior in specific situations. General examples of reference groups are political parties, religious groups, racial or ethnic organizations, clubs based on hobbies, and informal affiliations such as fellow workers or students.

For consumers, reference groups have three functions: (1) they provide information; (2) they serve as a means of comparison; and (3) they offer guidance. Sometimes the group norms have the *power* to require the purchase or use of certain products (uniforms, safety equipment). The reference group members may be so *similar* to you that you believe that any product or service the group members use is right for you too. Ads that feature typical users in fun or pleasant surroundings are using a reference-group strategy. You also may be *attracted* to a particular reference group and wish to be like the member of that group out of respect or admiration. Advertisers use celebrity endorsements to tap into this desire.

Think about all the groups you belong to, both formal and informal. Why do you belong to these groups? How do other members influence you or keep you informed? Have you ever bought anything specifically because it was required by a group you belonged to?

family *Two or more people who are related by blood, marriage, or adoption and live in the same household.*

household *All those people who occupy one living unit, whether or not they are related.*

lifestyle *The pattern of living that reflects how people allocate their time, energy, and money.*

demographics *The vital statistics about the human population, its distribution, and its characteristics.*

Family. A **family** consists of two or more people who are related by blood, marriage, or adoption and live in the same household. A **household** differs from a family in that it consists of all those who occupy a living unit, whether they are related or not.

Your family is critical to how you develop as an individual. It provides two kinds of resources for members: *economic,* such as money and possessions; and *emotional,* such as empathy, love, and companionship. The family is also responsible for raising and training children and establishing a lifestyle for family members. Your **lifestyle** determines how you spend your time and money and the kinds of activities you value.

It is important for advertisers to understand the structure and workings of the family. For example, the U.S. family structure is changing because of an increase in divorces, later marriages, one-parent and two-family households, and other alternative family systems. (These changing family structures are discussed in more detail later in the chapter.) Advertisers must create messages that appeal to the needs and lifestyles of these consumers. A family's purchase and consumption patterns offer some interesting challenges as well. For instance, most families have members, such as parents, who screen and evaluate product information. Other members, such as children, strongly influence which product or brand is purchased, although they are not necessarily the actual decision makers. The family is our most important reference group because of its longevity and intensity. Other reference groups, such as peers, coworkers, and neighbors, tend to change as we age and switch occupations or residency. Still, as the Saab ad illustrates, these references can be used in a generic or ideal manner, without specifying a particular peer group.

How has your family influenced you in your choice of schooling, lifestyle, and the way you spend your time and money? Now think about your best friend. Are the two of you different in any ways that can be traced to family differences?

PERSONAL INFLUENCES

Every consumer is a product of culture and society, social class, and family. Ultimately, however, a consumer is an individual. Individual characteristics strongly influence the way you think, decide, and behave as a consumer. These characteristics can be divided into two categories: demographic variables and psychographic variables. *Demographics* are the statistical representations of social and economic characteristics of people, including age, sex, income, occupation, and family size. In contrast, *psychographics* refer to people's psychological variables, such as attitudes, lifestyles, opinions, and personality traits.

Demographics

Demographics is the study of those social and economic factors that influence how you behave as an individual consumer. These factors serve as the basis for much of the advertising strategy. Knowing the age, sex, occupation, and race of the members of the target audience assists advertisers in message design and media selection.

Age. People in different stages of life have different needs. An advertising message must be understandable to the age group to which the product or service is targeted and should be delivered through a medium used by members of that group. How old are you? What products did you use 5 or 10 years ago that you don't use now? Look ahead 5 or 10 years—what products will you be in the market for then? What products do your parents buy that you don't? Do you read different publications and watch different programs than your parents do? If you were in the market for a car, would you look at the same features that your parents look at? In the United States several trends with respect to age have a direct bearing on advertising.

Baby Boomers   The baby boom includes all U.S. citizens born between 1946 and 1964. During that period 76.4 million people were born in the United States of whom approximately 68 million are still alive.* We have already described some of the characteristics of the baby boomers in Chapter 2. Recall that the majority of baby boomers are in blue-collar occupations, and they have fallen short of reaching the American Dream. Despite having a better education, higher-paying jobs, and more family members in the work force, baby boomers are experiencing a crisis of expectations due to increasing costs and excessive competition for higher-paying jobs. Younger baby boomers (ages 25 to 33), however, are enjoying the hard work of the older members of the group. This younger group is somewhat smaller and has found career opportunities and job advancement to be much easier and more readily available because the older boomers have expanded the size of the job market. It is this group that has been able to obtain many of the material possessions associated with the American Dream (see Ad 5.1.)†

The Elderly   As the baby boomers become more frustrated, the elderly market is growing in size and importance. By the turn of the century one person in eight will be 65 or older. Of great significance for marketers is the fact that this group is quite affluent, holding about half the discretionary buying power (the money available after paying taxes and buying necessities) of the nation and over three-quarters of its personal financial assets.‡ Marketers have responded to the new elderly population by introducing a host of products that appeal to affluent, healthy people who have free time. Advertisers no longer tend to portray the elderly as ill and dour, but rather as attractive and active. Even products difficult to advertise, such as adult diapers, have been positively portrayed through testimonials by former movie star June Allyson. In addition, several new media that are directed to the elderly have emerged. Examples are the Silver Pages directory, telemarketing, and magazines such as *Modern Maturity, New Choices,* and *Extended Vacations.*

Gender.   Gender, or sex, is an obvious basis for differences in marketing advertising. When we talk about gender differences, we consider both primary and secondary differences. *Primary* gender differences are physical or psychological traits that are inherent to males or females. The ability to bear children is a primary female trait. *Secondary* gender traits tend to be primarily associated with one sex more than the other. Wearing perfume and shaving legs are secondary traits associated with women. The primary gender characteristics of men and women create demands for products and

---

*"Growing Pains at 40," *Time* (May 19, 1986):22–41.
†Alan L. Otten, "Baby Boomer People Make Less but Make Do," *The Wall Street Journal* (July 5, 1990):B1.
‡Lenore Skenzay, "These Days, It's Hip to Be Old," *Advertising Age* (February 15, 1988):81.

It takes a pretty good TV to fool these experts.

No ordinary big screen television could deceive these discerning eyes. It takes a picture that's ultra-bright, ultra-clear and ultra-sharp. ∽ Like Hitachi's Ultravision.™ It looks so true to life because it's the first TV with 800 lines of resolution. ∽ Satisfy your own curiosity. Call 1-800-HITACHI and find out where to see Ultravision for yourself.

◎ HITACHI

AD 5.1
The baby boomers have popular-
ized the concept of the desire for
expensive, quality products, such
as this big-screen television.
(Courtesy of Hitachi.)

services directly associated with a person's sex. In the past there were many taboos regarding the marketing of such products. For example, marketers of tampons or sanitary pads were once restricted to advertising in media and retail outlets devoted strictly to women; and condoms, purchased almost exclusively by men, were behind-the-counter (or perhaps under-the-counter) items. Today these barriers have all but vanished, and primary female and male products are marketed in similar ways and in comparable media.

Marketing products related to secondary sexual characteristics has become more complicated. For example, hair, skin, and body type have long provided reliable clues to marketers. Skin-care products were the exclusive domain of women, and erotic magazines were restricted to men. Now skin-care products for men represent a $60 million market and *Playgirl* magazine is popular with women. Ad 5.2 for Clairol Option targets a product once considered "feminine" toward the new 1990s man.

BABY BUSTERS: THE GENERATION THAT CAN SAY NO

As of 1990, the youngest members of the baby-boom generation had been out of college for over 4 years and a new generation of consumers was coming to the forefront. They are the baby busters, aptly named for their dramatic rejection of the values of the baby boomers and workaholic yuppies of the last generation. The oldest members of this smaller generation were born in 1965. A few years out of college, they are establishing reputable careers, but unlike their predecessors, they have not turned into workaholics who sacrifice everything else in their lives for a six-figure salary and an impressive title.

The baby busters care more for personal interest—leisure, family, and lifestyle—than for the corporation. As a result, advertisers need to be aware of the needs and preferences of this new generation of consumers. Baby busters value quality of life. They put more emphasis on morals and religious values and would rather spend their money on travel and the arts than on sleek cars and expensive electronic toys. The environment is a major concern to this generation, and advertisers will have to be aware of this when they design, package, and push new product. As one Wharton MBA student states, "Hey, we need good tennis shoes, stuff to go camping—but not a BMW or an oceanfront condo."

The lifestyles the baby busters have chosen are more personalized and heterogenous than those of the past. Marriage is becoming more an option than a logical progression in life. In 1990, 46 percent of men aged 25 to 29 were never married. In 1970, this figure was only 19 percent. For women the change is even more dramatic: 30 percent versus 11 percent.

The novelty of the baby-buster generation makes the group something of a mystery to the advertising industry. So far, advertisers have failed to analyze and target the busters as a separate consumer market. When they do, they will be faced with the challenge of presenting messages of consumerism to an environmentally conscious, discriminating, and self-absorbed generation that rejects materialism as the equivalent of self-fulfillment.

Source: Alan Deutschman, "What 25-Year-Olds Want," *Fortune* (August 27, 1990): 42–50

AD 5.2
An example of a crossover ad of a traditionally female product targeted to male consumers.
(Courtesy of Clairol, Inc.)

So clean, so light, so fresh, it was made just for you.

New Ban® Body Fresh Scent.

Ban Body Fresh is a new anti-perspirant scent touched by subtle botanical essences. It works in harmony with your body.

Keep that shower fresh feeling

© 1990 Bristol-Myers Squibb Co.

AD 5.3
Ban is one of many companies advertising to distinctively masculine or feminine audiences. (Reproduced with the permission of Bristol-Myers Squibb Company.)

As prevalent as this crossover effect appears, many consumers still consider certain brands masculine or feminine. It is unlikely that men would use a brand of after-shave called White Shoulders. The Gillette Company found that women would not purchase Gillette razor blades, so they introduced new brands with feminine names such as "Daisy" and "Lady Gillette." Ad 5.3 for Ban Body Fresh Scent is an example of a product targeted at a feminine audience. Marketers of products formerly associated with one sex who want to sell them to both sexes find it necessary to offer "his and her" brands or even different product names for the same basic goods. What products do you buy that are unisex? What products do you use that are specifically targeted to your sex?

Family Status. Your purchasing patterns are affected by your family situation. People living alone buy different products, in different sizes, than do people living in families. Has your family's spending patterns changed since you went to college? Unless your parents were able to start a college fund when you were born, they have probably had to reduce their purchases of luxury items, vacations, and new cars.

Although the most common arrangements among U.S. families remains two parents with children, a number of alternative family arrangements have become more common. The prevalence of divorce—the number of divorces granted each year more than doubled from 1977 to 1990, although most divorces are followed by remarriage—has enlarged three other family categories: divorced with no children, single parent with children, and the "his, hers, and ours" family with children from different marriages living together in the same home with remarried parents. Each family system has its unique problems and offers special marketing opportunities.*

In addition, not everyone wishes to get married. According to experts, one-half of all U.S. households in 1990 included single men and women living alone.† However, generalizing about singles would be a mistake because they are a diverse group who experience a wide range of economic well-being and display varied spending patterns. Single people who have never married, for example, have a great deal of personal freedom and spend heavily on themselves. In contrast, divorced women with children often struggle financially and many of them represent a new poverty group. Unmarried couples who share a household (cohabitation) represent another alternative. This group, although estimated to be only 2 percent of the population, exhibits some interesting purchasing patterns. Uncertain how long their relationship will last, they are reluctant to purchase shared items and instead have duplicates of many household items (stereos, furniture, and small appliances).‡ Figure 5.1 illustrates some of the changes in the U.S. family structure from 1965 through 1989.

The final factor strongly affecting the American family is the increase in the number of women in the work force. By the mid-1990s approximately 45 percent of American families will have two wage earners.§ The wage-earning wife has caused a substantial realignment of family spending and role responsibilities. Families with two wage earners eat out more often, own more expensive cars, take more expensive vacations, and wear more expensive clothes. Husbands in many of these families participate in child care, housecleaning, food shopping and preparation, and laundry responsibilities. Do both of your parents work? Do you have friends whose

*Thomas Exter, "Look Ma, No Spouse," *American Demographics* (March 1990):63.
†Thomas Exter, "Alone at Home," *American Demographics* (April 1990):55.
‡Judith Waldrop, "Living in Sin," *American Demographics* (April 1990):12.
§Betsy Sharkey, "The Chameleon Decade," *Adweek: Marketing to the Year 2000* (September 11, 1989):16.

FIGURE 5.1
Trends in U.S. families, 1965–1989. Source: *Psychology Today.* May 1987, p. 64. Copyright © 1987 American Psychological Association.

	1965	1980	1985	1989
Marriage rate (number of marriages per 1000 population)[1]	9.3	10.6	10.2**	9.9
Median age at first marriage				
Men	22.5	23.6	25.0*	26.2
Women	20.4	21.8	22.9*	23.8
Divorce rate (number of couples divorcing per 1000 population)[1]	2.5	5.2	5.0**	7.5
Single-parent families (percentage of all families with children under age 18 having one parent)[2]	10.1	19.5	22.2	20.4
Births to Unmarried Women (percentage of all births)[1]	7.7	18.4	21.7*	22.0
Living alone (percentage of all households occupied by a single person)[2]	15.0	22.7	23.7	25.7

[1]National Center for Health Statistics.
[2]Bureau of the Census.
Psychology Today projection.
**Provisional data.

families are headed by only one wage earner? Do you see a difference in your lifestyles? How have your parents divided the family responsibilities?

Education. The level of education you have attained also influences your behavior as a consumer. Advertisers know they must market products differently to better-educated consumers than to the less-educated. Consumers with higher educations are often more responsive to technical-scientific appeals, prefer informative ads, and are better able to judge the relationship between the price and quality of a product. The trend toward a better-educated consumer is expected to continue through the 1990s. By the year 2000 nearly 30 percent of all Americans over age 25, male and female, will have a college degree.[*]

Occupation. Most people identify themselves by what they do. Even homemakers and students identify themselves this way. There has been a gradual movement from blue-collar occupations to white-collar occupations during the last 3 decades. There have also been shifts within white-color work from sales to other areas, such as professional specialty, technical, and administrative positions. Furthermore, the number of service-related jobs is expected to increase, especially in the health-care, education, and legal and business-service sectors. Much of this transition is a direct result of advanced computer technologies, which have eliminated many labor-intensive blue-collar occupations.[†] This shift has affected advertising in a number of ways. Most notably, blue-collar jobs are seldom portrayed in advertisements anymore, and ad copy tends to be more technical. Also, women are being depicted in more professional roles, as is evident in Ad 5.4 for American Express.

You belong to the student occupational category, but you are also in training for some other profession. Why did you choose that career objective? Obviously, your decision to go to college was affected by occupational considerations, as well as by the geographical area in which you live. What other decisions have you made on the basis of your occupation or profession—either past, present, or intended?

discretionary income *The money available for spending after taxes and necessities are covered.*

Income. You are only meaningful to a marketer if you have the resources to buy the product advertised. That means you must possess money and credit. It also means you must have some **discretionary income,** the money available to a household after taxes and basic necessities such as food and shelter are paid for. As your total income increases, the proportion that is considered discretionary income grows at a much faster rate. Some 26 million American households are thought to have significant discretionary income. Although this group represents only 29 percent of all households, it receives 53 percent of all consumer income before taxes:[‡]

The distribution of income among the population has a great impact on marketers. Essentially, the middle class, which represented 60 percent of U.S. households in the 1950s, is expected to decrease in the coming years. By the year 2000 only 30 percent of U.S. households will be middle class. The affluent will represent another 30 percent (compared to 10 per-

[*]Judith Waldrop and Thomas Exter, "What the 1990 Census Will Show," *American Demographics* (January 1990):30.

[†]Mark D. Hayward and William R. Grady, "The Worklife Patterns of a Cohort of Older Men in the U.S., 1966–1983," paper presented at the 1989 Annual Meeting of the Population Association of America (1988).

[‡]Bickley Townsend, "This Is Fun Money," *American Demographics* (October 1989):39–41.

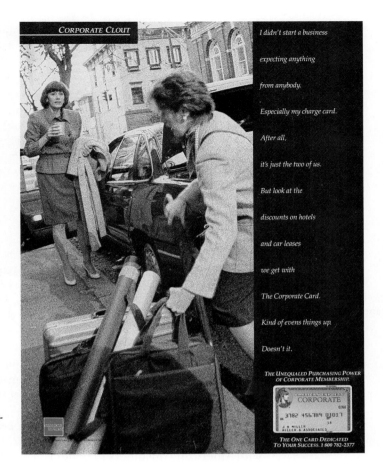

AD 5.4
The modern businesswoman is portrayed in a professional setting in this ad for American Express.
(Courtesy of American Express Company.)

cent in 1950), and the working class will account for the remaining 40 percent, with 20 percent of these households below the poverty level (compared to 30 percent of households in the working class in 1950, 8 percent of which were below the poverty level).* Clearly, the rich are getting richer and the poor are getting poorer (see Figure 5.2). Thus the bulk of demand in the 1990s will be for both premium products and low-end, no-frills items.

Can you think of any product that you wanted to buy recently but could not afford? Do you have a "wish list" of purchases you would like to make "someday"?

Race and Ethnicity. The United States has long been considered the "melting pot" of the world—an image implying that the diverse peoples who have settled here have adopted the same basic values and norms. This idea is probably less true than most people imagine. Race and ethnic background might not influence the consumer behavior of most white Anglo-Saxon Americans, simply because such considerations are not very important in their daily lives. However, there is evidence that this group actually has a strong tendency to adopt the behavior of outsiders. Witness the tremendous growth in the consumption of ethnic foods, especially Mexican, Chinese, Thai, Indian, and Vietnamese cuisines.

According to the 1990 Census, blacks remain the largest minority group, representing 12 percent of the population, the same percentage as

*Sharkey, "The Chameleon Decade," p. 32.

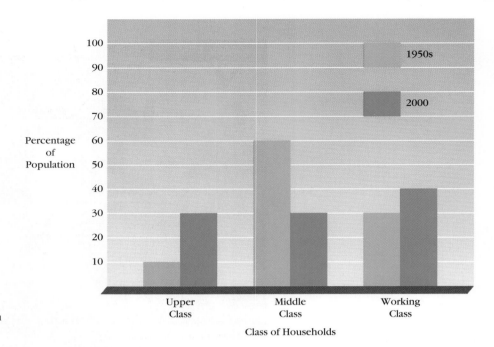

FIGURE 5.2
Distribution of the U.S. Population by Class (1950s and the year 2000).

in 1980. Hispanics represent 8 percent, a 3 percent increase since 1980, and their numbers are expected to grow even faster during the 1990s. Asians and other races represent only 3 percent of the total population, but this is a 65 percent increase since 1980.

A consumer survey conducted by Impact Resources of Columbus, Ohio, compared Asian consumers in four metropolitan areas in California with American consumers in general. The results showed that 54 percent of Asian Americans shop as a leisure activity compared with 50 percent of the general population. Asians also rank quality higher than price in choosing a store. Moreover, the survey indicated that Asian Americans are more comfortable with technology than is the general population. They are far more likely to use automated teller machines and to own VCRs, CD players, microwave ovens, home computers, and telephone answering machines.*

Racial and ethnic identities affect both self-image and consumer behavior of nonwhites and people with strong ethnic backgrounds. This is a complex area, however, because race and ethnicity are difficult to separate from such factors as family, language, and reference groups. For example, although in the United States we use the label "Hispanic" to identify members of many different ethnic groups, members of these groups do not identify with this umbrella term, but differentiate themselves as distinct cultures. Using the same ad in the Cuban community in Miami, the Puerto Rican community in New York, and the Mexican-American community in San Antonio could therefore prove disastrous for an advertiser.

Geographic Location

Knowing were people live is important to advertisers. Marketers study the sales patterns in different regions of the country to discover variations in the purchase behavior of consumers. People residing in different regions of the country have different needs for certain products or services. Someone living in the Midwest or Northeast is more likely to purchase products for

---

*Dan Fost, "California's Asian Market," *American Demographics* (October 1990):34–37.

TABLE 5.2
Population and change in population by region, 1980–1990

	1990 population	1980 population	1980–90 change	1980–90 percent change
United States	249,870	226,546	23,324	10.3%
NORTHEAST	50,911	49,135	1,776	3.6%
MIDWEST	59,939	58,866	1,073	1.8%
SOUTH	87,012	75,372	11,640	15.4%
WEST	52,008	43,172	8,836	20.5%

Source: Adapted from American Demographics (January 1990):24.

removing snow and ice, for example, whereas a Floridian would be more apt to buy suntan lotion or beach attire. There are also differences between urban areas and suburban or rural areas. Swimming pools that sell well in a residential suburban neighborhood would not be very much in demand in an urban neighborhood filled with apartment buildings.

In addition, marketers analyze different markets by population and growth rates. The population of different states and regions of the country will affect the weight of advertising placed in specific areas. For example, according to the 1990 Census, the Northeast had become the least populous region of the country, whereas the South, with 87 million people, had the highest population.*

The 1990 Census also showed that states in the South and West accounted for nearly 90 percent of the nation's 10-year population gain. Although the Midwest was the slowest-growing region, it was still the second most populous area in the nation. California gained more people than any other state—over 5 million since 1980. Texas and Florida gained more than 3 million residents each year during the 1980s, and Georgia gained over 1 million. In contrast, the populations of West Virginia, Iowa, and the District of Columbia decreased.† This kind of information is valuable to an advertiser in deciding where and to whom to target specific advertising messages. Table 5.2 illustrates the changes in the U.S. population from 1980 to 1990.

Psychographics

We have analyzed you as a member of social and reference groups and have looked at your personal characteristics. Now let's look at the internal elements that make you an individual. The variables that shape your inner self are referred to as your *psychological makeup.*

Advertisers use the term **psychographics** to refer to all the psychological variables that combine to shape our inner selves. Psychographics goes beyond demographics in attempting to explain complex behavior patterns. For example, why does one mother with a newborn infant use dispos-

psychographics *All the psychological variables that combine to shape our inner selves, including activities, interests, opinions, needs, values, attitudes, personality traits, decision processes, and buying behavior.*

---

*Waldrop and Exter, "What the 1990 Census Will Show," p. 24.
†Ibid., p. 24.

able diapers whereas another mother chooses reusable cloth diapers? And why does she use Pampers when others use generic brands or the brand for which they have a coupon? Why does one person drive a brand-new BMW, whereas a neighbor in the identical condo next door drives an old Volvo?

To explain these "true" motivations for behavior, advertisers look at a variety of dimensions, including activities, interests and hobbies, opinions, needs, values, attitudes, and personality traits. Taken together, these elements give a much broader picture of a person than do demographic data.

Although hundreds of different dimensions are encompassed under *psychographics,* the areas with the most relevance to advertising are: perception, learning, motives, attitudes, personality, lifestyles, and buying behavior.

perception *The process by which we receive information through our five senses and acknowledge and assign meaning to this information.*

Perception.   Each day you are bombarded by stimuli—faces, conversations, buildings, advertisements, news announcements—yet you actually see or hear only a small fraction. Why? The answer is perception. **Perception** is the process by which we receive information through our five senses and assign meaning to it. Perceptions are shaped by three sets of influences: the physical characteristics of the stimuli, the relation of the stimuli to their surroundings, and conditions within the individual. It is this last set of influences that makes perception a personal trait. Each individual perceives a given stimulus within a personal frame of reference. Factors that influence this frame of reference include learning experiences, attitudes, personality, and self-image. The process is further complicated by the fact that we are exposed to a great number of stimuli. Some of these stimuli are perceived completely, and some partially, some correctly, and some incorrectly. Ultimately, we select some stimuli and ignore others because we do not have the ability to be conscious of all incoming information at one time.

selective perception *The process of screening out information that does not interest us and retaining information that does.*

PRINCIPLE
An ad will be perceived only if it is relevant to the consumer.

Selective Perception   The process of screening out information that does not interest us and retaining information that does is called **selective perception.** Think about the route you take when driving to school every day. How many stimuli do you perceive? If you're like most people, you perceive traffic signals, what's going on in your car, other traffic, and pedestrians crossing in front of you. This is selective perception. This same process is repeated when we watch television or read a magazine. It also occurs when we look at an ad and perceive only the headline, a photograph, or a famous spokesperson. In addition to our tendency to select stimuli that are of interest to us, we also perceive stimuli in a manner that coincides with our reality. That is, your world includes your own set of experiences, values, biases, and attitudes. It is virtually impossible to separate these inherent factors from the way you perceive. For example, we naturally tend to seek out messages that are pleasant or sympathetic with our views and to avoid those that are painful or threatening. This is called **selective exposure.** Consumers tend to selectively expose themselves to advertisements that reassure them of the wisdom of their purchase decisions. Similarly, when we are exposed to a message that is different from what we believe, we engage in **selective distortion.** For example, a consumer may "hear" that an automobile gets good gas mileage, even though the salesperson has clearly indicated this is not so, because the consumer perceives other features of the car as perfect and therefore wants very much to buy it.

selective exposure *The ability to process only certain information and avoid other stimuli.*

selective distortion *The interpretation of information in a way that is consistent with the person's existing opinion.*

Advertisers are interested in these selective processes because they affect whether consumers will perceive an ad and, if so, whether they will remember it. Selective perception is also strongly influenced by our attitudes towards the person, situation, and idea. If we hold a strong positive attitude toward safety, for example, we will tend to perceive messages that deal with this subject. In turn, we will tend to remember details about the message, such as product features and the brand name, when perception is intense. More will be said about attitudes later in the chapter.

Our response to a stimulus has a direct bearing on advertising. A large part of what the brain processes is lost after only an instant. Even when we try very hard to retain information, we are unable to save a lot of it. **Selective retention** describes the process we go through in trying to "save" information for future use. Advertising can facilitate this process by using repetition, easily remembered brand or product names, jingles, high-profile spokespeople, music, and so forth. Its ability to stimulate and assist the consumer in selective retention often determines the success of an individual ad.

> **selective retention** *The process of remembering only a small portion of what a person is exposed to.*

Cognitive Dissonance   Another possible response to selective perception is a feeling of dissatisfaction or doubt. Seldom does a purchase produce all the expected positive results. According to the theory of **cognitive dissonance,** we tend to compensate or justify the small or large discrepancy between what we actually received and what we perceived we would receive. Research on this phenomenon has shown that people engage in a variety of activities to reduce dissonance.* Most notably, they seek out information that supports their decision and they ignore or distort information that does not. Advertising can play a central role in reducing dissonance. For example, car manufacturers anticipate where dissonance is likely to occur and provide supportive information, IBM uses testimonials by satisfied customers, and restaurants include discount coupons with their print ads.

> **cognitive dissonance** *A tendency to justify the discrepancy between what a person receives relative to what he or she expected to receive.*

The next time you watch television, study yourself as you view the ads. What do you select to pay attention to? Why? When do you "tune out"? Why? Did you find yourself disagreeing with a message or arguing with it? Can you see how your own selection processes influence your attention and response to advertising?

Learning.   Perception leads to learning—that is, we cannot learn something unless we have accurately perceived the information and attached some meaning to it. Because people often associate attempts at learning with real formal education, they tend to think of it as a conscious, deliberate, tedious, and painful process. In fact, learning is typically an unconscious activity; consumers don't usually even know when it's happening. It does happen, however, starting early in life and continuing throughout. If advertisers understand how learning takes place, they can design ads to optimize the learning of the key elements in the ad, such as brand name, location, product features, price, and so forth. Understanding how learning takes place is important for other reasons as well. Most notably, we can learn different attitudes, beliefs, preferences, values, and standards, all of which may lead to changes in purchase behavior.

Cognitive Learning   Various theories have been developed to explain different aspects of learning. Typically, two schools of learning are considered. The first is called the *cognitive* school. Cognitive interpretations emphasize the discovery of patterns and insight. Cognitive theorists stress the importance of perception, problem-solving, and insight. They contend that

---

*Leon Festinger, *A Theory of Cognitive Dissonance* (Evanston, IL: Row, Peterson, 1957):83.

most learning occurs not as a result of trial-and-error or practice but of discovering meaningful patterns that enable people to solve problems. These meaningful patterns are called "gestalts," and cognitive theories of learning rely heavily on the process of insight to explain the development of gestalts. This is comparable to the "ah ha" effect that occurs when we finally figured out how calculus worked.

When confronted with a problem, we sometimes see the solution instantly. More often we need to search for information, carefully evaluate what we learn, and make a decision. Cognitive learning characterizes people as problem solvers who go through a complex process of mentally processing information. Advertisers employing this perspective concentrate on the role of motivation in decision making and the mental processing consumers do when making decisions.

Connectionists   The second school of learning, the connectionists, argues that people learn connections between stimuli and responses. The connectionists school is further divided into classical conditioning and instrumental conditioning. Essentially, *classical conditioning* pairs one stimulus with another that already elicits a given response. Classical conditioning is often associated with experiments of Ivan Pavlov, in which a dog was taught to salivate at the sound of a bell.

Instrumental or *operant* conditioning depends on the voluntary occurrence of behaviors that are then rewarded, punished, or ignored. The greatest practical development of instrumental conditioning is attributed to B.F. Skinner and his followers. According to Skinner, most learning takes place in an effort to control the environment—that is, to obtain favorable outcomes. Control is gained by means of a trial-and-error process during which one behavior results in a more favorable response than do other behaviors. The reward received is instrumental in teaching the person about a specific behavior that provides more control. For advertisers, this process requires emphasizing repetition and discrimination in order to convince consumers that their brand provides greater rewards than do other brands.

For example, learning would include a stimulus such as needing a new pair of shoes. This stimulus—worn out shoes—is called a *need*. Next, a cue addresses that particular need, such as a local department store that is having a shoe sale. You may respond to this cue in a positive way because you have purchased shoes there before and have been very satisfied. Finally, *reinforcement* of learning occurs when the response is followed by satisfaction. Positive reinforcement strengthens the relationship between the cue and the response and therefore increases the probability that the response will be repeated.

Habit   When we have repeated a process many times and continue to be satisfied with the outcome, we reach a point called *habit*. Habit is a limitation on or total absence of information seeking and evaluation of alternative choices. Purchasing by habit provides two important benefits to the consumer: (1) it reduces risk; and (2) it facilitates decision making. Buying the same brand time and again reduces the risk of product failure and financial loss for important purchases. Habit also simplifies decision making by minimizing the need for information search. Obviously, advertisers would like consumers to be habitual users of their product. Achieving that requires a powerful message backed by a superior product. American automakers learned a hard lesson when they assumed that American consumers would continue habitually to purchase cars built in the United States even though they were inferior to Japanese cars. Once a habit is formed, the role

AD 5.5
Pepsi has been very successful in creating positive associations with its products. (Courtesy of Pepsi Cola Company.)

of advertising is to reinforce that habit through reminder messages, messages of appreciation, and actual rewards, such as coupons, premiums, and rebates. Breaking a consumer's habit is very difficult. Attacking a well-entrenched competitor may only make consumers defensive and reinforce their habit. Offering the consumer new relevant information about yourself or your competition is one successful approach. Providing an extra incentive to change, such as coupons, or free samples, has also proved effective.

Advertisers use a number of techniques to improve learning. Music and jingles improve learning because they intensify the repetition. Creating positive associations with a brand also enhances learning. Testimonials by well-liked celebrities and scenes of attractive people in attractive settings are used to intensify positive associations. Humor is employed because it gives the audience some reward for paying attention. Ad 5.5 is an example of advertising that creates a positive association with a product.

motive *An unobservable inner force that stimulates and compels a behavioral response.*

Motivation and Needs. A **motive** is an internal force that stimulates you to behave in a particular manner. This driving force is produced by the state of tension that results from an unfulfilled need. People strive—both consciously and subconsciously—to reduce this tension through behavior they anticipate will fulfill their needs and thus relieve the stress they feel.

At any given point you are probably being affected by a number of different motives, some of which may be contradictory. Some motives are stronger than others, but even this pattern changes from time to time. For example, your motivation to buy a new suit will be much higher when you start going out on job interviews.

What are your buying motives? Think back over all your purchases during the past week. Did you have a reason for buying those products that you might tell your mother or an interviewer, but also a hidden reason that you will keep to yourself? You can see how important the concept of buying motives is to an understanding of consumer behavior.

needs *Basic forces that motivate you to do or to want something.*

Needs are the basic forces that motivate you to do something. Each person has his or her own set of unique needs; some are innate; others are acquired. *Innate needs* are physiological and include the needs for food, water, air, shelter, and sex. Because satisfying these needs is necessary to maintaining life, they are referred to as *primary needs*. *Acquired needs* are those we learn in response to our culture or environment. These may include needs for esteem, prestige, affection, power, and learning. Because acquired needs are not necessary to our physical survival, they are considered *secondary needs* or motives. Abraham Maslow noted that needs exist in a hierarchy, and that we tend to satisfy our primary needs before our secondary needs. He identified five different need categories that can be arranged vertically, with the most primary at the bottom: (1) physical or biological needs, (2) safety and security needs, (3) love and affiliation needs, (4) prestige and esteem needs, and (5) self-fulfillment needs. Although it's very useful to examine this hierarchy, looking at needs from a cross-sectional point of view is also helpful. From a cross-sectional perspective, no one category of needs consistently takes precedence over the others. A list of general consumer needs is shown in Table 5.3.

TABLE 5.3
Consumer Needs

Consumer Needs	
Achievement	*Independence*
The need to accomplish difficult feats; to perform arduous tasks; to exercise your skills, abilities, or talents.	The need to be autonomous, to be free from the direction or influence of others; to have options and alternatives; to make your own choices and decisions; to be different.
Exhibition	*Recognition*
The need to display yourself, to be visible to others; to reveal personal identity; to show off or win the attention and interest of others; to gain notice.	The need for *positive* notice by others; to show your superiority or excellence; to be acclaimed or held up as exemplary; to receive social rewards or notoriety.
Dominance	*Stimulation*
The need to have power or to exert your will on others; to hold a position of authority or influence; to direct or supervise the efforts of others; to show strength or prowess by winning over adversaries.	The need to experience events and activities that stimulate the senses or exercise perception; to move and act freely and vigorously; to engage in rapid or forceful activity; to saturate the palate with flavor; to engage the environment in new or unusual modes of interaction.
Diversion	
The need to play; to have fun; to be entertained; to break from the routine; to relax and abandon your cares; to be amused.	*Novelty*
Understanding	The need for change and diversity; to experience the unusual; to do new tasks or activities; to learn new skills; to be in a new setting or environment; to find unique objects of interest; to be amazed or mystified.
The need to learn and comprehend; to recognize connections; to assign causality; to make ideas fit the circumstances; to teach, instruct, or impress others with your expertise; to follow intellectual pursuits.	*Affiliation*
Nurturance	The need for association with others; to belong or win acceptance; to enjoy satisfying and mutually helpful relationships.
The need to give care, comfort, and support to others; to see living things grow and thrive; to help the progress and development of others; to protect your charges from harm or injury.	*Succorance*
Sexuality	The need to *receive* help, support, comfort, encouragement, or reassurance from others; to be the *recipient* of nurturant efforts.
The need to establish your sexual identity and attractiveness; to enjoy sexual contact; to *receive* and to *provide* sexual satisfaction; to maintain sexual alternatives without exercising them; to avoid condemnation for sexual appetites.	*Consistency*
Security	The need for order, cleanliness, or logical connection; to control the environment; to avoid ambiguity and uncertainty; to predict accurately; to have things happen as you expect.
The need to be free from threat of harm; to be safe; to protect self, family, and property; to have a supply of what you need; to save and acquire assets; to be invulnerable to attack; to avoid accidents or mishaps.	

Source: Adapted from Robert B. Settle and Pamela L. Alreck, *Why They Buy* (New York: John Wiley & Sons, 1986):26–28.

attitude *A learned predisposition that we hold toward an object, person, or ideal.*

PRINCIPLE

Advertising tries to maintain existing positive attitudes and to change negative and neutral attitudes to positive ones.

AD 5.6
The American Cancer Society has spent many years and has used different appeals to teach us about cancer and influence our attitudes concerning good health. (Courtesy of American Cancer Society.)

Attitudes. An **attitude** is a learned predisposition, a feeling that you hold toward an object, a person, or an idea that leads to a particular behavior. An attitude focuses on some topic that provides a focal point for your beliefs and feelings. Attitudes also tend to be enduring. You can hold an attitude for months or even years.

We develop and learn attitudes, we are not born with them. Because attitudes are learned, we can change them, unlearn them, or replace them with new ones. Attitudes also vary in direction and in strength. That is, an attitude can be *positive* or *negative,* reflecting like or dislike.

Attitudes are important to advertisers because they influence how consumers evaluate products. A strong positive attitude might be turned into brand preference and loyalty. A weak attitude, even if it is positive, might not be enough to convince you to act. Changing an attitude is not impossible, but it is difficult.

Attitudes also reflect consumers' values. They tell the world what we stand for and identify the things and ideas we consider important. They also track our positive and negative reactions to things in our life. Opinion research is used to check how people feel about other people, products, brands, appeals, and contemporary trends. One of the most important areas for opinion research in advertising is product and brand perception. It is important to know how the consumer sees the product before developing an advertising strategy. Furthermore, advertisers must be aware of what the product is associated with in the consumer's mind (see Ad 5.6).

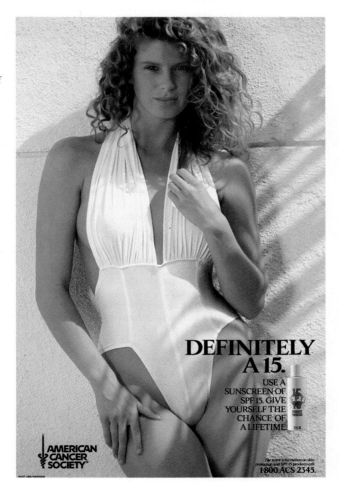

DEFINITELY A 15.

USE A SUNSCREEN OF SPF 15. GIVE YOURSELF THE CHANCE OF A LIFETIME.

AMERICAN CANCER SOCIETY

For more information on skin protection and SPF-15 products call 1-800-ACS-2345.

Personality. All of these personal and psychological factors interact to create your own unique personality. A **personality** is a collection of traits that makes a person distinctive. How you look at the world, how you perceive and interpret what is happening around you, how you respond intellectually and emotionally, and how you form your opinions and attitudes are all reflected in your personality (see Ad 5.7). Your personality is what makes you an individual.

personality *Relatively long-lasting personal qualities that allow us to cope with, and respond to, the world around us.*

Self-Concept Self-concept refers to how we look at ourselves. Our self-image reflects how we see our own personality and our individual pattern of strengths and weaknesses. Take a minute to think of the traits that best describe you. What do they tell you about your own self-concept? Are they basically positive or negative? Do you have high or low self-esteem? What image of yourself do you see?

Now consider yourself as a consumer. Explain how these same characteristics affect your response to different products, to advertising, and to your behavior as a consumer. Can you see how understanding personality is important in developing a relevant message?

Lifestyles. Lifestyle factors are often considered the mainstay of psychographic research. Essentially, lifestyle research looks at the ways people allocate time, energy, and money. Marketers conduct research to measure and compare people's activities, interests, and opinions—in other words, what they usually do or how they behave, what intrigues or fascinates them, and what they believe or assume about the world around them.

AD 5.7
MassMutual speaks to a young couple about to become parents, an event that will influence their personalities and lifestyles. (Courtesy of Mass Mutual and Bozell.)

A promise to dig the seat belts out from under the seats.

A promise to reserve comment on the latest additions to your wardrobe.

A promise that a safe world will mean more than night-lights and teddy bears.

Nothing binds us one to the other like a promise kept. Nothing divides us like a promise broken. At MassMutual we believe in keeping our promises. That way all the families and businesses that rely on us can keep theirs.

MassMutual
We help you keep your promises.™

value and lifestyles systems (VALS) *Classification systems that categorize people by values for the purpose of predicting effective advertising strategies.*

VALS The firm of SRI International is famous for its **Values and Lifestyles Systems (VALS)** conceptual models that categorize people according to their values and then identify the consumer behaviors associated with those values. VALS systems are used to show clients how consumer groups are changing and how these changes will affect the client's advertising strategy. The first model, VALS 1, was introduced in 1978 and contained nine categories that divided the American population along a hierarchy of needs. At the bottom of the hierarchy were the survivors and sustainers; at the top were the integrateds. Two separate paths led from the bottom to the top. One was outer-directed and included belongers, emulators, and achievers, who took their cues from the world around them. The other path was inner-directed, the I-am-me's, experientials, and societally conscious, who tended to make their own rules. The problem with using these segments is that they reflected a population of people who were in their twenties and thirties in the 1970s, and this population changed quite a bit in the 1980s. Moreover, businesses found it difficult to use these segments to predict buying behavior or to target consumers.

For these reasons SRI developed a new system in 1989. The firm dropped values and lifestyles as the basis for its psychographic segmentation scheme, having determined that the link between values and lifestyles and purchasing choices was less strong than it had once seemed. The new system—VALS 2—is based on a questionnaire that reveals unchanging psychological stances rather than shifting values and lifestyles, and is considered the superior system (see Figure 5.3). The psychographic groups in VALS 2 are arranged in a rectangle. They are stacked vertically by resources

FIGURE 5.3
Value and Lifestyles Systems (VALS 1 and VALS 2). Source: *American Demographics* (July 1989):26.

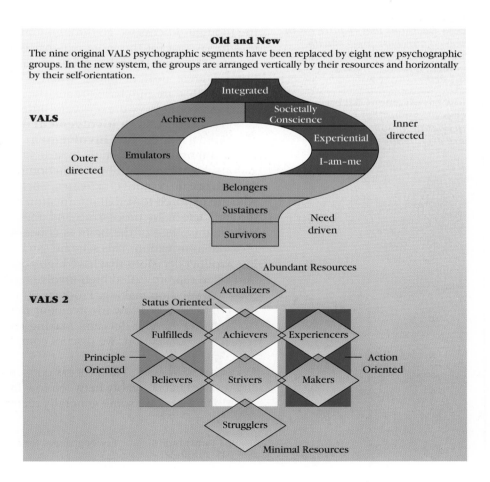

Old and New

The nine original VALS psychographic segments have been replaced by eight new psychographic groups. In the new system, the groups are arranged vertically by their resources and horizontally by their self-orientation.

(minimal to abundant) and horizontally by self-orientation (principle-, status-, or action-oriented). Resources include income, education, self-confidence, health, eagerness to buy, intelligence, and energy level.

A person's position along the resource/self-orientation axis determines which of eight classifications he or she falls into: actualizers, fulfilled, achievers, experiencers, believers, strivers, makers, or strugglers. Members of each group hold different values and maintain different lifestyles. Actualizers, for example, are located above the rectangle and have the highest incomes and such high self-esteem and abundant resources that they can indulge in any or all self-orientations. Image is important to these people. Because of their wide range of interests and openness to change, actualizers' purchases are directed at "the finer things in life."* Obviously, knowing the psychographic orientation of consumers is a valuable asset to an advertiser in deciding to whom messages should be targeted.

Buying Behavior

The information we have discussed thus far is used by advertisers to understand how the consumer decision-making process works—in other words, how the consumer goes about buying the product. Although at first it sounds like an individual process that cannot be generalized across consumers, there is evidence that most people engage in a similar decision process. Our understanding is also enhanced if we view decision making as either low-involvement or high-involvement.

high-involvement decision process *Decisions that require an involved purchase process with information search and product comparison.*

low-involvement decision process *Decisions that require limited deliberation; sometimes purchases are even made on impulse.*

Low- and High-Involvement Decision Making.   When we think about the thought process we go through in making product decisions, it is fairly safe to say that for the more expensive, personal, or emotion-laden products (such as automobiles, medical care, clothes, and vacations), we expend a great deal of effort, whereas for the inexpensive, less-exciting products that are purchased regularly, such as those found at supermarket checkout counters, we exert very little thought and effort. The former is called a complex, **high-involvement decision process,** whereas the latter is labeled a simple, **low-involvement decision process.** This concept of involvement originated in the research conducted on hemispheral lateralization—right-brain–left-brain functioning. The left hemisphere of the brain specializes in cognitive activities, such as reading and speaking. People who are exposed to verbal information cognitively analyze the information through left-brain processing and form mental images. Conversely, the right hemisphere of the brain is concerned with nonverbal, timeless, and pictorial information. This scheme can be applied to product decision making. Product decisions that have high personal relevance and contain a high perceived risk are called high-involvement purchases, and they necessitate complex decision making. Products at the opposite end of the relevance/risk continuum are low-involvement purchases that require simple decision making. Simple decision making requires very little information and virtually no evaluation. We discuss complex decision making next.

Decision Process.   The process consumers go through in making a purchase varies considerably between low-involvement and high-involvement situations. There are some generally recognized stages, however, and these

*Martha Farnsworth Riche, "Psychographics for the 1990s," *American Demographics* (July 1989):25–26, 30–32.

WHO ARE MOST LIKELY TO BUY CELLULAR CAR PHONES?

How can an advertiser identify the prospective purchasers of a new product? Cleverly designed market research can offer some good leads. For example, a cellular car phone company needed to find out more about its potential consumers at a time when only about 1 percent of U.S. adults had actually bought such phones. The problem was how to weed out such people for closer examination. By using the findings of a national survey of the activities, interests, and opinions of 5000 adults, the phone company was able to concentrate on the 259 people (about 7 percent of the total group in the survey) who thought they would be apt to buy a cellular phone within the next 4 years.

What are these self-styled potential consumers like, and how do they differ from Americans in general? Basically, people who are likely to buy cellular car phones are more adventurous. This was found to be true for both males and females. They are active people. Not only do they go out often, for instance, but they are quite bold about trying new things, visiting new countries, and taking chances on the unfamiliar.

The enthusiam these people have for active, fun, lifestyles extends to their jobs as well. They say that they work for the money to obtain goods and services, not for the security of the jobs. They characterize themselves as impulse buyers; they are quick to agree that they "are usually among the first to try new products," and they admit they "aren't very good at saving money." Indeed, on the contrary, they enjoy spending it impulsively. And though they earn higher-than-average incomes, these people are likely to end up spending more than they have.

Compared to the general sample, the potential cellular phone buyers are more optimistic about their futures because they are convinced that their greatest achievements still lie ahead and will indeed materialize through their own efforts. They are also confident that as they earn more (and they are sure they will), they will pay off their debts and buy other expensive goods and services. Not only are they distinctly self-confident about the future but they view themselves as leaders to whom other people turn for advice.

In demographic terms, the potential purchasers are more affluent than is the general sample. They are also better educated, more apt to be single (15 percent versus 9 percent), and typically are between the ages of 25 and 44. They work in professional or managerial occupations and tend to live in (or prefer to live in) urban environments.

In terms of media habits, cellular phone users read more newspapers and magazines and watch more television broadcast news, sports, and detective shows. They are also more likely to have cable television in their homes. Research indicates that they are already involved in the new technologies as well. A considerable proportion have bought such products as home computers, video tape recorders, portable phones, and either foreign or sporty American cars. In general terms, it seems that the potential cellular car phone user embodies the spirit of the entrepreneur—he or she is daring, adventurous, hard-working, outgoing, and more than willing to gamble on the future. These people are anything but cautious. They like their lifestyles, and they want to be different from the "run-of-the-mill" masses. Advertisers would be wise to regard the lifestyles and values of these people as favorable signs of future purchasing behavior and to target their advertising accordingly.

Exercise

What have you learned about the social and psychological makeup of cellular phone buyers that would help you design an advertising message? Think about the demographic and psychographic characteristics that distinguish them from the crowd. Now look for an existing ad (for any product) that seems to be the type of message that would win over cellular phone consumers.

Source: DDB Needham Worldwide, *Lifestyle and Demographic Profile of the Potential Cellular Car Phone User* (August 1986).

are highlighted in Figure 5.4. The stages are (1) need recognition, (2) information search, (3) evaluation and comparison, (4) outlet selection, (5) purchase decision, and (6) postpurchase evaluation.

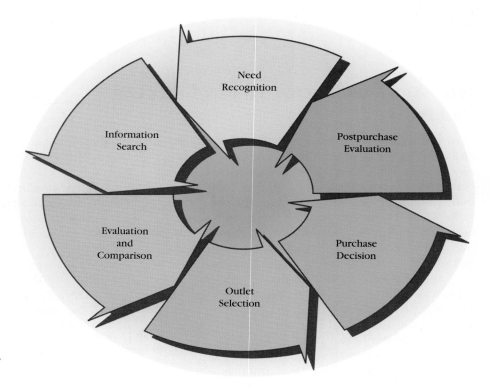

FIGURE 5.4
The major stages of the consumer purchase process.

Need Recognition   The first stage, *need recognition,* occurs when the consumer recognizes a need for a product. This need can vary in terms of seriousness or importance. The goal of advertising at this stage is to activate or stimulate this need. For example, the Burger King "Aren't you hungry?" campaign appeals to people's appetites and nutritional needs.

Information Search   The second stage is the *information search.* This search can be casual, such as reading ads and articles that happen to catch your attention, or formal, such as searching for information in publications like *Consumer Reports.* Another type of informal search is recalling information you have seen previously. Advertising helps the search process by providing information in the advertisement itself.

Evaluation and Comparison   The third stage is *evaluation and comparison.* Here we begin to compare various products and features and reduce the list of options to a manageable number. We select certain features that are important and use them to judge our alternatives. Advertising is important in this evaluation process because it helps sort out products on the basis of features.

Outlet Selection and Purchase Decision   The fourth stage is *outlet selection.* Is this product available at a grocery store, a discount store, a hardware store, a boutique, a department store, or a specialty store? Will the consumer select the brand first and then try to find a store that carries it, or will he or she select a store first and then consider the available brands? In-store promotions such as packaging, point-of-purchase displays, price reductions, banners and signs, and coupon displays affect these choices. (Sales promotion techniques will be discussed in more detail in Chapter 18). The outlet is the site of the fifth stage, which is the actual *purchase.*

Postpurchase Evaluation   The last step in the process is the point where we begin to reconsider and justify our purchase to ourselves. As soon as we purchase a product, particularly a major one, we begin to engage in postpurchase evaluation. Is the product acceptable? Is its performance satisfactory? Does it live up to our expectations? This experience determines whether we will repurchase the product.

Even before you open the package or use the product, you may experience doubt or worry about the wisdom of the purchase. This doubt is called *postpurchase dissonance.* Many consumers continue to read information even after the purchase in order to justify their decision to themselves. Advertising helps reduce postpurchase dissonance by restating the features and confirming the popularity of the brand or product.

*T*he Key to Effective Advertising: Understanding the Audience

Once a year, DDB Needham Worldwide mails questionnaires to a sample of 4,000 U.S. adults, covering various lifestyle topics from eating habits to attitudes toward neatness. The data is used to create in-depth profiles of client's target consumers. Betty Crocker wants to know who buys cake mixes, Wrigley's would be interested to know that 40 percent of Americans think people shouldn't chew gum in public, and Listerine and Scope want to know what percentage of the population thinks people should use mouthwash to fight bad breath.

The detailed profiles DDB Needham compiles are passed on to the creative people working on the specific accounts. A person responsible for the National Dairy Board campaign, for example needs to know who are the heavy users of cheese. These Lifestyle studies provide data on demographics, attitudes, beliefs, habits, needs, and opinions on all sorts of topics, from religion, family, and morals to the economy, law enforcement, and volunteerism—all the information necessary for developing and appropriately targeting campaigns.

Some of the questions asked may seem irrelevant, such as asking respondents to agree or disagree with the statement, "I like the look of a large lamp in a picture window," or "I would do better than average in a fistfight." These responses are valuable, however, and help to determine whether a person has traditional values, how he or she feels about sex roles, and help round out the profiles.

The Lifestyle studies also help to disprove some of the popular myths of so-called "trends" that seem to be appearing. For example, although it is believed that families don't eat together anymore, the Lifestyle data show that 75 percent of respondents say their whole family usually eats dinner together.*

Although it is impossible for us to know everything about the people with whom we communicate, the more we do know, the more likely our message will be understood. This same assumption is true for advertisers, although at a much broader level. Fortunately, advertisers have the resources to conduct extensive research that taps this information. Such research must not only be accurate, it must also be conducted constantly because people are always changing.

In this chapter we identified several key audience traits and behaviors that are relevant to the advertiser. There are more traits and behaviors that we have not discussed. Furthermore, those involved in the design and im-

*Joseph M. Winski, "Lifestyle Study: Who We Are, How We Live, What We Think," *Advertising Age* (September 24, 1990):25.

plementation of an advertisement may interpret these traits differently. We all have our own perceptions of things. The key to successful advertising is staying sensitive to the consumer. If all you know about your audience is what the computer printout tells you, you are unlikely to be an effective communicator. Creative advertising requires both basic awareness and empathy. In the next chapter we will turn to the specific research and planning strategies involved in achieving this kind of consumer awareness.

SUMMARY

- The social and cultural influences on consumers include society and subcultures, social class, reference groups, and family.
- Personal influences on consumers include age, gender, family status, education, occupation, income, and race.
- Psychological influences on the individual as a consumer include perception, learning, motivation, attitudes, personality, and self-concept.
- Advertisers identify audiences in terms of demographics and psychographics.
- Demographic profiles of consumers include information on population size, age, gender, education, family situation, occupation, income, and race.

- Psychographic profiles on consumers include information on attitudes, lifestyles, buying behavior, and decision processes.
- Your personality reflects how you look at the world, how you perceive and interpret what is happening, how you respond, and how you form opinions and attitudes.
- The decision process involves six stages: need recognition, information search, evaluation and comparison, outlet selection, purchase decision, and postpurchase evaluation.

QUESTIONS

1. How must advertisers adjust to the elderly? Do you think different adjustments will be required when the baby boomers enter this group? What kind?

2. Choose four VALS categories and find one or more print advertisements that appear to be targeted to individuals in each category. Explain why you think the ad addresses that audience.

3. What are the six stages in the consumer decision process? Give examples of how advertising can influence each stage. Find an ad that addresses the concern of consumers in each stage.

4. Sean McDonnell is the creative director for Chatham-Boothe, an advertising agency that has just signed a contract with Trans-Central Airlines (TCA). TCA has a solid portfolio of consumer research and has offered to let the agency use it. McDonnell needs to decide whether demographic, psychographic, or attitude/motive studies are best for developing the creative profile of the TCA target audience. If the choice were yours, which body of research would you base a creative strategy on? Explore the strengths and weaknesses of each.

5. Look at the social class segments illustrated in Table 5.1. Which two class segments would be most receptive to these product marketing situations:
   a. Full line of frozen family-style meals (for microwaving) that feature superior nutritional balances.
   b. Dairy product company (milk, cheese, icecream) with an exclusive packaging design that uses fully degradable containers.

6. If the projected U.S. age shifts forecasted for the next 20 years happen, what impact would these changes have on our current advertising practices (creative and media selection influences)?

7. Avon Products has established an admirable reputation for residence-to-residence personal selling. Now the corporation has seriously modified its marketing approach. What changes in consumer lifestyles have happened to prompt Avon's shift? How can Avon change with the times without giving up personal salesmanship?

FURTHER READINGS

BARD, B., "The Eighties Are Over," *Newsweek,* January 4, 1988, pp. 40–45.

MULLEN, BRIAN, AND CRAIG JOHNSON, *The Psychology of Consumer Behavior* (Hillsdale, NJ: Lawrence Erlbaum Associates, 1990).

SCHIFFMAN, LEON G., AND LESLIE LAZAR KANUK, *Consumer Behavior* (Englewood Cliffs, NJ: Prentice Hall, 1987).

SETTLE, ROBERT B., AND PAMELA L. ALBECK, *Why They Buy: American Consumers Inside and Out* (New York: John Wiley & Sons, 1986).

PRUS, ROBERT C., *Pursuing Customers: An Ethnography of Marketing Activities* (New York: Sage Publications, 1989).

VIDEO CASE

Teenage Angst: The "Jordache Basics" Campaign

The blue-jean and denim-apparel industry had been dominated by Levi Strauss and Company until the late 1970s. As the 1980s approached and Levi's recovered from a disastrous attempt to break into the high end of the men's fashion industry with suits, sports coats, and slacks under the Levi's brand name, several new and old apparel manufacturers took on Levi's flagship blue-jean product with their own jeans brands. Although Levi's equity in the jeans category was extremely strong, the company was not known as an innovator or a fashion leader. So as Levi's held on tightly to the traditional men's and women's jeans market, Calvin Klein, Jordache, and others took jeans uptown with different cuts, colors, and styles. Even as Levi's hurried to duplicate some of the less radical jeans transformations of its competitors, Wrangler was lining up famous rodeo stars to try to pick away at Levi's traditional source of strength as America's original jeans from the wild west.

As fashion began to win out over functionality in the jeans category, apparel makers that could carve out the most unique image for their products in their advertising experienced significant increases in sales. From the famous Brooke Shields "nothing comes between me and my Calvins" ads for Calvin Klein jeans to the ambiguous Guess? jeans campaign, image advertising has played a dominant role in the marketing of jeans and denim fashion products over the last decade.

Jordache initially jumped into the fray with the "Jordache Look" campaign. The campaign was the most primitive and obvious of the various image-oriented jeans campaigns of its time. The ads were dominated by close-up visuals of tight-fitting Jordache jeans while the lyrics of the repetitive jingle stated, "It's the Jordache look." The message seemed to work particularly well among teenagers because form-fitting jeans were an integral part of the junior-high, high school, and college dating scene at the time. As Calvin Klein and others made jeans fashionable for adults to wear to parties, restaurants, and other social gatherings, Jordache chose to build on its base strength among America's teenagers.

As the sophistication level of 1980s' teenagers was elevated by years of MTV and "brat pack" Hollywood feature films targeted to teens, Jordache could no longer rely on the relatively crude approach taken with the "Jordache Look" campaign. Learning from their more artful competition, Jordache developed the "Jordache Basics" campaign, which featured a variety of post-yuppie model/actors in a series of vignettes, discussing contemporary angst-ridden teen issues, such as the future, relationships, and parents. Part way through the campaign, the superimposed tag line "Jordache Basics" was joined by a superimposed subheadline "because life . . . is not." Prior to the superimposed tag lines at the end of the spots, the presence of Jordache products were only subtly conveyed by the actors and actresses donning Jordache apparel.

Subtle, almost unnoticeable product identification is not uncommon in advertising in the fashion and cosmetics industries. Generally, however, advertising media levels must be large enough for viewers to be aware of the product's identity from prior viewings. In this way, subsequent viewings of ads in the campaign are attributed to the correct product. Yet, even with a very focused media placement strategy on a single, very targeted station, such as MTV, the extreme subtlety of the Jordache product identification and the obtuse image message conveyed by the "Jordache Basics" campaign probably reduced the effectiveness of its expenditures.

Whereas subtle advertising can reduce the effectiveness of the media expenditures and the advertising itself, advertising that is considered controversial by the target audience can actually have a negative impact on product sales. Undoubtedly, several of the "Jordache Basics" campaign spots could have been considered controversial, at least by parents if not by the teenage target audience itself. For example, in one spot an attractive teenage girl claims she hates her mother because she believes her mother is more attractive than she is. In another spot, a teenage girl runs away from home to an uncertain fate and is shown to be unhappy with her life on the road in a later spot. The "Jordache Basics" campaign raises the issue of form over substance, which often plagues image-oriented advertising. In this case, parent bashing is used as an attempt to position Jordache jeans and denim apparel as hip and antiestablishment—a 1960s notion resurrected here to defuse parents' objections to the campaign.

It is obvious that the "Jordache Basics" campaign was somewhat groundbreaking, both in its use of an extremely subtle and obtuse image-based message as well as its subsequent use of self-parody. However, because the effectiveness of image-based advertising to generate product sales is often difficult to quantify, Jordache and its competitors may never determine with certainty if the creative breakthroughs exhibited in the "Jordache Basics" campaign were a progressive move forward in fashion advertising or a costly mistake.

QUESTIONS

1. Based on the "Jordache Basics" advertising, recreate what you think Jordache used as the copy platform for the campaign and justify your answer.
2. Because advertising media frequency is critical to an advertising campaign with a subtle selling message, what television dayparts, stations, or specific programs would you recommend to Jordache for their campaign? Justify your answer.

Appendix: Studying Consumer Trends

USING SOCIAL TRENDS FOR ADVERTISING DECISIONS

Courtesy of Marty Horn, Associate Director of the Delta Group, DDB Needham Worldwide.

Several years ago, Betty Crocker adopted the "Sweet Talker" advertising campaign to provide a fresher, more contemporary, and less traditional image to its line of baked goods. This image "makeover" was necessary in order to reflect the current lifestyle of Betty Crocker's target audience more accurately. (See Ad 1.)

When long-term trends indicated that consumers pressed for time couldn't afford the time to get their houses neat and clean, Rubbermaid designed an advertising campaign around a line of new products that were durable and highly effective in easing the burden and drudgery of housework. (See Ad 2.)

As these two examples suggest, major decisions about manufacturing, marketing, and advertising products to consumers are based, in part, on assumptions about how consumers' attitudes, beliefs, and behaviors are changing. In other words, business decisions are often predicated on assumptions about *trends* in American values and lifestyles.

Spotting Trends

Advertisers spot trends in values in at least four ways:

1. *Personal Observation.* Some advertising executives believe that spotting trends is simply a matter of observing what others are doing. They ask friends, neighbors, and acquaintances what they think, buy, read, watch, and listen to. In addition, they comb the popular press, books, and other literature to see what others say is happening.
2. *Qualitative Research.* Qualitative research, such as focus group discussions and in-depth interviews with "real people," is an extremely popular way businesses monitor what is going on in society.
3. *Trend Experts.* Another approach is to let experts identify trends. These "gurus" often use personal observation and qualitative research for much of their "expertise."
4. *Periodic Measurement.* The fourth approach is to survey large and representative samples of the population over time. These surveys typically include a lengthy battery of questions about people's attitudes, interests, and behavior on a wide range of subjects.

One such survey is the Lifestyle Study conducted by DDB Needham Worldwide. This survey, conducted annually since 1975, is made up as a sample of 4000 men and women nationwide.

Respondents are asked over 1000 questions on their attitudes and opinions on diverse topics, the activities in which they participate, the kinds of products and services they use, their media habits, and demographics.

Real Trends, Imaginary Trends

The first three approaches to spotting trends—personal observation, qualitative research, and trend experts—have one important element in common. All three depend on *stories.* Trend spotters who employ their own

AD 1
The Betty Crocker "Sweet Talker" campaign. (Courtesy of DDB Needham Worldwide).

personal observations depend on stories they tell to themselves. Moderators of focus groups and in-depth interviews, as well as trend gurus, depend mostly on stories others have told to them.

The benefit of stories is that they produce fascinating ideas and hypotheses that are easy to believe. An example comes from a brief excerpt from a *Newsweek* story about the Midwest:

> Kathy and Jack Ellis were not thrilled about moving to the Midwest from suburban New Jersey three years ago.
>
> Besides being separated from family and friends, there was the culture shock to consider. "My image was bib overalls," says Kathy, "that sort of thing."
>
> Now, Kathy and Jack can hardly say a bad word about Kansas City. When Jack returns home from a business trip back East, he feels as if he were going on vacation. "I take a big breath. I make a big sigh. It's just so wonderful to be back home."
>
> *Newsweek* (December 19, 1988).

On the basis of this and other stories, *Newsweek* concluded that the

Heartland is Hot!

This type of coherent detail makes us believe that the story must be true. We may even know people like Kathy and Jack. We are ready to believe that there is a trend towards more people moving to the Midwest and embracing heartland values and lifestyles.

The trouble with relying solely on stories to spot trends, however—be they from personal observation, qualitative research, or trend gurus—is that they often cannot distinguish real trends from imaginary trends. As convincing as the story is of Kathy's and Jack's love of Kansas City, it hardly constitutes a trend toward Midwest migration. A careful and systematic analysis of population changes conducted by the U.S. Census indicates that at the time the story was written metropolitan areas were growing everywhere *except* in the Midwest! Thus, the news magazine provided an excellent example of what might be called an imaginary trend.

Stories cannot help us distinguish real trends from imaginary trends because the samples are small and unrepresentative and there is no reliable history to compare with current findings. Sometimes an observation that appears to be a trend is just a unique and impressive case. Other times, the trend has been present all along but has gone unnoticed.

Compared to stories, periodic measurement has one unquestionable benefit: *accuracy*. Trends reported from periodic measurement rely on *data* drawn from large, representative samples of the population. Unfortunately, data—with its tables of percentages and clinical-looking trend lines—are less exciting and memorable than a well-told story. Nevertheless, periodic measurement provides the degree of accuracy advertising decision makers need.

Here are some other examples of trends generated from stories and posited by trend experts. Some of them are supported by periodic measurement, some are not.

Family Dinners. Many trend experts have said that today's family is so abuzz with activity that, as one expert put it, "it is nearly impossible for fam-

AD 2
The Rubbermaid "Workout" campaign. (Courtesy of DDB Needham Worldwide).

ilies to sit down together for dinner." Accordingly, some advertisers have portrayed family dinners as hit-or-miss affairs and have positioned their products as catering to this on-the-go lifestyle. Unfortunately, such advertising and product positioning may miss the mark.

According to the DDB Needham Lifestyle Study, 75 percent of Americans say their family "usually eats dinner together." Similar results have been obtained from surveys conducted by *The New York Times/CBS News* and *The Los Angeles Times.* Although this percentage has declined since 1975, the descent has not been as dramatic, nor the level as low, as some trend experts would have us believe.

Another supposedly widespread trend is "grazing," that is, eating small, quick meals on the run. Often these meals consist of foods normally thought of as snacks or appetizers. Sometimes grazing means skipping meals altogether and simply snacking during odd moments of the day. Many products positioned in advertising as "meals-on-the-run" for the time-pressed consumer are attempting to cash in on this trend. But can advertisers take this trend to the bank? Perhaps not.

First, the percentage of people who regularly eat breakfast, lunch, and dinner is pretty much the same today as it was in the early and mid-1980s.

Looking more closely at lunch, a time when grazing is said to be quite popular, the percentage of people who say they often skip lunch or just have a light snack at noon is not increasing at all, but is *declining*. There is no doubt that people are grazing. Some people may even graze a lot. But grazing hardly appears to be as large a social phenomenon as we may have heard.

Finally, only about one person out of three admits to eating mini-meals made up of snacks and appetizers—a percentage that is flat for women and declining for men.

Advertising strategy and advertising copy based on assumptions about trends easily can go wrong. Inaccurate estimates of the magnitude and direction of a trend can produce advertising campaigns that don't "ring true" to the target customer. Conversely, accurate estimates of the magnitude and direction of trends can greatly improve the chances of a successful advertising campaign.

Details. Details.

The above cases do not mean that all trends reported by the news media or offered up by trend "experts" are imaginary. Many are "real." For example, the news media and many trend experts have frequently highlighted the effects of inflation on consumer attitudes. In the DDB Needham Lifestyle Study, this effect also is easy to see.

As inflation grew in the late 1970s and early 1980s, people expressed deep concern about making ends meet. As inflation cooled during the remainder of the 1980s, so too did people's worries about losing their nest egg.

When trends are relatively easy to detect, periodic measurement can add important details on exactly how and among whom they are at work. For example, many media discussions of "the working woman" have remarked on how employment has affected the time available to prepare meals at home. The DDB Needham Lifestyle Study also has uncovered this trend, as shown by the steady increase among women who agree with the statement "Meal preparation should take as little time as possible."

Much of the media focus of this subject assumes that the increase in

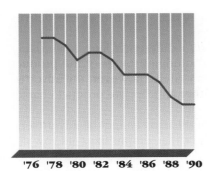

GRAPH 1
Our whole family usually eats dinner together.

this sentiment is due solely to the increase in the number of working women who must meet the demands of both their families and their jobs.

Yet, when we separate working women from homemakers, we see that sharply increasing proportions of women in *both* segments are seeking to reduce the amount of time spent on preparing meals.

The Unnoticed Trend

Possibly the most important contribution of periodic measurement is revealing a trend that was previously unnoticed but is both important and real. An advertiser that discovers such a trend has a decided advantage over the competition.

Let's put ourselves in the shoes of an advertising agency executive in charge of advertising a client's new line of healthy, microwaveable entrees. We know that during the 1970s and 1980s consumer concern about food and its relationship to health grew dramatically. As such, we are developing an advertising campaign that emphasizes the line's all natural, vitamin- and protein-rich, low-sodium food.

However, an unnoticed but real trend we may have missed is that some of the food concerns that were growing dramatically are now temporarily on hold or, in some instances, have been reversed.

The proportion of people who say they try to avoid foods with a high salt content reached its peak in the mid-1980s and has declined somewhat since.

Natural and additive-free foods have lost some of their appeal. Further, the proportion of people who try to select foods that are fortified with vitamins, minerals, and protein has steadily decreased throughout the second half of the 1980s.

Therefore, an advertising campaign based on the assumption that concerns about salt, additives, and vitamins would continue to increase would not reflect what is really going on.

All this is not to say that health and nutrition are no longer important issues for Americans. They are. Concern about cholesterol is growing, people are avoiding fat, and a high-fiber diet continues to be an important issue for many Americans.

These trends provide valuable knowledge about the environment in which advertising for nutritious products will appear. For example, an advertiser may decide to shift the emphasis from "all natural and low in sodium" to "low in fat and cholesterol," areas of increasing interest to

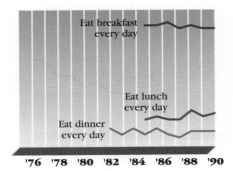

GRAPH 2
I eat breakfast/lunch/dinner every day.

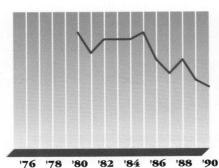

GRAPH 3
At noontime, I often skip lunch or just have a light snack.

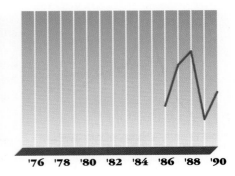

GRAPH 4
I find myself eating meals made up of food I would normally consider to be snacks or appetizers.

consumers. (Of course, this strategy assumes that the product can deliver the low-fat, low-cholesterol attributes.)

Or, the advertiser may decide to take a different route. Advertising copy can still refer to the all-natural, low-sodium attributes of the product line. In light of consumer trends in these two areas, however, the advertising may place greater emphasis on some other appropriate product characteristic, such as "superb taste."

These various advertising strategies might also change the advertiser's competition. The competition for a product that emphasizes its low-fat, low-cholesterol benefits may be other "diet" meals. With a strategy that focuses primarily on taste, the competition may be premium-priced, nondiet meals. Likewise, different strategies would call for different target audiences for the advertising. A "nutrition" advertising strategy might focus on older consumers who are concerned by their intake of fat and cholesterol. A taste strategy might be aimed at middle-aged consumers who are fussy about the taste of microwaveable entrees.

Beware of Pitfalls

It is important to emphasize that trend watching is not a solution for all advertising problems. Even when the data being analyzed are drawn from periodic measurement, the preferred choice, the marketer must beware of certain pitfalls.

First, the advertiser must realize that *attitudes can be put into action in many different ways.* Specific behaviors, such as buying a particular product, do not always follow general attitudes or values. For example, even though a large majority of Lifestyle respondents say they "like to buy new and different things," new product success rates are only about 10 percent. Simply being new isn't enough; the product has to satisfy a real consumer need.

A second point to which the advertiser must be sensitive is that *many things can come between an attitude and behavior.* The growing consumer interest in dietary fiber has not translated into huge market shares for those cereals that are *very* high in fiber. Although possessing the property that consumers seem to want—a lot of fiber—many high-fiber cereals simply do not taste as good as lower-fiber, sweeter cereals. Thus, "taste" has

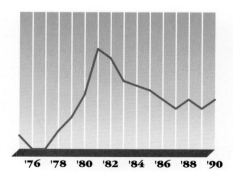

GRAPH 5
No matter how fast our income goes up, we never seem to get ahead.

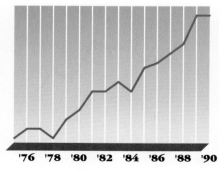

GRAPH 6
Meal preparation should take as little time as possible (women only).

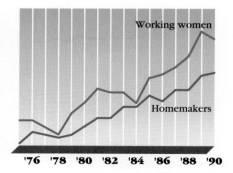

GRAPH 7
Meal preparation should take as little time as possible (working women vs. homemakers).

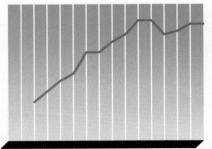

GRAPH 8
I try to avoid foods with a high salt content.

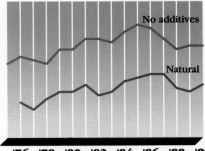

GRAPH 9
I try to avoid foods that have additives in them and I try to eat natural foods most of the time.

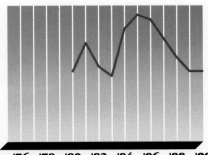

GRAPH 10
I try to select foods that are fortified with vitamins, minerals, and protein.

come between the attitude—a desire for high-fiber foods—and the behavior—the purchase of high-fiber cereals.

Finally, the advertiser should be aware that *trends can reverse at any time.* We have already seen a reversal of some major trends in diet and nutrition. Yesterday's trends are no guarantees of tomorrow's product triumphs.

If specific behaviors do not always follow trends in attitudes, or if social trends do not always parallel business trends, why do advertisers think it still is important to monitor trends?

The reason is simple. The savvy advertiser knows how to avoid, or at least be sensitive to, the pitfalls listed above. Having solid trend information at your disposal, even with its limitations, is a much more desirable alternative to having no trend information, or worse, having trend "information" that is largely or even partly wrong.

Almost all facets of marketing—including advertising, promotion, packaging, and price—are a form of communicating to a target consumer. The better advertisers know their targets, the more effectively they can communicate with them. Trend information about consumers' values and lifestyles provides advertisers with a much more detailed and thorough understanding of the target market than unaided judgment could provide. That knowledge can greatly increase the chances for campaigns that speak directly to what is on consumers' minds.

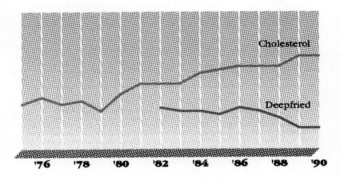

GRAPH 11
I try to avoid foods that are high in cholesterol and prepared deep-fried food.

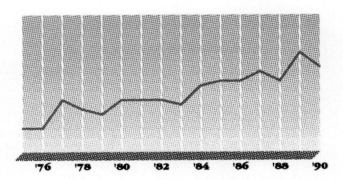

GRAPH 12
I make a special effort to eat enough fiber (bran) in my diet.

6

Strategic Research

Chapter Objectives

When you have completed this chapter, you should be able to:

- Explain the difference between qualitative and quantitative research
- Identify sources of exploratory research in government departments, trade associations, secondary and primary research suppliers, and advertisers' and agencies' research departments
- Develop a research program using the five parts of a strategy document
- Distinguish between primary and secondary research
- Understand how and when to use the six basic research methods: surveys, experiments, observation, content analysis, in-depth interviews, and focus groups
- Understand how research is used in the development of the creative message

COPPER MOUNTAIN'S RESEARCH ODYSSEY

During the 1986 ski season Copper Mountain Resort near Denver, Colorado, experienced a sharp decline in its number of front-range day skiers—skiers who came for the day from Colorado Springs, Boulder, and Denver. One possible reason for the decline was that skiing in general was losing out to other forms of outdoor recreation, not only at Copper Mountain, but everywhere. In that case, the managers of Copper Mountain might have wanted to join industry programs intended to lure people back to skiing; they did not have the resources to solve a problem of this size alone.

Another possibility was that Copper Mountain was losing share of the Denver-area ski business to Keystone and Breckenridge, Copper Mountain's closest neighbors. In that case, Copper Mountain's managers would have wanted to identify the reasons for the defections and see what they could do to regain the lost business.

Still another possibility was that the whole Denver ski area was losing skiers to Vail or Steamboat or to new resorts in Utah or California. If so, Copper Mountain would have wanted to know whether the problem was centered in Vail or Steamboat, or in Utah or California, or possibly in some combination of all four. If so, they would have wanted to join Keystone and Breckenridge in efforts to persuade skiers to ski near Denver instead.

Copper Mountain's managers had a lot of information available to guide their planning. Government surveys and forecasting studies and surveys and studies sponsored by the ski industry provided trend data on number and destinations of ski trips, attitudes toward skiing, and comparisons among skiing and other major forms of outdoor recreation. These surveys and studies could provide clues as to whether skiing was declining in popularity and what activities were replacing it. The surveys would also help identify the geographic, psychographic, and demographic groups among whom the declines were most precipitous, as well as provide some provisional assessment of the reasons why.

To supplement this very useful information Copper Mountain used findings from its own research program, which included an annual mail survey among past and potential customers. This survey asked questions about skiing practices and preferences, about skiing conditions and facilities at Copper Mountain and its principal competitors, and about reasons for choosing one skiing destination over another. In conjunction with the surveys by government and industry sources, this information could help Copper Mountain's managers determine where and why they were losing business.

Copper Mountain also conducted between 2,000 and 3,000 "chairlift" interviews each year—that is, interviewers rode the chairlift asking about skiing habits and preferences, about whether customers were skiing more or less this year than in previous years and why, about the skiing conditions, facilities, and personnel at Copper Mountain and its major competitors, and about awareness of and reaction to Copper Mountain's advertising and marketing programs. Finally, Copper Mountain sponsored periodic focus-group discussions with local skiers. These free-ranging in-depth interviews covered topics as specific as individual Copper Mountain advertisements and as general as the emotional reactions evoked by the skiing experience. They were also an important source for generating and testing campaign themes.

Taken together, the data collected from these surveys and interviews provided much food for thought. First, and most importantly, the findings supported management's initial belief that the decline in business was greatest among front-range day skiers and that front-range day skiers were but one of three important segments of the business, the other two being those skiers who spent a week or more at the resort and those who came to Copper Mountain from Keystone or Breckenridge in search of new skiing experiences.

The Copper Mountain surveys did point to a specific and potentially solvable problem close to home. Many skiers, especially front-range day skiers, said that although Copper Mountain was well known as a "skier's mountain," it was perceived as lacking the night life of its nearby competitors. At Copper Mountain the skiing was great, but there wasn't much to do after sundown. The surveys also indicated that cost was becoming an increasingly important factor.

Finally, Copper Mountain's surveys showed that although Keystone and Breckenridge did take shares of Copper Mountain's business, they also *contributed* to that business because many of Copper Mountain's day skiers came from Keystone or Breckenridge. More importantly, the surveys disclosed that the variety offered by the three different resorts attracted a significant number of highly profitable customers who might otherwise have gone to Utah or California.

This information was used in developing new advertising. The resort's previous campaign, called "Share Our Secret," had focused on Copper Mountain's already high reputation as a skier's mountain. The new campaign was called "White Hot" and featured plenty of downhill powder, but also provided for a shift in emphasis depending on the advertisement's intended audience (see Ad 6.1).

When the White Hot and Share Our Secret concepts were both presented to focus groups, the vote went to "Share Our Secret" because the campaign focused more single-mindedly on the skiing experience. When the White Hot concept was paired with a vivid illustration of a downhill skier, however, respondents said, "Oh, look at all that powder! I won't be disappointed if I go to ski there." Further, when references to night life were increased, responses became even more enthusiastic.

AD 6.1
One of the ads from Copper Mountain's White Hot campaign. (Courtesy of Copper Mountain Resort.)

Since the introduction of the White Hot campaign, Copper Mountain's ongoing research program has shown high awareness of the advertising and increases in the number of both front-range day skiers and longer-term visitors—all during a period when business in other areas was down dramatically.*

RESEARCH: THE QUEST FOR INTELLIGENCE

If an advertising agency were a factory, the products coming out the back door would be advertisements and media purchases. The raw material going in the front door would be information. Information is the basic ingredient from which all advertisements and all media purchases are made.

This information comes from two major sources. The first and most important source is the collective business and personal experience of the advertiser and the advertising agency. In the Copper Mountain case, for example, all of Copper Mountain's top executives had previous experience in the ski business. They also spent a great deal of their own time talking to managers of other resorts, both ski and nonski, such as cruise lines and amusements parks, reading about skiing and ski resorts, talking to customers, and communicating with their employees and with one another about management and planning problems. Many of Copper Mountain's managers were skiers themselves.

Every advertising campaign has similar personal input. For example, Shirley Polykoff, the copywriter who created the award-winning "Does she or doesn't she?" campaign for Clairol hair coloring, recounted this experience:

> In 1933, just before I was married, my husband had taken me to meet the woman who would become my mother-in-law. When we got in the car after dinner, I asked him, "How'd I do? Did your mother like me?" and he told me his mother had said, "She paints her hair, doesn't she?" He asked me, "Well do you?" It became a joke between my husband and me; anytime we saw someone who was stunning or attractive we'd say, "Does she or doesn't she?" Twenty years later, I was walking down Park Avenue talking out loud to myself, because I have to hear what I write. The phrase came into my mind again. Suddenly I realized, "That's it. That's the campaign."†

focus group *A group interview that tries to stimulate people to talk candidly about some topics or products.*

marketing research *Research that investigates all the elements of the marketing mix.*

market research *Research that gathers information about specific markets.*

The second source of information is formal research—surveys; in-depth interviews; **focus groups,** which are like in-depth interviews but involve a group rather than individuals, and all types of primary and secondary data. **Marketing research** is used to identify consumer needs, develop new products, evaluate pricing levels, assess distribution methods, and test the effectiveness of various promotional strategies. One type of marketing research, called **market research,** is much more specific and is used to gather information about a specific market. Although information of this sort plays a major role in every major advertising campaign, it is always assimilated into, combined with, altered by, and sometimes even overwhelmed by the professional and personal experiences of the writers, producers, and art directors who create the advertising and by the business

*Adapted from Joseph Hydholm, "Retaining Heat: Research and a Strong Marketing Program Keep Copper Mountain's Business Hot," *Quirks's Marketing Research Review* (March 1991):6–7, 40–41.
†Paula Champa, "The Moment of Creation," *Agency* (May–June 1991):31–37.

and personal experiences of the marketing executives who approve that advertising. Advertising is never the product of personal experience alone, however. Even as brilliant an inspiration as Shirley Polykoff's recollection of a 20-year-old experience was no doubt checked against the experiences of others and subjected to various forms of testing before it ever appeared in a magazine. All advertising campaigns are complex blends of fact and fiction, judgment, experience, inspiration, speculation, science, magic, and art.

Exploratory Research

exploratory research *Informal intelligence gathering, backgrounding.*

Exploratory research is informal intelligence gathering. When advertising people get a new account or a new assignment, they start by reading everything that is available on the product, company, and industry: sales reports, annual reports, complaint letters, and trade articles about the industry. What you are looking for with exploratory research is the problem —a problem that ultimately might demand more formal research and, perhaps, the development of a new strategy.

In an advertising agency the end users of exploratory research are the writers, art directors, and producers who create the advertisements and the media planners and buyers who select the media through which those advertisements reach the public. Before these end users begin their tasks, however, a great many other professionals play important roles in gathering, editing, and organizing research information. Among the most important are those professionals who work for government departments, trade associations, secondary research suppliers, primary research suppliers, and the research departments of advertisers and advertising agencies.

Government Organizations. Through its various departments the U.S. government provides an astonishing array of statistics that can be of great importance in making advertising and marketing decisions. Those statistics include census records and estimates of the U.S. population's size and geographical distribution, as well as highly detailed data on the population's age, income, occupational, educational, and ethnic segments. Demographic information of this kind is fundamental to decision making about advertising targets and market segmentation. An advertiser cannot aim its advertising at a target audience without knowing that audience's size and major dimensions.

In addition to basic population statistics, the U.S. government issues thousands of reports on topics of great interest to advertisers. For instance, the government publishes reports on food labeling and advertising, regulation of alcohol and tobacco marketing, auto safety, and sales and marketing of farm products and financial services. Table 6.1 offers a sampling of reports that can be obtained from the U.S. government.

Many state governments issue reports on the status of in-state business as well as trend data on business development, construction, tourism, education, retailing, and medical services. These reports, which would include information on tourism, ski resorts, and recreational facilities, would help Copper Mountain measure its performance against the performance of its competitors.

Foreign governments provide information roughly parallel to the information issued by the U.S. government. In other countries that information is just as useful as it is in the United States and is essential in planning and executing multinational advertising.

TABLE 6.1
U.S. Government Reports of Interest to Advertisers

Survey of Current Business: Basic operational statistics on U.S. business. (Bureau of Economic Analysis of the U.S. Department of Commerce)

Requirements of Laws and Regulation Enforced by the U.S. Food and Drug Administration: Laws and regulations affecting food and beverage advertising. (U.S. Department of Health and Human Services, Food and Drug Administration)

Economic Issues: How Should Health Claims for Foods Be Regulated? Regulation of health claims in food advertising. (Bureau of Economics, Federal Trade Commission)

Children's Information Processing of Television Advertising: How children react to television commercials. (National Technical Information Service, U.S. Department of Commerce)

Food Consumption: Households in the United States, Seasons and Year 1977–78, released in 1983: Detailed data on consumption of a wide range of foods. (Human Nutrition Information Service, U.S. Department of Agriculture)

Guidelines for Relating Children's Ages to Toy Characteristics: Rules that govern toy advertising. (U.S. Consumer Product Safety Commssion)

Vital and Health Statistics: Smoking and Other Tobacco Use: Consumption of tobacco products. (U.S. Department of Health and Human Services, National Center for Health Statistics)

Franchising in the Economy: Statistical review of franchised businesses. (U.S. Department of Commerce International Trade Administration)

Trade Associations. Many industries support trade associations that gather and distribute information of interest to association members. For instance, the American Association of Advertising Agencies (AAAA) issues reports on *The Advertising Agency of the Future, Patterns of Agency Compensation, Case Studies in Effective Advertising, Managing Your Agency for Profit, Executive Compensation and Employee Benefits, Analysis of Agency Costs,* and *Types of Insurance Carried by Agencies.* The major consumers of such reports are advertising agencies themselves, which use them in making salary and staffing decisions, monitoring their own performance, and keeping tabs on competitors. However, much of this information would also be useful to research suppliers, personnel recruiters, advertising media companies, and anyone else to whom advertising agencies are important customers. In a direct-marketing program designed to sell a service to agency executives, for example, basic knowledge of the industry would guide selection of the target to be addressed, the pricing and design of the service itself, and even the choice of words used to describe the offer.

As background for its own advertising and marketing decisions, Copper Mountain had access to a series of reports entitled *Sports Participation,* issued by the National Sporting Goods Association, *American Teenagers and Sports Participation,* issued by the Athletic Footwear Associations, and *Cost of Doing Business Survey for Ski Shops,* issued by the National Ski Retailers Association. Other major trade associations include the Radio Advertising Bureau, which publishes *Radio Facts,* an overview of the commercial radio industry in the United States; the Association of Home Appliance Manufacturers, which conducts research and reports industry statistics; the American Meat Institute, which publishes *Meat Facts,* an annual statistical review of the industry; the American Paper Institute, which gathers, compiles, and disseminates current information on the paper industry; and the National Soft Drink Association, which publishes *NSDA News* every month, covering legislative issues affecting soft-drink bottlers and suppliers to the soft-drink industry.

secondary research *Information that has been compiled and published.*

Secondary Research Suppliers.

Considering the overwhelming amount of information available from government reports, trade associations, and other sources of marketing data, it is not surprising that a mini-industry has sprung up to gather and organize this information around specific topic areas. Because this information was originally collected by some other organization (and usually for some other purpose), the research is called **secondary research,** and the firms that collect and organize the information are called *secondary research suppliers.* The two most important secondary research suppliers are FIND/SVP and Off-The-Shelf Publications, Inc.

In addition to firms that provide written reports, a new breed of secondary research supplier now provides information via computer terminal. Among the most important of these on-line vendors are Dialog Information Services, Inc., Lexis/Nexis, Dow Jones News/Retrieval, and Market Analysis and Information Database, Inc. With a connection to Dialog Information Service, Copper Mountain's managers could have used Dialog's Marketing and Advertising Information Service to access information on competitors' sales, market shares, and marketing activities. They could have used the Donnelley Demographics data base to retrieve mobility, housing, education, income, population, and household information for the local area and for other areas that might be sources of customers. The Prompt data base could have been used to identify hot trends in the leisure market in general and in the skiing industry in particular.

Primary Research Suppliers.

Much of the information that ultimately appears in the form of advertisements or media purchases is gathered by research firms that specialize in interviewing, observing, and recording the behavior of those who purchase, or influence the purchase of, industrial and consumer goods and services. Firms that collect and analyze this kind of **primary research** are called *primary research suppliers.*

primary research *Information that is collected from original sources.*

The primary research supplier industry is extremely diverse. The companies range from A. C. Nielsen, which employs more than 45,000 workers in the United States alone, to several thousand one-person entrepreneurs who conduct focus groups and individual interviews, prepare reports, and provide advice on specific advertising and marketing problems. The most comprehensive listing of primary research suppliers is the *International Directory of Marketing Research Companies and Services,* published by the American Marketing Association (AMA). Copper Mountain has relied heavily on primary research, information that is proprietary. Most of this research is conducted by an independent research firm specializing in the ski and leisure-time industry and is directed by a market research manager.

PRINCIPLE
Secondary research is information that has already been compiled for you; primary research is information you find out yourself.

Many advertising agencies subscribe to very large-scale surveys conducted by the Simmons Market Research Bureau (SMRB) or by Mediamark Research, Inc. (MRI). The surveys conducted by these two organizations employ large samples of American consumers (approximately 30,000 for each survey) and include questions on consumption or possession of a very wide range of products and services and usage of all the major advertising media. The products and services covered in the MRI survey range from toothbrushes and dental floss to diet colas and bottled water to camping equipment and theme parks.

Strictly speaking, both SMRB and MRI are secondary data sources; they are primarily intended to be used in media planning, which will be discussed in detail in Chapter 9. Because these surveys are so comprehensive, however, they can be mined for consumer information. Through a computer program called Golddigger, for example, an MRI subscriber can select a consumer target and ask the computer to find all the other products and services and all the media that members of the target segment use more than do consumers in general. The resulting profile provides a vivid and detailed description of the target as a person—just the information agency creatives need to help them envision their audiences.

Advertisers' Research Departments. Almost all large advertisers maintain marketing research departments of their own. These departments collect and disseminate secondary research data and conduct concept tests, product tests, test markets, package and pricing tests, and attitude and usage studies—all types of large- and small-scale consumer explorations. The immediate "clients" of advertisers' marketing research departments are the top officers of their respective companies and the line-product managers who are responsible for the pricing, promotion, advertising, distribution, sales, and profit of their brands. As we will discuss later in this chapter, much of this information ultimately finds its way into advertising.

The marketing research department of the Oscar Mayer Foods Corporation provides a good example. Oscar Mayer's marketing research department is divided into two groups: brand research and marketing systems analysis. The brand research group conducts primary and secondary consumer research and sales analysis, serves as a marketing consultant to product managers, reports and interprets broad consumer trends, and works on projects intended to improve marketing research methods. The marketing systems analysis group performs sales analyses based on shipment and store-scanner data, supports computer users within the marketing and sales departments, and manages Oscar Mayer's marketing information center.*

The product's performance, the performance and marketing activities of competing products, and the needs, wants, values, and attitudes of consumers are essential input to the strategy document described later in this chapter. For many advertising campaigns, the advertiser's marketing research department is the key source of such intelligence. Often this department is also responsible for one other activity that directly affects the marketer's advertising: It either conducts or supervises the testing procedures that determine whether an advertising campaign should run. These testing procedures, often called *copy tests,* are discussed in detail in Chapter 21. Copy tests are of great importance to the advertiser because they determine which advertising messages do and do not reach the public. They are therefore directly responsible for the success or failure of the advertising program.

Copy tests are possibly even more important to the advertising agency. In the course of developing a campaign an agency will create many alternatives, some or all of which may be tested by the advertiser's testing system. If that system rejects much of the work submitted, the account can require so much extra work that the agency cannot make a profit on it. Even more importantly, the agency's creative reputation (and the careers of its writers, art directors, and producers) depends on the ads that get through the testing system. Any system that persistently rejects the agency's "best" creative efforts is certain to become an object of bitter controversy.

The Inside Advertising box recounts a day in the life of professional researcher Jack Stratton, director of Consumer Research Services at General

---

*Charlie Etmekjian and John Grede, "Marketing Research in a Team-Oriented Business: The Oscar Mayer Approach," *Marketing Research: A Magazine of Management Applications* vol. *2,* no. 4 (December 1990):6–12.

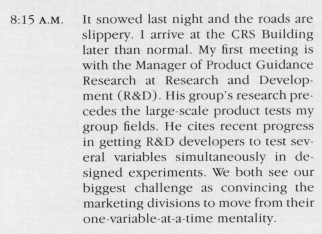

JACK STRATTON, DIRECTOR, CONSUMER RESEARCH SERVICES, GENERAL MILLS, INC.

8:15 A.M. It snowed last night and the roads are slippery. I arrive at the CRS Building later than normal. My first meeting is with the Manager of Product Guidance Research at Research and Development (R&D). His group's research precedes the large-scale product tests my group fields. He cites recent progress in getting R&D developers to test several variables simultaneously in designed experiments. We both see our biggest challenge as convincing the marketing divisions to move from their one-variable-at-a-time mentality.

9:30 A.M. Make phone calls.

10:00 A.M. Meet with my client service reps for the breakfast cereal division. We discuss client feedback on recent projects. Seems each of the business units in the division wants its research results in a different format. Whatever happened to standardization?

10:30 A.M. I walk through the building, stopping to talk with employees I don't see regularly, especially those in data processing.

11:30 A.M. At my request, a quantitative analyst takes me through some data tables she presented yesterday at a meeting I missed.

12:00 NOON Lunch with my Manager of Stimulus Testing. We walk next door to the R&D cafeteria.

1:00 P.M. Review progress on annual objectives with the Manager of Quantitative Analysis. We agree to repackage one of our product-testing techniques and market it more aggressively.

2:00 P.M. An outside supplier presents a new concept-testing method. It has advantages over what we can offer, but the price is steep. We are noncommittal about whether we will steer some business their way.

3:00 P.M. Read through in-basket.

3:30 P.M. The Vice President of Marketing Services (my boss) and the Director of Advertising come to CRS for an update on our copy-testing methods. We explain the mechanics of the adult and kid methods. The discussion quickly shifts to very fundamental issues. Are we "slavishly" following a system without understanding how the advertising really works? Is persuasion more important than recall? The session runs an hour late. Our visitors gain a better sense of how we test. We learn of recent examples where our findings have been interpreted too rigidly by divisional marketing researchers.

5:30 P.M. I leave to pick up my son from basketball practice.

Source: Courtesy of Jack Stratton.

Mills. In this account we see persistent concerns about the methods used in various types of consumer research and attempts to make sure that General Mills' Consumer Research Department is serving the information needs of other departments in the company. At the end of this particular day, a 2-hour discussion took place, which centered on the never-ending uncertainties surrounding evaluative copy research: Are the research methods now in use serving the purposes for which they were designed? Or are they being misused in ways that might do more harm than good? These are very important questions to both the advertiser and the agency.

Even when an advertiser is not large enough to support a marketing research department of its own, the information generated in the course of marketing activities can play an important part in determining how that firm will communicate with the public. For example, while revising the marketing program for its line of plant containers, the Weathashade division of the Gale Group—a manufacturer of outdoor lawn and garden supplies based in Apopka, Florida—conducted focus groups with potential customers, in-store observations of plant container purchasers, and both in-person and telephone interviews with retailers and distributors. This research led to the following recommendations:

- Integrate the indoor and outdoor offering under one umbrella, but develop a brand, name, and merchandising system in which either brand can stand alone.
- Take advantage of the planned purchase behavior and develop emotional appeals to both the novice and the expert gardener.
- Emphasize size, durability, and fade resistance in the outdoor offering. Emphasize size, color, style, value, and quality in the indoor offering. Emphasize lifestyle and performance convenience for both lines.
- Because of the potential opportunity, Weathashade should be the first company to create major brand recognition in this product category.
- The packaging and merchandising system will increase sales by creating excitement, attracting attention, stimulating interest with product ideas, and suggesting lifestyles. Information should be provided to maintain interest and aid purchase but this information should avoid being highly technical.
- The system should create a selling environment to take advantage of space through efficient stacking, to display the product, and to increase brand presence and awareness. A small on-product label denoting pot size and usage should be explored to reinforce brand awareness in the absence of the full merchandising system. Unique free-standing merchandisers could be incorporated into the design. The merchandising system must be flexible enough to allow use of one component, of multiple components, or of any combination.*

When these recommendations were followed, sales increased over 200 percent, surpassing even the most optimistic expectations. Thus strategic research, translated into effective communication, produced impressive results even in the absence of a budget that could support advertising in national magazines or on network television.

Advertising Agency Research Departments.   In the 1950s all the major advertising agencies featured large, well-funded, highly professional research departments. Agencies highlighted their research power in new-business presentations, and had a list been made of the most respected leaders in the advertising research field at that time, many of the names on that list would have been found on agency research department payrolls.

One of the reasons for this prominence was that profit margins in the 1950s allowed the agencies to provide expensive and impressive advertising and marketing research at no extra cost to their clients. Another was that many advertisers' own marketing research departments were relatively underdeveloped. In some cases, such as the Maxwell House Division of Gen-

---

*"Growing Indoors: Research Helps Makers Of Gardening Containers Expand," *Quirk's Marketing Research Review* (October 1990):6–7, 33–35.

eral Foods, the advertising agency research department supplied *all* the research used by the client.

In the 1960s both of these conditions began to change. Agency profit margins shrank to the level where agencies found it increasingly difficult to provide research at no extra cost. At the same time, partly as a result of agencies' declining research role, advertisers' own marketing research departments began to grow. By the end of the decade most major advertisers had developed effective research departments that bore primary responsibility for marketing research. In most cases, they took over the evaluative testing of advertisements as well.

Those trends continue today. Although some of the largest agencies, including Young and Rubicam, Grey Advertising, and the Leo Burnett Company, still invest heavily in their own research departments, others have sharply curtailed internal research activities and some have turned the research function over to account managers. Smaller agencies, which never had large research departments to begin with, now hire outside research suppliers on a case-by-case basis.

In those agencies that still have internal research departments, efforts now focus on projects that contribute directly to the development of advertising. These projects may range from two or three group interviews intended to show how consumers talk about a product or a brand, through small- or medium-scale surveys of consumers' opinions and attitudes concerning a specific product or service category, to relatively large-scale surveys, like the annual DDB Needham Lifestyle Study, intended to identify and measure activities, interests, and opinions within segments of the consumer population.

Those agencies that are too small to sustain internal research departments usually employ outside research suppliers when they need help. In some cases, these agency-supplier relationships become so productive that the supplier fulfills most of the roles of an internal research department even though it is not formally part of the firm.

Information Centers. All large advertising agencies, and even some relatively small ones, maintain specialized libraries (often called *information centers*) that provide access to reference volumes, such as dictionaries, encyclopedias, atlases, cookbooks, books of famous quotations, and trade and general newspapers and magazines. Writers, art directors, and producers use these sources when they need more information about a client, a product, or a brand, and when they are browsing in search of creative ideas. The information center is one of the most important features of the advertising agency research department. Even agencies that are not large enough to support a full-fledged research department usually have an information center of some kind. For a sample of the questions that come in to an information center, see Table 6.2.

Many information centers also maintain subject and picture files. Subject files contain clippings from magazines, newspapers, and government and trade reports, all classified by subject matter. The subjects may range from "advertisers," "airlines," "animal food," "auto care," and "baby market" to "video," "watch industry," "water softeners," "wine," and "women." Picture files may include "Americana," "amusements," "animals," "architecture," "art," "water," "waterfalls," "witches," "X-rays," and "zodiacs." The subject files provide quick synopses of subjects that may suddenly become important. The picture files provide images that jog creative work. Some of the pictures spark creative ideas and eventually inspire other pictures that finally appear in ads.

TABLE 6.2
A Sample of the Questions Answered by a Typical Advertising Agency Information Center

- What are the controversial issues involved in the Columbus Quincentennial celebration in 1992?
- Compile trends of the 1990s as they relate to diet and salt and the impact of salt on the environment.
- We plan to shoot in Sydney and northern Australia. What is the average temperature and rainfall there for mid-July? What are the famous places and landmarks?
- What information regarding the Fourth of July is available at the Information Center? I need both historic and fun ideas.
- I need pictures of birds flying in a flock, teens walking on a sandy beach, a close-up of shells on the beach, a close-up of a red rose, sand dunes with dramatic effect, and pictures of brightly dressed ladies—right away.
- Who are the leading marketers of frozen dinners and entrees? I need sales and market shares.
- Give me the number of families with children under 5 years old, the number of households with heads 25 to 45 years old, and the number of households with incomes over $25,000.
- What was the average Dow Jones Industrial Average in 1990?
- How much did Michael Jordan get for the Nike and Wheaties commercials? What was the package deal?
- Are people concerned about cholesterol in pancakes? Are people aware that pancakes have cholesterol? Do you have any articles on the Hungry Jack Panshakes?
- How many breakfast foods containing oats were introduced during the last 5 years?
- What is the weight of a hockey puck?
- How big is the foot-powder market?
- We need pictures of Simon and Garfunkel, the cast of *The Mary Tyler Moore Show*, President Jimmy Carter and his family, and the 1980 U.S. National Hockey Team. We also need their bios.
- We need pictures of brand characters—the original look and the revised ones. Examples: Betty Crocker, the Campbell Soup children, and the Morton Salt girl.

Many information centers are wired into Lexis, the Dow Jones Retrieval Service, and other computerized utilities that provide instant access to information in the general and trade press. To take just one example, a Lexis search on key words "Visa" and "1992 Olympics Sponsorship" might produce seven pages abstracting current articles on those related topics from *Mediaweek, Adweek's Marketing Week, Advertising Age, Euromarketing, ABA Banking Journal, Campaign, Bank Advertising News,* and *Tour and Travel News.* This file would give anyone interested in Visa's role in the 1992 Olympics a quick and current rundown on what is being written on the topic.

Who Organizes the Facts?

qualitative data *Research that seeks to understand how and why people think and behave as they do.*

quantitative data *Research that uses statistics to describe consumers.*

A typical advertising campaign might be influenced, directly or indirectly, by information from many sources, including the advertiser's marketing research department, one or more of the primary or secondary outside research suppliers, and the agency's research department itself. Surprisingly, the problem usually is not too little information, but too much. Someone must sift through the **qualitative data,** which seek to understand how and why consumers behave as they do, and the **quantitative data**—the numerical data such as exposures to ads, purchases, and other market-related events—that are available. This person must also separate the potentially relevant from the irrelevant material and put the outcome into a format that decision makers and creatives can use.

In advertising agencies with internal research departments that task usually falls to the research department staff. Indeed, the ability to organize huge amounts of information and to deliver that information in a useful form is one of the most important skills members of an advertising agency research department can have. In agencies without research departments the task of collecting and organizing information usually falls to members of the account group. Even in agencies with research departments members of the account group are likely to be highly involved in the final decisions as to what information will be passed on to those who will create the campaign. An account manager who is doing his or her job effectively will play a major role in every facet of the agency's work on his or her brand.

account planner *The person responsible for the creation, implementation, and modification of the strategy on which creative work is based.*

Account Planning. Boase Massimi Pollitt (BMP), an advertising agency in London, England, originated the concept of the **account planner,** a new way of thinking about the role of research within an advertising agency. Partly because of the consistently high recognition accorded to BMP's creative work, this concept has spread to other London agencies as well as to agencies in Europe, Asia, and the United States.

Charles Cannon, director of Studies at the Institute of Practitioners in Advertising, in London, defined account planning this way:

> The account planner is responsible for the creation, implementation, and modification of the strategy on which creative work is based. The planner will therefore be responsible for the generation, selection, and interposition of the research evidence at each stage of the advertising process, namely, in strategy development (such as the creation of the strategy), and in creative development (such as the implementation of the strategy), and in market evaluation (such as the assessment of effectiveness in the marketplace with a view to the maintenance or modification of the strategy for future work).

He went on to elaborate:

> (a) The core craft skill of planning is the translation of research evidence into advertising judgment.
> (b) In this sense, account planning is the integration of the research function into the account team.
> (c) Research relevant to advertising almost never speaks for itself and almost always requires interpretation which must be based on knowing about research *and* knowing about advertising, not one or the other on its own.*

When confronted with definitions of this kind, members of research departments of U.S. advertising agencies usually say, "That's what we've been doing all the time!" Indeed, if an advertising agency research department has not been performing many of these functions, it has probably ceased to exist.

Whether the information providers are called researchers, planners, or members of the account group, the most effective agency research parallels the planner model. Under one name or another, account planning is here to stay. The person who can pick out the most useful information from the suffocatingly large amount of data available, and who can make that information instantly relevant to the problem at hand, will always have an important role in the creative process.

*Charles Cannon, "The Role Of The Account Planner," paper presented at the Conference of the Institute of Canadian Advertising, London, England (June 1986).

THE STRATEGY DOCUMENT

The outcome of strategic research usually reaches agency creative departments in the form of a *strategy document* or *creative brief*. Although the exact form of this document differs from agency to agency and from advertiser to advertiser, most have five major parts: the marketing objective, the product, the target audience, the promise, and the brand personality.

Marketing Objective

The section of the document that deals with the marketing objective reviews the competitive situation and establishes a goal for the campaign. It includes both past and present sales figures; market shares of the brand and of its major competitors; competitors' advertising and promotional resources, tactics, and practices; and any other information about the brand that may lead to a prediction of early success or risk of failure. Although advertisers and agencies are acutely aware that marketing success depends on many factors besides advertising, advertisers do expect advertising to help them meet their marketing goals. It is therefore important that everyone involved in the development of the campaign understand exactly what those goals are. If the advertiser has an unspecified but totally unreasonable marketing objective, and the agency, through ignorance, implicitly agrees to meet that objective, the agency has unknowingly put itself in an extremely vulnerable position. In the strategy document the marketing objective should be specific; it should be agreed to at the outset.

AD 6.2
Research has found that two-thirds of MTV's audience are 18- to 34-year-olds, a fact the channel uses in its ads to attract advertisers interested in reaching a younger audience. (Courtesy of MTV Networks. © 1991 MTV Networks. All rights reserved. The MTV: MUSIC TELEVISION logo is a registered trademark of MTV Networks, a division of Viacom International Inc.)

The Product

The product section of the document includes the results of product tests, consumers' perceptions of the brand and its major competitors, and tests of or reactions to the brand's and its competitors' advertisements, promotions, retail displays, and packaging. In other words, any facts, opinions, perceptions, or reactions to the product that might fuel an advertising campaign are presented in this section of the strategy document.

The Target Audience

The next section of the document provides a demographic and psychographic description of the campaign's target audience. The demographic data come from secondary sources or from surveys that reveal the age, income, education, gender, and geographical distribution of the consumers who might be persuaded to adopt the brand. The psychographic information comes from attitude and opinion surveys, individual in-depth interviews, or focus groups, all of which help paint a portrait of the target as a person. The Lifestyle box entitled "Changes in Mothers of Children 2 Years of Age and Younger" examines how an advertiser attracts a specific target audience. Ad 6.2 for MTV is an example of an ad that is targeted at a specific audience.

Both the creative team, who must create communication, and the media planners, who must decide how and when to contact targets most efficiently, need to know as much as they can, in as much depth and detail as possible, about the people they are trying to reach.

Promise and Support

Advertising always promises some sort of reward the customer can obtain by buying or using the advertised product or service. This section of the strategy document tells writers and art directors which reward, out of many possibilities, the advertising should promise. The strategy document also indicates which facts about the product and its users are likely to make that promise most acceptable. Such insights into consumer motivations and purchasing decisions help solve the often difficult puzzle of selecting the most motivating promise and deciding how that promise will be supported.

Brand Personality

Brands, like people, have personalities. When a brand has a winning personality, its advertising should perpetuate and reinforce that personality. When a brand has a less than desirable personality, advertising should work to remedy the problem. Research that asks potential customers what the brand and its competitors would be like if they were people supplies the information needed to specify the brand's present personality and identifies the kind of improvements that are needed.

A strategy document is usually prefaced by a brief *strategy statement* that distills the document's main points. Following the strategy statement, the document itself presents the highlights of the most relevant research. Figure 6.1 is an example of a typical strategy statement.

Although formats vary considerably from advertiser to advertiser and from agency to agency, some way of conveying in writing what is known about the product, the brand, the competitive situation, and the prospective customer is as essential to an advertising campaign as a blueprint is to a construction project.

FIGURE 6.1
A strategy statement for milk.

1. Marketing Objective

Increase consumption of milk by members of the target audience by 10 percent.

2. The Product

Although milk is considered to be among the healthiest of beverages, milk drinking drops off sharply in the teenage years. Part of the problem is concern about fat and calories, part has to do with taste, and part has to do with milk's childish and unexciting image. Advertising can have its most direct effect on the image problem.

3. The Target Audience

Males and females 16 to 30 years old. Milk is a beverage they had to drink as children, and although they are still drinking it, they are choosing more often to drink other beverages. Milk has become less relevant to their lifestyle. They believe milk doesn't go as well with foods they like, such as pizza, Mexican cooking, and Oriental dishes. Females in particular are concerned about the calories and fat in milk.

Other beverages, such as soft drinks, are of greater interest to this group. Soft drinks are an exciting, versatile, and socially acceptable alternative to milk, which is practical, unexciting, and conservative.

These people are active and energetic. They want very much to be popular with their peers, to be attractive, and to look and feel fit.

4. Promise and Support

Today's milk can help you become the attractive, fun, dynamic person you want to be (promise). Milk has the nutrition your body needs to look and feel terrific. Today's most attractive and dynamic people drink milk. Ice-cold milk tastes great (support).

5. Brand Personality

Personality now: childish, practical, conservative. Needed personality: exuberant, contemporary, young adult.

MESSAGE DEVELOPMENT RESEARCH

For the sake of orderly exposition, it is convenient to speak as though research contributes to advertising in a logical, systematic, and linear way: Someone in the agency research department or the account group collects and organizes a vast array of facts, distills those facts into a strategy document, and hands that document over to previously uninformed writers and art directors, who then go off and create some advertising.

That impression is almost entirely wrong. Although facts do indeed play an important role in many advertising campaigns, they are always filtered through and evaluated against a system of ideas, experiences, prejudices, memories of past successes and failures, hierarchical relationships, and tastes and preferences within the advertiser's own company and within the advertising agency. Decisions as to what will go into the strategy document and how that document will be interpreted are never cut and dried.

Furthermore, as writers and art directors begin working on a specific creative project, they almost always conduct at least some informal research of their own. They may talk to friends—or even strangers—who might be in the target audience. They may visit retail stores, talk to salespeople, and watch people buy. They may visit the information center, browse through reference books, and borrow subject and picture files. They will conjure up old memories, as Shirley Polykoff did when thinking about the Clairol campaign. They will look at previous advertising (especially the competition's) to see what others have done, and in their heart of hearts they will become absolutely convinced that they are able to create something better than, and different from, anything that has been done before. This informal, personal research has a powerful influence on what happens later on.

CHANGES IN MOTHERS OF CHILDREN 2 YEARS OF AGE AND YOUNGER

How should a baby-food company modify its products and its advertising to attract today's young mothers? Or should it make any changes at all? One company commissioned a mail survey of women typical of Middle America; the study was designed to compare responses from a 1980 survey with those of 1989. Each participant in the research had at least one child 2 years of age or younger.

One major factor in the preferences of the 1989 respondents was the craze for healthy eating. These mothers felt that it's never too early to begin to eat healthy foods. They were quite receptive to buying baby foods that contain natural ingredients and are low in salt and cholesterol. Equally important, these respondents were willing to pay more for these products if necessary, even though they felt rather pinched for funds.

In contrast to the 1980 respondents, the 1989 mothers did not feel that their family income was sufficient to satisfy most of their important desires. In fact, one half of these mothers asserted that their families were already too heavily in debt. Fortunately, the newer mothers were optimistic that their family finances would improve markedly within 5 years.

Although the newer mothers didn't say that children are the most important element in a marriage, they did assert that in making family decisions, the children's needs should come first. This was a distinct difference from mothers in the prior decade. Compared to the mothers of 1980, the newer mothers weren't such fervent cooks and preferred that meal preparation require as little time as possible. The mothers themselves seemed to have healthier eating patterns than did the women in the earlier study. They were less likely to skip lunch, for example, or to feel they overate.

In general, the mothers of 1989 were seeking interesting, even adventurous, personal lives. Over the 9-year time span the more recent mothers were more likely to see themselves as people who would "try anything once." They bought on impulse and relished the fun of purchasing new products or different things for themselves and their families. However, they were just as concerned as the earlier mothers about checking on prices, shopping for specials, and making shopping lists before they set out. The newer mothers were also far less partial to store brands and instead tried to stick to well-known brand names. Unlike the earlier mothers, they did not feel that advertising insults the purchaser's intelligence, although both the 1980 and the 1989 mothers thought that advertising provides information that shapes better buying decisions.

The mothers of 1989 were more concerned with creating a distinctive appearance than were the earlier set of mothers, and they definitely wanted to feel attractive to males.

The women in the later survey were also more apt to feel that they worked hard and operated under a good deal of pressure. They didn't find much spare time in their days, and they were less likely to establish neighborhood friendships. Perhaps this was because a majority expected to be moving at least once within the next 5 years. All in all, they were not entirely content with their lives and would do things differently, given the chance.

Exercise: Now that you know something about how recent consumers, as compared to those of a decade earlier, feel about their lives, what kinds of research do you think might help you sharpen your advertising message?

Source: DDB Needham Worldwide, *Lifestyle Profile: Changes In Mothers Of Children 2 Years And Younger, 1980 vs. 1989* (July 1989).

Diagnostic Research and Concept Testing

diagnostic research *Research used to identify the best approach from among a set of alternatives.*

Diagnostic research is used to choose the best approach from among a set of alternatives. As creative ideas begin to take shape, writers and art directors bounce their ideas off each other and discuss them with their supervisors in the creative group. At this point, they may request some feedback from consumers, just to help them decide whether they are on the right track. **Concept testing** is the target audience's evaluation of alternative creative strategies. This feedback usually takes the form of loose, unstructured conversations with members of the target audience, either in individual interviews or in focus groups. Sometimes the people working on the advertising participate in these conversations; sometimes they only watch.

When advertising begins to approach a more finished form, diagnostic research becomes more clearly defined. Creative concepts are translated into rough comprehensives and storyboards—presentation pieces that show the artwork and print to be used in the final ad. Ideas begin to look more like print ads and television commercials. Consumers now have something specific to look at, and their reactions and evaluations to the concepts presented are taken more seriously.

Consumers aren't the only source of input at this stage, however. Supervisors within the creative department react favorably or unfavorably to early versions. Creative directors—the executives who are ultimately responsible for the agency's creative product—exercise editorial control. Creative review boards—groups of senior executives—might have the final word concerning what may and may not be submitted to the client.

In most cases, the advertiser also plays a part. Brand managers or their assistants review and comment on rough executions of the ad. They might request major changes. They might also pass the advertisement up the line so that higher-level executives can have input.

Whether from the agency or the client, these evaluations are all based on guesses about how consumers ultimately will react to the advertising. This is where diagnostic research can make a valuable contribution. Instead of *guessing* how prospects will interpret an advertisement, the agency and the advertiser can *hear* what real consumers think.

Contact Methods.   There are a number of ways to collect data from people. The contact can be in person, by telephone, or by mail. In a personal interview the researcher asks questions of the respondent in person. The questions can be either tightly structured in a questionnaire or they can be open-ended. Advertisers use *intercept surveys* to get a quick response on a strategy or creative idea. These interviews are often conducted in malls or downtown areas.

A telephone survey is used when the questions are relatively simple and the questionnaire is short. It is efficient and, depending on the number of interviewers, can reach many people quickly and easily. A mail survey can be longer and more in-depth than a telephone survey; however, it has to be absolutely clear because no interviewer is present to explain procedure or ambiguous questions.

Primary research data can be collected through a number of research methods. For example, you might conduct a survey to find out how many people prefer two-ply toilet paper. The results would be expressed *quantitatively* as a number and as a percentage of the total. If you also reported the spontaneous comments, or **verbatims,** given to explain the preference, then you would be reporting *qualitative* data.

Survey Research.   Several types of quantitative research are important in marketing and advertising. **Survey research** uses structured interview forms to ask large numbers of people the same questions. The questions can deal with personal characteristics, such as age, income, behavior, or at-

sample *A selection of people who are identified as representative of the larger population.*

experiments *A research method that manipulates a set of variables to test hypotheses.*

titudes. The people can be from an entire group, or **population,** or they can be a representative **sample** of a much larger group. Sampling uses a smaller number of people to represent the entire population.

Experimental Research. In **experiments** researchers attempt to manipulate one (and sometimes more than one) important variable while controlling all the other variables that might affect the outcome. For example, an agency might want to know which of two commercials works better for a particular audience. People who represent that audience would be divided into equivalent groups, and the first group would be shown one commercial while the second group would be shown the other. Both groups would then be questioned about whether they understood, liked, or were moved by the message. If the only important difference between the groups was the commercial, differences in response could be used to estimate which of the two commercials was more effective.

Direct Observation. Direct observation is a type of field research that takes researchers into a natural setting where they record the behavior of consumers. You might, for example, be asked to do an *aisle study* in a supermarket. Your assignment would be to note how people buy a particular product or brand. Do they deliberate or just grab a product and run? Do they compare prices? Do they read the labels? How long do they spend making the decision?

A pioneering study of the direct-observation technique concluded that "direct observation has the advantage of revealing what people actually do, as distinguished from what people say [they do]. It can yield the correct answer when faulty memory, desire to impress the interviewer, or simple inattention to details would cause an interview answer to be wrong."* The biggest drawback to direct observation is that it shows *what* is happening, but not *why*. Thus it is not very effective for evaluating attitudes and motives.

Content Analysis. Content analysis is a type of research that analyzes various dimensions of a message. In preparation for the development of a new advertising campaign, for example, the agency people might browse through magazines or listen to radio or television programming and code every advertisement by the competition. The print categories include such factors as size, use of color, type of layout, and type of headline. Television categories include length, number of scenes, use of music, types of shots, actors, characters, and product visuals. Content analysis can be used by advertising planners to suggest which message approaches have been most effective.

In-Depth Interview. A common type of qualitative research is the in-depth one-on-one interview. This technique is used to probe feelings, attitudes, and behaviors such as decision making. Because such interviews are not quantitative, researchers can't use statistical methods to project results to the consumer population. The insights, however, can be instructive about how a typical member of the target audience views some research question.

*William D. Wells and Leonard A. Lo Sciuto, "Direct Observation of Purchasing Behavior," *Journal of Marketing Research* (August 1966):227–33.

Focus groups have become increasingly important within the creative process.
(© 1987 by Prentice-Hall, Inc.)

Focus Groups. A **focus group** is another method used to structure quali-tative research. As we mentioned earlier, the focus group is like an in-depth interview, except that it involves a group rather than an individual. The ob-jective is to stimulate people to talk candidly about some topic with one an-other. The interviewer sets up a general topic and then lets conversation develop as group interaction takes over.

Perils of Qualitative Diagnosis. Although in-depth interviews and focus groups provide valuable feedback at early stages in the creative process, they are not without problems. The samples of consumers are usually very small, and they may not be truly representative of the whole audience. In the Copper Mountain case, for example, respondents living in the Denver area might underestimate many of the factors that encourage out-of-state skiers to choose Copper Mountain instead of California or Utah resorts.

Because the advertising ideas submitted to early qualitative evaluation are usually in very rough form, they might omit some important element that would make them work very well in the context of a full campaign. In the Copper Mountain focus groups, the "White Hot" idea was poorly re-ceived at first, until it was coupled with spectacular illustrations of snow.

FOCUS GROUPS

In a typical focus group, members of the target audience are invited to attend a group discussion at a central interviewing location.

When the group has been assembled and seated around a conference table, the "moderator" introduces the group members to one another and tries to make them feel at home. The moderator then leads the group through a preset list of topics, encouraging responses and attempting to make sure that all members of the group have opportunities to express what they think and how they feel.

Most focus group facilities provide a viewing room where observers can watch and listen to the discussion from behind a "one-way" mirror. Although respondents are told about the observers, they soon forget that they are there.

Focus groups are valuable because they bring decision makers into direct contact with consumers. Most marketing executives, and most members of advertising agency creative departments, live so differently from their customers that they have little direct day-to-day contact with how consumers think.

The outcome of a focus group depends heavily on the skill of the moderator. The moderator's responsibilities are to make sure that the most significant points are adequately covered and to follow up the most potentially useful ideas by asking insightful, probing questions. That task requires the ability to think quickly in a complex and rapidly changing interview. It requires sensitivity and good judgment, and it demands an understanding of what the client needs to know. Moderators with those skills are scarce and are therefore in constant demand.

After the interview the moderator usually meets with the observers to discuss and evaluate what has gone on. In this discussion the moderator might contribute observations derived from other interviews or from other research in which the problem was somewhat the same.

The moderator may prepare a report that summarizes and evaluates the results obtained from a series of groups. Often such reports contain extensive quotations from the group interactions so that readers who were not in attendance can get some feel for how consumers reacted and for the language they used to express their thoughts. Such information can prove extremely helpful to writers who must understand the thoughts and feelings of their audience.

Focus groups provide direct contact with consumers. Compared with many other research methods, they are more intimate and more personal, and they can be fast and cheap. Although focus groups have many obvious limitations, they are becoming more and more popular.

A third problem is that sometimes a small minority of respondents dominate a focus group, imposing their opinions on everyone else. Although a skilled moderator can moderate this kind of behavior, the loudest and most authoritative respondents often contribute more than their fair share. Furthermore, when interested parties witness qualitative interviews, they cannot help but single out and remember comments that support their special points of view. With a few off-hand remarks from a small sample of respondents, a copywriter, an art director, an account director, or a brand manager can become absolutely convinced that he or she had been on the right track all along. Sometimes even when better evidence presents itself at a later time these convictions can be very hard to shake.

In spite of the inevitable perils, however, the assets of diagnostic research outweigh its liabilities, and both individual in-depth interviews (sometimes called *one-on-ones*) and focus groups are widely used today. For a more detailed description of how focus groups are set up, conducted, and evaluated, see the box entitled "Focus Groups."

Communication Tests. The drawbacks of qualitative diagnosis have led many advertisers to use communication tests instead. These are one-on-one interviews, usually conducted in shopping malls that supply central interviewing facilities. Shoppers are recruited to fill out questionnaires on their age, sex, income, and product usage. They are asked to participate in a "study of consumers' opinions," and they are sometimes offered a small fee for their cooperation.

In the interviewing room respondents are shown advertisements one at a time and asked a standard list of questions such as:

- As you looked at the commercial, what thoughts or ideas went through your mind and what feelings did you have?
- In your own words, please describe what went on and what was said in the commercial.
- Besides trying to sell the product, what was the main point of the commercial?
- What was the name of the product advertised?
- Was there anything in this commercial that you found confusing or hard to understand?
- What, if anything, did you like or dislike about this commercial?

As the respondents answer the questions, the interviewer writes down the answers verbatim. The answers are later analyzed to determine how well respondents understood the message and how they reacted to the way the message was presented.

The verbatim comments are coded into categories such as:

- Main-point playback
- Spontaneous-claim recall
- Name recall
- Positive feelings
- Negative feelings
- Reactions to characters
- Believability
- Likes
- Dislikes

Communication–test samples are generally larger and usually somewhat more representative of the target audience than are the samples typically used for individual in-depth interviews or focus groups. Furthermore, although the coding of verbatim responses always requires a certain amount of judgment, it is not as casual and subjective as the interpretation of the more qualitative forms of diagnostic research.

Ratings. Many communication tests also include a set of scales intended to capture a wide range of reactions. These scales, designed to include most of the ways consumers can respond to advertisements, supplement the answers to the open-ended questions. They also help less articulate respondents express their opinions, and they sometimes suggest ideas that respondents have not thought to mention.

Even though the communication test has some obvious limitations, it can usually provide answers to three fundamental questions:

1. Did the advertisement convey the message it was intended to convey?
2. Did the advertisement convey any messages it was not intended to convey?
3. How did consumers react to the characters, the setting, the message, and the tone of the advertising?

The answers to these questions are valuable because they come at a time when it is still relatively easy to make changes. Changes will be much more difficult and expensive to make later in the advertising development process. For example, a commercial for a brand of spaghetti was intended to show, in a lighthearted way, that the advertised brand was better than spaghetti made from scratch. In the commercial a Mafia-type family was portrayed, and the character of the homemaker was a stereotypical "Italian mama." Although no one at the advertiser or the agency envisioned any particular problem with this execution, several communication-test respondents mentioned a possible implication that all Italians who love spaghetti are members of the Mafia. Alerted by this warning, the advertiser submitted the commercial to larger-scale testing directed specifically at the Mafia question. This research showed that although relatively few viewers made the Mafia association, some did, especially some Italian Americans. The plot was then dropped from further consideration.

Although not all communication-test results are that clear-cut, these tests can reveal that an advertisement is failing to deliver the message it was intended to deliver, or that it is succeeding in delivering a message never intended. Such findings can avoid a lot of problems later on.

As we noted early in this chapter, information is the raw material out of which advertising campaigns are made. Although much of this information comes from the professional and personal experiences of those who are responsible for creating and approving the advertising, a great deal of it comes from research of one type or another. In the end, these sources of information are intricately and untracably mixed. Examples like, "Does she or doesn't she?" and those in which one specific research finding led directly and unambiguously to one particular illustration or theme line are rare. And even in those cases, many other considerations play important parts in the development of the campaign, as we will show in the next chapter.

SUMMARY

- Information is the basic ingredient from which all advertisements and all media purchases are made.
- A very important part of advertising information comes from the personal and professional experiences of the men and women who are responsible for developing and evaluating the advertising. Another part of this information comes from formal research. In the development of any campaign these two information sources interact in complex ways.
- Formal research is provided by government departments, trade associations, secondary research suppliers, primary research suppliers, and the research departments of advertisers and advertising agencies.
- In the development of an advertising campaign the problem is seldom too little information but too much. Someone must identify, collect, and organize the most useful information and present it in a useful form. That task usually falls to members of the advertising agency research department, or, in the absence of a research department, to the account group.
- The most important research information usually goes into a strategy document that is, in a rough sense, a plan for the campaign.

- The difficult decisions as to just what information should go into the strategy document and how that information should be interpreted call for interactive judgments on the part of the advertiser and its agency. Within the agency, these judgments involve all those responsible for making sure that the communication works. These judgments are never automatic or obvious, nor are they cut and dried.
- Once creative work has started, the developing advertising ideas may be checked for effectiveness with the intended audience through relatively qualitative and informal diagnostic research.
- Although diagnostic research provides exposure to real consumers, it also opens the possibility that potentially excellent ideas may be rejected or that previous prejudices may be confirmed. Despite these risks, diagnostic research provides a valuable safeguard against the possibility that the finished advertising will fail to convey the intended message or that it will contain some message it was not intended to convey.

QUESTIONS

1. Every year Copper Mountain must decide how much emphasis to put on front-range day skiers versus skiers from the Denver market who stay overnight versus skiers from outside Copper Mountain's geographic area. What research information would help Copper Mountain's managers make those decisions? Where would they get that information?

2. Suppose you had the opportunity to develop a research program for a new bookstore serving your college or university. What kind of exploratory research would you recommend? Would you propose both qualitative and quantitative studies? What specific steps would you take?

3. The research director for Angelis Advertising always introduces her department's services to new agency clients by comparing research to a road map. What do maps and research studies have in common? How does the analogy of a map also indicate the limitations of research for resolving an advertising problem?

4. Judging from the chapter discussions, would you expect the following data bases to be developed from primary or secondary resources:
   a. national television ratings
   b. consumer brand's ad awareness scores
   c. household penetration levels for VCRs

5. Research professionals recommend using focus groups to help develop a campaign strategy or theme, but many are opposed to using focus groups to choose finished ads for the campaign. Is this contradictory? Why or why not?

6. A new radio station is moving into your community. Management is not sure how to position the station in this market and has asked you to develop a study with this decision.
   a. What are the key research questions that need to be asked?
   b. Outline a research program to answer those questions that uses as many of the research methods discussed in this chapter as you can incorporate.

7. In the course of diagnostic research a few focus-group respondents contradict an opinion based on years of professional and personal experience. Suppose that opinion is held by your client's top management. If you are a researcher, what do you do? Suppose that opinion is held by the creative director of your agency. What do you do? Suppose it is your opinion. What then?

FURTHER READINGS

DAY, GEORGE S., *Market-Driven Strategy: Processes for Creating Value* (New York: The Free Press, 1990).

EMORY, C. WILLIAM, *Business Research Methods,* 3rd. ed. (Homewood, IL: Irwin, 1985).

FLETCHER, ALAN, AND THOMAS BOWERS, *Fundamentals of Advertising Research,* 3rd ed. (Belmont, CA: Wadsworth, 1988).

GREEN, PAUL E., DONALD S. TULL, AND GERALD ALBAUM, *Research for Marketing Decisions,* 5th ed. (Englewood Cliffs, NJ: Prentice-Hall, 1988).

KERIN, ROGER A., VIJAY MAHAJAN, AND RAJAN VARADARAJAN, *Contemporary Perspectives on Strategic Market Planning* (Needham Heights, MA: Allyn and Bacon, 1989).

WEIERS, RONALD M., *Marketing Research,* 2nd ed. (Englewood Cliffs, NJ: Prentice Hall, 1988).

VIDEO CASE

ConAgra's Healthy Choice

Sales in the premium frozen dinner and entree category had been flat during 1990 and 1991 due to a lack of brand differentiation and an inability to identify meaningful new product benefits for consumers. Items in the category consisted primarily of regular-calorie and low-calorie dinners and entrees in a variety of recipes. Following the heart attack of ConAgra's Chairman, Mike Harper, however, the company recognized an opportunity to revolutionize the frozen dinner and entree category by offering consumers a unique and compelling benefit: healthy food.

The result was Healthy Choice, the first frozen dinner specially formulated within established dietary guidelines to be low in fat, sodium, and cholesterol. Consequently, ConAgra's advertising agency, Campbell-Mithun-Esty, was asked to establish a comprehensive brand franchise based on the premise of providing consumers with "heart healthy" alternatives to popular foods in a variety of different food categories. Estimated sales for the new product line were set at $100 million, which would give ConAgra the number two share position in the premium frozen dinner segment.

The creative strategy was to generate awareness for Healthy Choice by leveraging the product's unique heart healthy benefits of low fat, sodium, and cholesterol. The brand positioning, "Healthy Choice is great tasting food that is good for your heart," embodied both a health proposition and a necessary taste support. The theme line echoed this positioning: "Listen to your heart. Make the Healthy Choice," and conveyed both the personal and the emotional benefits of healthy eating.

After initially utilizing Mike Harper as a spokesperson for the brand, celebrity spokespersons were used to aid in building awareness and breaking through traditional advertising clutter. The celebrities were presented in a personalized interview format to maximize their credibility.

The target audience for Healthy Choice dinners was identified as adults 35 years of age and older who were interested in healthful activities and were current users of frozen convenience foods. The target audience for Healthy Choice entrees were identified as adult women 35 years of age and older who were interested in health as well as in low-calorie benefits and smaller portion sizes. Advertising spending for Healthy Choice dinners and entrees from October 1989 to September 1990 reflected over a 21 percent share of the total media spending in the premium frozen dinner and entree category and was the highest of any single competitor within the category.

The results of the roll-out category greatly exceeded ConAgra's expectations. Healthy Choice successfully created renewed vitality and brought in new users to a stagnant frozen dinner and entree category. Total premium frozen dinner category volume increased by 6 percent following the introduction of Healthy Choice dinner, versus a 22 percent decline projected by industry experts had Healthy Choice not been introduced. Within a year of the full national distribution of Healthy Choice dinners, the brand had surpassed the initial sales goals by 50 percent and had achieved a 36 percent share of the premium dinner segment, establishing it as the category leader. Similarly, after only 4 months of national distribution, Healthy Choice entrees achieved a 7 percent share of the premium entree segment, resulting in combined shares for the Healthy Choice brand, which represented over 17 percent of the total premium dinner and entree category.

The introduction of Healthy Choice also created an entirely new "health" segment within the frozen premium dinner and entree category. Health-oriented brands now account for over one-third of total frozen dinner volume, and sales of the health segment quadrupled within 2 years of Healthy Choice's introduction.

The success of Healthy Choice quickly encouraged other manufacturers to address the more broadly defined and growing health segment with new product introductions or existing brand repositionings. As a result, total media spending in the frozen premium dinner and entree category has increased by more than 70 percent since the introduction of Healthy Choice, and health-positioned consumer communications now account for approximately 40 percent of the total media spending in the category.

Healthy Choice has been recognized by the sales trade, consumers, and industry observers with many honors, including the AMA Edison Award for top new product in 1989. The success of Healthy Choice has convinced ConAgra to pursue aggressively a brand growth strategy for the future, including expansion into such product categories as shelf stable microwave cups and cans, egg substitutes, kids' meals, and other healthy food opportunities.

QUESTIONS

1. Although the advertising for Healthy Choice certainly contributed to its success, which do you think played a more critical role and why: the advertising or the product itself?
2. Despite the development of a fairly revolutionary concept in the frozen premium dinner and entree segment, ConAgra chose to pursue a relatively subdued, low-key advertising execution style. Why do you feel this was appropriate for the brand?
3. List the advantages and disadvantages of using ConAgra's Chairman as a post-heart attack spokesperson for Healthy Choice versus traditional celebrity spokespeople.

Source: Courtesy of Campbell-Mithun-Esty.

7

Strategy and Planning

Chapter Outline

The International Coffee War
Strategy and Planning
The Marketing Plan
The Advertising Plan
The Creative Plan and Copy Strategy

Chapter Objectives

When you have completed this chapter, you should be able to:

- Identify the key elements of a marketing plan and an advertising plan
- Understand how marketers allocate funds among advertising and other marketing functions
- Explain the difference between product-centered and prospect-centered strategies
- List the key elements of a creative platform

THE INTERNATIONAL COFFEE WAR

When you think of coffee, what country do you think of? When researchers asked that question in the 1960s, most U.S. consumers replied, "Brazil." The National Federation of Coffee Growers of Colombia found to their dismay that the country of Colombia received almost no mentions.

Obviously the Colombian coffee growers felt a major awareness campaign was needed. They also wanted U.S. consumers to identify brands with 100% Colombian coffee as quality or premium. This might sound like an impossible mission. Who, after all, cares which country grows the coffee beans?

The Colombian coffee growers' federation accepted the challenge. It developed the slogan "Richest Coffee in the World" and the character of Juan Valdez as a spokesperson who taught consumers how to identify

AD 7.1
Ads such as these, featuring the Juan Valdez logo and the campaign slogan, helped 100% Colombian coffee to compete effectively with Brazilian coffee in the U.S. market.
(Courtesy of The National Federation of Coffee Growers of Colombia.)

brands that contain 100% Colombia coffee (see Ad. 7.1). The Valdez character also explained the unique properties of Colombia that enabled it to grow the best coffee beans in the world.

DDB Needham ads established the premium image by featuring upscale settings with discriminating consumers enjoying 100% Colombian coffee. For example, one ad featured a businessman sitting in a lush grand parlor in front of a fireplace reading *The Wall Street Journal* and drinking a cup of Colombian coffee. The copy featured only the headline: "50% Tax Bracket, 100% Colombian Coffee," the Juan Valdez logo, and the campaign slogan.

By the early 1990s unaided awareness of Colombia as a coffee-producing country reached an all-time high of 61 percent compared to Brazil's 35 percent. Additionally, 66 percent of consumers believed that Colombia grows the best coffee, compared to 14 percent for Brazil. In the great coffee war Colombia took the offensive away from Brazil. In 1983 only 35 coffee brands featured the Colombia logo. Today 445 brands are in the program.*

STRATEGY AND PLANNING

Advertising is both an art and a science. The art comes from writing, designing, and producing exciting messages. The science comes from strategic thinking. Advertising is a disciplined art, and achieving the disciplined side of advertising is the focus of this chapter. Advertising messages aren't created by whimsy or a sudden flash of inspiration. Messages are formulated to accomplish specific objectives, and then strategies are developed specifically to achieve those objectives. This is all done through a process called *planning.*

Strategic Planning: Making Intelligent Decisions

Strategic planning is the process of determining *objectives* (which state what you want to accomplish), deciding on *strategies* (which tell you how to accomplish the objectives), and implementing the *tactics* (which make the plan come to life). All of this occurs within a specified time frame. Marketing and advertising strategies are chosen from an array of possible alternatives. Intelligent decision making means weighing these alternatives and sorting out the best approach. Often there is no *right* way, but there may be a *best* way to accomplish your objectives.

PRINCIPLE
Strategic thinking means weighing the alternatives and identifying the best approach.

It is sometimes difficult even for those experienced in advertising to tell the difference between an objective and a strategy. Both are important to the development of successful marketing and advertising plans; they are related to each other, but they are also different and serve different purposes. An objective is a *goal* or *task* to be accomplished. A strategy is the *means* by which the goal is accomplished.

For example, if the goal is to reinforce brand loyalty for the product, then any number of strategies could be employed to accomplish that task. Suppose, though that the advertiser wants to create brand loyalty by emphasizing that the brand delivers more of the benefit than do competing brands. The number of tactics that could be used with that strategy is almost infinite. For instance, the brand could be compared with its leading competitor. Other possible tactics to carry out the strategy are a demonstration, a testimonial, an emotional or funny story, or a straightforward fact-based approach.

*"Richest Coffee in the World," DDB Needham Case Study, unpublished document.

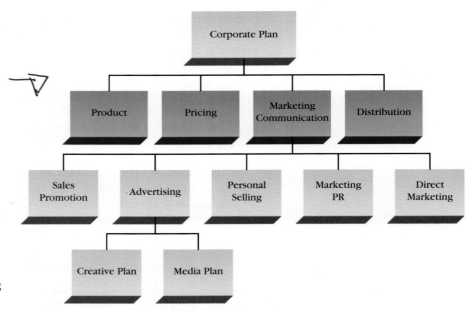

FIGURE 7.1
The relationship among advertising and planning areas.

Planning Documents.   Planning is usually summarized in a document that varies with the level and scope of the responsibility. Figure 7.1 illustrates a company's entire marketing communication planning program and shows where various types of advertising plans fit into the big picture. From the top down, these documents can represent a *corporate plan*, a *marketing plan*, an *advertising plan*, a *campaign plan*, or a *copy strategy* for a specific advertisement.

Briefly, the *corporate plan* states the company's profit objectives. As mentioned in Chapter 3, the *marketing plan* describes how all the elements of the marketing mix—product, distribution, pricing, and marketing communication—are coordinated. An *advertising plan* outlines a company's advertising program over a specified period of time, usually 1 year. A *campaign plan* describes a sustained advertising effort designed around a common theme that is carried across different media for a given time period. A *copy strategy* is the thinking behind the message strategy developed for a specific advertisement. Many of the decisions for these various types of plans are similar; objectives, for example, are developed for every level of planning. The difference lies more in the time frame and scope of responsibility.

*T*HE MARKETING PLAN

A **marketing plan** is a written document that proposes strategies for employing the various elements of the marketing mix to achieve marketing objectives. It analyzes the marketing situation, identifies the problems, outlines the marketing opportunities, sets the objectives, and proposes strategies and tactics to solve these problems and meet objectives. A marketing plan is developed and evaluated annually, although sections dealing with long-run goals might operate for a number of years. Some companies are finding that the marketplace changes so rapidly today that plans have to be updated more frequently than once a year—perhaps even quarterly.

marketing plan *A written document that proposes strategies for employing the marketing mix to achieve marketing objectives.*

The following is an outline for a typical marketing plan:

- Situation Analysis:
  1. Product
  2. Marketplace
  3. Distribution
  4. Pricing
  5. Marketing communication
  6. Consumer behavior
- Problems and Opportunities
- Objectives:
  1. Sales
  2. Dollars
  3. Share of market
- Strategies (will vary with the situation but include such areas as the following):
  1. Target markets
  2. Differentiation
  3. Branding
  4. Geographical emphasis BDI/CDI
  5. Channel: push or pull
  6. Pricing
  7. Cooperative promotions
- Implementation and Evaluation
  1. Schedule
  2. Budget
  3. Follow-up research

In terms of the internal logic of a marketing plan, the situation analysis section focuses on the past, whereas the problems and opportunities section is concerned with the present. Planning in the sense of identifying future actions begins with the objectives and continues through strategies, implementation, and evaluation. The overall outline is basically the same for an advertising plan, though the content will vary in each of these sections. We will discuss the basic concepts and sections of both advertising and marketing plans here.

Situation Analysis

situation analysis *The section of the marketing plan that analyzes the research findings.*

The **situation analysis** is a standard section in most plans. It summarizes relevant information about the product, marketplace, competition, demand, consumer behavior, distribution channels, costs, and environmental factors. This section will seek to answer questions like the following:

- *Product:* What are the product's features? Are any distinctive? What is the competitive advantage? Are there any new developments? What is the product's life-cycle stage?
- *Marketplace:* What are total sales (in units and dollars) for the product, the competition, and the category? What is the projected size of the market and the level of demand? What are the current market shares?
- *Promotion:* What is the advertising and promotion history for the firm and its competitors? What are the current advertising expenditures?
- *Distribution:* How do products get to the purchase location? Where do people buy the product—number and type of stores, locations?
- *Pricing:* What is the pricing picture? The history?
- *Consumers:* Who buys the product? How do they make the purchase decisions? Do they seek information? How do they perceive the brand? The competition?

Problems and Opportunities

The heart of strategic planning is analysis—the process of figuring out what all the information and data mean. After you have studied what sometimes seems to be a mountain of information, the problems and opportunities begin to emerge. Spotting the key problem is often very difficult. It takes experience, marketing sophistication, an analytical mind, and a unique way of looking at things. It has been said that a well-defined problem is more than half of the solution. Obversely, an ill-defined problem may not be capable of being solved at all.

It has also been said that a problem is merely an opportunity in disguise. Some problems that are identified can be solved or overcome. Some have to be circumvented. Others can be turned into opportunities by those with creative minds. Advertising can solve only *advertising* problems, however. If the problem does not have to do with advertising—that is, if it is not a *communication* problem—then no amount of advertising is going to solve it. Furthermore, pouring heavy doses of advertising into a nonadvertising problem is likely to make the problem worse. For instance, if brand sales are down because of poor distribution, then increasing brand advertising is not going to make it possible for people to find the product on the shelves any quicker.

Marketing Objectives

The primary objective for most marketing efforts is sales, or profit. In the marketing arena objectives are usually stated in terms of sales and market share, both of which should be specific and measurable. The objectives may also be given as short-term (annual) and long-term goals (up to 5 years).

Sales-volume objectives are specified in both units and dollars. **Share of market** describes how much of the market your product has garnered and is expressed as a percentage.

For example, let's say the marketing manager predicts a sales increase of 20 percent from 500,000 units this year to 600,000 units next year. If the units sold for $2 each, then the dollar volume would increase from $1 million to $1.2 million, also an increase of 20 percent. If the new sales level raised the product's share of market from 4.5 to 4.8 percent, that would represent an increase of 6 percent. These numbers are explained in Table 7.1.

Secondary objectives might focus on such areas as distribution levels and store traffic or on actions that need to be taken to solve specific problems. The success or failure of the marketing plan will be evaluated on the basis of how well these objectives are met, so they need to be realistic.

Marketing objectives and the strategies that accomplish them are related to both corporate and advertising objectives. The corporate objectives and strategies give direction to the marketing plan, and the marketing objectives and strategies give direction to the advertising plan.

Marketing Strategies

An important part of planning is identifying the key strategic decisions that will give the product or firm a competitive advantage in the marketplace. Strategies that are particularly important in terms of the direction they give the advertising program include decisions on targeting and segmentation, differentiation, branding, channel and distribution, pricing, and related elements in the marketing communication mix.

TABLE 7.1
Setting Marketing Objectives

I. Assumes the price and the total category sales remain the same:			
	Units	Dollars	Share of Market (%) (Market = 12.5 million units)
This year:	500,000	$1.0 million	4.5
Next year:	600,000	$1.2 million	4.8
Net difference:	100,000	$200,000	0.8
% Increase:	(20%)	(20%)	(6%)

II. Assumes price increases as well as increases in total category sales:				
	Units	Price	Dollars	Share of Market (%)*
This year:	500,000	$2.00	$1.0 million	4.0
Next year:	600,000	$2.10	$1.26 million	4.6
Net difference:	100,000	$ .10	$260,000	0.6
% Increase:	(20%)	(5%)	(26%)	(15%)

*This year's category sales = 12.5 million units; next year's estimated category sales = 13 million units.

---

market segments *Groups of people with characteristics in common who make up important subcategories of the population.*

market segmentation *The process of identifying segments to target.*

target market *A market segment with the most potential for purchase of the product.*

prospects *People who might buy the product or service.*

Targeting and Segmentation. In today's marketing arena a product with a truly homogeneous market—that is, a product that appeals to everyone—is rarely found. All markets, then, are divided into smaller groups, each with its own set of needs and desires for the product—homemakers, preteens, new mothers, senior citizens, rock climbers, or international business travelers, for example. These are called **market segments.** A market segment is a subgroup of the population that has characteristics that make it unique and therefore distinct from other groups who use the product. **Market segmentation** is the process of identifying these particular groups, singling out one group, and developing a unique marketing program aimed only at that group. This unique group is offered a marketing mix that meets its particular needs. Segmentation is an outgrowth of the consumer-oriented marketing concept.

Levi's for example, sells jeans to a variety of segments, including mothers of young boys, teenagers, farmers and other working men, young adults who are active and interested in the outdoors, and a fashion-oriented segment of teenage women. Every segment requires a different marketing-mix strategy, particularly in the areas of distribution and advertising.

Marketers select a **target market** by identifying the segment with the most potential for purchase of the product. A target market is a group of people who have been identified as **prospects** who might buy the product or service. The concept of targeting is very important. A target is something you aim at. The implication is that if you hit the target, your message will have a better chance of being understood and accepted than if it falls among random groups of consumers who are less likely to be interested. If you miss the target, the odds are high that you have wasted your marketing budget. Targeting doesn't mean ignoring multitudes of consumers; it simply means being more precise in developing your strategy.

An example of brilliant targeting comes from the media industry, where Whittle Communications is making a fortune publishing magazines and producing television programs targeted at narrow audience groups, such as college students, high-school students, customers waiting in beauty parlors, and patients in doctors offices. The company identifies these

PAULA S. AUSICK, DIRECTOR, CONSUMER RESOURCES, FOOTE CONE & BELDING, CHICAGO

For an account planner, the day-in–day-out charge is to come up with the *strategic consumer insight* that will inspire the creative development process or cause a client to say "Eureka!" Below is a slice of life from an account planner's day.

6:15 A.M. Turn off the alarm clock. Stagger out of bed and into the shower. Try a competitor's soap to see how I like it. Hmm, a little drying to my skin. Wonder if consumers, in general, feel that way about the brand. Turn on the television to CNN to catch up with the world. Switch to the *Today Show* for some fluff and to see what is being advertised on morning news programs. My friends think I watch television for the ads. Have a cup of coffee.

7:45 A.M. Arrive at the office and grab the folder with overheads of my presentation. Client is coming in at 8:30 for the AGENCY'S POINT OF VIEW on the future direction of our creative based on findings from the market structure study, tracking study, sales and brand-switching data, and the extensive copy-testing research on previous and current executions. No numbers in this presentation so we can better focus on the implications. It's sort of a *kansei* approach— "It just feels right."

8:20 A.M. Check to make sure that everything's in order. Make a few last-minute notes to myself. Call into my voice-mail system to change my greeting so that callers will know I'm out of my office for the morning.

8:30 A.M. Meet the client group, account, and creatives. Pour myself another cup of coffee and welcome everyone. The show begins. The presentation is going very well. Good interaction during the presentation with the brand manager and his associate. The group creative director is being very supportive and is showing examples of how the creatives can incorporate some of the findings into the next pool of creative. The brand people are tracking the presentation and are nodding in agreement.

10:30 A.M. Break in the meeting. The creatives are excited that, finally, they can explore another direction. The brand people are happy that, finally, the agency understands what they have been trying to explain to the creatives about a certain direction. And the account people are satisfied that we have accomplished our mission. Return to my office to access my voice mail and make a few phone calls— one account person, one creative person, and my insurance agent.

10:45 A.M. Return to the client meeting to discuss issues concerning a new campaign. Go over the script. Provide a viewpoint on how the consumer might respond to the execution. Discuss whether or not research is necessary. Brand wants some research. Agree with the client research director to go with him to the supplier to explore the feasibility of setting up research on this as soon as possible.

11:15 A.M. Client research director, supplier, a colleague, and I go to lunch. My colleague and I agree to follow up on some information for the research.

groups on the basis of demographics and psychographics. It also specializes in single-sponsored magazines targeted to carefully defined and controlled segments.

Descriptors A market may be identified—both segmented and targeted—by demographic, psychographic, or behavioral characteristics. Ideally, all three criteria will be used. For example, Close-Up toothpaste is aimed at a market segment that can be described demographically as both males and females, aged 15–24; psychographically as being concerned about appearance and appealing to the opposite sex; and behaviorally as being heavy users of toothpaste. The key of Close-Up's success is that it has directed all of its marketing efforts at this one particular segment without deviation since it first entered the marketplace. Obviously, the makers of

1:30 P.M. Return to the agency. Access my voice mail, change the greeting, and return call to a head-hunter and give him the name of a very good person to contact for the position available. Go through my in-box. Review materials for my next meeting.

2:15 P.M. Meet with account people on preliminary strategy exploration for a relaunch of an infrequently advertised brand in a heavily advertised category. Outline informational needs. Go over category and brand sales trends and brand-switching information over the past 3 years. Isolate some promising consumer segments to follow up on. Set next meeting in 3 days to brainstorm some strategic ideas and tactics. Agree to present some thoughts about the consumer at that time.

3:30 P.M. Review the sales data and brand-switching data more closely for clues. Begin to outline the issues and information needs for sections of the creative brief that I am responsible for—the consumer-needs section and the purchase-decision section. Call the media person on the account for input in determining target audience. Set up to meet with him in the morning.

4:15 P.M. Watch and study some competitive television advertising. Call the Information Center/Library for an information search on the category and on consumer segments. Read current and back issues of the major women's magazines to get an idea what our target is exposed to. Make sure that I get to see the current issue of *The Star*—it's the most popular rag circulating on the floor.

5:00 P.M. Check my calendar to see what I have listed for tomorrow. Chat with the secretary and thank her for all her work in getting things together for today's presentation. Catch up on hallway gossip. Stare out the window for a bit.

6:00 P.M. Shuffle the papers on my desk, turn off the lights, and head for home. Stop off at the grocery store to pick up stuff to cook for dinner. Casually observe what people are buying. Does work ever stop? Not when you love it.

Courtesy of Paula Ausick.
(FCB/Karen I. Hirsch.)

Close-Up wouldn't mind if people outside this targeted segment purchased their product, but they don't deliberately go after other groups.

Targeting is frequently done on the basis of product usage. Consumers are identified as *heavy users, light users,* or *nonusers*. There is an old adage in the industry called the 80:20 rule that says 20 percent of the consumers use 80 percent of the product. The goal of targeting is to zero in on that 20 percent. In other words, there's a certain group of *heavy users* who are very important to identify and target. From a strategic standpoint, marketers will usually either target the likeliest market (heavy users), who buy most of the product, or the largest market (light users), who may be convinced to increase their purchases. Converting nonusers is extremely difficult because you first have to sell them on the product category and then convince them to use your product. That doubles the difficulty of the mission.

All advertising is directed toward or at a particular audience.
(Courtesy of Owen Franken/Stock, Boston.)

benefit segmentation *Segments identified by the appeal of the product to their personal interests.*

Benefit Segmentation   **Benefit segmentation** marries the targeting decision to the product analysis. It is an approach that identifies segments of the audience in terms of the specific product benefits used to motivate them. Toothpaste advertisers, for example, know that different people buy different brands of toothpaste for different reasons. Some people buy a brand of toothpaste because it whitens their teeth, others buy a brand because it cleans their breath. Some buy a toothpaste to protect against cavities, others buy a different brand of toothpaste to fight plaque, and still others buy a brand because it tastes good. Different brands are segmented to appeal to these different audiences who want different things from a basic product like toothpaste.

An example of identifying segments in order to make the most strategic targeting decision is illustrated in a consumer study that was conducted for the Army National Guard. The Guard wanted to identify those groups that would be the most desirable to recruit and retain. Knowing more about the audience would enable the Guard to communicate better to these people. A study of 1,671 enlisted men in the Guard found four broad clusters of individuals:

- *The "Stable" group* (20 percent): Active, optimistic, content, politically active, open-minded, 26–45, some college, higher-than-average income. More likely than other groups to be married, to have prior service, and to want to stay in the Guard.
- *The "Misfits"* (26 percent): Pessimistic, fearful, angry, not ambitious or motivated, financially insecure, possess few educational or traditional values, lack self-confidence, have the least respect for the military, 18–25, single, minorities, high-school dropouts. Less likely to remain in the Guard.
- *The "Conservatives"* (28 percent): Homebodies, traditional, religious, not adventurous, don't like change, oldest group, been in the Guard longer, more likely to be in higher ranks, most likely to be married and have children, go out and entertain less, read less.
- *The "Swaggerers"* (25 percent): Active, optimistic, liberal, outgoing, adventurous, partiers and swingers, confident, lowest ranks, in the Guard the least amount of time, single, no prior service, enrolled in college, youngest (18–21), lowest income, read the most.

These results indicated that the "Stable" group were the most content in the Guard and the "Misfits" were the least happy. The "Swaggerers" were more likely to be attracted by the Guard's college benefits.

This analysis brought about a complete change in the Guard's advertising strategy. The agency recommended changing the Guard's priority target from young men right out of high school to an older group of men, especially those with prior service who have some college background and are active in their communities. It also suggested a change in media placement to more upscale, middle-of-the-road, and news-oriented publications. Another recommendation was to focus on young men in college or with college aptitude who would be interested in the tuition benefits.

Differentiation. Markets can be as broad as all the buyers of a particular type of product (snack foods) or as limited as a group of people defined by a very special interest (blue corn tortilla chips). Broad markets are sometimes referred to as **mass markets,** and narrowly defined markets are called **niche markets.** Clearly some products appeal to a wider audience than others—they have more *mass appeal.* For example, on the one hand, it is hard to identify "the" market for Coke because so many different types of people drink it. Pepsi, on the other hand, is more clearly targeted at young people and people who think young, as you can tell from the famous "Pepsi Generation" commercials. The decision on whether to target a broad market or a niche market is a very important aspect of marketing strategy and is an example of differentiation planning.

Niche strategies are developed to reach narrowly defined markets. In contrast, *undifferentiated strategies* are used for nationally marketed products that have universal appeal and are bought by a large number of people. Undifferentiated strategies ignore individual differences. The advertiser must have sufficient resources to support a massive marketing program to reach an undifferentiated market. In general, the latter strategy works for Coca-Cola, McDonald's, and Kodak, but not for many other products. Even mass-marketed products like Coke will occasionally target markets by age or region.

Differentiation strategies are also used in categories where the products are all the same or at least appear to be similar. Commodity products like gasoline and bread use differentiation to create brands that have some distinctive imagery. Many cars look the same, and their advertisements try hard to distinguish models that look like clones by associating the car with mountains, deserts, the top of a pinacle in the canyonlands, or spaceships.

Competitive Advantage If marketing is war, then there must be an enemy. If a product category has room for expansion, then everyone can grow and competition is often less intense. If, however, a particular category is static, then growth must come at someone else's expense and competition can be intense. Ad 7.2 is an example of competitive advertising. Identifying the competition is a way of targeting the vulnerable opposition.

You must decide where your **competitive product advantage** lies. The analysis of the product, the competition, and the target all happen simultaneously. These factors are interdependent because the concept of product advantage involves identifying what the consumer wants and comparing that with the competition's strengths and weaknesses as well as those of your product.

Advertisers analyze data on both direct and indirect competition to shed light on consumer behavior. **Direct competition** includes all other *brands* in the category, whereas **indirect competition** includes other *options,* perhaps outside the category. American Greetings, for example, is

mass markets *Broad undifferentiated markets.*

niche markets *Narrowly focused markets that are defined by some special interest.*

competitive product advantage *The identification of a feature that is important to the consumer where your product is strong and the competition is vulnerable.*

direct competition *A product in the same category.*

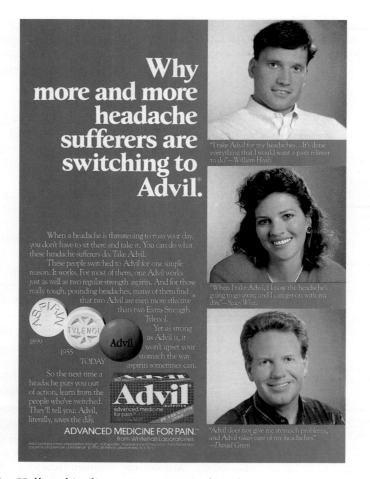

indirect competition *A product that is in a different category but functions as an alternative purchase choice.*

PRINCIPLE
The indirect competition may be more important than the direct competition.

PRINCIPLE
Your share of market can't increase unless a competitor's share shrinks.

Hallmark's direct competition, but the telephone company is an indirect competitor. Both Hallmark and the telephone company are after the consumer's "sentiment message." When an advertiser dominates its category, as Hallmark does, an indirect competitor can be more formidable than a direct competitor.

To identify these alternative choices, you need a knowledge of consumers and their purchasing decisions. As mentioned earlier, the competition is identified by the pattern of consumer alternatives rather than simply by listing the other brands and companies in the same category. A basic principle to remember is that even when you and your competition can grow in a growth market, you still might not be increasing market share. Because *market share* is a percentage of the whole market, you can't increase your own market share unless someone else's shrinks.

The problem is to identify which competitors are most vulnerable and on what basis. Does your product have an advantage over any of these competitors? Detecting a clear product advantage will give direction to the advertising message. If, for example, you find a distribution advantage, then geographical targeting might give you a competitive advantage.

Branding. Branding is discussed in Chapter 8 in terms of its psychology and creative implications. It is mentioned here because it is such a key strategic decision for marketing managers to reckon with. A manufacturer can sell products under store names, as generic products, as local brands, or as national brands. Obviously these different approaches will generate entirely different marketing and advertising strategies.

brand loyalty *Existing positive opinions held by consumers about the product or service.*

brand development index (BDI) *An index that identifies the demand for the brand within a region.*

category development index (CDI) *An index that identifies the demand for the category within a region.*

pull strategy *A promotional strategy that is designed to encourage consumers to ask for the product.*

push strategy *A promotional strategy that is directed to the trade in an attempt to move the product through the distribution channel.*

For those brands that are sold on their own name and image, branding is an important aspect of the targeting and segmenting decision. **Brand loyalty** indicates that there are existing positive opinions about a product or service, that customers like it well enough to buy it repeatedly. A brand's loyal customers make up its most important market, and marketing strategies are frequently developed to encourage these people to increase their consumption.

Geographical Emphasis: BDI/CDI. Where a brand sells or doesn't sell is also important to marketing and advertising managers. For example, iced tea is easier to sell during the winter in southern states than in northern ones. In contrast, Chapstick has a larger market in northern and mountain states.

On another level, marketing strategy combines branding with a product's marketing position and geographical sales picture to develop a type of opportunity analysis. Two terms are important for understanding the key elements in this type of strategic planning. The **brand development index** (BDI) and the **category development index** (CDI) are measures of sales potential by brand and by region. Using these indices, a brand's sales are compared to actual category sales to determine where the opportunities lie to increase sales and where to focus advertising dollars. An area with a high CDI has a strong demand for the category; an area with a high BDI has a strong demand for the brand. The ideal strategy is to find an area that has a high CDI and a low BDI. This information is used by marketing and advertising managers to target certain geographic areas for special emphasis in the placement of the advertising.

Channel: Push-Pull Strategies. Another decision that affects advertising planning is the strategic orientation to the distribution channel and the consumer. Marketing communication efforts that are directed to consumers, who then go to retailers and ask for the product, are described as using a **pull strategy.** Marketing communication that is directed to the wholesalers and retailers in an attempt to move the product through the distribution channel is said to use a **push strategy.**

Push strategies put more emphasis on trade, use heavy sales promotion, and are directed toward short-term results. Computers and software were originally *pushed* to dealers and retailers because the manufacturers relied on them to demonstrate, as well as to sell, these highly technical products. In contrast, pull strategies focus on the consumer, use heavy advertising, and try to create long-term brand image effects. Most package-goods products like shampoos and cereals are sold this way. It is important for marketing and advertising managers to understand the differences between push and pull strategies so they can determine how much emphasis to put on trade promotion and how much on consumer promotion.

Pricing Strategies. Although price appears obvious and easy to understand, it is a complex factor in both marketing and advertising strategy. Information about price is probably the most important message content that advertising can transmit. In *price advertising,* the price is obvious and is used as a peg for the advertising. This is particularly true for retail marketing and advertising. In other cases, such as national advertising for branded products, the price may not be stated, but signals about the price level are given so the consumer will know if it is expensive or a good value.

A *prestige pricing* strategy sets the price at a high level to signal to consumers that the product is unique, special, or a status symbol. A *price-*

reduction strategy reduces the price temporarily to encourage consumers to purchase the product. This strategy focuses on "sales," "specials," and other forms of discount pricing. Some stores use *loss leaders*—products advertised at prices below cost—to generate store traffic. A *customary pricing* strategy uses a single, well-known price for a long period of time. Movie theaters and candy manufacturers employ this strategy in the hope that the customer will become less sensitive to price.

Communication-Mix Strategies. As discussed earlier, different elements of the marketing communication mix accomplish different objectives. Advertising, for example, is particularly good at attitude change, increasing levels of awareness, and building a long-term brand image. In comparison, sales promotion can generate immediate increases in the sales curve by giving people an incentive to buy now. These two marketing communication tools are often used together to complement one another.

Likewise, retail advertising is short-term and is usually focused on stimulating store traffic on the local level. Manufacturers use cooperative advertising and promotions to help the retailer with local advertising and at the same time to build the national brand identity of the product. With co-op programs, the manufacturer agrees to pay part of the local advertising and promotion costs. Cooperative advertising is discussed in more detail in Chapter 22. These programs involve all types of marketing communications. For example, Panasonic is raising retailer participation in its ad program by tying campaigns to sponsorship of small-town sports. The strategic decision on how much emphasis should be on local and short-term advertising and how much on national brand building has major budget and advertising implications.

Implementation and Evaluation

The implementation section of the marketing plan focuses on the controls the firm has put in place to monitor the program—including the budgeting—and to test the effectiveness of various elements of the plan. In addition, this section includes details about implementation activities, such as scheduling. In other words, the various elements in the plan are analyzed in terms of time, money, and effectiveness. Evaluation is an important part of any marketing and advertising effort, and both types of plans will end with a discussion of the procedures to be used to see if the plan was successful in meeting its objectives and staying within budget. Evaluative research is discussed in more detail in Chapter 21.

*T*HE ADVERTISING PLAN

Advertising is only one element in the marketing communication mix, but it is the element we are most concerned with in this book. Advertising planning, which must dovetail with marketing planning, can occur at three levels. A firm may operate with an annual advertising plan. In addition to or instead of an annual advertising plan, a firm may develop a *campaign plan* that is more tightly focused on solving a particular marketing communication problem. Finally, a company may put together a copy strategy for an individual ad that runs independent of a campaign. The following discussion focuses on the elements of an advertising plan or a campaign plan because they are similar in outline and structure.

advertising plan *A plan that proposes strategies for targeting the audience, presenting the advertising message, and implementing media.*

An **advertising plan** matches the right audience to the right message and presents it in the right medium to reach that audience. In other words, three basic elements summarize the heart of advertising strategy:

- *Targeting the audience:* Who are you trying to reach?
- *Message strategy:* What do you want to say to them?
- *Media strategy:* When and where will you reach them?

The outline that guides the development of an annual or campaign advertising plan is similar in some ways to that for a marketing plan. There is a situation analysis section and objectives and strategies are identified, for example, in both marketing and advertising plans. The most important difference is found in the sections that focus on message and media strategies. A typical advertising or campaign plan can be outlined as follows:

- Situation Analysis:
    The advertising problem
    Advertising opportunities
- Key Strategy Decisions:
    Advertising objectives
    Target audience
    Competitive product advantage
    Product image and personality
    Product position
- The Creative Plan
- The Media Plan
- The Promotion Plan:
    Sales promotion
    Public relations
- Implementation and Evaluation
- Budget

The heart of an advertising or a campaign plan is found in the plans developed for the functional areas. The creative plan, for example, presents an analysis of the creative needs and proposed concepts and themes that will drive the advertising. The creative side of advertising is discussed in Chapters 13 through 15. Once the creative approach has been decided, the media team begins to develop the plan for buying and placing the ads in the various media that will be used. The media-planning and -buying side of advertising is discussed in Chapters 9 and 12. There are other functional areas that may or may not be included in an advertising plan depending on the needs of the product or the situation. For example, sales promotion, public relations, out-of-home media such as posters and billboards, and direct response are all important areas, particularly in an integrated marketing communications program, but how much any one of them will be used varies with the situation.

Situation Analysis

There is a group of key decisions that are made as part of the process of developing advertising strategy. Although these decisions are similar to sections of a marketing plan, they are focused on the *communication* aspects of marketing, including the communication problems and opportunities and the communication objectives to be achieved with the message. There is also a set of strategic considerations that come from the marketing plan but need to be analyzed in terms of their communication implications, such as the target audience and the product's features, image, personality, and position in the marketplace.

The Advertising Problem. Advertising is developed for strategic reasons: to deliver a message, to create some kind of effect on the consumer, and, ultimately, to solve some communication problem that affects the successful marketing of the product. Analyzing the situation and identifying the problem that can be solved with an advertising message are at the heart of strategic planning.

Different agencies employ different strategies. For example, BBDO uses a process called "Problem Detection" as the basis of its strategy building.* Problem Detection takes the question directly to consumers to find out what bothers them about the product or product category. Often the problems are not what the manufacturer expected to hear. A classic example involved the BBDO client Burger King. A Problem Detection study revealed that customers of fast-food hamburger restaurants objected to the fact that the hamburgers were all prepared the same way and then prepackaged. Thus a consumer with a particular preference—for example, no pickle or no onions—would have to wait while a special order was cooked. Burger King responded to this survey with its "Have It Your Way" campaign, in which the food was not packaged until the customer placed the order. Under this system, consumers could order hamburgers prepared especially for them without having to wait.

DDB Needham searches for "Barriers to Purchase."† These barriers are reasons why people are not buying any or enough of a product. The American Dairy Association asked DDB Needham to find out why the consumption of cheese was declining. A study identified the major barriers to increased consumption and eventually directed the agency toward the *one* barrier that was most easily correctable through advertising: the absence of *simple* cheese recipes for homemakers. The previous advertising used a campaign that focused on *elaborate* uses of cheese with *complicated* recipes.‡

Advertising can only solve message-related problems such as image, attitude, perception, and knowledge or information. It cannot solve problems related to the price of the product or its availability. A message can speak, however, to the perception that the price is too high. It can also portray a product with limited distribution as exclusive. In other words, although advertising does not determine the actual price or availability of a product, it can affect the way price and availability are perceived by consumers.

PRINCIPLE _____
Advertising turns problems into opportunities.

Advertising Opportunities. Advertising planners are adept at spotting problems and turning them into opportunities. For example, a high price can be turned into a status symbol. Likewise, limited distribution can be considered the sign of an exclusive product. Traditionally in advertising planning, problem identification is followed by a statement describing the opportunity. In other words, how can you turn this problem into an opportunity?

A DDB Needham strategy called the "Opportunity Quotient" tries to structure this process of identifying opportunities.§ The Opportunity Quotient combines acceptability and primary choice. For example, a major department store wanted to know which types of apparel from its diverse line of apparel items would offer the best advertising opportunity. After survey-

*E. E. Norris, "Seek Out the Consumer's Problem," *Advertising Age* (March 17, 1975):43–44.
†*Research for R.O.I.:1987 Communications Workshop,* DDB Needham, Chicago (April 10, 1987).
‡"In-Home Consumption of Natural Cheese," Chicago, unpublished report by DDB Needham Worldwide (1987).
§DDB Needham, *Research for ROI.*

ing the store's customers DDB Needham constructed the Opportunity Quotient for the various apparel lines by dividing the percentage of people who would consider the store for that item by the percentage who already most frequently bought the item there. Those apparel items with higher Opportunity Quotients represent the best advertising opportunities.

The crucial point to remember is this: *Use advertising to solve communication problems.* Not every product or brand can turn a high price into a status symbol. The opportunity must be based in reality and backed up by evidence. L'Oréal and Curtis Mathis, for example, can successfully use this approach because their products live up to the expectations generated by a status appeal. In contrast, it would be almost impossible to convince the gum-chewing public that a hard-to-find gum suffering from distribution problems should be sought after because it is distributed exclusively.

Advertising Strategy Decisions

advertising objectives *Statements of the effect of the advertising message on the audience.*

Advertising Objectives. Closely related to the identification of an advertising problem is the statement of the **advertising objectives.** Objectives are goal statements; they identify the effect the message is intended to have on the audience within a specified time frame. They are logically derived from the problem analysis. Ideally, if the advertising accomplishes its objectives, then the problem will have been solved.

Message Effects What can advertising do? No simple answer to this question exists. Different forms of advertising have different objectives. Direct-response advertising can stimulate an inquiry or directly generate sales. Newspaper advertising can build store traffic. Retail advertising may build an image of the store. These are action responses indicating some kind of behavioral impact. Coupon return also indicates an action response.

Most advertising, however, creates delayed action or indirect responses. Basically, advertising seeks to establish, modify, or reinforce attitudes, causing consumers to try a new product or switch brands. Brand advertising, for example, seeks to create an image or carve out a unique position for a product. Other advertisements try to call attention to a product feature or to associate a product with a certain lifestyle or typical user. The Colombian coffee campaign, for example, resulted in an attitude change, with 66 percent of the audience coming to believe that Colombia grows the best coffee as opposed to 14 percent believing that Brazil does.

Some advertisements attempt to stimulate an emotional respose, such as MCI's "friends and family" campaign. The Quaker Instant Oatmeal commercials try to create warm feelings for the product by showing parents that it's "the right thing to do."

hierarchy of effects *A set of consumer responses that moves from the least serious, involved, or complex up through the most serious, involved, or complex.*

Models for Objectives A number of models help advertisers analyze the effectiveness of their messages. Most of these models organize message effects from the simplest kind of impact to the most complex. Some of them present these effects as a series of steps in the process of moving consumers from initial awareness to final action. This series of steps is called a **hierarchy of effects.**[*]

One of the oldest advertising models is called the *AIDA* formula. It describes the process as beginning with *A*ttention, then moving to *I*nterest, then *D*esire, and finally *A*ction.

$$\text{Attention} \rightarrow \text{Interest} \rightarrow \text{Desire} \rightarrow \text{Action}$$

[*]John D. Leckenby, "Conceptual Foundations for Copytesting Research, *Advertising Working Papers,* No. 2 (February 1976).

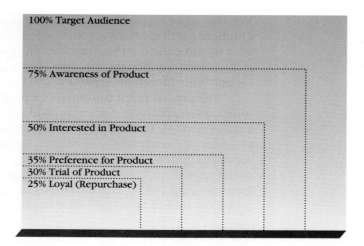

100% Target Audience

75% Awareness of Product

50% Interested in Product

35% Preference for Product

30% Trial of Product

25% Loyal (Repurchase)

FIGURE 7.2
Setting objectives using a hierarchy-of-effects model.

First the message captures the consumer's *attention.* Once the message has become recognizable, consumers become *interested,* meaning their curiosity is aroused and they are willing to hear more about the product. *Desire* suggests that the consumer has reached a decision point and would now like to try the product. Finally, *action,* the most difficult of all objectives to attain, occurs when the consumer responds to the message by actually doing something.

A similar four-step model was developed by the advertising theorist Russell H. Colley in his book *Defining Advertising Goals for Measured Advertising Results* (DAGMAR).* This DAGMAR model begins with awareness, then moves to comprehension, then conviction, and ends with action.

Awareness → Comprehension → Conviction → Action

The steps in Colley's model correspond to the *AIDA* formula. *Awareness* is a very important concept in advertising. It means that there has been some impact on the consumer's memory; in other words, consumers either remember having seen the ad or recall some of the information from it. *Comprehension* occurs when the consumer understands the information in the ad, and *conviction* when the consumer believes the information. When *action* occurs, the advertisement has affected the consumer's behavior.

Simpler effects, such as awareness, which are relatively easy to create, get higher levels of response. The more complex the effect, the lower the level of response. In other words, a lot of people may be aware of the product, but far fewer will actually try it. The hierarchy model in Figure 7.2 illustrates the relative impact of these various effects with the simplest, but broadest, response at the bottom and the most complex, but smallest, response at the top.

An example of an advertising campaign designed to stimulate action is one used by the California Almond Growers. Each ad ends with the suggestion to "Eat a can a week."

Some examples of a set of advertising objectives structured in a hierarchy are listed below. These objectives would all be established within a given time frame.

- To create an 80 percent *awareness* of the slogan (package, logo)
- To establish *knowledge* of the product's unique construction feature among 60 percent of the audience.

*Russell Colley, *Defining Advertising Goals for Measured Advertising Results* (New York: Association of National Advertisers, 1961).

- To create a positive *liking* among 50 percent of the targeted audience
- To create brand *preference* among 30 percent of the targeted audience
- To *convince* 20 percent that this product is the best in its category
- To elicit a 10 percent *response* to a coupon

Michael Ray developed the *learn-feel-do* model of message effects, which presumes that we approach a purchase situation using a sequence of responses.* In other words, we *learn* about something, then we form an opinion or attitude about it *(feel)*, and finally we take action and try it or buy it *(do)*. This model identifies three categories of effects called *cognitive* (mental or rational), *affective* (emotional), and *conative* (decision or action). Robert C. Lavidge and Gary A. Steiner associate these categories with the hierarchy of effects in the model depicted below.†

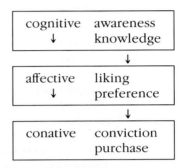

The learn-feel-do model is also called the *high-involvement* model because it depicts a series of standard responses typically found with consumers who are active participants in the process of gathering information and making a decision; they are "active" learners. This standard hierarchy is likely to be found with product categories and situations where there is a need for information, such as high-priced or major purchases, or where there is a lot of product differentiation, as in industrial products and consumer durables. This type of advertising usually provides many product details and is very informative.

In contrast, the *low-involvement* model changes the sequence of responses to learn-do-feel. According to this variation, consumers learn about a product, try it, and then form an opinion. This situation occurs when there is little interest in the product, such as with bath soap or detergent, and when there are minimal differences between the products. It is also descriptive of impulse purchasing. The idea of low involvement is based on Herbert Krugman's work explaining the effects of television advertising.‡ He theorized that television is basically a low-involvement medium and that is why a television commercial is able to produce high brand awareness and recall but have little impact on consumers' attitudes about the product.

Ray also proposed a third model for those situations where first something is tried, then there is a change in attitude, which results in learning. This is the "do-feel-learn" model, called the *dissonance/attribution hierarchy* by scholars. The idea is that the consumer selects from among several alternatives and then rationalizes the decision by developing strong positive attitudes about the product and strong negative attitudes about its com-

*Michael L. Ray, "Communication and the Hierarchy of Effects," in *New Models for Mass Communication Research,* P. Clarke, ed. (Beverly Hills, CA: Sage Publications, 1973):147–75.

†Robert C. Lavidge and Gary A. Steiner, "A Model for Predictive Measurements of Advertising Effectiveness," *Journal of Marketing 25* (October 1961):59–62.

‡Herbert E. Krugman, "The Impact of Television Advertising: Learning Without Involvement," *Public Opinion Quarterly 29* (Fall 1965):349–56.

petitors. Usually based on *selective perception and learning,* it explains how people deal with *postpurchase dissonance,* which refers to a state of psychological tension produced after a buying commitment is made. Dissonance is discussed in more detail in Chapter 5.

These models are important for advertising planners to understand because they identify the effects one can hope to achieve with an advertising message.

Targeting the Audience. As we mentioned earlier, marketing uses the term *target market* to identify prospects who might buy the product or service; advertising identifies a **target audience,** people who can be reached with a certain advertising medium and a particular message. The target audience can be equivalent to the target market, but it often includes people other than prospects, such as those who influence the purchase. For example, the target audience for an over-the-counter diet program might include doctors, pharmacists, dietitians, and government agencies concerned with health and nutrition, as well as consumers. If the product is new, another target audience might be the investment community.

Describing and Profiling Target audiences are described in terms of their demographic categories. Because these categories often overlap, the process of describing an audience is also the process of narrowing the targeting. Ad 7.3 for Lee Lites is aimed at a family audience. For example, you might use such descriptors as women 25 to 35 and suburban mall shoppers. These two categories would overlap because a certain percentage of women 25 to 35 are also in the suburban mall shopper category. Each time you add a descriptor, the targeted audience gets smaller because the group is more tightly defined. This kind of analysis lets the advertising planner pinpoint the target and zero in on the most responsive audience. Figure 7.3 illustrates how these descriptors zero in on a target. Demographic descriptions like these are particularly important to media planners who are comparing the characteristics of a targeted audience with the characteristics of the viewers, listeners, or readers of a particular medium.

AD 7.3
This ad for Lee jeans is aimed at a certain audience segment. The same ad would not appeal to all consumers of jeans. (Courtesy of Lee Jeans.)

Lee Lites. A new line of lightweight denim.

Light, cool, comfortable jeans with a remarkably soft hand. Perfect for all seasons. Available in two different finishes: Aged Stone and Aged Blue. Call your Lee sales representative today. Because Lee Lites are just what the market ordered. And they just might take off without you.

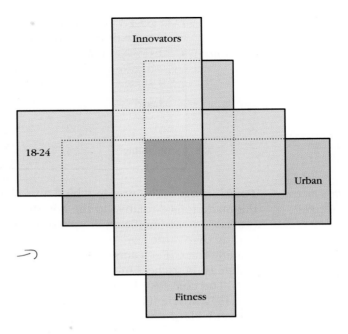

FIGURE 7.3
Targeting involves the use of overlapping descriptors to identify the most receptive audience.

profile *A personality sketch of a typical prospect in the targeted audience.*

feature analysis *A comparison of your product's features against the features of competing products.*

Profiles Audiences are also profiled in terms of the personality and lifestyle of the typical audience member. The attempt here is to identify a real person and make that person come to life for the creative people, who then try to write believable messages that will appeal to this person. For this reason, advertising research planners usually redefine the target as a **profile** of a typical user of the product. Writers then associate that general profile with someone they know. Creatives have a hard time writing moving messages to a pile of statistics. They can write much more easily and believably to someone they know who fits the description.

Product Features and Competitive Advantage. An important step in figuring out competitive advantage is to analyze your product in comparison to your competitors' products. **Feature analysis** is an easy way to structure this analysis.

If you are trying to figure out competitive advertising, first make a chart for your product and the competitor's products. Underneath each product list its features or attributes. The relevant features will vary for every product. Taste, for example, is important for sodas, horsepower and mileage are important for cars, and trendiness is important for fashion watches.

Next evaluate these lists on two dimensions. First rate how important each feature is to the target audience. (This requires primary research.) Then evaluate how well all the products perform on that feature. Your competitive advantage lies in that area where you have a strong feature that is important to the target and your competition is weak. Table 7.2 illustrates a sample analysis using a common set of hypothetical features. With parity, or undifferentiated products, the competitive advantage might lie with the image created by the advertising rather than with any specific feature.

Brand Personality. For branded products, advertising's major contribution is the development of a brand image or product personality. Familiar brands take on characteristics that we associate with people, such as warm, homey, trendy, sophisticated, and so on. These personalities are strictly added values created by the advertising.

TABLE 7.2
Feature Analysis

Feature	Importance to Prospect	Product Performance		
		Yours	X	Y	Z
Price	1	+	−	−	+
Quality	4	−	+	−	+
Style	2	+	−	+	−
Availability	3	−	+	−	−
Durability	5	−	+	+	+

positioning *The way in which a product is perceived in the marketplace by the consumers.*

PRINCIPLE
A product's position is located in the minds of the consumers.

Positioning. The way in which a product is perceived by consumers in the marketplace relative to the competition is called **positioning.** A position is a "niche" in the marketplace. A lot of strategic planning is directed at finding that "hole" or "home" in the market where a product can be positioned. The coffee campaign, for example, was able to position Colombian coffee as the richest in the world.

The concept of positioning was developed by Jack Trout and Al Ries in a 1972 article that appeared in *Advertising Age.** They pointed to an advertising classic, the "We try harder" campaign for Avis. The ad positioned the car-rental company as one that would serve its customers better because it had to work harder to compete with the number-one company, Hertz. Ad 7.4 for Suave is an example of a product that tries to position itself in the hair-care market.

*Jack Trout and Al Ries, "The Positioning Era," *Advertising Age* (April 24, May 1, 8, 1972).

AD 7.4
With intense competition in the hair-care market, Suave has carefully created a position for itself as the hair-care products that do what the expensive ones do but cost less. Notice the slogan at the bottom of the ad that reinforces the position Suave "owns." (Courtesy of Helene Curtis.)

"I LIKE WHAT SUAVE DOES. SO IT DOESN'T MAKE A WHOLE LOT OF SENSE FOR ME TO SPEND MORE."

WHEN YOU KNOW BEAUTIFUL HAIR DOESN'T HAVE TO COST A FORTUNE. Suave.

IT DOESN'T TAKE CODPIECES,
SPANDEX PANTS AND PYROTECHNICS
TO MAKE OUR MUSIC EXCITING.
(HOW FORTUNATE.)

As far as we know, Mozart never tried to ignite his piano. Beethoven passed on playing in studded leather.

Instead, they believed excitement should be drawn from something more pure. More simple. Namely, their music. You'll find this excitement, this passion, at a performance by The Houston Symphony.

Granted, you won't see any giant video monitors or laser lights. You'll see 100 musicians in formal wear.

However, watch as they play. Start with one musician, then one section, then the entire orchestra.

See how each part, each person, contributes to a greater whole. Listen. The music paints pictures no stage show can capture. It's excitement that's derived not from theatrics, but from the music. Radical notion.

For tickets, simply call 227-ARTS. The Houston Symphony. A higher form of music appreciation.

THE HOUSTON SYMPHONY
CHRISTOPH ESCHENBACH, MUSIC DIRECTOR

AD 7.5
The Houston Symphony increased their subscriptions dramatically with this creative print ad portraying classical music in a whole new light. (Courtesy of Houston Symphony Orchestra and Ogilvy & Mather.)

Establishing and moving positions requires a tremendous advertising effort. Both Marlboro cigarettes and Miller beer were originally sold to women at a time when market opportunities for cigarettes and beer for women were limited. Both were later repositioned as "macho" products through extensive costly advertising campaigns.

Ad 7.5 illustrates a case in which an advertiser repositioned a product as completely opposite from the prevailing perception of it. In this case the "product" is classical music as played by the Houston Symphony Orchestra. The campaign, created by Ogilvy & Mather of Houston, portrays classical music as exciting, dramatic, even sexy. According to Kathy Trautman, the account supervisor in charge of the campaign, Houston Symphony subscriptions went up substantially and the campaign "caused quite a stir around Houston." The campaign was recognized by *Adweek* magazine as one of the best print campaigns of 1990. The television campaign also won a Clio Award in 1991.

perceptual map *A map that shows where consumers locate various products in the category in terms of several important features.*

Perceptual Maps Positioning research begins with the feature analysis described previously. From this research you should be able to describe the most relevant attributes of your product. You can then create a *map of the marketplace* that locates the position of your product relative to the positions of all the competitors. A sample two-dimensional (using two attributes) **perceptual map** based on the preceding feature analysis appears in Figure 7.4.

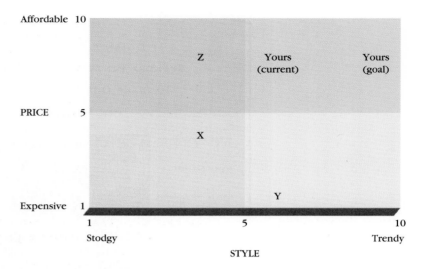

FIGURE 7.4
A two-dimensional perceptual map that examines two product attributes, price and style.

Strategically, the first step is to identify the current position of the product, if one exists using some form of perceptual mapping. For a new product, and for some established ones, a position must be established. For ongoing product lines, the decision is either to reinforce a current position or to move it.

Implementation and Evaluation

The last section of an advertising plan contains details of the implementation strategy, including scheduling and determining the budget, as well as techniques for evaluating the success of the advertising plan. We will talk in more detail about schedules in the media-planning and -buying chapters (Chapters 9 and 12). Evaluation is based on how well the plan meets its objectives, and a variety of research techniques can be used to monitor effectiveness. One specific type of control is copy testing, a scientific evaluation of the effectiveness of an advertisement. Copy testing is discussed in more detail in Chapter 21.

The Advertising Budget

The advertising budget is established by the company and is usually broken out from the overall marketing communication budget in the marketing plan. In other words, a certain percentage of the *marketing budget* is allocated to *marketing communication,* and within that budget a certain percentage is allocated to *advertising.* Budget decisions are based on the emphasis given to marketing communication within the marketing mix and to advertising within the marketing communication program.

As you can imagine, setting the budget is a major strategic decision. Typically, advertising is the biggest element in the marketing communication budget, although there is a major debate going on in the industry about just what percentage of this budget should be allocated to advertising and what percentage to sales promotion. Historically, advertising has received, on average, 60 percent of the budget, and sales promotion has received 40 percent. That split is shifting, however, because of the emphasis on short-term results, sales promotion is now receiving close to 60 percent of the communication dollars.

The budget level is important in terms of an advertising or campaign plan because it determines how much advertising the company can afford. In other words, a $50,000 budget will only stretch so far and will probably not be enough in most markets to cover the costs of television advertising. A $500,000 budget, however, will permit some television, and a $1.5 million budget will easily cover television costs. In addition to the television costs, the budget level also determines how many targets and multiple campaign plans a company or brand can support. McDonald's, for example, can easily carry on multiple campaigns designed to reach different target audiences. Likewise, certain types of advertisers—industrial and business-to-business, for example—typically operate on smaller advertising budgets than do consumer package-goods companies. Their media choices reflect their budget and narrow targeting strategies, and these companies often rely more on direct mail, trade publications, and telemarketing for their advertising.

The advertising budget may be spent by the advertising department within the company if advertising is an in-house function, or it may be assigned to the company's advertising agency. Most agencies receive commissions from the media with whom they have placed their advertising, although other reimbursement systems are becoming more popular. (Agency compensation is discussed in more detail in Chapter 4.) A typical advertising budget, then, is primarily for media expenses.

forecasting *Estimating sales levels and the impact of various budget decisions on sales.*

The big question at each of these levels (marketing mix, marketing communication mix) is: How much should we spend? Budgeting for the advertiser is essentially a **forecasting** operation. In other words, the advertiser is trying to figure out what level of sales will be generated by various levels of promotion budgeting.

Advertising planners use two primary approaches to establish the advertising budget. One is to work from the *top down*—in other words, set a figure and then allocate it among the various activities. The other way is to *build up* the budget by estimating how much each of the activities will cost and adding them up. Within these two general approaches are a number of specific procedures, some more formal than others.

task-objective method *A budgeting method that builds a budget by asking what it will cost to achieve the stated objectives.*

Task-Objective Method. The build-up approach is more commonly called the **task-objective method,** and this is probably the most common method for determining the budget level. This method looks at the objectives set for each activity and determines the cost of accomplishing each objective; what will it cost to make 50 percent of the people in your market aware of this product? How many people do you have to reach and how many times? What would be the necessary media levels and expenses?

Historical Method. History is the source for a very common top-down budgeting method. For example, a budget may simply be based on last year's budget with a percentage increase for inflation or some other marketplace factor.

percent-of-sales method *A technique for computing the budget level that is based on the relationship between cost of advertising and total sales.*

Percent-of-Sales Method. The **percent-of-sales method** is another type of top-down method. It compares the total sales with the total advertising (or promotion) budget during the previous year or the average of several years to compute a percentage. This technique can also be used across an industry to compare the expenditures of different product categories on advertising.

For example, if a company had sales figures of $5 million last year and an advertising budget of $1 million, then the ratio of advertising to sales would be 20 percent. If the marketing manager predicts sales of $6 million for next year, then the ad budget would be $1.2 million. The following explains how the percent-of-sales is computed.

$$\text{Step 1: } \frac{\text{Past advertising dollars}}{\text{Past sales}} = \text{\% of sales}$$

$$\text{Step 2: \% of sales} \times \begin{array}{c}\text{Next}\\\text{year's}\\\text{sales}\\\text{forecast}\end{array} = \begin{array}{c}\text{New}\\\text{advertising}\\\text{budget}\end{array}$$

Some categories spend a much higher percentage on promotion than others. And within the promotion budget some companies may spend more on one type of promotion and less on others—even within the same product category. For example, in the cosmetics industry Noxell, whose brands include Cover Girl and Noxzema, spends over 20 percent of its sales on advertising, whereas Avon spends only 1 percent on advertising. Avon has a much higher emphasis on personal sales in its promotional mix than Noxell does.

Competitive Methods. Budgeting often takes into account the competitive situation and uses competitors' budgets as benchmarks. *Competitive parity* budgeting relates the amount invested in advertising to the product's share of market. In order to understand this method, you need to understand the *share-of-mind* concept, which suggests that the advertiser's share of advertising—that is, the advertiser's media presence—affects the share of attention the brand will receive, and that, in turn, affects the share of market the brand can obtain.[*] The relationship can be depicted as follows:

$$\begin{array}{c}\text{Share of}\\\text{media voice}\end{array} = \begin{array}{c}\text{Share of}\\\text{consumer mind}\end{array} = \begin{array}{c}\text{Share of}\\\text{market}\end{array}$$

You should keep in mind, however, that the relationships depicted above are approximate and are used only as a rule of thumb. The actual relationship between share of media voice—an indication of advertising expenditures—and share of mind or share of market depends to a great extent on factors other than expenditures, such as the creativity of the message and the amount of clutter in the marketplace. In other words, a simple increase in the share of voice does not guarantee an equal increase in share of market.

Share of market is important to consider for certain types of advertising situations. For new products, for example, it is usually necessary to outspend competitors in order to make a dent in the market. In contrast, established brands generally don't have to spend at the level equivalent to their share of market. An example of comparitive budgeting comes from a *Wall Street Journal* article that reported that Audi's advertising and marketing costs rank among the highest in its category. In 1990, for example, the company's national advertising spending equaled an estimated $3,300 per car, more than 10 times the estimated $318 per car that General Motor's Cadillac division needs to spend annually on its national ads.[†] It is cheaper for a large company like GM to maintain its brand presence than it is for a smaller company like Audi.

Combination of Methods. In practice, many companies use a combination of budget approaches to determine a realistic budget level, comparing one benchmark or estimated budget level against another obtained from a different method.

---

[*]John J. Burnett, *Promotion Management,* 2nd ed. (St. Paul, MN: West Publishing, 1988).
[†]Bradley A. Stertz, "Audi Is Picking Up But Has Miles to Go," *The Wall Street Journal* (August 23, 1990):B1.

Three marketing professors have developed a budgeting-decision game that uses different factors and modifies the level according to the product's situation.* The underlying philosophy is to develop a base budget level using the percentage-of-sales method and then modify it for various situations. A limit is set, keeping in mind the advertising budgets of key competitors. The base budget is modified to increase or decrease the level after considering such factors as market share, product life cycle, market growth rate, product quality, and pricing strategy.

The important thing to understand about budgeting is that it reflects the marketing-mix and promotion-mix decisions. The level of the budget is determined by the emphasis that the company has decided to give to a certain area such as advertising.

*T*HE CREATIVE PLAN AND COPY STRATEGY

So far we've been discussing advertising planning in terms of an annual plan or a campaign plan, but planning goes on at another level, too. A copy strategy can also be developed for an individual advertisement, and this document focuses directly on the message and the logic behind its development.

Television and movie portrayals of copywriters often show them creating copy "on the fly." Usually this occurs during client meetings when the hard-nosed client absolutely hates the ideas presented by the robotic, button-downed account executive. The hero then leaps to his or her feet and saves the day with an idea for a brilliant ad that puts a smile on the client's face for the first time anyone can remember.

Although that scenario makes a nice drama, things rarely, if ever, happen that way in the real world of advertising. After the advertising plan has been developed and approved, the real business of creating the ads begins. Unless the creative personnel have been working on the account for a while and are intimately familiar with it, each of the ads will be developed from a plan that details the specifics of carrying out the prescribed objectives and strategies.

These plans go by various names—*creative* or *copy platform, creative work plan,* or *creative blueprint.* Not all agencies use such a document, but all copywriters work from some kind of systematic analysis of the problem to be solved. A **creative platform** is simply a way to structure this kind of analysis. It also serves as a guide to others involved in developing the advertisement so that everyone is working with the same understanding of the message strategy.

There are some general approaches to advertising message strategy. Advertisements can sell the *product* in a generic sort of way, or they can sell the *brand.* For example, Goodyear has recently moved away from its generic "Take Me Home" campaign to one that more aggressively sets the brand apart from others. The new campaign focuses on the premise that buying tires is difficult and that you should ask questions. The ads end with a slogan that focuses on brand identification: "Nobody Fits You Like Goodyear."

Another set of options looks at the information, associations, or emotions contained in the message. One approach is to focus on product *infor-*

*Amir Rashid, Hugh M. Cannon, and Edward A. Riordan, "Toward a Rule-Based Knowledge System for Making Advertising Budget Decisions in the Context of a Marketing Simulation Game," Annual Conference of the American Academy of Advertising, Chicago (April 11, 1988).

mation and provide a straightforward presentation of the product and its benefits. Another approach is to focus on the product or brand's image and try to *associate,* or link, celebrities and lifestyles with the product. A third approach is to tell a story in such a way that is moving and touches *emotions* in the audience. The Gap, for example, which has used celebrity advertising to associate its products with "individuals of style" in order to make its moderately priced clothes seem chic, is now changing its strategy to focus more on its clothes and, in particular, on the practical side of Gap jeans, workshirts, and casual clothes.

Most creative platforms combine the basic advertising decisions—problems, objectives, and target markets—with the critical elements of the sales message strategy, which include the selling premise, or main idea, and details about how the idea will be executed. Although outlines differ from agency to agency, the creative platform will include some or all of the following strategic decisions:

Creative Platform	
Advertising Strategy	**Message Strategy**
1. Problems and opportunities	1. Selling premise (claim, benefit, promise, reason why, or USP)
2. Objectives	2. Execution:
3. Target audience	Creative concept
4. Competitive advantage	Personality, tone, feel, or "look"
5. Brand image and personality	of the ad
6. Product position	

Selling Premises

Every salesperson has his or her own idea of how to approach the prospect. Different people and different situations require different strategies, and salespeople are generally more comfortable with certain approaches than with others. The same is true in advertising. The various approaches to the logic of the sales message are called **selling premises.** The most common premises are categorized as either product-centered or prospect-centered.

Product-Centered Strategies. Product-centered strategies refer to advertisements that focus on the product itself. These ads look at the attributes of the product and build a selling message around them.

A feature can be transformed into a selling point by stating what the product can do or has done. The **claim** is based on performance: how long the product lasts, how much it cleans, how little energy it uses. Torture tests, competitive tests, and before-and-after demonstrations can generate particularly strong claims. Often some scientifically conducted performance test supports such a claim.

Probably the least effective message strategy is one that focuses on the company and emphasizes the company's point of view, goals, and pronouncements with an overuse of the pronoun *we.* This kind of copy is boastful and egotistical. When you see copy with pompous headlines like "We're #1," "We've been in business for 50 years," or "We're reaching out in new directions," you know you are reading *brag-and-boast* advertising.

Prospect-Centered Strategies. The development of the marketing concept has led to a major increase in prospect-centered advertising strategies. Along with the change in marketing came a parallel switch in advertising, as message strategies focused on consumer needs rather than on product attributes. A number of message strategies use prospect-centered messages. They include (1) benefits, (2) reasons why, (3) promises, and (4) unique selling propositions (USPs).

benefits *Statements about what the product can do for the user.*

PRINCIPLE ⎯⎯⎯⎯⎯⎯⎯⎯⎯⎯
Focus on benefits, not features. Explain what the product can do for the prospect.

Benefits   At the heart of consumer-centered messages are **benefits.** In benefit strategies the product is promoted on the basis of what it can do for the consumer. Copywriters put themselves in the shoes of the prospect and ask themselves: "What does this mean to me? What can it do for me? Is the product a bargain? Will it make the prospect healthier, happier, more prosperous, more comfortable, more important, more secure, more attractive? Will it make work easier for the prospect? Will it save the consumer time or money?

To develop a benefit strategy, you must be able to turn an attribute into a benefit. Take a common product, like the shoe you're wearing. Ask yourself what each feature of that shoe does. Look at the sole—besides keeping your feet off the ground, what else does it do for you? Composition leather, for example, means it is durable and long-wearing; textured rubber may mean nonslip; different types of soles have shock-absorption features built in to help diminish the punishment of jogging or aerobics.

The following formula can be used to develop a benefit. First identify a feature, and then tell what it means to you. Fill in the blanks and you will have developed a benefit statement.

The ⎯⎯⎯⎯⎯⎯⎯⎯⎯⎯ feature is important because it will do ⎯⎯⎯⎯⎯⎯⎯⎯⎯⎯⎯⎯⎯⎯⎯⎯⎯ for me.

Note that the benefit is strictly in the mind of the consumer, not in the product. It is a subjective experience. Some sample benefit statements are:

- Crest's stannous fluoride means you don't have to worry about cavities.
- Du Pont's cordura nylon means backpacks can be light and yet tough.
- Noxzema's Clear Pink formula brings deep cleaning to sensitive skin; its Clear Green formula brings deep cleaning to oily skin.
- Hampton shoe's Bio Glide provides extra foot stability in each phase of the walking motion.

Ad 7.6 is an example of an ad that uses a benefit statement.

promise *A benefit statement that looks to the future.*

Promises   A **promise** is a benefit statement that looks to the future. It says something will happen if you use a given product. For example, if you use a certain type of toothpaste, then your breath will smell better, or your teeth will be whiter, or you will have extra cavity protection.

Furthermore, you can promise a benefit, so the two are interrelated. What makes a promise distinct is the idea of a future reward, an assurance or pledge that something will happen in the future as a result of product use.

To develop a promise, use the following formula. First specify how you use the product, and then follow with a statement of what it *will* do for you.

When I use   product , I will get   (what benefit) .

As you can see from the formula, what you promise is a benefit, so the two are related. Following are several examples of promises:

When I use Dial deodorant soap, I will feel more confident than when I use other brands.
When I take Amtrak, I will be more comfortable, better treated, and more valued (than when I take a plane).
When I take Excedrin for my headache, I will be better able to cope with the stresses in my life.
When I stay at Ramada, I will have fewer hassles than when I stay at other hotels.

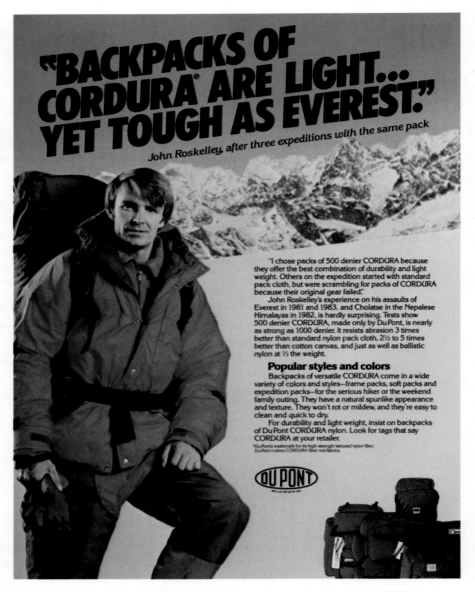

AD 7.6
This ad for Dupont's Cordura explains the qualities of this cloth.
(Courtesy of DuPont.)

---

reason why *A statement that explains why the feature will benefit the user.*

Reason Why   A **reason why** you should buy something is another form of a benefit statement. It differs from a promise in that it clearly states a reason for the benefit gained. In many benefit strategies this reason is unstated, implied, or assumed. The reason why you buy and use something is to get a certain benefit. A reason-why statement is based on logic and reasoning. The development of this form is highly rational. A reason-why statement usually begins with a benefit statement, then follows with a "because" statement that provides the "proof" or "support."

Ad 7.7 for Neutrogena Shampoo is an example of a reason-why ad. Even the headline begins with the word "why." The copy then goes on to provide all the reasons set up in the headline. To provide even more of an impression that the ad is fact-based, it is designed to appear like the editorial matter in the women's magazines in which it appears.

Other examples are: This shoe is comfortable *because* it has a unique padded interior. Or: This shoe is good for my foot *because* it has a special arch support. The padded interior and the arch support are both features. They are translated into benefits by the use of a reason-why statement that

AD 7.7
Neutrogena gives reasons for using their shampoo in this reason-why ad. (Courtesy of Neutrogena Corporation / Dailey & Associates / Photo / Bybee S.F.)

describes why the feature is important. The following are some sample reason-why statements. Notice how the "because" statement is used to give support to the argument in the examples.*

- When I take Amtrak from New York to Washington, I will feel more comfortable, better treated, and more valued than when I take a plane *because* Amtrak is a more civilized and less dehumanizing way to travel.
- When I use Dial deodorant soap, I will be more confident than when I use another brand *because* Dial has twice as much deodorant ingredient as the next-best-selling brand.

unique selling proposition *A benefit statement about a feature that is both unique to the product and important to the user.*

Unique Selling Proposition. The final consumer-oriented selling premise is the most complicated because it includes pieces of other premises such as claims, promises, and benefits. The concept of a **unique selling proposition,** or USP, was developed by Rosser Reeves, the head of the Ted Bates advertising agency.†

The heart of a USP is the *proposition,* a promise that states a specific benefit you will get from buying and using this product. This proposition must, however, be *unique.* If your product has a special formula, design, or feature protected by a patent or copyright, then you are assured that it is

*William D. Wells, *Planning for R.O.I.* (Chicago:DDB Needham Worldwide, 1987).
†Rosser Reeves, *Reality in Advertising* (New York:Knopf, 1963).

truly unique. In addition, the proposition has to be something that, in Reeves's words, will "move the mass millions." In other words, it has to be *relevant* to the prospect.

A USP, then, is a promise of a benefit that is both unique to the product and important to the prospect. A USP is frequently marked by the use of an "only" statement. This can be an outright statement or just implied. For example, the following is a USP taken from the copy for a camera:

> *USP:* This camera is the only one that lets you automatically zoom in and out to follow the action of the central figure.

Supporting Selling Premises. All of these message strategies are currently used by the industry. Different agencies favor different versions of these premises, but most of them use some structured approach to guide the development of the logic of the sales message.

Regardless of which selling premise an advertiser uses, you should be able to analyze the logic behind the premise. Most selling premises demand facts, proof, or explanations to support the claim, benefit, reason, or promise. A reason why includes the support in the "because" part of the statement. The rest of the selling premises are usually followed by copy that elaborates on the point. A claim, for example, demands some sort of proof or it won't be believed.

An example of a USP and its support is this excerpt from the strategy statement for Hubba Bubba bubble gum.‡

> *USP:* Hubba Bubba is the only chewing gum that lets you blow great big bubbles that won't stick to your face.
> *Proof:* Hubba Bubba uses a unique and exclusive nonstick formula.

PRINCIPLE _____
Support makes the selling premise believable.
_____

Support may be more important than any other part of the message strategy. Remember, support refers to everything in the message that lends credibility to the promise. If the message is to be believable or have impact, it must have support.

Volvo and Mercedes, for example, are locked in a battle on safety claims for their cars. Volvo focuses all of its advertising on car safety (see Ad. 7.8). Mercedes believes that it makes the safest cars and has used video

‡Wells, *Planning for R.O.I.*

AD 7.8
Support is a very important part of a message strategy. Volvo lends credibility to their claim that their cars are safe in their advertising.
(Courtesy of Volvo North America.)

film of its tests of rival models crashing into concrete barriers to provide convincing graphic support for its safety claims.

Execution Details

Execution of the strategy is the heart of the creative process in advertising. Developing the execution involves coming up with a creative idea variously called the *Big Idea,* or the *theme,* or the *creative concept.* This is where the creative people take the bare bones of a strategy statement and express that strategy in a way that is captivating and exciting. The execution is the creative team's "imaginative leap" that produces outstanding advertising that is both attention-getting and memorable. This creativity is discussed in detail in Chapter 13.

The details of the execution—how the advertisement "looks" and "feels"—are discussed in the chapters on creating ads for various types of media (Chapters 14 through 17). What we are talking about here is the tone of the ad—is it serious, funny, concerned, or sympathetic?

Before you can begin to understand how this creative process works, however, you must know how *advertising* works, which is the subject of the next chapter.

SUMMARY

- Strategy involves choosing the best approach for many alternatives.
- A marketing plan analyzes the situation, identifies the problems and opportunities, sets objectives, and proposes strategies.
- Advertising objectives focus on communication, or message-related, effects. Marketing objectives focus on sales.
- Advertising tries to turn problems into opportunities.
- Competitive advantage identifies those product features where you are strong and your competitors are vulnerable.
- Product personalities affect how consumers feel about products and brands.
- A position is where the consumer locates the product relative to the competition.
- An appeal is something that moves people.
- The selling premise states the logic of the sales message.
- A benefit states what the product will do for the user.

QUESTIONS

1. What do advertisers mean by "strategy"? What are the key considerations in an advertising strategy?
2. Think of a product you have purchased recently. How was it advertised? Which strategies can you discern in the advertising? Did the advertising help to convince you to purchase the product? Why or why not?
3. Day-Flo products sold 400,000 units in 1991. The total category sales (all competitors) for 1991 was 3.5 million units. What was Day-Flo's share of sales in 1991? In 1992 Day-Flo's objective is to increase unit sales by 15 percent; projections for total category sales are estimated at 10 percent. If these projections prove to be correct, what would Day-Flo's share of the market be at the end of 1992?
4. Advertising strategies are particularly sensitive to marketers who follow benefit-segmentation targeting. If you were marketing a new line of denim jeans for women, what are some of the logical benefit segments that consumer research would identify? How would advertising creative strategy shift according to segment priorities? Be as specific as possible.
5. The following is a brief excerpt from Luna Pizza's situation analysis for 1991. Luna is a regional producer of frozen pizza. Its only major competitor is Brutus Bros.

	Actual 1991	Est. 1992
Units sold	120,000	185,000
$ sales	420,000	580,000
Brutus $ sales	630,000	830,000

Estimate the 1992 advertising budgets for Luna under each of the following circumstances:

   a. Luna follows a historical method by spending 40 cents per unit sold in advertising with a 5 percent increase for inflation.

   b. Luna follows a fixed-percentage-of-projected-sales-dollars method, using 7.0 percent.

   c. Luna follows a share-of-voice method. Brutus is expected to use 6 percent of sales for its advertising budget in 1992.

6. A key to marketing-advertising strategy is the ability to convert attributes into customer-oriented benefits. Look at these attributes for an automobile for the future and change them to benefit statements.

   a. The "V" car computer-directed braking system that senses the exact pedal pressure needed for every road surface condition.

   b. The "V" has a special battery with a separate section that is climate insulated against any temperature extreme.

   c. The "V" has a programmed memory for the driver's seat that automatically positions height, distance from pedals, and steering wheel for each user.

FURTHER READINGS

AAKER, DAVID, RAJEEV BATRA, AND JOHN G. MYERS, *Advertising Management,* 4th ed. (Englewood Cliffs, NJ: Prentice Hall, 1992).

BELCH, GEORGE E., AND MICHAEL A. BELCH, *Introduction to Advertising and Promotion Management* (Homewood IL: Irwin, 1990).

ENGEL, JAMES F., MARTIN R. WARSHAW, AND THOMAS C. KINNEAR, *Promotional Strategy,* 6th ed. (Homewood, IL: Irwin, 1987).

ROSSITER, JOHN R., AND LARRY PERCY, *Advertising and Promotion Management* (New York: McGraw-Hill, 1987).

SCHULTZ, DON E., AND STANLEY I. TANNENBAUM, *Essentials of Advertising Strategy,* 2nd ed. (Lincolnwood IL: NTC Business Books, 1988).

SHIMP, TERENCE, *Promotion Management and Marketing Communications,* 2nd ed. (Chicago: Dryden, 1989).

Repositioning General Motors Automobiles: Part 2 Oldsmobile's "New Generation" Campaign

As the largest of the big three U.S. auto makers, GM stood to lose the most from increased Japanese competition. In response, in the mid-1980s GM embarked on an ambitious program to reposition its primarily mid-sized and large-sized automobiles to compete more favorably against the increasingly larger Japanese cars. At the same time the company began development of what would eventually become the Saturn subcompact car line to compete head-to-head with the smaller Japenese models.

After successfully striking a cord with American consumers with the popular "Heartbeat of America" campaign for Chevrolet, GM turned its attention to its Oldsmobile line. Improving Oldsmobile's position would be much more problematic, however, because the line lacked the type of sporty models that Chevrolet possessed, such as the Corvette and the Camaro. General Motors was also faced with the same problem facing many marketers of how to attract a younger market without alienating the aging, loyal Oldsmobile consumers.

General Motors chose to approach this dilemma by compromising. Rather than focusing exclusively on the growing younger-adult segment of the population or the aging loyal Oldsmobile consumers, GM and its agency devised a campaign they believed would appeal to both segments at the same time. Thus was born the Oldsmobile "new generation" campaign.

The spots in the campaign contained several key elements. The first was a jingle that reminded consumers that today's Oldsmobile "is not your father's Oldsmobile" and that consumers were now offered a purchase decision involving a "new generation" of cars. This central idea was visually communicated by casting the offspring of celebrities to tout the appeal of current Oldsmobile cars, only to be joined by their famous parent at the end of the spot, who would reinforce the allure of the Oldsmobile. Such celebrities as actor William Shatner and astronaut Scott Carpenter were featured in the campaign.

Unfortunately, the campaign could not achieve its objective for its two target audiences. The basic premise of a car that would not only be attractive and appealing to an aging celebrity parent but also to the celebrity's offspring is inherently self-contradictory. Although it may be reassuring to the aging Oldsmobile owner that the cars are in fact considered attractive by members of a younger generation, the opposite would almost certainly not be the case.

If today's Oldsmobiles are "not your father's," then the celebrity parents should not appear to be so comfortable riding in the cars at the end of the spot and should not be so impressed with the cars' appearance.

The campaign was also plagued with a common problem in translating storyboard concepts to final execution. In storyboard form, the campaign probably appeared to be powerful, persuasive, and perfectly capable of achieving its dual objective. The casting of untrained talent, however, even the children of famous actors, is typically a risky proposition. It was not surprising when the often stiff testimonials provided by celebrity offspring regarding the car's appearance and styling failed to add credibility to the spot's central idea in its finished form.

In fairness to the campaign itself, repositioning Oldsmobile cars to a more contemporary image was made a more difficult task because the cars themselves did not appear to be consistent with the new image. Perhaps because of its relatively large size compared to the other big domestic auto makers, GM in general and Oldsmobile in particular were slow to introduce contemporary body shapes and styles, as Ford had done. They were also slow to introduce innovative car, truck, and van models, as Chrysler had done. Consequently, the "not your father's Oldsmobile" claim was inherently difficult for the advertising to deliver because the cars themselves did not look that dissimilar from the automobiles of younger consumers' fathers.

General Motors did try to cover their bases by developing spots within the "new generation" campaign targeted specifically to the aging current Oldsmobile buyers and to the prospective young-adult market. The older consumers were targeted with high-end luxury cars by portraying elegant, silver-haired men and women on an evening out. The younger market was targeted in a spot that had the look and feel of a beer ad, complete with a soft-rock jingle and attractive young men and women interacting, with the cars as a backdrop for the frivolity.

Given an aging customer base and increasing competition from the Japanese, GM must find a more credible way to reposition Oldsmobile to appeal to a broader segment of the population. Until the cars themselves can effectively appeal to the younger-adult market, Oldsmobile will continue to be "your father's Oldsmobile."

QUESTIONS

1. Which of the "new generation" Oldsmobile spots do you believe most effectively appeals to the younger-adult market and why?
2. Which of the "new generation" Oldsmobile spots do you feel most effectively appeals to the current aging Oldsmobile market and why?
3. Assuming that major product line and body style revisions are cost prohibitive, what strategy do you believe would be most prudent for GM to employ in communications with Oldsmobile and why?

8

How Advertising Works

Chapter Objectives

When you have completed this chapter, you should be able to:

- Understand the barriers that an effective advertisement must overcome
- Be familiar with the different levels on which a viewer or reader will react to an ad
- Explain the different functions of an ad
- Explain what "breakthrough advertising" is and how it works

ZAPPROOFING THE ADS

When people don't care for a commercial, they have a new weapon to express their dislike—the remote control. Viewers are not reluctant to *zap* the ad by changing the channel. Researchers have found, for example, that Nissan's "yuppie engineer" ads were so disliked that nearly 80 percent of the viewers zapped them. These ads showed very earnest young engineers in presumably emotionally moving discussions of the cars' design. Viewers hated the Nissan ads so much they even zapped parody spots before realizing the spots were making fun of the Nissan commercials.

The remote control gives viewers a new power over advertising. This simple piece of technology lets them easily avoid messages and information that are of little or no interest to them. People have been flipping past print ads for years by turning pages; now, with the remote control, they can just as easily flip past television commercials. Moreover, they are doing it more frequently because the new viewing environment, with more networks, independents, and cable channels, offers so much more variety than ever before.

Zapping is one type of avoidance; another is *zipping,* which means fast-forwarding past the commercials on prerecorded videotapes. A related behavior is *grazing,* which means flipping around the channels, stopping now and then to look briefly at something, and then moving on. A person adept at grazing knows when a commercial break is about to begin and can time the cycle around his or her favorite channels in order to return to the original program just as the break ends.

The Pretesting Company of Englewood, New Jersey, analyzes commercials to determine at what point in a commercial audience members are likely to zap it. By knowing when and what turns people off, the company can tell which commercials stand a better chance of not being zapped. For example, Pretesting found that the word *period* in commercials for sanitary pads and tampons was embarrassing for women viewers. In laboratory studies some 60 percent of the women viewers, upon hearing that word, zapped the commercial before it was complete.

People are active viewers and watch only what interests them, frequently changing the channels to avoid messages they don't want to hear.   (Courtesy of Barbara Kirk/The Stock Market.)

The Pretesting Company has found other types of commercials that may be prone to zapping, including comparative ads and ads that leave out the brand name until the end. Parodies of other commercials are also vulnerable to zapping, especially if people didn't like the originals. A number of agencies are using the service to test their commercials, not only to isolate problems, but also to develop ads that are "zapproof," or at least zapresistant. The key to zapproofing is to develop ads with "stopping power," or "breakthrough advertising." Of course, once the ad arrests viewers' attention, it must keep that attention and address needs that are relevant to viewers.*

ADVERTISING IMPACT

Keith Reinhard, president of DDB Needham, has said, "Today, more than ever, if advertising is not relevant, it has no purpose. If it is not original, it will attract no attention. If it does not strike with impact, it will make no lasting impression."† Relevance, originality, and impact—ROI—these are the three key elements of effective advertising. Advertising that is relevant speaks to you about things you care about; advertising that is original catches your attention by its creativity; and advertising that has impact accomplishes the ultimate objective—it makes an impression.

In order to understand the importance of these ingredients and the environment within which they are created, this chapter will focus on the psychology behind advertising. It is important for you to know how advertising works—and doesn't work—in order to understand how advertising is created. First, let's discuss the environment in which advertising operates, and the audience's interaction with the advertisement.

The Advertising Environment

The advertising environment is very cluttered. Some 40,000 magazines and journals are published in the United States every year, and more than 10,000 radio stations crowd the airwaves. Sixty percent of American homes are now wired for cable television, and the average household can view 27 channels. Tied to the explosion in media outlets is the monumental increase in the number of commercial messages. Since 1965, for example, the number of network television commercials has tripled from approximately 1,800 to nearly 5,400 per year. This number is increasing by 20 percent annually as more advertisements are being run during commercial breaks. Networks often run five or six commercials in a row, and during prime time commercials average 10.5 minutes per hour.‡

As you can see, there is a lot of competition for people's attention. Advertising occurs within a glut of information-laden messages. Other media, ads, people, news stories, and random thoughts get in the way of advertisers' very expensive and carefully constructed commercial messages.

*Adapted from Jon Berry, "Zap Attack: How Audience Research Is Shaping Ads." *Adweek* (July 9, 1990):1; Carrie Heeter and Bradley S. Greenberg, *CableViewing* (Norwood, NJ: Ablex, 1988); and Sandra Moriarty, "Explorations into the Commercial Encounter," American Academy of Advertising Annual Conference, Reno, NV (April 1991).
†William D. Wells, *Planning for R.O.I.* (Englewood Cliffs, NJ: Prentice Hall, 1989):x–xi.
‡Peter F. Eder, "Advertising and Mass Marketing," *The Futurist* (May–June 1990):38–40.

The Audience

Given this cluttered environment, most people only give advertising their *divided attention*. A few ads may break through and receive total concentration, but that is very rare. At best an ad gets half the mind and one eye. Advertisers are also up against a *short attention span*. Human concentration happens in quick bursts. A compelling story may get a minute or two of concentrated time, but most media messages can only count on a few seconds. The actual information that gets attended to, then, is nothing more than a quick impression or a message fragment.

Information Processing.   Besides problems with attention, viewers have problems sorting out the information they are exposed to. Media messages become entangled in what psychologists call our *information processing*. Our minds are not tidy, and the approach we take to making sense of information is not as predictable or as thorough as an advertiser might like.

For example, most people reading a newspaper or magazine don't see much difference between editorial information and advertisements. They browse, scan, jump back and forth, and find snippets of useful information in both categories. Ads are often welcomed in newspapers and magazines because they are considered to be news of a sort. Furthermore, print ads are not forced on people. They can be scanned or ignored; the decision to follow through and read or to jump to another message is the reader's.

Similarly, every time you watch a television commercial, you must decide whether to attend to it or not. The decision is always yours, even though you may not be aware of it. If you make a commitment, it lasts only as long as the message maintains your interest. When you lose interest, your attention shifts and you move on to some other message.

Avoidance.   We have already mentioned that most people are very good at avoiding information that doesn't interest them. Bombarded with a huge number of commercials on television, you have no doubt become very good at avoidance. You probably don't even scan the commercials that don't interest you. If you are like most people, you will either change the channel, mute the sound, leave the room, or turn your attention elsewhere. Most people avoid most commercials in one way or another. Typical viewers may note the first commercial in a cluster, then, depending on whether it catches their attention, they do or do not stick around for the remaining message.* Actually, very few people watch all the way through a commercial break.

Furthermore, many consumers are scornful of advertising. A national survey found that 60 percent of consumers agreed that "advertising insults my intelligence," and over 70 percent said they "don't believe a company's ad when it claims test results show its product to be better than competitive products."† Disbelief, dislike, and irritation are very important aspects of the consumer response to advertising. The Concepts and Controversies box entitled "The Irritation Factor" takes a closer look at these aspects.

Breakthrough Advertising

This discussion dramatizes how few advertisements actually get read or watched. You may scan most of the stories and ads in the newspaper, but with limited concentration. Maybe half of all ads actually are noticed on a

*Sandra E. Moriarty, "The Commercial Encounter."
†Stephen J. Hoch and Young-Won Ha, "Consumer Learning: Advertising and the Ambiguity of Product Experience," *Journal of Consumer Research* (September 1986):221–33.

Dramatic, colorful, and unusual events can capture and maintain interest. (Dan Burns/Monkmeyer Press.)

"thinking" level. Perhaps 20 percent are read a little, and very few are read thoroughly.

Advertising that makes any impact at all breaks through this inattention and mindless scanning; it helps consumers sort out and remember what they see and hear; and it overcomes established patterns of avoidance and scorn. Such advertising is called *breakthrough advertising*. It is novel, compelling, and interesting. It speaks to the concerns of its audience on a personal level without being patronizing or phony.

THE PSYCHOLOGY OF ADVERTISING

How does advertising work? This is a very complex question. One thing we do know is that advertising may communicate a number of messages in a number of areas simultaneously. For example, at the same time you are trying to understand a copy point, you may also be forming a favorable or an unfavorable opinion of the product being advertised. The message's impact on both knowledge and liking can happen simultaneously.*

The following discussion will analyze how advertising works in terms of four basic psychological categories: *perception, awareness, understanding,* and *persuasion.*

Perception: Creating Stopping Power

When something has been perceived, it has been noted, and the message has registered. One of the biggest challenges for an advertiser trying to reach consumers with either a newspaper or a television ad is simply to get them to notice it. This is harder than it appears. Not only do consumers miss half the messages directed at them, there are all those other commercials on other channels and in other newspapers and magazines competing for their attention. The first step in perception, then, and one of the hardest to accomplish, is simple *exposure.*

*Sandra E. Moriarty, "Beyond the Hierarchy of Effects: A Conceptual Model," in *Current Issues and Research in Advertising,* James H. Leigh and Claude R. Martin, Jr., eds. (Ann Arbor: University of Michigan Graduate School of Business, 1983):45–56.

THE IRRITATION FACTOR

Everyone loves to hate the "ring around your collar" commercials, and more people make fun of Mr. Whipple than any other television celebrity. Why do advertisers use these techniques when viewers find them so irritating? Why do people like some commercials and despise others? Irritating ads are defined as those that cause displeasure and momentary impatience. The response is more negative than simple *dislike*.

Research has found that disliked advertising might work anyway because it generates high levels of attention and recall. Everyone does remember Mr. Whipple, after all. Even if consumers dislike these commercials, when they get to the store they remember the product name and forget their irritation at the ad. Still, it makes sense to assume that viewers' negative perceptions of the message usually do carry over to the product itself. One wonders if those irritating commercials are successful *in spite of* the message strategy rather than because of it.

Research into irritating advertising has found that a major source of irritation is the product itself; for example, feminine-hygiene products, underwear, laxatives, and hemorrhoid treatments. Regarding message strategy, irritation levels are higher when the situation is contrived, phony, unbelievable, or overdramatized. In the case of a sensitive product, the ads are more irritating when the product and its use are emphasized; indirect approaches seem to work better. Viewers also don't like to see people "put down" or forced into stereotypical roles. Neither do they like to see important relationships threatened, such as mother-daughter or husband-wife.

What do you think about the irritation factor in advertising? Can you remember any ads that you particularly disliked? Can you remember some that you liked? Why did you react that way? Are there products and situations where it isn't important for the commercial to be liked? If a particular commercial is irritating and unpopular but the product sells well, should that commercial be considered a success? Why or why not?

Source: David A. Aaker and Donald E. Bruzzone, "Causes of Irritation in Advertising," *Journal of Marketing* (Spring 1985):47–57.

Exposure.   Exposure is primarily a media-buying problem. First the message has to be placed in a medium that your target sees, reads, watches, or listens to. Then the message must survive the initial scan-and-avoid decision—in other words, exposure also depends on whether the message is attractive enough to keep the viewer or reader from changing the channel or turning the page. Exposure is therefore the minimum requirement for perception. If your target changes the channel, then no matter how great the message is, it will *not* be perceived.

Attention.   Once the audience has been exposed to the message, the next step is to keep their attention. Attention means the mind is engaged; it is focusing on something. Attention is aroused by a *trigger,* something that "catches" the target's interest. The trigger can be something in the message or something within the reader or viewer that makes him or her "lock onto" a particular message. In print it may be a sale price in large type, a startling illustration, or a strong headline. On television the trigger may be sound effects, music, a scene that is action oriented or visually interesting, or a captivating idea.

Getting attention involves more than just attracting the notice of the viewer or reader, however. When you are in the scanning mode, your attention is wandering. Nailing down attention requires some kind of *stopping power.* Ads that stop the scanning are usually high in intrusiveness or originality.

Intrusiveness. Advertisements are designed to be attention-getting, and that means they sometimes have to be intrusive—in other words, they have to force attention. Television commercials, especially, are designed to be intrusive, and viewers often resent the intrusion in the middle of their favorite program. As a result, viewers tend to leave the room or change the channel. Intrusive commercials are particularly important for products that have a small "share of mind"—those that are either not very well known or not very involving or interesting. In many cases there is little difference between competing brands, so the product interest is created solely by the advertising message.

What can you do to create this kind of impact? Many intrusive ads use loud, bold effects to attract viewer attention—they work by shouting. Others use captivating ideas or mesmerizing visuals. For print ads, for example, research has found that *contrast* can attract viewer attention. If every other ad in the medium is big and bold, then be small, quiet, and simple—use a lot of white space. If everything is tiny and gray (like type), then be bold and black or use color. If everything is colorful, then use black and white. Identify the characteristics of the medium environment and then do something different. The Energizer bunny campaign is an example of advertising that is intrusive, yet captivating. The pink bunny marches onto the scene beating its drum, interrupting a variety of 15-second parody television spots. In print the energetic bunny marches through a page of text, scattering lines of type in all directions (see Ad 8.1).

Originality. Creative advertising is unique, novel, or original. The function of originality is to capture attention. People will notice something that

AD 8.1
This magazine ad for Energizer batteries features the Energizer bunny disrupting a "story" in a magazine. The ubiquitous bunny has been parodied and satirized, but it has kept Energizer at the top of consumers' minds. (Courtesy of Energizer Corporation)

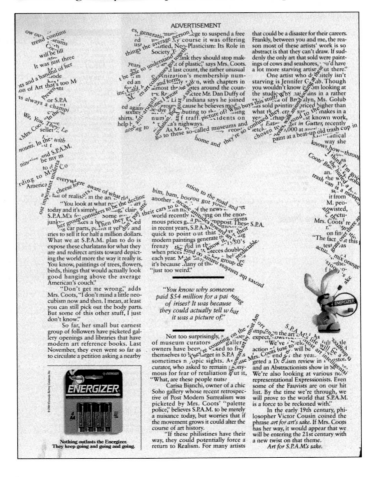

is new, novel, or surprising. Creative, or original, advertising breaks through the old patterns of seeing and saying without being irrelevant or too bizarre. The unexpectedness of the new idea is what creates stopping power.

Outrageous effects can also create impact. An article in *The New York Times* described an effort at the Young & Rubicam (Y&R) agency to push its creative people to take more risks to make their ads more distinctive. For an Irish Spring ad the agency used a fully clothed man with a bar of soap in his hand. By all appearances, he is about to launch into a standard pitch. Suddenly the ad turns slapstick. He loses control of the soap. It squirts him in the face and lathers up in his pocket. Such unorthodox ideas are being used successfully by Y&R to sell things like toothpaste, coffee, and ice cream.

To encourage this kind of freewheeling thinking Y&R set up a program called the Risk Lab that allowed copywriters and art directors to have their ideas informally tested by researchers in the early stages of concept development. The director of creative research, Dr. Stephanie Kugelman, took the title ''Dr. Risk'' and moved to the creative floors to work closely with the creative people.

As an example of daring to do something different, Y&R used a set of teeth 17 feet tall as an attention-getting device in a tartar-control ad for Colgate. During a research session a consumer described tartar as a ''wall'' and that image became the creative concept. The action showed a construction crew inside the ''mouth'' painting tartar on the teeth. The commercial was used first in England, and people were so intrigued they even asked to see it again. It also contributed to a huge increase in Colgate's share of the toothpaste market.*

Awareness: Making an Impression

Once a message has been perceived and has caught your attention, your perceptual process can move on to the next step, which is awareness. Awareness implies that the message has made an impression on the viewer or reader, who can subsequently identify the advertiser or product. Awareness is a low-level form of impact, but it is the goal of a great many ads. A simple recognition test can determine whether an ad has created product awareness.

Attention and awareness are message-design problems. The advertising message can, and must, compete with other messages in the same medium. Within a news medium, the advertising has to be able to compete with the intrinsically interesting nature of the news. In an entertainment medium like television, the advertising has to compete with the mesmerizing entertainment values of programming. Radio is almost always a background medium, and outdoor advertising is directed toward an audience whose attention, by definition, is directed elsewhere. Not only does outdoor advertising have to compete for attention, it also has to be able to win out over distractions such as other signs along the road, the car radio or tape deck, and conversations among passengers.

Relatively low levels of attention can create a minimal level of awareness for low-interest products. If the objective is simply brand or product reminder, then the attention level doesn't need to be as high as it does when the objective calls for the understanding of a copy point.

*Eileen Prescott, ''An Agency's Turn to Madcap Ads.'' *The New York Times* (June 7, 1987):1, 8–9.

Interest.   Awareness means you are tuned into the ad, and for that to happen, there has to be something in the message that interests you. Most people want to hear or read about themselves and the things they care about. They want to know how to improve their skills, look better, live longer, make more money, or save themselves time and expense. People will pay attention to advertising only if it's worth their while to do so. They make a deal with the advertiser: "Make it worth my time and I'll pay attention to your message as long as it doesn't bore me."

Selective perception, which we discussed in Chapter 5, is driven by interest. We pay attention to ads that speak to our wants and needs by providing information about such things as work, hobbies, roles, and relationships. Selection—being interested in one thing and not in something else—is also driven by our situations. When we are hungry or thirsty, for example, we pay more attention to food and drink ads.

Product Interest   There are many types of interest: You might be interested in the product advertised or in some element in the ad itself—the model or star, the promise made in the headline or by the announcer, or an unusual graphic or production technique. Different topics, product categories, and products have different levels of *built-in interest*. Some products are just inherently more interesting than others. Food and vacations, for example, are more interesting to most people than are toilet cleaners. Some products are of interest to specific groups of people. A man might look at an ad for tires but avoid an ad for diapers or a feminine-hygiene product.

Personal Interest   Interest is usually created by one of two things—personal involvement or something intriguing. You have some predispositions that affect what interests you—getting through school, hobbies, a trip you want to take, or a career goal. If a message applies to any of these elements in your life, then it affects you personally and you may have an interest in the message. Most people also respond to general "human-interest" items—a topic that strikes some universal chord, such as babies, kittens, and puppies, as well as tragedies and success stories.

Something that is intriguing stimulates your curiosity and makes you want to know more. Curiosity provides the "cognitive nudge" that engages your mind. Whenever you are confronted with something new, there is a period of curiosity, usually accompanied by doubt or some kind of questioning. New information is often greeted by phrases like "Can you believe it?" This confrontation of curiosity with doubt means you have entered the *interested* state.

Advertisers who are trying to develop a message that stimulates interest will speak to the personal interests of their target audience as well as do something to elicit curiosity. Ads that open with questions or dubious statements are designed to build interest and create awareness. For example, Ad 8.2 for Schick Personal Touch razors uses a provocative headline to pull readers into the ad. We discussed getting attention as the *stopping power* of an advertisement; keeping attention is the *pulling power* of an ad—it keeps pulling the reader or viewer through to the end of the message.

Maintaining Interest.   Interest is a momentary thing; it dies easily as attention shifts. A major challenge in advertising is to maintain interest until the point of the message is reached. Because of the scanning and browsing behavior of many readers and viewers, maintaining interest is more difficult than arousing it.

If you are worried about maintaining interest in an advertisement,

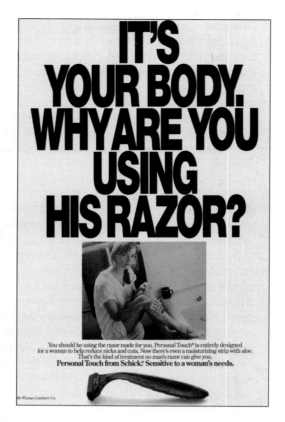

AD 8.2
This ad for Schick razors for women attracts attention with a bold headline, large type, and an involving question. (Courtesy of Warner-Lambert Co.)

then you must consider the pulling power of your message. This is primarily a sequencing problem: Does your copy pull the reader or viewer through to the end? How does the message develop? For example, if you start with a question, then the reader has to continue through the ad to find the answer. Storytelling is a good technique to hold the audience. Most people want to know how a story comes out. Suspense, drama, and narrative are good literary tools for maintaining interest.

Television has built-in sequencing because of the moving image. If skillfully used, the motion and action of a video message are very hard to ignore. A layout in a print ad can do the same thing. A layout can be designed with strong direction or movement cues that keep the eye of the reader engaged.

involvement *The intensity of the consumer's interest in a product.*

Involvement. We talked about relevance in the introduction to this chapter, and that is a key factor in the concept of **involvement,** which refers to the intensity of the consumer's interest in a product, medium, or message. *High involvement* means that a product—or information about it—is important and personally relevant. *Low involvement* means that the product or information is perceived as unimportant. Typically, people in a high-involvement situation—as when purchasing a new car, home, or European vacation—will be searching for information and critically evaluating it. Advertising for high-involvement products usually provides a lot of information about the product. In contrast, low-involvement purchases, such as chewing gum, toothpaste, and paper towels, are made without much searching and with little effort to think critically about the decision. Advertising for this type of product often focuses on simple key points, emotions, lifestyles, or images.

The word *involvement* is also used to describe an advertising technique that tries to get the audience to participate in how the message develops and evolves. Compelling readers or viewers to get involved in the message either physically or mentally is a strong persuasive technique. For example, some ads start with a question in order to draw people into constructing the answer. An oil company advertisement displays a big picture of a beautiful forest and asks the reader to find the oil well hidden somewhere among the trees to dramatize the point that oil drilling can be respectful of nature. The more involved the prospects are in developing the message, the more impact the message has.

Understanding: Making it Clear

Being aware of the message is not enough. The message must be understood as well. *Understanding* refers to a conscious mental effort to make sense of the information being presented. That is how we learn things. Whereas attention can be a relatively passive response, understanding demands an active response from the audience. It is an important part of the process of dealing with information. First we find ourselves interested, then we learn something about the subject of our interest, then we file it away in our memories. That is called *knowing*.

Understanding is particularly important for ads that present a lot of information—brand, price, size, how the product works, when and where to use it, and so on. When product differences exist, the features and how they translate into selling points are also important pieces of information to understand. An important requirement of informational advertising is that the explanation be clear and relevant to the prospect. Consumers have little patience with ads that are confusing, vague, or unfocused. The reader or viewer must be able to follow the logic, make discriminations, compare and contrast points of view, comprehend reasons and arguments, synthesize and organize facts, and, in general, make sense of things. If you are designing an advertising message where understanding is an objective, then you are probably dealing with factually based information, and you will be testing the effectiveness of your message by recall methods. Your ad must present the facts in a way that makes it easy for people to assimilate the information. Clarity is important.

Teaching and Knowing. Teaching is a very important element of advertising because most advertisers want people to know something after they have read, watched, or heard the message. Knowledge means the facts have been acquired through experience or study. In the case of new products, ads must bridge the gap in people's experience by teaching them how to recognize and use the product. Some brand advertising is primarily designed to teach people how to say the name and recognize the package. This may be simple identification, but it is learning nonetheless.

The literary tools of a message designed to stimulate understanding include definition, explanation, demonstration, comparison, and contrast. Definition and explanation are primarily verbal concepts, but demonstration, comparison, and contrast are often communicated in visuals. Any visual, whether print or video, can be used to compare two products or to show before-and-after scenarios. Television is particularly good for demonstration because it can show a sequence of operations.

Association. Another way to "know" something is to make a connection in your mind. When you link up two concepts—fall and football, for example—you have learned something. Association is used in advertising to

AD 8.3
This ad for the PostScript laser printer software links all the warm feelings we have about the cherry at the top of the dessert or the filling in the cake with the qualities that make this software "the best part" of the computer system. (Courtesy of Adobe Systems.)

build images. Advertisements that use association try to get you to know something by linking the product with something you aspire to, respect, value, or appreciate—like an envied lifestyle or person.

A metaphoric use of association appears in a campaign for the printer language called PostScript. This is a difficult concept to sell, so the creators of the advertising used a cherry to represent "the best part" of the computer system (see Ad 8.3).

Persuasion: Making Moving Messages

In addition to providing information, advertisements must persuade people to believe or do something. A persuasive message will try to establish, reinforce, or change an attitude, build an argument, touch an emotion, or anchor a conviction firmly in the prospect's belief structure. How do people feel about the product—do they like it or hate it? How do they feel about the ad?

Believability is an extremely important concept in advertising. Do consumers believe ads? Are the claims believable? Do spokespersons, particularly authority figures, have credibility? Consumers say they do not believe in advertising claims, but at the same time they find advertising helpful in making better decisions. Recent research has found that although consumers want proof of the validity of advertisers' claims, they do not require very convincing evidence to accept these claims.*

*Hoch and Ha, "Consumer Learning," pp. 221–33.

Support may be more important than any other part of the message strategy. Remember, support refers to everything in the message that lends credibility to the promise. If you want your message to be believable or to have impact, you must provide support.

appeal *Something that moves people.*

Appeals. Persuasion in advertising rests on the psychological appeal to the consumer. An **appeal** is something that makes the product particularly attractive or interesting to the consumer. Common appeals are security, esteem, fear, sex, and sensory pleasure. Appeals generally pinpoint the anticipated response of the prospect to the product and message.

Advertisers also use the word *appeal* to describe a general creative strategy. For example, if the price is emphasized in the ad, then the appeal is value, economy, or savings. If the product saves time or effort, then the appeal is convenience. A message that focuses on a mother or father making something for a child—like cookies or a rocker—might elicit an appeal of family love and concern. A *status appeal* is used to establish something as a quality, expensive product. *Appetite appeal* using mouth-watering visuals is used in food advertising.

Attitudes and Opinions. Beliefs, attitudes, and values structure our opinions, which in turn reflect how negatively or positively we feel about something. This is how we *evaluate* the information we receive.

People's opinions are built on a complex structure of attitudes. Every person has a different attitude structure based on individual experiences. Advertising that seeks to affect this complex structure of attitudes will usually attempt to accomplish one of three things:

1. Establish a new opinion where none has existed before
2. Reinforce an existing opinion
3. Change an existing opinion

New opinions need to be created when a new product is introduced. If this is your goal, then you can assume the slate is clean and that your advertising will be a primary force in the development of the target audience's initial opinion about your product. Consumer opinion concerning the product or service, of course, will be modified or confirmed as the product is used. No matter how strong your advertising, a bad experience with a new product will negate all of the positive attitudes your message has implanted.

The Saturn automobile advertisement is an example of advertising that is trying to change an attitude (see Ad 8.4). Its message is trying to rebuild consumer confidence in American automobile manufacturing by focusing on the people who make the cars and their enthusiastic participation in the building process.

Likability. Likability is an important indicator of positive attitudes toward a product or a message. An advertiser will try to build positive attitudes for new products and maintain existing positive attitudes for successsful mature products. When a product is liked well enough by consumers to generate repeat sales, that is called **brand loyalty.**

It is more unusual, and much harder, to try to change negative attitudes. If your product has a negative image—perhaps because the initial product or marketing strategy was faulty—then a major objective is to turn that consumer attitude around. This is very difficult and requires both a big budget and a major media blitz.

brand loyalty *Existing positive opinions held by consumers about the product or service.*

ALTON SMITH *has always loved cars. He first turned his backyard hobby into a full-time occupation in 1964, when he took a job on the line inspecting brake drums, fittings and gears. He remembers being gung-ho "because the guys depended on you." After nineteen years in the business, Alton talks about being gung-ho again. This time as a tool and die maker, building a brand new car called Saturn in Spring Hill, Tennessee.*

"...My best buddies in high school were twins. A couple of guys named Hugh and Hugo. We all had cars. And every Saturday we'd tear something down and put it back together just for the fun of it. So it's no big surprise that we all ended up in the car business.

But those guys wouldn't ever believe I just picked up and went to work for a car company that's never built a car before.

Well, what I'm doing now here at Saturn is something completely different.

Here, we don't have management and we don't have labor. We have teams. And we have what you call consensus. Everything's a group decision.

In the last seven months, I've only had a few days off here and there. But this is where I want to be. This is living heaven.

You work through breaks and you work through lunch. You're here all hours and even sometimes Saturdays. And you don't mind. Because no one's making you do it. It's just that here you can build cars the way you know they ought to be built.

I know the competition's stiff. I was out in California for a family reunion and everything was an import. Hondas, Toyotas. Well, now we're going to give people something else to buy.

I wouldn't be working all these hours if I didn't think we could...."

SATURN

A DIFFERENT KIND *of* COMPANY. A DIFFERENT KIND *of* CAR.
If you'd like to know more about Saturn, and our new sedans and coupe, please call us at 1-800-522-5000.

AD 8.4
By showing the dedicated employees who make the new Saturn automobile, the company hopes to change the negative attitudes that have developed about American automobiles. (Reprinted with permission of Saturn Corporation.)

Miller beer, for example, was originally seen as a woman's beer. Its slogan, "The champagne of bottled beer," spoke to that audience but turned off the male audience, which, in the 1950s and 1960s, consumed much more beer than women did. After the Philip Morris Company bought Miller, the beer was repositioned as a man's product, and subsequent advertising campaigns ignored that original slogan, using instead scenes of "macho" males in "tough guy" roles.

Twizzlers, a licorice candy, had a category problem. It had to compete against such big names as Tootsie Roll in the "chewy candy" subcategory of the candy market. The target for these candies is generally teens and children. Although most people like candy, licorice is not as well accepted. DDB Needham took on the challenge and created a strikingly visual campaign based on "singing mouths" that sang into a Twizzler microphone. Because the ads were so well liked, sales increased by 30 percent during the first year of the campaign. While all its competitors were losing share, Twizzler's share went up nearly 10 percent, to 37 percent of the market. The category grew at a rate of 7 percent, most of which represented Twizzler's growth.*

Arguments. Persuasive messages deal with more than basic attitude structure. People are persuaded by argument or reasoning. Reasons are

* "Twizzler Case Study," unpublished document by DDB Needham, Chicago (1986).

based on logic and the development of an argument. Argument in this sense refers not to a disagreement, but to a line of reasoning where one point follows from another, leading up to a conclusion. Your ad must focus on logic and proof when you are dealing with reasons. That is why the "reason-why" selling premise is a very common message strategy used in advertising.

Emotions. Persuasion is also concerned with emotions. How someone "feels" about your product, service, brand, or company is just as important as what that person knows about it. *Feeling* in this sense refers to an attitude, but it is an attitude surrounded by emotions. The intensity of the response comes from the emotions. If you touch someone's emotions with your message, he or she is more likely to remember the message. The telephone and greeting-card companies have been very successful with emotional campaigns because, after all, they are selling sentiment—warm feelings, love, missing someone, nostalgia, and so on. Ad 8.5 expresses the emotion behind a phone call.

Many of our buying decisions are emotional ones. We buy shoes because we don't want to go barefoot, but we buy a closetful of shoes for reasons other than necessity: different styles for different occasions and different moods. We often use "logical" surface reasons to justify emotional decisions that we seldom acknowledge.

AD 8.5
Ads such as this one for Southwestern Bell Telephone are designed to appeal to emotions rather than logic. Who is the target audience for this ad and what are they supposed to feel when they read it?
(Courtesy of Southwestern Bell Telephone.)

Conviction. Attitudes, reasons, logic, and emotion are all part of the persuasive package. What they lead to is belief. We believe something about every product we purchase; if we didn't, we wouldn't buy it. We believe it is good for us, it will make us look better or live better, or it will make us

I got this brother. He used to crack me up. When we were kids, he'd make up these jokes. Most of 'em didn't make much sense. But he'd always break out laughin', which made me laugh, and pretty soon we're both rollin' on the floor in tears. I called him today. Just to say hi. And you know what? That son of a gun did it again...

When you're far apart, long distance is the easiest way to let someone know how you feel. Just pick up the phone and dial 1+. And a little of you will go a long, long way.
The one to call on.

Southwestern Bell Telephone

richer or healthier. Even low-involvement products like chewing gum involve some belief system. I buy this brand of gum rather than another one because I believe this gum will taste better, freshen my breath, or do less damage to my teeth.

A conviction is a particularly strong belief that has been anchored firmly in the attitude structure. It is built of strong rational arguments that use such techniques as test results, before-and-after visuals, and demonstrations to prove something. Opinions based on convictions are very hard to change. Changing such a belief may mean completely rebuilding our entire attitude structure, which is a difficult and painful process. However, an advertiser who can build conviction in the target audience about a product or service achieves a virtually unassailable position.

Although building a convincing argument is an important part of persuasion, another technique used in advertising to build conviction is *demonstration*. According to the old adage, seeing is believing. Product performance that can be demonstrated tends to remove doubt and make it easy to believe the sales message.

Locking Power: Making it Memorable

Whereas perception and attention create stopping power, and maintaining awareness is the pulling power of an ad, ads that work effectively also have locking power—that is, they lock their messages into the mind. If you can't remember seeing the ad, or if you can remember the ad but not the brand, then you might as well not have seen it as far as the advertiser is concerned. When you go to the supermarket, it is important that you remember you saw the ad that announced soft drinks are on sale. It is also important that you remember the ad was for a certain brand. How does that process happen?

Our memories are like filing cabinets. You watch a commercial, extract those parts of it that interest you, and then find a category in your mental filing cabinet where you can store that fragment of information. The fragment, incidentally, may not look much like the original information as it was presented because your mind will change it to make it fit into your own system of concerns, preoccupations, and preconceptions.

A week later you may not remember that you have a fragment labeled "soft drink" filed away, or you may not be able to find it in the file. Most of us have messy mental filing systems. You have probably found yourself trying to remember something that you know. You can concentrate until your head hurts, and the thought just won't come to the surface. It does come back when it is cued, however. Maybe you remember the party you have planned for the weekend and that *reminds* you about the soft drink sale. That is how the *cueing* process works to pull things out of the file and back onto the top of our minds. A pink bunny reminds you that you need batteries and that they should be the Energizer brand.

Advertising research focuses on two types of memory—**recognition** and **recall**. Recognition means you can remember having seen something before; in other words, it has achieved *top-of-mind awareness*. Recall is more complex. It means you can remember the information content of the message. These concepts and research methods are discussed in more detail in Chapter 21.

Vampire Creativity.   One of the greatest challenges in the advertising world is to create memorability. It is easier to create a memorable advertisement than it is to create an advertisement that makes the product memorable. Testing has proved time and again that people often remember the commercial, but not the product. This problem, called **vampire creativity,** occurs primarily with advertisements that are *too* original, *too* entertaining, or *too* involving. The story of the commercial can be so mesmerizing that it gets in the way of the product. Celebrity advertising can have this problem. Ray Charles, M.C. Hammer, and Michael Jackson all appear in song-and-dance extravagances for soft drinks, but many viewers cannot remember which celebrity is associated with which product. It is essential that the commercial establish a strong link between the message and the product so that remembering the story also means remembering the product.

Repetition. There are several things you can do to ensure the memorability of your message. One technique is *repetition.* Psychologists maintain that you need to hear or see something a minimum of three times before it crosses the threshold of perception and enters into memory. The Yellow Pages ad uses visual as well as verbal repetition to establish the Yellow Pages identity (see Ad 8.6). **Jingles** are valuable memorability devices because the music makes it possible to repeat a phrase or product name without boring the audience.

jingles *Commercials with a message that is presented musically.*

Clever phrases are also useful not only because they catch attention, but also because they can be repeated to intensify memorability. Advertisements use **slogans** for brands and campaigns (a series of ads run under an umbrella theme). How many slogans can you identify in the Slogan Test box? **Taglines** are clever phrases that are used at the end of an ad to summarize the point of the ad's message in a highly memorable way such as: "Nothing outlasts the Energizer. They keep going and going and going." Both slogans and taglines are written to be highly memorable, often using *mnemonic* devices (techniques for improving memory) such as rhyme, rhythmic beats, and repeating sounds.

slogans *Frequently repeated phrases that provide continuity to an advertising campaign.*

taglines *Clever phrases used at the end of an advertisement to summarize the ad's message.*

Key Visuals. In addition to verbal memorability devices, most television commercials utilize a **key visual.** This is a dominant visual that the advertiser hopes will remain in the mind of the viewer. Remember that the memory's filing system usually stores fragments of information. Television is primarily a visual medium, and an effective commercial is built on some dominant scene or piece of action that conveys the essence of the message and can be easily remembered.

key visual *A dominant image around which the commercial's message is planned.*

There is also a structural dimension to memorability. Just as the beginning of an advertising message is the most important part for attracting attention, the end or closing of a message is the most important part for memorability. If you want someone to remember the product name, repeat it at the end of the commercial. Most print ads end with a **logo** (a distinctive mark that identifies the product or company) or a **signature** (the name of the company or brand written in a distinctive type style). Television commercials often **superimpose** the product name on the last visual, accompanied by the announcer repeating the name.

logo *Logotype; a distinctive mark that identifies the product, company, or brand.*

signature *The name of the company or product written in a distinctive type style.*

superimpose *A television technique where one image is added to another that is already on the screen.*

*H*OW BRAND IMAGES WORK

The ultimate test of the memorability function in advertising comes in the area of brand images. Brand personalities and brand images are developed to create a feeling of familiarity with a known product. Because this product is known, the consumer is reassured that it is appropriate to buy it again.

If Only It Were This Easy To Tell Wh en A Prospect Turns Into A Buyer.

Who knows when that switch goes on, and a prospect becomes a buyer. It could happen at any time. It could happen when he's flipping through a magazine and sees your ad. Perhaps it's when he sees your commercial. Or it could happen in the shower, the car, or when he's just out walking the dog. That's why your communications plan needs to include the one medium that attracts buyers at the most strategic time. That's why your plan needs the Yellow Pages. In the average week, an adult user reaches for the Yellow Pages at least three times. And in an average month, over 75% of all adults reach for the Yellow Pages. So go ahead and choose media that reach your audience. But don't leave out the medium *they're* going to reach for. For more information about the Yellow Pages and how a regional or national plan can be put to work for you, call the Yellow Pages Publishers Association at 1-800-325-8455, or if you prefer, write to us at the address below. We'd love to show you a number of different ways to be seen in the one place where people are really turned on. **The Yellow Pages.** **Be There When The Decision Is Made."**

AD 8.6
The use of a visual memory device is apparent in the copy of this ad for the Yellow Pages. The distinctive yellow image and the words ''Yellow Pages'' are repeated throughout the body copy. (Courtesy of NYNEX Yellow Pages)

That is the secret behind the phenomenal success of McDonald's over the years. The fast-food chain has a familiar and comfortable image, and consumers know from experience that it offers dependable quality at reasonable prices. Branding is used to create memorability, but it also establishes preferences, habits, and loyalties. In other words, it creates a platform on which a relationship is built between a product and its user.

Branding is particularly important for *parity products*—those products for which there are few, if any, major differences in features. The products are *undifferentiated* in the marketplace, but through the development of a brand image, they are differentiated in the minds of their users. A product such as soap is relatively indistinguishable. What makes for the difference between one soap and another is advertising. In such cases the *distinction* may be unreal, but the *difference* is not—because the difference lies in the perceived image and personality of the product. Product personalities were discussed in Chapter 7. Personality is important both in positioning a brand and in developing a brand image.

Brand Image

brand image *A mental image that reflects the way a brand is perceived, including all the identification elements, the product personality, and the emotions and associations evoked in the mind of the consumer.*

A brand identifies and represents a particular product, but it is much more than just a name. It is an image in customers' minds that reflects what they think and feel about a product—how they value it. A **brand image** is a mental image that reflects the way a brand is perceived, including all the identification elements, the product personality, and the emotions and as-

The following is a list of famous slogans. How many can you identify? What does this test tell you about the role of slogans in establishing product memorability?

_____	1. Like a good neighbor	a.	Prell
_____	2. Head for the mountains	b.	Secret
_____	3. Thank you for your support	c.	Kodak
_____	4. When you care enough to send the very best	d.	General Electric
		e.	Wheaties
_____	5. Own a piece of the rock	f.	Master Charge
_____	6. Be all you can be	g.	Merrill Lynch
_____	7. Taste as good as they crunch	h.	Doritos
_____	8. Carry the big fresh flavor	i.	Prudential
_____	9. A breed apart	j.	Bartles & Jaymes
_____	10. Let the good times roll	k.	State Farm
_____	11. We circle the world	l.	Chevrolet
_____	12. You deserve a break today	m.	Visine
_____	13. Breakfast of champions	n.	Johnson's Baby Shampoo
_____	14. Gets the red out	o.	Polaroid
_____	15. Strong enough for a man, but made for a woman	p.	_The Wall Street Journal_
		q.	Ford
_____	16. Gentle enough to use every day	r.	McDonald's
		s.	Kawasaki
_____	17. America's storyteller	t.	Wrigley Spearmint
_____	18. Today is the first day of the rest of your life	u.	Army
		v.	Hallmark
_____	19. We bring good things to life	w.	Busch
_____	20. Quality is Job 1	x.	Pringles

(_Answers:_ 1-k, 2-w, 3-j, 4-v, 5-i, 6-u, 7-h, 8-t, 9-g, 10-s, 11-f, 12-r, 13-e, 14-m, 15-b, 16-n, 17-c, 18-p, 19-d, 20-q)

sociations evoked in the mind of the consumer. _Product personality_—the idea that a product takes on familiar human characteristics, such as friendliness, trustworthiness, or snobbery—is an important part of an image.

A brand, then, has both a physical and a psychological dimension. The physical dimension is made up of the design of the package or logo—the letter, shapes, art, and colors that are used to define the graphics of the image. In contrast, the psychological side includes the emotions, beliefs, values, and personalities that people ascribe to the product. For example, when you talk about the _brand image_ of Hershey's, you are talking about the distinctive brown package and lettering of the name as well as the multitude of impressions and values conveyed by its slogan "the all-American candy bar."

Promise. A brand is also a _promise of value._ Because it seeks to establish a familiar image, a brand also creates an expectation level. Green Giant, for example, has built its franchise on the personality of the friendly giant who tells kids that vegetables are good for them. The name Green Giant on the package means there are no unexpected and unwanted surprises when you buy a Green Giant product. The idea of accumulating a reservoir of goodwill and good impressions is called _brand equity._

Building a Brand

brand equity *The use of a respected brand name to add value to a product.*

Brand Equity. **Brand equity** will be an extremely important concept in the 1990s. The idea that a respected brand name adds value to a product goes back to the dawn of modern marketing and poses many questions: How much value is added? Can that value be enhanced? Can it be transferred? Castle & Cook, Inc., for example, extensively researched its well-known Dole brand and discovered that the Dole name stood for much more than pineapple. As a result, Castle & Cooke launched Dole Fruit & Juice bars and other frozen desserts. Cheerios has expanded its brand name to embrace a variety of Cheerios cereals, including Apple Cinnamon and Honey Nut Cheerios. In contrast, Walt Disney Company discovered that any Disney film would be perceived as targeted to a young audience. Instead of looking for a way to extend the Disney name to films targeted at an adult audience, Disney launched Touchstone Films.

Branding is a way to assist the consumer's memory process. It identifies a product and also makes it possible to position the product relative to other brands. The tools used to lock brands into the memory include distinctive names, slogans, graphics, and characters.

Brand Names. Names have both denotative and connotative meanings. Denotative aspects tell what the brand is or does, like Head and Shoulders and Intensive Care. The connotative meaning contains a suggestion or association—a meaning that is supposed to carry over to the product, such as Bounce or Mustang. Some brand names don't say much, like Breck or Sony. Names like these take on meaning only through extensive advertising and the familiarity that comes from product use. Slogans work the same way, although they can carry more content than a simple name. Xerox, whose name has become practically synonymous with the copier product category, is trying to reposition itself with a new slogan: "the document company." It hopes to broaden its image beyond that of copy machines.

Research into names considers linguistics as well as associations. How does the name sound? What does it sound like, and what does it remind you of? Manufacturers must also be certain that the name does not convey any unintended meanings. When Esso renamed itself Exxon, it conducted years of study to find a distinctive name that did not have any unwanted meanings.

Interbrand, a linguistics company that charges as much as $100,000 per name, came up with Polaroid's Spectra and the analgesic Nuprin. The San Francisco-based company Namelab takes a linguistic approach, build-

Cheerios has maintained a very strong brand image even among its different flavors of cereals. (Rick Browne/Photo reporters.)

ing words from a table of 6,200 one-syllable sounds. Other namesmiths rely more on outside focus groups, which might include consumers, professional writers, or even Scrabble fanatics. Many firms also have computers that coin words by the bucketful or catalog millions of previous rejects.*

Graphic Elements. The brand's personality is displayed in distinctive graphics used in packaging and other forms of communication. A **logo** is a characteristic mark that identifies the maker. The graphic elements in the logo and the package design that define the graphic image include distinctive type, colors, and art.

A **trademark** is a distinctive visual brand that identifies a company's products. For example, distinctive detailing easily separates the bucking bronco used by Ford's Bronco from the prancing horse used by Ferrari (see Ad 8.7). Trademarks are an important part of brand image and reminder advertising programs.

Symbolic characters are used both to help identify a product and to associate it with a personality. The Marlboro cowboy and the Charlie woman are classic examples of symbols that represent an attitude with which the audience might want to identify. The Pillsbury Doughboy is a lovable character that associates warm, positive feelings with the company and with baking. Mr. Goodwrench is the kind of friendly, helpful repairman you can trust. His image counters the stereotype of the auto repairman as a swindler. The Maytag repairman is not only friendly, he's lonely because Maytag washing machines are so dependable that he never gets to see customers. All these symbols convey subtle, yet complex, meanings about the product's values and benefits, in addition to serving as an identity cue.

Because the effects of image advertising build up over time, consistency is critical to this process. You can't say one thing today and something different tomorrow. David Ogilvy, founder of Ogilvy and Mather, believed strongly in brand-image advertising. He said that every ad should contribute to the image. The message should focus on what that image is supposed to be, and should be consistent over a long time.†

Betty Crocker (a fictional character) made her advertising debut in 1936 as a symbol of General Mills. She went through five "face-lifts" as her character was updated to appeal to changing audiences. The sixth version was introduced in 1986 (see Ad 8.8).‡

Transformation Advertising

There is a big difference between a pair of K Mart jeans and a pair of Levi's 501s. Advertising has transformed Levi's 501s beyond the basic requirements of the category. Levi's has been endowed by advertising with the capacity to provide an experience different from the experience that comes from wearing any old pair of jeans. This concept of transformation was developed by Bill Wells of DDB Needham to explain how advertising, particularly brand-image advertising, works.§

The distinctions are very real because the experience of using the product is truly different. The experience of smoking a Marlboro is different from the experience of smoking a Pall Mall. The experience of using Coast is different from the experience of using Irish Spring or a generic bar

trademark *Sign or design, often with distinctive lettering, that symbolizes the brand.*

AD 8.7
Ferrari and Ford use a variation on the same symbol—the horse.
(Courtesy of Ford Motor Company and Ferrari North America.)

---

*B. G. Yovovich, "What Is Your Brand Really Worth?" *Adweek* (August 8, 1988).

† David Ogilvy, *Confessions of an Advertising Man* (New York: Dell, 1964).

‡"Betty Crocker Goes Yuppie." *Time* (June 2, 1986):63.

§William D. Wells, "How Advertising Works," a speech presented to St. Louis AMA, September 17, 1986.

transformation advertising
Image advertising that changes the experience of buying and using a product.

of soap. If you doubt the reality of such differences, try giving your mother a watch for her birthday in a box that comes from K Mart as opposed to giving the same watch in a box that comes from Tiffany. No doubt, you'll find the experiences of buying, giving, and wearing the watch are quite different.

Advertising provides information and at the same time transforms the experience of buying and using the product. Transformation is the secret to building a product personality and image. It is an expensive objective. One of the requirements for **transformation advertising,** or image advertising, is a big budget. Frequent exposure is the price of success. Furthermore, the process takes time because the effect is cumulative. It is a form of indirect advertising as opposed to direct-action advertising.

For transformation advertising to be effective in selling a product it should be *positive.* Its function is to make the experience richer, warmer, and more enjoyable. The Volkswagen "Fahrvergnügen" advertisement is an example of transformational advertising in that it tries to establish "driving excitement" as a characteristic of owning a Volkswagen.

Transformation may not be appropriate for certain products. Upbeat advertising messages might not work for products related to drudgery or unpleasant experiences because such a message would sound phony. It may not be possible to turn cleaning the oven, scrubbing the floor, or taking a laxative into a joyous occasion. Although some advertisements try to do this, they stretch believability.

It is possible to use transformation advertising to turn around perceived negatives. For example, the campaigns for the financial company HFC—"Never Borrow Money Needlessly" and "People Use Our Money to Make the Most Out of Life"—have taken some of the threat out of applying for a loan. The State Farm "agent" series—"Like a good neighbor, State Farm is there"—helped generate trust in a potentially brittle relationship. Transformation advertising for airlines has probably taken some of the anxiety out of flying.

Another requirement for transformation advertising is that it "ring true." Because it deals with images, it may not be technically verifiable in a literal sense, but it must *feel* true. The characters must act as the real people in that situation would act, and they must use the product as people would use it in real life.

A final requirement for transformation advertising is that it link the brand so tightly to the experience that people cannot remember one without remembering the other. One example where this did *not* occur involved a series of ads for a soap company that said:

"New blouse?"	"No, new bleach."
"New dress?"	"No, new bleach."
"New shirt?"	"No, new bleach."

That campaign created a strong link between the experience and the *product category,* but not the *actual product.* Almost everyone remembered the line. Almost no one remembered the advertiser.*

We know that most advertisements just "wash over" their audiences without any effect. Effective advertisements, in contrast, strike a responsive chord. In other words, they have impact, which means they overcome audience indifference and focus attention on the message. Furthermore, they catch attention without being irritating, and they keep attention while penetrating the mind. Advertisements that deliver impact have stopping power, pulling power, and lock the message into the mind of the target audience.

*Wells, *Planning for R.O.I.*

AD 8.8
The familiar face of Betty Crocker has actually changed several times since the 1930s. (Courtesy of General Mills, Inc.)

SUMMARY

- To be effective an ad must be able to penetrate the inattentiveness of the audience and compete in a cluttered environment.
- Advertising works on several levels: perception, awareness, understanding, and persuasion.
- Ads that work effectively have locking power that

locks the message into consumers' minds and makes it memorable.
- Effective advertising can make a product or brand stand out from the competition.
- Brand images are built through the use of distinctive names, slogans, graphics, and characters.

QUESTIONS

1. What is meant by breakthrough advertising? How is this accomplished?

2. What are some common methods of attracting and maintaining consumer interest?

3. How does the construct of perception-awareness-understanding-persuasion relate to advertising? What types of ads are appropriate at each level?

4. Mary Proctor is an associate creative director in an agency that handles a liquid detergent brand that competes with Lever's Wisk. Mary is reviewing a history of the Wisk theme "ring around the collar." It is one of the longest-running themes on television, and Wisk's sales share indicates that it has been successful. What is confusing to Mary is that the Wisk history includes numerous consumer surveys that all show consumers find "ring around the collar" a boring, silly, and altogether irritating advertising theme. Can you explain why Wisk is such a popular brand even though its advertising campaign is so disliked?

5. The chapter identifies four major operations in advertising creative strategy: perception, awareness, understanding, and persuasion. Emotional tactics are discussed under "persuasion," but emotion figures in the other operations as well. Identify how the creative use of emotion can enhance each operation. To bolster your position, select a current advertising campaign that supports your analysis.

6. Bill Thomas and Beth Bennett are a copywriter/art director creative team who often amuse themselves by arguing about famous ad campaigns. Their current subject is the Energizer bunny commercials. Bill says this is a perfect example of *vampire creativity*. Beth disagrees, stressing the theme's strength through "interest" and "ambiguity." Who is right? Why?

FURTHER READINGS

BOGART, LEO, *Strategy in Advertising: Matching Media and Messages to Markets and Motivation,* 2nd ed (Chicago: Crain Books, 1984).

OGILVY, DAVID, *Confessions of an Advertising Man* (New York: Atheneum, 1980).

PATTI, CHARLES H., and SANDRA E. MORIARTY, *The Making of Effective Advertising* (Englewood Cliffs, NJ: Prentice Hall, 1990).

RAYMOND, MINER, *Advertising That Sells: A Primer for Product Managers* (Cincinnati, OH: Black Rose, 1990).

REEVES, ROSSER, *Reality in Advertising* (New York: Alfred A. Knopf, 1963).

WELLS, WILLIAM D. *Planning for R.O.I.* (Englewood Cliffs, NJ: Prentice Hall, 1989).

VIDEO CASE

NEW YORK

Illinois State Tourism Board

Faced with existing perceptions as a low-preference vacation destination, the Illinois State Tourism Bureau contracted with McConnaughy, Stein, Schmidt & Brown (MSS&B) to craft an advertising campaign to create a positive image of Illinois as a vacation spot. Although the travel industry category had experienced dramatic growth over the previous 5 years, with total advertising spending exceeding $1 billion for the first time in 1989, the Illinois Tourism advertising budget had remained flat throughout the same period. In contrast, many other states had significantly increased spending since 1987, including Alaska, with a 430 percent increase, Colorado, with a 300 percent increase, Texas, with a 230 percent increase, Michigan, with a 92 percent increase, and New York, with a 42 percent increase.

The overall objective of the new advertising campaign was to create an image of Illinois as a great American institution, especially among upscale travelers and families with children. To evaluate the campaign, the State Tourism Bureau identified three quantitative objectives to be achieved as a result of the 1990 Illinois tourism advertising: 1) increase awareness of Illinois as a tourist destination by 10 percent on an annual basis; 2) increase consumer response to the Tourist 800 number by 10 percent in 1990; and 3) increase visitor spending dollars at least 10 percent over national spending level increases during 1990. In all cases, these objectives were assumed to be achieved via direct consumer response to State Tourism Bureau advertising and via improved economic impact on state revenues.

MSS&B's challenge was to create an advertising creative strategy that elevated the perception of Illinois to that of an important tourist destination based on the inherent values and substance of Illinois's attractions. Unfortunately, Illinois did not possess the built-in tourist magnets that other states enjoy, such as Nevada's gaming casinos, Florida's Disneyworld, and the allure of New York City. Therefore, the campaign had to establish interest in such existing Illinois landmarks as Abraham Lincoln's home town of Springfield, the Mississippi Territory, and the scenic beauty of the state's parks.

To accomplish this strategy, the agency created the "American Renaissance" theme because it was judged to be difficult for other states to pre-empt and it easily embodied the majority of existing Illinois tourism products. The support for this creative strategy stemmed in large part from a 1989 study completed by *Travel & Leisure* magazine, which indicated that over 40 percent of American travelers desired more than a suntan on their vacation. Specifically, they desired a tangible achievement of some kind to improve their knowledge and "improve their minds." Consequently, the "American Renaissance" campaign was developed to educate consumers about the value and substance a trip to Illinois could provide.

The primary target audience for the campaign included adult heads of households aged 25 to 54, with household incomes of at least $25,000 but skewed toward incomes of $35,000 or more. The geographic media target for the campaign included Areas of Dominant Influence (ADIs) within 1 day's drive of Illinois because the attractions that Illinois offered were well suited for long weekend trips by couples or families. Illinois' media budget had remained at $2.5 million dollars for the past 5 years, representing .02 percent of the total travel category advertising spending of $1.175 billion dollars in 1989, or 3.25 percent of the $100 million state tourism advertising budgets throughout the country.

Despite this relatively low share of voice, the Illinois State Tourism Bureau greatly exceeded its original campaign objectives. Awareness of Illinois as a tourist destination increased by over 17 percent in 1990 from 1989. Usage of the Tourism Bureau's 800 number increased by 20 percent in 1990 versus 1989, and one-third of 800-number callers cited the advertising as being influential in their travel decisions. Finally, Illinois realized a 17 percent increase in visitor spending in 1990 versus the prior year, almost double the 9 percent tourist spending increase for the nation as a whole.

QUESTIONS

1. What other general factors may have contributed to the increase in Illinois tourism besides the State Tourism Bureau's advertising effort?

2. Explain the advantages and disadvantages of the limited geographic media coverage area utilized by the Illinois State Tourism Bureau.

3. If the State Tourism Bureau's advertising budget were dramatically increased, allowing it to pursue a business target in addition to its existing target audience, what visuals should be included in the "American Renaissance" television campaign to attract business travelers and conventions?

Source: Courtesy of McConnaughy, Stein, Schmidt & Brown.

CASE STUDY

Discovering a New Credit Card

Charge accounts emerged in the 1950s when department stores began issuing "shopping plates" to their preferred customers as an alternative means of paying for retail purchases at their local stores. Introduced in the late 1950s, American Express provided a credit alternative for travel and entertainment purchases. BankAmericard (renamed VISA) and MasterCard were introduced in the 1960s to allow consumers to use one card to make purchases at stores across the country. American Express, VISA, and MasterCard continued to grow throughout the 1970s at the expense of department store cards.

As these cards moved beyond the primary goal of cardmember acquisition to increasing consumer usage, competition between the cards became fierce. To establish a competitive edge, cards began adding more features. Credit card issuers also began to recognize that they could distinguish themselves by using advertising to establish distinct brand images. Consequently, the first national, mass-marketed credit card advertising campaigns appeared in the late 1970s. As cards added features to remain competitive and spent more money on advertising, profit became an issue. Unfortunately for consumers, as a result VISA and MasterCard banks imposed annual fees to defray these increasing costs (American Express had always charged a fee).

By the mid-1980s the credit card category, historically an extremely competitive arena, was viewed by industry experts as a nearly saturated market. Approximately 80 percent of the population already held several cards each. MasterCard, VISA and American Express vied for the remaining 20 percent of American consumers who did not yet hold a major credit card. Competitors increased advertising spending as the battle to acquire and keep new cardmembers continued to escalate.

Although the credit card market appeared mature, opportunities were being overlooked. MasterCard and VISA had staked out a positioning strategy based on acceptance, which at the time was the consumers' primary reason for holding a credit card. Prestige was the domain of American Express. Value, however, remained an area relatively untouched by competitors. Getting more value from a credit card was becoming increasingly important to consumers who disliked paying annual fees and who felt that their loyalty to a particular card was going unrewarded, regardless of their social and economic status.

Sears Roebuck and Company was uniquely suited to take advantage of this opportunity, having a strong credit network already in place. Although VISA and MasterCard were strongly entrenched in the credit card category, there were limitations inherent in their structure. Because these cards consisted of an agglomeration of small issuing banks, they lacked consistent, solid features that could be marketed on a national basis. Sears recognized this structural weakness and, when considering the development of a credit card, chose to create a single issuer and therefore a completely new product. Single issuer status would allow Sears to speak with one voice about the product pricing and features, a clear advantage over competitors.

Features were then developed that addressed the area of opportunity—value. First, the card would be offered at no annual fee. Second, to reward consumers for their loyalty to the card, an annual cash rebate of up to 1 percent on purchases would be established as well as rebates on purchases at participating merchants, called ValueFinders® Coupons. Multisourced access to cash was also added.

Furthermore, an aggressive merchant program was mapped out to achieve widespread acceptance as early as possible. Finally, in 1985 Sears announced its plans to introduce a new all-purpose credit card—the Discover® Card—that would provide an important link in the Sears Financial Network chain of banking, investment, and insurance products. This was the first such national introduction since those of VISA and MasterCard in 1966.

In spite of its position as a retail marketing giant, Sears still faced two major challenges in introducing the Discover Card. Specifically, Sears would have to determine how to gain merchant acceptance, especially among Sears' retailer competitors, and how to entice consumers to acquire this card in addition to the many cards currently in their wallets.

In addressing the first challenge, Sears realized the importance of establishing the card with other merchants beyond Sears and anticipated reluctance among close competitors such as J.C. Penney and K Mart. In response, Sears devised an attractive fee structure for merchants, offering a rate much lower than that of American Express, VISA, and MasterCard. In addition, to encourage the display of Discover Card signage, a customized modular signage sign was developed in which the Discover Card, VISA, MasterCard, and American Express all appeared. Merchants could use one display to show all the cards accepted.

In addressing the second challenge, the consumer effort needed to establish a meaningful point of difference that would convince consumers to acquire the card. First, advertising needed to break through competitive clutter and begin to establish an image for the Discover Card. Advertising spending in the credit card category, historically very aggressive, was high in 1986 when Discover Card was introduced at $170,000,000. Competitive advertising targeted the affluent strata of the population, with all three major cards focusing their efforts on upper middle-class America. American Express used the "Do you know me?" campaign to perpetuate its prestigious image. The VISA card challenged American Express with its upscale, aspirational campaign, "It's everywhere you want to be." MasterCard also fueled an upscale image with its "Master the Moment" campaign. To differentiate Discover Card, the campaign focused on the segment of the population overlooked by the three key competitors: middle America. A newsworthy tone broke through competitive advertising via the "Dawn of Discover" tagline (see Exhibit A).

Second, Sears wanted to convey the fact that this card offered financial services unavailable from competitive credit cards. Consumers were unfamiliar with the concept of a financial services card, and therefore advertising needed to educate consumers about the Card's uses. Introductory advertising included several features that, when combined, conveyed a value message: a rebate on purchases, nationwide access to cash, high-yield savings account, and no annual fee.

By the end of 1987 the Discover Card had successfully accomplished the first phase of new product introduction: It had acquired initial distribution and a customer base. Performance surpassed the expectations of Sears as well as its competitors. Discover Card had acquired 12 million card members, signed over 550,000 merchants, and held charges totalling nearly $2 billion. Sears had managed to establish a solid card base and to convince even such tough competitors as K Mart to accept the card.

The advertising that was successful in helping to convince consumers to acquire the Discover Card was not as effective in motivating usage of the card. In the spring of 1987 many card members were not using the card on a monthly basis. In addition, some cardmembers were not using the card, they were using competitive cards. In fact, they used their other cards more frequently than did credit card users as a whole. Discover Card was clearly an additional, spare card, not one that replaced another credit card in the consumer's wallet or mind.

One key issue had to be addressed: What prevents Discover Cardmembers from using that card rather than VISA or MasterCard? Research was conducted to identify barriers to usage, which revealed three findings:

The Discover Card was not foremost in the minds of Cardmembers. Cardmembers did not perceive the card as widely accepted, and the Discover Card, viewed by Cardmembers as a new, optional card with limited acceptance, did not yet have a distinct image.

After determining the barriers to usage, three advertising objectives addressing the barriers were established:

- Measurably increase usage
- Significantly boost Discover Card awareness
- Foster a special, desirable, long-term image

To address the first objective of increasing card usage, the new advertising strategy required narrowing the advertising target to current Cardmembers and emphasizing the most compelling reason for this target audience to use the card. Research revealed that of the many features the card offered, the most relevant feature was the Cashback Bonus® received on all purchases. The advertising focused on this feature, and the tagline "It Pays to Discover" was devised to reinforce the value message.

Discover Card awareness was low, given that Cardmembers habitually chose a competitive card when reaching in their wallets to pay for a purchase. To overcome this barrier and increase awareness of the card among Card-

EXHIBIT A

ANNCR: Very few things cost you nothing to get and pay you back every day,

but now the Discover Card does

SONG: A WAY TO SAVE

SONG: THE DISCOVER CARD PUTS

MONEY IN A WHOLE NEW LIGHT.

ANNCR: From a member of Sears Financial Network,

members, the executional style of the campaign featured quick cuts of people making purchases on various retail and travel occasions. These purchases were interrupted at the actual moment when the customer is scanning the wallet to select a card. The competitive set was established by showing the VISA, MasterCard, and American Express cards in the person's wallet, as well as the Discover Card. The voiceover states, "We interrupt this transaction for a very important message." At that point, the Cashback Bonus benefit could be communicated in a clear and compelling way.

Media scheduling and programming were also revised to address the new strategy. To break the consumer habit of choosing competitive cards, a 52-week media plan was developed that provided daily, repeated exposure to the Discover Card message. To increase the relevancy of the message and address Cardmembers' interest in news, news-oriented television and radio were used.

Lastly, a special, desirable, long-term image was fostered through the use of aspirational situations. Attractive, successful people were shown making smart choices when they chose to use the Discover Card on vacation, when making retail purchases, and getting cash advances.

The new advertising campaign contributed to the overall success of the Discover Card marketing plan. As of year-end 1990, Discover Card had over 37,000,000 Cardmembers, was accepted at over 1,200,000 merchants, and performance had surpassed sales goals since 1988.

Courtesy of DDB Needham Worldwide.

9

Media Strategy and Planning

Chapter Outline

A Wall Comes Down: The New Age of Media and Creative Harmony
The Function of Media Planning in Advertising
The Aperture Concept in Media Planning
Media Planning Operations: Information Sources and Analysis
Media Planning Operations: Setting Objectives and Strategies
Media Planning Operations: Media Selection Procedures
Media Planning Operations: Staging a Media Plan

Chapter Objectives

When you have completed this chapter, you should be able to:

- Understand the central position of media planning in campaign development and how this function utilizes information from numerous sources, including product sales performance, competitor surveillance, and message creative strategy, to form the campaign design
- Understand the organization and purpose of the media plan, and see how each decision on selection and scheduling is coordinated with the client's sales objectives
- Explain how planners use communication aperture to give direction to media planning strategy
- Explain how the media's qualitative features (atmosphere and environment) are blended with their quantitative dimensions (reach, frequency, and efficiency) to provide the needed profile for selection

A WALL COMES DOWN: THE NEW AGE OF MEDIA AND CREATIVE HARMONY

What used to be a wall of misunderstanding and professional indifference between the media planners and those responsible for creating the advertising is now becoming a gateway to shared ideas. This revolution in cooperative spirit is all the more impressive when you consider the vocational distance between these major players in advertising. Media planners, known by some as "the bean counters" of advertising, deal in dollars and research probabilities, whereas the creative team, called "hippie dreamers" by some, concoct visual and verbal imagery. Unlikely collaborators, for sure, but many advertising agencies have been able to shove these personality differences aside in the quest for successful campaigns. The classic illustrations of role reversal depict media analysts proposing creative approaches to media use and writers and art directors recommending where the ads should appear.

Nowhere is this cooperation more apparent than in the work of TBWA, a New York–based agency, for Carillon Importers Absolut Vodka. The Absolut media strategy is concentrated in business and consumer magazines. With as many as 100 magazines involved in the campaign, the creative demand is enormous. Much of the burden is lessened, however, because the agency's media and creative departments work together on magazine selection and tailor advertising to each magazine's readership. The following are some examples of this innovative partnership (see Ad 9.1).

The media department suggested that the creative team design theater programs (playbills), to be followed up with a compatible theme. Agency creatives developed "Absolut Bravo," a photo of the Absolut bottle surrounded by roses.

Playboy was not on the media department's list of magazines until TBWA creatives dreamed up "Absolut Centerfold," a hilarious takeoff on the magazine's "Playmate of the Month" feature. The Absolut ad included a profile of the "centerfold model," complete with "Measurements" (11" × 11" × 11"), "Favorite Books or Plays" ("The Iceman Cometh" and "Soul on Ice"), and even a unique version of "Ambitions" ("To Always Be Cool, With or Without Ice").

Ads placed in Los Angeles–area magazines featured an LA-style swimming pool in the shape of the Absolut bottle. Similarly, for New York City–area readers, the advertisement showed a satellite photo of Manhattan, with Central Park assuming a new distinctive outline: the Absolut bottle.

Even trade publications were given unique treatment. When media planners recommended advertising in *Advertising Age* magazine, the Absolut art director responded with "Absolut Subliminal," with a glass filled with suspiciously encoded ice cubes.

When asked to discuss this creative mastery of a medium, Richard Costello, TBWA's president and chief executive officer, cited the force behind the cooperation between his media and creative staffs: "What Carillon has done for us is give us a more open mind and put more demand on all departments to be creative in their ideas than what otherwise would be the case." As a result, Carillon Importers sold 2.7 million cases of Absolut Vodka in 1990, compared to 12,000 cases in 1980, and claimed 58 percent of the imported vodka category.

In a period of soaring media costs, tighter budgets, and cluttered communication channels, the synergy provided by the new harmony between media and creative is a refreshing and needed change.*

*Adapted from Gary Levin, "Meddling in Creative More Welcome," *Advertising Age* (April 9, 1990):S-4, S-8.

AD 9.1
The media campaign for Absolut Vodka involved a creative print campaign that was targeted at the readers of various magazines. (Courtesy of Carillon Importers Ltd.)

THE FUNCTION OF MEDIA PLANNING IN ADVERTISING

media planning *A decision process leading to the use of advertising time and space to assist in the achievement of marketing objectives.*

Media planning is a problem-solving process that translates marketing objectives into a series of strategic decisions. The ultimate goal is to place the advertising message before a target audience. The planning decisions involved include: which audiences to reach, where (geographic emphasis), when (timing), for how long (campaign length), and how intense (frequent) the exposure should be. Media planning is a blend of marketing skills and familiarity with mass communication. Because it deals with the most significant portion of the advertiser's budget (cost for space and time), it is a crucial element in contemporary advertising.

Media planning was not always the sophisticated process it is today. In fact, it has undergone a substantial evolution in the last 25 years. What was once a clerical function of choosing media positions and contracting for them is now a central element in marketing strategy. Media department employees who once worked silently "behind the scenes" are now in the forefront directing marketing strategy.

This chapter is an introduction to media planning, with particular emphasis on its integral role in merging the science of marketing with the art of advertising. As you will see, the planner's role is twofold: He or she must act as both a marketing analyst and an expert appraiser of media channel effectiveness.

THE APERTURE CONCEPT IN MEDIA PLANNING

Each customer or prospect for a product or service has an ideal point in time and place at which he or she can be reached with an advertising message. This point can be when the consumer is in the "search corridor"—the purchasing mode—or it can occur when the consumer is seeking more information before entering the corridor. The goal of the media planner is to expose consumer prospects to the advertiser's message at these critical points.

aperture *The ideal moment for exposing consumers to an advertising message.*

This ideal opening is called an **aperture.** The most effective advertisement should expose the consumer to the product when interest and attention are high. Aperture can be thought of as the home-run swing in baseball: The ball meets the bat at the right spot and at the precise instant for maximum distance.

Locating the aperture opportunity is a major responsibility of the media planner. The planner must study the marketing position of the advertiser to determine which media opportunities will do the best job of message placement. This is a complex and difficult assignment. Success depends on accurate marketing research, appreciation of the message concept, and a sensitive understanding of the channels of mass communication.

MEDIA PLANNING OPERATIONS: INFORMATION SOURCES AND ANALYSIS

Media department people often believe they are the "hub" in the advertising wheel, the central point where each campaign element (spoke) is joined. In part, this belief is based on the amount of data and information

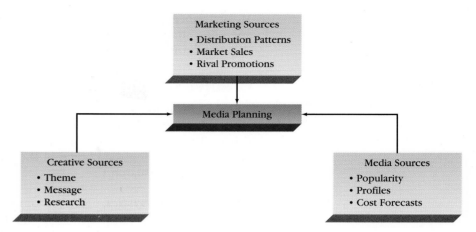

FIGURE 9.1
Sources of information in media planning.

that must be gathered, sorted, and analyzed before media decision making can begin. Figure 9.1 illustrates the sources of the required information. This chapter will explore how this information is used at subsequent stages in media planning.

Marketing Sources

Media analysis is described as the crucial bridge between product marketing and advertising strategy because so much of the activity in the marketplace has a direct bearing on media decisions. Territory, timing, distribution, and competition will all affect media planning.

Area Sales Patterns. Virtually no company that sells products or services in multiple markets has balanced or equal sales across all territories. The sales activity and sales rank often are different for each area. Because a major role of advertising is to support sales activity, media plans usually vary the amount of advertising designated to each sales territory. As a consequence, each market's sales reports are used to determine geographic dollar allocations. This concept of regionality has an important role in many media plans and is discussed later in the chapter (see BDI/CDI discussion).

Month-by-Month Sales Patterns. The timing of the advertising schedules is a vital strategy in media planning. Most sales for consumer products fluctuate. Media timing (when to start and stop a campaign) should reflect the sales calendar or seasonality for each advertiser. To do this accurately, planners carefully follow the consumer demand trends apparent from the monthly sales report.

Distribution Patterns. The success of most brands is heavily dependent on how many of each market's retailers carry (stock) the product. Marketers with poor or just-developing distribution may be unable to exploit even good market potentials until they improve their distribution. After all, there isn't much point in promoting a brand that consumers can't find on the shelves. Marketing people alert media planners to unsatisfactory distribution patterns so that ad spending can be modified accordingly.

Competitor's Advertising Patterns. Rival companies may compete heavily for certain markets or regions, whereas other markets may only be lightly considered. A study of recent advertising history will give the planner some idea of how much advertising to expect from the competition.

Heavy concentrations of competitive advertising may change a brand's spending strategy for a region or market. For more on this subject, see the "share of voice" (SOV) discussion later in this chapter.

Creative Sources

As the Absolut advertising campaign illustrated, close cooperation between media planners and those responsible for the creative decisions can produce brilliant results. Sharing information influences a number of media strategies, including the choice of the creative theme, the media vehicle, and consumer research.

Theme Characteristics. The recommended creative solution (what to say and how to say it) to an advertising challenge usually influences where the message should be placed. For example, creative strategies needing a product demonstration are best-suited for television. Complicated copy platforms, such as those for high-involvement products (running shoes or sports cars), might require the use of print media. Media planners must pay close attention to the thinking of the creative department.

Message Characteristics. Creative tactics can also affect media vehicle choices. Earlier we discussed how Absolut used different messages attuned to each magazine's audience. The tone of the message may indicate that one television program type is right and another one wrong for this creative approach. Media environments are discussed in more detail later in the chapter.

Creative Performance Research. Companies often monitor audience reaction to the advertising message (see Chapter 21). Although copy testing is primarily a measure of creative impact, media planners can use the data to make a number of decisions, including the number of messages to be used and the continuity pattern of the advertising.

Media Sources

The eventual selection of a medium (a single form of communication, such as television) and specific media vehicles (a single program, radio station, magazine title, and so on) depends on a stream of media research and information supplied to media planners and buyers on the size and profile of the audience and the media costs for space or time.

Media Popularity. Two obvious criteria for media selection are the size of the audience available for each media vehicle and how well the vehicle's audience matches the characteristics of the target market. Media planners and buyers have constant access to syndicated media audience research that estimates numbers of readers, viewers, and listeners from current audience studies. These data enable planners to forecast the future popularity of media positions.

Media Audience Characteristics. More important than the size of the audience are the social and economic profiles of audience members, including demographics, interests and lifestyles, purchasing patterns, and other characteristics that describe potential consumers.

Media Cost Forecasting. Forecasting media costs is as much an art as it is a science. Because media plans are developed long before the campaign

ISSUES AND APPLICATIONS

ORION INNOVATES MEDIA STRATEGIES

In November 1990 Orion Pictures released the film *Dances with Wolves,* starring and directed by Kevin Costner. The film is about a young soldier torn between his loyalties to the Union Army and the Sioux Indian tribe. In marketing *Dances with Wolves,* Orion joined the growing group of movie studios that target their advertising to more specific audiences. The company showed film trailers of *Dances with Wolves* on college campuses, in video stores, and on television screens in consumer electronics stores.

Universal Pictures' executive vice president of worldwide marketing, Simon Korblit, explained why movie studios have become attracted to media considered nontraditional for the film industry: "Just [like] the way you want to be different with creative, now we're trying to be different with media." The studios' objective is to differentiate themselves and their films from other movie studios. The hope is that using different targeted media will attract more moviegoers.

Orion Pictures faced two challenges in marketing *Dances with Wolves.* The first was the movie's 3-hour length, and the second was its subject matter. The company's response was to target the film at those moviegoers who were already interested in the subject matter and to get them to spread the word to others. As part of Orion's $8 million to $10 million budgeted media plan, Foote, Cone & Belding, the agency representing the studio, bought 60-second radio spots, which aired on November 9, 1990, on six American Indian stations. The commercial was written in English and then translated into American Indian languages appropriate for each station's audience. The strategy also included a very large network television buy. Many of the ads emphasized both Kevin Costner's starring role and the environmental issues the film invokes.

Media strategies targeted at upscale, well-educated adults included a sweepstakes promotion for the movie aired on cable's Discovery Channel and a special screening of the film to benefit the Nature Conservancy, a conservation group, that was advertised by public service announcements featuring Kevin Costner.

Orion also bought into Preview Tech, a company that distributes laser discs of film trailers to be aired on the 200 television monitors in each of the 165 consumer electronic outlets in Circuit City

Orion Pictures utilized various media strategies in advertising their 1990 film *Dances with Wolves,* starring Kevin Costner. (Photofest)

Stores. Each film distributed by Preview Tech runs for one month in this fashion. Universal's Simon Korblit explained the reason for such a media investment: "Whenever we can gain exposure for a trailer outside the traditional arena, we want to do that."

Orion is not the only movie studio to realize the value of targeted media planning. Warner Bros. used direct mail to promote *Memphis Belle,* its movie about War War II bomber pilots, to veterans, pilots, and readers of Time-Life Books' series on World War II. Mirimax Films created a campaign targeted at the handicapped to advertise its 1989 Oscar-winning movie *My Left Foot.* The trade-off for this kind of innovative media advertising is that funds are diverted from more standard television and newspaper advertising. As John Jacobs, vice president of media at Warner Bros., states: "As a studio, you can only [afford to] get involved with one or two of these things."

So far, the trend is going strong, but only time will tell if this new approach to targeting movie audiences will prove profitable.

Source: Adapted from Marcy Magiera, "*Dances'* Joins Film Efforts to Target Ads," *Advertising Age* (November 5, 1990):1, 67.

begins, a careful and accurate estimate of what the advertiser will pay for space and time is vital to successful planning. Media planning is a customized effort. Each situation dictates distinctive planning and application of sources.

The gathering, sorting, and analyzing of these and other data sources provide the foundation for the next stage in media planning: setting objectives and strategies.

MEDIA PLANNING OPERATIONS: SETTING OBJECTIVES AND STRATEGIES

Each media plan has a series of objectives that reflect some basic questions, the answers to which comprise a strategic plan of action.

The basic questions that direct media strategy are whom to advertise to, which geographic areas to cover, when to advertise, what the duration of the campaign should be, and what media environments are best for the advertiser's message.

Finding Target Audiences

Descriptions of people selected as the targets for a campaign are usually based on marketing research and given priority by the marketing management of the firm. Media planners do not create the profiles or the ranked value of these consumers. Their job, rather, is to translate the target descriptions into information that will fit the audience profiles provided by media research. In many cases the translation process is easy because the two descriptions are compatible. Often, however, the two descriptions are very dissimilar. In this case an accurate translation is vital. Suppose a marketer wanted to reach a group of consumers interested in ecological concerns. There are no media audience research sources that measure this attitude. Instead, audiences are usually measured by social and economic factors (age, income, occupation, and so on). Without audience research, the planner would have to sort through media opportunities looking for content that would attract special-interest consumers. The box entitled "Orion Innovates Media Strategies" discusses an example of this translation process.

Media planners have several categories of information to assist them in planning. These categories include demographic profiles, psychographics and lifestyles, and product-use segmentations.

Demographics. Demographics represents the most common "name tags" given to people. People are described by their age, income (personal and household), education, occupation, marital status, family size, and several other tags. Ad 9.2 for *The Sporting News,* for example, is targeted at men and is very gender-specific. For a more detailed discussion of demographics, refer to Chapter 5.

Psychographics. In contrast to demographics, psychographics looks for more sensitive measures of motivation and behavior. It attempts to classify people according to how they feel and act. For example, the lifestyle profile, one form of psychographic research, describes people by the way they view their careers and leisure/recreation pursuits (see Ad 9.3). A lifestyle

The way to a man's heart is through his sports.

For some men, sports is little more than a casual interest. But for others, it's a passionate love affair. And for 3.7 million of America's most avid sports enthusiasts, the magazine that fans the flames of their passion is *The Sporting News.*

The bible of sports for more than 100 years, *The Sporting News* is the only magazine that connects fans to every major sport every week of the year. Authoritative analysis. Insider reports. National perspective. When it comes to sports, no magazine delivers like *The Sporting News.*

The way to the hearts of 3.7 million avid sports fans is through *The Sporting News.*

The Sporting News' uncompromising weekly sports analysis attracts an audience of men who are active. Affluent. Well educated. And achievement oriented. In fact, *The Sporting News'* audience profile equals or exceeds that of *any* men's magazine—including *Sports Illustrated.*

But when it comes to the true measure of a magazine—the reading intensity that creates a dynamic ad environment—*The Sporting News* stands alone. As evidence, *The Sporting News'* 2.2 reading days is one of the highest in the men's category.

If you have a message you want men to take to heart, get serious. Serious about sports. Serious about men to whom sports is an integral part of their lives. Serious about the one magazine *real* sports fans love most.

The Sporting News.

	The Sporting News	Sports Illustrated
Male	91%	80%
Age 25-44 Index	131	119
IEI $40,000 + Index	181	150
College Graduate + Index	144	125
Professional/Mgrl. Index	126	128
Reading Days	2.2	1.9

The Sporting News

Get Serious

Times Mirror
1990 Simmons

AD 9.2
This *Sporting News* advertisement offers some very specific demographic information about its target **audience.** (Courtesy of The Sporting News)

profile provides perspective on people's *chosen* social and cultural environment. Preferences for products, services, and entertainment are identified from these consumer self-evaluations. Although this research is valuable, it is not always readily available to media planners.

Product-Use Segmentation. Audiences can also be classified according to their consumption habits (usage). Media planners obtain information on which products readers, viewers, or listeners buy and how often they use or consume these products. The *Rolling Stone* advertisement in Ad 9.4 incorporates this type of information on the consumption habits of its readers.

Where to Advertise: Geographic Areas

Sales geography is an important aspect of many advertising plans. As we mentioned earlier, although companies may distribute goods and services in many cities and states, sales are seldom consistent across areas. Even the most popular brands in sales leadership positions have serious differences

AD 9.3
This advertisement for *Family Circle* magazine emphasizes the nontraditional life-style of its female readers. (Courtesy of The Family Circle, Inc.)

across the country. In 1991, for example, the Gerber Baby Food Company, which has an outstanding 75 percent share of sales, decided to regionalize its advertising in order to match up its advertising effort to sales in each of its regions. For Gerber, this meant reducing its use of network television and consumer magazines in favor of more localized advertising media. Ad 9.5 is an example of a Sunday supplement promoting its geographic flexibility.

For the media planner, geographic specification means identifying markets to be considered and allocating a sum of dollars to each one. Priorities are invariably set so that each area receives a "fair share" of the allocation to achieve its goals. Such priorities can be based on a number of variables, including the size of the market (consumer population), brand sales in each area, distribution performance, media costs, and the relative strength of competitors in both sales and advertising pressure. There is no standard approach to market-by-market evaluation, but many consumer-products companies use the index system called brand and category development (BDI/CDI). The calculation of each BDI and CDI compares the sales of each market to the total sales of the company's brand (BDI) or compares the sales of *all* competitors in the market to total U.S. sales (CDI). These shares are then contrasted with each market's population share. The result is a comparative index that can assist planners in deciding how much to spend in each market:

$$BDI = \frac{Market\ X's\ \%\ of\ Brand's\ Total\ Sales}{Market\ X's\ \%\ of\ U.S.\ Population}(100)$$

For a new generation of Rolling Stone readers, there's more to living in harmony with our planet than sitting still for twenty minutes. And the readers of Rolling Stone are doing their part to recycle that message. If you want to reach socially responsible, highly educated consumers, you'll like the environment in the pages of Rolling Stone.

Rolling Stone

AD 9.4
This long-running *Rolling Stone* campaign emphasizes how the magazine and its readers have "matured." (By Straight Arrow Publishers, Inc. © 1990. All Rights Reserved. Reprinted By Permission.)

$$CDI = \frac{\text{Market X's \% of All Brand's Sales}}{\text{Market X's \% of U.S. Population}}(100)$$

Illustration: The Baltimore market has 1.0 percent of the U.S. population. It has 1.9 percent of Alpha brand's total U.S. sales, and 1.3 percent of category sales for all competitors.

$$\text{Baltimore BDI} = \frac{1.9}{1.0}(100) = 190$$

$$CDI = \frac{1.3}{1.0}(100) = 130$$

In other words, Alpha users in Baltimore use almost twice as much (190 percent) as do the brand's users in other markets. In terms of the CDI, there is almost a third more use (130 percent) of the product category in Baltimore as in other parts of the country. Note that it is possible for a product to have a high BDI in a low-CDI area and vice versa.

Timing: When to Advertise

When is the best time to place the message before the target audience? The concept of aperture suggests advertising is most effective when people are exposed at a time when they are most receptive to the product information. This is easier said than done. Media planners might have to juggle a number

When you've got to reach people in exactly the right places,

AD 9.5
Parade reminds marketers to use media vehicles that can geographically target audiences.　(Reprinted with permission of PARADE magazine © 1991 Parade Publications, Inc.)

you want a magazine that pinpoints markets.

Metro areas. Rural areas. Mountain states or coastal states. The Sunbelt or a snowbelt.
Growth, heavy-up or test markets. You name it. With Parade, you've got a choice of any or all of over
330 markets. So your ad always reaches people where you want to reach them. Precisely.

Over 330 markets or any combination.

of variables to make correct timing decisions: how often the product is bought, if it is used more in some months than others, and how heavily it is advertised by competitors month to month. Each combination of influences makes the timing strategy unique to each company and brand.

Seasonal Timing. The demand for many products and services is directly tied to changes in the weather. A good example is the Standard Oil Company of Ohio's (SOHIO) offer of a gasoline brand featuring a special seasonal additive for winter driving. The additive was designed to prevent fuel lines from becoming clogged with ice when temperatures dropped below freezing. Consumers used the special gas during serious cold spells, but sales suffered during warmer times when there was no threat of a frozen fuel system.

The oil company rejected the idea of a season-long campaign for two reasons. First, Ohio traditionally has uneven winters, with as many thaws as freezes and at least three distinct bands of temperature from north to south. Second, a long campaign would absorb funds better spent on other SOHIO products. The obvious solution was a series of short campaigns during cold spells. But how could the company know when temperatures would fall?

The problem was solved by the media planner for the SOHIO advertising agency. He recommended that prearranged radio station schedules be set up to use SOHIO "Freeze Alert" commercials *automatically* whenever the local weather bureau forecast below-freezing temperatures for a 24-hour period. The weather forecast was the "trigger" for the schedule. That winter, every time the mercury dipped, SOHIO was promoting its additive. Just when the consumer's need for protection opened the customer's aperture for the SOHIO message, SOHIO was on the air.

Holiday Timing. The timing of advertising schedules can also be coordinated with holidays and other national celebrations. Just as with seasonal planning, media planners must exercise careful judgment regarding when to use advertising to take advantage of the consumer's interest. Nowhere is this judgment more critical than in advertising children's toys and gifts.

Holiday toys and gifts for children pose a fairly tricky problem for

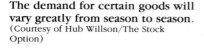

The demand for certain goods will vary greatly from season to season. (Courtesy of Hub Willson/The Stock Option)

media planners. There are two target audiences involved—the child (user) and the adult (buyer). Are both targets making a brand decision at the same time? If not (which is often the case), the planner must decide which target takes priority. Media planning based on the child's aperture may be wasteful in that it is too early. But planning based on the purchaser's action may be too late. The idea is to find the point where the child's interest in the product coincides with the parents' decision to shop.

Planners must also be aware of competitor scheduling—something the planner obviously has no control over. The effect of the best-timed message can be cramped by heavy use of the same media vehicle by competitors. The clutter created by advertising the same product in the same place simply confuses the prospective consumer.

Day-of-the Week Timing. Retail advertisers know their customers' shopping patterns first-hand. Shopping patterns are dictated by needs, work schedules, and payroll calendars; each day of the week is not equal in shopping traffic. Retail advertising is often used to create traffic during the normally slower times. For example, stores often advertise price specials during the midweek, when shopping is slower, rather than on Friday or Saturday, when it is already heavier. Another good example is restaurant advertising featuring discounts on weeknights, when people are inclined to eat in, rather than on weekends, when more people go out to eat.

Hour-of-the-Day Timing. Because many buying decisions are made on impulse, advertising in selected media should be scheduled when product need is high. This strategy is best accomplished with media that are capable of scheduling positions by the hour or even minute, such as television and radio. Examples of products that are advertised during certain parts of the day are fast-food restaurants (lunchtime), beer and wine products (evenings and weekends), convenience foods (end of the workday), and sleep-aid preparations (night).

Hour-of-the-day timing is also used by companies that target special consumer groups, such as children and teens (after-school hours and Saturday mornings), senior citizens (early morning rather than evening positions), and lifestyle groups, such as professionals and executives (early morning and weekends).

Duration: Finding the Best Campaign Length

How many weeks of the sales year should the advertising run? Strategies based on the answer to this question affect other plan elements. If there is a need to cover most of the weeks, the advertising will be spread rather thin. If the amount of time to cover is limited, advertising can be more heavily concentrated. The strategy employed to deal with duration is known as **continuity.** The selection of the best continuity pattern depends on a number of factors, including the advertising budget, consumer use cycles, brand loyalty, and competitive continuity strategies.

continuity *The strategy and tactics used to schedule advertising over the time span of the advertising campaign.*

The Advertising Budget. If their advertising allocations were unlimited, most companies would advertise every day. Not even the largest advertisers are in this position, however. All advertising budgets are limited, and this limitation forces firms to reduce month-after-month advertising in favor of shorter schedules with stronger levels of advertising.

Consumer-Use Cycles. Continuity should match consumer-use cycles (the time between purchase and repurchase), especially for products and services that demand high usage rates, such as soft drinks, toothpaste, candy and gum, fast-food restaurants, and movies. The marketer views these cycles as the number of times customers can be gained or lost.

Lack of Brand Loyalty. Marketing experts believe that consumer brand loyalty is much weaker in the 1990s than it once was. Loyalty means the consumer repeats the brand choice time after time. There is much evidence today that consumers are far more willing to change brands for any kind of small promotional incentive (coupons, price-offs). With lower or disappearing loyalty, advertisers feel obliged to use longer advertising durations to prevent decreased brand awareness when they aren't advertising.

share of voice *The percentage of advertising messages in a medium by one brand among all messages for that product or service.*

Competitive Advertising. In crowded product categories (household products, food, and durable goods) few advertisers are willing to ignore the advertising activity of competitors. In such situations scheduling decisions are made in response to the amount of competitive "traffic." The goal is to find media where the advertiser's voice is not suppressed by the voices of competitors. This concept, often called **share of voice** (percent of total advertising messages in a medium used by one advertiser), might mean scheduling to avoid the heavy clutter of competing advertising.

Continuity Scheduling Strategies

Depending on the length of the campaign, media planners will use one or more of three continuity strategies: continuous, pulsing, and flighting. All are designed to balance schedule length with impact. Each of these strategies is illustrated in Figure 9.2.

continuous *An advertising scheduling pattern in which spending remains relatively constant during the campaign period.*

Continuous Patterns. If the advertising is spread over the duration of the campaign in a fairly consistent way (only small variations), the pattern is called **continuous.** A continuous pattern may be chosen for advertising products used year-round, for retail services (barbers and hair salons, shoe repair shops, and plumbing services), and by firms that use advertising as a secondary support for other promotional tools (banks, utilities, and professional occupations). Media situations that support continuous strategies include sponsorship of television newscasts, outdoor billboard locations, and Yellow Pages advertising.

Fast-food restaurants use a pulsing schedule pattern for their advertising. (Peter Menzel/Stock Boston)

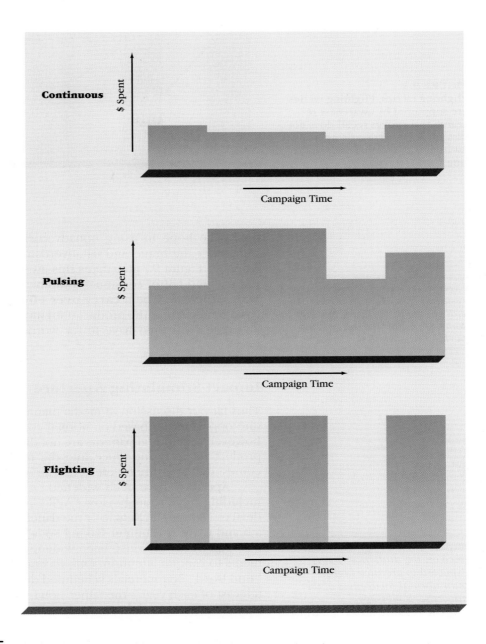

FIGURE 9.2
The three continuity tactics: continuous, pulsing, and flighting.

pulsing *An advertising scheduling pattern in which time and space are scheduled on a continuous but uneven basis; lower levels are followed by bursts or peak periods of intensified activity.*

flighting *An advertising scheduling pattern characterized by a period of intensified activity, called a* flight, *followed by periods of no advertising, called a* hiatus.

Pulse (Wave) Patterns. **Pulsing** is a popular alternative to continuous advertising. It is designed to intensify advertising prior to an open aperture, and then to reduce advertising to much lighter levels until the aperture opens again. The pulse pattern has peaks and valley.

Fast-food companies like McDonald's and Burger King use pulsing patterns. Although the competition for daily customers demands continuous advertising, they will greatly intensify activity to accommodate special events such as new menu items ("McRib Packs"), merchandise premiums ("Simpson Dolls"), and contests ("McDonald's Monopoly Games"). Pulsed schedules cover most of the year, but still provide periodic intensity.

Flight Patterns. The **flighting** strategy is the severest form of continuity adjustment. It is characterized by alternating periods of intense advertising activity and periods of no advertising (hiatus). This on-and-off schedule allows for a longer campaign without making the advertising schedule too

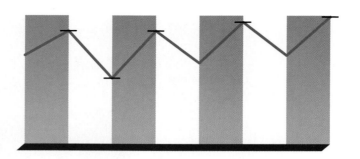

FIGURE 9.3
Flighting tactics. Flighting tactics are supported by awareness research that proves recall does not disappear once advertising stops. Awareness is shown by the single line.

carry-over effect *A measure of residual effect (awareness or recall) of the advertising message some time after the advertising period has ended.*

impact *A value of media influence on the audience that is expected to produce higher-than-normal awareness of the advertiser's message.*

light. The hope in using nonadvertising periods is that consumers will remember the brand and its advertising for some time after the ads have stopped. Figure 9.3 illustrates this awareness change. The line represents the rise and fall of consumer awareness of the brand. If the flight strategy works, there will be a **carry-over effect** of the past advertising that will sustain memory of the product until the next advertising period begins. The advertiser will then have fewer worries about low share-of-voice conditions.

Impact-Stimulating Aperture

Thus far our discussion of media planning has concerned the natural aperture opportunities based on normal consumer behavior patterns. Suppose, however, the normal patterns are not there. Perhaps an advertiser has a new product ready to introduce into the marketplace. The question then becomes: Can aperture be created? The answer is a qualified yes.

Apertures have been widened by a number of marketing techniques, including price strategy (low "APR" financing for cars), dramatic creative devices (Spuds MacKenzie or the dancing raisins), and new positioning for a brand (Arm & Hammer Baking Soda).

Apertures have also been widened by dramatic use of media environments to capture attention. One recent illustration of media **impact** is the "Bud Bowl" commercials scheduled during the most popular single sports telecast of each year—the Super Bowl. Ad 9.6 for Sassy is an example of an ad with impact.

A classic example of impact strategy involved a high-risk gamble taken by the J. R. Williams Company for a hand lotion called Rose Milk. Although Rose Milk was comparable to its competitors Jergens and Vaseline, it had nearly no consumer awareness and, even worse, poor distribution in drug and department stores. In 1975 Williams learned that the telecast of the Tournament of Roses Parade on January 1, 1976 was available for sponsorship from both the NBC and CBS television networks. This was the risk: Sponsorship would require committing nearly half the year's advertising budget to commercials that ran for a single day! Rose Milk flooded New Year's Day with its commercials, stressing the connection between the Tournament of Roses and Rose Milk. The impact was immediate, and Rose Milk went from being an also-ran competitor to a category leader. Rose Milk *created* an aperture instead of finding one.*

*Stephen A. Greyser, *Cases in Advertising and Communication Management,* 2nd ed. (Englewood Cliffs, NJ: Prentice Hall, 1981).

AD 9.6
Sassy advertising stresses reader devotion, an important feature of a product and media compatibility.
(Courtesy of *Sassy* magazine.)

Finding Acceptable Media Environments

Success in media planning depends on more than knowledge of the audience size, target profiles, and clever continuity strategies. Success also involves some intangibles that can influence the target consumer's reception of the advertising message. Intangibles include both positive and negative communication conditions. To many readers, viewers, or listeners, the advertising message is a seldom-desired intrusion. Although audiences only tolerate advertising (with the exception of shopping ads in newspapers), it is still risky for a company to run its advertising in an "alien" environment (a position of weaker communication potential). Three environmental areas deserve particular discussion: media content-product compatibility, media-created moods or atmospheres, and media clutter.

Media Content-Product Compatibility. Media content is said to be compatible with the product when the advertiser can find programming or editorial material that complements the message. Think of the sport and

AD 9.7
Leadership is demonstrated in the
Forbes magazine coverage of the
Donald Trump story. (Courtesy of
Forbes, Inc.)

recreation magazines that are filled with advertisements for clothing and
equipment. Think of televised golf and tennis matches, financial reports,
hunting and fishing shows, cartoon adventures, and cooking shows. All
offer advertisers a ready-made focus. One attraction of the opportunities is
audience characteristics. The other attraction is the special communication
between the customer and the content. When this environment is right, advertising becomes enjoyable rather than intrusive. Ad 9.7 for *Forbes* magazine is an example of compatibility between product and content.

Media-Created Moods. Moods or atmospheres are created by the programming or editorial content of the media vehicle. Audience members
react to content moods, and their emotional reaction is either good or bad
for the advertising message that follows. Television situation comedies,
such as *Murphy Brown* and *The Simpsons,* are designed to produce laughter
or good feelings. Other programs, such as *The Wonder Years,* mix happiness with sentimental feelings, whereas still others create tension or anxi-

ety (*In the Heat of the Night, Midnight Caller,* and *Rescue 911*). Companies sensitive to these variations in atmosphere demand that their commercials be run in atmospheres that will support brand and advertising acceptance by the audience. For example, General Foods (Jello Products) will not allow its commercials to run during programming that is not fully suitable for family audiences. Other firms are very cautious about advertising on programs that deal with controversial subjects or social issues.

Media Clutter. Most of the mass media allow too many promotional messages to compete for audience attention. Media planners cannot avoid all cluttered conditions, but they can reduce or limit the effect of clutter by isolating their messages from those of competitors and by advising against the use of the most cluttered media.

Judging medium clutter is a subjective process. Some people believe the commercial pod (a string of continuous broadcast messages run during program interruptions) is a severe form of clutter. Others feel that magazines that designate 50 percent of their pages to advertisements are cluttered. Every advertising media format is capable of becoming overcrowded to the point where communication is negatively affected.

*M*EDIA PLANNING OPERATIONS: MEDIA SELECTION PROCEDURES

Setting objectives and recommending strategies help to focus the media plan, but other factors must be considered in selecting the advertising media and the specific vehicles that will carry the message. These "yardsticks" measure the number of different people exposed to the message (reach), the degree of exposure repetition (frequency), and the efficiency (cost per thousand or CPM) of the selected vehicles. Each of these major dimensions of media planning will be examined in detail. In order to understand their contribution, however, you must first be familiar with the basic audience terms planners use to measure media impact.

Audience Measures Used in Media Planning

In the same way that a carpenter uses feet and inches and a printer uses points and picas, the media planner uses some special terms to evaluate a media plan.

A media supervisor presents a prospective media plan to a client.
(Courtesy of DDB Needham)

TABLE 9.1
Metro Company Gross Audience Impressions
August 1991 Schedule Hometown, U.S.A.

Media Vehicle	Audience Impressions	Number of Messages	Total Audience Impressions
Cheers	15,000	4	60,000
Times/Herald	8,400	6	50,400
You Magazine	6,300	1	6,300
		Total Gross Impressions	116,700

gross impressions *The sum of the audiences of all the media vehicles used within a designated time span.*

Gross Impressions. *Impression* represents one person's opportunity to be exposed to a program, newspaper, magazine, or outdoor location. Impressions, then, measure the size of the audience either for one media vehicle (one announcement or one insertion) or for a combination of vehicles as estimated by media research.

If *Late Night With David Letterman* has an audience of 100,000 viewers, then each time the advertiser uses that program to advertise a product, the value in impressions is 100,000. If the advertiser used an announcement in each of four consecutive broadcasts, the total viewer impressions would be 100,000 times 4, or 400,000. In practice, planners discuss **gross impressions**—the sum of the audiences of all the media vehicles used in a certain time spot—when dealing with multiple vehicles in a schedule. The summary figure is called *gross* because the planner has made no attempt to calculate how many *different* people viewed each show. Gross values simply refer to the number of people viewing, regardless of whether each viewer saw one, two, or all of the shows.

Total impressions are often calculated according to a "boxcar" figure, which represents the maximum exposure for all or part of the campaign. All the planner needs to do is find the audience figure for each vehicle used and multiply that figure by the times the vehicle was used. Then it is merely necessary to add the vehicle figures to get the sum of "gross impressions." Table 9.1 demonstrates the arrangement of data used to calculate the monthly gross impressions for a fictional company.

gross rating points *(GRP) The sum of the total exposure potential of a series of media vehicles expressed as a percentage of the audience population.*

Gross Rating Points. Gross impression figures tend to become very large and difficult to remember. The rating (percentage of exposure) is an easier method of measuring the intensity of schedules because it converts the raw figure to a percentage. The sum of the total exposure potential expressed as a percentage of the audience population is called **gross rating points.**

To demonstrate, in the previous example, *Late Night With David Letterman* had 100,000 viewer impressions. Suppose there were a total of 500,000 possible viewers (total number of households with televisions, whether the sets are on or off) at that hour. The 100,000 viewers watching *Letterman* out of the possible 500,000 would represent 20 percent of viewers, or a 20.0 rating. The gross rating point total on four telecasts would be 80 (20 rating × 4 telecasts).

Total rating values are calculated just as total impressions are. The sum of rating points can be used to calculate the total of gross rating points for any schedule, whether actual or proposed. In Table 9.2 the schedule for our fictional company is recalculated to reflect gross rating points.

Although gross rating points originated with broadcast-audience measurements, GRP is now used to represent print and out-of-home media

TABLE 9.2
Metro Company Gross Rating Points
August 1991 Schedule Hometown, U.S.A.

Media Vehicle	Audience Rating	Number of Messages	Total Rating Points
Cheers	13.6	4	54.4
Times/Herald	7.6	6	45.6
You Magazine	5.7	1	5.7
		Total Gross Rating Points	105.7

audiences as well. Gross rating points can also be calculated by multiplying two other audience measurements: *reach* (percentage) and *frequency* (integer).

Reach and Media Planning

An important aspect of an advertising campaign is how many *different members of the target audience* can be exposed to the message in a particular time frame. Different, or unduplicated, audiences are those that have at least *one* chance for message exposure. Most advertisers realize a campaign's success is due, in part, to its ability to reach as many prospects as possible.

reach *The percentage of different homes or people exposed to a media vehicle or vehicles at least once during a specific period of time. It is the percentage of unduplicated audience.*

    Reach is the percentage of the target population exposed at least once to the advertiser's message within a predetermined time frame. The reach of a schedule is produced according to research estimates that forecast the unduplicated audience. Most of the mass media are measured in this way, although for some media the estimate is only a statistical probability. This means the reach is not based on actual data but is calculated from the laws of chance. Reach can only be calculated when the planner has access to media audience research or projections from statistical models, however. It is not guesswork.

    To see how the reach calculation could work in television activity, we use a very simplified situation. Our fictional television market of Hometown, U.S.A., has a total of only ten television households. Table 9.3 is a television survey that shows home viewing for *Late Night With David Letterman* using a frequency analysis. The viewing survey is for 4 weeks during which the program ran once each week.

TABLE 9.3
Viewing Homes/Week for *Late Night With David Letterman*

Home	Week 1	Week 2	Week 3	Week 4	Total Viewings
1	▣	—	▣		3
2	—	▣	—		2
3	▣	—	—	—	1
4	—	▣	—		2
5	—	▣	▣		3
6	—	—	—	—	0
7	—	—	▣	—	1
8	▣	▣	▣	—	3
9	▣	—	—	—	1
10	—	—	—	—	0
Viewing/Week	4	4	4	4	16

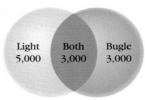

Total Poulation: 10,000
Total Light Readers: 5,000
Total Bugle Readers: 3,000
Read Both: 3,000

Unduplicated Readers: 5,000
(8,000 – 3,000 = 5,000) or 50 percent

FIGURE 9.4
Unduplicated audiences newspaper readership.

Each week 4 homes viewed *Late Night With David Letterman.* Because there are 10 homes in Hometown, the average program rating per week was 4 of 10, or 40.0. This viewing was done by all homes except home 6 and home 10. To be counted as "reached," the household only has to view *one* episode, and 8 of the 10 homes did that. The reach is then 8 of 10, or 80 percent.

Reach can also be demonstrated in print advertising. Bushville has a population of 10,000 households. It has two newspapers servicing the population. The *Light* has a circulation of 5,000 and the *Bugle* has a circulation of 3,000. If a media plan called for using both papers, the combined circulation would be 8,000. However, the unduplicated reach of the two newspapers is not 80 percent (8,000/10,000) because readership surveys show that some of the households subscribe to both papers. Figure 9.4 illustrates the reach as estimated from survey research.

Frequency and Media Planning

frequency *The number of times an audience has an opportunity to be exposed to a media vehicle or vehicles in a specified time span.*

As important as the percentage of people exposed (reach) is the number of times they are exposed. This rate of exposure is called **frequency.** Whereas the reach estimate is based on only a single exposure, frequency estimates the number of times the exposure is expected to happen.

To measure the frequency of a schedule, planners use two methods: either a "shorthand" summary called *average frequency* or the preferred frequency method that shows the percent of audience reached at each level of repetition (exposed once, twice, and so on). Both methods are illustrated below.

TABLE 9.4
Average Frequency Calculation Magazine Schedule
(Two Insertions Each) Total Insertions = Six

Magazine	Reader/Issue	Rating(GRP)	Unduplicated Readers
Today's Happiness	50,000	50.0	30,000
News Round-Up	40,000	40.0	15,000
Yuppie Life	18,000	18.0	11,000
Totals	108,000	108.0	56,000

Target Population: 100,000
Total Gross Impressions: 108,000
Gross Rating Points: 108.0
Unduplicated Readers: 56,000
Reach: 56.0 (56,000/100,000)
Average Frequency: 1.9 issues seen (108,000/56,000 = 1.9)
or (108 GRP/56 Reach = 1.9)

Average Frequency. To figure the "average" frequency you need only two numbers: the gross rating points (GRP) of a schedule and the reach estimate. The average frequency can also be calculated from the gross impressions and the unduplicated impressions if ratings are not available. Table 9.4 illustrates a situation involving a purchase of space in three magazines. For demonstration, the schedule is summarized in rating and impression values.

The schedule involves three magazines: *Today's Happiness, News Round-Up,* and *Yuppie Life.* Each magazine is listed by its total readership, readers expressed as a percent (rating), and the number of "unduplicated" readers (those who do not read either of the other two magazines). Note the formula calculations at the bottom of the table. Average frequency is calculated as follows:

$$\text{Average frequency} = \frac{\text{Gross rating points}}{\text{Reach (\%)}}$$

or

$$\text{Average frequency} = \frac{\text{Gross audience impressions}}{\text{Unduplicated impressions}}$$

Frequency Distribution. Averages can give the planner a distorted idea of the plan's performance. Suppose you had a schedule that could be seen a maximum of 20 times. If we figured the average from one person who saw 18 and another who saw 2 exposures, the average would be 10. But 10 exposures isn't close to the experience of either audience member. Therefore, planners who consider frequency in a functional way will choose to calculate *frequency distribution* whenever possible. The distribution will show the number of target audience members.

Table 9.5 demonstrates the principle for a magazine schedule of three news magazines: *Time, Newsweek,* and *U.S. News & World Report.* Each publication is to receive two insertions for a total of six advertising placements. The minimum exposure would be one insertion, and the maximum would be six.

The planner evaluating this distribution might consider alternative schedules because more than half of the target audience exposed would see three or fewer issues (33.5 percent of the 56 percent reached saw three or fewer).

The frequency distribution method is more revealing, and thus more valuable, than the average frequency method of reporting repetition. How-

TABLE 9.5
Magazine Frequency Distribution Table
Based on Three Magazines,
Two Insertions Each

Issues Read	Readers	Target Population (Percentage)
0	44,000	44.0
1	7,000	7.0
2	6,500	6.5
3	20,000	20.0
4	10,600	10.6
5	8,200	8.2
6	3,700	3.7
Totals	100,000	100.0

56,000 read at least one issue. Reach = 56.0

ever, frequency distribution data are only available from special research tabulations or from sophisticated math models, and this special research is expensive, so planners often have to settle for the average frequency method.

Combining Reach and Frequency Goals: Effective Frequency

effective frequency *A recent concept in planning that determines a range (minimum and maximum) of repeat exposure for a message.*

As we have just seen, the reach of an audience alone is not a sufficient measure of an advertising schedule's strength. Many media planners now feel that there should be a threshold or minimum level of frequency before any audience segment can be considered "exposed to the advertising message." In other words, for anyone to be considered part of the "reached" audience, he or she must have been exposed *more than once.* This theory essentially combines the reach and the frequency elements into one. This combination is known as **effective frequency.**

What is this level of repetition? There is no single standard in media planning today, and it is doubtful there will ever be one. True, some observers say that two or three is the minimum, but to prove an ideal level, all the brand's communication variables must be known (aperture, message content, consumer interest, and competitor intensity).

PRINCIPLE
Media are compared on the basis of their relative efficiency, which means cost and audience size.

Even without all the answers, planners can use their knowledge and experience to determine a probable range of effective frequency. The theory and technique behind these determinations is complex. Although the understanding of these questions is not complete, many planners are convinced that effective frequency is the essential planning dimension.

Cost Efficiency as a Planning Dimension

cost per thousand (CPM) *The cost of exposing each 1,000 members of the target audience to the advertising message.*

The media plan is not only evaluated in terms of audience impressions. As we mentioned earlier, the cost of time and space determines the number of message units that can be placed. These costs also influence the selection of media or of media vehicles. Inherent in media planning is the notion that media should be selected according to their ability to expose the largest target audience for the lowest possible cost. The key to this notion is the *target* audience because the advertiser wants prospects and not just readers, viewers, or listeners. The *target audience* is that proportion of a media audience that best fits the desired aperture. Therefore, the cost of each media vehicle proposed should be evaluated in relation to the medium's delivered target audience. The process of measuring the target audience size against the cost of that audience is called *efficiency*—or more popularly, **cost per thousand** (CPM) and **cost per rating point** (CPRP).

cost per rating point (CPRP) *A method of comparing media vehicles by relating the cost of the message unit to the audience rating.*

Cost per Thousand.   The CPM analysis allows the planner to compare vehicles within a medium (one magazine with another or one television program with another). It is also used to compare vehicles across media (the CPM of radio compared with the CPM of a newspaper), but this is a questionable practice because it compares "apples with oranges." Although the analysis can be done for the total audience, it is more valuable to base it only on that portion of the audience that has the target characteristics. To calculate the CPM you need only two figures: the cost of the unit (page or 30 seconds) and the estimated audience to be reached. The target audience's gross impressions are divided into the cost of the unit to determine the advertising dollars needed to expose 1,000 members of the target.

$$\text{CMP} = \frac{\text{Cost of message unit}}{\text{Gross impressions}} \times 1{,}000$$

Here are some examples from print and broadcast media to illustrate the formulas used in CMP analysis.

Magazines   Suppose an issue of *You* magazine has 10,460,000 readers who could be considered a target audience. The advertising unit is a four-color page and its rate is $42,000. The CPM is:

$$CPM = \frac{\text{Cost of page or fractional page unit}}{\text{Target audience readers}} \times 1,000$$

$$\frac{\$42,000 \times 1000}{10,460,000} = 4.015 \ (\$4.02)$$

Television   The show *Inside Gossip* has 92,000 target viewers. The cost of a 30-second announcement during the show is $850.

$$CPM = \frac{\$850,000}{92,000} \times 1000 = \$9.24$$

Cost per Rating Point.   Some planners prefer to compare media on the basis of rating points (ratings) instead of impressions. The calculation is parallel, with the exception that the divisor in CPRP is the rating percentage rather than the total impressions used in CPM.

$$CPRP = \frac{\text{Cost of message unit}}{\text{Program or issue rating}}$$

(*Note:* Because this is not on a per-thousand basis, the multiplication by 1,000 is not necessary.)

If the target audience rating for the program *Inside Gossip* were 12.0 and the cost were still $850, the CPRP would be 850/12, or $70.83.

Although both efficiency calculations are used, the CPRP is favored by planners for its simplicity. Both the CPM and the CPRP are relative values. The absolute numbers mean very little unless there are similar values to compare. A planner would not know if *Newsweek*'s CPM of $27.89 for the target audience were good or bad unless he or she had comparable figures for *Time* and *U.S. News & World Report.*

Although these efficiency analyses can be used across media (comparing one medium to another), such comparisons should be made with caution. When comparing the CPMs for radio and television, for example, you are comparing very different audience experiences, and if the experience is totally different, it is difficult to say that one medium is more efficient than the other. CPM and CPRP are more valid when used to compare alternatives *within* a medium.

*M*EDIA PLANNING OPERATIONS: STAGING A MEDIA PLAN

PRINCIPLE
Media plans are interwoven with all other areas of advertising: the budget, the target audience, the advertising objectives, and the message demands.

To control the flow of information to the plan and to ensure that each component makes a logical contribution to strategy, the planner uses a sequence of decision stages to form the media plan. The plan is a written document that summarizes the recommended objectives, strategies, and tactics pertinent to the placement of a company's advertising messages. Plans do not have a universal form, but there is a similar (and logical) pattern to the decision stages. To illustrate a style of presentation in a real-life setting, we use an actual media plan (excerpted) from the National Dairy

Brand: National Dairy Board—Cheese	**Media Budget:** 18,700M
Marketing Objective:	To increase in-home consumption of domestic cheeses.
Demographic Target:	Women Age 25–54 3+ Household Size Household Income of $30,000+
Target Universe:	22,710.0 (27% of all women)
Psychographics:	Middle class, sticks to basic foods, busy, active, family-oriented
Geographic Skew:	None
Seasonality:	Relatively flat, with increased sales in the November/December period.
Creative Executions:	Television: 15's Print Page 4/C Bleed

FIGURE 9.5
National Dairy Board overview.
(Courtesy of DDB Needham Worldwide)

Board. The National Dairy Board's mission is to strengthen the dairy industry's position in domestic and foreign marketplaces. The example used relates specifically to the cheese portion of the National Dairy Board's challenge.

A systematic direction of media plans would begin with the general and work down to the more specific questions. Similarly, it would begin with the most important decisions and work down to those of lesser priority. The following section offers a brief description of each stage.

Background/Situation Analysis

The background/situation analysis is the marketing perspective discussed in the beginning of the chapter. The National Dairy Board summarized overview includes consumer target profiles, geographic considerations, and seasonality (see Figure 9.5).

Media Objectives/Aperture Opportunities

A media objecitve is a goal or task to be accomplished by the plan. Objectives are pertinent to the brand's strategy, specifically detailed, and capable of being measured within a given time frame. The objectives listed in the media portion should be limited to goals that can be accomplished specifically from media directions (see Figure 9.6). Measurable media objectives usually focus on reach and frequency projections. Similarly, aperture guidance (though less specific) details the best opportunities of exposing the National Dairy Board's message. Observe that the objectives concentrate on target profile, geographic priorities, and scheduling requirements. Note the aperture importance of scheduling cheese advertising when consumers are most likely to grocery shop.

Strategy: Selection of Media

This section of the media plan explains why a single medium or set of media are appropriate for the campaign objectives. A sound strategy should be able to anchor each dimension to the recommendation.

Because planning occurs usually months before the campaign actually begins some detail is omitted. For the television portion of the National Dairy Board campaign (Figure 9.7), the planner cannot be assured of the

MEDIA OBJECTIVES:

Target advertising to medium/light cheese users, demographically defined as:

Women Age 25–54

3+ Household Size

$30,000+ Household Income

Provide national advertising support

Schedule 12 months of support recognizing greater consumption during the November/December period

Achieve comparable monthly W25–54 GRP levels vs. year ago

Aperture being sought

Every-week support
- Complements branded advertising activity
- Recognizes every-week usage and purchase opportunities

Emphasize biweekly pay periods
- Greater cheese sales opportunities due to increase in discretionary income

Best Food Day concentration
- Complements the higher incidence of grocery shopping

Audience Delivery:

# Weeks:	52 weeks of television
Geography:	National, with emphasis in cable homes due to higher incidence of cheese usage and advertising cost effiencies
Television:	40% Daytime
Daypart Mix:	25% Primetime
	20% Early Fringe
	15% Weekend

W25–54 GRPs

Television:	7500
Print:	1800
Total:	9300

Average Monthly Audience Delivery (W25–54)

	Cable Households	Non-Cable Households
Reach/Avg. Freq.	98/10.1	89/4.3
Reach at 4+:	83%	42%

Media Buying Tactics:

Daytime

Minimum of 70% of weight in above average rated programs.

Minimum of 75% of weight is soap opera programming.

Not more than one commercial in a single program.

Early Fringe Syndication

Emphasis on talk, sit-com and entertainment type programs vs. court shows.

A large mix of programs purchased on a weekly basis to maximize reach.

Primetime

Drama and news programming is the priority to complement greater audience attentiveness.

Cable

A large mix of networks purchased to maximize reach. Program sponsorships and billboards are highly desirable.

Magazines

Position advertising on the right hand page in the food section opposite 100% recipe edit.

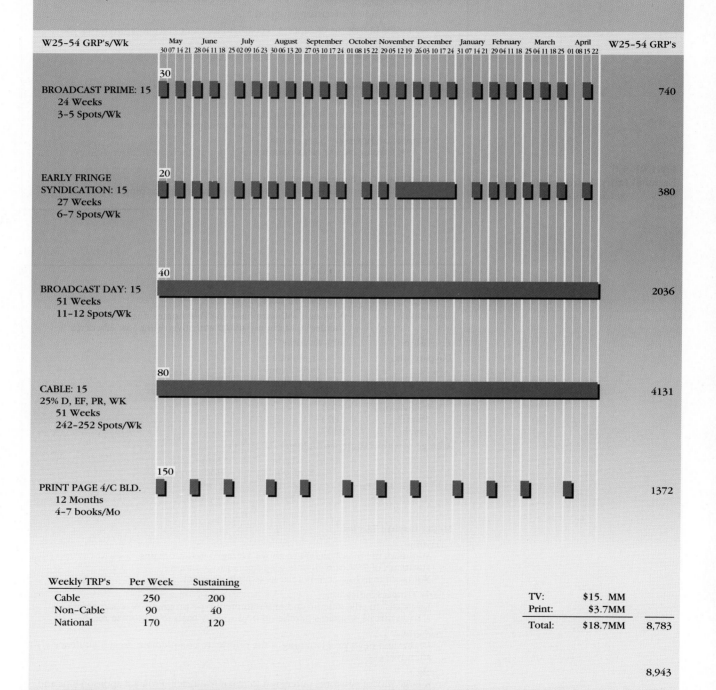

FIGURE 9.8
National Dairy Board consumer plan. (Courtesy of DDB Needham Worldwide)

program availability or specific pricing in television. In such situations the recommendation must deal with the overall characteristics without identifying specific locations. This isn't guesswork, as the anticipated performance of the television activity is shown in detail.

The Flow Chart: Scheduling and Budgeting Allocation

The graphic document depicted in Figure 9.8 is designed to illustrate most of the media recommendations. It shows the month-by-month placement of messages, details the anticipated impact through forecasted levels of GRPs, and illustrates how the campaign budget is allocated by medium and by month. In a concise fashion a flow chart is the "blueprint" of the media plan.

The media plan is a recommendation and must be accepted before any further steps are taken. In fact, planning is only the first stage in the advertising media operations. Once the plan directions are set, the actual selection, negotiation, and contracting must be done for time and space. These duties, known as media buying, are the subject of Chapter 12, which examines how buyers convert objectives and strategies into tactical decisions. Before the role of buyer is examined, however, you need to learn more about the advertising media. Chapters 10 and 11 will provide the foundation for a better understanding of the "seller" side of the media business.

SUMMARY

- Media planning involves the strategic use of marketing information to create an advertising schedule for a campaign.
- The ideal time to communicate with target prospects is called *aperture*.
- Media continuity refers to the scheduling of a campaign over a period of time. It does not mean that the ads run continuously or evenly.
- There are three possible scheduling strategies: continuous, pulsing, and flighting.
- Impressions measure the total audience exposure to an advertising message but do not take duplication into account.

- Planning decisions include whom to target, where, when, for how long, and how intense the exposure should be.
- Reach is more specific than impressions in that it measures the ability of a medium to attract different members of the target audience.
- Frequency refers to the number of times an audience member can be exposed to the advertising message.
- Media expenses are usually analyzed on a cost-per-thousand (CPM) basis. These costs can be compared within the same medium, but comparisons between different media are not as valid.

QUESTIONS

1. Why is the media planning function considered the bridge between sales marketing and the creative function of advertising?
2. Allan Johnson is a graduating senior from a mideastern journalism program. He is seeking some career advice from one of his professors. Allan has an interest in advertising, and wants to know what an advertising-journalism major with a business minor in marketing has prepared him for. In addition to ac-

count management positions, the professor urges Allan to consider media planning as a logical entry-level position. Why does the professor advise this? Why is marketing study so important for media planners?

3. Susan Ellet has just begun a new job as senior media planner for a relatively new automobile model from General Motors. Facing a planning sequence that will begin in 4 months, Susan's media director asks

her what data and information she needs for her preparation. What sources should Susan request? How will she use each of these sources in the planning function?

4. If the marketing management of McDonald's restaurants asked you to analyze the aperture opportunity for its breakfast entrees, what kind of analysis would you present to management?

5. The Pioneer account has accepted your recommendation for ten one-page insertions (ten issues) in a magazine known as the *Illustrated Press*. The magazine reaches an estimated 3,000,000 target readers per month, or a 10 percent rating per issue. The cost per page of the publication is $20,000. What are the total gross rating points delivered by this schedule? What is the cost per rating point and the CPM target readers?

6. If you were doing a frequency analysis composed of two magazines, a radio network schedule, and a national newspaper, would you rather use the average frequency procedure or a frequency distribution analysis? Defend your choice.

7. Explain why media planners try to *balance* reach, frequency, and continuity of proposed media schedules. What considerations go into this decision?

FURTHER READINGS

BARBAN, ARNOLD M., STEVEN M. CRISTOL, AND FRANK J. KOPECK, *Essentials of Media Planning: A Marketing Approach,* 2nd ed. (Lincolnwood, IL: NTC Business Books, 1987).

BRUVIC, ALLEN, *What Every Account Executive Should Know About Media* (New York: American Association of Advertising Agencies, 1989).

JUGENHEIMER, DONALD W., AND PETER B. TURK, *Advertising Media* (Columbus, OH: Grid Publishing, 1980).

SISSORS, JACK, AND LINCOLN BUMBA, *Advertising Media Planning,* 3rd ed. (Chicago: NTC Business Books, 1989).

Wellstone for U.S. Senate

When Paul Wellstone chose to run for senate in 1990, he was a political science professor at a small college in rural Minnesota and had never held an elected office. His decision to run for the U.S. Senate was made after seeing how few noteworthy Democratic candidates emerged after former-Vice President Walter Mondale's career in the Senate ended. Wellstone's opponent, Republican Rudy Boschwitz, was a two-term, 12-year incumbent considered virtually unbeatable due to his nationally renowned fund-raising ability and his long record for constituent service.

The base line poll commissioned by the Wellstone campaign at the end of July 1990 showed Boschwitz with a 98 percent name awareness among the state's voters and a 70 percent job approval rating, the highest of any politician in the state. Conversely, Wellstone had only 17 percent name awareness. Wellstone's task was made even more difficult because he had only meager campaign funds and little chance of raising anywhere near the amount of money his opponent possessed. At the time, Boschwitz's war chest contained $6 million, and he would eventually spend over $8 million throughout the course of the campaign.

The overall objective of the "Wellstone for Senate" campaign obviously was to elect Paul Wellstone to the U.S. Senate. Thus, the campaign would have to generate at least 51 percent of the vote on election day to achieve this objective. In order to do so, Wellstone's advertising agency, North Woods Advertising, identified several key strategies. Specifically, the campaign's principle goal was to raise Paul Wellstone's visibility and name awareness above the existing 17 percent level and to make his friendly, personable campaign style familiar to Minnesota voters. At the same time, the campaign was designed to undermine Boschwitz's 70 percent job approval rating by focusing on his legislative record, which included only one successfully sponsored piece of legislation in his 12 years in the Senate and a voting record that was not in keeping with his stated views, interests, and the concerns of most Minnesota residents.

In the highly charged and antiincumbent atmosphere of the 1990 election year, Paul Wellstone had to run a campaign of contrasts. Wellstone's populist, homespun, outsider image had to be contrasted with that of Boschwitz's elitist, Washington-insider image. The "no bucks" style of the Wellstone campaign was contrasted with Boschwitz's well-funded, media-intensive campaign. To emphasize this point, Wellstone used a converted school bus to travel around the state, and he stayed in supporters' homes rather than hotels, whereas Boschwitz, a millionaire himself, was frequently supported by big business. Lastly, Wellstone's energetic personal style of campaigning was contrasted with Boschwitz's removed, aristocratic style.

Typically, attempting to change existing public attitudes is a costly process, requiring significant media expenditures. However, the Wellstone campaign was to be outspent by his opponent by approximately 8 to 1 overall, and in media dollars by at least $6 million to $460,000. The Wellstone campaign represented less than 2 percent of total political dollars spent in the state. Given this spending disadvantage, the Wellstone campaign was forced to be more selective in its target audience definition, as well as more intelligent in its advertising execution style. Thus, the target audience for the campaign was identified as all voters over 18 years of age in the state, but was skewed particularly to women (because Wellstone was a pro-choice candidate), to younger, better-educated people between 25 and 49 years of age, and to voters in the typical democratic strongholds of northern Minnesota and the twin cities of Minneapolis/St. Paul. Stylistically, the executions were designed to engage voters' interest, to break through the clutter of traditional political advertising, and to force additional media coverage and responses from the Boschwitz camp.

Out of the 35 U.S. Senate races contested in 1990, only one seat changed hands. Incumbents won in every state except Minnesota, where Paul Wellstone defeated 12-year Senator Rudy Boschwitz by a 52 percent vote. It was one of the biggest political upsets in the nation. The campaign successfully raised Wellstone's name awareness to a respectable 72 percent, up almost five times from its base level of 17 percent and closer to the range of Boschwitz's 98 percent. The campaign also succeeded in exposing Boschwitz as an ineffective legislator who was not in touch with the interests of Minnesota residents, lowering his job approval rating from 70 percent to 42 percent by the end of the campaign. Despite being outspent by more than 8 to 1, the Wellstone campaign succeeded in making the financial disparity an issue in the race and a liability to the incumbent.

QUESTIONS

1. Although negative campaign advertising continues to be effective for candidates, what are the disadvantages to the American public?

2. Negative campaign advertising is certainly protected by freedom of speech laws, but the short duration of advertising campaigns coupled with the lack of regulation regarding truthfulness in campaign advertising could provide an unfair advantage to unscrupulous candidates. Describe these advantages.

3. Although North Woods Advertising successfully turned a budget disadvantage into a campaign benefit, in virtually every case larger media budgets versus competitors are preferable. What strategic errors do you believe Boschwitz's advertising agency made which could have allowed this advantage to become a liability?

Source: Courtesy of North Woods Advertising.

10

Broadcast Media

Chapter Outline

Chapter Objectives

When you have completed this chapter, you should be able to:

- Understand the basic nature of both radio and television
- Describe the audience for each medium and explain how that audience is measured
- List the advantages and disadvantages of using radio and television commercials

NINTENDO DIVIDES AND CONQUERS

In September 1990 Nintendo faced a serious dilemma with the advertising of its Game Boy hand-held video game, which offers a number of games comparable to the Nintendo system. Research indicated that approximately 40 percent of Game Boy sales were to adults, but previous television efforts had addressed adults only as parents who would purchase the game for their children. The company's advertising was not reaching the right target market. Furthermore, about 60 percent of the adults who buy Game Boy for their own use are males.

In response, Nintendo decided to develop three separate commercials (spots) for television. One would be targeted to 18- to 49-year-old men, whereas the other two would be targeted to the company's traditional 6- to 17-year-old male market. The entire campaign budget was $15 million. Television was chosen as the medium because it is able to show the excitement and action of the product. In addition, both target audiences can be reached more easily through television than print media because television draws a larger, more heterogenous audience.

The audience spot, called "Never Get Old," features men in a variety of professional situations playing with Game Boy. Symphonic music gives way to the wild sounds of an electric guitar as two messages appear on the screen: "You don't stop playing because you get old," followed by "But you could get old if you stop playing." The commercial aired nationally on the Fox network in ten spot markets (selected cities or areas rather than national coverage) during prime-time, late-night, and sports programs.

The other two spots were targeted at the younger market and let children do the talking. The fast-paced commercials feature adolescent jargon accompanied by animation illustrating the benefits of the product. The children's ads were mostly unscripted, allowing the children to react to the game-playing experience in a normal manner. The two spots directed at the younger crowd ran on syndicated programs, which are shown on local television stations, and cable.

Game Boy sales were expected to reach 5 million units in 1990, partly as a result of the new television campaign. (Nintendo had sold 1 million units in 1989 after the game's introduction in June of that year.) Nintendo is just one of thousands of advertisers that believe broadcast media are an effective system for delivering messages to a mass audience.*

Broadcast media, the process of transmitting sounds or images, includes both radio and television. Advertising experts contend that creating commercials for broadcast media is quite different from creating advertisements for print media. Certainly broadcast media tap into different human senses: sight (through movement and imagery) and sound.

Print is a *space* medium that allows the reader to digest information and images at his or her own speed. Broadcast is a *time* medium that affects the viewer's emotions for a few seconds and then disappears.

This chapter will explore broadcast media. Chapter 11 deals with print media. The overview contained in these chapters will provide the necessary background for Chapter 12, "Media Buying."

*Adapted from Cleveland Horton, "Nintendo Adopts Dual Strategy," *Advertising Age* (September 10, 1990):40.

*T*HE STRUCTURE OF TELEVISION

A great deal of change has taken place in the technical aspects of television. As a result, several different types of television systems are now available to advertisers for delivery of their messages to audiences.

Wired Network Television

Whenever two or more stations are able to broadcast the same program, which originates from a single source, a network exists. Networks can be "over-the-air" or cable.

affiliate *A station that is contracted with a national network to carry network-originated programming during part of its schedule.*

Currently there are four national over-the-air television networks—the American Broadcasting Company (ABC), the Columbia Broadcasting System (CBS), the National Broadcasting Company (NBC), and Fox Broadcasting Company. The first three own 15 regional stations, and the remaining 600 regional stations are privately owned **affiliates** (each network has about 200 affiliates). An affiliate station signs a contract with the national network (ABC, CBS, NBC, or Fox) whereby it agrees to carry network-originated programming during a certain part of its schedule. For example, WDIV-TV is NBC's Detroit affiliate. These major networks originate their own programs and are compensated at a rate of 30 percent of the fee charged for programs in a local market. In turn, affiliates receive a percentage of the advertising revenue (12 to 25 percent) paid to the national network and have the option to sell some advertising time during network programs and between programs. This is the primary source of affiliate revenues.

In over-the-air *network scheduling* the advertiser contracts with either a national or a regional network to show commercials on a number of affiliated stations. Sometimes an advertiser purchases only a portion of the network coverage, known as a *regional leg.* This is common with sports programming where different games are shown in different parts of the country. The top network advertisers are listed in Table 10.1, which also contains the 1989 expenditures for other mass media and will be a useful reference throughout our discussion on media.

Unwired Network Television

In contrast to the wired networks like ABC, NBC, CBS, and Fox, which do business directly with their affiliates in terms of programming, the unwired network station has nothing to do with programming and everything to do with advertising sales. Unwired networks are basically sales representative organizations that represent large market stations on a commission basis (15 percent). They simplify the buying process for the agency by designating one person at a network to handle the total buy. They also assist the client in media planning.*

Public Television

Although many people still consider public television to be "commercial-free," the Public Broadcasting Service (PBS) has engaged in advertising since the mid-1970s. Public television turned to advertising to compensate

*Cara S. Trager, "Unwired Networks Work to Unplug Rivals' Shares," *Advertising Age* (April 14, 1986):S-8.

TABLE 10.1
Top 15 U.S. Brands: Advertising Expenditures

RANK	Advertisers/ BRAND	PARENT	MAG	SMAG	NEWS	OUT	NET TV	SPOT TV	SYN TV	CATV NET	NET RAD	SPOT RAD	89 TOTALS (000)	88 TOTALS (000)
1	McDonald's	McDonald's Corp.	—	—	0.4	5.9	252.1	140.9	17.4	7.2	—	6.7	430,632.0	404,951.8
2	Sears	Sears Roebuck	3.1	4.3	123.1	0.4	102.9	35.3	1.8	5.0	36.9	32.1	349,099.5	209,054.2
3	Burger King	Grand Metropolitan	—	—	0.2	0.9	112.2	35.9	13.4	3.5	3.8	8.9	183,435.7	161,310.9
4	Kentucky Fried Chicken	Pepsico Inc.	—	—	—	0.2	63.6	48.6	—	3.5	1.5	0.3	117,746.4	100,523.1
5	Macy's	Macy, RH & Co.	1.4	0.3	105.0	—	—	7.0	—	—	—	0.2	113,816.6	113,666.8
6	Budweiser Beer	Anheuser-Busch	2.9	—	4.8	1.4	40.0	27.5	2.3	7.0	4.6	10.6	113,133.6	134,020.9
7	American Express Credit Card Service	American Express Co.	15.0	1.2	5.0	0.1	50.0	15.9	4.0	1.7	0.1	4.8	97,790.5	98,713.7
8	KMart Stores	KMart Corp.	10.6	6.4	15.4	—	7.0	2.8	0.3	0.7	12.1	10.8	96,971.0	94,858.4
9	Pizza Hut	Pepsico Inc.	—	—	0.8	0.4	35.1	55.6	—	2.2	0.1	1.1	95,850.2	83,283.3
10	American Airlines	American Airlines	9.7	1.0	40.3	0.4	10.5	18.1	—	0.3	0.5	13.6	94,531.1	101,205.8
11	AT&T Long Distance Business	AT&T	14.1	—	—	—	71.7	5.2	0.5	2.1	—	—	93,629.4	45,677.5
12	Wendy's Restaurant	Wendy's	—	—	0.1	1.4	47.9	36.5	3.8	2.7	—	0.6	93,108.3	86,836.4
13	Delta Air Lines	Delta Air Lines Inc.	3.1	—	28.4	1.7	29.3	4.1	—	2.0	—	17.3	85,892.3	77,754.7
14	United Airlines	United Airlines	10.8	0.2	11.6	0.8	40.6	9.9	—	2.5	1.6	—	84,746.4	71,937.9
15	AT&T Long Distance Lines	AT&T	23.0	0.9	—	—	25.8	18.5	5.0	3.3	6.0	12.2	82,383.9	73,123.2

Source: "The Top 200 Bands," Marketing & Media Decisions (July 1990): 36.

for the cutback in federal funding that occurred during the Nixon administration and to compete more effectively with cable television. PBS is an attractive medium for advertisers because it attracts a large upscale audience and because it adopted a much more consistent programming schedule beginning in the 1980s.

Current FCC guidelines allow ads to appear on public television only during the local 2.5-minute program breaks. Each station maintains its own acceptability guidelines. Some PBS stations accept the same ads that appear on paid programming, such as commercials for AT&T, one of the largest underwriters of PBS. Others will not accept any commercial corporate advertising, but only noncommercial ads that are "value-neutral." Such messages may include nonpromotional corporate and product logos and slogans, business locations and telephone numbers that are not used for direct-response selling, and brand names, service marks, and logos. In other words, there is no attempt to "sell" anything through these ads. For example, the Chubb Group of Insurance Companies, which spends more than $1 million to underwrite *American Playhouse,* chooses to simply show their name and the statement, "Brought to you by the Chubb Group of Insurance Companies."

Cable and Subscription Television

cable television *A form of subscription television in which the signals are carried to households by a cable.*

The initial purpose of **cable television** was to improve reception in certain areas of the country, particularly mountainous regions and large cities. However, alternative programming, with an emphasis on entertainment and information, has been primarily responsible for the rapid growth of

TABLE 10.2
Top 10 Cable TV Network Advertisers

Rank	Advertiser	Cable TV Network Spending			Total U.S. Ad Spending		Cable TV network as % of Total	
		1989	1988	% chg	1989	1988	1989	1988
1	Procter & Gamble Co.	$39.3	$31.5	24.5	$1,779.3	$1,655.8	2.2	1.9
2	Time Warner	35.5	24.4	45.4	567.5	505.6	6.3	4.8
3	Anheuser-Busch Cos.	26.3	21.7	21.3	591.5	645.9	4.4	3.4
4	General Mills	21.3	20.0	6.5	471.0	447.8	4.5	4.5
5	General Motors Corp	21.0	9.2	128.7	1,363.8	1290.6	1.5	0.7
6	Philip Morris Cos.	20.5	23.1	(11.2)	2,072.0	2,028.4	1.0	1.1
7	RJR Nabisco	19.1	13.9	37.4	703.5	740.9	2.7	1.9
8	Mars Inc.	14.0	10.0	39.9	293.3	334.5	4.8	3.0
9	Sears, Roebuck & Co.	13.3	4.7	186.9	1,432.1	1,031.4	0.9	0.5
10	Chrysler Corp.	11.8	10.7	9.7	532.5	476.4	2.2	2.3

Note: Dollars are in millions.
Source: Kevin Brown, *Advertising Age* (September 26, 1990):54. Copyright Crain Communications, Inc.

cable systems. According to the rating company A. C. Nielsen, as of February 1990, 58 percent of U.S. households (53.2 million) subscribed to cable television. This was not a drastic change from 1989, when 57.1 percent of the population (52.5 million) people subscribed, but it is a startling increase from 1980, when only 22.6 percent (approximately 17.6 million) of households subscribed to cable television.* Projections for 1995 and 2000 are 70 percent and 90 percent, respectively. Total cable advertising revenue rose to more than $2 billion in 1989, compared to $125 million in 1981. Growth is expected to continue at an annual rate of 17 percent, producing $10 billion in revenues by the year 2000.† Table 10.2 lists the top 10 cable network advertisers of 1989.

Some of these cable systems develop and air their own programs as well as pass along programs initiated by VHF stations, the 12 channels (2–13) located on the very high frequency band on the wavelength spectrum, or UHF (ultrahigh frequency) stations, such as WTBS. "Pay programming" is an option available to subscribers for an additional monthly fee. Ad 10.1 is an example of an advertiser-supported basic cable network. Pay programming normally consists of movies, specials, and sports under such plans as Home Box Office, Showtime, and The Movie Channel. In 1990, 12 million American homes were wired for pay cable.‡ Pay networks do not currently sell advertising time. Homes that do not subscribe to cable may purchase "subscription television" that is broadcast over the air with an electronically scrambled signal. Subscribers own a device that unscrambles the signal.

Origins of Cable Programs. Most of the programming shown on cable television is provided by independent cable networks such as Cable News Network (CNN), the Disney Channel, the Nashville Network, Music Television (MTV), the Entertainment and Sports Programming Network (ESPN), and a group of independent superstations whose programs are carried by satellite to cable operators (for example, WTBS-ATLANTA, WGN-CHICAGO, and WWOR-NEW YORK). Although approximately 80 percent of

*Joe Cappo, "Freedom of Choice Drives Cable Growth," *Advertising Age* (February 19, 1990):16.
†John Motavelli, "Cable TV," *Adweek* (September 1, 1989):158–162.
‡Sarah Polster, "Cable Gains 17.9%: Growth Pace Slows, Pay Cable Is Struggling." *Advertising Age* (June 25, 1990):36.

FREQUENT VIDEOTAPE RENTERS

Common sense might tell us that video rentals would cut into the profits of network television. That is, one medium competes with the other. To find out if this is really true we must first take a look at the lifestyles and media habits of video renters.

A national sample of heads of households reported that 29 percent of those surveyed are frequent videotape renters (rented 12 or more times a year). Some 37 percent of VCR owners alone are avid renters, and they account for 80 percent of videotaped movie rentals. The proportion of male to female renters is approximately the same.

Frequent videotape renters are younger than the general population. Over 75 percent are under age 45, whereas less than 50 percent of the comparison group (infrequent renters and nonrenters) are under 45. Frequent renters are also more likely to be married, with children living at home. Whereas 22 percent of the less dedicated renters are retired, only 3 percent of frequent renters are. Frequent renters earn a median income of $32,300, significantly higher than the median income of $26,400 of the comparison group. Differences in educational background between the two groups is relatively small.

Virtually all frequent video renters have bought blank videocassette tapes, and about 50 percent have videotaped at least one program on the VCR, double the number of infrequent renters or nonrenters who have done so. They are also sufficiently intrigued by new electronic products that, within the next few years, they plan to buy children's educational computer software, compact disc players, and personal computers. The infrequent renters and nonrenters are far less geared toward these future purchases.

The steady renters enjoy a broad range of television programming. In particular, they are more attracted by science fiction programs, *Saturday Night Live,* late night movies, and dramas than are members of the comparison group. As compared to the latter, frequent renters have a relaxed attitude toward television programming and advertising. They are less likely to complain about violence on television or to ask for more government control over television content. Although they spend a good amount of time in front of their television sets, they are also active sports participants and like to attend sporting events, entertain friends at home, barbeque, and work on do-it-yourself projects around the house. Furthermore, frequent renters do not only watch movies at home; they also enjoy going to movie theaters and are distinctly more enthusiastic about commercial films than are members of the comparison group.

With all these activities plus their jobs, frequent renters feel they and their families lead very

cable programming is provided through these systems, the cable operators themselves are originating more of their own programs.

interconnects *A special cable technology that allows local advertisers to run their commercials in small geographical areas through the interconnection of a number of cable systems.*

Cable Scheduling. *Cable scheduling* is divided into two categories: network and local. The system is the same as for the noncable systems. Network cable systems show commercials across the entire subscriber group simultaneously. Local advertisers are able to show their commercials to highly restricted geographic audiences through **interconnects,** a special cable technology that allows local or regional advertisers to run their commercials in small geographical areas through the interconnection of a number of cable systems. Interconnects are either "hard," in which different ads are distributed electronically by cable or microwave, or "soft," in which the same commercials are simply scheduled at the same time. Either way, they offer small advertisers an affordable way to reach certain local audiences through television.

Mergers. Once considered a high-risk industry with little potential for profit, the cable industry is now in the maturity stage of its life cycle. Even small cable operations have been quite profitable, and it is apparent that

hectic lives. The comparison sample is more inclined to feel that life is more even and predictable, although both samples feel they work hard most of the time.

In comparison to light renters and nonrenters, frequent renters purchase timesaving convenience foods, such as frozen pizza, packaged Mexican foods, or Hamburger Helper. They also serve them to their families without guilt. Frequent renters will turn to home-delivered meals or fast-food restaurants for relief more readily than will the comparison group. They also consume many of their meals in front of the television, but these eating habits do not worry the frequent renters too much. Perhaps because they are younger, they tend to be less concerned about health and food additives.

Dependable renters also want to appear attractive to the opposite sex so they do diet and exercise, and they consider themselves in as good physical condition as anyone else. They tend to shop for clothing more often than the others, and women's cosmetics are a popular item. Again, these habits may be a function of age.

Frequent renters tend to be more liberal on social and political issues than the general population, and they also have a more modern attitude toward sex roles. For example, they believe that husband and wife should share the responsibilities of marriage, and they are supportive of women's liberation. They do not assert that men are better at investing money than women.

Frequent renters enjoy risk. They like sports cars and motorcycles and the sensation of speed. Sometimes this preference for danger results in financial difficulties, but they are young and optimistic about their financial futures. They see themselves as leaders and as people whose opinions count for something.

Exercise:

Now that you know more about VCR enthusiasts, how would you increase VCR rentals by this group? For example, knowing that they are young with small children at home, what could you do to win over or retain the children as rental film fans? What do you think their parents would like in this regard? (*Hint:* It has been suggested that a free children's movie be included with every movie rental for adults). Where would you advertise? What could you do to make the rental process easier for the busy parent?

Source: Adapted from DDB Needham Worldwide, *Frequent Videotape Renters, Lifestyle Profile* (September 1988).

cable television is here to stay. Consequently, most of the small cable systems have been acquired by larger ones, and the major networks are now involved as well. The cable channel ESPN, for example, in which ABC has an 80 percent interest, is the most profitable programming venture in basic cable. In 1990 the channel earned $195 million in advertising revenues, a 16 percent increase over 1989. By the mid-1990s, cable programming could be dominated by a few key players: Tele-Communications, Inc., and its related companies, Time and Warner Communications, Viacom International (which owns MTV Networks and one-third of Lifetime), Turner Broadcasting, ABC, and NBC. In particular, NBC wholeheartedly invested in the cable business with its launch of two new channels in 1989, the Consumer News and Business Channel (CNBC) and Sports Channel America. In 1990 the network also moved into the direct-broadcast satellite business (DBS), which is capable of delivering up to 108 channels directly to homes that are not wired for cable service.

Cable seems to be partly responsible for a downward trend in the share ratings of the three major networks. In November 1990 the total network share for the Big Three was 63, down from 67 in 1989, 69 in 1988, and 71 in 1987. Various other factors have contributed to the Big Three's decline

AD 10.1

This ad for a cable channel demonstrates how targeted television has become in recent years. (Courtesy of The Travel Channel.)

They don't just fly. . .
they fly first class.

They don't spend two weeks
on vacation. . .
they spend four.

They didn't just go to college. . .
they have post graduate degrees.

and

They don't drive compacts. . .
they drive luxury cars.

**They are TRAVEL CHANNEL viewers
and they are serious about what
they do. . .
they live the good life.**

THE
TRAVEL
CHANNEL®

AMERICA'S ONLY CABLE TELEVISION NETWORK
DEVOTED TO THE ENTIRE WORLD OF TRAVEL.
For more information on advertising opportunities,
call Adrian T. Bogart III, (212) 603-4516.

in viewership, including the spread of the direct-broadcast satellite business and the growth of the Fox Television Broadcasting Network. It is changes in the cable industry, however, that have been largely responsible for the decrease in network shares. Although some people maintain that the higher caliber of network programming will allow the networks to stay well ahead of cable, the networks need to be wary of federal changes in cable regulation and the increasing growth of the cable industry. According to Doug McCormick, executive vice president of the Lifetime Network, "Cable has almost stolen the genre of made-for-television movies from network TV." He cites Lifetime's movie *Sudie and Simpson,* which led Los Angeles's KCBS-TV in local ratings in September 1990, as a case in point.*

Local Television

Local television stations are affiliated with a network and both carry network programming and program their own shows. Costs for local advertising differ, depending on the size of the market and the demand for the programs carried. For example, KHIO in Houston charges local advertisers $1,950 for a 30-second spot during prime time. This same time slot may cost $150 in a small town.

The local television market is substantially more varied than the national market. Most advertisers are local retailers, primarily department stores or discount stores, financial institutions, automobile dealers, restaurants, and supermarkets. Advertisers must buy time on a station-by-station basis. Although this arrangement makes sense for a local retailer, it is not an efficient strategy for a national or regional advertiser, who would have to deal individually with a large number of stations.

PRINCIPLE _____
*Network advertising schedules are
dominated by large national
advertisers.*

_____

*Cathy Taylor, "Waiting for Ratings to Hit Bottom," *Adweek* (December 10, 1990):16.

Specialty Television

Several alternative delivery systems have appeared recently. These systems attempt to reach certain audiences with television messages in a way that is more effective or efficient than network, cable, or local television. For example, low-power television (LPTV) is a privately owned broadcasting system with much smaller market coverage than conventional television, but it can reach local markets very inexpensively. The system can be picked up by homes through personal antennas and carries advertising for local retailers and businesses. Multipoint distribution systems (MDS) and subscription television (STV) both deliver limited programming without incurring the cost of cable installation. The former is used by hotels and restaurants to give guests access to special movies and other entertainment. The latter offers one-channel capabilities of pay-cable-type programming transmitted to individual homes through a signal decoder. Advertisers who use STV typically sell products related to the audience watching the STV program. All these specialty systems can carry advertisements.

A specialty type of advertising that remained in the experimental stage as of 1990 is an interactive television called ACTV, which is explained in more detail in the Issues and Applications box entitled "Interaction TV: Totally Customized."

Television Syndication

syndication *Television or radio shows that are reruns or original programs purchased by local stations to fill in during open hours.*

The **syndication** boom has been fueled mainly by the growth of independent stations that require programming. Syndicated shows are television or radio programs that are purchased by local stations to fill in open hours. Today both networks and independents have been forced to bid on these shows, referred to as "strips," to fill the many open hours in the morning, late afternoon, early evening, and late night. This open time is the result of the prime-time access rule (PTAR), which forbids network affiliates in the 50 major U.S. television markets from broadcasting more than 3 hours of prime-time programming in any one 4-hour slot.

Every winter hundreds of station directors attend the National Association of Television Program Executives (NATPE) meeting in order to bid on the many shows available for syndication. The top syndicated shows in 1989, along with their ratings and numbers of markets, are shown in Table 10.3. Revenue generated by syndication (licensing and advertising revenues) was $3.8 billion in 1990 and is projected to be $8.2 billion in the year 2000.*

Off-Network Syndication. There are two primary types of syndicated programming. The first is *off-network syndication,* which includes reruns of network shows. Examples are *M*A*S*H, The Bob Newhart Show, Star Trek,* and *Remington Steele.* The FCC imposes several restrictions on such shows. Most important, a network show must produce 65 episodes before it can be syndicated. The prime-time access rule prohibits large network affiliates from airing these shows from 7:30 P.M. to 8:00 P.M. Eastern time. These shows are often used as lead-ins to the local or network news.

The most expensive off-network show to date has been *The Cosby Show,* the most popular program in television history. Syndicator Viacom

*Ken Wylie, "Syndication Season Searching for Sizzle," *Advertising Age* (January 15, 1990):10.

TABLE 10.3
Leading Syndicated Television Shows of 1989

1989 Rank*	Syndicated Show	Rating† (% of households)		National Households (in thousands)	
		1989	1988	1989	1988
	Game Shows				
1	Wheel of Fortune	13.8	14.5	12,670	13,630
2	Jeopardy	12.2	12.1	11,250	11,370
9	Wheel of Fortune (Wknd)	7.9	8.6	7,270	9,080
14	Family Feud	5.2	5.4	4,800	5,000
16	Star Search	5.0	5.5	4,520	5,170
	Talk Shows				
5	Oprah Winfrey Show	9.6	9.8	8,820	9,210
12	Donahue Show	6.3	6.2	5,820	5,630
13	Geraldo	5.7	6.0	5,230	5,640
26	Sally Jesse Raphael	4.3	3.5	3,920	3,290
37	Arsenio Hall Show	3.2	NA	2,990	NA
	Sitcoms				
6	Cosby Show	9.5	11.2	8,790	10,530
14	Mama's Family	5.2	5.5	4,780	5,170
22	Charles in Charge	4.6	5.0	4,190	4,700
35	Out of this World	3.5	4.2	3,180	3,950
61	Munsters Today	2.2	3.5	2,010	3,290
	Information				
7	A Current Affair	8.4	5.8	7,710	5,450
8	Entertainment Tonight	8.1	6.5	7,450	6,110
11	National Geo on Assignment	6.5	8.2	5,990	7,710
23	Inside Edition	4.5	NA	4,170	NA
24	Hard Copy	4.4	NA	4,060	NA
	Children's				
19	Chip 'n Dale	4.7	NA	4,370	NA
26	DuckTales	4.3	4.6	3,960	4,320
40	Teenage Mutant Ninja Turtles	3.0	2.9	2,780	2,730
45	Super Mario Bros. Super Show	2.9	NA	2,670	NA
47	Muppet Babies	2.8	NA	2,560	NA
	Drama				
4	Star Trek	10.0	7.6	9,190	7,140
18	People's Court	4.3	5.9	4,370	5,360
19	Superboy	4.7	5.4	4,280	5,050
30	War of the Worlds	3.8	NA	3,520	NA
32	New Adventures of Lassie	3.7	NA	3,400	NA

*Rank among all first-run syndicated shows.

†Season national average for September 18–November 12, 1989, vs. September 4–November 13, 1988.

Note: An NA indicates the show did not exist in 1988.

Source: Advertising Age (January 15, 1990):S-10. Copyright Crain Communications, Inc.

Enterprises did not have much difficulty selling the show to 174 stations for an estimated $500 million to $600 million for rerun rights covering 4 years. In return, each station received 11 30-second spots to sell in each episode.

First-Run Syndication. Sometimes network shows that did not meet the minimal number of episodes, such as *Too Close for Comfort, It's a Living,* and *What's Happening!!,* are purchased from the networks and moved into syndication even as they continue to produce new episodes. This is referred to as "first-run" syndication. Such shows are now produced strictly for syndication, an arrangement that allows them to avoid the FCC's prime-time access rule. Syndicators also produce their own original shows. In

INTERACTION TV: TOTALLY CUSTOMIZED

McCann-Erickson Advertising is the first ad agency to sign on as a sponsor of the Massachusetts Institute of Technology's Media Lab, which is among the leading think tanks dedicated to developing new media technologies. Together with AT&T, Coca-Cola, and General Motors, McCann will participate in the test of an interactive television system called ACTV.

Three hundred cable households in the system have been equipped with special cable boxes that allow them to personalize television programming around each viewer's tastes. For example, viewers watching a sporting event like the Olympics have the option of selecting among four concurrent events. Moreover, they can select the specific camera angles that suit them. More than 300 hours of interactive programming have been produced already, including game shows in which television viewers are the contestants and an interactive music video show in which viewers pick the videos they want to see.

ACTV system allows advertisers to target their messages to specific viewers. Because ACTV uses an "intelligent" switching technology, the system is able to remember the demographic characteristics of each viewer and, in turn, deliver the appropriate commercial. "It has memory, so that it can keep track of what the viewer is watching," explains ACTV vice president Diana Gagnon. "For example, if I'm watching an exercise show, I let the system know that I'm a female and that I want to work my upper body and that I'm advanced in aerobics. The system will give me a personalized workout and it will remember that, so that when it comes time for me to get a commercial, I will get a commercial targeted to me." The system goes one step further by allowing viewers to "create" their own commercials by "choosing the information they want about a product, or what products they want commercials about."

As for the implications for advertising, according to McCann-Erickson's media director Gordon Link, "It doesn' take a brain surgeon to realize that interactive television systems are going to change advertising. The world we are going into will establish new relationships between the marketer, the consumer, and the media. And, hopefully, we will gain enough experience and know-how that it will take other agencies 5 years to catch up to us."

Source: Adapted from John Mandese, "McCann's Bet," *Marketing & Media Decisions* (February 1990):27–29.

1988, 25 first-run strips were introduced into the market. Over 90 percent of these shows failed.

Both network syndication and first-run syndication programs are purchased by barter, cash, or some combination of the two. With **barter syndication,** a show is offered to a station at a reduced price or free of charge, with presold national spots. For example, Procter & Gamble bought all the barter time for the first year's run of Orbis Communication's *The Joker's Wild* before the show was sold to any television stations. This amounted to 520 30-second commercial units valued at around $13 million, which translates into 1 minute of time per show, five shows per week for 52 weeks.

There are several problems with bartering. One is that advertisers expect the syndicated show to be sold to enough stations to cover at least 70 percent of the market, with a preferred rate of 80 to 85 percent. New shows often don't reach this level. Also, guaranteed ratings are not always met. Furthermore, because of the tremendous competition, a 2–3 share is not uncommon, meaning the syndicated program is only delivering 2 to 3 percent of the audience watching television during that time period. Finally, contracts with some stations stipulate that the national commercials—the barter spots—must run in the more desirable time slots, even if the show itself no longer is carried in that time period.

About half of the commercial time is presold to national spots, and

> **barter syndication** *Programs that are offered to a station at a reduced price or for fee, with presold national spots.*

half is available to be sold by the local station. This approach is popular because new independent stations have available commercial time but little cash. Sometimes, as was the case when *The Cosby Show* went into syndication, the independents wanted the show so desperately that they were willing to pay *cash*. Finally, a show like *The New Gidget Show* is sold under a *barter/cash* arrangement, in which the independents pay a reduced price and the show contains the bartered ads.*

*T*ELEVISION ADVERTISING

Like television programming, television ads can be aired through a number of different arrangements. Television advertisers can run their commercials through over-the-air network scheduling, local scheduling, cable scheduling, or unwired networks.

Forms of Television Advertising

The actual form of a television commercial varies depending on whether a network, local, or cable schedule is employed (see Figure 10.1). Networks allow either *sponsorships* or *participations,* and local affiliates allow *spot announcements* and *local sponsorships.*

sponsorship *An arrangement in which the advertiser produces both a television program and the accompanying commercials.*

Sponsorships. In **sponsorships,** which characterized most early television advertising, the advertiser assumes the total financial responsibility for producing the program and providing the accompanying commercials. Examples of early sponsored programs are *Bonanza* (sponsored by Chevrolet), *The Hallmark Hall of Fame,* and *The Kraft Music Hour.* Sponsorship has a powerful impact on the viewing public, especially because the advertiser can control the content and quality of the program as well as the placement and length of commercials. However, the costs of producing and sponsoring a 30- and 60-minute program make this option too expensive for most advertisers today. An alternative is for several advertisers to produce a program jointly. This plan is quite common with sporting events, where each sponsor receives a 15-minute segment.

participations *An arrangement in which a television advertiser buys commercial time from a network.*

Participations. Sponsorships represent less than 10 percent of network advertising. The rest is sold as **participations** in which advertisers pay for 15, 30, or 60 seconds of commercial time during one or more programs. The advertiser can buy any time that is available on a regular or irregular basis. This approach not only reduces the risks and costs associated with sponsorships but also provides a great deal more flexibility in respect to market coverage, target audiences, scheduling, and budgeting. Participations do not create the same high impact as sponsorships, however, and the advertiser does not have any control over the content of the program. Finally, the "time avails" (available time slots) for the most popular programs are often bought up by the largest advertisers, leaving fewer good time slots for the small advertiser. For example, in October 1990 Coca-Cola Company and General Mills, Inc., each agreed to pay NBC more than $40 million for commercial time on the 1992 Summer Olympics. Coca-Cola's deal was said to be worth between $42 million and $44 million, and GM's deal was closer to $40 million. As of late 1990, NBC projected a prime-time average Nielsen

*Alison Rogers, "What's New in Retro TV?" *Adweek* (January 20, 1987):26–27.

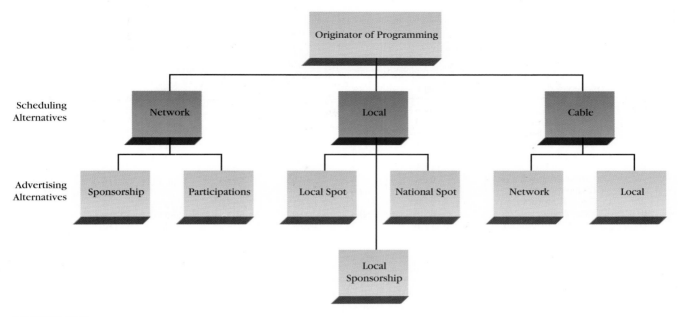

FIGURE 10.1
The figure illustrates the choices facing a television advertiser.

rating of 16.9 for advertisers, and the average household cost per thousand worked out to be approximately $17. (Nielsen ratings are discussed in more detail in the next section.) Furthermore, NBC offered its advertisers a 90 percent guarantee on its ratings projections.*

spot announcements *Ads shown during the breaks between programs.*

PRINCIPLE
Spot buys are dominated by local advertising.

Spot Announcements. The third form a television commercial can take is the **spot announcement.** (Note that the word *spot* is also used in conjunction with a time frame such as a "30-second spot," and this usage should not be confused with spot announcements.) Spot announcements refer to the breaks between programs, which local affiliates sell to advertisers who want to show their ads locally. Commercials of 10, 20, 30, and 60 seconds are sold on a station-by-station basis to local, regional, and national advertisers. The local buyers clearly dominate spot television. The leading advertisers of spot announcements are listed in Table 10.4.

The breaks between programs are not always optimal time slots for advertisers because there is a great deal of clutter from competing commercials, station breaks, public service announcements, and other distractions. Program breaks also tend to be time when viewers take a break from their television sets.

*T*HE TELEVISION AUDIENCE

With an estimated $26.7 billion in advertising revenues in 1989, television is big business.† Television has become a mainstay of American society. Nearly 33 million new television sets were sold in 1988, an all-time record. Thirteen million VCRs were sold in the same year, 300,000 less than the

---

*John McManus and Wayne Walley, "Coke, GM Plan $40M Deals for NBC's Olympics," *Advertising Age* (October 29, 1990):3, 62.
†Television Bureau of Advertising, Inc. (New York, 1990).

TABLE 10.4
Top 15 Spot Television Advertisers

Rank	Advertiser	Spot TV spending			Total U.S. Ad Spending		Spot TV as % of Total	
		1989	1988	% chg	1989	1988	1989	1988
1	PepsiCo Inc.	$264.6	$258.0	2.6	$786.1	$710.9	33.7	36.3
2	Procter & Gamble Co.	222.0	222.3	(0.1)	1,779.3	1,655.8	12.5	13.4
3	Philip Morris Cos.	180.5	158.4	14.0	2,072.0	2,028.4	8.7	7.8
4	General Mills	150.3	145.9	3.0	471.0	447.8	31.9	32.6
5	McDonald's Corp.	141.3	128.1	10.3	774.4	728.1	18.2	17.6
6	Nissan Motor Co.	113.5	64.1	76.9	300.6	224.9	37.8	28.5
7	Anheuser-Busch Cos.	94.8	97.6	(2.9)	591.5	645.9	16.0	15.1
8	Toyota Motor Corp.	91.0	68.6	32.7	417.6	732.0	21.8	25.1
9	General Motors Corp.	90.9	115.3	(21.1)	1,363,8	1,290.6	6.7	8.9
10	Time Warner	86.7	80.3	7.9	567.5	505.6	15.3	15.9
11	Grand Metropolitan PLC	75.7	127.0	(40.4)	823.3	754.6	9.2	16.8
12	Hasbro Inc.	71.9	90.6	(20.7)	151.9	176.7	47.3	51.3
13	Coca-Cola Co.	68.1	56.1	21.3	385.3	376.7	17.7	14.9
14	Hyundai Group	67.6	73.3	(7.7)	212.8	204.8	31.8	35.8
15	Walt Disney Co.	66.8	63.0	6.2	338.7	304.5	19.7	20.7

Note: Dollars are in millions.

Source: Kevin Brown, *Advertising Age* (September 26, 1990):38. Copyright Crain Communications, Inc.

record-setting level of 1987. In 1989, 70 percent of U.S. homes had remote control tuning capability.* In 1990 over 82 percent of U.S. households had a television set in the living room, over 65 percent had one in the bedroom, and over 20 percent kept a television in the family room.† People gather around the set day after day, night after night, to find a source of entertainment, an escape from reality. This dependency explains why a great number of advertisers consider television their primary medium. What do we really know about how audiences watch television? Are we a generation of zombielike television addicts? Or do we carefully and intelligently select what we watch on television?

A great deal of information describing the characteristics of television viewers has been gathered. For example, average household viewing time was approximately 50 hours per week in 1989. This number represents an increase of about 10 hours per week since the mid-1960s. In 1990 women were the heaviest daytime viewers, averaging over 19.5 hours per week. Women were also the heaviest prime-time viewers, averaging nearly 50 hours per week. Teenagers (ages 12 through 17) spent over an hour more time viewing television than did younger children (ages 6 through 11).‡

How People Watch Television

Further insights into the question of how people watch television were provided by a 5-month study done by Peter Collett, research psychologist at the University of Oxford in England. Collett used a video camera to examine the viewing behavior of 20 families. After studying 400 hours of videotape, Collett concluded that viewers often do anything but view. They read, talk, knit, vacuum, blow-dry their hair, and sometimes fight over the remote control. The study found two major responses to commercials: A large segment (approximately 45 percent) watched less than 10 percent of a given

*Alice K. Sylvester, "Controlling Remote," *Marketing & Media Decisions* (February 1990):54.
†*Adweek* (November 12, 1990):19.
‡*Media Trends,* DDB Needham Worldwide (February 1991):18.

commercial, and another segment (approximately 15 percent) watched more than 90 percent of a spot. Why this disparity? Collett believes it has to do with the following:

- The nature of the commercial, the way in which it is structured, or the nature of the product advertised.
- The makeup of the audience. Some viewers tend not to watch commercials at all; others are "commercial consumers."
- The positioning of commercials: What time of day they run, where spots fall in the commercial break.
- Viewer attention, perhaps related to the presence of others in the room. For example, the more people present, the fewer the commercials that are watched.
- The programming environment. If a break follows a popular, engaging program, viewers spend more time watching the commercial messages.

This study suggests that most people are not true television addicts. Actually, most people seldom give their full attention to the set. These facts must be kept in mind when considering television as an advertising medium.*

Measuring the Television Audience

Many of us have had our favorite television show taken off the air because of "poor ratings." Although we may have had some idea of how these ratings were derived, the "Nielsen family" and the rating process remain a mystery to most people.

Actually, the derivation of television ratings is a relatively simple process. Several independent rating firms periodically sample a portion of the television viewing audience, assess the size and characteristics of the audiences watching specific shows, and then make this data available to subscribing companies and agencies, which use it in their media planning. Two rating companies dominate this industry: Arbitron and A. C. Nielsen. Nielsen is the better known of the two, and the Nielsen Ratings provide the most frequently used measure of national television audiences. Table 10.5 offers an example of the statistics Nielsen provides.

Nielsen Indexes. Nielsen measures television audiences at two levels: network (Nielsen Television Index, NTI) and spot (Nielsen Station Index, NSI). In both cases, two measurement devices are used. The most famous is the Nielsen Storage Instantaneous Audimeter, or Audimeter for short. The Audimeter can record when the set is used and which station it is tuned to, but it cannot identify who is watching the program. Data on who is watching are provided by diaries mailed once every 3 weeks to approximately 2,600 households, of which about 850 are returned every week. However, evidence of sloppy record keeping has diminished the credibility of the diary technique.

People Meters In response, A. C. Nielsen, along with several other rating companies, has begun to measure not only what is being watched but who is watching. In the fall of 1987 Nielsen replaced its Audimeter and diary system with *people meters* that provide information on what television shows are being watched, the number of households that are watching, and which family members are viewing. The type of activity is recorded automatically; household members merely have to indicate their presence by

---

*Mary Connors, "Catching TV Viewers in the Act of Being Themselves," *Adweek* (March 9, 1987):30.

TABLE 10.5
Ratings and Share for Nielsen's Top Programs

Nielson Television Index
Top 20 Programs
Ranked by Average Audience Estimates (%)

Rank	Program Name	Telecast Date	Net.	Duration (minutes)	Avg. Aud. Rating (%)	Share	Avg. Aud. (000)
1	M*A*S*H Special	Feb. 28, 1983	CBS	150	60.2	77	50,150
2	Dallas	Nov. 21, 1980	CBS	60	53.3	76	41,470
3	Roots Pt. VIII	Jan. 30, 1977	ABC	115	51.1	71	36,380
4	Super Bowl XVI Game	Jan. 24, 1982	CBS	213	49.1	73	40,020
5	Super Bowl XVII Game	Jan. 30, 1983	NBC	204	48.6	69	40,480
6	Super Bowl XX Game	Jan. 26, 1986	NBC	231	48.3	70	41,490
7	Gone With the Wind-Pt. 1 (Big Event-Pt. 1)	Nov. 7, 1976	NBC	179	47.7	65	33,960
8	Gone With The Wind-Pt. 2 (NBC Mon. Mov.)	Nov. 8, 1976	NBC	119	47.4	64	33,750
9	Super Bowl XII Game	Jan. 15, 1978	CBS	218	47.2	67	34,410
10	Super Bowl XIII Game	Jan. 21, 1979	NBC	230	47.1	74	35,090
11	Bob Hope Christmas Show	Jan. 15, 1970	NBC	90	46.6	64	27,260
12	Super Bowl XVIII Game	Jan. 22, 1984	CBS	218	46.4	71	38,800
12	Super Bowl XIX Game	Jan. 20, 1985	ABC	218	46.4	63	39,390
14	Super Bowl XIV Game	Jan. 20, 1980	CBS	178	46.3	67	35,330
15	ABC Theater (The Day After)	Nov. 20, 1983	ABC	144	46.0	62	38,550
16	Roots Pt. VI	Jan. 28, 1977	ABC	120	45.9	66	32,680
16	The Fugitive	Aug. 29, 1967	ABC	60	45.6	72	25,700
18	Super Bowl XXI	Jan. 25, 1987	CBS	206	45.8	66	40,030
19	Roots Pt. V	Jan. 27, 1977	ABC	60	45.7	71	32,540
20	Ed Sullivan	Feb. 9, 1964	CBS	60	45.3	60	23,240

Note:
—Average Audience % Rankings based on Reports— July 1960 through January 25, 1987.
—Above data represent sponsored programs, telecast on individual networks; i.e., no unsponsored or joint network telecasts are reflected in the above listings.
—Programs under 30 minutes' scheduled duration are excluded.

Source: "The Coming Revolution in Television Measurement Research," *Nielsen Newscast,* No. 1 (1987): 17. Courtesy of Nielsen Newscast.

pressing a button. People meters have become the primary method for measuring national television audiences. For an illustration of the services the people meter provides see Figure 10.2.

People meters are quite controversial, however. Criticism of the people meter came to a head in the fall of 1990, when ABC, CBS, and NBC all refused to renew their contracts with Nielsen Media Research. The reason was a big unexplained drop in reported television usage during the first quarter of 1990 and the ensuing ratings shortfall that forced the networks to give away an estimated $150 million worth of advertising time to advertisers. The networks blamed Nielsen, alleging faulty methodology in compiling ratings. Nielsen replied that an internal investigation found nothing was amiss with its system.

One positive outcome of the debate was the establishment of the Committee on Nationwide Television Audience Measurement, a group made up of representatives from the Big Three networks and the National Association of Broadcasters. The committee issued a set of guidelines for the research industry and distributed it to advertisers, agency executives, and research companies. In particular, the document included guidelines for improving the cooperation rate of households chosen to become part of Nielsen samples, obtaining better representation by monitoring all television sets, and developing a way to deal with panelists who tire of pushing people-meter buttons.*

*Wayne Walley, "Nets Force Nielsen Showdown," *Advertising Age* (September 24, 1990):3, 60.

FIGURE 10.2

A description of the sample characteristics measured by the people meter. *Source:* "Nielsen Putting It All Together," *Nielsen Newscast,* no. 4 (1985):6. Courtesy of Nielsen Newscast.

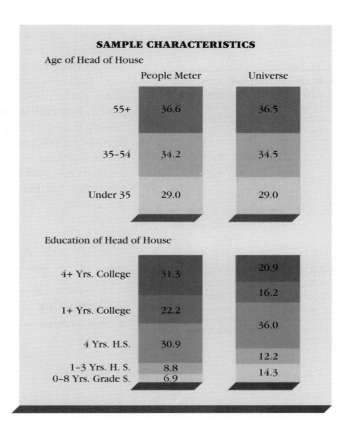

SAMPLE CHARACTERISTICS

Age of Head of House

	People Meter	Universe
55+	36.6	36.5
35–54	34.2	34.5
Under 35	29.0	29.0

Education of Head of House

4+ Yrs. College	31.3	20.9
		16.2
1+ Yrs. College	22.2	36.0
4 Yrs. H.S.	30.9	
		12.2
1–3 Yrs. H. S.	8.8	14.3
0–8 Yrs. Grade S.	6.9	

The A. C. Nielsen people meter.
Source: "Nielsen Putting It All Together," *Nielsen Newscast,* no. 4 (1985):6. Courtesy of Nielsen Newscast.

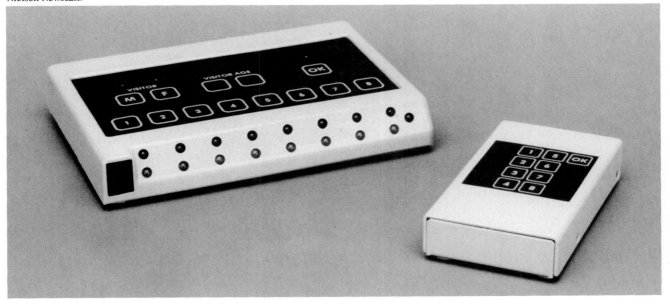

Arbitron. Arbitron's audience measurement service covers every television market four times each year. These ratings periods, when all 214 markets are surveyed, are known as "sweeps." In 201 markets Arbitron uses diaries exclusively to measure viewing. In 13 markets the service uses both household meters and diaries to measure set usage and audience identity. These markets are: New York, Chicago, Cleveland, Detroit, Miami, Washington, D.C., Boston, Philadelphia, Atlanta, Dallas/Ft. Worth, Los Angeles, San

Francisco, and Houston. In addition, Arbitron has a people-meter service in Denver called ScanAmerica that also collects household product purchase data from households in the panel. Figure 10.3 is a sample Arbitron page.

Both Nielsen and Arbitron publish their findings between four and seven times per year in a descriptive format called the *television market report.* A **television market** is an unduplicated geographical area to which a county is assigned on the basis of market size. One county is always placed in just one television market to avoid overlap. Arbitron refers to these television markets in which local stations receive the majority of the viewing hours as Areas of Dominant Influence (ADIs). Nielsen refers to comparable television markets as Designated Market Areas (DMAs).

FIGURE 10.3

A sample page from Arbitron, explaining how television markets are measured. *Source:* "How to Read Your Arbitron Television Market Report," *Arbitron Ratings* (1987):4. Copyright 1988 Arbitron Ratings Company.

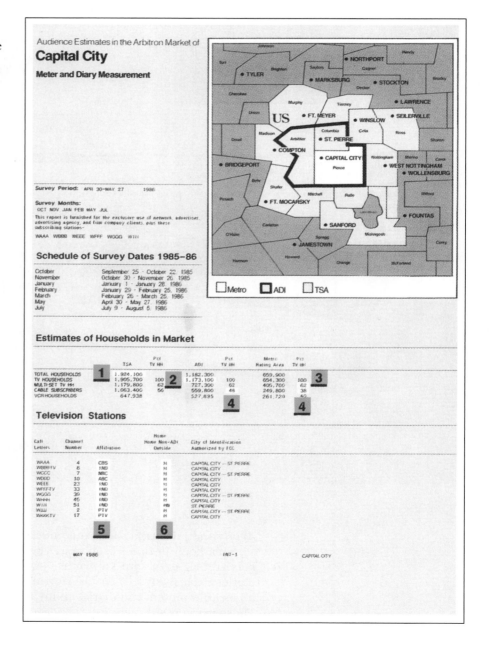

ADVANTAGES AND DISADVANTAGES OF TELEVISION

Advantages

Advertisers would not invest large sums of money in television commercials unless these ads were effective. The major strengths of television that make it appealing as an advertising medium are cost efficiency, impact, and influence.

PRINCIPLE _____
Television advertising reaches mass audiences and is very cost-efficient.

Cost Efficiency. Many advertisers view television as the most effective way to deliver a commercial message. The major advantage of television is its wide reach. Millions of people watch some television regularly. Television not only reaches a large percentage of the population, it also reaches people who are not effectively reached by print media. For example, NBC's *Today* show would average approximately $18,500 for a 30-second spot, and the household CMP would be $4.50. The cost of advertising on three evening news programs are shown in Figure 10.4. This mass coverage, in turn, is extremely cost-efficient. For an advertiser attempting to reach an undifferentiated market, a 30-second spot on a top-rated show may cost a penny or less for each person reached.

Impact. Another advantage of television is the strong impact created by the interaction of sight and sound. This feature induces a level of consumer involvement that often approximates the shopping experience, including interacting with a persuasive salesperson. Television also allows a great deal of creative flexibility because of the many possible combinations of sight, sound, color, motion, and drama. Television has tremendous dramatic capacity; it can make mundane products appear important, exciting, and interesting. In other words, television can create a positive association with the sponsor if the advertisement is "likable." But what is a likable television ad? This concept is discussed further in the Concept and Controversies box entitled "Attributes of Likable Television Commercials."

Influence. The final advantage of television is that it has become a primary facet of our culture. For most Americans television is a critical source of news, entertainment, and education. It is so much a part of us that we are more likely to believe companies that advertise on television, especially

FIGURE 10.4
Cost per 30-second split on the three major networks. *Source: Advertising Age* (May 28, 1990):39. Copyright Crain Communications, Inc.

No. 1 network news show
"ABC World News Tonight"
Rating—11.0
Cost per 30-second spot—$58,100
CPM, total households—$5.64

No. 2 network news show
"CBS Evening News"
Rating—10.1
Cost per 30-second spot—$46,700
CPM, total households—$5.10

No. 3 network news show
"NBC Nightly News"
Rating—9.9
Cost per 30-second spot—$50,700
CPM, total households—$5.46

sponsors of drama and educational programs like IBM, Xerox, and Hallmark Cards, than we are to believe those that don't. Sometimes this influence comes from a tie-in with a popular celebrity, such as Tommy Lasorda for Ultra Slim-Fast (see Ad 10.2).

Disadvantages

Despite the effectiveness of television advertising, problems do exist, including expense, clutter, nonselective targeting, and inflexibility.

Expense. The most serious limitation of television advertising is the extremely high *absolute* cost of producing and running commercials. Although the cost per person reached is low, the absolute cost can be restrictive. Table 10.6 shows the costs of airing a 30-second commercial on a prime-time network program in the 1989–1990 television season. Production costs include filming the commercial (several hundred to several hundred thousand dollars) and the costs of talent. For celebrities such as Bill Cosby, Bo Jackson, Michael Jackson, Candice Bergen, and Michael Jordan, the price tag can be millions of dollars (see Ad. 10.3). The prices charged for network time are simply a result of supply and demand. Programs that draw the largest audiences can charge more for their advertising space. A 30-second prime-time spot averages about $185,000, with *The Cosby Show* leading the market at $430,000, up from $300,000 in 1989.* Special shows, such as the Super Bowl, World Series, or Academy Awards, charge much more. Some experts estimate that only 50 U.S. companies can afford a comprehensive television media schedule at these costs. It has been said that television advertising is very cheap if you can afford it.

Clutter. Television suffers from a very high level of commercial clutter. The number of network television commercials increased by 35 percent from 1981 to 1989.† In the past the National Association of Broadcasters

*Joe Mandese, "The Biggest Game in Town," *Marketing & Media Decisions* (May 1990):35.
†*Media Trends,* DDB Needham Worldwide (February 1991):29.

TABLE 10.7
Prime-Time Network Television Costs for a 30-Second Commerical for Monday through Friday

	MONDAY				TUESDAY			WEDNESDAY			THURSDAY			FRIDAY		
	ABC	CBS	NBC	FOX	ABC	CBS	NBC	ABC	CBS	NBC	ABC	CBS	NBC	ABC	CBS	NBC
8:00	MacGyver 95K	Major Dad* 115K	Alf 200K	21 Jump Street** 85K	Who's the Boss? 260K	Rescue 911* 95K	Matlock 125K	Growing Pains 200K	Peaceable Kingdom* 75K	Unsolved Mysteries 155K	Mission Impossible** 60K	48 Hours 95K	Cosby 300K	Full House** 150K	Snoops* 105K	Baywatch* 90K
8:30	125K	People Next Door* 180K	Hogan Family	250K	Wonder Years		175K	Head of the Class				280K	Different World 125K	*Family Matters		
9:00	Football 235K	Murphy Brown 195K	Movie 160K	Alien Nation* 55K	Rosanne 375K	Wolf* 100K	Heat of the Night 145K	Anything But Love** 150K	Jack and the Fatman 100K	Night Court 195K	The Young Riders 90K	Top of the Hill* 105K	Cheers 330K	** Perfect Strangers 145K	Dallas 100K	Hardball* 120K
9:30		Famous Teddy Z 159K			Chicken Soup* 230K			Doogie Howser, M.D.* 115K		Nutt House* 130K			Dear John 250K	Just the Ten of Us 115K		
10:00		Designing Women** 180K	Movie		thirty-some-thing	Island Son	Midnight Caller	China Beach	Wiseguy	Quantum Leap	Prime Time Live*	Knots Landing	LA Law	20/20	Falcon Crest	Mancuso FBI*
10:30		Newhart** 135	75K		200K	65K	140K	150K	145K	110K	110K	155K	260K	140K	95K	125K

*New program **Time period change.

Source: Verne Gay, "Unit Costs Soar 25–30% for November Prime," *Variety* (August 30–September 5, 1989):73–74.

AD 10.3
A famous celebrity endorsement enhances the advertising of a product, but the expense of hiring the talent can be limiting. (Courtesy of DDB Needham Worldwide, Inc.)

(NAB) restricted the amount of allowable commercial time per hour to approximately 6 minutes. In 1982 the Justice Department found this restriction illegal. Although the networks now continue to honor the NAB guidelines, this could change as their needs for revenue increase. The Justice Department ruling could eventually increase the number of 30-second commercials, station-break announcements, credits, and public service announcements, which in turn would diminish the visibility and persuasiveness of television advertisements. Although in recent years the growth of the 15-second spot (:15) was responsible for much of the clutter in televi-

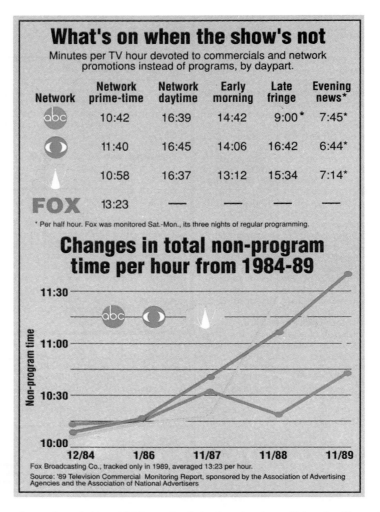

FIGURE 10.5
Network clutter on the rise *Source:*
Reprinted with permission from *Advertising Age* (July 2, 1990):17. Copyright Crain Communications, Inc. 1990.

sion advertising, 1990 marked the beginning of the decline of these shorter commercials since their introduction in 1983. According to the Television Bureau of Advertising, approximately 35 percent of network commercials were 15-second spots through October 1990, down from nearly 38 percent in 1989. Fewer :15s were used in nonnetwork television as well, averaging only 5.7 percent though October 1990, a .3 percent decrease from the same time period in 1989.* Fifteen-second spots represented 31 percent of all television commercials in 1990, down from 35 percent in 1989.† Finally, much of the clutter is also a result of the many network and local stations promoting their own programming. The extent of network clutter is illustrated in Figure 10.5.

Nonselective Audience. Despite the introduction of various technologies that better target consumers, television remains nonselective. Network television still attracts about 75 percent of the U.S. audience. Although the networks attempt to profile viewers, their descriptions are quite general, offering the advertiser little assurance that appropriate people are viewing the message. Thus television advertising includes a great deal of *waste coverage*—that is, communication directed at an unresponsive (and often un-

---

*Wayne Walley. "Popularity of :15s Falls," *Advertising Age* (January 14, 1991):3, 41.
†Joanne Lipman, "Short TV Spots Lose Supporters as Length Frustrates Some Firms," *The Wall Street Journal* (June 20, 1990):B-5.

interested) audience that may not fit the advertiser's target market characteristics.

Inflexibility. Television also suffers from a lack of flexibility in scheduling. Most network television is bought in the spring and early summer for the next fall season. If an advertiser is unable to make this up-front buy, only limited time-slot alternatives will remain available. It is difficult to make last-minute adjustments in terms of scheduling, copy, or visuals.

THE STRUCTURE OF RADIO

signals *A series of electrical impulses that compose radio and television broadcasting.*

frequency *The number of radio waves produced by a transmitter in 1 second.*

Radio can be classified according to transmission and power. The actual range of the station depends on the height of the antenna, the quality of the equipment, and so forth. Radio is a series of electrical impulses called **signals** that are transmitted by *electromagnetic waves.* Radio signals have a height (amplitude) and a width. The width dictates the frequency of the radio signal. A **frequency** is the number of radio waves a transmitter produces each second. The wider the signal, the lower the frequency, and the narrower the wave, the higher the frequency. Frequency is measured in terms of thousands of cycles per second (kilohertz) or millions of cycles per second (megahertz). Thus a radio station assigned a frequency of 930,000 cycles per second would be found at 93 on your radio dial. The Federal Communications Commission (FCC) assigns these frequencies to ensure that station signals do not interfere with one another.

AM Radio

Radio stations are designated either AM or FM. An AM, or *amplitude modulation,* station has the flexibility to vary the height of its electromagnetic signal so that during the daytime it produces waves, called *ground waves,* that follow the contour of the earth. At night the station transmits waves into the sky, called *sky waves,* that bounce back to earth and are picked up by receivers far beyond the range of the station's ground waves.

The actual power or strength of an AM signal depends on the power allowed by the FCC. Stations with a broadcast range of approximately 25 miles are considered *local stations.* Most local stations are allowed 100 to 250 watts of power. In contrast, *regional stations* may cover an entire state or several states. The most powerful stations are called *clear channel stations* and may use up to 50,000 watts. The relative power of each type of station will vary, depending on the frequency assigned. Generally, the lower the frequency, the farther the signal will travel.

FM Radio

An FM, or *frequency modulation,* station differs from AM in that the band width (frequency) is adjusted rather than the height (amplitude), which remains constant. Because the signal put out by an FM station follows the line of sight, the distance of the signal depends on the height of the antenna. Typically, 50 miles is the maximum signal distance. However, the tonal quality of an FM signal is superior to that of AM.

AM radio revenue is growing at approximately 1 percent annually, but the growth on FM stations exceeds 7 percent. In 1989 FM stations accounted for 76 percent of all radio listeners and 60 percent of all radio advertising revenue.* The loss of AM listenership, due to the perception that FM offers better sound quality, is likely to put more AM stations out of business.

As radio's importance as a local medium increases, more of its programming will be satellite-delivered from radio networks. Aaron Daniels, president of ABC Radio Networks, predicts that 30 percent of the country's 10,000 stations will use satellite-delivered programming by the middle of the 1990s. In addition, more stations will use satellite networks to reduce their programming costs.†

*R*ADIO ADVERTISING

network radio *A group of local affiliates providing simultaneous programming via connection to one or more of the national networks through AT&T telephone wires.*

Radio advertising is available on national networks and on local markets. **Network radio** refers to a group of local affiliates connected to one or more of the national networks through telephone wires and satellites. The network provides simultaneous network programming, which is quite limited compared with network television programming. Therefore many local or regional stations belong to more than one network, with each network providing specialized programming to complete a station's schedule. Ad 10.4 is an example of a radio network. Each station then sends out the network's signal through its own antenna. There are also regional networks (for example, Intermountain Network and the Groskin Group) that tend to serve a particular state or audience segment, such as farmers. The top 15 network radio advertisers are listed in Table 10.7.

*Stephen Battaglio, "Radio," *Adweek* (September 11, 1989):184.
†*Ibid.,* 185.

AD 10.4
Radio networks often provide specialized programming, such as BRN all-business radio. (Courtesy of Business Radio Network.)

AD 10.5
This ad for Unistar lists its advantages to potential advertisers.
(Courtesy of Unistar.)

TABLE 10.7.
Top Network Radio Advertisers

	Top network radio advertisers ($000,000) first quarter 1990, and percentage change from first quarter 1989.		
1	Sears, Roebuck & Co.	$14.75	0.5%
2	Volkswagen AG	9.80	*
3	Campbell Soup Co.	6.18	50.4
4	Procter & Gamble Co.	5.40	−22.3
5	AT&T Co.	5.05	90.9
6	City Investing Corp.	5.00	−4.0
7	General Motors Corp.	4.69	−44.8
8	Bayer AG	4.64	111.3
9	Chrysler Corp.	4.61	23.8
10	Hershey Foods Corp.	4.20	17.9
11	Warner-Lambert Co.	3.82	25.6
12	U.S. Government	3.81	−22.3
13	Marriott Corp.	3.34	*
14	Philip Morris Cos.	3.16	153.0
15	Cotter & Co.	2.50	−21.0

*Company did not buy network radio spots in first quarter 1989.

Source: Wayne Walley, "Radio: Special Report," *Advertising Age* (September 10, 1990):S-2. Copyright Crain Communications, Inc.

Network Radio

Complete market coverage combined with quality programming has increased the popularity of network radio. Over 20 national radio networks program concerts, talk shows, sports events, and dramas. Satellite transmission has produced important technological improvements. Satellites not only provide a better sound but also allow the transmission of multiple programs with different formats. Network radio is viewed as a viable national advertising medium, especially for advertisers of food, automobiles, and over-the-counter drugs.

In the 1980s network radio went through a period of consolidation that produced four major radio networks: Westwood One, CBS, ABC, and Unistar (see Ad 10.5). The Radio Advertising Bureau reported revenues of $424 million for network radio in 1989. Over $1.5 billion was spent on national spot advertising out of a total of $8.4 billion in advertising revenues. The growth of network radio is also attributed to the increase in syndicated radio shows and unwired networks.*

Syndication. As the number of affiliates has boomed, so has the number of news syndicated radio shows, creating more advertising opportunities for companies eager to reach new markets. In fact, syndication and network radio have practically become interchangeable terms. Syndication has been beneficial to network radio because it offers advertisers a variety of high-quality specialized programs. Both networks and private firms offer syndication. Essentially a syndication offers a complete catalogue of programming to the local affiliate. For example, Transtar Radio Network, located in Colorado Springs, claims about 600 affiliates. Its only direct competitor is Satellite Music Network, Dallas, which claims 800 affiliates. Both networks offer 24-hour programming daily, which could provide a station with all its programming needs. With this kind of arrangement a broad-

*Stephen Battaglio, "Radio," *Adweek* (October 30, 1989):M.O. 44.

caster needs nothing but a satellite dish and a sales staff. The station remains, but much of the operating costs disappear.

Unwired Networks. The final reason for the growth of network radio is the emergence of unwired networks. Network radio has always been at a disadvantage because of the difficulty of dealing with the many stations and rate structures available in large markets. This system was discussed earlier in connection with unwired television networks.

Spot Radio

spot radio advertising *A form of advertising in which an ad is placed with an individual station rather than through a network.*

PRINCIPLE
Spot advertising dominates radio scheduling.

In **spot radio advertising** an advertiser places an advertisement with an individual station rather than through a network. Although networks provide prerecorded national advertisements, they also allow local affiliates open time to sell spot advertisements. Table 10.8 lists the leading spot radio advertisers. Spot radio advertising represents nearly 80 percent of all radio advertising. Its popularity is a result of the flexibility it offers the advertiser. With over 8,000 stations available, messages can be tailored for particular audiences. In large cities such as New York, Chicago, or Los Angeles, 40 or more radio stations are available. Local stations also offer flexibility through their willingness to run unusual ads, allow last-minute changes, and negotiate rates. Buying spot radio and coping with its nonstandardized rate structures can be very cumbersome, however.

Radio advertising revenue is divided into three categories: network, spot, and local. Network revenues are by far the smallest category, accounting for approximately 5 percent of total radio revenues. National spot advertising makes up the remaining 5 percent.

*T*HE RADIO AUDIENCE

PRINCIPLE
Radio is a highly segmented medium.

Radio is a highly segmented medium. Program formats offered in a typical market include hard rock, gospel, country and western, "Top 40" hits, and sex advice. Virtually every household in the United States (99 percent) has a radio set (527 million radios in total, with an average 5.6 sets per household), and most of these sets are tuned in to a vast array of programs.[*]

Market researcher Michael Hedges separates radio listeners into four segments: station fans, radio fans, music fans, and news fans. Station fans make up the largest segment of radio listeners, at 46 percent. They have a clear preference for one or two stations and spend up to 8 hours or more each day listening to their favorite. Most station fans are women between the ages of 25 and 44. Radio fans represent 34 percent of the population. They may listen to four to five different stations per week, and they show no preference for one particular station. Most are under 35 years of age, though many women aged 55 and older are radio fans. Only 11 percent of the population are music fans—people who listen exclusively for the music being played. Men between the ages of 25 and 45 are most likely to be music fans, although many elderly adults also fit the profile. Finally, a percentage of radio listeners choose their station based on a need for news and informa-

[*]J. Thomas Russell and Ronald Lane, *Kleppner's Advertising Procedure,* 11th ed. (Englewood Cliffs, N.J. Prentice Hall, 1990):208.

TABLE 10.8
Top 10 Spot Radio Advertisers

Rank	Advertiser	Spot Radio Spending			Total U.S. Ad Spending		Spot Radio as % of Total	
		1989	1988	$ chg	1989	1988	1989	1988
1	Philip Morris Cos.	$42.7	$40.1	6.5	$2,072.0	$2,028.4	2.1	2.0
2	Anheuser-Busch Cos.	42.1	42.7	(1.5)	591.5	645.9	7.1	6.6
3	Chrysler Corp.	40.3	19.4	107.4	532.5	476.4	7.6	4.1
4	General Motors Corp.	39.5	40.2	(1.8)	1,363.8	1,290.6	2.9	3.1
5	Sears, Roebuck & Co.	36.1	25.4	41.8	1,432.1	1,031.4	2.5	2.5
6	PepsiCo Inc.	33.4	28.2	18.4	786.1	710.9	4.2	4.0
7	Southland Corp.	33.2	22.1	50.3	NA	NA	NA	NA
8	Grand Metropolitan PLC	26.6	21.1	26.0	823.3	754.6	3.2	2.8
9	News Corp.	24.8	13.4	85.3	128.9	130.2	19.2	10.3
10	Delta Air Lines	18.3	19.9	(8.3)	116.0	104.9	15.8	19.0

Note: Dollars are in millions. *Source:* Kevin Brown, *Advertising Age* (September 26, 1990):64. Copyright Crain Communications, Inc.

tion. They have one or two favorite stations, listen in short segments, and are almost exclusively aged 35 or older.*

Measuring the Radio Audience

Advertisers considering radio are most concerned with the number of people listening to a particular station at a given time. The radio industry and independent research firms provide several measures considered useful to the advertiser.

The most basic measure is the station's *coverage.* This is simply the geographical area (which includes a given number of homes) that can pick up the station clearly, whether or not they are actually tuned in. A better measure is *circulation,* which measures the number of homes that are actually tuned in to the particular station. This figure is influenced by such factors as the competing programs, the type of program, and the time of day or night.

Arbitron. Several major audience rating services operate in the advertising industry. One, the Arbitron Ratings Company, estimates the size of radio audiences for over 250 markets in the United States. The primary method used by Arbitron is a 7-day self-administered diary that the person returns to Arbitron at the end of the week.

RADAR. A second radio rating service is Radio's All-Dimension Audience Research, or RADAR. This service deals with local and network radio. Using a random dial system, respondents are contacted as many as nine times during a 7-day period in order to assess radio usage. Final reports are based on data collected over 48 weeks.

Birch/Scarborough-VNU. Birch radio audience surveys measure station listenership in the 80 largest U.S. markets and in smaller markets when specifically requested. Birch uses telephone interviews to construct profiles of listener habits based on major demographic categories and selected product-usage categories. The frequency of these reports varies according to the size of the market.

*"Radio Days," *American Demographics* (November 1988):18.

ADVANTAGES AND DISADVANTAGES OF RADIO

Radio is not for every advertiser, and it is important to understand the relative strengths and weaknesses of this medium.

Advantages

Target Audiences.   The most important advantage offered by radio is that it reaches specific types of audiences by offering specialized programming. In addition it can be adapted to different parts of the country and can reach people at different times of the day. Radio, for example, is the ideal means of reaching people driving to and from work.

Speed and Flexibility.   The *speed and flexibility* of radio have been noted already. Of all the media, radio has the shortest *closing period,* in that copy can be submitted up to airtime. This flexibility allows advertisers to adjust to local market conditions, current news events, and even the weather. For example, a local hardware store can quickly implement a snow shovel promotion the morning after a snowstorm.

Costs.   Radio may be the least expensive of all media. Because airtime costs are relatively low, extensive repetition is possible. In addition, the cost of producing a radio commercial can be low, particularly if the message is read by a local station announcer. Radio's low cost and high reach of selected target groups make it an excellent supporting medium. In fact, the most appropriate role for most radio advertising is a supportive one.

Mental Imagery.   An important advantage of radio is the scope it allows for the listener's imagination. Radio uses words, sound effects, music, and tonality to enable listeners to create their own picture of what is happening. For this reason radio is sometimes referred to as the "theater of the mind." The ad for John Moore Plumbing (Ad 10.6) demonstrates how radio effectively creates mental pictures.

High Levels of Acceptance.   The final advantage of radio is its high acceptance at the local level. Partly because of its passive nature, radio normally is not perceived as an irritant. People have their favorite radio stations and radio personalities, which they listen to regularly. Messages delivered by these are more likely to be accepted and retained.

Disadvantages

Inattentiveness.   Radio is not without its drawbacks. Because radio is strictly a listening medium, radio messages are fleeting and commercials may be missed or forgotten. Many listeners perceive radio as pleasant background and do not listen to it carefully.

Lack of Visuals.   The restrictions of sound may also hamper the creative process. Clearly, products that must be demonstrated or seen to be appreciated are inappropriate for radio advertising. Creating radio ads that encourage the listener to see the product is a difficult challenge. Experts believe that the use of humor, music, and sound effects may be the most effective way to do this.

John Moore Plumbing

(*A telephone rings twice. A man groggily answers:*)

He: John Moore Plumbing.

She: It's 2 A.M. and I'm not asleep . . .

He: I'm not either.

She: Are you having insomnia too?

He: No, I'm having a phone conversation.

She: When I can't sleep I read the Yellow Pages. Do you ever do that?

He: No.

She: Anyway, I saw that John Moore Plumbing is open 24 hours a day. So I thought I'd call . . .

He: Well, John Moore Plumbing has a 24-hour emergency service. Do you have an emergency?

She: Well, I'm desperate. Does desperate count?

He: Are you desperate about plumbing?

She: Sometimes.

He: How 'bout tonight?

She: Sorry, I have plans for tonight.

He: No, no. I mean do you have leaking pipes or a backed-up toilet or something?

She: Hold on a second, I'll check.

Announcer: When you have a plumbing emergency in the middle of the night or middle of the day, call John Moore. Call 590-5555. 24 hours a day. And you'll always get prompt service when you call John Moore Plumbing. Even at 2 A.M.

She: Toilets are fine. I can't see the pipes.

He: Why not?

She: They're underwater.

He: I'll be right over.

She: I'll set a place for you . . .

Announcer: John Moore Plumbing. 590-5555. Call John. And get more.

Clutter.   The proliferation of competing radio stations, combined with the opportunity to engage in heavy repetition, has created a tremendous amount of clutter in radio advertising. Coupled with the fact that radio listeners tend to divide their attention among various activities, this clutter greatly reduces the likelihood that a message will be heard or understood.

PRINCIPLE
Radio should be used as a support medium when the target audience is clearly defined and visualization of the product is not critical.

Scheduling and Buying Difficulties.   The final disadvantage of radio is the complexity of scheduling and buying radio time. The need to buy time on several stations makes scheduling and following up on ads very complicated. The bookkeeping involved in checking nonstandardized rates, approving bills for payment, and billing clients can be a staggering task. Fortunately, computers and large-station representatives have helped alleviate much of this chaos.

SUMMARY

- Broadcast media include both radio and television. Whereas print media are bound by space, broadcast media convey transient messages and are bound by time.

- Among the different television systems that an advertiser can use are network, cable, subscription, local, specialty, and public television. Network television is still the dominant form.

- The size of the television audience is measured in a number of ways, including the use of diaries and people meters.
- Television offers advertisers cost efficiency, impact, and influence.
- Advertisers have a choice of scheduling their commercials on a network, local, or cable scheduling basis.
- Television commercials can take the form of sponsorships, participations, or spot announcements.

- Radio is classified as either AM or FM according to transmission and power.
- The audience for radio can be measured in terms of a station's coverage or its circulation.
- The advantages of radio include specialized programming, speed and flexibility, low cost, the use of mental imagery, and high levels of acceptance. Its disadvantages include inattentiveness, lack of visuals, clutter, and scheduling and buying difficulties.

QUESTIONS

1. What are the major differences between broadcast and print media? How are the two media similar?
2. Describe television syndication. Contrast off-network syndication with first-run syndication. What is barter syndication? How does syndication affect the advertiser?
3. What are the primary advantages and disadvantages offered to advertisers by cable television? How do interconnects affect the decision to advertise on cable?
4. You are a major agency media director who has just finished a presentation to a prospective client in convenience food marketing. During the Q and A period a client representative asks you this question, "We know that television's viewer loyalty is nothing like it was 10 or even 5 years ago with cable and VCRs. There are smaller audiences per program each year, yet television time-costs continue to rise. Do you still believe we should consider commercial television as a primary medium for our company's advertising?" How would you answer?
5. Local market radio audiences are primarily measured by the diary (Arbitron) and the telephone interview (BIRCH). If you, as a media sales director for a radio station, had to choose one service to measure station popularity, which one would you subscribe to? Assume that the cost of each service is roughly the same.
6. Message clutter affects both radio and television advertising. Advertisers fear audiences react to long commercial pods by using the remote control for the television set or the push button on the radio. Some have proposed that advertisers should absorb higher time costs to reduce the frequency and length of commercial interruptions. Others argue that broadcasting should reduce the number of commercials sold and also reduce program advertising even if it means less profit for broadcasters. Which of these remedies would be the best to take in the 1990s?
7. One of the interesting ways to combine the assets of radio and television is to use the sound track of television commercials for the radio creative. Why would an advertiser consider this media/creative strategy? What limitations would you mention?

FURTHER READINGS

Broadcasting/Cable Yearbook 1992 (Washington DC; Broadcast Publications, Inc.).

KALISH, DAVID, "Bad Reception," *Marketing & Media Decisions,* August 1988, pp. 63–65.

Television: The Critical View, 4th ed. (New York: Oxford University Press, 1987).

WHETMORE, EDWARD J. *Mediamerica,* 4th ed., (Belmont, CA: Wadsworth Publishing Co., 1989).

WILLIAM, MARTIN, *TV: The Casual Art,* (New York: Oxford University Press, 1982).

Taking Sneakers Uptown

What Adidas began in the 1960s and Nike, Reebok, and others finished in the 1980s was nothing less than the total repositioning of the sneaker/athletic-shoe market. From its humble beginnings as the footwear of choice for children and teens and an essential component of basketball and tennis players' equipment, the sneaker or athletic shoe has since become a true fashion statement. This transformation not only dramatically expanded the market by making sneakers acceptable for all age groups and for virtually all occasions, it also allowed manufacturers to charge over $100 for items that previously had hovered below $25 per pair.

The idea behind the repositioning of the sneaker category is not a new one to marketing professionals. Strategically minded consumer-products firms often scan other categories for similar opportunities. Typically, these firms are looking for product categories that operate largely on a commodity basis and thus are ripe for the creation of powerful branded products and the corresponding ability to charge premium prices. For example, the Clorox Company was able to expand and dominate the charcoal briquette category with the introduction of the Kingsford brand, after recognizing that the charcoal category had primarily been controlled by small regional brands that competed largely on a price basis.

Consumer-products firms also look for opportunities within categories in which strong brands exist but key quality and/or price niches have yet to be exploited. For example, Breyer's, Haagen-Dazs, and others revolutionized the ice cream category with the introduction of premium-quality ice creams because the category had been primarily dominated by smaller regional dairies that produced relatively common and undifferentiated flavors for the consumer market. This transformation completely rewrote the rules of the game for ice cream marketers, creating a subcategory known as "frozen novelties" and initiating the dramatic increase in new product introductions.

For Nike, Reebok, and, to a lesser extent, L.A. Gear and others, the running boom offered a window of opportunity in which they could attempt to convert the sneaker/athletic-shoe category from one that was positioned primarily on functionality to one that placed at least as much emphasis on fashion. Just as the ice cream category was revolutionized by a dramatic increase in quality and the corresponding explosive growth in new product introductions, the athletic-shoe category was transformed from a relatively uncompetitive one in which older brand names vied for market share to one in which style, per-

formance, and status primarily influenced purchases. The simple introduction of color into the traditionally black or white athletic shoe paved the way for teens and others to purchase sneakers to match a variety of outfits.

For true athletes or those who wished to appear athletic, however, athletic shoes were still required to maintain some legitimacy in terms of performance. Thus, Nike's revolutionary "air" system initially gave the firm an advantage over other athletic shoe competitors. Reebok responded with the "pump" system that allowed athletes to fill small bladders in their shoes with a small air pump built into the tongue of each sneaker. These features allowed Nike and Reebok to justify even higher price increases in their athletic shoes, which was important because the earlier rise in sneaker pricing had left many consumers wondering if they were really getting more substance for their money or simply more style.

Among those athletic-shoe manufacturers that emphasize style and fashion, product sales have followed more of a traditional fashion/fad curve. For example, L.A. Gear, which had rapidly risen to fame on the heels of its flamboyant founder, Sandy Saemann, experienced a dramatic drop in sales in recent months, prompting its board of directors to call for Saemann's resignation.

Thus, many battles in the "sneaker wars" must still be fought over the performance issue as well as fashion. Consequently, Reebok, Nike, and others often woo college and professional athletic teams and coaches with free shoes and cash in exchange for wearing their shoes during games. This practice certainly benefits coaches and saves athletic-department budgets but, perhaps most importantly, it also provides truly credible aspirational role models for young and old sports viewers alike.

As the demographics in the United States shift with the aging of the baby-boomer segment, sneaker manufacturers are anticipating a rough road ahead. With flat to declining population growth projected for the future and the existing population aging beyond peak athletic participation years, demand for the traditional performance-based benefits of athletic shoes will almost certainly decline. Whether sneaker ads of the future will feature aging athletes still maintaining peak athletic performance in their hi-tech Nikes or will revert to portraying nonathletes who select Nikes for their comfort and convenience remains to be seen. What is known is that the sneaker/athletic-shoe category will become more competitive in the future as the battle for shares in a flat market becomes even more intense.

QUESTIONS

1. Why is it important for sneaker/athletic-shoe manufactures to maintain a link to athletic performance rather than focusing exclusively on fashion-based appeals?

2. Besides pure comfort and the convenience of Velcro fasteners versus laces, what other tangible or intangible benefits do you believe athletic-shoe manufacturers will be able to offer to an aging population?

3. Recent discussions regarding the regulation of the advertising industry have focused on the utilization

of on-screen superimposed disclaimers to identify products portrayed in movies as the result of paid considerations. Why do you think it would be beneficial or unnecessary for similar advertising disclaimers to be included in sports broadcasts in which athletic shoes are worn in response to manufacturer's payments to coaches, players, or schools?

Source: ABC News, *Business World,* Show #175, (March 11, 1990); and *20/20,* "Sneaker Wars."

11

Print Media

Chapter Objectives

- Understand the similarities and differences between newspapers and magazines
- Explain the advantages and disadvantages of newspaper, magazine, and other forms of media advertising
- Explain the major trends in print advertisements

FINDING COLLEGE STUDENTS WHERE THEY LIVE

One thing is certain—college students read. In addition to classroom assignments, the 12.3 million U.S. college students read newspapers and magazines. According to a 1989 *Advertising Age* survey, college students spend nearly 2 hours a day reading newspapers and magazines. Furthermore, 86 percent read the college newspaper daily, and 50 percent read campus magazines. It's not surprising, therefore, that the number of newspapers and magazines targeted at college students has grown dramatically since the early 1980s.

Campus newspapers remain primarily a local medium, carrying mostly ads for local retailers, and only occasionally running a few national ads. There are a few exceptions, however. For example *U.* is a national college newspaper that has been particularly successful (see Ad 11.1). This full-color tabloid is a compendium of articles, editorials, photos, and cartoons compiled from more than 260 U.S. college newspapers that are members of the American Collegiate Network, *U.*'s publisher. Controlled circulation is approximately 1.4 million students on 349 campuses. National advertisers include American Express, AT&T, Anheuser-Busch, the U.S. Army, General Foods, and Miller Brewing.

The development of college magazines has been rather turbulent. Although several magazines were introduced in the early 1980s, poor distribution caused the demise of many by the end of the decade. Then, taking advantage of direct-mail delivery, a host of new magazines appeared in the late 1980s. For example, *CV: The College Magazine* ("CV" stands for "career vision" and "campus vision") is distributed to 250 colleges, including 60 traditionally black colleges. *Volume* appears twice each semester and offers both male and female demographic editions. Each issue of *Volume* is based on one of four themes considered "universally important to the generation"—sex, humor, photojournalism, and "interaction." *Eyes* is a "serious monthly newsmagazine," and *Great Opportunities for Today's Collegian* is essentially a catalog of ads with coupons that is published once a semester.*

*Adapted from Patrick Reilly, "College Magazines—The Next Generation," *Advertising Age* (February 6, 1989):S-1, S-2; and Ruth Stroud, "Other National Paper Adds Sense of Community," *Advertising Age* (February 6, 1989):5–9.

AD 11.1
U. **is an example of a successful national college newspaper that attracts large national advertisers.** (Courtesy of *U. The National College Newspaper.*)

PRINT MEDIA

Throughout most of the history of mass communication, print was the only readily accessible means of storing information and retrieving it at will. Print is the keeper of records, great literature, and accomplishments. It differs from broadcast media in several ways. For example, print media deliver messages one topic at a time and one thought at a time, whereas television and electronic media use a simultaneous approach, delivering a great deal of information in a rapid-fire manner. Furthermore, print advertising has a history and credibility unmatched by broadcast advertising. These differences have important consequences for advertisers and media planners to consider.

Advertisers benefit from the selective targeting print media provide as well. For example, those wishing to capture a college-age audience may be inclined to advertise in *U.* or one of the other popular college newspapers or magazines. For an advertiser trying to target college students, print is preferable because it utilizes a very structured information-processing style. Essentially, college students are constantly reading and absorbing information with intensity and credibility. Can we assume that this concentration carries over to print media? Probably. Can we assume that people tend to trust print more than broadcast and absorb it more carefully? Definitely.* In a 1986 study sponsored by *Audits and Surveys,* both men and women indicated a higher attention-level score for magazines than for television. Reasons given revolved around the fact that reading requires a more intensive involvement, whereas television can be taken in more passively.† In another study Jacoby, Hoyer, and Zimmer found that print was better *comprehended* than either television or audio presentations of the same material.‡ Nevertheless, print media makers have had to recognize that their appeal is not universal. In general, we have become a broadcast-oriented society. Print does not work with all people. Consequently, it is not relevant to all advertisers. It is a viable alternative for certain advertisers under certain conditions, however. These conditions, along with the history, structure, and advantages and disadvantages of newspapers and magazines, will be the focus of this chapter.

NEWSPAPERS

PRINCIPLE
Newspapers serve the local market.

For centuries advertising appeared in three basic formats: handbills and circulars, outdoor signs, and newspapers. Whereas the first two have greatly diminished in importance as advertising media, newspapers remain the leading local medium. Maintaining this dominant position has not been easy, however. Newspapers were forced to compete with magazines in the late 1800s, with radio in the 1920s, and with commercial television since the 1950s.

A century ago, there were 18 daily newspapers (dailies) published in New York City alone. As of 1990, only five existed; one was in Spanish, and

*Edward Jay Whetmore, *Mediamerica,* 4th ed. (Belmont, CA: Wadsworth Publishing Co., 1989):20.
†"Study of Media Involvement," *Audits and Surveys* (November 1986).
‡Jacob Jacoby, Wayne D. Hoyer, and Mary R. Zimmer, "To Read, View or Listen? A Cross-Media Comparison of Comprehension," in *Current Issues & Research in Advertising,* James H. Leigh and Claude R. Martin, Jr., eds. (Ann Arbor: The University of Michigan, 1983):201–18.

three were tabloids that were fighting among themselves. Most U.S. cities are surviving now with only one daily paper. Once the only source of information—and even recently the dominant source—newspapers are now just another alternative.

> The immediate problem is the rapid drop in household penetration from a time 3 decades ago when many homes were receiving more than one paper (hence a penetration rate of more than 100 percent) to today's more vulnerable 70 percent. But a focus on penetration paints over the ultimate reality: This may not be a battle to reclaim domination, but a fight for survival. And to survive, the industry may need to recognize that it must find its niche.*

The initial response of the newspaper industry to this fierce competition was to develop new technologies to alleviate the most glaring deficiencies of the medium, which included poor reproduction and lack of sound, movement, and color. Examples are the move from hot metal to cold type, text editing, offset printing, on-line circulation information systems, electronic libraries, data-base publishing, and, most recently, satellite transmission and computerization. There have also been attempts to match the advantages offered by magazines and radio (market selectivity) and television (total market coverage). Examples of market selectivity are free-standing inserts and special-interest newspapers. The latter strategy is reflected in nationally distributed newspapers such as *The Wall Street Journal* and *USA Today*. Finally, the high cost of competition, combined with the increased costs of newspaper production, has resulted in a general consolidation in the newspaper industry. The major owners have become publishing empires, such as Gannett, Knight-Ridder, and Times-Mirror. Other newspaper conglomerates are Newhouse Newspapers, the Tribune Company, and the New York Times Company.

Statistics for 1989 indicated that total daily and Sunday circulation had increased to 64.1 million and 60.4 million, respectively, compared to a daily circulation of 57.1 million and a Sunday circulation of 54.6 million in 1980. Although these numbers may seem high, they represent a rather unimpressive growth rate of slightly more than 10 percent in nearly a decade. *The Wall Street Journal* led the way with a circulation of over 1.9 million, followed by *USA Today* (nearly 1.5 million) and the *Los Angeles Times* (over 1.2 million). Of the top 100 newspapers, 21 had declining circulations.† According to the Newspaper Advertising Bureau (NAB), total advertising revenue, which accounts for 50 percent of newspaper revenue, stood at an estimated $32.5 billion in 1989.‡ Table 11.1 lists the top 20 national newspaper advertisers.

Despite the massive reforms in the newspaper industry, several problems still exist: Does everybody read the same newspaper? Is it practical for the industry to support several different papers? Do we need a new definition of literacy? A study conducted by the Socio-Economic Research Institute of America suggests a partial solution: "During the next decade, better-educated people will be the newspaper readers. They will want high-quality information about current events. . . . Newspapers that provide this will have the greatest chance of growth".§

---

*Gary Hoenig, "Newspapers," *Adweek Supplement* (September 1, 1989):175.

†Ira Teinowitz, "Circulation Up at Most Papers on Top 100 List," *Advertising Age* (May 7, 1990):20.

‡Janet Meyers, "Dressing Up the National Buy," *Advertising Age* (February 19, 1990):S-1.

§Gary Hoenig, "Newspapers," *Adweek Supplement* (September 1, 1989):175.

TABLE 11.1
The Top 20 Newspaper Advertisers

Rank	1989 Investments [000]	1988 Investments [000]	Percent Change
1. News Corp. Ltd.	$247,450.1	272,056.5	−9.0
2. Valassis Inserts	226,653.3	203,170.2	11.6
3. Texas Air Corp.	72,208.6	82,197.2	−12.2
4. General Motors Corp.	55,653.5	83,250.6	−33.1
5. AMR Corp.	40,957.9	28,488.4	43.8
6. American Telephone & Telegraph Co.	39,715.0	30,329.8	30.9
7. Automobile Tires Local Dealers	37,436.5	35,229.3	6.3
8. Pan American World Airways Inc.	35,264.8	28,466.0	23.9
9. MCA Inc.	30,361.0	23,904.2	27.0
10. Warner Communications Inc.	30,149.6	32,734.0	−7.9
11. Philip Morris Companies Inc.	29,678.8	40,421.0	−26.6
12. Go Go Tours	29,353.2	22,835.3	28.5
13. Delta Air Lines Inc.	28,471.0	25,325.1	12.4
14. Trans World Airlines Inc.	28,179.6	27,640.0	2.0
15. Ford Motor Co.	26,725.7	24,468.3	9.2
16. Columbia Pictures Entertainment Inc.	26,403.7	24,930.2	5.9
17. NWA Inc.	25,408.1	10,445.9	143.2
18. Walt Disney Co.	24,627.9	23,967.3	2.8
19. Paramount Communications Inc.	24,066.4	26,773.6	−10.1
20. Daimler-Benz AG	21,414.5	21,027.1	1.8

Source: M & MD (June 1990): 46.

The Structure of Newspapers

Newspapers can be classified by three factors: frequency of publication, size, and circulation.

Frequency of Publication. Newspapers are published either daily or weekly. There are approximately 1,650 dailies and 8,000 weeklies in the United States.* Daily newspapers are usually found in cities and larger towns.

Dailies have morning editions, evening editions, or all-day editions. Daily papers printed in the morning deliver a relatively complete record of the previous day's events, including detailed reports on local and national news as well as on business, financial, and sports events. Evening papers follow up the news of the day and provide early reports of the events of the following day. Evening papers also tend to depend more on entertainment and information features than do morning papers. The *San Francisco Examiner* is an example of a daily evening paper. Approximately 30 percent of the dailies and a few of the weeklies also publish a Sunday edition. The *Chicago Sun-Times* is a daily paper that publishes both a morning and a Sunday edition. In 1990 there were 834 Sunday papers in circulation, nearly twice as many as had existed 50 years earlier.† Sunday newspapers are usually much thicker and contain a great deal of news, advertising, and special features. The circulation of Sunday papers is usually greater than that of dailies because they contain more information and because they appear on a day when readers have more leisure time to spend reading a paper.

Weekly papers appear in towns, suburbs, and smaller cities where the volume of hard news and advertising is not sufficient to support a daily newspaper. These papers emphasize the news of a relatively restricted area;

*Jon Berry, "There Are the Good Old Days," *Adweek Supplement* (April 23, 1990):6–9.
†Berry, "These Are the Good Old Days," pp. 6–9.

they report local news in depth but tend to ignore national news, sports, and similar subjects. Weeklies are often shunned by national advertisers because they are relatively high in cost, duplicate the circulation of daily or Sunday papers, and generate an administrative headache because ads must be placed separately for each newspaper. *The Hegwich News* is an example of a weekly circulated in a Chicago neighborhood.

tabloid *A newspaper with a page size five to six columns wide and 14 inches deep.*

Size. Newspapers are typically available in two sizes. The first, referred to as the **tabloid,** consists of five or six columns, each about 2 inches wide, and a total length of approximately 14 inches. This form makes tabloids look similar to an unbound magazine. The *Chicago Sun Times* employs this size, as does the New York *Daily News,* the *National Enquirer,* and *The Star.* The *standard size,* or **broadsheet,** newspaper is twice as large as the tabloid size, usually eight columns wide and 300 lines deep, or 22 inches deep by 14 inches wide. For both pragmatic and aesthetic reasons, however, many standard-sized newspapers have recently reduced their layouts to six columns wide. More than 90 percent of all newspapers use standard size. *The New York Times* is an example of a standard-size newspaper.

AD 11.2
The Chicago Tribune newspaper has varied its format in recent years. (Copyright 1991 Chicago Tribune Company, all rights reserved, used with permission.)

The newspaper format is not fixed and frozen. The success of *USA Today* indicates that newspapers can and will adjust to changing consumer tastes. *USA Today* stories are brief and breezy, dressed up with splashy graphics and full color in every section, and include an array of charts and graphs to simplify the day's events for the reader. Ad 11.2 is an example of a newspaper with a novel format, influenced by the success of *USA Today,* and designed to attract young readers.

Advertisers' major criticism of the newspaper industry was not as much about the lack of standardization of news format as about the standardization of advertisement format. Historically, national advertisers were discouraged from using newspapers because each paper had its own size guidelines for ads, making it impossible to prepare one ad that would fit every newspaper. This problem was resolved in 1981 with the introduction of the Standard Advertising Unit (SAU) system designed by the American Newspaper Publishers Association and the Newspaper Advertising Bureau. The present version was introduced in 1984 and is shown in Figure 11.1. It is now possible for an advertiser to select one of the 56 standard ad sizes and be assured this ad will work in every newspaper in the country.

FIGURE 11.1
The expanded Standard Advertising Unit system. (*Source: Guide to Quality Newspaper Reproduction,* joint publication of the American Newspaper Publishers Association and Newspaper Advertising Bureau, 1986.)

Depth in Inches	1 col. 2-1/16"	2 col. 4-1/4"	3 col. 6-7/16"	4 col. 8-5/8"	5 col. 10-13/16"	6 col. 13"
FD*	1xFD	2xFD	3xFD	4xFD	5xFD	6xFD
18"	1x18	2x18	3x18	4x18	5x18	6x18
15.75"	1x15.75	2x15.75	3x15.75	4x15.75	5x15.75	
14"	1x14	2x14	3x14	4x14	N 5x14	6x14
13"	1x13	2x13	3x13	4x13	5x13	
10.5"	1x10.5	2x10.5	3x10.5	4x10.5	5x10.5	6x10.5
7"	1x7	2x7	3x7	4x7	5x7	6x7
5.25"	1x5.25	2x5.25	3x5.25	4x5.25		
3.5"	1x3.5	2x3.5				
3"	1x3	2x3				
2"	1x2	2x2				
1.5"	1x1.5					
1"	1x1					

1 Column 2¹/₁₆"
2 Columns 4¹/₄"
3 Columns 6⁷/₁₆"
4 Columns 8⁵/₈"
5 Columns 10¹³/₁₆"
6 Columns 13"

Double Truck 26³/₄"
(There are four suggested double truck sizes:)

13xFD 13x18 13x14 13x10.5

*FD (Full Depth): Can be 21" or deeper. Depths for each broadsheet newspaper are indicated in the Standard Rate and Data Service. All broadsheet newspapers can accept 21" ads, and may float them if their depth is greater than 21".

Tabloids: Size 5 x 14 is a full page tabloid for long cut-off papers. Mid cut-off papers can handle this size with minimal reduction. The N size measuring 9³/₈ x 14 represents the full page size for tabloids such as the New York Daily News and Newsday and other short cut-off newspapers. The five 13 inch deep sizes are for tabloids printed on 55 inch wide presses such as the Philadelphia News. See individual SRDS listings for tabloid sections of broadsheet newspapers.

AD 11.3
The leading Spanish-language daily newspaper, *La Opinion,* is an example of a popular newspaper directed at a specific foreign-language group. (Courtesy of *La Opinion.*)

circulation *A measure of the number of copies sold.*

Circulation.   For the most part, newspapers are a mass medium, attempting to reach either a regional or a national audience. Industry people use the word **circulation** to refer to the number of newspapers sold. A few newspapers have a *national* circulation, such as the *London Times* and *USA Today;* a far greater number are restricted to a *regional* circulation. Some newspapers, however, have attempted to reach certain target audiences in other ways. Most common among these are newspapers directed at specific ethnic or foreign-language groups, such as *La Opinion,* a Spanish daily published in Los Angeles (see Ad 11.3). Over 200 newspapers in the United States are aimed primarily at black Americans. In New York City alone papers are printed in Chinese, Spanish, Russian, Yiddish, German, and Vietnamese.

Special newspapers also exist for special-interest groups, religious denominations, political affiliations, labor unions, and professional and fraternal organizations. For example, *Stars and Stripes* is the newspaper read by millions of armed services personnel.

The Readers of Newspapers

Newspaper readers encompass all income brackets, educational levels, age groups, and ethnic backgrounds. They live in cities, suburbs, towns, resorts, and rural areas. By all demographic standards, the newspaper is a solid mass-market medium.

In 1990 over 63 million people subscribed to newspapers. This figure does not include the 12 percent of the population that buys single copies. Frequent readers of daily newspapers tend to be the most regular readers of the Sunday paper. Nearly half of all adults receive home delivery of a Sunday or weekend newspaper; delivery levels are highest in middle-size cities and lowest in rural locations and the largest metropolitan areas. The average reader spends 62 minutes reading the Sunday edition, compared with an average of 45 minutes on the weekday paper. Gender differences also exist. Men tend to read the "hard news" section of the Sunday paper, which includes the political, financial, and front-page sections. They also tend to read the sports section, whereas women do not have a particular preference. There are age differences as well. Those 35 and older are more likely than young readers to read news sections; those under 35 regularly read the comics, television booklet, entertainment and fashion sections, and inserts.*

Recently, the trend has been toward more regular and more upscale readerships. In 1990 the penetration rate of newspapers was at 70 percent, compared to 65 percent in 1987 and 67 percent in 1982. This percentage reflects 63 million readers, close to an all-time high.† Furthermore, these better-educated adults with higher incomes tend to read newspapers more often and more thoroughly than other people do.

Measuring the Newspaper Audience

The most useful way to assess newspaper readers is in terms of how they use the newspaper. In 1988 the newspaper industry sponsored a study supporting industry assertions that consumers rely more on newspapers than television in deciding what to buy or where to shop. The results showed that, on the average weekday, 67 percent of all the newspaper pages in readers' hands were opened, providing ad exposure. Furthermore, regardless of their age, income, or level of education, readers opened at least 60 percent of newspaper pages. The study also showed that 66 percent of readers looked through the classified advertising and that 56 percent had clipped coupons from a newspaper in the last 3 months.‡

The Audit Bureau of Circulations. Statements regarding newspaper circulation are verified by the Audit Bureau of Circulations (ABC), an independent auditing group that represents advertisers, agencies, and publishers. Members of the ABC include only paid-circulation newspapers and magazines. The ABC reports have nothing to do with setting the rates that a newspaper charges. They simply verify the newspaper's circulation statistics and provide a detailed analysis of the newspaper by state, town, and county. The newspaper can charge whatever it desires. Advertisers may decline to pay, however, if the rate is out of line with the paper's relative circulation figures as reported by ABC. Other companies, such as the Advertising Checking Bureau, provide newspaper research data and information on competitive advertising.

Newspapers that do not belong to an auditing organization must provide either a "publisher's statement" or a "Post Office statement" to prospective advertisers. The former is a sworn affidavit, and the latter is an annual statement given to the Post Office.

Simmons-Scarborough. The research firm Simmons-Scarborough Syndicated Research Associates provides a syndicated newspaper readership study that annually measures readership profiles in approximately 70 of the nation's largest cities. The study covers readership of a single issue as well as the estimated unduplicated readers for a series of issues. Scarborough is the only consistent measurement of popular audiences in individual markets.

Advertising in Newspapers

Although newspapers are not formally classified by the type of advertising they carry, this is a useful way of thinking about newspapers. There are three general types of newspaper advertising: classified, display, and supplements.

*"The Sunday Newspaper and Its Readers," *Newspaper Advertising Bureau* (October 1988).
†Gary Hoenig, "Newspapers," *Adweek Supplement* (September 11, 1989):180.
‡Patrick Reilly, "Reader Study Shows Newspaper as Power," *Advertising Age* (September 12, 1988):80.

KENNETH O. HUSTEL—VICE PRESIDENT, NEWSPAPER ADVERTISING BUREAU, INC.

Organizations such as the National Advertising Bureau (NAB) are responsible for the economic health of the newspaper industry. As noted in this box, people like Kenn Hustel spend a very active life trying to make sure newspapers prosper. The following is a look at the morning schedule of a vice president of NAB.

Prior to the Thanksgiving holiday, I must meet with my newspaper Future of Advertising (FOA) teammates in Minneapolis—next Tuesday or Wednesday would be ideal. The FOA project is a team-selling project designed to convince a major advertiser to plan a sustaining newspaper program in a broad list of daily newspapers. The team involves a member of the NAB and two members of a specific newspaper —generally the senior marketing executive and the national advertising manager. The Bureau provides marketing services support, and in the event creative work is required, either the NAB or the creative services department of the member newspaper will be involved. Preparation of the advertising plan, presentation, et al. are in the hands of the three-person sales team.

Our category is ready-to-eat cereals (R-T-E). Following a thorough marketing review of this business we determined the category leader as our target account. The analysis includes not only secondary data sources, but also personal fact-finding sessions with appropriate advertising principles at each company and each of their agencies.

In our second presentation we encountered some resistance from the advertising agency, who suggested we target our effort toward the promotional budget rather than the consumer media budget. This means we need to see the client, since they control the promotional funds.

We have been persistently trying to schedule a meeting with the client's director of marketing services. We carefully explained our purpose and agenda as we requested a short 45 minutes of time. This morning we were "officially" advised that she has no interest in reviewing our concepts and ideas. I find this appalling. I always thought companies would be highly interested in learning of proposals/ ideas that could conceivably move their business ahead. Most companies subscribe to this principle, but not all. I suppose we could go a level or two higher to force a meeting, but to what avail? That would only guarantee a hostile atmosphere and a negative response to our recommendation. Not to worry. We have another target that will be far more receptive.

I must remember to call the other major Chicago-based agency on the client's cereal business to review our complete proposal. These people provided us with helpful information during a fact-finding session, so it is appropriate for us to share the

---

classified advertising *Commercial messages arranged in the newspaper according to the interests of readers.*

Classified. Historically, **classified advertising** was the first type of advertising found in newspapers. Classified ads generally consist of all types of commercial messages arranged according to their interest to readers, such as "Help Wanted," "Real Estate for Sale," and "Cars for Sale." Classified ads represent approximately 40 percent of total advertising revenue. *Regular classified* ads are usually listed under a major heading with little embellishment or white space. *Display classified* ads use borders, larger type, white space, photos, and, occasionally, color. Often newspapers will also include legal notices, political and government reports, and personals in the classified section.

display advertising *Sponsored messages that can be of any size and location within the newspaper, with the exception of the editorial page.*

Display. **Display advertising** is the dominant form of newspaper advertising. Display ads can be of any size and are found anywhere within the newspaper, with the exception of the editorial page. Display advertising is further divided into two subcategories—local (retail) and national (general).

program with them. I'll try to schedule for mid-December. This also provides us with an opportunity to show the strong thinking and comprehensive program we can apply to other accounts controlled by the agency. You never know where business might emanate from, so it's important to take advantage of all opportunities.

Next week in the Twin Cities, our sales team will review our strategic sales plan for our new target. Because some time has elapsed since our initial fact-finding session with the client, we might well reexamine the status and direction of the client's cereal advertising program. If the client dictates, we will be prepared to visit with the New York-based ad agency responsible for the R-T-E cereal business within 2 weeks. Following those sessions, we will write the plan developing creative strategy, have NAB-NY prepare some conceptual creative units, and try to get back to the client in early January 1991.

As the R-T-E cereal project rolls ahead, I need to push ahead on a similar project for an Indianapolis-based major household cleaner/food protection company. The ad director of the consumer-products division listened to our target account proposal and quickly accepted our challenge. Since her company is under a mandate to search and examine media alternatives (to network television), our proposal struck a positive chord. Ad director advised media directors to contact at principal New York-based

agency and the agency on household cleaners based in South Carolina.

Our project has now reached the point where we are prepared to discuss it in detail with both agencies. I will call company ad director tomorrow to advise of our plans to meet with both agencies late the first week of December. I'll write the letters in Columbus and fax to my office for processing.

Courtesy of Kenneth O. Hustel.

Local display advertising is placed by local businesses, organizations, or individuals who pay the lower, local advertising rate. The difference between what is charged for local display advertising and national display advertising is referred to as the *rate differential*. In a study conducted by the American Association of Advertising Agencies, which traced the rate differential over time, the national rate was found to be more than 66 percent higher than the local rate in 1987 and 90 percent higher for newspapers with circulations greater than 250,000.* Approximately 85 percent of all display advertising is local, placed by local businesses. Ad 11.4 for the Glendale Galleria is an example of a local display ad.

This higher cost is justified by several factors. First, newspapers contend that national advertisers ask for more assistance from newspapers, especially with special promotions, such as coupons and free-standing inserts. Second, they argue that national advertisers are less reliable than local

*"A History of Rate Differentials Since 1933," *American Association of Advertising Agencies* (1988):14–16.

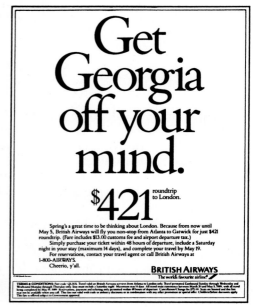

AD 11.4
This local ad for the Glendale Galleria presents the mall as a friendly, inviting place to shop. (Courtesy of Glendale Galleria, Glendale, California.)

AD 11.5
Airlines, such as British Airways, are offered hybrid rates when advertising in newspapers. (Courtesy of British Airways.)

advertisers, often placing no ads for weeks or months at a time. Finally, newspapers believe that the national advertiser is unlikely to change the number of ads placed in a given newspaper regardless of whether the rate goes up or down.

As a result of these higher rates, national advertisers have been reluctant to use newspapers or have looked for ways to get around the rate differential. One alternative that allows the national advertiser to pay the local rate is cooperative (co-op) advertising with a local retailer. Co-op advertising refers to an arrangement between the advertiser and the retailer whereby both parties share the cost of placing the ad. The exact share is negotiated between the two parties. Co-op advertising is discussed in more detail in Chapter 22. Some newspapers have created "hybrid" rates that are offered to regular national advertisers, such as airlines, car-rental companies, and hotels. Ad 11.5 is an example of a company that receives hybrid rates.

National display advertising is run by national and international businesses, organizations, and celebrities to maintain brand recognition or to supplement the efforts of local retailers or other promotional efforts.

supplements *Syndicated or local full-color advertising inserts that appear in newspapers throughout the week.*

Supplements. Both national and local advertising can be carried in newspaper supplements. **Supplements** refer to syndicated or local full-color advertising inserts that appear throughout the week and especially in the Sunday edition of newspapers. One very popular type is the magazine supplement, of which there are two kinds—syndicated and local.

Syndicated supplements are published by independent publishers and distributed to newspapers throughout the country. The logo for the publisher and the local paper appear on the masthead. The best-known syndicated supplements are *Parade* and *USA Weekend. Local supplements* are produced by either one newspaper or a group of newspapers in the same area. Whether syndicated or locally edited, magazine supplements resemble magazines more than newspapers in content and format.

Another type of newspaper supplement is the **free-standing insert advertisement** (FSIA), or "loose insert." These preprinted advertisements range in size from a single page to over 30 pages and may be in black and white or full color. This material is printed elsewhere and then delivered to the newspaper. Newspapers charge the advertiser a fee for inserting the material plus a special rate for carrying the ad in a particular issue. This form of newspaper advertising is growing in popularity with retail advertisers for two reasons: (1) It allows greater control over the reproduction quality of the advertisement; and (2) the multipage FSIA is an excellent coupon carrier. Newspapers are not necessarily happy about the growth of free-standing inserts because they make less revenue from this form of advertising.

The Advantages of Newspapers

There are numerous advantages to advertising in newspapers. These include market coverage, comparison shopping, positive consumer attitudes, flexibility, and interaction of national advertising and local retailers.

Market Coverage. Undoubtedly the most obvious asset is the extensive market coverage provided by newspapers. When an advertiser wishes to reach a local or regional market, newspapers offer an extremely cost-efficient way to do so. Even special-interest groups and racial and ethnic groups can be reached through newspapers.

Comparison Shopping. Consumers consider newspapers valuable shopping vehicles. Many use newspapers for comparison shopping. Consumers can also control when and how they read the paper. As a result, they view newspaper ads very positively.

Positive Consumer Attitudes. Consumers maintain positive attitudes toward newspapers in general. Readers generally perceive newspapers—including the advertisements—to be very immediate and current, as well as highly credible sources of information.

Flexibility. Flexibility is a major strength of newspapers. Newspapers offer great geographic flexibility. Advertisers using them can choose to advertise in some markets and not in others. Newspapers are often flexible in the actual production of the ads as well. Unusual ad sizes, full-color ads, free-standing inserts, different prices in different areas, and supplements are all options for a newspaper advertiser.

Interaction of National and Local. Finally, newspapers provide an excellent bridge between the national advertiser and the local retailer. A local retailer can easily tie in with a national campaign by utilizing a similar advertisement in the local daily. In addition, quick-action programs, such as sales and coupons, are easily implemented through local newspapers.

Charlotte Weisinberger, J. Walter Thompson's media director, summarizes the benefits of advertising in newspapers: "There are a number of things—from representing a local retailer, to breaking a last-minute campaign, to couponing, to telling a detailed story that won't fit in a 30-second spot—that newspapers simply do better than any other medium."*

---

*Warren Berger, "What Have Your Done for Me Lately?" *Adweek* (April 23, 1990):13.

The Disadvantages of Newspapers

Like every other advertising medium, newspapers also have their disadvantages. The issues that are most problematic in newspaper advertising are a short life span, clutter, limited reach of certain groups, product criteria, and poor reproduction.

Short Life Span. Although a great many people do read newspapers, they read them quickly and they read them only once. The average life span of a daily newspaper is only 24 hours.

Clutter. High clutter is a serious problem with most newspapers. This is particularly true on supermarket advertising days and on Sundays, when information overload reduces the impact of any single advertisement.

Limited Coverage of Certain Groups. Although newspapers have wide market coverage, certain market groups are not frequent readers. For example, newspapers do not reach a large part of the under-20 age group. The same is true of the elderly and those speaking a foreign language who do not live in a large city.

Product Criteria. Newspapers suffer the same limitations shared by all print media. Certain products should not advertise in newspapers. Products that require demonstration would have a difficult time making an impact in the newspaper format. Similarly, products that consumers do not expect to find advertised in newspapers might easily be overlooked.

Poor Reproduction. With the exception of special printing techniques and preprinted inserts, the reproduction quality of newspapers is comparitively poor and limiting, especially for color advertisements, although color reproduction has improved thanks to the popularity of *USA Today.* In addition, the speed necessary to compose a daily newspaper prevents the detailed preparation and care in production that is possible when time pressures are not so great.

MAGAZINES

The earliest American magazines were local journals of political opinion. Most were monthly and did not circulate far beyond their geographic origins. Andrew Bradford's *American Magazine* was the first to appear in the colonies in 1741, arriving 3 days earlier than Benjamin Franklin's *General Magazine and Historical Chronicle.* Both publications folded within 6 months. Since that time, magazines have come and gone. All have been aimed at specific audiences; most sell advertising and are published monthly.* Ad 11.6 offers a pictorial view of the evolution of magazines throughout history. Despite the high risks associated with the magazine business, there appears to be no decline in the number of new magazines introduced each year. One study estimates that 491 new magazines were introduced in 1989. Over 50 percent failed within the first year.† In addition, publishers are investing more money than ever in existing titles. Individual magazines have become bigger and brighter. Heavy paper stocks, lush pho-

*John McDonough, "In Step with History," *Advertising Age* (May 24, 1989):23.
†Iris Cohen Slenger, "Consumer Magazines," *Adweek* (September 11, 1989):191.

AD 11.6
The evolution of magazines from 1883 through 1990. (Reprinted with permission from *Advertising Age,* May 24, 1989. Copyright Crain Communications, Inc. 1989.)

In 1930, Henry Luce launched *Fortune,* which weighed three pounds and cost the then-staggering price of $1.

When *Time* magazine burst forth in 1923, it had no correspondents, no bureaus. But it had "attitude."

Like its mass audience brethren, *Collier's* had a huge circulation before its demise, while *The New Yorker* flourished on a much smaller base.

The Ladies' Home Journal, founded in 1883, was among the earliest magazines to accept advertising and make it work for them.

One of the great post-World War II magazine success stories, *Playboy* embodied the dilemmas of its age, praising intelligent women in its "philosophy" while stressing other attributes in its photographs.

tographs, and sophisticated graphics are used to create beautiful, eyecatching editorial environments that entice both readers and advertisers.

Upscale magazines seem to have an edge over mass consumer magazines in attracting advertisers. Upscale advertisers don't look to promotion spending as an alternative to advertising. Instead, they tend to turn to the image advertising that upscale magazines provide. For example, magazines such as *Gourmet, Architectural Digest,* and *Condé Nast Traveler* all increased their ad pages in 1990. Steve Forbes, president and CEO of *Forbes* magazine, attributes this increase to gains in the "luxury category" of advertising, such as Rémy Martin Amérique, Cadillac, and Jaguar. *Elle* senior vice president/publisher Anne Sutherland Fuchs says that her magazine's "strong push to shore up [its] position with upscale advertisers has helped it buck the tide of ad page decline facing many women's magazines."*

The magazine industry has entered the "age of skimming," where readers acquire 80 percent of their information from the story titles, subheadings, captions, and pictures rather than from the editorial content. Although magazine advertising revenue in 1989 was $7.1 billion, magazines are still unsure of which format to adopt and which audiences to target.† This is a medium that advertisers tend to view cautiously. Table 11.2 lists the 1989 rankings of the top 10 magazines by advertising revenue.

*Iris Cohen Selenger, "Mags with Upscale Ads Show Gains," *Adweek* (November 12, 1990):19.
†Jon Berry, "Trade Magazines," *Adweek Supplement* (September 1, 1989):196.

TABLE 11.2
Magazines Ranked by 1989 Ad Revenue, With Rankings by Total Ad Pages

	1989 Ad Revenue		1988 Ad Revenue		1989 Ad Pages		1988 Ad Pages	
	Million $	Rank	Million $	Rank	Pages	Rank	Pages	Rank
Time	373.4	1	349.7	1	2734	11	2506	11
Sports Illustrated	336.7	2	323.9	3	2982	10	2978	9
People Weekly	326.2	3	305.3	4	3771	5	3826	3
TV Guide	323.0	4	335.4	2	3255	8	3507	4
Parade	314.5	5	266.5	5	718	101	665	106
Business Week	260.6	6	227.3	7	4914	1	4586	1
Newsweek	255.9	7	241.7	6	2495	12	2479	12
Fortune	167.3	8	137.4	9	3775	4	3237	7
Forbes	157.7	9	128.7	12	3906	3	3459	5
U.S. News & World Report	152.8	10	128.1	13	2053	19	1873	20

Source: Adweek (February 12, 1990):34. Reprinted with permission of *Adweek.*

The Structure of Magazines

The Standard Rate and Data Service classifies magazines according to their frequency of publication and their audience. The magazine industry also classifies magazines by *geographic coverage, demographics,* and *editorial diversity.*

Audience. Three types of magazines are categorized by the audiences they serve. The first category, *consumer magazines,* is directed at consumers who buy products for their own consumption. These magazines are distributed through the mail, newsstands, or stores. Examples are *Reader's Digest, Lear's, Time,* and *People.* The second category is *business magazines.* These magazines are directed at business readers and are further divided into *trade papers* (read by retailers, wholesalers, and other distributors; for example, *Chain Store Age*), *industrial magazines* (read by manufacturers; for example, *Concrete Construction*) and *professional magazines* (read by physicians, lawyers, and others; for example, *National Law Review*). Business magazines are also classified as being vertical or horizontal publications. A *vertical publication* presents stories and information about an entire industry. *Women's Wear Daily,* for example, discusses the production, marketing, and distribution of women's fashion. A *horizontal publication* deals with a business function that cuts across industries, such as *Direct Marketing. Farm magazines* represent a third category. They go to farmers and those engaged in farm-related activities. *Peanut Farmer* is an example of a farm magazine.

Geography. Magazines generally cover certain sections or regions of the country. The area covered may be as small as a city (*Los Angeles Magazine* and *Boston Magazine*) or as large as several contiguous states (the southwestern edition of *Southern Living Magazine*). Geographic editions help encourage local retail support by listing the names of local distributors in the advertisement.

Demographics. Demographic editions group subscribers according to age, income, occupation, and other classifications. *McCall's* for example, publishes a ZIP edition to upper-income homes. A ZIP edition is a special version of the magazine which is sent to subscribers who live in a specific zip code. A zip code presumably tells something about the people living in an area. They typically share common demographic traits, such as income. *Newsweek* offers a college edition, and *Time* sends special editions to students, business executives, doctors, and business managers.

Editorial Content. Various magazines emphasize certain types of editorial content. The most widely used categories are: general editorial (*Reader's Digest*), women's service (*Family Circle*), shelter (*House Beautiful*), business (*Forbes*), and special interest (*Ski*).

Physical Characteristics. The structure of the magazine industry is also reflected in the terminology used to describe the physical characteristics of a magazine. The most common magazine page sizes are 8½ x 11 inches and 6 x 9 inches.

Distribution and Circulation. The method used to distribute a magazine partly reflects its structure. **Traditional delivery** is either through *newsstand purchase* or *home delivery* via the U.S. Postal Service. **Nontra-**

traditional delivery *Delivery of magazines to readers through newsstands or home delivery.*

nontraditional delivery *Delivery of magazines to readers through such methods as door hangers or newspapers.*

ditional delivery systems include hanging bagged copies on doorknobs, delivery within newspapers, and delivery through professionals. Magazines distributed through nontraditional delivery systems are provided free. This is referred to as *controlled circulation* as opposed to *paid circulation.* Rodale Press, located in Pennsylvania, is one of the most active publishing houses in developing controlled circulation. Two Rodale Magazines, *Prevention* and *Men's Health,* are often placed in doctors' waiting rooms.

The Readers of Magazines

Currently, 92 percent of all adults read at least one magazine per month. This is true of both males and females. On average, adults read nine different issues of magazines per month. The average magazine is read over a period of 2 days, for 54 minutes in total reading time, by an average of four adults per copy.* It is therefore safe to conclude that the American public has a voracious appetite for magazines and the unique and specialized information they provide. *Sports Illustrated* is an example of a magazine that is targeted at a specific audience.

Readers also appear to have a positive attitude toward magazine advertising. Approximately 79 percent of adults consider magazine advertising "helpful as a buying guide." Roughly 75 percent express positive attitudes toward various aspects of magazine advertising, including the amount of information carried, the use of color; and the provision of coupons. Women tend to have slightly more positive attitudes than men do. In general, people pay relatively more attention to magazine advertising than to television advertising.†

Measuring Magazine Readership

Magazine rates are based on the number of readers, which correlates with the circulation that a publisher promises to provide—that is, the *guaranteed circulation.* Table 11.3 lists the 15 largest magazines by circulation. As

*Mediamark Research Inc., *Doublebase 1988 Study:*19.
†"Study of Media Involvement," *Audits & Surveys* (March 1988).

TABLE 11.3
Magazines Ranked by Circulation

	Total Circulation 1989	Total Circulation 1988	Percent Change
1 Modern Maturity*	20,326,933	17,924,783	13.4
2 NRTA/AARP News Bulletin*	20,001,538	17,623,715	13.5
3 Reader's Digest	16,434,254	16,964,226	− 3.1
4 TV Guide	16,330,051	16,917,545	− 3.5
5 National Geographic	10,829,328	10,518,837	3.0
6 Better Homes & Gardens	8,027,010	8,152,478	− 1.5
7 Family Circle	5,212,555	5,900,794	−11.7
8 McCall's	5,150,814	5,146,554	0.1
9 Ladies' Home Journal	5,117,712	5,013,761	2.1
10 Good Housekeeping	5,114,774	5,027,865	1.7
11 Woman's Day	4,401,746	5,138,280	−14.3
12 Time	4,393,237	4,737,912	− 7.3
13 Guideposts	4,239,396	4,371,861	− 3.0
14 National Enquirer	4,222,755	4,303,631	− 1.9
15 Redbook	3,906,453	4,007,584	− 2.5

*Association magazine
Source: Michael Winkleman, "Hot, Hot, Hot," *Adweek* (February 12, 1990): 35.

with newspapers, the ABC is responsible for collecting and evaluating these data to ensure that guaranteed circulation was obtained. The ABC audits subscriptions as well as newsstand sales. It also checks the number of delinquent subscribers and rates of renewal.

Magazine circulation refers to the number of copies of an issue sold, not to the readership of the publication. A single copy of a magazine might be read by one person or by several people, depending on its content.

The Simmons Market Research Bureau (SMRB) goes one step further by relating readership patterns to purchasing habits. The Bureau provides data on who reads which magazines and which products these readers buy and consume. Most advertisers and agencies depend greatly on SMRB estimates of magazine audiences. Other research companies, such as Starch and Gallup and Robinson, provide comparable information about magazine audience size and behavior. More is said about these research firms in Chapters 10 and 12.

MRI. A company known as MediaMark provides a service called MRI that measures readership for most popular national and regional magazines (along with other media). Reports are issued twice a year and cover readership by demographics, psychographics, and product usage.

Advertising in Magazines

Magazines are a valuable medium for reaching many demographic groups. By their nature, magazines must fill a niche with unique editorial content in order to satisfy specific groups of readers. As a result, they are extremely diverse in terms of their characteristics, readers, and reader interaction. In evaluating a magazine, it is important for advertisers to examine the full range of characteristics that distinguish one magazine from all others.

Technology. New technologies have enabled magazines to distinguish themselves from one another. For example, *selective binding,* and *ink-jet imaging* allow publishers to construct and personalize issues for individual subscribers one signature or insert at a time. Selective binding combines information on subscribers kept in a data base with a computer program to produce a magazine that includes special sections for subscribers based on their demographic profiles. Ink-jet printing permits a magazine such as *U.S. News & World Report* to personalize its renewal form so that each issue contains a renewal card already filled out with the subscriber's name, address, and so on. Personalized messages can be printed directly on run-of-book ads (the technology that is used for the entire magazine) or on inserts.

Desktop publishing is another mainline technology used by many magazines. This method, when combined with satellite transmission, allows magazines to close pages just hours before presstime—eliminating the long lead time that has traditionally been a serious drawback of magazine advertising. A final technology that has improved the advertising effectiveness of magazines is the adoption of sophisticated data-base management. This lets publishers combine the information available from exact subscriber lists with other public and private lists to create complete consumer profiles for their advertisers.

Format. Each magazine or magazine category uses its own terminology to describe its format. Nevertheless, all magazines share some characteristics. For example, the front cover of a magazine is called its *first cover page.* The inside of the front cover is called the *second cover page,* the inside of the back cover the *third cover page,* and the back cover the *fourth cover*

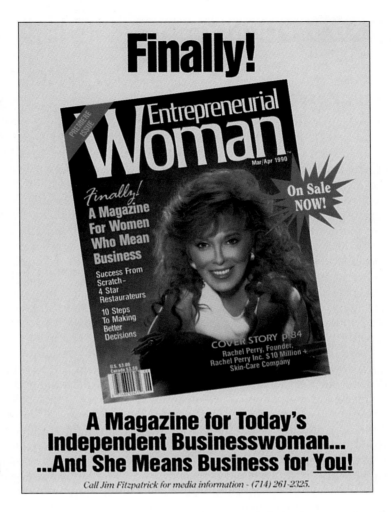

page. Normally the double-page spread is the largest unit of ad space sold by magazines. The two pages usually face each other. When a double-page ad is designed, it is critical that the *gutter* (the white space between the pages running along the outside edge of the page) be bridged or jumped—meaning that no headline words run through the gutter and that all body text is on one side or the other. A page without outside margins, in which the color extends to the edge of the page, is called a *bleed page.* Magazines can sometimes offer more than two connected pages (four is the most common number). This is referred to as a *gatefold.* Finally, a single page or double page can be broken into a variety of units called *fractional page space* (for example, vertical half-page, horizontal half-page, double horizontal half-page, half-page double spread, and checkerboard). The box entitled "Positions on Positioning" discusses the implications of ad-page positioning.

The Advantages of Magazines

The benefits of magazine advertising include the ability to reach specialized audiences, audience receptivity, a long life span, visual quality, and the distribution of sales promotion devices.

PRINCIPLE
Magazines are becoming more specialized.

Target Audiences. The overriding advantage of magazines in the 1940s and 1950s was their ability to reach a wide, general audience. This is no longer true. As noted, the greatest areas of growth are expected to be in

POSITIONS ON POSITIONING

In October 1990 the advertising agency BBDO Chicago compiled an overview of 40 years of research concerning the effects of positioning on the amount of exposure of magazine advertising and the ability of consumers to recall magazine ads. The study was organized in response to an *Advertising Age* editorial by one magazine publisher stating that requests for positions are increasing to the point where it is difficult to satisfy all his accounts. According to BBDO, some ad positions do affect the recall of an ad, but positioning is only one of many factors that influence the success of an ad.

The BBDO agency presented research findings that dispute two popular myths of magazine ad-page positioning. According to the first myth, the front of the magazine is better than the back. Research does not support this theory. In fact, recall scores for the back of a magazine are the same as those for the front, partly because nearly 40 percent of readers do not start at the beginning of a magazine. The second myth, that right-hand pages are better than left, has never been proved in over 30 years of research. Despite this fact, many magazines continue to place three times as many ads on the right as on the left.

Although the research does not support either of these myths, some positions, such as high-traffic areas, are shown to enhance recall better than others. High-traffic areas include the table of contents and popular editorial and magazine covers. A 1987 study by the research firm Starch INRA Hooper revealed that ads opposite the table of contents, featured articles, pictures of people, and articles with recipes scored the highest. A half-page spread at the top of the page has also proved advantageous over the bottom of the page. Perception Research used eye-tracking studies to measure readership patterns. These tests indicated that the eye typically goes to the top of the page first. These studies were based on tests of full-page ads, however, so the findings are hard to generalize.

Starch has also shown that covers do attract greater readership. Findings indicate that readership scores increase by 10 to 18 percent for ads placed on the second and third covers. The back cover accounts for a 20 to 30 percent increase. Furthermore, these findings have been consistent for over 20 years.

Other influences besides positioning affect the recall of an ad, however. A 1935 article in the *Journal of Applied Psychology* showed that clutter negatively affects the recall of an ad. This is still true today. Current research indicates that having multiple ads in the same category or a high ad-to-editorial ratio can cause reader confusion.

The format of the ads themselves can also affect their impact. According to Daniel Starch, readership increases by approximately 13 percent for bleed ads, although the premium charged for these ads (up to 15 percent) may not justify the practice. Unusually shaped ads have proved to be attention-getters as well. These ads rely on the novelty of the presentation, however, and once the innovation wears off, readers may quickly avert their attention. The magazine itself also plays a role. A magazine that follows the same format month to month may become too predictable. Regular readers will learn where their favorite features are and turn to them directly, avoiding the ads. Some ads are just as interesting as the editorial content, however, such as ads for clothing and cosmetics in fashion magazines.

The bottom line is this: There are no hard-and-fast rules. Some positions may prove better than others for certain ads, some may not. Covers continue to outscore inside positions, and editorial adjacencies can help increase recall and exposure. Most importantly, however, the ad must be creative and the readers must be interested in its message. The media planner must know both the target audience and the strengths and weaknesses of the magazine to ensure the best advertising opportunities for his or her client.

Source: Adapted from Garnet Pike, "Left or Right: The Ad Positioning Fight," *Marketing & Media Decisions* (October 1990):54–57.

special-interest magazines and special editions of existing publications. The ability to reach specialized audiences has become a primary advantage (see Ad 11.7). The Lifestyles box entitled "Men Speak Out on Men" discusses how magazines are targeting the new male of the 1990s.

MEN SPEAK OUT ON MEN

During the 1980s *The New York Times* began running a column called "About Men" in its Sunday magazine, giving male readers a chance to discuss the personal side of their lives. Hundreds of men immediately submitted essays. The opportunity squelched a number of popular misconceptions about the male sex. It provided an outlet for men—who had long been stereotyped as breadwinning, sports-watching, beer-swilling creatures—to share their feelings and experiences.

Several magazine publishers are relying on this new, more liberal outlook to provide new advertising opportunities. They say the "modern American man" is not a Neanderthal interested only in typically male magazines, such as *Sports and Field, Esquire,* and *Playboy.* Men of the 1990s have expanded their horizons and their interests, so advertisers will be wise to look past *GQ* and *Sports Illustrated* and toward lifestyle magazines that address the widespread interests of middle-aged male baby boomers.

According to the 1990 U.S. Census report, the number of men age 30 to 49 has grown 37 percent to approximately 37 million since 1980. By 1995 this segment is expected to exceed 40 million. This is a sizable population that cannot be ignored. Moreover, these aging boomers are perhaps not as physically active as they used to be and are more inclined to relax with a magazine, especially one that encompasses a variety of topics. Furthermore, the increase in the number of married women in the work force has jostled men into a more active domestic role. In the 1990s men will increasingly participate in buying decisions and childrearing. They have therefore become targetable for nontraditionally male ad categories. For example, according to the Food Market Institute, over 40 percent of supermarket shoppers are men. In addition, men are said to be more brand-loyal than women. As a result, packaged-goods manufacturers such as Stouffers are now advertising in men's magazines.

Source: Adapted from Michael Garry, "Men, Men, Men," *Marketing & Media Decisions* (September 1990): 38–42.

Audience Receptivity. The second advantage of magazines is their high level of audience receptivity. The editorial environment of a magazine lends authority and credibility to the advertising. Many magazines claim that advertising in their publication gives a product prestige. Clearly an ad in *Fortune* would impress business audiences, just as an ad in *Seventeen* would impress teenagers.

Long Life Span. Magazines have the longest life span of all the media. Some magazines, such as *National Geographic* or *Consumer Reports,* are used as ongoing references and might never be discarded. Other publications, such as *TV Guide,* are intended to be used frequently during a given period of time. In addition, magazines have very high reach potential because of a large *pass-along,* or secondary, audience of family, friends, customers, and colleagues.

Finally, people tend to read magazines at a relatively slow rate, typically over a couple of days. Therefore, magazines offer an opportunity to use long copy. The magazine format also allows more creative variety through multiple pages, inserts, and other design features.

PRINCIPLE
Magazines offer excellent reproduction of quality visual images such as color photographs.

Visual Quality. The visual quality of magazines tend to be excellent because they are printed on high-quality paper stock that provides superior photo reproduction in both black and white and color. This production quality often reflects the superior editorial content. Feature stories are frequently written by well-respected writers.

AD 11.8
This ad illustrates two primary advantages of magazines: the ability to reproduce color and the capacity to carry sales promotions. (Courtesy of Campbell Soup Company.)

Sales Promotions. Magazines are an effective medium through which to distribute various sales promotion devices, such as coupons, product samples, and information cards. A 1987 Post Office ruling allowed magazines to carry loose editorial and advertising supplements as part of the publication provided the magazine is enclosed in an envelope or wrapper.* Ad 11.8 illustrates a magazine that carries a sales promotion.

The Disadvantages of Magazines

Magazines are limited by certain factors. The most prominent disadvantages are limited flexibility, high cost, and difficult distribution.

Limited Flexibility. Although magazines offer many benefits to advertisers, long lead time and lack of flexibility and immediacy are two of their drawbacks. Ads must be submitted well in advance of the publication date. For example, advertisers must have engravings for full-color advertisements at the printer more than 2 months before the cover date of a monthly publication. As noted earlier, however, magazines that have adopted desktop

*DDB Needham, *Media Trends* (1987):55.

publishing and satellite transmission are able to avoid this limitation and can close just hours before presstime. Magazines are also inflexible in respect to available positions. Prime locations, such as the back cover or inside front cover, may be sold months in advance. Some readers do not look at an issue of a magazine until long after it has reached their homes; therefore, impact builds slowly.

High Cost. The second disadvantage associated with magazines is their relatively high cost. In 1990 the cost for a full-page four-color ad in *Newsweek* magazine's national edition was $116,490. For a general-audience magazine such as *Newsweek,* the cost per thousand (CPM) is quite high, and magazines of this type do not compare favorably with other media on this score. However, magazines with carefully segmented audiences, such as *Byte,* can be very cost-efficient because a tightly targeted audience is more expensive to reach than a mass audience.

Distribution. The final disadvantage associated with magazines is the difficulty of distribution. Many magazines, such as *Woman's Day* and *People,* are purchased primarily through newsstands. Yet there is no way that 2,500 different magazines can all appear on store racks. Some magazines are simply not available to all possible target audiences.

SUMMARY

- Print media are static and visual. They are superior to broadcast media in respectability, permanence, and credibility.
- Newspapers, which are still the leading local medium, have improved their technology owing to increased competition from broadcast and direct mail, but they are diminishing in number.
- The structure of newspapers is determined by frequency of publication, size, and circulation.
- There are three general types of newspaper advertising: classified, display, and supplements.
- The greatest advantage of advertising in newspapers

is extensive market coverage. The biggest disadvantages are a short life span, clutter, and poor reproduction.
- Magazines have the greatest ability to reach preselected or tightly targeted audiences. This selectivity is exhibited through the elaborate structure found in the industry.
- Magazines are categorized by audience, geography, demographics, and editorial content.
- Advertising in magazines does have drawbacks, including limited flexibility, high costs, and difficult distribution.

QUESTIONS

1. Discuss the various characteristics of newspapers readers. What are the implications for an advertiser considering newspapers?

2. You are the head media planner for a small chain of upscale furniture outlets in a top 50 market that concentrates most of its advertising in the Sunday magazine supplement of the local newspaper. The client also schedules display ads in the daily editions for special sales. Six months ago a new high-style, metropolitan magazine approached you about advertising for your client. You deferred a decision by saying you'd see what reader acceptance would be. Now the magazine has shown some steady increases (its circulation is now about one quarter of the newspaper's). If you were to include the magazine on the ad schedule, you'd have to reduce the newspaper

linage. What would be your recommendations to the furniture store?

3. Many magazines have editorial environments that are well-suited to certain products and services (home service, entertainment, sports, recreation, and financial magazines). Compatibility between the advertising and the reader's editorial interest is a plus. However, editorial "compatibility" will attract your competitors' ads too. Would having a number of competitors' ads in an issue where your ad appeared cause you to consider less compatible publications? Explain your reasons.

4. Discuss the advantages and disadvantages of advertising in newspapers and magazines from the viewpoint of the advertising directed for GE small appliances.

5. Peter Wilcox, a display salesman for the *Daily Globe*, thought he had heard all the possible excuses for not buying newspaper space until he called on the manager of a compact disc store that sold new and preowned discs. "I've heard about newspaper reader studies that prove how wrong the audience is for me. Readership is too adult—mostly above 35 years of age," he said. "And besides, readers of newspapers are families with higher incomes—the wrong market for our used disc business," he continued. If the Globe is a typical metropolitan daily, could the store manager be correct? In any event, how should Wilcox try to counter the manager's views?

6. A terrific debate is going on in Professor Morrison's retail advertising class. The question is: "Why do na- tional advertisers refuse to seriously consider news- papers in media plans?" The advertising manager for a home products company argues that despite newspaper's creative limitations, more firms would buy newspaper space if the medium did not practice rate discrimination against national companies. The sales manager for a small chain of newspapers admits the price difference, but says it is justified by the extra attention, and commissions (sales rep and agency) newspapers have to pay for each national order. The sales manager also claims the price issue is a "smokescreen" for advertisers to hide their con- tinuing "love affair" with television. Which position would you accept? Is price difference an issue large enough to restrict marketer's interest? How does co- operative advertising figure into the debate?

FURTHER READINGS

ALSON, AMY, "The Search for National Ad Dollars," *Mar- keting & Media Decisions* (February 1989):29–30.

ANGELO, JEAN MARIE, "One Out of Four Mags Goes Off Rate Card," *Inside Print* (December 1988):21.

DAMIANO, STEVE, "For Women, Business and Pleasure," *Marketing & Media Decisions* (April 1990):14.

HUHN, MARY, "Breaking the Black-and-White Habit," *Ad- week Special Report—1988* (April 26, 1988):27.

MATOVELLI, JOHN, "Toward an Age of Customized Maga- zines," *Adweek Special Report—Magazine World 1989* (February 13, 1989):36–37.

PERRY, DAVID, "Performance Advertisers Practice What They Preach," *Business Marketing* (March 1988):86.

STRAUSS, STEVE, *Moving Images: The Transportation Poster in America* (New York: Fullcourt Press, 1984).

VIDEO CASE

 ## Marketing in the Age of Social Responsibility

While the 1990s have heralded a renewed interest in social concerns and the environment, few marketers have successfully been able to attract and retain consumers with a staunchly "pro-world" stance. Currently, several firms are attempting to capitalize on this renewed interest in the environment by reducing packaging materials for products and utilizing recycled paper and/or biodegradable ingredients. This trend has come to be known as "green marketing."

Perhaps no firm has successfully leveraged its social marketing positioning as well as Ben & Jerry's Ice Cream. The firm's home-spun social and environmental points of view are often printed on packaging materials for consumers to read. One of the company's more recent flavors is even named after the cause for which a portion of its proceeds are dedicated: rain forests.

Cofounder Ben Cohen says he judges the success of his firm by how much good it has done for the community. This radical, almost anticorporate philosophy made Ben & Jerry's the darling of the business media during the 1970s and 1980s. Although some reporters argued that the founders' social beliefs were part of an elaborate fabrication to elicit free publicity, the majority have accepted Ben & Jerry's ideals as genuine, often praising them for their uniquely successful blending of savvy marketing with social welfare concerns.

To date, however, fickle American consumers have proven to be difficult to attract with ideals alone. Consumers still prefer value and performance in the majority of their household product purchases, particularly in poor economic times, such as a recession. Consequently, sophisticated marketers have recognized that a given product's social and/or environmental benefit alone will not serve as the primary purchase incentive in the foreseeable future. However, products that are "kinder and gentler" to the environment can elicit consumer preference if all else is equal. For example, if two brands of facial tissue are priced comparably and offer equal performance in terms of scent, softness, and packaging graphics, the one made by recycled paper may be purchased more by environmentally sensitive consumers. Conversely, few mainstream consumers would be tempted to buy a brand of facial tissue that costs more, is rougher on the skin, and

has tacky packaging graphics that fail to blend into most consumers' home decors, regardless of its environmental benefits.

Marketers would categorize green marketing issues in product or packaging design as the "absence of a negative." This refers to a manufacturer's conscious elimination of a known consumer concern that often has little or nothing to do with a product's basic consumer benefit. For example, when Procter & Gamble introduced unscented Tide, the product's basic laundry cleaning benefit remained unchanged; however, a product feature, the scent, was eliminated. Undoubtedly, this was done because Procter & Gamble had received complaints from consumers regarding the objectionable scent of original Tide and/or concerns regarding allergic reactions. More importantly, Procter & Gamble recognized that an unscented version of Tide represented a potential for increased sales from a small segment of the population, but because the product delivered comparable performance to the original version, the absence of a negative for those consumers who viewed scent as a product problem actually become a positive feature.

Similarly, Ben & Jerry's primarily benefited from an extremely high-quality product. Flying in the face of the movement by the major ice cream producers to create low-calorie, low-cholesterol ice creams, Ben & Jerry's produced almost sinful combinations of enriched ice cream and other various ingredients. With such flavors as Cherry Garcia, Heath Bar Crunch, Chunky Monkey, and Chocolate Chip Cookie Dough, Ben & Jerry's ice cream would undoubtedly have been a success regardless of its founders' ideals. However, the media interest generated by the company's unique social stance undoubtedly helped reduce some of the guilt associated with high-calorie ice cream consumption among consumers. As Ben & Jerry's struggles to expand and hire people with similar ideals, other manufacturers are trying to prove that they too care about our world. However, unless product value and quality are kept competitive with less environmentally sensitive products, the green marketing movement may be a very short one, leaving only those firms like Ben & Jerry's, which appear to be in it for moral rather than for profit motives.

QUESTIONS

1. The majority of national surveys among consumers indicate that dieting and the consumption of low-calorie foods are primary concerns; however, grocery product sales fail to support this trend to the same extent. This dichotomy has certainly aided Ben & Jerry's success, but how can you explain the discrepancy?
2. Many have characterized environmental concerns as a luxury for rich nations and rich consumers. Explain why you believe this statement is accurate or inaccurate as it relates to the green marketing of consumer products.
3. Explain the differences and similarities between Paul Newman's Own line of food products and Ben & Jerry's ice cream in terms of how their social benefit is positioned to the public.

Source: ABC News, *Business World,* Show #141 (July 2, 1989).

12

Media Buying

Chapter Objectives

When you have completed this chapter, you should be able to:

- Explain how media buying is different from media planning and how it complements media planning
- Understand the major duties of a media buyer: research analyst, expert evaluator, negotiator, and troubleshooter
- Explain how buyers translate media plan objectives into target-directed advertising schedules
- Understand why media pricing and negotiating skills will have even greater roles in the advertising strategies of the 1990s

REEBOK PUMPS UP FOR MEDIA BUYING

In 1991 Reebok International, marketers of sport and recreation shoes, captured the attention of the advertising agency business by removing the media-buying function of its $40 million advertising account from its advertising agency, Hill, Holiday, Connors, Cosmopulos in Boston, and hiring DeWitt Media of New York to handle all of its media-buying activities. The Boston agency will continue to handle the advertising planning and creative work for Reebok, but now Reebok has a firm specializing in the buying function. Although advertising agencies traditionally perform all media duties as part of the "full-service" concept, some marketers do not find this fully satisfactory. "The word is out that unbundling services [separating duties between companies] works. Clients are beginning to realize that they can get a better job going to two different specialists," says Roy Muro, president of Vitt Media International, a major media-buying company.

Not too long ago advertising media buying was thought to be a drab and tedious process that simply involved "filling in the lines" of the media plan by choosing the media placements and signing the paperwork. It was considered just another service provided by agencies under the commission system. As the Reebok story suggests, however, the days of taking media buying for granted are over.

Media-buying companies, which began in the 1960s, have a single purpose: to find the desired space or broadcast positions for the lowest available price and to do this better than the typical ad agency media-buying department. To accomplish this, specialty buying firms use experienced media buyers, full media audience research services, and "leading-edge" computers and software. In a dollar-sensitive advertising economy where media costs have become a key pocketbook issue, Reebok and a growing list of other advertisers see media buying as a vital part of marketing success in the 1990s.*

Furthermore, advertisers can get a larger target audience for each dollar spent when the buying is done by skilled experts. Expertise in media is demanded in this era of new media sources, open pricing, and a general wheel-and-deal atmosphere. Ad 12.1 for VideOcart is an example of a new opportunity in media buying. To understand media buying we first need to see how it fits with media planning.

The media planning and media buying functions overlap to a certain degree. For example, when planners recommend magazines as a target medium, they specify which titles to use as well as the schedule for the publications. The buyer then negotiates prices, placement positions, and merchandising possibilities. With other media, however, the planners are much less specific. How specific a media planner gets depends on the planning timetable. Media plans are usually developed well before the beginning of the advertising campaign, so early that the choice of media placement often is not yet available. Broadcast programs, for example, now change significantly; some programs may even be eliminated from the station's or the network's schedule. Even the available positions of renewed programs may be sold to other advertisers before the client's campaign begins. In such situations the media planner's suggestions for placements must be fairly general. In contrast, the media buyer who works much closer to the campaign calendar, will make all the specific decisions on where and when the advertising will run. This shared responsibility between planner and buyer is just one of the features of a professional media department.

*Adapted from: Cynthia Rigg, "Buying Gets Hot," *Advertising Age* (November 12, 1990):24.

AD 12.1
Media-buying expertise involves a constant search for unique media vehicles, such as the shopping cart technology. (Courtesy of VideOcart, Inc., Chicago, IL.)

MEDIA-BUYING FUNCTIONS

A media buyer has a number of distinct responsibilities and duties, which we will describe here in an operational sequence. We will discuss some of the most important buyer functions in more detail later in the chapter.

Providing Inside Information to the Media Planner

Media buyers are close enough to day-to-day variations in media popularity, pricing shifts, and media organizational changes to be a constant source of inside information to media planners. For example, a newspaper buyer discovers that a key newspaper's delivery staff is going on strike, a radio-time buyer learns a top disk jockey is leaving a radio station, or a magazine buyer's source reveals that the new editor of a publication is going to seriously change the editorial focus. All of these things can influence the strategy and tactics of current and future advertising plans.

Media performance (audience reaction) is also very changeable. In many advertising agencies the media buyers are specialists who carefully monitor changes in audience patterns as reflected in field research. One of the more active media areas is in spot or market-by-market television. Buyers who specialize in negotiating spot schedules constantly check the rating reports from each television market. Time buyers also discuss programming changes with sales representatives in order to anticipate how schedule shifts might affect current and future schedules.

Media Vehicle Selection

One essential part of buying is choosing the best media vehicles to fit the target audience's aperture. The media planner lays out the direction, but

AD 12.2
CNN Headline News portrays itself as a vehicle to reach an audience that network programming cannot. (Courtesy of Turner Broadcasting System, Inc.)

the buyer is responsible for choosing the specific media. Armed with the media plan directives, the buyer seeks answers to a number of difficult questions. Does the vehicle have the right audience profile? Will the program's current popularity increase, stabilize, or decline? How well does the magazine's editorial format fit the brand? Does the radio station's choice of music offer the correct atmosphere for the creative theme? How well does the newspaper's circulation pattern fit the advertiser's distribution? The answers to those questions bear directly on the campaign's success.

For example, Ad 12.2 for CNN Headline News offers advertisers a vehicle for reaching an audience interested in a type of programming different from that carried on the major networks. In 1991 CNN established itself as a major news station with its coverage of the Gulf War.

Media buyers expect CNN's standing as an advertising vehicle to improve. On January 16, 1991, the day war broke out, CNN achieved a 7.3 cable rating, its highest rating ever. Each rating point represents 568,000 households. The network's prime-time rating increased to an average 16.5 for January 17. According to Louis Schultz, executive vice president–director of media services for Lintas:USA, New York, the war coverage "help[ed]" CNN a lot, both for image and future sales."* (For more information on media coverage of the Persian Gulf War, see the Issues and Applications box in Chapter 4.)

*Crain News Service, written by Wayne Walley and the *Electronic Media* staff, "CNN Gulf Coverage Shines," *Advertising Age* (January 21, 1991):1, 52.

Negotiating Media Prices

In the 1990s nothing is considered more crucial in media buying than securing the lowest possible price for placements. Because time and space charges make up the largest portion of the advertising budget, there is continuing pressure to keep costs as low as possible. To accomplish this, buyers operate in a world of transaction or negotiation. Media buyers are expected to bargain for every possible dollar, and it takes all their skill to do this for every schedule.

Monitoring Vehicle Performance

In an ideal world every vehicle on the campaign schedule would perform at or above expectations. Likewise, every advertisement, commercial, and posting would run exactly as planned. In reality, underperformance and schedule problems are facts of life. The buyer's response to these problems must be swift and decisive. Poorly performing vehicles must be replaced or costs must be modified. Production and schedule difficulties must be rectified. Delayed response could hurt the brand's sales.

Postcampaign Analysis

Once a campaign is completed, the buyer's duty is to review the plan's expectations and forecasts against what actually happened. Did the plan actually achieve GRP, reach, frequency, and CPM objectives? Did the newspaper and magazine placements run in the positions expected? Such analysis is instrumental in providing the guidance for future media plans. For a full discussion of postcampaign research see Chapter 21.

These five tasks provide highlights of media buying. For a better understanding of buying operations, however, we need to look at some of these duties in closer detail.

SPECIAL SKILLS: EXPERT KNOWLEDGE OF MEDIA OPPORTUNITIES

If you were to ask media buyers what they need to know in order to do their jobs, they would probably say "Everything I can." Buying media has a great many dimensions, and many of these are subject to change. Network and local television stations are constantly changing and rearranging programs. Radio stations alter their music formats. Media audiences change their habits. Even media prices are fluid and increase or decrease at different times.

To keep up with all these shifts and changes, media buyers must develop a deep and specialized knowledge. They need experience to anticipate how changes will affect the advertiser's plans. Many agencies insist that media buyers concentrate on a single medium. For example, television buyers do nothing but buy television time. Whereas media planners work with a broad range of opportunities, media buyers develop narrow but deep expertise in one medium. This expertise involves several areas, including media contact, audience characteristics, and research evaluation.

Media Content

As we emphasized in Chapter 9, media placement strategy is more than a popularity contest of choosing the media vehicles with the largest target au-

NEW MEDIA ALTERNATIVES

In a world of constant technological innovation media buyers are continually exposed to new alternatives for presenting their clients' messages to the public. Betsy Frank, senior vice president–director of television information and new media for Saatchi & Saatchi Advertising, New York, discusses some of the creative alternatives available to media buyers today.

All of the opportunities discussed in this box expand the creativity that has come to be associated with media. Each must prove itself, however, and success is gauged in terms of audience measurement. A new medium must do two things: It must show how the opportunity fits in, and it must offer something that other opportunities do not. In shaky economic times, in particular, advertisers tend to stay with traditional media and avoid new opportunities. Media buyers must weigh the "gut feeling" that a new opportunity is valuable against the rational likelihood that it will be profitable for their clients.

Most media innovations involve the use of television because it is such a pervasive medium. Whereas people have cut down on other media-related activities, they have increased their television viewing in the last two decades from 10.5 hours a week, or 30 percent of total leisure time, to over 15 hours a week, or 38 percent of leisure hours.

Cross-Media Deals. Media buyers must know their clients' needs and either take this information to the sellers who have developed opportunities or suggest the opportunities to the sellers themselves. This kind of interaction helps sellers create more client-specific deals.

Place-Based Media. Place-based media are those that expose users to messages where these messages are most likely to be received—in schools, doctors' offices, waiting rooms, and the like. Consumers are not a "captive audience" who stay home all the time, so the media must seek them out wherever they go. Because television is the most important source of entertainment and information, it is typically used for place-based media.

Checkout Channel in Supermarkets. ActMedia and Turner Broadcasting System (TBS) realized the value of putting a television set "where people stand for a period of time." As of early 1991 the Checkout Channel was still being tested in selected supermarkets. Its main challenge is to distinguish itself from the other in-store media, such as aisle displays and shopping carts.

Interactive Media. Interactive media offer a way to target an audience and talk one-on-one with consumers. Telephones have become a direct-marketing tool; computers are used to advertise products and services. The Fox network is even considering producing an interactive game show.

Source: Adapted from "Alternative Media Worth Watching," *Advertising Age* (January 21, 1991):42.

dience. Often the buyer must also judge the message environment. Does it have the right mood or style for the advertiser's message? Is the media vehicle overcrowded with other ads or commercials? Is it careful in its production of messages? The answers to these questions cannot be found in reader surveys or broadcast ratings. Buyers monitor sample copies of publications, listen to off-the-air tapes, and study analyses of media content.

For their part, the media know how interested buyers are in areas beyond audience members. *USA Today,* for example, affirms a particular connection with its readers by telling buyers "People get into it because they get so much out of it".

Audience Habits

Audiences' media preferences are neither stable nor consistent. People are fickle about how they spend their leisure time. Their interests change with the seasons. They grow tired of one entertainment mode and shift to another. Buyers cannot afford to wait until the shift is obvious; they must

The Seal that sells the seal.

Your ordinary run-of-the-sea seal doesn't have it. Only the Dakin seal carries the Good Housekeeping Seal. The Dakin seal earned it by conforming to the requirements of Good Housekeeping magazine. Now Dakin proudly displays our Seal on its seals and lions and tigers and giraffes and the rest of the kingdom.

A recent study by Simmons shows retailers and advertisers agree that the Good Housekeeping Seal helps sell their products. Consumers say it helps them decide which products to buy. Call it part of a label if you want. We like to think of it as a performing Seal.

Good Housekeeping

Good Housekeeping is a publication of Hearst Magazines, a division of The Hearst Corporation. © 1987 The Hearst Corporation.

AD 12.3
In this ad *Good Housekeeping* emphasizes its ability to reach a particular audience. (Courtesy of *Good Housekeeping.*)

sense it coming and select accordingly. Fresh and interested media options provide the best opportunities for aperture. Buyers who can judge where media audiences are headed will have their messages prepared. What images are being used in Ad 12.3 for *Good Housekeeping?* What types of advertisers would want to appeal to this audience?

Research Evaluation

Besides their constant exposure to standard audience research (such as Arbitron and SMRB), media buyers are inundated with research and special analyses by media salespeople. This information may be special interpretations of standard research, or it may be a special research study ordered by the station or publication. Because such research is less than objective, buyers must carefully judge its accuracy and fairness. Did it follow statistical guidelines? Was the sample size adequate? Were the survey questions unbiased rather than leading? Buyers are responsible for deciding if sales-presented research is valuable to the client.

SPECIAL SKILLS: KNOWLEDGE OF MEDIA PRICING

Advertisers bear many costs in the advertising campaign. They must pay for the talent that develops the message, the production to create the message, and, above all, the media costs to place the message before the target audience. With few exceptions, media costs are the largest area of advertising investment.

Media Cost Responsibilities

Media buyers must be experts in all aspects of media pricing. They not only conduct current price negotiations, but are also responsible for gathering historical price experiences and projecting future changes.

The buyer's cost training begins with an understanding that the advertiser and the media are adversaries when it comes to pricing. Marketers want the lowest possible price, and the media try to charge as much as they can. As the advertiser's representative, the buyer is expected to use all possible leverage to secure the lowest prices. At the same time, they must not sacrifice target audience profiles or reach objectives just to meet price goals. Buying television spots that run at 3 A.M. might be cheap but may not fit the advertiser's needs. The price paid must be balanced against the size and quality of the audience delivered.

Media buyers must develop skills in three cost areas: charting media cost trends, learning to use media rate cards, and balancing audience to cost efficiency (CPM). The following discussion describes each of these areas in more detail.

average cost trends *A history of changes in the average unit (per message) prices for each medium that is used in cost forecasting.*

Average Cost Trends. The average prices paid in the recent past for each medium are **average cost trends**. Trends can be compiled in different ways: national trends for each medium, summaries of key marketing areas, or trends for particular media vehicles, such as sports programs.

The most recent national trends for some of the major media are shown in Table 12.1. The price averages reflect many variables, such as the rate of inflation and the consumer price index, but media costs increase at higher rates than do these other variables.

TABLE 12.1
Measured media spending in 1990

Rank	Media	Top 200 brands			All measured brands		
		1990	1989	% chg	1990	1989	% chg
1	Network TV	$6,181.0	$5,477.4	12.8	$10,132.3	$9,559.0	6.0
2	Spot TV	3,149.5	2,906.2	8.4	9,293.3	9,030.4	2.9
3	Newspaper*	2,063.2	1,987.6	3.8	9,679.1	9,514.5	1.7
4	Magazine	2,023.4	1,971.2	2.7	6,737.7	6,594.9	2.2
5	Syndicated TV	856.8	592.5	44.6	1,587.6	1,286.7	23.4
6	Cable TV networks	458.4	353.2	29.8	1,110.2	952.5	16.6
7	National spot radio	363.8	322.5	12.8	1,143.3	889.0	28.6
8	Network radio	357.1	346.4	3.1	766.4	696.2	10.1
9	Outdoor	150.8	137.8	9.4	688.8	705.8	(2.4)
	Subtotal print media	4,086.6	3,958.8	3.2	16,416.7	16,109.4	1.9
	Subtotal broadcast media	11,366.6	9,998.2	13.7	24,032.9	22,413.9	7.2
	Total	15,604.0	14,094.8	10.7	41,138.5	39,229.1	4.9

Notes: Dollars are in millions.

*Includes newspaper-distributed Sunday magazines.

Source: Reprinted with permission from *Advertising Age,* May 20, 1991, p. 19, p. 7a.

Copyright Crain Communications Inc., 1991.

Media Price Formats (Rate Cards).   Each media-buying company has its own way of charging for its services. Some, such as national cable and network television, prefer not to use set pricing at all. Instead, they allow complete negotiation with each advertiser to determine the price. (Open pricing will be discussed in more detail later in the chapter.) Those media that wish formally to present price schedules do so through a published format called a *rate card,* which includes the price for each message unit (size or length), the types of incentive discounts available, and scheduling and production requirements.

Although companies using rate cards follow general patterns, there is no standard for prices, discounts, or scheduling. Each rate card is unique. Buyers must learn to understand each format and how it can be used to the maximum benefit for the advertiser. The variety of rate cards and formats may seem overwhelming to beginning media buyers, but through steady experience the buyer learns to master each approach. To give you some idea of how the rate cards are organized, here are two illustrations—one for magazines and one for television.

Consumer Magazines.   Figure 12.1 is an excerpt from a rate card used in the past by *Rolling Stone* magazine. Notice that rates for black-and-white and color advertisements are listed separately and that the various unit sizes are priced individually.

Rolling Stone's discount structure is based on frequency (the number of ad units contracted for within a contract year). In other words, the more units used by an advertiser within the contract, the lower the price charged for each ad. To illustrate, look at the one-page "black/white rate." If the advertiser bought only one ad, the price for a page would be $22,825. If, however, the advertiser bought a total of 13 advertisements, the page cost would drop to $21,225, or a discount of $1,600 ($22,825 − $21,225).

Advertisers can receive these discounts in advance (before they run the full schedule) or as a lump sum at the end of the schedule contract (a *rebate*). If discounts are taken in advance and the advertiser does *not* complete the schedule, the advertiser has to pay the difference between the discount taken and the discount earned (called a *short rate*).

Discounts are only a small portion of the magazine's rate card. Other parts of the card cover geographic portions of the circulation for sale, issue closing dates, and mechanical (production) requirements. Some magazines have extremely detailed rate cards that amount to a small book of rates and discounts.

Rolling Stone

FIGURE 12.1
Rolling Stone **Rate Card**   *Source: Rolling Stone* magazine.

5. BLACK/WHITE RATES

	1 ti	7 ti	13 ti	25 ti	39 ti
1 page	22,825.	22,140.	21,225.	20,085.	19,630.
3/4 page	18,265.	17,715.	16,985.	16,075.	15,710.
1/2 page	13,690.	13,280.	12,730.	12,045.	11,775.
1/4 page	7,990.	7,750.	7,430.	7,030.	6,870.
1/8 page	4,570.	4,435.	4,250.	4,020.	3,930.
Spread	45,650.	44,280.	42,455.	40,170.	39,260.
1/2 Spread	27,380.	26,560.	25,465.	24,095.	23,545.

	50 ti	75 ti	100 ti
1 page	18,715.	18,030.	17,345.
3/4 page	14,975.	14,430.	13,880.
1/2 page	11,225.	10,815.	10,405.
1/4 page	6,550.	6,310.	6,070.
1/8 page	3,745.	3,610.	3,475.
Spread	37,435.	36,065.	34,695.
1/2 Spread	22,450.	21,630.	20,810.

FREQUENCY DISCOUNT

Frequency discounts available only when a regular advertising schedule is adhered to; otherwise, frequency discounts computed at end of advertising year and a rebate or shortrate made to advertiser at that time to the nearest applicable discount.
Frequency discounts to non-contract advertisers given as earned in any 12-month period.

MULTIPLE PAGE DISCOUNTS

Advertisers purchasing 4 or more pages for one brand in a single issue will be granted a 5% multiple page discount. Pages may run consecutively, in a single printed form, or throughout the issue. Regular frequency discounts apply in addition to the special multiple page discount with each page counting as 1 insertion.

COLOR RATES
2 color:

	1 ti	7 ti	13 ti	25 ti	39 ti
1 page	29,370.	28,490.	27,315.	25,845.	25,260.
3/4 page	23,495.	22,790.	21,850.	20,675.	20,205.
1/2 page	17,625.	17,095.	16,390.	15,510.	15,160.
1/4 page	10,280.	9,970.	9,560.	9,045.	8,840.
Spread	58,740.	56,980.	54,630.	51,690.	50,515.

	50 ti	75 ti	100 ti
1 page	24,085.	23,200.	22,320.
3/4 page	19,265.	18,560.	17,855.
1/2 page	14,455.	13,925.	13,395.
1/4 page	8,430.	8,120.	7,815.
Spread	48,165.	46,405.	44,640.

4 color:

	1 ti	7 ti	13 ti	25 ti	39 ti
1 page	33,405.	32,405.	31,065.	29,395.	28,730.
3/4 page	26,725.	25,925.	24,855.	23,520.	22,985.
1/2 page	20,045.	19,445.	18,640.	17,640.	17,240.
1/4 page	11,690.	11,340.	10,870.	10,285.	10,055.
Spread	66,810.	64,805.	62,135.	58,795.	57,455.
1/2 Spread	40,090.	38,885.	37,285.	35,280.	34,475.

	50 ti	75 ti	100 ti
1 page	27,390.	26,390.	25,390.
3/4 page	21,915.	21,115.	20,310.
1/2 page	16,435.	15,835.	15,235.
1/4 page	9,585.	9,235.	8,885.
Spread	54,785.	52,780.	50,775.
1/2 Spread	32,875.	31,670.	30,470.

Summer Double and Year-End Double Issues will have a rate increase based on a higher rate base guarantee.

```
SPOT ANNOUNCEMENTS
          30 SECONDS—DAYTIME
                                    F    P1   P2   P3
MON THRU FRI, AM:
6-8, CBS News/Morning Program ......   35   30   25   20
8-9, Wil Shriner Show .................   45   40   35   30
9-noon, CBS Morning Rotation ........   55   50   45   40
PM:
Noon-12:30, News .....................   75   70   65   60
12:30-3, CBS Afternoon Rotation .....   45   40   35   30
3-5, Early Fringe Rotator ............   95   85   75   65
3-3:30, Love Connection ..............   70   60   50   40
3:30-4, Newlywed Game ...............   70   60   50   40
4-4:30, Superior Court ...............   85   75   65   55
4:30-5, People's Court ...............  120  110  100   90
5-5:30, News .........................  100   90   80   70
5:30-6 Mon thru Sun, CBS Evening
   News ..............................  160  150  140  130
6-6:30, News .........................  230  220  210  200
6:30-7 ...............................  160  150  140  130
10-10:30 Mon thru Sun, News .........  230  220  210  200
10:30-11:30, CBS Late Movie I .......   70   60   50   40
10:30 pm-midnight, Late Movie II .....   70   60   50   40
10:30 pm-1 am, Late Night III ........   45   40   35   30
1-2 Fri, Friday The 13th-The Series ...   35   30   25   20
SAT, AM:
6-7, All Star Wrestling ...............   35   30   25   20
7-noon, CBS Kids Rotation ...........  120  100   80   60
PM:
Noon-6 Sat/Sun, CBS Sports/Various  150  130  110   90
6-7, Hee Haw .........................  200  190  180  170
10:30-11:30, Universal Wrestling
   Federation ........................   85   75   65   55
11:30 pm-12:30 am, WWF Wrestling ..   75   65   55   45
12:30-1 am, TBA ......................   35   30   25   20
SUN, AM:
7-noon, Religious Rotation ...........   60   50   40   30
PM:
10:30-11:30, To Strengthen Our
   Wings .............................   60   50   40   30
11:30 pm-12:30 am, Jimmy Swaggert   60   50   40   30
12:30-1 am, TBA ......................   35   30   25   20
1-6 am Mon thru Sun, Country Music
   TV/CBS Nightwatch ................   35   30   25   20
```

FIGURE 12.2
Local Television Rate Card

Local Television. Individual television stations have a difficult task preparing published prices and discounts because of the constant change in their audience size and composition. Time costs are based on program popularity, which is anything but stable.

Some local stations, following the practice of national networks, have eliminated rate cards in favor of "quoted" prices when the time buyers request commercial availabilities. Those stations that still use rate cards believe that buyers need to know the range of prices the station offers. The challenge to the station is to present a rate card that offers program-related time prices with enough flexibility to cover changes in audience and advertiser demand.

Figure 12.2 offers an excerpt of a rather popular format of a local television rate card. It is designed to give the buyer some idea of pricing while keeping the opportunity for negotiation open.

The station can use any of the four prices (F, P1, P2, P3) depending on certain conditions. Furthermore, the time buyer is often allowed to choose the price the client will pay for the program position as long as the schedule requirements, set by the station, are followed. These conditions are known as *preemptibility*. Preemptive prices (identified by the letter "P") involve some risk for the time buyer. For example, suppose a buyer wants to use the "P2" price in buying time on *CBS News/Morning Program* because it is less than the "P1" or the "F" price. If another advertiser decides to pay a higher price, such as "P1," for the same program, the station can move the buyer's client out of that program. This moving of advertisers is known as *preempting*. On rate cards of this design, "P1" means a move with 2 weeks' notice—that is, the schedule can stay for 2 weeks before the preemption takes place. The "P2" and the "P3" carry a 1-week notice and 48-hour notice, respectively.

Preemptibility creates a gamble for the time buyer. Will the station have enough demand at the higher rate to move the buyer's client? If no movement occurs during the length of the schedule, the buyer has succeeded in getting the program position at a lower price. The buyer who does not want to risk schedule changes can choose the "F" level price which means no chance of preemption ("F" stands for fixed). Pay more or risk a schedule change—that is the risk with preemptible rate cards. Experienced buyers are valuable because they are able to balance the risk and low prices to the advertiser's advantage.

TABLE 12.2
Major Media Cost-per-Thousand Percentage Changes, 1989–1991

Medium	1989–1990	1990–1991
Television		
Prime evening, network	+10.9	+7.7
Daytime, network	+ 8.4	+6.8
Spot market	+ 5.6	+5.4
Daily newspaper	+ 6.5	+5.8
Consumer Magazines	+ 5.6	+5.7
Outdoor	+ 4.0	+3.0
Spot market radio	+ 4.5	+4.7

Note: All 1990 and 1991 figures are based on agency estimates.

Source: "Media Cost," *Marketing & Media Decisions* (August 1990):23.

Cost-per-Thousand (CPM) Trends

CPM trend analysis *Longitudinal (long-term) history of average cost-per-thousand tendencies of advertising media that is used to assist in forecasting future CPM levels.*

The CPM trends are a more sensitive mirror of change in media costs. In Chapter 9 we showed that the CPM is affected by either a change in audience size or a change in unit prices. In Table 12.2 notice that the CPM increase for prime-time network television is greater than the increase in prime unit costs. This is an example of a dual change: Although units costs for prime time increased, the audience popularity of prime time dropped. The **CPM trend analysis** shows the historical fluctuations in price and audience. It is also valuable in forecasting future changes.

SPECIAL SKILLS: MEDIA VEHICLE SELECTION AND NEGOTIATION

A buyer's knowledge and expert preparation are tested when he or she represents the client in the media marketplace. It is here that execution of the plan takes place. The key questions are: Can the desired vehicles be located, and can a satisfactory schedule be negotiated?

These buying tasks are often anxiety-producing. In many circumstances media selection and negotiation is a high-stakes competition. The challenge is simple: Find the best possible audience vehicles and secure them for the lowest possible price. So easy to say—so hard to do.

The Boundaries: Working Within Plan Requirements

The boundaries of media negotiation are set by the advertising plan (Chapter 7). How many dollars are available? Who is the target audience? When does the advertising run? What atmosphere is desired? What is the duration of scheduling? Question after question must be answered in the construction of the advertiser's schedule. The following paragraphs detail some of the critical considerations.

PRINCIPLE
Negotiation involves getting the best schedule at the best price.

allocations *Divisions or proportions of advertising dollars among the various media.*

Dollar Allocations. The budget in an advertising campaign limits the dollars available to achieve plan objectives. **Allocations** are all the other money decisions concerning how to divide the budget. Allocations of dollars will determine how much money each medium will receive, how much will be spent per month or per week, how many dollars each geographic area will receive, and so on. Media buyers follow the allocation recommendations as closely as possible.

Here is a simple illustration of budgeting, allocation, and balancing. A local tire company budgets $100,000 for advertising in 1991. The media plan objectives can be achieved by allocating $50,000 for newspaper advertising and $50,000 for local radio advertising. When the buyer negotiates the schedule and prices, the costs for one medium may be higher than the anticipated $50,000. This may be acceptable if the goals for the other media can be achieved for less than $50,000. The skill lies in balancing costs with goals. Negotiating costs and scheduling is discussed in more detail later in the chapter.

Target Audiences. The media plan will give the buyer a clear profile, with media-sensitive characteristics, of the target prospect. Research services, such as Simmons, offer data on particular audience markets, such as the media preferences of children (see Ad 12.4). If multiple targets are

AD 12.4
Characteristics of target audiences are used to determine which vehicle is most appropriate for advertising certain products or services.
(Courtesy of Simmons Market Research Bureau.)

weighted audience values *Numerical values assigned to different audience characteristics that help advertisers assign priorities when devising media plans.*

specified by the plan, the plan should also specify a weight or priority for each characteristic.

Airline advertising offers a good illustration. Some adults fly much more than others. Suppose an airline profiled a key prospect as an adult traveler, between 25 and 54 years old, with a sales/managerial occupation. This profile specifies two elements: age and occupation. But which dimension is more important?

Target audience research from the media plan will often reveal the *relative* importance of each profile characteristic. Suppose the audience research for the airline indicated that although both the age and the occupation of prospects were important, occupation (professional or managerial) was twice as important as age. In such a situation the buyer would assign these audience priorities as value weights. The buyer does not simply count the audience because each member may have a different target audience value to potential airline sales. For each media vehicle evaluated, the portion of the media audience having the goal occupation would be doubled, whereas the age segment would be used as it appears (one time). Once the **weighted audience values** are calculated, they would be added together to determine which vehicle is best for the target audience needed. Table 12.3 demonstrates this process for two television shows, *60 Minutes* and *Nightline*.

TABLE 12.3
Target Audience Evaluation of Television Program Opportunities for Professionals and Managers, 25–54 Years Old

	Viewers per Program (in Thousands)				
Program	Prof./Mgrs.	Weighted Value	Age: 25–54	Weighted Value	Total Aud. Value
60 Minutes	45.0	90.0	125.2	125.2	215.2
Nightline	30.0	60.0	80.0	80.0	140.0

MARIE NETOLICKY, NATIONAL TELEVISION BUYER, DDB NEEDHAM/CHICAGO

I'm running late this morning—late enough so that I must phone in a "hold" to ABC before I leave home. A "hold" on two :30 units in *The American Comedy Awards* will reserve it at the negotiated price until I can get an order from the client. This was unexpected. We recommended a two-night sponsorship in the miniseries *The Bourne Identity,* based on the Robert Ludlum novel. Can you believe it? The ratings projection is good, but the client will not purchase it because they "don't like the leading man and woman." When will professional people learn to keep their personal feelings out of a sound business decision? Anyway, the last thing the client said last night was they *definitely* wanted two :30's in the awards show.

With that phoned in, I proceed to the office. When I get in, there are already five messages waiting for me. As I grab a cup of tea and look through my morning mail, the network calls me back to inform me that only one :30 unit is left in the awards show. They are holding that one :30 for me, but this changes everything. I now must go back to the drawing board and reconstruct another recommendation, because one :30 will not achieve the media plan goals.

While I try to rethink and rework, my two associates—planners on our accounts—pop in and out of my office with questions, problems, solutions, and jokes for comic relief. I could use them! Meanwhile I try to reach the media supervisor to discuss the changes to the recommendation, and we keep playing phone tag. My boss steps into my office to tell me he would like to meet with me and a few other supervisors in our group to discuss long-term national cable TV negotiations. The agency purchases all the following year's cable TV for all our clients in order to leverage the combined dollars for an efficient corporate rate. These negotiations can take months when you have as many as 15 cable networks with which to negotiate. I finally reach the media supervisor on the changes and we discuss the alternatives. She asks if I am available for a conference call with the client and, of course, I am. I wait until 12:40 P.M. to get a call back from her saying that I will not be needed for the conference call. Her boss is sending her over to the client to speak to them directly and to sell the new alternative recommendation.

By now it is 2:00 P.M. and I have to deal with the traffic problem. I speak to the associate media director on this account and we decide which of the other brands will cover the spots for the unfinished creative. I call a meeting with the broadcast traffic manager and the planner, and we agree on what is to be done. I really feel for the planner because his job is to change all the brand codes against the spots so that traffic can reschedule. Network and syndication are not bad, but the cable television changes involve several hundred units.

Finally, I receive the phone call I have been waiting for—the media supervisor calls and tells me that the alternative recommendation sold and that the client was happy. All that is left now is to get some promotional posters ordered with the client's logo imprinted on them.

It's getting near the end of the day, and I go through the rest of my mail. And the mail is endless . . . trade magazines to read, client correspondence that outlines new projects, contracts that must be checked and filed, and interoffice memos that need to be acted upon. And it starts all over again tomorrow.

(Courtesy of Marie Netolicky.)

Target audience weighting is common because many advertisers have either more than one prospect audience or one audience with several profile characteristics. As you might imagine, evaluating media vehicles means analyzing them through multiple audience examinations.

Timing and Continuity. Many schedules must work within a tight time frame. Buyers are expected to follow any flight or pulse pattern required by the media plan (see Chapter 9). The buyer must adjust the number of message placements to reflect the desired campaign calendar. This may mean arranging an on-off schedule to reflect a flight pattern. The greater the changes in intensity and in advertising periods, the more difficult the scheduling is for the buyer.

Gross Rating Point Levels. Many plans dictate weighting messages according to goals based on desired repetition (frequency) or exposure (reach). Often the rating point levels are used primarily for budget guidance. These levels are then translated by the buyer into insertion frequencies (print) or into announcement frequencies (broadcast). The buyer's task is to use the GRP guides (with the dollar allocation) to develop schedules that can also match frequency and reach objectives.

For example, imagine this situation for a fast-food company. The plan calls for a special month-long schedule for June in selected markets. The buyer's instruction might look like this:

- Markets: As listed.
- Desired GRP Level: 460
- Medium: Spot Television
- Dayparts: 25 percent of GRP in Evening-Fringe (5–7:30 P.M. E.S.T.) and
- 75 percent in Prime Evening (8:00–11:00 P.M. E.S.T.)
- High Reach Dispersion Needed

The buyer for each market would negotiate schedules for 4 weeks at an average target GRP of 115 per week (4 weeks × 115 AVG. GRP = 460). The placements must follow the dayparts and the proportions. Evening fringe should have 115 (25 percent of 460) must be scheduled. Prime evening should have 345 (75 percent of 460 GRP).

Media buyers may disperse their messages to increase their reach. **Dispersion** refers to a media policy that places the message in as many different programs and spots or publications as possible to avoid duplicating the audience. The request for *maximum dispersion* means that reach is to have a priority over frequency. In this case the buyer should avoid duplicating programs or publications as much as possible. Using different shows increases the opportunity for different or unduplicated audiences.

Negotiation: The Art of a Buyer

Just as a labor union transacts with management for pay raises, security, and work conditions, so does a media buyer pursue special advantages for clients. The following are some of the key areas of negotiation.

Vehicle Performance. Selection through negotiation is especially important where the medium offers many options and where the buyers might need to use forecasted audience levels. One typical example is network television.

Nighttime programming is particularly fluid or changeable. Because of the dollars at risk, networks are very quick to rearrange programs, to can-

dispersion *The use of as many different stations and programs as possible to avoid duplicating the message audience.*

AD 12.5
Buyer evaluation of advertising schedules is very dependent on research services such as those offered in this testimonial to **Nielsen**. (Courtesy of Nielsen Media Research.)

cel them and replace them with new ones, and to make other sorts of shifts. Buyers of time in network television are usually faced with selecting programs that (1) are new, (2) are not new but have been scheduled on a different night, or (3) have new lead-in programs. Selection must be made with little or no guarantee of audience popularity. Buyers deal with these uncertainties through careful research on the type of program (action, situation comedy), the rating history of the time slot, the audience flow patterns of competing programs, and a close examination of the content of the program itself, including scripts, talent, and all other elements. For all this research, buyers still need good "instincts" to make successful selections. Ad 12.5 for Nielsen is an example of a visually appealing media research ad.

Unit Costs.   Getting a low price has always been a goal for media buyers, but in the 1990s it appears to have become a rule. The published or opening price is no longer acceptable to advertisers. Rather, the so-called earned rate is now the starting point in negotiations.

fixed pricing *A traditional method of media pricing where rates are published and are applied equally to all advertisers.*

open pricing *A method of media pricing in which prices are negotiated on a contract-by-contract basis for each unit of media space or time.*

   Fixed pricing is a standard policy that treats all advertisers alike. Television executives decided that this price structure was too restrictive and limited profit potential. As a result, network television shifted to **open pricing,** in which each buyer or buying group negotiates a separate price for each program. Spot television followed, and some magazines are leaning in this direction.

   Open pricing makes buyer negotiation both important and risky. The balance or trade-off between price and audience objectives must be fully understood before an all-out pursuit of open pricing is attempted. Some media experts believe that pricing will replace all other values, and media will eventually be treated like a bag of grain or a barrel of oil. Buyers fear that placing too much emphasis on negotiating a low price will diminish the effectiveness of the media campaign.

They know there is a very important balance to maintain between cost and value. In other words, "you don't get something for nothing." No matter what pressure the buyer is under for low prices, he or she must balance a vehicle's quality with its cost. Talented buyers will not sacrifice impact for a cheap price.

preferred positions *Sections or pages of magazine and newspaper issues that are in high demand by advertisers because they have a special appeal to the target audience.*

Preferred Positions. In magazines there are assumed readership advantages in having the advertising message placed next to well-read pages or in special editorial sections. These placements are known as **preferred positions.** Imagine the value to a food advertiser of having its message located

AD 12.6
In addition to providing advertising space and time, the media must offer merchandising and sales support to advertisers.

A WORLD OF MEREDITH MERCHANDISING/SALES SUPPORT OPPORTUNITIES

We can also help create a customized merchandising/sales support program that maximizes the effectiveness of your advertising with your sales staff, distributors and dealers. Some of the many possibilities:

▲ Producing special videos for promotional use.
▲ Using consumer direct mail lists (35 million names in all) for specialized direct marketing.
▲ Creating special publications to maintain contact with your customers or with your distribution network.
▲ Using Meredith books as consumer premiums or in sales incentive programs.
▲ Conducting quantitative or attitudinal marketing research.
▲ Using our real estate network to reach homebuyers.

These and other programs can be used individually or in combination.

MEREDITH'S
CUSTOM
COVERAGE
PROGRAM

in a special recipe section that can be detached from the magazine for permanent use by the homemaker. How many additional exposures might that ad get? An ideal position in newspapers might be opposite the editorial page or a location in the food, financial, or sports section. With so many competing "voices," buyers are very anxious to find the most widely read sections.

Because they are so visible, preferred positions often carry a premium surcharge, usually 10 to 15 percent above standard space rates. In these days of negotiation space buyers are not hesitant about requesting that such charges be waived. Buyers will offer publications a higher number of insertions if the special positions are guaranteed without extra cost.

Merchandising Support for Advertisers. In the age of promotion, most of the major media are willing to assist advertisers with additional sales support activities. This has become a major focus for negotiation, and the activities themselves have become more elaborate and costly. In Ad 12.6 the Meredith company lists the support activities it offers to advertisers.

Consider a typical promotion that buyers for major soft-drink firms use in major markets. Radio stations are offered substantial summer schedules. In return, the station agrees to cosponsor a season-long promotional contest. Each day the station will send out a van specially painted with the advertiser's colors and logo. The audience is urged to find the van to receive prizes consisting of cases of soft drinks and cash. The station is also obliged to promote the contest on the air with a specific number of announcements per week, each announcement to include the name of the advertiser. All of these extras are offered free to the advertiser.

The pressure on buyers to gain extra leverage ("more bang for the buck") has grown enormously. Agencies, which once felt it unprofessional to squeeze the media for special concessions, are now willing to press very hard for this special treatment. Media buying is entering a new era of negotiation because so many media companies can offer all sorts of combinations.

SPECIAL SKILLS: MAINTAINING PLAN PERFORMANCE

Today a media buyer's responsibility to a campaign does not end with the signing of space and time contracts. Buys are made in advance on the basis of forecasted audience levels—the expectation that the audience for a vehicle will be at a certain level. If this happens—fine. But what if vehicles underperform? What happens if unforeseen events affect scheduling? What if newspapers go on strike, if magazines fold, if a television show is canceled? The buyer is responsible for monitoring audience research as well as for fixing any schedule problems.

Monitoring Audience Research

guarantees *Agreements in which the medium promises to compensate the advertiser should the audience fall below a specified level.*

When campaigns begin, the forecasts in the media plan are checked against actual performance. Whenever possible, buyers check each incoming research report to determine whether the vehicle is performing as promised. To offset the risk of forecasted performance, buyers seek concessions from the media in the form of "insurance." **Guarantees** offer the buyer some sort of protection if media audiences fall below projected expectations.

In broadcasting, the arrangement might mean that the network or station will add free placements to the schedule to offset audience decline. In print, particularly magazines, the guarantee may mean returning some of the contract cost to the advertiser if the circulation falls below a certain level.

Network Television. Network programming is under constant research scrutiny. Nielsen's National Television Index (NTI) reports are issued on nearly a continuous basis. "Overnight" surveys give performance ratings in a day or two. The frequency of these reports encourages close scrutiny of client schedules.

Spot Radio/Television. Stations and programs are selected, in part, on *past* rating reports. Whenever the rating report schedule cooperates, buyers will check on the spot schedule's current audiences. The sources are Arbitron and Nielsen Station Index (NSI) for television and Arbitron and Birch Reports for radio (see Chapter 10).

Outdoor Postings. Major users of billboards know from experience that it is prudent to check outdoor showings. This means sending buyers to at least the larger markets to *ride the showing*—that is, to check the condition of the billboards, the presence of obstructions (new buildings or trees), and any other situation that might impair traffic flow.

Magazines and Newspapers. Research reports on readership for magazines and newspapers are limited in frequency, but buyers also monitor issues to determine if advertisement positions are correctly placed.

Schedule and Technical Problems

makegoods *Compensation given by the media to advertisers in the form of additional message units that are commonly used in situations involving production errors by the media and preemption of the advertiser's programming.*

There are all sorts of temporary snags in scheduling and in the reproduction of the advertising message. For missed positions or errors in handling the message presentation, buyers must be alert to make the needed changes to reconcile difficulties. Most adjustments involve either replacement positions at no cost or money refunds. This policy of various forms of substitution is called *making good on the contract.* The units of compensation are known as **makegoods.** Here are some examples.

program preemptions *Interruptions in local or network programming caused by special events.*

Program Preemptions. Special programs or news events often interrupt regular programming. When this happens, the commercial schedule is also interrupted. **Program preemptions** occur nationally and locally. In the case of long-term interruptions—for example, congressional hearings or the coverage of the Persian Gulf War—the disruption can be very serious. Buyers have difficulty finding suitable replacements before the schedule ends.

Missed Closings. Magazines and newspapers have clearly set deadlines, called *closings* for each issue. Sometimes the advertising materials do not arrive in time. If the publication is responsible, it will make some sort of restitution. If the fault lies with the client or the agency, there is no restitution by the publication.

Technical Problems. Technical difficulties are responsible for the numerous "goofs," "gliches," and "foul-ups" that haunt the advertiser's schedule. In a classic example the buyer for a major airline received a call from the sales representative of the *Washington News,* who was most apologetic. A very unfortunate mistake had been made. It seemed the makeup staff at the newspaper had missed the intended position for the airline's ad and had run it instead on the *obituary page.* A makegood was forthcoming. In another case the buyer for a new consumer brand accidentally learned that someone in production at the television station had inserted a "super" (an optical phrase superimposed on the film or tape) informing viewers the product was only available in two small area towns. In truth those towns accounted for less than 10 percent of the brand's distribution. The damage was beyond calculation, and the station did more than make good. It settled out of court.

Most technical problems are not quite so disastrous. "Bleed-throughs" and out-of-register colors for newspapers, torn billboard posters, broken film, and tapes out of alignment are more typical of the problems that plague media schedules.

SUMMARY

- Media buying involves a series of duties and functions that are separate from media planning.
- Media buyers are responsible for executing the media plan recommendations. To do this they must find and select the media vehicles that best fulfill the advertiser's needs.
- The media buyer must observe activity in the media marketplace, analyze audience research, negotiate for positions and price, and monitor schedule performance.

- Price negotiation has become more important as media have shifted from fixed to flexible pricing. Buyers are under strong pressure to get the lowest possible rates without sacrificing desired audience values.
- Buyers are also responsible for maintaining the performance standards established by the media plan throughout the campaign. Changes that lower the value of the message placements must be rectified quickly and efficiently.

QUESTIONS

1. Explain the job-related differences between media planning and media buying. Which job do you feel would be more challenging and satisfying? Assume that both positions offer equal compensation.

2. Mavis Cord is the senior buyer-negotiator for network television for her agency. Through "insider" production contracts she has learned that a key program in the upcoming Willow Foods campaign is having serious production problems (star-director conflict). The start of the schedule is still 2 months away. Because this new program is projected to be one of the hits of the fall season, Willow management has been very excited about merchandising opportunities using the show's star. What should Mavis do, if anything, about this situation? How should she use her confidential information?

3. Your client is a major distributor of movie videotapes. Its yearly plan for magazines has been settled and you are in negotiation when you learn that a top publishing company is about to launch a new magazine dedicated to movie fans and video collectors.

Although the editorial direction is perfect, there is no valid clue as to how the magazine will be accepted by the public. Worse, there won't be solid research on readership for at least a year. The sales representative offers a low charter page rate if the advertiser agrees to appear in each of the first year's issues (monthly). There is no money to add the publication to the existing list. To use it you will have to remove one of the established magazines from your list. Is the risk worthwhile? Should the client be bothered with this information considering that the plan is already set? What are your recommendations?

4. Bob Maples is the head buyer on the Killer Cola account. One portion of the soft drink's media plan involves a news programming buy in Columbus for radio advertising. The plan's primary goal is to develop frequent exposure against the target audience. Below are the highlights of two competing proposals. Only one can be selected. Which station should Bob recommend and why?

Station	Monthly Cost ($)	Announcements per Month	Target Impressions per Month
WOOK	2000	50	307,000
KLOD	1992	83	285,000

5. *Environmental Weekly* is one of the fastest-growing publications in the consumer sector. It has just announced that it will adopt an open-pricing program for space rates. The sales manager of EW has warned, however, that each magazine buy will be negotiated separately (if one of the agency clients gains a low page rate, it will not set a standard for others). As the head of the magazine buying group, what problem(s) does this approach suggest to you? What will you recommend to the department's director?

6. Discuss the difference between open and fixed media pricing. How does the use of these price policies affect the buying process?

FURTHER READINGS

ARNOLD M., DONALD W. JUGENHEIMER, and PETER B. TURK, *Media Research Sourcebook and Workbook* (Lincolnwood, IL: NTC Business Books, 1989).

WALL, ROBERT W., *Media Math: Basic Techniques of Media Evaluation* (Lincolnwood, IL: NTC Business Books, 1987).

VIDEO CASE

Public Service Announcements: Skin Savers

Virtually all media companies must set aside a certain portion of their paid advertising time for public service announcements, or PSAs. PSAs are essentially free advertising provided to organizations that provide some public benefit, such as the American Cancer Society, the Society for a Drug-Free America, and others. Often the creative development time itself is donated at no cost by advertising agencies in what is called "pro bono," or "for free," work.

Although advertising agencies derive no revenue from pro bono work, many enjoy the opportunity to work on such projects because the clients usually lack the expertise of paid advertisers and, thus, give creatives much more leverage to do the kind of work they like to do with minimal interference. The result is often among the most memorable advertising in any media and the opportunity for creatives to work for a cause in which they personally believe.

When the Massachusetts division of the American Cancer Society identified that the rate of skin cancer in the state was increasing faster than anywhere else in the nation, it turned to Mintz & Hoke, Incorporated for assistance in creating an advertising campaign to raise the public's awareness of the problem. Not only was skin cancer the fastest growing type of cancer among men in the Bay State and second fastest among women, it was also one of the most common new cancers, with virtually one in three new cases diagnosed as skin cancer. Thus, there were two objectives to accomplish: to educate the public about skin cancer, including its causes and methods of prevention, and, more importantly, to get the public to advocate a free skin cancer screening test sponsored by the American Cancer Society. One of the measurable objectives for the campaign was to increase the number of people in the state signing up for the skin screening program because the largest number the society had ever tested in a single year was 1,500. The campaign was also designed to communicate to the public that although skin cancer is the most common form of cancer, it is also the most preventable.

The creative strategy primarily focused on raising the public's awareness to the dangers of sun exposure by attacking peoples' perceptions of the sun and tanning. However, the education effort was complicated by the need to show what skin cancer looks like, how to identify the early warning signs, and to teach the public what to look for in identifying skin cancers.

The target audience for the campaign was identified as women 25 to 45 years old because it was believed that, as the primary family care givers, women would pass along the message of skin cancer risks to fathers, husbands, and other family members. The secondary target was identified as people in high-risk categories, such as those with fair hair and light skin. As with any public service advertising, however, it was difficult to rely on adequate media weight to achieve the communications and campaign goals because virtually all of the media time was donated.

Nonetheless, the results of the "Flowers" campaign for the American Cancer Society achieved excellent results. The skin cancer screening program experienced a 465 percent increase in tests performed to over 7,000 people, and a total of 400 cases of skin cancers were detected. Based on a survey of screening participants, 65 percent were women and 45 percent within the target age group of 25 to 45-year-olds. Almost 75 percent of the screening participants indicated they had initially heard about the program via some form of the American Cancer Society's advertising campaign. Additionally, 85 percent of those participating in the screenings reported that they had followed at least some of the Society's guidelines to avoid sun exposure.

Although many media buyers are trained to negotiate with media companies for the lowest rates possible, it is much more difficult to "negotiate" for the limited amount of available free public service announcement time. As was the case with the American Cancer Society's "Flowers" campaign, however, producing and placing PSAs can often be the most rewarding aspect of advertising work.

QUESTIONS

1. What type of clout do you believe an agency's media buyer could possess that would increase his or her ability to procure public service announcement time from media companies?

2. Besides the more creative advertising that may be produced for PSAs, what other characteristics do you believe contribute to their "memorability"?

3. List five ads that you believe were produced as public service announcements.

Source: Courtesy of Mintz & Hoke, Inc.

CASE STUDY

Don't Let "Bambi" Get Away

Home Video Is a New and Dynamic Industry

As consumer industries go, home video is very young, having begun with the availability of videocassette recorders (VCRs) around 1980. Over the next 10 years, prerecorded videocassette (PRC) growth was driven by an explosion in VCR penetration, which grew from 29 percent in 1985 to 70 percent in 1990. By 1990 the PRC industry was enormous, with retail sales of over $10 billion.

After 1990 this seemingly automatic growth of PRCs based on new households with VCRs slowed, and the entire video market rapidly started to mature. Most industry sources expect VCR penetration to top out at 80 percent of households within the next few years. Furthermore, the VCR is no longer such a novelty in most homes, so usage has settled into consistent, but somewhat less frequent, use. In 1990 average household rental of videocassettes was about four to five cassettes per month; average PRC purchase was about four per year.

Sellthrough Versus Rental

The videocassette industry typically is broken down into two categories: rental and sellthrough, or purchase. In 1990 about 65 percent of retail sales were rental and about 35 percent were sellthrough, with sellthrough growing more rapidly and rental becoming flat.

After a film has a theatrical run, the video division of a studio uses box office results and audience research to assess its video potential as a rental-only or as a sellthrough release. This decision must be made carefully. Sellthrough titles are usually priced at about $10 to $30 each at retail. Good sellthrough titles typically will have sales from 3 million to 5 million units; a great title will have sales from 5 million to 9 million units. In 1991 only three titles had ever sold over 10 million units: *E.T.* (12.5 million, released in video in October 1988), *Bambi* (10.5 million, released in September 1989), and *Batman* (10.0 million, released in November 1989).

If a film is judged to have a more limited appeal, it is released as a rental-only title and priced to appeal to video-store owners, who will gradually pay off the cost over the rental life of the cassette. Rental titles are priced between $75 to $100, with the most successful achieving sales of about 600,000 units to retailers.

Although potential retail revenue on a successful sellthrough title is obviously much higher than a rental title, there are few titles with the consumer demand to be successful sellthrough titles. In addition, marketing and distribution costs associated with a sellthrough title are significant, much greater than costs to market and distribute a rental title.

Home Video Is a Hit-Driven Business

The engine of home video is the blockbuster movie. Typical new blockbuster hits move most of their total volume within the first 60 days of release. All marketing efforts and retailer energy are forced into very short windows, which has led to a fickle environment: When a title is "hot," it's on everyone's "must-have" list, and when it is only "lukewarm," it goes unwanted. Although home video is becoming a year-round business, traditionally 35 to 65 percent of sellthrough volume has moved into the fourth quarter of the year.

Nearly every target group rents PRCs. However, the best titles are those that appeal to the whole family or to children, *The Little Mermaid* and *Teenage Mutant Ninja Turtles,* for example.

Buena Vista Home Video Is the Industry Leader

Buena Vista Home Video (BVHV), the home video distribution, sales, and marketing arm of Disney Studios, has been number one in share for the past several years. BVHV markets 1) Disney animated classic movies, cartoons, and live-action films (such as *Son of Flubber*), which are primarily targeted at families with children, 2) Touchstone movies, which are often targeted at nonfamily, adult audiences, and 3) acquired materials, such as *Bullwinkle.* Most of BVHV's sellthrough titles are Disney products because Touchstone movies typically are sold as rental titles, with the exception of mega-hits, such as *Pretty Woman.*

Disney is very careful in its release strategy for its classic animated movies. Each year, the company chooses only one or two titles to be released from the vaults, usually for the fourth-quarter gift-buying season. After the holiday season no new orders are taken, and unsold copies can actually be returned to BVHV. That title is then returned to the vault, usually for about 7 years, until the next theatrical release. Past releases have included *Lady and the Tramp* (see Exhibits A-1 and A-2), *Pinocchio, Cinderella, Bambi, Peter Pan,* and *Jungle Book.* Although these classics are truly timeless, they are released into this hit-driven environment, where even these titles can get cold quickly because of the fast-paced sales environment. Within about 90 days, every movie, no matter how big, is old news to the retailer and even to most consumers, all of whom are waiting for the next big release.

Bambi Was Released for Christmas 1989

The heartwarming story of *Bambi,* with unforgettable characters, such as Thumper and Flower, and memorable lines like, "If you don't have nothin' nice to say, don't say nothin' at all," was released in September 1989 to capture maximum fourth-quarter video sales. It is clearly one of Disney's all-time great classics (see Exhibit B). Volume predictions—and hopes—were very high.

During 1989 the only big competitive movie was *Batman,* Warner's record-breaking summer release. Rumors were rampant at the annual video trade show in August (Video Software Dealers Association). Would

Warner release *Batman* on videocassette so close to its theatrical run? Probably not, as it wouldn't even be released for theaters in Europe until November. But if Warner waited until 1991, the *Batman* fever would be over.

It would appear that *Bambi* and *Batman* would not compete for the same consumer dollars—one is a young children's movie that is warm and wonderful, and the other is targeted to older children and adults and is, frankly, dark and sinister. However, the key target for Bambi is families with children, the key quality for any sellthrough title is repeatability, and the key ingredient for success is trade support: floor space for displays, window space for posters, and advertising space with low-price offers. Although BVHV and the trade had expected *Bambi* to be *the* hot item for 1989, *Batman* would be a fierce competitor in all these key areas. The release of a hit as

big and as "hot" as *Batman* would impact the sales of *Bambi* to retailers, and eventually to consumers.

There were other fourth-quarter competitors as well. *Wizard of Oz* (MGM/United Artists) was restored and rereleased with new footage and a consumer rebate from several Procter & Gamble products. *Who Framed Roger Rabbit?* (BVHV) came out with a special price rebate. In addition, *All Dogs Go to Heaven* (MGM/UA), *Land Before Time* (MCA), and a number of others were all competing for the same floor space, ad space, and space under a Christmas tree.

The marketing plan and advertising strategy for *Bambi* was based on BVHV's extensive consumer research. An intent-to-purchase study revealed enormous potential with especially high interest among mothers and kids under 12. BVHV's annual Attitude and Usage Study provided insights into the targets, demographics, and psychographics. BVHV knew the title would appeal to mothers because of their memories of the film, what it meant to them as they grew up, and their desire to share that part of their childhood with their own children. They also knew the story, the characters, and the values *Bambi* teaches about friendship and growing up were key to a persuasive advertising message. Finally, the fact that *Bambi* videocassettes were available for a limited time before being returned to the vault would create urgency for purchase.

The *Bambi* advertising strategy was to touch mothers' hearts by demonstrating how this classic story about growing up can touch their own children's hearts

EXHIBIT A-1

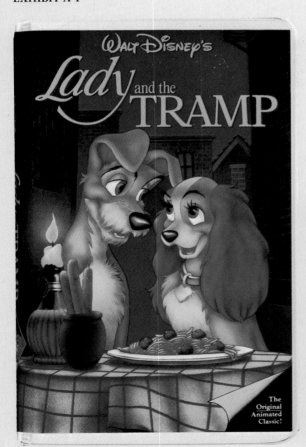

EXHIBIT A-2

EXHIBIT B

(see Exhibit C). The consumer benefit was, "When I buy *Bambi* on videocassette now, I will ensure that my loved ones will always be able to enjoy this most beloved Disney masterpiece."

In September BVHV's sellin to the trade for *Bambi* was unprecedented—over 10 million units, which could make *Bambi* the largest selling animated video of all time. *Bambi*'s marketing/advertising efforts for the holiday were strong, and typical for BVHV in 1990. They included advertising, primarily television and radio, a trade program for distributors and retailers, and a consumer rebate from Crest.

In October Warner made its announcement. *Batman* would be released immediately for sellthrough with a huge marketing program. *Bambi,* only out for a month, was at risk of becoming old news much too fast. The race was on.

In December consumer sales on *Bambi* sales were solid. Despite the diversion of trade attention and in-store space to *Batman,* over 7 million units of *Bambi* videocassettes had been sold to consumers before Christmas. *Bambi* had become one of the largest videocassette sellers of all times in the toughest video market in history. Overall consumer appetite had been big enough for two megahits and several other strong titles. Although early reports put *Batman* ahead of *Bambi* in consumer sales, BVHV ended the year as number one in overall sales. But the final chapter was still unfinished.

There was a big decision yet to be made. It was January; *Bambi* was no longer news and the pre-Christmas buying season had passed. BVHV management knew that despite strong *Bambi* sales there was more business to be had—more consumers had expressed interest in owning *Bambi* than had actually purchased it. The pre-Christmas competition probably meant that both films had not

EXHIBIT C

DISNEY HOME VIDEO
Bambi
:30 TV

<u>**"Eyes"**</u>   22 Aug 89 DR   **AS PRODUCED**

AVO:	Do you know what happens when these eyes meet these?
	And these?
	Love at first sight.
	Here at last, Walt Disney's Bambi.
OWL:	This is quite an occasion!
AVO:	With characters loved by generations.
FLOWER:	Garsh.
AVO:	One of the greatest movies of all time.
	The masterpiece everyone will watch with wonder, can finally be yours to treasure forever. On videocassette. It's Bambi.
	Only $23.99 after $3 refund with additional purchase.
	No one should grow up without Bambi.

reached their home-video potential. Should BVHV wait for the next hit title or risk investing costly additional marketing and sales efforts against a potentially cold title? A decision had to be made.

The company decided to risk a second marketing wave—a surprising move in the industry. The challenge was to communicate new urgency to trade and consumers in a compelling way on a title that had been out for 4 months. After March, unsold cassettes could be returned by retailers to BVHV and *Bambi* could be returned to the vaults. Further, no new videocassettes could be reordered until after the next theatrical rerelease, which usually happens every 7 years. The opportunity for reaching *Bambi's* potential would be gone. BVHV took a chance that consumers might be persuaded to buy an after-Christmas videocassette if they knew the truth—that *Bambi* could soon disappear from the shelves.

"Disappearing Classics" Was a Tough Retail Message
The advertising challenge was not an easy one: How to communicate to consumers that *Bambi* could become unavailable if families didn't buy now. No one knew how truly "unavailable" *Bambi* videos would become, or how fast. Furthermore, it would be difficult to create a commercial in keeping with a warm and friendly Disney and Bambi's character, with a potentially negative message.

A new advertising strategy was written with a direct, hard-hitting benefit: "If I don't buy Bambi now, I may miss the chance to share this Disney masterpiece with my children." The support was that 1) Bambi is an unforgettable story that all children love, and 2) it was a limited edition release that may become hard to find.

As a result of the new "Disappearing Classics" campaign, *Bambi* became the second-highest seller in the history of the industry—roughly 500,000 units ahead of *Batman!* Copies of other Disney classics, which were already on the shelf, began to sell as well. The disappearing classics idea worked so well for *Bambi* that is was repeated in January 1991 to make sure that all consumers who wanted *Peter Pan,* the 1990 Disney classic release, were reminded to purchase it before *Peter Pan* was put into the vault again. And, once again, BVHV was number one in share.

Courtesy of DDB Needham Worldwide and Buena Vista Home Video.

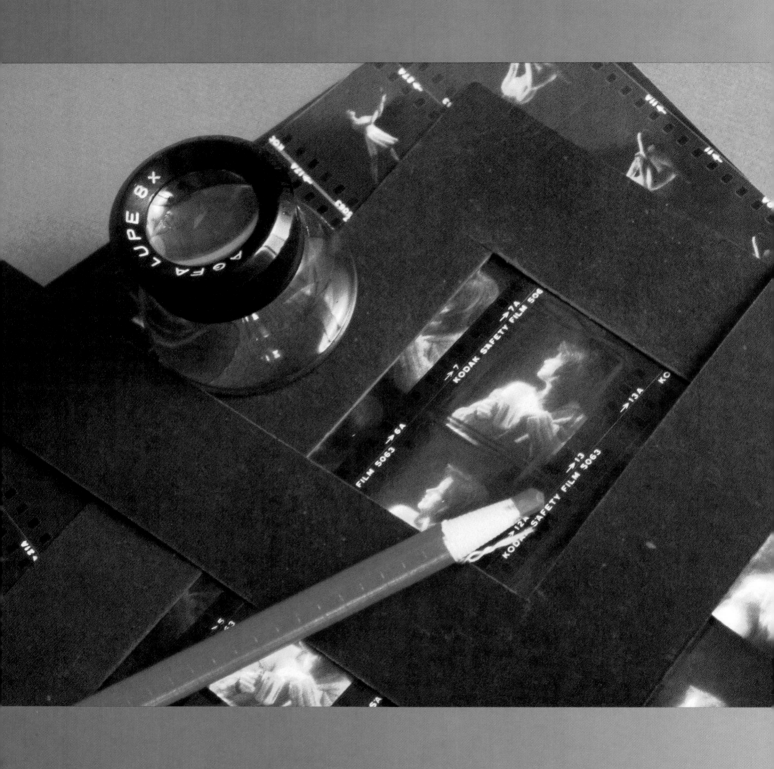

13

The Creative Side of Advertising

Chapter Objectives

When you have completed this chapter, you should be able to:

- List various characteristics of creative people
- Explain what advertisers mean by a creative concept
- Describe the various stages involved in creating an advertisement
- Understand how the various elements in an advertisement work together to create impact
- Distinguish between effective copywriting and adese

*T*AKE MY IDEA . . . PLEASE

Ads are easy to create, right? How many times have you watched a commercial and said, "I could come up with a better idea than that"? Joshua Levine, a columnist for *Forbes,* got that opportunity when he was invited by the Martin Agency in Richmond, Virginia, to join a creative team working on a new commercial for Mariott's Residence Inn hotel chain.

The objective of the assignment was to come up with an idea that would pull guests in on weekends. Compared to other hotels, Residence Inns have bigger rooms, full kitchens, and fireplaces, all designed to appeal to business travelers who stay an average of 4 to 14 days. The hotels lack room service, however, which makes them a hard sell for tourists and couples looking for a runaway weekend.

The first step in the assignment is the *creative briefing* given by the account executives (called "suits" by the creative team), who serve as liaisons with the client. This account team figures there is no way to sell a weekend getaway without room service, so the copy strategy is to focus on Residence Inn as a guesthouse in which to stash visiting relatives. The suits, worried the creatives will go off on some self-indulgent tangent, caution that it shouldn't become a commercial for "in-law haters."

The creative team, Levine included, hole up in an office and begin "concepting"—thinking out loud. This stage can take days or weeks, often nights and weekends as well. Levine explains the process: "We're supposed to think of an image, a line, or an idea and just say it." In creative sessions like this nothing is considered too off-the-wall. Even the lamest idea can spark someone else's brainstorm.

The Residence Inn session produces images of hordes of obnoxious nephews, blue-haired aunts, and bottom-heavy brothers-in-law. The copywriter describes the ultimate visiting relative nightmare: gypsies camped in the living room and pigs roasting on spits. Levine observes, "Cute, but it won't sell hotel space." The copywriter then throws out a line: "It's that time of year when friends and relatives drop in unexpectedly. And stay." The art director draws pictures: in-laws dropping out of the sky in parachutes with hatboxes, beach umbrellas, and suitcases. "We all like it," Levine notes, "but no one can figure out where to go with it." The rest of the day yields some good lines and amusing images, but nothing jells. The copywriter wants to do something with the line, "Rid your house of pests," but everyone knows the suits won't buy it.

The next day the art director has a flash: Use Henny Youngman, the comedian who knows more relative jokes than there are relatives. The team plays with one-liners and ways of picturing Youngman as he does 30 seconds of nonstop jokes. But how does he tie in with Residence Inn? The product is in danger of getting lost, a major problem with ads that are too creative or too funny.

Levine admits that his contributions up to this point have been marginal at best and says, "This advertising business is much tougher than it looks." Suddenly he gets an idea using Youngman's signature line and pipes up tentatively: "Take your visiting relatives to Residence Inn. Please." Bingo. The pieces fall together.

The job is not over, however. The next week the team runs the idea by the agency's creative director, who giggles at the jokes and instinctively completes the line before anyone else does. Youngman turns out to be available and affordable on the Residence Inn budget. Then the team has to get the idea past the suits, who have one objection: They want more sales message. The senior account executive wants to add more words to the closing line, but the creative team protests that it will throw the pacing off and make it sound like a joke with bad timing. As a compromise they agree to add the phrase "All the Comforts of Home" on screen under the Residence Inn logo at the end of the commercial.

There is still one more group to sell—the client. The creative and account team fly to Washington, D.C., where the idea is developed, explained, and justified to all the various executives involved with approving advertising and marketing ideas. As a member of the creative team lays out the spot, it is clear from the grins on the clients' faces that the idea has made it past the biggest hurdle of all.*

CREATIVE CONCEPT: THE BIG IDEA

creative concept *A "Big Idea" that is original and dramatizes the selling point.*

PRINCIPLE
Effective ads are built on strong creative concepts.

Behind every good advertisement is a **creative concept,** a "Big Idea" that makes the message distinctive, attention-getting, and memorable. Usually a Big Idea is simple and, after it has been developed, seems to be the "obvious" solution. You know a successful Big Idea when you find yourself saying "I wish I had thought of that."

This step is what advertising giant Otto Kleppner called "The Creative Leap."† To come up with the Big Idea, you have to move away from the safety of the strategy statements and leap into the creative unknown. The creative team's mission is to find an idea that has not been used before in order to communicate what might otherwise be a dull sales message.

Usually the concept is developed by a copywriter/art director team. These two people work together to generate as many ideas as they can, hoping that one of them will turn out to be the Big Idea. Both people are good at thinking in words and pictures, so they work as a team rather than as individual specialists.

Although the strategy statement may say everything we want said, it is not distinctive, attention-getting, and memorable. Strategy statements are dull outlines, platforms for in-house discussion and agreement, not messages that will persuade a consumer audience to buy or believe something.

The concept may come to mind as a visual, a phrase, or a thought that uses both visual and verbal expression. If it begins as a phrase, the next step is to try to visualize what the concept looks like. If it begins as an image, the next step is to come up with words that express what the visual is saying. The ideal concept is expressed simultaneously through both the visual and the verbal elements. Words and pictures reinforce one another, as in the Dial ad pictured in Ad 13.1.

What Makes an Idea Creative?

Creative ideas aren't limited to advertising. People such as Henry Ford, who created and then advertised his Model T, and Steven Jobs, the inventor of Apple Computers, are highly creative. They are idea men, creative problem solvers, and highly original thinkers. Creative people are found in business, in science, in engineering, even in advertising.

Although definitions of creativity vary, all agree that the focus of creativity is the end result—the idea that comes out of creative thinking. Stein says that creativity results in a "novelty that is accepted as useful, tenable, or satisfying by a significant group of others. . . . The result represents a 'leap,'

---

*Adapted from Joshua Levine, "Inside Ad Land," *Forbes* (October 15, 1990):180–81.
†Thomas Russell and Glenn Verrill, *Otto Kleppner's Advertising Procedure,* 11th ed. (Englewood Cliffs, NJ: Prentice Hall, 1990):457.

For both mildness and effectiveness, Dial is the anti-bacterial soap you can recommend with confidence.

That's why more hospitals use Dial than any other bar soap. And why doctors have been recommending Dial for over 40 years.

The next time you recommend a soap to your patients, recommend Dial. You can't find a better all-family soap.

No. 66258   Dr. Troiani
Bill Brichta
For a mild, effective anti-bacterial program; lather, rinse, and repeat as necessary.
Dial Soap

AD 13.1
This Dial ad demonstrates how words and pictures can work together to create impact. (Courtesy of DDB Needham Worldwide.)

not merely a step away from that which existed before but a good distance away."*

The creative leap is what sets the advertisement apart. The springboard for the leap is a solid strategy statement. Advertising has to be creative, but it must also be strategic. The nature of this relationship is expressed in the philosophy of DDB Needham Worldwide, summarized as relevance, originality, and impact (R.O.I.).

relevance *That quality of an advertising message that makes it important to the audience.*

Relevance.   Advertising is a disciplined, goal-oriented field that tries to deliver the right message to the right person at the right time. The goal is persuasion that results in either a change of opinion or a sale. Ideas have to mean something important to the audience. In other words, they must have **relevance.**

Advertising is a tough, problem-solving field where you don't have the luxury of waiting for a creative concept to appear. According to former advertising executive Gordon White, "It is creativity on demand, so to speak. Creating within strict parameters. Creativity with a deadline."†

empathy *Understanding the feelings, thoughts, and emotions of someone else.*

Advertising is directed at convincing people to do something. Unlike a painting, a building, or a technological breakthrough, creativity in advertising requires **empathy,** a keen awareness of the audience: how they think and feel, what they value, and what makes them take notice. A creative idea has to speak to the right audience with the right sales message. The purpose of advertising is first and foremost to sell the product, service, or idea. No matter how much the creative people or the client or the account executive may like an idea, if it doesn't communicate the right message or the right product personality to the right audience, then it won't work. Liking the idea simply isn't enough.

PRINCIPLE ————————
If it doesn't conform to strategy, reject it.

*Morris I. Stein, "The Investment Analyst: An Intermediary in the Creative Process," *Wall Street Transcript* (April 20, 1981):61.
†Gordon E. White, "Creativity: The X Factor in Advertising Theory," in *Strategic Advertising Decisions: Selected Readings,* Ronald D. Michman and Donald W. Jugenheimer, eds. (Columbus, OH: Grid, Inc., 1976):212.

Originality. An advertising idea is considered creative when it is novel, fresh, unexpected, and unusual. **Original** means one of a kind. Any idea can seem creative to you if you have never thought of it before, but the essence of a *creative* idea is that no one else has thought of it either.

In classes on creative thinking, a teacher will typically ask students to come up with ideas about, for example, what you can build with ten bricks. Some ideas—like a wall—will appear on many people's lists. Those are obvious and expected ideas. The original ideas are those that only one person thinks of.

An unexpected idea can be one with a twist, an unexpected association, or catchy phrasing. A familiar phrase can become the raw material of a new idea if it is presented in some unusual or unexpected situation. An ad for Bailey's Irish Cream, for example, shows the product being poured into a wine glass over ice cubes. The twist is in the headline that reads: "Holiday on Ice." A play on words is also a good way to develop something unexpected. The American Cancer Society used the headline "Fry Now, Pay Later" for its safe-tanning message (see Ad 13.2).

Clichés Unoriginal advertising is not novel or fresh; it is the common or obvious idea. Look-alike advertising copies somebody else's great idea. Unfortunately, a great idea is only great the first time around. When it gets copied and overused, it becomes a **cliché.** Even though professionals continually disparage copycat advertising, it remains a dominant advertising form. Although everyone is searching for a great idea, not everyone is lucky or talented enough to find one.

AD 13.2
This ad by the American Cancer Society illustrates creative use of a play on words. What other ads can you think of that use this device?
(Courtesy of DDB Needham Worldwide. Photography, Jeff Turnau)

One of the most copied advertising ideas in history is the "Perception/Reality" campaign for *Rolling Stone* magazine created by the Fallon McElligott agency The campaign, which began running in 1985, pairs people's "perceptions" of the magazine as a publication for hippies with the reality of who the early hippie readers of *Rolling Stone* have become. Using visual and verbal puns, the ad's perception side will show a picture of a map of Canada, for example, and the reality side will show a picture of an army recruitment brochure. The campaign has become so popular within the advertising community that every time a creative team has an assignment that asks them to change a perception, they are tempted to create a copycat ad. An example of the *Rolling Stone* campaign is shown in Chapter 9.

impact *The effect that a message has on the audience.*

Impact. To be creative, the ideas must also have **impact.** Most advertisements just "wash over" the audience. A commercial with impact can break through the screen of indifference and focus the audience's attention on the message and the product. An idea with impact helps people see themselves or the world in a new way. The classic campaign for V-8 vegetable juice demonstrates the impact of a creative idea when the various characters hit themselves on the forehead in the familiar gesture that says "Why didn't I think of that" while saying aloud, "I could have had a V-8." That ad expresses the impact and power of a relevant, new idea.

An ad with impact has the stopping power that comes from an intriguing idea—something you have never thought about before. An example of how a startling thought can stop you and make you think is Ad 13.3 for Lexus, with its powerful slogan, "The relentless pursuit of perfection."

AD 13.3
An advertisement with impact like this one for Lexus can stop the audience with an intriguing idea.
(Courtesy of Team One Advertising.)

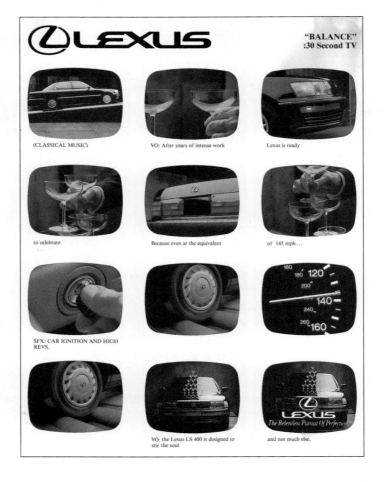

CONCEPTS AND CONTROVERSIES

THE CURSE OF THE CLIO

One of the great classic ads is the "I can't believe I ate the whole thing" commercial for Alka Seltzer. The industry loved it and it won all kinds of creative awards, but the client reported product sales actually went down during the period the commercial ran and, ultimately, the agency lost the account. The major advertising award in the United States—the Oscar for ads—is the Clio. The loss of clients by Clio-winning agencies has been referred to as the "curse of the Clio." Harry McMahan, who has written extensively on television, analyzed the Clio winners one year and reported that:

- Four of the agencies that won Clios lost the accounts.
- Another Clio winner was out of business.
- Another Clio winner eliminated its television budget.
- Another Clio winner gave half the account to another agency.
- Another Clio winner refused to put the winning entry on the air.
- Of the 81 television classics picked by the Clio festival in previous years, 36 were by agencies that had either lost the account or gone out of business.

To put it mildly, winning an award for creativity does not guarantee success for an agency.

The "curse of the Clio" has given rise to a heated debate in the advertising world about the function of award programs. Are award-winning advertisements winners for the client as well as for the creative team? Some people argue that the creative team views advertising differently than does the account executive or the client. Whereas creatives are concerned with originality, management has only one criterion for judging an ad: Does it increase sales?

This difference in perspective has been documented by Elizabeth Hirschman in a study in which she interviewed agency participants in the ad-making process. Hirschman found that these different perspectives are derived from the various ways people in agencies advance their careers. Creative players advance by developing "books" (portfolios) that demonstrate their ability to produce unique, high-quality creative ideas. In contrast, managers advance by demonstrating that they can manage the client's resources effectively and efficiently. "The copywriter succeeds by winning awards for creative commercials; the product manager succeeds by improving the client's market share and profitability."

The "curse of the Clio" raises several difficult questions for people concerned with advertising. Does creativity matter? Who should judge creativity and how should it be measured? How important are artistic standards? Which would you rather create, an ad that wins an award or an ad that increases sales for the client?

Sources: David Ogilvy, *Ogilvy on Advertising* (New York: Vintage Books, 1985):24; Harry McMahan and Mack Kile, "In TV Sports, One Picture Worth 10,000 Words," *Advertising Age* (April 27, 1981):50; and Elizabeth C. Hirschman, "Role-Based Models of Advertising Creation and Production," *Journal of Advertising 18,* no. 4 (1989):42–53.

Effective Creativity. Many advertising professionals believe that an ad is creative only if it meets the sponsor's objectives. The philosophy of one major worldwide agency is, "It isn't creative unless it sells." The Concept and Controversies box entitled "The Curse of the Clio" focuses on the debate about whether creative awards really measure anything of value. There are some advertising scholars, however, who feel that effective advertising can have a tremendous impact on public taste and make a positive aesthetic contribution as well as ringing up sales at the cash register.*

There is a real danger in focusing too heavily on the marketing objectives and ignoring the need for original, novel ideas. *Strategy hypnosis,* an extreme concentration on strategy, can stifle creative thinking. The environment can also block creative thinking. Bureaucracy, specialization, and time clocks can all hinder the spirit of exploration and playfulness necessary for creative thinking.

*Carl F. Walston, *The Aesthetic Dimension Of Advertising,* unpublished master's thesis, University of Colorado (1991).

Leonardo da Vinci, Albert Einstein, and Pablo Picasso all excelled in different fields, but all three qualify as creative geniuses. (Leonardo da Vinci and Albert Einstein courtesy of The Bettmann Archive and Pablo Picasso courtesy of UPI/Bettmann Newsphotos.)

Perhaps the environmental factor most inhibiting to creative advertising is the *risk-aversive* nature of many large organizations. Typically, a creative person will use a proven formula for an ad, knowing that the approach is safe and the ad probably won't fail, even though it may not be highly successful either. A new approach is always a gamble. The creative person who tries a new idea may be dismissed as lucky if the ad is successful or incompetent if it fails. Creative people often choose to play it safe when working with a multimillion-dollar investment.

The Creative Personality

Is creativity a personality trait we are born with, or can we be trained to be creative? Geneticists studying the issue contend that we are all born somewhat creative, able to combine complex and unrelated ideas and to solve problems. However, creativity tests show that a person's score invariably drops about 90 percent between the ages of 5 and 7. At the age of 40, the average adult has only about 2 percent of the creativity he or she possessed at age 5.*

Being Different. What causes this enormous creative loss? Several factors are responsible. Most notably, creativity is smothered in the growing-up process. We are rewarded for complying and punished for being different. Human beings are taught from birth to use their minds to accomplish certain tasks in specific ways. Parents and teachers are often more concerned with keeping children "well behaved" and "under control" than with developing their creative abilities. Thus both our culture and our education can stifle our capacity to be different.

Personal Characteristics. Although everyone has some problem-solving abilities, certain traits seem to be typical of creative problem solvers. The first is that they soak up experiences like sponges. They have a huge personal reservoir of material: things they have read, watched, or listened to, places they have been and worked, and people they have known.

Research has found that creative people tend to be independent, self-assertive, self-sufficient, persistent, and self-disciplined, with a high toler-

*Richard Bencin, "The Psychology of Creativity," *Marketing Communications* (December 1983):43.

CHARACTERISTICS OF CREATIVE PEOPLE

Creative people in advertising tend to score high on the following personal characteristics, although not every person on the creative side scores high on every factor. How do you rate yourself?

	High	Medium	Low
• Intuitive	—	—	—
• Risk taker	—	—	—
• Enthusiastic	—	—	—
• Open to your feelings	—	—	—
• Motivated	—	—	—
• Nonconformist	—	—	—
• Hard worker	—	—	—
• Goal-directed	—	—	—
• Imaginative	—	—	—
• Self-confident	—	—	—
• Enjoy toying with ideas	—	—	—
• Think ideas are a dime a dozen	—	—	—
• Persuasive	—	—	—
• Express feminine interests (for men)	—	—	—
• Express masculine interests (for women)	—	—	—
• Like the unknown	—	—	—
• Do not mind being alone	—	—	—
• Curious	—	—	—
• Interested in aesthetics	—	—	—
• Perceptive	—	—	—
• Self-demanding	—	—	—
• Observant	—	—	—
• Good-natured	—	—	—
• Independent	—	—	—
• Resourceful	—	—	—
• Original	—	—	—

Source: Adapted from a study by Roxanne Hovland, Gary Wilcox, and Tina Hoffman, "An Exploratory Study of Identifying Characteristics of Advertising Creatives: The Creative Quotient Test," 1988 Annual American Academy of Advertising Conference, Chicago (April 11, 1988).

ance for ambiguity. They are risk takers, and they have powerful egos. In other words, they are *internally driven.* They don't care much about group standards and opinions. They are less conventional than are noncreative people and have less interest in interpersonal relationships.

Creative people typically have an inborn skepticism and very curious minds. They are alert, watchful, and observant, and reach conclusions through intuition rather than through logic. They also have a mental playfulness that allows them to make novel associations. They find inspiration in daydreams and fantasies, and they have a good sense of humor.

In general, creative people tend to perform difficult tasks in an effortless manner and are unhappy and depressed when they are not being creative. In addition to having many positive characteristics, however, they have also been described as abrasive, hard to deal with, and withdrawn.

What characteristics do creative thinkers *not* exhibit? They are not dogmatic (although they can be stubborn), and they have little patience with authoritarian people. These people don't follow the crowd, and they like being alone. They aren't timid, and they don't care much about what other people think. The box entitled "Characteristics of Creative People" offers a rating system of creativity.

Visualization Skills. Most copywriters have a good visual imagination as well as excellent writing skills. Art directors, of course, are good visualizers, but they can also be quite verbal. Stephen Baker, in his book *A Systematic Approach to Advertising Creativity,* describes "writers who doodle and designers who scribble" as the heart of the advertising concept team.*

*Stephen Baker, *A Systematic Approach to Advertising Creativity* (New York: McGraw-Hill Book Co., 1979).

AD 13.4
The visual of the airplane tails is an important element in developing the idea of an airline with a person-ality. (Courtesy of Alaska Airlines.)

HAS YOUR AIRLINE LOST ITS PERSONALITY?

Over the last few years, a lot of bright, spunky west coast airlines have been replaced by a few huge, national carriers. Airlines that are very efficient. Very businesslike. And about as inter-esting as a tax form.

One airline, however, hasn't lost its identity: Alaska Airlines, the one with the smiling Eskimo on the tail.

Hop on an Alaska Airlines flight and you'll still find bright, energetic people who take great pride in doing everything they can to serve their customers. With flair, spirit, and their own individual style. So the next time you're traveling up or down the west coast, fly Alaska Airlines.

And see if our attitude toward flying doesn't change yours.

Alaska Airlines

visualization *The ability to see images in the mind, to imagine how an ad or a concept will look when it is finished.*

Writers as well as designers must be able to visualize. Good writers paint pictures with words; they describe what something looks like, sounds like, smells like, and tastes like. They use words to transmit these sensory impressions. Most of the information we accumulate comes through sight, so the ability to manipulate visual images is very important for good writers. In addition to seeing products, people, and scenes in their "minds eye," good writers are able to visualize a mental picture of the finished ad while it is still in the talking, or idea, stage.

Visualization is not a skill limited to print advertising, however. Copywriters, art directors, and producers work together to create radio and television commercials. Copywriters for radio commercials have to be par-ticularly good at painting pictures with words and sounds to create an image in the listener's mind. In television, visualizing means being able to think in terms of staging, movement, and story development. The ability to imagine how the ad or commercial will look is critical to people on the cre-ative side of advertising.

For example, imagine you are creating an advertisement for Alaska Airlines and come up with the idea of attributing a personality to the airline. How would you turn that idea into a visual? Ad 13.4 shows how Alaska Air-lines' creative people accomplished that mission.

Creative Thinking

How do creative ideas appear? There is a tendency to think that only certain people are creative. That is one of the myths of the advertising business, and people who work on the "creative side" in advertising deliberately maintain it. Actually, creativity is a special form of problem solving, and everyone is born with some talents in that area. Research has consistently shown that all people are creative to some extent and can increase their abilities by learning to think creatively.

Furthermore, creativity is not limited in advertising to the "creative side." Advertising is a very creative business that demands imagination and problem-solving abilities in all areas. Media planners and researchers, for example, are just as creative as copywriters and art directors in searching for innovative solutions to the problems they face.

Juxtaposition. An **idea,** according to James Webb Young, a legendary advertising executive, is "a new combination" of thoughts. In his classic book *A Technique for Producing Ideas,* Young claimed that "the ability to make new combinations is heightened by an ability to see relationships."* An idea is a thought that is stimulated by placing two previously unrelated concepts together. The juxtaposition sets up new patterns and new relationships and creates a new way of looking at things. This phenomenon has been described as making the familiar strange and the strange familiar.

Creative thinking uses a psychological technique called **free association.** Young's definition of a new idea calls for the juxtaposition of two seemingly unrelated thoughts. That is what happens in associative thinking. In free association you think of a word and then describe everything that comes into your mind when you imagine that word. Associative thinking can be visual or verbal—you can start with a picture or a word. Likewise, you can associate by thinking of either pictures or words.

Divergent Thinking. Creative thinking is different from the way you think when you try to balance your checkbook or develop an outline for an essay in English class. Most of the thinking that students do in classrooms is rational and is based on a linear logic whereby one point follows from another, either inductively or deductively.

Creative thinking uses an entirely different process. J. P. Guilford, a well-known cognitive psychologist, distinguished between convergent thinking and divergent thinking.† **Convergent thinking** uses linear logic to arrive at the "right" conclusion. **Divergent thinking,** which is the heart of creative thinking, searches for all possible alternatives.

Convergent thinking neatly and systematically pursues a logical route to an answer. It follows from the past and leads to predictable conclusions on the basis of what has gone before. In contrast, divergent thinking seeks alternative approaches rather than a correct or right answer. It makes a series of breaks with the past and leads to surprising or unexpected alternatives.

Right and Left Brain. In current neurophysiology the two types of thinking have been associated with different hemispheres of the brain. Left-brain thinking is logical and controls speech and writing; right-brain thinking is intuitive, nonverbal, and emotional. Most people use both sides of their brains, depending on the task.

There are personality types, however. An artist is generally more oriented to right-brain thinking, whereas an accountant is more left-brained. A person who is left-brain dominant is presumed to be logical, orderly, and verbal. In contrast, a person who is right-brain dominant deals in expressive visual images, emotion, intuition, and complex interrelated ideas that must be understood as a whole rather than as pieces.‡

The Creative Process

There is a tendency to think of a creative person as someone who sits around waiting for an idea to strike. In comic books that is the point where

---

idea *A mental representation; a concept created by combining thoughts.*

free association *An exercise in which you describe everything that comes into your mind when you think of a word or an image.*

convergent thinking *Thinking that uses logic to arrive at the "right" answer.*

divergent thinking *Thinking that uses free association to uncover all possible alternatives.*

---

*James Webb Young, *A Technique for Producing Ideas,* 3rd ed. (Chicago: Crain Books, 1975).
†J. P. Guilford, "Traits of Personality," in *Creativity and Its Cultivation,* H. H. Anderson, ed. (New York: Harper & Brothers, 1959).
‡Betty Edwards, *Drawing on the Right Side of the Brain* (Los Angeles: Tarcher, 1979).

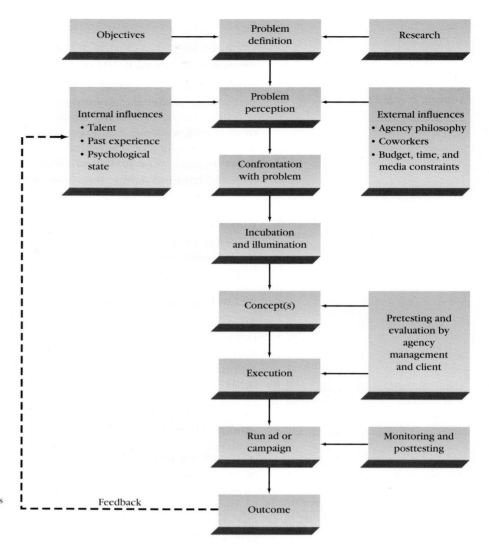

FIGURE 13.1
The creative process in advertising. *Source:* Reprinted from *Marketing News,* published by the American Marketing Association. Bruce Vanden Bergh, "Take This 10-Lesson Course on Managing Creatives Creatively," *Marketing News* (March 18, 1983):22.

the light bulb comes on above the character's head. In reality, most people who are good at thinking up new ideas will tell you that it is hard work. They read, they study, they analyze, they test and retest, they sweat and curse and worry, and sometimes they give up. Major breakthroughs in science or medicine may take years, decades, even generations. That unusual, unexpected, novel idea doesn't come easily.

Despite differences in terms and emphasis, there is a great deal of agreement among the different descriptions of the creative process. The creative process is usually portrayed as following sequential steps (see Figure 13.1). As long ago as 1926 an English sociologist named Graham Wallas first put names to the steps in the creative process. He called them: *preparation, incubation, illumination,* and *verification.**

A more comprehensive process is suggested by Alex Osborn, the former head of the BBDO agency, who established the Creative Education Foundation, which runs workshops and publishes a journal on creativity:

1. Orientation: pointing up the problem
2. Preparation: gathering pertinent data
3. Analysis: breaking down the relevant material
4. Ideation: piling up alternative ideas

*Graham Wallas, *The Art of Thought* (New York: Harcourt, Brace & World, Inc., 1926).

5. Incubation: letting up, inviting illumination
6. Synthesis: putting the pieces together
7. Evaluation: judging the resulting ideas*

Although their steps vary somewhat and their names differ, all creative strategies seem to share several key points. Researchers consistently have found that ideas come after the person has immersed himself or herself in the problem and worked at it to the point of giving up. *Preparation* is that essential period of hard work when you read, research, investigate, and learn everything you can about the problem.

After preparation comes a time of playing with the material, of turning the problem over and looking at it from every angle. This is also a period of teasing out ideas and bringing them to the surface. Most creative people develop a physical technique for generating ideas, such as doodling, taking a walk, jogging, riding up and down on the elevator, going to a movie, sharpening pencils, or eating strange foods. It is a highly personal technique used to "get in the mood," to start the wheels turning. The objective of this stage is to generate as many alternatives as possible. The more ideas that are generated, the better the final concepts.†

The processes of analysis, juxtaposition, and association are mentally fatiguing for most people. You may hit a blank wall and find yourself giving up. This is the point that Young describes as "brainfag." It is a necessary part of the process.

Incubation is the most interesting part of the process. This is the point where you put your conscious mind to rest and let your subconscious take over the problem-solving effort. In other words, when you find yourself frustrated and exasperated because the ideas just won't come, try getting away from the problem. Go for a walk, go to a movie, do anything that lets you put the problem "out of your mind," because that is when the subconscious will take over.

PRINCIPLE
Ideas come at the most unexpected times—but only after hard work.

Illumination is that unexpected moment when the idea comes. Typically, the solution to the problem appears at the least expected time: not when you are sitting at the desk straining your brain, but later that evening just before you drop off to sleep or in the morning when you wake up. At an unexpected moment the pieces fit together, the pattern is obvious, and the solution jumps out at you.

One of the most important steps is the *verification* or evaluation stage, where you step back and look at the great idea objectively. Is it really all that creative? Is it understandable? Most of all, does it accomplish the strategy? Most people working on the creative side of advertising will admit that many of their best creative ideas just didn't work. They may have been great ideas, but they didn't solve the problem or accomplish the right objective. Copywriters will also admit that sometimes the idea they initially thought was wonderful does not project any excitement a day or a week later.

brainstorming *A creative-thinking technique using free association in a group environment to stimulate inspiration.*

Brainstorming. **Brainstorming** is a technique developed in the early 1950s by Alex Osborn.‡ Brainstorming uses associative thinking in a group context. Osborn would get a group of six to ten people together in his agency and ask them to come up with ideas. One person's ideas would stimulate someone else, and the combined power of the group associations

*Alex F. Osborn, *Applied Imagination,* 3rd ed. (New York: Scribners, 1963).

†Bruce G. Vanden Bergh, Leonard N. Reid, and Gerald A. Schorin, "How Many Creative Alternatives to Generate," *Journal of Advertising 12* (1983):4.

‡W. J. J. Gordon, *The Metaphorical Way of Learning and Knowing* (Cambridge: Penguin Books, 1971).

stimulated far more ideas than any one person could think of alone. For example, the copywriter for the Residence Inn campaign described in the beginning of the chapter came up with a line about friends and relatives dropping in unexpectedly and staying. This thought triggered the art director's idea to use Henny Youngman, which led to Levine's idea to use Youngman's signature line.

PRINCIPLE _____

In brainstorming, seek quantity but defer judgment.

The secret to brainstorming is to remain positive. Try to elicit the maximum number of ideas without any evaluation of their effectiveness. The rule is to defer judgment. Negative thinking during a brainstorming session can destroy the informal atmosphere necessary to achieve a novel idea.

Another type of divergent thinking uses such comparisons as analogies and metaphors. Young's definition of an idea also called for the ability to see new patterns or relationships. That is what happens when you think in analogies. You are saying that one pattern is like or similar to another totally unrelated pattern. William J. J. Gordon, a researcher in the area of creative thinking, discovered in his research that new ideas were often expressed as analogies. He has developed a program called *Synectics* that trains people to approach problem solving by applying analogies.*

Developing the Skills.   Understanding the creative process is the biggest step in learning to be more creative. Most people who think they aren't creative simply don't work hard enough. You must accumulate a great deal of information to produce good ideas. Be alert, be perceptive, observe everything that's happening around you. Read, wonder, and question. You can consciously develop a creative mind.

The mental digestion process takes time and effort. Develop your own getting-started techniques like doodling with words and pictures. Creative people often fill pads with what seems to be aimless doodling. They even sleep with notepads by their beds. In fact, these half-sketched ideas and phrases are the raw materials of ideas. This stage often leads to what seems to be a blind wall. Don't give up too easily; take a walk instead. Too many people give up too soon.

Another way to become more creative is to develop your associative thinking skills. You can practice free association by yourself. Just look around the room, pick out an object, relax, open your mind, and see what thoughts come into it. The more often you do this, the more comfortable you will be with the process. You will find that the number and variety of associations increase. Strive for the funniest, silliest, craziest associations you can think of—that is how you develop the ability to come up with original associations.

Analogies are also useful exercises. Look around the room and pick out something. Ask yourself what that item is like—what it resembles, either physically or functionally. Functional analogies compare processes such as how something works or how something is used. A vacuum cleaner is like . . . an anteater, the tentacles of an octopus, a swimmer gasping for air. Keep playing with the images—once again, the crazier the better. The creative mind is a muscle that can be strengthened through exercises like making associations and analogies, but it takes practice.

The Creative Leap: A Case Study.   The hardest part of advertising is making the leap from research and strategy to the novel creative concept. It is easy to become so hypnotized by the logic that it gets in the way of the cre-

*Ibid.

ative thinking, thinking that is propelled by illogical jumps to unexpected and surprising associations. To show you how the creative leap works, we will consider how DDB Needham creatives made the jump from data derived from an annual lifestyle study to an interesting and sound creative concept for Southwestern Bell Mobile Systems.*

Standard data on the cellular telephone market focuses on predictable demographics. According to these data, cellular telephone users tend to be male, between the ages of 25 to 45 years old, who earn more than $35,000 a year, travel a lot, and spend 1 to 7 hours a week in the car for business or commuting. The lifestyle study, however, found that the cellular phone user was also outgoing, hard-working, physically active, self-confident, ambitious, and liked to exert influence over associates and friends.

DDB Needham did not want to do another "yuppie-in-car-on-phone" campaign for Southwestern Bell, so the agency creatives had to make a "creative leap" to translate this lifestyle information into a new but interesting and memorable idea. They came up with a humorous campaign in which a variety of animals were portrayed as cellular phone users. Under each drawing were headlines that addressed the appeals identified in the study. For example, one ad, headlined "Lead or Follow," showed a string of elephants linked tail to trunk, with the lead elephant sporting a cellular antenna. Another ad featured giraffes, all eating except for one alert, cellular-equipped giraffe. The headline read, "When the situation changes, you're the first to know." The campaign won a number of awards, but more importantly, the ads have worked and Southwestern Bell is quoted as "very pleased."†

*T*HE MESSAGE DESIGN

The creative side of a message strategy involves figuring out what to say and how to say it. This is referred to as *designing the message*. There is no one right way to create an ad; there are many ways, and the art of advertising involves knowing which strategy will create an ad with the most relevance, originality, and impact.

Hard and Soft Sell

hard sell *A rational, informational message that emphasizes a strong argument, and calls for action.*

Advertisements are designed to touch either the head or the heart. These two approaches are also called *hard sell* and *soft sell*. A **hard sell** is a rational, informational message that is designed to touch the mind and create a response based on logic. The approach is direct and emphasizes tangible product features and benefits. Hard-sell messages try to convince the consumer to buy because the product is very good, better, or best.‡ An example of this approach is a commercial for Cheer laundry detergent, which shows a mother and her teenage son arguing about the laundry. The son concedes to his mother when he sees how All-Temperature Cheer removes the dirt from his shirts of different colors and different fabrics.

Soft sell uses an emotional message and is designed around an image intended to touch the heart and create a response based on feelings and at-

---

*Joseph M. Winski, "Research + 'Creative Leap' = Award-Winning Ads," *Advertising Age* (September 24, 1990):24.
†Ibid.
‡"The Hard Sell: How Is It Doing?" *Topline* (August 1986).

soft-sell *An emotional message that uses mood, ambiguity, and suspense to create a response based on feelings and attitudes.*

titudes. The subtle, intriguing, and ambiguous commercials Jordache, Calvin Klein, and Guess jeans produce illustrate how advertisers sell moods and dreams more than product features. The ads for Obsession for Men, with their stark images and puzzling story lines, are an example of the strange images created by Calvin Klein for his products.

A soft sell can be used for hard products. For example, if you were designing an ad for an auto-parts store, you might be inclined to take a rational, informative approach. However, NAPA auto parts ran an emotional ad that showed a dog sitting at a railroad-track crossing, forcing a truck to break hard to avoid hitting him as a train bears down on the scene. The slogan puts the heart-stopping visual story into perspective: "NAPA because there are no unimportant parts." (see Ad 13.5).

The research firm McCollum/Spielman has found that although the emphasis today is on soft-sell advertising, hard-sell messages have not become extinct. In a random 2-hour viewing of afternoon soap operas, researchers counted 36 hard-sell commercials out of a total of approximately 42 commercials run during the period. In a different study the company found that although hard-sell commercials might be less arresting than soft-sell, nearly two-thirds of those studied enjoy acceptable levels of brand awareness. They also discovered that hard sell was clearly more persuasive than soft sell.

Lectures and Dramas

lecture *Instruction delivered verbally to present knowledge and facts.*

drama *A story built around characters in a situation.*

Most advertising messages use a combination of two basic literary techniques: lecture and drama. A **lecture** is serious structured instruction given verbally by a teacher. A **drama** is a story or play built around characters in some situation. Both techniques are used in broadcast advertising. Print advertising makes less use of drama and more use of an anonymous voice engaged in presenting a written lecture.

Lectures.   Lectures are a form of direct address. Stylistically, the speaker addresses the audience from the television or written page. The audience receives the message "at a distance." A television-commercial lecture is like a platform speech. In a lecture the speaker presents evidence (broadly speaking) and employs such techniques as an argument to persuade the audience.

Some lectures work by borrowing expertise from authority figures or experts in certain technical areas, such as Michael Jordan for Nike, Chuck Yaeger (a former test pilot) for Delco automobile parts, and "Marcus Welby, M.D." for decaffeinated Maxwell House coffee. Compared with unknown presenters, such "authorities" are more likely to attract audience respect and attention.

Because advertising lectures work by presenting facts, they face the same kinds of problems schoolteachers face. The audience often becomes distracted by other matters, discounts part or all of the evidence, makes fun of the source, or disputes every point. In many cases these responses dilute or even cancel the message the advertiser wants to convey. Lectures do not have to be dull, however. Ad 13.5 for natural gas, for example, personalizes the problems of air pollution and presents the story in an interesting and creative way.

Despite the power of dramas, lectures are still the dominant commercial message format. One advantage of lectures is that they cost less to produce. Another is that they are more compact and efficient. A lecture can deliver a dozen selling points in seconds, if need be. Because the current

AD 13.5
This fact-filled ad on air pollution
is interesting to read because of the
conversational style and the intriguing artwork. (Courtesy of American
Gas Association.)

trend is toward shorter commercials, lectures may become more common
because they are so efficient—it takes time to set up a dramatic scene and
introduce characters. A third advantage of lectures is that they get right to
the point. A lecture can be perfectly explicit, whereas drama relies on the
viewer to make inferences.

Dramas. A drama is a form of indirect address, like a movie or a play. In a
drama the characters speak to each other, not to the audience. In fact, they
usually behave as though the audience were not there. Members of the audience observe and sometimes even participate vicariously in the events
unfolding in the story. They are "eavesdroppers."

Like fairy tales, movies, novels, parables, and myths, advertising
dramas are essentially stories about how the world works. Viewers learn
from these commercial dramas by inferring lessons from them and by applying those lessons to their everyday lives. The key word here is *infer*. Audiences learn from dramas by observation and inference, just as they learn
from stories they hear and from other things that happen to them every day.

Use of the term "drama" is not intended to imply an intense emotional experience. Some drama ads are comic sketches, some are cartoons,
and some are conversations about household products, medicines, or trivial
everyday events. Some simply tell a story. Ad 13.6 for Nissan is an example
of a drama that tells the story of a Nissan driver's fantasy.

A commercial drama can be very powerful. The source of the power is
the viewer's involvement. When a drama rings true, the viewer "joins" in it,
draws conclusions from it, and applies those conclusions to his or her own
life. From the viewer's perspective, conclusions drawn from dramas are
"mine," whereas conclusions urged in lectures are "ideas that other people
are trying to impose on me."

To have this involving effect, a drama must appear realistic to the audience. If it is contrived or unrealistic, the viewer will reject both the drama
and the message. When this happens, the inferences the advertiser counted
on being made will not be made.

One important thing to remember is that the drama should be intrin-
sic to the product. In other words, don't tell a cute or funny story just to be

PRINCIPLE
*Stress the inherent drama of the
product.*

"If I had a 240SX"
Music: Light, upbeat jazz.
240SX Woman Dreamer: If I had a Nissan
240SX...
(Dark coupe appears)
240SX Dreamer: I'd get a red coupe.
(The car changes to a silver fastback)
240SX Dreamer: ...No! A silver fastback. And I'd
go for a spin up Route 7...
(Driving footage, then flutter cuts of road signs,
their numbers changing, then stopping on "7");
240SX Dreamer: ...the twisty part.
(Point of view shot of driver looking over to
passenger seat. An Airedale dog sits in the
passenger seat, ears flapping in the breeze)
240SX Dreamer: Just me and Elvis...
(Dog pops out, attractive man pops in)
240SX Dreamer: ...maybe Mark.
(Mark pops out, Ken Wahl pops in)
240SX Dreamer: Heck, why not Ken Wahl?!
(Driving shot, quick cut of Ken in
passenger seat smiling seductively)
240SX Dreamer: ...in my silver
(Silver car changes to red)
240SX Dreamer: ...no red 240 SX
(An obviously fake sun sets quickly)
240SX Dreamer: ...driving into the sunset.
Super: Nissan (R) Logo
Built for the Human Race. TM
Music: Jazz vocal comes in and fades out.

AD 13.6
**This ad for Nissan uses drama to
tell a comical story about a Nissan
driver's fantasy.** (Courtesy of Nissan
Motor Corporation in U.S.A.)

entertaining. There is a drama in every product, and the product must be central to the drama. The tendency in using drama is to forget or downplay the point of the ad. Even with dramatic forms, you still need a solid selling premise.

Combinations. Many television commercials combine lecture and drama. One common format begins as a drama, which is then interrupted by a short lecture from the announcer, after which the drama concludes. One example of this form is the classic Charlie the Tuna ads. Charlie is a cartoon character who is always being placed in some situation where he aspires to "good taste." The commercials then turn to real-life product shots of tuna fish being used in meals while the announcer explains the quality of Starkist tuna. The commercials close with Charlie once again realizing he is not good enough for Starkist, but vowing to keep trying.

Another common version of the combination is a commercial that is almost all drama until the end, when a tiny lecture, like the moral of a story, is added as a tag. In still another common version the message is mostly lecture, but the lecture is illustrated with minidramas that amplify the information.

Formats and Formulas

In addition to these basic approaches, advertisers use a number of common formats, or formulas, for advertising messages. These include straightforward and factual messages, demonstrations, comparisons, humor, problem-solution, slice of life, and spokesperson.

Straightforward Factual. One of the most common formats is a straightforward factual message. These advertisements usually convey information without using any gimmicks or embellishments. They are rational rather than emotional. Cigarette advertisements that make claims about low tar, for example, are usually presented in a straightforward manner. Business-to-business advertising also is generally factual in tone.

Volvo, BMW, and Saab use straightforward factual copy for their cars. For example, in one BMW ad, the headline simply reads: "How purists tell a future classic from a contemporary antique." The focus of the body copy is on the advanced technologies used in its manufacture. In contrast, other car companies use pictures of their cars against pretty backgrounds such as mountains, deserts, or beaches.

Demonstrations and Comparisons. Two other types of message formats that are usually straightforward and rational in tone are demonstrations and comparisons. The demonstration focuses on how to use the product or what it can do for you. The product's strengths take center stage. In demonstration seeing is believing, so conviction is the objective. Demonstration can be a very persuasive technique.

A comparison contrasts two or more products and usually finds the advertiser's brand to be superior. The comparison can be direct, in which a competitor is mentioned, or indirect, with just a reference to "other leading brands." Advertising experts debate the wisdom of mentioning another product in comparative advertising, particularly if it is a category leader. A direct comparison has to be handled carefully, or you may find your expensively purchased time or space is simply increasing your competition's awareness level.

Humor. The copy strategy behind making people laugh is the hope they will transfer the warm feelings they have as they are being entertained to the product. Humor is hard to handle, however. Although everyone appreciates a good joke, not everyone finds the same joke funny. Some advertising experts advise against using humor because of the danger it will overpower the brand identification—people will remember the punch line and forget the product name. This was the long-time philosophy of David Ogilvy, although he has changed his opinion in recent years and is now saying some humor, if deftly handled, is acceptable.

For a humorous ad to be effective, the selling premise must center around the point of the humor. Humor should *never* be used to poke fun at the product or its users. Stan Freeberg, who has used classic humor in advertising Chun King products and prunes, is one of the proponents of humor in advertising. Hal Riney has used a soft, gentle form of humor in his

AD 13.7
Wrigley's uses a metaphor to explain why its spearmint chewing gum should replace a cigarette as carry-on luggage on an airplane.
(Courtesy of Wm. Wrigley Jr. Company.)

THE JOLLY GREEN SPOKESGIANT

In 1926 a drawing of a giant appeared on the label of the Minnesota Valley Canning Company's extra-large sweet peas. Two years later the giant was colored green, and when Leo Burnett opened his ad agency, with Minnesota Valley Canning as his first client, he added the word "jolly." Thus was born the Jolly Green Giant, the spokesperson for Pillsbury's Green Giant vegetables for over 65 years.

The Green Giant first appeared in print ads in the 1930s and was finally taken to television in the early 1960s. A man of few words, all the giant has ever uttered is the widely known phrase "Ho Ho Ho." To balance the Giant's silence, the Little Green Sprout was created, "chatting up a storm" and imparting his inside knowledge of the Green Giant products to consumers. The Sprout communicates the necessary product knowledge, allowing the Giant to retain his status as the strong, silent overseer of the valley. The giant is always in the background of the ads, his features obscured, and he moves and speaks very little. This portrayal is consistent across foreign markets, where the Giant receives the same positive response from consumers.

According to Gary Klengl, president of Green Giant Company in Minneapolis, "The giant gives consumers a reason to believe." The character is "bigger than life" and is able to connect with people's emotions, touching "the child within the consumer." The character also has years of consistency on his side and continues to stand for high quality and reasonable prices.

A 1991 study of food-product characters, however, indicates that the Giant's Q ratings (measures of overall appeal) are not as high as they could be. Of those consumers surveyed, 91 percent said they were familiar with the Green Giant, but the character's Q rating was 19. (Little Sprout had a Q rating of 29). This rating is average—the average food-product character had a familiarity rating of 72 percent and a Q score of 19—indicating that the Giant is a good fit for the product line but he doesn't generate

a lot of enthusiasm. Higher Q scores went to Poppin' Fresh (36), the California Raisins (37), Tony the Tiger (28), and the Dominos Pizza Noid (23).

Some suggest that the company needs to do something to make the Green Giant more modern, humanistic, authoritative, or educational. Greg Lincoln, director of advertising services at Pillsbury, disagrees. He feels the character's consistency is what appeals to consumers: "It's a known entity." The company is expanding on the Green Giant concept, however. In newer ads for Green Giant mushrooms, for example, Sprout is seen outside of the valley, and the Giant is absent altogether. But he'll be back, and the company does not intend to introduce any new characters. As Huntley Baldwin, executive vice president of creative services at Leo Burnett, says, the campaign has been so durable because "the advertising has been characterized by an innocent charm that has made it fun to watch." The Green Giant has successfully stood for freshness, quality, and consistency for over 65 years and continues to offer consumers an emotional connection with the company and its products.

Source: Adapted from Cyndee Miller, "The Green Giant: An Enduring Figure Lives Happily Ever After," *Marketing News* (April 15, 1991):2.

(Courtesy of Green Giant.)

spots for Bartles and James. One campaign character who consistently scores well with the public is the Energizer bunny who keeps showing up in the middle of other television spots, commercials that are actually parodies of commercials.*

Another humorous ad that has been well-received is an ad for Dorman's cheese, titled "Cowrobics." The commercial shows cows decked out in full exercise regalia—headbands, leg warmers, towels, and so on. The cows go through a rigorous routine of exercise. They are "busting our hooves," as the announcer explains it. The point being made is that Dorman's offers low-fat cheeses, and the tagline wraps up this idea by stating, "No one works harder to give you less."

Problem-Solution. There are several dramatic formats that you will hear referred to in analyzing advertising messages. One is the problem-solution, also known as the *product-as-hero* technique. The message begins with some problem, and the product is presented as the solution to that problem. This is a common technique used with cleansers and additives that make things run smoother. Automotive products often use problem-solution. The Wrigley's ad (Ad 13.7) highlights a problem for smokers on airplanes—smoking is prohibited—and proposes a solution: Chew gum instead.

A variation on this technique is the *problem-avoidance* message where the problem is avoided because of product use. This is a form of threat appeal. It is often used to advertise insurance and personal-care products.

slice of life *A problem-solution message built around some common, everyday situation.*

Slice of Life. The much maligned **slice of life** is really just an elaborate version of a problem-solution message presented in the form of a playlet. It uses some commonplace situation with "typical people" talking about the problem. Procter & Gamble (P&G) is particularly well known for its reliance on the slice-of-life technique. The P&G version puts the audience in the position of overhearing a discussion wherein the problem is stated and resolved. There is something very compelling about listening in on a conversation and picking up some "tip." The tip, of course, is a P&G product.

PRINCIPLE

The spokesperson should not over-power the product.

Spokesperson. Using a person to speak on behalf of the product is another popular message technique. Spokespersons and endorsers are thought to build credibility. They are either celebrities we admire, experts we respect, or someone "just like us" whose advice we might seek out. One of the problems with a spokesperson strategy is that the person may be so glamorous or so attractive that the message gets lost. The spokesperson should be associated with the product, but the product should still be the center of attention; that may be difficult with glamorous endorsers.

Although anyone can be a spokesperson, endorsers usually fall into one of four categories:

1. A created character like the Pillsbury Doughboy or Madge the manicurist
2. A celebrity like Ray Charles for Diet Pepsi or Bill Cosby for Jell-O
3. An authority figure like a doctor for an over-the-counter drug product
4. A typical user who represents as closely as possible the targeted audience

The box entitled "The Jolly Green Spokesgiant" takes a closer look at the use of a created character to advertise a product.

* Craig Bloom, "Madison Avenue, Where Humor Can Get Some Respect," *The New York Times* (August 19, 1990):F5.

HEALTH CLUB USERS AND HOME EXERCISERS

You're a fledgling copywriter, and you've just been assigned to the Higher Horizons Health Club account. You happen to have some dreams of your own—you'd like to come up with the Big Idea. The first thing you're given is a study of lifestyle profiles of health club users as compared to home exercisers. Will you be able to create any magic ideas from these findings?

The Higher Horizons Club is concentrating on attracting professional men and women in their late thirties, with incomes of about $40,000 or more. The Club thinks it is important to find out something about how health club users in general compare to people who don't join health clubs and how people who exercise at home compare with those who exercise at clubs.

First of all, you, as copywriter, learn that though only 14 percent of U.S. adults have attended health clubs within the past year, almost 75 percent exercised at home within that year. Are you surprised?

Now read further about the comparisons of men and women with $40,000+ incomes who use and don't use health clubs. Here is a summary of the major findings.

Americans have learned to be concerned about weight and nutrition, particularly, about blood cholesterol levels and salt intake. Health club patrons have not only absorbed the lessons, but they are more likely to *do* something about changing their diets, checking labels, drinking sugarless beverages, and eating low-calorie yogurt and high-fiber bran cereals. The women, like all American women, are intensely preoccupied with their weight. They've tried reducing, and they do eat low-fat and low-calorie products, but now and again, they indulge in super-premium ice cream or frozen yogurt! The men, in particular, tend to smoke less than the males who do not use health clubs.

It seems reasonable, then, that health club members would have fewer health complaints, such as sleep difficulties or indigestion, than would nonmembers. And indeed, the club clients are more likely to consider themselves in good general health. Consequently, they are less likely than non-members to have consulted physicians about treatment and are more willing to pay for advice on diet, nutrition, and stress reduction.

As you might guess, club members are much more concerned about their physical appearance. The men want to be strong and look youthful. To maintain that masculine appearance, they pamper themselves and are good customers for frequent haircuts and for hand and body lotions, face moisturizers, hair conditioners, sunscreens, and deodorant soaps. The women are equally determined to look young and attractive. They use local department stores to buy such cosmetics as eye liners, hair-styling gels, and blemish concealers. Both the men and women are dedicated to dressing well, and they patronize specialty shops and boutiques.

Health club users seem to be more self-confident and optimistic about their lives than non-members. The members say they anticipate increases in their earnings; they feel their greatest achievements still lie ahead; and they think positively about the future instead of pining for the "good old days." Most of them are quite willing to take personal and financial risks. They like adventure and shun routine. For instance, they travel by plane a good deal for both personal and business reasons, and they like to visit exotic, out-of-the-way spots. They see themselves as leaders and will give their friends advice about products and brands and new films and the latest electronic products such as personal computers or VCRs (which they, the club people, are the first to buy.)

Members of health clubs are more liberal in their social views than are nonpatrons. They think couples should live together before marriage, and they are more in favor of legalized abortion. They are also less likely to be worried about the threat of communism.

Health club members enjoy socializing with people and having fun together. Their social calendars include dinner parties, picnics, rock or pop concerts, sporting events, and vacation trips. Fun for them also means visits to art galleries or museums. If given a choice, they'd rather go out than entertain at home. Maybe they'll go to bars or taverns, or maybe they'll decide to go camping and visit national parks. In either case, they'd like to have other people with them.

Health club members are not only interested in sports but they are active participants as well. They like such activities as tennis, golf, jogging, swimming, and cycling; the male clubbers are also involved in such team sports as softball and volleyball.

As compared to nonmembers, health club members lean toward products and services that offer convenience and no bother. Thus, club members eat at restaurants for breakfast or for dinner; they also purchase more convenience foods and home-delivered meals or fast foods than do nonmembers. Club users don't hesitate to purchase housecleaning services.

Members certainly don't expect to have everything prepackaged for them. For instance, they more frequently read the lifestyle, travel, and editorial sections of the newspapers than do nonmembers. They are also more interested in publications that keep them informed about business—*The Wall Street Journal* or *Money,* for instance. They're not avid television watchers, but when they do watch, it's apt to be late at night.

How do these club participants compare with people who exercise at home? Not surprisingly, they share the concern with health and physical fitness. The home exercisers carry out their programs because they think exercise is part of the healthy life. Yet the home exerciser is more of a worrier about health and tends to exaggerate minor problems, consult physicians, and use prescription medicines more readily that do health club patrons.

As contrasted with the adventure-seeking person who uses the clubs, the home exerciser dotes on routine. He or she eats at the same time every day, exercises on a regular basis, and doesn't leave much to chance or whim. For example, the home exerciser draws up a complete shopping list before setting out for the store. In a different realm, we find that the home exerciser prefers safety to high return in financial investments. One wouldn't say the typical home exerciser is very impulsive.

But there are certain distinct similarities between the club users and the home exercisers. Both are friendly and sociable; both are willing to work hard at building their careers, and both feel that this effort has paid off. Both like watching sports, and although the home exerciser may not go off jogging or camping, both are sports enthusiasts.

The home is distinctly the exerciser's base; it is an anchor for his or her life. Exercisers entertain at home, feel content to spend time there, and only occasionally venture far afield. They envision themselves staying in their present homes in their present towns for the rest of their lives.

The home exercisers feel pretty satisfied with their accomplishments and think they have things under control. They aren't going to rush out and buy European cars or sports cars, nor are they terribly worried about their clothing and cosmetics. Boutiques or hair salons are not vital to them. They tend to choose items that are acceptable rather than fashionable. Similarly, home exercisers are less likely to be interested in buying such new products as personal computers, VCRs, and cellular car phones.

Like the club users, home exercisers aren't enthusiastic television fans, but they certainly do not choose late night television for their occasional viewing. Overall, as compared to club members, home exercisers prefer the simple things in life.

Now that you have some impressions of how health club users and home exercisers lead their lives and see their lives, can you come up with some creative way of attracting new customers to a health club that wants very much to expand its enrollment?

Source: DDB Needham Worldwide, *Lifestyle Profiles of Upscale Male/Female Health Club Users and Upscale Male/Female Home Exercisers* (December 1989).

A **testimonial** is a variation of the spokesperson message format. The difference is that people who give testimonials are talking about their own personal experiences with the product. Their comments are based on personal use, which has to be verifiable or the message will be challenged as deceptive. Slim-Fast uses a number of famous people, including Tommy Lasorda and Christina Ferrare, to testify to the success of the diet shake in losing weight.

All of these formats are commonly used in advertising. There are other ways to package the message—this list is not complete. Some advertising professionals would like to ban many of these techniques because they are so overused. Because they are so common, however, they do provide a way to analyze advertising messages.

Burnett's "Structural Analysis"

So far we have focused on the creative concept—the Big Idea that inspires attention-getting and memorable advertising. The creative idea is only half of the advertising message, however. The other half is the strategy, which we discussed in Chapter 7. As we mentioned earlier, advertising is a disciplined art, and both the discipline of strategic thinking and the impact of creative thinking are necessary for effective advertising.

The Leo Burnett agency has developed an approach to analyzing the message design that keeps both strategy and creativity in perspective. This structural analysis first looks at the power of the narrative or story line and then evaluates the strength of the product claim. Finally, it looks at how well the two aspects are integrated—that is, how the story line brings the claim to life. The creative team checks to see if the narrative level is so high that it overpowers the claim or if the claim is strong but there is no memorable story. Ideally, these two elements will be so seamless that it is hard to tell whether the impact derives from the power of the story or the strength of the claim.

IMAGES AND ADVERTISING

Which is more important in an advertisement—the words or the picture? In print as well as in broadcast advertising a decision has to be made to emphasize either the images or the words. In the past the words tended to dominate, with the visual used as a supporting element, particularly in print. Contemporary advertising, however, has made more effective use of the visual as an important contributor to the content of the message.

Message Objectives

Before deciding whether to emphasize words or pictures, a creative team has to consider the underlying strategy for the ad. For example, if the message is complicated, if the purchase is deliberate and well considered, or if the ad is for a high-involvement product, then the more information the better, and that means using words. If you are doing reminder advertising or trying to establish a brand image, then you may want to put less emphasis on words and more on the visual impression. Undifferentiated products with low inherent interest are often presented with an emphasis on the visual message.

Actually, words and pictures are both important, and the best advertising uses the two to reinforce each other. They do tend to do different things, however. Visuals are thought to be better at getting attention, although words can be strong if they are bold and don't have to compete with the visual. Pictures also communicate faster than words. A picture is seen instantaneously, but verbal communication must be deciphered word by word, sentence by sentence, line by line.

PRINCIPLE _____
Words and pictures work in combination to create a concept.

Visuals are thought to be easier to remember, although some verbal phrases can make a long-term impression, like "Where's the beef?" Many people remember messages as visual fragments. These are key images that they lock into their minds. You probably remember the word _home_ in terms of the image of a specific house in which you have lived. Most people file memories using a visual index, although some people who are highly verbal may have difficulty remembering images. Most of us remember a print ad in terms of how it generally looked. We would have a difficult time describing all the details. Likewise a television commercial is remembered for some key visual image that is just a section or fragment of the entire commercial. It is the power of this visual image that makes an ad easy to remember and creates an effective impact.

The Power of the Visual

PRINCIPLE _____
What you show can speak more effectively than what you say.

An ad for Saab demonstrates the power of the visual by deliberately avoiding nearly all copy. The picture is taken from inside a car on a winding highway, looking over the driver's hands. The headline reads: "What we could tell you about the Saab 900 in the space below is no substitute for ten minutes in the space above." The "space below" where the body copy would normally be found was left blank in the layout.

The Benetton ads are great examples of strong visuals that make a lasting impression as well as an editorial statement. In 1989 Benetton used a controversial campaign that featured a picture of a white man's hand and a black man's hand handcuffed together. The global marketer's in-house agency is known for using strong visuals to draw symbolic parallels between its multicolor and multicultural apparel and larger world issues, such as racial harmony. These parallels are confirmed through the company's slogan, "United Colors of Benetton." In 1990 Benetton toned down the campaign with a series of ads that promoted brotherhood. The campaign used more subtle and safe imagery, such as cute black and white children and a white dog paw-in-paw with a black cat. Later that year Benetton ads became less subtle, however. One ad showed test tubes filled with blood, labeled with the names of world leaders, to show that all people are the same.* Benetton's 1991 campaign moved into other issue-oriented areas such as AIDS and overpopulation, as the company continued to make a statement about being socially conscious.

**Visual Impact.** Different people respond to words and pictures in different ways. When you think of a car, do you think of an image or a word? Some people are highly visual and automatically think and remember in images; others are more verbal and would respond with a word like Ford or Ferrari.

The strength of the visual is demonstrated in an ad by the Burroughs company. It simply shows a brick wall. The impact comes after reading the headline: "Does talking to your computer company's service department conjure up a certain image?"

* "What's New Portfolio," _Adweek's Marketing Week_ (April 9, 1990):52; and Alison Fahey, "Benetton's Latest," _Advertising Age_ (February 11, 1991):16.

Research involving print advertising has found that more than twice as many magazine readers are captured by a picture in an ad as by the headline. Furthermore, the bigger the illustration, the higher the attention-getting power of the advertisement. Ads with pictures are noticed more than are ads composed entirely of type. Ads with pictures also tend to pull more readers into the body copy. In other words, the initial attention is more likely to turn to interest with a strong visual.

Similar research with television has found that the pictorial elements of a television commercial are better remembered than are the words. One study ranked the elements according to how well people remembered them. People tended to remember the picture first, then type on the screen, then voices, and finally other sounds.

Purpose of the Visual

Obviously the most important functions of the visual are to capture attention and to illustrate the benefit of the product or service. Beyond that, look at a print ad and analyze how the visual communicates the essence of the message. Although the visual is illustrative, notice how it also expresses the central point, the pivotal idea.

Narration. In some advertisements the picture itself tells much of the story. The legendary campaign for Hathaway shirts is an example ("The Man in the Hathaway Shirt"). David Ogilvy created the elegant Hathaway man with his eye patch in 1951, suggesting a fascinating, but mysterious, lifestyle. The campaign continues to this day with contemporary men such as sportscaster Bob Costas and artificial-heart designer Robert Jarvik. It is a visual image—with relatively little reliance on words. The story development is left to the imagination of the reader.

Illustration. In other ads the idea is carried more by the words, and the visual illustrates the point or the product. In retail advertising, for example, a department store may feature housewares in an ad. The visual shows the line of dishes, what they look like, and what pieces are available. That is an illustrative function. The emphasis of the visual is on tangible product details.

Demonstration. With a new product, the visual may be used to demonstrate how it works or how to use it. Demonstrations are primarily visual, because it can be extremely difficult to show how something works with only verbal instructions. The picture, and particularly a series of pictures showing the steps, is a critical element in a demonstration.

Symbolization. Intangibles such as quality, economy, value, speed, and flexibility are difficult to express in visuals. These abstractions are easier to communicate with words. Internal states like happiness, confidence, and satisfaction are also difficult to visualize. How do you show somebody looking "satisfied"? The answer is through symbols.

symbolism *Words and images that represent, or cue, something else.*

Symbols are images that represent something, usually by association. They substitute a *cue* for a concept. If you want to communicate stress, you can show a picture of a person snapping a pencil in half. Quality usually means something upscale like a fancy car, a mink coat, or a formal dinner. Associative thinking skills are important for people who communicate using abstractions and symbols.

Artistic creativity is essential to successful advertising. (Courtesy of Comstock.)

Art Direction

As discussed in Chapter 4, the person who is primarily responsible for the graphic image of the advertisement is the **art director.** The art director "composes" the visuals in both print and video and "lays out" the ad elements in print. Artists may do the specific illustrations or renderings, but the art director is the chief arranger of these elements. He or she is responsible for the visual "look" of the message.

art director *The person who is primarily responsible for the visual image of the advertisement.*

Photography versus Artwork. One of the primary decisions made by an art director is whether to use photography or artwork. Photography is the mainstay of the advertising business because it is "real" and adds credibility to the message. Seeing is believing, after all. Probably three-fourths of all advertising visuals are photographic. Of the photographs, around 80 percent are realistic. Illustrations in print and animation on television are used for fashion, fantasy, and exaggerated effects.

Styles of Photography. If the decision is to use photography, then there are different styles of images to choose from. A reportorial style uses dramatic black-and-white images to try to imitate photojournalism. Documentary style also uses black and white, but the style is more stark. Most products and product scenes, however, are shot in realistic full color, either in a studio, on a set, or on location.

Different photographers specialize in different types of shots. Some are great with fashion, others shoot buildings, some are good at landscapes, others know all the difficulties of shooting food, and still others specialize in photographing babies or animals. Each area demands specialized knowledge of how to handle lighting, staging, props, and models.

Styles of Artwork. If the layout calls for illustrations, the art director must decide which artist to use. Every artist has a personal style, although most good artists are able to shift styles somewhat to reflect the nature of the message. There is a big difference between a *loose* style, which is somewhat rough, primitive, or casual in appearance, and a *tight* style, which is detailed, perhaps even technical. Some artists are good at realistic effects, whereas others are better at abstract or highly stylized effects, as in fashion advertising. Some are good cartoonists.

Artists use a variety of techniques to create different effects, such as pen-and-ink sketches, oils, pastels, watercolor, wash drawings, scratchboards, and felt-tip pens. Computergraphics can be used to create almost any effect. Art created on a sophisticated computer is limited only by the artist's imagination and willingness to experiment.

Words and Advertising

Advertising writing is a special art form. It has an entirely different style than that found in English essays or journalistic new stories. The structure is different; the language is different. In some ways advertising writing is more similar to poetry than to the usual styles of prose writing.

Copywriting

copywriter *The person who writes the text for an ad.*

Advertising writing is called *copy,* and the person who shapes and sculpts the words in an advertisement is called a **copywriter.** Copywriters are preoccupied with language. They listen to how people talk. They read everything they can get their hands on, from technical documents to comic books. They are tuned in to current expressions and fads. They understand technical communication as well as street language.

Versatility is the most common characteristic of copywriters. They can move from toilet paper to Mack trucks and shift their writing style to match the product and the language of their target. Copywriters don't have a style of their own because the style they use has to match the message and the product. Some veteran copywriters specialize in certain types of writing, but beginners find themselves advertising all types of products. Except in a few rare cases, advertising copy is anonymous, so people who crave a byline generally would not be very happy as copywriters.

Stylistics

There is good writing and there is bad writing in advertising, just as there is in every other area of expression. Some of the characteristics discussed here are features of good advertising writing, although all ads are not written this way.

PRINCIPLE
Keep it simple.

Simple. Advertising has to win its audience, and usually it is in competition with some other form of programming or editorial matter. For that reason, the copy should be as easy to understand as possible. Unless the rewards are exceptional, most people will shun advertising copy that taxes them. Simple ads avoid being gimmicky or too cute. They don't try too hard or reach too far to make a point. The Soloflex campaign is a good example of a simple concept simply expressed. The visual is of a well-built man taking off his shirt. There is no headline, but the short body copy is set in large type and serves as a long headline. The copy reads: "To unlock your body's potential, we proudly offer Soloflex. Twenty-four traditional iron pumping exercises, each correct in form and balance. All on a simple machine that

fits in a corner of your home." The short slogan is a play on words: "Body by Soloflex."

Advertising copy uses short, familiar words and short sentences (see Ad 13.8). If a technical term is used, it is defined immediately. Advertising copy avoids long, complex sentences and paragraphs. You will probably notice in print advertising that some of the paragraphs are only one sentence long.

Every attempt is made to produce copy that looks or sounds easy to understand. Long blocks of copy in print, which are too "gray" or intimidating for the average reader, are broken up into short paragraphs with many subheads. The equivalent of a long copy block in television advertising is a long speech by the announcer. Television monologues can be broken up by visual changes, such as shots of the product. Sound effects can also be used to break up the heaviness of the monologue.

Specific. The more specific the message, the more attention-getting and memorable it is. The better ads won't say "costs less" but will spell out exactly how much less the product costs. There isn't a lot of time to waste on generalities.

Concise. Advertising copy is very tight. Every word counts because both space and time are expensive. There is no time or room for ineffective words. Copywriters will go over the copy a hundred times trying to make it as concise as possible. The tighter the copy is, the easier it is to understand and the greater its impact will be.

Conversational. The best advertising copy sounds natural, like two friends talking to one another. It is not forced; it is not full of generalities and superlatives; it does not brag or boast. Conversational copy is written the way people talk. It uses incomplete sentences, fragments of thoughts, and contractions.

Because it is written as if it were a conversation, advertising copy can also be described in terms of *tone of voice*. In developing a statement of message strategy, copywriters are often asked to describe the tone of the ad. Hard-sell and soft-sell message approaches reflect a tone of voice. Look through some magazines and notice how the tone varies from ad to ad. Most ads are written as if some anonymous announcer were speaking. Even with anonymity, however, there may be an identifiable tone of voice. Some ads are angry, some are pushy, some are friendly, others are warm or excited.

In order to get the right tone of voice, copywriters usually move away from the target audience description and concentrate on the typical user. If they know someone who fits that description, then they write to that person. If they don't, then they may go through a photo file, select a picture of the person they think fits the description, and develop a profile of that personality. They may even hang that picture above their desk while they write the copy.

Personal and Informal. One way that advertising differs from newswriting is in the use of pronouns. It is perfectly acceptable in copywriting to use "you" in direct address. In fact, a conscious attempt to use "you" will force copywriters to be more natural and less affected in their writing. It also forces them to think about the product in terms of the prospect and benefits.

"We" copy is advertising that is written from the company's point of view. It tends to be more formal, even pompous. It is also called **brag-and-boast copy.** Research has consistently found that this is the weakest of all forms of ad writing. "I" copy is used occasionally in testimonials or in dramas such as slice of life where a leading character speaks about a personal experience.

"Adese." Unfortunately, advertising does have a style that is so well known that it is parodied by comedians. It is a form of formula writing, called **adese,** that violates all the preceding guidelines. Adese is full of clichés, superlatives, stock phrases, and vague generalities. For example, would you ever say things like this to a friend: "Now we offer the quality that you've been waiting for—at a price you can afford"? "Buy now and save." Can you hear yourself saying that aloud?

An ad by Buick for its Somerset line is full of adese. The headline starts with the stock opening: "Introducing Buick on the move." The body copy includes superlatives and generalities such as:

> "Nothing less than the expression of a new philosophy."
>
> "It strikes a new balance between luxury and performance; a balance which has been put to the test."
>
> "Manufactured with a degree of precision that is in itself a breakthrough."
>
> "Two coats of clear paint are added for an almost unbelievable luster."

The problem with adese is that it looks and sounds like what everyone thinks advertising should look and sound like. Because people are so conditioned to screen out advertising, messages that use this predictable style are the ones that are the easiest to notice and avoid.

Strategy and Originality

To be creative, an idea must be both *different* and *right* for the product and target. Novelty alone is not enough. The U.S. Patent Office is crammed with

PRINCIPLE

Write to someone you know and match the tone of voice to the situation.

brag-and-boast copy *Advertising text that is written from the company's point of view to extol its virtues and accomplishments.*

adese *Formula writing that uses clichés, generalities, stock phrases, and superlatives.*

new but useless devices, such as "Boomerang Bullets" and "Automatic Hat Tippers." Television is strewn with the wreckage of ads gone wrong. Good advertising is both original and strategically sound—it is both an art and a problem solution. Creative people in advertising must answer to both masters, which makes creative advertising extremely difficult.

Undisciplined creatives who lack an understanding of strategy are frequently at a loss for words when asked how well their advertising fared in the marketplace.* They are more interested in winning awards than in achieving sales objectives. The legendary Bill Bernbach reminds the creative person to make the product—not the author—shine:

> Merely to let your imagination run riot, to dream unrelated dreams, to indulge in graphic acrobatics and verbal gymnastics is *not* being creative. The creative person has harnessed his imagination. He has disciplined it so that every thought, every idea, every word he puts down, every line he draws, every light and shadow in every photograph makes more vivid, more believable, more persuasive the product advantage.†

*Carl F. Walston, "The Aesthetic Dimension of Advertising," unpublished master's thesis, University of Colorado, 1991.
†Bill Bernbach, *Bill Bernbach Said* (New York: Doyle Dane Bernbach International).

SUMMARY

- The "Big Idea" is the creative concept around which the entire advertising campaign revolves.
- A creative concept must have relevance, originality, and impact.
- All people are born with creative skills, but most people lose these skills in the course of their lives.
- Creative people tend to be right-brain, rather than left-brain, dominant. These differences correspond roughly to divergent versus convergent thinking.

- The two basic literary techniques used in advertisements are lectures and dramas. Some ads use a combination of the two.
- Common advertising formats include humor, problem-solution, slice of life, spokesperson, straightforward factual, and comparisons and demonstrations.
- Effective copywriting is informal, personal, conversational, and concise. Forced, unnatural writing is referred to as *adese*.

QUESTIONS

1. What are some of the major traits of creative people? Which characteristics of the advertising world do you think enhance creativity? Which discourage it?

2. Find a newspaper or magazine advertisement that you think is bland and unexciting. Rewrite it, first to demonstrate a hard-sell approach, and then to demonstrate a soft-sell approach.

3. One of the challenges for creative ad designers is to demonstrate a product whose main feature cannot be seen by the consumer. Suppose you are an art director on an account that sells shower and bath mats with a patented system that ensures the mat will not slide (the mat's underside is covered with tiny suction cups that grip the tub's surface). Brainstorm for some ways to demonstrate this feature in a television commercial. Find a way that will satisfy the demands of originality, relevance, and impact.

4. In the past Diet Pepsi ran a commercial involving the famous blind musician and vocalist Ray Charles, in which, as a practical joke, someone switched Diet Coke for the sponsored drink. The joke was reversed when Ray Charles immediately discovered the switch once he tasted Pepsi's competitor. Was Mr. Charles's role in that commercial one as a spokesperson or a testimonial? Was there a symbolic idea behind the strategy? Which of the formats and formulas discussed in the chapter best fits this Diet Pepsi commercial?

5. Peter Madison, a sophomore in advertising, is speaking informally with a copywriter from a local advertising agency following the writer's class presentation. Peter states his strong determination to be some sort of creative professional once he gets his degree. "My problem is that I'm a bit shy and reserved. I'm interested in all sorts of stuff, but I'm not

really quick in expressing ideas and feelings. I'm not sure my personality is suited for being an advertising creative. How do I know if I've picked the right career direction?" What advice should that writer give Peter?

6. Some time ago a copywriting analyst warned writers that they should be aware of the "ignorance distance" between the writer and the audience. He meant avoiding copy that is either over the heads of the audience or well below the audience's knowledge of the product. What are the copy dangers in speaking above the audience's frame of reference? What are the dangers of underestimating the audience's knowledge? Which of the elements discussed in the "stylistics" section of the chapter would reduce these threats of "ignorance distance"?

FURTHER READINGS

BAKER, STEPHEN, *A Systematic Approach to Advertising Creativity* (New York: McGraw-Hill Book Co., 1979).

BARBAN, ARNOLD A., and C. H. SANDAGE, eds., *Readings in Advertising and Promotion Strategy* (Homewood, IL: Irwin, 1968).

DE BONO, EDWARD, *Lateral Thinking: Creativity Step by Step* (New York: Harper and Row, 1970).

GORDON, W. W. J., *The Metaphorical Way of Learning and Knowing* (Cambridge, MA: Penguin Books, 1971).

MARRA, JAMES L., *Advertising Creativity: Techniques for Generating Ideas.* (Englewood Cliffs, NJ: Prentice Hall, 1990).

MORIARTY, SANDRA, *Creative Advertising,* 2nd ed. (Englewood Cliffs, NJ: Prentice Hall, 1990).

YOUNG, JAMES WEBB, *Technique for Producing Ideas,* 3rd ed. (Chicago: Crain Books, 1975).

VIDEO CASE

NEW YORK

Clearasil— "Doo Run"

By 1989 the cream segment of the acne remedy category had experienced 5 consecutive years of volume losses to such products as nonsoap cleansers and acne pads, which offered a preventative solution to acne problems. During this time, cream's share of acne remedy category dollar volume declined from 54 percent to 41 percent. The cream segment share leader, Richardson-Vicks' Clearasil, also experienced share losses each year from 1985 to 1989.

Competitive activity compounded Clearasil's share-loss trend when Richardson-Vicks' main competitor, Oxy, introduced a new cream product, Oxy Night Watch, in early 1990. Night Watch increased Oxy's overall share by approximately 20 percent in 6 months time. Oxy further benefited from a more contemporary image than Clearasil and, thus, was perceived as being more in touch with contemporary teenage attitudes and culture, whereas Clearasil was viewed as somewhat more old-fashioned.

The acne remedy category also suffered from a long-term credibility problem among teenagers because acne advertising had consistently promised or implied that products could get rid of pimples virtually instantaneously, something no nonprescription product could deliver. Thus, Richardson-Vicks's advertising agency, D'Arcy, Masius, Benton & Bowles (DMB&B) identified three campaign objectives for Clearasil creams: 1) reverse Clearasil creams' 5-year unit share decline by building creams and overall franchise business for successive share periods (in spite of the introduction of Oxy Night Watch); 2) begin to reposition Clearasil as a more contemporary, less old-fashioned product; and 3) reestablish credibility with teenagers by communicating a strong sense that Clearasil is honest and can be trusted.

DMB&B recognized that teenagers did not think acne products worked, but they used them just in case they *might* work and to reassure themselves that they were doing everything they could to fight acne. Thus, DMB&B identified a creative strategy that centered on an honest performance claim of "fewer pimples in 5 days". Although 5 days seemed like a long time for a teenager to wait for a pimple medicine to work, the 5-day promise was considered to be a compelling advantage over other products, whose performance teens may not have believed. Furthermore, the tangibility of the 5-day promise allowed teen-

agers to forego their skepticism about whether or not the product would work immediately. To reduce skepticism further among teenagers, Richardson-Vicks introduced a money-back guarantee regarding Clearasil's performance. This was the first time a money-back guarantee had been offered in television advertising in the acne remedy category.

Richardson-Vicks's traditional teen target focused on the 13- to 19-year-old segment, and its cumulative media budget represented 28 percent of total acne remedy media spending, comparable to previous years. DMB&B ultimately created the "Doo Run" campaign and submitted it for copy testing, conducted by McCollum Spielman. The results confirmed that the "Doo Run" campaign was more believable than both previous Clearasil advertising and the current Oxy campaign, suggesting that teenagers were indeed perceiving the more honest approach in Richardson-Vicks's advertising claims. Specifically, 74 percent of copy-test respondents rated Clearasil's "Doo Run" campaign as very believable, whereas only 53 percent of respondents rated Clearasil's "Fast Forward" ad and Oxy's current spot as believable. Teenagers participating in the study also indicated that they could relate better to the "Doo Run" spot than they could to Oxy's current advertising, suggesting that DMB&B had successfully projected a more contemporary image. For example, 76 percent of teenagers reported that the "Doo Run" spot was "talking to someone like me," whereas only 54 percent of teens felt that the Oxy ad was talking to them.

As with any advertising campaign, the true measure of its effectiveness is how it affects product sales. During each of the 5 months prior to the initial airing of "Doo Run," Scantrack Data reported dollar-share declines for the creams segment compared to the prior year. For each of the 5 months the "Doo Run" ad aired, however, dollar share of the creams segment was up, compared to the prior year. Similarly, Nielsen unit share data for the 2 consecutive months after the start of the "Doo Run" advertising reported an increase of 1 percent and 7 percent, respectively, representing the first evidence of category growth for a consecutive bimonthly period in over 3 years. Share for the Clearasil cream brand increased by 6 percent and 9 percent respectively, for the same two periods.

QUESTIONS

1. Identify at least three significant elements that distinguish advertising for teenagers from advertising for the adult market.
2. Advertising for a product which makes a stronger claim than advertising for competitive products is generally more effective. The "Doo Run" campaign,

however, actually increased effectiveness by diluting Clearasil's claim versus prior efforts by Richardson-Vicks. Explain why this situation violates the rule.

Source: Courtesy of D'Arcy, Masius, Benton & Bowles.

14

Creating Print Advertising

Chapter Objectives

When you have completed this chapter, you should be able to:

- Distinguish between the key features of newspaper and magazine advertising
- List the various elements of a print ad and their function
- Understand the process by which print ads are created
- Distinguish between letterpress, offset, gravure, and silk-screen printing

THE INFINITI TEASER

One of the biggest debates in advertising broke over Nissan's use of Zen-like ads to introduce its new Infiniti luxury cars in 1990. The campaign featured stylized landscapes and copy philosophizing about the harmony between humanity and nature. Although created by an American team at the Hill, Holliday agency, the ads trade heavily on Japanese aesthetics, which is a very unusual creative strategy for an automotive advertising campaign.

Magazines were used first for the teaser and launch ads because they are a good medium for image advertising, which was the creative strategy behind this unusual campaign. The landscapes featured in the ads—rocks with tracings of moss, leaves floating on a pond, a waterway framed by tall grass—were all carefully composed images reminiscent of Japanese gardens. The ads devoted either one or two pages to the striking visual, followed by a single page with a small amount of copy. The body copy referred to the timelessness of the quality and beauty of fine engineering and how that related to nature. Headlines such as "A luxury car that resists time" were used. The copy in one ad explained:

> An automotive designer looks at the shapes of nature . . . and these lines suggest an automotive design that is honest and natural. Where the driver is more important than the car itself. And what is discovered just watching nature is an ancient Japanese notion of what is beautiful.

These teaser ads did not show a picture of the $38,000 car. Dealers complained about the controversial campaign initially, competitors laughed at it, and critics took potshots at it. Seven weeks after the launch only 1,700 cars had been sold, which was lower than Nissan's projections. Dealers admitted, however, that the campaign did have an impact and people were showing up at the new dealerships even before they were open. Many dealers reported heavy traffic in the showrooms during the first week. A Chicago dealer observed, "The number of people coming in here has been tremendous. It's been like the Auto Show here."

Some hailed the campaign as "new" and "different," a revolutionary experiment in image advertising. After the first 2 months of running the teaser ads, Infiniti was the best-recalled advertiser in the nation, according to the Gallup Organization's AdWatch monthly survey conducted for *Advertising Age.* Furthermore, tracking research found that 80 percent of the Infiniti's target audience could identify the car's logo just 6 weeks into the launch. Defenders of the campaign pointed out that the ads not only had high recall scores but pulled record numbers of consumers into the showrooms. If the car wasn't selling as fast as Nissan had projected, maybe it wasn't the fault of the ads, which seemed to be doing what car ads are supposed to do—getting attention and creating showroom traffic.*

PRINT ADVERTISING

The foundation of modern advertising message strategy and design lies in the early print formats. The earliest mass-produced commercial messages either appeared in newspapers or as handbills. Thus many advertising

---

*Adapted from Cleveland Horton, "No Cars, Just Nature Scenes for Infiniti TV," *Advertising Age* (August 29, 1989):3; Cleveland Horton, "Infiniti Ads Pull in Traffic," *Advertising Age* (November 27, 1989):2; Scott Hume, "Infiniti Shoots to Top of Best-Recalled Ads," *Advertising Age* (January 8, 1990):10; and Betsy Sharkey, "Taking the Hot Seat at Infiniti: Peter Bossis Defends Hill, Holliday's Zen Ads," *Adweek* (January 15, 1990):22–23.

copy *The written elements in an ad, including headlines, underlines and overlines, subheads, body copy, captions, slogans, and taglines.*

art *The visual elements in an ad, including illustrations, photos, type, logos and signatures, and the layout.*

PRINCIPLE
Advertising is news too.

newsprint *An inexpensive, tough paper with a rough surface, used for printing newspapers.*

in register *A precise matching of colors in images.*

PRINCIPLE
Illustrations reproduce better than photos in newspapers.

freelance artists *Independent artists who work on individual assignments for an agency or advertiser.*

guidelines originated with print, and print techniques, such as headline writing, are still considered basic concepts. Many things have changed over the years. Television has had a tremendous impact on advertising. Visuals, which were limited in the early press to infrequent woodcuts, are now as important as words. Print advertising continues to be important, however, and still serves as a foundation in that its techniques are the easiest to understand and analyze. We will therefore begin our discussion of media and their creative characteristics with newspapers and magazines.

The key elements of print advertising are divided between copy and art. The **copy** elements include headlines, underlines and overlines, subheads, body copy, captions, slogans, and taglines. **Art** refers to the visual elements, which include illustrations or photography, the type, logotypes (logos) and signatures, and the *layout* itself, which is the arrangement of all the elements.

Newspaper Advertisements

Most people see newspaper advertising as a form of news. In fact, newspaper advertising is one of the few forms of advertising that is not considered intrusive. People consult the paper as much to see what is on sale as to find out what is happening in City Hall. For this reason, newspaper advertisements do not have to work as hard as other kinds of advertising to catch the attention of an indifferent audience.

In addition, because the editorial environment of a newspaper is generally more serious than entertaining, newspaper advertisements don't have to compete as entertainment, as television ads do. Therefore, most newspaper advertising is straightforward and newslike. It announces what merchandise is available, what is on sale, how much it costs, and where you can get it.

Production Characteristics. Daily newspapers are printed at high speed on an inexpensive, rough-surfaced, spongy paper, called **newsprint,** that absorbs ink on contact. The demands of speed and low cost have traditionally made newspaper reproduction rather low-quality printing.

Newsprint is not a great surface for reproducing fine details, especially photographs and delicate typefaces. Most papers offer color to advertisers, but because of the limitations of the printing process, the color may or may not be **in register** (aligned exactly with the image).

We are accustomed to seeing news photographs that are somewhat "muddy," but most of us expect better quality in advertising. Although photographs are used in newspaper advertising, illustrations generally reproduce better. Illustrations in newspaper advertisements, like the Bullocks Wilshire ad pictured in Ad 14.1, are bold, simple, and specifically designed to reproduce well within the limitations of the printing process.

Most newspapers subscribe to an artwork service, called a *mat service,* that sends general and seasonal illustrations directly to the advertising department. This generic art satisfies the needs of most local advertisers. Larger newspapers may have their own graphic artists who are available to local advertisers. Some major advertisers have their own art services through their trade associations, such as banks and savings and loan associations. Large department stores often have an in-house advertising staff that includes artists. Stores also hire **freelance artists,** who provide original art for the store's ads.

This scene is changing, however. *USA Today* has pioneered much better quality reproduction for daily newspapers. Because the paper itself is of better quality, photographs and color reproduction are considerably better

BW

Ralph Lauren

A modern classic. Give her the quiet elegance of Ralph Lauren, mastered here in pure white linen.
Shawl collar robe with navy trim and signature crest, two patch pockets, self belt.
8-10(s) or 12-14(m), $310.
Loungewear, at all seven BW stores.

B U L L O C K S W I L S H I R E

3050 WILSHIRE BOULEVARD (213) 382-6161   PALM SPRINGS (619) 325-1571   WOODLAND HILLS (818) 887-5151   NEWPORT BEACH (714) 759-1211   LA JOLLA (619) 455-7111   PALOS VERDES (213) 377-3838   PALM DESERT (619) 568-6900

AD 14.1
Despite the limitations of reproducing illustrations in newspapers, this ad manages to appear both artistic and informative. (Courtesy of Bullocks Wilshire.)

than are those found in most newspapers. Significant use of color is an important part of the *USA Today* formula. Many newspapers are upgrading their technology to catch up with *USA Today,* so quality color is more easily available to advertisers today.

Even fancy printing techniques are now possible. Some newspaper advertisements include decals and logos that have been printed with a special heat-transfer ink. These can be cut out of the paper and then ironed onto T-shirts. These techniques will be discussed in more detail later in the chapter.

Magazine Advertisements

PRINCIPLE _____
In magazine advertising, speak to their special interest.

Advertising that ties in closely with the magazine's special interest may be valued as much as the articles. For example, skiers read the ads in the ski magazines to learn about new equipment, new technology, and new fashions. Readers of professional publications may cut out and file ads away as part of their professional reference library. For this reason magazine ads are often more informative and carry longer copy than do newspapers ads. Still, despite this built-in interest, ads must catch the attention of the reader who may be more absorbed in an article on the opposite page. To do that, magazine advertising tends to be more creative than newspaper advertising,

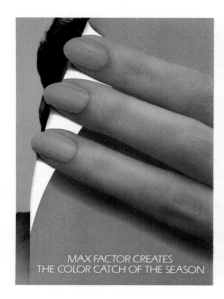

MAX FACTOR CREATES
THE COLOR CATCH OF THE SEASON

DIAMOND HARD
FORMULA
MAX
FACTOR
CREME NAIL ENAMEL 1/2 FL OZ

SHRIMP

THE INCREDIBLE NEW SHADE OF SOFTNESS AND LIGHT.

Color that captures the warmth and glow of the springtime sun. Bathes you in it. And stays so completely neutral, it goes with everything. Whatever your skin tone. Whatever you're wearing.

Any time of the night or day. Catch it. In Diamond Hard™ Nail Enamel and Moisture Rich Lipstick.

MAX FACTOR

AD 14.2
Max Factor uses a gimmick to draw the magazine readers into turning the page and reading about its makeup. (Courtesy of Max Factor & Co.)

using beautiful photography and graphics with strong impact. Magazines are also particularly useful for image advertising, as noted in the opening story on the Infiniti campaign.

Production Characteristics. Magazines have traditionally led the way in graphic improvements. The paper is better than newsprint; it is slick, coated, and heavier. Excellent photographic reproduction is the big difference between newspapers and magazines. Magazines do use illustrations, but they employ them to add another dimension, such as fantasy, to the visual message.

Magazine advertisements are also turning to more creative, attention-getting devices such as pop-up visuals, scent strips, and computer chips that play melodies when the pages are opened up. Ad 14.2 for Max Factor shows how a three-page insert can be used to tease readers into opening up a fold-out *spread* (a layout designed across two pages).

*W*RITING FOR PRINT

display copy *Type set in larger sizes that is used to attract the reader's attention.*

body copy *The text of the message.*

In Chapter 13 we talked in general about advertising copywriting. In this chapter we will examine the specific demands of print advertising. There are two categories of copy: display and body copy, or text. **Display copy** includes all those elements that the reader sees in his or her initial scanning. These elements, usually set in larger type sizes, are designed to get attention and to stop the viewer's scanning. **Body copy,** the text of the message, includes the elements that are designed to be read and concentrated on.

Headlines

headline *The title of an ad; it is set in large type to get the reader's attention.*

Most experts on print advertising agree that the headline is the most important display element. The **headline** works with the visual to get attention and communicate the creative concept. This Big Idea is usually best communicated through a picture and words working together. For example, an ad for Bekins, a moving and storage company, showed a photograph of a personal check torn in half. The picture made sense when combined with the headline: "If a mover only does part of the job well, that's all he should be paid for."

The headline is the most important element of a print ad because most people who are scanning read nothing more. Researchers estimate that only 20 percent of those who read the headline go on to read the body copy.*

Because headlines are so important, there are some general guidelines for their development and particular functions that they serve. A headline must *select* the right prospect, *stop* the reader, *identify* the product and brand, *start the sale,* and *lure* the reader on into the body copy.

PRINCIPLE
Tell as much of the story in the headline as possible.

Selecting Prospects.
Ideally, a good headline will attract only those who are prospects; there is no sense attracting people who are not in the market for the product. A good headline selects out target audience members by speaking to their interests. An old advertising axiom is: "Use a rifle, not a shotgun."

An example of an ad that pinpoints its audience is one for Metropolitan Life that tries to sell insurance to women who are single parents. This is a very specific audience. Life insurance is not an easy product to sell to anyone, but this headline spoke to a person who might not have wanted to even think about life insurance: "Children growing up without their fathers should be able to live without their mothers too."

Gaining Viewer Attention.
Once the prospects have been selected, stopping and grabbing their attention is critical. As discussed in Chapter 8, this responsibility, shared with the visual, is a measure of the strength of the creative concept. An advertisement by General Motors that focused on its automotive testing used a picture of a car driving on rough cobblestones. The headline was unexpected. It read: "One way or another we will destroy this car."

One way to stop and grab readers is to involve them in completing the message. Involvement techniques can have tremendous impact. Questions can be puzzling, make you think, and invite you to participate in the development of the message. Furthermore, you feel compelled to read on to find out the answer.

A different kind of involvement technique was used by Kraft for its Macaroni & Cheese Dinner. The ad used an incomplete headline, "Kraft Macaroni and ___," that the reader had to complete after looking at the visual, which included a chunk of cheddar cheese. This is a psychological principle called *closure* in which the reader completes the thought.

PRINCIPLE
Name the brand, if you can, in the head.

Identifying the Product.
Product and brand identification is very important. At the very least, the headline should make the product category clear to the reader. The headline should answer the question: "What kind of product is this?" The more the brand is tied into the concept, the more likely you are to leave some minimal identification with the 80 percent of the audience who look at the ad, read the headline, and then move on.

A series of ads for Goodyear Eagle radial tires was able to develop the association with high-performance vehicles and, at the same time, link the name of the brand to well-known sports cars. For example, one of the ads

PRINCIPLE
Telegraph the selling premise in the headline.

*Philip Ward Burton, *Which Ad Pulled Best?* (Chicago: Crain, 1981).

had two pictures of Formula One racing cars with a Ferrari Testarossa in between. The headline said: "The fact that all of these Ferraris are on Goodyear Eagle radials is no coincidence."

Introducing Selling Premises. Another function of a good headline is to introduce the selling premise. If the strategy calls for a benefit, a claim, a unique selling proposition (USP), a promise, or a reason why, that message should be telegraphed in the headline. If you have a strong sales point, lead with it. For example, Tylenol advertised its Extra Strength Tylenol Gelcaps with an advertisement that showed the pain reliever being held in a person's hand. The gelcap was boxed off with a white border, drawing attention to the product. The headline emphasized the strength of the pain reliever by stating: "Tylenol Gelcaps. The Power to Stop Pain." The ad illustrates how a headline can both identify the product and state the selling premise while leading into the body copy.

Introducing Body Copy. Finally, a good headline will lead the reader into the body copy. In order for that to happen, the reader has to stop scanning and start concentrating. This need to change the perceptual mode is the reason only 20 percent of scanners become readers.

Types of Headlines. Headlines can be grouped into two general categories: direct and indirect action. *Direct headlines* are straightforward and informative, such as the Tylenol headline about "The Power to Stop Pain." They select the audience with a strong benefit, promise, or reason why. They identify the product category, and they link the brand with the benefit. Direct headlines are highly targeted, but they may fail to lead the reader into the message if they are not captivating enough.

Action techniques include news announcements, assertions, and commands. News headlines obviously are used with new-product introductions, but also with changes, reformulations, new styles, and new uses. An assertion is used to state a claim or a promise. A command headline politely tells the reader to do something. The headline used in Ad 14.3A for Oil of Olay is an example of an ad that speaks directly to the target audience.

Indirect headlines are not as selective and may not provide as much information, but they may be better at luring the reader into the message. They are provocative and intriguing, and they compel people to read on to find out the point of the message. Indirect headlines use curiosity and ambiguity to get attention and build interest. Ad 14.3B for Allstate, for example, uses a provocative photo of a pair of colorful boxer shorts and an indirect headline to grab attention and stimulate interest. The headline reads: "Renters. Insure your boxer shorts against fire, theft, lightning, windstorm, vandalism, explosion, falling objects, riot, or hail."

Techniques for indirect headlines include questions, how-to statements, challenges, and puzzlements. A question headline can be effective if it addresses an important, powerful message because it makes it possible for people to accomplish or achieve something on their own. Challenges and puzzling statements are used strictly for their provocative power. Safeway used a picture of an egg with a puzzling headline to introduce its testing procedures. The headline read: "You can't judge an egg by its cover."

All these techniques require the reader to examine the body copy to get the answer or explanation. Sometimes these indirect headlines are referred to as "blind" because they give so little information. A blind headline is a gamble. If it is not informative or intriguing enough, the reader may move on without absorbing any product name information.

Now you can get soap clean without soap.

New
100%
soap-free
Foaming
Face
Wash
from
Oil of Olay

Forget about dry. New Foaming Face Wash cares for your face better than any soap. This rich lather even removes eye makeup without being irritating. 100% oil-free, it rinses clean. Leaving skin refreshed yet silky soft. Even a bit younger looking. Change the way you wash your face. Forever.

Renters. Insure your boxer shorts against fire, theft, lightning, windstorm, vandalism, explosion, falling objects, riot, or hail.

Allstate

AD 14.3A
An example of a direct headline.
(Courtesy of Oil of Olay.)

AD 14.3B
An example of an indirect headline. (Courtesy of Allstate.)

Headline Writing. Writing a headline is tremendously challenging. Writers will cover notepads with hundreds of headlines and spend days worrying about the wording. Headlines are also carefully tested to make sure they can be understood at a glance and that they communicate exactly the right idea. *Split-run tests* (two versions of the same ad) in direct mail have shown that changing the wording of the headline, while keeping all other elements constant, can double, triple, or quadruple consumer response. That is why the experts, such as David Ogilvy, state that the headline is the most important element in the advertisement.*

Other Display Copy

Subheads and Captions. Most people, if their interest is aroused by the visual and the headline, will scan the body of the advertisement to see if it looks interesting enough to read. Subheads and photo captions help to make that decision easier. Ad 14.4 for the Beef Industry Council and Beef Board, for example, incorporates a number of types of display copy elements such as subheads, captions, slogans, and taglines.

Subheads are sectional headlines. They are smaller in size than headlines but larger than body copy. They are sprinkled throughout the body copy to break up the gray type, to tease the reader's interest, and to identify the major points of the advertisement. They should be written just as carefully as the main headline. The Beef Industry ad uses a series of four subheads to reinforce the nutritional value of beef.

Captions, or cutlines, are used with the art because photos and illustrations can be interpreted in a number of ways. Captions not only help prevent misunderstanding but also are the next copy read after the headline. Because of the power of the visual, captions have very high readership. David Ogilvy insists that every photo should have a caption.†

Overlines and Underlines. An **overline** is a subhead that leads into the headline; an **underline** is a subhead that leads from the headline into the

subheads *Sectional headline used to break up masses of type.*

captions *Short descriptions of the content of a photograph or an illustration.*

overline *A subhead that leads into the headline.*

---

*David Ogilvy, *Ogilvy on Advertising* (New York: Vintage Books, 1985).
†Ogilvy, *Ogilvy on Advertising*.

AD 14.4
The copy package for the beef advertisement includes a number of display copy elements designed to attract and keep the reader's attention. (Reprinted by permission of the Beef Industry Council and Beef Board.)

underline *A subhead that leads from the headline into the body copy.*

tagline *A memorable phrase that sums up the concept or key point of the ad.*

body copy. They are used to compensate for the limitations of direct and indirect headlines. The overline, for example, is a teaser. It may be used with a straightforward headline to spark some interest. An underline is a transition, a bridge, and it is used with indirect headlines. The underline provides the information that was missing in the "blind" headline. These supplemental headings are useful with complex multipage layouts.

Slogans and Taglines. Product and campaign slogans are also part of the copy package. Slogans were discussed in Chapter 8 as an important element in creating memorability. A **tagline** is a particularly memorable phrase from an individual advertisement that is repeated at the end of a single ad. It captures some key point of the ad. If it is repeated from ad to ad, then it becomes a slogan.

An example of a tagline that is used to wrap up the creative concept is found in the Beef Industry ad. The tagline at the bottom of the ad reads: "Beef. Real Food For Real People."

Copywriters employ a number of literary techniques to enhance the memorability of slogans and taglines. Some slogans use a startling or unexpected phrase; others use rhyme, rhythm, alliteration (repetition of sounds), or parallel construction (repetition of the structure of a sentence or phrase). This repetition of structure and sounds contributes to memorability. Notice the use of these techniques in the following slogans:

- BMW: "The Ultimate Driving Machine"
- Army: "Be all that you can be"
- *The Wall Street Journal:* "The daily diary of the American dream"

Body Copy

The body copy is the text of the ad, the paragraphs of small type. The content develops the sales message and provides support, states the proof, and gives the explanation. This is the persuasive heart of the message. You excite consumer interest with the display elements, but you win them over with the argument presented in the body copy.

Candy bars, for example, might be seen by some writers as a difficult product about which to write an interesting message. However, the copy for Take Five* candy bar is fun, interesting, and easy to read all the way through. The headline asks:

"When to Take Five."
The body copy answers:

"• When you total up your dog's veterinarian bills and discover he's getting better medical care than you.
• When your credit card balance makes you the fourth biggest deficit spender after Argentina, Mexico and Brazil.
• When the number of candles on your birthday cake makes it necessary to blow them out with a fan.
• Whenever you bring work home on the weekend and actually do it.
• When you have a flat and the spare is in the garage.
• When you arrive in Toledo and your bags arrive in Taipei.
• Whenever the car repair bill is under $100.
• When your mother informs you she's taking up break-dancing.
• After taking 1st prize at a costume party and you didn't wear one.
• Anytime on Monday.
• When you discover that the CPA who found all those loopholes for you last year, is working for the IRS this year.
• After you finish reading all these reasons to take five and you're dying to try a Take Five bar.
• When you want light wafers, silky peanut creme, covered with Hershey's milk chocolate . . .
• When you want the richness of a candy bar without the heaviness of one, try a Take Five bar."

Types of Body Copy. There are as many different kinds of writing styles as there are copywriters and product personalities. Some body copy is *straightforward* and written in the words of an unknown or unacknowledged source. A *narrative* style may be used to tell a story, which may be either in the first person or the third person. A *dialogue* style lets the reader "listen in" on a conversation.

The liquor Sambuca Romana uses historical stories in its advertising campaign. The following example started with a headline, followed by an underline:

Lord Byron's Dilemma† (or, the lady or the Sambuca Romana)
The story tells of Lord Byron's adventures with Sambuca Romana in Venice:

The story is told that it was in a Venetian cafe, early for a rendezvous, that he first ordered the two drinks at one time. His coffee arrived and, just as he saw his contessa stepping from her gondola, the liqueur. As he started to his feet, somehow jostling the waiter, the Sambuca Romana spilled into the coffee. There was time for only one sip. He sipped, considered a moment, then sat down to finish the cup at his leisure.

It was plain the lady would have to wait. The attraction of this sensuous new taste was greater than even hers.

For the rest, we know Byron left Italy soon afterwards for Greece and his ultimate destiny. As for Sambuca Romana and coffee, the taste is history.

Dialogue is a little harder to write. It takes an ear for the language used by the target audience. An example of copy that reflects the witty ur-

---

*The TAKE FIVE candy bar material is reprinted by permission of the copyright owner, Hershey Foods Corporation, Hershey, Pennsylvania, U.S.A. TAKE FIVE and HERSHEY'S are registered trademarks of Hershey Foods Corporation.
†Courtesy of Sambuca Romana, Morgan Furze, Ltd., Ft. Lee, NJ.

AD 14.5
The body copy in this ad for Paco Rabanne demonstrates the use of a dialogue style. (Courtesy of Compar, Inc. Agency: Ogilvy & Mather.)

banity of a contemporary couple has appeared in a series of ads for Paco Rabanne, a men's cologne. Notice how the dialogue is set up in Ad 14.5.

Craftsmanship. Body copy is very well crafted. Copywriters will spend hours, even days, on one paragraph. They will write a first draft, revise it, then tighten and shorten it. After many revisions the copy gets read by others, who critique it. It then goes back to the writer, who continues to fine-tune it. Body copy for most major ads is revised over and over again.

Notice the craftsmanship in the following advertisement for the computer software product Lotus 1-2-3. This copy is unusual in that it doesn't have a headline. Possibly the body copy is intended to be one long headline. At any rate, the emphasis is definitely on the text of the message. As you read it, notice the use of natural language, personal address, parallel structure, and alliteration:

> If you've ever scribbled on a yellow pad, a napkin, a tablecloth, a notebook or a memo pad,
>
> If you've ever used even the simplest tools of business to prepare a budget, predict a trend, plan a schedule or to analyze information of any kind.
>
> If you deal in straight lines, curved lines, credit lines or bottom lines,
>
> If you've ever asked "what if," "why not," or "how come?"
>
> If you've ever taken into account a variable, a sudden change of plans, a mid-course correction or the weather,
>
> If you work in any kind of business, anywhere in the world, then you can use 1-2-3 software from Lotus.
>
> That's what makes the world's most powerful analytical tool the world's most popular.

The copy ends with a tagline that functions as a headline: "More people use it because it does so much more."

Structure. Two paragraphs get special attention in body copy: the *lead-in* and the *close*. The first paragraph of the body copy is another point where people test the message to see if they want to read it. Magazine article writers are particularly adept at writing lead paragraphs that pull the reader into the rest of the copy.

Closing paragraphs in body copy are difficult to write because they have to do so many things. Usually the last paragraph refers back to the creative concept and wraps up the Big Idea (see Chapter 13). Often the closing will use some kind of "twist," an unexpected tie-in with the concept. In addition, direct-action messages include some kind of *call to action* with instructions on how to respond. Even indirect-action advertisements, like brand-reminder ads in magazines, may use some kind of call to action, perhaps a reminder of where the product can be found.

DESIGNING FOR PRINT

Layout and Design

Architects design buildings in their minds and then translate the details of the structure onto paper in a form known as a *blueprint*. The blueprint guides the construction of a building. It tells the builder what size everything is and what goes where.

COPY CHECKLIST

- Pictures and words work together to create impact and meaning.
- Write to someone you know who fits the characteristics of the target audience. Put that person's picture above your typewriter while you write—it will make your copy more believable.
- Write the way people talk. Don't use an essay style, and avoid the marketing lingo you find in strategy statements.
- Read the copy aloud and imagine you're saying this to a friend. If you're uncomfortable saying the copy aloud, then rewrite it until it sounds like something you would say.
- Advertising copy is developed as thoughts, and thoughts are usually expressed in short, succinct expressions.

- Use the present tense, active voice, and simple sentence constructions.
- Short paragraphs are easier to read and less intimidating than long ones.
- Advertising personalizes copy by using personal address with lots of "you's."
- Avoid using the corporate "we"; it sounds pompous and indicates "brag-and-boast" copy.
- Avoid a pedantic, preachy, or negative tone of voice; you want your reader to like your product and have good feelings about it.

Source: Adapted from Sandra E. Moriarty, *Creative Advertising,* 2nd ed., (Englewood Cliffs, NJ: Prentice Hall, 1991):Chapter 8.

The same thing happens in advertising. The art director takes the creative concept that has been developed with the copywriter and visualizes in his or her mind how the final ad will look. This visual inventiveness is characteristic of good designers.

layout *A drawing that shows where all the elements in the ad are to be positioned.*

Art directors manipulate the elements on paper to produce a **layout,** which is a plan that imposes order and at the same time creates an arrangement that is aesthetically pleasing. A layout is a map, the art director's equivalent of a blueprint. The art director positions and sizes the elements. These include the visual or visuals, the headline and other supplemental display copy, copy blocks, captions, signatures, logos, and other details such as boxes, rules, and coupons.

A layout has several roles. First, it is a communication tool that translates the visual concept for others so that the idea can be discussed and revised before any money is spent on production. After it has been approved, the layout serves as a guide for the production people who will eventually handle the typesetting, finished art, photography, and pasteup. In some cases the layout acts as a guide for the copywriter who writes copy to fit the space. It is also used for cost estimating. Figures 14.1A through 14.1C demonstrate some of the major steps involved in creating a print ad.

Layout Styles. The most common layout format is one with a single dominant visual that occupies about 60 to 70 percent of the area. Underneath it is a headline and a copy block. The logo or signature signs off the message at the bottom. A variation on that format has a dominant visual and several smaller visuals in a cluster. A panel or grid layout uses a number of visuals of certain sizes.

Less frequently you will see layouts that emphasize the type rather than art. Occasionally you will see an all-copy advertisement where the headline is treated as type art. A copy-dominant ad may have art, but it is either embedded in the copy or positioned at the bottom of the layout.

thumbnail sketches *Small preliminary sketches of various layout ideas.*

semicomp *A layout drawn to size that depicts the art and display type; body copy is simply ruled in.*

comprehensive *A layout that looks as much like the final printed ad as possible.*

mechanicals (keylines) *A finished pasteup, with every element perfectly positioned, that is photographed to make printing plates for offset printing.*

Developing Layouts. There are several steps in the normal development of a print layout. Most art directors—and sometimes copywriters at this stage—work with a form known as **thumbnail sketches.** These are quick miniature versions of the ad, preliminary sketches (more like doodles) that are used for developing the concept and judging the positioning of the elements. In the early stages of development an art director may fill page after page with these thumbnail sketches, trying to decide what the ad will look like and where the elements will be positioned.

The second step is a *rough layout.* Roughs are done to size but not with any great attention to how they look. Once again, a rough layout is for the art director's use in working out size and placement decisions. It is sometimes called a *visualization.* In newspaper ads the "rough" may be the only step before the layout goes to production.

In order to show the idea to someone or to test various concepts, the art director will usually move to the next step, which is a **semicomp** ("comp" is short for comprehensive). A semicomp is done to the exact size of the ad, and all the elements are exactly sized and positioned. It is done by hand, but because it is going to be presented to others, extra care is taken to make it look good.

In a semicomp the art is sketched in, usually with felt-tip markers. Color is added where appropriate. Shading for black and white is done with various gray markers to indicate tonal variations. The display type is lettered in to resemble the style of type in the final ad. The body copy is indicated by ruling in parallel lines that indicate the size of the body type and the space it will fill. Most advertising layouts are presented in either the rough layout or semicomp stage. The semicomp is used for most routine presentations.

On special occasions a full-blown **comprehensive** may be developed. This is an impressive presentation piece. Type may be set, particularly for the display copy. Body copy is often just nonsense type (also called *Greeking* type), either commercially available or cut out of another publication. It is supposed to be the right size and resemble the actual typeface specified for the ad. The art may be a rendering by an artist who specializes in realistic art for comps, or it may be cut out of another publication. The idea is to make the comp look as much as possible like the finished piece. It is used for presentations to people who cannot visualize what a finished ad will look like from a semicomp. It is also used in important situations like new business presentations and agency reviews.

The last stage in the production process is the development of **mechanicals,** also called **keylines.** These are extremely carefully prepared pasteups intended for the printer. They are strictly for production use. Mechanicals are disappearing as more agencies and printers move to electronic publishing. With computer composition and layout, everything is done on the screen and the computer prints out an electronically assembled image—or sometimes a page negative that is one step closer to printing plates.

Design Principles

A layout begins with a collection of miscellaneous elements, usually a headline (and perhaps an overline or underline), one or more pieces of art and maybe some accompanying captions, body copy complete with subheads, a brand or store signature, and perhaps a trademark, a slogan, or a tagline. Local retail advertising will also include reminder information such as address, hours, telephone number, and credit cards accepted. Arranging

FIGURE 14.1A
A rough layout. The rough contains little detail—note the nonsense type—and is used for size and placement decisions.

FIGURE 14.1B
The mechanical. Used in offset printing, the mechanical is a photo-ready original with all of the elements properly placed. The various instructions are printed on transparent overlays.

FIGURE 14.1C
The final proof. (Courtesy of Maybelline USA.)

Gütenberg Diagonal *A visual path that flows from the upper left corner to the lower right.*

all of these elements so that they make sense and attract attention is a challenge. These decisions are both functional and aesthetic. The functional side of a layout makes the message easy to perceive; the aesthetic side makes it attractive and pleasing to the eye.

Organization. The challenge to the designer is to impose some order on all this chaos. We know from research into perception that organized visual images are easier to recognize, perceive, and remember than are visual images without any order.*

By order, we mean organization—imposing some pattern on the placement of the elements. Behind every layout is a pattern. If you take a piece of tracing paper and convert the major elements of any good ad to geometric shapes, a pattern will emerge. *Pattern* is a way of talking about the relationship of various elements to one another. A layout without any order lacks visual coordination of the elements.

Direction. The next thing you will notice when you study the tracing paper is that your eye follows some kind of path when it scans the elements. This path is determined by the ordering of the elements. The elements seem to follow one another according to some very carefully planned strategy.

In Western countries most readers scan from top to bottom and from left to right. That motion from upper left to lower right was tagged the **Gütenberg Diagonal** (see Figure 14.2) by graphics expert Edmund Arnold. Ad 14.6 for Lubriderm Lotion illustrates this visual path. Most layouts try to work with these natural eye movements, although directional cues can be manipulated in a layout to cause the eye to follow an unexpected path. The biggest problem occurs when the visual path is unclear.

*Gerald Murch, *Visual and Auditory Perception* (Indianapolis: Bobbs-Merrill Co., 1973).

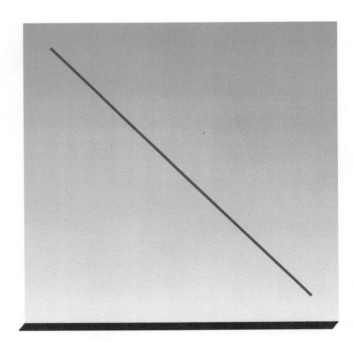

FIGURE 14.2
The Gütenberg Diagonal.

focal point *The first element in a layout that the eye sees.*

visual path *The direction in which the reader's eye moves while scanning a layout.*

PRINCIPLE
Use graphic signposts to make the visual path obvious.

PRINCIPLE
Think unity. Keep things together that go together.

Dominance   Most good layouts have a starting point, called the *dominant element.* Within the design process, someone must determine the relative importance of the various elements in order to decide which one should be dominant. Normally the dominant element is a visual, but it can be a headline if the type is sufficiently big and bold to overpower the other elements. By definition there can be only one dominant element; everything else must be subordinate. This element is the **focal point** of the ad; it is the first thing you see.

Visual Path   In most ads this starting point will be the upper half of the layout, and frequently the upper left quarter. That is the natural point of entry for the eye. Likewise the natural ending point is the lower right corner, which is where you will often find a brand logo or store signature.

The **visual path** that your eye follows in scanning the ad is a function of the pattern created by the arrangement. Built into the arrangement are signposts that tell you where to look next. Sometimes they are very obvious, like the direction of a model's gaze or a pointing hand. The alligator's tail in the Lubriderm ad provides direction, down and to the right, where the product is shown. More often the pattern itself creates the order. Your eye will move from one element to another depending on the descending visual importance of the element.

Unity.   A layout begins with a collection of discrete elements. It ends with a design in which all the elements have been fused into one coherent image: The pieces become a whole. For that to happen, the relationships have to be strong. The art and the headline must work together to create a concept. The selling premise and creative concept must work together to touch the right chord in the target. On a visual level the content of the message must fuse with the form of the presentation. The ad's appearance should match its message. You wouldn't use delicate letters for an ad about Mack trucks, nor would you use fanciful art for an ad targeted to truck drivers.

AD 14.6
This layout demonstrates the visual power of the Gütenberg Diagonal. (Courtesy of Warner-Lambert Company.)

Consistency   Consistency is important to unity. Using one typeface rather than several is a good technique for creating unity, particularly for display copy. If there is a dominant artistic style, stick to it. Ultramodern type doesn't fit with an illustration that looks Victorian.

Contiguity   Neighboring elements that touch and align are another important aspect of unity. An old axiom in layout states: "Keep things together that go together." Captions need to adjoin the pictures to which they refer. Headlines lead into the text, so the headline should be over the body copy. Pictures providing a different view of the same thing should be grouped.

White Space   White space is not simply an area where nothing happens. It can be massed and used as a design element. It works in one of two ways: It either frames an element in a sea of white, which gives it importance; or it separates elements that don't belong together. Because it sets things apart, white space is used as a prestige cue in layouts for upscale stores and products.

margin *White space used to frame the ad content.*

Margins   Margins are an important part of unity. A **margin** is simply white space designed to frame the ad and separate it from everything surrounding it. When layout artists begin an ad, the first thing they do is draw the ad size (for a newspaper) or the page size (for a magazine); then they draw a second set of faint guidelines that indicate the four internal margins of the ad.

Margins are critical in newspapers, where ads frequently abut one another. In magazines, for a special charge, a full-page ad may **bleed** to the trim edge of the page, eliminating the margins altogether. Bleed pages are used for ads that are dominated by photographs. You wouldn't want the copy to run right to the trim edge because it might be trimmed off. Even bleed ads use an internal set of margins that determine the edge of the copy blocks.

bleed *An ad in which the printed area runs to the trim edge of the page.*

Contrast.   Contrast indicates the importance of the various elements. Contrast makes one element stand out because it is different. People notice opposites, the unexpected. Contrast is also used to separate an ad from its surroundings. Because the newspaper environment is mostly black and white, an ad that uses color will stand out in contrast. In magazines, where most of the ads and editorial materials use color, a black-and-white ad might stand out. Black-and-white ads, by definition, are high in contrast. They can create dramatic, high-contrast images. A small ad or illustration can dominate if it contrasts effectively with its surrounding.

Balance. When an artist decides where to place an element, he or she is manipulating balance. A layout that is not in a state of visual equilibrium seems to be heavier on one side than the other. A layout that is out of balance is visually unpleasing and looks like a mistake.

There are two types of balance—formal and informal. *Formal balance* is symmetrical, left to right. Everything is centered. Formal balance is conservative and suggests stability. *Informal balance* is asymmetrical and creates a more visually exciting or dynamic layout. Informal balance is much harder to achieve because it requires manipulating and counterbalancing visual weights around an imaginary optical center. Counterbalancing uses the teeter-totter principle: Larger figures are positioned closer to the fulcrum than are smaller figures.

The concept of optical center is critical to informal balance. The **optical center** is the point on a page that our eyes see as the center. Because we tend to overemphasize the top half of the page, the optical center is slightly above the mathematical center (the point where the diagonals cross). This is an imaginary point. Sometimes the designer uses it to position the actual focal point of the ad, but more often it is just the point around which the elements are balanced.

Proportion. Proportion is both an aesthetic and a mathematical principle that concentrates on the relative sizes of the elements. The basic idea is that equal proportions are visually uninteresting because they are monotonous. Two visuals of the same size fight with one another for attention, and neither provides a point of visual interest. Copy and art, for example, should be proportionately different. Usually the art dominates and covers two-thirds to three-fifths of the page area. The worst sin aesthetically is to use a layout that divides the page in half.

Simplicity. The architect's axiom applies here: Less is more. The more elements that are crowded into a layout, the more the impact is fragmented. Don't overload the layout. The fewer the elements, the stronger the impact. *Clutter* is the opposite of simplicity. It comes from having too many elements and too little unity.

It is possible, however, to create busy ads with numerous elements and still control the organization. Discount store advertising typically uses a form called an *omnibus* ad that is crammed with many items and big prices as a signal to the reader that the store has plenty of merchandise at good prices. This layout style can work if the elements are carefully organized, the pattern is obvious, and the visual path is logical.

Local retail advertising often tries to crowd as many elements as possible into a limited advertising space because the advertiser is trying to get maximum advertising out of a limited budget. Such ads can be a waste of the advertiser's money if the layout is not skillfully organized. Then the art looks like postage stamps, and the clutter makes the layout so unappealing that is is frequently ignored by most of its prospective readers. Those who lay out ads know that when you "feature" something in an ad, it has to stand out. People won't fight through clutter and disorganization. Make it hard for them to read and they won't bother to.

optical center *A point slightly above the mathematical center of a page.*

PRINCIPLE
Less is more, so when in doubt, delete.

AD 14.7
Smuckers uses colors to associate warm feelings with its spreadable fruit. (Courtesy of © The J.M. Smucker Company.)

Color

Color is used in advertising to *attract attention, provide realism, establish moods,* and *build brand identity.* Research has consistently shown that ads with color get more attention than do ads without color. Full-color photos are more interesting than are black-and-white photos. In newspapers, where color reproduction may not be very accurate, *spot color,* in which a second accent color is used to highlight important elements, has proved to be highly attention-getting.

Realism is important for certain message strategies, where full-color photographs may be essential. Some things just don't look right in black and white: pizza, flower gardens, beef stroganoff, and rainbows, for example. Color is needed to do justice to the content.

Color has a psychological language that speaks to moods and symbolic meanings. Warm colors, such as red, yellow, and orange, are bright and happy. These colors are used by Smucker's in Ad 14.7 to associate warm feelings with its fruit flavors. Pastels are soft and friendly. Earth tones are natural and no-nonsense. Cool colors, such as blue and green, are aloof, calm, serene, reflective, and intellectual.

Yellow and red have the most attention-getting power. Red is used to symbolize alarm and danger, as well as warmth. Yellow combined with black is not only attention-getting but also dramatic because of the stark contrast in values between the two colors. Black is used for high drama and can express power and elegance.

Metallic ink is popular with advertisers. Automotive advertising often uses a silver metallic ink. The gold industry ran a campaign that used 18-karat gold foil that was applied by heat.

Color association can be an important part of a brand image. Johnnie Walker Red has built a long-running campaign on all the warm associations we have with red, such as sunrises and sunsets, a fireplace, and a red setter. Kool cigarettes has used the color green so extensively that you can recognize the ad even when the product image is obliterated. IBM uses the color blue so extensively that the company is sometimes referred to by people in the computer industry as "Big Blue."

*P*RINT PRODUCTION

The Type

Most people don't even notice the letters in an ad, which is the way it should be. Good typesetting doesn't call attention to itself because its primary role is functional—to convey the words of the message. As George Lois, chairman and creative director at Lois Pitts Gershon Pon/GGK, stated: "It's important the typography doesn't get in the way of an idea."* Type also has an aesthetic role, however, and the type selection can, in a subtle way, contribute to the impact and mood of the message, as in Ad 14.8 for Celestial Seasonings.

font *A complete set of letters in one size and face.*

Typeface Selection. The basic set of typeface letters is called a **font.** A type font contains the alphabet for one typeface in one size plus the numerals and punctuation (see Figure 14.3). The alphabet includes both capital letters, called *uppercase,* and small letters, called *lowercase.* You may

*Noreen O'Leary, "Legibility Lost," *Adweek,* (October 5, 1987):D7.

want to specify *all caps,* which means every letter is a capital, or *U&lc* (upper and lower case), which means the first letter is capitalized and the others are lowercase.

Categories of Type. Most people don't realize that designers must choose among thousands of typefaces to find the right face for the message. Within each category of type are type families, which are made up of typefaces of similar design.

Two of the major categories are serif and sans serif. The **serif** is the little flourish that finishes off the end of the stroke. "Sans" means "without" in French, which is how **sans serif** letters are identified: They are missing the serif. Most of the sans serif typefaces are clean, blocky, and more contemporary in appearance (see Figure 14.4).

Type is organized into type *families,* which are groups of typefaces with similar characteristics. For example, *sans serif* is a category of typeface that includes such faces as Futura, Helvetica, and News Gothic. The serif faces are called *romans,* and that category includes such faces as Cheltenham, Goudy, Caslon, and Bodoni.

Other categories include *cursive,* or *script,* typefaces, which look like handwriting, and *black letter* or Old English. These faces are copies of the kinds of letters in use when Gutenberg made his first type. They look like the lettering in medieval manuscripts or early printed Bibles. There are also hundreds of ornamental typefaces designed to look like everything from logs to lace.

Family Variations. In addition to the thousands of typefaces in the various categories, there are variations within the typeface family itself. For example, any one typeface comes in a range of sizes. Figure 14.5 shows a typeface reproduced in different sizes.

The posture, weight, and width of a typeface also vary. Posture can vary from the normal upright letters to a version that leans to the right, called **italic.** The weight of the typeface can vary depending on how heavy the strokes are. Most typefaces are available in *boldface* or *light,* in addition to the normal weight. Variation in width occurs when the typeface is spread out horizontally or squeezed together. These variations are called *extended* or *condensed.*

14 pt

ABCDEFGHIJKLMNOPQRSTUV
abcdefghijklmnopqrstuvwxyz
1234567890

FIGURE 14.3
This is an example of the widely used Times Roman typeface.

ABCDEFGHIJKLMNOPQRSTUVWXYZ ABCD
ABCDEFGHIJKLMNOPQRSTUVWXYZ ABCD

FIGURE 14.4
The top line is printed in serif letters; the bottom line in sans serif.

6 POINT

ABCDEFGHIJKLMNOPQRSTUVWXYZABCDEFGHIJKLMNOPQRSTUVWXYZABC
abcdefghijklmnopqrstuvwxyzabcdefghijklmnopqrstuvwxyzabcdefghijklmnop   1234567890

12 POINT

ABCDEFGHIJKLMNOPQRSTUVWXYZ A
abcdefghijklmnopqrstuvwxyzabcd 1234567890

18 POINT

ABCDEFGHIJKLMNOPQRSTUVWXYZ   ABCDEFGHIJ

abcdefghijklmnopqrstuvwxyz abcdefghijklmnopqrstuvwxyz abc

1234567890

FIGURE 14.5
Examples of the different sizes available for the Times Roman typeface.

---

point *A unit used to measure the height of type; there are 72 points in an inch.*

pica *A unit of type measurement used to measure width and depth of columns; there are 12 points in a pica and 6 picas in an inch.*

justified *A form of typeset copy in which the edges of the lines in a column of type are forced to align by adding space between words in the line.*

Printers' Measures. To understand type sizes, you must understand the printers' measuring system. Type is measured in **points,** which are the smallest unit available. There are 72 points in an inch, so 72-point type is 1 inch high and 36-point type is one-half inch high. The space between lines of type, called *leading* (pronounced "ledding"), is also measured in points. Normally, 1 to 2 points of leading separate lines of body copy. Most designers consider type set in 14 points or larger to be display copy and type set 12 points or smaller to be body copy.

The width of columns, also called *line length,* is measured in **picas.** The pica is a bigger unit of measurement than the point. There are 6 picas in an inch and 12 points in a pica. So 12-point type is exactly 1 pica high, or one-sixth of an inch. Column lengths are usually measured in inches. Figure 14.6 illustrates a pica ruler. The most common sizes for body copy are 9-, 10-, and 11-point.

Justification. One characteristic of typeset copy as opposed to typewriter copy is the forced alignment of the column edges. With **justified** copy, such as you are reading here, every line ends at exactly the same point. Because lines don't normally end so neatly, there has to be a system to force this alignment. It consists of taking the extra space at the end of the last

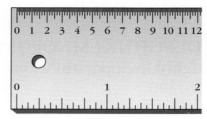

FIGURE 14.6
72 points = 1 inch
12 points = 1 pica
6 picas = 1 inch
This ruler shows the relationship
between points, picas, and inches.

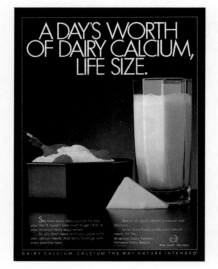

AD 14.9
**An example of reverse type that
works because it is big and bold.**
(Courtesy of National Dairy Board.)

---

reverse type *A style of typesetting
in which letters appear to be white
against a darker background.*

---

surprinting *Printing type over
some other image.*

---

word in the line and redistributing it back through the line at all the word breaks. Thus the spacing between words varies from line to line.

Justified copy is aligned at both the right and left column edges. Other options are available to advertisers. One variation is to let the right line endings fall where they will. This is called *ragged right.* You can also specify the opposite, *ragged left,* although that is a very unusual way to set type. If you want to specify that either edge be justified, then the phrase *flush left* or *flush right* is used. Another option is to set everything *centered,* which means neither the right nor the left edges align, but instead everything is centered around a vertical mid-point axis.

Legibility. As previously mentioned, type selection is primarily functional. The objective of *legibility* is to convey the words as clearly as possible. Because reading is such a complex activity, the type should make the perceptual process as easy as possible. If the type is difficult to read, most people will turn the page. Research has discovered a number of type practices that can hinder the reading process.*

All Caps One of the biggest problems that shows up consistently in legibility research is type set in all capitals. All caps slows down reading and causes many readers to give up. Although art directors like all caps because it gives a clean, rectangular look to the type, line after line of it will chase away all but the most dedicated readers.

Reverse Type Another legibility problem is **reverse type,** a technique that creates letters that appear to be white against a dark background. If the letters are big, bold, and few in number, then most people won't have any problem with reverse type (see Ad 14.9). If the letters are small and delicate, however, and if there is a lot of type to be read, most people will give up.

Ornamentals Unusual typefaces can also create legibility problems. Cursives and black-letter typefaces are particularly difficult to read. Ornamental faces are also difficult. Overly manipulated faces can also cause problems. Jeff Level, director of type research at Monotype Inc., has said: "A lot of people are thoroughly abusing typefaces today. They're stretching them, condensing them, and running them up against each other."†

Surprinting **Surprinting** is a technique that prints the type over or across some other image. If the background is clear, surprinting might not cause a problem. However, background patterns of any sort can fight with the letter forms and actually obliterate them. Big and bold surprinting dis-

---

*Rolf Rehe, *Typography: How to Make It Most Legible* (Indianapolis: Design Research Publications, 1974).

† O'Leary, "Legibility Lost," p. D7.

TYPE CLASSIFICATION SYSTEM

Some of the most commonly used categories of type
are the following:

Sans Serif:
This line is set in Futura.
This line is set in Helvetica.
This line is set in News Gothic.
This line is set in Avant Garde Gothic Book.

Romans:
Oldstyle Romans:
This line is set in Cheltenham Book.
This line is set in Goudy Old Style.
This line is set in Garamond Book.

Transitional Romans:
This line is set in Times Roman.
This line is set in Century Book.
This line is set in Baskerville.

Modern Romans:
This line is set in Bodoni.

Inscribed Serif:
This line is set in Optima.
This line is set in Americana Light.
This line is set in Serif Gothic.
This line is set in Palatino.
This line is set in Korinna.

Square Serif:
This line is set in Clarendon.
This line is set in Lubalin Graph Book.
This line is set in Memphis Medium.

Round Serif:
This line is set in Souvenir Medium.
This line is set in Cooper Black.

Script:
This line is set in English Script.

Black Letter:
This line is set in Old English.

Ornamentals:
THIS LINE IS SET IN LEMONADE.

SPECIFYING TYPE VARIATIONS

This is set in a light typeface.
This is set in a normal weight.
This is set in boldface.
This is set in italic.
This is set in an expanded typeface.
This is set in a condensed typeface.

PRINCIPLE
Play it safe. Don't fool around with the type.

play type is generally acceptable. The problem comes when small, delicate type is surprinted over a discernible pattern.

The most useful rule for gauging legibility is: Don't play games with type.

Typesetting. Most type is set, or composed, electronically using computer typesetting equipment that prints out a "slick" on photographic paper or a negative on film. The old methods of typesetting using metal type made of molten lead gave way in the 1950s and 1960s to photographic typesetting using punched tape to drive the composition process. The new computer typesetting still creates a photographic image, but the instructions and copy are delivered via computer rather than punched tape. Computerized photocomposition has freed typesetting from the limitations of metal and made it more flexible, as well as cheaper, cleaner, and more creative.

Before type is sent to a typesetter it has to be specified and the copy marked up. That means the art director chooses the type—in all of its variations and sizes—for the various pieces of copy. These specifications are then written on the original typewritten manuscript, along with any other editing and formatting information. This is called *copy markup*. For example, in order to set headlines, the typesetter needs to know the typeface, including any variations such as italic or boldface, and the size of the type. For body copy the typesetter needs the same information plus instructions on the line length (which is also referred to as the *column width*) and the amount of spacing between the lines.

Usually the copy is accompanied by a layout so the typesetter can verify the specifications and better fit the type to the space. Fitting the type to the space is a complicated process known as *copyfitting* that involves estimating how long the copy will run in picas or inches after it has been typeset into the specified typeface and size.

The Art

The word *art* refers to the graphics, whether an illustration or a photograph. Although art directors lay out the ad, they rarely do finished art. If an illustration is needed, then an artist who works in the appropriate style is hired, usually freelance. Fashion illustration is different from cartooning, for example. If a photo is needed, then a photographer is hired. Both artists and photographers tend to have personal styles or specialties, and the right person has to be found for the visual. An article in *Adweek* reported that specialized freelancers are being used more frequently as advertising agencies move into unusual media.*

The layout guides the execution of the illustration or photograph. The photographer uses it to compose the image. **Composition** is a term used to describe how the elements in the picture are arranged and framed. It is different from a layout, which arranges all the elements in an ad, including the type as well as the visual.

The problem faced in composition is how to position the elements in a picture; the problem in layout is how to arrange all the diverse elements in an ad—photographs, illustrations, headlines, body copy, and other typographic elements. The Smucker's ad demonstrates how a photographer positioned the elements in a picture; the Celestial Seasonings ad illustrates how an art director approached the layout problem.

Art Reproduction

There are two general types of images that are reproduced in print. A simple drawing is called **line art** because the image is just solid black lines on a white page. Photographs, however, are much more complicated because they have a range, or shades, of gray tones between the black and white. The phrase *continuous tone* is used to refer to images with this range of gray values.

Because printing is done with black ink, designers must be able to create the illusion of a range of grays. Continuous-tone art and photos must be converted to **halftones** in order to be printed. The *halftone process* begins when the original photograph is shot by another camera after a fine screen has been placed over the original (see Figure 14.7). That screen looks just like the screen on your window, only finer. If the area on the original is dark, then the dot will fill the space; if the original is light, then the dot will be surrounded by empty white space. The image, in other words, is converted to a pattern of dots that gives the illusion of shades of gray, the

composition *The process of arranging the elements in a photograph or an illustration.*

line art *Art in which all elements are solid with no intermediate shades or tones.*

halftones *Images with a continuous range of shades from light to dark.*

* Casey Davidson, "Agencies Learn the Art of Farming Work Out," *Adweek* (October 5, 1987):D14.

FIGURE 14.7
This figure contrasts the same image reproduced as line art (left) and a halftone (right).

shades being replicated by the various sizes of the dot pattern. If you look at a photograph in most newspapers, you may be able to see the dot pattern with your naked eye. If you can't, look at the image through a magnifying glass.

Screens. The quality of the image depends on how fine the screen is that is used to convert the original picture to a dot pattern. Because of the roughness of newsprint, newspapers use a relatively coarse screen, usually 65 lines per inch. (This is referred to as 65-line screen.) Magazines use finer screens, which may be 90, 110, 120, and on up to 200 lines per inch. The higher the number, the finer the screen and the better the quality of the reproduction.

Screens are also used to create various tint blocks, which can either be shades of gray in black-and-white printing or shades of color. A block of color can be printed solid or it can be *screened back* to create a shade. These shades are referred to as a range of percentages such as 100 percent (solid) down to 10 percent (very faint). Examples of screens are found in Figure 14.8.

Color Reproduction

Besides reproducing halftones, the other major problem for printers is the reproduction of full color. When you look at a slide, you see a full range of colors and shades. It would be impossible to set up a printing press with a separate ink roller for every possible hue and value. How, then, are these colors reproduced?

FIGURE 14.8
These figures show the different screens for black and white and for color.

process colors *Four basic inks—magenta, cyan, yellow, and black—that are mixed to produce a full range of colors found in four-color printing.*

color separation *The process of splitting a color image into four images recorded on negatives; each negative represents one of the four process colors.*

Process Colors. The solution to this problem is to use a limited number of base colors and mix them to create the rest of the spectrum. Full-color images are reproduced using four distinctive shades of ink, called **process colors.** They are magenta (a shade of pinkish red), cyan (a shade of bright blue), yellow, and black.

Printing inks are transparent, so when one ink color overlaps another, a third color is created. Red and blue create purple, yellow and blue create green, yellow and red create orange. The black is used for type and, in *four-color printing,* adds depth to the shadows and dark tones in an image.

Color Separations. The process used to reduce the original color image to four halftone negatives is called **color separation.** The negatives replicate the red, yellow, blue, and dark areas of the original. The separation is done photographically, beginning with original full-color images on slides. (Slides, or transparencies, produce the most accurate and grain-free images.) Color filters are used to screen out everything but the desired hue. A separate color filter is used for each of the four process colors. Lasers are now used to scan the image and make the separations. Figure 14.9 illustrates the process of color separation.

Computerized Color. New technologies have made it possible for a color piece to go directly from computer to film. Some agencies don't create mechanicals at all anymore. Instead, ads are created on the computer and transmitted to a service bureau or color separation by modem or floppy disks. There they can go directly to film.

Using computers for illustrations is relatively simple. The difficulty is in photography. In theory, a transparency can be scanned into a traditional high-end prepress system, then data can be sent to a Macintosh, for example, and assembled into an ad and then returned to the system for output on film. In reality, such files use up huge amounts of memory and time, and color calibration is not yet sophisticated enough to guarantee that what you see is what you get. What actually happens is that art directors work with low-resolution scans for positioning purposes only. The prepress operators then assemble the ad electronically, replacing the position-only scans they've made from transparencies in the traditional way.

As these methods are perfected, the time-consuming, labor-intensive assembling of ad pieces will be replaced with desktop color imaging. Color matching can be expensive, but it can also save companies money in stripping costs and typesetting, and the industry is optimistic about computerized color graphics.*

*Cathy Madison, "Ads Brought To You In Computerized Color" *Adweek* (January 14, 1991):24.

FIGURE 14.9 (Cont.)
Red plate.

FIGURE 14.9
The following photos illustrate the process of four-color separation.
Yellow plate.

FIGURE 14.9 (Cont.)
Yellow and red plates.

FIGURE 14.9 (Cont.)
Blue plate.

FIGURE 14.9 (Cont.)
The finished ad with all four process colors. *(Courtesy of Redbook.)*

FIGURE 14.9 (Cont.)
Black plate.

445

PRINTING PROCESSES

Letterpress

Four major printing processes are used in advertising (see Figure 14.10). The oldest method, **letterpress,** is a form of relief printing, which means it prints from a raised surface. The old "hot metal" typesetting methods produced type with such raised images. A rubber stamp is a cheap form of relief printing. Letterpress is seldom used today except for sequential numbering and specialty printing effects.

Offset Lithography

When **offset** printing emerged in the 1960s, many newspapers and magazines converted to this form of printing. Offset prints from a flat, chemically treated surface that attracts ink in the printing areas and repels it elsewhere.

A *camera-ready* original is shot photographically onto a thin aluminum *plate,* one plate for each color. The plate is chemically treated so that the image-carrying surfaces attract oil while the rest of the surface is covered with water. The plate is wrapped around a roller that revolves through a water bath and presses against an ink roller. The ink is greasy and doesn't

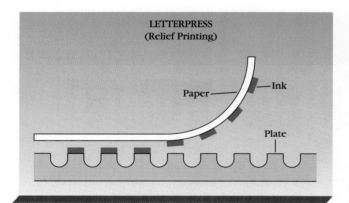

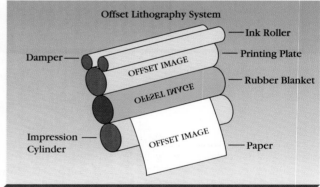

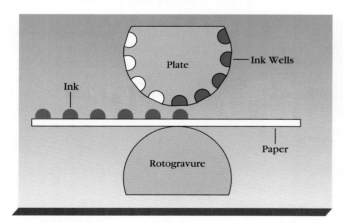

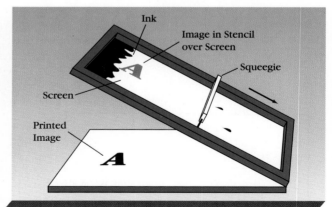

FIGURE 14.10
The major types of printing presses.
Top left: letterpress printing. *Top right:* offset printing.
Bottom left: rotogravure. *Bottom right:* screen printing.

stick to the water-covered nonprinting parts of the image. The next step explains why this process is called "offset." The inked image is transferred to a rubber blanket on an adjoining roller and from that roller to paper.

Offset is now used for most printing jobs. It is clean and involves no heavy molten lead, as did older presses. Anything that can be photographed can be printed. The camera-ready original, variously called a *mechanical* or a *keyline,* is a pasteup of all the elements. In advertising agencies people who prepare the camera-ready materials are called *keyliners.*

Rotogravure

gravure *A type of printing that uses an image that is engraved, or recessed, into the surface of the printing plate.*

Gravure printing is the exact opposite of relief printing; the images are engraved into the surface of the plate. The printing is done from a recessed image composed of tiny inkwells. Have you ever wiped your feet when you were wearing tennis shoes and then walked across a clean floor? You probably noticed that even though the surfaces of your shoes were clean, they still left a tread mark. That's because there was something in the treads that left an image on the floor. Gravure works well for photographic reproduction and for long runs because there is no wear on the printing surface. Quality magazines often use gravure printing, as do some Sunday newspaper photo sections and advertising inserts.

Flexography

A printing technique that is growing in popularity is flexography because it can print on any surface. *Flexography* is similar to offset in that it uses a rubber blanket to transfer the image to the page. It differs in that the ink is water-based and there is a different blanket setup on the press. Newspapers use flexography because the image is sharper and there is little ink ruboff.

Silk Screen

silk screen *A form of printing in which the nonimage areas, represented by a "blockout" film or lacquer, are adhered to a porous fabric while ink is forced through the image areas that aren't blocked out.*

A relatively simple printing method based on a stencil process, **silk screen** is used to make small runs of posters and greeting cards. Beyond that, more complicated automatic equipment is now used by commercial printers for printing posters, T-shirts, decals, banners, point-of-sale materials, and advertising specialties such as pens and coffee mugs.

In silk screen a fine meshlike fabric, similar to silk, is tautly fastened across a frame. A design is drawn on a lacquer film that is then adhered to the screen. The printing areas are cut away with a knife or washed away chemically. A heavy opaque ink is then forced through the screen with a squeegee. It passes through the open areas but the film holds back the ink in the nonprinting areas.

Duplicating Ads

If an ad is going to run in a number of publications, there has to be some way to distribute a reproducible form of the ad to all of them. For letterpress, a *mat* made from a kind of papier-mâché is sent, along with a *proof* made from the original engraving. For gravure printing, film positives are sent to the publications. The duplicate material for offset printing is a "slick" proof of the original mechanical. These proofs are called *photoprints* or *photostats,* which are relatively cheap images. *Veloxes* or *C-Prints* are better-quality prints.

CREATIVE ADVERTISING IN THE COMPUTER AGE

Introducing the computer into the production stream of agencies has had an unexpected effect and elicited a variety of reactions. Assembling a mechanical, or a pasteup, of all the elements of an advertisement was once the work of the studio artists or an art director who was particularly adept at this skill. The studio might charge $75 per hour, and the exacting effort might require more than 1 hour of work for each different size or variation of the advertisement.

Enter the computer, with all the elements scanned into memory. The first mechanical might take 20 to 30 minutes. Each successive variation, although a completely separate mechanical, might take only 5 to 10 minutes.

In the last few years creatives at BBDO have found themselves turning to computers for more and more of their needs. They use Apple Macintosh computers to help in the production of creative ideas, particularly in the Los Angeles office, which handles a lot of print advertising. Along with the assets of computer production come some problems, however. For example, in the real world, when light passes through glass, it bends. In producing images of some form of glass, such as soda bottles, this visual effect cannot, so far, be replicated by computer. Damian Pezzano, BBDO senior vice president and director of computer systems, is working on ways to make this possible, however.

Pezzano and his group have also set to work designing a "studio" within the computer—a program that would allow a producer to sit in front of the computer and manipulate all the elements that go into producing a spot.

The Mac has also saved the agency money by allowing slides to be produced in-house. Computerization has helped many agencies save both time and money.

According to a 1990 survey conducted for *Adweek* and Mead Data Central by M/A/R/C Inc. of Pittsburgh, computers have become an accepted and appreciated part of agency life. Of 100 agencies surveyed, 97 have bought or leased computers in quantity. The average ratio is one computer to every two employees. Some 27 percent of agencies use their computers to create finished art, and a small number

—2 to 3 percent—are experimenting in graphics, desktop publishing, presentations, and slides.

The survey found that the most popular programs used in creative departments ranged from the leaders in desktop publishing, such as Page Maker, Persuasion and FreeHand programs, and Adobe Illustrator, to Quark XPress, the Cricket Line, Letraset Ready-Set-Go, Claris MacDraw to Microsoft PowerPoint and Silicon Beach's Super Paint. The result is a tool box of programs that are drawn for specific, individual tasks.

Many agencies have come to rely on the many facets and capabilities of these programs. For example, because Pepsi's agency, BBDO, also handles Apple Computer, it used the Mac to create advertising for the soft drink. In an ad that shows nine cans of Pepsi in different languages, for example, the computer enabled the creative team to replace one country's version, say Taiwan, with another, say China. By making this change with the computer, both speed and crispness of execution are gained. Computers were also used to scan in the foreign logos around each can rather than having to take photographs of the actual cans.

Computers were also used in the popular *fahrvergnügen* campaign for Volkswagen. The commercials integrated live-action photography with graphics: The fahrfel logo dissolved into the classy, modern Eurographic of a driver, which then dissolved into a roadway. High-tech techniques allowed the spot to combine a real car and a surreal background into a seamless whole.

Smaller agencies and clients are using computer graphics as well. Cramer-Krasslet, the agency for The Cat Practice, an Illinois veterinary hospital specializing in cat care, created a computer-generated ad that used four yarn balls in the corner, each unravelling to form the ad's borders. The yarn ball was first hand-drawn then scanned into the computer and manipulated so that each of the four balls was unique. Using the computer enabled the creative team to try a number of different revisions on the spot, quickly and efficiently.

Source: Adapted from Jon Berry, "Playing For Keeps," *Adweek's Marketing Week* (August 6, 1990):24–38; and Betsy Sharkey, "Mac-in-Touch: Apple Shines in Linking BBDO Offices," *Adweek* (May 1, 1989):30.

Binding and Finishing

A number of special printing effects are created at the end of the production process. These are mechanical techniques that embellish the image using such methods as embossing or foil stamping. The last step in production is the binding, where the pages of a publication are assembled.

Newspapers are folded, and the fold holds the sheets together. Magazines are folded, stapled or sewn, and trimmed. Sometimes a separate cover is glued on. During this binding process separate preprinted ads provided by the advertiser can be glued in. Such ads are called **tip-ins.** They are used when an advertiser wants particularly fine printing or wishes to include something that can't be accommodated in the normal printing process. Most perfume manufacturers, for example, are tipping in perfume samples that are either scratch-and-sniff or scented strips that release their fragrance when pulled apart.

Advertisers are searching for even more novel effects to add interest and impact to their magazine ads. Recent ads have included such novelty techniques as a sailboat that unfolds, called a *pop-up,* in the middle of a Merit cigarette ad that ran in *Time.* Honeywell used a similar pop-up to present an entire factory/office complex in *Business Week.* Maybelline has used a "peel 'n' brush" blusher sample in *Glamour.* Both Absolut vodka and Canadian Mist liquor have played holiday music in magazine ads via a tiny microchip. Probably the ultimate novelty was created for a Toyota ad to dramatize the slogan, "The new dimension in driving." Detachable cardboard binoculars gave a Viewmaster-like 3-D image of a Toyota Corolla on the road.*

New Technology

A new technology, based on computers and transmission by phone line using fiber optics or by satellite, has generated a revolution in print media. Computerized typesetting now makes it easy to transmit type electronically. Art can be *digitized* (broken into tiny grids, each one coded electronically for tone or color) and then transmitted. Fiber optics can send type, art, or even complete pages across a city for local editions of newspapers. Satellites make national page transmission possible for regional editions of magazines and newspapers such as *U.S.A. Today.*

Printing by personal computer, utilizing easy-to-use software, is taking over the low end of the typesetting function. In addition to typesetting, page layouts as well as advertising layouts can be done on a personal computer. This new approach to typesetting and layout is called *desktop publishing.* Graphics that can be drawn and modified on computers are now being used in many newspapers. The box entitled "Creative Advertising in the Computer Age" takes a closer look at new production technology.

At the higher end of the typesetting function, many quality typesetting systems use some kind of computer-based *pagination* equipment that combines sophisticated computer typesetting with page layout capabilities.

Inkjet printing, which is a type of printing directed by computer, is becoming more common. It can speed up the entire printing process by eliminating many of the technical steps in printing, such as negatives and plate-making. It will soon be possible to go directly from the computer to a printed publication. This may make it feasible to customize the content of a

tip-ins *Preprinted ads that are provided by the advertiser to be glued into the binding of a magazine.*

---

*Bob Garfield, "Don't Gimme Gimmicks: Novelty Ads Flood Media," *Advertising Age* (November 9, 1987):41.

publication, advertising as well as articles, to the interest of the reader, thus creating a new world of one-on-one publishing and, eventually, personalized target marketing. *Time* used this to print subscribers' names on each cover.

SUMMARY

- Newspaper ads are more informative and less entertaining than other types of advertising.
- Magazines provide better reproduction of color and photographs than newspapers do.
- Headlines target the prospect, stop the reader, identify the product, start the sale, and lure the reader into the body copy.
- A layout arranges all the elements to provide a visual order that is aesthetically pleasing.
- Color is used in advertising to attract attention, provide realism, establish mood, and build brand identity.
- Typefaces convey meaning beyond the words; they help to create mood and impact.
- Color is reproduced as either spot color or process color, which involves a complicated process of color separation.
- The common printing processes are letterpress, offset, gravure, and silk screen.

QUESTIONS

1. What are the major features of a print ad? What is the purpose of each one?
2. Collect a group of ads for department and discount stores. Compare their layouts. What does the layout "say" about the type of store and the merchandise it carries?
3. Think of ads you have seen in newspapers and magazines over the past 10 years. What trends, if any, do you notice? How do you account for these trends?
4. We read from left to right and top to bottom. This pattern forms the natural "Z" shape. What does the chapter call this pattern of direction? Now look at some advertising in a favorite magazine. Do any of the ads *not* follow this pattern? Trace the visual direction used. What shape does it take? Why would the designer choose this direction pattern?
5. A student struggles with a layout assignment involving informal balance. She has a dominant vertical illustration element placed at the right side of her page. Her difficulty is finding some other element (copy block or small illustration) to balance the size and strength of the key visual. When she asks her instructor for help, he tells her, "You've forgotten one of the simplest principles of equilibrium: You don't always need other copy and design pieces to balance the dominant object." What does he mean?
6. Search your area newspapers for ads for clothing stores. Sort these into expensive stores and those that feature lower-priced apparel. Now compare the design aspects of each type of store. How many differences do you see in design, art, type, and other elements? Do any of these differences produce a store personality or image? Identify those print concepts in the ad that provide a special "signature" for the store.
7. More and more newspaper advertising departments and advertising agency creative staffs are using personal computer software to produce "comp" and "semicomp" layouts. Why is this "desktop" approach becoming so popular? Be specific in listing advantages.

FURTHER READINGS

ADLER, KEITH, *Advertising Resource Handbook* (East Lansing, MI: Advertising Resources, Inc., 1989).

BURTON, PHILIP WARD, *Which Ad Pulled Best?* (Chicago: Crain, 1981).

KEDING, ANN, and THOMAS H. BIVINS, *How to Produce Creative Advertising* (Lincolnwood, IL: NTC, 1991).

MORIARTY, SANDRA E., *Creative Advertising,* 2nd ed. (Englewood Cliffs, NJ: Prentice Hall, 1991).

MURCH, GERALD, *Visual and Auditory Perception* (Indianapolis: Bobbs-Merrill, 1973).

O'LEARY, NOREEN, "Legibility Lost," *Adweek,* October 5, 1987.

REHE, ROLF, *Typography: How to Make It Most Legible* (Indianapolis: Design Research Publications, 1974).

Dannon Yogurt: Dannon Light "Reflections" Campaign

Dannon has been the market leader in the refrigerated-yogurt category during its entire 40-year history in the United States. When the FDA approved the use of aspartame as a sweetener in yogurt, however, other yogurt producers quickly entered the "light-yogurt" market. The competition beat Dannon's entry by 6 months because Dannon had taken longer to develop a high-quality product consistent with its brand image. Consequently, when Dannon's light product entered the market in June 1989, Yoplait had already obtained a 51 percent share of the new segment, Weight Watchers held 22 percent of the market, and Light N' Lively held 11 percent.

Thus, Dannon's agency, Lord, Dentsu & Partners, faced an uphill battle to bypass competitive brands and gain sales leadership in the light segment of the yogurt market. The campaign objectives were primarily to generate rapid awareness and trial for Dannon Light and to establish its preeminence as the high-quality leader in the light-yogurt segment. The creative strategy was to convince weight-conscious yogurt users that new Dannon Light would help them control their diet and feel better about themselves because it had no fat and only 100 calories. This strategy was identified after extensive research, including psychographic data, qualitative focus groups, and quantitative and attitude-usage studies. Lord, Dentsu & Partners also designed the creative to appear executionally different from that of the competition by using consumer-relevant life situations to show product benefits rather than taking the informational, attribute-based approach of the other yogurt brands. The advertising included other executional considerations designed to convince consumers that new Dannon Light had the same high quality as traditional Dannon yogurt had.

The target audience for the campaign was identified as weight-conscious yogurt users, primarily women ages 18 to 49. These women tended to be better educated, with incomes over $40,000. Quantitative research also confirmed that 85 percent of light-yogurt consumers would come from existing yogurt users. The audience was further defined psychographically as inner-directed individuals acting to satisfy their self images. Media spending for Dannon Light accounted for approximately 23 percent of total media spending for the light-yogurt category, from introduction through the first 6 months of Dannon Light's sales.

The success of the Dannon Light launch exceeded the ambitious objectives set for the brand. By June 1990 Dannon Light had achieved a commanding lead in the light segment of the yogurt market, 6 months earlier than planned. Between January and June 1990 Dannon Light achieved a 32 percent share of light-yogurt sales, almost double the share for the Yoplait Light, Light N' Lively, and Weight Watchers products. The "Reflections" Dannon Light campaign also performed well in consumer attitude and behavior research conducted in April 1990. Specifically, unaided brand awareness for Dannon Light reached 76 percent, compared to 53 percent for Yoplait Light, the next closest competitor. Aided advertising awareness for the Dannon Light "Reflections" campaign also reached 76 percent, ten points above Yoplait Light. Approximately 80 percent of research participants reportedly had tried Dannon Light, compared to 64 percent who had tried Yoplait Light, and 36 percent indicated that Dannon Light was the brand of light yogurt they ate most often, almost double the level for Yoplait Light.

With the highest brand and advertising awareness levels in the category, market leadership on a sales basis, and quality leadership on a image basis, Dannon Light was the single most successful new product introduction in the long, profitable history of the Dannon Company.

QUESTIONS

1. Typically, brands with strong-quality images need only to reflect their brand names in advertising for line extensions to transfer their quality perception. What else did Dannon do to achieve a high quality rating among consumers in its "Reflections" campaign for Dannon Light?

2. How do you think the "Reflections" campaign would have looked different had it been created by a company new to the yogurt category?

Source: Courtesy of Lord, Dentsu & Partners.

15

Creating Broadcast Advertising

Chapter Objectives

When you have completed this chapter, you should be able to:

- Understand the roles of the various people associated with television commercials, including the producer, director, and editor
- List the various stages in the production of a television commercial
- Identify the critical elements in radio and television commercials
- Read and understand a radio script and a television script
- Compare and contrast radio ads and television commercials

LIGHTS, CAMERA, FISH?

Producing television commercials is the glamour side of the business. It's Hollywood. It's working with big budgets and big stars. It's lights, camera, action!

Well, not always. Often the "star" of the commercial is the product, and the "actors" you're working with may be babies or—even worse—animals. Creative director Frank Haggerty of Carmichael Lynch (CL), a Minneapolis-based agency, works with some mighty strange animals—fish. It comes with the territory when one of your accounts is Normark, a distributor for Blue Fox Tackle Company of Cambridge, Minnesota. Haggerty is a 10-year veteran of this account.

One of Haggerty's recent television commercials for Blue Fox, called "Na-na," showed underwater shots of a lure taunting fish with chants of "You can't get me!" The spot won many awards and increased sales. So what did the creative director do when Normark asked him to advertise a lure called Vibrax that has a bell resonator that attracts the attention of fish underwater? He combined the "Na-na" idea with the fact that fish yawn, and he created a spot, called "Yawning Fish," cowritten with CL writer Kerry Casey. In this spot fish yawn to human sound effects while the lure, which sounds like an alarm clock, goes off and "wakes" them up.

Filming took place in Ocala, Florida, at Glen Lau Productions, a production house that specializes in "critters and fish." For 8 days a cameraman sat under a black baggie watching and filming ten largemouth bass in an 8,000-gallon tank of water. The cameraman then just sat back and waited for them to yawn. He noticed after a while that three or four of the fish yawned more than the others, and one yawned most of all. One particular problem Haggerty encountered was the fact that fish "like to yawn and poo at the same time." Thanks to the patience of the cameraman, however, after more than a week of filming, he ended up with about 45 good shots and another successful commercial (see Ad 15.1).*

THE TELEVISION ENVIRONMENT

Like most Americans, you probably have a love-hate relationship with television commercials. On the one hand, you may have a favorite commercial or campaign. The Bartles and Jaymes wine cooler commercials by the Hal Riney Agency have been amazingly successful using two elderly men to sell wine coolers to an audience composed primarily of young women because the characters are so captivating. On the other hand, you can probably identify a dozen commercials that you resent so much that you turn the channel or leave the room the minute they appear. You might hate the product or see the characters in the commercial as stupid and the message as insulting. Your reaction may be personal—different people like different things; strategic—you are not in the target for that particular product and the message isn't addressed to you; or factual—there are, after all, a number of dreadful commercials on television.

*Source: Adapted from Cathy Madison, "CL Trawls for More Awards With a Yawner of a Campaign, *Adweek* (July 9, 1990):4.

4
"Yawning Fish"
Music: Goes from light and sleepy to tense and violent.
(Open on a big bass. He yawns. Cut to another bass, same routine; yawns get bigger and funnier)
SFX: Yaawn ho hum.
Anncr. (VO): Some days, you just have to wake 'em up.
SFX: Yeeeeeeeeeawnnnnnnnn yum yum!
(Cut to product shot)
Anncr. (VO): The Super Vibrax. It creates bell vibrations that get fish....
SFX: Distant alarm clock, getting louder, louder yet.
(Cut to fish yawning, mouth agape. It clomps down on passing Vibrax lure.
SFX: Distant alarm clock, getting louder, louder yet. Clomp. Muffled alarm clock ringing.
Anncr. (VO): ...up and at 'em.
Title card: (out of black) Blue Fox
SFX: Muffled alarm clock ring under, out.

Frank Haggerty, art director
Kerry Casey, writer
Jack Supple/Frank Haggerty, creative directors
Glen Lau, producer/director
Glen Lau Productions, production company
Carmichael Lynch (Minneapolis), agency
Blue Fox, client

AD 15.1
Filming fish yawning took time, patience, and some clever production techniques.
(Courtesy of Blue Fox Tackle Company.)

Characteristics of Television Commercials

Television commercials are characterized in two ways: They can achieve audience acceptance if they are well done, and they can minimize viewers' patterns of avoidance if they are intriguing as well as intrusive.

Acceptance. People do like to watch commercials if the ads are well done. They watch excerpts from the annual Clio awards given for television advertising when they appear as an item on news broadcasts. Television shows on famous ads and advertising bloopers consistently get high ratings. Lines from commercials can even take on a life of their own, such as "Do you know me?" from the American Express campaign and "Thanks, I needed that" from a Mennon Skin Bracer commercial. The Wendy's line "Where's the beef?" went from an immensely popular commercial to a catch phrase used by one political candidate, Walter Mondale, against another, Gary Hart, in the 1984 presidential primaries.

Intrusiveness. Most people pay more attention to television than they do to radio programming. People watching a program they enjoy are frequently absorbed in it. Their absorption is only slightly less than that experienced by people watching a movie in a darkened theater. Advertising is considered an unwelcome interruption because it disrupts concentration. This intrusiveness can be disconcerting and can cause the viewer to be even less receptive to the commercial message.

Another problem confronting television advertisers is the tendency of viewers to switch channels or leave the room during commercial breaks. Because of television viewers' strong patterns of avoidance, commercials have to be intriguing as well as intrusive.

THE NATURE OF COMMERCIALS

Message Strategy

Every advertising medium is different, and copywriters are adept at writing messages that take advantage of each medium's particular set of strengths. Television is unlike radio or print in many ways, the most important of which is it is a medium of moving images.

Action and Motion. Television is a visual medium, and the message is dominated by the impact of visual effects. But, you might observe, newspapers and magazines also use visuals. So what makes the difference in impact between television and print visuals? It is the moving image, the action, that makes television so much more mesmerizing than print. When you watch television you are watching a walking, talking, moving world that

AD 15.2
Illinois uses the Huckleberry Finn story to capture nostalgia in a tourism commercial. (Courtesy of Illinois Department of Tourism.)

"Riverboat"
Music: Orchestral soundtrack.
(Open on golden scene of a rock skipping across a river several times, cut to shot of two boys on the shore skipping rocks)
Huck (VO): There was heavy timber on the Illinois side so me and Tom weren't afraid of anybody runnin' across us.
(Cut to riverboat, boys watch it pass)
Huck (VO): We laid there all day and watched the rafts and steamboats spin down the shore ... and upbound steamboats fight the big river in the middle.
(Close-up shot of paddle wheel, then long shot of riverboat)
Anncr. (VO): You've read the book. Now see the river.
Super: Illinois. The American Renaissance. 1-800-223-0121.

even gives the illusion of being three-dimensional. Good television advertising uses the impact of action and motion to attract attention and sustain interest.

Storytelling.   Stories can be riveting if they are well told, and television is our society's master storyteller. Most of the programming on television is storytelling. But stories do more than just entertain—they express values, teach behavior, and show us how to deal with our daily problems. Television shows like *The Cosby Show, L.A. Law, Thirtysomething,* and *Life Goes On* all include discussions of ethics or morals.

Effective television advertisements also use storytelling, both for entertainment value and to make a point. These little stories can be funny, warm, silly, or heart-rending, just as in real life. Slice of life is simply instruction in a soap opera format. Emotion is also best expressed in a narrative form (see Ad 15.2).

Emotion.   More than any other advertising medium, television has the ability to touch emotions, to make people feel things. This ability to touch the feelings of the viewer makes television commercials entertaining, diverting, amusing, and absorbing. Real-life situations with all their humor, anger, fear, pride, jealousy, and love come alive on the screen. Humor, in particular, works well on television. The Boatmen's Bank ad (Ad 15.3) demonstrates the use of a comical character and situation to get attention.

These emotions are pulled from natural situations that everyone can identify with. Hallmark has produced some real tear-jerker commercials

PRINCIPLE _____
*Television uses stories to entertain
and to make a point.*

AD 15.3
A deadpan character and a funny line create attention for Boatmen's Bank.   (Courtesy of Boatmen's Bank and TBWA, St. Louis.)

"Eligible Tellers"
(Open on Interviewer and Lorraine)
Interviewer: Lorraine, how would you improve banking?
(Cut to close-up of Lorraine)
Lorraine: I would like to see more eligible tellers.
(Cut to Interviewer and Lorraine. Interviewer is thrown by Lorraine's response)
Interviewer: Uh-huh. Well, uh, what about Boatmen's new policy, the "No Runaround" policy? That's where if ... if you call Boatmen's and the person who answers the phone...
(Cut to Lorraine, who is expressionless)
Interviewer: ...doesn't have the answer, they'll find someone who ... who... does have the answer.
(Cut to Interviewer and Lorraine)
Interviewer: Pretty nice of 'em, huh? They'll call you back and...
(Cut to close-up of Lorraine, who remains stone-faced. Cut to Interviewer and Lorraine)
Interviewer: You pretty much have your heart set on the ... more eligible tellers.
(Interviewer, perplexed, looks at camera)
Camera card: Boatmen's. How You'd Run A Bank.

Becky Cohen, art director
Brad Fels, writer
Lloyd Wolfe, creative director
Tony Windler, producer
Mark Story, director
Story Piccolo Guliner, production company
TBWA Kerlick Switzer (St. Louis), agency

BOATMEN'S
How You'd Run A Bank.

about those time of our lives that we remember by the cards we get and save. Kodak and Polaroid have used a similar strategy for precious moments that are remembered in photographs.

The copy for a commercial for Dreyer's Grand Ice Cream (known as Edy's in some markets) illustrates the use of emotion. Peter Murphy, creative director at Hal Riney & Partners, who wrote the ad, explained: "We didn't want to show why Edy's is superior to other brands. We wanted to show how ice cream makes people feel." The writer interviewing Murphy observed that "the view of human nature brought out in that commercial comes from a place much deeper in his soul."* The copy is as follows:

> When we introduced Edy's Grand Ice Cream to towns and villages, some extraordinary things happened. A meter maid smiled and gave someone who needed a quarter a quarter. Baseball players asked the fans for their autographs. Hardly anyone forgot a birthday or an anniversary. All the flowers in all the flower shops were sold. The average age of someone with a balloon was 43. And generally speaking, it was the happiest people have been in a long time.

PRINCIPLE _____
Demonstrations are persuasive on television because we believe what we see.

Demonstration.   Demonstration was discussed in Chapter 7 as an important message strategy. If you have a strong sales message that lends itself to demonstration, then television is the ideal medium for that message. Its realism makes the demonstration persuasive. Believability and credibility are high because we believe what we see with our own eyes.

Sight and Sound.   Television is an audiovisual medium—that is, it uses both sight and sound—and an effective television commercial fuses the audio and visual elements. One of the strengths of television is its ability to reinforce verbal messages with visuals or visual messages with verbal (see Ad 15.4).

Hooper White, who has been making television commercials since the 1950s, says in his book *How to Produce an Effective TV Commercial* that "The idea behind a television commercial is unique in advertising." He explains that it is a combination of sight and sound: "The TV commercial

*Art Kleiner, "The Culture of Marketing and the Marketing of Culture," *Whole Earth Review* (Spring 1987):74–80.

AD 15.4
This Dannon yogurt ad uses sight gags to strengthen the impact of its message. (Courtesy of The Dannon Company.)

consists of pictures that move to impart fact or evoke emotion and selling words that are not read but heard." He concludes: "The perfect combination of sight and sound can be an extremely potent selling tool."*

Advertising professionals have long known that memorability is much higher when commercials show the product and say the name at the same time. The long-running Bud Light campaign shows all the incredible number of things that come to mind when you think of the word "light" and at the same time dramatically fuses the name Budweiser with the word "light." Rather than focusing on a product benefit, it simply combines the brand name with the "light" category by dramatizing the word "light" with these unexpected visuals.

The point of audiovideo fusion is that words and pictures must work together or else commercials will show one thing and say something else. Researchers have found that people have trouble listening and watching at the same time unless the audio and visual messages are identical.

PRINCIPLE
Sight and sound should reinforce one another.

Elements

Various elements work together to create the visual impact of television commercials. Audiovisual elements do not stand alone. They must be put into the right setting and surrounded by appropriate props. The right talent must be chosen, and appropriate lighting and pacing are critical, along with other elements.

Video. The visual dominates the perception of the message in television, so copywriters use it as the primary carrier of the concept. The *video* elements include everything that is seen on the screen. Copywriters use visuals, the silent speech of film, to convey as much of the message as possible. Emotion is expressed most convincingly in facial expressions, gestures, and other body language. Good television writers try not to bury the impact of the visual under a lot of unnecessary words.

A tremendous number of visual elements must be coordinated in successful television ads. Because television is theatrical, many of the elements, such as characters, costumes, sets and locations, props, lighting, optical and computerized special effects, and on-screen graphics, are similar to those you would use in a play, television show, or movie. Because of the number of video and audio elements, a television commercial is the most complex of all advertising forms.

voice-over *A technique used in commercials in which an off-camera announcer talks about the on-camera scene.*

Audio. The audio dimensions of television and radio ads are the same—music, voices, and sound effects—but they are used differently in television commercials because they are related to a visual image. An announcer, for example, may speak directly to the viewer or engage in a dialogue with another person who may or may not be on-camera. A common manipulation of the camera-announcer relationship is the **voice-over,** in which some kind of action on the screen is described by the voice of an announcer who is not visible. Sometimes a voice is heard *off-camera,* which means it is coming from either side, from behind, or from above.

talent *People who appear in television commercials.*

Talent. A television commercial has all the ingredients of a play. The most important element is people, who can be announcers (either on- or offstage), presenters, spokespersons, "spokesthings" (like talking butter dishes), character types (old woman, baby, skin diver, policeman), or ce-

*Hooper White, *How to Produce an Effective TV Commercial* (Chicago: Crain Books, 1981).

AD 15.5
Michael J. Fox has become a popular spokesperson for Pepsi. (Courtesy of the Pepsi Cola Company)

set *A constructed setting where the action in a commercial takes place.*

PRINCIPLE
The most important prop is the product.

crawl *Computer-generated letters that move across the bottom of the screen.*

lebrities, like Michael J. Fox (see Ad 15.5). People in commercials are called **talent.** Some commercials use just parts of people, such as hands, feet, or the back of the head.

Depending on what kind of people are being used, *costumes* and *makeup* can be very important. Historical stories, of course, need period costumes, but modern scenes may also require special clothing such as ski outfits, swim suits, or cowboy boots. The script should specify which costumes are essential to the story. Makeup may be important if you need to create a skin problem or to change a character from young to old.

Props. In most commercials the most important *prop* is the product. The ad should reflect the essential properties of the product. Does it come in a package? Does it have a distinctive logo? How should it be depicted? Can you show it in use? What other props are necessary to make the story come together? Sometimes props are critical to the action, like a tennis racket in a tennis scene. Sometimes they are used just to set the scene, like the patio table and tray of drinks in the background behind the tennis players. The script should identify every important element in the scene.

Setting. The setting is where the action takes place. It can be something in the studio—from a simple table top to a constructed **set** that represents a storefront. Commercials shot outside the studio are said to be filmed *on location.* In these cases the entire crew and cast are transported somewhere. The location could be an alley or a garage down the street, or it could be some exotic place like New Zealand.

Lighting. Lighting is another critical element that is usually manipulated by the director. Special lighting effects need to be specified in the script. For example, you might read "Low lighting as in a bar," or "Intense bright light as though reflected from snow," or "Light flickering on people's faces as if it were reflecting from a television screen."

Graphics. There are several types of visuals that are filmed from a flat card or generated electronically on the screen by a computer. Words and still photos are shot from a card. Words can also be computer-generated right on the screen. The **crawl** is computer-generated letters that appear to be moving across the bottom of the screen.

Stock footage is a previously recorded image, either video, still slides, or moving film, that is used for scenes that aren't accessible to normal shooting. Examples are shots from a satellite or rocket and World War II scenes.

Pacing. The speed of the action is another important factor in a television commercial. Pacing describes how fast or how slow the action progresses. Some messages are best developed at a languid pace; others work better done upbeat and fast. If the pacing is an important part of the message, then it needs to be explained in the script.

Filming and Taping

Producing a major national commercial may take the work of hundreds of people and cost as much as half a million dollars. The "1984" commercial for Apple Computers that ran only once during the 1985 Super Bowl used a cast of 200 and is estimated to have cost half a million dollars.* Since that

*David Carey, "Advertising in the '80s: A Roaring Comeback," *Financial World* (March 20, 1985):8–9.

time even more expensive commercials have been produced. The expense only makes sense if the ads will reach large numbers of people.

There are a number of ways to produce a message for a television commercial. It can be filmed live or it can be prerecorded using film or videotape. It can also be shot frame by frame using animation techniques.

Live. In the early days of television most commercials were shot live. The history of advertising includes numerous stories about refrigerator doors that wouldn't open and dogs that refused to eat the dog food. These traumatic experiences explain why most advertisers prefer to prerecord a commercial rather than gamble on doing it live.

You will occasionally see live commercials using spokespersons such as Ed McMahon on the Johnny Carson show. These commercials project a warmth and an immediacy that prerecorded commercials lack. But the chance remains that something will go wrong. The most skilled announcer can still forget a line or mispronounce the name of the product.

Film. Today most television commercials are shot on 16 mm or 35 mm film. The film is shot as a negative and processed, after which the image is transferred to videotape. This transferring technique is called *film-to-tape transfer.*

film *A strip of celluloid with a series of still images, called frames.*

Film consists of a series of frames on celluloid that, for advertising, is usually 35 mm wide. Actually, each frame is a still shot. The film passes through a projector, and the small changes from frame to frame create the illusion of motion. Film is shot at 24 frames per second. In film-to-tape transfer the film has to be converted to videotape that uses 30 frames per second.

cut *An abrupt transition from one shot to another.*

Editing on film is done by cutting between two frames and either eliminating a segment or attaching a new segment of film. The term **cut,** which comes from this editing procedure, is used to describe an abrupt transition from one view of a scene to another.

videotape *A type of recording medium that electronically records sound and images simultaneously.*

Videotape. Until the 1980s **videotape** was thought of as an inferior alternative to film. It was used primarily by the news side of the television industry because it records sound and images instantly, without a delay for film processing, and the videotape can be replayed immediately. Videotape's ''cheap cousin'' image has changed dramatically in the last decade. First of all, the quality of videotape has improved. The film-to-tape transfer has seen significant improvements. Also, a number of innovations in editing have made the process more precise and faster; computer editing has improved accuracy and made special effects possible.

animation *A type of recording medium in which objects are sketched and then filmed one frame at a time.*

Animation. **Animation,** which uses film rather than videotape, records drawn images one at a time, frame by frame. Cartoon figures, for example, are sketched and then resketched with a slight change to indicate a small progression in the movement of an arm or a leg or a facial expression (see Ad 15.6). Animation is traditionally shot at 12 or 16 drawings per second. Low-budget animation uses fewer drawings, and consequently the motion looks jerky.

Because of all the hand work, animation is labor-intensive and expensive. It takes a long time to create an animated commercial because of the drawing time, though the introduction of computers is speeding up the process. Now illustrators need draw only the beginning and the end of the action sequence; the computer plots out the frames in between.

stop motion *A technique in which inanimate objects are filmed one frame at a time, creating the illusion of movement.*

A variation on animation is called **stop motion,** a technique used to film inanimate objects like the Pillsbury Doughboy, which is a puppet. The

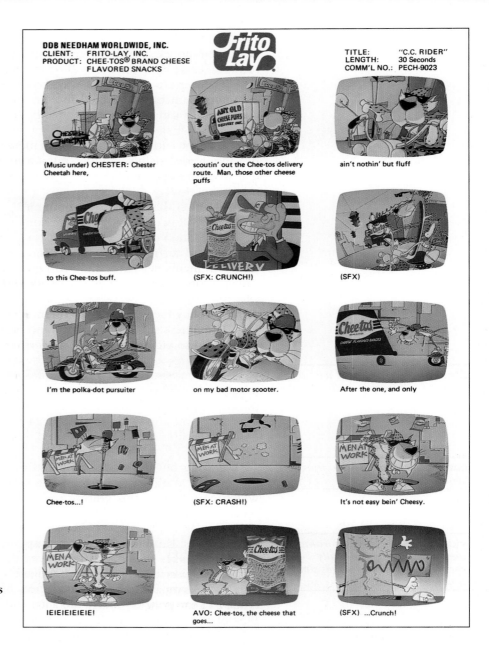

(Music under) CHESTER: Chester Cheetah here,

scoutin' out the Chee-tos delivery route. Man, those other cheese puffs

ain't nothin' but fluff

to this Chee-tos buff.

(SFX: CRUNCH!)

(SFX)

I'm the polka-dot pursuiter

on my bad motor scooter.

After the one, and only

Chee-tos...!

(SFX: CRASH!)

It's not easy bein' Cheesy.

IEIEIEIEIEIE!

AVO: Chee-tos, the cheese that goes...

(SFX) ...Crunch!

AD 15.6
Cheetos uses an animated character, Chester Cheetah, and his antics to get attention for the brand.
(Courtesy of DDB Needham Worldwide and Frito-Lay, Inc.)

claymation *A technique that uses figures sculpted from clay and filmed one frame at a time.*

little character is moved a bit at a time and filmed frame by frame. The same technique is used with **claymation,** which involves creating characters from clay and then photographing them. The dancing raisins in the "Heard It Through the Grapevine" commercial by the National Raisin Board are the product of the claymation technique.

PLANNING AND PRODUCING COMMERCIALS

Planning Television Commercials

In planning a television commercial, there are many considerations. The producers of the Blue Fox commercial we discussed at the beginning of the chapter had to plan how long the commercial would be, what shots would appear in each scene, what the key visual would be, and where to shoot the commercial.

Lengths. As we discussed in Chapter 10, the most common length for a commercial on broadcast television today is 30 seconds. Because of the increasing costs of air time, 60-second commercials are becoming rare. Some network commercials now run in 20-second and 15-second formats. An advertiser may buy a 30-second spot and split it in half for two related products in the line. If the two messages are interdependent, the strategy is called *piggybacking*. An example of piggybacking is a 15-second cake mix ad sharing a 30-second spot with a 15-second frosting ad.

Scenes. A commercial is planned in scenes. These are segments of action that occur in a single location. Within each scene there may be a number of shots from different angles. A 30-second commercial is usually planned with four to six scenes, though a fast-paced commercial may have many more.

key frame *A single frame of a commercial that summarizes the heart of the message.*

Key Frames. The writer and art director begin the planning together. The television equivalent of a thumbnail sketch is called a **key frame.** Because television is a visual medium, the message is developed from a key visual that contains the heart of the concept. The last frame in the Blue Fox commercial, which shows the company logo, is the key frame. The various concepts are devised, tested, and revised as key visuals. When a concept seems promising, the writer and art director move to a rough script and storyboard.

Local Productions. Most local retail commercials are simple, relatively inexpensive, and are shot at the local station or production facility on videotape. The sales representative for the station may work with the advertiser to write the script, and the station's director handles the filming of the commercial. They may not have extravagant production techniques, but these commercials can be just as effective as any big-budget production.

Scripts and Storyboards

A print advertisement is created in two pieces: a copy sheet and a layout. Commercials are planned with two similar documents. A script is the written version with all the words, dialogue, lyrics, instructions, and description; the storyboard shows the number of scenes, the composition of the shots, and the progression of the action.

script *A written version of a radio or television commercial.*

Television Scripts. A television **script** is a detailed document. It includes the visual plan of the commercial plus all the descriptions necessary to assist the director or producer in finding the location or building the set, the talent agency in casting the talent, the composer/arranger in creating the music, and the producer in budgeting and scheduling the entire project.

The script is written in two columns with the audio on the right and the video on the left. Ad 15.7 for State Farm Insurance is an example of a television script with key frames from the commercial. The key to the structure of a television script is the relationship between the audio and the video. The video is typed opposite the corresponding audio. Sometimes these are numbered to correspond to the frames on the storyboard.

storyboard *A series of frames sketched to illustrate how the story line will develop.*

Storyboards. The **storyboard** is the visual plan, the layout, of the commercial. It uses selected frames to communicate how the story line will develop. It depicts the composition of the shots as well as the progression of action and the interaction of the audio with the video. A 30-second commercial will be planned with six to eight frames. These frames, of course, are stills. They don't show action; they can only suggest it by a pictorial pro-

JAY DANDY, SENIOR COPYWRITER, FOOTE, CONE AND BELDING, CHICAGO

Having a job in advertising is a lot like being in the circus. When you're not on the high wire doing a balancing act between what your agency wants and what your client wants, you do a lot of juggling. And juggling is exactly what I was doing while finishing up a job in New York not too long ago.

I started my day by waking up with a terrific hangover. Now, don't get the wrong idea. This hangover wasn't from some fun-filled night on the town. I got it from the two Excedrin PM's I had taken the night before. You see, when you've just spent the previous 14 hours in an editing room ingesting nothing but sugar and caffeine and staring at the same 30 seconds of film over and over and over again, the development of a splitting headache is not an uncommon occurrence.

Anyway, my phone rings and it's my producer. She wants to know if I'm coming downstairs to join her in a workout before we go to the studio to do our final sound mix. I grumble that I'm having problems working on getting out of bed and that I'll meet her downstairs in about an hour.

Two minutes later the phone rings again. This time it's the director. He wants to know if I can come down to his office with my art director and look at casting tapes and go over locations. This is all good and fine, but this guy is not the director of the current spot I'm working on. He's the director of another commercial we're going to be shooting in a couple of weeks. So I explain the situation and he says he can meet me at my sound mix later that afternoon.

Somehow I manage to take a shower and pack my bags. But not without a few more phone calls from my producer wanting to know if I've taken a shower and packed my bags. By the time we check out of the hotel and get up to the mix, I'm a little mixed up myself.

A sound mix is where you make sure your announcer, your music, and your sound effects all line up and don't fight each other. The spot we're doing is going to run on Saturday morning television. It involves a pretty fast track, an announcer voice-over, and a bunch of sound effects. You always add your sound effects last so you can cue them to the picture.

Now here's where it gets interesting. While the sound engineer is getting set up we start talking about what and where our sound effects should go. Since there are eight different people in the room there are eight different opinions. There are also eight times as many phone calls and other assorted interruptions.

At this point, the director of our upcoming spot shows up. My producer and art director leave to speak with him. This is right in the middle of our discussion of whether to use a "bonk" or a "boink," and if we do use a "boink," what kind of "boink" do we use.

Before a decision can be reached, my producer comes back and says I have to talk to this other director to clear up a few things. So I run upstairs and start to go over casting tapes and locations. But this is all rather difficult because I still have this whole "bonk"/"boink" issue on my mind.

---

gression. The art director must determine which visuals convey the most information. Underneath the frame will be a short version of the audio, just enough to locate the dialogue in relation to the video. The storyboard is a very important tool for showing the basic concept of the commercial to the client and other agency members.

animatic *A preliminary version of a commercial with the storyboard frames recorded on videotape along with a rough sound track.*

photoboard *A type of rough commercial, similar to an animatic except that the frames are actual photos instead of sketches.*

Animatics and Photoboards. As the concept is revised and finalized, the script becomes more detailed and the storyboard art more finished. A finished storyboard is equivalent to a comprehensive in print. To make the storyboard even more realistic, the frames may be shot on slides for presentation to the client. If the frames are recorded on videotape along with a rough sound track, the storyboard is called an **animatic.** Animatics are frequently used for client presentations and market research sessions. If frames are actual photographs of the action, which are more realistic, they

When I get back downstairs we strike a compromise. We will use the "boink" that I like if we can use the "bonk" that the director likes somewhere else in the spot.

Soon after that crisis has passed, another one arises. I get a frantic phone call from one of my account executives back in Chicago. She is wondering what happened to the copy for a print ad that needed to be rewritten. It seems she sent it along with my art director, and whadya know—he forgot to give it to me.

Three hours later we finish up our mix with just enough time to get to the airport and catch our flight back to Chicago. I stumble into work the next day and crank out the copy for the print ad. I sit back and catch my breath. In the last 24 hours I've done my sound mix with one director, gone over casting and locations with another, settled the "bonk"/"boink" issue, rewritten my print copy, and acquired an additional 733 frequent flyer miles.

I start going through the stack of mail on my desk thinking that I've got everything under control. Then I come across this note that says, "Gee Jay, I know you've been out on production, but if you're not too busy could you write a short article on what it's like being a copywriter. It would be a terrific opportunity, but the only problem is we need it by the end of the day. So if it's not too much trouble . . ." So much for life under the big top.

Source: Courtesy of Jay Dandy.

are called **photoboards.** You have been looking at photoboards in many of the ads depicted throughout this book.

The Team

A locally produced commercial uses the station's personnel for most of the production roles. In addition to a lot of time and a great deal of money, however, producing a major national advertisement requires a number of people with specialized skills. The agency crew usually includes the copywriter, art director, and producer. The outside people include a production house, a director and shooting crew, a talent agency, a music arranger/director plus musicians, and a film or video editor. The client's advertising manager is also involved throughout the planning and production.

The copywriter, art director, and possibly a creative director and pro-

STATE FARM INSURANCE
9/18/89
RURAL
:30 TV

__"Hoffrogge/Rural"__

VIDEO		AUDIO

I'm their State Farm Agent . . .

OPEN ON RURAL MINNESOTA FARM.- DAWN
CUT TO SCENES OF AGENT WITH:
    LOCAL RESIDENTS,
    FAMILIES
    TOWN SHOPKEEPERS
INTERCUT WITH SCENES OF:
    FAMILY LIFE
    CHILDREN PLAYING
    LEAF RAKING ETC.

CUT TO DENNIS IN HIS OFFICE, CU AT DESK

AGENT: I grew up on a farm just down the road. I know 'most everybody in town, and handle the insurance for quite a few.
I'm their State Farm agent... Dennis Hoffrogge.
My job is to help my neighbors. To help 'em protect their families, and the things they've worked for.
It's a job I take seriously.
Every State Farm agent does.
Y'know, State Farm started out in small towns just like this.... people trying to help their neighbors.
We're _still_ helpin'.

SOLO SINGER (VO): AND LIKE A GOOD NEIGHBOR,

CUT TO WIDE SHOT OF TOWN FROM EXTREME HIGH ANGLE

SING: LIKE A GOOD NEIGHBOR,
STATE FARM IS THERE.

STATE FARM IS THERE.

AD 15.7
Example of a television script and key frames. (Courtesy of State Farm Insurance Companies and DDB Needham Worldwide.)

ducer work together to develop the idea and translate it into a script and a storyboard. The copywriter writes the actual script, whether it involves dialogue, narrative, lyrics, announcement, or descriptive copy. The art director develops the storyboard and establishes the "look" of the commercial, whether realistic, stylized, or fanciful.

producer *The person who supervises and coordinates all of the elements that go into the creation of a television commercial.*

The **producer,** usually an agency staff member, is in charge of the production. He or she handles the bidding and all of the arrangements, finds the specialists, arranges for casting the talent, and makes sure the budget and the bids all come in together.

The production house usually coordinates the entire shoot, working closely with the agency staff. The production house normally provides the director, but may choose to use a freelance director instead, particularly if that director's special "look" is desired for the commercial. The production house provides most of the technical expertise and equipment needed to produce the commercial. The **director** is in charge of the actual filming or taping: the look of the set and lighting; how long the scenes and pieces of

director *The person in charge of the actual filming or taping of the commercial.*

action are; who does what and moves where; and how the lines are spoken and the characters played. The director manages the flow of action and determines how it is seen and recorded by the camera.

The music **composer** writes original music; the music **arranger** orchestrates that music for the various instruments and voices to make it fit a scene or copy line. The copywriter usually writes the lyrics or at least gives some idea of what the words should say. A composer who does a lot of commercials, like Barry Manilow, might write the lyrics along with the music. Musicians are hired as needed, from a complete orchestra to a marching band to a vocalist.

In a film production the **editor** becomes involved toward the end of the process and puts everything together. Film is shot from a number of different cameras, each representing a different angle. The audio is recorded on multiple tracks. The editor's job is to decide which are the best shots, how to assemble the scenes, and how the audio tracks work best with the assembled video.

Producing a Television Commercial

Commercials for local stores are relatively inexpensive to produce because they use the facilities and staff of the local station. The production process for a major national television commercial, however, is long and expensive. It is also involved and complex. The script and storyboard are reviewed and approved by the client and become the basis for the production planning. The producer and staff first develop a set of *production notes,* describing in detail every aspect of the production. These are important for finding talent and locations, building sets, and getting bids and estimates from the specialists.

Preproduction. Before the commercial can be filmed or taped, a number of arrangements need to be handled. Once the bids have been approved, a preproduction meeting of the creative team and the producer, director, and other key players is held. The meeting attempts to outline every step of the production process and anticipate every problem that may come up. A detailed schedule is also finalized and agreed to by all parties.

The talent agency is in charge of casting, which is accomplished through a series of auditions. A location has to be found and arrangements made with owners, police, and other officials to use the site. If sets are needed, then they have to be built. Finding the props is a test of ingenuity, and the prop person may wind up visiting hardware stores, second-hand stores, and maybe even the local dump. Costumes may have to be made.

The Shoot. Although the actual filming takes a rather short time, the setup and rehearsal can take incredible amounts of time. It may seem as though nothing is happening when actually everyone is busy setting up and checking specialized responsibilities.

The film crew includes a number of technicians, all of whom have to know what is happening and what they are supposed to do. Everyone reports to the director. If the sound is being recorded at the time of shooting, the recording is handled by a *mixer,* who operates the recording equipment, and a *mic* or *boom* person, who sets up the microphones. For both film and video recording, the camera operators are the key technicians.

Other technicians include the *gaffer,* who is the chief electrician, and the *grip,* who moves things such as the sets. The grip also lays track for the dolly on which the camera is mounted and pushes the camera on the dolly

TELEVISION TERMINOLOGY

Distance (camera to image): Long shot (LS), full shot (FS), medium shot (MS), wide shot (WS), close-up (CU), extreme close-up (ECU or XCU).

Camera Movement

- Zoom in or out: The lens on the camera manipulates the change in distance. As you zoom in, the image seems to come closer and get larger; as you zoom back, it seems to move farther away and get smaller.
- Dolly in and out: The camera itself is wheeled forward or backward.
- Pan right or left: The camera is stationary but swings to follow the action.
- Truck right or left: The camera itself moves right or left with the action.

Transitions

- Cut: An abrupt, instantaneous change from one shot to another.
- Dissolve: A soft transition where one image fades to black while another image fades on.

- Lap dissolve: A slow dissolve with a short period in which the two images overlap.
- Superimposition: Two images held in the middle of a dissolve so they are both on-screen at the same time.
- Wipe: One image crawls across the screen and replaces another.

Action

- Freeze frame: Stops the scene in midaction.
- Stop motion: Shots are taken one at a time over a long period. Used to record animation, claymation, or something that happens over a long period of time, like a flower blooming.
- Slow motion: Suspends the normal speed of things by increasing the number of frames used to record the movement.
- Speeded-up motion: Increases the normal speed by reducing the number of frames used to record the movement.
- Reverse motion: The film is run backward through the projector.

---

along the track at the required speed. The *script clerk* checks the dialogue and other script details and times the scenes. All of the technicians are supported by their own crew of assistants. A set is a very busy, crowded place. The box entitled "Television Terminology" offers a concise definition of terms commonly used in television commercial production.

The commercial is shot scene by scene, but not necessarily in the order set down in the script. Each scene is shot and reshot until all the elements come together. If the commercial is filmed in videotape, the director plays it back immediately to determine what needs correcting. Film, however, has to be processed before the director can review it. These processed scenes are called *dailies.*

Rushes are rough versions of the commercial assembled from cuts of the raw film footage. They are viewed immediately after the filming to make sure everything necessary has been filmed.

If the audio is to be recorded separately in a sound studio, it is often recorded after the film is shot to **synchronize** (sync) the dialogue to the footage. Directors frequently wait to see exactly how the action appears before they write and record the audio track. If the action occurs to music, then the music may be recorded prior to the shoot and the filming done to the music.

Postproduction. For film, much of the work happens after the shoot. That is when the commercial begins to emerge from the hands and mind of the editor. In film a **rough cut** is a preliminary edited version of the story. The editor chooses the best shots and assembles them to create a scene. The scenes are then joined together. After the revision and reediting is completed, an **interlock** is made. The audio and film are separate, but they are timed, and can be listened to, simultaneously. The final version with the sound and film recorded together is called an **answer print.**

rushes *Rough versions of the commercial assembled from unedited footage.*

synchronize *Matching the audio to the video in a commercial.*

rough cut *A preliminary rough edited version of the commercial.*

interlock *A version of the commercial with the audio and video timed together, although the two are still recorded separately.*

answer print *The final finished version of the commercial with the audio and video recorded together.*

Shooting a television commercial is an expensive and complicated process. (Courtesy of DDB Needham Worldwide.)

dubbing *The process of making duplicate copies of a videotape.*

release prints *Duplicate copies of a commercial that are ready for distribution.*

In order for the commercial to run at hundreds of stations around the country, duplicate copies have to be made. This process is called **dubbing,** and the copies are called **release prints.** Release prints are distributed on 16 mm film or videotape. Because the industry now uses the film-to-tape transfer process, most production is done on videotape, thereby avoiding much of the film-laboratory work.

*T*HE RADIO ENVIRONMENT

Imagine you are writing a musical play. This particular play will be performed before an audience whose eyes are closed. You have all the theatrical tools of casting, voices, sound effects, and music available to you, but no visuals. Imagine having to create all the visual elements—the scene, the cast, the costumes, the facial expressions—in the imagination of your audience. Could you do it?

PRINCIPLE
Radio creates images in the imagination of the listener.

This is how radio works. It is a theater of the mind in which the story is created in the imagination of the listener. The listeners are active participants in the construction of the message. How the characters look and where the scene is set come out of their personal experience. Radio is the most personal of all media.

Characteristics of the Radio Environment

Writing for radio is fun, but it is also very challenging because of the need to create an imaginary visual. Successful radio writers and producers have excellent visualization skills and a great theatrical sense. In addition, radio has some unique characteristics that make it a challenging medium for advertisers.

Personal. Radio is the most intimate of all media. It functions as a good friend in our culture, particularly for teenagers. Radio has one wonderful advantage over print media and that is the human voice, whether it is a newscaster's, a sportscaster's, a talk-show announcer's, or a singer's. The "boombox" on the shoulder or the earphones on a jogger reflect this intimate relationship.

Programming is oriented toward the tastes of particular groups of people. In that sense radio is a very specialized type of medium.

Most people who are listening to the radio are doing something else at the same time. (Courtesy of J. F. Kainz/The Stock Option.)

Inattention.   There is one serious problem, however. Although radio is pervasive, it is seldom the listener's center of attention. Most people who are listening to the radio are doing something else at the same time, like jogging or driving. The listener's attention can focus on radio, particularly during programming that demands concentration like news and weather, but generally radio is a background medium.

Even though most people listen to radio with a divided mind, they remember the songs and words they hear. Sounds that are heavily repeated, like songs, can overcome inattentiveness. Evening drive time is a great time to reach people, when they are thinking about eating. The primary challenge for radio advertisers is to break through the various distractions and get the audience to focus attention on the message. People tune in as something catches their attention and tune out when it loses it. But understanding an advertising message requires more than just tuning in. Radio ads lack the equivalent of a newspaper ad headline that carries the heart of the message. Thus, for a message to have impact, the audience must be induced to listen with some measure of concentration. How many times have you stopped what you were doing to listen to a radio ad?

Intrusive.   Radio advertising seeks to capture audience attention with one of two strategies. Some advertisements are primarily musical; they use a catchy tune and heavily repeated lyrics to embed the message in an inattentive mind.

The other strategy is to be intrusive. As we mentioned in our discussion of television, an intrusive message is one that forces itself on the audience, like the Oxy-5 commercials whose commanding voice has incredible recognition among teenagers around the country. Both television and radio use intrusive messages because of the inattention problem. Most people dislike intrusive messages, however, which causes a dilemma for those who create advertising and who know that intrusive techniques are essential.

Message Strategy

PRINCIPLE _____
Repeat product information as often as possible.

The radio message is ephemeral—it is here one moment and gone the next. You cannot tune in to the middle of an ad and then go back to the headline, as you can with print. You can't "reread" a radio message. Repetition is used to overcome that problem. Key points are repeated, the product name is repeated, and any kind of numerical information that has to be included is also repeated.

PRINCIPLE _____
Avoid giving numbers and complex information in radio commercials.

Numbers are difficult to remember when they are given verbally. Phone numbers and addresses, for example, have to be repeated several times if they are to sink in. That is why advertisers avoid using phone numbers in radio commercials. People driving cars or walking down the street have a hard time finding a pencil to write down the number. Addresses are better conveyed as mental maps, such as "on Broadway across from K Mart."

Complicated information is also difficult to convey on the radio. An inattentive audience is not likely to understand the logic of a sophisticated sales argument or a list of copy points. For that reason print advertisements, which are often complex, seldom translate easily to radio. Radio calls for different message tactics.

Radio is an ideal medium for reminder messages. Simple messages can promote product awareness and identification. Jingles are an effective means of repeating a name or slogan. Radio is also good for image advertising because of its ability to create pictures in the mind. Lifestyle associations can be reinforced through the theater of the mind.

WRITING FOR AUDIO

Writing radio copy requires a particular style and certain tools. Like television scripts, radio copy is written for a certain time frame and according to a particular form and code.

Style

vernacular *Language that reflects the speech patterns of a particular group of people.*

PRINCIPLE _____
For radio, write as you speak, not as you write.

Radio copywriters write in a conversational style using **vernacular** language. Spoken language is different from written language. We talk in short sentences, often in sentence fragments and run-ons. We seldom use complex sentences in speech. We use contractions that would drive an English teacher crazy. Spoken language is not polished prose, as demonstrated in the PacTel commercials:*

> **Man:** I go to a PacTel Cellular agent the other day and I buy a PacTel Cellular phone and as I'm leavin' the guy gives me a free portable CD player as a promotional gift and I'm thinkin' this is a nice thing, this is a good thing, a little touch of humanity from a busy corporation, when all of a sudden I get this sharp pain deep inside me where my conscience used to live before I got an M.B.A. degree and I realized I was havin' a problem acceptin' a gift for doin' somethin' I needed to do anyway, so I went back to the phone guy and said, "Look, we're both businessmen here, you charge a fair price for your product and I decide to buy your product based on how that phone matches my needs for the product,

*Courtesy of PacTel Cellular, Los Angeles.

you don't have to give me a free portable CD player just for buyin' a Pac-Tel cellular phone, I appreciate it but I can't take it" and I was almost completely out the door before that M.B.A. degree kicked in and I was able to snatch the CD player back out of the guy's stunned, clutching hands.

Anncr.: Buy a PacTel Cellular phone before December 31st, with no money down and no payments for 90 days, and get a free, portable CD player. Call 1-800-PacTel 1. On approved credit. Financing for individuals only. Service activation is not included or required. Call 1-800-PacTel 1. A Pacific Telesis company.

Word choice should reflect the speech of the target audience. Slang can be hard to handle and sound phony, but copy that picks up the nuances of people's speech can sound natural when carefully written. Each group has its own way of speaking, its own phrasing. Teenagers don't talk like 8-year-olds or 80-year-olds. A good radio copywriter has an ear for the distinctive patterns of speech that identify social groups.

Tools

Radio uses three primary tools to develop messages: *voice, music,* and *sound effects.* These can be manipulated to create a variety of different effects.

Voice. Voice is probably the most important element. Voices are heard in jingles, in spoken dialogue, and in straight announcements. Most commercials have an announcer, if not as the central voice, at least at the closing to wrap up the product identification. Dialogue uses character voices to convey an image of the speaker—a child, an old man, an executive, a Little League baseball player, or an opera singer.

Music. Music is another important element of radio. Don Wilde of SSC&B said at a symposium that "Music has been found to be more effective in persuasiveness than celebrity endorsements, product demos, or hidden camera techniques." He explained: "It falls just a little under humor or kids. If you write a humorous jingle on kids, you've got it made."*

So-called "jingle houses" are companies that specialize in writing and producing jingles for radio and television. The people who work in this side of the music industry prefer the term "commercial music." A custom-made jingle—one that is created for a single advertiser under strict specifications—can cost $10,000 or more. In contrast, many jingle houses create "syndicated" jingles made up of a piece of music that can be applied to different lyrics and sold to several different advertisers in different markets around the country. These jingles may only cost around $1,000 or $2,000.

In Chapter 8 we mentioned the use of jingles—catchy songs about a product that carry the theme and product identification. These finger-snapping, toe-tapping songs have tremendous power because they are so memorable. Jingles are good for product identification and reminder messages, but they do not effectively convey complex thoughts and copy points.

Jingles can be used by themselves as a musical commercial, or they can be added to any other type of commercial as a product identification. A

*Aliza Laufer, "Agency Panel Mulls the Impact of :15s on Jingle Biz at SAMPAC Symposium," *Back Stage* (February 7, 1986):1.

straight announcer commercial, for example, might end with a jingle. Musical forms can be easily adapted to the station's programming. Most major campaigns that use radio produce a number of different versions of the jingle, each one arranged to match the type of music featured in the programming, whether it is country and western, rock, reggae, or easy listening.

Music can also be used behind the dialogue to create mood and establish the setting. Any mood, from that of a circus to that of a candle-lit dinner, can be conveyed through music. Music can be composed for the commercial or it can be borrowed from an already recorded song. There are also a number of music libraries that sell stock music. This music is not copyrighted, however, so there is no guarantee that other ads will not use the same music.

PRINCIPLE _____
The simpler the jingle, the higher the memorability.

sound effects *(SFX) Lifelike imitations of sounds.*

Sound Effects. **Sound effects** (SFX) are also used to convey a setting. The sounds of sea gulls and the crash of waves, the clicking of typewriter keys, and the cheers of fans at a stadium all create images in our minds. Sound effects can be original, but more often they are taken from records.

Scripting

Timing. As we discussed in Chapter 10, radio commercials are written for a limited time frame. The common lengths are 10, 20, 30, and 60 seconds. The 10-second and 20-second commercials are used for reminders and product or station identification. More elaborate messages are usually 30 or 60 seconds. The 60-second spot is quite common in radio, although it has almost disappeared in television, where the more common length is 30 seconds.

Forms. Like television scripts, radio scripts use a common form and code. The scripts are typed double-spaced with two columns. The narrow column on the left describes the source of the sound, and the wider column on the right gives the actual content of the message, either words or a description of the sound and music.

The typing style is important because typed cues tell the producer and announcer instantly what is happening. For example, anything that isn't spoken is typed in capital letters. This includes the source identification in the left column and all instructions and descriptions that appear in the right column. Underlining is used to call attention to music and sound effects in the right column so the announcer can see instantly that those instructions are not to be read over the microphone as if they were copy. If you write radio scripts often, you will probably use a preprinted form that sets up the columns and the identification information for the commercial at the top. Ad 15.8 is an example of a radio script.

PRODUCING A RADIO COMMERCIAL

Radio commercials are produced in one of two ways: They are either taped and duplicated for distribution, or they are recorded live. The more common form is the taped radio commercial.

Project Help   11/17/87   DR/jks
"No Place Like Home"
:60 Radio
"INTRUSION ALARM"

ANNCR: There's someone walking around right next to me.

                        You probably don't hear him. That's the way he likes

                        it. Because he's an intruder. And an intruder in

                        your home steals much more than just your valuables...

                        He steals your privacy. Your security. Your sense

                        of home.

                        And no insurance check can begin to replace that.

SFX: ALARM

ANNCR: Now you definitely hear this.

                        This is the sound of the new Eversafe Intrusion Alarm.

                        It mounts easily on a door or a window. To keep

                        intruders out. And what you value in.

                        The Eversafe Intrusion Alarm is part of a full-line

                        of home safety and security products that you'll

                        find at the Eversafe Center. One place with all

                        the elements you need to create an entire security

                        system. To protect your home. From intruders, fire,

                        or even power blackouts.

                        So visit your Eversafe Center. You'll find it at

                        _____. And protect what's yours. With

                        Eversafe.

                        Cause there's no place like home.

AD 15.8
An example of a radio script.
(Courtesy of DDB Needham Worldwide.)

---

producer *The person in charge of all the arrangements for a commercial, including settings, casting, arranging for the music, and handling bids and budgets.*

---

mixing *Combining different tracks of music, voices, and sound effects to create the final ad.*

Taped Commercials

The radio **producer** is in charge of getting the commercial casted, recorded, mixed, and duplicated. All the sound elements are recorded separately or *laid down* in stages. Voices can be double- and triple-tracked to create richer sounds. There may be as many as 24 separate tracks for an ad. **Mixing** occurs when the tracks are combined, with appropriate adjustments made in volume and tone levels.

National radio commercials are produced by an advertising agency, and duplicate copies of the tape are distributed to local stations around the country. Commercials for local advertisers might be produced by local stations, with the station's staff providing the creative and production expertise. The recording is done in house using the station's studio.

An example of editing using an audiotape editing machine. (© 1988 by Prentice Hall, Inc. All rights reserved.)

Live Spots

An unusual experiment in "live" radio was conducted in Chicago in 1987, when the *Chicago Tribune* hired two of the city's top radio personalities to ad-lib commercials while they bantered on the air. The approach was the idea of Hal Riney & Partners. Media columnists criticized the ads for not sounding like ads. The "extemporaneous ad-lib announcement" involved reading an item—whether personal ad, column, or news story—from the *Tribune* and mentioning the paper's name. The ads were paid for and listed as 60-second commercials in the station's program log.*

*M*ESSAGE TRENDS

What does the future have in store for broadcast advertising? Cable and videocassettes are having a tremendous impact on television commercials. The nature of the advertising message has changed dramatically, and the percentage of the audience that watches and listens to the commercials has diminished. Clutter on the networks, the increasing costs of commercials, and smaller audiences have forced television commercials to become ever more competitive.

Length and Content

There are two observable trends in the length of television messages. As previously explained, network commercials are getting shorter, with 15-

*Julie Liesse Erickson, "Riney, *Tribune* Spark Interest in Radio Ad(Lib)," *Advertising Age* (November 9, 1987):3.

second spots becoming more and more common. In alternative media such as cable, videocassettes, and movie theaters, advertising messages are getting longer—often lasting 2 to 5 minutes. A new term, *infomercials,* has been introduced to refer to even longer commercials—some lasting 30 or 60 minutes—that provide extensive product information.

The informative commercials playing on cable and videotext and in theaters allow room for the development of longer messages. At the same time, the creative demands of the shorter commercials on network television call for simpler messages that are as concise and pointed as the messages on outdoor boards. Reminder ads with to-the-point brand imagery seem to work best in these short formats. The trends in message design, then, are to be more informative in the alternative media and more concise on traditional network television.

Zapproofing

As we discussed in Chapter 8, the threat of zapping commercials makes the creative side of the message even more important. To survive in this new era when control over the message is in the hands of a viewer holding a remote-conrol device requires an "awesome creative effort" that will make "the commercials even better than the programs."* Len Sugarman, executive vice president and creative director at Foote, Cone & Belding, says that zapproofing calls for "advertising that is more intriguing up front . . . more intriguing and beautiful."†

Arthur Meranus, executive vice president and creative director at Cunningham & Walsh, separates ads into those that use a traditional tell-it-up-front approach, sometimes referred to as the P&G (Proctor & Gamble) approach, and those that use "some sort of likability in the beginning." The traditional commercials start by telling the viewer what the product is and what it promises. Meranus feels, however, that the trend is toward commercials that start with likability devices, such as the Bud Light sight gags.‡ *Zapproofing* commercials means designing them to be entertaining—dramatic, funny, puzzling, or emotional.

An example of zapproof commercials on cable television is General Food's "shortcuts" series, which has kept fidgety audiences glued to the tube. A typical spot opens with a hostess promising to reveal a recipe for baked Brie cheese. The picture then dissolves to a 30-second commercial for some other GF product. Then comes the payoff as the commercial moves back to the cheese and shows how to insert the wheel of cheese into a precut hole in the french bread. The hostess explains that you bake it for 30 minutes. *Voila!* Instant success.§

Embeds

Another technique used to beat the zipping and zapping is to embed the commercial message in some kind of programming. For example, during

---

*Richard Christian, "Can Advertising Survive Split 30s, Zapping, Globalization, High tech, Million Dollar Minutes, Narrowcasting, and Even More Accountability?" *Back Stage* (May 31, 1985):12, 24.

†"Can Ad Agency Creativity Combat Zapping, Zipping?" *Television/Radio Age* (November 11, 1985):63–65.

‡"Can Ad Agency Creativity Combat Zapping, Zipping?"

§"Advertisements That Aren't," *Marketing & Media Decisions* (July 1987):24–25.

the Texas Sesquicentennial, Media Drop In Productions produced a series of true tales about Texas featuring Willie Nelson. Included within the 45 vignettes were commercials for Wrangler jeans.

Image Manipulation

Sophisticated computergraphic systems, such as those used to create the *Star Wars* special effects, have pioneered the making of fantastic original art on computers. At the same time, MTV has generated some of the most exciting video techniques to be seen anywhere on television. The messages are filled with action, unexpected visuals, and, most of all, imaginative special effects.

In the new computer-animated world, television images are changing dramatically. Already the Quantel Paint Box system is being used by computergraphic specialists to create and manipulate video images. Eventually, as costs decrease, these systems will find their way into the art director's office and will expand the graphic capabilities of the agency and production houses—both for print and for video.

Computergraphic artists brag that they can do anything with an image using a computerized "paintbox"—they can make Mel Gibson look 80 or Ronald Reagan look 30. They can look at any object from any angle or even from the inside out. Photographs of real objects can be seen on television as they change into art or animation and then return to life.

An example of computergraphics is a commercial by the computer production company Charlex for Pringles potato chips that shows six children munching on Pringles that appear to come out of their computers. The set is a collection of real elements, including desks, chairs, computers, students, and bookcases, but the scene is "perfectly colorized, cloned, and totally paintboxed, right down to shadows and lighting effects." The wide-angle pan reveals six children plucking Pringles from their computer screens. However, two of these youngsters were created via paintbox. Likewise only three computers actually existed in the original scene; the rest were cloned by paintbox.*

Television Radio Age (November 11, 1985).

SUMMARY

- Broadcast advertisements must be intrusive to overcome audience inattention.
- Television uses stories to entertain and make a point.
- The production of a television commercial begins with preproduction planning and continues through rehearsal, the shoot, and the postproduction editing.

- The three tools used in radio commercials are voice, music, and sound effects.
- Radio copy is simple, avoids complex information, and uses conversational language.

QUESTIONS

1. Think of an effective television commercial you have seen recently. Why was it effective? What types of creative efforts do you think went into producing this commercial? How long do you think it took to produce? How much do you think it cost?

2. How has the emergence of cable television and

VCRs affected the nature of commercials? How might they affect advertising in the future?

3. What are the major characteristics of radio ads? How do these characteristics reflect the use of voice, music, and sound effects?

4. Professor Strong has set up a lively debate between the advertising sales director of the campus newspaper and the manager of the campus radio station, which is a commercial operation. During the discussion the newspaper representative says that most radio commercials sound like newspaper ads, but are harder to follow. The radio manager responds by claiming that radio creativity works with "the theater of the mind," something that no newspaper ad can do. Can you explain what these creative positions mean? Do you agree with either one?

5. Jingles are a popular creative form in radio advertising. Even so, there are probably more jingles that you don't want to hear again than ones that you do. Identify several short musical bits that you really dis-

like. Consider the reasons why you do not like them. Do they reflect on the advertiser? Write some descriptive statements on why these jingles don't work in your case.

6. Rough ideas for television commercials are often tested on selected members of the target audience. Sometimes tests use key visuals or storyboards; other times they use photoboards or even animatics. If you were deciding which testing style to use, would the type of product help you decide? Give some examples of products that would be better tested with animatics than with storyboards.

7. Television is primarily a visual medium. However, very few television commercials are designed without a vocal element (actors or announcers). Even the many commercials that visually demonstrate products in action use an off-screen voice to provide information. Why is there a need to use the voice to provide continuity and information?

FURTHER READINGS

BALDWIN, HUNTLEY, *Creating Effective TV Commercials* (Chicago: Crain Books, 1972).

HEIGHTON, ELIZABETH J., AND DON R. CUNNINGHAM, *Advertising in the Broadcast Media* (Belmont, CA: Wadsworth Publishing Co., 1976).

ORLIK, PETER B., *Broadcast Copywriting* (Boston: Allyn and Bacon, 1982).

TERRELL, NEIL, *The Power Technique of Radio-TV Copywriting* (Blue Ridge Summit, PA: Tab Books, 1971).

WHITE, HOOPER, *How to Produce an Effective TV Commercial* (Chicago: Crain Books, 1981).

ZEIGLER, SHERILYN K., AND HERBERT H. HOWARD. *Broadcast Advertising* (Columbus, OH: Grid, 1978).

VIDEO CASE

The AT&T Universal Card

The credit-card market was already an extremely competitive one in 1990 when AT&T introduced its Universal Card. The fierce competition stemmed in large part from the difficulty in maintaining unique product features for any length of time because new innovations were rapidly copied by other credit-card firms. The result was an influx of up to 20 pieces of direct-mail credit-card offers each year to consumers, who were also inundated with credit-card advertising.

AT&T's Universal Card was truly unique, however. It functioned both as a credit card—either a VISA or a Mastercard—as well as an AT&T calling card. The card was available in either classic or gold versions and offered 10 percent off AT&T's calling-card rates. Despite attractive promotional offers accompanying the card's launch, including no annual fees for life for 1990 charter members, AT&T's advertising agency, Lord, Dentsu & Partners (LD&P), faced major hurdles in the development of its communication programs for the Universal Card. AT&T's launch of the Universal Card into the saturated credit-card market had to be communicated in a manner that would set it apart from the competition by clearly establishing both its superiority over other card offerings and its innovation in the category.

Because AT&T's Universal Card Services Division had set extremely aggressive account acquisition goals for the launch of the card, high awareness, good comprehension of card benefits and features, and strong interest levels were critical in order to stimulate the level of purchase intent necessary to achieve the card's objectives. Furthermore, given the importance of credit-card revenues to large banks, major competitors were expected quickly to match key elements of the Universal Card's offer. Therefore, LD&P had to establish the uniqueness of the card's features and benefits and to maintain AT&T's favorable image among consumers and transfer that image to the financial-services arena.

Consequently, the campaign objectives for AT&T's Universal Card focused on two key areas: First, Universal Card advertising had to generate mass awareness and create brand preference while also pre-emptively positioning the Card's benefits and features. Second, the campaign had to establish clearly the Universal Card's unique selling proposition while providing an incentive for accounts to enroll in the program.

The creative strategy itself focused on communicating the fact that the AT&T Universal Card would make it simple for users to connect with their world. Support for this message dealt with AT&T's communication-services expertise, combined with the resources and purchasing power of VISA and Mastercard. Secondary creative considerations called for the inclusion of card features relating to its value, such as no annual fees for life for charter members, 10 percent discounts on calling rates, and other credit-card enhancements. The creative concept was summarized in the tagline, "One World. One Card."

The target audience for the Universal Card was defined as all telephone and credit-card consumers, primarily adults 25 to 44 years of age. The audience was further defined psychographically as those who sought products to help control and manage their lives. AT&T committed media funds to the Universal Card launch, which represented over 25 percent of total credit-card category media spending, ranking it first of any credit card during the first 3 months of its launch. To further accelerate awareness for the Universal Card, advertising was launched on the March 26, 1990, Academy Awards broadcast, one of the highest-rated network broadcasts of the year.

The launch of the AT&T Universal Card met or exceeded all business and advertising objectives in its first year. The 4-month account enrollment goal of 2.5 million retail locations was easily surpassed and reached 4.7 million accounts by the year end. By mid-year the Universal Card was ranked as the sixth largest credit-card issuer in the nation and was named one of *Fortune* magazine's products of the year. Even though the advertising did not initially carry an 800 number, over 250,000 calls were received by AT&T within the first 24 hours of advertising, and over 2 million total calls were received by AT&T over the course of the campaign.

Qualitative research conducted in October 1990 revealed that the AT&T Universal Card had in fact developed a unique brand image. Research participants indicated that the card does indeed do many more things than other credit cards and offers greater value, high quality, and excellent service. The card's personality was characterized as young, dynamic, and exciting but also reliable and dependable—a card you can count on.

QUESTIONS

1. Based on your knowledge of existing advertising for VISA, Mastercard, and American Express credit cards, what does the "One World. One Card" message say that is unique from advertising for the other cards?

2. Given the plethora of credit-card and calling-card advertising that exists today, what elements of the "One World. One Card" campaign do you believe clearly convey that the Universal Card is both a credit card and a calling card?

Source: Courtesy of Lord, Dentsu & Partners.

16

Creating Direct-Response Advertising

Chapter Outline

Chapter Objectives

When you have completed this chapter, you should be able to:

- Define direct-response advertising
- Distinguish between direct-response advertising, direct marketing, and mail order
- Evaluate the various media that direct-response advertising can utilize
- Explain how modern technology has transformed the nature of direct response
- List the three types of firms that produce direct-response advertising

BUICK SUBSCRIBES TO NEW TECHNOLOGY

If you subscribe to any magazines, it may not be long before you start seeing ads in them that are personalized to you, the subscriber. Imagine seeing your name in the headline and copy of an ad in one of your favorite magazines. Although the technology hasn't quite gotten to that point, current technology does allow an advertiser to run an ad and tip in a reply card personalized with the subscriber's name. The technology that enables this to take place includes the ink-jet printer and the computer—the most valuable tool the direct advertiser has. The ink-jet printer prints near-typeset-quality print very quickly, and the computer can store massive amounts of data and access them in a fraction of a second to direct the printer.

Subscriber lists are the starting point. These computerized lists of all those who subscribe to a magazine can be sorted by demographic information gathered from the subscribers and/or by zip code. Sorting by zip code is based on the notion that "birds of a feather flock together." Thus, in theory, people living in the same zip code areas resemble one another in a great many ways.

During Spring 1991 Buick used this new technology to personalize advertisements to subscribers of *Time, Newsweek, U.S. News & World Report, People, Sports Illustrated, Entertainment Weekly,* and *Money.* Buick was introducing its Roadmaster station wagon and wanted to target advertising to families living in upscale neighborhoods, primarily in the Northeast and Midwest. By using the computer, the ink-jet printer, and zip code data, Buick was able to direct a personalized, tipped-in card inviting the subscriber to send for more information. This was more precise targeting than would have been possible using the magazines' own specialized subscriber lists. This unique media buy enabled Buick to reach 20 percent of the 50 percent of U.S. households that are buyers of large station wagons.*

DIRECT MARKETING

A revolution is taking place in marketing and advertising as marketers are moving to more direct forms of communication with their customers. In the past marketing communication was a monologue, with advertisers talking to anonymous consumers through the mass media. Now communication is becoming a one-on-one dialogue through computers, the mail, video, and the Touch-tone telephone.

data bases *Lists of consumers with information that helps target and segment those who are highly likely to be in the market for a certain product.*

PRINCIPLE _____
Traditional advertising targets groups of people; data-base advertising targets the individual.

With the advent of computers and the development of extensive **data bases**—files of information that include names, addresses, telephone numbers, and demographic and psychographic data—it is becoming possible for an advertiser to develop one-on-one communication with those most likely to be in the market for a certain product. That is the ultimate in "tight" targeting because the information allows advertisers to understand consumers more thoroughly and zero in on primary prospects. In other words, although traditional advertising targets groups of people, data-base advertising targets the individual. For example, Buick did not want its advertising to reach everybody—only those individuals most likely to buy large station wagons.

*Adapted from Raymond Serafin and Cleveland Horton, "Buick Ads Target ZIP Codes," *Advertising Age* (April 1, 1991):1.

AD 16.1
Amtrak uses a coupon for a free copy of a travel guide to encourage customer interest. (Courtesy of Amtrak.)

Direct-response marketing uses data bases both to reach consumers and to collect information about them. This type of marketing uses direct-response advertising and other marketing communication techniques, such as sales promotion, to contact consumers directly, without a retailer or personal sales, and solicit a response. Direct-marketing experts Stan Rapp and Tom Collins note in their book *The Great Marketing Turnaround* that there is widespread carelessness in the use of direct-response terms. The following discussion adapts their definitions and will help clarify the different terminology applied to direct marketing.*

Direct-Response Advertising

Direct-response advertising is a direct-response marketing tool that achieves an action-oriented objective—such as an inquiry, visiting a showroom, answering a questionnaire, or purchasing a product—as a result of the advertising message and without the intervention of a sales representative or retailer. Ad 16.1 for Amtrak, for example, looks like a traditional advertisement except that it is promoting a coupon to encourage inquiry. Direct-response advertising can use any medium—magazines, newspapers, radio, television, or direct mail. The focus on the objective contrasts with *brand or image advertising,* where the desired response to the advertising message is typically awareness, a favorable attitude, or a change of opinion. With brand or image advertising, the actual sale is made by a retailer in a store or a sales representative who calls at the office or home.

Obviously direct response can be a very efficient form of sales communication because it eliminates that second sales step. Historically, however, it has been seen as less efficient because it didn't reach as many

*Stan Rapp and Tom Collins, *The Great Marketing Turnaround: The Age of the Individual and How to Profit from It* (Englewood Cliffs, NJ: Prentice Hall, 1990):46–47.

people as did mass-media advertising, or if it did, the cost of reaching them individually was very high. Today this argument is being reconsidered. Direct response is now seen as reaching a prime audience—people who are more likely than the average person, for some reasons related to their demographics or lifestyles, to be interested in the product. In other words, although it costs more per impression, direct-response advertising has less waste than mass-media advertising. Furthermore, although it lacks personal contact, which is an important element in closing some types of sales, the newer forms of interactive media are beginning to solve that problem as well.

Direct mail is an advertising medium that uses the postal service to deliver the message. This is an older term that is frequently and confusingly used to refer to the broader areas of direct-response advertising and marketing. Direct-mail advertising includes letters, brochures, and catalogs—anything mailed to the home or office. **Direct-order marketing,** a new term that is replacing **mail order,** is a form of direct marketing that focuses attention on distribution; it delivers the goods to the customer's address by mail, fax, or some other package delivery system. Direct mail will be discussed in more detail later in the chapter.

Data-Base Marketing

As we mentioned earlier, the growth of extensive data bases has contributed to more targeted communication with consumers. CCX, for example, is a data-base program that stores more than 1 billion names and allows list users to mix and match information. Stan Rapp explains that nearly 90 percent of major airlines, car rental companies, hotels, resorts, retailers, and marketers of financial services, package goods, agricultural equipment, and cars have or are developing data bases to derive their communication programs.[*] This new development is also referred to as *data-base marketing, relationship marketing,* or *"MaxiMarketing."*[†] More and more marketers are moving to this new form of direct marketing as a way to develop a deeper and longer-lasting relationship with their customers. Auto companies, for example, are using data-base marketing systems to link national marketing, service, and dealer organizations with customers. Data bases allow companies to call new customers within 30 days of delivery of their cars to get their impressions of the product and to take care of any problems. Such systems can also be used to profile customers and research their purchasing behaviors.

List brokers have thousands of lists tied to demographic, psychographic, and geographic breakdowns. They have classified their data on America's households down to the carrier routes. For instance, one company has identified 160 zip codes it calls "Black Enterprise" clusters, inhabited by "upscale, white-collar, black families" in major urban fringe areas. If you want to target older women in New England who play tennis, most major firms would be able to put together a list for you by combining lists, called **merging,** and deleting the repeated names, called **purging.**

Nintendo has a 2-million-name data base it uses when it introduces more powerful versions of its video game system. The names and addresses were gathered from a list of subscribers to its magazine, *Nintendo Power.*

---

[*]Lauro Loro, "Data bases Seen as 'Driving Force,' " *Advertising Age* (March 18, 1991):39.
[†]Stan Rapp and Tom Collins, *MaxiMarketing* (New York: McGraw-Hill Book Co., 1987).

direct mail *A medium of advertising that uses the mail to carry the message.*

direct-order marketing or **mail order** *A form of marketing that uses mail or some other delivery system to deliver the product.*

merging *The process of combining two or more lists of prospects.*

purging *The process of deleting repeated names when two or more lists are combined.*

The company believes that many of its current customers will want to "trade up" and this direct communication will make it possible for Nintendo to speak directly to its most important target about new systems as they become available. Nintendo began its data base in 1988 and credits data-base marketing with helping it to maintain its huge share of the $4.7 billion video game market.

Interactive Technology. The new interactive technology, however, is what makes this area of direct marketing so exciting. Interactive means the consumer can respond back to the message. The telephone is the prime example of a media vehicle that both delivers and receives messages. For example, Pepsi planned a call-in sweepstakes for the 1991 Super Bowl but postponed the effort because it feared the nation's telecommunication capacity could not handle the response. Interactive technology is being developed, possibly using toll-free 800 numbers or 900 pay-for-call numbers, that will be able to generate 30,000 simultaneous calls and take detailed messages, like answers to a trivia quiz or a credit card order. Such systems will be capable of handling up to 300,000 phone calls in 30 minutes. At present, this system still envisions using a bank of clerks to transcribe names and addresses spoken by callers, but computer voice recognition will eliminate that need when that technology becomes available.

Ann Klein II's nontraditional marketing communication has pioneered both data-base and interactive communication.* In 1989 the company established a program to generate names for its data base and mailing lists that has since created an entirely new approach to retailing. The company now sends out some 8 million mailers to interest women in its merchandise. Customers receive season fashion tip sheets and "minimagazines" that also give fashion advice and display the new lines of clothing. In addition, the company mails seasonal "paper doll books" that show how consumers can coordinate separate articles of Ann Klein II clothing. The cornerstone of the interactive program is the "At Your Service" 800-number that allows customers to receive fashion tips and shopping information over the phone. Some 1,800 women across the country call the number every week. Men are also encouraged to call the line for advice on buying clothes for their wives or girlfriends, and ads announcing the service ran in such publications as *GQ* and *Business Week*. Customers can also access a national search network of 972 stores to track down Anne Klein II items anywhere in the country.

The secret to the success of data-base marketing is the power of the computer to manage the incredible wealth of descriptive data that are now being accumulated along with prospect lists. Most list brokers have standard lists for sale, but in addition they can sort, merge, and purge lists to custom-design one to fit a particular prospect profile.

Stan Rapp and Tom Collins see the computerized data base as revolutionizing marketing. In their book *MaxiMarketing* they explain: "The trend is as clear as the name on your checkbook. From mass marketing to segmented marketing to niche marketing to tomorrow's world of one-to-one marketing—the transformation will be complete by the end of the eighties."†

---

*Cara Applebaum, "Anne Klein II Blitzes Direct Marketing," *Adweek's Marketing Week* (October 8, 1990):20.

† Rapp and Collins, *MaxiMarketing,* p. viii.

*T*HE DIRECT-RESPONSE INDUSTRY

Direct response has been an important advertising area for over a century. The first major venture by an important national company into mail order was the publication of the Montgomery Ward catalog in 1872.* The Direct Mail/Advertising Association was founded in 1917. Currently known as the Direct Marketing Association (DMA), it has long been active in industry research and professional training programs. One of DMA's most successful programs is a seminar for college students sponsored by its Direct Marketing Educational Foundation.

Direct response has been a fast-growing segment of the advertising industry in recent years. In the early 1980s annual growth averaged 30 percent. Total 1990 U.S. direct-response volume rose only 18.3 percent to $2.1 billion, but it is still a healthy industry, particularly compared to the 9.5 percent growth predicted by advertising agency executives for that year and the gains of 12 percent in 1989 and 9.6 percent in 1988. Commissionable billings for direct-response media rose about 19.5 percent to $780 million in 1990.†

Direct marketing is one of the selling methods applied in virtually every consumer and business-to-business category. For example, direct marketing is used by IBM, Digital Equipment, Xerox, and other manufacturers selling office products. It is used by almost every bank and insurance company. It is used by airlines, hotels, and cruise lines, as well as by resorts and government tourist agencies. It is used by packaged-goods marketers, such as General Foods, Colgate, and Bristol Myers; by household product marketers, such as Black and Decker; and by automotive companies, such as Ford, Buick, and Cadillac. Direct marketing is also employed for membership drives, fund raising, and solicitation of donations by nonprofit organizations such as the Sierra Club, Audobon Society, and political associations.

PRINCIPLE
Busy people often prefer to shop directly from their home or office.

Reasons for Growth

Direct-response advertising is growing for both social and technological reasons. The influx of women into the work force in recent decades and the rise in the number of single-parent homes are two societal factors. Furthermore, both men and women are very busy today and find shopping a nuisance. They would rather not spend their precious leisure time looking for a place to park at the mall.

Technological advances have made direct response more efficient for marketers and more beneficial for shoppers. Zip codes and toll-free numbers have made it easier for consumers to respond (see Ad 16.2). Another major factor has been the credit card. With an automated billing system, a customer can call in an order and give a number for billing. The order is filled immediately; the company does not have to wait for a check to be mailed and cleared by the bank. These technological improvements have created the "armchair shopper" who would just as soon shop from the easy chair at home as drive to a store.

The Computer. The technology that has had the biggest impact on direct marketing is the computer. Advertisers use the computer to manage lists of names, sort prospects by important characteristics such as zip code or pre-

*Kenneth C. Otis II, "Introduction to Direct Marketing," DMMA Manual Release 100.1 (April 1979):1.
†Kenneth Wylie, "Recession Felt, But Direct Shops Gain," *Advertising Age* (May 20, 1991):32.

AD 16.2
This direct-response ad includes a toll-free number that makes it easy for customers to order the product if there isn't a store that carries it nearby. (Courtesy of Godiva Chocolatier.)

vious ordering patterns, handle addressing, and feed personalized addresses into the printing process. Consumers are also beginning to use their personal computers at home to reach marketers through computerized home-shopping services.

Computers and their programs are getting smarter. On-line services, such as Prodigy, run by Sears, not only provide the user with on-line buying services but also remember purchases and, over time, build a purchase profile of each user. This kind of information is very valuable to marketers, resellers, and their agencies. Already some grocery stores have computerized their grocery carts with displays that show advertised specials as the customer moves from one aisle to another. Customers at a few of these stores have been issued bank cards to use in making purchases at these particular stores. When a customer makes a purchase using the card, the store's computer provides an item-by-item list of that customer's purchases and adds this to the demographic and income information on the customer's card application. The banks are so interested in this information that they are willing to waive the usual fees and charges to the store in trade for the data.

Personalized advertising in a variety of media may become the norm in the near future. Smart computers, used with videotext systems and cable broadcast facilities, will be able to tailor messages precisely to each of us as individuals. Imagine hitting a milestone birthday or obtaining a new job and finding that all of the advertisements you now receive are tailored to these new characteristics about yourself. For instance, one day you turn 40 and all the cereal ads you receive on your television are for cereals heavy in bran and vitamins.

CHARACTERISTICS OF DIRECT RESPONSE

Direct response is different from other types of advertising because it uses some form of two-way communication and a reply device. Action objectives make it possible to measure the response and determine what works and what doesn't. The targeted audience tends to be smaller than for other forms of media advertising. One reason for this is that direct-response advertising is tightly targeted to people who are already identified as serious prospects. It is a more expensive, but also a more efficient, form of advertising. We will now summarize the essential characteristics of direct-response advertising.

Tightly Targeted

PRINCIPLE _____
Direct-response advertising is tightly targeted to people who have been identified as prospects.

The most important characteristic of direct-response advertising is that it can be tightly targeted. With some media, such as mail or telephone, it can even be targeted directly to an individual rather than to a population. This advantage allows the marketer to personalize the message to a far greater degree than is possible with other advertising forms.

With computers and extensive data bases on prospects, direct mail, for example, can be targeted to very specific types of people—not just to consumers but also to potential customers—who are actually in the market for the product. Furthermore, the letter can be personally addressed, and the message can be tailored to that person's interests. In their book on direct marketing Mary Lou Roberts and Paul Berger call this "precision targeting."* The box entitled "Direct Marketing and the Privacy Issue" discusses some of the implications of precision targeting.

Interactive

interactive *Advertising that uses personal interaction between the advertiser and the customer.*

Another characteristic that distinguishes direct-response advertising from other types of promotion is that it is **interactive.** A transaction takes place between the advertiser and the customer. Direct response is the most personal of all types of advertising. There is a direct communication link between advertiser and target. In direct mail it is a letter; in telemarketing it is a phone call; in conventional media it is an ad with a response device.

Direct response always includes at least one reply technique, either a telephone number (usually toll-free for national advertising), an order card or inquiry form, or a return envelope. Ad 16.3 for Lands' End includes a toll-free number and a reply form.

Measurable Action Objectives

Direct advertising usually includes stated action objectives—generally a purchase or a request for additional information. Not only is the response direct, it is usually immediate. Other forms of advertising are limited to indirect communication objectives like awareness or attitude change.

One benefit of having specific action objectives is that direct-response advertising is measurable. In fact, it is one of the most frequently tested areas in all of advertising. Advertisers often use split-run techniques and variations on the message to test the strength of the offer and the creative strategy.

Drawbacks and Disadvantages

Direct-response advertising is growing as a result of the need to reach more tightly targeted audiences as well as the interest by consumers in more convenient shopping methods. There are, however, some problems with this

_____
*Mary Lou Roberts and Paul B. Berger, *Direct Marketing Management: Text and Cases* (Englewood Cliffs, NJ: Prentice Hall, 1989).

type of marketing. Direct-response advertising by phone—telemarketing—is particularly irritating to consumers. Direct mail is popularly termed "junk mail," a term that expresses the negative feelings some people have toward mailings that come to them unsolicited. This negativity will only increase as environmentalist concerns spread and people become more worried about wasting natural resources (paper is made from trees) and the waste-management problem.

Although it does offer the opportunity to target tightly with the least amount of waste, direct mail has the highest cost per thousand of any form of advertising. The cost differential will continue to rise as the cost of both postage and paper increases. Bulk mailing, although cheaper than first class, offers no guarantees on time of delivery, and delays are common. Thus, sale mailers by retailers may arrive after the sale is over.

*T*HE PLAYERS

Three main players are involved in direct-response marketing: *advertisers* who use direct response to sell products or services by phone or mail; certain *agencies* that specialize in direct-response advertising; and *consumers* who are the recipients of direct-mail and phone solicitations.

AD 16.3
A toll-free number and a reply form make it easy for interested consumers to order a Lands' End catalog.   (Courtesy of Lands' End.)

CONCEPTS AND CONTROVERSIES

DIRECT MARKETING AND THE PRIVACY ISSUE

An innovative—and controversial—direct-mail campaign was developed to advertise the Porsche 300,000. The campaign was aimed at 300,000 carefully screened affluent prospects who were invited to test-drive the sports car. Multiple versions of the letter were sent out, all referring specifically in the copy to the prospect's "preeminent position" as a doctor or some other respected and upscale profession and the type of car he or she owned. The campaign planners were able to obtain data-base information about the prospects' professions and income range, the type of cars they currently drove and what they used to drive, as well as where they lived and the type of neighborhood they lived in.

The campaign was controversial because some members of the targeted audience were shocked that Porsche had assembled all this information about them. This raised a serious privacy issue. The auto maker insisted that it was acting entirely within federal and state regulations regarding direct marketing. Actually, Porsche had access to a lot more information than it could legally use in an unsolicited communication, so the company was aware that it was treading a fine line.

Other ethical questions arise with automatic phone messages. Every day an estimated 7 million Americans receive automatic telephone sales messages from some 180,000 solicitors. Typically, people are more annoyed by unsolicited phone calls than by unsolicited mail. Telemarketers also run up against the privacy question. So many consumer complaints about telemarketing have been lodged with the U.S. Office of Consumer Affairs that several federal legislators have proposed legislation to curb telemarketing. In addition, more than 500 bills affecting direct marketers have been proposed in state legislatures. The Direct Marketing Association (DMA) is actively promoting self-regulation to head off such actions; however, only half of the direct marketers in the United States belong to the DMA.

Source: Adapted from John Osbon, "Abuses Draw Congress' Fire," *Advertising Age* (September 25, 1989):S8–S9; and Cleveland Horton, "Porsche 300,000: The New Elite," *Advertising Age* (February 5, 1990):6.

The Advertisers

There are more than 12,000 firms engaged in direct-response marketing whose primary business is selling products and services by mail or telephone.* This number does not include the many retail stores that use direct marketing as a supplemental marketing program. Traditionally, the product categories that have made the greatest use of direct marketing have been book and record clubs, publishers, insurance, collectibles, packaged foods, and gardening firms. A study sponsored by the DMA identified the most common users of direct-response advertising.†

Direct-response consumer categories include:

1. Apparel (including jewelry)
2. Home furnishings
3. Periodicals
4. Appliances
5. Books
6. Records
7. Gardening

Direct-response business categories include:

1. Computer technology
2. Books
3. Office supplies
4. Computer supplies

* Roberts and Berger, *Direct Marketing Management.*
† Neil Doppelt, "Measuring Direct Marketing: DMA's Industry Statistics Survey," *DMA Focus* (January–February 1987):7.

TABLE 16.1
The Top 10 Direct-Marketing Agencies

Agency	Headquarters	Total Worldwide Billings (In Thousands)		
		1990	1989	% Change
1. Ogilvy & Mather Direct	New York	$354,180	$304,980	+16.1
2. Rapp Collins Marcoa	New York	243,160	226,000	+7.6
3. FCB Direct	Chicago	214,278	210,438*	+1.8
4. Wunderman Worldwide	New York	197,504	181,490*	+8.8
5. The Direct Marketing Group	New York	146,200	149,600	−2.3
6. Kobs & Draft	Chicago	134,300	116,900	+14.9
7. Bronner Slosberg Humphrey	Boston	127,209	79,800	+59.4
8. Grey Direct	New York	120,000	119,000	+0.8
9. Barry Blau & Partners	Fairfield, Conn.	100,916	101,175	−0.3
10. Chapman Direct	New York	100,097	48,198	+107.7

*Restated estimate, mostly due to an agency merger or acquisition. (Courtesy of *Adweek*)

Some of the largest direct-marketing firms are well known because they are major retail firms that use national advertising, but others are not as familiar because they only engage in direct marketing. Among the largest U.S. direct marketers are Sears, J. C. Penney, Time, and the American Automobile Association.*

The Agencies

Three types of firms are involved in direct-response advertising: advertising agencies, independent direct marketing agencies, and service firms.

Advertising Agencies. First are the *advertising agencies,* whose primary business is general media advertising. These agencies might have a department that specializes in direct response or they might own a separate direct-response company. Many major advertising agencies that want to provide integrated, full-service promotional programs for their clients are buying direct-response companies because this is such an important part of the corporate promotional program.

Independent Agencies. The second category is the *independent, full-service, direct-marketing agency.* These companies specialize in direct response, and many of them are quite large. Table 16.1 lists the top ten direct-market agencies. The largest direct-marketing agencies include some firms that specialize only in direct response and others that are affiliated with major agencies.

Service Firms. The third category is the *service firms* that specialize in supplying such services as printing, mailing, and list brokering.

The Consumers

Most people have a love-hate relationship with direct-response advertising. They complain about the "junk mail" that clutters their mailbox. They hate to get telephone calls at dinnertime asking for donations, no matter how good the cause. They ridicule the salesperson on television who is demonstrating a new screwdriver. However, they respond. They buy through di-

* Arnold Fishman, "The 1986 Mail Order Guide," *Direct Marketing* (July 1987):40.

A woman ordering merchandise directly from a catalog. (Courtesy of Teri Stratford.)

rect-mail letters and catalogs, they listen to the personal sales pitch over the telephone, and they call in orders after watching television ad pitches.

New Shoppers. Although people might dislike the intrusiveness of direct-response advertising, they appreciate the convenience. Former Postmaster General Preston Tisch observed that it is "a method of purchasing goods in a society that is finding itself with more disposable income but with less time to spend it."*

Stan Rapp described this new consumer in his speech to the annual DMA conference a few years ago as "a new generation of consumers armed with push-button phones and a pocket full of credit cards getting instant gratification by shopping and doing financial transactions from the den or living room." He pointed to the tremendous success of Domino's Pizza, with its home-delivery service, as the fastest-growing sector of the $12 billion pizza market.†

The push-button shopper is a new breed. It takes some daring to order a product you can't see, touch, feel, or try out. It is not like shopping at a retail store. This new breed of consumer is self-confident and willing to take a chance but doesn't like to be disappointed.

PRINCIPLE
The push-button shopper is self-confident and willing to take chances on a product that can't be seen, touched, or tried on.

Expectations. Barbara Berger Opotowsky, president of the Better Business Bureau of Metropolitan New York, describes direct response as "an act of faith." She explains: "If the company does not meet the expectations created by the promotion, the customer may lose faith, not only in that firm, but in all direct-marketing offers. You know what happens when you've

---

* "Outlook '87," *Target Marketing* (January 1987):25–28.
† "Looking into the Future of Direct Marketing," *Direct Marketing* (May 1987):144–45, 153.

been burned. You tend to say, 'I've learned my lesson, I'll never try that again.' " She comments that "There is no industry in which strong customer relations are more important than the direct-marketing industry."*

The biggest problem identified by Opotowsky is unrealistic expectations. Sometimes the shopper just doesn't read the ad carefully enough. Sometimes the ad doesn't tell enough of the story to give a good picture of the product. Sometimes the puffery and hype soar so out of control that the description bears little resemblance to the actual product.

One recent case involved a miniature electronic piano. It was really a toy, about the size of a cassette. Two of the firms offering it described it as being like an instrument: "Easiest-to-play model, fully electronic, soft-touch keyboard." Their customers complained that they had been deceived. Two other firms sold the identical product for a similar price but included a picture and the size specifications. They received no complaints.

Spiegel, a catalog marketer that is now adding new customers at a rate of 1 million per year, is very conscious of the need for a good customer-service program. Henry A. Johnson, vice chairman of Spiegel, describes the company's three levels of service. The first is accuracy—every product is described and depicted realistically. The second is immediate correction of any error. The third level is a strong customer-relations program—trained people answer questions, take orders, and handle complaints.[†]

THE MEDIA OF DIRECT RESPONSE

Direct response is a multimedia field. All conventional advertising mass media can be used, as well as others that you might not think of as advertising media, such as the telephone and the postal service. Sometimes media are used in combination. A mail offer, for example, may be followed up with a telephone call. Advertisers are allocating increasing sums of money to direct-response media.

Telemarketing is clearly the growth area in direct response. It includes both incoming and outgoing calls—in other words, any telephone call related to direct marketing comes under this category, including offers, orders, inquiries, and service calls. The calls placing orders may be in response to ads in any of the media. Direct mail through television is expensive because of the costs of production and airtime.

Direct Mail

Direct mail provides the historical foundation for the direct-response industry. A direct-mail piece is a complex, self-standing advertising message for a single product or service. It may be as simple as a single-page letter or as complex as a package consisting of a multipage letter, a brochure, supplemental flyers, and an order card with a return envelope.

Direct mail continues to be the main medium of direct-response messages. It accounted for nearly 66 percent, or $1.4 billion, of total direct response media spending in 1990.[‡]

* Barbara Berger Opotowsky, "Consumer Confidence: The Future of Direct Marketing," *Directions* (March–April 1987):6, 12.
† "Outlook '87," pp. 25–28.
‡ Wylie, "Recession Felt, But Direct Shops Gain," p. 32.

Most direct mail is sent using the third-class bulk mail permit, which requires a minimum of 200 identical pieces. Third class is cheaper than first class, but it takes much longer to be delivered. Estimates of nondelivery of third-class mail run as high as 6 to 8 percent.

Assistant Postmaster General John R. Wargo estimates that the volume of third-class mail may surpass first class sometime during the 1990s. He also notes that a typical household receives an average of 17 pieces of third-class mail each week. Even this number does not tell the whole story because not all direct-mail ads are sent third class. In fact, as much as 10 percent of all first-class mail is direct response.* The Issues and Applications box entitled "The Price of a Stamp" discusses factors affecting the direct-mail industry.

Characteristics. Direct mail, more than any other medium, demonstrates how a message can sell a product without the help of a salesperson. Because direct mail is a self-contained sales message, it has to deliver all the information and all the incentives necessary to make a sale. If it didn't work, it wouldn't have been used all these decades. Response rates for direct mail are generally higher than those for any other medium used in direct marketing.†

Tight targeting is one of direct mail's strengths. Although media advertising is limited to the circulation of the publication or the audience of the station, direct mail can select its own group of prospects. This selectivity is matched by direct mail's flexibility. Messages can be sent to any postal address at any time of the year in any size or shape acceptable for mailing. Anything, including product samples, computer discs, and videocassettes, can be included.

Message Format. Direct mail can be anything and look like anything, but most pieces follow a fairly conventional format. The packaging usually includes an outer envelope, a letter, a brochure, supplemental flyers or folders, and a reply card with a return envelope.

The Outer Envelope   One of the most important elements in direct mail is the outer envelope. The critical decision by the target is whether to read the mailing or throw it out, and that decision is made on the basis of the outer envelope. Actually, the industry estimates that three-fourths of the pieces do get read. Ad 16.4 gives examples of outer envelopes.

Advertisers use a number of techniques to get people to open the envelope. One is to state the offer on the outside: "Save $50 on a set of china." If an incentive is part of the offer, then that might be used: "Order now and get a free telephone." A *teaser* statement or question might be used to spark curiosity: "What is missing from every room in your house?" A "peek-through window" may be used to show part of the product; a "show-through envelope" can call attention to the message design of the brochure and the quality and colorfulness of its graphics.

The Letter   The letter is second in importance because it is the next thing seen after the envelope. The letter highlights and dramatizes the selling premise and explains the details of the offer. Most letters are two to four

---

*"Print Executives Say Direct Mail Growth is Strong Draw, Although It's Still Healthy," *DM News* (July 1, 1987):8; and Herbert Katzenstein and William S. Sachs, *Direct Marketing* (Columbus, OH: Merrill Publishing Co., 1986):254–55.
†Katzenstein and Sachs, *Direct Marketing.*

AD 16.4
Examples of direct-mail envelopes. What characteristics of these envelopes would encourage recipients to examine the contents? (Courtesy of Time-Life Music, Better Homes and Gardens, and Crest Fruit.)

PRINCIPLE
Direct-response letters have to do the work of hundreds of people.

broadsheets *Large brochures that unfold like a map.*

pages long, although many are longer. Research has found that people with any interest in the product will read everything in the letter. The letter has to carry the full weight of the marketing, advertising, and sales effort.

Bill Jayme, one of the best copywriters in direct-response advertising, has commented that people "often ask why we in direct marketing are so verbose. Letters that can run to eight pages. Brochures the size of a bedsheet." He explains why: "Because a single mailing package must in one fell swoop do the work, in more conventional selling, of many hundreds of people."*

The style of the letter is personal. It usually begins with a personal salutation that includes the target's name. The tone is a little different from that of traditional media advertising. It points out things about the offer as a friend might. The first paragraph works like a headline to convince the reader to stay with the message all the way through. It may dramatize the selling premise, spark curiosity, or make some incredible statement as a way to build interest.

The body of the letter provides support, explanation, proof, documentation, and details. This is serious hard-sell copy. One critical part of the letter is the postscript (P.S.). Because the postscript is highly attention-getting, most writers use it to wrap up or restate the offer.

The Brochure Accompanying the letter may be a brochure that features the product in glowing color. The letter uses words; the brochure uses graphics to create impact. The product is displayed in as many attractive settings as possible. Demonstrations and how-to-use visuals are included, if appropriate. These can be one-page flyers, multipanel folders, multipage brochures, or spectacular **broadsheets** that fold out like maps to cover the top of a table. Smaller, supplemental pieces may also be used as postscripts or for additional details or incentive offers (see Ad 16.5).

The Order Card Usually an order card with its own envelope is included. The order form may also contain a toll-free number to give the customer a choice in how to respond. Order cards sometimes have involvement devices such as tokens, stickers, stamps, and scratch-off boxes.

Message Functions. The functions of a direct-mail message are similar to the steps in the sales process. The mailing plays many roles. First it has to get the attention of the targeted prospect. Then it has to create a need for

*John Francis Tighe, "Complete Creative Checklist for Copywriters," *Advertising Age* (February 9, 1987):24, 69.

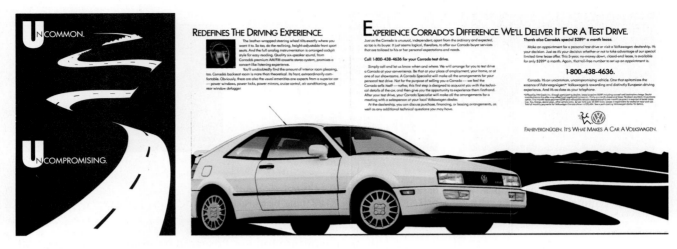

AD 16.5
This brochure for Volkswagen's Fahrvergnügen campaign was mailed to
prospects with income and car ownership qualifications. (Courtesy of
Volkswagen United States.)

the product, show what it looks like, and demonstrate how it is used. Furthermore it has to be able to answer questions like a good salesperson and reassure the buyer. It might have to provide critical information about product use. It must inspire confidence, minimize risk, and establish that the company is reputable. Finally, it has to make the sale, which involves explaining how to buy, how to order, where to call, and how to pay or charge the purchase. There may even be an incentive to encourage a fast response.

The List. Direct-mail advertising can only be effective if the mailing list targets the appropriate customers. If the prospects are not in the market of the product, then even the best direct-mail package will be thrown away. The biggest problem with computer-generated lists is accuracy. Updating mailing addresses is a constant problem in a mobile society. Other errors include addressing a woman as a man (and vice versa) and misspelling names.

The mailing list is really a segmentation tool. The list is usually categorized in terms of certain consumer characteristics, such as demographics (young mothers), professions (accountants, hair stylists, engineering professors), interests (sailing, jogging, cat or dog owner), or buying behavior (buys from upscale catalogs). As with all other forms of advertising, the more selective and upscale the list, the more it will cost.

Lists can be purchased or rented from *list managers,* people who work for companies that offer lists of group memberships that they want to market, or from list brokers. A *list broker* handles a variety of lists from many different sources and can act as a consultant to help you find a list or compile your own list from several different sources.

There are three types of lists: house lists, response lists, and compiled lists. *House lists* are lists of customers maintained by a company, store, or association. Most retailers know that their most important target audience is their own customers, so it is important to identify these people and keep in touch with them. Stores offer their own credit plans in order to maintain this link. They also offer things like service plans, special sale announcements, and contests that require customers to sign up. Some stores fill in the customer's name and address at the cash register on the sales slip, and the carbon copy becomes a source of names for the list. This is probably the most valuable list available to a store or company.

THE PRICE OF A STAMP

According to direct marketing executives, the 25 percent higher third-class postal rates that went into effect in February 1991 will cut down on the amount of "junk mail" consumers can expect to receive. Third-class mail is typically used to send millions of direct-mail ad pieces to private homes and businesses. It is also used to send out magazines and catalogs. In response to the increased postal rates, advertisers plan to send direct-mail ads only to people who have requested them. In addition, many executives say they will concentrate more of their marketing on cable television.

Companies were projected to spend approximately $25 billion on direct marketing in the United States in 1991, an increase from $7.6 billion in 1980. The postal rate increase is expected to affect the direct-response industry, however. According to George Wiedemann, president of Grey Direct, the direct-marketing division of Grey Advertising, "It is going to force direct marketers to rediscover mass media." Many executives agree that the biggest change will be a substantial increase in television commercials that use toll-free numbers to get the names of prospective customers, who are then mailed product information.

Because cable television already targets specific audiences, it is likely to be the medium of choice for such advertising. For example, ESPN at-

tracts more male viewers than female, Lifetime network is targeted at women more than at men, and MTV is popular with teenagers and young adults. Cable has been used for years to sell magazine subscriptions, records, and inexpensive household items by advertising a toll-free number to call. Now larger companies, such as Colgate and Procter & Gamble, are using these kinds of commercials to encourage consumers to call for free samples of their products.

As advertisers turn to the more traditional mass media for direct marketing, direct-marketing agencies will probably lose business to advertising agencies. A direct-marketing agency that uses television, radio, newspapers, or magazines to get its messages across will have to rely on advertising agencies to create the ads and buy the media placements. After all, many direct-marketing firms are not set up to create the kinds of ads appropriate for television. For example, Hal Brierly, president of Brierly & Partners, a Dallas-based direct-marketing company, anticipates having to acquire a small advertising agency: "I want to be perceived as capable of providing total advertising."

Source: Adapted from Kin Foltz, "Postal Rise May Cancel a Direct-Marketing Edge," *The New York Times* (February 19, 1991):C8.

A *response list* is derived from people who respond to something such as a direct-mail offer or solicitation from a group whose members are similar to the advertiser's target audience. For example, if you sell dog food, you might like a list of people who have responded to a magazine ad for a pet identification collar. These lists are usually available for rent from the original direct-mail marketer. This type of list is very important because it indicates a willingness to buy by direct mail.

A *compiled list* is one that is rented from a direct-mail list broker who represents a company that has a house list for sale or who works for a direct-mail company that is in the business of building lists. These are usually lists of some specific category, such as sports car owners, new home buyers, graduating seniors, new mothers, association members, or subscribers to a magazine, book club, or record club.

Lists can be further combined using a computer that has the ability to merge several lists and purge the duplicate names. For example, you may want to develop a list of people who are in the market for upscale fine furniture in your city. You could buy a list of new home buyers and combine that with a list of people who live in a desirable census tract. These two lists

AD 16.6
J. Crew produces one of the best-known catalogs. (Courtesy of J. Crew.)

together would let you find people who have bought new homes in upscale neighborhoods. The merge/purge capability is very important to avoid using several lists that have the same names, in which case people may receive multiple copies of the same mailing. This is annoying to the recipient and expensive to the mailer.

The Catalog Marketplace

A catalog is a multipage direct-mail publication that shows a variety of merchandise. The big books are those produced by such retail giants as Sears Roebuck, Montgomery Ward, and J. C. Penney. The Spiegel company is a major catalog merchandiser that doesn't have a retail outlet (see Ad 16.6). Saks Fifth Avenue, Neiman-Marcus, and Bloomingdale's are major retailers that support their in-store sales with expensive catalogs.

The catalog business went through a decade of explosive growth, increasing 25 to 30 percent in the mid-1980s, but the industry has settled down in the 1990s and is coming to grips with saturated markets. The postal increase in 1991 was one factor in the slowdown. A slowing economy is another. Catalog experts estimate that sales in 1990 totaled $30 billion to $35 billion and are now growing only at a rate of 8 to 12 percent a year.

Specialty Catalogs. The real growth in this field is in the area of specialty catalogs. There are catalogs for every hobby, as well as for more general interests, such as men's and women's fashions, sporting goods, housewares, gardening, office supplies, and electronics. There are catalogs specifically for purses, rings, cheese and hams, stained-glass supplies, garden benches, and computer accessories—to name just a few. For example, Balducci's fruit and vegetable store in Greenwich Village, New York City, produces a catalog promising overnight delivery of precooked gourmet meals.

Some of these retailers have their own stores, such as L. L. Bean, Williams-Sonoma, and Banana Republic. Others, such as Hanover House and FBS, offer their merchandise only through catalogs or other retailers. Levi's, for example, has always depended on other retailers to distribute its

AD 16.7
This catalog from American Express Merchandise Services advertises many upscale products. (Courtesy of American Express.)

products, but it is now planning a catalog that will make the entire Levi's line available to its customers. Some of the merchandise is relatively inexpensive, like the Hanover line, which is usually $10 or less. Others are much more upscale. Neiman-Marcus, Sakowitz, Steuben, and Tiffany all offer items priced in the thousands of dollars. The catalog in Ad 16.7 is an example of upscale advertising.

Catalogs are the chief beneficiaries of the social changes that are making armchair shopping so popular. In fact, catalogs are so popular that direct-response consumers receive mailings offering them lists of catalogs available for a charge. People pay for catalogs the way they pay for magazines: an increasing number of catalogs can now be purchased at newsstands.

Designing the Catalog Message. The most important part of the catalog message is the graphics. Products are displayed in attractive settings showing as many details and features as possible. People scan through a catalog, looking at the pictures. Only after they have been stopped by the visual do they read the copy block. Thus copy is usually at a minimum and provides such details as composition, fabric, color, sizes, and pricing.

Some catalogs are low-budget, particularly those in special-interest areas such as hobbies and professional supplies. A catalog for woodworkers or plumbers might be printed on cheap paper in black and white. Most general-interest catalogs, however, are moving to quality reproduction with slick paper and full-color printing. The fashion catalogs are often shot at exotic locations, and the reproduction values are excellent.

Some catalogs are designed to create an image, such as the Banana Republic and Caswell-Massey catalogs, which come in unusual sizes and use distinctive illustrative styles. Caswell-Massey is an apothecary that dates back to Colonial days and carries an unusual assortment of soaps, brushes, after-shave lotions, and colognes. Banana Republic specializes in the "jungle look" in fashion, and each of its catalogs features a story about some expedition to an exotic location. Ad 16.8 is an example of two specialty catalogs.

AD 16.8
Specialty catalogs are available for many different interests. *Hold Everything* is for home organization, and *Gardener's Eden* is for people who love gardens. (Left: Courtesy of *Hold Everything*; right: courtesy of *Gardener's Eden*.)

Electronic Catalogs. Catalogs are becoming available in videocassette and computer disk formats. Buick developed an "electronic catalog" on computer disk. The message is interactive and features animated illustrations. It presents graphic descriptions and detailed text on the Buick line, including complete specifications, and lets you custom-design your dream car.* The electronic catalog has been marketed to readers of computer magazines.

Video catalogs are being considered by a number of advertisers. Video offers a dynamic live presentation of the product, its benefits, and its uses. With more than half of American homes owning VCRs, this medium is becoming increasingly important. Cadillac developed a video brochure for Allante, its new luxury car. Air France and Soloflex have also investigated videos for in-home promotions.

Print Media

Ads in the mass media are less directly targeted than are direct mail and catalogs. However, they can still provide the opportunity for a direct response. Ads in newspapers and magazines can carry a coupon, an order form, an address, or a telephone number for customers to respond to. The response may be either to purchase something or to ask for more information. In many cases the desired response is an inquiry that becomes a sales lead for field representatives.

One of the most interesting experiments with personal targeting using magazines was *Time* magazine's cover in 1990 that incorporated each reader's name into its cover design. The covers read, "Hey __(subscriber's name here)__ don't miss our really interesting story on the junk mail explosion" (see Ad 16.9). Newsstand copies read: "Hey, you at the newsstand." The article, incidentally, noted that 92 million Americans responded to direct-marketing in 1989, a 60 percent increase in 6 years.

In *MaxiMarketing* Rapp and Collins discuss the power of *double-duty advertising* that combines brand-reinforcement messages with a direct-response campaign to promote a premium, a sample, or a coupon. Giorgio perfume, Cuisinart, and Ford all use multifunctional advertising in magazines that works two or more ways, including direct response.†

* "Software Beats Hard Sell at Buick," *Advertising Age* (November 24, 1986):59.
† Rapp and Collins, *MaxiMarketing,* p. 171.

American Express is using this double-duty concept in its attempt to combine magazine and direct marketing. The company has launched *Your Company,* a quarterly mailed to more than 1 million American Express corporate card members who own small businesses. *Your Company* was launched by four sponsors—IBM, United Parcel Service, Cigna Small Business Insurance, and American Express Small Business Services. American Express also mails a magazine, *Connections,* to college students. Such efforts combine the editorial direction of a magazine with direct advertising's ability to target a narrow audience based on demographics and lifestyle. Magazines have been trying to do this with demographic editions and selective binding as well.

Reply Cards. In magazines the response cards may be either *bind-ins* or *blow-ins.* These are free-standing cards that are separate from the ad. Bind-in cards are stapled or glued right into the binding of the magazine adjoining the ad. They have to be torn out to be used. Blow-in cards are blown into the magazine after it is printed by special machinery that "puffs" open the pages. These cards are loose and may fall out in distribution, so they are less reliable.

Broadcast Media

Television and radio have also become involved in direct-marketing advertising.

Television. Television is a major medium for direct marketers who are advertising a broadly targeted product and who have the budget to afford the ever-increasing costs of television advertising. Direct-response advertising on television used to be the province of the late-night hard sell with pitches for vegematics and screwdrivers guaranteed to last a lifetime. As more national marketers such as Time Inc. move into the medium, the direct-response commercial is becoming more general in appeal.

Direct-response television advertising has come a long way since the vegematic and hair restoration ads. An award-winning campaign for Ryder Truck Rental included a 2-minute television spot illustrating one family's humorous, but happy, experience with Ryder trucks, which boosted the company's visibility dramatically. The spot generated 150,000 requests for a free step-by-step moving guide. The U.S. Postal Service used a commercial on the home-video release of MCA's *The Land Before Time* to generate interest in its dinosaur stamp release.

Cable Television   Cable television lends itself to direct-response commercials because the medium is more tightly targeted to particular interests. For example, ads on MTV for products targeted to the teenage audience can generate a tremendous response. Sales are soaring on the Home Shopping Network (HSN), a cable network that displays merchandise in living color. The QVC network, a home-shopping channel, and HSN reported more than 57 million subscribers in 1990.

J. C. Penney is the first major retailer to go on air via a cable hookup. The company invested $40 million in its new interactive home-shopping service called Teleaction. Through this "video catalog" service, customers can order the merchandise on screen by using their push-button phones.*

Radio.   Radio has not been a dynamic medium for direct-response advertising because most experts believe the radio audience is too preoccupied with other things to record an address or a telephone number. Home listeners, however, are able to make a note and place a call, and local marketers have had some success selling merchandise this way.

Radio's big advantage is its targeted audience. Teenagers, for example, are easy to reach through radio. There has even been some success selling products such as cellular phones and paging systems specifically to a mobile audience.

*T*ELEMARKETING

telemarketing *A type of marketing that uses the telephone to make a personal sales contact.*

The telephone system is a massive network linking almost every home and business in the country. More direct-marketing dollars are spent on telephone ads using **telemarketing** than on any other medium. The telephone combines personal contact with mass marketing, which is an important factor in relationship marketing.

Costs

Personal sales calls are very expensive but very persuasive. Telemarketing is almost as persuasive, but a lot less expensive. A personal sales call may cost anywhere from $50 to $100 when you consider time, materials, and transportation. A telephone solicitation may range from $2 to $5 per call. That is still expensive, though, if you compare the cost of a telephone campaign to the cost per thousand of an advertisement placed in any one of the mass media. Telemarketing is four to five times as expensive as direct mail.†

* "Penney Says Teleaction to Start by September," *Advertising Age,* (June 8, 1987):82.

† Katzenstein and Sachs, *Direct Marketing.*

If this medium is so expensive, why would anyone use it? The answer is that the returns are much higher than those generated by mass advertising. Telemarketing has to be efficient to be justifiable. The revenue has to justify the bottom-line costs.

Characteristics

Telemarketing is personal; that is its primary advantage. The human voice is the most persuasive of all communication tools. Although many people regard a telephone solicitation as an interruption, there are still large numbers who like to talk on the telephone. Some people are flattered by receiving a telephone call, even if it is just a sales pitch.

Two-way. Telephone conversations are also two-way. There is a conversation in which the prospect can ask questions and give responses. This conversation can be tailored to individual interests. Furthermore, if the person isn't a prospect, the caller can find out immediately and end the call.

There is another important aspect of this two-way communication system. Just as the marketer can call the prospect, the customer can call the company. When you think of telemarketing, you probably just think of the telephone solicitation, but that is only half the picture. The telephone is also used by the consumer to place orders and to call with questions and complaints. The telephone is a very important tool in *customer service* as well as in getting and taking orders.

wide area telephone service (WATS) *A system of mass telephone calling at discount rates.*

Technology. Two technological changes have spurred the use of telemarketing. The first is the **wide area telephone service** (WATS line), a system provided by the telephone company that is similar to bulk mail. The price is discounted with use; the more calls made from a single location, the cheaper the cost of each individual call.

The WATS line has made it possible for telemarketers to set up "phone factories" with multiple lines, banks of telephones, and hundreds of trained callers. This mass production of telephone calls has made telemarketing economically feasible.

The other innovation is the incoming WATS line, which we have referred to previously as the 800 number or toll-free number. The number isn't free, of course; the charges go to the company being called rather than to the caller.

Telemarketing Firms. Most companies that use telemarketing hire a specialized company to handle the solicitations and order taking. They do this because most of the activity occurs in bunches. If a company advertises a product on television, for example, the switchboard will be flooded with calls for the next 10 minutes. Companies that do occasional direct-response advertising don't have the facilities to handle a mass response. A service bureau that handles a number of accounts is more capable of coping with the bursts of activity that follow promotional activities.

The Message

The most important thing to remember about telemarketing solicitations is that the message has to be simple enough to be delivered over the telephone. If the product requires a demonstration or a complicated explanation, then the message might be better delivered by direct mail.

The message also needs to be compelling. People resent intrusive telephone calls, so there must be a strong initial benefit or reason-why statement to convince prospects to continue listening. The message also needs to be short; most people won't stay on the telephone longer than 2 to 3 minutes for a sales call. That, of course, is still a lot longer than a 30-second commercial.

SUMMARY

- Direct marketing always involves a one-on-one relationship with the prospect. It is personal and interactive.
- The growth in direct-response advertising has been stimulated by technologies such as computers, zip codes, toll-free numbers, and credit cards.
- Direct-response advertising can use any advertising medium, but it has to provide some type of response or reply device.
- Direct-response advertising has benefited from the development and maintenance of a data base of customer names, addresses, telephone numbers, and demographic and psychographic characteristics.

- The new push-button consumer is busy and appreciates the convenience of shopping at home or at the office.
- A direct-mail advertising piece is a complex package using an outer envelope to get attention, a cover letter, a brochure, an order card, and a return envelope.
- Catalogs are so popular that some consumers will pay to get their names on the mailing lists.
- Telemarketing is the biggest direct-response area; it combines the personal contact of a sales call with mass marketing.

QUESTIONS

1. What are the major advantages of direct response compared to other forms of advertising? The major disadvantages?
2. What types of firms produce direct-response advertising?
3. Hildy Johnson, a recent university graduate, is interviewing with a large garden-products firm that relies on television for its direct-response advertising. "Your portfolio looks very good. I'm sure you can write," the interviewer says, "but let me ask you a serious question. What is it about our copy that makes it more important than copy written for Ford, or Pepsi, or Pampers?" How should Hildy answer that question? What can she say that would help convince the interviewer she understands the special demands of direct-response writing?
4. We know that copy and illustration are vital parts of a successful direct-mail campaign, but there must be some priorities. Review the Chapter 13 section on

"What Makes an Idea Creative." All of the components are important, but which one is the first consideration for direct-response creativity? Defend your choice.

5. One of the smaller privately owned bookstores on campus is considering a direct-response service to cut down on its severe in-store traffic problems at the beginning of each semester. What ideas do you have for setting up some type of direct-response system to decrease "traffic overload"?

6. Suppose you are the marketing director for a campus service organization dedicated to assisting needy people and families in the immediate area. What are your ideas for developing a telemarketing program to promote campus fund raising? Would it be better to solicit money directly or indirectly by having people attend specially designed events? Your primary targets are students, faculty, and staff.

FURTHER READINGS

KATZENSTEIN, HERBERT, AND WILLIAM S. SACHS, *Direct Marketing* (Columbus, OH: Merrill Publishing Co., 1986).

"Looking into the Future of Direct Marketing," *Direct Marketing,* May 1987, pp. 144–45, 153.

RAPP, STAN, AND TOM COLLINS, *MaxiMarketing* (New York: McGraw-Hill Book Co., 1987).

RAPP, STAN, AND TOM COLLINS, *The Great Marketing Turnaround* (Englewood Cliffs, NJ: Prentice Hall, 1990).

ROBERTS, MARY LOU, AND PAUL D. BERGER, *Direct Marketing Management: Text and Cases* (Englewood Cliffs, NJ: Prentice Hall, 1989).

Home Shopping: Direct-Mail Catalogs

The 1980s were considered the golden years for catalog marketers. Once envisioned as a low-cost way to reach new markets, catalogs soon emerged as the perfect retail experience for modern consumers. They allowed dual-income households strapped for time to shop to their heart's content without ever stepping foot outside their own front doors. Retailers also benefited from the catalog boom because the cost to produce and ship catalogs was much less than the cost to build and maintain a network of retail store locations.

Unfortunately, the proliferation of catalogs in recent years has oversaturated the marketplace and stalled the explosive sales growth experienced in the 1980s, forcing the catalog industry to recognize that it is not immune to economic influences. With the rapid growth from new sales no longer evident, the catalog industry was faced with declining sales for the first time during the 1990-1991 recession.

Fortunately, the catalog industry possesses several key advantages that have allowed it to weather the rough economic times. Specifically, with increasingly sophisticated direct-mail data bases to target narrower demographic groups, the catalog industry was able to tailor its catalog distribution and product mix to better insulate itself from the recession. Although retailers dependant on retail store locations for sales can modify their product mixtures within 3 to 6 months, the long lead time required to relocate or to open new locations limits their ability to adapt to rough economic times. In contrast, direct-mail catalog retailers can focus catalog distribution on more upscale households and/or modify product lines to include either lower cost or more durable and practical goods within a few months' time.

Although this greater flexibility allows the catalog industry to react to economic conditions more rapidly than can traditional retailers, it does little to protect catalog producers from the ravages of increased competition within the industry itself. As the amount of available demographic data has increased and more sophisticated computer software has emerged to manipulate the data, catalog retailers have found it possible to match customized products to smaller and smaller customer niches more easily than ever before. Consequently, catalog retailers have found it increasingly necessary to update catalogs, finetune customer mailing lists, and procure more innovative product offerings more rapidly than ever before.

This heightened competition within the catalog industry has dramatically increased the cost of doing business, leading to what many industry experts anticipate could be a shake-out of players in the coming years. Whereas in the early days of catalog retailing, one version of a catalog could serve many markets for several years with little or no changes and, thus, relatively low production costs, the industry environment today requires an adequate capital base to allow for frequent catalog makeovers in order to remain competitive.

This is particularly critical for catalog retailers who lack an in-house produced line of products or the exclusive rights to a line of another manufacturer's products because direct competition for such products is limited. However, for catalog retailers who simply package a collection of commonly available products with a specific theme or to appeal to a specific demographic group, frequent catalog makeovers are often the only way to ward off direct competition from other catalogs. In such circumstances, price discounts may also become more critical to differentiate items in one catalog from another.

QUESTIONS

1. Whereas early catalogs featured primarily black-and-white photographs or illustrations of products, lengthy delivery times, and limited return policies, modern catalogs offer full-color photographs of items, quick delivery, and often unconditional return policies. What demographic and/or attitudinal changes have taken place over the last 20 years to have allowed catalog marketers to charge the higher prices necessary to provide the heightened service levels found in todays catalogs?

2. Whereas early catalogs were distributed by retailers with existing store locations, such as Sears and Montgomery-Wards, today many catalog marketers have opened retail store locations following the success of their catalog businesses. List the advantages and disadvantages for traditional retailers offering catalogs and for catalog retailers opening stores.

3. Because much of the success of modern catalog marketing is due to the ability to target narrow demographic segments in the population, explain which, if any, traditional advertising media options could be utilized to promote catalog sales for targeted households.

Source: ABC News, *Business World,* Show #212 (November 25, 1990).

17

Creating Directory and Out-of-home Advertising

Chapter Objectives

When you have completed this chapter, you should be able to:

- Understand how consumers use the Yellow Pages to search for information about stores, products, and services
- Describe the characteristics of a well-written and well-designed Yellow Pages ad
- Explain the importance of graphics in poster design
- Understand the effect of a moving audience on the design of a billboard
- Explain the difference between interior and exterior transit advertisements
- Identify innovative media to use to deliver sales, reminder, and action messages

REPORTING ON THE YELLOW PAGES

An advertising professor was sitting across from a newspaper reporter at lunch during a journalism conference both were attending. The following conversation actually took place.

"I'm a reporter. What do you do?" asked the reporter of the professor.

"I'm an advertising professor."

"Oh, advertising?" said the reporter smugly. "Well, I never pay any attention to advertising. I never look at the ads."

"Never?"

"Nope. I don't need to. They don't tell you anything anyway."

"Let met ask you something, then," said the professor. "Suppose you went home this afternoon and discovered that your washing machine had broken down, what would you do?"

"I'd call a repair shop," the reporter answered.

"How would you know which one to call?"

"I'd look in the phone book, of course," responded the reporter while looking at the professor incredulously.

"What part of the phone book would look in?" the professor prodded.

"The Yellow Pages," answered the reporter with dawning awareness that he had been trapped.

"You mean the section with all the ads?" asked the professor innocently.

"Those aren't ads!" the reporter sputtered. "The Yellow Pages is just information—it's not advertising."

"Does the phone company just give away the space in the Yellow Pages to the companies?"

"No."

"Then someone has to buy the space and puts whatever they want to in it, right?"

"Yes."

"I'd call that advertising, wouldn't you? I'd also say that when you say that you 'never look at ads' that that isn't exactly true, is it?

The reporter took a bite of his salad and chewed it thoroughly. "I still say it's not the same thing. It's not *really* advertising."

"Actually," said the professor, "I'd say it's advertising at its best—it offers essential information to those who need it, when they need it."

The reporter took another bite of his salad and quickly became absorbed in the conversation going on further down the table.

DIRECTORY ADVERTISING

Directories are books that list the names of people or companies, their phone numbers, and their addresses. In addition to this information, many directories publish advertising from marketers who want to reach the people who use the directory. The most common directories are produced by a community's local phone service. Of course, the Yellow Pages is also a major advertising vehicle, particularly for local retailers. The Yellow Pages

exclude

revenues for 1990 were $8.8 billion, making it the fourth-largest advertising medium, with growth that outpaced advertising expenditures in other media by almost one-third.*

But that is just the beginning of the directory business. There are an estimated 7,500 directories available, and they cover all types of professional areas and interest groups. In advertising, for example, the *Standard Directory of Advertisers* and *Advertising Agencies* (known as the red books) take advertising, as does *The Creative Black Book,* which takes ads for photographers, illustrators, typographers, and art suppliers. Similar publications are available in cities that have large advertising communities.

The ads in trade and professional directories are usually more detailed than those in consumer directories because they address specific professional concerns, such as qualifications and scope of services provided. Trade directories also use supplemental media such as inserts and tipped-in cards (glued into the spine) that can be detached and filed. Although many different kinds of directories take advertising, this chapter will focus on Yellow Pages advertising.

directional advertising *Advertising that directs the buyer to the store where the product or service is available.*

Yellow Pages advertising is described as **directional advertising** because it tells people where to go to get the product or service they are looking for. There is one important difference between this kind of advertising and brand-image advertising, which attempts to create a desire to buy: Directory advertising reaches prospects—people who already know they have a need for the product or service. If you are going to move across town and you want to rent a truck, you will consult the Yellow Pages. That is why U-Haul spends more than $10 million a year for directory listings. Directory advertising is the primary form that is actively consulted by prospects who need or want to buy something.

Yellow Pages Advertising

The Yellow Pages directory lists all local and regional businesses that have a telephone number. In addition to the phone number listing, retailers can also buy display space and run a larger ad. The industry's core advertisers are service providers—restaurants, travel agents, beauty parlors, and florists, for example—rather than retailers, which have been hard hit by the economic slowdown of the late 1980s and early 1990s. For some small businesses, the Yellow Pages is the only medium of advertising. Over 88 percent of Yellow Pages advertising is generated from local businesses.

Although there has always been a certain amount of competition among businesses in the same category listings, the competition has become more intense and complex since the breakup of AT&T in 1984. With deregulation, the local Bell companies and their directories are faced with competition from many independent sources. Most major cities now have a number of alternative and competing local directories. Many of these are aimed at general consumers, but there are also books that specialize by providing listings for certain regions or neighborhoods or by targeting certain consumer groups, such as the Silver Pages for senior citizens or Spanish-language books for Hispanics. The Bell Atlantic Yellow Pages (Ad 17.1) is an example of regional Yellow Pages directories.

---

*Monte Williams, ''Shielded from Recession,'' *Advertising Age* (March 18, 1991):S1; ''The Yellow Pages Tackle the Other Media,'' *Link 2* (September/October 1990):23.

Before you advertise in the Bell Atlantic Yellow Pages, ask for references.

50 times a second, on an average, 3,000 times a minute. That's how often people in the Mid-Atlantic region refer to their Bell Atlantic Yellow Pages. And 52% of those shopping references result in sales.

The One That Works!

AD 17.1
Since the breakup of AT&T the number of Yellow Pages directories has increased, which has led to greater competition. (Courtesy of Bell Atlantic Yellow Pages.)

The Audience

The behavior of consumers using the Yellow Pages is considerably different from that of consumers using other forms of mass-media advertising. For this reason directory advertisements are designed differently than other ads. The Yellow Pages is consulted by consumers who are interested in buying something. They know what they want, they just don't know where to find it. Almost 90 percent of those who consult the Yellow Pages follow up with some kind of action.* Because a Yellow Pages ad is the last step in the search for a product or service by a committed consumer, the ads are not intrusive.

According to a survey by the Gallup organization for *Advertising Age*, the Yellow Pages are used primarily for comparison shopping. Of the consumers surveyed, 40 percent said they use the Yellow Pages to compare different stores and suppliers. Another 32 percent use the directory to find the business closest to their residence, 10 percent use it to check store hours, and 6 percent use it for local maps.†

*"How to Write an Ad for the Yellow Pages," ad by Southwestern Bell Telephone that ran in local community newspapers.
† Williams, "Shielded from Recession," S–1.

Creating the Yellow Pages Ad

Although the advertisement doesn't have to attract the attention of an indifferent audience, it does have to stand out in a competitive environment. Once they locate the category, most consumers tend to "browse" through the listings. The decision about which store to call or visit will be based on certain criteria, the first being the size of the ad. Larger ads typically get more attention than smaller ads.

Another decision factor is *convenience,* especially location and hours. Most people prefer to shop at the nearest store. Large directories in major metropolitan areas often group businesses by geographical area. Other factors that affect the consumer's decision are the scope of the services or product lines available and the reputation or image of the store.

Index and Headings. The most important feature of Yellow Pages advertising is the category system. Because consumers must be able to find the product, store, or service in the directory, category headings are extremely important.

NYNEX used a sweepstakes promotion to anchor these headings in its consumers' memories. Cash prizes were given to residents who knew both the advertised "heading of the day" and its corresponding page number in the Yellow Pages. NYNEX also won awards for its creative commercials that featured visual puns built on headings such as "Civil Engineers." The commercial showed a group of railroad engineers in overalls with caps and bandanas sitting in a parlor setting and having tea. The NYNEX ad in Ad 17.2 uses that same concept to attract advertisers.

If there is any doubt about where people would be likely to look, then the best practice for an advertiser is to use multiple ads that cover all possible headings. For example, a store selling radios may be listed under "Appliances" or even under "Television." It is critical for an advertiser to know how people search for the store or service and to make sure information is found under every possible heading that they might use.

Critical Information. Certain pieces of information are critical to a Yellow Pages ad. In addition to location and hours of operation, the telephone number must be included. The Yellow Pages, after all, is a directory of

AD 17.2
NYNEX ads used a series of puns in their headings. (Courtesy of Yellow Pages Association)

AD 17.3
This ad for IBM contains a great deal of valuable information, including several telephone numbers for various services. (Courtesy of IBM)

AD 17.4
This ad develops a strong brand image. (Courtesy of Great Bear Spring Co.)

AD 17.5
This ad for a chain of retail florist shops uses stylized flowers and a tasteful layout to create a visually attractive ad. (Courtesy of Conroy's Flowers.)

phone numbers, and many consumers will call to see if the product is available before making a trip. Note the multiple telephone numbers listed in Ad 17.3 for IBM.

Writing. Yellow Pages specialists advise using a real headline that focuses on the service or store personality rather than a label headline that just states the name of the store. The ad should describe the store or the services it provides, unless the store's name is a descriptive phrase like "Overnight Auto Service" and "The Computer Exchange." In Ad 17.4, because "Great Bear" gives no clue to the product, the advertiser uses descriptive phrases and a drawing.

Complicated explanations and demonstrations don't work very well in the Yellow Pages. Any information that is timely or changeable can become a problem because the directory is only published once a year.

The Design. Among the key design elements of Yellow Pages ads are size, image, and graphics.

Size When people browse through the ads in a category, their choice of a company or product is often influenced by the size of the ad. One study reported that the larger the ad, the more favorable the consumer perception.*

Image People make decisions based on the reputation and image of the store. This unique personality should be reflected in the design of the ad. Is it a high-quality, upscale, expensive store? Is it nostalgic or classy or exclusive? When you look through the Yellow Pages for restaurants, women's clothing stores, or hair stylists, can you tell something about the personality of the store from the ad? This personality is communicated through the headline, the illustration, the layout, and the use of type (see Ad 17.5).

Graphics In addition to communicating a store image, the design performs several other functions. In a competitive market design helps an ad stand out. An illustration, for example, can make an ad more visible. The at-

*Dennis Hinde and Gary Scofield, "Is Bigger Better in Yellow Pages Ads?" *Journalism Quarterly* (Spring 1984):185–87.

tention-getting elements should also be big and bold. Spot color, which is becoming available at an additional cost, contributes tremendously to the impact of the ad.

Simplicity is very important. Specialists advise advertisers to keep the number of elements to a minimum. If you must use a lot of pieces, then organize the layout carefully so that the visual path is clear and things that belong together are grouped together. A fanciful display type may be used for the headline to communicate an image, but try to avoid using a variety of faces in a variety of sizes. Use *bullets* (a series of dots) rather than an extended piece of body copy to list important points.

Photographs don't reproduce well in phone books, given the quality of the paper and printing. Line drawings work better, although a high-contrast photo may be acceptable. Avoid any graphic that has a lot of detail. Full-color art and photos also don't reproduce well. Maps are very important, but they need to be simplified to show only major streets in the immediate neighborhood.

Electronic Directories

A recent development in directories is the electronic Yellow Pages, a data base accessed by computer. These data bases are used primarily in business-to-business communication, although the idea is becoming popular among consumers who have computers hooked up to telephone modems and who subscribe to such on-line services as Prodigy. We mentioned Prodigy, the joint venture between IBM and Sears, in the previous chapter as a form of direct marketing; however, it also carries electronic directories.

The concept of electronic directories was pioneered in France by Minitel, which provides consumers there with access to telephone listings, news, and sports through a network of 5 million small video terminals located throughout the country. As of Spring 1991, the regional Bell companies were prohibited from entering into this type of electronic publishing. The U.S. government feels that a dominant carrier of information (technical transmission) should not also be the source of information because that would give it too much control (although this is changing). These services therefore were primarily provided by independent publishers who were actively exploring the depth and breadth of this new type of information and advertising.

OUTDOOR ADVERTISING

PRINCIPLE *Strong graphics are central to the design of posters.*

Outdoor advertising is a big industry. It is seen all day, every day. It can't be turned off or tuned out. Because of its continuous presence, it is a constant reminder. The primary objectives of outdoor messages are awareness, announcement, and reminder. Detailed explanations are not possible, and there is no time for elaboration of copy points. Outdoor advertising is found primarily in three main formats: posters, billboards, and painted bulletins. Figure 17.1 shows how outdoor billboard ad revenues have grown throughout the years.

Posters

A poster is a large placard or sign that is posted in a public place to announce or publicize something. Almost every culture throughout history has left behind some form of public message (see Chapter 1). For this rea-

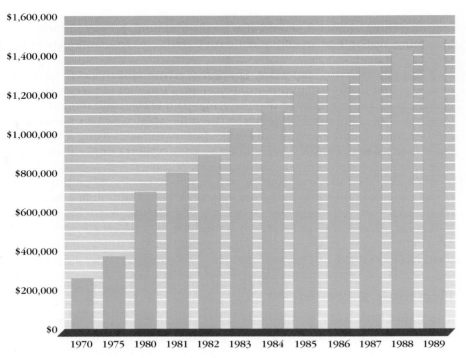

Years	Billions
1970	$259,529.3
1975	$370,553.0
1980	$701,301.3
1981	$799,483.4
1982	$887,911.1
1983	$1,027,559.0
1984	$1,128,259.8
1985	$1,221,905.4
1986	$1,275,669.0
1987	$1,329,247.0
1988	$1,416,676.5
1989	$1,487,540.5

Source: DDB Needham Woldwide, *Media Trends* (February 1991): 83.

FIGURE 17.1
Outdoor billboard ad revenues continue to climb.
(Courtesy of Institute of Outdoor Advertising.)

son posters have been called the oldest form of advertising. Even after a culture has disappeared, its messages have remained.

Early posters and signs were primarily pictorial or symbolic because most of the population couldn't read. A sculptured wooden shoe over the door indicated a shoemaker; a sign of a lady with a crown indicated the Queens Crown pub. Graphics remain central to the design of posters as well as other forms of outdoor advertising. Even if a poster is predominantly type, the type will be designed artistically for maximum impact. The key to most posters, however, is a dominant visual with minimal copy.

Aesthetics.   Posters and other advertising signs have achieved "art" status and are collected and valued for their aesthetics. Posters became masterpieces following the invention of lithography. During the nineteenth century such artists as Manet, Toulouse-Lautrec, and Beardsley produced posters advertising events such as plays and bicycle races.

Poster competitions for artists are popular even today. Posters, both historic and contemporary, are found on display in galleries and museums. The Swiss and English governments have sponsored programs to encourage posters as art. Posters are probably the only advertising medium that has received such encouragement.*

Outdoor Poster Panels.   The design for an outdoor board is supplied by the advertiser or agency. For poster panels, the art is printed on a set of large sheets of paper. Thousands of copies can be printed and distributed around the country. The sheets are then pasted like wallpaper on existing boards by the local outdoor advertising companies that own the boards.

*Sally Henderson and Robert Landau, *Billboard Art* (San Francisco: Chronicle Books, 1981); and *The Big Outdoor* (New York: The Institute of Outdoor Advertising).

The standard sizes of poster boards are the *30-sheet poster,* with a printed area 9 feet 7 inches by 21 feet 7 inches surrounded by margins of blank paper; and the *bleed poster,* with a printed area 10 feet 5 inches by 22 feet 8 inches that extends all the way to the frame. Smaller eight-sheet posters are 5 feet high and 11 feet wide. These "junior posters" are used by groceries and local advertisers.

Location.   Posters are found on buildings, walls, lampposts, and bulletin boards, in hallways, subway platforms, and bus shelters—anywhere people congregate or pass by in great numbers. *Station posters* are a form of transit advertising that uses posters in bus shelters and subway platforms. In Europe and on university campuses special structures called **kiosks** are designed for public posting of notices and advertisements. Some of these locations are places where people walk by; others are places where people wait. The location has a lot to do with the design of the message.

If people are moving, then the design needs to be simple and easy to read instantly. If people are waiting, then the advertiser has a captive audience, and the poster can present a more complicated message.

Billboards

Billboards are oversized versions of posters. They are designed to be seen by people traveling by in cars. This is a most unusual situation in that the audience is moving and the advertising is stationary. The word *billboard* goes back to the nineteenth century. At that time advertising posters were called "bills." Entrepreneurs began leasing space on wooden boards in high-traffic areas where these bills could be posted—hence "billboards." The implications of the great number of billboards is examined in the box entitled "Should Outdoor Advertising Be Banned?"

Format.   The format of all outdoor advertising has a tremendous impact on its message design. The format is extremely big and extremely horizontal, and visuals and layouts are forced to accommodate to these dimensions. Television screens are slightly horizontal, and magazine and newspaper pages are vertical. A design for a magazine or newspaper page doesn't transfer very well to a billboard because of the elongated horizontal dimension.

Extensions.   Extensions can be added to painted billboards to expand the scale and break away from the limits of the long rectangle. The extensions are limited to 5 feet 6 inches at the top and 2 feet at the sides and bottom. These embellishments are sometimes called **cutouts** because they present an irregular shape that reflects something like a mountain range or a skyscraper.

As part of a campaign against drunk driving, a billboard was created using the remnants of an actual car a family of four was killed in by a drunk driver (see Ad 17.6). This billboard is distinctive and memorable both because of its message and because of the way it is communicated outside the confines of the flat surface of the billboard. Figure 17.2 shows the top ten categories in billboard advertising in 1989.

Painted Bulletins

Painted bulletins are prepared by artists working for the local outdoor advertising company. They are hand-painted either on location or in the shop on removable panels that can be hoisted up and attached to the billboard

kiosks *Multisided bulletin board structures designed for public posting of messages.*

billboards *Large structures erected on highways and roads for the display of huge advertising posters.*

PRINCIPLE
The huge horizontal format of outdoor affects the design of the message.

cutouts *Irregularly shaped extensions added to the top, bottom, or sides of standard outdoor boards.*

PRINCIPLE
Because viewers are traveling past the billboard, outdoor billboards must deliver the message with "quick impact."

AD 17.6
Mothers Against Drunk Driving (MADD) used a powerful 3-D image to get its message across in this billboard. (Courtesy of MADD, MN.)

frame. All three of the standardized poster panel sizes maintain a basic 2¼:1 proportion. The painted bulletin used for local advertising is even more horizontal than poster panels; the proportion is 3½:1.

The standard size of painted bulletins is 14 feet by 48 feet. Some use a *rotary plan* and are moved to different places every 30, 60, or 90 days for greater exposure. Others are *permanent* and remain at one location.

Painting a large-scale image takes an unusual eye because the details are so much larger than life. Up close the work looks like an impressionistic painting because the colors, contrasts, and shading patterns are so exaggerated. From a distance the details blend together to create a recognizable image.

Categories	$(000)	% of Total
Cigarettes	$200,013.8	13.4%
Retail	$155,515.9	10.5%
Business, Consumer Services	$129,909.5	8.7%
Automotive, Auto Access/Equip.	$126,673.3	8.5%
Travel, Hotels and Resorts	$111,191.5	7.5%
Publishing, Media	$107,551.7	7.2%
Entertainment, Amusements	$106,294.3	7.1%
Beer, Wine, Liquor	$91,326.5	6.1%
Insurance, Real Estate	$68,535.9	4.6%
Healthcare	$37,400.0	2.5%

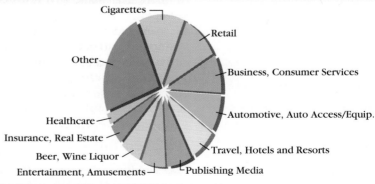

FIGURE 17.2
The top ten categories in outdoor billboard advertising. (Courtesy of Institute of Outdoor Advertising.)

Source: DDB Needham Woldwide, *Media Trends* (February 1991): 84.

ADVANTAGES AND DISADVANTAGES OF OUTDOOR ADVERTISING

Advantages

- *Impact:* Outdoor is big, colorful, hard to ignore, and larger than life.
- *Strategy:* An excellent reminder medium, outdoor can also be used to trigger an impulse.
- *Message:* Outdoor can showcase a creative concept.
- *Cost:* Outdoor is the least expensive of all major advertising media based on CPMs.
- *Long Life:* Outdoor is good for messages that need to be repeated.

Disadvantages

- *Message:* Because the message must be simple and brief, you can't develop an involved story or copy points.
- *Exposure:* The average driver is exposed to an outdoor message for only a few seconds.
- *Criticism:* Some critics feel outdoor advertising is visual pollution.
- *Availability:* Because of criticism of outdoor advertising, some areas restrict or ban billboards.

Message Design

Outdoor messages differ from other advertising messages. Some of the key elements are discussed below.

PRINCIPLE

Effective outdoor advertising is built on a strong creative concept that can be understood instantly.

Concept. Effective outdoor advertising is built on a strong *creative concept* that can be instantly understood. The idea needs to be creative because the message has to get attention and be memorable. Most of all, it has to make the point quickly. For example, a billboard for a doughnut store announcing that it now sells cookies featured a huge, one-word headline filling the entire board that read: "Goody." The two O's in the middle were both round cookies. The underline read: "Winchell's has gone cookies." The concept was expressed in both words and visuals.

PRINCIPLE

Outdoor advertising uses short, catchy phrases.

Copywriting. The copy on a billboard is minimal. Usually there is one line that serves both as a headline and as some kind of product identification. The most important characteristic is *brevity*. The words are short, the phrases are short, and there are no wasted words. Some books suggest that no more than six to seven words be used. The headline is usually a phrase, not a sentence. There is nothing equivalent to the body found in a print ad. The best copy for outdoor is a short, catchy phrase. It needs to catch attention, but it also needs to be captivating in order to be memorable. Often the phrase will be a play on words or a twist on a common phrase. For example, a billboard for Orkin pest control showed a package wrapped up with the word "Orkin" on the tag. The headline read: "A little something for your ant." A billboard for Best Food mayonnaise showed a butcher block with tomatoes, lettuce, cheese, and rye bread sitting next to the mayonnaise bottle. The headline read: "Best on the block."

The Design. Because billboards must make a quick and lasting impression, design is critical to their effectiveness.

AD 17.7
The words and visuals in the Mercury Outboards billboard work together to form a single creative concept. (Courtesy of Mercury Marine.)

Layout   The integration of art and headline is critical for the development of a strong concept. The layout is compact, with a very simple visual path, usually beginning with a strong graphic, followed by a catchy headline, and ending with some kind of product identification. The relationships should be so clear and so integrated that the elements are perceived as one whole concept. Ad 17.7 for Mercury Outboards is an example of a good layout.

Graphics   The most important feature of billboard design is high visibility. *Visibility* means that a billboard is conspicuous; it is noticeable; it bursts into view. The illustration should be an eye-stopper.

What makes something visible? Size is one factor. A billboard is the world's biggest advertising medium. It offers a grand scale, much larger than life, and therefore can create tremendous impact. You can depict a 25-foot-long pencil or a pointing finger that is 48 feet long. The product or the brand label can be hundreds of times larger than life. Most elements on a billboard are big and bold—the type as well as the illustrations.

Bold, bright color is another characteristic of impact. The outdoor industry has done significant research on color and color combinations. It has found that the greatest impact is created by maximum contrast between two colors. The strongest contrast, for example, comes from dark colors against white or yellow. Yellow adds tremendous impact as well as contrast. Other bright colors also add impact. The visibility problem is compounded by the fact that outdoor boards are seen at all times of the day and night under all kinds of lighting conditions. The most visible billboards use bright, contrasting colors.

Another aspect of visibility is the clarity of the relationship between foreground and background. In outdoor advertising the best practice is to make this distinction as obvious as possible. A picture of a soft drink against a jungle background will be very hard to perceive when viewed from a moving vehicle at a distance. The background should never compete with the subject.

Typography.   Type demands unusually sensitive handling. It has to be easy to read at a distance by an audience in motion. The outdoor industry has researched type legibility on billboards. Among its conclusions is to avoid all-capital letters because that is the hardest typographical form to read. Ornamental letters, depending on how fanciful they are, can also be hard to read, as can script and cursive letters. Anything that is unusual can create legibility problems. Experts in outdoor advertising advise using simple, clean, and uncluttered type.*

A Creative Guide to Outdoor Advertising (New York: Institute of Outdoor Advertising).

SHOULD OUTDOOR ADVERTISING BE BANNED?

What's down the road for the outdoor advertising industry? Billboards are criticized for being unsightly; that was the reason for the restrictions sketched out in the Highway Beautification Act of 1965. Environmentalists consider them a blight on the landscape, and many people agree that although some highway information may be important, most billboards just add clutter to the urban landscape. The problem is defining "clutter." Is clutter merely the perception of poorly designed billboards, which stirs up a cauldron of questions about aesthetics, or is it based solely on the number of billboards within a given area?

New bills with more stringent regulations, up to and including outright bans on outdoor advertising, are constantly being proposed in Washington, D.C., and in many state capitals. In 1991 the Bush administration proposed expanding the number of roads and highways where outdoor boards might be banned and granting individual states the power to ban them. The bill would either ban new boards along the 150,000-mile national highway system and on nearly 300,000 miles of rural secondary highways or give states the authority to ban or regulate them. A study by the Department of Transportation's inspector general and the General Accounting Office indicates that new billboards are being erected at least three times faster than old billboards are coming down.

In some local communities such as Boulder, Colorado, and Peoria, Illinois, city councils have voted to ban outdoor advertising within the city limits, although Peoria did revote after an outcry by local businesses and concerned citizens. Businesses worry that eliminating billboards will hurt them in the local marketplace. A survey of business owners in Blue Springs, Missouri, for example, where opponents are calling for an end to signs within the city limits, found that although there are concerns that the billboards may be unsightly, most believed that billboards attract new business.

In addition to their unsightliness, billboards are also criticized for communicating unsocial messages to the wrong audiences. A study in Baltimore found that about 70 percent of the city's 2,015 billboards were located in economically depressed inner-city neighborhoods. Of those billboards, 76 percent advertised liquor and cigarettes. Baltimore is not unusual. When the Metropolitan Outdoor Advertising Company of New York City replaced a beer ad with the message "God makes house calls," local Harlem residents cheered. Metropolitan has also announced that it will remove all liquor and cigarette billboards within five blocks of schools, play areas, and churches.

Industry defenders say restrictions and bans violate advertisers' free speech rights and their right to advertise. When the Bush administration proposed banning new billboards along the national highway system, Outdoor Advertising Association of America (OAAA) spokespersons reiterated their argument that outdoor advertising is protected by the U.S. Constitution.

Regarding the desirability of the product messages, a four-state study by OAAA found that less than 10 percent of the total outdoor boards available were devoted to tobacco advertising. The states (and their percentages) were Florida (6.8 percent), Texas (7 percent), Indiana (11 percent), and California (14.5 percent).

And so the debate continues.

Source: Adapted from Eric Weissenstein, "Bush Widens Outdoor Ad Ban Bill," *Advertising Age* (February 25, 1991); and "Outdoor Advertising: What's Down the Road?" *Outdoor Advertising,* a publication of Custom Ad Planner Systems (Spring 1990):6–7.

Distance. Planning for reading at a distance is an important aspect of billboard design. The Institute for Outdoor Advertising has developed a poster distance scale viewer that designers use in planning the layout. Designers realize that a layout on a desk has a very different impact than a billboard by the side of a highway. The viewer lets them evaluate the design as it would be seen at a distance from a moving car.

AD 17.8
The little red tab toting Levi's name and the single phrase 'Sit on it' are all the jeans company needs to establish product identification in this billboard. (Courtesy of Levi Strauss & Company.)

spectaculars *Billboards with unusual lighting effects.*

holography *A technique that produces a projected three-dimensional image.*

Product Identification. Product identification is another important aspect of the design of outdoor advertising. Most billboards focus attention on the product. The distinctive label on a cold, dripping Perrier bottle filled the entire space on one billboard. Underneath was the headline: "It's only natural." The red Smirnoff label with its distinctive typeface appeared on another board next to an olive and a lemon peel. The headline was a play on words: "Olive 'R Twist." The Levi's billboard in Ad 17.9 is a good example of strong product identification. Table 17.1 lists the top ten billboard advertisers of 1989.

Production of Outdoor

As a result of modern technology, outdoor ads can now utilize a number of special effects.

Lighting. Lighting is a very important aspect of outdoor advertising. Illuminated billboards against a nighttime sky can create a compelling visual. In urban areas illuminated boards may be combined with special lighting effects that blink and change colors. Neon may even be added. These displays are called **spectaculars.** Las Vegas and Times Square in New York display many examples of lighted spectaculars.

A new *backlighting* technique used for nighttime showings appears to make the background of the board disappear so that the image pops out against the black sky. Another experiment involves the use of an internally illuminated transparent polyvinyl that gives the appearance of a luminous image projected onto a screen. Some advertisers are experimenting with **holography,** which can project a three-dimensional image from a board or onto a board.

Shape. Designers have been searching for decades for techniques to break away from the rectangular frame of most boards. Extensions help, but advertisers are also experimenting with designs that create the illusion of 3-D effects by playing with horizons, vanishing lines, and dimensional boxes.

Inflatables are even closer to 3-D. Giant inflatable liquor bottles and cigarette packs made of a heavyweight stitched nylon inflated by a small electric fan have been added to outdoor boards. An especially impressive billboard for Marineland shows a 3-D creation of Orca, Marineland's killer whale, bursting through the board.

TABLE 17.1
The Top 10 Billboard Advertisers

	1989 Billboard Dollars	Total Dollars	Billboards as % of Budget	% of Total Billboard Dollars
Philip Morris Cos.	70.9	2,072.0	3.4	6.4%
RJR Nabisco	49.1	703.5	7.0	4.4%
Loews Corp.	34.2	143.0	23.9	3.1%
B.A.T. Industries PLC	27.7	196.4	14.1	2.5%
American Brands	10.7	204.2	5.3	1.0%
Seagram Co.	9.0	136.8	6.6	0.8%
Grand Metropolitan	8.1	823.3	1.0	0.7%
Guinness PLC	6.4	NA	NA	0.6%
Anheuser-Busch Cos.	6.1	591.5	1.0	0.5%
McDonald's Corp.	5.9	774.4	0.8	0.5
Total	228.1			20.5%

Note: Dollars in millions.
Source: DDB Needham Worldwide, *Media Trends* (February 1991):86.

Times Square in New York offers many examples of the elaborate outdoor ads known as spectaculars. (Courtesy of Comstock.)

kinetic boards *Outdoor advertising that uses moving elements.*

Motion. Revolving panels, called **kinetic boards,** are used for messages that change. These two-, three-, or four-sided panels can contain different messages for different products or they can be used to develop a message that evolves. Two- or three-sided stationary panels can be used to create a message that changes as the viewer passes by—different angles giving different versions of the message.

Motors can be added to boards to make pieces and parts move. Disk-like wheels and glittery things that flicker in the wind have all been used to create the appearance of motion and color change. Special effects include techniques to make images squeeze, wave, or pour.

*T*RANSIT ADVERTISING

Transit advertising is primarily an urban advertising form that uses vehicles to carry the message to people. The message is on wheels, and it circulates through the community. Occasionally you might see trucks on the highway that carry messages. Many semitrailer trucks carry graphics to identify the company that owns them. Some of these graphics are beautiful, such as the designs on the sides of the Mayflower Moving trucks and the Steelcase trucks. In addition to this corporate identification, the sides of trucks may also be rented out for more general national advertising messages. Trucks are becoming moving billboards on our nation's highways.

Transit advertising also includes the posters seen in bus shelters and train, airport, and subway stations. They are targeted at commuters and travelers. Most of these posters must be designed for quick impressions, although posters on subway platforms or bus shelters are often studied by people who are waiting and thus may present a more involved or complicated message.

Transit advertising is reminder advertising; in other words, it is a high-frequency medium that lets advertisers get their name in front of a local audience at critical times such as rush hour and drive time. Frito-Lay used a transit campaign to promote its Smartfoods, the white cheddar cheese popcorn. The campaign's objective was to demonstrate that Smartfood is everywhere and to make the image a powerful presence in a local market. Other companies are making use of this type of advertising, as discussed in the box entitled "Taking Advertisers Along for a Ride."

The Audience

interior transit advertising
Advertising on posters that are mounted inside vehicles such as buses, subway cars, and taxis.

exterior transit advertising *Advertising posters that are mounted on the sides, rear, and top of vehicles.*

There are two types of transit advertising—interior and exterior. **Interior transit advertising** is seen by people riding inside buses, subway cars, and some taxis. **Exterior transit advertising** is mounted on the sides, rear, and top of these vehicles, and it is seen by pedestrians and people in nearby cars.

Targeting. Transit messages can be targeted to specific audiences if the vehicles follow a regular route. Buses that are assigned to a university route will have a higher proportion of college students, whereas buses that go to and from a shopping mall will have a higher proportion of shoppers.

Message Design

car cards *Small advertisements that are mounted in racks inside a vehicle.*

Interior Transit. Interior advertising in buses and subways uses a format called **car cards.** These cards are mounted in racks above the windows and in panels at the front and back of the vehicle. The car cards are horizontal, usually 11 inches high by either 28, 42, or 56 inches wide.

Interior advertising is radically different from exterior transit advertising. People sitting in a bus or subway car are a captive audience. Their ride averages 20 to 30 minutes. Some read books or newspapers, but most watch other riders, look out the window, and read and reread the ads. In addition, most people who commute on mass transit ride both ways, so the messages get studied twice.

PRINCIPLE
Interior transit advertising uses longer and more complex messages because it can be studied.

As a result, car cards can have longer and more complex messages than outdoor or exterior panels. The only problem with length is visibility. The messages are read from a distance and frequently at an angle. The type must be big enough to be legible given this seating problem.

Car cards offer other opportunities for extending the message. Many cards come with *tear-offs* and *take-ones.* Tear-offs are pads of coupons or other information that are glued to the car card. Take-ones are pockets filled with flyers or leaflets. Both can be used for coupons, recipes, or just to provide more in-depth information.

PRINCIPLE
Exterior transit advertising is designed like small billboards with simple, bold, and catchy messages.

Exterior Transit. Exterior advertising panels are very similar to outdoor boards and the same guidelines are used in their design. The only difference is that the vehicle carrying the message, as well as the reader, may be in motion. This makes the perception of the message even more difficult. Exterior panels are designed like small billboards: simple, bold, catchy, and legible.

TAKING ADVERTISERS ALONG FOR A RIDE

Colgate-Palmolive was offered a choice of media to include in its advertising campaign for Ajax. Among 15-second television commercials, women's magazines, and transit ads, the company chose transit, and ads showing one sparkling clean house among a row of gray houses were plastered on buses in five major U.S. cities. Clay Timon, Colgate's vice president of worldwide advertising, explained the decision: "Simply because we wanted a high-frequency campaign to get the Ajax name out there."

Colgate is faced with the same situation as many other package-goods marketers. Most members of their target audiences work during the day, so these marketers have found that they can get more mileage from a transit campaign than from television advertising.

According to Jodi Yegelwel, vice president of sales promotion and research at Gannett Transit, package goods is becoming a major category for transit advertising. In 1972 transit ad spending totaled $43 million; by 1989 an estimated $225 million was being spent annually. One transit ad company, Transit Displays, sells ad space on and inside buses, commuter railroads, taxis, telephone kiosks, and San Francisco's cable cars. The company attributes its success to the willingness of more companies to try new media and to the increasing costs of television advertising. Transit Displays has sold space to Frito-Lay's Smartfoods, Kraft General Foods Group's Entenmann's Fat-Free cakes and pastries, and H. J. Heinz Company's Weight Watchers.

Source: Adapted from Laurie Freeman and Alison Fahey, "Package Goods Ride with Transit," *Advertising Age* (April 23, 1990):28.

MOVIE ADVERTISING

trailers *Advertisements that precede the feature film in a movie theater.*

Most movie theaters will accept filmed commercials to run before the feature. Called **trailers,** these advertisements are similar to television commercials but are generally longer and better produced. Theater messages are usually 45 seconds or 1 minute in length. This gives more time for message development than the typical 30-second television spot. There is even talk of 2-minute minifilms for theater showings.

The Audience

There may be some limited targeting of these messages in terms of location and the type of audience attracted by various kinds of movies. The important audience factor, however, is the attention and concentration generated by the theater environment. The projection of larger-than-life images in a darkened theater is totally unlike the experience of watching television. The impact of the large screen makes for a compelling image that commands total attention. It is very difficult for the audience to turn off or tune out whatever is happening on that screen.

PRINCIPLE
Theater advertising is the most compelling form of advertising because of the impact of larger-than-life images in the dark on the big screen.

Message Design

The critical feature of theater advertising is that it must function as entertainment. People in theaters have a low tolerance for hard-sell messages. Dramas and MTV techniques, with their music and intense imagery, have been particularly effective with theater advertising.

exclude

THE MALE GOLFER

In our society professional sports and advertising have become inseparable. Every major sporting event from the Super Bowl to the Indy 500 has its commercial sponsors. In turn, sports figures are often used as spokespersons because so many people identify with them. By examining a lifestyle study of male golfers, we can decide whether the endorsement of a sports celebrity and other promotional techniques are likely to help sell a product.

Profile

The study focuses on men who played golf 12 times or more within the previous year. Male golfers are a distinct group who constitute only 7 percent of the total male population. According to the study, male golfers are more likely than men in general to be over the age of 45 and to be retired, and they are less likely to have children living at home. They more frequently have attended college and have household incomes higher than $30,000. Golfers are also self-confident and consider themselves leaders.

Because golfers earn a high income, they tend to be less price-conscious than men in general. Most golfers are more concerned with the quality of a product than with its price. They are less likely than men in general to pay cash for all their purchases, to check prices, and to shop for specials.

Golfers are also more active than men in general. They take part in social activities, including dinner parties, sporting events, and cultural activities, such as visiting museums and libraries. They are also more physically active, taking part in exercise and sports activities.

Golfer Bernhard Langer endorsing certain brands of sporting goods.
(Courtesy of Dave Cannon/Allsport.)

Golfers tend to have liberal views on television and advertising. They are less concerned about the amount of sex and violence on television, and they are less likely to oppose television advertising of alcoholic beverages or ads directed toward children.

Exercise

What types of special advertising techniques would appeal to male golfers? Do you think they would use sporting goods that are endorsed by a professional golfer? Does it make sense to spend money promoting these products to male golfers, given the fact that so few men fit into this category?

Source: Needham Harper Worldwide, "Lifestyle Profile: The Male Golfer," prepared by Diana Kinzie (October 1985).

The Controversy

Movie advertising isn't universally appreciated. Moviegoers have been known to picket outside movie theaters to express their displeasure that advertisements are being shown before the feature movies. Walt Disney refuses to let its movies be shown in movie houses that run commercials before the films. People have also been known to boo and hiss in the theater when these commercials come on. Most people who resent these ads explain that they have paid money to attend the movie and therefore they shouldn't be subjected to commercials.

The decision to run ads is usually not up to the individual theater but is made by the motion picture companies and the distributors who handle the films. Theaters typically limit the commercials to no more than three per film. Ads will be run for everything from cars to credit cards to the Marine Corps, but the mix usually depends on the type of audience perceived as watching that particular film. Movies thought to appeal to teenagers, for example, will often open with MTV-like advertisements. As with most advertising, some theater ads are irritating and some are entertaining.

INNOVATIVE MEDIA

Sales Messages

New and novel media are constantly being utilized as vehicles for advertising messages. Pay telephones are beginning to carry advertising space. This can be a highly targeted medium. If you want mall shoppers, then you can reach them at telephone booths in malls; if you want travelers, use the airport telephones; if you want college students, advertise on campus pay telephones.

indicia *The postage label printed by a postage meter.*

Companies that have their own postage meters use the **indicia** for printed messages on the envelopes of the correspondence. Some people have even suggested that the government sell space on postage stamps for advertising messages.

Even garbage and trash cans on the city streets are being used for short messages. These advertisements can carry short copy lines and product symbols. Bus-stop benches are also available for short copy such as slogans, although visuals don't work well on benches.

Reminder Messages

Blimps have been around for decades and, of course, the Goodyear Blimp is a classic example of brand-reminder advertising. Planes pulling banners have been used over major outdoor events such as fair and football games. More recently, hot air balloons have carried commercial messages.

Athletic competition makes heroes, and heroes are good message endorsers. Consequently, almost every sports event is a display for special-interest advertising. All the tennis, skiing, swimming, and golf equipment manufacturers prominently display their brands on the course or on the athletes' clothing.

Other sponsors, such as beer companies, simply like to affiliate with an attention-getting event such as the Indy 500 or the Super Bowl. The Indy cars are covered with decals for the sponsors who underwrite the cost of getting the car into the race and onto the track.

Blimps offer a creative way to advertise. (David Wells/The Image Works.)

Action Messages

Grocery carts now have placard space that can be rented. These are reminder messages, but they function like point-of-purchase advertising (see Chapter 18). They confront the shopper at the moment when he or she is ready to make a purchase.

Coupons are being printed on the back of tickets to major events like college football games. Coupons are also showing up on the back of grocery store receipts.

SUMMARY

- The Yellow Pages is the most universal advertising medium.
- Yellow Pages ads focus on the service offered or the store personality.
- Posters are the oldest form of advertising.
- Posters are graphic, and the focus of the message is the visual.
- Outdoor advertising delivers messages to moving audiences using "quick-impact" techniques such as strong graphics and short, catchy phrases.

- A billboard is the largest advertising medium.
- National billboards are distributed as preprinted posters; local billboards are original, hand-painted art.
- Interior transit messages can be studied; exterior messages must be seen in a glance.
- Theater advertising is the most compelling form of advertising because of the impact of larger-than-life images on the big screen.

QUESTIONS

1. Why is Yellow Pages advertising described as "directional"?
2. Outdoor advertising is described as "quick impact." What does that mean? How do you design effective messages for this medium?
3. Since his freshman year in college, Phil Dawson, an advertising major, has waited on tables at Alfredo's, a small family-operated restaurant featuring excellent food and an intimate atmosphere. The owner has been approached by a Yellow Pages representative to run a display ad. He asks Phil for advice on whether a display would help, and if so, what the ad should look like. What should Phil recommend?
4. You are constantly exposed to poster advertising all over your campus. If you had authority over all poster advertising, what would you do to improve the effectiveness of poster advertising on campus?

5. There is some extraordinary outdoor billboard technology under development that will allow advertising images to be projected onto the board space. The same technology could also provide public information (in addition to the advertising) from each board location. The creative possibilities of computer-controlled projection are obvious, but what about the ability to convert each location into a special message board? What sort of services could key locations provide that would contribute to public service? Do you feel that such ideas would improve public opinion toward outdoor billboards?
6. One of the most logical opportunities for new advertising methods is to expand the communication options found inside stores. What are some store-level activities that could be used in (a) supermarkets and (b) department stores?

FURTHER READINGS

The Big Outdoor (New York: The Institute of Outdoor Advertising).

A Creative Guide to Outdoor Advertising (New York: The Institute of Outdoor Advertising).

FLETCHER, ALAN D., *Yellow Pages Advertising* (Chesterfield, MO: American Association of Yellow Pages Publishers, 1986).

HENDERSON, SALLY, AND ROBERT LANDAU, *Billboard Art* (San Francisco: Chronicle Books, 1981).

"Multiple Directories: A Publisher's Point of View," *Update,* Summer 1986, pp. 2–3.

"Yellow Pages Co-op Advertising: The $2 Billion Advertisers Bonanza," *Update,* Summer 1986, pp. 4–5.

VIDEO CASE

Down to Earth Problems for General Motors' Saturn Project

In the mid-1980s, when General Motors (GM) first showed off the prototype for what would eventually become the Saturn small car project, the concept seemed like an appropriate response to the invasion of high-quality, low-cost compact and subcompact cars from Japan. Five years later, behind schedule and plagued by production problems, GM launched Saturn in the domestic marketplace. Within months, Saturn had experienced its first recall, and by mid-1991 the dream of Roger Smith, General Motors' Chairman during the birth of the project, was rapidly evolving into a costly nightmare for Smith's successor.

The apparent failure of the Saturn project adds another dismal chapter to the gloomy saga of the Big Three domestic auto makers' fall from grace. In fact, within the last year, Honda Motors of Japan displaced the Chrysler Corporation as the third largest producers of automobiles in the world. The causes behind the apparent failure of the Saturn project are too numerous and complex to address within the scope of a single case, so the following discussion will focus primarily on the advertising for the Saturn car and the associated strategic decisions that spawned it.

In the late 1980s, in a move that shocked both the automotive and the advertising industries, GM assigned the Saturn account to Hal Riney & Partners, of San Francisco. Riney had previously leveraged his deep baritone voice and his unique creative skills to developing successful campaigns for Gallo and other clients. With his own agency barely 2 years old and with little automobile advertising experience, Riney got the Saturn account. GM's rationale was that Riney could bring the kind of fresh new perspective to the Saturn line that was needed to "break the clutter" of traditional automobile advertising.

Riney's staff was undoubtedly daunted by the task of identifying effective creative solutions for a product that provided few, if any, benefits over important small-car alternatives other than the obvious "Made in the U.S.A." appeal. The agency was also given perhaps too much time to think about the campaign as production delays on the Saturn project dragged on for over 2 years. The result was an often inscrutable campaign typified by outdoor billboards with such headlines as "Made Fresh Daily."

Historically, advertising strategies for automobiles have run the gamut from very tangible price or performance-based claims for economy cars and trucks to purely intangible, emotional claims for sports cars and recreational vehicles. With the notable exception of the classic Volkswagen Beetle campaigns of the 1960s and 1970s, however, successful economy-car advertising has traditionally focused on value rather than emotional satisfaction.

Consequently, when Saturn was launched with a largely emotion-based advertising positioning, it was crucial for the automobile itself to provide some performance or aesthetic benefit that could make the emotional claims credible. In reality, the Saturn lacked any readily apparent innovation in style, design, performance, or features. Thus, without the help of a truly unique selling proposition, Riney's quirky, offbeat ads lacked relevance for the product and appeared gimmicky.

The apparent failure of the Saturn project also further undermines the credibility of domestic auto makers' claims to be more competitive than ever against Japanese quality. Saturn was, perhaps, the last major attempt by a domestic producer to battle for share in the compact and subcompact car arena, forcing the company to focus more on the midsize and luxury-car markets. However, with the successful launch of the Acura line by Honda, the Infinity line from Nissan, and the Lexus line from Toyota, domestic auto producers are now being squeezed from both ends, leaving them to battle with each other more aggressively than ever for the midsize, medium-priced segment of the automobile category.

If the current trends continue, industry observers can only expect one or more of the Big Three to teeter once again on the edge of bankruptcy, with little hope of a federal government bailout, similar to the Chrysler cash infusion of the late 1970s, because the federal government now has debt problems of its own. As long as voluntary import restriction quotas remain in effect, however, domestic auto producers may be saved by joint ventures with their Japanese competitors because such agreements can benefit U.S. firms by providing access to technology and low-cost labor and benefit the Japanese with greater access to U.S. markets.

QUESTIONS

1. With consumer confidence in U.S. automobile quality at low levels and with look-alike body styles utilized in Saturn's design, what benefits other than "Made in the U.S.A." could Hal Riney & Partners have pursued for the Saturn launch?

2. What would "Made Fresh Daily" connote about Saturn cars to the naive consumer, as used in the automobiles outdoor billboard?

3. Describe the advantages and disadvantages of using an advertising agency with extensive experience in the category for which they are assigned to develop creative versus an agency with little or no experience in the assigned category.

Source: ABC News, *Business World,* Show #170 (February 4, 1990).

CASE STUDY

Lands' End: Advertising with a Direction

Over the past 30 years Lands' End has become one of the most successful direct merchants of "cut-and-sewn" products in the United States. Customers can use Lands' End catalogs to order traditionally styled recreational and informal clothing for men, women, and children, shoes, accessories, and soft luggage without leaving their homes (see Exhibit A). The company's success stems in part from its policy of supplying quality merchandise at reasonable prices, backed by excellent customer service. However, customers might never have heard of Lands' End had it not been for an aggressive—and effective—advertising campaign.

Lands' End was founded in 1963 by former copywriter Gary Comer. The company was started in a basement along the river in Chicago's old tannery district. Comer and his staff were all sailors and initially the company supplied sailboat hardware and equipment by mail. Early catalogs included a clothing section to complement

EXHIBIT A

other products. Incidentally, the misplaced apostrophe in the company's logo is explained rather simply—it was a typo in the first printed piece, and it was too expensive to reprint and correct it.

In 1976 Lands' End decided to focus its efforts on selling "soft goods"—clothing and soft luggage. By 1979 the company had moved to Dodgeville, Wisconsin, expanded the clothing offerings in its catalog, and began recruiting personnel experienced in the area of fabrics and clothing manufacturing. The company had been a leader in the integration of consumer advertising techniques with mail-order practices. By 1980 Lands' End was offering its line of quality cut-and-sewn clothing and luggage to about 400,000 customers, and sales were growing at better than 50 percent annually.

Despite this success, Comer remained convinced that his company had not realized its full potential. He consulted consumer-media specialist Richard C. Anderson, who recommended an ambitious, 5-year consumer-advertising plan that would focus on building a national reputation for quality, value, and service. The strategy ultimately called for placing Lands' End ads in the medium best suited to the targeted audience of upscale, professional people Comer's philosophy attracted—consumer

magazines such as *New York, Smithsonian,* and *Travel and Leisure.* Exhibit B is the first ad ever run by Lands' End. The ads were full-page, black and white, with simple artwork (no photography) and detailed descriptive copy. Black-and-white ads were both cost-efficient and distinctive, and they typified the company philosophy of substance over flash. Ads included an address and a toll-free number that consumers could use to order a free catalog.

By 1981 Lands' End had begun its national advertising campaign to describe its business philosophy and expand its reputation for quality, value, and service. The campaign introduced the phrase "direct merchant" to illustrate the company's approach to its business.

This long-range image-building approach was a major departure from conventional mail-order advertising, which measured success by such short-term results as cost per inquiry and revenue per ad. Direct-mail advertising traditionally is relegated to small spaces in the back of books or the mail-order section of magazines where a coupon is offered for a catalog request. Lands' End advertising is more like product advertising. It always takes up an entire page and focuses on the company image and reputation.

The campaign proved so successful that it was ex-

EXHIBIT B

EXHIBIT C

tended beyond the "5-year mark" right through to the present. As indicated by Exhibit C, the style of the campaign is essentially unchanged. Note the consistency of style in this ad compared with Exhibit B. How effective has the campaign been in recent years? Net income for the fiscal year ended January 31, 1991 was $14.7 million on net sales of $604 million, about 70 times what they were before the campaign was initiated in 1980. Figure 1 lists the company's sales growth since 1985.

In order to establish a relationship with its customers, Lands' End encloses a get-acquainted piece in catalogs sent to first-time customers. Exhibit D is an example of a Dodgeville piece that is enclosed in catalogs, which details the company's history and sets forward the Lands' End philosophy of quality, value, and service. The underlying message of the advertising is that the Lands' End people wouldn't sell anything they wouldn't wear themselves. Exhibit E is an example of a recent catalog. Exhibit F lists the Lands' End business principles Comer established from the very beginning, which became the foundation for the company's marketing philosophy.

The Lands' End Market

Recent market research has revealed a great deal of information about the 5.5 million Lands' End customers spread across the United States (a smaller number reside in Canada or overseas). Relatively larger concentrations live in metropolitan areas, in the major lake regions, and along the coastlines. Research has found that nearly nine out of ten customers have some level of college education. In comparison, this is only true for about 35 percent of the U.S. population. Lands' End customers are five times more likely than the general population to have some level of postgraduate education. High education is reflected in the occupations of Lands' End customers. A high percentage are in professional and managerial positions, and many of the women are employed outside the home. Lands' End consumers fall primarily within the 25 to 54 year-old age group, with the largest portion between 35 to 44 years of age.

As a result of their professional and educational achievements, Lands' End customers are relatively affluent. Over two-thirds of Lands' End households have annual incomes above $35,000. Lands' End customers also tend to be participants and are involved in a broad range of personal interests. They tend to travel far more than the average American both for pleasure and business. They participate in a wide variety of active sports and differentiate themselves most from the general population by their interest in tennis, sailing, skiing, and gardening.

In order to appeal to these consumers, Lands' End has primarily relied on print advertising, particularly ads in upscale magazines. The company rents lists to look for potential customers. In addition, it includes subscription cards in catalogs for referrals of new customers. Lands' End was a well-kept secret for a long time, but it is now an outstanding example of how a well-managed company that produces quality goods can use a creative advertising approach to create a success story.

Courtesy of Lands' End.

EXHIBIT D

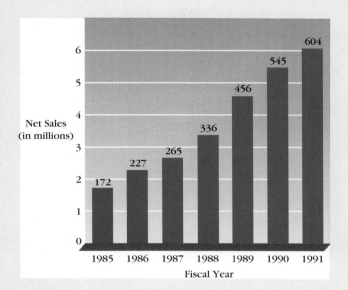

FIGURE 1
Lands' End sales growth 1985 to 1991.

EXHIBIT E

EXHIBIT F

18

Sales Promotion

Chapter Objectives

When you have completed this chapter, you should be able to:

- Distinguish between sales promotion and advertising
- Explain how promotion and advertising work together within the marketing mix
- List several types of promotions, both for consumers and for resellers
- Understand why advertisers are spending increasing sums of money on sales promotion
- Explain the advantages and disadvantages of sales promotion as compared to advertising

JOINT PROMOTIONS LEAD THE WAY

Cross promotions—or joint promotions—are becoming a way of life for two of the major television networks. In 1990 NBC teamed up with McDonald's and Toys 'R' Us for two separate cross promotions tied into the network's fall season.

The NBC/Toys 'R' Us joint promotion was targeted to children watching Saturday morning shows. The effort involved all of the toy retailer's 400-plus stores and revolved around a contest "where every kid's a winner." The NBC/McDonald's joint promotion involved a nationwide game-like promotion supporting the network's prime-time lineup. The effort reached over 60 million people each day through network spots and traffic at the fast-food chain's 8,400 restaurants.

That same year CBS and K Mart repeated a 1989 program entitled "Get Ready Giveaway" sweepstakes. Although this tie-in ran only three weeks, the CBS/K Mart effort was a success by all accounts. Premiere program episode ratings increased an average of 28 percent from a year earlier. The sweepstakes program was quite complex. K Mart offered CBS game cards in circulars to 72 million households and tuned all television sets in K Mart's 2,275 stores to CBS schedules and premiere inserts. In return, CBS gave K Mart extensive on-air exposure. The game's 6 million prizes included 12 1990 Dodge Caravans and Plymouth Voyagers (a trade with Chrysler for media exposure), family trips to Hollywood, televisions and VCRs from K Mart, and limited-edition CBS mugs. Maxell was also involved in the promotion, carrying CBS's new-season brochure in 5 million videotape packages during the summer. In return, CBS mentioned Maxell in some of the network's fall premiere print ads by including the line "If you can't be home to watch it, record it on Maxell tape." Media support included radio, print, outdoor, cable television, and in-flight videos on American Airlines and Trans World Airlines. The estimated media budget was $20 million to $30 million.

Given the increased recognition that advertising combined with sales promotion produces powerful results, these types of joint promotions are likely to grow in frequency. The CBS network planned at least a dozen such events for 1991 alone. John Miller, executive vice president of marketing at NBC, notes that the joint sales promotion tie-ins with key advertisers will be a regular element in launching future fall seasons.*

Advertising agencies, already faced with higher client expectations and cost problems (see Chapter 4), have been hit by 30-to-40-percent reductions in media budgets by their major clients. Agencies initially reacted to this trend by arguing that advertising was a far more effective communication device than sales promotion. Some still believe this is true. Others have come to realize that sales promotion is here to stay, and they are learning how to incorporate it into the advertising campaign. Yet there is still a great deal of confusion about the definition of sales promotion, its role in marketing, and how it should interact with advertising.

*Adapted from Wayne Walley, "Networks Prime Joint Promotions," *Advertising Age* (April 16, 1990):45; and Alison Fahey, "Get Ready Again," *Advertising Age* (April 16, 1990):45.

DEFINING SALES PROMOTION

sales promotion *Those marketing activities that add value to the product for a limited period of time to stimulate consumer purchasing and dealer effectiveness.*

The evolution of **sales promotion** has also changed the way experts define the practice. At one point, the official definition of sales promotion proposed by the American Marketing Association (AMA) was: "Marketing activities, other than personal selling, advertising, and publicity, that stimulate consumer purchasing and dealer effectiveness, such as displays, shows, exhibitions, demonstrations, and various nonrecurrent selling efforts not in the ordinary routine."[*]

In 1988 the AMA offered a new definition: "Sales promotion is media and nonmedia marketing pressure applied for a predetermined, limited period of time in order to stimulate trial, increase consumer demand, or improve product quality".[†] The Council of Sales Promotion Agencies offers a somewhat broader perspective: "Sales promotion is a marketing discipline that utilizes a variety of incentive techniques to structure sales-related programs targeted to consumers, trade, and/or sales levels that generate a specific, measurable action or response for a product or service".[‡] All these definitions present sales promotion as a set of techniques that prompt members of the target audience to take action—preferably immediate action.

PRINCIPLE
Sales promotion offers an extra incentive for consumers to take action.

Sales promotion offers an "extra incentive" for consumers to act. Although this extra incentive is usually in the form of a price reduction, it may be additional amounts of the product, cash, prizes, premiums, and so on. Furthermore, sales promotions usually include specified limits, such as an expiration date or a limited quantity of the merchandise. Finally, sales promotion has three somewhat different goals, which relate to its three target audiences: (1) to increase immediate *customer* sales, (2) to increase support among the marketer's *sales force,* and (3) to gain the support of *intermediaries* (resellers) in marketing the product.

THE SIZE OF SALES PROMOTION

Determining the actual size of the sales promotion industry is difficult; estimates vary according to which agency or research firm collects the data. For example, the research firm Donnelley Marketing estimates that spending on sales promotion reached $135 billion in 1989[$] (see Table 18.1). This figure does not include an estimated $24 billion spent on telemarketing and other promotional expenditures, such as packaging. (Note the discrepancy with earlier estimates of media expenditures listed in Chapter 1 of approximately $120 billion. This discrepancy is a result of the different research criteria used by organizations that provide this information.) Current trends suggest that more dollars are being spent on sales promotion than on adver-

---

[*]American Marketing Association, *Marketing Definitions: A Glossary of Marketing Terms* (Chicago, 1960):20.
[†]Russ Brown, "Sales Promotion," *Marketing & Media Decisions* (February 1990):74.
[‡]"Shaping the Future of Sales Promotion," *Council of Sales Promotion Agencies* (1990):3.
[$]Russ Brown, "Sales Promotion," *Marketing & Media Decisions* (February 1990):74.

TABLE 18.1
1989 Advertising and Promotion Expenditures*

Advertising	$(000)	1989 % of Total	% vs. Prev.	Total Yr.
Television	$25,478	36%	+	4%
Radio	7,906	11%	+	7%
Business Publications	2,763	4%	+	6%
Consumer Magazines	6,380	9%	+	10%
Newspapers	26,868	38%	+	6%
Farm Publications	212	†	+	8%
Outdoor	1,111	2%	+	4%
TOTAL	$70,718	100%	+	45%
Sales Promotion				
Direct mail	$21,945	16%	+	4%
POP/Display	18,474	14%	+	10%
Premiums & Incentives‡	17,814	13%	+	8%
Meetings & Conventions	37,610	28%	+	12%
Trade Shows & Exhibits	8,844	6%	+	10%
Promotional Advertising	11,374	8%	+	5%
Print/AV/Miscellaneous	13.098	10%	+	10%
Coupon Redemption	6,320	5%	+	9%
TOTAL	$135,479	100%	+	68%

GRAND TOTAL $206,197
SALES PROMOTION = 65.7% SHARE
ADVERTISING   = 34.3% SHARE

*Based on previously defined categories of marketing to establish consistent trend data.

†Less than 1%. ‡ Includes sweepstakes, contests & games

Types of Promotion	Percent of Respondents in Each Year				
	1986	1987	1988	1989	1990
1. Couponing Consumer Direct	91%	96%	92%	93%	95%
2. Money Back Offers/Cash Refunds	85	87	85	74	72
3. Premium Offers	58	74	68	73	62
4. Sweepstakes	72	66	72	70	68
5. Sampling New Products	64	71	68	66	75
6. Cents-Off Promotions	70	69	74	64	88
7. Couponing in Retailers' Ad	45	57	63	63	57
8. Sampling Established Products	57	65	63	57	62
9. Pre-Priced Shippers	58	56	52	44	35
10. Contests	40	38	46	41	31

Source: Donnelley Marketing Thirteenth Annual Survey of Promotional Practices for 1986, 1987, 1988, 1989, and 1990.

tising (roughly 65 percent versus 35 percent; see Figure 18.1). Sales promotion is growing at an annual rate of 9 percent, compared to only 6 percent for advertising.* Finally, with the growth of sales promotion has come the growth of organizations supporting sales promotion. Virtually all major advertising agencies have acquired a sales promotion subsidiary or have brought sales promotion in-house. Table 18.2 lists the top independent sales promotion agencies of 1989.

*Robert D. Buzzell, John A. Quelch, and Walter J. Salmon, "The Costly Bargain of Sales Promotion," *Harvard Business Review* (March–April 1990):141–149.

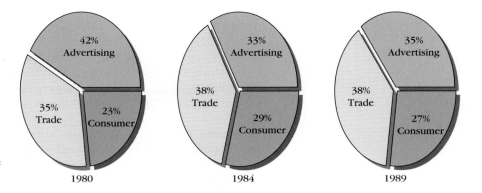

FIGURE 18.1
Advertising/promotion allocations: 1980, 1984, 1989. *Source:* Donnelley's Annual Survey.

Reasons for the Growth of Sales Promotion

The statistics presented thus far pose one question: Why are companies spending more and more money on sales promotion? The chief reasons are the pressure for short-term profits, the accountability factor, economic factors, changes in the marketplace, and the increasing power of retailers.

Short-Term Solutions. Most U.S. companies have a drive for immediate profits and progress, which sales promotion satisfies. Vincent Sottasanti, president and CEO of the consulting firm Comart-KLP, states: "There's pressure on the brand manager and senior management as well for short-term profits as well as long-term goals."* Others agree that product managers are under pressure to generate quarterly sales increases. Because advertising's benefits are often apparent only in the long term, companies are investing more money in sales promotion, which generates immediate results.

TABLE 18.2
Top 20 Sales Promotion Agencies

Rank 1989	Agency, Headquarters	Gross Sales Promotion Revenues 1989	1988
1	**D.L. Blair Corp.,** Garden City, N.Y.	$25,700	$24,200
2	**Alcone Promotion,** Irvine, Calif.	23,700	15,430
3	**Frankel & Co.,** Chicago	23,193	19,605
4	**Cato Johnson Worldwide,** New York	22,800	16,700
5	**Clarion Marketing & Communications,** Greenwich, Conn.	18,804	16,425
6	**Comart-KLP,** New York	18,200	13,700
7	**Saugatuck/FKB,** Westport, Conn.	15,765	7,523
8	**Strottman Marketing,** Irvine, Calif.	14,800	10,500
9	**U.S. Communications Corp.,** Minneapolis	14,000	13,000
10	**American Consulting Corp.,** New York	13,900	11,500
11	**Niven Marketing Group,** Scottsdale, Ariz.	13,428	13,676
12	**Flair Communications Agency,** Chicago	12,884	12,700
13	**Impact,** Chicago	11,500	12,150
14	**Sims Freeman O'Brien,** Elmsford, N.Y.	11,234	8,368
15	**Siebel/Mohr,** New York	10,724	12,071
16	**Communications Diversified,** New York	9,100	6,400
17	**Richman Sales Promotion,** Bala Cynwyd, Pa.	9,000	8,500
18	**QLM,** Princeton, N.J.	8,800	7,000
19	**KSJ Promotions,** St. Louis	8,700	NA
20	**Columbian Advertising,** Chicago	8,550	7,595

Source: Advertising Age (April 30, 1990):S–2. Copyright Crain Communications, Inc.

* "Sales Promotion: What's Ahead?" *Advertising Age* (May 8, 1989):38.

Need for Accountability. Another reason for the growth is the account-ability of sales promotion techniques. It is relatively easy to determine whether a given sales promotion strategy accomplished its stated objectives. Moreover, this assessment can be done rather quickly. Providing accountability is critical at a time when marketers want to know exactly what they are getting for their promotional dollars.

Economic Factors. Advertisers also cite economic reasons for the shift. Media costs have escalated to the point where alternatives must be thoroughly explored. The cost of mass-media advertising increased approximately 4 percent in 1991, compared to sales promotion cost increases of only 2 percent.* But as the networks have been raising their prices, their share of prime-time television viewing has been dropping (to approximately 70 percent in 1988 from 92 percent in 1979).† Advertisers therefore are exploring fresh new media forms that cost less and produce immediate, tangible results, and sales promotion is able to produce the desired results.

Consumer Behavior. Other reasons for the move toward sales promotion reflect changes in the marketplace. For instance, shoppers today are better educated, more selective, and less loyal to brand names than in the past. In addition, many new markets are developing because of demographic shifts. The affluent "gray" market, the "new man," the "yuppie," and the working woman are all markets that appear responsive to the benefits of sales promotion. For example, in the spring of 1989 Polaroid targeted a sales promotion entitled "The Cutest Little Baby Face" at black consumers. Print ads in *Ebony* and *Essence* invited consumers to send in baby pictures in one of three categories—dinner, fun time, and special occasion (see Ad 18.1). The prize consisted of a $10,000 annuity worth $30,000 at maturity and $2,500 for child care. Over 100,000 entries were received in 90 days.‡

From the consumer's perspective, sales promotion reduces the *risk* associated with purchase because promotions typically offer the consumer "more for less." This attitude was reinforced during the recession of the 1970s, when people were desperately looking for opportunities to save. That economic downturn introduced many consumers to the benefits of sales promotion, and they apparently enjoyed the experience. More is said about consumers' attitudes and reactions to sales promotions in the Lifestyle box entitled "Consumers' Use of Sales Promotion."

Lack of New-Product Categories. Although we are constantly bombarded with the terms "new" and "improved," very few entirely new product categories have emerged since World War II. Today's marketplace is characterized by mature product categories and considerable consumer experience and knowledge. In most industries, the battle is for market share rather than general product growth. In many instances advertising remains the best tool for launching new products, especially when the need for brand awareness is important. However, sales promotion is often the most effective strategy for increasing share and volume for an existing product.

The Pricing Cycle. Retail pricing has also been influential in creating opportunities for the increased use of sales promotion, particularly in the

AD 18.1
Companies are targeting their sales promotion advertising at particular demographic markets, such as Polaroid's contest targeted at black consumers. (Courtesy of Polaroid)

---

*Junu Kim, "Lid to Clamp Down Hard on Media Pricing," *Advertising Age* (November 26, 1990):S-1.

†Joseph P. Flanagan, "Sales Promotion: The Emerging Alternative to Brand-Building Advertising," *The Journal of Consumer Marketing 5* (Spring 1988):45–48.

‡Peg Masterson, "Should Marketers Target Blacks More?" *Advertising Age* (July 2, 1990):20.

CONSUMERS' USE OF SALES PROMOTION

In late 1989 a study on consumer attitudes toward sales promotion tactics conducted by United Marketing Services for the Promotion Marketing Association of America concluded that consumers will change their shopping habits and brand preferences to take advantage of promotions, especially those that cut purchase prices or provide rebates. The survey was conducted by phone among 500 people who said they were the primary shoppers in their household and who had participated in some type of sales promotion. Over 85 percent of the participants were women.

Manufacturers' coupons were the most popular of the four promotions studied, with 98 percent of respondents saying they had used at least one coupon in the previous 6 months. Rebates were second (54 percent of respondents used them), followed by sweepstakes (26 percent), and premiums (17 percent). Eight of ten people surveyed said they regularly check newspaper ads for coupons, and nearly half said that they also look for the other three types of promotional efforts (rebates, sweepstakes, and premiums).

The survey found that in addition to being the most popular, coupons have the most influence on consumers' buying habits and brand switching. Asked if they ever bought a new product never before used simply because of a promotional offer, 70 percent of the respondents said they had done so because of a coupon offer. Premium offers had enticed 40 percent of respondents, whereas 20 percent had been influenced by a sweepstakes offer, and 38 percent had been lured by a rebate.

Coupons also proved to be the most compelling promotional enticement to change brands within a product category. Almost 75 percent of respondents said that a coupon had caused them to switch at least once in the previous 6 months. Fifty percent said a rebate had made them change brands, 40 percent were enticed by a premium, and 20 percent had switched brands because of a sweepstake offer.

More than 60 percent of respondents cited batteries as the product category most vulnerable to brand switching because of an offer. Brand loyalty was weak when it came to several other product categories, including coffee, personal appliances, shampoo, and toothpaste. More than half of the respondents said they are likely to switch brands in these categories because of promotional offers.

These survey findings indicate a fundamental change in the thinking of the consumer toward a variety of products. Potential and actual savings—particularly through coupon redemption—are a strong motivation for product trial and continued purchase. Sales promotions that offer price reductions are more powerful than product quality, relevant product information, or even emotional appeals.

Source: Adapted from Scott Hume, "A Penny Saved Is a Penny Spent," *Advertising Age* (April 2, 1990):33.

---

highly volatile supermarket environment. Prices soared during the inflationary 1970s as the result of increased costs of labor, raw materials, and manufacturing. This situation led to the growth of low-priced private-label brands and the emergence of generic products. Having adjusted to these lower-priced goods, consumers have come to expect constant short-term price reductions such as coupons, sales, and price promotions.

The Power of the Retailer.   The final reason for the growth of sales promotion is the increasing power of the modern retailer. Dominant players, such as Safeway, Wal-Mart, K Mart, Toys 'R' Us, and Home Depot, demand a variety of promotional incentives before allowing products into their stores. Obtaining desirable shelf location requires special in-store merchandising support. Procter & Gamble, for example, estimates that 25 percent of sales time and approximately 30 percent of brand-management time are spent in designing, implementing, and overseeing promotions.*

* Robert D. Buzzell, John A. Quelch, and Walter J. Salmon, "The Costly Bargain of Sales Promotion," *Harvard Business Review* (March–April 1990):141.

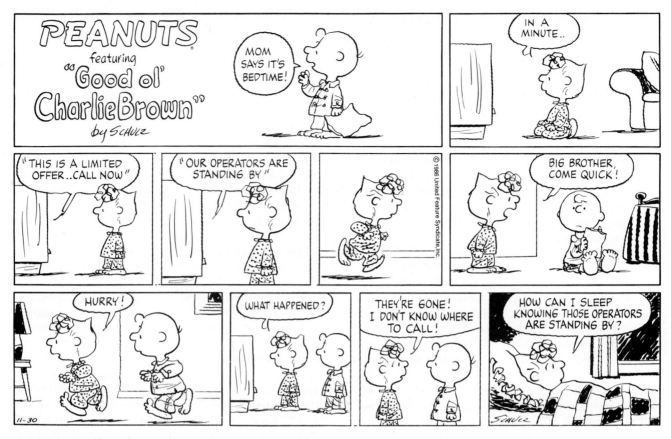

PEANUTS reprinted by permission of UFS, Inc.

It is estimated that quite soon just a few retailers will dominate retail distribution. The increased concentration of buying power among fewer and fewer retail accounts has enabled retailers to demand the financial support of manufacturers through sales promotion techniques.

TYPES OF SALES PROMOTION

Sales promotion strategies are divided into three primary types: end-user or consumer, reseller or trade, and salesforce strategies. The first two have direct implications for advertising and will be discussed in some detail. Salesforce sales promotions are simply activities directed at the firm's salespeople to motivate them to strive to increase their sales levels. These activities are classified in two ways. The first set of activities includes programs that better prepare salespeople to do their jobs, such as sales manuals, training programs, and sales presentations, as well as supportive materials like films, slides, videos, and other visual aids. The second set of activities is concerned with promotional efforts or incentives that will motivate salespeople to work harder. Contests dominate this category.

Consumer Sales Promotion

Consumer sales promotions are directed at the ultimate user of the good or service. They are intended to "presell" consumers so that when people go into a store they will look for a particular brand. Most often, consumer sales

PRINCIPLE

Consumer sales promotion is most effective if the product or service is presold by advertising.

price deal *A temporary reduction in the price of a product.*

coupons *Legal certificates offered by manufacturers and retailers that grant specified savings on selected products when presented for redemption at the point of purchase.*

promotions are the responsibility of the product manager, along with the advertising campaign planner, the advertising department, or a sales promotion agency or advertising agency.

The primary strengths of consumer sales promotions are their variety and flexibility. There are a large number of techniques that can be combined to meet almost any objective of the sales promotion planner. This flexibility means that sales promotion can be employed by all kinds of businesses.

Price Deals. A temporary reduction in the price of a product is called a **price deal.** Price deals are commonly used to encourage trial of a new product, to persuade existing users to buy more or at a different time, or to convince new users to try an established product. They are effective only if price is an important factor in brand choice or if consumers are not brand loyal.

There are two principal types of consumer price deals: cents-off deals and price-pack deals. A *cents-off deal* is a reduction in the normal price charged for a good or service (for example, "was $1,000, now $500," or "50 percent off"). Cents-off deals can be announced at the point of sale or through mass or direct advertising. Point-of-sale announcements include the package itself and signs near the product or elsewhere in the store. Advertising includes sales flyers, newspaper ads, and broadcast ads. Both types of cents-off deals can be initiated by the manufacturer, the wholesaler, or the retailer.

Price-pack deals provide the consumer with something extra through the package itself. There are two types of pack deals: bonus packs and banded packs. *Bonus packs* contain additional amounts of the product free when the standard size is purchased at the regular price. For example, Purina Dog Food may offer 25 percent more dog food in the bag. Often this technique is used to introduce a new large-size package of the product. When one or more units of a product are sold at a reduced price compared to the regular single-unit price, a *banded pack* is being offered. Sometimes the products are physically banded together. The Pillsbury Company has been banding three cans of their biscuits together for many years. In most cases the products are simply offered as two-for, three-for, five-for, and so on.

Coupons. Legal certificates offered by manufacturers and retailers that grant specified savings on selected products when presented for redemption at the point of purchase are called **coupons.** *Manufacturer-sponsored coupons* can be redeemed at any outlet distributing the product. *Retailer-sponsored coupons* can only be redeemed at the specified retail outlet. The primary advantage of the coupon is that it allows the advertiser to lower prices without relying on cooperation from the retailer.

There are several disadvantages associated with coupons, however. Most notably, there is serious coupon clutter. Over 90 percent of consumer product marketers used coupons in 1989, but the redemption rate was only 3 percent. More than 88 percent of coupons are delivered through free-standing inserts. Insert fees (the fees newspapers charge for inserting FSIs) are increasing dramatically, making coupon distribution very expensive. A final problem is misredemption (accidentally misredeeming coupons) and fraud (counterfeit coupons).*

Manufacturer-sponsored coupons can be distributed directly (direct

---

* Russ Bowman, "Coupons Come of Age," *Marketing & Media Decisions* (February 1990):74.

mail, door-to-door), through media (newspaper/magazine ads, free-standing inserts), in or on the package itself, or through the retailer (co-op advertising). Manufacturers also pay retailers a fee for handling their coupons. Ad 18.2 for Checkout Coupon is an example of a recent innovation in tracking coupon redemption.

According to the Summary Scan division of the Advertising Checking Bureau, marketers of packaged goods distributed 263 billion coupons through print media in 1989, an increase of 4 percent from 1988. In 1989 marketers spent $979 million on print ads with coupons and $207 million on print ads supporting promotions but not carrying coupons. Coupon redemption saved consumers almost $4.6 billion that year.* Ad 18.3 shows a combination coupon for A&W diet root beer and diet cream soda.

Contests and Sweepstakes.   The popularity of contests and sweepstakes grew dramatically during the 1980s. These strategies create excitement by promising "something for nothing" and offering impressive prizes. **Contests** require participants to compete for a prize or prizes on the basis of

*Scott Hume, "Coupons Go In-Store," *Advertising Age* (May 21, 1990):45.

contests *Sales promotion activities that require participants to compete for a prize on the basis of some skill or ability.*

sweepstakes *Sales promotion activities that require participants to submit their names to be included in a drawing or other type of chance selection.*

AD 18.2
New technology now allows companies to issue coupons to specific consumers, cutting back on waste and clutter. (Courtesy of Catalina Marketing.)

ONLY TWO OF THESE RICH, CREAMY
TREATS WON'T BLOW YOUR DIET.

If you're not careful, you might mistake our A&W diet drinks for dessert.
That's because diet A&W Root Beer and A&W diet Cream Soda have a rich, satisfying flavor that other diet drinks can't match. And with only one calorie and no caffeine, they make the perfect treat.
So give them a try. You'll find they only taste fattening.

A&W. THERE'S JUST MORE TO IT.

SAVE 25¢
on
1 six-pack
or
1 two-liter
bottle of
A&W diet
Cream Soda
or
diet A&W
Root Beer

Manufacturer's Coupon   Expires June 30, 1990

SAVE 55¢
on any
combination of
2 six-packs or
2 two-liter
bottles of
A&W diet
Cream Soda
or
diet A&W
Root Beer

AD 18.3
Coupons are a popular type of consumer sales promotion. (Courtesy of A&W Brands, Inc.)

game *A type of sweepstake that requires the player to return to play several times.*

refund *An offer by the marketer to return a certain amount of money to the consumer who purchases the product.*

some sort of skill or ability. **Sweepstakes** require only that participants submit their names to be included in a drawing or other chance selection. A **game** is a type of sweepstake. It differs from a one-shot drawing-type of sweepstake in that the time frame is much longer. A continuity is established, requiring customers to return several times to acquire additional pieces (such as bingo-type games) or to improve their chances of winning.

A good contest or sweepstakes generates a high degree of consumer involvement, which can revive lagging sales, help obtain on-floor displays, provide merchandising excitement for dealers and salespeople, give vitality and a theme to advertising, and create interest in a low-interest product. Contests are viewed favorably by advertising designers because the copy tends to write itself as long as it is supported by background enthusiasm and excitement.

Refunds and Rebates. Simply stated, a **refund** is an offer by the marketer to return a certain amount of money to the consumer who purchases the product (see Ad 18.4). Most refunds encourage product purchase by creating a deadline. The details of the refund offer are generally distributed through print media or direct mail. General information may be delivered through broadcast media. Refunds are attractive because they stimulate sales without the high costs and waste associated with coupons. The key to success is to make the refund as uncomplicated and unrestrictive as possible. The refund may take the form of a cash *rebate* plus a low-value coupon for the same product or other company products, a high-value coupon alone, or a coupon good toward the brand purchased plus several other brands in the manufacturer's line.

AD 18.4
Refunds are very popular in the automobile industry. (Courtesy of Chrysler Corporation. AD: Ron Bacsa. Copy: Don McKechnie. This ad prepared by Bozell, NY.)

premium *A tangible reward received for performing a particular act, such as purchasing a product or visiting the point of purchase.*

Refunds have proved to be a very effective promotional device. According to Shopper's Pay Day, a research firm, money refund offers generate five times as much business as product coupons for comparable values.*

Premium Offers. A **premium** is a tangible reward received for performing a particular act, usually purchasing a product or visiting the point of purchase. The toy in Cracker Jacks, glassware in a box of detergent, and a transistor radio given for taking a real estate tour are examples of premiums. Premiums are usually free. If not, the charge tends to be quite low. Over $15 billion was spent on premiums in 1989.†

Direct Premiums There are two general types of premiums: direct and mail. *Direct premiums* award the incentive immediately, at the time of purchase. There are four variations of direct premiums:

1. Store premiums: given to customers at the retail site
2. In-packs: inserted in the package at the factory
3. On-packs: placed on the outside of the package at the factory
4. Container premiums: the package is the premium

Mail Premiums In contrast, *mail premiums* require the customer to take some action before receiving the premium. The original mail premium is called a *self-liquidator*. Self-liquidators usually require that some proof of purchase and payment be mailed in before receiving the premium. The amount of payment is sufficient to cover the cost of the item, handling, mailing, packaging, and taxes, if any. The food industry is the largest user of self-liquidating premiums. Country Pride Fresh Chicken, for example, offers an apron in exchange for the proof-of-purchase of their product (see

*Ronnie Telzer, "Rebates Challenge Coupons' Redeeming Values," *Advertising Age* (March 23, 1987):S-18, S-20.
†*Incentive Marketing* (September 1990):38.

Get this BBQ apron for chicken feed.

A fresh idea from Country Pride® Fresh Chicken. BBQ your best in our wild and crazy chicken apron. It's fresh, it's funny, it's fabulous. Order information below.

AD 18.5
Self-liquidating premiums require the consumer to mail in proof-of-purchase before receiving the premium. (Courtesy of Country Pride Chicken.)

Ad 18.5). The *coupon plan* or *continuity-coupon plan* is the second type of mail premium. It requires the customer to save coupons or special labels attached to the product that can be redeemed for merchandise. This plan has been used by cigarette and diaper manufacturers. The final type of mail premium is the *free-in-the-mail* premium. In this case the customer mails in a purchase request and proof of purchase to the advertiser. For example, Procter & Gamble offered a discount on a down comforter premium with proof of purchase of White Cloud toilet paper.

One advantage of premiums is their ability to enhance an advertising campaign or a brand image. The best examples of this strategy are those brands or companies that are symbolized by characters such as the Campbell Soup Kids, Charlie the Tuna, Tony the Tiger, Cap'n Crunch, Ronald McDonald, and the Pillsbury Doughboy.

Specialty Advertising. Advertising specialties are similar to premiums, except that the consumer does not have to purchase anything in order to receive the specialty item. These items normally have a promotional message printed on them somewhere. Although specialties are often given away as year-end gifts (the calendar hanging in the kitchen), they can be used throughout the year in particular sales situations. For example, some specialties, including pens, pencils, and organizers, are ideal for desktops.

Specialty items can be effective memory devices if they are useful and reasonably well made.
(Courtesy of Teri Stratford.)

Other items work well because they are attention-grabbing novelties. Balloons, fans, litter bags, and tote bags fall into this category. The ideal specialty item is something that is kept out in the open where a great number of people can see it, such as a calendar or penholder displaying the company's name.

The 15,000-plus specialty items that are manufactured by companies are used for a variety of marketing purposes: thanking customers for patronage, reinforcing established products or services, generating sales leads. Specialty advertising has numerous advantages, but it also has some disadvantages.

Advantages Thanks largely to improved printing processes, specialty items can be extremely inexpensive. An advertiser's message can be imprinted on 5-cent pencils and little packets of popping corn with a message thanking customers. The trend is toward more expensive gifts, however. At the Specialty Advertising Association (SAA) annual meeting, advertisers have the opportunity to select Pierre Cardin calf-leather binders, silk jackets, and business cards in a bottle for the customers and prospects they really want to impress.

The most important advantage of specialty advertising is its long life. In a survey of consumer audiences A. C. Nielsen Company found that almost one-third of respondents were still using at least one specialty item they had received 12 months earlier.* Another advantage is the positive attitude recipients have toward specialty items, especially if they are useful. The third advantage of specialty advertising is the ability to preselect the audience so that there is very little waste circulation. The final advantage is the flexibility offered by this industry. Not only do specialty houses store thousands of existing items, but they will also design specific items on request.

Disadvantages On the negative side, specialty advertising tends to be quite expensive on a per-prospect basis. There is also the "junk" image associated with poor-quality specialty merchandise. Although better-quality items do get used, poor-quality merchandise is often quickly discarded.

---

continuity program *A program that requires the consumer to continue purchasing the product or service in order to receive a reward.*

Continuity Programs. A **continuity program** requires the consumer to continue purchasing the product in order to receive the benefit or reward. The purpose of any type of continuity program is to tie consumers to the organization by rewarding them for their loyalty. Typically, the higher the purchase level, the greater the benefits. In the 1950s and 1960s the popular type of continuity program was trading stamps. Today continuity programs are synonymous with the word "frequent." Frequent-flier clubs sponsored by airlines are the model of a modern continuity program. They offer a variety of rewards, including seat upgrades, free tickets, and premiums based on the number of frequent-flier miles accumulated. Continuity programs work in very competitive situations where the consumer has difficulty perceiving real differences between brands. For example, in a joint continuity program American Airlines offered College Savings Bank's College Sure certificate of deposit (CD) as a premium for the airline's A Advantage frequent-flier members. The CD, designed to help parents save for their children's college educations, has a lower price (about $16,400 per unit, rather than $18,000) and higher yield (a minimum interest rate of 5 percent) than the bank's standard CDs (4 percent).†

*"Specialty Advertising Fact Sheet," *Specialty Advertising Association International* (Irving, TX: Marketing Communications Department, 1990).

†Alison Fahey and Bradley Johnson, "Frequent Shopper Programs Ripen," *Advertising Age* (August 6, 1990):21.

AD 18.6
Purina provides a sample in conjunction with an advertisement.
(Courtesy of Ralston Purina Company.)

PRINCIPLE
Sampling, which allows the consumer to try the product or service free, is effective for new-product introductions.

Consumer Sampling. Allowing the consumer to experience the product or service free of charge or for a small fee is called **sampling.** It is a very effective strategy for introducing a new or modified product or for dislodging an entrenched market leader. To be successful, the product sampled must virtually sell itself on the basis of a certain uniqueness and ability to create a strong positive impact with minimal trial experience.

Samples can be distributed to consumers in several ways. The most common method is through the mail. An alternative is to hire companies specializing in door-to-door distribution. Advertisers can design ads with coupons for free samples, place samples in special packages, or distribute samples at special in-store displays. Ad 18.6 for Purina Pro Plan offers a sample of the company's line of pet food.

Warner-Lambert developed two successful programs for sampling the company's Schick Slim Twin razor system. In the first program Schick became the official razor of the National Basketball Association (NBA) and free razors containing the names and colors of local NBA teams were distributed to team members. In the second program colleges were given free razors stamped with the schools' names and colors.*

---

*Alison Fahey, "Schick, Wilkinson Slash at Sensor," *Advertising Age* (March 19, 1990):1.

AD 18.7
Nestlé Foods is one of many companies to use more than one promotional technique to sell its products. (Courtesy of Nestlé Chocolate & Confection Co.)

In general, retailers and manufacturers maintain that sampling can boost sales volume as much as five to ten times during a product demonstration and 10 to 15 percent thereafter. Sampling is generally most effective when reinforced on the spot with product coupons. Most consumers like sampling because they do not lose any money if they do not like the product.*

Although all of these consumer sales promotion techniques can be effective alone, they can also be combined to create a tremendous impact. The Nestlé Foods Corporation did just this with the material shown in Ad 18.7. The company positioned three of its products—Raisinets®, Goobers®, and Crunch™—as the "Home Video Candy" in a promotion where consumers could redeem a mail-in certificate with any VCR movie rental receipt along with proof-of-purchase and receive a $2 cash rebate. The certificate was available in free-standing inserts and at point-of-purchase displays, and the three candy products were packaged in a take-home pack. The promotion was developed by Saxton Communications Group, New York.

Reseller (Trade) Sales Promotion

Resellers, or intermediaries, are the 1.3 million retailers and 338,000 wholesalers who distribute the products made by manufacturers to other resellers and ultimate users. The manufacturer usually is certain the product is acceptable only if resellers are willing to carry and *push* it. Sales promotion is used to bring resellers to that point of conviction.

Reseller sales promotions are intended to accomplish four overall goals:

1. Stimulate in-store merchandising or other trade support (for example, feature pricing, superior store location, and/or shelf space)
2. Manipulate levels of inventory held by wholesalers and retailers
3. Expand product distribution to new areas of the country or new classes of trade

* *The Wall Street Journal* (August 28, 1986):19.

4. Create a high level of excitement about the product among those responsible for its sale

The ultimate gauge of a successful reseller promotion is whether sales increase among ultimate users.

A great many promotional devices that are designed to motivate resellers to engage in certain sales activities are available to the manufacturer. The major ones are discussed in the following paragraphs.

Point-of-Purchase Displays. A **point-of-purchase display** (P-O-P) is designed by the manufacturer and distributed to retailers in order to promote a particular brand or group of products. Although the forms vary by industry, P-O-P can include special racks, display cartons, banners, signs, price cards, and mechanical product dispensers. Point of purchase is the only advertising that occurs when all the elements of the sale—the consumer, the money, and the product—come together at the same time. As we move toward a self-service retail environment in which fewer and fewer customers expect help from sales clerks, the role of point of purchase will continue to increase. According to the Point of Purchase Advertising Institute (POPAI), 66 percent of purchase decisions are made in the store rather than before entering the store.*

Point of purchase is a big-business effort ($18 billion in 1989) that must be well thought out if it is to be successful.† Advertisers must consider not only whether P-O-P is appealing to the end user but also whether it will be used by the reseller. Retailers will use a P-O-P only if they are convinced that it will generate greater sales.

A P-O-P should be coordinated with the theme used in advertisements. This not only acts as a type of repetition, it also creates a last-minute association between the campaign and the place of decision. The RC Cola P-O-P display in Ad 18.8 was part of a seasonal print and television advertising campaign.

*Cyndee Miller, "P.O.P. Gains Followers as 'Era of Retailing' Dawns," *Marketing News* (May 14, 1990):2.
†*Donnelly Marketing Thirteenth Annual Survey of Promotional Practices* for 1986, 1987, 1988, 1989, and 1990.

AD 18.8
RC created a nautical P-O-P display to tie in with its summer promotion. (Courtesy of RC Cola.)

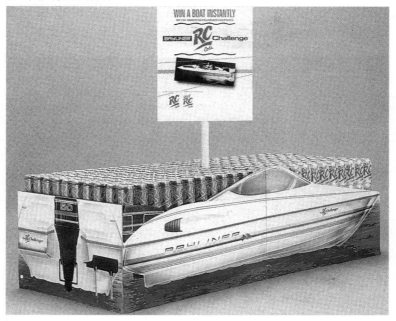

Dealer Contests and Sweepstakes.   As in the case of consumer sales promotion, contests and sweepstakes can be developed to motivate resellers. Contests are far more common, primarily because contest prizes are usually associated with the sale of the sponsor's product. A sales quota is set, for example, and the company or individual who exceeds the quota by the largest percentage wins the contest.

The need to create the desired amount of excitement and motivation has forced designers to develop spectacular contests with very impressive prizes. Frequent contests quickly lose their excitement, however. Contests are effective only if they take place periodically. If conducted properly, contests can provide short-term benefits and can improve the relationship between the manufacturer and the reseller.

Trade Shows and Exhibits.   Many industries present and sell their merchandise at trade shows and exhibits that allow demonstrating the product, providing information, answering questions, comparing competing brands, and writing orders. In turn, trade shows permit manufacturers to gather a great deal of information about their competition. In an environment where all the companies are attempting to give a clear picture of their products to potential customers, competitors can easily compare quality, features, prices, and technology.

Because of the tremendous importance of trade shows, companies spend a great deal of money each year (approximately $8 billion) planning and staging them.* For some companies, this expense represents most of their promotional expenditure.

Trade Incentives.   There are instances when a contest is not appropriate or the goal may be to gain extra shelf space or to increase use of promotional material rather than to increase sales. In such cases trade incentives are offered to the reseller by the marketer for accomplishing certain tasks. The only requirement is that the reseller demonstrate in some way that the object was displayed. For example, a retailer might send the manufacturer a photograph of the display he or she promised to use. Incentive programs are very common when attempting to introduce a new product into a market, gain shelf space, or get retailers to stock more of a product. For example, a manufacturer may offer a substantial prize of cash or merchandise to a retailer who orders a certain amount of product or a certain product. Most incentive programs are customized for each reseller and each situation. However, there are two types of trade incentive programs that are somewhat standard—push money and dealer loaders.

push money (*spiffs*) *A monetary bonus paid to a salesperson based on units sold over a period of time.*

Push Money   Push money, or *spiffs,* is a monetary bonus paid to a salesperson based on units sold over a period of time. For example, a manufacturer of air conditioners might offer a $50 bonus for the sale of model EJ1, $75 for model EJ19, and $100 for model EX3 between April 1 and October 1. At the end of that period each salesperson sends in evidence of total sales to the manufacturer and receives a check for the appropriate amount.

dealer loader *A premium given to a retailer by a manufacturer for buying a certain quantity of product.*

Dealer Loader   A dealer loader is a premium (comparable to a consumer premium) that is given to a retailer by a manufacturer for buying a certain amount of a product. The two most common types of dealer loaders are *buying loaders* and *display loaders.* Buying loaders award gifts for buy-

* *Ibid.*

ing a certain order size. Budweiser offered store managers a free trip to the Super Bowl if they sold a certain amount of beer in a specified period of time before the event. Display loaders award the display to the retailer after it has been taken apart. For example, Dr. Pepper built a store display for the July 4th holiday, which included a gas grill, picnic table, basket, and so forth. The store manager was awarded these items after the promotion ended. Both techniques can be effective in getting sufficient amounts of a new product into retail outlets or in getting a point-of-purchase display into a store. The underlying motivation for both arrangements is to sell large amounts of the product in a short period of time.

trade deals *An arrangement in which the retailer agrees to give the manufacturer's product a special promotional effort in return for product discounts, goods, or cash.*

Trade Deals. **Trade deals** are the most important reseller sales promotion technique. A retailer is "on deal" when he or she agrees to give the manufacturer's product a special promotional effort that it would not normally receive. These promotional efforts can take the form of special displays, extra purchases, superior store locations, or greater promotion in general. In return, retailers sometimes receive special allowances, discounts, goods, or cash.

No one knows exactly how much money is spent on trade deals; experts estimate approximately $8 billion to $12 billion annually.* In some industries, such as grocery products, electronics, computers, and automobiles, trade deals are expected. A manufacturer would find it impossible to compete in these industries without offering trade discounts. In fact, the requirement to "deal" has become so prevalent that many advertisers fear it is now more important in determining which products receive the greatest promotion than either the value of the product or the expertise of the manufacturer. In the grocery field, for example, approximately 60 percent of all manufacturers' sales are accompanied by a trade deal averaging about 12 percent of the asking price.†

Buying Allowances   There are two general types of trade deals. The first is referred to as *buying allowances* and includes situations in which a manufacturer pays a reseller a set amount of money for purchasing a certain amount of the product during a specified time period. All the retailer has to do is meet the purchase requirements. The payment may be given in the form of a check from the manufacturer or a reduction in the face value of an invoice.

Advertising Allowances   The second category of trade deals includes advertising and display allowances. An *advertising allowance* is a common technique employed primarily in the consumer-products area in which the manufacturer pays the wholesaler or retailer a certain amount of money for advertising the manufacturer's product. This allowance can be a flat dollar amount or it can be a percentage of gross purchases during a specified time period. *Cooperative advertising* involves a contractual arrangement between the manufacturer and the resellers whereby the manufacturer agrees to pay a part or all of the advertising expenses incurred by the resellers. A *display allowance* involves a direct payment of cash or goods to the retailer if the retailer agrees to set up the display as specified. The manufacturer requires the retailer to sign a certificate of agreement before being paid.

* Kevin T. Higgins, "Sales Promotion Spending Closing in on Advertising," *Marketing News* (July 4, 1986):8.
†Keith M. Jones, "Held Hostage by the Trade?" *Advertising Age* (April 27, 1987):18.

THE ROLE OF SALES PROMOTION IN MARKETING

As explained in Chapter 3, sales promotion is just one element of the marketing communication mix available to the marketer, the other three being personal selling, advertising, and public relations. Because of its unique characteristics, however, the various sales promotion techniques we just discussed can accomplish certain communication goals that the other elements cannot. For example, research suggests that sales promotion excels at the following:

1. Obtaining trial of a new product
2. Establishing a purchasing pattern by persuading triers to rebuy
3. Increasing consumption of a product
4. Neutralizing competitive promotions
5. Affecting the sales of companion products

Conversely, sales promotion cannot:

1. Build brand loyalty
2. Reverse a declining sales trend
3. Convert rejection of an inferior product into acceptance*

Sales promotion should be incorporated into the company's strategic marketing planning, along with advertising, personal selling, and public relations. This means establishing sales promotion goals and selecting appropriate strategies. A separate budget should be set up for sales promotion. Finally, management should evaluate the sales promotion performance.

Although all these elements are important, setting promotional objectives is particularly important. Our definition of sales promotion implied three broad objectives:

1. To stimulate demand by industrial users or household consumers
2. To improve the marketing performance of resellers

*Don E. Schultz, Dennis Martin, and William P. Brown, *Strategic Advertising Campaigns,* 2nd ed. (Lincolnwood, IL: Crain Books, 1984):388–90.

AD 18.9
Northwest Airlines offers a free ticket as an incentive to encourage customers to fly their airlines more often. (Courtesy of Northwest Airlines)

3. To supplement and coordinate advertising, personal selling, and public relations activities

The more specific objectives of sales promotion are quite similar to those of advertising. For example, in order to *get customers to try a new product,* companies, such as Del Monte, Ralph Lauren, Wilkinson Sword, and VLI's Today sponge, distribute over 500,000 free samples in Daytona Beach each spring break. To *encourage increased spending during the holiday season,* Kraft food products and Hasbro toys participated in a joint promotion through a nationally distributed free-standing newspaper insert that included cents-off coupons and rebates on toys. To *encourage present customers to use the product more often,* Northwest Airlines developed a two-for-one frequent-flier program that provided one free trip for every ticket purchased (see Ad 18.9).

Thus sales promotion has become an important element in the strategy of many marketers. Like advertising, it is not right for everyone, however, and it will be effective only if it is carefully managed.

*T*HE RELATIONSHIP BETWEEN SALES PROMOTION AND ADVERTISING

As we mentioned earlier, advertising and sales promotion are two of the elements that make up the promotional mix. These two elements have a number of similarities and often work together toward a common goal, but they also differ in many ways.

Differences and Similarities

Differences. The major differences between advertising and sales promotion concern their methods of appeal and the value they add to the sale of the product or service. Whereas advertising is interested in creating an image and will take the time to do so, sales promotion is interested in creating immediate action, preferably a sale. In order to accomplish this immediate goal, sales promotion relies heavily on rational appeals, whereas advertising relies on emotional appeals to promote the product's image. Advertising also tends to add intangible value to the good or service and makes a moderate contribution to profitability. In contrast, sales promotion adds tangible value to the good or service and contributes greatly to profitability (see Table 18.3).

Similarities. Advertising and sales promotion also have much in common. According to Leonard Lodish, an international expert on sales promo-

TABLE 18.3
The Differences Between Advertising and Sales Promotion

Advertising	Sales Promotion
• Creates an image over time	• Creates immediate action
• Relies on emotional appeals	• Relies on rational appeals
• Adds intangible value to the product or service	• Adds tangible value to the product or service
• Contributes moderately to profitability	• Contributes greatly to profitability

tion, the two share the same roles: to increase the number of customers and to increase the use of the product by current customers. Both tasks attempt to change audience perceptions about the product or service, and both attempt to make people do something.* Of course, the specific techniques used to accomplish these tasks differ.

Introducing a New Product

One area in which advertising and promotion work well together is the introduction of new products and services. Suppose we are introducing a new corn chip named Corn Crunchies. Our first challenge is to create awareness of this product. This is the real strength of advertising. However, sometimes advertising should be combined with an appropriate sales promotion device calling attention to the advertising and the brand name. Possibilities

*Leonard M. Lodish, *The Advertising and Promotion Challenge* (New York: Oxford University Press, 1986):18.

AD 18.10
Advertisers often offer coupons as part of the ad to enhance the sales promotion message. (Courtesy of Rubbermaid Incorporated.)

are colorful point-of-purchase displays, a reduced introductory price, and a special tie-in with a well-known chip dip company.

Creating awareness will only take the product so far, however. Corn Crunchies must also be perceived as offering some clear benefit compared to the competitors' to convince consumers to purchase it. Advertising promotes this perception through informational and transformational executions. Recall from Chapter 8, informational advertising provides meaningful facts to the consumer when needed, whereas transformational advertising moves the consumer emotionally to a point of greater acceptance. Sales promotion enhances the message by offering coupons as part of the ad (known as an *overlay* ad), mailing free samples of Corn Crunchies to households, and conducting a contest in conjunction with the product introduction during the July 4th holiday. Ad 18.10 for Rubbermaid food containers is an example of an overlay ad. If we have successfully implemented this *pull strategy,* consumers will be convinced of the value of Corn Crunchies and go to their supermarkets and demand that the product be stocked. By asking for it, they will *pull* it through the channel of distribution.

Unfortunately, creating awareness and desire means nothing unless the product is available where the consumer thinks it should be. Somehow resellers (the trade) must be convinced that the product will move off the shelves before they will stock it. Therefore, a *push promotional strategy* is used to convince members of the distribution network to carry and market Corn Crunchies. We literally *push* the product through the channel. This is accomplished through two devices, *trade advertising* and *trade sales promotion.* Trade advertising directed at wholesalers and retailers can be effective in providing resellers with important information. In addition, trade sales promotion techniques, especially price discounts, point-of-purchase displays, and advertising allowances, help to gain shelf space.

After the initial purchase we want the customer to repeat purchase, and we also want retailers to allocate more shelf space to Corn Crunchies. This means that advertising copy is changed to remind customers about the positive experience they had with the product, and sales promotion is used to reinforce their loyalty with coupons, rebates, and other rewards. Retailers will be rewarded as well, with a predictable customer who will not only buy the product being promoted but will also purchase other products while in the store.

Can Sales Promotion Build Brands?

For several years now there has been a heated debate between the advertising industry and the sales promotion industry concerning brand building. Advertisers claim that the strength of advertising is creating and maintaining brand image and that sales promotion negates all their hard work by diverting the emphasis from the brand to the price. The result is a brand-insensitive consumer. Critics of sales promotion cite the price-cutting strategies followed by Coke and Pepsi as an example of two brands that are now interchangeable in the minds of many consumers. On any given weekend, especially holiday weekends, Coke and Pepsi product displays are located on end-of-the-aisle caps or island displays featuring per-case prices as low as $4 and six-pack prices as low as $1.29, down from the regular price of $5.50 and $2.69, respectively. Procter & Gamble's division manager of advertising and sales promotion, V. O. "Bud" Hamilton, describes the situation as follows: "Too many marketers no longer adhere to the fundamental premise of brand building, which is that franchises aren't built by cutting price but rather by offering superior quality at a reasonable price and clearly communicating that value to consumers. . . . The price-cutting patterns began in the early 1970s continue today, fostering a short-term orientation that has caused long-term brand building to suffer."*

Experts in sales promotion respond to this criticism in two ways. First, they argue that the claim that sales promotion destroys brand image is greatly exaggerated. They refer to many cereal brands, rental car companies, airlines, and hotels that have used a variety of well-planned sales promotion strategies to enhance their brand image. Hertz, for example, uses price promotions regularly, yet they have increased sales and market share both during and after these promotions. Second, they acknowledge that *continuous* promotion—particularly continuous price promotion—does not always work. They point to situations in which an entire advertising/promotion budget had been committed to a single promotion technique, causing the brand to self-destruct. Sear's predictable price reductions is a classic example of a company that destroyed its brand name through poor promotion planning. Conversely, continuous sales promotion can and does work if it is part of a well-analyzed and well-executed strategy. Furthermore, such promotion works most efficiently when it is part of a well-integrated advertising/promotion plan. Sales promotion pioneers William Robinson and Alan Maites outlined several key promotional techniques to use in the 1990s that will increase both consumer interest and brand image:

- New technology, such as the use of computer floppy discs by General Motors and Ford to give new car prospects "test drives"
- "Continuity plus" programs, such as the buyer assurance program that replaces merchandise bought with the American Express card and subsequently broken or stolen
- Special events, such as Phillip Morris's sponsorship of a Virginia Slims tennis tour or the College Comedy Tour sponsored by AT&T.
- Marketing synergy, like Anheuser-Bush's "Bud Bowl" campaigns during the Super Bowl, which combine promotions with television spots†

*T*HE FUTURE OF SALES PROMOTION

It should be obvious by now that sales promotion is a very diverse area. Trying to become an expert on all aspects of sales promotion may be unrealistic, and special skills in certain areas may be best learned on the job.

Experts predict that sales promotion will experience the following trends in the 1990s:‡

- More targeted promotions
- Increased co-op or "account-specific" tie-ins
- Greater use of hi-tech P-O-P and direct mail

*Scott Hume, "Rallying to Brands' Rescue," *Advertising Age* (August 13, 1990):3.
†Scott Hume, "Rally to Brands Rescue," *Advertising Age* (August 13, 1990):3, 52; Scott Hume, "Redefining Promotion Role," *Advertising Age* (August 13, 1990):54; and W. E. Philips and Bill Robinson, "Continuous Sales (Price) Promotion Destroys Brands: Yes or No," *Marketing News* (January 16, 1989):4.
‡Russ Bowman, "Sales Promotion," *Marketing & Media Decisions* (July 1990):21.

- Continuing concern over price versus value added
- Expansion of frequency (loyal user) plans
- Longer-term planning (with flexibility)
- More group promotions and tie-ins

It is apparent that sales promotion will continue to grow as a promotional alternative. Whether it will diminish the importance of advertising is still debatable, but certainly the varieties and styles of sales promotion are changing the world of advertising.

SUMMARY

- Sales promotion offers an "extra incentive" to take action. It gives the product or service additional value.
- Sales promotion is growing rapidly for many reasons. It offers the manager short-term solutions; the extent to which sales promotion has achieved objectives can be assessed; sales promotion is less expensive than advertising; it speaks to the current needs of the consumer to receive more value from products; and it responds to the new power acquired by modern retailers.
- Sales promotion has three broad roles: to stimulate

demand by users or household consumers; to improve the marketing performance of resellers; and to supplement and coordinate advertising, personal selling, and public relations activities. In turn, sales promotion can move the consumer to purchase.
- Sales promotions directed at consumers include price deals, coupons, contests and sweepstakes, refunds, premiums, specialty advertising, continuity programs, and sampling.
- Reseller sales promotion includes point-of-purchase displays, contests and sweepstakes, trade shows, trade premiums, and trade deals.

QUESTIONS

1. What is sales promotion? What are the broad goals of sales promotion in terms of its three target audiences, and how do these goals differ from those of advertising? How are they the same? Discuss when sales promotion and advertising should be used together.

2. One agency executive was quoted as saying the following: "Advertising is on its way out. All consumers want is a deal. Sales promotion is the place to be." What do you think this executive meant? Do you agree or disagree?

3. You have just been named product manager for Bright White, a new laundry detergent that will be introduced to the market within the next 6 months. What type of sales promotion strategy would work best for this product? What types of advertising would enhance this strategy?

4. The chapter discussion says that sales promotion has made significant strides in marketing investment at the expense of advertising. Many companies show more confidence in direct sales stimulation. Why has this happened? Try to identify which explanations fit in each of these categories: a) changes in advertising, b) changes in consumer needs/wants, and c) changes in marketing strategy. Does some change in any of these signal a shift back to more advertising emphasis?

5. Tom Jackson's promotional strategy professor is covering some sales promotion methods explaining that in selecting the consumer sales promotion, planners must know the brand situation and objectives *before techniques* are chosen; some ways are for increased product usage, and some are for getting new consumers to try the product. "Which methods belong with which objective and why?" the professor asks. How should Tom answer this question?

6. Janice Wilcox is a brand manager for a very new line of eye cosmetics. She is about to present her planning strategy to division management. Janice knows her company has been successful in using sales promotion plans lately, but she has strong misgivings about following the company trend. "This new line must create a consumer brand franchise—and promotion isn't the best way to do that," she thinks to herself. What is a weakness of sales promotion in "brand franchising"? Should Janice propose no promotion or is there a reasonable compromise for her to consider?

7. Jambo Product's promotion manager, Sean Devlin, is calculating the cost of a proposed consumer coupon drop for March. The media cost (FSI) and production charges are $125,000. The distribution will be 4 million coupons with an expected redemption

of 5 percent. The coupon value is 50 cents, and Devlin has estimated the handling and compensation (store) to be 8 cents per redeemed coupon. Based on these estimates, what will be the cost to Devlin's budget?

FURTHER READINGS

LODISH, LEONARD M., *The Advertising and Promotion Challenge* (New York: Oxford University Press, 1986).

HALEY, DOUGLAS F., "Industry Promotion and Advertising Trends: Why Are They Important?" *Journal of Advertising Research* (December 1987–January 1988): RC-6.

FITZGERALD, KEN, "Ad Support Builds for Tools," *Advertising Age* (August 28, 1989):20.

MCCANN, THOMAS, "Promotions Will Gain More Clout in the '90s," *Marketing News* (November 6, 1989):4, 24.

HUME, SCOTT, "Premiums & Promotions: After Buying-Binge, What?" *Advertising Age* (September 12, 1988): S1–S5.

BABAKUS, EMIN, PETER TAT, and WILLIAM CUNNINGHAM, "Coupon Redemption: A Motivational Perspective," *Journal of Consumer Marketing* (Spring 1988):40.

VIDEO CASE

Sales Promotions and the Death of Brands

For the marketing executives at Procter & Gamble and other consumer packaged goods firms during the early part of the century, advertising was a sacred cow. Although many would have agreed with the retail advertising adage "I know half of my advertising is wasted, but I don't know which half," they nonetheless recognized that advertising could create, build, and maintain brand equity, something no other marketing tool could reliably achieve.

Those early marketers would undoubtedly be stunned by the shift in advertising expenditures to sales promotion expenditures over the last 15 years. Their shock would result not from their ignorance of the value of sales promotion as a sales-building technique, but simply because they would easily recognize sales promotion as the dangerous threat to brand equity that it represents today.

Whereas the ultimate goal of brand advertising is to establish loyalty for a given product due to the product's unique selling proposition (USP), the most common goal of sales promotion is to "incentivize" consumers into switching brands in exchange for a price discount of some kind, a gift or premium, or some other form of purchase incentive. However, the power of sales promotion to foster brand switching is such that few firms can risk lost sales by avoiding the trap of sales promotion wars. Just as price discounting is often answered by price discounts from competitors, high-value coupons must often be responded to with comparably valued coupons or similar value-added promotions to avoid losing business to the competition.

Unfortunately, as the sales promotion wars have escalated and the distribution of cents-off coupons has increased into the hundreds of billions annually, most firms have been forced to divert advertising dollars into sales promotion expenditures. Consequently, brand equity has become an early casualty as advertising support has generally been withdrawn from products. This situation has been compounded by escalating media costs that, together with the proliferation of viewing alternatives to traditional network television, have left brand equity vulnerable for many firms.

Perhaps the most extreme example of sales promotion's ability to foster brand-switching can be found in the hi-tech Coupon Solutions system created by Catalina Marketing. The system interfaces with cash registers in supermarkets and can be instructed to generate instantly a high-value coupon for a Catalina Marketing client's brand if a shopper buys a competitor's product.

Other short-sighted, profit-generating tactics of consumer packaged goods firms have also conspired to weaken the position of brands in the U.S. marketplace during the last 15 years. Primary among them was the dramatic proliferation of new products that failed to represent truly meaningful improvements over benefits offered by existing brands and products. As this wave of new products pressed itself into the limited shelf space of retail locations, and as ownership of retail locations consolidated, retailers were able to pressure manufacturers into providing more trade promotion monies in exchange for their cooperation. Thus, not only were advertising dollars for brands reduced to fund increased sales promotion expenditures, but retailer pressure necessitated further advertising reductions to fund increased trade promotion expenditures as well.

In addition to the erosion of brand equity, the net result of this shift in marketing support from advertising to sales and trade promotions has been an erosion in manufacturers' profitability. Although some manufacturers have responded by acquiring or merging with other packaged goods firms to reduce their competition, this too has proven costly.

In any event, the only clear winners to emerge thus far in the promotion war have been consumers and retailers. The increased use of sales promotions has afforded the savvy consumer with additional opportunities to reduce product prices via cents-off coupons and other means. Retailers have benefited from the wholesale shift in advertising spending to trade promotions, earmarked to ensure stocking and merchandising support for new products but also to enlist their cooperation for the increased consumer sales promotion activity.

If this trend continues, it is conceivable that the domestic manufacturer/retailer division of power will shift to resemble a more European scenario, similar to that observed in Germany. There, only a few retailers account for the vast majority of retail sales in the country, so retailers have adequate negotiation power to require large trade promotion spending from manufacturers. With the resulting shift in profitability to retailers, store brands are often the premium-priced items in the store, and independent manufacturers' brands are often the discount, or bargain, products. It is generally believed that this situation developed because manufacturers were left with insufficient funds to advertise the unique benefits of their own products and were forced to pursue a pricing strategy that is less dependent on advertising for its success.

Whether or not the U.S. manufacturer/retailer relationship will evolve to this state is still unclear. However, as long as manufacturers pursue shorter-term solutions for improving profitability, and as long as control of the retail environment falls into fewer and fewer hands, it is likely that only those manufacturers with a broad assortment of products and with brands whose equities have been established over generations will continue to justify charging price premiums. For the remainder, their brand equities may continue to suffer a slow death.

QUESTIONS

1. Explain why the "value-adding" of sales promotions can be viewed as analogous to a price decrease.
2. Why do you think many manufacturers refer to trade promotions as "reduced revenue"?
3. Why do you think consumers will lose in the long run if retailers only can afford to advertise their own brands and independent manufacturers are forced to compete on price alone?

Sources: ABC News, Business World, Show #120 (January 29, 1989); and Advertising Age (July 1, 1991).

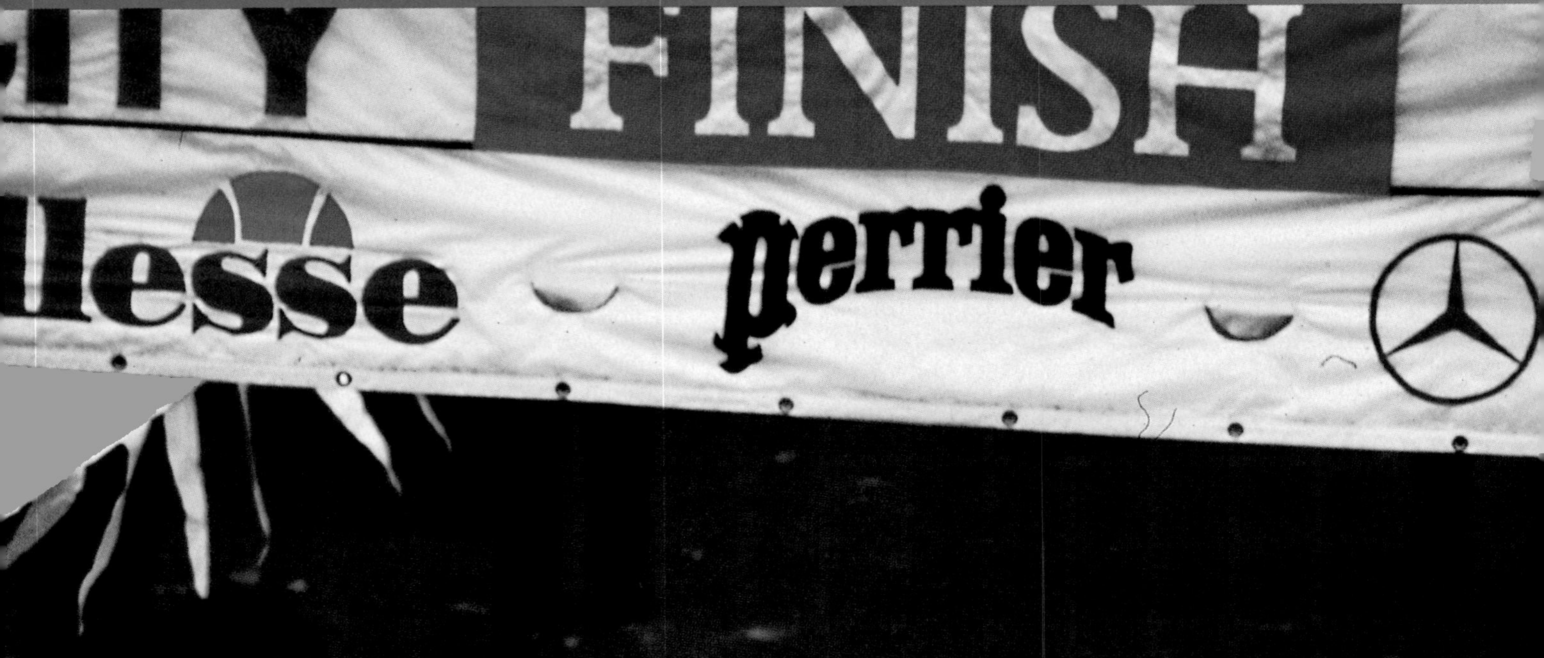
FINISH
perrier
ellesse
MANUFACTURERS

19

Public Relations

Chapter Outline

Chapter Objectives

When you have completed this chapter, you should be able to:

- Understand what public relations is, how it differs from advertising, and what its advantages are
- Explain how public relations, advertising, and other marketing communications can work together to achieve greater benefit for an organization
- Identify the areas in which public relations operates and some of the activities performed in those areas
- Understand the value and importance of measuring the results of public relations efforts

RETAILERS GET DOWN TO EARTH

Wal-Mart Stores, a chain of discount retail stores, is leading a crusade in support of environmental protection. On August 15, 1989, a full-page ad appeared in both *The Wall Street Journal* and *USA Today* announcing, "We're looking for quality products that are guaranteed not to last." The ad went on to explain, "We're challenging our manufacturing partners to improve their products to help prevent lasting environmental problems." Wal-Mart's ad was intended to encourage the store's suppliers to support the cause and help prevent environmental abuse.

According to Brenda Lockhart, Wal-Mart Stores public relations coordinator, Wal-Mart is the only discount retailer actively campaigning for this cause. All Wal-Mart divisions, including Sam's Wholesale Club, found in the southern and southwestern states, and Hypermart, located in the Southwest, will be involved in this effort, she explained. The stores will feature environmentally improved products and packaging, which will be promoted through clear shelf tagging notifying consumers of packaging that is environmentally safe.

Wal-Mart decided to back the environmental cause with such vigor in response to numerous letters from customers expressing concern over the growing environmental problem. According to Lockhart, the environment is "one of the most important issues today . . . We're not trying to be a hero. We think Wal-Mart is of significant size that we should be doing something to make a difference." The body copy of the Wal-Mart ad states the company's objectives: "We are all linked to our environment by the products we manufacture, sell, and consume. We encourage you, our manufacturers, to look for ways to provide Wal-Mart and our customers with more merchandise and packaging that is better for the environment in manufacturing, use, and disposal."

To promote their efforts, Wal-Mart has circulated letters to vendors asking them to use recyclable materials or reusable packages. According to Lockhart, manufacturers have begun to respond. Procter & Gamble, for example, packages its Spic and Span cleaner in recycled plastic. Wal-Mart's Texas-based advertising agency, GSD&M, has responded by forming an "environmental action team" to look for ways to protect the environment and intends to choose suppliers according to the attention they give to environmental concerns.*

THE CHALLENGE OF PUBLIC RELATIONS

The goodwill of the public is the greatest asset any organization can have. A public that is well-informed is not only important; it is critical to the survival of an organization. Informing the public is the responsibility of public relations.

Although there is no universally accepted definition of **public relations**, the First World Assembly of Public Relations Associations in Mexico City offered the following definition in 1978: "The art and social science of analyzing trends, predicting their consequences, counseling organizational

public relations *A management function enabling organizations to achieve effective relationships with their various audiences through an understanding of audience opinions, attitudes, and values.*

*Adapted from Lisa Parkowski, "Wal-Mart Voices Its Concern for Environment," *Adweek* (August 21, 1989):4.

TABLE 19.1
The top 10 public relations firms

Firm	1989 Fee Income (in millions)	% Fee Change
1. Shandwick	$180.0	+48
2. Hill and Knowlton	164.0	+13.1
3. Burson-Marsteller	159.8	+10.4
4. Ogilvy PR Group	57.7	+21.2
5. Rowland Worldwide	50.0	+19.5
6. Omnicom PR Network	48.5	+42.3
7. Fleishman-Hillard	38.0	+17
8. Ketchum PR	35.7	+35.2
9. Edelman PR Worldwide	35.7	+13.6
10. Manning Selvage & Lee	26.7	−0.5

Source: O'Dwyer's P. R. Services, vol. 4, no. 5 (New York: J. R. O'Dwyer Co., May 1990):1.

leaders, and implementing planned programs of action which will serve both the organization and the public interest." A much simpler definition is offered by Dilenschneider and Forrestal in the *Public Relations Handbook:* "Public relations is the use of information to influence public opinion."*

Both definitions treat public relations as a management function that is practiced by companies, governments, trade and professional associations, nonprofit organizations, the travel and tourism industry, the educational system, labor unions, politicians, organized sports, and media. Its audiences (publics) may be external (customers, the news media, the investment community, the general public, the government) and also internal (stockholders, employees).

Public relations is a growing industry. It is estimated that the public relations industry employs 145,000 people and that its billings are increasing by 18 to 20 percent annually.† Virtually every city in the United States contains at least one public relations practitioner serving clients of every size and interest. Annual fees paid by these clients range from a few hundred dollars to several million. Table 19.1 lists the 10 largest public relations firms and their annual incomes. In addition, many companies, such as Texas Instruments, have their own in-house public relations departments and do not contract with public relations agencies. Others, such as Exxon, consult with agencies only about specific activities.

Public relations, advertising, and sales promotion together present the marketing communication strategy of an organization. What a company's advertising says, how it says it, and what medium it uses have a direct bearing on the company's public relations strategy and vice versa. Thus advertising agencies need to understand what public relations is and how it works with advertising to benefit both public relations and advertising. Furthermore, advertising strategists, especially copywriters and media specialists, often play a major role in the design and placement of public relations messages in mass media. Accordingly, this chapter attempts both to provide an overview of public relations and to show its direct applications to advertising.

Before we enter into this discussion, however, we must distinguish advertising from public relations.

*Robert L. Dilenschneider and Dan J. Forrestal, *Public Relations Handbook,* 3rd rev. ed. (Chicago, IL: The Dartnell Corporation, 1987):5.
†Public Relations Society of America, *Careers in Public Relations* (1990):1.

COMPARING PUBLIC RELATIONS AND ADVERTISING

Designing ads, preparing their written messages, and buying time or space for their exposure are the primary concerns of advertising people. Although advertising should complement a total public relations program, it is really a separate function. Advertising and public relations differ in the way they employ the media and control the messages they convey.

Media Approach

publicity *Cost-free public relations that relates messages through gatekeepers.*

To begin with, public relations practitioners have a different approach to the media than do advertisers. Whenever possible, they avoid purchasing time or space to communicate messages. Instead, they seek to persuade media "gatekeepers" to carry their information. These gatekeepers include writers, producers, editors, talk show coordinators, and newscasters. This type of public relations is labeled **publicity** and is characterized as cost-free because there are no direct media costs. There are indirect costs, however, such as production expenses and getting the cooperation of the gatekeepers.

corporate/institutional advertising *Advertising used to create a favorable public attitude toward the sponsoring organization.*

Even when public relations uses paid-for media, the nature of the message tends to be general with little or no attempt to sell a brand or product line. The goal is to change the attitudes of the public in favor of the sponsoring organization. This type of advertising is referred to as **corporate or institutional advertising.** When the gasoline crunch of the 1970s caused prices at the pump to skyrocket, Texaco, Phillips Petroleum, and Exxon all introduced a series of ads designed to curb public anger toward the petroleum industry. A similar situation occurred in 1990 with the Iraqi invasion of Kuwait. The copy in one ad for the Amoco Oil Company shows how one company affected by the political situation responded to this crisis:

> President Bush asked Amoco and other U.S. oil companies to do their fair share regarding gasoline prices as they are affected by the turmoil in the Persian Gulf. Throughout this critical period, Amoco is determined to act reasonably and responsibly.
>
> We support President Bush's efforts to resolve the Middle East conflict as soon as possible, because no commodity is of greater value to all of us than world peace.

Corporate advertising will be discussed in more detail later in the chapter.

advocacy advertising *A type of corporate advertising that involves creating advertisements and purchasing space to deliver a specific, targeted message.*

The American Association of Retired Persons (AARP), the nation's largest organization of people aged 50 and older, engages in both publicity and corporate advertising. The AARP has recently attempted to develop a national program to reduce health-care costs without sacrificing the quality of the care. Part of this program involves educating older consumers about these issues. To reach this large audience the AARP advertises its program —that is, it creates print advertisements and purchases space in newspapers to carry the ads. This special type of corporate advertising tends to be targeted and delivers a pointed message. It is labeled **advocacy advertising.** The organization also persuades television talk shows to invite AARP spokespersons to appear and encourages radio call-in programs to air the association's views of the issues.

Control and Credibility

Amount of control is the second inherent difference between advertising and public relations. In the case of publicity, the public relations strategist is at the mercy of the media representative. There is no guarantee that all or even part of the story will appear. In fact, there is the real risk that the story may be rewritten or reorganized so that it no longer means what the strategist intended. In contrast, advertising is paid for, so there are many checks to ensure that the message is accurate and appears when scheduled.

The difficulty in measuring the results of public relations is another problem. It may take months or even years to change public opinion. In addition, it is hard to measure accurately the components that reflect public opinion.

Public relations does offer a credibility not usually associated with advertising, however. For example, a 2-minute story delivered by Tom Brokaw on the *NBC Evening News* about an Eli Lily Drugs medical breakthrough is far more credible than a print ad sponsored by Eli Lily. Another benefit of public relations is the longer length of publicity compared to a typical television commercial. A story delivered by Tom Brokaw or published in *Fortune* magazine is longer than the typical 30- or 60-second spot or one-page print ad.

The fundamental differences between advertising and public relations are widely accepted but the role played by public relations within the advertising strategy is still being debated. However, with more emphasis on integrated marketing communication, public relations is beginning to be recognized as an important element in the marketing mix.

THE COMPONENTS OF PUBLIC RELATIONS

Public relations, like advertising, is a managed activity. It begins with a thorough understanding of its publics and is guided by objectives. In turn, a message strategy or campaign is developed relative to these objectives. Although the process is similar to the advertising process, the particular elements differ.

Measuring Public Opinion

publics *Those groups or individuals who are involved with an organization, including customers, employees, competitors, and government regulators.*

Traditionally in public relations, the term **public** has been used to describe any group who has some involvement with an organization, including customers, employees, competitors, and government regulators. The public relations strategist researches the answers to two primary questions. First, which publics are most important to my organization, now and in the future? Second, what do these publics think? In identifying important publics, public relations follows the same process as advertising does in identifying a target market, which is simply the group of people or institutions we wish to receive our message (see Chapter 7). Determining what these publics think, however, is often quite challenging. **Public opinion,** the label used to denote what people think, is defined as "a belief, based not necessarily on fact but on the *conception* or *evaluation* of an event, person, institution, or product."*

public opinion *People's beliefs, based on their conceptions or evaluations of something rather than on fact.*

The power of public opinion cannot be denied. It created the dictatorial influence of Adolf Hitler, made a hero of John F. Kennedy and a villain of Gary Hart, and has prompted countries to go to war. However, as many celebrities, politicians, and major corporations have found, public opinion is very fickle because of its fragile base in perceptions. Such per-

*Doug Newsom, Alan Scott, and Judy Van Slyke Turk, *This Is PR: The Realities of Public Relations,* 4th ed. (Belmont, CA: Wadsworth Publishing Co., 1989):99.

ceptions are difficult to control, and often the public keys in on cues that are either negative or easily misinterpreted. Hot words, such as "abortion," "taxes," and "equal rights," can be taken out of context or overshadow the real message. Physical appearance, mannerisms, or one poorly handled event can influence public opinion.

Despite the critical need to understand public opinion, there is still no one system of measurement of the "climate of public opinion." Polls only measure public opinion on a particular issue at a given time. Different people maintain different values; likewise, a person's values can change over time. Clients of public relations agencies may rely on the research capabilities of the firm to evaluate public opinion, but they are more likely to rely on professional pollsters such as Louis Harris, George Gallup, and the Opinion Research Corporation.

Green Marketing

Measuring subtle movements in public opinion is very difficult. Most shifts in public opinion are not very obvious. The decade of the 1990s appears to be characterized as a time when there is a general concern for the environment, however, and this proenvironment movement has become very widespread. Destruction of the rain forests; air, water, land, and noise pollution; and the use of nonrenewable natural resources reflect a public opinion to which businesses, such as Wal-Mart, have responded. This concern of businesses for the environment has been labelled "green marketing," and has been implemented through advertising that emphasizes a concern for the environment (see Ad. 19.1). For a closer look at the implications of green marketing, see the Issues and Applications box entitled "Sponsoring Earth Day."

Some of the most obvious advertisers to concern themselves with green marketing are suppliers of lawncare products, such as O.M. Scott & Sons and Ringer Corporation. In 1991 Ringer doubled its advertising budget to $6 million annually and significantly increased its number of organic-based products. Ringer's advertising included two 30-second television spots featuring John Cleese promoting Lawn Restore, a new natural fertilizer. Scott introduced a new print campaign in 1991 for its lawncare products, which also included a new organic fertilizer. The problem for these advertisers is the wide-ranging definition of the term "organic," which is being reexamined by the U.S. Senate's Subcommittee on Toxic Substances and the Federal Trade Commission.*

Green Claims. Lawn and garden suppliers are not the only companies to concern themselves with advertising environmentally safe products. On April 8, 1991, Mobil Chemical Company introduced a multimillion-dollar national campaign for its "improved" Hefty Steel-Sak trash and tall kitchen garbage bags. The commercials did not include any mention of environmental benefits, however. The company was charged by state attorneys general in seven states with deceptive advertising over environmental claims for degradable trash bags when it touted the source-reduction benefits of its thinner bags. In reality, the bags did use 30 percent less material, making them thinner, but they were found to be just as strong and difficult to decompose as their predecessors, therefore not making them any more environmentally safe. As a result, Mobil took its environmental claims out of all advertising until national green standards become established.

*Kate Fitzgerald, "Ripe for Growth," *Advertising Age* (April 1, 1991):4.

THE NEW TRADITIONALIST.

SHE WANTS MUCH MORE THAN A CLEAN HOUSE.
SHE WANTS A CLEANER WORLD.

Our readers, the New Traditionalists who feel a renewed commitment to improving the environment, look to Good Housekeeping to help lead the way.

Here is what we're doing to guide the millions of people who want to do their part:

•Good Housekeeping US and UK have joined forces to create a landmark, two-nation publishing venture, "Green Watch -

the World of Good Housekeeping" to appear in March, 1991.

•The Good Housekeeping Institute established the Bureau of Chemistry and Environmental Studies.

•The Good Housekeeping "Green Watch" awards have been established to honor those making significant contributions to the environment.

•The Good Housekeeping "Green Watch" pages - a monthly editorial section.

•"The Environmental Moments" - special public service announcements on cable TV.

Healing the earth is a responsibility we all share. Good Housekeeping will make it our continuing priority throughout the "Decency Decade" of the 90's.

THE EARTH BELIEVES IN GOOD HOUSEKEEPING

AD 19.1
Advertisers have become environmentally conscious in their advertising. (Courtesy of *Good Housekeeping* Magazine, a publication of Hearst Magazines, a division of the Hearst Corporation.)

Competing companies are becoming more bold in their advertising, however. First Brands Corporation, for example, claim in its ads for "improved" Glad open-mouth trash bags that, "Although very small, this reduction is a continuing effort on the part of Glad to help reduce solid waste." Carlisle Plastics introduced new Ruffies Sure Strength bags, advertised as "A better choice for our environment—made with 40% less plastic." In addition, new green product lines have emerged, including Webster Industries' Renew bags, which are made from 80 percent recycled plastic. This new line of bags is supported by a $2 million ad budget, including television, print, and trade ads, as well as coupons and sampling. Topco Associates, a private label-buying cooperative owned by 30 supermarket chains, introduced the GreenMark line of products, which includes trash bags, degradable compost bags, and bags for holding trash for recycling. All of these products contain reduced material for environmental benefits.*

*Christy Fisher, "Mobil Avoids Hefty Green Claim," *Advertising Age* (April 1, 1991):4.

SPONSORING EARTH DAY

Earth Day 1991 had fewer sponsors than did the first celebration of environmental awareness the previous year, due to more relaxed attitudes about sponsors' qualifications and quieter media attention to the event. Procter & Gamble, Gillette, and Hardee's Food Systems were the only sponsors of Earth Day 1991, each of whom bought magazine space or helped distribute magazines offering environmental tips. Procter & Gamble bought three and one-half ad pages in "Every Day: The Earth Day 1991 Lifestyle Guide," a 64-page booklet of environmental facts, figures, stories, and product reviews. Gillette bought one half-page ad, and Hardees agreed to distribute 1 million copies to customers. Each color page advertising costs $25,000.

According to Bruce Anderson, president of Earth Day USA, scrutinizing the potential sponsors of the 1990 event to make sure their environmental programs were "worthy of the cause" contributed to the scarcity of sponsors in 1991. Many companies feared "getting targeted" by groups accusing sponsors of being hypocritical based on past environmental performance. Anderson also cited the recession, the Persian Gulf War, and a change in or-ganizing groups from the Earth 1990 temporary Palto-Alto, California-based group to the new Earth Day USA organization based in Manchester, New Hampshire, as other causes.

Plans for the April 1992 Earth Day include a major concert tour of Paris and Eastern Europe, tentatively called Earth Express. Sponsors for the event will be allowed to ride the train through the region's capitals and meet dignitaries while spreading "the environmental message." Among those who have agreed to perform at the concerts are Bob Dylan, Joni Mitchell, and Neil Young.

Besides Earth Day, advertisers are getting involved in environmental developments in other ways as well. As of April 1991 McDonald's restaurants began giving away more than 9 million tree seedlings in conjunction with the American Forestry Association's Global ReLeaf Program. Tambrands introduced its own promotion, giving away a paperback entitled "50 Simple Things You Can Do To Save The Earth" with every purchase of its 40-tampon box.

Source: Adapted from Gary Levin, "Earth Day Digs Up Few Sponsors For '91," *Advertising Age* (April 1, 1991):4.

AD 19.2
The American Lung Association runs strong public service announcements to educate the public about the dangers of pollution. (Courtesy of American Lung Association.)

Let's not pollute our ocean of air like we polluted theirs.

AMERICAN LUNG ASSOCIATION®
The Christmas Seal People®

Space contributed by the publisher as a public service.

PUBLIC RELATIONS TECHNIQUES

The arsenal of tools available to the public relations practitioner is vast and diverse. One way of organizing the available material is to divide it into two categories: controlled media and uncontrolled media. Controlled media include house ads, public service announcements, corporate (institutional) advertising, in-house publications, and visual presentations. These techniques are paid for by the sponsoring organizations. In turn, the organization maintains total control over how and when the message is delivered. The two exceptions to the paid-for criteria are house ads and public service announcements.

House Ads

A house ad is an ad that is prepared by the organization for use in its own publication or a publication over which it has some control. Consequently, no money changes hands, even though a particular organization may use some sort of billing mechanism. For instance, a local television station may run a house ad announcing its new fall programming.

Public Service Announcements

public service announcement (PSA) *A type of public relations advertising that deals with public welfare issues and is typically run free of charge.*

Public service announcements (PSAs) are announcements designed by charitable and civic organizations and broadcast on television or radio or placed in print media free of charge. The United Way, the American Heart Association, and the local arts council all offer public service announcements. These ads are prepared just like commercials, and in many instances ad agencies donate their expertise to the design of PSAs. Ad 19.2 is an example of a public service announcement developed by the American Lung Association. The Advertising Council is a private nonprofit organization that conducts public service advertising campaigns in the public interest. The Advertising Council follows a prescribed procedure in evaluating and producing PSA campaigns (see Figure 19.1). Essentially, all public service announcements appearing on network television have been produced by the Advertising Council.

Unfortunately, networks and publishers have been so inundated with requests to run public service announcements that many are never aired or are run during very low viewing times or printed at the end of magazines. This severe competition has forced nonprofit organizations to do a better job designing PSAs or to run them as paid-for commercials. For a more in-

FIGURE 19.1
The organization of the Advertising Council. *Source: The Advertising Council: Report to the American People 1988–1989.*

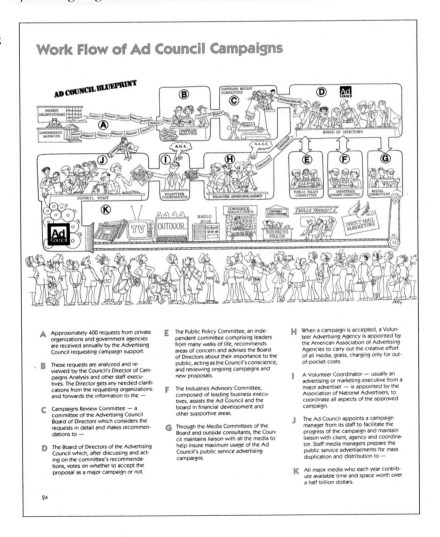

depth look into public service announcements, see the box entitled "Public Service Announcements or Paid Ads?"

Corporate (Institutional) Advertising

As we mentioned earlier, corporate advertising is designed and paid for by the organization to enhance or change the image of the firm. There is no attempt to sell a particular product. This type of advertising sometimes takes the form of position statements directed at the public. Companies seeking public support for corporate policies and programs have begun to invest more in this type of advertising, called *advocacy advertising*. For example, during the breakup of AT&T in the early 1980s, the Pacific Telesis Group had a negative image with the financial community, which viewed the firm as a high-risk investment. Among its other problems, Pacific Telesis had the lowest earning record of the seven Regional Bell Holding Companies that began operation independently on January 1, 1984. In preparation for the AT&T divestiture, however, Pacific Telesis embarked on a strategic plan to turn the firm around. Convinced that the strength of the plan, combined with the company's vastly improved financial condition, would more than compensate for poor earnings in the past, the company believed that all that remained to be accomplished was to communicate these changes to the financial community. Pacific Telesis did this through institutional advertising. The first print ad laid out the whole story—from the company's financial health, to its marketing strategy, to the strength of its top management team.*

corporate identity advertising
A type of advertising used by firms to establish their reputation or increase awareness.

Corporate identity advertising is another type of advertising used by firms that want to enhance or maintain their reputation among specific audiences or to establish a level of awareness of the company's name and the nature of its business. For example, to increase awareness of what 3M stood for among younger (ages 25 to 34) middle managers who purchased its products, 3M used the positioning strategy "One thing leads to another" shown in Ad 19.3. Companies that have changed their names, such as Nissan (formerly Datsun) and Exxon (formed from Esso, Humble Oil, and Standard Oil of New Jersey), have also employed corporate identity advertising.

A Case Study: Dun & Bradstreet. A classic example of what a well-planned public relations program can do for an organization involves the firm of Dun & Bradstreet (D&B). Research indicated that D&B's world leadership in providing credit information to businesses dominated the business market's perception of the company. As a result, many businesses were unaware of D&B's other informational capabilities. To promote D&B's publishing, marketing, and business information services, D&B and its agency aimed a public relations program at present and potential customers, government economists, the financial community, and the media. They created a flow of business information to promote the company's other "brand names," including Moody's Investor Service and A. C. Nielsen Research. News releases, regional economic forecasts, and a spokesperson program (using a media-trained chief economist) secured extensive media coverage in the United States, Canada, Great Britain, and West Germany. Major stories emphasizing D&B's leadership role in the business information industry appeared in *Fortune, The New York Times*, and *The Wall Street*

*William R. Brittingham, "How a Brand New $16 Billion Company Assesses Its Communication Needs," *Sixth Annual ARF Business Advertising Research Conference* (Advertising Research Foundation:Grand Hyatt Hotel, New York City, October 4, 1984).

AD 19.3
This 3M ad was designed to increase brand awareness among younger consumers. (Courtesy of 3M.)

Journal. The media coverage reached an estimated 890 million readers during the program's first year, and calls to D&B's economic analysis department for business information increased by 280 percent.

In-House Publications

There is an almost endless list of publications provided by organizations to their employees and other publics. Examples are pamphlets, booklets, annual reports, books, bulletins, newsletters, inserts and enclosures, position papers, and information racks. In-house publications differ from house ads in that the latter are not distributed in-house. Rather, house ads are carried by a medium owned by the organization that conveys information outside the organization. For example, NBC might broadcast a commercial about a new television program or *Sports Illustrated* might run an ad about its Swimsuit edition. An example of an in-house publication is the free booklet Corning Fiberglass Insulation offers on home insulation "do's and don'ts" as an integral part of its promotion effort, which is highlighted in its advertising campaign. A company's financial report, especially the annual report, may be the single most important document the company distributes. Millions of dollars are spent on the editing and design of annual reports.

Speakers, Photographs, and Films

Maintaining visual contact with the various publics is a big part of public relations. Many companies have a speakers' bureau of articulate people who are made available to talk about topics at the public's request. Apple Com-

CORPORATE PERFORMANCE

DUN & BRADSTREET REDEPLOYS THE RICHES

In a flurry of acquisition and divestiture, Dun & Bradstreet has sold five companies and bought 33. It still has cash for more. To whatever it buys, the company brings the technological muscle that makes it a leader in the business of business information.   ■ by Stuart Gannes

Joyce "the Voice" Gordon records messages in a New York studio for Dun's Voice, an automated service customers phone for credit information.

Reprinted through the courtesy of the Editors of FORTUNE
© 1985 TIME INC.

Dun & Bradstreet public relations campaign resulted in widespread publicity for the company's varied informational services, as illustrated in this edition of *Fortune* Magazine.   (Courtesy of Doremus Porter Novelli.)

puter, Harvard University, and the Children's Hospital in Houston, Texas, all have speakers' bureaus.

Pictures of people, products, places, and events may all be desired by some publics. It is important for an organization that receives such requests to maintain a picture file and make sure these photographs are accurate, in good condition, and delivered promptly.

Films, especially videotapes, have become a major public relations tool for a great many companies. At $1,000 to $2,000 per minute, these videos are not cheap. However, for a company like Cunard Cruise Line, mailing videotapes that show the beauty of a newly developed Caribbean paradise to 10,000 travel agents is a worthwhile investment.

Displays, Exhibits, and Staged Events

There is no clear distinction between displays, exhibits, and staged events, though display is thought of as the simplest technique of the three. A picture of a new store being built and a presentation of a company's product line at a regional fair are examples of displays. Exhibits tend to be larger, may have moving parts, sound, or video, and are usually manned by a company representative. Booth exhibits are very important at trade shows, where many companies take orders for a majority of their annual sales. Parade floats, museum exhibits, and historic exhibits are other common types.

There are various kinds of staged events, such as open houses and plant tours. However, the use of more elaborate staged events has seen the most growth. Corporate sponsorship of various sporting events has evolved as a favorite public relations tactic. It is hard to identify a golf tournament,

PUBLIC SERVICE ANNOUNCEMENTS OR PAID ADS?

Critics charge that the line between public service and corporate promotion is becoming blurred and that some cause-oriented spots are actually commercials in disguise. "The lines are being blurred by for-profit organizations who are trying to profit from nonprofits, wrapping themselves in the cloak of 'public service' for corporate benefit," said Don Schultz, professor at Northwestern University's Medill School of Journalism.

In October 1990, for example, McDonald's planned to sponsor a 30-minute public service television special, "Stay in School," to be aired in February 1991, produced in association with the National Basketball Association, NBC, Turner Network Television, and Nickelodeon. The special was to be run in donated network television time and include spots for the nonprofit Ronald McDonald Children's Charities. The question that results from such sponsorship is whether marketers are pushing cause marketing into ethical gray areas in their search for effective nontraditional marketing tools.

Dan Langdon, senior vice president at the Advertising Council, presents the issue this way: "Is there self-interest on the part of McDonald's? If you looked at [Ronald McDonald Children's Charities] without the 'McDonald' attached, sure, it's legitimate public service advertising. But does the company accrue benefit from this program? Sure." In response, McDonald's Children's Charities counter that it is not their intention to advertise McDonald's but to fund worthwhile projects that help the children.

McDonald's is not the only company to come under fire. Quaker Oats was refused air time by some broadcasters for including its public service announcements for the American Medical Association, starring Wilford Brimley, as part of the com-

pany's media plan for Quaker oatmeal. Philip Morris was criticized for funding the National Archives' celebration of the Bill of Rights bicentennial when critics charged that the campaign was "an attempt to subvert the ban on broadcast cigarette advertising."

Nike's "Don't be Stupid, Stay in School" campaign, Anheuser-Busch's "Know When to Say When" promotion—are these public service announcements or commercials in disguise? Advertisers are being approached more frequently by nonprofit organizations to sponsor cause-oriented programming, and they are getting more equal billing for doing so. When does such cause-related marketing become suspect?

According to Phil Schuman, vice president-associate creative director at Burson-Marstellar in New York, "a cause-marketing effort needs to be appropriate and tasteful—and viewed as legitimate—or run the risk of backfiring. The public will reject any form of disguised commercial." There is also the very real danger of negative backlash if the sponsoring organization overtly acts in the interest of making a profit.

The arguments are strong on both sides. Critics maintain that the growth in paid public service announcements may eliminate opportunities for some organizations that can't afford to advertise and don't have access to the Nikes and Quakers of the world. Furthermore, they feel that overexposure will lead to consumer apathy to charitable organizations in general. In contrast, those who favor such paid announcements argue that nonprofit organizations are eager for visibility and funding and that buying television time gives them more control over their message.

Source: Adapted from Julie Liesse, "Line Between Public Service, Paid Ads Blurs," *Advertising Age* (October 8, 1990):26.

tennis tournament, or automobile race that isn't sponsored by one or more corporations. For example, in 1988 RJR Nabisco sponsored the Salem Pro Sail race series featuring boat races in Miami, San Francisco, and Newport, Rhode Island, in order to promote Winston, the company's number-two brand of cigarettes. The newly designed package features a sail image on the box, and the event was deemed an appropriate vehicle for promoting the new image.*

*Wayne Friedman, "No Burnout Here," *Adweek Special Report* (September 19, 1988):24.

Public Relations Implemented Through Uncontrolled Media

As we mentioned earlier, there are instances when an organization has no direct control over how the media will report on corporate activities. Sometimes the company will initiate the publicity and even provide pertinent information to be used by the media. In other cases the media will report a news event (good or bad) without guidance from the company. In order for either scenario to turn out favorably for the company, it is necessary for the public relations practitioner to become an expert at *press relations*.

The relationship between the public relations person and the media representative is tenuous at best and often adversarial. The reporter is motivated by the public's right to know, and the public relations practitioner's loyalty is to the client or company. A successful relationship between public relations and media is built on a reputation for honesty, accuracy, and professionalism. Once this reputation is tarnished or lost, the public relations person cannot function.

news release *Primary medium used to deliver public relations messages to the media.*

The News Release.   The **news release** is the primary medium used to deliver public relations messages to the various media editors and reporters. It must be written differently for each medium, accommodating space and time limitations. The more carefully the news release is planned and written, the better the chance it has of being accepted and published as written. Being a good writer is considered a prerequisite for going into public relations. The news release is the primary reflection of this skill. Note the tight and simple writing style in the news release from Plumbing-Heating-Cooling Information Bureau, the official spokesperson for that industry.

An example of a news release. The language is concise and simple.

NEWS RELEASE

PLUMBING · HEATING · COOLING
INFORMATION BUREAU

303 East Wacker Drive • Chicago, Illinois 60601 • Phone (312) 372-7331

CONTACT: Susan Birkholtz or Lynette Duncan

FOR IMMEDIATE RELEASE
October, 1989

Is Your Home Ready For Winter?

PRECAUTIONS KEEP PIPES FROM FREEZING

Is your plumbing ready for the icy blasts of sub-zero wind chill factors?

The combination of low temperatures and high winds can freeze pipes in your home, possibly causing them to burst. However, preventing this common winter problem is not difficult, according to David Weiner, executive director of the Plumbing-Heating-Cooling Information Bureau.

"If a pipe has frozen in the past, keep heat close to it," he advised. "Leave the cabinet door open to let warm air from the house get in.

"People who use wood-burning stoves to save on heating bills during cold snaps often have problems with frozen pipes because the outside walls don't get enough heat," Weiner continued. "Don't shut off your furnace or boiler completely. Fuel costs less than a major plumbing repair."

-more-

FROZEN PIPES -- add 1

If a pipe does freeze, an electric hair dryer will defrost it. For safety, be sure the dryer is grounded and never hold the pipe while operating an electric appliance.

Larger pipes will probably require professional attention. To prevent them from bursting, turn off the water supply. However, if you have hydronic heat, remember the boiler must have a continual water supply while operating.

Another way to prevent freezing is to keep faucets in problem areas running in a low-to-moderate stream during a cold snap. If all else fails, the Bureau recommends having a licensed plumbing contractor relocate the pipes.

The Plumbing-Heating-Cooling Information Bureau is the consumer information arm of the plumbing-heating-cooling industry.

-30-

AT&T held a press conference to anounce its new company logo.
(Randy Matusow.)

press conference *A public gathering of media people for the purpose of establishing a company's position or making a statement.*

The Press Conference. One of the riskiest public relations activities is the **press conference.** Although some companies, such as Polaroid and Chrysler Motors, have been very successful in introducing new products through press conferences, there have been many disasters. For example, in the fall of 1990 Victor Kiam, president of Remington Razors and owner of the New England Patriots football team, called a press conference concerning the allegations against his players over the improper treatment of a female reporter in the locker room. Protesters were refusing to buy Remington products, and questions raised by reporters and answers given by Kiam had serious repercussions on the sale of his razors.

Companies worry about various issues when planning a press conference. Will the press show up? Will they ask the right questions? Will they ask questions the company cannot or will not answer? One way to avoid some of these problems is to design an effective press kit. A press kit, normally in a folder form, provides all the important background information to members of the press either before they arrive or when they arrive at the press conference. The risk in offering press kits is that they give reporters all the necessary information so that the press conference itself becomes unnecessary.

Crisis Management. The 1980s seemed to be a decade of corporate disasters. Insider trading scandals, oil spills, plane crashes, and management improprieties made it difficult *not* to characterize American business as corrupt and poorly managed. This image is due in part to our efficient mass communication system and in part to the media's desire to publish sensational news. Handling bad news is the responsibility of public relations. The public relations strategist must anticipate the possibility of a crisis and establish a mechanism for dealing with it and ensuring that it will not happen again. Johnson & Johnson demonstrated the correct way to handle a crisis when in 1982 an unknown person(s) contaminated dozens of Tylenol capsules with cyanide, causing the death of eight people and a loss of $100 million in recalled packages for Johnson & Johnson. In 1986 a second poisoning incident forced J&J to withdraw all Tylenol capsules from the market at a loss of $150 million. The company abandoned the capsule form of medication and consequently had to redesign its production facilities. It also ran a series of ads informing the consumer of these changes, gave away free packages of the new product, and endeared the consumer through its honesty and quick action.

One of the results of the tragic Exxon Valdez oil spill. (Gamma-Liaison.)

In contrast, Exxon has suffered tremendous losses in revenue and good will because of the way it handled the Valdez spill, which occurred on March 24, 1989. Exxon antagonized its customers by denying responsibility for the Valdez oil spill. When the company finally admitted its guilt, it still failed to act responsibly by denying the severity of the disaster. Over 40,000 customers overtly responded by cutting up their Exxon gas credit cards and mailing the pieces to Exxon in protest. Various monetary settlements were proposed, ranging from the hundreds of millions of dollars to $1.1 billion dollars in an out-of-court settlement in April 1991. The state of Alaska did not want to accept even the latter.

Sometimes, in the case of natural disasters, prevention is not possible. However, there are instances when a carefully planned strategy is appropriate. A case in point is the $500,000 public relations campaign sponsored by Philip Morris USA warning marketers of children's products not to use Philip Morris trademarks. Philip Morris employed this strategy in an attempt to counter charges by antismoking groups that the company encourages young people to smoke.*

Lysol: Crisis Management in Action. Another example of a company that developed a strong public relations campaign to counter negative publicity is Lehn & Fink, the manufacturer of Lysol products. For 10 years beginning in 1978, Sterling Drug, Inc., and its Lehn & Fink Division struggled to protect their "Lysol" brand name of household disinfectants from claims that Lysol products contained dangerous chemicals. The problem began when a railroad tank car containing chemicals spilled into the backyards of dozens of homes near Belleville, Illinois. In the ensuing class action suit against Monsanto, the maker of the chemicals, a lawyer for the plaintiffs dramatized the danger of the chemicals by saying in court that they contained dioxin, "which is used in Lysol."

Lehn & Fink did not use dioxin in the manufacture of Lysol. To prove this, the company commissioned an independent laboratory to test its products and to verify that they did not contain dioxin. While these tests were being conducted, the company turned to its public relations agency to develop a program for dealing with the media. The concern was that statements about dioxin in Lysol would severely injure product sales.

The public relations plan identified a number of situations that might arise and set forth strategies for dealing with each one. Many statements and question-and-answer documents were prepared to address any possible results from the testing. As the case dragged on, the agency developed follow-up plans for possible new charges against Lysol.

The case finally went to summation in the fall of 1987. The Lehn & Fink public relations agency covered the closing arguments at the trial and provided each reporter at the proceedings with a statement correcting the misinformation about Lysol products.

The agency then tracked media stories about the trial to ascertain whether dioxin was still being connected with Lysol. Where this was the case, the company initiated additional media contacts to correct the misinformation. As a result, although the trial was covered by national media, every mention of Lysol included a statement that its manufacturer had conducted independent tests showing there was no dioxin in any Lysol products.

*Judann Dagnoli, "PM Warns Kids' Marketers," *Advertising Age* (July 16, 1990):41.

NONCOMMERCIAL ADVERTISING

noncommercial advertising *Advertising that is sponsored by an organization to promote a cause rather than to maximize profits.*

Thus far we have discussed public relations advertising employed by corporations and organizations that are motivated to increase profits or create a positive company image. This is not the only type of public relations. **Noncommercial advertising** is advertising that is sponsored by business or organizations that are not motivated by the maximization of profits. The emphasis in this type of advertising is on changing attitudes or behaviors relative to some idea or cause. This is not to say that these organizations operate cost-free. There are often pleas for donations in order to keep the organization going, but acquiring money is not the ultimate goal. Noncommercial advertising is typically sponsored by nonprofit organizations. Ad 19.4 is an example of a noncommercial ad that was sponsored by Aetna.

Nonprofit Organizations

Placing an organization in the nonprofit category is not simple. Although the Red Cross and the Salvation Army are clearly considered nonprofit, organizations such as the U.S. Postal Service are not as easy to classify. Ultimately, the only important classification dimension is a legal one. Section 501 of the Revenue Code grants tax-exempt status to 23 categories of organizations. Thirty-nine percent of these are covered under Section 501(c)(3), which includes charitable, religious, scientific, and educational institutions. Section 501(c)(4) of the tax code includes civic leagues; Section

AD 19.4
Noncommercial advertising is used to promote a cause, such as education through public television.
(Courtesy of Aetna Life & Casualty.)

501(c)(6) covers business leagues; and Section 501(c)(7) includes social clubs.

The government's rationale for giving these organizations special status is twofold. First, the concept of "public goods" argues that nonprofit organizations provide services, such as health care, education, and basic research, that would not be provided were it not for the tax subsidy. Second, nonprofit organizations provide "quality assurance" in that they furnish services in areas in which consumers are ordinarily ill-equipped to judge quality, such as health care and education.

In their book *Strategic Marketing for Nonprofit Organizations* Philip Kotler and Alan Andreasen contend that all advertising sponsored by nonprofit organizations falls into one of six categories:

1. Political advertising (local, state, federal)
2. Social-cause advertising (Drug-Free America, Planned Parenthood)
3. Charitable advertising (Red Cross, United Way)
4. Government advertising (parks and recreation departments, U.S. Armed Forces)
5. Private nonprofit advertising (colleges, universities, symphonies, museums)
6. Association advertising (American Dental Association, The American Bankers Association)*

Each of these six categories reflects a slightly different approach toward advertising. Political advertising, for example, has reached a very high level of sophistication and is guided by in-depth research and highly creative minds. Conversely, charitable and private organizations have limited funding and expertise and rely heavily on outside assistance and public service announcements. Ad 19.5 for the Army National Guard is an example of nonprofit advertising.

California Antismoking Campaign: A Case in Point. According to reports by California's chief health official, a 1990 antismoking campaign appears to have been successful. The total budget for the antismoking campaign was approximately $221 million, with $29 million designated for advertising. The series of ads that ran in the campaign were emotional as well as educational. Many of the ads depicted smoking as a nasty, filthy habit and portrayed tobacco industry officials as "merchants of death." These ads were part of a larger marketing campaign that health officials call the biggest offensive ever against smoking. The campaign was also the first to use marketing techniques funded by cigarette taxes to try to reduce and eventually eliminate tobacco use.

One of the commercials used the slogan, "The tobacco industry in its own words," and depicted industry officials talking about their products. The commercial ended by showing a sticker similar to the warning label found on cigarette packs, which read, "Warning: Some people will say anything to sell cigarettes." Other ads railed against vending machines and their use by children and teenagers. One in particular entitled "Smash Kids" was aimed at children between the ages of 6 and 10. The ad informed children that they are smarter than their parents because they don't smoke.

As of October 1990, the percentage of Californians who smoke had dropped from 25 to 21 percent since the antismoking campaign was implemented. A survey of 6,500 youngsters indicated that the percentage of students intending to smoke had decreased from 24.6 to 21.8 percent as well.[†]

*Philip Kotler and Alan R. Andreasen, *Strategic Marketing for Nonprofit Organizations*, 3rd ed. (Englewood Cliffs, NJ: Prentice Hall, 1987):544–545.
†Sonia L. Nazario, "California Anti-Cigarette Ads Seem to Reduce Smoking," *The Wall Street Journal* (October 31, 1990):B1.

AD 19.5
Military branches rely on nonprofit advertising to attract recruits.
(Courtesy of Army National Guard.)

*E*VALUATING PUBLIC RELATIONS

Measuring the effectiveness of public relations has been a problem, which is a major reason that public relations has not been accepted as an efficient and effective approach to behavior change. We need better standards for gauging the effectiveness of public relations efforts.

Evaluating public relations differs in several ways from evaluating advertising. One major difference relates to the lack of control public relations practitioners exercise over whether their message appears in the media and what it will look like if it does appear. Advertisers at least know the exact nature of their messages and the schedule of exposure to target audiences. Public relations practitioners must devote significant effort just to identifying and tracking the output of a campaign.

Public relations measurement may be divided into two categories: *process evaluation* (what goes out) and *outcome evaluation* (effect on the audience).

Process Evaluation

Process evaluation examines the success of the public relations program in getting the message out to the target audiences. It focuses on media and nonmedia approaches with such questions as:

- How many placements did we get? For example, how many articles were published? How many times did our spokesperson appear on talk shows? How much airplay did our public service announcements receive?
- Has there been a change in audience knowledge, attitudes, or reported behavior (as measured in the pre- and posttracking)?
- Can we associate actual behavior change (for example, product trial, repeat purchase, voting, or joining) with the public relations effort?

RECRUITING BLOOD DONORS

When the Blood Center of Southeastern Wisconsin found itself in peril of losing most of its donors, the Center was forced to reconsider how to conduct its operations. For some time, the Blood Center had conducted very successful mobile blood drives at local corporations. But a major shift in the economy of the region impelled many of the firms to move out of the area. How was the Center to obtain the blood it so urgently needed? It was clear that the Center would need to set up some permanent sites where donors could give blood. But what kinds of appeals would attract and retain the donors?

By good luck, the Blood Center was able to take advantage of a major lifestyle study about to be launched in the field. The Center asked the surveyors to include one special question: "How often in the past 3 years have you donated blood?" The Center was pretty convinced that sheer convenience of a site (at work versus away from work) was not really the key factor for regular donors. The hunch was that those people who would take the trouble to donate blood would turn out to be very different kinds of people from those who did not do so. The study compared the demographics, habits, attitudes, and outlooks of the willing donors with those of infrequent or nondonors. The results were intended to help the Blood Center design multiple campaigns to hold on to present donors and net a large number of new ones.

From a nationwide survey containing 1000 questions, it turned out that 80 percent of the respondents were nondonors; approximately 11 percent gave blood occasionally; and only 9 percent donated as frequently as 3 or more times a year.

What characteristics distinguished the faithful donors from the other two groups? And, in a very practical sense, what did these differences imply for the Center's outreach efforts?

The demographic profile revealed that frequent donors were younger, better off financially, better-educated, and more likely to live in two-income households with children than were infrequent or nondonors.

How did the steady donors invest their time and energy? It probably came as no surprise to the Blood Center to learn that those people were more involved in volunteer work, community and social activities, and more receptive to contributing money to local charities. All in all, these were busy, adventurous, self-confident individuals, who were politically and socially liberal. Unlike the two comparison groups, frequent donors saw themselves as leaders, as risk takers, and as people who weren't frightened by changes in the world around them. They liked adventure, movies, sports, shopping, cultural events, and do-it-yourself projects. And strangely enough, despite the fact that they were far more active than the infrequent or nondonors, the donor group felt far less pressed for time. Apparently, their myriad activities were quite satisfying to them.

With few exceptions, frequent donors were not very addicted to television programs, and they preferred to get their news from the papers and radio.

With the study data in hand, the Blood Center formulated some new policies that were intended to retain the more committed donors and to attract the more reluctant ones. It was clear that the lifestyle of the frequent donors *was* distinctly different from

Outcome Evaluation. Several difficulties are encountered in evaluating the outcome of public relations efforts. As with advertising, it is hard to assess the public relations contribution within a larger marketing communications mix. In fact, because public relations programs have smaller budgets and, presumably, more modest effects, results are even more difficult to isolate and measure than they are for advertising. In addition, unless the program is directly aimed at changing a specific audience behavior, such as product purchase, "success" is ambiguous and hard to ascertain. This is also true of "image" campaigns, such as corporate communications or community relations. How do you determine whether a public relations campaign has changed popular attitudes toward a product or an organiza-

that of the others, and certainly the Center didn't want to lose these people once the mobile stations had disappeared. Therefore, they set out to contact each of these donors personally to assure them how much their services were needed. Secondly, the nurses were given a special training program to make the whole experience a more personal and comfortable one. Thirdly, because the study had indicated that frequent donors had a predilection for greeting cards, the Center mailed thank-you cards to each person after the blood was taken.

How, then, to activate the people who weren't giving? One strategy was to design recruitment materials that would interest well-educated people because, according to the study, they would be good prospects. Instead of continuing to distribute simple and "cutesy" literature, the Blood Center prepared some more serious materials. For example, a brochure was circulated explaining what happened to blood after it was donated; another one described how specific children had survived emergencies only because sufficient blood had been available. With working couples in mind, the Blood Center instituted other measures: Donation hours were extended beyond the business day, specific appointments were offered, and the whole process was streamlined to cut down time required at the donation site. The Center also targeted such institutions as law firms, universities, and accounting firms, where better-educated people were likely to be employed.

In an effort to attract new sources of donors, the Blood Center turned to local high schools and encouraged the students to organize blood drives and recruit donors—not only fellow students, but their teachers and parents as well. Similarly, because steady donors envisioned themselves as leaders, the Center asked them to bring in their own friends and families to participate.

Local radio stations were persuaded to carry public service announcements. Direct mailings were sent to higher-income households and to employed workers. In view of the fact that frequent donors watched M*A*S*H (despite their predilection for radio), Alan Alda, star of the show, was asked to film donation appeals. He agreed to do so.

The results of these combined strategies were eminently satisfactory. Soon, the Center was supplying blood to other districts instead of depending on outside sources itself. The special effort to follow up and retain donors proved to be a useful tactic. Alda's participation produced an unusually favorable response. The appeal to leadership on a one-to-one basis brought in almost twice the number of donations. The Center had weathered the crisis and was sailing smoothly ahead.

Exercise: Can you think of any other factors or issues that would affect the public's willingness to give blood today? How about AIDS, for example? What specific fears and worries might the public have in mind? How could the recruitment drive handle these?

Source: *Use of Life Style Profiles for Recruiting Blood Donors*, DePaul University (December 12, 1988).

tion? And even if a positive change in awareness and attitudes is achieved, it is difficult to know whether these changes will lead to desired behaviors, such as receptivity to salespeople, donations, or a purchase.

Despite the problems associated with evaluating public relations, there is little doubt that carefully planned public relations works. The key here is to move public relations into the realm of professional management. Major public relations firms leave nothing to chance. They carefully identify target markets, establish appropriate objectives, and design and implement public relations strategies that are equivalent to the best advertising strategies. It is under these conditions that public relations complements advertising and vice-versa.

SUMMARY

- Public relations is a management function practiced by companies, governments, trade and professional associations, and nonprofit institutions.
- Advertising and public relations are separate activities, but the two work best when they are integrated.
- Both advertising and public relations use a number of different media. Public relations practitioners often have less control over their messages than do advertisers.
- Public relations activities can be performed by a department within a large organization or by a public relations agency.
- Public relations techniques can be divided into controlled media and uncontrolled media.
- Corporate advertising is implemented by organizations to enhance or change the firm's image.
- Managing crises is the responsibility of public relations.
- Public relations is similar to advertising in that it must be evaluated, although its direct effects on the audience are difficult to establish.

QUESTIONS

1. How does public relations differ from advertising? Does public relations offer advantages not available through advertising? Explain.
2. Define the concept of public opinion. Why is it so important to the success of public relations?
3. Dynacon Industries is a major supplier of packaging containers for industrial and food-service companies. Its research labs have developed a foam-polymer container with revolutionary environmental characteristics. The public relations department learns the trade and consumer press is unwilling to give the product the coverage the company needs. Public relations proposes that paid space (news and trade magazines) be used. The message will feature product background and the story about the environmental implications. Public relations argues that half the media and creative costs should be shared from the advertising budget. If you were in charge of these budgets, what would you recommend?
4. The chapter makes clear that prescription drug companies are supposed to be forbidden by law to advertise directly to consumers. However, Upjohn has run a campaign on hair-loss on commercial television. Similarly, CIBA-GEIGY has promoted an oral medication as an alternative to gallbladder surgery in daily newspaper ads. Is this considered legal because it is public relations (despite using paid space and time)? What difference should it make whether the consumer is reached through advertising or public relations?
5. Wendy Johnson and Phil Draper are having a friendly career disagreement before class. Wendy claims that she is not interested in advertising because she dislikes the "crass-commercialism" of promoting products and services that many people don't need. Phil counters by saying that public relations is doing the same thing by "selling ideas and images," and its motives are usually just as economic as advertising. If you overheard this discussion would you take Wendy's or Phil's side? Could you offer advice on ethical considerations of both careers?
6. Suppose your fraternity, sorority, or other campus group was planning a special weekend event on campus to raise public support and funds for a local charity. This will cost your organization time and money. Although contributions at the event will be some measure of the effectiveness of your public relations program, what other things could you do to evaluate the public relations activities?

FURTHER READINGS

CANTOR, BILL, *Inside Public Relations: Experts in Action* (New York: Longman, 1984).

KLIPPER, MICHAEL, *Getting Your Message Out: How to Get, Use, and Survive Radio and TV Air Time* (Englewood Cliffs, NJ: Prentice Hall, 1984).

LOVELL, RONALD, *Inside Public Relations* (Boston: Allyn & Bacon, 1982).

NAGER, NORMAN R., AND RICHARD H. TRUITT, *Strategic Public Relations Counseling* (New York: Longman, 1987).

WALSH, FRANK, *Public Relations Writer in the Computer Age* (Englewood Cliffs, NJ: Prentice Hall, 1985).

Green Consumerism: Trend or Fad?

Throughout the 1960s, 1970s, and 1980s U.S. firms grudgingly modernized production plants to reduce air and water pollution under the watchful eye of the Environmental Protection Agency (EPA). Throughout this period, companies generally resisted the government's attempts to reduce their air and water emissions because doing so generally increased production costs with no noticeable product benefit to the public and, thus, limited opportunities to justify price increases to recover the higher costs.

This situation has begun to change in the early 1990s. For those marketers who had not already recognized the potential of "environmentally sensitive" products, the broad popularity of the Earth Day anniversary and other ecologically-themed events reinforced the need to do more than just comply with government laws and regulations regarding environmental protection. Some of the more progressive firms, like Procter & Gamble and others, have begun not only to modify their products and packaging to be "kinder and gentler" to the environment, but they have actually begun to promote and advertise those changes to the public.

For the most part, these changes have been met with open arms by the public and the media. Procter & Gamble's downsizing of packages and concentration of products was an immediate hit, not only with consumers but also with the grocery industry, which found the products to be more cost-effective to warehouse and stock on shelves due to their smaller sizes. Even some grocery chains have publicly embraced the new "green consumerism," and many envision supermarkets of the near future with a "green aisle," stocked exclusively with products considered more beneficial to the environment.

Some marketers, however, have run into controversy and competition as they have pursued green-marketing strategies. For example, McDonald's, still smarting from critical media coverage of its revised, more nutritious menu, boldly announced to the press that it was removing all styrofoam containers from its restaurants in favor of paper containers. Arch rival Burger King responded with nationwide ads in newspapers sarcastically welcoming McDonald's to the environmental bandwagon, while noting Burger King had been utilizing purely paper-based packaging materials since the 1960s.

As more and more firms consider the costly capital investments necessary to make their products and packaging more environmentally sensitive, they are asking themselves if the green-consumerism movement will be a true long-term consumer trend or simply a fad. Marketing theorists generally describe four categories of consumer acceptance: styles, fashions, trends, and fads.

A *style* is a basic and unique method of public expression, such as tudor- or ranch-styles of homes and modern or abstract styles of art. Once a style is developed, it may last for a long period of time, often going "in and out of style."

A *fashion* is the currently accepted or popular style in a given area of expression. For example, rap music may be considered a fashion in today's popular music scene. Fashions tend to develop gradually, remaining popular for a period of time before beginning a gradual decline.

A *trend* is a long-duration fashion, one that is particularly good at addressing a public need or value. Recent examples of trends in U.S. consumer attitudes include the desire for nutritious, healthful foods and the fitness craze. Concern for the environment would also classify as a trend among the American public, although green consumerism is a relatively new phenomenon and thus, it is difficult to predict its longevity with accuracy.

Fads are fashions that come and go quickly in the public eye. They are usually adopted with great enthusiasm; however, they peak early and decline very rapidly. Fads are often adopted by individuals who wish to distinguish themselves from others or simply to have something to talk to others about. Fads generally do not survive because they do not satisfy a strong need or do not satisfy one very well.

Marketers can often inadvertently influence the pattern of these consumer-acceptance categories, similar to the situation currently developing in the healthy/nutritious food product categories. Specifically, many marketers anxious to capitalize on consumers' desire for healthy and nutritious foods have utilized liberal interpretations of the FDA's guidelines for food-product claims. Although the FDA is currently stepping up its response to firms it believes are violating their standards, the proliferation of "fresh," "no cholesterol," and "all natural" claims —many of which are unsubstantiated—may damage the credibility of all such claims in the food industry.

In the much less regulated area of environmental claims, the opportunity for a dramatic expansion of unsubstantiated claims exists. If this were to take place, it could help ensure that green consumerism does not survive beyond the fashion stage to become a true trend in and of itself.

QUESTIONS

1. Identify the key characteristics of a fad, a fashion, a style, and a trend, and provide current examples of each.

2. What are some of the characteristics of green consumerism, which could make it a trend?

3. What are some of the characteristics of green consumerism you believe will prevent it from becoming a true trend?

Sources: ABC News with Peter Jennings (January 23, 1990); and Philip Kotler, *Marketing Management,* 5th ed. (Englewood Cliffs, NJ: Prentice Hall, Inc., 1985).

20

Advertising Campaigns

Chapter Outline

RCA: Revitalizing a Brand
The Structure of a Campaign Plan
RCA: Changing Entertainment. Again
Evaluating the Campaign

Chapter Objectives

When you have completed this chapter, you should be able to:

- Understand the role of the situation analysis in identifying key problems to be solved by the advertising
- Understand how the basic strategy decisions are developed for an advertising campaign
- Analyze how the message strategy solves the key problem
- Explain how the media plan relates to advertising objectives and message needs
- Explain how the effectiveness of an advertising campaign is evaluated

RCA: REVITALIZING A BRAND

The RCA brand is the biggest seller of televisions in America, but it was threatened throughout the 1980s by Sony. Consequently, in 1986 RCA brand managers decided to begin a long-term effort to rebuild the brand's image by redesigning and redefining the entire product line and by bringing back Nipper the dog, the best-loved corporate icon in America. This "Threshold of Change" repositioning effort is just beginning to have an impact on the marketplace in the 1990s, so you can watch it as it develops.

In the 1960s and early 1970s RCA dominated the television market with its product innovations, high quality, and moderate prices. RCA was the undisputed market leader in consumer electronics. Its leadership was defined by the brand's invention of color television, its sheer size and presence in the marketplace, and its universal distribution and command of shelf space. In contrast, Japanese electronics companies were seen as making low-quality copycat products.

In the 1970s and 1980s RCA remained the absolute volume leader in televisions. However, its market share was steadily declining in a growing marketplace increasingly dominated by "Japan, Inc." RCA products were still selling well, but they were perceived as old-fashioned—the kind of televisions your grandparents would buy. Knowing that a company can't lose its technological and product-design edge and still maintain market leadership, in the mid-1980s RCA managers faced up to the fact that the company that had introduced television to America was stodgy and desperately needed resuscitation.

That is the local half of the RCA story; the other half is global. In 1985 General Electric and RCA announced a merger with the intention of helping to improve American competitiveness in worldwide markets. RCA's video-electronics business was two and a half times the size of GE's; the combined electronics division had sales of more than $3 billion, making it the largest consumer-electronics business in the country.

Then, in 1987, Thomson S.A., the French electronics giant, purchased GE's consumer-electronics business, including both the GE and RCA brands. Thomson is a major consumer-electronics company, with a $3 billion European business. Ultimately, however, to be big in television a company has to be big in the U.S. market because the U.S. video industry is still the dominant force in global electronics. By buying the GE and RCA brands, Thomson became a major player in the United States as well as in Europe and one of the largest color television companies in the world. It achieved a worldwide presence and the ability to compete head to head with Philips and products from the Far East in the rapidly changing European marketplace.

This chapter will use the RCA experience as an extended case study to explain the elements and steps in campaign planning. It will explain how the RCA brand managed its repositioning effort and will look specifically at the development of the 1990s' "Changing Entertainment" campaign that is part of a bigger effort to make the RCA brand more competitive in the global consumer-electronics market.

THE STRUCTURE OF A CAMPAIGN PLAN

In Chapter 7 we talked about the use of military metaphors for advertising planning. The word *campaign* is another military term adopted by the advertising industry. An **advertising campaign** is a comprehensive advertising plan for a series of different but related ads that appear in different media across a specified time period. The campaign is designed strategically to meet a set of objectives and to solve some critical problem. It is a short-term plan that usually runs for a year or less.

A campaign plan summarizes the marketplace situation and the strategies and tactics for the primary areas of creative and media, as well as the supporting areas of sales promotion, direct marketing, and public relations. The campaign plan is presented to the client in a formal business presentation. It is also summarized in a written document called a *plansbook*.

Scope of the Project. The Threshold of Change project represented a long-term effort by Thomson to bring together a new marketing strategy for the RCA brand. It involved analyzing and identifying the problems, setting up the infrastructure, designing and producing new products, and developing new marketing-communication programs.

The effort started in 1986 and continued through 1987. Phase I involved streamlining operations, reducing inventory, and generally fixing the business fundamentals. The goal was to stop share erosion. Phase II (1988–1989) involved heavy research and development (R&D) plus investment in manufacturing and engineering. The goal was to engineer a market-share turnaround. The hope in Phase III (1990–1992) was that, with the introduction of a new marketing-communications program, the impact of the turnaround would be seen in revitalized brands, a stronger consumer franchise, and the regaining of the industry leadership role for the RCA brand.

Situation Analysis

The first section of most campaign plans is a **situation analysis** that summarizes all the relevant information the agency has compiled on the product, the company, the competitive environment, the industry, and the consumers. This information is obtained using primary and secondary research techniques.

Consumer Analysis. The RCA brand was faced with a situation in which changing consumer lifestyles, attitudes, and interests had affected both how people watch television and what types of video products they use. The consumer profile of television buyers is changing. The largest segment of the U.S. population—the baby boomers—are now in their prime spending years (see Figure 20.1). The lifestyles of these home television viewers are changing dramatically in various ways:

- *Time:* As spare time shrinks, its value escalates. People increasingly want leisure options that give them optimum convenience, control, and flexibility.

advertising campaign *A comprehensive advertising plan for a series of different but related ads that appear in different media across a specified time period.*

situation analysis *The section of an advertising campaign plan that summarizes the relevant research findings about the company, the product, the competition, the marketplace, and the consumer.*

FIGURE 20.1
The 1990s consumer profile.
(Courtesy of Thomson Consumer Electronics, Inc.)

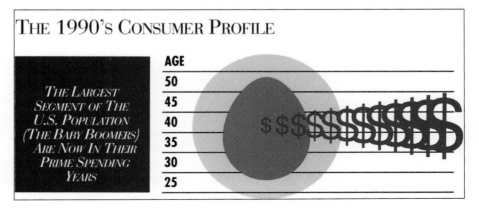

THE 1990'S CONSUMER PROFILE

THE LARGEST SEGMENT OF THE U.S. POPULATION (THE BABY BOOMERS) ARE NOW IN THEIR PRIME SPENDING YEARS

AGE
50
45
40
35
30
25

$ $$$$$$$$$$$

- *Fragmented Lives:* The increased number of two-worker and single-parent households means that people get involved in more volunteer activities and do-it-yourself projects. Americans today find themselves wearing a growing number of hats, with each activity demanding time and energy.
- *The Chore of Shopping:* Consumers don't want to deal with poorly informed, unenthusiastic salespeople who can't translate technobabble.
- *Quality and Service:* Consumers do want products that don't break down. And if they do break down, consumers want their products fixed fast, the first time, and at a time convenient to them.

Overall, today's consumers want a brand they know will perform up to their expectations and that won't require a degree in electrical engineering to operate. "User-friendly" has become the byword of consumer electronics. Simplified, easily understood controls are an absolute must. Size and storage convenience are also important.

There has been dramatic growth in home entertainment as well. Whereas the 1980s focused on redoing kitchens and bathrooms, the 1990s will emphasize media rooms: According to RCA research, 46 percent of consumers prefer staying home versus 28 percent who prefer going out. Of home activities, renting movies received the most votes, and there was $9 billion in movie rental business in 1989 compared to $5 billion in theater business. Furthermore, television viewing has increased 50 percent over the last 25 years.

Table 20.1 illustrates the facts of twentieth-century life. These data are important for marketers like RCA, who are trying to serve the needs of contemporary consumers.

Industry Trends. The size of the consumer-electronics industry tripled in the United States in the 1980s. The boom ended in the 1990s; however, future growth will come from niche products, such as outdoor televisions and bedside and other ultra-small televisions, as well as from emerging markets in other parts of the world. Although the 1980s saw enormous price increases for many major purchase categories in the United States, such as houses and cars, the price of televisions actually declined by 27 percent relative to the Consumer Price Index. Therefore, not only is the market declining, but consumer electronics are not as profitable as they were in the 1980s.

Furthermore, as lifestyles change, so do the products people buy. As people increasingly concentrate on in-home entertainment, sales of VCRs and camcorders are expected to continue to climb. Although sales of televisions are expected to remain approximately level, the *kind* of television

TABLE 20.1
The Facts of Twentieth-Century Life

Category	1900–1929	1930–1959	1960–1989	1990
How we entertain	Dinner party	Bridge party	Barbecue	VCR party
Where we shop	Main Street shops	Downtown department stores	Suburban malls	Catalogs
Essential appliances	Electric iron	Refrigerator/freezer	Dishwasher	Microwave oven
What changed home life	Automobiles	Television	Air conditioning	Electronics
Favorite gadget	Potato peeler	Can opener	Food processor	Remote control
Photography	Box camera	Brownie	Polaroid®	Camcorder
Leisure activity	Radio	Movies	Television	VCR
Favorite toy	Wind-up train	Electric train	Board games	Video games
Favorite game	Checkers	*Monopoly*	Scrabble	Nintendo
What schools emphasize	The 3 "R's"	Humanities	Science	Computers

purchased will shift dramatically to the larger table models and big-screen home theaters (see Figure 20.2). Already, nearly two-thirds of VCRs purchased are used primarily as playback devices for rented movies. As the quality and performance expectations of the home entertainment experience rise, more fully featured VCRs will play an important role.

In 1990 camcorder sales had increased nearly 30 percent over 1989 sales, with all the growth occurring in the compact formats. Convenient, fully featured, full-size RCA brand VHS and compact 8 mm camcorders are expected to meet the consumer demands of the 1990s.

The truth is that Americans consume more television than does any other population. The U.S. television viewer is the most knowledgeable in the world. That is why it is so important to dominate the U.S. market in order to maintain global leadership in the industry.

Perception of RCA.   The Threshold of Change repositioning effort involved a number of studies of both consumers' and dealers' perceptions of the RCA brand. The following list summarizes the research efforts made by Thomson to better understand RCA brand's position in this market.

- Television consumer brand awareness and reputation survey (October 1985).
- A qualitative study of brand imagery (June 1987).
- Color television dealership study (September 1987).
- Consumer-electronics brand-name research (October 1987).
- A qualitative study of RCA dealers' attitudes (February 1988).
- Brand-image study among consumers (February 1988).
- Home video dealer attitude survey (May 1988).
- Brand rub-off analysis: cross-product impact (September 1988).
- Dealer attitude study about television manufacturers (May 1989).
- RCA new-image campaign creative development (June 1990).
- Motivations and attitudes of early Proscan buyers (February 1991).

The studies found that during the late 1970s and early 1980s the RCA brand image was strong with older, traditional television buyers. Typically, these

FIGURE 20.2
Color television industry unit sales.   (Courtesy of Thomson Consumer Electronics, Inc.)

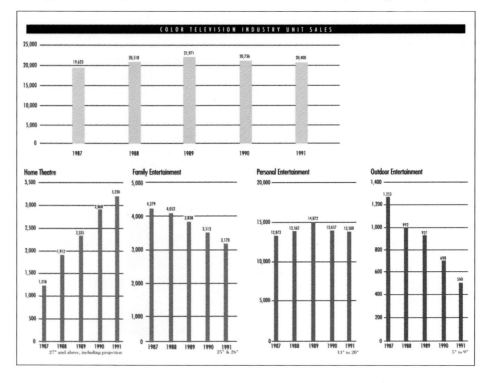

Simple Touch remote control.
RCA's new Simple Touch compact
remote offers control of all the
basic television functions in a
small, easy-to-hold shape. (Courtesy
of Thomson Consumer Electronics, Inc.)

buyers wanted a larger piece of furniture (described by many as Mediterranean-style wood consoles) rather than a television that was part of a larger media system. RCA's image was weaker with younger buyers, particularly those interested in more technologically advanced systems.

The studies also found that Sony had been successful in repositioning RCA as a mass-market, conservative, old-fashioned product, particularly among males, who were more interested than females in the advanced technological and engineering features of consumer electronics. Video enthusiasts and sophisticated buyers who like to assemble their own home-entertainment systems were particularly unimpressed by the old RCA. Because the bulk of video purchases in the 1990s will be by younger, predominately male buyers, the RCA brand decided it had to change its appeal and address the design and engineering concerns of the more technologically sophisticated buyer.

New Products. Research also found that consumers were looking for simplified operation, convenience, and enhanced performance. Consequently, Thomson created an entire line of easy-to-use consumer-electronics products for the RCA brands that would also give consumers state-of-the art technology. According to Louis Lenzi, manager of industrial design for Thomson, to enhance usability, the company worked with cognitive psychologists and a human factors design group to identify and solve the problems consumers have with technology. Some of the leading-edge products that evolved for RCA brand from this research were:

- The new, compact remote that offers all the basic functions of a remote in a small, easy-to-hold shape.
- RCA's convenient integrated storage system that complements many RCA Home Theatre and large-screen televisions, with matching built-in or optional storage systems.
- VCRs with VCR Plus+™ that can be programmed just by entering a simple code from the television listings section.
- RCA's SRS™ (Sound Retrieval System) that creates a fuller, richer, three-dimensional sound without the need for additional speakers.

**RCA televisions and storage
systems.** (Courtesy of Thomson
Consumer Electronics, Inc.)

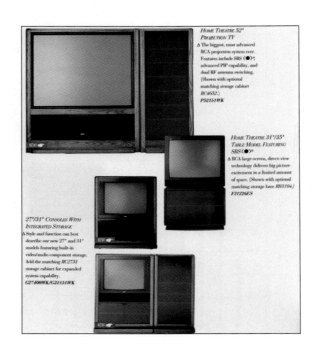

Now that the entire RCA brand reflected an increased focus on market-and consumer-drive product cues, such as ease of use, the product literature and advertising needed to reflect this new view of product marketing.

Trade. Nationally, RCA brand generates 50 percent more consumer traffic for retailers than does any other brand. Research shows that approximately one out of four consumers are considering RCA when they enter a store. That should have given RCA brand considerable clout in dealing with retailers, but there were some problems.

The consumer-electronics industry suffers from the same type of bloody war the food and grocery industry is undergoing. In these intensely competitive industries the retail environment is "overstored": There are too many stores and not enough customers. As a result, many department stores and independent stores are failing, and many of the hot retailers of the 1980s are in trouble. In spite of—or because of—this intense competitiveness, certain dominant retailers have become extremely powerful, and they are trying to "engulf and devour" their suppliers by demanding preferential treatment based on the volume of the business they generate.

RCA brand's retailers include Circuit City, Highland, and Silo. The RCA brand also receives strong support from department stores such as Sears, Wards, Federated, Allied, and May companies. Discount stores, such as K Mart and WalMart, carry the brand as well. Other support comes from wholesale clubs and warehouse merchants like Service Merchandise and Best, and mom-and-pop stores and small independent retailers have been traditionally strong supporters of the RCA brand.

Strengths, Weaknesses, Opportunities, and Threats (SWOT). The concluding section of the situation analysis is where the significance of the research is analyzed. Some plans include a section called "Problems and Opportunities"; others call it a SWOT analysis and look at the plan's *s*trengths, *w*eaknesses, *o*pportunities, and *t*hreats. The strengths-and-weaknesses discussion compares the product or brand with the competition, and the opportunities-and-threats discussion analyzes the brand's situation in the marketplace. These sections serve as a transition that leads directly into the key strategic decisions that will form the foundation of the campaign plan.

In terms of strengths and opportunities, consumer research has shown that a large percentage of consumers who own a brand that has served them well stick with that brand because of their positive experiences. The RCA brand, therefore, is in an enviable position. It has the largest consumer base in the color television industry (nearly 25 percent of the market) and in the VCR industry (nearly 12 percent of the market). Furthermore, as Figure 20.3 shows, more RCA owners repurchase RCA than any other brand.

The key marketing communication problem, then, is how to rebuild the brand's image to make the biggest and best-selling consumer-electronics brand appeal to a younger, more technologically sophisticated audience without losing the traditional market. RCA was viewed as the leader by consumers 40 and over, but those under 40—the opinion leaders and volume buyers—perceived RCA as behind the Japanese brands in technology and design. Furthermore, retailers often emphasized Japanese brands over RCA to consumers.

The strategy for the Threshold of Change repositioning effort and the Changing Entertainment campaign was to focus on a multifaceted marketing challenge. Competition dictated that RCA brand update its product in terms of design and technology. The brand would also need to bring this

FIGURE 20.3
Color television/VCR brand repurchase. Source: Trendata.

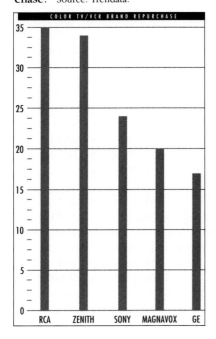

perception of change to both its loyal, older customers and influential, younger customers, as well as to rally retailers behind its new efforts.

Campaign Strategy

After the situation analysis and the SWOT analysis, most advertising campaign plans focus on the key strategic decisions that will guide the campaign. These decisions were discussed in detail in Chapter 7; they include such activities as specifying the objectives, targeting the audience, identifying the competitive advantage, and locating the best position for the product or brand. They are fundamental decisions that are relevant for all areas of marketing-communication planning, from the creative plan to the media, sales promotion, and public relations plans.

Selling Strategy. Consumers are changing, the industry is changing, and the RCA brand has responded by changing its entertainment offerings. Today's video user wants more than just the latest gadget at a good price. Consequently, RCA brand needed to focus its message on the needs of the marketplace, selling customers on how its video products provide the enhanced entertainment options suited to their lifestyles.

Objectives. The objective of this campaign strategy, then, was to position the RCA brand as providing new directions in entertainment for today's consumer. To fulfill this objective, the advertising's goals were to maintain and extend RCA's key strength—its image of warm, traditional reliability—while at the same time updating this image to be immediately relevant to the important younger electronics consumer.

Target Audience. The RCA brand target audience for the Changing Entertainment campaign was specifically defined. Demographically, the target audience consists of adults aged 35 to 54, with a household income of $30,000 and over and some college education. Psychographically, these consumers are audio/video enthusiasts and entertainment seekers, who lead activity-filled, time-pressured lives and maintain a global perspective on issues.

There are some differences between television and camcorder buyers, with older males more likely to buy Home Theatre televisions and younger, slightly more affluent consumers more likely targets for camcorders. The media buys reflect these differences.

Competitive Advantage and Positioning. A product's position refers to how it is seen in the marketplace by the target audience. This perception is based on the product's position in the consumer's mind relative to the competition and is strongest when built on an important competitive advantage. *Competitive advantage* lies in those product features that are important to consumers—areas where the product or brand is strong and its competition is weak.

Research determined that the RCA brand leads in consumer awareness and brand preference for both color televisions and VCRs. Furthermore, the brand has the largest customer base in the industry, with approximately 25 percent of the market. This translates into a strong competitive advantage for the RCA brand, based on both past experience with the brand and its perceived image of quality and long-time leadership. In other words, the RCA brand name and all that it stands for is a more important competitive advantage than design, engineering, technology, and product features.

Because of this long-time favorable brand image, RCA brand holds a strong position in consumers' minds. Thirty percent of consumers think of RCA when they think of color television or VCR; half of these consumers are likely to buy RCA. The brand is high on most consumers' list of choices or evoked set of brands, but the brand image is primarily one of conservative and traditional quality.

The position statement of the newly redesigned and redefined RCA brand product line—"we are selling enjoyment"—reflected the change from product-oriented to consumer-oriented marketing. This philosophy moved the brand's position beyond quality—which was no longer the tie-breaker but now merely the price of admission to the category—to what video products really mean to the consumer, which is entertainment and enjoyment.

*R*CA: CHANGING ENTERTAINMENT. AGAIN

Creative Plan

Finding the right creative approach is the most important part of the advertising plan. The creative approach is expressed through the message strategy—the campaign theme or creative concept, as well as the way the theme is developed across various executions for different features, product lines, and media.

Message Strategy. The RCA campaign during the 1990s focuses on the changing environment of home entertainment. The copy emphasizes consumer benefits, like enjoyment, rather than product features, and is intended to focus attention on things like convenience and ease of use, which appeal most to consumers. The campaign also addresses specific copy points, such as innovative but user-friendly technology (VCR Plus, Master Touch remote control, Simple Touch remote control) and new, technologically advanced product lines (the Home Theatre series, Laser disc player, 8 mm Camcorder). Ad 20.1 is an example of copy that addresses these particular points.

With the RCA brand, high-technology consumer electronics have at last become user-friendly for the average person. Thomson's global research and development resources have concentrated on making the RCA brand consumer electronics not only the most technologically advanced, but also the easiest to use.

Campaign Theme. The Changing Entertainment campaign developed by the Ammirati & Puris advertising agency uses several strong brand-building devices. The famous RCA symbol of Nipper the dog—used as the corporate logo since 1929 with the old Victrola illustration and the slogan "His master's voice"—embodies the best of RCA's imagery. According to Bruce Hutchison, the national advertising manager for Thomson, Nipper was brought back to reassert the RCA market leadership image. The problem was *how* to bring the symbol back. Although it represents quality and trust, it can also say "old-fashioned" and "out-of-date"—which is a problem for a brand that is trying to reposition itself as a leader in technology and design. The decision was to use Nipper as a symbol of expertise and at the same time to develop a new symbol to represent the spirit of change.

The result was a pup identical to Nipper, only smaller, as a symbol of the new generation of innovation. The cute pup has all of the visual charm

AD 20.1

The 8mm Giant. This ad for the RCA Pro 850 8mm Camcorder emphasizes simplicity and advanced technology in the copy.

(Courtesy of Thomson Consumer Electronics, Inc.)

traditionally associated with puppies and kittens. At the same time, it represents the future—the new RCA and the new product lines—as well as optimism and excitement. It immediately communicates to consumers that something is different. It also appeals to the element of playfulness that is an important aspect of the "enjoyment" position (see Ad 20.2).

In addition, the new campaign slogan "Changing Entertainment. Again" was used to crystalize the message and reinforce the image of RCA brand as innovative. The phrasing was very important: It is a line that only a leader would or could use. In other words, it is a statement of preemptive leadership, which represents all the innovations that RCA has brought to the television industry—for example, introducing consumer television in the 1930s and color television in the 1950s.

Executions. Five 30-second television commercials were included in the Changing Entertainment campaign, each focusing on a different product or feature. All were made available as regular commercials or as 25-second local television spots that could be customized by the dealer to add store names and locations. All of the ads depicted the product as hero. They shouted "Technology!" and the dogs provided a touch of humor.

The campaign also included five radio spots that described various products and product features. These could also be customized with a local dealer tag. One of the radio spots, which tied in with a special promotion, announced the "Name That Pup" contest for Nipper's sidekick, which will be described in more detail later in the chapter.

The tie-in opportunities of Nipper and friend provided an unexpected bonus. Sears, for example, has used the dogs in its own consumer electronics spots. (The pup was named Chipper in late 1991.)

In addition to the broadcast advertising, ads were run in major con-

AD 20.2
Nipper and pup. Nipper was joined by a new friend in the early 1990s to symbolize the new generation of innovation. (Courtesy of Thomson Consumer Electronics, Inc.)

sumer magazines. Strong graphics and copy focused readers' attention on product benefits. Each ad featured Nipper and his sidekick with some quip or playful comment. The ads all concluded with the campaign slogan, "Changing Entertainment. Again."

Calendar

In terms of annual campaign planning, RCA's product year is from August to August. The sell-in (introduction to sales staff and distributors) begins in May with the national sales meeting and continues through the summer for the new line that becomes available in the fall. The first numbers indicating the campaign's success become available after December, when the retailers begin reordering.

Media Plan

In 1991 approximately $25 million to $30 million was allotted for the media budget, nearly twice as much as was spent on advertising in 1990. Because of the need to support new-product introductions as well as to communicate the leadership positioning message, RCA's media plan was designed to emphasize reach first, then frequency. Two strategic peaks in flighting the media schedule were called for in the media plan to provide continuity throughout the strongest consumer electronics sales periods:

- *September:* Get retailers excited after the long summer hiatus; introduce the new product line.
- *Post-Thanksgiving:* Establish Christmas-shopping frame of mind.

Vehicles The media strategy was to concentrate on high-profile sports and entertainment vehicles for the following reasons:

- Sports effectively delivers the male audience.
- Sports can filter down through all aspects of advertising and promotion.
- Entertainment vehicles provide a balance of female consumers.
- Sports and entertainment are merchandisable and will capture retailer attention as well.

Broadcast commercials ran in conjunction with sports events, such as the NCAA basketball tournament in May, the fall football coverage of NFL and NCAA college games, and sports programming on cable from January through March. Ad 20.3 is an example of an ad designed to appeal to sports enthusiasts. The print schedule called for ads in *USA Today, Business Week, People, Sports Illustrated, U.S. News & World Report, National Geographic, Omni, Entertainment Week, American Baby,* and *Parenting.* Trade publications included *Blockbuster, HFD, Dealerscope Merchandising, Video Magazine, Video Review,* and *A/V Interiors.* Details of the vehicle selection and activity are shown in the media flow chart in Figure 20.4.

Delivery Analysis Breakdowns showing the reach, frequency, and impressions for both television and print during the two strategic peaks are shown in Table 20.2.

Integrated Marketing Communications

The RCA brand Threshold of Change plan is a fully integrated marketing communications effort that carries through several subcampaigns. In the words of the RCA brand general manager, "the campaign is seamless." It

AD 20.3

Sports publications were a primary vehicle of the Changing Entertainment media plan. (Courtesy of Thomson Consumer Electronics, Inc.)

FIGURE 20.4

Thomson Consumer Electronics RCA division 1991 media plan. (© 1985–1990 Media Plan, Inc.:14.)

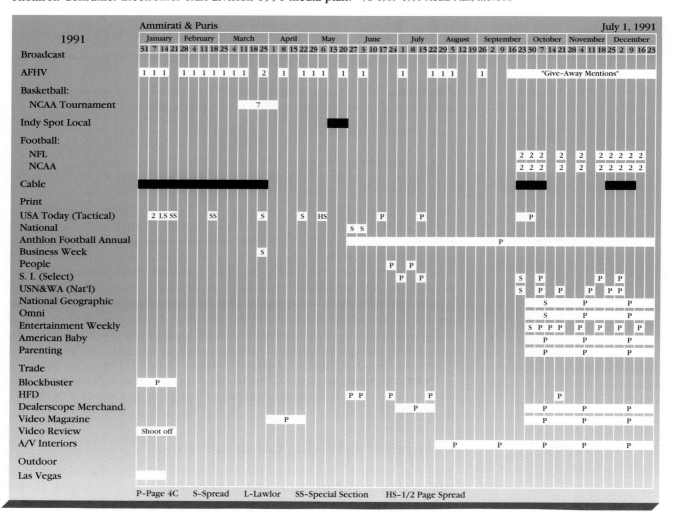

TABLE 20.2
RCA Delivery Analysis

September–December: Adults 35–54 with Income of $30,000+			
	Television	Print	Combined
Reach / Frequency ratio	50/7.0	49/3.7	75/7.1
Impressions (thousands)	159,352	76,488	235,840
Male / Female ratio*	64/36	57/43	62/38
January–December (Cumulative): Adults 34–54 with Incomes of $30,000+			
	Television	Print	Combined
Reach / Frequency ratio	78/11.0	62/4.4	92/12.3
Impressions (thousands)	392,460	113,853	506,313
Male / Female ratio*	55/45	56/44	55/45
*Goal: 60/40.			

has one message—RCA is changing home entertainment—and a coordinated strategy that is conveyed through all media (consumer and trade advertising, sales promotions, public relations, catalogs, point-of-sales materials, and sales training and support materials). The Changing Entertainment campaign also makes one graphic statement: All the support materials for the different areas were designed by the Pentagram design firm to reinforce the campaign message visually.

Special Promotions. To build consumer identification a contest was designed around the familiar image of Nipper and his lovable puppy sidekick. Nearly everyone loves a pup, so this contest was expected to have strong positive appeal. The RCA "Name That Pup" contest associated the brand with the exciting new spirit of RCA Home Theatre products, ease of use, and family entertainment and fun. The national contest was conducted through the spring and summer of 1991, using print and radio advertising, and all those who entered received a stuffed pup as a premium.

The RCA brand retailers were able to boost floor traffic by tying in to the national contest. Sales-support materials contained the "Name That Pup" merchandising kit, entry cards, and other point-of-sales materials, including stuffed animal likenesses of both Nipper and the pup, to generate customer interest.

The drama of home theater was showcased with tie-ins with major national sporting events, such as the Indy 500, the PGA tournament, major league baseball, and NFL football. These events generate excitement and sales opportunities for seasonal promotions. By choosing major sporting events for advertising and merchandising focus, the campaign was expected to reach a large audience with the right demographics to be attracted to the technologically innovative but easy-to-use line of RCA consumer electronics. Sponsoring an Indy 500 team, for example, matched the brand with the excitement, intensity, and technology of modern car racing.

Public Relations. During the campaign the RCA brand consumer-electronics products were the subject of the most intensive public relations coverage the company had ever experienced, in both print and broadcast media. Opportunities included stories on NBC's *Today Show* as well as features in *The Wall Street Journal, USA Today, Chicago Tribune, Home Furnishings Daily,* and *Business Week,* among others. The "Name That Pup"

Nipper and the pup— immortalized. (Courtesy of Thomson Consumer Electronics, Inc.)

FIGURE 20.5
RCA's free brochure on how to
build a home theater. (Courtesy of
Thomson Consumer Electronics, Inc.)

contest generated a great deal of media coverage as well as a barrage of consumer responses. The number of entries jumped from 6,000 to 24,000 after a publicity campaign that included, among other things, a 5-minute segment on the *Today Show* in May 1991.

Direct Response. A special promotion built around the Home Theater product line invited people to respond to a television spot by calling an 800 number and asking for a free brochure. The brochure explained what it takes to build a home theater—in other words, how to integrate other equipment into an RCA system (see Figure 20.5).

Merchandising and Dealer Support. Trade advertising in electronics industry journals was used to tell retailers how the RCA brand is changing. These ads focused on the products' ease-of-use features. The ads also explained the marketing support, point-of-sales materials, national promotions, advertising support, instruction manuals, and the interactive video store displays.

The interactive video display called Info Theatre was a first for the industry. Info Theatre is a point-of-sales display that uses the product itself—the 35-inch large-screen television—with a laser-disc player with a microprocesser to demonstrate the capabilities of the Home Theatre Series. The program works from a menu, and the customer selects various features to explore using either of the new Master Touch or Simple Touch remote controls.

The RCA Merchandising Planner
(Courtesy of Patrick Reynolds.)

Sales Support. In order to be successful a campaign must have tremendous impact on all of the employees behind the new product lines. The most critical group of employees is the sales staff, of course, and a complete sales support campaign was developed as part of the Changing Entertainment campaign.

An impressive multidimensional sales piece called "Strategy in a Box" was created to capture the entire marketing and advertising strategy of the Changing Entertainment campaign for the sales staff to use in explaining the program to retailers. The box contained three full-color brochures summarizing the brand strategy, product highlights, and marketing communication program. Another set of full-color brochures explained the various product lines, such as Family Entertainment and Home Theatre. Also included were spec sheets, merchandising planners, and order sheets. A series of small brochures called PockeTalk summarized the details and specifications of the product features and other products not explained in the product line brochures. In addition, the box contained slicks of the print ads and a videotape and audiotape of the television and radio commercials.

*E*VALUATING THE CAMPAIGN

The Changing Entertainment campaign was accomplished by constant monitoring, including monthly tracking studies by phone. Every element was tested in development and evaluated after it ran. The real test, however, according to RCA brand general manager Mehrotra, would be the number of RCA products placed on dealers' floors and, ultimately, carried into consumers' homes.

As of the summer of 1991, the campaign had completed the most successful sell-in in the brand's history. Initial consumer feedback indicated that the commercials significantly outperformed previous RCA advertising, as well as advertising by key competition, with the following results:

- 90 to 95 percent unaided recall

- 72 to 80 percent opinion about brand improved
- 72 to 91 percent total "liking" of the spots

The Thomson Consumer Electronics marketing communication commitment behind the RCA brand is the most comprehensive, well-coordinated, and impactful program the company has ever put together. It had to be if it was to have any chance of succeeding in its goal of turning the brand around. As never before, RCA brand is trying to create a sales, advertising, and merchandising approach that links products, dealers, and consumers in a way that redefines the entire concept of home entertainment. The RCA brand hopes this new campaign will erase its old stodgy image and reposition the brand as innovative and as a leader in producing products that meet the needs of consumers.

SUMMARY

- The situation analysis includes primary and secondary research findings about the company, product, competition, marketplace, and consumers.
- The strategy section of a campaign plan identifies the key problem, the advertising objectives, the target audience, the competitive advantage, and the position.
- The creative plan includes a theme, or creative concept, and variations, or executions, for different media, situations, and times of the year.
- The media plan includes media objectives, media selection, geographic strategy, timing schedules, and a budget.
- Research for an advertising campaign includes concept and execution testing, as well as postevaluation that evaluates the campaign against its objectives.

QUESTIONS

1. Develop a research proposal in outline form for a program that you would recommend to evaluate the effectiveness of the most current campaign for Pepsi, Coca-Cola, Burger King, or McDonald's.

2. A key element in any situation analysis is previous research. It appears that much of the RCA background was based on primary research done with dealers. Why would the emphasis be in trade research rather than consumer research?

3. The target audience for the RCA brand is described as "adult" (men and women). Do the strategies and tactics appear to be directed to both? Creatively, which elements are male-oriented, and which are female oriented? Why isn't there greater female emphasis in the media selections?

4. The RCA brand shows a strong determination to stress product benefits instead of product attributes or consumer-need orientation (motives). Which are the benefits emphasized? Do you agree that the ben-

efit segment is the strongest way for RCA to reposition itself?

5. Strategically, the RCA campaign walks a "tightrope." This difficult position means that, on one hand, it seeks to assure RCA brand loyals that the company intends to maintain its traditional reputation (quality and dependability). At the same time, it also wants to present a new (leading-edge) image to those who feel that RCA is behind the times. Were both themes used in the creative strategy? Explain with examples. Were both handled effectively?

6. The obvious way to evaluate the effectiveness of this campaign would be to monitor sales results. What other evaluation activities should the agency recommend for the advertising and public relations efforts? Specifically, what measure would you recommend to determine if the new creative did reposition the RCA image?

FURTHER READINGS

AAKER, DAVID A., AND JOHN G. MYERS, *Advertising Management,* 3rd ed. (Englewood Cliffs, NJ: Prentice Hall, 1987).

ANDREWS, KIRBY, "Communications Imperatives for New Products," *Journal of Advertising Research* 26 (1986): 29–32.

HOGAN, BOB, "Print's Place in the Media Mix," *Inside Print,* March 1987, pp. 39–42.

SCHULTZ, DON E., *Strategic Advertising Campaigns,* 3rd ed. (Chicago: Crain Books, 1990).

VIDEO CASE

NEW YORK

Virgin Market for Virgin Atlantic Airways

Despite the failure of several small transatlantic airlines based in Britain, British entertainment mogul Richard Branson created Virgin Atlantic Airways with a single 747 plane in 1984 and began service from Newark to London. From 1984 to 1990 Virgin expanded its routes to include Miami and other major airport routes. By late 1989 Virgin identified Los Angeles International Airport (LAX) as a key expansion route. Unlike the east coast airport introduction, however, few west coast flyers had ever heard of the airline and even fewer knew that Virgin flew to London. Furthermore, London was not as frequent a destination for west coast leisure and business travelers as it was for easterners, and London-bound travelers from the west coast already had an existing choice of more established carriers, such as American Airlines, British Airways, Continental, Pan Am, and TWA.

To crack the tough Los Angeles market, Virgin Atlantic asked its advertising agency, Korey, Kay & Partners, to create awareness and generate word-of-mouth about Virgin Atlantic Airways' new LAX to London route. The airline's key goal was to achieve load factors—the occupancy rate of existing seats on an aircraft—equal to the 65 percent industry average within the first 12 weeks of operation.

The creative strategy was designed to introduce Virgin as the "entertainment capital of the sky to the entertainment capital of the world"—Los Angeles. To stand out, the ads were also designed to be totally unlike those for conventional airlines. The creative capitalized on Virgin's essentially unknown founder and his unique and adventuresome character as a trend-setting, entertainment entrepreneur. While never revealing Branson's identity, the creative addressed the airline's origin in the entertainment industry and how it translated into the art of entertaining Virgin's passengers. Thus, the agency attempted to position Virgin as a new flying experience, one that would bring new excitement to international travel.

The target audience for Virgin was identified as adults 25 to 54 years of age, with household incomes of over $25,000, who are business travelers and/or leisure travelers to London. The target was further defined as trend-setters in the Los Angeles area. Virgin's annual share of total airline advertising in the Los Angeles market was estimated to be about 5 percent. By condensing the media exposure into a 12-week introductory period, however, Virgin was projected to achieve a 30 percent share of voice during its introduction.

The campaign results were overwhelmingly successful. Virgin exceeded its goal of 65 percent load factors during the first week of operation and consistently hovered above the 90 percent mark after approximately 6 weeks. Within 3 weeks of the campaign's start in March 1990, telephone calls to Virgin's reservation agents were up by 1,000 calls per day, a 40 percent increase. Because overall seating capacity in the United States increased by only 30 percent during this period, load factors for Virgin increased by an adjusted 78 percent during the first 4 weeks of the operation's start.

Advertising tracking study results revealed that after 4 months of advertising in the Los Angeles market, one in four transatlantic passengers were aware of Virgin's advertising. Approximately one-third of the target audience recalled that Virgin flew to London. After only 3 months, advertising awareness attained levels reached in prior expansion route regions after 3 years of media exposure.

QUESTIONS

1. Based on your existing knowledge of traditional airlines advertising, what key elements separate Virgin's advertising from those of other airlines?

2. What elements of the Virgin advertising campaign in Los Angeles would be appropriate for use in other markets, and which elements do you believe would be inappropriate for use in other markets?

3. Given that Virgin's primary emphasis was on transatlantic passengers and its ads emphasized the entertainment value of the flying experience over reliability, service, or other traditional airline benefits, do you feel the demographic target defined by Virgin was appropriate?

Source: Courtesy of Korey, Kay & Partners.

21

Evaluative Research

Chapter Objectives

When you have completed this chapter, you should be able to:

- Explain why advertisers devote time and money to research
- Distinguish between evaluative and diagnostic research
- Identify the eight major evaluative research methods and what each one claims to test
- Evaluate the strengths and weaknesses of various forms of testing
- Understand the concerns surrounding the issues of validity and reliability

WHY CAN'T CANNES AGREE?

Every year the International Advertising Film Festival (also known as the Cannes festival) attracts more than 3,700 entries from all over the world. Because it confers the most prestigious awards in all of advertising, and because it is held in Cannes, on the French Riviera, it also attracts most of advertising's creative stars.

The 23 Cannes judges are leaders of major international advertising agencies, who narrow the entries to a short list, then select winners in each product category through lengthy, sometimes acrimonious debate. The top commercial in each category receives a "Gold Lion." The Grand Prix, the "best of show," of all categories is advertising's most coveted award.

Although the Cannes festival is the world's top advertising competition, it is punctuated by disagreement. The judges disagree with one another. The attendees disagree with the judges' decisions; sometimes they even throw vegetables at the screen. For weeks after the festival the advertising trade press prints caustic comments from critics who didn't like the outcome of the contest.

The Cannes festival is not atypical. A judge of the One Show—a U.S.-based event similar to the Cannes festival—had this to say about the entries:

> It was like going through thousands of garbage cans looking for something to eat.
>
> Judging is always painful. But this year, it made you sick to your stomach.
>
> There was little, if any, movement creativity. With a few minor exceptions, the work was a bad imitation of what has gone before.
>
> The same old ground, the same old foot-prints. You read this stuff, watched this stuff, hour after hour, day after day, and you got mad.
>
> It was insulting. A horrendous waste of money.*

Disagreements among creative directors are matched by disagreements between agencies and their clients. Agencies insist that their work merits at least an A+. Typically, clients are not so sure. They want the most effective advertising they can get. Maybe some other approach would work even better. Maybe the present approach will not work at all.

evaluative research *Research intended to measure the effectiveness of finished or nearly finished advertisements.*

Faced with such conflicts of opinion, many advertisers turn to evaluative research. Here, the term **evaluative research** means research used to make final go/no-go decisions about finished or nearly finished ads, as distinguished from the *strategic research* described in Chapter 6, which is used to test strategies and different versions of a concept or approach. Advertisers who use evaluative research hope that it will provide a definitive measure of effectiveness, and that it will eliminate the risks and conflicts inevitable with decisions based on judgment alone.

The stakes are high. By the time an average 30-second commercial is ready for network television, it has cost more than $200,000.† If the commercial is run nationally, its sponsor puts several million dollars behind it. Furthermore, careers are on the line. Brand managers and advertising managers are rewarded for successes and punished for failures. At the agency the reel—a collection of commercials "authored" by an individual writer, art director, or producer—(or in the case of print ads, the portfolio) is both the key to salary increases and the passport to professional respect.

*Dan Wieden, "Blue Penciling a Year of Creative," *Adweek* (June 10, 1991):12.
† Stuart Elliott, "Advertising," *The New York Times* (June 13, 1991).

Ideally, the results of evaluative research would be available before large sums of money have been invested in finished work. Failing that, the best alternative is a test that predicts effectiveness before millions of media dollars have been spent in purchasing space or time. Test results may even be useful after an advertisement has been placed. Sales may fall, or they may not increase as rapidly as expected. Is the advertising at fault? Would sales be better if the advertising were "working harder"? Although earlier is always better, advertisers may feel a need to test their advertising anywhere along the line.

*E*VALUATIVE RESEARCH SUPPLIERS AND METHODS

Evaluative research suppliers are listed in the American Marketing Association's *International Directory of Marketing Research Companies and Services,* which we described in Chapter 6. Most major advertisers have a favorite supplier and a favorite research method; a few use proprietary methods of their own (methods that have been developed by, and are used exclusively by, one advertiser). Some of the best-known evaluative research suppliers are listed in Table 21.1

This list is by no means exhaustive. Many other research companies offer some form of copy testing, including qualitative, in-depth interviews, and focus groups. The question is: Which (if any) of the evaluative research methods really work?

Although every supplier is in some way unique, all use copy-testing methods that fall into eight major categories: (1) memory tests, (2) persuasion tests, (3) direct-response counts, (4) communication tests, (5) focus groups, (6) physiological tests, (7) frame-by-frame tests, and (8) in-market tests. Of these eight types, memory, persuasion, communication, and focus groups are the most widely employed.

*M*EMORY TESTS

Memory tests are based on the assumption that for an advertisement to affect behavior, it must leave a mental "residue" with the person who has been exposed to it. One way to measure an advertisement's effectiveness,

TABLE 21.1
Suppliers of Evaluative Research

Supplier	Medium	Methods
ASI Market Research, Inc. New York, NY	Television, print	Recall Persuasion
Bruzzone Research Co. Alameda, CA	Television	Recognition
Burke Marketing Research Cincinnati, OH	Television, print	Recall Persuasion In-market sales
Communications Workshop, Inc. Chicago, IL	Television, print, radio	Communications Test
Diagnostic Research, Inc.	Television, print, radio	Communications Test
Gallup and Robinson, Inc. Princeton, NJ	Television, print	Recall Persuasion
Information Resources, Inc. Chicago, IL	Television	In-market sales
Starch INRA Hooper, Inc. Mamaroneck, NY	Print	Recognition

therefore, is to contact consumers and find out what they remember about it. Memory tests fall into two major groups: *recall tests* and *recognition tests*.

Recall Tests

recall test *A test that evaluates the memorability of an advertisement by contacting members of the advertisement's audience and asking them what they remember about it.*

The company most commonly associated with recall tests is Burke Marketing Services, which conducts day-after recall (DAR) tests. Gallup and Robinson's In-View Service is another recall test designed to show which ads best capture and hold attention. In a traditional **recall test** a finished commercial is run on network television within a regular prime-time program. The next evening interviewers in three or four cities make thousands of random phone calls until they have contacted about 200 people who were watching the program at the exact time the commercial appeared. The interviewer then asks a series of questions:

- Do you remember seeing a commercial for any charcoal briquettes?
- (If no) Do you remember seeing a commercial for Kingsford charcoal briquettes? (Memory prompt)
- (If yes to either of the above) What did the commercial say about the product? What did the commercial show? What did the commercial look like? What ideas were brought out?

The first type of question is called *unaided recall* because the particular brand is not mentioned. The second question is an example of *aided recall,* where the specific brand name is mentioned. The answers to the third set of questions are written down verbatim. The nature of these questions is important. Interviewers do not ask, "Please tell me about all the commercials you remember seeing on television last night" or "Please tell me about any charcoal briquette commercials you remember." The test requires that the respondent link a specific brand name, or at least a specific product category, to a specific commercial. If the commercial fails to establish a tight connection between the brand name and the selling message, the commercial will not get a high recall score.

The traditional recall test has many variations. In one variation interviewers prerecruit people to watch a specified program and recontact only those respondents the following day. This method saves research costs and eliminates the need to make a huge number of random phone calls to find 200 viewers who happen to have been watching the program on which the test commercial appeared. Another method exposes respondents to commercials in a theater setting. The respondents are then telephoned at home 24 or 72 hours later. In a third variation respondents are prerecruited to watch a program telecast on local cable television. The latter two methods are popular because, unlike recall tests that employ network television, they can be used to test rough executions.

Analyzing Test Results. Recall test results are analyzed by examining the verbatim responses (verbatims) to determine how many viewers remembered something specific about the ad. If an answer indicates that the viewer was merely guessing or remembering other advertising, that viewer is not counted toward the recall score. Furthermore, even though some recall test verbatims are surprisingly detailed, many are so sketchy that it is hard to be sure the respondent was remembering a specific ad. Here are four typical verbatims. Which prove recall of the specific commercial being tested?

1. The guy was in his backyard, I think, and he was using them. I'm not really sure about that. The guy was using them in his grill.

2. I think they grilled a steak. I just remember it was Kingsford. They were grilling a steak.

3. They showed the bag of charcoal. It was fast lighting. I think it said it burned evenly.

4. I remember numerous grills in the commercial.

5. I remember, I think it was the one with big letters, with reference to the professionals, what the professionals use. I thought it was a pretty good advertising scheme. Amateur chefs like to think they're professionals. It was mostly the big letters. I remember a guy with a chef's hat on, smiling real big. I think the guy had dark hair. It was sort of a quick, not a subliminal thing but everything flashed real quick, the big letters, sort of a rapid fire approach. Just all I remember was that line, what the pros use.

Typically, anywhere from zero to 60 to 70 percent of viewers are counted as having proved recall. The average recall score for a 30-second commercial across a range of product categories is about 20 percent. In other words, about one in five of those who view a commercial can recall something about it the following day.*

Print Ad Recall Tests. When recall tests are used to evaluate magazine advertisements, respondents who have read the magazine go through a deck of cards containing brand names. If the respondent says, "Yes, I remember having seen an advertisement for that brand," the interviewer asks the respondent to describe everything he or she can remember about the ad. As in a television recall test, answers are taken down verbatim and studied later to determine whether the respondent was remembering the specific advertisement being tested.

Assessing Recall Tests. Recall tests have several advantages over other memory methods. First, they have been around for a long time, almost since the beginning of national advertising. Advertisers are accustomed to using them—for some advertisers, they have become part of the corporate culture, an ingrained tradition.

Second, because recall tests have been so popular, research companies that conduct them have accumulated *norms*—records of results that serve the same purpose as batting averages. Norms allow the advertiser to tell whether a particular advertisement is above or below the average for either the brand or its product category. Without norms the advertiser would not know whether a score of 23, for example, is good, bad, or average. Like students, commercials are graded with reference to others in the category being tested.

Reliability   A third advantage of recall tests is **reliability.** In this context, the term *reliable* means that the commercial gets essentially the same score every time it is tested. Reliability is important because, like all test scores, recall test scores incorporate a certain amount of random measurement error. Measurement errors are due to differences among interviewers and among the programs or magazines that carry the advertisements, as well as a host of other factors that influence test results and vary from time to time. When the amount of measurement error is high, as it is in some of the more qualitative methods of evaluating advertisements, scores vary from test to test—a high score this time, a low score the next time, a medium score the time after. When results are inconsistent, the test obviously is not dependable.

Although recall tests are not perfectly reliable, they are more reliable

reliability *A characteristic that describes a test that yields essentially the same results when the same advertisement is tested time after time.*

*David W. Stewart and David H. Furse, *Effective Television Advertising* (Lexington, MA: DC Heath & Co., 1986).

than most tests. That fact alone helps to explain why they remain popular with advertisers.

Validity   Reliability is only one measure of the value of a copy test. An advertiser who uses a recall score is assuming that the score reflects the ad's ability to sell the product. At first glance, it might seem obvious that the most effective advertisements would make the most indelible impressions. Yet everyone can remember advertisements for brands they never use, and everyone uses some brands without being able to remember any advertising for them. The real question is whether there is a strong positive relationship between the ad's overall score and some later assessment of its sales effectiveness.

validity *The ability of a test to measure what it is intended to measure.*

The technical term for what we are discussing is **validity.** When an advertiser uses a recall test, the advertiser is assuming that the recall score is a valid indication of the advertisement's sales effectiveness. Many researchers, and most of advertising's creative leaders, however, believe that this assumption is incorrect.

In general, when recall tests are used to measure an ad's effectiveness, most research executives are not as outraged as creative executives might be. However, many research leaders have expressed their own doubts about the relationship between recall and effectiveness, and some believe that this relationship cannot possibly be high:

> "We know that recall data are inherently weak. We know that the theory on which recall data are based is shaky. We know that the evidence for the validity of recall is—to be charitable—checkered. We may not know the answer to the longest playing controversy in all of marketing research, but we know what the answer is not—and it's not recall."*

Cost   Recall tests are not inexpensive. On the average, television recall tests cost from $9,000 to $17,000 per commercial; and print recall tests cost from $7,000 to $13,000 per ad. These costs limit the number of advertisements that an advertiser can afford to test.

PRINCIPLE
In spite of much research, the relationship between day-after recall scores and sales effectiveness is still unknown.

Recall Tests and Decision Making.   If recall tests are costly and if their validity is unknown (to say the least), why do so many advertisers use them? One reason is that recall is a relatively reliable measure of *something*, and many advertisers believe—despite all evidence to the contrary—that that something must be related to advertising effectiveness. It just seems logical that a well-remembered advertisement will, on average, be more effective that will an advertisement that leaves little detectable impression in the viewer's mind.

But the most fundamental reason that advertisers continue to use recall tests is that they help them make decisions. As we noted earlier, the decision to run or not to run an advertisement affects the careers of everyone involved and triggers the expenditure of very large marketing resources. Aware of the consequences, and beset on all sides by doubts and conflicting opinions, decision markers need something to help them justify their decisions. In so tense a setting, a recall test—or any other test that has been sanctified as part of corporate dogma—can play a decisive role even when no one is really sure that the test is any good.

*Lawrence D. Gibson, "If The Question Is Copy Testing, The Answer Is Not Recall," *Journal of Advertising Research* 23 (1983):39–46.

Recognition Tests

One way to assess an advertisement's effectiveness is to ask people to recall it. Another way is to show the advertisement to people and ask them if they remember having seen it. The latter kind of test is generally called a **recognition test.** Like recall tests, recognition tests were first used to evaluate print advertising. One of the earliest, and still one of the most popular, is named after its inventor, Daniel Starch. Ad 21.1 is an example of a test the Starch Advertisement Readership Service conducted to test two different approaches to automobile advertising.

The Starch Test. The Starch test can test only print ads that have already run. After verifying that the respondent at least looked through the magazine being studied, the interviewer proceeds page by page, asking whether the respondent remembers having seen or read each ad.

In the magazine used in the interview, each ad is assigned an item number and is broken down into component parts (such as illustration, headline, logo, or main body of print) that are identified by codes. Figure 21.1 shows the various components as they are measured by the Starch test. If the respondent says he or she remembers having seen a specific ad in that particular issue, the interviewer then asks a prescribed series of questions to determine exactly how much of the ad the respondent saw or read. The Starch procedure produces three scores:

AD 21.1
The Starch test revealed that Ad A (left) was remembered better than Ad B (right) when these two versions of the same ad were placed in separate issues of *Business Week.* (Courtesy of Starch INRA Hooper.)

1. *Noted:* The percentage of respondents who say they noticed the ad when they looked through the magazine on some previous occasion.
2. *Associated:* The percentage of respondents who said they noticed a part of the ad that contains the advertiser's name or logo.
3. *Read Most:* The percentage of respondents who reported reading 50 percent or more of the ad copy.

FIGURE 21.1
An example of a Starch test of a well-known ad. (Courtesy of Starch INRA Hooper and IBM.)

Assessing the Starch Test. Compared with a recall test, the Starch test has some valuable advantages. First, because the questions are easier, the Starch interview proceeds more rapidly. A faster interview allows more advertisements to be tested, which in turn lowers the cost per advertisement. Starch tests cost $500 per ad, much less than the cost of recall tests. Lower cost implies a better investment of the advertiser's research resources.

Norms Like recall tests, the Starch test has been in use for many years, and the research supplier has accumulated norms that help interpret individual test scores. The Starch test's norms now include many different product categories. This specificity makes interpretation more precise.

Reliability The Starch procedure is very reliable. Repeated evaluations have shown that Starch scores are remarkably consistent. In fact, in the print medium Starch tests are substantially more reliable than are recall tests.

FOREIGN AND DOMESTIC CAR OWNERS

A nationwide study on car ownership revealed some basic data about the population of car owners. The study found that 72 percent of Americans owned domestic cars only, 19 percent possessed foreign cars only, and just 9 percent owned both types of cars at the same time. What do the personal opinions, activities, purchasing styles, media habits, and background characteristics of these people tell us about the differences between foreign and domestic car owners?

Research reveals quite a few surprises about the foreign car owner. This person is apt to be female, under 35, and either single or divorced. Not only has she graduated from college, but she has most likely attended graduate school as well. Most probably, she lives in a large metropolitan area in the Pacific region. She sees herself as a career woman and works full time in a professional or managerial position, earning a pretty good salary. Two out of three of these women earn at least $30,000 a year, and one out of two has an income over $40,000. Being more affluent than the typical domestic car owner does not mean that she necessarily feels content with her salary. However, she does assume that in the future she will probably be more financially comfortable that she is at present. In fact, she has a pretty positive outlook on life in general and is convinced that her greatest achievements are yet to come.

The foreign car owner's buying style is not a cautious one. She will be the first to buy that new electronic product, perhaps even on a whim, although she is far more careful about buying major items. She would by no means restrict either small or large purchases to American-made products. She has no compunctions about using a bank credit card; unlike the domestic car owner, she doesn't feel she should necessarily pay cash for her purchases.

This woman is willing to take calculated risks in the investment realm. High interest rates are considerably more appealing to her than is the sheer safety of an investment. She relishes the speed of the sports car, but she is neither a wild driver nor a wild purchaser. On the contrary, she is a thorough shopper, searching for the best price. She is also far more concientious about using her seat belt than is the domestic car buyer. Although she will probably have mufflers, shock absorbers, and spark plugs changed at a specialty shop, she's not adverse to doing some of this work herself.

She is generally more liberal than the American car buyer. For instance, she thinks television advertising for contraceptive products is quite desirable, and she is in favor of legalized abortion. Moreover, she does not agree with the domestic car owner that the government should excise more control over television content. As you might predict, the foreign car owner is not a believer that a woman's place is in the home. She is all for the women's liberation movement.

Not surprisingly, the foreign car owner likes to travel and to see foreign places, and she travels more frequently than do domestic car owners. Television is not her primary mode of entertainment, but she does like to watch rented movies on her VCR. She enjoys all types of music, with the exception of country-western. Active sports, such as cycling and swimming, appeal to her, and she is likely to attend exercise classes or work out at a health club. No matter what her chronological age, she has a youthful, adventurous, and optimistic outlook.

Exercise

1. Knowing what you do about foreign car owners, which of the two versions of the Peugeot ad in Ad 21.1 do you think would be more effective? Why?

2. If you were marketing auto parts or auto services, how would you tailor your advertising specifically to female foreign-car owners? How would you evaluate its effectiveness?

Source: Adapted from DDB Needham Worldwide, *A Lifestyle Profile of Foreign and Domestic Car Owners* (July 1989).

Validity   In experiments on the Starch method some respondents have claimed recognition of unpublished advertisements they could not have possibly seen. These experiments show that claimed recognition is not a perfectly valid measure of memory and that something else is probably at work.

Subsequent investigations have suggested that when a Starch respondent says, "Yes, I looked at that ad when I went through the magazine," he or she is really saying, "Ads like that usually attract my attention." When the Starch respondent says, "I didn't look at that ad," he or she is saying. "I usually ignore that kind of advertising." If that interpretation is correct, as many researchers believe, a Starch score actually represents a kind of consumer vote on whether that advertisement is worth more than a passing glance.* Therefore, although the Starch test is not solely a measure of memory, it is an unusually reliable measure of something. That something is probably attractiveness, a quality most advertisers want in their advertising. Given that conclusion, and given the cost of the Starch procedure, the Starch test continues to be widely used.

The Bruzzone Test. A television analogue of the Starch test is offered by the Bruzzone Research Company (BRC). The Bruzzone test is conducted through the mail. Consumers receive questionnaires that show scenes from television commercials along with the scripts, but minus the brand names (see Figure 21.2). The questionnaire asks whether they remember having seen each commercial before. If the answer is "yes," the respondents are asked to identify the brand and to rate the commercial on the basis of a short checklist of adjectives. This procedure produces a recognition score for each commercial, along with a brief assessment of how many respondents liked it and how many thought it said something relevant to their needs.

The Bruzzone test has many of the same advantages as the Starch test. The scores it produces are quite reliable. Compared with other television copy-testing methods, it is relatively inexpensive—about $1,450 per ad. The research supplier also has accumulated norms that help the advertiser interpret scores. The Bruzzone test also shares the Starch test's principle drawback, however: It cannot be used until after all the costs of final production and placement in the media have already been incurred.

PERSUASION TESTS

persuasion test *A test that evaluates the effectiveness of an advertisement by measuring whether the ad affects consumers' intentions to buy a brand.*

The basic format for a **persuasion test,** or attitude-change test, is this: Consumers are first asked how likely they are to buy a specific brand. Then they are exposed to an advertisement for that brand. After exposure, they are again asked about what they intend to purchase. Results are analyzed to determine whether intention to buy has increased as a result of exposure to the advertisement.

Types of Persuasion Tests

Research companies that conduct persuasion tests often invite consumers to a theater to see a "preview of a new television show." They use this pretense because they do not want respondents to pay undue attention to advertising before coming to the testing session and because they want to minimize artificial attention to the commercials once the testing session has begun.

Before the audience members see the program, they fill out a questionnaire that asks about their preferences for various brands. They then watch a television program, complete with commercials, after which they

*Herbert E. Krugman, "Point Of View: Limits Of Attention To Advertising," *Journal of Advertising Research* 38 (1988):47–50.

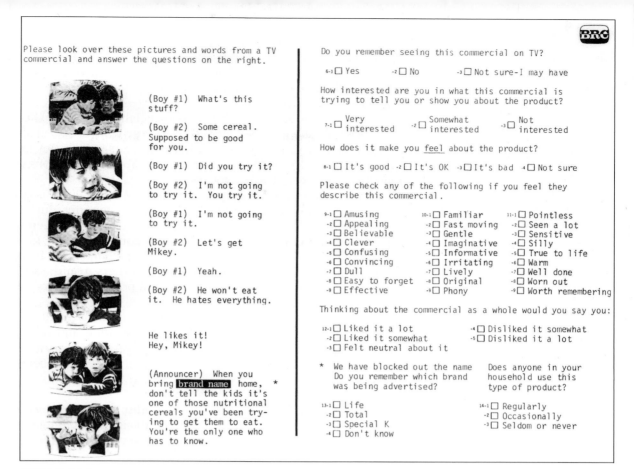

Please look over these pictures and words from a TV commercial and answer the questions on the right.

(Boy #1) What's this stuff?

(Boy #2) Some cereal. Supposed to be good for you.

(Boy #1) Did you try it?

(Boy #2) I'm not going to try it. You try it.

(Boy #1) I'm not going to try it.

(Boy #2) Let's get Mikey.

(Boy #1) Yeah.

(Boy #2) He won't eat it. He hates everything.

He likes it! Hey, Mikey!

(Announcer) When you bring brand name home, * don't tell the kids it's one of those nutritional cereals you've been trying to get them to eat. You're the only one who has to know.

Do you remember seeing this commercial on TV?

6-1 ☐ Yes   -2 ☐ No   -3 ☐ Not sure-I may have

How interested are you in what this commercial is trying to tell you or show you about the product?

7-1 ☐ Very interested   -2 ☐ Somewhat interested   -3 ☐ Not interested

How does it make you feel about the product?

8-1 ☐ It's good -2 ☐ It's OK -3 ☐ It's bad -4 ☐ Not sure

Please check any of the following if you feel they describe this commercial.

9-1 ☐ Amusing	10-1 ☐ Familiar	11-1 ☐ Pointless
-2 ☐ Appealing	-2 ☐ Fast moving	-2 ☐ Seen a lot
-3 ☐ Believable	-3 ☐ Gentle	-3 ☐ Sensitive
-4 ☐ Clever	-4 ☐ Imaginative	-4 ☐ Silly
-5 ☐ Confusing	-5 ☐ Informative	-5 ☐ True to life
-6 ☐ Convincing	-6 ☐ Irritating	-6 ☐ Warm
-7 ☐ Dull	-7 ☐ Lively	-7 ☐ Well done
-8 ☐ Easy to forget	-8 ☐ Original	-8 ☐ Worn out
-9 ☐ Effective	-9 ☐ Phony	-9 ☐ Worth remembering

Thinking about the commercial as a whole would you say you:

12-1 ☐ Liked it a lot   -4 ☐ Disliked it somewhat
-2 ☐ Liked it somewhat   -5 ☐ Disliked it a lot
-3 ☐ Felt neutral about it

* We have blocked out the name   Does anyone in your
  Do you remember which brand   household use this
  was being advertised?   type of product?

13-1 ☐ Life   14-1 ☐ Regularly
-2 ☐ Total   -2 ☐ Occasionally
-3 ☐ Special K   -3 ☐ Seldom or never
-4 ☐ Don't know

FIGURE 21.2
Bruzzone Test Questionnaire. (Courtesy of Bruzzone Research Company.)

answer questions concerning their reactions to the entertainment. They then respond to the brand-preference questions again.

At the beginning of the session most members of the audience believe that their major task will be to evaluate the entertainment. Before the session is over, however, most respondents have figured out that the commercials are the research company's principle interest. Although some respondents react negatively when they realize their cooperation has been secured through false pretenses, most go along with the instructions and give their opinions willingly.

Like recall tests, persuasion tests come in several varieties. In one variation, respondents are telephoned at home and requested to watch a program at a certain time. During the course of the recruitment interview they are asked about their brand preferences. After the program has been telecast, they are recontacted and asked about their brand preferences again. Another method exposes respondents to commercials only, without program material. The procedure is basically the same in all such variations: pretest–exposure–retest, with a comparison of purchasing intentions before and after exposure to the advertisement.

Assessing Persuasion Tests

Audience Composition.   The validity of a persuasion test depends in part on whether participants in the experiment constitute a good sample of the prospects the advertiser is trying to reach. A dog-food advertiser, for example, would not be interested in responses from people who do not own dogs. That requirement creates a problem because, unless the audience has been specially recruited to contain only dog owners, many of the responses in a typical persuasion test audience will come from people who are not purchasers of the product.

Audience composition becomes especially important when the target audience is relatively small. Denture wearers, heavy users of pain relievers, and potential buyers of expensive European cars will be tiny minorities of the audience in any normal persuasion test. Yet their reactions are the only reactions the advertiser really wants.

In addition to control costs, persuasion test suppliers usually evaluate five or six commercials in different product categories during the same testing session. This means that even if the audience has been recruited to match the requirements of one product category—dog food, for example—it will not match the requirements of the other commercials being tested. It is highly unlikely that an audience of dog owners would also be denture wearers, heavy users of pain relievers, and potential buyers of expensive European cars.

Because perfectly appropriate samples are so difficult to get, advertisers are tempted to ignore audience composition and to take findings from the entire group, regardless of how many people in it are really potential buyers. An understandable decision, but to anyone concerned with validity, wrong.

The Environment.   Further threats to validity are created by the exposure situation. The theater setting is a highly artificial environment. To what degree do reactions in the theater setting correspond to reactions that would occur at home?

Brand Familiarity.   When the advertisement being tested is for a well-known brand, the amount of change created by one exposure to one commercial is almost always very small, and small changes tend to be unreliable. When changes are small, the advertiser cannot tell whether the difference between two commercials is small but real or is due to some random combination of factors that accidentally affected the results.

The small size and consequent unreliability of persuasion test scores for well-known brands is an important limitation. Advertisers of well-known brands are heavy users of evaluative testing. Yet the better known the brand, the less likely the persuasion test will be a dependable measure of its advertising's effect.

Cost.   Persuasion tests are usually expensive. A typical persuasion test costs between $11,000 and $15,000, and if special efforts to recruit a hard-to-find sample are required, the cost can go much higher. Some persuasion test suppliers provide recall test scores and information about attitudes toward the advertisement for the overall cost of a persuasion testing session, however, so the advertiser can get useful information in addition to the ad's persuasion score.

Protest.   Naturally, creative directors do not like persuasion tests any more than they like recall tests. When, for example, the Carnation company decided to compensate its agencies through a formula based in part on persuasion test scores, creative directors predicted the end of the world. One said, "It's the end of creativity, the end of anything meaningful or right in the advertising business if this isn't laughed out of the business quickly." Another said, "I think it's insane. There's going to be a lot more commercials that are good for [research companies] and less that are good with the consumer."*

Research executives have been less vehement. Although audience composition, the environment, and brand familiarity pose serious threats to persuasion test validity, evidence has shown that, when persuasion tests are competently conducted, scores are positively related to sales effectiveness —especially for advertisements that have something new and important to say about the brand.†

Despite all the arguments against persuasion tests, advertisers continue to use them for the same basic reason they continue to use recall tests: The tests help them make very difficult and very important decisions. Advertisers reason that even though the tests are not perfect, they provide some objective information. When conflicting arguments intrude from every side, some objective information is a lot more reassuring than none at all.

DIRECT-RESPONSE COUNTS

direct-response counts *Evaluative tests that count the number of viewers or readers who request more information or who purchase the product.*

Some advertisements request a direct response, via an 800 number in a television commercial or an 800 number, a coupon, or an offer embedded in the body copy of a print ad. Instead of depending on memory or persuasion, the advertiser relies on a direct count of the number of viewers or readers who request more information or who actually buy the product. **Direct-response counts** are sometimes called *inquiry tests.* This name is not quite accurate, however, because, increasingly, the counts are of actual sales rather than of inquiries.

In some cases, direct-response advertisements are split run—different versions bound into alternate copies of newspapers or magazines. Because each version has its own code on the reply coupon or its own box number in the return address, the advertiser can tell exactly which ad produced the best results. Compared with recall tests and persuasion tests, few reliability or validity problems plague this type of evaluative research.

Of course, direct-response counts cannot be used to test all advertisements. Most ads are intended to encourage purchase at a retail outlet—an automobile showroom, a supermarket, or a department store, for example. When the purchase is a retail purchase, the direct connection between ad and purchase is lost, and no one can tell which purchaser responded to which, if any, of the advertiser's ads. The box entitled "Television's Longest-Running Spot" takes a closer look at how direct-response evaluation saved one ad.

COMMUNICATION TESTS

The communication test described in Chapter 6 is sometimes used for final evaluation as well as for diagnostic research. Advertisers who are not convinced that recognition, recall, or persuasion are adequate measures of an ad's effectiveness, and who can't rely on direct-response counts, may settle

*Marcy Magiera, "Admen Question Carnation Plan," *Advertising Age* (March 13, 1989):4.
†Anthony J. Adams and Margaret Hendersen Blair, "Persuasive Advertising and Sales Accountability: Past Experience and Forward Validation," Advertising Research Foundation 35th Annual Conference, New York City, April 1989.

TELEVISION'S LONGEST-RUNNING SPOT

Because direct-response counts provide an exact measure of an ad's effectiveness, they can keep a very effective advertisement in circulation long after the ad might ordinarily be judged to have worn out.

A good example of an extremely long-running direct-response television advertisement is a commercial for "150 Music Masterpieces," first aired in 1968. It made a profit for 15 years for the client, Vista Marketing, and its agency, Wunderman, Ricotta & Kline, grossing $25 million and garnering 2.5 million orders of the five-record sets of abbreviated musical themes. (The average direct-marketing album commercial sells a half million sets.) The commercial cost only $5,000 to produce.

In "150 Musical Masterpieces" actor John Williams says, "I'm sure you recognize this lovely melody, 'A Stranger in Paradise,' but did you know the original theme is from the 'Polovetsian Dance No. 2' by Borodin? Ah, it's a priceless introduction to the classics that will enrich every home." Directed at fans of Lawrence Welk, Roy Rogers and Dale Evans, and Jackie Gleason, the 2-minute commercial remained relatively unchanged over the years, with the exception of the tagline announcing the price. Originally offered at $5.95, by the mid-1980s the albums sold for $12.95 and the tapes for $14.95. John Williams's part of the taping took only 3 to 4 hours, for which the late actor received residuals for the next 15 years, amounting to between $250,000 and $500,000.

The history of this commercial has become a case study in the use of direct marketing. In the New York market it first ran about 150 times a week for 2 years. Spot time was bought in all major markets. After the fifth year, research revealed that the commercial was no longer receiving the kind of response it had been getting, so it was shelved for a

The late John Williams: His commercial lives on.   Courtesy of *Adweek* (May 16, 1983):20.

few months. Direct-response evaluation indicated, however, that there were certain times of the day and stations that still worked well for the ad, and so it was brought back into particular spots and advertised on such shows as the syndicated *Merv Griffin Show* and other programs that appealed to older women, such as daytime game shows.

Had this commercial been an advertisement intended to encourage retail purchases, it probably would have been judged "worn-out" after its first few months. Because Vista had an exact record of the ad's effectiveness, however, it stayed on the air and continued to work. This case raises an interesting question: How many commercials that have not had the advantage of direct-response evaluation have been discarded while they were still in the prime of life?

Source: Adapted from Maria Fisher, "TV's Longest-Running Spot: 15 Years and Still Selling," *Adweek* (May 16, 1983):20.

for answers to the three basic communication questions: Did the ad deliver the message it was intended to deliver? Did the ad deliver any messages it was *not* intended to deliver? How did the representatives of the target audience react to the message, the characters, the situation, and the tone? Although the answers to these questions are a far cry from definitive measures of sales effectiveness, they obviously are important. Some major advertisers have decided that answers to these questions are about the best evaluation they can get.

Memory test scores, persuasion test scores, and direct-response counts are final grades that can be quickly interpreted as good, bad, or indifferent, pass or fail. In contrast, communication tests do not give single scores, but rather patterns of findings, which require detailed analysis and interpretation of consumers' reactions to the advertisement. This quality is both a disadvantage and an advantage. On the one hand, it increases the unreliability caused by subjective interpretation. On the other hand, it provides richer, more detailed information about how consumers reacted to the ad.

FOCUS GROUPS

Focus groups, described in detail in Chapter 6, are sometimes used to make final go/no-go decisions about television commercials and print ads. The results of focus group testing can be virtually instantaneous—three or four groups can be conducted and reported on in less than a week. Furthermore, compared with recall tests, persuasion tests, and even communication tests, focus groups are relatively inexpensive, costing usually less than $5,000 per ad.

Focus groups can be extremely unreliable, however. Because the events that transpire during an informal conversation depend on the particular individuals who happen to be in the group, and because group moderators differ so widely in interviewing tactics and leadership style, different groups can arrive at entirely different evaluations of the very same advertisement. In principle, this randomness could be balanced out by conducting a large number of focus groups with independent moderators. In practice, because conducting a large number of groups would cancel out the time and cost advantage of this method, advertisers often settle for only one or two. This practice leaves the fate of the advertisement up to the luck of the draw.

This shortcoming is especially dangerous when focus groups are used for final evaluation. When focus groups are used for diagnosis, as described in Chapter 6, their outcomes are combined with many other elements, including the collective experience of the agency and the client and other campaign research. When focus groups are used for final evaluation, having the results of a few possibly erroneous groups may be decisive, and their seemingly convincing findings may be entirely wrong. Advertisers who use focus groups for final evaluation put far too much weight on weak evidence. Although focus groups for final go/no-go decisions is a growing practice, it is a very dangerous one.

PHYSIOLOGICAL TESTS

All of the methods discussed thus far require consumers to make verbal responses: Do you remember seeing a commercial for a detergent? As you were looking at the commercial, what thoughts or ideas went through your mind? Which brand do you intend to buy? The value of those questions depends on the respondents' ability to observe their own reactions and to report those responses accurately and thoroughly.

Aware of the shortcomings of verbal response, investigators have tried to use **physiological tests** to evaluate emotional reactions to ads. They

physiological tests *Tests that measure emotional reactions to advertisements by monitoring reactions such as pupil dilation and heart rate.*

SOME THINGS I THINK I KNOW ABOUT STUDYING TELEVISION COMMERCIALS

JOHN S. COULSON

John Coulson is a former vice president in charge of research at the Leo Burnett agency and a partner in Communication Workshop, Inc., a creative and marketing research company that specializes in developing and evaluating new products and corporate communications. In both capacities he has evaluated numerous television commercials. The following observations are based on his research experiences.

Courtesy of John S. Coulson.

1. No single set of measurements will serve to evaluate all commercials. A commercial is a very complex communication with many different goals. It is part of a total advertising program that is part of a total marketing program. Studying it out of context can produce highly irrelevant information.

2. A key element in the results of a commercial test is the type of people among whom the commercial is being studied. Some people are more receptive to a particular brand's advertising than are others. For example, product and brand users are generally more receptive to a message about that brand than are nonusers. Trier-rejecters show even less interest and acceptance. Generally women are more accepting than men, older adults are more accepting than younger adults, and children are more accepting than adults.

3. The most basic rule for achieving a successful commercial is that its viewers be able to identify the product and brand being advertised. Occasionally a competitive brand is misidentified as the advertiser. To be sure that the brand is correctly identified, it must be an integral part of the story line of the commercial rather than an element that is out of synch with the rest of the commercial.

4. The commercial's ability to create brand or product recall is largely independent of its effect on the viewer's attitudes toward the brand or product. Recall is a measure of how well the commercial is communicating its message. It is related to the commercial's *efficiency* rather than to the *effectiveness* of its communication.

5. One effective commercial format is to provide news that is relevant and important to viewers. Information about a product can be news to the public for a long time, particularly if it can be given a fresh twist. Advertisers frequently feel that news is stale long before the public does.

6. When the objective of the commercial is to provide news, the news should be seen as important and relevant to the way the consumer uses the product, it should be believable, and it should be unique to the brand being advertised. Otherwise the commercial will be less effective.

7. The measurement of believability is tricky. If there is no news in the commercial, it tends to be rated as believable. Also, the believability of the message in the commercial is not always important to the commercial's success. If the product is relatively low priced, consumers might purchase it just to test the claim that they found difficult to believe in the commercial.

8. A basic problem of advertising with the goal of providing news is trying to cover too many ideas. It is more than twice as difficult to deliver two ideas as it is to deliver one, and the attempt to deliver three or four ideas almost always produces a jumble that is quickly forgotten.

9. An attractive spokesperson who is appropriate for the product or brand attracts attention and makes the message more believable and compelling.

10. Viewers are wary about the use of celebrity spokespeople in advertising. If the spokespeople are not appropriate to the commercial, viewers do not believe them and reject the message.

11. In addition to informative commercials, another widely used approach to television advertising is a mood or emotional commercial designed to create greater awareness of, and favorable reaction to, the product or the brand. Many commercials successfully combine the two approaches.

12. When a commercial is delivering news of real interest to its viewers, liking the commercial or empathizing with its situation is generally not critical to its effectiveness. Instead, clarity and simplicity are important. For mood commercials, on the other hand, likability and empathy are far more important than clarity and simplicity.

13. Appropriate music can enhance the mood of a commercial. Music can make a commercial more memorable and improve consumer attitudes toward the product.

reasoned that physiological measurements might pick up responses that the person was unable or unwilling to report. Some physiological measurements that have been tried are:

- *Heart rate:* The heart speeds up during an emotional response.
- *Pupil dilation:* The pupil of the eye dilates when a person sees something especially interesting.
- *Galvanic skin response:* Emotional reactions produce measurable changes in the elctrical conductivity of the skin.
- *Electroencephalographic (EEG) response:* Electrical activity in the brain changes as the brain processes information.

Assessing Physiological Tests

Despite some apparent advantages, physiological measurements have not yet fulfilled their promise. Validity has been a problem because physiological reactions are often caused by things that have little or nothing to do with the content of the ad, such as minor changes in the testing environment, changes in brightness or color as a commercial unfolds, or random thoughts. Such instability leads to questions about what exactly is being measured. It also produces reliability problems—inconsistent findings when the same ad is tested more than once.

The Test Environment. Most physiological tests require that respondents report to a laboratory, a setting that is hardly conducive to natural responses. Also, many of the tests require that respondents be attached to unfamiliar laboratory instruments, sometimes for extended periods of time. These requirements reduce the representativeness of samples because many potential respondents cannot be persuaded to submit to such unusual and possibly threatening procedures. They also reduce the representativeness of the environment in which the advertisement is shown.

Further, no one is entirely sure how to interpret any of the physiological reactions. A change in emotional response may mean that the consumer

PRINCIPLE

Many physiological tests are so sensitive to outside influences that their test-retest reliability is unacceptably low.

Physiological tests measure emotional responses to advertising. (Tim Davis/Photo Researchers.)

likes the advertisement or the product. Then again, it may mean that the consumer is irritated or upset by something in the advertisement or by something in the testing situation itself. Researchers have had a hard time deciding what bearing any of that might have on the advertisement's intended effect.

Because physiological measurements show so much theoretical promise, investigators have gone back to them again and again. However, every attempt to put them into commercial practice has run aground on the reliability and validity difficulties just described. As a result, although physiological tests continue to attract intermittent attention and interest, they are not now in general use in evaluative research.

FRAME-BY-FRAME TESTS

A great deal goes on while a television commercial unfolds. Even though the commercial may be very brief, it is always made up of separate parts. As those episodes progress, viewers' responses to the commercial change as well.

Researchers have attempted to track those changes in several different ways. In one form of **frame-by-frame test,** viewers turn a dial or press numbers on an electronic keypad to indicate their moment-to-moment reactions to what they are seeing on the screen. That procedure produces a "trace"—a continuous record of ups and downs. When the trace is correlated with the commercial frame by frame, it provides a record of which parts of the commercial increased attention (or liking of whatever is being measured) and which parts reduced it.

One of the best-known frame-by-frame tests is VIEWFACTS' PEAC test, in which respondents in a minitheater setting punch buttons on hand-held keypads to indicate how much they like or dislike what they are seeing on a television screen. The test commercial is embedded in a series of commercials, and respondents indicate their reactions to each one. As respondents are reacting, a computer collects and averages the responses and translates them into a continuous trace line keyed to the commercial's scenes.

After respondents give their initial reactions, they use their keypads to answer a set of questions that resemble those asked in a communication test. The computer collects the answers and tabulates them for discussion later on.

In the second half of a PEAC session the computer superimposes the response line over the test commercial on the screen (see Figure 21.3). An interviewer stops the commercial at key turning points and asks the audience members why their evaluations went up or down. Toward the end of the sessions the interviewer reviews the communication questions and asks the respondents to explain why they reacted the way they did.

Thus the PEAC test combines the advantages of moment-to-moment response with an opportunity to ask and discuss questions about the respondents' reactions. Although the PEAC test is relatively expensive, this combination provides useful diagnostic information that cannot be accumulated in any other way.

In another form of frame-by-frame test viewers wear tiny electrodes that measure the electrical conductivity of the skin. As various parts of the commercial provoke an emotional response, electrical conductivity changes, producing an "emotional reaction" trace line. Unlike the PEAC

frame-by-frame tests *Tests that evaluate consumers' reactions to the individual scenes that unfold in the course of a television commercial.*

FIGURE 21.3
The PEAC test. (Courtesy of VIEWFACTS.)

test, which produces a voluntary measure of liking, electrical conductivity tests measure involuntary, emotional reactions. Although this method is still in the early stages of development, it shows considerable promise. It combines the advantages of frame-by-frame analysis with the advantages of involuntary emotional response.

Assessing Frame-by-Frame Tests

Frame-by-frame tests can be useful because they provide some guidance as to how the commercial might be improved. When a commercial gets a low recall score or a low persuasion score, no one can really be sure what will bring that score up. In contrast, because the trace line in frame-by-frame tests goes up in response to some scenes and down in response to others, it provides direct clues as to which parts of the commercial need further work.

As usual, reliability and validity are difficult to establish. Traces can be unstable from person to person and from group to group, especially when physiological measures are involved. Further, the relationship between the trace's form or level and the advertisement's ultimate effect is uncertain. Even in those investigations in which the trace can be shown to be reliable, the question remains: Exactly what is the trace a reliable measurement of?

Nevertheless, frame-by-frame analysis brings something to advertising research that other methods do not. It provides an opportunity to look inside a commercial, and it offers clues as to what scenes produce what kind of response. Because that is such a valuable advantage, the PEAC test and its direct competitors are becoming more widely used.

*I*N-MARKET TESTS

in-market tests *Tests that measure the effectiveness of advertisements by measuring actual sales results in the marketplace.*

In-market tests evaluate advertisements by measuring their influence on sales. In view of all the problems discussed thus far, a sales-impact measurement might appear to be the only measurement that an advertiser should accept. However, the practical difficulties of conducting in-market tests are so great that, with the exception of direct-response counts, full-scale in-market tests are seldom attempted in evaluating individual ads.

One problem is that sales of any brand are produced by a tightly interwoven net of factors, including economic conditions, competitive strategies, and all of the marketing activities in which the advertiser is engaged. Within that complicated set of interrelationships the effect of any single advertisement is extremely difficult to detect. Even with the benefit of a carefully designed, large-scale (and therefore costly and time-consuming) experiment, the effect of a single advertisement may be entirely lost.

Another reason sales is not a popular criterion is that by the time sales figures become available, most of the important investments have already been made: The advertisement has been produced, and media costs have all been incurred. For purposes of evaluating an advertisement, sales results become available very late in the game.

Simulated Test Markets

Some of those problems can be avoided by using **simulated test markets.** In a simulated test market the research company conducting the test ex-

simulated test market *Research procedure in which respondents are exposed to advertisements and then permitted to shop for the advertised products in an artificial environment where records are kept of their purchases.*

poses respondents to advertising and then asks them to choose among competing brands. Later the researchers recontact respondents who have used the advertiser's brand to ask if they would purchase the same brand again. The two numbers produced by that pair of interviews are *trial*—the proportion of respondents who chose to try the brand after seeing it advertised—and *repeat*—the proportion of respondents who, having tried the product, chose to purchase the same brand again.

Despite the artificiality of simulated test markets, research companies that conduct them have developed formulas using trial-and-repeat numbers that have proved to be remarkably accurate predictors of later in-market success. One of the reasons for this accuracy is that the trial-and-repeat numbers collected in simulated test markets are much closer to what happens in the real marketplace than are the other tests discussed earlier in this chapter.

In a simulated test market, however, the advertisement's effect is combined with the effects of packaging and pricing, and of course with reactions to the product itself. Therefore, although simulated test markets can predict the success of a marketing program as a whole, they cannot give more than a rough indication of the advertisement's independent influence on sales.

In principle, this problem could be solved by conducting multiple simulated test markets in which only the advertisements were varied and everything else remained the same. This solution runs into the problem of cost. The cost of conducting a single simulated test market runs from $50,000 to $75,000. The cost of conducting multiple test markets is higher than most advertisers believe they can afford.

Single-Source Data

In another major substitute for a full in-market test, the research company conducting the test arranges to control the television signal received by the households in a community. The company divides the households into equivalent matched groups. It then sends advertisements to one group of households but not to the other and collects exact records of what every household purchases. Because advertising is the only variable being manipulated here, the method permits an unambiguous reading of cause and effect. The data collected in this way are known as *single-source data* because exposure records and purchasing records come from the same household.

Single-source data can produce exceptionally dependable results. Real advertisements are used, and they are received under natural conditions in the home. The resulting purchases are real purchases made by real consumers for their own use. The method is very expensive, however—$200,000 to $300,000 per test. Furthermore, the method usually requires more than 6 months to produce usable results. It is therefore not usually considered an acceptable method for routine testing of individual ads.

*I*MPLICATIONS OF EVALUATIVE RESEARCH

PRINCIPLE
The most realistic tests of an advertisement's effectiveness are too expensive for routine use.

In evaluative copy testing, the advertiser must make trade-offs. In-market tests, which come closest to duplicating the most important features of the natural environment, are too expensive and too time-consuming to be used on a regular basis. Tests that are fast and affordable have so many obvious defects that their reliability and validity are very much in doubt. Added to all that, creative "experts" within the company and—especially—within the advertising agency fight all kinds of copy testing at every step. Faced with such problems, advertisers must either depend on unaided judgment, which may be less reliable and less valid than any of the research techniques, or supplement judgment with research findings that, although far from perfect, can be much more reassuring than no help at all.

In this dilemma the advertiser joins the government official, the military leader, the business executive, the economist, the physician, and the educator. When decisions are hard-fought, complex, and important, research cannot tell the decision maker what to do. However, it can provide guidance, and when that guidance is used rationally, decisions generally turn out better than they would have if based on intuition alone.

The same principles apply to selection and purchase of advertising media. Whereas research can be a valuable guide, decisions as to how much to spend—and when, where, and how to allocate those funds—always include an element of hard data and an element of hunch.

SUMMARY

- Creative experts disagree with one another, and agencies disagree with their clients. Faced with these conflicts of opinion, advertisers often resort to evaluative research in the hope that it will provide a reliable and valid prediction of an advertisement's sales effectiveness.

- The major evaluative research methods fall into eight major groups: (1) memory tests, (2) persuasion tests, (3) direct-response counts, (4) communication tests, (5) focus groups, (6) physiological tests, (7) frame-by-frame tests, and (8) in-market tests.

- Although memory tests have a long history in advertising research, no one knows whether they predict sales. Many creative leaders and many research leaders believe that they do not.

- Persuasion tests are relatively good predictors of effectiveness when the ad has something new and interesting to say. However, when brands are well known, and when all messages are similar, persuasion findings may be largely due to chance.

- Direct-response counts show exactly how many consumers responded to each ad. Although this method is highly accurate, it can be used only with advertisements that request a direct response. It cannot be

used with television commercials or print ads intended to encourage purchases at retail stores.

- Communication tests do not produce simple pass–fail results. Rather, they provide a detailed analysis of consumers' subjective reactions to the advertisements being tested. This quality makes them less useful for go/no-go decisions but more useful for understanding how the advertisement works.

- Focus groups are the least reliable of the major evaluative research methods. Advertisers who use them for this purpose are leaving too much to chance.

- Although physiological tests show considerable theoretical promise, low reliability and high cost have excluded them from routine use in evaluative research.

- Frame-by-frame tests allow advertisers to examine viewers' reactions as a television commercial unfolds. Because they link reactions to specific scenes, frame-by-frame tests provide especially useful clues as to how a commercial may be improved.

- When properly conducted, in-market tests are the most valid of all types of evaluative research. However, they are so expensive and so time consuming that they are not practical options for testing individual ads.

QUESTIONS

1. Make a list of the assets and liabilities of each of the copy-testing methods reviewed in this chapter. Considering this list, if you were an advertiser with a $100 million advertising budget, which method would you use? Why? Would your answer change if you had a $1 million budget? In what way?

2. Suppose you are in charge of advertising a student production of a Broadway play and that an advertis-

ing class has developed several quite different ads. How would you decide which ad to use? How would you know whether you made the right choice?

3. The problems an advertiser encounters in trying to evaluate an individual advertisement resemble the problems a college administrator encounters in trying to evaluate an individual college course. In what

ways are the two sets of problems similar? In what ways are they different?

4. Professor Fletcher is illustrating research principles by describing a case in which he was involved. A marketer of men's cologne was testing its advertisement for recognition. Ten sample groups of men aged 25 to 40 were tested, and the recognition scores for each sample were in the 25 to 35 percent range. Fletcher tells the class that the data were clearly reliable but very likely invalid. Then he asks the class two questions: Why is it that a result has to be reliable in order to be valid, but a reliable result doesn't prove validity? Why was the cologne testing probably invalid?

5. One of the methods used for testing television commercial impact is the theater test. Approximately 100 people are invited to view television programs being considered by the networks, and the commercials are embedded in the programs. Prior to the viewing, the audience is asked to select products that would like to receive if they were a door-prize winner. After the viewings (and drawings), the audi-ence repeats its choices. The tested products (and competing brands) are on the selection lists. What dimension of consumer effect is being tested in this way? Is this a valid method of testing for this effect?

6. The chapter discusses one weakness of physiological testing by pointing out that results from these experiments are very hard to interpret for eventual sales effectiveness. A number of researchers claim the same sort of weakness affects many recall and attitude procedures used in copy testing. Why would these very popular tests be criticized this way? What is the best way to measure the persuasion of an advertising message?

7. Through advanced technology (UPC scanning), research companies are able to speed up results from field tests on advertising effectiveness. Although companies do not have to wait several months for results, many are still fearful of real-life field testing. In part, this fear explains the continued popularity of simulated test market studies. What is this fear about? What serious validity threat to test marketing can be relieved by a market simulation?

FURTHER READINGS

CLANCY, KEVIN J., AND LYMAN E. OSTLUND, "Commercial Effectiveness Measures," *Journal of Advertising Research* 16, (1976):29–34.

FLETCHER, ALAN D., AND THOMAS A. BOWERS, *Fundamentals of Advertising Research,* 3rd ed. (Belmont, CA: Wadsworth Publishing Co., 1988).

KALWANI, MANOHAR U., AND ALVIN J. SILK, "On the Reliability and Predictive Validity of Purchase Intention Measures," *Marketing Science* 1, (1980):243–86.

STEWART, DAVID W., "Measures, Methods, and Models in Advertising Research," *Journal of Advertising Research* 29, (1989):54–60.

STEWART, DAVID W., AND DAVID H. FURSE, *Effective Television Advertising* (Lexington, MA: D.C. Heath and Co., 1986).

WALKER, DAVID, AND MICHAEL F. VON GONTEN, "Explaining Related Recall Outcomes: New Answers from a Better Model," *Journal of Advertising Research* 29 (1989):11–21.

YOUNG, SHIRLEY, "Copy Testing Without Magic Numbers," *Journal of Advertising Research* 12 (1972):3–12.

VIDEO CASE

NEW YORK

"Perfect" Navy by Cover Girl

The women's fragrance category accounts for over $2 billion and has experienced annual growth rates of approximately 4 percent. Unlike traditional consumer products, however, the women's fragrance category has hundreds of competitors, many with fractional shares. The category is, therefore extremely fragmented and is further segmented by "mass versus class" channels of distribution. Approximately half of the women's fragrances are sold through broad (mass) distribution channels, such as drug and mass merchandisers. The remaining products are sold through higher priced, more exclusive (class) locations, such as department and specialty stores.

Cover Girl developed the Navy fragrance for introduction in Spring of 1990. The product was designed for introduction in mass-distribution outlets, where advertising is considered a key determinant of success. In such a highly fragmented category full of brands with short life expectancies, strong initial success is considered critical for long-term trade acceptance and support. Thus, Cover Girl's ultimate goal for advertising was to achieve sales and share for Navy among the top ten brands in mass distribution within 3 years of its introduction. The overall objective of the resulting "Perfect" campaign for Navy was to communicate strongly a highly desirable brand personality so that Navy would become a major brand in the women's fragrance category. Cover Girl also established objectives related to awareness, trial, purchase intent, and brand image/personality. These were determined based on the levels achieved for similar successful, heavily advertised brands in the women's fragrance category. The specific image/personality goal was to create an "aspirational" brand image that would establish Navy as a clean, classic fragrance, with a personality that would be viewed as stylish, smart, sexy, and confident—"perfect" for any occasion.

The challenge of the creative strategy was to establish a distinctive and classic Navy brand personality that would set it apart from the myriad of products in the category. Because Cover Girl wanted women to consider Navy appropriate for all-day, year-round usage, the main promise for the new campaign was "You always feel perfect in Navy." Cover Girl defined Navy's user group psychographics as stylish, smart, sexy, and confident; thus, Navy users would feel comfortable in any situation—glamorous or casual. Demographically, Navy's target audience was identified as women 18 to 34 years of age who are regular users of fragrance, who currently include mass-market brands among their "wardrobe" of personal fragrances, and for whom fashion is an important consideration. Navy's introductory media spending amounted to approximately 7.5 percent of the total media expenditures in the women's fragrance category, and media vehicles included a 30-second television commercial and four-color, full-page magazine ads with scent strips.

Navy's initial success surpassed the objectives established by Cover Girl. After 3 months of introductory advertising, the brand's share of unit volume established it as the number two mass-distributed brand in the category, trailing the number one brand by only a narrow margin. It ranked third in terms of dollar sales, behind two well-established major brands. Consumer awareness of Navy's advertising immediately following the launch of the campaign was in the same range as the strongest brands in the category, whose campaigns had run for several years. Further consumer tracking study data indicated that Navy easily exceeded all of its awareness, trial, purchase intent, and attitudinal objectives. Among the brand's target group, Navy's purchase intent scores ranked second in the category, and its advertising ranked first in terms of recall. Cover Girl also reported that the advertising successfully communicated its brand image objectives, as consumers characterized the product as "stylish, confident, and sexy," a scent that can be worn at any time.

QUESTIONS

1. What visual characteristics seem to separate the Navy "Perfect" spot from other women's fragrance advertising you have seen in the past?

2. With the shortened product life cycles common in the women's fragrance category, why do you think it is essential for brands to establish strong rapid trial and awareness during their introductory periods?

3. Manufacturers in the women's fragrance category have successfully positioned their products as analogous to apparel styles in that they should ideally be unique for any woman, ever-changing, and always current and up-to-date. Explain how this success has fostered increased new product competition, shortened product life cycles, and increased product development and advertising costs.

Source: Courtesy of Lotas Minard Patton McIver, Inc.

CASE STUDY

Cancer Treatment Centers of America

After having watched his mother die from what he felt was ineffective treatment of her cancer, Richard Stephenson, with the help of a group of investors, bought the failing Zion Community Hospital in 1975, which had a specialty program in cancer treatment. He gathered together a professional staff with the objective of finding better and more successful ways of treating cancer and founded Cancer Treatment Centers, a chain of hospitals specializing in the treatment of many forms of cancer. This is the story of how that hospital built itself into an internationally recognized cancer specialty operation, drawing its patients from across the nation and outside the country through a combination of a comprehensive team approach to cancer treatment and a level of service within the hospital unmatched by any.

The initial hospital building had a 95-bed capacity. When the private investors bought the property, they agreed with the community to set aside 25 percent of the beds to maintain community service. Because a specialization in cancer had been his dream, Mr. Stephenson (currently Chairman of the Board) set about to staff the cancer unit with the best physicians, laboratory technicians, radiologists, surgeons, and chemotherapy professionals he could find. From the beginning, the hospital practiced a team approach, involving the patient in all of the meetings at which potential treatments were discussed and determined. Family members were encouraged to remain with the patient and even to participate in the decision. The three classic approaches to treating cancer—surgery, radiation therapy, and chemotherapy—were supplemented with nutrition programs, psychological counseling, and attentive and personal nursing care. The ratio of staff to patients is six to one, nearly twice that of the typical hospital.

As the average daily census (ADC) began to grow in the hospital, the management observed that many of the patients who were attracted to the hospital were unusually well-read about their disease, they understood it better than did patients of other diseases, and they responded better to the natural-food diet that was part of the hospital's regimen. Early marketing efforts involved distributing pamphlets to health-food stores around the country. The pamphlets were developed in-house and were distributed by marketing staff members or by agents retained to call on health-food stores.

As word of mouth grew, it was observed that an increasing number of patients had been referred by chiropractors. Because many chiropractors use X-rays in their work, a special campaign thanking chiropractors for their early detection of cancer and encouraging them to refer patients to the Zion hospital was initiated. This campaign was advertised in chiropractor journals and via direct mail, personal contact, and specialized follow-ups.

These early marketing efforts saw rapid and dramatic results. In 1985 the ADC of cancer patients in the hospital was five. The next year this number had jumped to 11. With increasing direct marketing, the ADC rose to 22 in 1987 and by 1990 it was 45.

Advertising was begun in 1986 and is done in-house by a freelance creative and design team. Media management has been assigned to CPM, Incorporated, of Chicago. One of the first advertisements developed, "Relentless" (see Exhibit A) was developed in-house and ran in such publications as *Prevention* and other smaller magazines aimed primarily at a health-conscious public. Almost from the beginning any advertising was reviewed by a focus group of patients then at the hospital. Although the "relentless" copy rang true ("Cancer can be relentless, so can we"), it seemed to lack the warmth and personal testimonials that were part of the experience of so many patients as they returned to the hospital for check ups. This finding was consistent in repeated focus groups.

In 1988 the hospital began using stories of patients who had been treated. The results indicated that the per-

EXHIBIT A

In 1986, about one million people will be diagnosed as having cancer. The survival for these people is contingent on two factors — time and treatment.

Time: Accurate and early diagnosis.

Treatment: For more than a decade, American International Hospital has striven to help patients place cancer in remission with some of the most innovative — yet medically proven — therapies available. As a patient with cancer, you owe it to yourself to explore treatment alternatives.

Hyperthermia, for example, is a therapy that raises the body temperature to kill or weaken cancer cells making it possible for other therapeutic agents to completely destroy the remaining disease.

Our oncology team knows that your own immune system and your spirit are the most important weapons in the fight against cancer. We're prepared to back you all the way.

Cancer need not be a hopeless battle. At American International Hospital, we — and our patients — are fighting back. Relentlessly.

Call or write for a free information packet. Ask about our free patient travel program.

DIAL 1-800-FOR-HELP
(Toll-Free)

American International Hospital and Clinic

Professional Care with a Personal Touch

1911 27th Street, Zion, Illinois 60099
(312) 872-8722 (Just 40 Miles North of Chicago)

American International Hospital
Information Center
1911 27th Street
Zion, Illinois 60099

☐ Yes, I want to know more about American International Hospital's cancer treatment programs. Please send me this information right away.

☐ Also include the free patient travel program information.

Name _____
Address _____
City _____
State _____ Zip _____
Phone ( ) _____

PHLPA586

sonal style added to the warmth and drawing power of the campaign. Exhibit B is an example of the personal style of these ads. By 1990 additional focus groups within the hospital and results from advertising placed in various print media showed that one of the most successful ads ever run was the story of Flossie Dishong. Flossie's story was also made into an unscripted television commercial, with Flossie talking about her favorable experience at Cancer Treatment Centers of America. The making of this commercial set the pattern for future commercials. Although it might take 8 hours of shooting to get 60 seconds of material, the effort produced very believable advertising.

Just as every treatment at the Cancer Treatment Centers of America hospitals is carefully reviewed by a board of medical, professional, and ethical experts (the hospital was one of the pioneers in the use of ethicists on its review board), so too all the advertising is reviewed by the medical staff and by attorneys. This ensures that every statement can be verified and that none of the copy is inadvertently missing.

As the creative, media placement, and media buying were further refined by experts in the field, the response rate to the advertising continued to grow and at a more efficient rate. Figure 1 indicates the number of responses to the advertising over the years 1987 through 1990. The rate

of response went from nearly 3000 in 1989 to 13,000 in 1990, more than doubling between 1989 and 1990, with a budget increase of 60 percent. Efficiency continued to climb each month.

With units in Zion, Illinois, and Tulsa, Oklahoma, Cancer Treatment Centers of America (the name adopted for national marketing in 1990) now plans to open additional units around the country at a rate of roughly one per year. Local, regional, and national marketing efforts will be used to support this extension of service.

Locally, newspaper, outdoor, local television, and staff media appearances have been used, especially to advertise the Tulsa unit. Regional marketing has consisted of advertising in regional editions of *Parade, USA Weekend, People, TV Guide,* and *National Geographic,* among other publications. Television advertising is concentrated in cities within 600 to 700 miles of Tulsa or Chicago. National marketing includes insertions in *Prevention, American Health, Health,* and *Coping.* Cable television is used sparingly, including Discovery Channel, Prevue Channel, Lifetime, and Turner Broadcasting System. Each medium or publication has its own 800 number so that responses can be tracked precisely by city, day, and hour. As the number of hospitals expands, Cancer Treatment Centers will continue to refine its marketing with focus-group research on creative plans, statistical analysis or response rates, demographic analysis of responding patients, and by testing new ways to reach cancer victims in smaller areas.

Source: Courtesy of Cancer Treatment Centers of America.

EXHIBIT B

FIGURE 1
Increasing response to advertising 1987–1990.

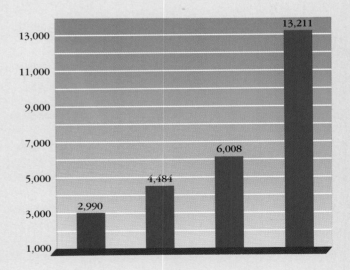

22

Business-to-Business and Retail Advertising

Chapter Outline

A Special Retailer

Business-to-Business Advertising

Business-to-Business Advertising Media

Retail Advertising

Retail Advertising: Creativity, Media, and Research

Chapter Objectives

When you have completed this chapter, you should be able to:

- Explain business-to-business advertising objectives
- List the different markets in the business arena and the various media used in business advertising
- Understand how local retail advertising differs from national brand advertising
- Understand how cooperative advertising works

A SPECIAL RETAILER

There is no other retail store exactly like Barneys New York. On any given day it would not be unusual to spot Sigourney Weaver shopping for boxer shorts in the men's underwear department or Michelle Pfeiffer buying gloves. The fascination with Barneys is shared by these and many other celebrities. This success is even more impressive when you consider the fact that Barneys started off as a modest Seventh Avenue discount men's shop, distinguished by its hand-painted sign in the window reading "Home of Famous Brands." Today this retailer encompasses 170,000 square feet of selling space, accounting for more than $100 million in annual sales.

Among those responsible for this unbelievable turnaround is former photography student Neil Kraft. Kraft is in charge of Barneys' in-house advertising department, BNY Advertising. He and his group of seven talented individuals have produced ads as original and innovative as those developed by the best Madison Avenue agencies. The use of classic black-and-white photographs has become a Barneys hallmark. For example, original works by William Claxton, Roy Dacaraua, and Garry Winogrand have been combined with taglines borrowed from Barneys' ads of years past. One famous Elliot Erwitt shot of two men brawling on a city street, for instance, has been used in a two-page print ad with the shots on one page and the words "tastes differ" printed in lowercase lettering on the opposite page (see Ad 22.1). Another print ad shows an old Mercedes parked on a deserted dirt road, accompanied by the single word "Dream."

The retail store's founder, Barney Pressman, has always been an advertising rebel. In 1933, for example, Barneys was the first U.S. retailer to advertise on radio programming, proclaiming, "Calling all men! Calling all men to Barneys!" In 1947 Barneys was the first to advertise on television, using the slogan "Select, Don't Settle." Pressman's son Fred joined him in 1946, increasing store space to 100,000 square feet, but keeping Barneys as a discount store.

Business had begun to decline when Fred's sons Gene and Robert entered the business in the 1970s. They introduced Giorgio Armani to America, added a small women's department to the store, and expanded the

AD 22.1
Retailers, such as Barneys New York, often use their own in-house advertising departments to create successful advertising campaigns.
(Courtesy of Barneys.)

store another 70,000 square feet. The Pressman brothers, seeking to find an ideal advertising "voice" to reflect their new image, had the wisdom to hire Kraft in 1984. Within a year Kraft had given them that voice. In his first commercial, shot in grainy black and white, a jerky camera zoomed in on supermodel Paulina Porizkova as she sashayed around her apartment, changing clothes to a rock tune. It was an instant smash, and imitators sprang up almost overnight. Kraft's next big success was a series of celebrity profiles starring famous Barneys customers, including Joseph Papp, John Irving, Jeremy Irons, and Sandra Bernhard. The ads were quickly copied by The Gap, Dunhill, and other retail chains.*

Equally impressive as Barneys' sales success is its original and creative advertising. This chapter deals with two special types of advertising—business-to-business and retail—that are not known for producing great advertising. In fact, words such as "dull" and "uninspiring" typically describe ads found in these two categories. Such labels are unfair, however, given the limitations and special circumstances with which both types of advertising must cope. These factors, as well as the special adjustments necessary to create effective business-to-business and retail advertising, will be discussed in this chapter.

*B*USINESS-TO-BUSINESS ADVERTISING

business-to-business advertising
Advertising directed at people who buy or specify products for business use.

Business-to-business advertising is directed at people in business who buy or specify products for business use. As Figure 22.1 shows, these people work in a variety of business areas, such as commercial enterprises (retailing and manufacturing), government agencies (federal, state, and local), and nonprofit institutions (universities and hospitals), and purchase many different types of products. Although personal selling is the most common method of communicating with business buyers, business advertising is used to create product awareness, enhance the firm's reputation, and support salespeople and other channel members. A purchaser in the business market, just as a consumer, "gathers information about alternatives, processes this information, learns about available products, determines which alternatives match the perceived needs most closely, and carries through by making a purchase."†

In the business arena, however, many people can be involved in the purchasing decision—people from different functional areas, such as marketing, manufacturing, or purchasing, who have varying information needs. For example, when a purchasing decision might result in a product change, such as altering the product's materials or packaging, marketing interest centers on product salability; manufacturing or production costs. Thus business advertising is also used to (1) reach the various influencers involved and (2) communicate the different information needs.

Types of Business-to-Business Advertising

Information needs also depend on the type of business market the business advertiser is trying to reach. The business arena comprises five very distinct markets, each of which tends to purchase products and services quite dif-

---

*Adapted from Benjamin Svetky, "Retail's Art and Kraft Movement," *Adweek* (April 2, 1990): 26–27, 30.
†Edward F. Fern and James R. Brown, "The Industrial/Consumer Marketing Dichotomy: A Case of Insufficient Justification," *Journal of Marketing 48* (Spring 1984):68–77.

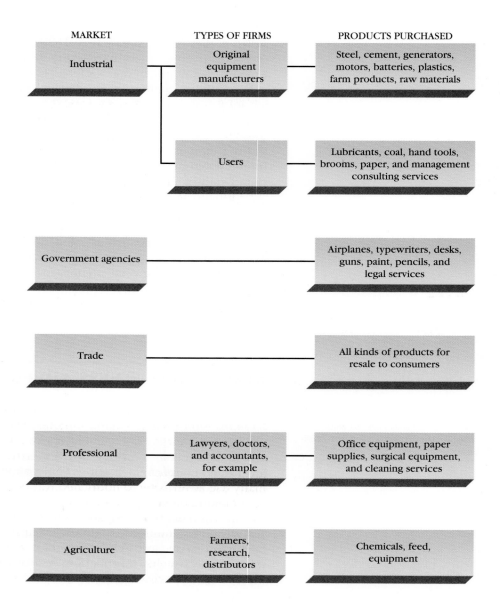

MARKET	TYPES OF FIRMS	PRODUCTS PURCHASED
Industrial	Original equipment manufacturers	Steel, cement, generators, motors, batteries, plastics, farm products, raw materials
	Users	Lubricants, coal, hand tools, brooms, paper, and management consulting services
Government agencies		Airplanes, typewriters, desks, guns, paint, pencils, and legal services
Trade		All kinds of products for resale to consumers
Professional	Lawyers, doctors, and accountants, for example	Office equipment, paper supplies, surgical equipment, and cleaning services
Agriculture	Farmers, research, distributors	Chemicals, feed, equipment

FIGURE 22.1
The diversity of business markets and products purchased.

ferently. These markets are most frequently referred to as the *industrial, government, trade, professional,* and *agricultural* markets.

industrial advertising *Advertising directed at businesses that buy products to incorporate into other products or to facilitate the operation of their businesses.*

Industrial Advertising. Original equipment manufacturers (OEMs), such as IBM and General Motors, purchase industrial goods and/or services that either become a part of the final product or facilitate the operation of their businesses. Information needs, then, depend on the reason for the purchase of the product. **Industrial advertising** is directed at such businesses. *Business Week, Auto World,* and *Fortune* may all be used for industrial advertising. For example, when General Motors purchases tires from Goodyear, information needs focus on whether the purchase will contribute to a quality finished product. When Goodyear purchases packaging material to ship the tires it manufactures, information needs focus on prompt, predictable delivery. Ad 22.2 for W. E. Andrews Company, Inc., advertises the company's dedication to quality.

Last night, I performed for the Metropolitan Ballet.

AD 22.2
Industrial advertising may use humor to relate a valued service or product. (Courtesy of W.E. Andrews Company, Inc.)

Government Advertising. The largest purchasers of industrial goods in the United States are federal, state, and local governments. These government units purchase virtually every kind of good—from $437 hammers to multimilliondollar Polaris missiles. Such goods may be advertised in *Federal Computer Week, Commerce Business Daily,* or *Defense News.* Interestingly, however, you seldom see advertisements targeted directly to government agencies. Perhaps this is because government agencies normally use advertising to notify potential suppliers that they are in the process of taking bids. Supplier reputation, however, plays an important role in the selection decision. Because government buyers are responsible to, and influenced by, numerous interest groups that specify, legislate, evaluate, and use the goods and services that governments purchase, corporate image advertising is one way of influencing the government market.* Such interest groups include the Congress, the office of Management and Budget, and external watchdogs, such as the Consumer Union.

trade advertising *Advertising used to influence resellers, wholesalers, and retailers.*

Trade Advertising. **Trade advertising** is used to persuade resellers, wholesalers, and retailers in the consumer market to stock the products of the manufacturer. *Chain Store Age, Florist's Review,* and *Pizza and Pasta* are examples of trade publications. Because resellers purchase products for resale to ultimate consumers, they want information on the profit margins they can expect to receive, the product's major selling points, and what the producer is doing in the way of consumer advertising and other promotional support activities.

professional advertising *Advertising directed at people such as lawyers, doctors, and accountants.*

Professional Advertising. **Professional advertising** is directed at a diverse group of people such as lawyers, accountants, management consultants, doctors, funeral directors, and marketing research specialists. Advertisers interested in attracting professionals advertise in publications such as the *Music Educator Journal* or *Advertising Age.* Information needs depend on both the advertiser's product and the desired audience.

*"Selling to the Government Market: Local, State, and Federal," *Government Products News* (Cleveland, OH: Government Product News, 1977).

AD 22.3
This life insurance company is targeting employee benefits managers. (Courtesy of Northwestern National Life Insurance Company.)

agricultural advertising *Advertising directed at large and small farmers.*

Agricultural Advertising. **Agricultural advertising** promotes a variety of products and services, such as animal-health products, farm machinery and equipment, crop dusting, and fertilizer. Large and small farmers alike want to know how industrial products can assist them in the growing, raising, or production of agricultural commodities. They turn to publications such as *California Farmer* or *Trees and Turf* for such assistance.

Business versus Consumer Marketing

There are several inherent characteristics that differentiate business marketing from consumer marketing, including the market concentration, decision makers, strategy, and purchasing objectives. As a result, the process of creating business-to-business advertising, as well as the expertise of the people involved, differs from that involved in consumer marketing. For example, in Ad 22.3, Northwestern National Life Insurance Company is directing its appeal to benefits managers in large companies.

Market Concentration. The market for a typical business good is relatively small compared to the market for a consumer good. In some cases, particularly where an original equipment manufacturer (OEM) is concerned, the market may even be geographically concentrated. For example, the auto industry is located primarily in Detroit, the steel industry in Pennsylvania and Illinois, and the furniture industry in North Carolina. These concentrations have direct ramifications for media selection and the ability to target media. For example, businesses selling special computer hardware and software used in stock-and-bond purchases can run their ads in media concentrated in cities, such as New York and Chicago, or zone additions of magazines that reach these markets.

In addition to geographic concentration, businesses can be grouped according to the *Standard Industrial Classification (SIC) System.* The U.S. government established the SIC system in order to group organizations on the basis of major activity or major product or service provided. It enables the federal government to publish the number of establishments, number of employees, and sales volume for each group, designated by a commercial code. Geographic breakdowns are also provided where possible. The

SIC system classifies more than 4 million manufacturers into ten major categories that are each subdivided into more specific groups. For example, food SIC is 20, meat products is 201, and canned food is 2032. The SIC system permits an advertiser to find the SIC codes of its customers and then obtain SIC-coded lists that also include publication usages by SIC classifications. This publication usage information allows the advertiser to select media that will reach the businesses in a certain SIC.

Decision Makers. In general, those involved in making decisions for businesses are professionals who utilize rational criteria when comparing choices. Many times these professionals possess technical knowledge and expertise about the products and services being advertised. Moreover, it isn't uncommon for as many as 15 to 20 people to be involved in a particular purchase decision. Unfortunately, little is known about the inner workings of the decision process or the people involved. Dillard B. Tinsley, a professor of marketing at Stephen F. Austin State University, suggests that we must understand a firm's organizational culture before we can know how decisions are made at that firm. Organizational culture includes the stories and anecdotes employees tell about their company, how they feel about their competitors, and how they feel about being (for example) the industry leader, as well as company procedures, policies, rules, job descriptions, and other formalized guidelines for employee activities.[*]

According to a study sponsored by the newspaper *Australia Post,* there are four types of business decision makers: (1) *information seekers* (25 percent), who are very receptive to both advertising and sales representatives; (2) *hesitants* (19 percent), who are concerned about the quality of both the advertising and the sales representatives; (3) *innovators* (31 percent), who are particularly positive toward advertising efforts, but negative toward sales representatives; and (4) *doubters* (25 percent), who are negative toward both the advertising and sales representatives.[†] Advertisers may create separate messages and media strategies to reach each of these diverse groups.

Strategic Orientation. Unlike the typical consumer who makes decisions based on partial information and irrational criteria, businesses tend to be guided by a specific strategy. This strategy eliminates much of the autonomy available in other kinds of decision making. Factors such as cost pressures, measures of advertising effectiveness, the agency-client partnership, company-customer linkages, and distribution may dictate what a business must do regardless of the advertising message. Therefore, advertisers must understand the components of a businesses strategy and adjust their own strategies accordingly.[‡]

One major adjustment is simply accepting the time frame of a typical business strategy. Buying decisions, as well as advertising decisions, are often made by committees and are influenced by others within the organization. This process can take days, weeks, or months. Furthermore, creative efforts and media buys may no longer be valid when approval is finally given. Each of the other functional areas may also have its own timetable. The product-development people will not be willing to introduce the

---

[*]Dillard B. Tinsley, "Understanding Business Customers Means Learning About Its Culture," *Marketing News* (March 14, 1988):5, 15.

[†]Tony Rambaut, "Getting Through to Business Consumers," *Direct Marketing* (March 1989):78–81.

[‡]Richard A. Kozak, "Business-to-Business Ad Trends," *Marketing News* (March 19, 1990):32.

product until test results have achieved certain scores; finance won't fund the effort until certain conditions prevail; and the marketing director will closely monitor the chosen market segment, looking for strategic opportunities that signal a successful product launch.

Purchasing Objectives. As you can see in the BP America advertisement, (Ad 22.4), purchasing objectives in the business market for the most part center on rational, pragmatic considerations such as price, service, quality, and assurance of supply. The BP America ad assures business purchasers that the company offers a "complete business portfolio," an affirmation it backs up with detailed data about the various resources it employs.

1. **Price** Buyers in the business arena are more concerned than ordinary consumers are with the cost of owning and using a product. Most notably, the large volume of a particular product purchased, or the high per-unit cost, means that businesses spend thousands or millions of dollars with each purchase decision. In evaluating price, therefore, businesses consider a variety of factors that generate or minimize costs, such as: What amount of scrap or waste will result from the use of the material? What will the cost of processing the material be? How much power will the machine consume?

2. **Services** Business buyers require multiple services, such as technical assistance, availability of spare parts, repair capability, and training information. Thus the technical contributions of suppliers are highly valued wherever equipment, materials, or parts are in use.

3. **Quality** Organizational customers search for quality levels that are consistent with specifications. Thus they are reluctant to pay for extra quality or to compromise specifications for a reduced price. The crucial factor is uniformity or consistency in product quality that will guarantee uniformity in end products, reduce the need for costly inspections and testing of incoming shipments, and ensure a smooth blending with the production process.

4. **Assurance of Supply** Interruptions in the flow of parts and materials can shut down the production process, resulting in costly delays and lost sales. To guard against interruptions in supply, business firms rely on a supplier's established reputation for delivery.

Business-to-Business Advertising Objectives

The average cost of an industrial sales call is approximately $179.* Business-to-business advertising enables a business marketer to reach a large portion of the market at a lower cost. For example, according to one study, the *adjusted* cost per thousand for ads by Minolta, IBM, and Toshiba in the same issue of *Time* magazine ran from $49.71 to $51.78.†

Although business advertising is an economical means of reaching large numbers of buyers, it is primarily used to assist and support the selling function. Thus business advertising objectives center on creating company awareness, increasing overall selling efficiency, and supporting distributors and resellers.

Creating Company Awareness. Effectively planned business advertising assists the industrial salesperson by increasing customer awareness of, and interest in, the supplier's product. When buyers are aware of a company's reputation, products, and record in the industry, salespeople are more effective.

---

*"From a Reporter to a Source: A New Survey of Selling Costs," *Sales & Marketing Management* (February 16, 1987):12.

†Joan Treistman, "Where the Reader Eye Roams," *Business Marketing* (April 1984):110–18.

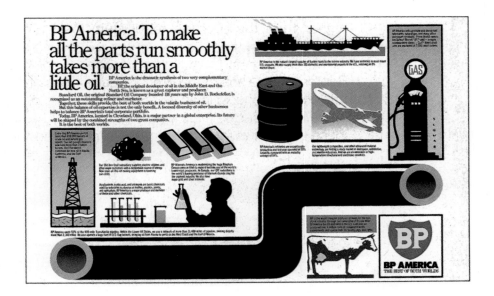

AD 22.4
This ad for BP America illustrates several rational purchasing objectives, including quality and assurance of supply. (Courtesy of BP America.)

Increasing Overall Selling Efficiency. Salespeople are frequently unaware of people within a firm who are in a position to exert influence on a purchasing decision. Such influencers could be engineers who design the product, production experts who manufacture the product, or financial people who maintain cost controls. These influencers, however, do read trade magazines and general business publications, and they can be reached through advertising. By responding to these ads, unknown influencers often identify themselves, making it possible for salespeople to contact them. Such advertising, therefore, generates leads for the salesforce. Furthermore, for some producers, particularly those of industrial supplies, advertising may be the only way of reaching broad groups of buyers efficiently.

Supporting Channel Members. Business advertising frequently provides an economical and efficient supplement to personal selling by providing information to distributors and resellers as well as to end users. It can reassure intermediaries that the end users are aware of the company's products. At the same time, it can answer the most common resellers' questions, such as what profit they can expect on a product and what the producer is doing in the way of consumer advertising and other promotional support. Rarely can a salesforce be deployed to reach all potential distributors and resellers often enough to satisfy all of these information needs.

Creating Business-to-Business Ads

As in consumer advertising, the best business-to-business ads are relevant, understandable, and strike an emotion in the prospective client. There are, however, adjustments that must be made in light of the differences discussed earlier. According to Steve Penchina, creative director of Penchina, Selkowitz of New York, effective business-to-business ads must establish an emotional connection between the product and the prospective client, and the ad should sell to people, not to companies. The classic Xerox Leonardo da Vinci ad is an example (see Ad 22.5). Penchina is bothered by boring or ridiculous visuals, trite taglines, and irrelevant or insulting metaphors, such

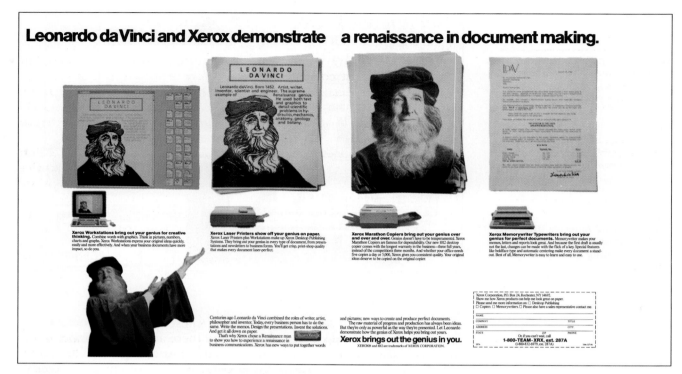

AD 22.5
This Xerox ad uses a series of subheadings to attract and hold the reader's interest.
(Courtesy of Xerox Corporation. Photography by Lamb & Hall, Inc.)

as "the power of ideas" used in Apple Computer ads.* Another expert, Sandra Tenney, posits that the two keys to successful business-to-business advertising are headlines and art. "Headlines should demonstrate specific benefits in language readers understand. Excellent photography and clear illustrations increase readership while strengthening headlines or elaborating on them," she notes.† Finally, John Graham, president of John R. Graham, a public relations/advertising agency, provides three guidelines for business-to-business advertising: (1) Make it easy for the prospect to respond or to pursue further information; (2) send reprints of ads with a personal letter to current customers and prospects explaining why you are advertising and where your ads will appear; and (3) combine advertising with media stories and a newsletter and mail these to prospects.‡

BUSINESS-TO-BUSINESS ADVERTISING MEDIA

Although some business advertisers use traditional consumer media, most rely on general business or trade publications, industrial directories, direct marketing, or some combination thereof.

*Patricia Winters, "Business-to-Business: Trite Is Blight," *Advertising Age* (August 28, 1989):48.
†Sandra M. Tenney, "For Good Business Ads, Apply Some Simple Rules," *Marketing News* (March 14, 1988):12.
‡John R. Graham, "Business-to-Business Ads Can Work," *Marketing News* (March 13, 1989):7.

General Business and Trade Publications

General business and trade publications are classified as either horizontal or vertical. **Horizontal publications** are directed to people who hold similar jobs in different companies across different industries. For example, *Purchasing* is a specialized business publication that is targeted to people across industries, who are responsible for a specific task or function. The magazines read by accountants or computer programmers are other examples of horizontal publications.

In contrast, **vertical publications,** such as *Iron Age* and *Steel,* are targeted toward people who hold different positions in the same industries. Some general business publications, such as *Fortune, Business Week,* and *The Wall Street Journal,* tend to be read by business professionals across all industries because of the general business news and editorials they provide. Advertisers select publications on the basis of whom they want to reach and what their goals are. Other specialized business publications, such as *Iron Age* and *Steel,* however, are targeted to people in a specific industry and are therefore classified as vertical publications.

Directory Advertising

Every state has an industrial directory, and there are also a number of private ones. One of the most popular industrial directories is the New York–based *Thomas Register.* The *Register* consists of 19 volumes that contain 60,000 pages of 50,000 product headings and listings from 123,000 industrial companies selling everything from heavy machine tools to copper tubing to orchestra pits.

Direct Marketing

In addition to trade magazines and general business publications, business advertisers use various other vehicles, such as direct mail, catalogs, and data sheets, to reach their markets. Business advertisers often use direct mail to prepare the groundwork for subsequent sales calls. Catalogs and **data sheets** support the selling function by providing technical data about the product as well as supplementary information concerning price and availability.

Direct mail emerged as a primary medium for several business-to-business advertisers during the last decade. Thanks to the evolution of computer software, direct mail can be designed in a manner that personalizes the message to specific customers, includes highly technical information, and provides top-notch photography and designs. Long copy, illustrations, diagrams, or any other device can be carried through direct mail. In addition, dramatic improvements in the accuracy of mailing lists have reduced the waste historically associated with direct mail. Direct mail has the capacity to sell the product, provide sales leads, or lay the groundwork for subsequent sales calls.

Consumer Media

Consumer media, despite their wasted circulation, can sometimes be very effective owing to the lack of competition from other business advertisers. Because the message exposure occurs away from the office, it also encounters less competition from the receiver's other business needs. Although consumer media are also an excellent means of reaching a market where market coverage is limited geographically, they are still not used much. According to a survey sponsored by the Business/Professional Advertising Association, consumer publications received about 3 percent of the total dollar amount spent on business-to-business advertising, and spot radio and spot television each picked up only 1 percent, whereas network television accounted for under 1 percent.*

In addition to the use of traditional consumer media, there has been a tremendous growth in business television programming that is targeted at both businesspeople and consumers who are interested in business-related topics. For example, FNN not only produces its own business shows, it also provides the syndicated business shows *This Morning's Business* and *First Business.* Introduced in 1989, CNBC was conceived with the consumer in mind, and its programming focuses more on personal finances and health.†

Recent Trends in Service Media

Today there are more media choices available to the business-to-business advertiser than ever before. Consequently, media that can offer advertisers a competitive advantage in reaching their customers will be quite appealing. In some instances an existing medium has developed a unique service unmatched by its competitors. For example, *Business Week* offers a Federal Express service so subscribers can get their issues on Friday instead of waiting for the Monday mail. New media have also emerged. Responding to the desire of readers to receive financial news sooner, *Financial World,* in conjunction with UPI and State News Service, put out *The Latest News,* an hourly newspaper distributed free between 2:30 and 7:30 P.M. on Pan Am's East Coast shuttle.‡

The videocassette industry has also entered the fray as a reliable business-to-business medium. Videocassettes can be sent to customers requesting product information or a product demonstration. They can also be mailed unsolicited as an exciting selling tool. Entire catalogs can be put on video, called video logs. This is affordable owing to the development of disposable videocassettes that have a life of 10 to 12 plays and cost just pennies to produce.

Does Business Advertising Sell?

Although few business marketers today rely exclusively on their salesforces to reach potential buyers, the effectiveness of business advertising has been questioned by many people. However, in 1987 the Advertising Research Foundation (ARF) and the Association of Business Publishers (ABP) undertook to study the link between business advertising and industrial product sales and profits. The researchers monitored product sales and the level and frequency of their advertising schedules for a period of 1 year. To ensure that the study's findings could be applied to a wide range of industries and products, three very different products were monitored: a portable safety device that sold for less than $10, a commercial transportation component package that sold for around $10,000, and highly specialized laboratory equipment priced between $5,000 and $10,000. Despite the diversity

*Andrew Jaffe, "The Big Guys Get Serious," *Adweek Special Report* (May 23, 1988):B.M.6.
†Debra Goldman, "Is More News Good News?" *Adweek* (May 21, 1990):B.M.29.
‡"Faster Than a Speeding Bullet," *Adweek* (May 21, 1990):B.M.7.

TEN STEPS TO SUCCESSFUL BUSINESS ADVERTISING

The Laboratory of Advertising Performance (LAP), New York, a division of McGraw-Hill Research, published ten guidelines for building sound advertising programs for firms selling to the business-to-business markets:

1. Don't stop advertising during a recession. Although the temptation is there, LAP studies of the 1981–1982 recession found that sales increased 59 percent in 1981 alone and a cumulative 275 percent by the end of 1985 for those who continued or increased advertising during the recession. In contrast, sales dropped 12 percent in 1981 and were up only 19 percent by the end of 1985 for those who cut or ended advertising during the recession.

2. Those who don't advertise can lose two-thirds of their market. Studies found that 65 percent of buyers do see advertising, whereas less than 10 percent are ever contacted by a salesperson.

3. Plan advertising on a year-round basis. Continuing advertising improves product awareness among both new prospects and existing customers while keeping product benefits fresh in the minds of every potential buyer.

4. Pave the way for the salesforce. Good advertising initiates the sales process by creating awareness, arousing interest, and building preference.

5. Use bigger and more colorful ads. A study of nearly 800 ads found that full-page ads, or those spread over two pages, drew nearly twice the response of fractional ads. Use of color drew 26 percent more responses than black-and-white ads.

6. Organize salespeople's time better. The LAP study found that salespeople spent only 25 percent of their time in face-to-face selling, with the rest spent traveling, waiting, writing reports, in meetings, or on the phone.

7. Follow up on leads. Eighty-six percent of 1,500 salespeople used leads generated from advertisements; 70 percent used reprints, tear sheets, or other examples of product advertising in sales presentations.

8. Keep the best people. Proper selection, training, supervision, and a carefully crafted compensation plan help build a productive salesforce.

9. Train workers. Nearly 30 percent of 1988 sales executives reported that their salespeople do not effectively bring exact product and benefits information to buyers.

10. Keep the company's message out there. Sales increased and remained significantly higher when advertising frequency was increased.

Source: "Business Marketers Can Take 10 Steps to Building Strong Marketing, Ad Programs," *Marketing News* (March 14, 1988):18–19.

---

in price, product life, purchase complexity, and distribution channels, the study found that, for all three products:

- Business-to-business advertising created more sales than would have occurred without advertising.
- Increased advertising frequency resulted in increased product sales.
- It paid to advertise to both dealers and end users when the product was sold through dealers.
- Increased advertising frequency increased sales leads and generated higher profits.
- It took 4 to 6 months to see the results of the advertising program.
- The use of color in the advertising made a dramatic difference.
- The advertising campaign was effective long after the campaign had ended.
- Advertising favorably affected purchasers' awareness of, and attitudes toward, industrial products.*

The Issues and Applications box that follows lists the findings of one study that suggests ten steps to successful business-to-business advertising.

*"From a Reporter to a Source: A New Survey of Selling Costs," *Sales & Marketing Management* (February 16, 1987):12.

The Integrated Business Advertising Plan

People in business advertising departments typically participate more heavily in the actual creation and placement of advertising strategy than do their counterparts in consumer organizations. This is because most business advertising and sales promotion, such as direct mail, catalogs, and trade show exhibits, are noncommissionable to advertising agencies. Additionally, business advertising tends to be technical and thus requires experts within the firm to prepare the copy and artwork.

A well-written action plan, as developed in the box entitled "Anatomy of a Business Advertising Plan," should cover specifically what is to be communicated, when it is to be communicated, and through what media it is to be implemented. It should also incorporate all promotional plans included in the overall advertising strategy.

RETAIL ADVERTISING

retail advertising *A type of advertising used by local merchants who sell directly to consumers.*

Most discussions of advertising focus on commercials that run on the Super Bowl, full-page ads in *Time* magazine, and copy strategies used by companies like Procter & Gamble. Often overlooked is **retail advertising,** which is used by local merchants to sell their products and services directly to consumers and which accounts for nearly half of all the money spent on advertising.

The amount spent on advertising varies by retail category. Recent figures indicate that discount stores spend about 3.2 percent of sales, apparel retailers 2.2 percent, department stores 4.0 percent, and supermarkets about 1.1 percent.*

Just as advertising is part of the marketing mix for nationally promoted products and services, it also plays an important role in the marketing or merchandising mix for retailers. Therefore, to understand retail advertising, it is first necessary to see how it differs from national advertising.

Retail Advertising versus National Advertising

Retail advertising is often called *local advertising* because the target market is frequently local in nature. However, institutions that may advertise locally, such as banks, financial services, and real estate organizations, are not considered part of the retail trade by the Bureau of the Census. Moreover, some retailers, such as Sears and J. C. Penney, advertise nationally. Thus when we talk about retail advertising, we are referring to advertising disseminated by retail institutions. Although retailers try to create a local presence, a great deal of retail advertising is standardized across regions of the country or even nationally. Retail advertising is designed to perform several universal functions: selling a variety of products, encouraging store traffic, delivering sales promotion messages, and creating and communicating a store image or "personality."

Retail advertising differs from national advertising in various ways. First, retail advertising, whether sponsored by a national chain or a local retailer, is targeted at people living in the local community. Such advertising is customized to match the needs, wants, culture, and idiosyncrasies of

*Michael F. Smith, "Mass Retail and Its Mass Markets," *Market & Media Decisions* (April 1990):88.

VOLKSWAGEN

- FOX • GOLF
- JETTA • GTI
- QUANTUM
- SCIROCCO
- CABRIOLET
- VANAGON
- VANAGON CAMPER

"WHERE TO BUY THEM"

AUTHORIZED DEALERS

MASSAPEQUA
LEGEND VOLKSWAGEN LTD
Merrick Rd & Clocks Blvd E Maspqa.......795-5790

NEW HYDE PARK
VOLKSWAGEN G C MOTORS
1 Jericho Trnpk Nw Hyd Pk....................488-2420

OCEANSIDE
ISLAND VOLKSWAGEN INC
2555 Long Bch Rd Ocnsid....................536-0010

QUEENS VILLAGE
WEIS VOLKSWAGEN CORP
Authorized Body & Paint Shop
218-25 Hmpstd Av Qns Vlg
Call.........................Lynbrook Tel No 599-6900

AD 22.6
This Volkswagen ad is an example of cooperative advertising. (Courtesy of Volkswagen, Ltd.)

cooperative advertising *A form of advertising in which the manufacturer reimburses the retailer for part or all of the advertising expenditures.*

these people. In comparison, national advertisers must deliver a standardized message that often deals with generalities that do not address the needs of individuals. Second, national advertising supports the brand(s) of the sponsor, whereas retail advertising may promote several different brands or even competing brands. The retailer's loyalty gravitates to whichever brand is selling best. Retail advertising also has an inherent urgency. Everything about the ad pushes the consumer toward a behavior such as visiting the store. Consequently, the retail ad includes price information, conditions of sales, color, sizes, and so on. National advertising is more concerned with image and attitude change. As a result, there tends to be less copy and fewer specifics. The third difference is that retail advertising is customized, to some extent, to reflect the local store. Typically, it includes basic information such as the store's name, address, telephone number, hours open for business, and so forth.

To build and maintain store traffic, a retailer must meet four objectives: build store *awareness,* create consumer *understanding* of items or services offered, *convince* consumers that the store's items and services are high-quality or economical, and create *consumer desire* to shop at this particular store. In addition, most retailers use advertising to help attract new customers, build store loyalty, increase the amount of the average sale, maintain inventory balance by moving out overstocks and outdated merchandise, and help counter seasonal lows.

With a few exceptions, retail advertising is less sophisticated and more utilitarian than national advertising. There are several reasons for this. First, retail advertising is more *short-term* than national advertising. Most retail ads deal with price and run for only a few days, whereas a national ad may be used for months or years.

In addition, retailers can't justify high production costs for advertising. National advertisers can easily justify spending $5,000 to produce a newspaper ad when they are paying $200,000 to run it in 100 large markets. A local retailer who places an ad in the local newspaper might have a media cost of only $400, making it difficult to justify spending $5,000 on production.

Most retailers have little formal training in advertising and therefore are often uncomfortable making professional advertising decisions. Consequently they rely on their media sales representatives to design and produce their ads. Most media advertising departments turn out several dozen ads a day, rather than working on one ad for 2 to 3 days as ad agencies do. Also, print media generally use *clip art* rather than custom art. Clip art services provide books of copyright-free pieces of art, which can be clipped and used as the advertiser sees fit. The ads work, but they are generally less "creative" than national brand advertising.

Cooperative Advertising

One way retailers can compensate for their smaller budgets and limited expertise is to take advantage of **cooperative advertising,** in which the manufacturer reimburses the retailer for part or all of the advertising expenses. Most manufacturers have some type of ongoing promotional program that provides retailers with advertising support in the form of money and advertising materials. Funds for cooperative advertising are available subject to certain guidelines and are generally based on a percentage of sales to the retailer. Ad 22.6 is an example of co-op advertising.

Co-op funds, which are sometimes referred to as *ad allowances,* are no longer just "a little something extra" from the manufacturer. In 1987

Marketing objective	Increase Acme's market share in the industry from 12 to 18 percent over the next 12 months, beginning January 19xx.	Run six two-page, four-color spreads every other month in *Widgeting World.*
Advertising objectives	Increase awareness in existing market of Acme Widgets from 35 to 55 percent over the next 12 months. Create awareness in new market of Acme Widgets from 0 to 20 percent over the next 12 months.	Run one half-page black-and-white ad each month in *Widgeting Product News* offering free technical manual "Widgeting Cross Sectional Dimensionality." Insert "800" toll-free number. Run four four-color spreads in June, July, September, and October issues of *ABC Monthly Roundup* and *ABC Process Times* announcing widgeting "breakthrough" cost superiority, without maintenance or quality deficiency, compared to ABC process. Emphasize Acme Widget new wider size range, technical top line, and free offer of "Widgeting Versatility" technical manual.
Target market and audience	Widget processing industry, plant engineers, product designers, and purchasing agents.	
Communication strategies		
Advertising	Prepare advertising copy to emphasize the production and purchasing benefits of one source of Widget product applications. Develop headline and illustrations to draw attention to the problems of multiple sourcing.	
Direct Mail		Rewrite "The Acme Widget Advantage" product brochure, emphasizing new wider range of sizes. Complete rewrite,

such payments totaled nearly $11 billion.* Ad allowances have become so widespread, in fact, that most retailers won't even consider taking on a new brand, especially one in a heavily advertised category, without receiving some support.

"Ad money," as it is also called, generally comes to retailers in one of three ways. An ad allowance is an amount that can change from month to month for each unit of purchase. The higher the amount, the more the retailer is expected to do. With an *accrual fund* the manufacturer automatically "accrues," or sets aside, a certain percentage of a retailer's purchases that the retailer may use for advertising at any time within a specified period.

Vendor support programs are developed by retailers themselves. Large drug and discount chains, for example, will periodically schedule a special advertising supplement. Their suppliers are offered an opportunity to "buy" space in this supplement. Suppliers are generally promised that no competing brands will be included.

To receive co-op money retailers must send the manufacturer a **tear sheet,** which is proof that the ad ran, and an invoice showing the cost of the

tear sheet *The pages from a newspaper on which an ad appears.*

*Ken Hustel, Newspaper Advertising Bureau, Chicago (April 1988).

editing, approval, and production by March 20, 19xx. Mail brochure and letter to customer list in April 19xx and to sales department's "hit list" the same month. Distribute brochure in bulk to district sales offices and distributor list in February.

Telemarketing   Hire telemarketing consultant in January to set up incoming telephone program. Complete upgrade by March.

Sales promotion   Schedule trade show for new market prospects for July 19xx at Cleveland Widget Expo. Promote trade show through invitations mailed with technical manual to new market sales leads. Complete invitation and trade show schedule outline by March 31. Complete trade show planning by June 15. Offer free "Widgeting Versatility" manual in nine fractional ads, April through December, in *Production Unlimited* and *Factory Engineering Extra,* inserting "800" toll-free phone number. Run same ad in *Perfect Plant* postcard mailing in September.

Publicity   Write and distribute press release and product brochure to *Widget Industries'* editorial department in January, emphasizing user and purchasing benefits of new larger-size range of Acme Widget Line. Distribute technical manual and press releases with a short synopsis to *Factory Engineering* editorial department in June. Research and write application case history, emphasizing the role of the wide range of widget sizes available from single-source Acme, for presentation to editor of *Widgeting World* in April for possible late spring or early summer publication.

Source: Adapted from Robert A. Kriegel, "Anatomy of a Marketing Communications Plan," *Business Marketing Magazine* (July 1983):72–78.

---

advertising. For broadcast ads, stations will provide the retailer with a letter, or *affadavit,* stating when the ad ran.

Manufacturers also make artwork available, which can be used for preparing catalogs and other print ads. Some manufacturers also provide a **dealer tag,** in which the store is mentioned at the end of a radio or television ad. Also available are window banners, bill inserts, and special direct-mail pieces, such as four-color supplements that carry the store's name and address.

The Robinson-Patman Act prohibits a manufacturer from offering one retailer a price or promotion incentive that will give that retailer an advantage over competitors in the same trading area. This restriction becomes especially delicate in food and pharmaceutical retailing, where almost all advertising is price advertising.

dealer tag *Time left at the end of a broadcast advertisement that permits identification of the local store.*

Trends in Retailing

The good old days of the mom-and-pop retailers who knew all their customers personally and who could count on their continued loyalty are gone. During the last 40 years there have been dramatic changes in retailing, many of which have had a direct impact on retail advertising.

TABLE 22.1
The Top 10 Specialty Chains

Rank	Company Chain (Headquarters)	Parent	Type	Sales (000,000)	% Gain (Decrease)	Units	% Gain (Decrease)
1.	Toys "R" Us[a] (Rochelle Park, N.J.)	Ind	Toys	$4,788	19.7	404	12.8
2.	The Limited (Columbus, Ohio)	Ind	Apparel	4,648	14.2	3,168	(6.3)
3.	Kinney Shoe (New York)	Wool	Shoe/Apparel	3,042	18.2	3,604	4.1
4.	Radio Shack[b] (Fort Worth)	Tan	ConsEl	2,940	2.5	4,821	0.2
5.	Circuit City (Richmond, Va.)	Ind	ConsEl	2,097	21.8	149	22.1
6.	Marshall's (Woburn, Mass.)	Mel	Apparel	1,939	10.6	347	12.3
7.	T.J. Maxx (Framingham, Mass.)	TJX	Apparel	1,677	12.9	352	14.3
8.	Gap Inc.[c] (San Bruno, Cal.)	Ind	Apparel	1,587	26.8	960	6.7
9.	Petrie Stores (Secaucus, N.J.)	Ind	Apparel	1,258	3.2	1,569	(0.1)
10.	U.S. Shoe (Cincinnati)	USS	Apparel	1,234	7.2	1,721	(2.1)

Source: STORES (August 1990):10.

Location.   One of the most significant changes in retailing has been the relocation of retail activity from city centers to suburbs. With the growth of the suburbs has come the development of shopping centers and malls. Merchants located in these complexes benefit from group promotions for the entire shopping center as well as from their own individual advertising.

Consolidation.   Ownership consolidation, especially among department stores and specialty chains, has brought mass merchandising to many stores that formerly operated on a smaller scale (see Tables 22.1 and 22.2). This consolidation of power among fewer retailers has changed the nature of the relationship between manufacturers and retailers. Retailers now dictate terms of sale, delivery dates, and product specifications. Wal-Mart, for example, had enough clout to force manufacturers such as Procter & Gamble and Colgate Palmolive to change over to biodegradable packaging (see Chapter 19). Consolidation has also given retailers a much greater interest in mass advertising. For example, Pier 1 Imports, a once-small specialty retailer, now spends $40 million annually on billable media (see Ad 22.7). Retailers such as Wal-Mart have also been able to dictate the creative strategy of many manufacturers. In addition, they have created tremendous growth in the use of different media, such as free-standing-inserts, in lieu of traditional newspaper space.

Nonstore Retailing.   Nonstore retailing is when the exchange between the manufacturer/retailer and the consumer takes place outside the traditional retail store. In the case of Mary Kay Cosmetics and Lands' End, the companies produce the product and sell it through door-to-door and catalog selling, respectively. Lillian Vernon, in contrast, purchases products from a variety of manufacturers and sells the products through her catalog. Nonstore retailing has grown in popularity for a variety of reasons. Most notably, the time-conscious consumer is no longer inclined to spend hours shopping for goods and services. Simultaneously, the quality and selection of the merchandise sold through nonstore retailing has greatly improved. Warranties and guarantees remove the risk associated with purchasing unseen merchandise. Finally, improvements of mailing lists have better matched the marketer with potential customers. The use of nonstore retailing has shifted a great deal of retail advertising toward direct marketing and direct mail.

TABLE 22.2
The Top 10 Department Store Divisions

Rank	Company Division (Headquarters)	Affil.	Units	Sq. Ft. (000)	Volume (000,000)
1.	J.C. Penney (Dallas, Tex.)	(Ind)	1,325	112,800	$14,469
2.	Mervyn's (Hayward, Cal.)	(DH)	221	17,486	3,858
3.	Macy's Northeast (New York)	(RHM)	46	14,937	3,350
4.	Dillard's (Little Rock, Ark.)	(Ind)	146	20,898	2,769
5.	Nordstrom (Seattle)	(Ind)	59	6,890	2,671.1
6.	Macy's South (Atlanta)	(RHM)	48	10,138	1,875
7.	Dayton Hudson (Minneapolis)	(DH)	37	7,711	1,801
8.	Macy's California (San Francisco)	(RHM)	25	5,846	1,545
9.	Bloomingdale's (New York)	(Cmp)	17	4,518	1,295
10.	Saks Fifth Avenue (New York)	(Bat)	45	NA	1,244

Source: STORES (July 1990):10.

Demographics. Several demographic changes in our society have a bearing on retail advertising. These changes include time compression, the aging of the population, geomarketing, and market fragmentation.

For families in which both spouses work, time is a valuable commodity. As a result, creative avenues must be found to reach consumers with messages that are short and sweet.

The population is made up of more elderly people, who are knowledgable and adept at shopping and have definite opinions on the value of brand names and the relationship between price and quality. Advertising copy must facilitate such comparisons.

In targeting consumers, a retailer's first concern is geography: Where do my customers live? How far will they drive to come to my store? The next concern is consumer taste. Geomarketing is a phenomenon geared to the increasing diversity in tastes and preferences. Retailers are attempting to develop offers that appeal to consumers in different parts of the country as well as in different neighborhoods in the same suburb. For example, H.E.B. Supermarkets operates its stores in both central and south Texas. In

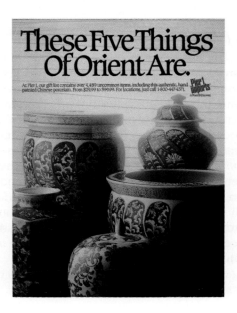

AD 22.7
Pier 1 Imports' use of four color, good photography, and catchy headlines shows how a retailer can create a positive image. (Courtesy of Pier 1 Imports.)

San Antonio, the stores located in Mexican-American neighborhoods carry a very different merchandise assortment than do those located in neighborhoods dominated by upscale apartments and condominiums. In contrast, national advertising targeting is more concerned with other factors such as age, income, education, and lifestyle.

Markets will continue to decrease in size as competitors segment them according to values, lifestyles, demographics, geographics, and product benefits. Advertising strategies must place greater emphasis on developing the appropriate image to match the consumer's lifestyle and less emphasis on price promotions.

Product Specialization. Many retailers have begun to specialize in merchandising products, such as electronics, running shoes, tennis equipment, baked potatoes, toys, and the like. In these cases retail advertising has become more like manufacturer advertising in that fewer products are highlighted and the emphasis is on image rather than a quick sale. Benetton, a clothing company that specializes in Italian sportswear, is an example of this type of retailing. Its ads often feature founder Luciano Benetton touting two or three of his new designs. Originality, quality, and image are always emphasized over price. However, as will become apparent in the discussion that follows, price copy is still prevalent because of growing competition in retailing and an uncertain economy.

Price Advertising. In recent years retail advertising has focused on price —more specifically on sale or discounted prices. Many retailers now use any reason they can find to have a sale (Presidents' Day, Tax Time, Overstocked). There are also EOM (end-of-month) sales and even hourly sales (Ayre's 14-Hour Sales, K mart's Midnight Madness Sale). This trend has led to retailers' complaints about the disappearance of consumer loyalty as people move from store to store searching for the best price.

As strange as it may seem, the items that retailers advertise at reduced prices are often not the ones they really want to sell. In order to offer a reduced price, retailers generally have to sacrifice part of their profit on each of these products. Sometimes stores even offer items for less than they paid for them merely to attract consumers to the store. These items are called **loss leaders.**

loss leader *Product advertised at or below cost in order to build store traffic.*

Types of Retail Advertising

Despite the great diversity in retailing, the nature of the advertising employed can be placed in one of two categories: product or institutional. *Product advertising* presents specific merchandise for sale and urges customers to come to the store immediately to buy it. This form of advertising helps to create and maintain the store's reputation through its merchandise. Product advertising centers around themes relating to merchandise that is new, exclusive, and of superior quality and designs (called *nonpromotional* advertising), as well as around themes relating to complete assortments and merchandise events (called *assortment* advertising). Sales announcements, special promotions, and other immediate-purpose ads are other forms of product advertising. When the sale price dominates the ad, it is called *promotional* or *sales* advertising. When sales items are interspersed with regular-priced items in the ad, it is referred to as *semipromotional advertising.*

Institutional retail advertising sells the store as an enjoyable place to shop. Through institutional advertising, the store helps to establish its image as a leader in fashion, price, and wide merchandise selection, as well as superior service, or quality, or whatever image the store chooses to cultivate.

RETAIL ADVERTISING: CREATIVITY, MEDIA, AND RESEARCH

Creating the Retail Ad

The primary difference between national and retail ad copy is the emphasis retail advertising places on *prices* and *store name*. Store image should be as important to a retailer as brand image is to a manufacturer. In order to build store traffic, ads are designed either to emphasize a reduced price on a popular item or to promote the store image by focusing on such things as unusual or varied merchandise, friendly clerks, or prestige brands.

Image or Price. For retail operations that sell products and services where there is little product differentiation, such as gasoline, banking, and car rentals, a positive, distinctive image is a valuable asset. The retailer can only convey this image through advertising. Pier 1 Imports, for example has maintained a very positive image through its high-quality print ads.

Price also can be a factor in establishing a store's image. Most discount stores signal their type of merchandise with large, bold prices. Several specialty retailers, emphasize price by offering coupons in much of their print advertising. Featuring prices doesn't necessarily apply only to ads that give the store a bargain or a discount image, however. Price can help the consumer comparison-shop without visiting the store. This basic information is appreciated by many consumers.

Executing Retail Ads. Because the main objective of retail ads is to attract customers, store location (or telephone number, if advertising a service) is essential. For merchandise that is infrequently purchased, such as cars, furniture, wallpaper, and hearing aids, the ad should include a map or mention a geographical reference point (for example, 3 blocks north of the state capitol building) in addition to the regular street address.

A creative mistake some retailers make is wanting to be the star or key spokesperson in their advertising. This is especially noticeable in broadcast commercials, where a presenter needs acting talent or training. Although hiring the acting superstars of advertising is beyond the budgets of most retailers, competent and affordable actors abound in most cities. In fact, local celebrities typically have greater attention-getting potential than does imported talent.

Small- and medium-size retailers often save money by using stock artwork. All daily newspapers subscribe to clip art services that provide a wide range of photographs and line drawings. Ad 22.8 is an example of stock artwork.

Larger retailers generally have their art custom-designed, which gives all of their ads a similar look and helps confer a distinctive image. Retailers have also found ways to make their television production more efficient by using a "donut" format in which the opening and closing sections are the same, whereas the middle changes to focus on different merchandise.

The recent trend in shopping center advertising is to produce a slick four-color "magazine" that carries editorial material, such as recipes, a calendar of local events, and other topics of local interest, in addition to ads

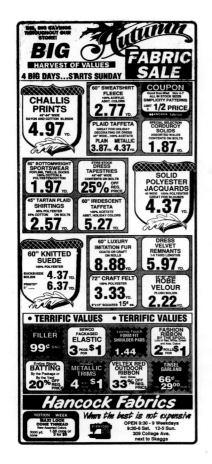

AD 22.8
This ad illustrates the use of stock artwork in retail advertising. (Courtesy of Hancock Fabrics.)

A PORTRAIT OF TWO FAMILIES WITH CREDIT CARDS

The Borrowers

The Borrowers and their two children and pets are real middle Americans. They are a young couple, both of whom work in full-time positions, she as a clerk, he as a blue-collar employee. They think they'll probably be changing those jobs within the next 2 years or so. They work hard; their combined income adds up to something under $40,000.

They're really having a difficult time making ends meet, partly because they feel they don't actually manage their money well, and they are constantly in debt. However, they're pretty sure that 5 years from now, their financial situation will be much easier. Ideally, they'd certainly like to pay cash for everything they buy, but for the present, they're quite dependent on their credit cards.

The Borrowers look for a credit card with the lowest interest rate because they already know they won't be paying the bill in full each month. An extended payment plan is essential. They also are well aware of and eager to use the cash advance services feature; they use the advances for paying large or unexpected bills. They don't much care whether the card is accepted by all the finest restaurants or fashionable stores or looks prestigious. Nor does the cash rebate feature mean much to them. They want to know the card can be used for any type of purchase, is accepted by small stores as well as discount stores, and will be promptly replaced within 24 hours if lost or stolen.

They don't feel guilty about their credit card use because they know they are trying to do the best they can for their families. With both parents working, life is busy and stressful enough. Why should they have to wait for years to buy the things they desire for themselves and their children?

As consumers, the Borrowers are quite distinctive. They are impulsive shoppers and not very well informed about the products and services they will buy. They intend to purchase some rather expensive items within the next few years, and of course, they also constantly need to buy clothes for their children. Even with their credit card borrowing, they certainly don't have the funds for investments or exotic travel, much as they might like the idea of adventure.

The Borrowers would rather spend a quiet evening at home than go out to a party. It's definitely more relaxing at home, once they actually get there. They like to have cookouts or rent video movies, and they love to watch television. In fact, with *TV Guide* beside them, the screen is apt to be their primary form of entertainment. They are likely to watch prime-time movies, *The Cosby Show, Cheers, Family Ties,* and national talk shows. They are not too inter-

for the retail stores in the shopping center. Centers interested in projecting a status image to upscale consumers make the greatest use of this magazine concept.

Who Does the Creative Work? Most retail advertising is created and produced by one or a combination of the following: in-house staff, media, ad agencies, and freelancers. The larger the retail operation, the more likely it is to have an in-house advertising staff. An in-house agency can guarantee a consistent look and can react on short notice. One disadvantage of the in-house agency is lack of creativity, as many good creative people prefer working for a multiclient agency where the work is more diversified and the pay is often higher.

All local media create and produce ads for retailers. With the exception of television, most provide this service free. The medium- and larger-size newspapers and stations often have people whose only job is to write and produce ads.

ested in Public Broadcasting System (PBS) programs. Television is a good form of escape for them, and they take advantage of it. They have a kind of relaxed attitude toward television content and toward the appearance of propriety. Thus, they're not too worried about people chewing gum in public, or men wearing too much jewelry, or the fact that the husband happens to be the one who does the family laundry.

Their real worries are in the financial realm. Will they ever seem to get ahead? Will they ever be able to pay off those credit cards once and for all?

The Payers

The Payers are a middle-aged, middle-class couple who lead a comfortable suburban existence. They are both in their early fifties, their children no longer live at home, and they do have pets. The husband is a college graduate who works full time in an administrative job and earns approximately $45,000. His wife is a homemaker. He is seriously thinking about his retirement years, at which time they'll just stay right where they are for the rest of their days.

The Payers are quite satisfied with the way things are going for them. He feels he works hard but is not under stressful conditions. They like to be in their home, but they also enjoy eating in restaurants, visiting museums, and taking vacation trips abroad. Even after expenditures like these, they still have money left for savings and investments.

They think they manage their money quite well and can avoid financial emergencies. Their family income seems to be sufficient to satisfy almost all of their important desires. In fact, they suspect that may have more to spend on extras than most of their neighbors. They will probably make a major household purchase within the next year, quite possibly with a credit card. They don't see themselves resorting to paying off that card over time, however. Instead, they'll pay the full amount when the statement arrives. They don't really like to embark on major purchases without knowing they'll have the money available, and, conversely, they're not very willing to pay interest simply in order to have things right away. They are careful shoppers and seek out information before buying expensive items. They do not in the least consider themselves impulsive buyers.

The Payers use their credit cards more frequently and for larger amounts than the Borrowers do. They want credit cards with a low fee and widespread acceptability by hotels, motels, fine restaurants, and major airlines. They don't especially care about such features as extended payment schedules or immediate increases in credit limits.

Retail stores often advertise which credit cards are accepted (Mike Mazzaschi/Stock, Boston.)

Although some professional retail ads are created by agencies, this is the most costly way to produce ads. Also, because agencies work for many different clients, they cannot always respond as quickly as an in-house agency can. Mary Joan Glynn, former marketing vice president at Bloomingdale's, who became the managing director of BBDO Merchants Group, claims that no agency is prepared to handle the large number of day-to-day copy changes that are characteristic of major retail advertising. She says that what an agency can best do for a retailer is develop an image or position that can then "be set and implemented in-house for newspapers with the agency handling the electronic media."*

Freelancers often provide a good compromise between an in-house staff and an ad agency. They generally charge a lower hourly rate than do ad agencies because they work out of their home and therefore have minimal overhead.

*"Retail Report," *Television/Radio Age* (September 29, 1986):59.

Buying and Selling Local Media

Perhaps the most rapidly changing area in retail advertising is the buying and selling of local media time and space. On the buying side, retailers are becoming more sophisticated about media as they are being forced to work with tighter budgets, are getting more advertising help and advice from their suppliers, are being exposed to more media ideas at association workshops and seminars, and are being educated by a growing number of media salespeople.

At the same time, local media competition has significantly increased. Nearly all major markets now have, in addition to network affiliates, at least one local independent plus a public television station (which now solicits underwriting, a type of soft-sell advertising). These stations, along with local advertising that is now being sold by the national cable networks, have created many more television opportunities for the retailer. Most of the top 50 markets have at least one local magazine offering retailers high-quality four-color ads to reach the upscale consumer. Examples are *Los Angeles Magazine, Southwest,* and *Palm Springs Life.*

The increase in competition for the retailers' advertising dollar has resulted in a different type of selling. Salespeople increasingly emphasize advertising and promotion ideas rather than just rate cards and circulation figures. Unfortunately, many retailers still buy advertising strictly on price or number of spots. Some retailers don't realize that five spots during morning-drive time on the market's leading radio station can sometimes reach more people than can 50 spots that run between 2:00 A.M. and 4:00 A.M.

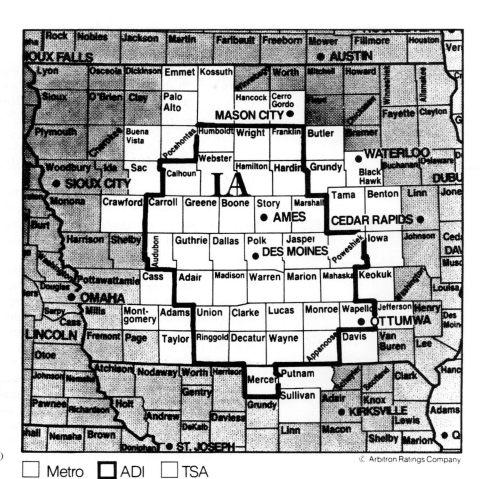

FIGURE 22.2
This ADI map illustrates how you might be buying more coverage than you need when you buy television. The Des Moines ADI, for example, includes 32 counties.
(Copyright 1988 Arbitron Ratings Company.)

☐ Metro ☐ ADI ☐ TSA

Retail Media Strategy. Unlike national advertisers, retailers generally prefer reach over frequency. A retailer with a "⅓ Off All Women's Casual Shoes" ad doesn't have to tell this more than once or twice to women interested in saving money on a pair of casual shoes. In contrast, a national advertiser with an image campaign like Coke continually needs to remind soft drink users that "Coke is it."

Because retailers can choose from many local media, they must be careful not to buy a lot of wasted circulation (see Chapter 9). Take, for example, an ordinary bakery in an area of dominant interest (ADI) like Des Moines, Iowa, that has approximately 380,000 households and 24 other bakeries. Over 80 percent of this bakery's business will come from within a 3-mile radius that contains only 6 percent of the ADI's households, as shown in Figure 22.2. If this bakery uses television advertising that covers the total ADI, the bakery will be wasting over 90 percent of its advertising dollars. Successful retailers use media that minimize waste. Direct mail, which is narrowly targeted, is now the second-largest advertising medium used by retailers. Also, many newspapers can zone the delivery of advertising circulars and inserts, offering geographical targeting to neighborhoods, counties, or even zip codes.

Media Alternatives

Retailers may choose from the entire arsenal of media alternatives. Both local and national retailers may use an identical media mix to reach a particular local target market. In general, however, local retailers are interested only in local media and stay clear of media that reach an audience beyond their immediate markets. There are several media that are more relevant to retailers.

Newspapers. Newspapers have always made up the bulk of the retailer's advertising, probably because the local nature of newspapers fits the retailer's desire for geographic coverage, prestige, and immediacy. In addition, newspapers are a participative medium that people read in part for the advertising. In fact, many people use newspapers as a shopping guide. Also, retailers can gain some measure of audience selectivity by advertising in specific sections of the paper, such as the sports, society, and financial pages.

Most retailers that advertise regularly make *space contracts* with the newspaper. In the contract the retailer agrees to use a certain amount of space over the year and pay a certain amount per line, which is lower than the paper's open rate for the same space. The lower rate is simply a quantity discount.

In addition to special rates, newspapers have developed several other products or services to remain competitive. Many newspapers will provide retail advertisers with their zip/postal code circulation reports, which identify the circulation level for that newspaper in the various zip codes. This information, combined with zone editions of the paper (certain versions of the paper go to certain counties, cities, and so on), greatly reduces the wasted circulation often associated with large newspapers. Special advertising sections, such as preprints, can be inserted in these various papers. Specialty-type papers, such as shoppers, have also emerged.

Shoppers and Preprints. Free-distribution newspapers (shoppers) that are dropped off at millions of suburban homes once or twice each week are becoming increasingly popular advertising outlets for retailers. More than

3,000 such papers are published in the United States, such as *Center Island Pennysavers,* distributed in Long Island, New York.*

Preprints are advertising circulars furnished by a retailer for distribution as a *free-standing insert* in newspapers. In recent years preprinted inserts have also become popular with retailers striving for greater market coverage. For example, preprints account for 81 percent of Wal-Mart's advertising budgets.†

Magazines. Many magazines have regional or metropolitan editions. They enable local retailers to buy exposure to the audience within their trading area only. Sears, K mart, and J. C. Penney advertise in monthlies targeted to particular audience segments and in weeklies to accommodate short-term sales patterns. Grocery retailers use magazines primarily for institutional or image ads.

Broadcast Media. Local retailers advertise on television and radio as well, but broadcast media are used primarily to supplement newspaper advertising. Both offer important advantages over print media. Radio has a relatively low cost and a high degree of geographic and audience selectivity. It also provides high flexibility in spot scheduling, and this flexibility carries over into creativity. Radio will help retail advertisers write the ads, provide live hookups from the store or any other location, and is able to take advantage of last-minute events. For example, a station in Colorado Springs helped a hardware store sell hundreds of snow shovels when an unexpected storm dumped 7 inches of snow one April morning.

Many of the same advantages are found in local television. The cost of television is higher, however, as is the creative expertise needed to produce satisfactory commercials. Television stations will produce commercials for a fee. The expense problem has been reduced somewhat by the advent of cable television with its ability to show a retail commercial in the local market only. Cable also offers the retailer the kind of selectivity that network television cannot. Undoubtedly, as more and more homes are hooked up to cable, retailers will view television as an affordable, effective media alternative.

Directories. Telephone directories (the Yellow Pages) are important advertising media for retailers. In the Yellow Pages the retailer pays for an alphabetical listing (and a larger display ad, if desired) within a business category. The overwhelming majority of retailers advertise in the Yellow Pages (refer to Chapter 17). The advantages are widespread customer usage and long life (1 year or more). The disadvantages include limited flexibility and long lead times for new ads. Retailers who don't get their ads to the Yellow Pages in time (for example, a camera-ready ad must often be mailed by May or June for the September directory) will have to wait an entire year.

Direct Response. Direct response is a medium retailers use extensively to communicate their product offerings to a select group of consumers. In direct-response advertising, the retailer creates its own advertisement and distributes it directly to consumers either through the mail or through the personal distribution of circulars, handbills, and other printed matter. Although direct-response advertising is expensive in terms of cost per thou-

*"Free-Distribution Shopper's Are Posing Serious Threat to Daily Newspapers," *The Wall Street Journal* (June 19, 1984):31.
†Susan Caminiti, "What Ails Retailing," *Fortune* (January 30, 1989):61–62.

sand, it is actually the most selective medium because the ads are read only by people the retailer selects. It is also a personal form of advertising and extremely flexible. Direct-response advertising can include pictures, letters, records, pencils, coins, coupons, premiums, samples, and any other gifts the retailer chooses.

Retail Market Research

Information about the local market is becoming more and more valuable to retailers. Although retail stores that belong to a national chain often receive research findings from their parent company, most independent retailers must depend on the media and their suppliers for local marketing research information. Many commercial research companies like Simmons and PRIZM provide information on the top markets.

One of the most valuable, yet inexpensive, types of research a retailer can conduct is to identify its customers. This can be done by analyzing charge-card files or by sponsoring a contest or sweepstakes. Businesses that issue their own charge cards report that two-thirds of their sales come from their charge-card customers. Smart retailers send up to a dozen direct-mail pieces to these customers each year in addition to their regular advertising. The purpose of sweepstakes is to use an entry form that asks for customer name, address, age, income, or whatever information is desired.

Retailers can also conduct focus groups to help determine their store's image. These are best if arranged and conducted by an outside trained research service. To help test ad copy, one furniture retailer had a direct-mail piece made up for a mattress sale and sent it to a limited number of households. When he found it had a relatively good response, he then placed the same copy and artwork in a newspaper ad.

Just as most retailers can't justify spending large sums on ad production, neither can they for marketing research. Retailers have direct consumer contact and can quickly determine which ads work. That's one advantage they have over national advertisers.

SUMMARY

- Business-to-business advertising is used to influence demand and is directed at people in the business arena who buy or specify products for business use. Its objectives include creating company awareness, increasing selling efficiency, and supporting channel members.
- Compared to the consumer market, the market for business goods is relatively limited, decision making tends to be shared by a group of people, and purchasing decisions center around price, services, product quality, and assurance of supply.

- Business-to-business media consist of general business and trade publications, directories, direct mail, catalogs, data sheets, and consumer media.
- Compared to national advertising, retail advertising is less concerned with brand awareness and more concerned with attracting customers.
- Retail advertising uses various media alternatives, from shoppers and preprinted inserts to television and radio.
- Identifying customers is one of the most valuable kinds of research a retailer can conduct.

QUESTIONS

1. You are developing an ad to reach chemists in the oil industry. Would you place this ad in a general business magazine or in a trade publication? Why?
2. How does retail advertising differ from national advertising?

3. Think of a restaurant in your community. What types of people does it target? Would you recommend that its advertising focus on price or image? What is (or should be) its image? Which media should it use?

4. Biogen Corporation's corporate mission is to become a leading company in genetic research and development for health industries. Privately held at time of incorporation, it has decided to go public and have its stock traded. How would corporate advertising assist Biogen in its mission? What audience targets should be priorities for its communication programs? Should it develop more than one campaign?

5. Although personal selling is a vital marketing tool for industrial (business to business) companies, advertising also has a significant role in many marketing situations. What if a limited budget means expanding one at the sacrifice of the other, however? Suppose you were making a decision for a company that is beginning a marketing effort for a new set of products; you'll need approximately six new salespeople. If an advertising campaign to introduce the firm would mean hiring four salespeople instead of six, is the advertising worth it? Explain the strengths and weaknesses of this idea.

6. Tom and Wendi Promise have just purchased a frozen-yogurt franchise. They found a good lease in a neighborhood shopping center, but the cost of franchising, leasing, and other charges have left them very little for advertising. With limited dollars, Tom and Wendi can only afford one of the following options: a) Yellow Pages display ad, b) a series of advertisements in the area's weekly "shopper" newspaper, c) advertising in the area's college newspaper (the campus is six blocks from the store). Which of these opportunities will best help Tom and Wendi get the awareness they need?

7. Abby Wilson, the advertising manager for a campus newspaper (published four times per week) is discussing ways to increase advertising revenues with her sales staff. She asks opinions on using sales time to promote a co-op program to interest campus-area businesses. One salesperson says the retailers won't be bothered with all the "paperwork." Another explains that newspaper reps really have to understand co-op to sell it, and that none of Wilson's staff has experience. Would you be persuaded that promoting cooperative advertising is more trouble than it is worth?

FURTHER READINGS

BEISEL, JOHN L, *Contemporary Retailing* (New York: Macmillan, 1987).

BERMAN, BARRY, AND JOEL R. EVANS, *Retail Management: A Strategic Approch,* 3rd ed. (New York: Macmillan, 1986).

BOLEN, WILLIAM H., *Contemporary Retailing,* 3rd ed. (Englewood Cliffs, NJ: Prentice Hall, 1988).

DIAMOND, JAY, AND GERALD PINTEL, *Retailing Today* (Englewood Cliffs, NJ: Prentice Hall, 1988).

FERN, EDWARD F., and JAMES R. BROWN, "The Industrial/Consumer Marketing Dichotomy: A Case of Insufficient Justification," *Journal of Marketing 48* (Spring 1984): 68–77.

HALL, S. ROLAND, *Retail Advertising and Selling* (New York: Garland Publications, 1985).

MASON, J. BARRY, and MORRIS L. MAYER, *Modern Retailing: Theory and Practice,* 4th ed. (Plano, TX: Business Publications, Inc. 1987).

VIDEO CASE

Price Chopper: "Best Foods/Best Price"

NEW YORK

As the largest grocery retailer in the Kansas City area Price Chopper continually faced increasing competition from both new and existing retail grocery operations. As the volume leader, Price Chopper stood to lose the most in terms of market share, particularly because the Kansas City area was experiencing no significant population growth.

To combat this increased competition, Noble & Associates, Price Choppers' advertising agency, recommended a new creative strategy for its client in 1989. The principle campaign objective was to maintain Price Chopper's share of market leadership while fighting off the increased competition from new and existing retail grocery competitors in the Kansas City market. The creative strategy itself offered shoppers the dual benefits of low price and high quality. Thus, it positioned Price Chopper as the retail grocery that sold the best and the freshest perishable foods.

This approach was not unusual in the grocery industry; the large national branded products such as Kellogg, Heinz, and Pepsi are essentially "commodities" that are carried in all stores with virtually the same selection of items. Consequently, branded products can only be differentiated on a price basis. However, items that have traditionally been viewed as commodities, such as fresh fruits, vegetables, and meats, as well as freshly prepared foods such as bakery items, currently afford retail grocers the best opportunity to distinguish themselves from one another: These items can truly be "branded" and vary from store to store. This is particularly important because fresh foods are typically ranked by consumers as the most important criteria in selecting a grocery store.

Price Chopper and Noble & Associates summarized the consumer benefits of this creative strategy as follows: Price Chopper brings consumers the best and the freshest food at the best price. Hence, consumers could obtain the best food value in Kansas City at Price Chopper. All effective creative strategies include "support" statements that justify the consumer benefit and, thus, enhance its credibility. The support for Price Chopper's consumer benefit include the following: 1) Price Chopper buys and makes the best food in Kansas City; 2) Price Chopper buys more food than any other retail grocery operation in Kansas City; 3) Price Chopper's large volume purchasing results in the lowest prices in Kansas City; and 4) Price Chopper's large volume purchasing and high turnover results in the freshest food.

Price Chopper primarily targeted women between the ages of 18 and 54 and identified men between 18 and 54 as a secondary target. This is a fairly traditional retail grocery target audience because women still represent the most common grocery shoppers. The target audiences were further defined as men and women who are concerned about both good value and good quality. Noble & Associates also knew from syndicated data that Price Chopper held the largest share of voice in the Kansas City Area of Dominant Influence (ADI). Specifically, Price Chopper's media expenditures accounted for 30 percent of all retail grocery television advertising media weight in the Kansas City area, followed by Food Barn with 20 percent, Food For Less with 12 percent, Bob's IGA with 10 percent, and Hy-Vee Markets with 8 percent. This large share of voice put Price Chopper in the best position to create or modify consumer's perceptions about the chain via its advertising efforts.

Early market research results indicated that the campaign successfully enhanced Price Chopper's image among grocery shoppers in the Kansas City market. Within the first year of the campaign's introduction in October 1989, Price Chopper's market share had increased by 5 points to 36 percent, more than double the share increase experienced in the prior year. This was achieved during a period of flat population growth in the Kansas City area and less than a 1 percent increase in all-commodity grocery sales volume (ACV) and no new Price Chopper store openings.

Additional research results indicated that consumer recall of the campaign tagline "Best Food/Best Price" was 80 percent among Price Chopper customers and 43 percent among total Kansas City residents. Research conducted just 2 months after the campaign started indicated that the "Jammin Nanas" spot successfully communicated the overall message of "Price Chopper sells more quality fruit at a lower price than any other store."

Thus, in a very competitive, no-growth environment, Price Chopper and Noble & Associates were able to increase grocery sales significantly, due almost exclusively to the power of advertising. Although the success of any advertising effort is intimately linked to the product's or service's ability to deliver the advertising claims, creative advertising with a sales-oriented message still represents one of the most powerful competitive tools available for companies today.

QUESTIONS

1. Typically grocery retailers emphasize either food price or food quality in their advertising. Explain what additional demographic factors besides age and sex should be included in a grocery retailer's target audience definition for a price-based advertising strategy and for a food quality-based advertising strategy.

2. Explain why it would be difficult for a smaller grocery retailer in the Kansas City market to success-

fully employ a "Best Food/Best Price" advertising strategy.

3. Based on your existing knowledge of traditional retail grocery advertising, what general characteristics in addition to those discussed above make "Jammin Nanas" different from the bulk of existing grocery advertising?

Source: Courtesy of Noble & Associates.

23

International Advertising

Chapter Objectives

When you have completed this chapter, you should be able to:

- Distinguish between local, regional, international, and global brands
- Explain how international advertising is created and executed
- Understand how international agencies are organized
- List the special problems that international advertisers face
- Observe changes in Eastern Europe advertising with greater comprehension

*T*HE SOFTNESS NO ONE COULD BEAT

In early 1987 Cellox was the best-selling brand of toilet tissue in Thailand, with a market share of over 30 percent, followed by Scott and Delsey. At that time, both Cellox (the local brand) and Scott (the international brand) were manufactured by the same factory and were in the standard-price segment of toilet tissue, the largest segment. For no reported reason, Cellox was forced to withdraw the brand from the market in September 1987. One month later Scott, taking advantage of an opportunity, broadcast its first television commercial with the message that "Cellox is now changed to Scott." Within a few months Scott had taken over the Cellox market share and become the market leader, as most Cellox users switched to Scott when they were unable to find Cellox on the shelf. Without any real competitors, Scott had become the only seller in the standard-price segment.

In October 1988 armed with improved product quality and a stronger distribution network, Cellox was reintroduced to Thai consumers in the same old package as before. Research indicated that the Cellox name had remained in the minds of most consumers and that the brand was perceived quite favorably. As a result, Cellox's advertising strategy was built around two themes: "The return of Cellox" and, capturing a market position favored by consumers, "The softness that no one can beat."

Cellox broadcast two television commercials during a period of 2 weeks, the first asking, "Where has the missing Cellox been?" and the second answering, "The good old Cellox is now coming back!" This initial advertising was followed by the thematic television commercial, "The Naked Little Kid," which was supported by billboard advertising and point-of-purchase materials (see Ad. 23.1). Six months later Cellox had regained its market share and its position as the market leader in the standard-price seg-

AD 23.1
The "Naked Little Kid" campaign succeeded in reviving a local brand-name product that had been ousted by an international competitor. (Courtesy of Cellox.)

CHILD : BUT THEN...MOM'S SHIRT IS ALSO SOFT.　CHILD : SO WHAT COULD BE...

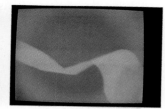

CHILD : IT'S CELLOX!　　　　　SOFTER...MORE COMFORTABLE.

FEMALE ANNCR : CELLOX ROLL TISSUES...

THE SOFTER, MORE COMFORTABLE TOUCH.

ment of toilet tissue. As of 1990, Cellox had maintained that position and had a market share of more than 30 percent.

As a local brand, Cellox employed many of the same advertising and marketing skills in its comeback as Scott had used to take over the brand in an international market. Cellox had a task to accomplish ("gain back product position"), a purpose ("persuade the target audience to specify Cellox instead of Scott every time they buy toilet tissue"), and a media plan that included identifying the target audience (female housewives age 20 and up) and identifying the media to be used (television, the Thai daily newspaper, billboards, and supermarket shopping carts).* These are all specific parts of any advertising program.

In this case a local company fought back against an international company, employing its resources even more effectively than its larger competitor did. The marketplace is increasingly international in scope, but each market is its own facet of the larger mosaic. This chapter will deal with aspects of advertising that are now relevant wherever free or relatively free markets exist.

EVOLUTION OF INTERNATIONAL MARKETING

Since Wendell Willkie coined the phrase "One World" in his 1940 presidential campaign, the distance between the concept and the reality has narrowed. The top 25 worldwide marketers spent approximately 45 percent of their advertising dollars outside the United States in 1989, and only nine of those marketers were headquartered in the United States. Table 23.1 lists the top 20 international advertisers of 1989. The evolution of advertising from the home country to a foreign country to regional blocs to a worldwide audience is the subject of this chapter. Included in this discussion are the tools of international management, the means of organizing for interna-

*DDB Needham Worldwide, *Case Study: Cellox Toilet Tissues.*

TABLE 23.1
Top 20 Global Advertisers: 1989 Ranking of World Advertising Spending by Company

Rank		Advertiser	Headquarters	Primary Business	Worldwide Spending ($ million)	% Non-U.S.
World	Non-U.S.					
1	2	Procter & Gamble	U.S.A.	Soaps	2,713.3	34.4
2	5	Philip Morris Cos.	U.S.A.	Food, tobacco	2,502.1	17.2
3	1	Unilever NV	U.K./Netherlands	Soaps, food	1,744.2	65.4
4	13	General Motors Corp.	U.S.A.	Automobiles	1,687.7	19.2
5	3	Nestlé SA	Switzerland	Food	1,143.0	46.8
6	43	McDonald's	U.S.A.	Restaurants	934.1	17.1
7	48	Pepsico, Inc.	U.S.A.	Food	913.8	14.0
8	20	Ford Motor Co.	U.S.A.	Automobiles	870.7	30.9
9	31	Kellogg Co.	U.S.A.	Food	823.7	25.7
10	14	Toyota Motor Corp.	Japan	Automobiles	739.8	43.6
11	9	Nissan Motor Co.	Japan	Automobiles	649.3	53.7
12	17	Mars	U.S.A.	Food	583.6	49.7
13	7	Matsushita Electric	Japan	Electronics	568.9	68.1
14	32	Sony Corp.	Japan	Electronics	560.8	36.4
15	23	Honda Motor Co.	Japan	Automobiles	546.4	45.3
16	11	Mazda Motor Corp.	Japan	Automobiles	529.7	62.9
17	22	Colgate-Palmolive Co.	U.S.A.	Soaps	503.4	51.1
18	10	Volkswagen AG	Germany	Automobiles	467.5	71.8
19	4	Renault SA	France	Automobiles	432.0	100.0
20	6	Fiat SpA	Italy	Automobiles	403.5	99.9

Source: *Advertising Age* (November 19, 1990):S-4. Copyright Crain Communications Inc.

local brand *A brand that is marketed in one specific country.*

regional brand *A brand that is available throughout an entire region.*

international brand *A brand of product that is available in most parts of the world.*

international advertising *Advertising designed to promote the same product in different countries and cultures.*

tional advertising, creating and planning international advertising campaigns, and special problems encountered in the field.

In most countries markets are composed of local, regional, and international brands. A **local brand** is one marketed in a single country. A **regional brand** is one marketed throughout a region—for example, North America or Europe. An **international brand** is available virtually everywhere in the world. This chapter deals with regional and international brands, products, and services, and with the advertising that supports them.

International advertising is a relatively recent development within international commerce. It did not appear in any organized manner until the late nineteenth century. Ancient records in Egypt, Persia, Greece, and Rome refer to metals, spices, fabrics, gemstones, and other materials "of value" that were exchanged over extensive distances. This commercial intercourse was, except for tribute or taxes, based on the "trading" of goods from one region to another.

By the Middle Ages, Holland was trading tulip bulbs internationally in exchange for various products and services. English, French, Spanish, and Dutch companies procured spices, tea, and silk in the Orient for European consumers. This was not considered "marketing" as we define it, however, because the old trading companies were not developing products for the European market, nor were producers in Turkey, China, the Philippines, and Indonesia seeking to stimulate demand for their goods in Europe.

Marketing emerged with the emphasis changed from importing products (tea, spices, silk, gold, and silver) to exporting products. Advertising was used to introduce, explain, and sell the benefits of a product—especially a branded product—in markets outside the home country. Stanley Tools and S. C. Johnson were two of the earliest companies to advertise internationally. The current patterns of international expansion emerged in the mid-twentieth century. Understanding these patterns will help us to appreciate both how international advertisers have operated and some of the restrictions that custom and history have imposed on them throughout the years.

Home-Country Production

Figure 23.1, although hypothetical, illustrates the development of products from companies such as S. C. Johnson, Nestlé, and Stanley Tools outside their home markets. It starts with a product that is beginning to reach saturation in its home market and cannot grow faster than the population. At this point, management seeks to recapture the sales gains of the growth pe-

FIGURE 23.1
The typical S-curve life cycle of a product.

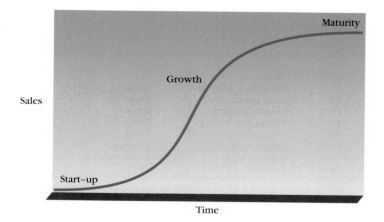

riod. This can be accomplished in one of two ways. The company can introduce new products or it can expand into foreign markets. International expansion involves the following steps:

- Production of goods in the home country
- Export of goods to another country and appointment of an importer or a local distributor
- Transfer of management from the home-country export manager to on-site management
- Local manufacture of the imported products and of new products for the product lines; acquisition of local companies
- Coordinated regional manufacturing, marketing, and advertising
- Coordinated global marketing

The progression from exporting to the development of a regional trading bloc and finally to global marketing and advertising is far smoother in theory than in reality. Wars, currency fluctuations, product shortages, and restrictions on the flow of capital (such as those in the United States in the late 1960s) affect planning. It is not the saturation of the home-country market alone that causes companies to move products outside their home markets. After World War II market research was used to evaluate the potential of foreign markets, acquisitions put companies into new national markets and brought products whose potential could be exploited into neighboring countries, and companies moved into foreign markets to preempt development by competitors.

The sequence of steps outlined above can be used for understanding the growth and intensity of international marketing and advertising.

Export

The physical exportation of a product requires a means of inserting that product into the distribution system of another country. The exporter typically appoints a distributor or an importer who assumes responsibility for marketing and advertising in the new country.

As volume grows, the complexity of product sizes, product lines, pricing, and local adaptation increases. The exporter might send an employee to work with the importer to handle details, to verify that promised activities are being carried out, and to solve communication problems. This employee serves as a facilitator between the exporter and the importer. Some companies prefer to appoint a local distributor who knows the language and the distribution system and can therefore handle customers and the government better than a foreigner could.

The Japanese followed this route in their export drive after World War II. Although they set up their own companies in some major countries, they relied heavily on local ad agencies, particularly U.S. agencies, which built relationships with Japanese managements and learned Japanese business customs. For example, Grey Advertising serves Canon in the United States, Canada, and 11 countries in Europe and Asia. The FCB Publicis Agency works for Mazda Motors in North America and three other nations, BBDO handles Sony in the United States and four other markets, and Saatchi & Saatchi handles Toyota in North America and eight other countries, but not in the agency's home market, the United Kingdom.

The large Japanese agencies typically have not been given global assignments by their clients in the home islands. Both Dentsu and Hakuhodo, the leading Japanese agencies, are looking for opportunities to expand in Europe and North America, however, Kouichi Segawa, deputy director of

Dentsu's overseas operations planning division, has said, "We need our own network to meet the [international] needs of our clients. We will develop [an international presence] through acquisition rather than starting new agencies."*

Exporting is still the first step in international marketing. In 1989, for example, Lands' End tested the European and Japanese markets by shipping directly from its home office in Dodgeville, Wisconsin. The company generated orders by placing small space advertising in English in both Japan and Europe, encouraging Americans to order their products by fax.

Transfer of Management

As the product or product line grows in export markets, it receives greater attention from the exporter. This process may involve sending someone from management to work in the importer's organization or to supervise the importer from an office in the importing country. At this point, the company still considers itself a domestic producer that is exporting products to other markets. As long as this is true, the transferred employee must still secure approval of plans, obtain funds for operations, and defend sales forecasts to a company management that is primarily concerned with the domestic market. Until just recently, this was the pattern for farm-equipment manufacturers. However, some are now moving their manufacturing to low-wage areas closer to markets in order to compete better in the 1990s.

Nationalization

A Citibank Office in Hong Kong. How would international status affects a company's advertising strategies? (John Lei/Stock, Boston.)

As the local importer-distributor grows with the imported line, the exporter may want greater control over the product or a larger share of the profits. As a result, he or she may buy back the rights contracted to the importer or set up assembly (or even manufacturing) facilities in the importing country. The result is the transfer of management and manufacturing to what was the importing country. The resourceful transferee will seek means of increasing sales and profits. At this point, the key marketing decisions focus on the acquisition or introduction of products especially for the local market. For example, Japanese car makers are now developing cars specifically for the United States from design studios located in California to be built in their "transplants" in Middle America.

Regionalization

As the exporter's operations become nationalized in a regional bloc, the company establishes an international regional management center and transfers responsibilities for day-to-day management from the home country to the regional office. The regions are the major trading areas: Europe, Latin America, Asia-Pacific, and North America. Numerous American companies followed this pattern after World War II: exporting, establishing local subsidiaries, and acquiring local companies. Corporations such as ITT, S. C. Johnson, Procter & Gamble, and IBM all had European management centers by the 1960s, and most major companies have them now. When a company is regionalized, it still focuses on the domestic market, but international considerations are becoming more important.

---

*David Kilburn, "Dentsu Pushing Non-Japan Growth," *Advertising Age* (May 21, 1991):41.

THE GLOBAL PERSPECTIVE

global perspective *A corporate philosophy that directs products and advertising toward a worldwide rather than a local or regional market.*

After a company has regionalized its operations, it faces the ultimate decision: If the home office is in the United States, should it now create a North American division and separate its corporate management from identification with any one country or region? Once this separation occurs, it will take time—perhaps even a business generation—for a global perspective to emerge. A **global perspective** directs the advertising of a product to a worldwide market. This change has been made by such companies as Unilever, Shell (both of which have headquarters in the United Kingdom and the Netherlands), Arthur Andersen, IBM, Nestlé, and Interpublic. The achievement of a global perspective requires internationalizing the management group because as long as management is located exclusively in one country, a global perspective will be difficult to achieve.

As we mentioned earlier, virtually every product category can be divided into local, regional, and international brands. *International* brands are those that are marketed in two or more of the four major regional blocs: North America, Latin America, Europe, and Asia-Pacific. (China is becoming a major part of the Asia-Pacific bloc.) Table 23.2 lists the top agencies in the Latin American, European, and Asia-Pacific blocs. The fifth bloc, Eastern Europe, has changed substantially since 1989 and is increasingly participating in European commerce. Although it will exist as a trading region for some years to come, the Eastern European bloc seems likely to be subsumed into the European bloc eventually. The sixth bloc—Africa, the Middle East, and Southern Asia—is so much smaller economically than the others that it is usually attached to Europe or even Asia-Pacific.

TABLE 23.2
Top Agency Standings in the Major Regional Blocs

		Who's on Top in Latin America			
Rank	Agency	1989 Lat. Amer. Gross Income by Equity	1989 Lat. Amer. Gross Income as % of Worldwide	1989 Lat. Amer. Billings by Equity	1989 Lat. Amer. Billings as % of Worldwide
1	McCann-Erickson Worldwide	$73,464	10.3	$490,006	10.3
2	J. Walter Thompson Co.	58,092	9.3	342,795	7.8
3	Ogilvy & Mather Worldwide	42,888	6.1	295,622	6.1
4	Lintas:Worldwide	40,698	6.9	271,453	6.9
5	Duailibi, Petit, Zaragoza	34,616	NA	139,550	NA
6	Young & Rubicam	25,887	3.0	172,142	2.6
7	Leo Burnett Co.	24,732	5.1	190,568	5.9
8	Foote, Cone & Belding	17,695	3.5	118,024	3.5
9	BBDO Worldwide	14,533	2.2	73,843	1.6
10	Saatchi & Saatchi Advertising	12,645	1.4	89,276	1.5
11	Grey Advertising	8,999	1.8	55,005	1.7
12	D'Arcy Masius Benton & Bowles	4,580	1.0	29,408	0.8
13	Scali, McCabe, Sloves	4,364	3.4	24,935	2.9
14	Bozell	3,317	1.7	22,110	1.6
15	DDB Needham Worldwide	1,516	0.3	10,113	0.2

Note: Figures are in thousands. Percentages of change from 1988 to 1989 are not given for gross income and billings because of the volatility of the Latin American financial markets; J. Walter Thompson Co.'s figures include data for CBBA/Propeg, São Paulo, 100% owned by JWT; since a requirement to be listed as a network is at least one office outside the home country, the following four Brazilian shops do not appear in the chart: MPM Propaganda, São Paulo, No. 1 in Brazil, affiliated with Grey Advertising. Gross income and billings in 1989 $83.9 million and $220.7 million. ALMAP/BBDO, São Paulo, No. 2. BBDO holds 19.9% equity. Gross income and billings $38 million and $144.1 million. Norton Publicidade, São Paulo, No. 7. Gross income and billings $24.2 million and $96.8 million. Salles/Inter Americana, São Paulo, No. 8. Gross income and billings, $22 million and $110 million.

TABLE 23.2
Top Agency Standings in the Major Regional Blocs
(continued)

				Who's on Top in Europe			
Rank	Agency	1989 European Gross Income by Equity	% Change over 1988	1989 European Gross Income as % of Worldwide	1989 European Billings by Equity	% Change over 1988	1989 European Billings as % of Worldwide
1	Publicis FCB	$354,773	10.2	98.9	$2,374,738	9.4	98.7
2	Young & Rubicam	337,494	20.6	39.0	2,345,992	26.7	37.5
3	Saatchi & Saatchi Advertising	332,708	14.6	37.4	2,269,871	7.9	37.5
4	McCann-Erickson Worldwide	278,062	10.5	38.9	1,854,826	10.5	38.8
5	Backer Spielvogel Bates	264,626	3.9	34.8	1,796,142	10.2	34.9
6	Ogilvy & Mather Worldwide	260,999	12.6	37.3	1,822,075	18.2	37.7
7	Lintas:Worldwide	226,518	7.3	38.2	1,510,880	7.3	38.2
8	HDM	222,618	15.0	60.5	1,489,328	15.6	58.3
9	J. Walter Thompson Co.	210,725	8.8	33.6	1,479,152	8.1	33.6
10	Grey Advertising	197,349	14.5	39.6	1,333,566	16.1	40.8
11	EWDB	195,574	14.5	51.3	1,316,274	15.6	48.7
12	D'Arcy Masius Benton & Bowles	185,239	7.7	39.3	1,382,369	11.1	36.3
13	DDB Needham Worldwide	174,238	48.0	31.5	1,204,325	50.3	29.4
14	BBDO Worldwide	156,267	12.8	23.8	1,018,844	13.9	22.4
15	Lowe International	142,391	11.4	62.1	949,266	11.4	62.1
16	RSCG Group	121,444	11.5	69.3	839,010	9.0	68.0
17	Leo Burnett Co.	108,285	13.1	22.4	721,954	14.1	22.2
18	TBWA	90,378	21.7	73.1	605,043	16.8	73.2
19	BDDP Group	84,931	37.4	71.4	566,233	29.5	71.6
20	Collett Dickenson Pearce	67,888	47.3	85.1	479,525	48.5	83.9

Note: Figures are in thousands. Publicis FCB, headquartered in Paris, is a combination of the mutual European holdings of the two organizations into a single, jointly owned network; Young & Rubicam's European percentage ownership in HDM is not included in Y&R's totals: EWDS is Eurocom WCRS Della Femina Bell, a network created late in 1989.

				Who's on Top in Asia-Pacific			
Rank	Agency	1989 Asia-Pacific Gross Income by Equity	% Change over 1988	1989 Asia-Pacific Gross Income as % of Worldwide	1989 Asia-Pacific Billings by Equity	% Change over 1988	1989 Asia-Pacific Billings as % of Worldwide
1	Dentsu	$1,314,400	11.9	NA	$10,063,184	12.6	NA
2	Hakuhodo	585,457	12.1	NA	4,449,166	12.9	NA
3	Dai-Ichi Kikaku	155,795	9.8	NA	1,052,953	7.7	NA
4	Daiko Advertising	152,064	8.9	NA	1,214,107	7.8	NA
5	Asatsu	113,879	10.8	NA	837,272	13.1	NA
6	I&S Corp.	94,734	13.9	NA	770,203	11.2	NA
7	Backer Spielvogel Bates Worldwide	93,908	26.7	12.4	627,702	30.7	12.2
8	McCann-Erickson Worldwide	93,637	12.6	13.1	624,561	12.6	13.1
9	HDM	88,834	88.7	24.1	618,445	82.7	24.2
10	J. Walter Thompson Co.	66,562	26.2	10.6	439,326	25.6	10.0
11	Cheil Communications, Seoul	64,018	43.1	NA	247,471	27.5	NA
12	Ogilvy & Mather Worldwide	55,617	36.1	7.9	379,580	43.6	11.5
13	Leo Burnett Co.	55,386	34.0	11.4	366,153	34.6	11.3
14	Saatchi & Saatchi Advertising	51,906	20.5	5.8	327,614	36.4	5.4
15	Chuo Senko Advertising	50,615	7.6	NA	376,396	8.9	NA

Note: Figures are in thousands. Since a requirement to be listed as a network is at least one office outside the home country, the following three Tokyo-based shops were not listed; Tokyo Agency, Tokyo, No. 3 in Japan, with gross income and billings in 1989 of $156.2 million and $1.3 billion, respectively; Yomiko Advertising, Tokyo, No. 7, with gross income and billings of $100.3 million and $753.5 million; and Asahi Advertising, Tokyo, No. 10, with gross income and billings of $82.9 million and $509.4 million. Young & Rubicam did not qualify for the chart because it uses HDM's network in Asia and maintains separate offices only in Australia and New Zealand.

Source: Advertising Age.

Global Brands

Substitute the world *global* for *international* and the controversy begins. A **global brand** is one that has the same name, design, and creative strategy everywhere in the world. The product that is almost always used as an example of a global brand is Coca-Cola (see Ad 23.2). Coke clearly is an international brand. The global definition breaks down slightly, however, because Classic Coke appears only in the United States and a few other markets. Elsewhere Coke is Coke, and it is marketed virtually the same way everywhere.

Other global brands are emerging, including Revlon, Marlboro, Xerox (including Rank Xerox and Fuji Xerox), Avis, Chanel, Gillette, BMW, Mercedes-Benz, products from Pepsi Cola Foods, Rolex, Toyota, Nissan, Ford, and Henkel. The controversy is not so much over the *concept* of a global brand, but how and whether it will be realized.

The Global Debate

PRINCIPLE
Ideas are global; products or services that embody those ideas might not be.

The global controversy was ignited by an article by Theodore Levitt, professor of business administration and marketing at the Harvard Business School, in the May–June 1983 issue of *Harvard Business Review*. In his article Levitt argued that companies should operate as if there were only one

AD 23.2
Because of the positive reactions to the Mean Joe Greene commercial in the United States and the universality of sports, Coke made the television commercial available in international markets. In this ad, Thai soccer star, Niwat, tosses his jersey to a grateful young fan.
(Courtesy of Coca-Cola Corporation)

THE COMMUNIST BLOC MOVES TO A MARKET ECONOMY

The epic events of 1989 in the Communist bloc produced waves of changes and reactions, especially in Europe. In his book *The New Realities,* published in 1989, Peter Drucker predicted that the market economy would prevail. The impact of the changes and the difficulties Western companies encountered in attempting to enter Eastern Europe were unforeseen, however.

In 1990 unemployment in Poland, a country that went "cold turkey" off a planned market and into a market economy, reached 25 percent in 6 months. Advertising virtually stopped, and the few advertising agencies that existed went bankrupt or cut back severely. Consumer marketing froze.

In Hungary, the most market-oriented country in the Eastern bloc, Western companies jostled for position. A few joint ventures or acquisitions were approved, most notably the U.S. General Electric acquisition of control of Osram, an electrical manufacturing company already exporting to Europe and the United States but in need of capital and technology. In this case the Hungarian government was able and willing to approve the transaction. But what of other entities?

In Hungary, as in other former Communist economies, Western advertising agencies and publishing firms seeking partners were confronted with what was a novel problem for them: There was no basic law of private property. Almost a year after the revolution such a law was still being drafted, starting with definitions for such concepts as property, rights of shareholders, and profits—concepts that had been out of use in the Communist bloc for 40 years. Even more cumbersome was one aspect of the process of privatization: electing management. The existing managers, sometimes Communist functionaries, could not negotiate deals with Western companies until the workers voted, and voting could not take place until the laws were codified. One international agency network was on the verge of signing an agreement with a Budapest agency only to be told the workers had thrown the management out.

In October 1990 East Germany solved its transition problem by merging with West Germany. Czechoslovakia is expected to follow a path similar to Hungary's. Romania and Bulgaria are progressing very slowly, the latter having voted the renamed Communist Party into power. Russia is eager for showcase deals, which it has been negotiating through government agencies. Moscow relaxed currency regulations and laws to sign Fiat, General Motors, Coca-Cola, Pizza Hut, and McDonald's. Young & Rubicam, BBDO, McCann-Erickson, and other global agencies have made various arrangements to open offices in Moscow, either alone or in partnership with state entities.

The opening of the largest McDonald's in the world in Moscow in 1990 was the result of negotiations that had originated in an encounter between Canadian McDonald's management and Russian representatives during the 1976 Montreal Olympics. The two signatories were the City of Moscow and McDonald's of Canada for a 51 percent/49 percent equity split. One of the controversial points in the long negotiation was McDonald's desire to extend its franchising principle and eventually appoint individual owner-managers. Because Russian law still has no provision for private property, the deal ended

(global) market. He felt that differences among nations and cultures were diminishing and those that remained should be ignored because people throughout the world are motivated by the same desires and wants. Furthermore, Levitt argued, businesses will be more efficient if they plan for a global rather than a multinational market.

Advertising Agencies and the Global Debate.   The London-based Saatchi & Saatchi company adopted this philosophy in a bid to become the first global advertising agency. On June 3, 1984, the agency ran a two-page ad in both *The New York Times* and the *Times* of London with the headline, "The Opportunity for World Brands." This ad applied Levitt's global proposition to advertising and the service to be expected of global agencies.

in a compromise: A cooperative could become a franchise, and the definition of a cooperative was reduced to "three or more people."

Western and Japanese companies have moved rapidly to establish themselves in Eastern Europe. These were some of the news reports of late 1990:

- Mars will move its confectionery and pet food into Hungary and Poland.
- The music video channel MTV will become available in the Soviet Union, reaching 88 million households with 8 minutes of advertising per hour. Early sponsors are Wrangler jeans, L.A. Gear shoes, and Benetton sweaters.
- J. Walter Thompson was researching Soviet citizens' responses to 12 television spots broadcast to 200 million viewers.
- "We're there to protect our brand name," said the Xerox Eastern European manager.*

Just as the Eastern bloc has been shedding the stifling weight of a planned economy, abolishing regulations and freeing businesses to compete, the opposite trend is appearing in the European Community and North America: New regulations have been proposed and more restrictions have been written into law. Draft provisions for a unified European Community after 1991 so alarmed the advertising industry that normally warring parties reached some common ground at the International Advertising Association (IAA) world convention in Hamburg, Germany, in June 1990. The IAA, under the leadership of its director-general, Norman Vale, former Grey Advertising executive, was able to convince the three segments of the industry—the advertisers, the media, and the agencies—to put aside their differences and begin a coordinated effort to maintain more freedom and individual rights in consumer markets in Europe and elsewhere.

Michel Reinarz, director of Visual Communications at IAA, noted the irony of a simultaneous breakdown of the restrictive Communist system in the Eastern countries and an increase in legislative control and censorship in the West.

> For both the West and the East it is the loss of power to the people. Once people are informed—have tasted freedom and can choose freely their religion, political party, newspaper, TV channel, supermarket, or spaghetti brand—that freedom cannot be taken away. And if people have the choice and therefore the power, one must "sell" them a specific ideology, religion, newspaper, TV channel, supermarket, or spaghetti brand. This means politicians, religious leaders, media owners, distributors, and manufacturers all have to do "marketing."*

Consequently, Reinarz stated, competition is the key to any successful economic system. A free-market economic system is not only preferable, it is mandatory for a thriving economy. His solution to the growing changes in Eastern and Western thought is simple: "All goods and services which are legally in the marketplace should enjoy the same freedom of commercial speech." Now that the Eastern countries have begun to acknowledge this philosophy, we must make sure that the West does not forget it.†

*International Advertising Association Perspectives (November 20, 1990):3.

*Michel Reinarz, "Will the West Liberate Itself After the East?" IAA Perspectives (August 24, 1990).
†Ibid.

Under the subheading "Impact on Agency Structure," Saatchi & Saatchi stated:

> What are the implications of these trends for the advertising industry? . . .

> Most observers believe that the trend to pan-regional or global marketing will have a marked impact on the structure of advertising agencies . . . because world brands require world agencies.

> A HANDFUL OF WORLDWIDE AGENCY NETWORKS WILL HANDLE THE BULK OF $140 BILLION IN WORLD ADVERTISING EXPENDITURE FOR MAJOR MULTINATIONALS.*

*Courtesy of Saatchi & Saatchi.

Other agencies also tried to incorporate the global concept. A typical response was that of Grey Advertising, which took the position "Global Vision with Local Touch." As one of Grey's presentations in 1986 stated:

> Every idea needs a champion and Global Vision with Local Touch needs several at both the client company and its agencies.... The role of these Grey champions is to:

- Provide the global vision
- Look for the positive signals that point to global applications
- Ward off the NIH (not invented here) factor and develop mutual trust and respect with local client managers
- Employ all of Grey's tools, knowledge, and considerable resources to achieve global application.*

Philip Kotler, marketing professor at Northwestern University, disagreed with Levitt's philosophy. According to Kotler, Levitt misinterpreted the overseas success of Coca-Cola, PepsiCo, and McDonald's. "Their success," he argued, "is based on variation, not offering the same product everywhere."†

The key to this debate is *perspective*. Neither Levitt's nor Kotler's position is totally correct. Global advertising is presently restricted by language, regulation, and local media, but the direction is inescapably toward globalization. Will true global advertising ever be achieved? Probably not—at least, probably not soon. Already, however, ideas are global, and management thinking is increasingly global. The challenge in advertising is to marry the careful and sophisticated use of Kotler's national and regional "variations" to a basic Levitt-style global plan.

*T*OOLS OF INTERNATIONAL MANAGEMENT

As soon as a second country is added to a company's operations, management practices begin to change. Experience has shown that, regardless of the company's form or style of management, internationalization requires new management disciplines or tools. These tools include one common language or "lingua franca" (usually English), one control mechanism (the budget), and one strategic plan (the marketing strategy).

Lingua Franca

It is not difficult to understand why English is the language of choice of international management. The expansion of international marketing was accomplished chiefly by American companies within the Common Market. To succeed within the company, and sometimes even to be hired, a person needed a working knowledge of English.

The American companies brought with them standardized forms of accounting, law, and banking. As a result, local lawyers, accountants, and bankers found it necessary to speak English in order to serve local clients and to have a hope of securing business from local companies owned or operated by Americans.

Language also affects the creation of the advertising itself. English requires less space in printed material or airtime than do most other languages. Its range of words (estimated at over 900,000) and the ease with

*Courtesy of Grey Advertising.
†"Colleague Says Levitt Wrong," *Advertising Age* (June 25, 1984):50.

which English adopts words from other languages make it more exact and more economical than other languages. This creates a major problem when the space for copy is laid out for English and one-third more space is needed for French or Spanish.

Headlines in any language often involve a play on words, themes that are relevant to one country, or slang. The images called to mind in the originating language are distorted or poorly communicated in another. Unintentional meanings, slang, and national styles must be removed from the advertising unless the same meaning or intent can be recreated in other languages. For this reason, international campaigns are not translated, they are written by a copywriter into a second language. Every international advertiser has an example of how a word translated into another language produced a disaster. An example is Coca-Cola's use of "Coke adds life" in China. The Chinese translation reportedly came out "Coke brings your ancestors back from the dead." On the same note, translations of languages into English have the same problem. From a Japanese hotel: "You are invited to take advantage of the chambermaid." From a Bangkok dry cleaner: "Drop your trousers here for best results."*

Some languages simply do not have words equivalent to English expressions. Computer words and advertising terms are almost universally of English derivation. The French have a government agency to prevent English words from corrupting the French language. "Marketing" and "weekend," unacceptable to the French government agency, are translated literally as "study of the market" and "end of the week," respectively. Neither captures the essence of the English word. As if to prove how difficult it is to dislodge the most appropriate word, the French functionary who announced the above equivalents for "marketing" and "weekend" was pressed at the news conference why the agency head was not present. Without thinking, he replied, "Monsieur is gone for *le weekend.*"

Bilingual Copywriting. Experience has shown that the only reasonable solution to language problems is to employ bilingual (meaning English and the local language) copywriters who understand the full meaning of the English text and can capture the essence of the message in the second language. It takes a brave and trusting international creative director to approve copy he or she doesn't understand but is assured is right. A back translation into English is always a good idea, though it never conveys a cultural interpretation.

The language problem is intensified in bilingual countries, such as Canada or Belgium, and even more so in Switzerland, which has three main languages, and China, which has more than 20 dialects. Multiple back translations can produce sharply different messages in English, even if they have the desired strategic focus in the language used.

Budget Control

The budget has become almost another language—in this instance one of control. Centralized companies typically distribute responsibility to branch operations. As a result, techniques for forecasting, dealing with currency fluctuations, and rapidly monitoring performance have improved, especially with more extensive use of computers. The global banks, ITT, and IBM have led in this area. Companies refine budget steps, standardize bud-

A Häagen-Dazs store in Tokyo. American tourists with no knowledge of the Japanese language would have no problem recognizing the brand. (Jeffrey Blackman/The Stock Market.)

*Courtesy of Hood, Light & Geise Advertising, Spring 1990 Newsletter:1.

ALS U EXPORTEERT, KUNT U HIERMEE KAPITALEN BESPAREN

Met die "ene" markt binnen handbereik, zal het zakendoen binnen Europa volslagen anders gaan. De directe beschikbaarheid van gedetailleerde export informatie kan wel eens het verschil uitmaken tussen succes en falen.

Om die reden heeft INTRUM JUSTITIA–de grootste Credit Management groep in Europa–een nogal bijzonder hulpmiddel ontwikkeld.

De gids over internationale betalingen en incasso geeft een overzicht van de meest gebruikte termijnen en procedures in Europa. De gids is helder van opzet en helpt u om een maximaal resultaat uit uw export te bereiken. Hij kost u geen cent.

Knip vandaag nog de bon uit of bel voor uw gratis exemplaar.

EN HET KOST U GEEN CENT

The European Credit Management Corporation.

Ja, stuur mij de gratis International Payment en Collection Guide toe.
INTRUM INTERNATIONAL B.V.
Strawinskylaan 603, 1077 XX AMSTERDAM. Tel: 020-6625881

Naam _____   *Adres* _____

Functie _____   _____

Bedrijf _____   *Tel no* _____

Intrum International is lid van de Intrum Justitia Groep

get philosophies, and tie performance to achievement. Local management negotiates final budgets.

Strategic Plan

The strategic plan is prepared in conjunction with the budget. Basically, the plan outlines the marketing strategy, whereas the budget allocates the funds. If one is changed, the other must change as well. This principle is especially important in international management. Ad 23.3 is an example of an international campaign Smee's, a London-based agency, developed for Intrum Justitia, Europe's largest group in credit management and debt-recovery services. The campaign consisted of brochures, direct-mail pieces, promotional items, and advertisements, which were distributed throughout Europe. For a closer look at the work of Smee's Advertising, see the Inside Advertising box on Anthony Smee.

Two major models of assessing how to advertise in foreign cultures have been developed, one market-oriented and the other culture-oriented.

Market Analysis. As the opening example of Cellox suggests, local conditions often dictate action. Markets share common characteristics ranging from the slightest similarities to substantial ones. For example, bread is made from similar grains all over the world, but varies widely in texture, size, shape, use, packaging, and distribution because of local customs, attitudes, habits, and religious beliefs. In contrast, technological products such as pocket calculators, laptop computers, and cellular phones can be targeted to people in virtually any market economy.

A headquarters marketing manager must look not only at share but also at market size, growth rates, and opportunities for growth through new products or increased expenditures.

For example, cola-flavored soft drinks are not nearly as dominant in Germany as they are in the United States. To generate sales in Germany, therefore, a soft-drink company would have to develop orange and lemon-lime entries. In addition to the traditional Big Macs, fish sandwiches, and French fries, McDonald's serves beer in Germany, wine in France, a local fruit-flavored shake in Singapore and Malaysia, and even a Portuguese sausage in Hawaii to cater to local tastes.

Such "variations" in the uniform global-brand strategy are adjusted by market, by season, and by company. Wise global companies employ a flexible global strategy and allow local management to test new local brands, realizing that almost every successful global or multinational brand started as a local brand somewhere. In contrast, Gillette launched the Sensor razor virtually worldwide in 1990, without first establishing it in one country. The product was so successful that Gillette had difficulty fulfilling early demand.

The largest agencies have benefited from the increasing volume of global planning. In the 13 years from 1976 to 1989, the market share of the multinational agencies rose from 14 percent to 30 percent of worldwide billings, as advertisers aligned brand advertising with the same agencies across Europe, Asia, and North America.*

The Culture-Oriented Model. The second model of international advertising emphasizes the cultural differences among peoples and nations. This

*"The Advertising Industry" *The Economist* (June 9, 1990).

ANTHONY SMEE, MANAGING DIRECTOR, SMEE'S ADVERTISING LTD., LONDON

Anthony Smee is Managing Director of Smee's Advertising Ltd. in London, England. A typical day for Smee involves working at his desk from 7:00 a.m. to 7:00 p.m. With Europe 1 hour ahead and the United States 5 to 7 hours behind, Smee dedicates his morning hours to European clients and the afternoon and evening hours to U.S. clients, continuing his business with the United States by car phone on the way home. He typically spends 20 percent of his time out of England working on European client business.

One of Smee's clients is Intrum Justitia, a Swedish credit-rating service similar to Dun & Bradstreet in the United States. Because Sweden is not in the European Community, which is moving to one coordinated marketplace, Intrum Justitia was faced with two problems. First, should the company move out of Sweden to gain the benefit of the easy movement of capital and ideas? Second, how should it expand rapidly into other European countries to provide Community-wide service in the 1990s?

In 1990 the company moved its headquarters to Holland and began advertising aggressively in Germany, Switzerland, the United Kingdom, and Scandinavia. Its advertising was backed by direct mail throughout the rest of Europe, with a full data base being worked up from scratch. As a result, awareness of the Intrum Justitia name increased dramatically, and the direct-mail response was over 30 percent in some countries. The marketing effort was completely designed and coordinated by Smee's Advertising on an integral unit basis, which allowed it to be tailored accurately and consistently to each market. Ads went out in every European language.

Another Smee's client is Lovell España, the Spanish branch of an important development and

Source: Courtesy of Anthony Smee.

construction company in the United Kingdom. The low prices and warm climate of Spain have long attracted the English to spend summer vacations on the Spanish Mediterranean coast, where many families have bought homes and condominiums. Smee's research indicated an opportunity to build a planned vacation community on the Costa del Sol. Initial sales were strong but flagged when the UK economy faltered in the late 1980s. Smee's recommended offering seminars and advertising to upscale prospects all over Europe and the east coast of the United States, with videos, brochures, and media all in local languages. In this way, Smee's was able to increase the client's market from 56 million British consumers to over 400 million European and American consumers on the same budget. Sales increased dramatically, with European and American sales increasing from 20 percent of the original market to 80 percent of the total market.

---

school of thought recognizes that people worldwide share certain needs, but it stresses that these needs are met differently in different cultures.*

Although the same emotions are basic to all humanity, the degree to which these emotions are expressed publicly varies from culture to culture. The camaraderie typical of an Australian business office would be unthinkable in Japan. The informal, first-name-basis relationships between supervisors and workers that are common in North America are frowned upon in

* The following summary of this analysis is based on work by William Wells of DDB Needham Worldwide, Inc., and is used with the author's permission. It is fully contained in a paper published by the agency entitled "What's Global, What's Not." The high-context/low context distinction is adapted from two books by Edward T. Hall, *The Silent Language* (New York: Doubleday, 1973) and *Beyond Culture* (New York: Doubleday, 1977).

Germany, where even coworkers often do not address each other by their first names. In Japan the gulf between management and staff is submerged in uniforms and group dynamics but is actually wider than in most Western nations. The ways in which we categorize information and the values we attach to people, places, and things depend on where we were raised.

High-Context versus Low-Context Cultures   How do cultural differences relate to advertising? According to the culture-oriented model, although the *function* of advertising is the same throughout the world, the *expression* of its message varies in different cultural settings. The major distinction is between *high-context cultures,* in which the meaning of a message can be understood only within a specific context, and *low-context cultures,* in which the message can be understood as an independent entity. The following list is a grading of cultures from high to low context, with Japanese being the highest-context culture: Japanese, Chinese, Arabic, Greek, Spanish, Italian, English, French, North American, Scandinavian, and German.

As we mentioned earlier, an issue that cannot be overlooked in international advertising is language. The differences between Japanese and English are instructive. English is a low-context language. English words have very clearly defined meanings that are not highly dependent on the words surrounding them. In Japanese, however, a word can have multiple meanings. Listeners or readers do not understand the exact meaning of a word unless they clearly understand the preceding or following sentences —that is, the context in which the word is used.

For example, many Japanese words are pronounced the same but use totally different characters. Also, one character may have several different meanings and may differ in pronunciation according to the context. Phonetically, the Japanese word *hana* sounds the same no matter how it is written, but is written differently depending on the context. It can mean flower, flour, nose, tip for service, or edge. The word *koh* is always written the same but has different meanings: school, to do research, to think, to compare, to correct. Even the word for Chinese character, *kanji,* can mean Chinese character (ideograph), feeling or sense, manager, committee, or inspector.

Advertising messages constructed by writers from high-context cultures might be difficult to understand in low-context cultures because they do not get right to the point. In contrast, messages constructed by writers from low-context cultures may be difficult to understand in high-context cultures because they omit essential contextual detail.

In discussing Japanese advertising, Takashi Michioka, president of DYR, a joint-venture agency of Young & Rubicam and Dentsu, said, "In Japan, differentiation among products does not consist of explaining with words the points of differences among competing products as in America. Differentiation is achieved by bringing out the people appearing in the commercial—the way they talk, the music, the scenery, etc.—rather than emphasizing the unique features and dissimilarities of the product itself."

*O*RGANIZATION OF INTERNATIONAL ADVERTISING AGENCIES

The Scope of International Advertising

Starch INRA Hooper, in cooperation with the International Advertising Association, tabulates world advertising spending, converted to U.S. dollars. Table 23.3 lists the top countries by advertising expenditures. Although the

TABLE 23.3
Top 15 Countries by Advertising Expenditure* ($ Million at Current Prices)

Rank	Country	1980	Country	1990	Country	1993
1	U.S.A.	35,501	U.S.A.	82,817	U.S.A.	94,362
2	Japan	16,043	Japan	34,357	Japan	42,588
3	Germany	5,888	U.K.	12,662	U.K.	15,092
4	U.K.	4,189	Germany	10,604	Germany	13,022
5	Canada	2,552	France	7,875	Spain	11,732
6	France	2,091	Spain	6,721	France	9,801
7	Netherlands	1,385	Canada	6,055	Italy	7,643
8	Australia	1,338	Italy	5,809	Canada	7,361
9	Switzerland	1,063	Australia	4,062	South Korea	4,839
10	Italy	905	South Korea	2,806	Australia	4,743
11	Spain	702	Taiwan	2,048	Taiwan	3,034
12	Sweden	519	Netherlands	2,046	Sweden	2,311
13	Belgium	417	Switzerland	2,012	Switzerland	2,201
14	Austria	396	Sweden	1,676	Netherlands	2,194
15	Denmark	391	Finland	1,186	India	2,035

*Major media only.

Source: Zenith Media Worldwide, *Advertising Expenditure Forecasts* (December 1990):6.

United States still dominates world advertising spending, advertising growth rates outside the United States, reinforced by a weaker dollar since 1985, have outstripped U.S. growth. Table 23.4 lists the top 10 agencies worldwide in 1989. Among the largest international marketers are Unilever, Procter & Gamble, Philip Morris, General Motors, Nestlé, and RJR Nabisco.

Most international advertisers can be analyzed according to the model presented in Figure 23.2. Most companies fall on the axis from similar products and centralized managements (quadrant 1) to different or localized products and decentralized managements (quadrant 3). There are exceptions, however. For example, McDonald's products are largely standardized, and its international management is decentralized. Nestlé allows substantial local autonomy but markets a large number of common products.

TABLE 23.4
Top 10 Agencies Worldwide by Gross Income

Rank	Agency, Headquarters	Worldwide Gross Income			Worldwide Billings		
		1989	1988	% Change	1989	1988	% Change
1	**Dentsu,** Tokyo	$1,316.4	$1,176.2	11.9	$10,063.2	$8,939.3	12.6
2	**Saatchi & Saatchi Advertising Worldwide,** New York	890.0	740.5	20.2	6,049.9	5,053.9	19.7
3	**Young & Rubicam,** New York	865.4	757.6	14.2	6,250.5	5,390.3	16.0
4	**Backer Spielvogel Bates Worldwide,** New York	759.8	689.8	10.2	5,143.2	4,677.9	9.9
5	**McCann-Erickson Worldwide,** New York	715.5	656.8	8.9	4,772.3	4,381.0	8.9
6	**Ogilvy & Mather Worldwide,** New York	699.7	635.2	10.1	4,828.0	4,110.1	17.5
7	**BBDO Worldwide,** New York	656.6	585.9	12.1	4,550.0	4,051.2	12.3
8	**J. Walter Thompson Co.,** New York	626.4	559.3	12.0	4,407.5	3,857.5	14.3
9	**Lintas:Worldwide,** New York	593.3	537.6	10.4	3,957.6	3,585.6	10.4
10	**Hakuhodo,** Tokyo	585.5	522.2	12.1	4,449.2	3,939.1	12.9

Note: All figures are U.S. dollars in millions.

This table is an updated version from the Agency Income Report (AA, March 26).

Source: Advertising Age (December 24, 1990). Copyright Crain Communications Inc.

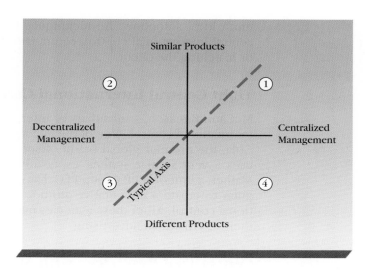

FIGURE 23.2
The product-management axis.

Each company develops its own policy to guide its application of resources in regional or global marketing. Henkel, a large German manufacturer of household and cleaning products, provides an example of how centralized management with similar products works. Henkel's international strategy was designed to accomplish three goals: to eliminate duplication of effort among their national companies, to provide central direction for new products, and to achieve efficiency in advertising production and impact. It included these steps:

- Identify the need to be fulfilled or the function of a product.
- Determine the commonality of that need or its benefit in Europe or a larger area.
- Assign that specific need or benefit to one product with one brand name.
- Assign that brand to one brand manager and one advertising agency to develop and market.
- Prohibit the benefit, the name, or the creative campaign of that brand from being used by any other brand in the company.

Agencies have to develop techniques to service brands that are marketed around the world. Some agencies exercise tight control, others allow

U.S. Gross Income			U.S. Billings		
1989	1988	% Change	1989	1988	% Change
NA	NA	NA	NA	NA	NA
$395.2	$326.3	21.1	$2,778.9	$2,209.6	25.8
409.5	372.8	9.9	3,114.8	2,791.8	11.6
310.7	282.7	9.9	2,158.0	1,964.2	9.9
209.1	197.0	6.1	1,394.8	1,314.0	6.1
305.1	281.1	8.6	2,104.4	1,874.9	12.2
373.6	340.5	9.7	2,656.0	2,414.3	10.0
266.5	257.5	3.5	1,851.0	1,787.9	3.5
224.9	201.7	11.5	1,499.9	1,345.4	11.5
NA	NA	NA	NA	NA	NA

more local autonomy. All techniques fall into one of three groups: tight central international control, centralized resources with moderate control, or matching the client.

Tight Central International Control

McCann-Erickson, a subsidiary of Interpublic Group, relies on tight central international control. One of the clients McCann-Erickson handles is Coca-Cola, the premier global brand of soft drinks. The Leo Burnett Company uses a very similar system, especially for Marlboro cigarettes. Ogilvy & Mather, a unit of WPP Group PLC, has used a highly respected training program to create a cooperative attitude that actually helps achieve international control. All of these agencies maintain rigid centralized control over their international advertising.

Centralized Resources with Moderate Control

Agencies such as BBDO Worldwide (for Gillette and Apple Computers), Grey Advertising (for Clairol and Playtex), and DDB Needham (for Volkswagen and American Airlines) centralize their resources for clients but allow their agencies local autonomy in executing centrally planned strategies (see Ad 23.4).

AD 23.4
Premier Maldonado and Associates handles advertising for Northbound American Airlines directly from Puerto Rico. (Courtesy of American Airlines.)

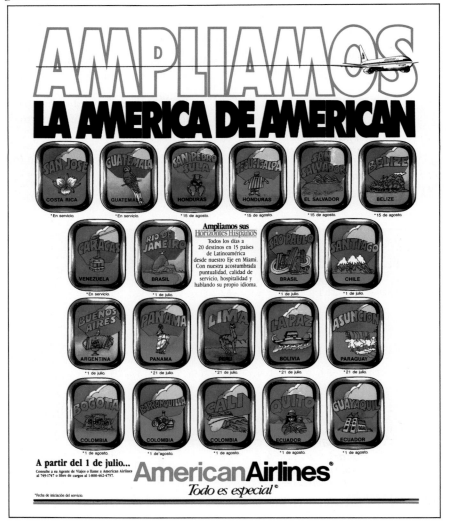

Matching the Client

Matching the client must be part of any international support system for a client. Companies with few international clients can easily offer each one personalized services. Those with more clients must decide whether each client will receive tailored service or some features will be standardized to establish a pattern of service.

The more centralized the client, the more likely the agency is to have a headquarters group assigned to the client with a tactical team ready to fly anywhere a problem needs to be solved. In the future international agencies will increasingly base this team outside the United States and will have multiple centers of service. McCann-Erickson, among others, uses tactical teams to support local and national offices worldwide.

In analyzing how clients work, the J. Walter Thompson agency, a unit of WPP Group PLC, identified three strata of support for international campaigns: exchange, encouragement, and enforcement. At the first level, the agency office at client headquarters (the lead agency) *exchanges* information, advertising campaigns, and material with its other international offices. At the next level, agency management more actively *encourages* local offices to follow the international direction. At the third level, agency management is asked to *enforce* international direction throughout the agency's network.

CREATING AND PLANNING INTERNATIONAL ADVERTISING CAMPAIGNS

According to an old axiom, "All business is local." This proverb should be modified to "Almost all *transactions* are local." Advertising itself is intended to persuade local readers or listeners to do something (buy, vote, phone, order). That "something" is a transaction that is usually completed at home, near home, or at least in the same country if by direct mail. (This will change as multinational direct-mail campaigns become possible in a unified Common Market and in the emerging Canada–United States–Mexico free-trade area.)

How are advertising campaigns that have near-global application created? International advertising campaigns use one of two basic starting points: (1) success in one country; or (2) a centrally conceived strategy, a need, a new product, or a directive.

The patterns identified in this section are not only applicable to U.S. products or U.S. advertisers. Global marketers based in Japan, Germany, the United Kingdom, Holland, France, Sweden, Switzerland, and elsewhere use these same techniques. Personnel from one country can move to another company in a different country and find common ground with the advertising managers and agencies that work on international brands. Although the examples are largely American, the principles are not.

Expanding a National Success

In the first case a successful advertising campaign, conceived for national application, is modified for use in other countries. The acclaimed Avis campaign "We try harder," began in the United States and then spread extensively. Wrigley, Marlboro, IBM, Waterman Pen, Seiko Watches, Philips Shavers, Ford, Hasbro, and many other companies have taken successful campaigns originated in one country and transplanted them around the world. A strong musical theme (McDonald's, for example) makes the transfer even smoother because music is an international language.

Centrally Conceived Campaigns

The second form, a centrally conceived campaign, was pioneered by Coca-Cola and now is used by many other companies in their global strategies. Although the concept is simple, the application is difficult. A work team, sometimes called a *task force* or an *action group,* is assembled from around the world. Usually a basic strategy is presented. That strategy is debated, modified if necessary, and accepted (or imposed) as the foundation for the campaign. Some circumstances require that a strategy be imposed even if a few countries object.

Cost is a primary factor for choosing the centrally conceived campaign. If the same photography and artwork can be used universally, the company can save the $10,000 or more each local variation might cost. Or if television programs or magazines can cross from one country to its neighbors, international management may insist that the same campaign be used in neighboring countries. Colgate faced this problem before its red dentifrice package and typography were standardized. Because distributors in Asia bought shipments from either the United States or Europe, depending on currency rates and shipping dates, a variety of packages for the same product appeared on store shelves. Colgate now uses the same basic design for its dentifrice worldwide.

This procedure varies when a promising new product is being developed. In this case the assembled team might begin its work by developing a common global strategy. Once the strategy is developed, the members of the team responsible for creative execution go to work. For one Coke campaign the multinational group was sequestered until a campaign emerged. In other cases the team members return to their home countries, develop one or more approaches or prototype campaigns, reassemble in a matter of weeks, review all the work, and decide on one or two executions to develop into a full campaign. Such a campaign would include television, radio, newspaper, magazine, cinema, and outdoor advertising, as well as collateral extensions (brochures, mailings, counter cards, in-store posters, handouts, and take-one folders). The team can stay together to finish the work, or it can ask the writer or developer of the campaign to complete or supervise the completion of the entire project.

In order to communicate their positions clearly and cope with rapidly changing conditions, several major advertisers gather their agencies for strategy sessions periodically. McDonald's does this every year in August or September to announce the forthcoming year's plans. In early 1990 Eastman Kodak called its agencies together to discuss the need to economize and "get more bang for the buck." Nestlé convened its five major agencies —J. Walter Thompson, Ogilvy & Mather, McCann-Erickson, Lintas:Worldwide, and Publicis-FCB—to discuss agency alignments by product group and how a more market-driven and consumer-driven Nestlé will respond to change. Barry Day, Lintas's assistant to the chairman and an attendee, said, "I believe agencies have to match the client organization. They must mold to [the client] philosophy and respond in kind."*

*Laurel Wentz, "Nestlé Calls Summit," *Advertising Age* (September 10, 1990):87.

Variations on Central Campaigns

Variations of the centrally conceived campaign do exist. For example, Rank Xerox may handle its European creative development by asking the European offices of Young & Rubicam to develop a campaign for a specific product—a word processor, a copier, whatever. The office that develops the approved campaign is designated the "lead agency." That agency office then develops all the necessary pattern elements of the campaign, shoots the photography or supervises the artwork, and prepares a standards manual for use in other countries. This manual includes examples of layouts, patterns for television (especially the treatment of the logo or the product), and design standards for all elements. Individual offices may either order the elements from the lead agency or produce them locally if this is less expensive. Because photography, artwork, television production, and color printing are very costly, performing all of these in one location and then overprinting or rerecording the voice track in the local language saves money.

McDonald's, Coca-Cola, and other companies record basic music for campaigns and make various sound tracks available for local use. This work is not necessarily done in the home country. Superb sound stages and musicians and printing companies are available in Spain, for example, where costs are significantly lower than in the United States.

Local Application and Approval.   Beyond central approval is local application and approval. Every ad in every country cannot be sent to regional and world headquarters for approval. Local application is simplified when common material originates from a central source. Within a campaign framework, most companies allow some degree of local autonomy. Some companies insist on approving only pattern ads (usually the two or three ads that introduce the campaign) and commercials and allow local approval of succeeding executions. Others want to approve only television commercials and allow local freedom for other media. In any case, free-flowing communication is necessary. Senior officers travel, review work, and bring with them the best of what is being done in other countries. Seminars, workshops, and annual conventions all serve to disseminate campaign strategies, maintain the campaign's thrust, and stimulate development of new ideas.

Selecting Media for International Campaigns

Though advertising practitioners debate the applications of global theories to their profession, one fact is inescapable: No global media currently exist. Television can transmit the Olympics around the globe, but no one network controls this global transmission. Therefore, an advertiser seeking global exposure has to deal with different networks in different countries. Satellite transmission now places programs with advertising into many European homes, but its availability is not universal because of the "footprint" (coverage area of the satellite), technical limitations, and regulations on transmission by the various European governments.

For example, as a series of events seized the world's attention in the late 1980s and early 1990s, Cable News Network (CNN) became the medium for the exchange of news for most of the world. When the Foreign Ministry in Moscow wants to be sure the State Department in Washington understands its position, it calls CNN because CNN is monitored in every major capital. Advertisers were quick to see this network as a means of reaching influential consumers even before CNN was available in homes. The Persian Gulf War in 1991 heightened CNN's recognition and increased its influence as a nearly global electronic medium.

As other satellites are launched, they will beam signals to more than one country in Europe, the Asian subcontinent, North America, and the Pacific, but they will be regional, not global. Because most governments in Southeast Asia—Malaysia and Singapore, in particular—restrict the reception of satellite signals, the strict censorship found in this area presents another barrier to global transmission.

Still, satellites are leaping borders with advertising messages. One company reported an order from Spain for a product only offered by Sky Channel, a European multinational satellite. At the time there was only one satellite dish in Spain—in the Royal Palace.

Execution of International Campaigns. Media planning for an international campaign follows the same principles used for reaching a national target audience. The execution, however, is more complex. Table 23.5 lists the world advertising expenditures by media.

International campaigns are not always centrally funded. The global corporation has operating companies locally registered in most major countries. Advertising might have to be funded through these local entities for maximum tax benefits or to meet local laws of origination. Therefore, the media planner might only be able to establish the media definition of the target audience, lay down a media strategy, and set the criteria for selecting media. Greater latitude is allowed in media application than in creative variation. For example, a media campaign in the southern hemisphere, especially for consumer goods and seasonal items, requires major changes from a northern hemisphere campaign. In the southern hemisphere, summer, Christmas, and back-to-school campaigns are all compressed into the "summer season" that lasts from November through January. National media directors must examine local research on audience characteristics and use judgment in executing media strategies.

Media Choices. Once the basic global media strategy and plan have been created and approved, the central media planner looks for regional or mul-

TABLE 23.5
World Advertising Expenditure Summary ($ millions at current prices)

Major Media*	1989	1990	1991	1992	1993
North America	85,965	88,872	92,498	97,236	101,723
Europe	51,570	55,916	60,914	67,184	73,425
Asia-Pacific	43,044	47,999	52,267	56,979	62,195
Latin America	6,424	6,854	7,313	7,876	8,443
Africa-Middle East	1,866	1,991	2,124	2,288	2,453
Subtotal	188,869	201,632	215,116	231,563	248,239
Direct Mail					
North America	23,943	25,199	26,477	27,830	29,252
Europe	8,731	9,398	10,172	11,106	11,966
Japan	1,494	1,719	1,890	2,041	2,205
Miscellaneous Media†					
U.S.A.	23,715	24,901	26,146	27,453	28,826
Japan	3,443	3,960	4,356	4,704	5,080
Grand Total	250,195	266,809	284,157	304,597	325,568

*TV, print, radio, cinema, and outdoor.

†Includes point-of-sale/sales promotion expenditure.

Source: Zenith Media Worldwide, *Advertising Expenditure Forecasts* (December 1990):4.

tinational media. If magazines are part of the plan, advertising space in *Time, Fortune, Newsweek, The Economist, Reader's Digest,* and other magazines with international editions may be bought. (The box entitled "*Zhenjia* Is Just Another Word for Capitalism" discusses international magazines in more detail.) With the exception of *Reader's Digest,* all these publications are available in English only. The *International Herald Tribune* and *The Wall Street Journal* are published simultaneously in a number of major cities using satellite technology. Magazines published by international airlines for their passengers are another option. Multinational satellites, such as British Satellite Broadcasting in Europe, provide opportunities to place the same message before a target audience at the same time across national boundaries.

In large measure, however, such media reach only an international, English-speaking segment of the target audience. If the audience being targeted is for a consumer product, local planning and purchase are required. This is usually accomplished in one of two ways: through an international advertising agency (or international consortium of agencies) or through an international media-buying service. If neither of these methods is used, the media executive must execute the plan through a multitude of local, national, or regional media-buying services or advertising agencies. The Issues and Applications box discusses how well advertising crosses borders.

International Advertising Agencies. If the campaign is handled by one of the international advertising agencies, the senior media officer in the office that works for client headquarters will be in charge. He or she will supervise the efforts of that agency's offices in cities around the world in executing the media plan. Media orders will be placed locally, with copies sent to the coordinating agency office for review and compilation. In other cases the plan will be reviewed centrally and placement will be handled locally without reporting to headquarters.

International networks of independent agencies have been formed to provide their members with global reach and to prevent the loss of clients to the international corporate agencies. Examples are Affiliated Advertising Agencies International, Advertising and Marketing International Network, and International Federation of Advertising Agencies. Ad 23.5 for Lacoste shows an international version of an ad developed by IFAA. Similar groups are forming in regional blocs, such as the National Advertising Agency Network in the United States and the Association for European Marketing, Advertising, and Public Relations in Europe. These groups provide multinational media buying for their clients.

International Media-Buying Services. The other primary option in media placement is to use international media-buying services. These services usually work for smaller international companies that do not have well-developed agency relationships in each country in which they operate.

International Production. The Wace Group PLC, the world's largest producer of the color separations used in printing, provides advertisers and media with a satellite-linked network of printing facilities. This will allow for global print advertising transmission in the same way that satellites have made multinational television commercials possible in most parts of the world.*

*Scott Hume, "Global Pre-Press Network Set," *Advertising Age* (September 17, 1990):30.

ZIBENJIA IS JUST ANOTHER WORD FOR CAPITALISM

In February 1991 Forbes Inc. and Capital Communications (based in Hong Kong) launched a Chinese-language monthly called *Zibenjia,* modeled after the English-language magazine *Forbes.* The second foreign-language publication for Forbes (the first is a German edition, *Forbes von Burda,* published by Forbes and Burda Publications), *Zibenjia* is targeted at the 40 million Chinese people living outside mainland China. The English, Chinese, and German editions will be packaged as a single buy. According to Albert Cheng, publisher at Capital Communications, 10,000 copies were already targeted for the United States and Canada at the end of 1990, with 70,000 distributed in Southeast Asian capitals.

Zibenjia, translated as *Capitalist,* is targeted at a specific audience, primarily through direct marketing. Mailing lists of prestige credit card owners and membership lists of private Chinese businessmen's clubs around the world were used to promote subscriptions as part of the $1.5 million campaign that was created in-house. The magazine was also advertised in local Chinese business newspapers, including *The Asian Wall Street Journal* and the *International Herald Tribune.* According to Cheng, making money for Forbes is not the issue as much as improving the company's presence in Asia and the Chinese community. The place to make money would be in China, and as of November 1990, the Chinese government had not allowed the circulation of *Zibenjia* on the mainland.

Just as the German edition adjusted the *Forbes* formula to the German market, *Zibenjia* focuses on Chinese businesses and entrepreneurs around the world. A color page advertisement costs $6,000, but a character rate of $4,800 was given to advertisers who booked their ads before December 31, 1990. As of late 1990, 96 pages of editorial matter and 40 pages of advertising were predicted for first edition. Forbes is continuing to look into other foreign markets as well, including Japan and two other markets in Europe.

Source: Adapted from Andrew Geddes and Scott Donaton, "Forbes Targets Chinese Audience," *Advertising Age* (November 19, 1990).

AD 23.5
An example of a Lacoste ad in French developed by IFAA.
(Courtesy of Lacoste, Inc.)

SI LA MER N'AVAIT QU'UNE COULEUR, IL N'Y AURAIT QU'UN BLEU LACOSTE.

LACOSTE

HOW WELL DOES ADVERTISING CROSS BORDERS?

One of the most interesting studies to examine the question of how effectively advertising crosses borders was conducted in 1990 by Alice, a French advertising agency, and IPSOS, a French research group. "Rather than measuring what is acceptable in all markets (and lowering creative standards), we have taken the most competitive advertising in each local market and found out how competitive it remains in the other markets." The top 87 commercials from France, Germany, Holland, Italy, Spain, and the United Kingdom were judged by 100 consumers in each of those countries. Each commercial was adapted into each of the six languages. At the end of each commercial, an explanation or further translation appeared. The conclusions of this research were:

1. *Local nationality characteristics dominate in a market.* The most competitive commercials in each market, those that garnered the strongest responses, were local commercials. The Dutch Amstel beer commercial ranked 18th in Holland but only 43rd overall. A British telecom spot was third in the United Kingdom but 25th overall.

2. *There are genuine national advertising cultures.* Local creation and production recognize these local cultures. Usually, what makes a commercial strong in its home market is precisely what makes it difficult to understand outside the local market. A French commercial (Mamie Nova) was 11th in France but 86th overall.

3. *Basic creative approaches explain the capacity of some commercials to cross frontiers.* The key deter-

minates of commercials both "liked" and "convincing" were the strength of their emotional appeal, the quality of their entertainment value, and the simplicity of the human situations they portrayed. The most liked and convincing commercial, the Spanish TVE spot, was ranked 1st in form in all six countries.

Three commercials that met this last standard were entertaining, action-packed films. They were TVE, a Spanish Television network commercial, a United Kingdom Levi's commercial, and a condom campaign from the United Kingdom. They scored as follows:

Rank	France	Germany	Holland	Italy	Spain	U.K.
1	1	2	1	1	*	1
2	2	1	2	2	1	*
3	3	3	4	3	2	*

*Not one of the top four commercials in this country.

The major conclusions of the French research reinforce the importance of national characteristics, the weight of local culture, and the power of emotional appeals. As the report stated, "decentralized advertising appears to be the most competitive approach because of the importance of national cultures; [however] globalization is possible but in the most extreme way, benefiting [from] the strongest ideas. Supranational can only be creative."

Source: Adapted from "Europe: Can Creative Advertising Cross Frontiers?" Alice and IPSOS, 1990.

*I*NTERNATIONAL CONSIDERATIONS

International advertising has a worldly glamour about it—extensive travel, cultural opportunities, exotic places and cuisines, and the excitement of spending a weekend half a world away from home. It is also tough work, involving long days, jet lag, insomnia, and dysentery. The business itself has some peculiar problems. We already discussed the problems that language creates. Other concerns relate to laws, customs, time, and inertia, resistance, rejection, and politics.

Laws

International advertisers do not fear actual laws; they fear *not knowing* those laws. For example, television advertising directed toward children under 12 is not permitted in Sweden or Germany. Restaurant chains cannot be advertised in France, and advertising of any kind is forbidden on Sundays in Austria. Until recently, a model wearing lingerie could not be shown on television in the United States. In contrast, nudity is acceptable in France. In Malaysia jeans are considered Western and decadent, and are therefore prohibited. A commercial can be aired in Australia only if it is shot with an Australian crew. A contest or promotion that is successful in one country might be illegal in another.

Customs

Customs can be even stronger barriers than laws. When advertising to children age 12 and over was approved in Germany, the local feeling against it was so strong that companies risked customer revolt if they took advantage of the new law. In many countries naming a competitor is considered bad form.

Customs are often more subtle than laws, and therefore easier to violate. Quoting an obscure writer or poet is risky in the United States because most Americans would not respond to an unknown author. In Japan, however, the audience would respect the advertiser for using the name or become embarrassed at not knowing a name they were expected to recognize. Thus, in the United States the audience might be turned off, whereas in Japan consumers might search out the meaning of the message. In one case the communication might be terminated, and in the other it would be reinforced.

Time

Time is the enemy in international advertising. Everything takes longer internationally. The New York business day overlaps for only 3 hours with the business day in London, for 2 hours with most of Europe, and for 1 hour with Greece. Normal business hours in New York do not overlap at all with those in Japan, Hong Kong, the Middle East, or Australia. Overnight parcel service is dependable to most of Europe, if the planes are able to take off and land, but chancy elsewhere. Therefore, telecopy transmission is now the mode for international communication. Facsimile, or "fax," numbers have become almost as universal as telephone numbers on stationery and business cards in international companies. No matter what the activity, it always seems to take longer in another country, even if that second country is the United States.

PRINCIPLE _____
Everything takes longer internationally—count on it.

Time is an enemy in other ways. France and Spain virtually close down in August for vacation. National holidays are also a problem. Most U.S. corporations average 12 to 14 paid legal holidays a year. The number escalates to over 20 in Europe and over 30 in Italy. Some countries have patron saints for industry sectors. For example, no business is conducted in Spain on St. Barbara's day. St. Barbara is the patron saint of advertising and artillery.

Inertia, Resistance, Rejection, and Politics

Inertia, resistance, rejection, and politics are sometimes lumped together as "not-invested-here situations." Advertising is a medium for change, and change sometimes frightens people. Every new campaign is a change. A highly successful campaign in one country might or might not be successful in another country. (Experience suggests the success rate in moving a winning campaign to another country is about 60 percent.) Creative directors resist advertising that arrives by mail rather than from within the local agency. This resistance is partly the result of a very real problem in international agency offices: an inability to develop a good creative team or a strong creative reputation when most of the advertising emanating from the office originates elsewhere. Government approval of television commercials can also be difficult to secure in some countries. Standards may seem to be applied more strictly to international than to national products.

Flat rejection or rejection by delay or lack of support must be anticipated with every global strategy and global campaign. Typical responses are, "We do not do it that way here," "You do not understand how different we are in this country," and "We tried that once and it did not work." The best solution to this kind of rejection is to test a locally produced version of the advertising.

Overcoming Inertia and Resistance. At times the resistance and rejection are political, the result of office politics or an extension of international politics. Trying to sell a U.S. campaign in a foreign country, for example, can be difficult if relations between the two nations are strained. Being politic in the diplomatic sense of the word is the only practical way to overcome local resistance. International advertising involves the forging of consensus. This cannot be accomplished by mail. Successful international companies have frequent regional and world conferences, maintain a constant flow of communication, transfer executives, and keep their executives well informed through travel, videotapes, teleconferences, and consultation. They have learned that few actions are as flattering as asking for advice. When local managements are asked to comment on a developing strategy or campaign, their involvement often becomes support.

Another proven axiom states: Always go to a problem, do not bring it to headquarters. Solutions worked out in the country that has the problem are seldom what either party anticipated and are frequently better than either could have hoped. The adrenalin that precedes an "international confrontation" can often be directed to very positive solutions.

Despite its complexities and difficulties, international advertising is growing and will continue to grow in an increasingly interconnected world economy. Two of the largest agency groups are British-owned Saatchi & Saatchi and WPP, and the largest single agency is Japanese (Dentsu), indicating that international advertising is no longer under American control. Students in the United States need to understand how international advertising works if they wish to succeed in this ever-changing industry. In fact, the United States is the only major country that still distinguishes between business and international business. Most of the Western world has already made the transition.

SUMMARY

- The United States accounts for approximately half of all advertising in the world, but this percentage is dropping. Fewer than one-third of the 25 highest-spending world advertisers are headquartered in the United States.
- The market structure in most countries consists of local brands, regional brands, and international brands. Regional brands operate in the market blocs of North America, Europe, Latin America, and Asia-Pacific.

- International advertisers organize their operations on the basis of their attitude toward centralization and the similarity of their brands as marketed in various countries. The more central the management and the more similar the products, the more common their advertising will be around the world.
- International advertising agencies have three organizational options: tight international control, centralized resources but moderate control, and matching individual client needs.

- The lack of global media forces advertisers to plan regionally or globally but to execute plans locally or regionally.
- The conflict between market freedom and regulation is accentuated as Eastern Europe moves toward a market economy and the European Community and North America impose or propose new regulations on products, marketing, and advertising.
- Market structures, based on the relative strength of local, regional, and international brands, and cultural differences shape international brands. Cultural differences shape international advertising strategy and execution.

- International advertising campaigns usually evolve from a success in one country or a centrally conceived plan, although recent global launches are changing these approaches.
- Placement of international advertising can be supervised centrally or delegated according to a centrally approved plan.
- When advertising internationally, laws, customs, time constraints, and problems of inertia, resistance, rejection, and politics must be taken into account.

QUESTIONS

1. How does a local brand achieve international status? What are the main steps in this process?

2. Think of a product that has international appeal. How would you market this product in South America? Germany? Japan? What factors would you have to consider within your strategic plan?

3. Williams and Boynton (WB), a Midwestern advertising agency, is in the midst of "soul searching" over an international opportunity. It seems that an existing client that features a full line of garden chemicals (vegetables and flowers) is determined to begin export activities to Europe. The marketer has urged the agency to also develop an "international operation" to assist in international advertising but is worried that a refusal would send this marketer into the arms of another agency that has international offices in operation. What should the agency think about in making its decision? Is there some compromise position WB could take, something between a refusal and setting up a series of European offices for one client?

4. Jane Trapper, the U.S. based creative director on a global food company account, is stunned by an ad that is being proposed by the agency's London office. The ad deals with a mustard preparation that has had great selling success in the institutional market (such as restaurants), but has had trouble in selling to home consumers. The ad layout shows a man sitting in a pub being served the mustard by a waitress. The headline, however, bothers Jane. It reads

"He can get it here, why can't he get it at home?" Jane is supposed to present this to the food company for approval. Should she allow this possible off-color idea to be seen by the client?

5. There were a lot of smiles around a large West Coast agency when it learned that their top account (soft drinks) had secured an export opportunity for Australia. Tim Weston, the agency's senior creative head, called a long-time business friend in Sydney to get a reading on the drink's creative. "We have just finished filming some tour footage of Phil Collins. They're dynamite commercials by our standards. How do you think they'll play in Sydney?" Tim asked. His Aussie friend replied—"Well, mate, there's good news and bad news on that. The good news is that Collins is as solid on the charts here as he has ever been." Do you know what bad news Tim was about to hear? What should Weston consider as a strategy?

6. Karen Lockhart has wanted to work overseas in advertising as long as she can remember. Her second language is an above-average level of French. She will graduate with a dual major in advertising and international business. Karen doesn't know if this will help her find a position leading to a European assignment. What can you recommend to Karen that may improve her international horizons? Should she move overseas and eventually try there? Would it be better to earn some experience in the United States first?

FURTHER READINGS

MARIEKE K. DEMOOIJ, *Advertising Worldwide* (London: Prentice Hall International, 1991).

"Multinationals Take Global Marketing," *Advertising Age* (June 25, 1984):50.

"The Opportunity for World Brands," *The New York Times,* June 3, 1984.

"Targeting the Globe," *Target Marketing* (January 1987): 12.

WELLS, WILLIAM D., "What's Global; What's Not," published by DDB Needham Worldwide.

Big Mac Attack on the Soviet Union

Attempts by U.S. firms to break into international markets are littered with horror stories of translational gaffs and unintentional cultural slurs. When Perdue Chicken attempted to translate its famous tagline "It takes a tough man to make a tender chicken" into Spanish for Hispanic markets, the phrase was literally translated as "It takes a sexually aroused man to make a chick excited." Similarly, Anheuser-Busch's "King of Beers" Budweiser slogan ended up as the "Queen of Beers" in Spanish.

Such examples are all too common as companies attempt to master the marketing strategies necessary not only to overcome language barriers but to address cultural differences. Some of the hard-won lessons of international advertising and marketing include the hiring of local marketing and advertising staff to develop and implement the plans to achieve the broader business objectives defined by the corporate parent. Consequently, if domestic sacred cows, such as long-used advertising taglines or positionings, are inappropriate for use in foreign countries, they should not be considered unless budgetary considerations mandate it.

Despite the promise of multinational, mega-merger agencies resulting from the acquisition frenzy of the 1980s, few domestic campaigns have translated into truly international efforts to date. Only very simple graphic images for fashion and other intangibly based product benefits have succeeded in developing international appeal, such as the "United Colors of Benetton" campaign.

Given these obstacles, when McDonald's secured the rights to open its first restaurant in the Soviet Union after decades of negotiation, it was committed to doing it right. With competition escalating and domestic fast-food sales flattening, the international market represents one of the most promising areas for revenue expansion in the industry. So, when McDonald's began planning its largest restaurant for Pushkin Square in Moscow, it devoted a great deal of time to studying the culture, hiring and training local staff, and procuring local sources of ingredients. In some cases, when the quality of local ingredients was below McDonald's standards, arrangements were made to contract-produce an adequate supply of ingredients exclusively for McDonald's use.

Although state-run restaurants in the Soviet Union were famous for bad food and service, their prices were extremely low. Without state subsidization, McDonald's recognized that a typical meal at the Golden Arches would require a princely fee from Soviet citizens. Consequently, they focused on the other critical elements of successful fast-food operations: quality and service. Thoroughly screened Soviet youths were hired and trained to be courteous to all patrons, a novelty in Moscow restaurants. With over 700 seats, the Moscow Golden Arches location would be among the first to offer fast food with consistent quality and friendly service.

To date, McDonald's sales in Moscow have exceeded expectations, with Muscovites continuing to endure lengthy waits for a chance to dine on a Big Mac and fries and to sample capitalist enterprise at close range. Despite 400 percent increases in food prices, sales have scarcely been affected. In fact, waiting in line at McDonald's has become the premiere people-watching spot in Moscow, with youths emulating western fashions seen in fashion magazines from Europe and the United States.

QUESTIONS

1. Traditionally, international marketers identify current cultural norms and attempt to mimic them in the presentation of their product or service in other countries. Why did McDonald's choose to deviate from the existing cultural norms for restaurant service in Moscow?

2. What characteristics common to Soviet shopping practices actually offer advantages for McDonald's over its domestic operations?

3. The basic elements of food-service success are quality, service, and value. Without state subsidies, McDonald's could not address the value component via meal prices as effectively as state-run restaurants. Why was the company still able to create a high perceived value among Soviet consumers?

Source: ABC News, *Prime Time Live* (January 25, 1990).

CASE STUDY

Brooke Bond PG Tips

In 1955 Brooke Bond, an English tea company, relaunched its PG Tips tea. Before 1955 the number four brand had been called ''Pre-Gestive'' tea, referring to its dietary and medicinal properties. The relaunch modernized the tea's image, but it did not increase the brand's market share until the end of 1958, when it became the dominant brand leader, increasing its volume share from 10 percent in early 1956 to 23 percent the end of 1958.

How did PG Tips achieve and maintain this success for over 35 years? A combination of factors have been responsible, including changes in the nature of what the British eat and drink and in the fashions in the tea market. The most important contributor to this success story, however, was the introduction of a new campaign that hasn't changed since it was first advertised in 1956 and the high level of media support given to the brand ever since.

What do you think of when you think of tea? Not many people would think of chimps, but one copywriter visiting Regent's Park zoo in 1956 observed chimpanzees enjoying a tea party in front of a large crowd and decided to use the image to sell tea. A few months later, the first Chimps commercial was shot in a stately home, featuring a chimps tea party accompanied by a voiceover by actor Peter Sellers (see Exhibit A). The 60-second commercial first appeared on British television in Fall 1956 and was designed to boost awareness of PG Tips and to develop an original and unique property for the brand. It was also hoped that the commercial would establish a stronger relationship between the brand, advertisers, and consumers by bringing the enjoyment of the crowd at the zoo into the homes of viewers.

Within 2 years the chimps advertising had surpassed all expectations. It replaced Typhoo from the number one spot, and overtook other tea giants such as Brook Bond Dividend and Lyon. The chimps campaign soon became so popular that Brooke Bond began conducting film shows in cinemas around the country. The key to the enormous success of the campaign has been the consistency it has maintained ever since its introduction. Similar creative executions have continued to run over the entire 35-year life span of the campaign. By 1986, the thirtieth anniversary of the Chimps advertising, over 100 commercials had been made. Consistency has been maintained not only in the creative style of the advertising but in its media presence as well. PG Tips has always retained the dominant share of voice in the tea market. Whereas its competitors have greatly fluctuated their advertising spending from year to year, PG Tips has varied its spending by a relatively small proportion.

Maintaining such consistency has presented PG Tips with many challenges. The first is to keep viewers excited by new ideas. In addition, many social changes have occurred in the last 35 years, and the Chimps have had to reflect these trends in society so as not to become dated. For example, in the late 1960s the commercials were designed to reflect the self-expression of the times by portraying the Chimps as a photographer in one commercial and an artist in another. In the 1970s the chimps commercials reflected topical events such as the oil crisis. Throughout all these years, clearly observed sketches on the British character have always attracted consumer interest in the commercials. In the 1972 commercial ''Mr. Shifter'' the title character coined the phrase ''You hum it son, I'll play it'' (see Exhibit B), and the Tour de France cyclist asked ''Avez-vous un cuppa?'' which has also become part of the common vernacular.

The campaign has also been adapted to counter competition. For example, in response to Tetley's emphasis on the advantages of their teabags' ''2000 perforations,'' Brooke Bond relaunched PG Tips with new ''Flavour Flow'' teabags in 1981. In these ads, ''Brooke Bond,'' a character based on James Bond, guarded the new teabags' secret.

Between 1983 and 1985, ''Ada and Dolly'' formed

EXHIBIT A

Music: 'Greensleeves'
VO. The clock strikes four. In millions of English homes that means it's tea time

Tea time time with its gleaming silver and tinkling tea cups

What a happy time it is and how fortunate the hostess who knows that her favourite tea is also the favourite of her friends

For no matter how elegant the manners or charming the company

no guest is ever really happy without the right kind of tea –

good tea, fresh tea, tea you can taste to

the last delicious drop

"He means Brooke Bond PG Tips. B-B-B-Brooke Bond"

Sound of laughter from other chimps

the core campaign, moving back to the more traditional "kitchen sink" image. Ada characterized the traditional packet tea user, and Dolly was the more modern teabag user. The appeal of old favorites was still strong, and the Mr. Shifter and Tour de France ads continued to be shown as well. More recently the chimps are depicted in modern-day scenarios as jet-setters flying off to Spain on vacation, as health conscious, visiting health farms, and as corporate executives making board room decisions and using computers.

The Challenges

Since the 1960s tea companies have been faced with declining sales as a result of the new appeal of coffee to the younger generation and the growth of other substitutes (see Exhibit C). Two major structural changes occurred in the last 35 years to combat this challenge: the introduction of the teabag in 1963 and the importance of own label teas. PG Tips, the largest brand, has lost least to its own

label over the past 34 years; own label has eaten into the other brands in both packet and bags sectors. Throughout the years, PG Tips has also been faced with intense competitive pressures. Rival brands have been relaunched (such as Quickbrew 1986) and have intermittently outspent PG Tips. Furthermore, every conceivable promotional weapon has been used by rival companies to try and wrest away some of the brand's market share.

The Response

PG Tips has been able to maintain its leadership position throughout the years in light of the challenges it has faced and has given the brand long-term added value. This success is attributed almost exclusively to the product's advertising. A paper written by BMP DDB Needham Worldwide, the British agency responsible for the chimps campaign, analyzed the possible causes of the brand's success and concluded that the chimps campaign was the sole contributor to the explosive growth PG Tips experienced

EXHIBIT B

"Getting the hang of it, mind the bannisters son"

"Ooh, I can't hold it dad"

"Don't worry son, I've shifted more pianos than you've had hot dinners"

"Cooee, cooee Mr Shifter, light refreshments"

"Thankyou most kindly madam"

(Piano crashes down the stairs)

"One way of shifting it!"

VO. When a good cup of tea really counts you're right to drink Brooke Bond PG Tips - it's the tea you can really taste

"Dad, do you know the piano's on my foot?"

"You hum it son and I'll play it"

EXHIBIT C

TRENDS IN DRINKS CONSUMPTION
Average Daily Intake

Coffee
Fruit Juice
Carbonates
Tea

Source: NDS

in the late 1950s and continues to experience today. Other possible causes were suggested but disputed as causal variables for the brand's success.

The Product. PG Tips has always been an excellent product and is blended to a standard set by Brooke Bond's chief tea blender, but it is not distinguished from its competitors in blind taste tests.

Name Change. Pre-Gestive Tea was already being called PG by consumers prior to 1955 because the "P" and "G" were in bold type on the package. Therefore, changing the name is not attributed to the great success the brand experienced.

Taste Change. The blend used in the tea was not changed at the time of the first chimps commercial and therefore had no influence on its popularity.

Distribution Change. Even as the number four brand, PG Tips was already in very strong distribution, aided by Brooke Bond Dividend's preeminence. In addition, in March 1990 PG Tips, Tetley, and Typhoo all enjoyed 90 percent distribution, so distribution gains can be excluded.

Price Change. PG Tips was sold at the same price premium (1 percent) over both Tetley and Typhoo both before and after the chimps advertising broke, so the growth was not caused by advantageous pricing. Furthermore, PG Tips has actually increased its price premium against own label over time from 24 percent to 57 percent higher. Indeed, the data suggests that the brand has been able to enjoy a consistent price premium as a result of the added value.

Promotions. There is no evidence to suggest that PG Tips has been more promoted than its rivals or that the promotions have carried greater value. Furthermore, if the promotions have been more effective than the competitors', then this is a *result* of the brand's perceived value, not a cause.

Packaging. Although the consistency of the tea picker, red and green color coding, and "PG Tips" block letter has played a part in building brand recognition for PG Tips, both Tetley and Typhoo packaging elements are strong as well.

The Concept of Added Value

Brooke Bond has had the marketing foresight to continue to invest rather than just milk a strong brand. The company has invested the brand with "added value" that prompts consumers to continue buying even when more functional qualities of the brand suggest that other brand choices would be at least as satisfactory. Without the chimps advertising or with advertising only as effective in the long-term as other tea brands, it seems unlikely that PG Tips would have been able to fight off the kind of competitive activity it has faced.

The concept of added value was measured in various ways. Blind taste tests revealed that consumers have a

hard time distinguishing between the major brands by taste alone. Throughout the years these tests have indicated that the average consumer response for the top 5 brands was very similar, varying by only 1 or 2 percent. In recent branded tests, however, PG Tips was greatly preferred and perceived as the best-tasting tea. PG Tips was also found to have added value in that a price increase did not affect consumers' preference for the brand. An analysis of recent data from the teabag sector indicated that PG Tips is much less sensitive than Tetley to price changes by both branded and own label competitors. In other words, consumers are more likely to ignore price in favor of other "values" when it comes to purchasing PG Tips.

Furthermore, the concept of added value suggested that the brand should be less sensitive to short-term declines in the level of its advertising support, and this proved to be the case. When less is spent on the chimps advertising, only a small decline in share is found in the short term. Similarly, when Tetley advertises on television there is found to be only a small impact on PG Tips share, a small proportion of what Tetley gains from spending that amount. It is impressive that PG Tips can survive off air for a few months without suffering any significant fallback in share even when Tetley's advertising is capable of stealing significant share from other brands.

The chimps campaign has also been responsible for creating the longer-term added value the brand now possesses. Compared to its competitors, most of whom have declined, PG Tips has maintained resilience. Differences in the creative content and the level of advertising investment is responsible for this success. The major decline in other brand of tea is further evidence of this in that the declining fortunes of each of the brands correlates with a strategy of chopping and changing the content of the advertising and the lower support for the advertising.

How the Advertising Works

The chimps campaign has been shown to have the highest level of awareness of all tea campaigns. It is also the most efficient campaign in terms of generating awareness. According to a study by Millward Brown, PG Tips advertising index is the highest in the market. Given that consumers tend to talk about the chimps as part of the brand, it is also plausible that the advertising is at least partly responsible for the brand's emotional appeal, which is what the added value of the brand is built on. The chimps advertising also claims in some form that "There is no other tea to beat PG . . . It's the taste." It is the entertaining and lovable nature of the advertising that enables this message of extra quality to be accepted. Lastly, many consumers describe the advertising almost as a "pick-me-up." The brand and the chimps have almost become one. In other words, the appeal of the advertising translates into appeal for the brand.

Source: Courtesy of BMP DDB Needham Worldwide Limited.

APPENDIX: CAREERS IN ADVERTISING

The American Association of Advertising Agencies publishes a brochure entitled "Go For It: A Guide to Careers in Advertising," which provides detailed job descriptions and advice for pursuing a career in advertising. The material found in this appendix provides a more in-depth look at agency positions, their requirements and career opportunities, as well as helpful information on preparing a résumé and for a job interview.

JOBS IN AN ADVERTISING AGENCY

As you have seen in these chapters, agencies handle a broad range of tasks requiring people with experience and ability in overall management as well as specialized fields. In a small agency, one person may wear several hats, such as media planner and buyer, whereas at a large agency some people will tend to specialize, such as a network television buyer. In all agencies, however, the jobs usually fall into five categories:

- Account management
- Creative
- Media
- Market research
- Support services and administration

ACCOUNT MANAGEMENT

At an agency, the client and its business are usually called "the account." One advertiser may offer many products or services and ask separate agencies to handle each one. Another may use a single agency to handle several products or services. No matter what the particular situation, the account management department is where the resources of the agency and the needs of the client connect.

The account manager oversees the advertising business that has been assigned to the agency and is ultimately responsible for the quality of service the client receives. The account manager serves as the client's representative at the agency and the agency's representative at the client's organization. It is his or her job to get the client its money's worth—to get the best possible work from the agency for the client—but at a profitable return for the agency. This means knowing how to handle people at the agency so that they give the client their best effort without spending more time than the income from the client's business justifies.

The effective account manager develops a thorough knowledge of the client's business, the consumer, the marketplace, and all aspects of advertising, including creative, media, research, and commercial production. As team leader and strategist, the account person must communicate the client's needs clearly to the agency team, plan effectively to maximize staff time and energy, and present the agency's recommendations candidly to the client. He or she must also know all about the agency: who are the most qualified people in each department and how to get their attention when it is needed.

The account manager must also know all about the client, enthusiastically learning every aspect of the client's business—ideally, from product development through the entire marketing operation—well enough to command the client's respect when presenting the agency's recommendations. In the final analysis, the account person must be able to foster productive communication between client and agency staffs, identify common goals, and make sure that the final product is profitable and effective for the client and the agency.

Entry-Level Positions

Assistant Account Executive (Manager). The typical assistant account executive reports directly to an account executive and has a wide range of responsibilities. Some common duties include reporting client billing and forecasting agency income, analyzing competitive activity and consumer trends, writing conference reports from meetings, and coordinating creative, media, research, and production projects.

Successful candidates have strong general business skills: the ability to write and spell effectively, demonstrated leadership experience, a capacity for statistical analysis, and developed organizational skills. In addition, it is important to be able to work well under pressure, handle a variety of tasks simultaneously, and coordinate the work and energy of diverse types of people, as well as to have creative sensibility and an intense interest in advertising and marketing.

Candidates for this position should have a bachelor's degree and, in some cases, a master of business administration. A degree in advertising or marketing is not a prerequisite. Within the agency business, agency account management and media departments hire the greatest number of entry-level candidates. Some of the large agencies offer entry-level training programs in account management.

Career Opportunities An entry-level position in account management usually leads to account executive and then to more senior positions, with responsibility for more than one account and for the work of several account executives. Ultimately, account management can assume broader office and corporate positions. Currently the largest percentage of top agency management positions are filled from the ranks of the account management department.

CREATIVE

The creative department of an advertising agency is responsible for developing the ideas, images, and words that make up commercials and ads. Although many people contribute to the process, the invention and production of advertising is mainly the responsibility of copywriters and art directors.

When a copywriter and art director are assigned to an account, they must learn about the product or service to be advertised, marketing strategy, consumer or potential consumer, media to be used, advertising by competitors, production budget, and the client personnel (such as brand managers) with whom the agency deals. The research, account management, and media departments provide basic information on all these topics. However, the creative people will most likely want to gain first-hand experience with the client's product.

After the creative people assimilate as much information as possible, they agree on a general direction. The art director and copywriter work as a team trying out ideas first on each other, on the creative director, and on the other agency groups working on the account. These executions are reviewed by senior members of the agency (including legal counsel), sometimes called the review board, to evaluate whether they match the goals of the marketing and advertising strategy.

The reviewed creative executions are presented to the client for approval. Once the client approves, the art director and copywriter work with print and broadcast production people to produce the final version of the advertisement. Magazines and newspapers require camera-ready copy. To prepare such print advertisements, agencies rely on outside services, from photographers to typesetters. Agency specialists in print production oversee this contracted work. Television stations require videotape; radio stations must have audio tape. Broadcast commercials often involve a large cast of outside specialists. Agency producers oversee the completion of television and radio commercials. They hire directors, production studios with film crews, and actors. In addition, producers administer the budget, work with composers and musicians, and participate in the review and editing of the rough film or videotape into the final version.

CREATIVE

CREATIVITY IS THE
BASIS OF THE AGENCY'S
ABILITY TO USE THE
UNEXPECTED AND
DEVELOP STRENGTH
FROM THE SURPRISE.

Entry-Level Positions

Junior Copywriter. A junior copywriter assists one or more copywriters in editing and proofreading ad copy, writing body copy for established print campaigns, and developing merchandising and sales promotion materials. With proven ability and experience, assignments might include generating ideas for product or company names and writing dialogue for television commercials and scripts for radio ads.

A successful candidate not only has outstanding skills in writing but has a "love affair" with words and symbols and their use in communication. Interest in a wide range of subjects and an insatiable sense of curiosity are assets. Candidates should have some knowledge of marketing and how words and visuals have been used in advertising.

Agencies expect job candidates to demonstrate their talent by showing portfolios of previous creative work, seminal ideas, and "rough" designs of potential campaigns, even if they were done in the classroom or on your own. Although a bachelor's degree is not required, most agencies look for candidates with proven intellectual ability and emotional maturity. Degrees in English, journalism, or advertising and marketing can be helpful. Opportunities for candidates who have no writing experience are limited. Some of the largest agencies offer entry-level training programs in copywriting.

Junior or Assistant Art Director. The junior art director assists one or more art directors in preparing paste-ups, rough lettering, and layouts for print ads and television storyboards, developing visual concepts and designs, and overseeing photo sessions and the filming of television commercials.

A successful candidate will have strong visual concept skills and good basic drawing and design ability. Although an assistant art director must be capable of handling day-to-day lettering and matting tasks, agencies are also interested in identifying candidates with visual imagination and an interest in applying that ability to marketing and advertising problems.

Agencies expect candidates to show portfolios displaying their basic drawing skills and roughs of ideas for potential advertising campaigns. Although a bachelor's degree is not required, most agencies look for candidates with at least a 2-year degree from an art or design school. Entry-level opportunities are very limited for candidates with only some related business experience, such as in a retail advertising department.

Career Opportunities An entry-level position as junior copywriter leads to copywriter. An entry-level position as a junior art director leads to art director. In these more senior positions, each is given more responsibility and freedom in developing the visual and copy ideas for campaigns and may work on more than one account or on accounts that make special demands.

The position of art director or copywriter can lead to creative supervisor, the professional responsible for the work of a group of copywriters or art directors. More senior positions usually include creative group head, responsible for supervising teams of art directors and copywriters as well as production functions; creative director, responsible for all creative work produced by the agency for either all clients or a groups of clients; and chief or executive creative director, responsible for overall creative work in a division, region, or company-wide. Senior creative people are important to the overall management of an agency. Many of them reach top agency management positions.

MEDIA

Even the most innovative and highly creative advertising in the world can fail if it is presented to the wrong audience or if it is presented at the wrong time or in the wrong place. The media department of an advertising agency is responsible for placing advertising where it will reach the right people in the right place and do so in a cost-effective way.

To bring advertising messages to the public, agencies must use a carrier, called a medium of communication or simply a medium. The four most commonly used media are television, radio, magazines, and newspapers. Some other media include billboards, posters, printed bulletins, and even skywriting.

Planning and buying media at an advertising agency is exciting and challenging because ways of communicating are constantly changing and becoming more complex. Such technological advances as cable television or videotext make an impact on what media are available for advertising and how viewership is calculated. A recent increase in the number of specialty publications enables more precise targeting of consumers. Today, more than ever, agencies and clients are recognizing the importance of creative and innovative media planning and buying.

When working on a particular advertising campaign, the media planners discuss, with the client and other agency people, the goals of the marketing strategy as well as a description of the potential consumer. As planners, they think about the kinds of media the target group might read, listen to, or watch. They compare the content, image, and format of each medium with the nature of the product or service, its image, and the goals of the advertising campaign. In discussions with the creative department and account team, planners suggest which media can be used most effectively to reach the target audience.

The media department is responsible for developing a plan that answers the question: How can the greatest number of people in the target group be reached often enough to have the advertising message seen and remembered—and at the lowest possible cost? Once the media plan has been developed, presented to the client, and approved, the department's media buyers start negotiating for space and time. Buyers purchase space in which to display their messages in print media. They buy time in the broadcast media.

Buyers must not only find and reserve available space and time, but also negotiate the best price. Will a station offer a lower price if more time slots are bought? Will prime time be discounted if the buyer is willing to purchase, in addition, some less desirable time in the morning or late at night? Buyers who have outstanding negotiating skills are valuable assets to any agency's media department.

After the space and time have been purchased, the department must monitor the media to make sure that the advertising actually appeared, in the proper form and at the proper time as it was ordered. If a discrepancy occurs, the department negotiates an adjustment to the billing or accepts a credit for additional time or space.

Entry-Level Positions

Assistant Media Planner. The typical assistant media planner reports to a media planner and gathers and studies information about people's viewing and reading habits, evaluates editorial content and programming of various media vehicles, calculates reach and frequency for specific target groups and campaigns, learns all there is to know about the media in general (magazines, newspapers, radio, television) and about media vehicles in particular *(Time, The Wall Street Journal),* and becomes thoroughly familiar with media data banks and information sources.

Accomplishing these tasks requires the ability to find and analyze data, apply computer skills, ask innovative questions, and interpret or explain findings with attention to quantitative and qualitative considerations. In short, a planner must gain knowledge of what information is important and where to find it. By assisting in gathering statistics to support a variety of plans, he or she eventually becomes familiar with broader characteristics and trends in all media.

Assistant Media Buyer.   The typical assistant media buyer reports directly to a media buyer and knows when and where space and time are available for purchase, reconciles agency media orders with what actually appears, calculates rates, usage, and budget, learns buying terminology and operating procedures, develops skills in negotiation and communication with media sales representatives, and becomes familiar with the media market. Accomplishing these tasks requires ease at working with numbers and budgets, outstanding communication skills, and the ability to work under pressure. Skills in negotiation and sales are especially advantageous.

Successful candidates have strong general business skills: the ability to write and speak effectively, developed organizational skills, aptitude for working with numbers and statistics, and basic computer skills. In addition, other important attributes are working well under pressure, maintaining priorities while handling a variety of tasks simultaneously, the ability and desire to interact with a wide range of personalities at the agency, the client, and within the media industry, an intense curiosity and interest in all types of media and their role in the marketing process, and understanding of sales and negotiation concepts (leverage, timing, and positioning), and a winning personal attitude.

Candidates should have a bachelor's degree. A degree in advertising or marketing is not a prerequisite. In most agencies, the media department, along with account management, hires the greatest number of entry-level candidates. Most larger agencies offer entry-level training programs in media.

The organization of a media department varies with the size of the agency. In large agencies, a person may specialize by medium, whereas in small and medium-sized agencies each person may handle all media. The media function is headed by a media director, who usually reports to the highest level of management.

Career Opportunities   An entry-level position as an assistant media planner usually leads to media planner, the person responsible for developing a media plan. An entry-level position as an assistant media buyer usually leads to media buyer, responsible for negotiating time and space. It is common for the planner and buyer to develop expertise in specific media categories, such as magazine or network or spot television. In a small agency, the two jobs may be combined.

The next step is supervisory. The media planning supervisor coordinates the work of planners and presents recommendations to the account group and client. The broadcast buying supervisor oversees buying operations.

With greater knowledge and experience, media people advance to any of several positions—associate media director, manager of media research, network supervisor, director of spot broadcast, groups media director, director of programming and negotiations, and media director. Many agencies have top media people represented in senior management and as members of their boards of directors.

MARKET RESEARCH

The basic role of the market research department in an advertising agency is to understand the wants, desires, thoughts, concerns, motivating forces, and ideas of the consumer. By researching secondary information, conducting focus groups or one-on-one interviews, testing people's reactions to new advertising copy, tracking sales volume, or studying buying trends, the advertising agency researcher becomes an expert on consumer behavior.

Most researchers are assigned to specific accounts and work as advisors to the account, creative, and media people. They help develop, refine, and evaluate potential strategies and are called on to react to possible creative approaches based on their understanding of the consumer. This might be done with the creative team during the process or with account managers as evaluators of creative alternatives.

Some agencies also employ researchers who specialize in specific areas of quantitative or qualitative research. Consumer trends and lifestyle research are two areas in which most large agencies maintain continuing studies. Findings from these specialized studies tend to have an impact on all agency clients as well as on the process of creating advertising. In addition, the research department oversees projects that are subcontracted to "out-of-house" research firms. A typical example is surveys of shoppers at malls. The agency researchers design the questionnaire and interpret results, but a private firm conducts the interviews and summarizes the data so the researcher can write a report on the survey.

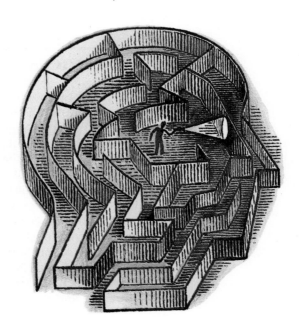

Entry-Level Positions

Assistant Research Executive. The typical assistant reports directly to a research executive. Duties usually include compiling data from secondary resources, following the progress of research projects, assisting in the development of primary research tools, and learning to analyze facts and numbers, interpreting and explaining what these really mean.

Successful candidates have strong quantitative skills and the aptitude for analyzing and interpreting qualitative as well as quantitative data. Computer literacy is also advantageous. In addition, candidates should be able to write and speak effectively, work well under pressure, and organize work priorities. They should have an interest in forecasting trends and patterns and a fascination with human behavior and motivation.

A bachelor's degree is the minimum requirement, but it is not unusual to find people who have master's or doctorate degrees employed in agency research departments. Although a specific major is not a prerequisite, many employers are attracted to candidates whose coursework is related to research. Some academic disciplines fitting this category are sociology, psychology, marketing, marketing research, economics, journalism, quantitative methods, anthropology, and mass communications.

Entry-level positions in agency research departments are relatively rare, especially in medium- and small-sized agencies. Candidates who have only bachelor's or master's degrees and no experience might find some opportunities at the largest agencies or at research firms.

Career Opportunities An entry-level position as an assistant research executive usually leads to a supervisory position with responsibility for managing research on individual accounts or brands overseeing the work of assistant research executives. During this stage a person might identify a personal interest in a specific research area and seek to specialize. The next step is management of a specialized research function or responsibility for all research on more than one account. Ultimately, a research person may have the opportunity to move into more general corporate management or marketing functions.

SUPPORT SERVICES

Like any well-run business, the advertising agency must maintain a full complement of people who handle accounting, personnel, clerical, and office services. In addition, agency traffic managers make sure that, once started, an ad or commercial moves smoothly through the agency, additions and corrections are obtained, and the whole job arrives at the publication or the broadcast station on time.

Cost controllers monitor agency costs, making sure that work stays within budget or that everyone is aware of, and approves, any needed changes in the budget. Other agency employees may include lawyers, librarians, and certain specialists. For example, agencies with big food or packaged-goods accounts sometimes keep nutritionists and home economists on staff. Those with healthy products or medical accounts may employ physicians. Such diversity is one more aspect that makes agency work such a fascinating and rewarding career choice.

PREPARING FOR A CAREER IN ADVERTISING

Breaking into advertising is not easy. Most jobs require a college degree. Internships and related work experience can be helpful. Retail selling experience is also excellent preparation. In addition to all this, however, getting a job in an advertising agency requires determination for two reasons. First, there are few job openings, and second, a lot of other bright people, like yourself, want those jobs, too. This year alone many agencies will receive thousands of inquiries for entry-level opportunities. Of this number, a very large agency might hire only 30. In short, there are many more people interested in working at agencies than there are openings. Nothing guarantees a job with an agency, but there are seven basic steps you should consider.

1. Educate Yourself About the Business

Find out as much as possible about the advertising business, what an agency does, and the career area or department in which you would like to work. Read every bit of relevant material you can find—articles, books, and such trade journals as *Advertising Age, Mediaweek,* and *Adweek.*

Talk to people. Track down any contacts or friends you have in the business. Sit down with your college instructors and career counselors. Make inquiries at such professional organizations as the American Association of Advertising Agencies, Advertising Women of New York, the American Advertising Foundations, or your local advertising club. Find out about seminars and attend them. One source of information can lead you to ten others. The more you know about your chosen area, the better you can present yourself as a first-rate candidate.

2. Target Your Prospects

Decide what factors are important to you about a company and evaluate prospective employers on that basis. Make use of the *Standard Directory of Advertising Agencies,* popularly known as the "Agency Red Book." It is available at most libraries and lists all the agencies worldwide. It gives names and titles of key people, size of the agency (in dollar billings, number of offices, and total personnel), the agency's accounts, and a breakdown of the media in which the agency invests its clients' money.

Read the trade press to learn more about specific agencies you want to target. For example, *Advertising Age* prints a special issue each year that provides profiles of individual agency business activity during the previous 12 months. It also selects an "agency of the year" and publishes an in-depth description.

3. Develop a Strategy

With all the competition for jobs in advertising, you must develop your own "unique selling proposition" to communicate your own unique qualities. It is not enough that you are interested in advertising, or that you made dean's list eight times, or that you wrote for the school newspaper. So did most of your competition. You have to connect what you have done in the past, in a unique way, to what you will do for the agency in the future. Developing a strategy gets your commitment, imagination, and analytical thinking out in the limelight. It is the key to making you stand out from other candidates.

4. Create a Good Résumé

The primary purpose of a résumé is to get you an interview. Used correctly, it can open doors. Used incorrectly, it slams them shut. A good résumé connects your experience to your job goal. Support your candidacy by highlighting relevant skills, such as writing, speaking, managing, and so on. Include any activities, jobs, or internships directly related to advertising. Did you sell space for the school's newspaper? Were you yearbook editor? Or stage manager for the college theater group? Add less-related activities only if they are outstanding. Be selective. Your résumé is a selling tool, not a life history. Keep it neat, clear, precise, and all on one page. Try to make it unique and interesting but not gimmicky.

5. Take Pains with Each Cover Letter

A cover letter works hand in hand with your résumé. Together they create a first impression of you. Your cover letter should work as a connecting tool between you and the agency you are writing to. Don't let it read like a form letter. Instead, include real knowledge of the agency, its clients, its work, and its position in the industry. Tell the agency why you are interested in them and why you think you'd be right for them. Then make sure that you are prepared to discuss in your interview whatever you say in the cover letter. Remember, you are being judged on communicative skill, Watch spelling, grammar, and typing. Most importantly, be clear, crisp, and brief.

6. Assemble a Portfolio

To help you get a job in an agency creative department, you must prepare a portfolio that shows your thinking and imagination. If you are an aspiring art director, this clearly has to include ample demonstration of your design ability and graphic sense. If you want to be a copywriter, visuals are less critical than is demonstration of your writing ability and marketing sense.

In either case, show your very best work. If you have not had any experience, pick some currently running campaigns, determine their objectives, and interpret them in your own way. It doesn't matter if your "ads" are not professional. Your prospective employer wants to see fresh concepts and new ideas that prove you have potential. Then keep making changes to improve your portfolio. For more specific suggestions, see Maxine Paetro's book on building portfolios, entitled *How to Put Your Book Together and Get a Job in Advertising.*

7. Prepare for Your Interview

At most agencies, an invitation to be interviewed reflects more than casual interest in a candidate. If you have made it this far, you're at least in the quarterfinals. And if you've done your homework, you should have nothing to worry about.

Before the interview, organize your thinking. Review your résumé and the cover letter you sent the agency. Decide what key selling points you should communicate about yourself. Think how you can best do this. Review the information you have about the agency. Be aware of its current campaigns and any fast-breaking developments. Commenting on these can help you make an immediate connection with the interviewer.

Be ready to discuss your point of view on advertising in general and your area of interest in particular. Be articulate. Be self-confident and enthusiastic, but relax and do it naturally. Don't try to recite everything you know. Selectivity shows you are thinking.

Remember, someone is interested enough in your background to invest 30 minutes or more in you. That person wants you to succeed.

Source: Courtesy of The American Association of Advertising Agencies.

GLOSSARY

A

Account management The function in an agency which serves as a liaison between the agency and the client.

Account planner The person responsible for the creation, implementation, and modification of the strategy on which creative work is based.

Adese Formula writing that uses clichés, generalities, stock phrases, and superlatives.

Advertiser The individual or organization that initiates the advertising process.

Advertising Paid nonpersonal communication from an identified sponsor using mass media to persuade or influence an audience.

Advertising campaign A comprehensive advertising plan for a series of different but related ads that appear in different media across a specified time period.

Advertising objectives Statements of the effect of the advertising message on the audience.

Advertising plan A plan that proposes strategies for targeting the audience, presenting the advertising message, and implementing media.

Advocacy advertising A type of corporate advertising that involves creating advertisements and purchasing space to deliver a specific, targeted message.

Affiliate A station that is contracted with a national network to carry network-originated programming during part of its schedule.

Agent Someone who acts on behalf of someone else, usually for a fee.

Agricultural advertising Advertising directed at large and small farmers.

Allocations Divisions or proportions of advertising dollars among the various media.

Animatic A preliminary version of a commercial with the storyboard frames recorded on videotape along with a rough sound track.

Animation A type of recording medium in which objects are sketched and then filmed one frame at a time.

Answer print The final finished version of the commercial with the audio and video recorded together.

Aperture The ideal moment for exposing consumers to an advertising message.

Appeal Something that moves people.

Arranger The person who orchestrates the music, arranging it for the various instruments, voices, and scenes.

Art The visual elements in an ad, including illustrations, photos, type, logos and signatures, and the layout.

Art director The person who is primarily responsible for the visual image of the advertisement.

Attitude A learned predisposition that we hold toward an object, person, or ideal.

Average cost trends A history of changes in the average unit (per message) prices for each medium that is used in cost forecasting.

B

Barter syndication Programs that are offered to a station at a reduced price or for fee, with presold national spots.

Benefit segmentation Segments identified by the appeal of the product to their personal interests.

Benefits Statements about what the product can do for the user.

Billboards Large structures erected on highways and roads for the display of huge advertising posters.

Bleed An ad in which the printed area runs to the trim edge of the page.

Body copy The text of the message.

Brag-and-boast copy Advertising text that is written from the company's point of view to extol its virtues and accomplishments.

Brainstorming A creative-thinking technique using free association in a group environment to stimulate inspiration.

Brand development index (BDI) An index that identifies the demand for the brand within a region.

Brand equity The use of a respected brand name to add value to a product.

Brand image A mental image that reflects the way a brand is perceived, including all the identification elements, the product personality, and the emotions and associations evoked in the mind of the consumer.

Brand loyalty Existing positive opinions held by consumers about the product or service.

Branding The process of creating an identity for a product using a distinctive name or symbol.

Broadsheet A newspaper with a size of eight columns wide and 22 inches deep.

Business-to-business advertising Advertising directed at people who buy or specify products for business use.

C

Cable television A form of subscription television in which the signals are carried to households by a cable.

Captions Short descriptions of the content of a photograph or an illustration.

Car cards Small advertisements that are mounted in racks inside a vehicle.

Carry-over effect A measure of residual effect (awareness or recall) of the advertising message some time after the advertising period has ended.

Category development index (CDI) An index that identifies the demand for the category within a region.

Cease-and-desist order A legal order requiring an advertiser to stop its unlawful practices.

Channel of distribution People and organizations involved in moving products from producers to consumers.

Circulation A measure of the number of copies sold.

Claim A statement about the product's performance.

Classified advertising Commercial messages arranged in the newspaper according to the interests of readers.

Claymation A technique that uses figures sculpted from clay and filmed one frame at a time.

Cliché A trite expression, an over-used idea.

Cognitive dissonance A tendency to justify the discrepancy between what a person receives relative to what he or she expected to receive.

Color separation The process of splitting a color image into four images recorded on negatives; each negative represents one of the four process colors.

Commission A form of payment in which an agent or agency receives a certain percentage (often 15 percent) of media charges.

Competitive product advantage The identification of a feature that is important to the consumer where your product is strong and the competition is vulnerable.

Composer The person who writes the music.

Composition The process of arranging the elements in a photograph or an illustration.

Comprehensive A layout that looks as much like the final printed ad as possible.

Concept testing The audience's evaluation of alternative creative strategies.

Conflict of interest An agency dilemma of having a client's two competing companies.

Consent decree An order given by the FTC and signed by an advertiser, agreeing to stop running a deceptive ad.

Consolidation The appointment of one agency to handle all the advertising of a client's divisions.

Consumers People who buy or use products.

Contests Sales promotion activities that require participants to compete for a prize on the basis of some skill or ability.

Continuity The strategy and tactics used to schedule advertising over the time span of the advertising campaign.

Continuity program A program that requires the consumer to continue purchasing the product or service in order to receive a reward.

Continuous An advertising scheduling pattern in which spending remains relatively constant during the campaign period.

Convergent thinking Thinking that uses logic to arrive at the "right" answer.

Cooperative advertising A form of advertising in which the manufacturer reimburses the retailer for part or all of the retailer's advertising expenditures.

Copy The written elements in an ad, including headlines, underlines and overlines, subheads, body copy, captions, slogans, and taglines.

Copywriter The person who writes the text for an ad.

Corporate identity advertising A type of advertising used by firms to establish their reputation or increase awareness.

Corporate/institutional advertising Advertising used to create a favorable public attitude toward the sponsoring organization.

Corrective advertising A remedy required by the FTC in which an advertiser who produced misleading messages is required to issue factual information to offset these messages

Cost per rating point (CPRP) A method of comparing media vehicles by relating the cost of the message unit to the audience rating.

Cost per thousand (CPM) The cost of exposing each 1,000 members of the target audience to the advertising message.

Coupons Legal certificates offered by manufacturers and retailers that grant specified savings on selected products when presented for redemption at the point of purchase.

CPM trend analysis Longitudinal (long-term) history of average cost-per-thousand tendencies of advertising media that is used to assist in forecasting future CPM levels.

Crawl Computer-generated letters that move across the bottom of the screen.

Creative concept A "Big Idea" that is original and dramatizes the selling point.

Creative platform A document that outlines the message strategy decisions behind an individual ad.

Cultural and social influences The forces that other people exert on your behavior.

Culture The complex whole of tangible items, intangible concepts, and social behaviors that define a group of people or a way of life.

Cut An abrupt transition from one shot to another.

Cutouts Irregularly shaped extensions added to the top, bottom, or sides of standard outdoor boards.

D

Data bases Lists of consumers with information that helps target and segment those who are highly likely to be in the market for a certain product.

Data sheets Advertising that provides detailed technical information.

Dealer loader A premium given to a retailer by a manufacturer for buying a certain quantity of product.

Dealer tag Time left at the end of a broadcast advertisement that permits identification of the local store.

Demographics The vital statistics about the human population, its distribution, and its characteristics.

Diagnostic research Research used to identify the best approach from among a set of alternatives.

Direct competition A product in the same category.

Direct mail A medium of advertising that uses the mail to carry the message.

Direct-order marketing or mail order A form of marketing that uses mail or some other delivery system to deliver the product.

Direct-response advertising A type of marketing communication that achieves an action-oriented objective as a result of the advertising message.

Direct-response counts Evaluative tests that count the number of viewers or readers who request more information or who purchase the product.

Direct-response marketing A type of marketing that uses media to contact a prospect directly and elicit a response without the intervention of a retailer or personal sales.

Directional advertising Advertising that directs the buyer to the store where the product or service is available.

Director The person in charge of the actual filming or taping of the commercial.

Discretionary income The money available for spending after taxes and necessities are covered.

Dispersion The use of as many different stations and programs as possible to avoid duplicating the message audience.

Display advertising Sponsored messages that can be of any size and location within the newspaper, with the exception of the editorial page.

Display copy Type set in larger sizes that is used to attract the reader's attention.

Divergent thinking Thinking that uses free association to uncover all possible alternatives.

Drama A story built around characters in a situation.

Dubbing The process of making duplicate copies of a videotape.

E

Editor The person who assembles the best shots to create scenes and who synchronizes the audio track with the images.

Effective frequency A recent concept in planning that determines a range (minimum and maximum) of repeat exposure for a message.

Empathy Understanding the feelings, thoughts, and emotions of someone else.

Evaluative research Research intended to measure the effectiveness of finished or nearly finished advertisements.

Experiments A research method that manipulates a set of variables to test hypotheses.

Exploratory research Informal intelligence gathering, backgrounding.

Exterior transit advertising Advertising posters that are mounted on the sides, rear, and top of vehicles.

F

Family Two or more people who are related by blood, marriage, or adoption and live in the same household.

Feature analysis A comparison of your product's features against the features of competing products.

Federal Communications Commission (FCC) A federal agency that regulates broadcast media and has the power to eliminate messages, including ads, that are deceptive or in poor taste.

Federal Trade Commission (FTC) A federal agency responsible for interpreting deceptive advertising and regulating unfair methods of competition.

Fee A mode of payment in which an agency charges a client on the basis of the agency's hourly costs.

Film A strip of celluloid with a series of still images, called frames.

Fixed pricing A traditional method of media pricing where rates are published and are applied equally to all advertisers.

Flighting An advertising scheduling pattern characterized by a period of intensified activity, called a flight, followed by periods of no advertising, called a hiatus.

Focal point The first element in a layout that the eye sees.

Focus group A group interview that tries to stimulate people to talk candidly about some topics or products.

Font A complete set of letters in one size and face.

Food and Drug Administration (FDA) A federal regulatory agency that oversees package labeling and ingredient listings for food and drugs.

Forecasting Estimating sales levels and the impact of various budget decisions on sales.

Frame-by-frame tests Tests that evaluate consumers' reactions to the individual scenes that unfold in the course of a television commercial.

Free association An exercise in which you describe everything that comes into your mind when you think of a word or an image.

Freelance artists Independent artists who work on individual assignments for an agency or advertiser.

Free-standing insert advertisements Preprinted advertisements that are placed loosely within the newspaper.

Frequency The number of radio waves produced by a transmitter in 1 second; The number of times an audience has an opportunity to be exposed to a media vehicle or vehicles in a specified time span.

G

Game A type of sweepstakes that requires the player to return to play several times.

Generic products Products that are marketed without any identifying brand; they are usually less expensive than branded products.

Global brand A brand that has the same name, design, and creative strategy everywhere in the world.

Global perspective A corporate philosophy that directs products and advertising toward a worldwide rather than a local or regional market.

Gravure A type of printing that uses an image that is engraved, or recessed, into the surface of the printing plate.

Gross impressions The sum of the audiences of all the media vehicles used within a designated time span.

Gross rating points (GRP) The sum of the total exposure potential of a series of media vehicles expressed as a percentage of the audience population.

Guarantees Agreements in which the medium promises to compensate the advertiser should the audience fall below a specified level.

Gütenberg Diagonal A visual path that flows from the upper left corner to the lower right.

H

Halftones Images with a continuous range of shades from light to dark.

Hard sell A rational, informational message that emphasizes a strong argument and calls for action.

Headline The title of an ad; it is set in large type to get the reader's attention.

Hierarchy of effects A set of consumer responses that moves from the least serious, involved, or complex up through the most serious, involved, or complex.

High-involvement decision process Decisions that require an involved purchase process with information search and product comparison.

Holding company A company that owns the stocks of other corporations.

Holography A technique that produces a projected three-dimensional image.

Horizontal publications Publications directed to people who hold similar jobs in different companies across different industries.

Household All those people who occupy one living unit, whether or not they are related.

I

Idea A mental representation; a concept created by combining thoughts.

Impact A value of media influence on the audience that is expected to produce higher-than-normal awareness of the advertiser's message; the effect that a message has on the audience.

In register A precise matching of colors in images.

In-house agency An advertising department on the advertiser's staff that handles most, if not all, of the functions of an outside agency.

In-market tests Tests that measure the effectiveness of advertisements by measuring actual sales results in the marketplace.

Indicia The postage label printed by a postage meter.

Indirect competition A product that is in a different category but functions as an alternative purchase choice.

Industrial advertising Advertising directed at businesses that buy products to incorporate into other products or to facilitate the operation of their businesses.

Integrated marketing communications Promotional planning that focuses on integrated communication based on an analysis of consumer behavior.

Interactive Advertising that uses personal interaction between the advertiser and the customer.

Interconnects A special cable technology that allows local advertisers to run their commercials in small geographical areas through the interconnection of a number of cable systems.

Interior transit advertising Advertising on posters that are mounted inside vehicles such as buses, subway cars, and taxis.

Interlock A version of the commercial with the audio and video timed together, although the two are still recorded separately.

International advertising Advertising designed to promote the same product in different countries and cultures.

International brand A brand of product that is available in most parts of the world.

Involvement The intensity of the consumer's interest in a product.

Italic A type variation that uses letters that slant to the right.

J

Jingles Commercials with a message that is presented musically.

Justified A form of typeset copy in which the edges of the lines in a column of type are forced to align by adding space between words in the line.

K

Key frame A single frame of a commercial that summarizes the heart of the message.

Key visual A dominant image around which the commercial's message is planned.

Kinetic boards Outdoor advertising that uses moving elements.

Kiosks Multisided bulletin board structures designed for public posting of messages.

L

Layout A drawing that shows where all the elements in the ad are to be positioned.

Lecture Instruction delivered verbally to present knowledge and facts.

Letterpress A type of printing that prints from an image onto a raised surface.

Lifestyle The pattern of living that reflects how people allocate their time, energy, and money.

Line art Art in which all elements are solid with no intermediate shades or tones.

Line extensions New products introduced under existing brand names.

Local brand A brand that is marketed in one specific country.

Logo Logotype; a distinctive mark that identifies the product, company, or brand.

Loss leader Product advertised at or below cost in order to build store traffic.

Low-involvement decision process Decisions that require limited deliberation; sometimes purchases are even made on impulse.

M

Makegoods Compensation given by the media to advertisers in the form of additional message units, which are commonly used in situations involving production errors by the media and preemption of the advertiser's programming.

Margin White space used to frame the ad content.

Market An area of the country, a group of people, or the overall demand for a product.

Market philosophy The general attitude of the marketer toward the customer.

Market research Research that gathers information about specific markets.

Market segmentation The process of identifying segments to target.

Market segments Groups of people with characteristics in common who make up important subcategories of the population.

Marketing Business activities that direct the exchange of goods and services between producers and consumers

Marketing mix A plan that identifies the most effective combination of promotional activities.

Marketing plan A written document that proposes strategies for employing the marketing mix to achieve marketing objectives.

Marketing research Research that investigates all the elements of the marketing mix.

Mass markets Broad undifferentiated markets.

Mechanicals (keylines) A finished pasteup, with every element perfectly positioned, that is photographed to make printing plates for offset printing.

Media The channels of communication used by advertisers.

Media planning A decision process leading to the use of advertising time and space to assist in the achievement of marketing objectives.

Megamergers Combinations of large international agencies under a central holding company.

Merging The process of combining two or more lists of prospects.

Mixing Combining different tracks of music, voices, and sound effects to create the final ad.

Motive An unobservable inner force that stimulates and compels a behavioral response.

N

Needs Basic forces that motivate you to do or to want something.

Network radio A group of local affiliates providing simultaneous programming via connection to one or more of the national networks through AT&T telephone wires.

News release Primary medium used to deliver public relations messages to the media.

Newsprint An inexpensive, tough paper with a rough surface, used for printing newspapers.

Niche markets Narrowly focused markets that are defined by some special interest.

Noncommercial advertising Advertising that is sponsored by an organization to promote a cause rather than to maximize profits.

Nontraditional delivery Delivery of magazines to readers through such methods as door hangers or newspapers.

Norms Simple rules for behavior that are established by cultures.

Offset A type of printing that prints from a flat surface on the printing plate. The image is transferred to a rubber blanket that carries the impression to the paper.

Open pricing A method of media pricing in which prices are negotiated on a contract-by-contract basis for each unit of media space or time.

Optical center A point slightly above the mathematical center of a page.

Original One of a kind; unusual and unexpected.

Overline A subhead that leads into the headline.

P

Participations An arrangement in which a television advertiser buys commercial time from a network.

Percent-of-sales method A technique for computing the budget level that is based on the relationship between cost of advertising and total sales.

Perception The process by which we receive information through our five senses and acknowledge and assign meaning to this information.

Perceptual map A map that shows where consumers locate various products in the category in terms of several important features.

Personality Relatively long-lasting personal qualities that allow us to cope with, and respond to the world around us.

Persuasion test A test that evaluates the effectiveness of an advertisement by measuring whether the ad affects consumers' intentions to buy a brand.

Photoboard A type of rough commercial, similar to an animatic except that the frames are actual photos instead of sketches.

Physiological tests Tests that measure emotional reactions to advertisements by monitoring reactions such as pupil dilation and heart rate.

Pica A unit of type measurement used to measure width and depth of columns; there are 12 points in a pica and 6 picas in an inch.

Point A unit used to measure the height of type; there are 72 points in an inch.

Point-of-purchase display A display designed by the manufacturer and distributed to retailers in order to promote a particular brand or line of products.

Population Everyone included in a designated group.

Positioning The way in which a product is perceived in the marketplace by the consumers.

Preferred positions Sections or pages of magazine and newspaper issues that are in high demand by advertisers because they have a special appeal to the target audience.

Premium A tangible reward received for performing a particular act, such as purchasing a product or visiting the point of purchase.

Press conference A public gathering of media people for the purpose of establishing a company's position or making a statement.

Price deal A temporary reduction in the price of a product.

Primary research Information that is collected from original sources.

Process colors Four basic inks—magenta, cyan, yellow, and black—that are mixed to produce a full range of colors found in four-color printing.

Process evaluation Measuring the effectiveness of media and nonmedia efforts to get the desired message out to the target audience.

Producer The person in charge of all the arrangements for a commercial, including settings, casting, arranging for the music, and handling bids and budgets.

Product life cycle The history of the product from its introduction to its eventual decline and withdrawal.

Professional advertising Advertising directed at people such as lawyers, doctors, and accountants.

Profile A personality sketch of a typical prospect in the targeted audience.

Program preemptions Interruptions in local or network programming caused by special events.

Promise A benefit statement that looks to the future.

Promotion The element in the marketing mix that encourages the purchase of a product or service.

Promotion mix The combination of personal selling, advertising, sales promotion, and public relations to produce a coordinated message structure.

Prospects People who might buy the product or service.

Psychographics All the psychological variables that combine to shape our inner selves, including activities, interests, opinions, needs, values, attitudes, personality traits, decision processes, and buying behavior.

Public opinion People's beliefs, based on their conceptions or evaluations of something rather than on fact.

Public relations A management function enabling organizations to achieve effective relationships with their various audiences through an understanding of audience opinions, attitudes, and values.

Public service announcement (PSA) A type of public relations advertising that deals with public welfare issues and is typically run free of charge.

Publicity Cost-free public relations that relates messages through gatekeepers.

Publics Those groups or individuals who are involved with an organization, including customers, employees, competitors, and government regulators.

Puffery Advertising or other sales representation that praises the item to be sold using subjective opinions, superlatives, and similar mechanisms that are not based on specific fact.

Pull strategy A promotional strategy that is designed to encourage consumers to ask for the product.

Pulsing An advertising scheduling pattern in which time and space are scheduled on a continuous but uneven basis; lower levels are followed by bursts or peak periods of intensified activity.

Purging The process of deleting repeated names when two or more lists are combined.

Push money (spiffs) A monetary bonus paid to a salesperson based on units sold over a period of time.

Push strategy A promotional strategy that is directed to the trade in an attempt to move the product through the distribution channel.

Q

Qualitative data Research that seeks to understand how and why people think and behave as they do.

Quantitative data Research that uses statistics to describe consumers.

R

Reach The percentage of different homes or people exposed to a media vehicle or vehicles at least once during a specific period of time. It is the percentage of unduplicated audience.

Reason why A statement that explains why the feature will benefit the user.

Recall The ability to remember specific information content.

Recall test A test that evaluates the memorability of an advertisement by contacting members of the advertisement's audience and asking them what they remember about it.

Recognition An ability to remember having seen something before.

Recognition test A test that evaluates the memorability of an advertisement by contacting members of the audience, showing them the ad, and asking if they remember it.

Reference group A group of people that a person uses as a guide for behavior in specific situations.

Refund An offer by the marketer to return a certain amount of money to the consumer who purchases the product.

Regional brand A brand that is available throughout an entire region.

Release prints Duplicate copies of a commercial that are ready for distribution.

Relevance That quality of an advertising message that makes it important to the audience.

Reliability A characteristic that describes a test that yields essentially the same results when the same advertisement is tested time after time.

Reposition Changing the consumer's perception of a product.

Retail advertising A type of advertising used by local merchants who sell directly to consumers.

Reverse type A style of typesetting in which letters appear to be white against a darker background.

Rough cut A preliminary rough edited version of the commercial.

Rushes Rough versions of the commercial assembled from unedited footage.

S

Sales promotion Those marketing activities that add value to the product for a limited period of time to stimulate consumer purchasing and dealer effectiveness.

Sample A selection of people who are identified as representative of the larger population.

Sampling An offer that allows the customer to use or experience the product or service free of charge or for a very small fee.

Sans serif A typeface that does not have the serif detail.

Script A written version of a radio or television commercial.

Secondary research Information that has been compiled and published.

Selective distortion The interpretation of information in a way that is consistent with the person's existing opinion.

Selective exposure The ability to process only certain information and avoid other stimuli.

Selective perception The process of screening out information that does not interest us and retaining information that does.

Selective retention The process of remembering only a small portion of what a person is exposed to.

Selling premises The sales logic behind an advertising message.

Semicomp A layout drawn to size that depicts the art and display type; body copy is simply ruled in.

Serif A typeface with a finishing stroke on the main strokes of the letters.

Set A constructed setting where the action in a commercial takes place.

Share of market The percentage of the total category sales owned by one brand.

Share of voice The percentage of advertising messages in a medium by one brand among all messages for that product or service.

Signals A series of electrical impulses that compose radio and television broadcasting.

Signature The name of the company or product written in a distinctive type style.

Silk screen A form of printing in which the non-image areas, represented by a "blockout" film or lacquer, are adhered to a porous fabric while ink is forced through the image areas that aren't blocked out.

Simulated test market Research procedure in which respondents are exposed to advertisements and then permitted to shop for the advertised products in an artificial environment where records are kept of their purchases.

Situation analysis The section of an advertising campaign plan that summarizes the relevant research findings about the company, the product, the competition, the marketplace, and the consumer.

Slice of life A problem-solution message built around some common, everyday situation.

Slogans Frequently repeated phrases that provide continuity to an advertising campaign.

Social class A way to categorize people on the basis of their values, attitudes, lifestyles, and behavior.

Societal marketing concept A concept that requires balancing the company, consumer, and public interests.

Soft-sell An emotional message that uses mood, ambiguity, and suspense to create a response based on feelings and attitudes.

Sound effects (SFX) Lifelike imitations of sounds.

Spectaculars Billboards with unusual lighting effects.

Sponsorship An arrangement in which the advertiser produces both a television program and the accompanying commercials.

Spot announcements Ads shown during the breaks between programs.

Spot radio advertising A form of advertising in which an ad is placed with an individual station rather than through a network.

Stereotyping Presenting a group of people in an unvarying pattern that lacks individuality and often reflects popular misconceptions.

Stop motion A technique in which inanimate objects are filmed one frame at a time, creating the illusion of movement.

Storyboard A series of frames sketched to illustrate how the story line will develop.

Subheads Sectional headline used to break up masses of type.

Subliminal message A message transmitted below the threshold of normal perception so that the receiver is not consciously aware of having viewed it.

Superimpose A television technique where one image is added to another that is already on the screen.

Supplements Syndicated or local full-color advertising inserts that appear in newspapers throughout the week.

Surprinting Printing type over some other image.

Survey research Research using structured interview forms that ask large numbers of people exactly the same questions.

Sweepstakes Sales promotion activities that require participants to submit their names to be included in a drawing or other type of chance selection.

Symbolism Words and images that represent, or cue, something else.

Synchronize Matching the audio to the video in a commercial.

Syndication Television or radio shows that are reruns or original programs purchased by local stations to fill in during open hours.

Target audience People who can be reached with a certain advertising medium and a particular message.

Target market A market segment with the most potential for purchase of the product.

Task-objective method A budgeting method that builds a budget by asking what it will cost to achieve the stated objectives.

Tear sheet The pages from a newspaper on which an ad appears.

Telemarketing A type of marketing that uses the telephone to make a personal sales contact.

Television market An unduplicated geographical area to which a county is assigned on the basis of the highest share of the viewing of television stations.

Testimonial An advertising format in which a spokesperson describes a positive personal experience with the product.

Thumbnail sketches Small preliminary sketches of various layout ideas.

Tip-ins Preprinted ads that are provided by the advertiser to be glued into the binding of a magazine.

Trade advertising Advertising used to influence resellers, wholesalers, and retailers.

Trade deals An arrangement in which the retailer agrees to give the manufacturer's product a special promotional effort in return for product discounts, goods, or cash.

Trademark Sign or design, often with distinctive lettering, that symbolizes the brand.

Traditional delivery Delivery of magazines to readers through newsstands or home delivery.

Trailers Advertisements that precede the feature film in a movie theater.

Transformation advertising Image advertising that changes the experience of buying and using a product.

T

Tabloid A newspaper with a page size five to six columns wide and 14 inches deep.

Tagline A memorable phrase that sums up the concept or key point of the ad.

Talent People who appear in television commercials.

U

Underline A subhead that leads from the headline into the body copy.

Unique selling proposition A benefit statement about a feature that is both unique to the product and important to the user.

V

Validity The ability of a test to measure what it is intended to measure.

Value and lifestyles systems (VALS) Classification systems that categorize people by values for the purpose of predicting effective advertising strategies.

Values The source for norms, which are not tied to specific objects or behaviors.

Vampire creativity An advertising problem in which an ad is so creative or entertaining that it overwhelms the product.

Verbatims Spontaneous comments by people who are being surveyed.

Vernacular Language that reflects the speech patterns of a particular group of people.

Vertical publications Publications directed to people who hold different positions in the same industries.

Videotape A type of recording medium that electronically records sound and images simultaneously.

Visual path The direction in which the reader's eye moves while scanning a layout.

Visualization The ability to see images in the mind, to imagine how an ad or a concept will look when it is finished.

Voice-over A technique used in commercials in which an off-camera announcer talks about the on-camera scene.

W

Weighted audience values Numerical values assigned to different audience characteristics that help advertisers assign priorities when devising media plans.

Wide area telephone service (WATS) A system of mass telephone calling at discount rates.

Data bases, 181, 482–84
Data sheets, 639
Datril ad, 82
Davids, Meryl, 107*n*
Davidson, Casey, 440*n*
da Vinci, Leonardo, 390
Day-after recall (DAR) tests, 606
Day, Barry, 680
Day-of-the-week timing, of advertising
schedules, 279
DDB Needham Worldwide, 2, 30, 84, 87,
102, 106, 112, 116, 125, 126, 127, 203,
216–17, 258, 369, 386, 397, 474
Life Style studies, 165
Dealer contests/sweepstakes, 550
Dealer loader, 550–51
Dealerscope Merchandising, 595
Dealer tag, 645
Deceptive advertising, 55
remedies for, 59–62
Bureau of Alcohol, Tobacco, and
Firearms action, 61–62
cease-and-desist orders, 59
consent decrees, 59
consumer redress, 61
corrective advertising, 59–60
Federal Communications Commission
(FCC) action, 61
Food and Drug Administration (FDA)
action, 61
legal responsibility of agency, 60
substantiation of claims, 61
U.S. Postal Service action, 61
Decision making:
advertising budget, 224–25
in business arena, 635
consumer, 140–44
ethical, 37
low-/high-involvement decision
making, 162
recall tests and, 608
Decision Research Corporation, 119
Decline stage, product life cycle, 77
De Deo, Joe, 268
*Defined Advertising Goals for Measured
Advertising Results* (DAGMAR)
(Colley), 217, 218
Della Femina, Travisano & Partners
agency, 9
Demographics, 144–52, 272
age, 144–45
data bases, 181
education, 150
family status, 148–50
gender, 145–48
income, 150–51
race/ethnicity, 151–52
and retail advertising, 647–48
Demonstrations, 58–59
television commercials, 458
and visuals, 408
Denotative aspects, of brand name, 257
Dentsu agency, 126, 663, 675
Department store divisions, 647
Design:
message, 397–406
print advertising, 427–35
color, 435
layouts, 427–29
principles, 429–34
research, 186–87
Yellow Pages advertising, 511–13

Designated Market Areas (DMAs), 316
Designing Women, 44
Desktop publishing, 348, 442, 448, 449–50
Deutschman, Alan, 147*n*
DeVoe, Merrill, 24*n*
Dewar's ads, 37–38
Diagnostic research, 191–92
Dial ad, 386
Dialog Information Services, Inc., 181
Dialogue-style body copy, 426–27
Di Chiro, Patrick, 150
Diddley, Bo, 7
Differentiation strategies, 211–12
Digital Equipment Corporation, 486
Digitized art, 449
Dilenschneider, Robert L., 563*n*
Direct-action advertising, 13
Direct-broadcast satellite business (DBS),
305
Direct competition, 211
Direct headlines, 423
Direct mail, 484, 493–98
characteristics of, 494
mailing lists, 496–98
compiled lists, 497
house lists, 496
list brokers, 496
list managers, 496
merging/purging, 497–98
response lists, 497
message format, 494–95
brochures, 495
letters, 494–95
order cards, 495
outer envelopes, 494
message functions, 495–96
Direct Mail/Advertising Association, 486
Direct marketing, 81, 482–85, 639
data-base marketing, 484–85
data bases, 482–84
direct-response advertising, 483–84
Direct Marketing Association (DMA), 486
Direct-marketing department, 121
Direct Marketing magazine, 346
Direct observation, 193
Director, television commercials, 466–67
Direct-order marketing, 484
Directories, and retail advertising, 654
Directory advertising, 11, 508–13, 639
electronic directories, 513
Yellow Pages advertising, 509–12
audience, 510
creating, 511–13
Direct response, and retail
advertising, 654–55
Direct-response advertising, 11, 72,
481–505
characteristics of, 487–89
drawbacks/disadvantages, 488–89
interactive nature, 488
measurable action objectives, 488
tight targeting, 488
data bases, use of, 483
direct marketing, 482–85
industry growth, 486–87
media of, 493–502
broadcast media, 501–2
catalogs, 498–500
direct mail, 493–98
print media, 500–501
players, 489–93

advertisers, 490–91
agencies, 491
consumers, 491–93
telemarketing, 489
See also Data bases; Direct
marketing; Telemarketing
Direct-response counts, 615
Disclaimers, 58
Discretionary income, 150
Disney Channel, 303
Dispersion, 370
Display advertising, newspapers, 340–42
Display allowances, 551
Display classified ads, 340
Display copy, 340–42
Dissolve, 468
Dissonance/attribution hierarchy, 219
Distribution:
exclusive distribution, 81
frequency distribution, 289–90
intensive distribution, 81
magazines, 346–47, 353
patterns, 269
selective distribution, 81
Distribution channel, 74, 79–81
Diversified Agency Services, 125
Doak Tar dandruff shampoo ad, 157
Dole brand, 257
Dollar allocations, 367
Dolliver, Mark, 44*n*
Dolly in/out, 468
Dominant element, layouts, 432
Donaton, Scott, 48*n*, 684*n*
Dooner, John, 105
Doppelt, Neil, 490*n*
Dorman Cheese, "Cowrobics" ad, 403
Double-duty advertising, 500–501
Dow Jones News/Retrieval, 181, 186
Doyle Dane Bernbach, *See* DDB Needham
Worldwide
Dramas, 399–400
Drexel Burnham Lambert, Inc, 58
Dubbing, 469
Duplicating ads, 447
Duration, 279–80
and advertising budget, 279
and consumer-use cycles, 279–80
and lack of brand loyalty, 280
Durot, Donahoe & Purohit agency, 107

Earned rate, 371
Eastman Kodak ads, 458, 680
Ebony magazine, 538
*Economic Issues: How Should Health
Claims for Foods Be Regulated?,*180
Economic role of advertising, 12
Economist, The, 683
Eder, Peter F., 239*n*
Editing on film, 461
Editor, television commercials, 467
Education, categorization by, 150
Edwards, Betty, 393*n*
Edy's Ice Cream ads, 458
Effective Advertising Copy (DeVoe), 24*n*,
27*n*, 29*n*
Effective creativity, 389–90
Effective frequency, 290
Einstein, Albert, 391
Elderly market, *See* Senior citizens
Electromagnetic waves, 321
Electronic catalogs, 500
Electronic directories, 513